Why Do You Need This New Edition?

If you're wondering why you should buy this new edition of *Literature: A Pocket Anthology*, here are five good reasons!

1. The fiction collection now includes **Washington Irving's "Rip Van Winkle,"** one of the most beloved stories of all time, as well as compelling new selections from masters of the genre, including **Edgar Allan Poe's "The Cask of Amontillado."**

2. **Short story authors new to this collection** include award winners **Tobias Wolff, Helen Simpson, and Susan Perabo,** as well as the Pulitzer-prize winning Indian-American, **Jhumpa Lahiri.**

3. The poetry collection brings **new selections from classic and contemporary authors,** including **John Keats, e.e. cummings, Langston Hughes, Elizabeth Bishop,** and **Richard Wilbur,** as well as fresh models from **poets new to this edition** including **Amy Gerstler, Rebecca Foust, Craig Arnold, Ernest Hilbert** and **Erica Dawson,** whose work brings poetry into the 21st century.

4. The drama section includes **Yasmina Reza's Tony-winning comedy *The God of Carnage,*** produced on Broadway with a cast including James Gandolfini and Jeff Daniels and reflecting the robust strength of today's Broadway and of contemporary comedy, as well as **Shakespeare's *Twelfth Night,*** which brings a classic comedy to this collection for the first time.

5. And as always, *Literature: A Pocket Anthology* offers a comprehensive collection of poetry, short fiction, and drama at an affordable price and an appealing length.

PEARSON

about the author

R.S. GWYNN has edited several other books, including *Drama: A Pocket Anthology; Poetry: A Pocket Anthology; Fiction: A Pocket Anthology; Inside Literature: Reading, Responding, Writing* (with Steven Zani); *The Art of the Short Story* (with Dana Gioia); and *Contemporary American Poetry: A Pocket Anthology* (with April Lindner). He has also authored five collections of poetry, including *No Word of Farewell: Selected Poems, 1970–2000.* He has been awarded the Michael Braude Award for verse from the American Academy of Arts and Letters. Gwynn is University Professor of English and Poet-in-Residence at Lamar University in Beaumont, Texas.

PENGUIN ACADEMICS

LITERATURE

A POCKET ANTHOLOGY

PENGUIN ACADEMICS

LITERATURE

A POCKET ANTHOLOGY

FIFTH EDITION

Edited by

R. S. Gwynn
Lamar University

Longman
Boston   Columbus   Indianapolis   New York   San Francisco
Upper Saddle River   Amsterdam   Cape Town   Dubai   London   Madrid
Milan   Munich   Paris   Montreal   Toronto   Delhi   Mexico City
São Paulo   Sydney   Hong Kong   Seoul   Singapore   Taipei   Tokyo

Senior Sponsoring Editor: Virginia L. Blanford
Senior Marketing Manager: Joyce Nilsen
Assistant Editor: Rebecca Gilpin
Production Project Manager: Clara Bartunek
Project Coordination, Text Design, and Electronic Page Makeup: Nitin
    Agarwal, Aptara®, Inc
Creative Art Director : Jayne Conte
Cover Designer: Bruce Kenselaar
Cover Illustration/Photo: Fotolia
Printer and Binder: Courier/Westford
Cover Printer: Lehigh/Phoenix-Hagerstown

For more information about the Penguin Academics series, please contact us
by mail at Pearson Education, attn: Marketing Department, 51 Madison
Avenue, 29th Floor, New York, NY 10010, or visit us online at
www.pearsonhighered.com/english.

For permission to use copyrighted materials, grateful acknowledgment is
made to the copyright holders on page 1347 which are hereby made part of
this copyright page.

Library of Congress Cataloging-in-Publication Data
Literature : a pocket anthology / edited by R.S. Gwynn.—5th ed.
        p. cm.—(Penguin academics)
    Includes bibliographical references and index.
    ISBN-13: 978-0-205-03219-8 (alk. paper)
    ISBN-10: 0-205-03219-2 (alk. paper)
    1. English literature.   2. American literature. I. Gwynn, R. S.

PR1109.L57 2010
808.8—dc22   2010043751

1 2 3 4 5 6 7 8 9 10—CRW—14 13 12 11
Longman
is an imprint of

www.pearsonhighered.com

ISBN-13: 978-0-205-03219-8
ISBN-10:   0-205-03219-2

gender social issue 474

contents

POETRY

Introduction to Poetry   427

CONTENTS

CONTENTS

xxi

preface

When the *Pocket Anthology* series first appeared, our chief aim was to offer a clear alternative to the anthologies of fiction, poetry, and drama that were available at the time. *Literature: A Pocket Anthology*, Fifth Edition, incorporates many of the features of three genre-based anthologies: *Fiction: A Pocket Anthology*, Seventh Edition; *Poetry: A Pocket Anthology*, Seventh Edition; and *Drama: A Pocket Anthology*, Fifth Edition. Designed to be used in a wide range of courses, this relatively brief anthology can be packaged with one or more of a rich selection of Penguin titles, which Pearson Longman offers at significantly reduced prices. Your Pearson Arts and Sciences representative can supply full details about the available Penguin titles.

What's New in This Edition

As with earlier editions of *Literature*, our goal has been to provide variety and flexibility within the parameters of a brief, affordable anthology. Contemporary fiction writers new to this anthology include Jhumpa Lahiri, Tobias Wolff, and Susan Perabo. The fiction section also includes new selections from masters of the form ranging from Poe to contemporary writers such as Tim Gautreaux. The Fifth Edition of *Literature* also includes the work of contemporary poets Brian Turner, Allison Joseph, Sophie Hannah, Emily Moore, Ernest Hilbert, and Erica Dawson. As well as new selections from a range of poets. We have added two plays to this edition—Shakespeare's *Twelfth Night* and Yasmine Reza's *The God of Carnage*. More than a third of the selections overall represent voices of women, people of color, and writers from cultures outside the United States, and a strong effort has been made to include work that reflects contemporary social questions and will stimulate classroom discussion.

Goals of This Anthology

Literature addresses the four wishes and concerns most commonly expressed by both instructors and students. First, of course, is the variety of selections it contains. Admittedly, a pocket anthology has to be very selective in its contents, so we are especially proud that the stories, poems, and plays in this book represent canonical writers such as Shakespeare, Sidney, and Donne; Poe, Faulkner, and O'Connor; and Sophocles and Tennessee Williams, as well as newer voices that represent the diversity of gender, ethnic background, and national origin that is essential to any study of contemporary literature. The contents of *Literature* have been shaped both by the advice of experienced instructors, who have cited authors and works that are most often taught and that possess proven appeal to students, and by the editor's own experience as a critic, poet and teacher of literature and creative writing.

Our second goal was flexibility. We wanted a book that could be used as both a primary and a supplemental test in a wide range of courses, from introduction to literature courses, to classes in research methods and application of literary theory, to mixed-genre courses in writing. *Literature* contains, in addition to its generous selection of stories, poems, and plays, biographical headnotes for authors, introductions that cover the techniques and terminology of each of the three major literary genres, and a concise section on writing about literature and research procedures. As an aid to student writing assignments, *Literature* also contains three appendixes that group works from all three genres thematically and provide suggestions for the application of a range of critical approaches.

Third, we wanted an affordable book. Full-size introductory literature books now cost well over $70, and even the compact editions of these books represent a significant expense to students. Pearson Longman is committed to keeping the price of the *Pocket Anthology* series reasonable without compromising on design or typeface. We hope that readers will find the attractive layout of *Literature* preferable to the cramped margins and minuscule fonts found in many literature textbooks. Because of its relatively low cost, this volume may be easily supplemented in individual courses with handbooks of grammar and usage, manuals of style, introductions to critical theory, textbooks on research methods, or instructional texts in creative writing. The relatively low price of *Literature* reflects the original claims of the *Pocket Anthology* series—that these books represent "a new standard of value."

Finally, we stressed portability. Many instructors have expressed concern for students who must carry literature books comprising 2,000 or more pages in backpacks already laden with book and materials for other courses. A semester is a short time, and few courses can cover more than a fraction of the material that may full-size collections contain. Because the focus of *Literature* is on primary texts, we are able to offer roughly the same number of poems, stories, and plays as much larger books. Although *Literature* may still be a snug fit in most pockets, we trust that sympathetic instructors and their students will appreciate a book that does not add a physical burden to the intellectual one required by college courses.

Acknowledgments

No book is ever created in a vacuum. We would like to express our gratitude to the instructors who reviewed the current edition of this volume and offered invaluable recommendations for improvement. They are: Shazia Ali; Eastfield College; Tony Ardizzone, Indiana University, Bloomington; Mark G. Aune, California University of Pennsylvania; Lucas Carpenter, Oxford College of Emory University; Michael J. Chappell, Western Connecticut State University; Jo Cochran, Klamath Community College; David Holper, College of the Redwoods; Norman W. Jones, Ohio State University, Mansfield Campus; William E. Matsen, North Hennepin Community College; Elizabeth M. Sloan, Northeast State Community College; Karla Stouse, Indiana University Kokomo; E. Bert Wallace, Campbell University;Royal Ward, Albion College; Portia Weston, Point Park University.

We are also grateful to those who reviewed earlier editions, including Ruth Anne Baumgartner, Fairfield University; Franz Blaha, University of Nebraska; Allan Braden, Tacoma Community College; Paul Castagno, University of North Carolina/Wilmington; Thomas C. Crochunis, Shippensburg University; Laura Early, University of Louisville; Randy Hendricks, University of West Georgia; James Hoggard, Midwestern State University; Patricia S. Kennedy, University of North Carolina; Donald Kenneth Pardlow, Georgia Highlands College; Derek Sheffield, Wenatchee Valley College; Matha Silano, Edmonds and Bellevue Community College; Stephen Tuttle, Brigham Young University; and Jeanne Yeasting, Western Washington University.

The editor also acknowledges the invaluable assistance of Rachel Klauss in assembling this edition.

R. S. Gwynn
Lamar University

introduction to literature

Experience, Experiment, Expand: Three Reasons to Study Literature

It is a good day in Belton Hall 105. The instructor has assigned a short story by a well-known contemporary American writer, and even though spring is making its presence felt among the campus trees and shrubs, no one is gazing wistfully out the open windows. Some interest is stirring in the classroom, hands go up quickly, and, instead of lecturing, all the instructor has to do is field one question and raise another. The days when her teaching technique consisted of a recitation of details for note-taking—the parts of a plot, the structure of a sonnet, the origins of tragedy—seem like memories of gray winter afternoons, and the students' eyes, some of them flashing with anger, focus on one another instead of on the pages of their notebooks. One student complains that the story places women in a subordinate role and turns them into objects of the narrator's lustful eye; another counters that such behavior is exactly what one should expect from the story's protagonist, a teenage boy working at a dull job in a supermarket. The instructor is clearly enjoying herself, feeling lucky to be playing the role of referee in the debate, which has grown animated as the members of the class add their opinions and take sides. On occasions like this, discussing and arguing about literature seems as natural as talking about sports, campus gossip, or the movies. It is a good day in Belton Hall 105.

1

But on the other days—the days of lectures, inscrutable diagrams on the chalkboard, eyes that would rather look at anything other than a piece of lined paper—instructors and students alike ponder the toughest questions of all: What's the point of this? Why do we have to study literature? What value is this study to me? As a way of introducing *Literature: A Pocket Anthology* (5th ed.), I have chosen three words—experience, experiment, expand—to suggest some good reasons why the study of literature is invaluable to any education.

Experience

"We are such stuff / As dreams are made on; and our little life / Is rounded with a sleep," says Shakespeare's great magician Prospero. Our experience of the world is limited by time and place, and even the most resolute traveler can only superficially come to know the complex blends of cultures that make up our world. The act of reading literature provides us with a means of imaginatively entering minds and civilizations that may seem distant to us but actually are only as remote as a turn of the page. To read *Antigone* is to recapture something of the awe with which the Athenians of Sophocles' day witnessed the dramatic reenactments of their ancient history. In reading such a play, we may also realize that the questions the ancient Greeks asked about human destiny are the same ones we still ponder today. True, we may never travel to Africa, but by reading a story by Chinua Achebe we can learn something about customs that in some ways resemble our own but in others seem foreign and strange. A poem by a contemporary American poet such as Ellen Bryant Voigt may bring with it the shock of recognition we reserve for those experiences that touch us most deeply. In literature we are allowed the possibility of inhabiting, for a brief time, lives and minds that are not our own. Men can learn from Adrienne Rich's "Rape" what it feels to be a victim of a sexual assault; women can learn how the protagonist of Raymond Carver's "Cathedral" overcomes both jealousy and prejudice in coming to know an old friend of his wife, a blind man. We can see the world through the eyes of people of genders, races, historical eras, and social classes that may resemble or vastly differ from our own. The perspectives and subjects we experience in literature are as varied and sometimes as troubling as life itself, but in investigating them we can broaden our understanding of life in ways that other fields of academic study cannot equal. We might eventually agree that the insight that we gain from a literary work is equal or even superior to the experience that we may personally identify with in it. "How frugal is the Chariot / That bears the Human soul," said Emily Dickinson, speaking of the readily available pleasures of reading.

Experiment

Literature does not write itself, and even the most vivid experience does not automatically translate into a memorable poem, story, or play. To the writer, every event that he or she considers as a likely subject presents a problem in literary form. Which of the genres—drama, fiction, or poetry—can best depict an experience, and which of each genre's innumerable subtypes—comedy or tragedy, short story or novel, open-form poem or sonnet—will work best? To study literature is to learn that every play, story, or poem that has ever been written involves some kind of experiment in literary technique, and much of the study of literature must be given over to questioning why artists make the choices that they do. Edgar Allan Poe once wrote an essay, "The Philosophy of Composition," about how he came to write his famous poem "The Raven," in which he explained in detail the decisions that he made about rhythm, language, setting, and even the sounds of individual words. But many readers have found that "The Raven," or for that matter any successful piece of literature, adds up to more than the sum of its parts; not even the creator has the last word on what the experiment has uncovered. As serious readers, our job is often to go beneath the surface to reveal the underlying structures and meanings. We may never write a short story, poem, or play ourselves, but in being entertained and perhaps instructed by a writer's skill with words, we gain some insight into one of the greatest human mysteries—the motives and methods of those who make art literally out of nothing. To read literature with the goal of learning how it is made is to understand literature not as life itself but as an artful imitation of it. As Richard Wilbur, observing his own daughter's attempts to write a short story, says to her, "It is always a matter, my darling, / Of life or death. . . ." And then he adds, ". . . as I had forgotten."

Expand

We expand our understanding by reading, by discussing what we have read, and by writing about it. When talking about a poem in a classroom group, students are often surprised to find that the way one reads a certain passage is not quite the same as a classmate's interpretation and that both differ from the instructor's. Literature is not a science, and many of the meanings we attach to individual works remain largely matters of speculation. This is not to claim that all interpretations, no matter how far-fetched, are equally valid; it is only an observation that complex works of literature offer different channels of interpretation for readers, as any survey of available criticism of a given text will quickly demonstrate. The student's chance to speak his or her piece most often takes the form of the essay answer on an examination, the theme or thesis paper, or the research project. The job of making assertions, backing them up with references to the text, and locating support from outside sources may not be the most exciting aspect of literary study, but it remains the primary way through which students may demonstrate that their initial attempts to understand a story, poem, or play have grown and deepened. In analyzing, researching, and writing about literature, we expand our minds as we realize that none of us has the final word. As in life, the qualifications and adjustments we make as we respond to literary works teach us something about the necessity of not taking things at face value; there is always one more question to ask, one more possibility to weigh and test.

It is no coincidence that the three words that I have chosen all begin with the prefix ex-, which means "out of." One of the most common questions from students that I have heard over the years is "What are we supposed to get *out of* this (story, poem, play)?" I may be turning the phrase slightly, but if you have really savored the full experience that good literature offers, then the first thing you should get "out of" will be your own skin—when you do that you will answer your own question. For a few moments you may lose your own identity and see through the eyes of an ancient Greek, a modern Nigerian, or a contemporary American woman, and you may just find that in some significant way your own manner of looking at the world will never be quite the same again.

In beginning our study of literature, we must first look at the different literary genres—fiction, poetry, and drama—and discuss their different methods and techniques. Each genre, or type, of literature has its own history and terminology, some of which may be shared with other genres. In the introductory discussions of fiction, poetry, and drama that follow, certain important terms appear in boldface type. An index of critical terms is found at the end of this book.

Introduction to Fiction

The Telling of the Tale

The memory begins with a scene like this: the circle contains about thirty boys and girls, all in their preteen years and dressed identically in khaki shorts and t-shirts, who sit on upended sections of logs around a leaping fire. The sun has just dropped beneath the rim of a nearby mountain, and a hint of damp chill steals into the August woods. It is the last night of camp, and they have gathered to sing songs and receive awards. Now one of the counselors, a college student who could pass for an older brother of any of the campers, puts away his guitar and nods to his colleague, a young woman who steps into the ring of firelight and begins to speak. "Many, many years ago," she begins, her solemn voice describing three characters—a brave warrior, a maiden with a beautiful laugh, a wolf cub raised as a pet—"on a night not too different from this . . . ." The surrounding woods seem to grow darker as the campers lean forward toward the rise and fall of her voice and the blaze of the flames. Caught in the spell of her words, they have momentarily left text-messaging, and television behind, enacting one of the human race's oldest rituals as they respond to the simple magic of the storyteller's art.

Before we can begin to examine the elements of literary fiction we must bear in mind that literature in its written form is historically a recent innovation; indeed, its two most common modern forms, the short story and the novel, have been in existence for little more than two centuries. Yet long before the invention of writing, for thousands of years ancient peoples developed complex **oral traditions** of literature; these primitive stories, dealing with the creation of the cosmos and the origins of gods and goddesses, formed a body of **myths,** supernatural narratives widely believed to be true by the people of a given culture, and **legends,** popular stories about characters and events that may contain trace elements of historical truth. Even in modern societies, elements of this primitive folklore survive in regional or ethnic tales passed on through the generations, most often taking the written form of **folk tales** collected by literary scholars; **fairy tales,** like Charles Perrault's "Beauty and the Beast" or Hans Christian Andersen's "The Little Mermaid"; **beast fables,** stories with animal characters such as those of Aesop (c. 550 B.C.) or Joel Chandler Harris (1848–1908); or **parables,** short realistic tales like those found in the Gospels. Many of these, especially the last two types, are to some degree **didactic,** with the narrative events illustrating a **moral** that is either stated or implied.

Even in modern societies other ancient forms of oral literature still enjoy a good state of health. These include **anecdotes,** accounts of single incidents usually involving a well-known person, and **riddles** and **jokes** of all types, which often seem to spring into circulation overnight and often unwittingly mirror the basic situations and coarse humor of venerable **fabliaux**—short, realistic tales from the Middle Ages that often turn on a bawdy situation. Recently, much attention has been given to **urban legends,** so named by folklorist Jan Brunvand, which are short narratives involving grotesque incidents that are widely accepted as true. The title of one of Dr. Brunvand's collections, *The Vanishing Hitchhiker,* refers to a ghost tale that virtually every American has heard in one of its many versions.

When myths and legends are assembled around the exploits of a great hero, the result is the **folk epic,** a long narrative in elevated style that is generally considered a starting point for any culture's literary history. Like most types of oral folk literature, epics were originally composed in verse for the sake of memorization, but they otherwise contain the same elements as modern literary forms like the short story and novel. For example, the individual **episodes** of Homer's *Odyssey*—Odysseus's outwitting the Cyclops or his adventures with the sorceress Circe—can stand alone as exciting tales and also can fit into the larger structure of the epic, like chapters in a novel. Later authors, living in societies which had invented writing, consciously imitated the style of folk epics in composing **literary epics.** The *Aeneid* by Virgil (70–19 B.C.) and *The Divine Comedy* by Dante (1265–1321) are two famous examples. In the Middle Ages, **romances,** written in both verse and prose, gained great popularity among all classes. These tales of chivalry—involving a knightly hero and a series of exciting, if improbable, adventures—were ridiculed by Miguel de Cervantes (1547–1616) in *Don Quixote,* a realistic account of an impoverished Spanish gentleman driven mad by reading too many romances. The eventual form that Cervantes gave Don Quixote's adventures was perhaps influenced by **picaresque novels** like the anonymous *Lazarillo of Tormes* (c. 1450), which involved a young orphan (or *picaro,* Spanish for "rascal") in a series of loosely connected adventures. These picaresque tales are rightly considered the ancestors of modern realistic fiction. Many novels, from Henry Fielding's *Tom Jones* to Mark Twain's *The Adventures of Huckleberry Finn* to J. D. Salinger's *The Catcher in the Rye* and Jack Kerouac's *On the Road,* borrow their structure from picaresque novel, and the modern short story is indebted to their often stark level of realism.

The Short Story Genre

There is no agreement on the precise origins of the modern short story. One important influence in its development was the Italian **novella** of the late Middle Ages and Renaissance. The most famous collection of these realistic prose narratives is *The Decameron* by Giovanni Boccaccio (1313–1375). *The Decameron,* in which the individual stories are narrated by young men and women who have taken to the country to escape the Black Death, is an example of a **frame tale,** in which the stories are "framed" by a larger narrative. The famous Arabian collection *A Thousand and One Nights* is one of the earliest examples of this genre. In translation, these tales were popular in other countries and widely imitated. In writing his plays, Shakespeare borrowed from Italian writers frequently; his tragedy *Othello* takes its plot from a sensational novella by Giraldi Cinthio. We still use the term "novella" for short stories that are long enough (usually over 15,000 words) to be published separately in book form. Count Leo Tolstoy's *The Death of Ivan Ilyich* is a classic Russian example, and Ernest Hemingway's *The Old Man and the Sea* is one of the best-known novellas in English.

The first half of the nineteenth century is the great period of the growth of the short story as a distinct **literary genre,** or type, and its rise takes place in many countries at roughly the same time. Many reasons for this rapid development could be put forth, but perhaps the most important was the literary market established by newspapers and magazines aimed at middle-class audiences. The United States, with its increasingly high rate of literacy and expanding middle class, led the way in this period; Washington Irving's tales such as "Rip Van Winkle" and "The Legend of Sleepy Hollow" were among the first American writings to attain international popularity. Edgar Allan Poe, the first great theorist of the short story and one of its notable practitioners during this period, supported himself primarily (although not very prosperously) as a magazine editor and contributor and thus had a large personal stake in promoting short fiction. Poe's influential review of Nathaniel Hawthorne's *Twice-Told Tales* in 1842 first stated the theory that a short story ought to be a unified artistic creation, as carefully shaped as a sonnet. Poe said:

> A skillful literary artist has constructed a tale. If wise, he has not fashioned his thoughts to accommodate his incidents; but having conceived, with deliberate care, a certain unique or single effect to be wrought out, he then invents such incidents—he then combines such events as may best aid him in establishing this preconceived effect. If his very initial sequence tend not to be the outbringing of this effect, then he has failed in his first step. In the whole composition there should be no word written, of which the tendency, direct or indirect, is not to the one pre-established design. And by such means, with such care and skill, a picture is at length painted which leaves in the mind of him who contemplates it with a kindred art, a sense of the fullest satisfaction.

This idea of the *single effect* is perhaps Poe's most important contribution to the development of the short story as a serious literary genre.

Most of Hawthorne's and Poe's stories are perhaps more properly termed **tales,** if by that term we mean narratives that contain elements that are exotic or supernatural and that to some degree depart from the level of ordinary experience. Poe himself established many of the conventions of the horror, science fiction, and detective tales still being written and read today; **formula fiction,** which rigidly follows the clichés and conventions of a particular genre, is sometimes half-affectionately called **pulp fiction,** a reminder of the low grade of paper once used in inexpensive magazines. Still, the tale remains a lively tradition among serious artists as well. Among the contemporary stories in this book, selections by Faulkner, Oates, and others show their debt to the tradition of the tale.

The short story in its present form, on the other hand, developed somewhat later, and its evolution was part of the larger literary movement of **realism,** which profoundly influenced the arts in the mid-nineteenth century with its "slice of life" approach to subject matter that, in early centuries, would have been deemed inappropriate for serious treatment. It has been rightly noted that realism simply represents the effect of democracy on literary history. Celebrating its appearance as early as 1837, Ralph Waldo Emerson noted, "The literature of the poor, the feelings of the child, the philosophy of the street, the meaning of household life, are the topics of the time." **Naturalism,** an outgrowth of realism that emerged in the second half of the century, also proved influential, for it joined realistic treatments of everyday life with understandings of human behavior drawn from the new sciences of psychology and sociology. Both realism and naturalism remain vital currents in contemporary short fiction, as stories here by Raymond Carver, Alice Walker, and Bobbie Ann Mason will attest.

The twentieth century saw the short story rise to its highest level of popularity and just as rapidly decline in its influence as a literary form. During the first half of the century, when many magazines like *Collier's* and the *Saturday Evening Post* paid large sums for short stories by important authors, the genre flourished. F. Scott Fitzgerald, a frequent contributor to these magazines, kept a meticulous ledger in which he noted, in one six-month period in 1922–1923, that he earned over $15,000 from magazine sales alone. A decade later, in the depths of the Great Depression, Fitzgerald complained that stories that earlier would have sold for prices in excess of $4,000 now commanded only $2,500. If these amounts do not seem exorbitant, remember that we are talking about times when a new automobile sold for under $1,000 and a gallon of gasoline cost a dime! Today, when virtually every college in the country employs one or more writers-in-residence whose primary income comes not from publishing but from teaching, we tend perhaps to underestimate the impact that economic realities have had on the history of literature.

In the second half of the twentieth century, many of the established magazines that regularly ran serious fiction ceased publication. Search a typical magazine rack and you will find only one weekly magazine, *The New Yorker*, and a handful of monthlies containing short stories. Reading tastes have changed, and increased competition from television and other forms of entertainment has made the writing of short stories an expensive pastime for writers. Still, the pages of little magazines and literary quarterlies continue to provide outlets for publication, and new writers seem undeterred by the prospect of being paid with little more than what one disgruntled writer has called "two free copies of what I've already got." Almost every writer of short fiction who is prominent today first appeared in small-circulation periodicals of this type, and many have continued to publish in magazines that can offer, instead of money, prestige and a discriminating readership numbering in the hundreds. Indeed, the little magazines have traditionally been hospitable to many kinds of **experimental fiction** that editors of commercial magazines would never have considered. Also, recent decades have seen a rise in so-called **"short-short"** stories or **"flash fiction."** If the quantity of contemporary short fiction being published has shrunk from what it was in previous decades, the quality, one might argue, has remained the same or even improved. When we look at lists of recent winners of the Pulitzer or Nobel prizes, we discover many writers who have counted the short story as their first genre.

Reading and Analyzing Short Fiction

We read for many reasons. In our daily lives most of our reading is strictly utilitarian—it is part of our jobs or education—or informational, as we scan the headlines of a daily newspaper or drudge.com for current events, business trends, or sports scores. We read short stories and other types of fiction for differing reasons. Sometimes our motives are simply to be entertained and to pass the time. Reading matter of this type is usually termed **escapist literature** and includes such popular categories as romance and detective novels, science fiction tales, and westerns. Or we might consciously choose to read "inspirational" fiction that is obviously didactic and contains messages or moral lessons that apply to our own lives. Literary reading, however, occupies a position between the two extremes. Serious literature should certainly entertain us, but on a deeper level than, say, a half-hour episode of a television comedy show does. Similarly, it may also contain an ethical theme with which we can identify, even if it does not try to "preach" its moral message to the reader. A short story that we can treat as a serious work of art will not yield all of its subtlety at first glance; in order to understand and appreciate its author's achievement fully we may have to examine its components—its plot, characterization, point of view, theme, setting, style, and symbolism—noting how each part contributes to the story's overall effect. With that purpose in mind, let's read a very brief example by a modern American master of the genre, John Cheever's "Reunion" on page 190.

Plot

In his discussion of tragedy in the *Poetics*, Aristotle (384–322 B.C.) gives first importance to **plot** as an element of a play, and most readers would agree that it holds a similar position in a work of fiction. Indeed, if we tell a friend about a short story we have enjoyed, we will probably give a **synopsis** or brief summary of its incidents. In the case of a very brief story like "Reunion," this synopsis is only a few sentences long:

> In "Reunion," the narrator, a teenaged boy, meets his estranged father between trains in New York City. Over the course of an hour and a half the father's alcoholism and potentially abusive personality are revealed. The story ends with the narrator boarding his train, indicating that this was the last time he saw his father, possibly by choice.

Plot may be defined as a story's sequence of incidents, arranged in dramatic order. One is tempted to insert the word "chronological," but doing so would exclude many stories that depart from this strict ordering of events. Although its use is more characteristic in longer works like novels, many stories employ the **flashback** to narrate incidents in the past. For example, Bobbie Ann Mason's "Shiloh" uses a flashback to describe the death of Leroy and Norma Jean's infant son. Margaret Atwood's "Happy Endings" dispenses with a single plot line entirely, offering numerous possibilities for the fates of her characters. In opposite fashion, writers sometimes use **foreshadowing** to provide hints of future actions in the story; an effective use of foreshadowing prevents a story's outcome from seeming haphazard or contrived. Of course, the manner in which stories handle time is largely illusory.

During scenes with dialogue and action, time is slowed down by descriptive and explanatory phrases. In other places, stories cover gaps in chronology or leap over uneventful periods with transitional phrases and passages; the opening sentence of the second paragraph of "Reunion" compresses into a second or two an action that in reality would have taken at least several minutes. Even though "Reunion" does not take serious liberties with chronological time as we experience it, the hour or so of action in the story is compressed into about ten minutes of the reader's time. A plot like this, in which the action is more or less continuous within a single day, is called a **unified plot;** one which stretches over weeks or even longer periods and thus consists of isolated scenes connected by a thin tissue of transitional devices is called an **episodic plot.**

When we speak of the **dramatic structure** of a story, we refer to the exact way in which our emotional involvement in its plot is increased and relaxed. As Janet Burroway observes of the short story in *Writing Fiction,* "*Only* trouble is interesting." If we are not quickly engaged by the situation of a story and caught up in its plot, we pronounce the cruelest of all critical verdicts on it by closing the book. The first part of this dramatic structure is the **exposition,** which provides the reader with essential information—who, what, when, where—he or she needs to know before continuing. While writers of sophisticated fiction may try to disguise the fact, they often begin their stories with a variation of the "Once upon a time" opening common to fairy tales. A different type of beginning, called the **in medias res** ("in the middle of things") opening after the conventions of the old epic poems, may actually open with a "blind" bit of action before supplying its context. The exposition of "Reunion" is fairly straightforward; in the first paragraph we learn who (Charlie and his father), what (a lunchtime meeting between trains), when (noon to 1:30 P.M.), and where (in and near Grand Central Station in Manhattan). Cheever might have begun the story with a slightly more "dramatic" sentence ("At twelve o'clock sharp I saw him coming through the crowd."), but he would have to have provided the essential contextual information in short order to avoid unnecessarily confusing the reader.

Exposition in a story usually describes a stable situation, even if it is not an entirely happy one. Charlie tells us that his parents' divorce is three years old and that he has not seen his father in that time. If he had not taken the step of writing the letter arranging the "reunion," that state of affairs might have gone on indefinitely. The appearance of "trouble" constitutes the second part of a plot, the **complication,** the appearance of some circumstance or event that shakes up the stable situation and begins the **rising action** of the story. Complication in a story may be either external and internal, or a combination of the two. A stroke of fortune such as illness or accident which affects a character is a typical example of an external complication, a problem that the characters cannot ignore, while an internal complication might not be immediately apparent, the result of a character's deep-seated uncertainties, dissatisfactions, and fears. The external complication in "Reunion" is the father's series of confrontations with waiters; the internal complication is Charlie's growing sense of pity and revulsion. Typically, the complication of a plot is heightened by **conflict** between two characters who have different personalities and goals. Charlie is overjoyed to see his father at the beginning of the story, but despite his knowledge that he will grow up to "be something like him," he is more than eager to escape his company at the end, even if he is unconsciously trying to run away from his own "future and . . . doom."

The body of a story is called the rising action and usually comprises a number of scenes, containing action and dialogue, which build to **moments of crisis,** points in the story where a resolution of the complication momentarily seems at hand but quickly disappears. Aristotle used the term **peripety** for these moments of reversal, as the hopes of the characters rise and fall. Thus, in "Reunion" all that needs to be resolved, at least on the surface, is for the characters to order lunch, eat, and return in time for the departing train. The father's increasingly obnoxious behavior, however, keeps postponing this resolution until the reunion has turned from a happy occasion to something very different. Unlike most stories, "Reunion" has a rising action as rigidly structured as a joke with its four similar restaurant scenes gradually escalating in absurdity as the father's senseless rage increases.

The central moment of crisis in a plot is the **climax,** or moment of greatest tension, which inaugurates the **falling action** of the story, in which the built-up tension is finally released. Some stories, particularly those involving a heavy use of suspense, have a steep "dramatic curve" and the writer uses all of his or her skills to impel the reader toward the final confrontation. Among the writers included here, Edgar Allan Poe is the master of this kind of plot construction. Often one encounters the **trick ending** (also called the **O. Henry ending,** after the pen name of

William Sidney Porter, a popular writer of the nineteenth century). A climax like this depends on a quick reversal of the situation from an unexpected source; its success is always relative to the degree to which the reader is surprised when it occurs. More typically, modern short stories instead rely on climactic devices that are somewhat subtler than unexpected plot twists. Many modern writers have followed James Joyce's lead in building not to a climactic event but to a moment of spiritual insight or revelation, or what Joyce termed an **epiphany.** In the hands of a melodramatic writer insistent on sentimental happy endings, "Reunion" might have concluded with Charlie delivering a "tough love" sermon to his father, who would then fall to his knees and beg his son's forgiveness, having seen the error of his ways. Cheever's more realistic method of climax is, in this case, to avoid the confrontation altogether as Charlie escapes to his train.

The final part of a plot is the **dénouement** (or **resolution**). The French term literally refers to the untying of a knot, and we might compare the emotional release of a story's ending with a piece of cloth that has been twisted tighter and tighter and is then untwisted as the action winds down. The dénouement returns the characters to another stable situation. Just as fairy tales traditionally end with "And they lived happily ever after," many stories conclude with an indication of what the future holds for the characters. In the case of "Reunion," we return to the estrangement between Charlie and his father that existed at the beginning of the story, although this time all indications are that it will be a permanent one. A story's dénouement may be termed either closed or open. A **closed dénouement** ties up everything neatly and explains all unanswered questions the reader might have; a typical example is the "Elementary, my dear Watson" explanation of any remaining loose ends that is provided by the sleuth Sherlock Holmes in the final paragraphs of Arthur Conan Doyle's famous tales. On the other hand, an **open dénouement** leaves us with a few tantalizing questions. The last phrase of "Reunion," which consciously mirrors the story's opening sentence, does not explicitly state *why* Charlie never sees his father again. Was it strictly his own choice? Or did the father die soon after their meeting? Or were other factors involved? We do not know, of course, and such an ending invites us to speculate.

One final word about plots: the fledgling writer attempting to invent a totally original plot is doomed to failure, and it is no exaggeration to say that there is nothing new under the sun where plots of short stories are concerned. These plots often draw on what psychologist Carl Jung called **archetypes,** universal types of characters and situations that all human beings carry in their unconscious minds. Plots deriving from these archetypes may be found in ancient mythologies, fairy tales, and even in contemporary fiction. Among a few of the most familiar are the triangle plot, a love story involving three people; the quest plot, which is unified around a group of characters on a journey; and the transformation plot, in which a weak or physically unattractive character changes radically in the course of the story. "Reunion" is an example of one of the most widely used of all archetypal plots, the **initiation story.** In a plot of this type the main character, usually a child or adolescent, undergoes an experience (or **rite of passage**) that prepares him or her for adulthood. In this book, such stories as Sarah Orne Jewett's "A White Heron" and Joyce Carol Oates's "Where Are You Going, Where Have You Been?" share the same archetype, although they differ in almost every other respect.

Characterization

Every story hinges on the actions undertaken by its main character, or **protagonist,** a term drawn from ancient Greek tragedy (literally "first debater") that is more useful in discussions of fiction than such misleading terms as hero or heroine. Additionally, stories may contain an opposing character, or **antagonist,** with whom the protagonist is drawn into conflict. In many modern stories, there is little, in any traditional sense, that is heroic about the protagonists; it may be more accurate to use a negative term, **anti-hero,** to designate one who occupies center stage but otherwise seems incapable of fitting the traditional heroic mold. Indeed, modern writers have often been so reluctant to seem didactic in presenting characters who are "moral beacons" that they go to the opposite extreme in presenting protagonists whom we regard with pity or even disgust instead of with admiration.

A character in a short story may be termed either a **flat character** or a **round character,** depending on the depth of detail the writer supplies. In "Reunion," the father is essentially a flat character, rendered with a few quick strokes of the pen and reduced to a single personality trait, his alcoholic rudeness. Flat minor characters in stories are often **stock characters,** stereotypes who may be necessary to advance the plot but otherwise are not deserving of more than the barest outlines of description. Round characters, on the other hand, are given more than one trait, some of which may even seem contradictory, and are explored in depth as the author delves into the character's past and even into his or her unconscious mind. Characters of this type, usually the protagonists of stories, begin to approach the level of complexity that we associate with real human beings.

Development and **motivation** are also important in any consideration of a story's characters. Characters can be termed either **static** or **dynamic,** depending on the degree to which they change in the course of the story. In "Reunion," the father is a static character. His personality was fixed long before the story opens, and Cheever holds out no likelihood that he will ever alter his course. But Charlie does attain some understanding in the course of the story, even if it is at the cost of his own disillusionment with what he wants his father to be. If development in a character is usually clear in a story, then motivation, the reasons the reader is given for a character's actions, may not be so obvious. In many cases, an author will simply tell us what is going on in a character's mind, but in others we are denied access to this level of understanding. Although we can speculate, playing the amateur psychiatrist, about Charlie's father's strange behavior, we are not given any direct insight into his own view of his actions. In some stories, writers may try to plug directly into a character's thoughts by using **interior monologue,** a direct presentation of thought that is somewhat like a soliloquy in drama, or **stream-of-consciousness,** an attempt to duplicate raw sensory data in the same disordered state that the mind receives it. As useful as these devices can be in explaining motivation, they sometimes place excessive demands on readers and are thus comparatively rare.

Description of characters also helps us to understand the author's intent. In real life we are told from an early age not to judge people by external appearance, but in fiction the opposite is more often the case: physical description is invariably a sign of what lurks beneath the surface. Given the brevity of most short stories, these physical details may be minimal but revealing in their lack of particulars. Cheever has Charlie describe his father at first as only "a big, good-looking man." Remarkably, the author here uses his protagonist's sense of smell to make the character vivid: Charlie breathes in "a rich compound of whiskey, after-shave lotion, shoe polish, woolens, and the rankness of a mature male." In that burst of imagery, we may momentarily overlook the most important item in the list, the evidence that Charlie's father has been drinking in the morning.

Other elements may add to our understanding of its characters. Many writers take particular care in naming their characters in such a way as to draw attention to aspects of their personalities. This device (**characternym** is a coined term that is often employed for it) is sometimes obvious; in her story "Good Country People," Flannery O'Connor calls an unscrupulous seducer Manley Pointer, a name that a moment's thought reveals as an outrageous pun. Similarly, actions in the story, such as speech patterns and mannerisms, may also disclose personality traits. A character's misuse of grammar or stilted vocabulary can *show* us a great deal more about background and self-image than a whole page of background information or analysis. Charlie's father's gestures and loud attempts at ordering in various foreign languages grow more embarrassing until his tongue-tied request for two "Bibson Geefeaters" (a "Beefeater Gibson" is a potent martini made from a well-known brand of gin) comes as the punchline to a grotesque joke on himself.

Point of View

When we speak of a politician's **point of view** on an issue, we mean his or her attitude toward it, pro or con. In fiction, however, the term point of view is employed in a specialized sense, referring to the question of *authority* in the story. Every story has a **narrator,** a voice or character that provides the reader with information about and insight into characters and incidents, but in some cases the identity of this voice of authority is not immediately apparent. Being too literal-minded about the matter of point of view is usually a mistake, and we usually have to accept certain **narrative conventions** without questioning them too seriously if we are to enjoy reading stories. Thus, when we finish reading a detective story narrated by the sleuth himself, we should not worry ourselves too much about when such a busy character found time to jot down the events of the story. Similarly, we accept as a convention the fact that a narrator may suddenly jump from simply recording a conversation to telling us what one of its participants is thinking. Very early in our lives we learn how stories are told, just as we have been conditioned to make a mental transition, while watching a movie, when our perspective shifts in the blink of an eye from one character's frightened stare, to the flashing barrel of a gun, to a hand clutching a chest, to another actor's sneer of triumph.

Almost all narrative points of view can be classified as either first person or third person. In **first-person narration,** the narrator is a **participant** in the action. He or she may be either a major character (which is the case with Charlie in "Reunion") or a minor character and may be close to the event in time or distant from it. Although it is never directly stated, the adult Charlie is probably narrating an account of something that happened years before; thus, his repeated phrase about the last time he saw his father has a finality about it that goes far beyond a simple statement like, "The last time I saw my father was a week ago in Grand Central Station." In general, first-person stories may seem more immediate than third-person stories, but they are limited by the simple fact that the narrator must be present at all times and must also have some knowledge of what is going on. If, for example, an attempt had been made to tell "Reunion" from the point of view of one of the waiters, the narrator might have to resort to eavesdropping on Charlie and his father in order to report their circumstances. The ability of the narrator to tell the story accurately is also important. An **unreliable narrator,** either through naïvete, ignorance, or impaired mental processes, relates events in such a distorted manner that the reader, who has come to recognize the narrator's unreliability, must literally turn his reporting on its head to make sense. Imagine how we would read "Reunion" if it had been told from the boozy, self-deluding point of view of Charlie's father.

Third-person narration, by definition, employs a **nonparticipant** narrator, a voice of authority which never reveals its source and is capable of moving from place to place to describe action and report dialogue. In third-person stories, the question of reliability is rarely an issue, but the matter of **omniscience,** the degree to which the "all-knowing" narrator can reveal the thoughts of characters, is. **Total omniscience** means just that—the narrator knows everything about the characters' lives, their pasts, presents, and futures—and may reveal the thoughts of anyone in the story. An **editorial point of view** goes even further, allowing the god-like author to comment directly on the action (also called **authorial intrusion**).

Most contemporary authors avoid total omniscience in short fiction, perhaps sensing that a story's strength is dissipated if more than one perspective is used. Instead, they employ **limited omniscience,** also called **selective omniscience** or the **method of central intelligence,** limiting themselves to the thoughts and perceptions of a single character. This point of view is perhaps the most flexible of all because it allows the writer to compromise between the immediacy of first-person narration and the mobility of third person. A further departure from omniscience is the **dramatic point of view** (also called the **objective point of view**). Here the narrator simply reports dialogue and action with minimal interpretation and no delving into characters' minds. The dramatic point of view, as the name implies, approximates the experience of reading a play; readers are provided only with set descriptions, stage directions, and dialogue, and thus must supply motivations that are based solely on this external evidence.

Technically, other points of view are possible, although they are rarely used. Stories have been told in the second person. Note the use of the imperative verbs and an implied "you" in Lorrie Moore's "How to Become a Writer." A plural point of view also may be employed, but such points of view are difficult to sustain and may quickly prove distracting to readers. Also, there is an unwritten rule that point of view should be consistent throughout a story, although occasionally a writer may utilize multiple perspectives to illustrate how the "truth" of any incident is always relative to the way in which it is witnessed.

Theme

We have already discussed the manner in which fables and other types of didactic literature make their purposes clear by explicitly stating a moral or interpretation at the end of the story. Literary fiction, however, is usually much more subtle in revealing its **theme,** the overall meaning the reader derives from the story. Most of the reading we did as children probably fell into two distinct categories—sheer entertainment or overt didacticism—with very little middle ground. Thus, many readers, coming to serious fiction for the first time, want either to avoid the tedious search for a "message" or to complain: "If the author was trying to say that, then why didn't she just come right out and *say* it?" To further complicate matters, the theoretical manner in which we analyze stories and the preconceptions we bring to bear on them may result in multiple interpretations of meaning. No single statement of theme is likely to be the "correct" one, although it is fair to say that some seem more likely than others.

What, then, is the theme of "Reunion"? A reader insistent on a moral might denounce Charlie's father, inveighing against "demon rum" and its destructive effect on "family values." Another reader, slightly more charitable, might recognize alcoholism as a disease and feel some amount of sympathy for the father. Yet another, perhaps entirely too self-righteous, might fault Charlie for running away from his father, interpreting the older man's actions as a subconscious cry for help. If we investigate Cheever's own troubled biography and note his own serious problems with both parenthood and alcoholism, we may read the story as a psychological confession, with Cheever himself simultaneously playing the roles of father and son. With so many possibilities before us, it is often best to state a story's theme as broadly as possible: "'Reunion,' like most initiation stories, is about growth through loss of innocence. Children have to learn, often through painful experience, that they are not responsible for their parents' well-being, and sometimes they must distance themselves from their parents in order to survive." Such a statement does not encompass every possible nuance of the story's theme, but it does at least provide us with a starting point for arguing about the finer points of Cheever's meaning.

All this is not to say that modern authors are always reticent in revealing their themes. Flannery O'Connor perceives her characters' shortcomings and judges them according to her own Roman Catholic moral standards. Alice Walker has investigated social themes like female genital mutilation in her fiction. Margaret Atwood's feminism is rarely hidden in her stories and poems. Many modern stories are in fact **allegorical tales,** in which the literal events point to a parallel sequence of symbolic ideas. In many stories the literal setting of the story, say a doctor's waiting room or a crowded city bus, is a **microcosm,** a "small world" that reflects the tensions of the larger world outside. Thus, despite their outward sophistication, many of the stories in this anthology reveal their debt to the ancient ethical functions of fables and parables.

Setting

Novelists can lavish pages of prose on details of setting, just as they can *describe* characters down to such minutiae as the contents of their pockets. But short story writers, hemmed in by limitations of space, rarely have such luxury and must ordinarily limit themselves to very selective descriptions of time and place. When a writer like Edgar Allan Poe goes into great detail in his descriptions, it is likely that **atmosphere,** the emotional aura surrounding a certain setting, is more important to him than the actual physical locale.

Setting is simply the time and place of a story, and in most cases the details of description are given to the reader directly by the narrator. A story may employ multiple locations in its different scenes, and its time frame may encompass only a few hours or many years. "Reunion" is a story with relatively few details of setting. Because Cheever wrote his stories almost exclusively for *The New Yorker,* it is not necessary for him to describe the interior of Grand Central Station to an audience doubtless familiar with it, nor do we feel at much of a loss. Similarly, he spends no more than a sentence or two describing each of the restaurants: one has "a lot of horse tack on the walls," one is "Italian," and the other two are not described at all. The time setting is also relatively unimportant here. We know that the action is taking place during the lunch hour on a weekday, probably in the summer, but as far as a more specific time is concerned, we know little or nothing. "Reunion" could be taking place in 2007 or fifty years ago or, for that matter, twenty years from now.

Some stories, however, depend on their **locale** or general setting in time and place much more heavily and thus demand fuller exposition of setting. **Historical fiction** usually pays great attention to the altered landscapes and customs of bygone eras. A writer who carelessly lets an electric alarm clock go off in a story set in the early 1800s has committed an anachronism that may be only slightly more obvious than another writer's use of contemporary slang in the same setting. **Local color fiction** depends heavily on the unique characteristics of a particular area, usually a rural one that is off the beaten path. Such places have become increasingly rare in contemporary America, but the deep South and Alaska still provide locales that possess intrinsic interest. Some writers, like William Faulkner or Flannery O'Connor, first established their reputations as practitioners of **regionalism,** setting most of their work in one particular area or country. A contemporary American writer like Bobbie Ann Mason shows, in virtually every one of the stories in her first collection, her deep roots in her native Kentucky. A South American writer like Gabriel García Márquez continually draws us into the strange world of Colombian villages cut off from the contemporary world, places where past and present, history and folklore, natural and supernatural, seamlessly join in what has been labeled **magic realism.**

Stories contain both specific and general settings. The specific setting is the precise time(s) and place(s) where the action takes place. The general setting of a story, its **enveloping action,** is its sense of the "times" and how its characters interact with events and social currents in the larger world. We have already mentioned how the specific setting of a story often is a microcosm that reflects the doings of society at large. It is impossible to read stories by Flannery O'Connor or Alice Walker and not be made aware of the social changes that have transformed the rural South in the last fifty years. Stories sometimes depend on readers' ability to bring their knowledge of history and culture to bear on the events taking place. In reading a story like Ralph Ellison's "A Party Down at the Square," younger readers may be unaware of the widespread horrors of lynchings in an America that older readers can vividly recall.

Style and Symbol

Style in fiction refers equally to the characteristics of language in a particular story and to the same characteristics in a writer's complete works. The more individual a writer's style is, the easier it is to write a **parody,** or satirical imitation, of it, as the well-publicized annual "Faux Faulkner" and "International Imitation Hemingway" contests attest. A detailed analysis of the style in an individual story might include attention to such matters as diction, sentence structure, punctuation (or the lack thereof), and use of figurative language. In English we usually make a distinction between the differing qualities of words—standard usage versus slang, Latinate versus Germanic vocabulary, abstract versus concrete diction, and so on. While such matters are most meaningful only in the context of an individual story, there is obviously a difference between one character who says, "I have profited to a great degree from the educational benefits of the realm of experience," and another who says, "I graduated from the school of hard knocks." However, in analyzing style we must be sensitive to the literary fashions of periods other than our own; it is senseless to fault Poe for "flowery diction" when comparing his use of language to that of his contemporaries, who may have similarly lush styles. The prevailing fashion in fiction today is for the unadorned starkness of writers like Bobbie Ann Mason and Raymond Carver—what has been disparagingly called "K-Mart realism" by one critic—but one should not be surprised if, in the new century, fashions shift and writers compete to outdo Faulkner at his most ornate.

The style of "Reunion" is, for the most part, straightforward, with few flourishes of vocabulary (if we disregard the foreign phrases) or sentence structure. About the only significant departure from this plain style is in the opening paragraph, where Charlie momentarily rises to a slightly elevated rhetorical plateau: ". . . as soon as I saw him I felt that he was my father, my flesh and blood, my future and my doom." The **tone** of the story, or what we can indirectly determine about the author's own feelings about its events from his choice of words, is also carefully controlled. Cheever avoids the twin pitfalls of sentimentality on the one hand and cynicism on the other by deftly walking an emotional tightrope. After the opening paragraph, at no point does Charlie tell us how he feels; instead, he lets his father's actions speak for themselves. There are points in "Reunion" where we may laugh, but it is an uncomfortable laugh at which we probably feel a little guilty. The range of possible tones available for use in any given story may run through the whole range of human emotions, from outright comedy or satirical contempt to pathos of the most wrenching sort. It may be possible for an unwary reader to fail to appreciate the keen edge of Flannery O'Connor's irony or the profound philosophical skepticism of Ursula Le Guin, but this failure should not be laid at the feet of the writers, who have taken great pains to make their own attitudes clear.

That symbolism in stories is often a troublesome affair for students is indicated by the oft-heard phrase "hidden meanings," as if authors were doing their best to conceal, rather than reveal, the significance of actions and things in their works. Symbolism may occur in any of the elements discussed above: a plot or character or setting may have some symbolic value. There is little heavy symbolism in "Reunion," but if we think about the title, with its suggestions of emotional warmth, and the setting, a busy train station, we can see that Cheever has chosen his title carefully, and it has both ironic and symbolic overtones.

If the details of a plot seem consistently symbolic, with each detail clearly pointing the way to some obvious larger meaning, then we are reading **allegory.** An allegorical reading of Hawthorne's "The Minister's Black Veil" (which he calls a "parable") might focus on the veil as a symbol of human hypocrisy, showing that the story's critique of human behavior is much more important that the intriguing "mystery" of its plot. Many stories do not use symbolism in so schematic a way, however. In a given story, an author may employ a **traditional symbol,** a thing that most members of a culture instantly recognize as possessing a shared symbolic meaning. We may recognize a white gown or a red rose symbolizing, on the one hand, innocence, and on the other, romantic love, without having to think very deeply. Familiarity with an individual author's works may also help us to recognize a **private symbol,** a symbol that the author has made his or her own by repeated use. To cite one example, Flannery O'Connor's use of bursts of bright light generally herald some kind of dawning spiritual revelation in the mind of one of her characters. Another writer may use certain colors, situations, and actions repeatedly; it is hard to read much of Poe's fiction without becoming aware of the personal horror that small, confined spaces represent for the author or his consistent use of *doppelgänger* characters, "doubles" who mirror each other in significant ways. Finally, we may identify an **incidental symbol** in a story. This may be a thing or action that ordinarily would have no deeper meaning but acquires one in a particular story. How can we learn to spot these symbols? Paying close attention to the way an author repeats certain details or otherwise points to their significance is the key. (Repeated words or phrases are called *motifs.*) Deciding what a symbol *means* is often less important than merely realizing that it *exists.* The meaning of incidental symbolism is usually subject to multiple interpretations that do not necessarily contradict one another.

WASHINGTON IRVING ■ (1783–1859)

Irving was born in Manhattan, the son of a prosperous merchant, and began submitting letters to New York newspapers as a teenager, under the pseudonym "Jonathan Oldstyle." After living abroad, Irving returned to New York to study law, entering the bar and completing his first major work, a satirical history of the Dutch colony by Diedrich Knickerbocker, another pseudonym. Returning to England to live at the home of Walter Scott, Irving wrote the tales that comprise The Sketch Book of Geoffrey Crayon Gent., *which included "Rip Van Winkle," a story Irving claimed to have written in a single evening. Determined to continue as a writer, Irving traveled widely in Europe, settling for a time in Spain, where he wrote histories and collected his experiences of Spanish folklore and life in* Tales from the Alhambra. *After diplomatic service in London, he returned to the United States, where he traveled widely, wrote, and became a champion of legislation regulating copyrights. In later life, Irving served as Minister to Spain and published a five-volume biography of his namesake, George Washington. The first American writer to gain an international reputation, Irving was a sophisticated man of the world who never forgot his American roots. In "Rip Van Winkle," a story that most Americans are familiar with whether they have read it or not, Irving drops sly hints throughout that Rip's fantastic explanation for his twenty year's absence may not quite be the whole story of his adventures in the wider world.*

Rip Van Winkle

A Posthumous Writing of Diedrich Knickerbocker

(THE FOLLOWING tale was found among the papers of the late Diedrich Knickerbocker, an old gentleman of New York, who was very curious in the Dutch history of the province, and the manners of the descendants from its primitive settlers. His historical researches, however, did not lie so much among books as among men; for the former are lamentably scanty on his favorite topics; whereas he found the old burghers, and still more their wives, rich in that legendary lore so invaluable to true history. Whenever, therefore, he happened upon a genuine Dutch family, snugly shut up in its low-roofed farmhouse, under a spreading sycamore, he looked upon it as a little clasped volume of black-letter, and studied it with the zeal of a bookworm.

The result of all these researches was a history of the province during the reign of the Dutch governors, which he published some years since. There have been various opinions as to the literary character of his work, and, to tell the truth, it is not a whit better than it should be. Its chief merit is its scrupulous accuracy, which indeed was a little questioned on its first appearance, but has since been completely established; and it is how admitted into all historical collections as a book of unquestionable authority.

The old gentleman died shortly after the publication of his work, and now that he is dead and gone it cannot do much harm to his memory to say that his time might have been much better employed in weightier labors. He, however, was apt to ride his hobby in his own way; and though it did now and then kick up the dust a little in the eyes of his neighbors and grieve the spirit of some friends, for whom he felt the truest deference and affection, yet his errors and follies are remembered "more in sorrow than in anger"; and it begins to be suspected that he never intended to injure or offend. But however his memory may be appreciated by critics, it is still held dear among many folk whose good opinion is well worth having; particularly by certain biscuit bakers, who have gone so far as to imprint his likeness on their New Year cakes, and have thus given him a chance for immortality almost equal to the being stamped on a Waterloo medal or a Queen Anne's farthing.)

> By Woden, God of Saxons,
>
> From whence comes Wensday, that is Wodensday,
>
> Truth is a thing that ever I will keep
>
> Unto thylke day in which I creep into
>
> My sepulchre—
>
> CARTWRIGHT.

Whoever has made a voyage up the Hudson must remember the Catskill Mountains. They are a dismembered branch of the great Appalachian family, and are seen away to the west of the river, swelling up to a noble height, and lording it over the surrounding country. Every change of season, every change of weather, indeed, every hour of the day, produces some change in the magical hues and shapes of these mountains, and they are regarded by all the good wives, far and near, as perfect barometers. When the weather is fair and settled, they are clothed in blue and purple, and print their bold outlines on the clear evening sky; but sometimes, when the rest of the landscape is cloudless, they will gather a hood of gray vapors about their summits, which, in the last rays of the setting sun, will glow and light up like a crown of glory.

At the foot of these fairy mountains the voyager may have descried the light smoke curling up from a village whose shingle roofs gleam among the trees, just where the blue tints of the upland melt away into the fresh green of the nearer landscape. It is a little village of great antiquity, having been founded by some of the Dutch colonists, in the early times of the province, just about the beginning of the government of the good Peter Stuyvesant (may he rest in peace!), and there were some of the houses of the original settlers standing within a few years, with lattice windows, gable fronts surmounted with weathercocks, and built of small yellow bricks brought from Holland.

In that same village, and in one of these very houses (which, to tell the precise truth, was sadly time-worn and weather-beaten), there lived many years since, while the country was yet a province of Great Britain, a simple, good-natured fellow, of the name of Rip Van Winkle. He was a descendant of the Van Winkles who figured so gallantly in the chivalrous days of Peter Stuyvesant, and accompanied him to the siege of Fort Christina. He inherited, however, but little of the martial character of his ancestors. I have observed that he was a simple, good-natured man; he was, moreover, a kind neighbor and an obedient, henpecked husband. Indeed, to the latter circumstance might be owing that meekness of spirit which gained him such universal popularity; for those men are most apt to be obsequious and conciliating abroad who are under the discipline of shrews at home. Their tempers, doubtless, are rendered pliant and malleable in the fiery furnace of domestic tribulation, and a curtain lecture is worth all the sermons in the world for teaching the virtues of patience and long-suffering. A termagant wife may, therefore, in some respects, be considered a tolerable blessing; and if so, Rip Van Winkle was thrice blessed.

Certain it is that he was a great favorite among all the good wives of the village, who, as usual with the amiable sex, took his part in all family squabbles, and never failed, whenever they talked those matters over in their evening gossipings, to lay all the blame on Dame Van Winkle. The children of the village, too, would shout with joy whenever he approached. He assisted at their sports, made their playthings, taught them to fly kites and shoot marbles, and told them long stories of ghosts, witches, and Indians. Whenever he went dodging about the village, he was surrounded by a troop of them, hanging on his skirts, clambering on his back, and playing a thousand tricks on him with impunity; and not a dog would bark at him throughout the neighborhood.

The great error in Rip's composition was an insuperable aversion to all kinds of profitable labor. It could not be from the want of assiduity or perseverance; for he would sit on a wet rock, with a rod as long and heavy as a Tartar's lance, and fish all day without a murmur, even though he should not be encouraged by a single nibble. He would carry a fowling piece on his shoulder, for hours together, trudging through woods and swamps, and up hill and down dale, to shoot a few squirrels or wild pigeons. He would never even refuse to assist a neighbor in the roughest toil, and was a foremost man at all country frolics for husking Indian corn, or building stone fences. The women of the village, too, used to employ him to run their errands, and to do such little odd jobs as their less obliging husbands would not do for them; in a word, Rip was ready to attend to anybody's business but his own; but as to doing family duty, and keeping his farm in order, it was impossible.

In fact, he declared it was of no use to work on his farm; it was the most pestilent little piece of ground in the whole country; everything about it went wrong, and would go wrong, in spite of him. His fences were continually falling to pieces; his cow would either go astray or get among the cabbages; weeds were sure to grow quicker in his fields than anywhere else; the rain always made a point of setting in just as he had some outdoor work to do; so that though his patrimonial estate had dwindled away under his management, acre by acre, until there was little more left than a mere patch of Indian corn and potatoes, yet it was the worst-conditioned farm in the neighborhood.

His children, too, were as ragged and wild as if they belonged to nobody. His son Rip, an urchin begotten in his own likeness, promised to inherit the habits, with the old clothes of his father. He was generally seen trooping like a colt at his mother's heels, equipped in a pair of his father's cast-off galligaskins, which he had much ado to hold up with one hand, as a fine lady does her train in bad weather.

Rip Van Winkle, however, was one of those happy mortals, of foolish, well-oiled dispositions, who take the world easy, eat white bread or brown, whichever can be got with least thought or trouble, and would rather starve on a penny than work for a pound. If left to himself, he would have whistled life away, in perfect contentment; but his wife kept continually dinning in his ears about his idleness, his carelessness, and the ruin he was bringing on his family. Morning, noon, and night, her tongue was incessantly going, and everything he said or did was sure to produce a torrent of household eloquence. Rip had but one way of replying to all lectures of the kind, and that, by frequent use, had grown into a habit. He shrugged his shoulders, shook his head, cast up his eyes, but said nothing. This, however, always provoked a fresh volley from his wife, so that he was fain to draw off his forces, and take to the outside of the house—the only side which, in truth, belongs to a henpecked husband.

Rip's sole domestic adherent was his dog Wolf, who was as much henpecked as his master; for Dame Van Winkle regarded them as companions in idleness, and even looked upon Wolf with an evil eye, as the cause of his master's so often going astray. True it is, in all points of spirit befitting an honorable dog, he was as courageous an animal as ever scoured the woods—but what courage can withstand the everduring and all-besetting terrors of a woman's tongue? The moment Wolf entered the house his crest fell, his tail drooped to the ground, or curled between his legs; he sneaked about with a gallows air, casting many a sidelong glance at Dame Van Winkle, and at the least flourish of a broomstick or ladle would fly to the door with yelping precipitation.

Times grew worse and worse with Rip Van Winkle as years of matrimony rolled on; a tart temper never mellows with age, and a sharp tongue is the only edged tool that grows keener by constant use. For a long while he used to console himself, when driven from home, by frequenting a kind of perpetual club of the sages, philosophers, and other idle personages of the village, which held its sessions on a bench before a small inn, designated by a rubicund portrait of his majesty George the Third. Here they used to sit in the shade, of a long lazy summer's day, talking listlessly over village gossip, or telling endless sleepy stories about nothing. But it would have been worth any statesman's money to have heard the profound discussions which sometimes took place, when by chance an old newspaper fell into their hands, from some passing traveler. How solemnly they would listen to the contents, as drawled out by Derrick Van Bummel, the schoolmaster, a dapper, learned little man, who was not to be daunted by the most gigantic word in the dictionary; and how sagely they would deliberate upon public events some months after they had taken place.

The opinions of this junto were completely controlled by Nicholas Vedder, a patriarch of the village, and landlord of the inn, at the door of which he took his seat from morning till night, just moving sufficiently to avoid the sun, and keep in the shade of a large tree; so that the neighbors could tell the hour by his movements as accurately as by a sun-dial. It is true, he was rarely heard to speak, but smoked his pipe incessantly. His adherents, however (for every great man has his adherents), perfectly understood him, and knew how to gather his opinions. When anything that was read or related displeased him, he was observed to smoke his pipe vehemently, and send forth short, frequent, and angry puffs; but when pleased, he would inhale the smoke slowly and tranquilly, and emit it in light and placid clouds, and sometimes taking the pipe from his mouth, and letting the fragrant vapor curl about his nose, would gravely nod his head in token of perfect approbation.

From even this stronghold the unlucky Rip was at length routed by his termagant wife, who would suddenly break in upon the tranquillity of the assemblage, and call the members all to nought; nor was that august personage, Nicholas Vedder himself, sacred from the daring tongue of this terrible virago, who charged him outright with encouraging her husband in habits of idleness.

Poor Rip was at last reduced almost to despair; and his only alternative, to escape from the labor of the farm and clamor of his wife, was to take gun in hand and stroll away into the woods. Here he would sometimes seat himself at the foot of a tree, and share the contents of his wallet with Wolf, with whom he sympathized as a fellow-sufferer in persecution. "Poor Wolf," he would say, "thy mistress leads thee a dog's life of it; but never mind, my lad, while I live thou shalt never want a friend to stand by thee!" Wolf would wag his tail, look wistfully in his master's face, and if dogs can feel pity, I verily believe he reciprocated the sentiment with all his heart.

In a long ramble of the kind on a fine autumnal day, Rip had unconsciously scrambled to one of the highest parts of the Catskill Mountains. He was after his favorite sport of squirrel shooting, and the still solitudes had echoed and reëchoed with the reports of his gun. Panting and fatigued, he threw himself, late in the afternoon, on a green knoll, covered with mountain herbage, that crowned the brow of a precipice. From an opening between the trees he could overlook all the lower country for many a mile of rich woodland. He saw at a distance the lordly Hudson, far, far below him, moving on its silent but majestic course, the reflection of a purple cloud, or the sail of a lagging bark, here and there sleeping on its glassy bosom, and at last losing itself in the blue highlands.

On the other side he looked down into a deep mountain glen, wild, lonely, and shagged, the bottom filled with fragments from the impending cliffs, and scarcely lighted by the reflected rays of the setting sun. For some time Rip lay musing on this scene; evening was gradually advancing; the mountains began to throw their long blue shadows over the valleys; he saw that it would be dark long before he could reach the village, and he heaved a heavy sigh when he thought of encountering the terrors of Dame Van Winkle.

As he was about to descend, he heard a voice from a distance, hallooing, "Rip Van Winkle! Rip Van Winkle!" He looked around, but could see nothing but a crow winging its solitary flight across the mountain. He thought his fancy must have deceived him, and turned again to descend, when he heard the same cry ring through the still evening air: "Rip Van Winkle! Rip Van Winkle!"—at the same time Wolf bristled up his back, and giving a low growl, skulked to his master's side, looking fearfully down into the glen. Rip now felt a vague apprehension stealing over him; he looked anxiously in the same direction, and perceived a strange figure slowly toiling up the rocks, and bending under the weight of something he carried on his back. He was surprised to see any human being in this lonely and unfrequented place, but supposing it to be some one of the neighborhood in need of assistance, he hastened down to yield it.

On nearer approach, he was still more surprised at the singularity of the stranger's appearance. He was a short, square-built old fellow, with thick bushy hair, and a grizzled beard. His dress was of the antique Dutch fashion—a cloth jerkin strapped around the waist—several pair of breeches, the outer one of ample volume, decorated with rows of buttons down the sides, and bunches at the knees. He bore on his shoulders a stout keg, that seemed full of liquor, and made signs for Rip to approach and assist him with the load. Though rather shy and distrustful of this new acquaintance, Rip complied with his usual alacrity, and mutually relieving one another, they clambered up a narrow gully, apparently the dry bed of a mountain torrent. As they ascended, Rip every now and then heard long rolling peals, like distant thunder, that seemed to issue out of a deep ravine, or rather cleft between lofty rocks, toward which their rugged path conducted. He paused for an instant, but supposing it to be the muttering of one of those transient thunder showers which often take place in mountain heights, he proceeded. Passing through the ravine, they came to a hollow, like a small amphitheater, surrounded by perpendicular precipices, over the brinks of which impending trees shot their branches, so that you only caught glimpses of the azure sky and the bright evening cloud. During the whole time, Rip and his companion had labored on in silence; for though the former marveled greatly what could be the object of carrying a keg of liquor up this wild mountain, yet there was something strange and incomprehensible about the unknown that inspired awe and checked familiarity.

On entering the amphitheater, new objects of wonder presented themselves. On a level spot in the center was a company of odd-looking personages playing at ninepins. They were dressed in a quaint, outlandish fashion: some wore short doublets, others jerkins, with long knives in their belts, and most had enormous breeches, of similar style with that of the guide's. Their visages, too, were peculiar: one had a large head, broad face, and small, piggish eyes; the face of another seemed to consist entirely of nose, and was surmounted by a white sugar-loaf hat set off with a little red cock's tail. They all had beards, of various shapes and colors. There was one who seemed to be the commander. He was a stout old gentleman, with a weather-beaten countenance; he wore a laced doublet, broad belt and hanger, high-crowned hat and feather, red stockings, and high-heeled shoes, with roses in them. The whole group reminded Rip of the figures in an old Flemish painting, in the parlor of Dominie Van Schaick, the village parson, and which had been brought over from Holland at the time of the settlement.

What seemed particularly odd to Rip, was that though these folks were evidently amusing themselves, yet they maintained the gravest faces, the most mysterious silence, and were, withal, the most melancholy party of pleasure he had ever witnessed. Nothing interrupted the stillness of the scene but the noise of the balls, which, whenever they were rolled, echoed along the mountains like rumbling peals of thunder.

As Rip and his companion approached them, they suddenly desisted from their play, and stared at him with such fixed statue-like gaze, and such strange, uncouth, lack-luster countenances, that his heart turned within him, and his knees smote together. His companion now emptied the contents of the keg into large flagons, and made signs to him to wait upon the company. He obeyed with fear and trembling; they quaffed the liquor in profound silence, and then returned to their game.

By degrees, Rip's awe and apprehension subsided. He even ventured, when no eye was fixed upon him, to taste the beverage, which he found had much of the flavor of excellent Hollands. He was naturally a thirsty soul, and was soon tempted to repeat the draught. One taste provoked another, and he reiterated his visits to the flagon so often, that at length his senses were overpowered, his eyes swam in his head, his head gradually declined, and he fell into a deep sleep.

On awaking, he found himself on the green knoll from whence he had first seen the old man of the glen. He rubbed his eyes—it was a bright sunny morning. The birds were hopping and twittering among the bushes, and the eagle was wheeling aloft and breasting the pure mountain breeze. "Surely," thought Rip, "I have not slept here all night." He recalled the occurrences before he fell asleep. The strange man with a keg of liquor—the mountain ravine—the wild retreat among the rocks—the woe-begone party at ninepins—the flagon—"Oh! that flagon! that wicked flagon!" thought Rip—"what excuse shall I make to Dame Van Winkle?"

He looked round for his gun, but in place of the clean, well-oiled fowling piece, he found an old firelock lying by him, the barrel incrusted with rust, the lock falling off, and the stock worm-eaten. He now suspected that the grave roysters of the mountain had put a trick upon him, and having dosed him with liquor, had robbed him of his gun. Wolf, too, had disappeared, but he might have strayed away after a squirrel or partridge. He whistled after him, shouted his name, but all in vain; the echoes repeated his whistle and shout, but no dog was to be seen.

He determined to revisit the scene of the last evening's gambol, and if he met with any of the party, to demand his dog and gun. As he rose to walk, he found himself stiff in the joints, and wanting in his usual activity. "These mountain beds do not agree with me," thought Rip, "and if this frolic should lay me up with a fit of the rheumatism, I shall have a blessed time with Dame Van Winkle." With some difficulty he got down into the glen; he found the gully up which he and his companion had ascended the preceding evening; but to his astonishment a mountain stream was now foaming down it, leaping from rock to rock, and filling the glen with babbling murmurs. He, however, made shift to scramble up its sides, working his toilsome way through thickets of birch, sassafras, and witch-hazel, and sometimes tripped up or entangled by the wild grape vines that twisted their coils and tendrils from tree to tree, and spread a kind of network in his path.

At length he reached to where the ravine had opened through the cliffs to the amphitheater; but no traces of such opening remained. The rocks presented a high, impenetrable wall, over which the torrent came tumbling in a sheet of feathery foam, and fell into a broad, deep basin, black from the shadows of the surrounding forest. Here, then, poor Rip was brought to a stand. He again called and whistled after his dog; he was only answered by the cawing of a flock of idle crows, sporting high in air about a dry tree that overhung a sunny precipice; and who, secure in their elevation, seemed to look down and scoff at the poor man's perplexities. What was to be done? the morning was passing away, and Rip felt famished for want of his breakfast. He grieved to give up his dog and gun; he dreaded to meet his wife; but it would not do to starve among the mountains. He shook his head, shouldered the rusty firelock, and, with a heart full of trouble and anxiety, turned his steps homeward.

As he approached the village, he met a number of people, but none whom he knew, which somewhat surprised him, for he had thought himself acquainted with every one in the country round. Their dress, too, was of a different fashion from that to which he was accustomed. They all stared at him with equal marks of surprise, and whenever they cast their eyes upon him, invariably stroked their chins. The constant recurrence of this gesture induced Rip, involuntarily, to do the same, when, to his astonishment, he found his beard had grown a foot long!

He had now entered the skirts of the village. A troop of strange children ran at his heels, hooting after him, and pointing at his gray beard. The dogs, too, none of which he recognized for his old acquaintances, barked at him as he passed. The very village was altered: it was larger and more populous. There were rows of houses which he had never seen before, and those which had been his familiar haunts had disappeared. Strange names were over the doors—strange faces at the windows—everything was strange. His mind now began to misgive him; he doubted whether both he and the world around him were not bewitched. Surely this was his native village, which he had left but the day before. There stood the Catskill Mountains—there ran the silver Hudson at a distance—there was every hill and dale precisely as it had always been—Rip was sorely perplexed—"That flagon last night," thought he, "has addled my poor head sadly!"

It was with some difficulty he found the way to his own house, which he approached with silent awe, expecting every moment to hear the shrill voice of Dame Van Winkle. He found the house gone to decay—the roof fallen in, the windows shattered, and the doors off the hinges. A half-starved dog, that looked like Wolf, was skulking about it. Rip called him by name, but the cur snarled, showed his teeth, and passed on. This was an unkind cut indeed—"My very dog," sighed poor Rip, "has forgotten me!"

He entered the house, which, to tell the truth, Dame Van Winkle had always kept in neat order. It was empty, forlorn, and apparently abandoned. This desolateness overcame all his connubial fears—he called loudly for his wife and children—the lonely chambers rung for a moment with his voice, and then all again was silence.

He now hurried forth, and hastened to his old resort, the little village inn—but it too was gone. A large rickety wooden building stood in its place, with great gaping windows, some of them broken, and mended with old hats and petticoats, and over the door was painted, "The Union Hotel, by Jonathan Doolittle." Instead of the great tree which used to shelter the quiet little Dutch inn of yore, there now was reared a tall naked pole, with something on the top that looked like a red nightcap, and from it was fluttering a flag, on which was a singular assemblage of stars and stripes—all this was strange and incomprehensible. He recognized on the sign, however, the ruby face of King

George, under which he had smoked so many a peaceful pipe, but even this was singularly metamorphosed. The red coat was changed for one of blue and buff, a sword was stuck in the hand instead of a scepter, the head was decorated with a cocked hat, and underneath was painted in large characters, GENERAL WASHINGTON.

There was, as usual, a crowd of folk about the door, but none whom Rip recollected. The very character of the people seemed changed. There was a busy, bustling, disputatious tone about it, instead of the accustomed phlegm and drowsy tranquillity. He looked in vain for the sage Nicholas Vedder, with his broad face, double chin, and fair long pipe, uttering clouds of tobacco smoke instead of idle speeches; or Van Bummel, the schoolmaster, doling forth the contents of an ancient newspaper. In place of these, a lean, bilious-looking fellow, with his pockets full of handbills, was haranguing vehemently about rights of citizens—election—members of Congress—liberty—Bunker's Hill— heroes of '76—and other words, that were a perfect Babylonish jargon to the bewildered Van Winkle.

The appearance of Rip, with his long grizzled beard, his rusty fowling piece, his uncouth dress, and the army of women and children that had gathered at his heels, soon attracted the attention of the tavern politicians. They crowded around him, eying him from head to foot, with great curiosity. The orator bustled up to him, and drawing him partly aside, inquired "on which side he voted?" Rip stared in vacant stupidity. Another short but busy little fellow pulled him by the arm, and raising on tiptoe, inquired in his ear, "whether he was Federal or Democrat." Rip was equally at a loss to comprehend the question; when a knowing, self-important old gentleman, in a sharp cocked hat, made his way through the crowd, putting them to the right and left with his elbows as he passed, and planting himself before Van Winkle, with one arm akimbo, the other resting on his cane, his keen eyes and sharp hat penetrating, as it were, into his very soul, demanded, in an austere tone, "what brought him to the election with a gun on his shoulder, and a mob at his heels, and whether he meant to breed a riot in the village?" "Alas! gentlemen," cried Rip, somewhat dismayed, "I am a poor quiet man, a native of the place, and a loyal subject of the king, God bless him!"

Here a general shout burst from the bystanders—"A Tory! a Tory! a spy! a refugee! hustle him! away with him!" It was with great difficulty that the self-important man in the cocked hat restored order; and having assumed a tenfold austerity of brow, demanded again of the unknown culprit, what he came there for, and whom he was seeking. The poor man humbly assured him that he meant no harm; but merely came there in search of some of his neighbors, who used to keep about the tavern.

"Well—who are they?—name them."

Rip bethought himself a moment, and then inquired, "Where's Nicholas Vedder?"

There was silence for a little while, when an old man replied in a thin, piping voice, "Nicholas Vedder? why, he is dead and gone these eighteen years! There was a wooden tombstone in the churchyard that used to tell all about him, but that's rotted and gone, too."

"Where's Brom Dutcher?"

"Oh, he went off to the army in the beginning of the war; some say he was killed at the battle of Stony Point—others say he was drowned in a squall, at the foot of Antony's Nose. I don't know—he never came back again."

"Where's Van Bummel, the schoolmaster?"

"He went off to the wars, too, was a great militia general, and is now in Congress."

Rip's heart died away, at hearing of these sad changes in his home and friends, and finding himself thus alone in the world. Every answer puzzled him, too, by treating of such enormous lapses of time, and of matters which he could not understand: war—Congress—Stony Point!—he had no courage to ask after any more friends, but cried out in despair, "Does nobody here know Rip Van Winkle?"

"Oh, Rip Van Winkle!" exclaimed two or three, "Oh, to be sure! that's Rip Van Winkle yonder, leaning against the tree."

Rip looked, and beheld a precise counterpart of himself, as he went up the mountain: apparently as lazy, and certainly as ragged. The poor fellow was now completely confounded. He doubted his own identity, and whether he was himself or another man. In the midst of his bewilderment, the man in the cocked hat demanded who he was, and what was his name?

"God knows," exclaimed he, at his wit's end; "I'm not myself—I'm somebody else—that's me yonder—no—that's somebody else, got into my shoes—I was myself last night, but I fell asleep on the mountain, and they've changed my gun, and everything's changed, and I'm changed, and I can't tell what's my name, or who I am!"

The bystanders began now to look at each other, nod, wink significantly, and tap their fingers against their foreheads. There was a whisper, also, about securing the gun, and keeping the old fellow from doing mischief; at the very suggestion of which, the self-important man in the cocked hat retired with some precipitation. At this critical moment a fresh, likely woman pressed through the throng to get a peep at the gray-bearded man. She had a chubby child in her arms, which, frightened at his looks, began to cry. "Hush, Rip," cried she, "hush, you little fool, the old man won't hurt you." The name of the child, the air of the mother, the tone of her voice, all awakened a train of recollections in his mind. "What is your name, my good woman?" asked he.

"Judith Gardenier."

"And your father's name?"

"Ah, poor man, his name was Rip Van Winkle; it's twenty years since he went away from home with his gun, and never has been heard of since—his dog came home without him; but whether he shot himself, or was carried away by the Indians, nobody can tell. I was then but a little girl."

Rip had but one question more to ask; but he put it with a faltering voice:—

"Where's your mother?"

"Oh, she too had died but a short time since; she broke a blood vessel in a fit of passion at a New England peddler."

There was a drop of comfort, at least, in this intelligence. The honest man could contain himself no longer.—He caught his daughter and her child in his arms.—"I am your father!" cried he—"Young Rip Van Winkle once—old Rip Van Winkle now!—Does nobody know poor Rip Van Winkle!"

All stood amazed, until an old woman, tottering out from among the crowd, put her hand to her brow, and peering under it in his face for a moment, exclaimed, "Sure enough! it is Rip Van Winkle—it is himself. Welcome home again, old neighbor.—Why, where have you been these twenty long years?"

Rip's story was soon told, for the whole twenty years had been to him but as one night. The neighbors stared when they heard it; some where seen to wink at each other, and put their tongues in their cheeks; and the self-important man in the cocked hat, who, when the alarm was over, had returned to the field, screwed down the corners of his mouth, and shook his head—upon which there was a general shaking of the head throughout the assemblage.

It was determined, however, to take the opinion of old Peter Vanderdonk, who was seen slowly advancing up the road. He was a descendant of the historian of that name, who wrote one of the earliest accounts of the province. Peter was the most ancient inhabitant of the village, and well versed in all the wonderful events and traditions of the neighborhood. He recollected Rip at once, and corroborated his story in the most satisfactory manner. He assured the company that it was a fact, handed down from his ancestor the historian, that the Catskill Mountains had always been haunted by strange beings. That it was affirmed that the great Hendrick Hudson, the first discoverer of the river and country, kept a kind of vigil there every twenty years, with his crew of the *Half-Moon*, being permitted in this way to revisit the scenes of his enterprise, and keep a guardian eye upon the river, and the great city called by his name. That his father had once seen them in their old Dutch dresses playing at ninepins in a hollow of the mountain; and that he himself had heard, one summer afternoon, the sound of their balls, like long peals of thunder.

To make a long story short, the company broke up, and returned to the more important concerns of the election. Rip's daughter took him home to live with her; she had a snug, well-furnished house, and a stout cheery farmer for a husband, whom Rip recollected for one of the urchins that used to climb upon his back. As to Rip's son and heir, who was the ditto of himself, seen leaning against the tree, he was employed to work on the farm; but evinced an hereditary disposition to attend to anything else but his business.

Rip now resumed his old walks and habits; he soon found many of his former cronies, though all rather the worse for the wear and tear of time; and preferred making friends among the rising generation, with whom he soon grew into great favor.

Having nothing to do at home, and being arrived at that happy age when a man can do nothing with impunity, he took his place once more on the bench, at the inn door, and was reverenced as one of the patriarchs of the village, and a chronicle of the old times "before the war." It was some time before he could get into the regular track of gossip, or could be made to comprehend the strange events that had taken place during his torpor. How that there had been a revolutionary war—that the country had thrown off the yoke of old England—and that, instead of being a subject of his Majesty, George III, he was now a free citizen of the United States. Rip, in fact, was no politician; the changes of states and empires made but little impression on him; but there was one species of despotism under which he had long groaned, and that was—petticoat government; happily, that was at an end; he had got his neck out of the yoke of matrimony, and could go in and out whenever he pleased, without dreading the tyranny of Dame Van Winkle. Whenever her name was mentioned, however, he shook his head, shrugged his shoulders, and cast up his eyes; which might pass either for an expression of resignation to his fate, or joy at his deliverance.

He used to tell his story to every stranger that arrived at Dr. Doolittle's hotel. He was observed, at first, to vary on some points every time he told it, which was, doubtless, owing to his having so recently awaked. It at last settled down precisely to the tale I have related, and not a man, woman, or child in the neighborhood but knew it by heart. Some always pretended to doubt the reality of it, and insisted that Rip had been out of his head, and this was one point on which he always remained flighty. The old Dutch inhabitants, however, almost universally gave it full credit. Even to this day they never hear a thunderstorm of a summer afternoon, about the Catskills, but they say Hendrick Hudson and his crew are at their game of ninepins; and it is a common wish of all henpecked husbands in the neighborhood, when life hangs heavy on their hands, that they might have a quieting draught out of Rip Van Winkle's flagon.

NOTE.—The foregoing tale, one would suspect, had been suggested to Mr. Knickerbocker by a little German superstition about the Emperor Frederick and the Kypphauser Mountain; the subjoined note, however, which he had appended to the tale, shows that it is an absolute fact, narrated with his usual fidelity.

"The story of Rip Van Winkle may seem incredible to many, but nevertheless I give it my full belief, for I know the vicinity of our old Dutch settlements to have been very subject to marvelous events and appearances. Indeed, I have heard many stranger stories than this, in the villages along the Hudson; all of which were too well authenticated to admit of a doubt. I have even talked with Rip Van Winkle myself, who, when last I saw him, was a very venerable old man, and so perfectly rational and consistent on every other point, that I think no conscientious person could refuse to take this into the bargain; nay, I have seen a certificate on the subject taken before a country justice and signed with a cross, in the justice's own handwriting. The story, therefore, is beyond the possibility of a doubt.

"D. K."

POSTSCRIPT 1.—The following are traveling notes from a memorandum book of Mr. Knickerbocker:—

The Kaatsberg, or Catskill Mountains, have always been a region full of fable. The Indians considered them the abode of spirits, who influenced the weather, spreading sunshine or clouds over the landscape, and sending good or bad hunting seasons. They were ruled by an old squaw spirit, said to be their mother. She dwelt on the highest peak of the Catskills, and had charge of the doors of day and night to open and shut them at the proper hour. She hung up the new moon in the skies, and cut up the old ones into stars. In times of drought, if properly propitiated, she would spin light summer clouds out of cobwebs and morning dew, and send them off from the crest of the mountain, flake after flake, like flakes of carded cotton, to float in the air; until, dissolved by the heat of the sun, they would fall in gentle showers, causing the grass to spring, the fruits to ripen, and the corn to grow an inch an hour. If displeased, however, she would brew up clouds black as ink, sitting in the midst of them like a bottle-bellied spider in the midst of its web; and when these clouds broke, woe betide the valleys!

In old times, say the Indian traditions, there was a kind of Manitou or Spirit, who kept about the wildest recesses of the Catskill Mountains, and took a mischievous pleasure in wreaking all kinds of evils and vexations upon the red men. Sometimes he would assume the form of a bear, a panther, or a deer, lead the bewildered hunter a weary chase through tangled forests and among ragged rocks; and then spring off with a loud ho! ho! leaving him aghast on the brink of a beetling precipice or raging torrent.

The favorite abode of this Manitou is still shown. It is a great rock or cliff on the loneliest part of the mountains, and, from the flowering vines which clamber about it, and the wild flowers which abound in its neighborhood, is known by the name of the Garden Rock. Near the foot of it is a small lake, the haunt of the solitary bittern, with water snakes basking in the sun on the leaves of the pond lilies which lie on the surface. This place was held in great awe by the Indians, insomuch that the boldest hunter would not pursue his game within its precincts. Once upon a time, however, a hunter who had lost his way, penetrated to the Garden Rock, where he beheld a number of gourds placed in the crotches of trees. One of these he seized, and made off with it, but in the hurry of his retreat he let it fall among the rocks, when a great stream gushed forth, which washed him away and swept him down precipices, where he was dashed to pieces, and the stream made its way to the Hudson, and continues to flow to the present day; being the identical stream known by the name of Kaaterskill.

NATHANIEL HAWTHORNE ■ (1804–1864)

Nathaniel Hawthorne was born in Salem, Massachusetts, and could trace his heritage back to the earliest settlers of New England. He attended Bowdoin College, where his schoolmates included Henry Wadsworth Longfellow and future president Franklin Pierce, for whom Hawthorne later wrote an official campaign biography. For twelve years after his 1825 graduation, Hawthorne lived at his parents' home, devoting himself solely to learning the craft of writing. An early novel, Fanshawe *(1828), attracted no attention, but a collection of short stories,* Twice-Told Tales *(1837), was the subject of an enthusiastic review by Edgar Allan Poe (see page 4 in "Introduction"). Hawthorne traveled in Europe in his later years and served as American consul at Liverpool during the Pierce administration. Unlike his friend Ralph Waldo Emerson, whose optimism was a constant in his transcendentalist credo, Hawthorne was a moralist who did not shrink from depicting the dark side of human nature, and his often painful examinations of American history and conscience have set the tone for many subsequent generations of writers. His ambivalent attitude toward his Puritan ancestors' religious beliefs (one of his forebears, John Hathorne, was a magistrate who assisted the prosecution during the infamous Salem witch trials) supplied material for his novel* The Scarlet Letter *(1850) and many of his short stories. "The Minister's Black Veil" was based, to some degree, on the life of the Rev. Joseph Moody, a Maine clergyman who covered his face after accidentally shooting a friend. A descendant, contemporary writer Rick Moody, wrote* The Black Veil: A Memoir with Digressions *(2002), detailing his fascination with his ancestor's story.*

The Minister's Black Veil

A Parable

The sexton stood in the porch of Milford meeting-house, pulling busily at the bell-rope. The old people of the village came stooping along the street. Children, with bright faces, tripped merrily beside their parents, or mimicked a graver gait, in the conscious dignity of their Sunday clothes. Spruce bachelors looked sidelong at the pretty maidens, and fancied that the Sabbath sunshine made them prettier than on week days. When the throng had mostly streamed into the porch, the sexton began to toll the bell, keeping his eye on the Reverend Mr. Hooper's door. The first glimpse of the clergyman's figure was the signal for the bell to cease its summons.

"But what has good Parson Hooper got upon his face?" cried the sexton in astonishment.

All within hearing immediately turned about, and beheld the semblance of Mr. Hooper, pacing slowly his meditative way towards the meeting-house. With one accord they started, expressing more wonder than if some strange minister were coming to dust the cushions of Mr. Hooper's pulpit.

"Are you sure it is our parson?" inquired Goodman Gray of the sexton.

"Of a certainty it is good Mr. Hooper," replied the sexton. "He was to have exchanged pulpits with Parson Shute, of Westbury; but Parson Shute sent to excuse himself yesterday, being to preach a funeral sermon."

The cause of so much amazement may appear sufficiently slight. Mr. Hooper, a gentlemanly person, of about thirty, though still a bachelor, was dressed with due clerical neatness, as if a careful wife had starched his band, and brushed the weekly dust from his Sunday's garb. There was but one thing remarkable in his appearance. Swathed about his forehead, and hanging down over his face, so low as to be shaken by his breath, Mr. Hooper had on a black veil. On a nearer view it seemed to consist of two folds of crape, which entirely concealed his features, except the mouth and chin, but probably did not intercept his sight, further than to give a darkened aspect to all living and inanimate things. With this gloomy shade before him, good Mr. Hooper walked onward, at a slow and quiet pace, stooping somewhat, and looking on the ground, as is customary with abstracted men, yet nodding kindly to those of his parishioners who still waited on the meeting-house steps. But so wonder-struck were they that his greeting hardly met with a return.

"I can't really feel as if good Mr. Hooper's face was behind that piece of crape," said the sexton.

"I don't like it," muttered an old woman, as she hobbled into the meeting-house. "He has changed himself into something awful, only by hiding his face."

"Our parson has gone mad!" cried Goodman Gray, following him across the threshold.

A rumor of some unaccountable phenomenon had preceded Mr. Hooper into the meeting-house, and set all the congregation astir. Few could refrain from twisting their heads towards the door; many stood upright, and turned directly about; while several little boys clambered upon the seats, and came down again with a terrible racket. There was a general bustle, a rustling of the women's gowns and shuffling of the men's feet, greatly at variance with that hushed repose which should attend the entrance of the minister. But Mr. Hooper appeared not to notice the perturbation of his people. He entered with an almost noiseless step, bent his head mildly to the pews on each side, and bowed as he passed his oldest parishioner, a white-haired great-grandsire, who occupied an arm-chair in the centre of the aisle. It was strange to observe how slowly this venerable man became conscious of something singular in the appearance of his pastor. He seemed not fully to partake of the prevailing wonder, till Mr. Hooper had ascended the stairs, and showed himself in the pulpit, face to face with his congregation, except for the black veil. That mysterious emblem was never once withdrawn. It shook with his measured breath, as he gave out the psalm; it threw its obscurity between him and the holy page, as he read the Scriptures; and while he prayed, the veil lay heavily on his uplifted countenance. Did he seek to hide it from the dread Being whom he was addressing?

Such was the effect of this simple piece of crape, that more than one woman of delicate nerves was forced to leave the meeting-house. Yet perhaps the pale-faced congregation was almost as fearful a sight to the minister, as his black veil to them.

Mr. Hooper had the reputation of a good preacher, but not an energetic one: he strove to win his people heavenward by mild, persuasive influences, rather than to drive them thither by the thunders of the Word. The sermon which he now delivered was marked by the same characteristics of style and manner as the general series of his pulpit oratory. But there was something, either in the sentiment of the discourse itself, or in the imagination of the auditors, which made it greatly the most powerful effort that they had ever heard from their pastor's lips. It was tinged, rather more darkly than usual, with the gentle gloom of Mr. Hooper's temperament. The subject had reference to secret sin, and those sad mysteries which we hide from our nearest and dearest, and would fain conceal from our own consciousness, even forgetting that the Omniscient can detect them. A subtle power was breathed into his words. Each member of the congregation, the most innocent girl, and the man of hardened breast, felt as if the preacher had crept upon them, behind his awful veil, and discovered their hoarded iniquity of deed or thought. Many spread their clasped hands on their bosoms. There was nothing terrible in what Mr. Hooper said, at least, no violence; and yet, with every tremor of his melancholy voice, the hearers quaked. An unsought pathos came hand in hand with awe. So sensible were the audience of some unwonted attribute in their minister, that they longed for a breath of wind to blow aside the veil, almost believing that a stranger's visage would be discovered, though the form, gesture, and voice were those of Mr. Hooper.

At the close of the services, the people hurried out with indecorous confusion, eager to communicate their pent-up amazement, and conscious of lighter spirits the moment they lost sight of the black veil. Some gathered in little circles, huddled closely together, with their mouths all whispering in the centre; some went homeward alone, wrapt in silent meditation; some talked loudly, and profaned the Sabbath day with ostentatious laughter. A few shook their sagacious heads, intimating that they could penetrate the mystery; while one or two affirmed that there was no mystery at all, but only that Mr. Hooper's eyes were so weakened by the midnight lamp, as to require a shade. After a brief interval, forth came good Mr. Hooper also, in the rear of his flock. Turning his veiled face from one group to another, he paid due reverence to the hoary heads, saluted the middle aged with kind dignity as their friend and spiritual guide, greeted the young with mingled authority and love, and laid his hands on the little children's heads to bless them. Such was always his custom on the Sabbath day. Strange and bewildered looks repaid him for his courtesy. None, as on former occasions, aspired to the honor of walking by their pastor's side. Old Squire Saunders, doubtless by an accidental lapse of memory, neglected to invite Mr. Hooper to his table, where the good clergyman had been wont to bless the food, almost every Sunday since his settlement. He returned, therefore, to the parsonage, and, at the moment of closing the door, was observed to look back upon the people, all of whom had their eyes fixed upon the minister. A sad smile gleamed faintly from beneath the black veil, and flickered about his mouth, glimmering as he disappeared.

"How strange," said a lady, "that a simple black veil, such as any woman might wear on her bonnet, should become such a terrible thing on Mr. Hooper's face!"

"Something must surely be amiss with Mr. Hooper's intellects," observed her husband, the physician of the village. "But the strangest part of the affair is the effect of this vagary, even on a sober-minded man like myself. The black veil, though it covers only our pastor's face, throws its influence over his whole person, and makes him ghostlike from head to foot. Do you not feel it so?"

"Truly do I," replied the lady; "and I would not be alone with him for the world. I wonder he is not afraid to be alone with himself!"

"Men sometimes are so," said her husband.

The afternoon service was attended with similar circumstances. At its conclusion, the bell tolled for the funeral of a young lady. The relatives and friends were assembled in the house, and the more distant acquaintances stood about the door, speaking of the good qualities of the deceased, when their talk was interrupted by the appearance of Mr. Hooper, still covered with his black veil. It was now an appropriate emblem. The clergyman stepped into the room where the corpse was laid, and bent over the coffin, to take a last farewell of his deceased parishioner. As he stooped, the veil hung straight down from his forehead, so that, if her eyelids had not been closed forever, the dead maiden might have seen his face. Could Mr. Hooper be fearful of her glance, that he so hastily caught back the black veil? A person who watched the interview between the dead and living, scrupled not to affirm, that, at the instant when the clergyman's features were disclosed, the corpse had slightly shuddered, rustling the shroud and muslin cap, though the countenance retained the composure of death. A superstitious old woman was the only witness of this prodigy. From the coffin Mr. Hooper passed into the chamber of the mourners, and thence to the head of the staircase, to make the funeral prayer. It was a tender and heart-dissolving prayer, full of sorrow, yet so imbued with celestial hopes, that the music of a heavenly harp, swept by the fingers of the dead, seemed faintly to be heard among the saddest accents of the minister. The people trembled, though they but darkly understood him when he prayed that they, and himself, and all of mortal race, might be ready, as he trusted this young maiden had been, for the dreadful hour that should snatch the veil from their faces. The bearers went heavily forth, and the mourners followed, saddening all the street, with the dead before them, and Mr. Hooper in his black veil behind.

"Why do you look back?" said one in the procession to his partner.

"I had a fancy," replied she, "that the minister and the maiden's spirit were walking hand in hand."

"And so had I, at the same moment," said the other.

That night, the handsomest couple in Milford village were to be joined in wedlock. Though reckoned a melancholy man, Mr. Hooper had a placid cheerfulness for such occasions, which often excited a sympathetic smile where livelier merriment would have been thrown away. There was no quality of his disposition which made him more beloved than this. The company at the wedding awaited his arrival with impatience, trusting that the strange awe, which had gathered over him throughout the day, would now be dispelled. But such was not the result. When Mr. Hooper came, the first thing that their eyes rested on was the same horrible black veil, which had added deeper gloom to the funeral, and could portend nothing but evil to the wedding. Such was its immediate effect on the guests that a cloud seemed to have rolled duskily from beneath the black crape, and dimmed the light of the candles. The bridal pair stood up before the minister. But the bride's cold fingers quivered in the tremulous hand of the bridegroom, and her deathlike paleness caused a whisper that the maiden who had been buried a few hours before was come from her grave to be married. If ever another wedding were so dismal, it was that famous one where they tolled the wedding knell. After performing the ceremony, Mr. Hooper raised a glass of wine to his lips, wishing happiness to the new-married couple in a strain of mild pleasantry that ought to have brightened the features of the guests, like a cheerful gleam from the hearth. At that instant, catching a glimpse of his figure in the looking-glass, the black veil involved his own spirit in the horror with which it overwhelmed all others. His frame shuddered, his lips grew white, he spilt the untasted wine upon the carpet, and rushed forth into the darkness. For the Earth, too, had on her Black Veil.

The next day, the whole village of Milford talked of little else than Parson Hooper's black veil. That, and the mystery concealed behind it, supplied a topic for discussion between acquaintances meeting in the street, and good women gossiping at their open windows. It was the first item of news that the tavern-keeper told to his guests. The children babbled of it on their way to school. One imitative little imp covered his face with an old black handkerchief, thereby so affrighting his playmates that the panic seized himself, and he well-nigh lost his wits by his own waggery.

It was remarkable that of all the busybodies and impertinent people in the parish, not one ventured to put the plain question to Mr. Hooper, wherefore he did this thing. Hitherto, whenever there appeared the slightest call for such interference, he had never lacked advisers, nor shown himself averse to be guided by their judgment. If he erred at all, it was by so painful a degree of self-distrust, that even the mildest censure would lead him to consider an indifferent action as a crime. Yet, though so well acquainted with this amiable weakness, no individual among his parishioners chose to make the black veil a subject of friendly remonstrance. There was a feeling of dread, neither plainly confessed nor carefully concealed, which caused each to shift the responsibility upon another, till at length it was found expedient to send a deputation to the church, in order to deal with Mr. Hooper about the mystery, before it should grow into a scandal. Never did an embassy so ill discharge its duties. The minister received them with friendly courtesy, but became silent, after they were seated, leaving to his visitors, the whole burden of introducing their important business. The topic, it might be supposed, was obvious enough. There was the black veil swathed round Mr. Hooper's forehead, and concealing every feature above his placid mouth, on which, at times, they could perceive the glimmering of a melancholy smile. But that piece of crape, to their imagination, seemed to hang down before his heart, the symbol of a fearful secret between him and them. Were the veil but cast aside, they might speak freely of it, but not till then. Thus they sat a considerable time, speechless, confused, and shrinking uneasily from Mr. Hooper's eye, which they felt to be fixed upon them with an invisible glance. Finally, the deputies returned abashed to their constituents, pronouncing the matter too weighty to be handled, except by a council of the churches, if, indeed, it might not require a general synod.

But there was one person in the village unappalled by the awe with which the black veil had impressed all beside herself. When the deputies returned without an explanation, or even venturing to demand one, she, with the calm energy of her character, determined to chase away the strange cloud that appeared to be settling round Mr. Hooper, every moment more darkly than before. As his plighted wife, it should be her privilege to know what the black veil concealed. At the minister's first visit, therefore, she entered upon the subject with a direct simplicity, which made the task easier both for him and her. After he had seated himself, she fixed her eyes steadfastly upon the veil, but could discern nothing of the dreadful gloom that had so overawed the multitude: it was but a double fold of crape, hanging down from his forehead to his mouth, and slightly stirring with his breath.

"No," she said aloud, and smiling, "there is nothing terrible in this piece of crape, except that it hides a face which I am always glad to look upon. Come, good sir, let the sun shine from behind the cloud. First lay aside your black veil: then tell me why you put it on."

Mr. Hooper's smile glimmered faintly.

"There is an hour to come," said he, "when all of us shall cast aside our veils. Take it not amiss, beloved friend, if I wear this piece of crape till then."

"Your words are a mystery, too," returned the young lady. "Take away the veil from them, at least."

"Elizabeth, I will," said he, "so far as my vow may suffer me. Know, then, this veil is a type and a symbol, and I am bound to wear it ever, both in light and darkness, in solitude and before the gaze of multitudes, and as with strangers, so with my familiar friends. No mortal eye will see it withdrawn. This dismal shade must separate me from the world: even you, Elizabeth, can never come behind it!"

"What grievous affliction hath befallen you," she earnestly inquired, "that you should thus darken your eyes forever?"

"If it be a sign of mourning," replied Mr. Hooper, "I, perhaps, like most other mortals, have sorrows dark enough to be typified by a black veil."

"But what if the world will not believe that it is the type of an innocent sorrow?" urged Elizabeth. "Beloved and respected as you are, there may be whispers that you hide your face under the consciousness of secret sin. For the sake of your holy office, do away this scandal!"

The color rose into her cheeks as she intimated the nature of the rumors that were already abroad in the village. But Mr. Hooper's mildness did not forsake him. He even smiled again—that same sad smile, which always appeared like a faint glimmering of light, proceeding from the obscurity beneath the veil.

"If I hide my face for sorrow, there is cause enough," he merely replied; "and if I cover it for secret sin, what mortal might not do the same?"

And with this gentle, but unconquerable obstinacy did he resist all her entreaties. At length Elizabeth sat silent. For a few moments she appeared lost in thought, considering, probably, what new methods might be tried to withdraw her lover from so dark a fantasy, which, if it had no other meaning, was perhaps a symptom of mental disease. Though of a firmer character than his own, the tears rolled down her cheeks. But, in an instant, as it were, a new feeling took the place of sorrow: her eyes were fixed insensibly on the black veil, when, like a sudden twilight in the air, its terrors fell around her. She arose, and stood trembling before him.

"And do you feel it then, at last?" said he mournfully.

She made no reply, but covered her eyes with her hand, and turned to leave the room. He rushed forward and caught her arm.

"Have patience with me, Elizabeth!" cried he, passionately. "Do not desert me, though this veil must be between us here on earth. Be mine, and hereafter there shall be no veil over my face, no darkness between our souls! It is but a mortal veil—it is not for eternity! O! you know not how lonely I am, and how frightened, to be alone behind my black veil. Do not leave me in this miserable obscurity forever!"

"Lift the veil but once, and look me in the face," said she.

"Never! It cannot be!" replied Mr. Hooper.

"Then farewell!" said Elizabeth.

She withdrew her arm from his grasp, and slowly departed, pausing at the door, to give one long shuddering gaze, that seemed almost to penetrate the mystery of the black veil. But, even amid his grief, Mr. Hooper smiled to think that only a material emblem had separated him from happiness, though the horrors, which it shadowed forth, must be drawn darkly between the fondest of lovers.

From that time no attempts were made to remove Mr. Hooper's black veil, or, by a direct appeal, to discover the secret which it was supposed to hide. By persons who claimed a superiority to popular prejudice, it was reckoned merely an eccentric whim, such as often mingles with the sober actions of men otherwise rational, and tinges them all with its own semblance of insanity. But with the multitude, good Mr. Hooper was irreparably a bugbear. He could not walk the street with any peace of mind, so conscious was he that the gentle and timid would turn aside to avoid him, and that others would make it a point of hardihood to throw themselves in his way. The impertinence of the latter class compelled him to give up his customary walk at sunset to the burial ground; for when he leaned pensively over the gate, there would always be faces behind the gravestones, peeping at his black veil. A fable went the rounds that the stare of the dead people drove him thence. It grieved him, to the very depth of his kind heart, to observe how the children fled from his approach, breaking up their merriest sports, while his melancholy figure was yet afar off. Their instinctive dread caused him to feel more strongly than aught else, that a preternatural horror was interwoven with the threads of the black crape. In truth, his own antipathy to the veil was known to be so great, that he never willingly passed before a mirror, nor stooped to drink at a still fountain, lest, in its peaceful bosom, he should be affrighted by himself. This was what gave plausibility to the whispers, that Mr. Hooper's conscience tortured him for some great crime too horrible to be entirely concealed, or otherwise than so obscurely intimated. Thus, from beneath the black veil, there rolled a cloud into the sunshine, an ambiguity of sin or sorrow, which enveloped the poor minister, so that love or sympathy could never reach him. It was said that ghost and fiend consorted with him there. With self-shudderings and outward terrors, he walked continually in its shadow, groping darkly within his own soul, or gazing through a medium that saddened the whole world. Even the lawless wind, it was believed, respected his dreadful secret, and never blew aside the veil. But still good Mr. Hooper sadly smiled at the pale visages of the worldly throng as he passed by.

Among all its bad influences, the black veil had one desirable effect, of making its wearer a very efficient clergyman. By the aid of his mysterious emblem—for there was no other apparent cause—he became a man of awful power over souls that were in agony for sin. His converts always regarded him with a dread peculiar to themselves, affirming, though but figuratively, that, before he brought them to celestial light, they had been with him behind the black veil. Its gloom, indeed, enabled him to sympathize with all dark affections. Dying sinners cried aloud for Mr. Hooper, and would not yield their breath till he appeared; though ever, as he stooped to whisper consolation, they shuddered at the veiled face so near their own. Such were the terrors of the black veil, even when Death had bared his visage! Strangers came long distances to attend service at his church, with the mere idle purpose of gazing at his figure, because it was forbidden them to behold his face. But many were made to quake ere they departed! Once, during Governor Belcher's administration,[1] Mr. Hooper was appointed to preach the election sermon. Covered with his black veil, he stood before the chief magistrate, the council, and the representatives, and wrought so deep an impression, that the legislative measures of that year were characterized by all the gloom and piety of our earliest ancestral sway.

In this manner Mr. Hooper spent a long life, irreproachable in outward act, yet shrouded in dismal suspicions; kind and loving, though unloved, and dimly feared; a man apart from men, shunned in their health and joy, but ever summoned to their aid in mortal anguish. As years wore on, shedding their snows above his sable veil, he acquired a name throughout the New England churches, and they called him Father Hooper. Nearly all his parishioners, who were of mature age when he was settled, had been borne away by many a funeral: he had one congregation in the church, and a more crowded one in the churchyard; and having wrought so late into the evening, and done his work so well, it was now good Father Hooper's turn to rest.

Several persons were visible by the shaded candle-light, in the death chamber of the old clergyman. Natural connections he had none. But there was the decorously grave, though unmoved physician, seeking only to mitigate the last pangs of the patient whom he could not save. There were the deacons, and other eminently pious members of his church. There, also, was the Reverend Mr. Clark, of Westbury, a young and zealous divine, who had ridden in haste to pray by the bedside of the expiring minister. There was the nurse, no hired handmaiden of death, but one whose calm affection had endured thus long in secrecy, in solitude, amid the chill of age, and would not perish, even at the dying hour. Who, but Elizabeth! And there lay the hoary head of good Father Hooper upon the death pillow, with the black veil still swathed about his brow, and reaching down over his face, so that each more difficult gasp of his faint breath caused it to stir. All through life that piece of crape had hung between him and the world: it had separated him from cheerful brotherhood and woman's love, and kept him in that saddest of all prisons, his own heart; and still it lay upon his face, as if to deepen the gloom of his darksome chamber, and shade him from the sunshine of eternity.

---

[1] 1730–1741

For some time previous, his mind had been confused, wavering doubtfully between the past and the present, and hovering forward, as it were, at intervals, into the indistinctness of the world to come. There had been feverish turns, which tossed him from side to side, and wore away what little strength he had. But in his most convulsive struggles, and in the wildest vagaries of his intellect, when no other thought retained its sober influence, he still showed an awful solicitude lest the black veil should slip aside. Even if his bewildered soul could have forgotten, there was a faithful woman at his pillow, who, with averted eyes, would have covered that aged face, which she had last beheld in the comeliness of manhood. At length the death-stricken old man lay quietly in the torpor of mental and bodily exhaustion, with an imperceptible pulse, and breath that grew fainter and fainter, except when a long, deep, and irregular inspiration seemed to prelude the flight of his spirit.

The minister of Westbury approached the bedside.

"Venerable Father Hooper," said he, "the moment of your release is at hand. Are you ready for the lifting of the veil that shuts in time from eternity?"

Father Hooper at first replied merely by a feeble motion of his head; then, apprehensive, perhaps, that his meaning might be doubtful, he exerted himself to speak.

"Yea," said he, in faint accents, "my soul hath a patient weariness until that veil be lifted."

"And is it fitting," resumed the Reverend Mr. Clark, "that a man so given to prayer, of such a blameless example, holy in deed and thought, so far as mortal judgment may pronounce; is it fitting that a father in the church should leave a shadow on his memory, that may seem to blacken a life so pure? I pray you, my venerable brother, let not this thing be! Suffer us to be gladdened by your triumphant aspect as you go to your reward. Before the veil of eternity be lifted, let me cast aside this black veil from your face!"

And thus speaking, the Reverend Mr. Clark bent forward to reveal the mystery of so many years. But, exerting a sudden energy, that made all the beholders stand aghast, Father Hooper snatched both his hands from beneath the bedclothes, and pressed them strongly on the black veil, resolute to struggle, if the minister of Westbury would contend with a dying man.

"Never!" cried the veiled clergyman. "On earth, never!"

"Dark old man!" exclaimed the affrighted minister, "with what horrible crime upon your soul are you now passing to the judgment?"

Father Hooper's breath heaved; it rattled in his throat; but, with a mighty effort, grasping forward with his hands, he caught hold of life, and held it back till he should speak. He even raised himself in bed; and there he sat, shivering with the arms of death around him, while the black veil hung down, awful, at that last moment, in the gathered terrors of a lifetime. And yet the faint, sad smile, so often there, now seemed to glimmer from its obscurity, and linger on Father Hooper's lips.

"Why do you tremble at me alone?" cried he, turning his veiled face round the circle of pale spectators. "Tremble also at each other! Have men avoided me, and women shown no pity, and children screamed and fled, only for my black veil? What, but the mystery which it obscurely typifies, has made this piece of crape so awful? When the friend shows his inmost heart to his friend; the lover to his best beloved; when man does not vainly shrink from the eye of his Creator, loathsomely treasuring up the secret of his sin; then deem me a monster, for the symbol beneath which I have lived, and die! I look around me, and lo! on every visage a Black Veil!"

While his auditors shrank from one another, in mutual affright, Father Hooper fell back upon his pillow, a veiled corpse, with a faint smile lingering on his lips. Still veiled, they laid him in his coffin, and a veiled corpse they bore him to the grave. The grass of many years has sprung up and withered on that grave; the burial stone is moss-grown, and good Mr. Hooper's face is dust; but awful is still the thought that it mouldered beneath the Black Veil!

—1836, 1837

EDGAR ALLAN POE ■ (1809–1849)

Edgar Allan Poe has become so much the captive of his own legend that his name summons up visions of a mad genius who has little in common with the meticulous craftsman of criticism, fiction, and poetry whose influence on world literature has been immense. Born in Boston, Poe was the child of actors and orphaned at age 2. Nevertheless, he lived a privileged childhood as the ward of John Allan, a wealthy Richmond merchant who gave Poe his middle name. After a profligate year at the University of Virginia, successful military service (under an assumed name), and an abortive stay at West Point, Poe broke with his foster father, married his young cousin, and set about a literary career, succeeding as editor of several prominent magazines. However, his irregular habits and a drinking problem, which grew more pronounced following the death of his wife in 1847, led to his mysterious death in Baltimore at the age of 39. Poe's poetry and short fiction have influenced writers as diverse as Charles Baudelaire and Stephen King; genres like the horror tale and the detective story must list Poe stories like "The Tell-Tale Heart" or "The Murders in the Rue Morgue" among their earliest important examples. Similarly, Poe's literary criticism has been extremely influential; his theory of the "single effect" is quoted and discussed in the introduction.

The Cask of Amontillado

The thousand injuries of Fortunato I had borne as I best could, but when he ventured upon insult, I vowed revenge. You, who so well know the nature of my soul, will not suppose, however, that I gave utterance to a threat. *At length* I would be avenged; this was a point definitively settled—but the very definitiveness with which it was resolved precluded the idea of risk. I must not only punish, but punish with impunity. A wrong is unredressed when retribution overtakes its redresser. It is equally unredressed when the avenger fails to make himself felt as such to him who has done the wrong.

It must be understood that neither by word nor deed had I given Fortunato cause to doubt my good will. I continued as was my wont, to smile in his face, and he did not perceive that my smile *now* was at the thought of his immolation. → to kill by fire.

He had a weak point—this Fortunato—although in other regards he was a man to be respected and even feared. He prided himself on his connoisseurship in wine. Few Italians have the true virtuoso spirit. For the most part their enthusiasm is adopted to suit the time and opportunity to practise imposture upon the British and Austrian millionaires. In painting and gemmary, Fortunato, like his countrymen, was a quack, but in the matter of old wines he was sincere. In this respect I did not differ from him materially; I was skilful in the Italian vintages myself, and bought largely whenever I could.

tells about Fortunato

It was about dusk, one evening during the supreme madness of the carnival season, that I encountered my friend. He accosted me with

excessive warmth, for he had been drinking much. The man wore motley. He had on a tight-fitting parti-striped dress and his head was surmounted by the conical cap and bells. I was so pleased to see him, that
I thought I should never have done wringing his hand.

I said to him—"My dear Fortunato, you are luckily met. How remarkably well you are looking to-day! But I have received a pipe of
what passes for Amontillado, and I have my doubts."

"How?" said he, "Amontillado? A pipe? Impossible? And in the middle of the carnival?"

"I have my doubts," I replied; "and I was silly enough to pay the full
Amontillado price without consulting you in the matter. You were not
to be found, and I was fearful of losing a bargain."

"Amontillado!"

"I have my doubts."

"Amontillado!"

"And I must satisfy them."

"Amontillado!"

"As you are engaged, I am on my way to Luchesi. If any one has a
critical turn, it is he. He will tell me"—

"Luchesi cannot tell Amontillado from Sherry."

"And yet some fools will have it that his taste is a match for your
own."

"Come let us go."

"Whither?"

"To your vaults."

"My friend, no; I will not impose upon your good nature. I perceive
you have an engagement Luchesi"—

"I have no engagement; come."

"My friend, no. It is not the engagement, but the severe cold with
which I perceive you are afflicted. The vaults are insufferably damp.
They are encrusted with nitre."

"Let us go, nevertheless. The cold is merely nothing. Amontillado!
You have been imposed upon; and as for Luchesi, he cannot distinguish Sherry from Amontillado."

Thus speaking, Fortunato possessed himself of my arm. Putting on
a mask of black silk and drawing a *roquelaire* closely about my person, I
suffered him to hurry me to my palazzo.

There were no attendants at home; they had absconded to make
merry in honour of the time. I had told them that I should not return

until the morning and had given them explicit orders not to stir from the house. These orders were sufficient, I well knew, to insure their immediate disappearance, one and all, as soon as my back was turned.

I took from their sconces two flambeaux, and giving one to Fortunato bowed him through several suites of rooms to the archway that led into the vaults. I passed down a long and winding staircase, requesting him to be cautious as he followed. We came at length to the foot of the descent, and stood together on the damp ground of the catacombs of the Montresors.

The gait of my friend was unsteady, and the bells upon his cap jingled as he strode.

"The pipe," said he.

"It is farther on," said I; "but observe the white webwork which gleams from these cavern walls."

He turned towards me and looked into my eyes with two filmy orbs that distilled the rheum of intoxication.

"Nitre?" he asked, at length.

"Nitre," I replied. "How long have you had that cough?"

"Ugh! ugh! ugh!—ugh! ugh! ugh!—ugh! ugh! ugh!—ugh! ugh! ugh!—ugh! ugh! ugh!

My poor friend found it impossible to reply for many minutes.

"It is nothing," he said, at last.

"Come," I said, with decision, "we will go back; your health is precious. You are rich, respected, admired, beloved; you are happy as once I was. You are a man to be missed. For me it is no matter. We will go back; you will be ill and I cannot be responsible. Besides, there is Luchesi"—

"Enough," he said; "the cough is a mere nothing; it will not kill me. I shall not die of a cough."

"True—true," I replied; "and, indeed, I had no intention of alarming you unnecessarily—but you should use all proper caution. A draught of this Medoc will defend us from the damps."

Here I knocked off the neck of a bottle which I drew from a long row of its fellows that lay upon the mould.

"Drink," I said, presenting him the wine.

He raised it to his lips with a leer. He paused and nodded to me familiarly, while his bells jingled.

"I drink," he said, "to the buried that repose around us."

"And I to your long life."

He again took my arm and we proceeded.

"These vaults," he said, "are extensive."

"The Montresors," I replied, "were a great numerous family."

"I forget your arms."

"A huge human foot d'or, in a field azure; the foot crushes a serpent rampant whose fangs are imbedded in the heel."

"And the motto?"

"*Nemo me impune lacessit.*"

"Good!" he said.

The wine sparkled in his eyes and the bells jingled. My own fancy grew warm with the Medoc. We had passed through walls of piled bones, with casks and puncheons intermingling, into the inmost recesses of the catacombs. I paused again, and this time I made bold to seize Fortunato by an arm above the elbow.

"The nitre!" I said: "see it increases. It hangs like moss upon the vaults. We are below the river's bed. The drops of moisture trickle among the bones. Come, we will go back ere it is too late. Your cough"—

"It is nothing," he said; "let us go on. But first, another draught of the Medoc."

I broke and reached him a flagon of De Grave. He emptied it at a breath. His eyes flashed with a fierce light. He laughed and threw the bottle upwards with a gesticulation I did not understand.

I looked at him in surprise. He repeated the movement—a grotesque one.

"You do not comprehend?" he said.

"Not I," I replied.

"Then you are not of the brotherhood."

"How?"

"You are not of the masons."

"Yes, yes," I said "yes! yes."

"You? Impossible! A mason?"

"A mason," I replied.

"A sign," he said.

"It is this," I answered, producing a trowel from beneath the folds of my *roquelaire.*

"You jest," he exclaimed, recoiling a few paces. "But let us proceed to the Amontillado."

"Be it so," I said, replacing the tool beneath the cloak, and again offering him my arm. He leaned upon it heavily. We continued our route in search of the Amontillado. We passed through a range of low arches, descended, passed on, and descending again, arrived at a deep crypt, in which the foulness of the air caused our flambeaux rather to glow than flame.

At the most remote end of the crypt there appeared another less spacious. Its walls had been lined with human remains piled to the vault overhead, in the fashion of the great catacombs of Paris. Three sides of this interior crypt were still ornamented in this manner. From the fourth the bones had been thrown down, and lay promiscuously upon the earth, forming at one point a mound of some size. Within the wall thus exposed by the displacing of the bones, we perceived a still interior recess, in depth about four feet, in width three, in height six or seven. It seemed to have been constructed for no especial use in itself, but formed merely the interval between two of the colossal supports of the roof of the catacombs, and was backed by one of their circumscribing walls of solid granite.

It was in vain that Fortunato, uplifting his dull torch, endeavoured to pry into the depths of the recess. Its termination the feeble light did not enable us to see.

"Proceed," I said; "herein is the Amontillado. As for Luchesi"—

"He is an ignoramus," interrupted my friend, as he stepped unsteadily forward, while I followed immediately at his heels. In an instant he had reached the extremity of the niche, and finding his progress arrested by the rock, stood stupidly bewildered. A moment more and I had fettered him to the granite. In its surface were two iron staples, distant from each other about two feet, horizontally. From one of these depended a short chain; from the other a padlock. Throwing the links about his waist, it was but the work of a few seconds to secure it. He was too much astounded to resist. Withdrawing the key I stepped back from the recess.

"Pass your hand," I said, "over the wall; you cannot help feeling the nitre. Indeed it is *very* damp. Once more let me *implore* you to return. No? Then I must positively leave you. But I must first render you all the little attentions in my power."

"The Amontillado!" ejaculated my friend, not yet recovered from his astonishment.

"True," I replied; "the Amontillado."

As I said these words I busied myself among the pile of bones of which I have before spoken. Throwing them aside, I soon uncovered a quantity of building stone and mortar. With these materials and with the aid of my trowel, I began vigorously to wall up the entrance of the niche.

I had scarcely laid the first tier of my masonry when I discovered that the intoxication of Fortunato had in a great measure worn off. The earliest indication I had of this was a low moaning cry from the depth of the recess. It was *not* the cry of a drunken man. There was then a long and obstinate silence. I laid the second tier, and the third, and the fourth; and then I heard the furious vibrations of the chain. The noise lasted for several minutes, during which, that I might hearken to it with the more satisfaction, I ceased my labours and sat down upon the bones. When at last the clanking subsided, I resumed the trowel, and finished without interruption the fifth, the sixth, and the seventh tier. The wall was now nearly upon a level with my breast. I again paused, and holding the flambeaux over the mason-work, threw a few feeble rays upon the figure within.

A succession of loud and shrill screams, bursting suddenly from the throat of the chained form, seemed to thrust me violently back. For a brief moment I hesitated—I trembled. Unsheathing my rapier, I began to grope with it about the recess; but the thought of an instant reassured me. I placed my hand upon the solid fabric of the catacombs, and felt satisfied. I reapproached the wall. I replied to the yells of him who clamoured. I reechoed—I aided—I surpassed them in volume and in strength. I did this, and the clamourer grew still.

It was now midnight, and my task was drawing to a close. I had completed the eighth, the ninth, and the tenth tier. I had finished a portion of the last and the eleventh; there remained but a single stone to be fitted and plastered in. I struggled with its weight; I placed it partially in its destined position. But now there came from out the niche a low laugh that erected the hairs upon my head. It was succeeded by a sad voice, which I had difficulty in recognising as that of the noble Fortunato. The voice said—

"Ha! ha! ha!—he! he!—a very good joke indeed—an excellent jest. We will have many a rich laugh about it at the palazzo—he! he! he!—over our wine—he! he! he!"

"The Amontillado!" I said.

"He! he! he!—he! he! he!—yes, the Amontillado. But is it not getting late? Will not they be awaiting us at the palazzo, the Lady Fortunato and the rest? Let us be gone."

"Yes," I said; "let us be gone."

"*For the love of God, Montresor!*"

"Yes," I said, "for the love of God!"

But to these words I hearkened in vain for a reply. I grew impatient. I called aloud—

"Fortunato!"

No answer. I called again—

"Fortunato!"

No answer still. I thrust a torch through the remaining aperture and let it fall within. There came forth in return only a jingling of the bells. My heart grew sick—on account of the dampness of the catacombs. I hastened to make an end of my labour. I forced the last stone into its position; I plastered it up. Against the new masonry I reerected the old rampart of bones. For the half of a century no mortal has disturbed them.

In pace requiescat!

SARAH ORNE JEWETT ■ (1849–1909)

Sarah Orne Jewett was born in the harbor village of South Berwick, Maine, the granddaughter of a sea captain and daughter of a doctor who taught at Bowdoin College and also served as a general practitioner among the local fishermen and farmers. Often ill as a child, Jewett received little formal education and did not attend college, but was introduced to literature by her well-read father. Jewett's publishing career began early, with children's stories and poems appearing in her teens and acceptances in the Atlantic Monthly as she entered her twenties. Jewett's early sketches of Maine people and places owe much to the popular "local color" tradition of the nineteenth century, but her stories largely avoid the moralizing and sentimentality common to popular fiction of its day. Although she traveled widely in later life, Jewett remained throughout her career a writer inextricably connected with her region. Her realism, common sense, and attention to detail were chiefly brought to bear on a type of American rural life that was quickly disappearing.

A White Heron

I

The woods were already filled with shadows one June evening, just before eight o'clock, though a bright sunset still glimmered faintly among the trunks of the trees. A little girl was driving home her cow, a plodding, dilatory, provoking creature in her behavior, but a valued companion for all that. They were going away from whatever light there was, and striking deep into the woods, but their feet were familiar with the path, and it was no matter whether their eyes could see it or not.

There was hardly a night the summer through when the old cow could be found waiting at the pasture bars; on the contrary, it was her greatest pleasure to hide herself away among the huckleberry bushes, and though she wore a loud bell she had made the discovery that if one stood perfectly still it would not ring. So Sylvia had to hunt for her until she found her, and call Co'! Co'! with never an answering Moo, until her childish patience was quite spent. If the creature had not given good milk and plenty of it, the case would have seemed very different to her owners. Besides, Sylvia had all the time there was, and very little use to make of it. Sometimes in pleasant weather it was a consolation to look upon the cow's pranks as an intelligent attempt to play hide and seek, and as the child had no playmates she lent herself to this amusement with a good deal of zest. Though this chase had been so long that the wary animal herself had given an unusual signal of her whereabouts. Sylvia had only laughed when she came upon Mistress Moolly at the swamp-side, and urged her affectionately homeward with a twig of birch leaves. The old cow was not inclined to wander farther, she even turned in the right direction for once as they left the pasture, and stepped along the road at a good pace. She was quite ready to be milked now, and seldom stopped to browse. Sylvia wondered what her grandmother would say because they were so late. It was a great while since she had left home at half-past five o'clock, but everybody knew the difficulty of making this errand a short one. Mrs. Tilley had chased the horned torment too many summer evenings herself to blame any one else for lingering, and was only thankful as she waited that she had Sylvia, nowadays, to give such valuable assistance. The good woman suspected that Sylvia loitered occasionally on her own account; there never was such a child for straying about out-of-doors since the world was made! Everybody said that it was a good change for a little maid who had tried to grow for eight years in a crowded manufacturing town, but as for Sylvia herself, it seemed as if she never had been alive at all before she came to live at the farm. She thought often with wistful compassion of a wretched geranium that belonged to a town neighbor.

" 'Afraid of folks,' " old Mrs. Tilley said to herself, with a smile, after she had made the unlikely choice of Sylvia from her daughter's houseful of children, and was returning to the farm. " 'Afraid of folks,' they said! I guess she won't be troubled no great with 'em up to the old place!" When they reached the door of the lonely house and stopped to unlock it, and the cat came to purr loudly, and rub against them, a deserted pussy, indeed, but fat with young robins, Sylvia whispered that this was a beautiful place to live in, and she never should wish to go home.

The companions followed the shady woodroad, the cow taking slow steps and the child very fast ones. The cow stopped long at the brook to drink, as if the pasture were not half a swamp, and Sylvia stood still and waited, letting her bare feet cool themselves in the shoal water, while the great twilight moths struck softly against her. She waded on through the brook as the cow moved away, and listened to the thrushes with a heart that beat fast with pleasure. There was a stirring in the great boughs overhead. They were full of little birds and beasts that seemed to be wide awake, and going about their world, or else saying goodnight to each other in sleepy twitters. Sylvia herself felt sleepy as she walked along. However, it was not much farther to the house, and the air was soft and sweet. She was not often in the woods so late as this, and it made her feel as if she were a part of the gray shadows and the moving leaves. She was just thinking how long it seemed since she first came to the farm a year ago, and wondering if everything went on in the noisy town just the same as when she was there; the thought of the great red-faced boy who used to chase and frighten her made her hurry along the path to escape from the shadow of the trees.

Suddenly this little woods-girl is horror-stricken to hear a clear whistle not very far away. Not a bird's-whistle, which would have a sort of friendliness, but a boy's whistle, determined, and somewhat aggressive. Sylvia left the cow to whatever sad fate might await her, and stepped discreetly aside into the brushes, but she was just too late. The enemy had discovered her, and called out in a very cheerful and persuasive tone, "Halloa, little girl, how far is it to the road?" and trembling Sylvia answered almost inaudibly. "A good ways."

She did not dare to look boldly at the tall young man, who carried a gun over his shoulder, but she came out of her bush and again followed the cow, while he walked alongside.

"I have been hunting for some birds," the stranger said kindly, "and I have lost my way, and need a friend very much. Don't be afraid," he added gallantly. "Speak up and tell me what your name is, and whether

SARAH ORNE JEWETT

you think I can spend the night at your house, and go out gunning early in the morning."

Sylvia was more alarmed than before. Would not her grandmother consider her much to blame? But who could have foreseen such an accident as this? It did not seem to be her fault, and she hung her head as if the stem of it were broken, but managed to answer "Sylvy," with much effort when her companion again asked her name.

Mrs. Tilley was standing in the doorway when the trio came into view. The cow gave a loud moo by way of explanation.

"Yes, you'd better speak up for yourself, you old trial! Where'd she tucked herself away this time, Sylvy?" But Sylvia kept an awed silence; she knew by instinct that her grandmother did not comprehend the gravity of the situation. She must be mistaking the stranger for one of the farmer-lads of the region.

The young man stood his gun beside the door, and dropped a lumpy game-bag beside it; then he bade Mrs. Tilley good-evening, and repeated his wayfarer's story, and asked if he could have a night's lodging.

"Put me anywhere you like," he said. "I must be off early in the morning, before day; but I am very hungry, indeed. You can give me some milk at any rate, that's plain."

"Dear sakes, yes," responded the hostess, whose long slumbering hospitality seemed to be easily awakened. "You might fare better if you went out to the main road a mile or so, but you're welcome to what we've got. I'll milk right off, and you make yourself at home. You can sleep on husks or feathers," she proffered graciously. "I raised them all myself. There's good pasturing for geese just below here towards the ma'sh. Now step round and set a plate for the gentleman, Sylvy!" And Sylvia promptly stepped. She was glad to have something to do, and she was hungry herself.

It was a surprise to find so clean and comfortable a little dwelling in this New England wilderness. The young man had known the horrors of its most primitive housekeeping, and the dreary squalor of that level of society which does not rebel at the companionship of hens. This was the best thrift of an old-fashioned farmstead, though on such a small scale that it seemed like a hermitage. He listened eagerly to the old woman's quaint talk, he watched Sylvia's pale face and shining gray eyes with ever growing enthusiasm, and insisted that this was the best supper he had eaten for a month, and afterward the new-made friends sat down in the door-way together while the moon came up.

Soon it would be berry-time, and Sylvia was a great help at picking. The cow was a good milker, though a plaguy thing to keep track of, the hostess gossiped frankly, adding presently that she had buried four children, so Sylvia's mother, and a son (who might be dead) in California were all the children she had left. "Dan, my boy, was a great hand to go gunning," she explained sadly. "I never wanted for pa'tridges or gray squer'ls while he was to home. He's been a great wand'rer, I expect, and he's no hand to write letters. There, I don't blame him, I'd ha' seen the world myself if it had been so I could."

"Sylvy takes after him," the grandmother continued affectionately, after a minute's pause. "There ain't a foot o' ground she don't know her way over, and the wild creaturs counts her one o' themselves. Squer'ls she'll tame to come an' feed right out o' her hands, and all sorts o' birds. Last winter she got the jaybirds to bangeing[1] here, and I believe she'd 'a' scanted herself of her own meals to have plenty to throw out amongst 'em, if I hadn't kep' watch. Anything but crows, I tell her, I'm willin' to help support—though Dan he had a tamed one o' them that did seem to have reason same as folks. It was round here a good spell after he went away. Dan an' his father they didn't hitch,—but he never held up his head ag'in after Dan had dared him an' gone off."

The guest did not notice this hint of family sorrows in his eager interest in something else.

"So Sylvy knows all about birds, does she?" he exclaimed, as he looked round at the little girl who sat, very demure but increasingly sleepy, in the moonlight. "I am making a collection of birds myself. I have been at it ever since I was a boy." (Mrs. Tilley smiled.) "There are two or three very rare ones I have been hunting for these five years. I mean to get them on my own grounds if they can be found."

"Do you cage 'em up?" asked Mrs. Tilley doubtfully, in response to this enthusiastic announcement.

"Oh no, they're stuffed and preserved, dozens and dozens of them," said the ornithologist, "and I have shot or snared every one myself. I caught a glimpse of a white heron a few miles from here on Saturday, and I have followed it in this direction. They have never been found in this district at all. The little white heron, it is," and he turned again to look at Sylvia with the hope of discovering that the rare bird was one of her acquaintances.

[1]**bangeing** loitering

But Sylvia was watching a hop-toad in the narrow footpath.

"You would know the heron if you saw it," the stranger continued eagerly. "A queer tall white bird with soft feathers and long thin legs. And it would have a nest perhaps in the top of a high tree, made of sticks, something like a hawk's nest."

Sylvia's heart gave a wild beat; she knew that strange white bird, and had once stolen softly near where it stood in some bright green swamp grass, away over at the other side of the woods. There was an open place where the sunshine always seemed strangely yellow and hot, where tall, nodding rushes grew, and her grandmother had warned her that she might sink in the soft black mud underneath and never be heard of more. Not far beyond were the salt marshes just this side the sea itself, which Sylvia wondered and dreamed much about, but never had seen, whose great voice could sometimes be heard above the noise of the woods on stormy nights.

"I can't think of anything I should like so much as to find that heron's nest," the handsome stranger was saying. "I would give ten dollars to anybody who could show it to me," he added desperately, "and I mean to spend my whole vacation hunting for it if need be. Perhaps it was only migrating, or had been chased out of its own region by some bird of prey."

Mrs. Tilley gave amazed attention to all this, but Sylvia still watched the toad, not divining, as she might have done at some calmer time, that the creature wished to get to its hole under the door-step, and was much hindered by the unusual spectators at that hour of the evening. No amount of thought, that night, could decide how many wished-for treasures the ten dollars, so lightly spoken of, would buy.

The next day the young sportsman hovered about the woods, and Sylvia kept him company, having lost her first fear of the friendly lad, who proved to be most kind and sympathetic. He told her many things about the birds and what they knew and where they lived and what they did with themselves. And he gave her a jack-knife, which she thought as great a treasure as if she were a desert-islander. All day long he did not once make her troubled or afraid except when he brought down some unsuspecting singing creature from its bough. Sylvia would have liked him vastly better without his gun; she could not understand why he killed the very birds he seemed to like so much. But as the day waned, Sylvia still watched the young man with loving admiration. She had never seen anybody so charming and delightful; the woman's heart, asleep in the child, was vaguely thrilled by a dream of love. Some premonition of that great power stirred and swayed these young creatures who traversed the solemn woodlands with soft-footed silent care. They stopped to listen to a bird's song; they pressed forward again eagerly, parting the branches—speaking to each other rarely and in whispers; the young man going first and Sylvia following fascinated, a few steps behind, with her gray eyes dark with excitement.

She grieved because the longed-for white heron was elusive, but she did not lead the guest, she only followed, and there was no such thing as speaking first. The sound of her own unquestioned voice would have terrified her—it was hard enough to answer yes or no when there was need of that. At last evening began to fall, and they drove the cow home together, and Sylvia smiled with pleasure when they came to the place where she heard the whistle and was afraid only the night before.

II

Half a mile from home, at the farther edge of the woods, where the land was highest, a great pine-tree stood, the last of its generation. Whether it was left for a boundary mark, or for what reason, no one could say; the woodchoppers who had felled its mates were dead and gone long ago, and a whole forest of sturdy trees, pines and oaks and maples, had grown again. But the stately head of this old pine towered above them all and made a landmark for sea and shore miles and miles away. Sylvia knew it well. She had always believed that whoever climbed to the top of it could see the ocean; and the little girl had often laid her hand on the great rough trunk and looked up wistfully at those dark boughs that the wind always stirred, no matter how hot and still the air might be below. Now she thought of the tree with a new excitement, for why, if one climbed it at break of day could not one see all the world, and easily discover from whence the white heron flew, and mark the place, and find the hidden nest?

What a spirit of adventure, what wild ambition! What fancied triumph and delight and glory for the later morning when she could make known the secret! It was almost too real and too great for the childish heart to bear.

All night the door of the little house stood open and the whippoorwills came and sang upon the very step. The young sportsman and his old hostess were sound asleep, but Sylvia's great design kept her broad awake and watching. She forgot to think of sleep. The short summer night seemed as long as the winter darkness, and at last when the whippoorwills ceased, and she was afraid the morning would after all come too soon, she stole out of the house and followed the pasture path through the woods, hastening toward the open ground beyond, listening with a sense of comfort and companionship to the drowsy twitter of a half-awakened bird, whose perch she had jarred in passing. Alas, if the great wave of human interest which flooded for the first time this dull little life should sweep away the satisfactions of an existence heart to heart with nature and the dumb life of the forest!

There was the huge tree asleep yet in the paling moonlight, and small and silly Sylvia began with utmost bravery to mount to the top of it, with tingling, eager blood coursing the channels of her whole frame, with her bare feet and fingers, that pinched and held like bird's claws to the monstrous ladder reaching up, up, almost to the sky itself. First she must mount the white oak tree that grew alongside, where she was almost lost among the dark branches and the green leaves heavy and wet with dew; a bird fluttered off its nest, and a red squirrel ran to and fro and scolded pettishly at the harmless housebreaker. Sylvia felt her way easily. She had often climbed there, and knew that higher still one of the oak's upper branches chafed against the pine trunk, just where its lower boughs were set close together. There, when she made the dangerous pass from one tree to the other, the great enterprise would really begin.

She crept out along the swaying oak limb at last, and took the daring step across into the old pine-tree. The way was harder than she thought; she must reach far and hold fast, the sharp dry twigs caught and held her and scratched her like angry talons, the pitch made her thin little fingers clumsy and stiff as she went round and round the tree's great stem, higher and higher upward. The sparrows and robins in the woods below were beginning to wake and twitter to the dawn, yet it seemed much lighter there aloft in the pine-tree, and the child knew she must hurry if her project were to be of any use.

The tree seemed to lengthen itself out as she went up, and to reach farther and farther upward. It was like a great main-mast to the voyaging earth; it must truly have been amazed that morning through all its ponderous frame as it felt this determined spark of human spirit wending its way from higher branch to branch. Who knows how steadily the least twigs held themselves to advantage this light, weak creature on her way! The old pine must have loved his new dependent. More than all the hawks, and bats, and moths, and even the sweet voiced thrushes, was the brave, beating heart of the solitary gray-eyed child. And the tree stood still and frowned away the winds that June morning while the dawn grew bright in the east.

Sylvia's face was like a pale star, if one had seen it from the ground, when the last thorny bough was past, and she stood trembling and tired but wholly triumphant, high in the treetop. Yes, there was the sea with the dawning sun making a golden dazzle over it, and toward that glorious east flew two hawks with slow-moving pinions. How low they looked in the air from that height when one had only seen them before far up, and dark against the blue sky. Their gray feathers were as soft as moths: they seemed only a little way from the tree, and Sylvia felt as if she too could go flying away among the clouds. Westward, the woodlands and farms reached miles and miles into the distance; here and there were church steeples, and white villages, truly it was a vast and awesome world!

The birds sang louder and louder. At last the sun came up bewilderingly bright. Sylvia could see the white sails of ships out at sea, and the clouds that were purple and rose-colored and yellow at first began to fade away. Where was the white heron's nest in the sea of green branches, and was this wonderful sight and pageant of the world the only reward for having climbed to such a giddy height? Now look down again, Sylvia, where the green marsh is set among the shining birches and dark hemlocks; there where you saw the white heron once you will see him again; look, look! a white spot of him like a single floating feather comes up from the dead hemlock and grows larger, and rises, and comes close at last, and goes by the landmark pine with steady sweep of wing and outstretched slender neck and crested head. And wait! wait! do not move a foot or a finger, little girl, do not send an arrow of light and consciousness from your two eager eyes, for the heron has perched on a pine bough not far beyond yours, and cries back to his mate on the nest and plumes his feathers for the new day!

The child gives a long sigh a minute later when a company of shouting cat-birds comes also to the tree, and vexed by their fluttering and lawlessness the solemn heron goes away. She knows his secret now, the wild, light, slender bird that floats and wavers, and goes back like an arrow presently to his home in the green world beneath. Then Sylvia, well satisfied, makes her perilous way down again, not daring to look far below the branch she stands on, ready to cry sometimes because her fingers ache and her lamed feet slip. Wondering over and over again what the stranger would say to her, and what he would think when she told him how to find his way straight to the heron's nest.

"Sylvy, Sylvy!" called the busy old grandmother again and again, but nobody answered, and the small husk bed was empty and Sylvia had disappeared.

The guest waked from a dream, and remembering his day's pleasure hurried to dress himself that might it sooner begin. He was sure from the way the shy little girl looked once or twice yesterday that she had at least seen the white heron, and now she must really be made to tell. Here she comes now, paler than ever, and her worn old frock is torn and tattered, and smeared with pine pitch. The grandmother and the sportsman stand in the door together and question her, and the splendid moment has come to speak of the dead hemlock-tree by the green marsh.

But Sylvia does not speak after all, though the old grandmother fretfully rebukes her, and the young man's kind, appealing eyes are looking straight in her own. He can make them rich with money; he has promised it, and they are poor now. He is so well worth making happy, and he waits to hear the story she can tell.

No, she must keep silence! What is it that suddenly forbids her and makes her dumb? Has she been nine years growing and now, when the great world for the first time puts out a hand to her, must she thrust it aside for a bird's sake? The murmur of the pine's green branches is in her ears, she remembers how the white heron came flying through the golden air and how they watched the sea and the morning together, and Sylvia cannot speak; she cannot tell the heron's secret and give its life away.

Dear loyalty, that suffered a sharp pang as the guest went away disappointed later in the day, that could have served and followed him and loved him as a dog loves! Many a night Sylvia heard the echo of his whistle haunting the pasture path as she came home with the loitering cow. She forgot even her sorrow at the sharp report of his gun and the sight of thrushes and sparrows dropping silent to the ground, their songs hushed and their pretty feathers stained and wet with blood. Were the birds better friends than their hunter might have been,—who can tell? Whatever treasures were lost to her, woodlands and summertime, remember! Bring your gifts and graces and tell your secrets to this lonely country child!

—1886

*Guy de Maupassant did not consider a literary career until he was almost 30
years of age. After military service he worked as a French government clerk until 1882. The great influence on his development as a writer was the novelist
Gustave Flaubert, who introduced him to other Parisian literary figures, including Émile Zola, the leader of the naturalists. "Boule-de-suif," the story of a
prostitute (the title, literally "grease-ball," is her nickname) whose generosity is
gratefully accepted by a group of war refugees until they reach safety and revert
to their former contempt, made Maupassant a celebrity when it was published
in 1880 in an anthology of stories about the Franco-Prussian War of 1870.
This humiliating defeat for France also provides the background for "Mother
Savage." Maupassant died young, a victim of a self-destructive lifestyle that
led to syphilis, attempted suicide, and madness, but during his most productive
decade (1880–1890) he produced over three hundred stories, six novels, poetry,
travel writing, and a play. Like his American contemporary O. Henry (William
Sidney Porter), Maupassant first reached a large popular audience through
mass-circulation magazines. Maupassant's focus on the unglamourous realities of both rural and urban life mark him as one of the masters of literary
naturalism, and his careful plot construction and attention to detail set high
standards for later writers of short fiction.*

Mother Savage

Translated by Lafcadio Hearn; edited and revised by R. S. Gwynn

I

It had been fifteen years since I had visited Virelogne. One autumn I
returned to do some hunting and stayed with my friend Serval, who
had finally rebuilt the château that the Prussians had destroyed.

I was madly in love with the area. It is one of those delightful corners of the world that possess a sensual appeal for the eyes. This is almost a physical kind of love. Those of us who are easily seduced by
landscapes retain fond memories of certain springs, certain woods,
certain streams, and certain hills which have become familiar to us and
which can move our hearts like happy events. Sometimes our daydreams return to a wooded spot, or a riverbank, or an orchard bursting
into blossom, seen only once on a lovely day but held in our hearts like

images of women strolling the streets on a spring morning with fresh, clean faces, stirring body and soul with unrequited desire, with the unforgettable sensation of fleeting joy.

At Virelogne, I loved the whole countryside, dotted with little woods and traversed by streams that course though the soil like veins carrying blood to the earth. We fished for crawfish, for trout and eels. Such blessed happiness! There were spots to swim, and we could flush snipe from the tall weeds that grew along the banks of these narrow ribbons of water.

I walked along, lightly as a goat, watching my two dogs range in front of me. Serval, a hundred meters to my right, beat through a field of high grass. As I came around the bushes that mark the border of the Saudres Forest, I saw a thatched cottage in ruins.

Suddenly I recalled that I had seen it before, the last time in 1869, well kept up, covered with vines, and with a few chickens around the front door. What can be sadder than a dead house with its skeleton still standing, ruined and sinister?

I also recalled that the good woman who lived there had asked me in, one day when I was bone-tired, for a glass of wine, and that Serval had later told me the family history. The father, an old poacher, had been shot by the police. The son, whom I had seen before, was a tall, wiry fellow who also had a reputation as a fierce killer of game. They were called the Savages.

Was this their name or nickname?

I called out to Serval. He walked over to me with his long, ambling stride.

I asked him:

"What's become of the people who lived here?"

And he told me this story.

II

When the war broke out, Mother Savage's son, who was then thirty-three years old, volunteered, leaving his mother all alone. However, no one felt sorry for the old woman because everybody knew that she had money.

So she lived by herself in her isolated cottage, far from the village at the edge of the forest. But she was not a bit afraid, being made of the same stuff as the men of the countryside—a hardy old woman, tall and gaunt, who seldom laughed and whom nobody dared to cross.

The women of the countryside do not laugh much. That's the men's business! The souls of these women are melancholy and narrow, for their lives are dismal and rarely brightened by an hour of joy. The peasant husbands or sons enjoy a little noisy gaiety in taverns, but their wives or mothers remain serious, with perpetually severe expressions. The muscles of their faces have never learned the movements of laughter.

Mother Savage continued to live as she always had in her cottage, which was soon covered with snow. Once a week she used to come to the village to buy bread and meat, after which she would return home. As there was quite a bit of talk about wolves, she never went out without a gun slung on her shoulder, her son's rifle, a rusty weapon whose stock was quite worn from the hands that had rubbed against it; she made a strange sight, that tall old woman, a little stooped by age, walking with slow steps through the snow with the barrel of the gun sticking up behind the black scarf which covered her head and concealed the white hair that no one had ever seen.

One day the Prussians came. They were billeted with the people of the area, according to the wealth and resources of each family. The old woman had to take four of them because she was known to have money.

These were four big fellows with fair skin, blond beards, and blue eyes who had not grown thin in spite of all the wear and tear they had endured; they seemed to be good boys, even though they were in a conquered country. Finding themselves alone with the old woman, they took pains to show her all possible consideration and did everything they could to save her trouble or expense. You could see them every morning, all four of them, washing up at the well in their shirt sleeves, pouring great quantities of cold water over that fair, rosy Northern skin of theirs even on the days when it was snowing most heavily—while Mother Savage came and went, getting their soup ready. Later they could be seen cleaning up the kitchen, washing windows, chopping wood, peeling potatoes, washing linen—in short, doing all the chores like four good boys working for their own mother.

But the old woman was always thinking of her own son—her tall, gaunt boy with his hooked nose and brown eyes and thick mustache that seemed to cover his upper lip like a pelt of black fur. And every day she used to ask the four soldiers quartered in her home, "Do you know where that French regiment is, the 23rd of the line? My son is in it."

They would reply, "No, not know, not nothing." And sensing her pain and fear, they, who had mothers far away themselves, showed her a thousand little courtesies. She liked them well enough, too, those four enemies of hers; for country people do not as a rule feel patriotic hatred—those feelings are reserved for the upper classes. The humble folk—those who pay the most because they are poor and are always being weighed down with new burdens, those who are slaughtered wholesale, those who make up the real cannon fodder because there are so many of them, those who, to tell the truth, suffer most hideously from the miserable atrocities of war because they are the most vulnerable and the least powerful—such people do not understand war fever or the fine points of military honor or, even less, those so-called political necessities which exhaust two nations in six months, both victor and vanquished alike.

Speaking of Mother Savage's Germans, folks in the area would say, "Well, those four landed in a safe enough spot."

One morning while Mother Savage was at home alone, she caught sight of a man far off across the fields, hurrying towards her gate. He soon came near enough for her to recognize him: it was the rural postman. He handed her a sheet of folded paper, and she took her glasses, which she always wore when sewing, out of their case, and read:

Madam Savage,

This letter has a sad story to tell you. Your boy Victor was killed yesterday by a cannonball, which cut him practically in two. I was right there when it happened, for we stood next to each other in line and he was always talking to me about you so that I could let you know at once if he had any bad luck.

I took his watch out of his pocket to bring to you when the war is over.

Cordially,

Césaire Rivot,
Private Second Class in the
Twenty-third Regiment of the Line

The letter was dated three weeks earlier.

She did not cry. She remained motionless, so overwhelmed, so stupefied by the blow that she did not immediately feel anything. She thought, "There's Victor, and now he's been killed." Then, little by little, tears slowly rose in her eyes, and sorrow invaded her heart. Thoughts came to her, one after the other—frightful, torturing ones. She would never kiss him again, her only child, her big, tall boy—never! The police had killed his father, and now the Prussians had killed the son . . . he had been cut in two by a cannonball. And it seemed to her she could see it all, the whole horrible thing: his head falling with his eyes wide open, his teeth still gnawing the corners of his thick mustache the way he used to do when he was angry.

What had they done afterward with his body? Couldn't they have brought her son back the same way they brought her husband back to her, with a bullet hole in the middle of his forehead?

But then she heard the sound of loud voices. It was the Prussians returning from the village. Quickly she hid the letter in her pocket and met them very calmly with her usual expression, for she had managed to wipe her eyes.

All four of them were laughing, quite delighted that they had been able to bring home a fine rabbit—doubtless stolen—and they made signs to the old woman that they were all going to have something really good to eat.

She set to work at once to prepare their dinner, but when the time came to kill the rabbit she did not have the heart to do it. Yet surely this wasn't the first rabbit she had ever been given to kill! One of the soldiers knocked it out by striking it behind the ears with his hand. Once it was dead she pulled the red body out of its skin, but the sight of the blood she was handling, which covered her fingers—the warm blood that she could feel cooling and coagulating—made her tremble from head to toe; all the while she kept seeing her tall son, cut in two and all red just like the body of the still quivering animal.

She sat down at the table with her Prussians, but she could not eat, not so much as a mouthful. They devoured the rabbit without paying any attention to her. Meanwhile she watched them from the corners of her eyes, not speaking—turning an idea over and over in her head, but with such an impassive face that none of them noticed anything unusual.

All of a sudden she said, "I don't even know your names, and we've been together for a whole month." They understood, with some difficulty, what she wanted and told her their names. But that was not enough; she made them write them down on a piece of paper along with the addresses of their families, and, placing her reading glasses on her big nose, she looked over the foreign writing; then she folded up the paper and put it into her pocket, next to the letter which had told her about the death of her son.

When the meal was over she said to them:

"Now I'm going to do something for you."

And she started carrying straw up into the loft where they slept.

They thought this was rather strange, but when she explained to them that it would keep them warmer they helped her. They stacked the bales all the way up to the thatched ceiling and made themselves a sort of large room with four walls of forage, warm and fragrant, where they could sleep peacefully.

At supper one of them became worried that Mother Savage still had not eaten anything. She told him that she had stomach cramps. Then she lit a good fire to warm herself, and the four Germans climbed up into their loft on the ladder they used every evening.

As soon as they had closed the trapdoor, the old woman took away the ladder, and, going outside without a sound, she began to collect straw and filled her kitchen with it. She walked barefoot through the snow—so softly that no one could hear her. From time to time she heard the loud and fitful snoring of the four sleeping soldiers.

When she decided that her preparations were complete, she thrust one of the bundles of straw into the fire, then flung the burning handful on top of the others and went outside to watch.

In several seconds a fierce glare lit the inside of the cottage; then the whole thing became a terrible furnace, a gigantic oven whose violent light blazed through the single narrow window and sent a bright ray reflecting over the snow.

Loud cries rang out from the upper part of the house. Then they were followed by a clamor of human screams full of agony and terror. Then, the trapdoor having been lifted, a storm of flame roared up into the loft, burnt through the roof of straw, rose up to the heavens like a vast bonfire, and the whole cottage went up in flames.

Nothing could now be heard but the crackling of the fire, the crumbling of the walls, the falling of the beams. The last fragments of the roof fell in, and the red-hot shell of the dwelling flung a huge shower of sparks skyward through clouds of thick smoke.

The snow-covered fields, lit up by the fire, shone like a sheet of silver tinged with crimson.

Far away, a bell began to ring.

Old Mother Savage stood at attention in front of the ruins of her home, armed with a gun, her dead son's rifle, to make sure that none of them could escape.

When she saw that it was all over, she threw the weapon into the fire. A single shot rang out.

People came running to the scene—the neighbors, the Prussian soldiers.

They found the old woman sitting on a tree stump, calm and satisfied.

A German officer, who spoke French like a son of France, asked her: "Where are your soldiers?"

She stretched out her skinny arm towards the smoldering mass of ruins where the fire was dying down at last and answered in a strong voice: "There! Inside!"

Everyone gathered around her. The Prussian asked:

"How did the fire start?"

She answered:

"I started it."

They could not believe her, and they thought that the disaster had driven her mad. Then, when everyone had moved closer to listen to her, she told the whole story from beginning to end—from the arrival of the letter down to the final screams of the burning men inside her house. She did not leave out a single detail of what she had felt and what she had done.

When she finished, she took two pieces of paper out of her pocket and, so she could tell one from the other by the last light of the fire, adjusted her glasses and announced, holding up one piece of paper, "This one is Victor's death." Holding up the other, she added, nodding her head towards the still-red ruins, "This one has their names on it so you can write home about them." She calmly handed the white sheet to the officer, who was now holding her by the shoulders, and she continued:

"You can write them how this all happened, and you can tell their parents that I was the one who did it—I, Victoire Simon, The Savage! Never forget it."

The officer screamed some orders in German. They seized her and pushed her up against the still-warm walls of her house. Then a dozen men lined up in front of her, twenty meters away. She never blinked an eye. She knew what was coming, and she waited.

An order rang out, followed by a loud volley. One shot echoed all by itself after the others.

The old woman did not fall. She sank straight down as though her legs had been cut away from under her.

The Prussian officer approached to look. She had been cut almost in two, and her stiffened fingers still clutched the letter, bathed in blood.

III

My friend Serval added, "In reprisal, the Germans destroyed the local château, which I owned."

For my own part, I thought about the mothers of those four poor boys who had burned inside, and of the terrible heroism of that other mother, shot dead against that wall.

And I picked up a little stone, which still bore the scorch marks of the fire.

—1884

KATE CHOPIN ■ (1851–1904)

Kate Chopin was virtually forgotten for most of the twentieth century. She was rarely mentioned in histories of American literature and was remembered primarily as a chronicler of life among the Louisiana Creoles and Cajuns. Her works had long been out of print, when they were rediscovered in recent decades, initially by feminist critics and subsequently by general readers. Her most important novel, The Awakening *(1899), today appears frequently on college reading lists and was filmed in 1992 as* Grand Isle. *Born in St. Louis, Chopin spent the 1870s in rural Louisiana, the wife of Oscar Chopin, a cotton broker from New Orleans. Later she lived with her husband on a plantation near Natchitoches, an area that provides the setting of the stories collected in* Bayou Folk *(1894) and* A Night in Arcadie *(1897) and from which she absorbed a rich mixture of French and black cultures. After her husband's death in 1883, Chopin returned to St. Louis with her six children and began her literary career, placing stories and regional pieces in popular magazines. Much of her later work is remarkable for its frank depiction of women's sexuality, a subject rarely broached in the literature of the era, and Chopin became the subject of controversy after the appearance of* The Awakening. *The negative reception of that work caused Chopin to suffer social ostracism and effectively ended her active career as a writer.*

The Story of an Hour

Knowing that Mrs. Mallard was afflicted with a heart trouble, great care was taken to break to her as gently as possible the news of her husband's death.

It was her sister Josephine who told her, in broken sentences, veiled hints that revealed in half concealing. Her husband's friend Richards was there, too, near her. It was he who had been in the newspaper office when intelligence of the railroad disaster was received, with Brently Mallard's name leading the list of "killed." He had only taken the time to assure himself of its truth by a second telegram, and had hastened to forestall any less careful, less tender friend in bearing the sad message.

She did not hear the story as many women have heard the same, with a paralyzed inability to accept its significance. She wept at once, with sudden, wild abandonment, in her sister's arms. When the storm of grief had spent itself she went away to her room alone. She would have no one follow her.

There stood, facing the open window, a comfortable, roomy armchair. Into this she sank, pressed down by a physical exhaustion that haunted her body and seemed to reach into her soul.

She could see in the open square before her house the tops of trees that were all aquiver with the new spring life. The delicious breath of rain was in the air. In the street below a peddler was crying his wares. The notes of a distant song which some one was singing reached her faintly, and countless sparrows were twittering in the eaves.

There were patches of blue sky showing here and there through the clouds that had met and piled one above the other in the west facing her window.

She sat with her head thrown back upon the cushion of the chair, quite motionless, except when a sob came up into her throat and shook her, as a child who has cried itself to sleep continues to sob in its dreams.

She was young, with a fair, calm face, whose lines bespoke repression and even a certain strength. But now there was a dull stare in her eyes, whose gaze was fixed away off yonder on one of those patches of blue sky. It was not a glance of reflection, but rather indicated a suspension of intelligent thought.

There was something coming to her and she was waiting for it, fearfully. What was it? She did not know; it was too subtle and elusive to name. But she felt it, creeping out of the sky, reaching toward her through the sounds, the scents, the color that filled the air.

Now her bosom rose and fell tumultuously. She was beginning to recognize this thing that was approaching to possess her, and she was striving to beat it back with her will—as powerless as her two white slender hands would have been.

When she abandoned herself a little whispered word escaped her slightly parted lips. She said it over and over under her breath: "Free, free, free!" The vacant stare and the look of terror that had followed it went from her eyes. They stayed keen and bright. Her pulses beat fast, and the coursing blood warmed and relaxed every inch of her body.

She did not stop to ask if it were not a monstrous joy that held her. A clear and exalted perception enabled her to dismiss the suggestion as trivial.

She knew that she would weep again when she saw the kind, tender hands folded in death; the face that had never looked save with love upon her, fixed and gray and dead. But she saw beyond that bitter moment a long procession of years to come that would belong to her absolutely. And she opened and spread her arms out to them in welcome.

There would be no one to live for during those coming years; she would live for herself. There would be no powerful will bending her in that blind persistence with which men and women believe they have a right to impose a private will upon a fellow creature. A kind intention or a cruel intention made the act seem no less a crime as she looked upon it in that brief moment of illumination.

And yet she had loved him—sometimes. Often she had not. What did it matter! What could love, the unsolved mystery, count for in face of this possession of self-assertion which she suddenly recognized as the strongest impulse of her being.

"Free! Body and soul free!" she kept whispering.

Josephine was kneeling before the closed door with her lips to the keyhole, imploring for admission. "Louise, open the door! I beg; open the door—you will make yourself ill. What are you doing, Louise? For heaven's sake open the door."

"Go away. I am not making myself ill." No; she was drinking in a very elixir of life through that open window.

Her fancy was running riot along those days ahead of her. Spring days, and summer days, and all sorts of days that would be her own. She breathed a quick prayer that life might be long. It was only yesterday she had thought with a shudder that life might be long.

She arose at length and opened the door to her sister's importunities. There was a feverish triumph in her eyes, and she carried herself unwittingly like a goddess of Victory. She clasped her sister's waist, and together they descended the stairs. Richards stood waiting for them at the bottom.

Some one was opening the front door with a latchkey. It was Brently Mallard who entered, a little travel-stained, composedly carrying his gripsack and umbrella. He had been far from the scene of the accident, and did not even know there had been one. He stood amazed at Josephine's piercing cry; at Richards' quick motion to screen him from the view of his wife.

But Richards was too late.

When the doctors came they said she had died of heart disease—of joy that kills.

—1894

CHARLOTTE PERKINS GILMAN ■ (1860–1935)

Charlotte Perkins Gilman was born in Hartford, Connecticut, and, on her father's side, was related to Harriet Beecher Stowe, the author of the great anti-slavery novel Uncle Tom's Cabin. *Gilman's father abandoned the family when she was an infant, and her early education was spotty, but she eventually studied at the Rhode Island School of Design. Following marriage and the birth of a daughter, she suffered from severe depression, an experience that she recreates in "The Yellow Wallpaper." In a 1913 essay on the story's autobiographical basis, Gilman relates how, following a "rest cure," her doctor, Weir Mitchell, ordered her "never to touch pen, brush, or pencil again." This advice proved almost catastrophic, and Gilman soon discovered that happiness and emotional stability could be found only in "work, the normal life of every human being; work, in which is joy and growth and service, without which one is a pauper and a parasite." In later life, Gilman became an important public spokesperson for various feminist causes. After she discovered that she had inoperable breast cancer, she chose to end her own life.*

The Yellow Wallpaper

It is very seldom that mere ordinary people like John and myself secure ancestral halls for the summer.

A colonial mansion, a hereditary estate, I would say a haunted house and reach the height of romantic felicity—but that would be asking too much of fate!

Still I will proudly declare that there is something queer about it.

Else, why should it be let so cheaply? And why have stood so long untenanted?

John laughs at me, of course, but one expects that.

John is practical in the extreme. He has no patience with faith, an intense horror of superstition, and he scoffs openly at any talk of things not to be felt and seen and put down in figures.

John is a physician, and *perhaps*—(I would not say it to a living soul, of course, but this is dead paper and a great relief to my mind)—*perhaps* that is one reason I do not get well faster.

You see, he does not believe I am sick! And what can one do?

If a physician of high standing, and one's own husband, assures friends and relatives that there is really nothing the matter with one but temporary nervous depression—a slight hysterical tendency—what is one to do?

My brother is also a physician, and also of high standing, and he says the same thing.

So I take phosphates or phosphites—whichever it is—and tonics, and air and exercise, and journeys, and am absolutely forbidden to "work" until I am well again.

Personally, I disagree with their ideas.

Personally, I believe that congenial work, with excitement and change, would do me good.

But what is one to do?

I did write for a while in spite of them; but it *does* exhaust me a good deal—having to be so sly about it, or else meet with heavy opposition.

I sometimes fancy that in my condition, if I had less opposition and more society and stimulus—but John says the very worst thing I can do is to think about my condition, and I confess it always makes me feel bad.

So I will let it alone and talk about the house.

The most beautiful place! It is quite alone, standing well back from the road, quite three miles from the village. It makes me think of English places that you read about, for there are hedges and walls and gates that lock, and lots of separate little houses for the gardeners and people.

There is a *delicious* garden! I never saw such a garden—large and shady, full of box-bordered paths, and lined with long grape-covered arbors with seats under them.

There were greenhouses, but they are all broken now.

There was some legal trouble, I believe, something about the heirs and coheirs; anyhow, the place has been empty for years.

That spoils my ghostliness, I am afraid, but I don't care—there is something strange about the house—I can feel it.

I even said so to John one moonlight evening, but he said what I felt was a *draught*, and shut the window.

I get unreasonably angry with John sometimes. I'm sure I never used to be so sensitive. I think it is due to this nervous condition.

But John says if I feel so I shall neglect proper self-control; so I take pains to control myself—before him, at least, and that makes me very tired.

I don't like our room a bit. I wanted one downstairs that opened onto the piazza and had roses all over the window, and such pretty old-fashioned chintz hangings! But John would not hear of it.

He said there was only one window and not room for two beds, and no near room for him if he took another.

He is very careful and loving, and hardly lets me stir without special direction.

I have a schedule prescription for each hour in the day; he takes all care from me, and so I feel basely ungrateful not to value it more.

He said he came here solely on my account, that I was to have perfect rest and all the air I could get. "Your exercise depends on your strength, my dear," said he, "and your food somewhat on your appetite; but air you can absorb all the time." So we took the nursery at the top of the house.

It is a big, airy room, the whole floor nearly, with windows that look all ways, and air and sunshine galore. It was a nursery first, and then playroom and gymnasium, I should judge, for the windows are barred for little children, and there are rings and things in the walls.

The paint and paper look as if a boys' school had used it. It is stripped off—the paper—in great patches all around the head of my bed, about as far as I can reach, and in a great place on the other side of the room low down. I never saw a worse paper in my life. One of those sprawling, flamboyant patterns committing every artistic sin.

It is dull enough to confuse the eye in following, pronounced enough constantly to irritate and provoke study, and when you follow the lame uncertain curves for a little distance they suddenly commit suicide—plunge off at outrageous angles, destroy themselves in unheard-of contradictions.

The color is repellent, almost revolting: a smouldering unclean yellow, strangely faded by the slow-turning sunlight. It is a dull yet lurid orange in some places, a sickly sulphur tint in others.

No wonder the children hated it! I should hate it myself if I had to live in this room long.

There comes John, and I must put this away—he hates to have me write a word.

We have been here two weeks, and I haven't felt like writing before, since that first day.

I am sitting by the window now, up in this atrocious nursery, and there is nothing to hinder my writing as much as I please, save lack of strength.

John is away all day, and even some nights when his cases are serious.

I am glad my case is not serious!

But these nervous troubles are dreadfully depressing.

John does not know how much I really suffer. He knows there is no *reason* to suffer, and that satisfies him.

Of course it is only nervousness. It does weight on me so not to do my duty in any way!

I meant to be such a help to John, such a real rest and comfort, and here I am a comparative burden already!

Nobody would believe what an effort it is to do what little I am able—to dress and entertain, and order things.

It is fortunate Mary is so good with the baby. Such a dear baby!

And yet I *cannot* be with him, it makes me so nervous.

I suppose John never was nervous in his life. He laughs at me so about this wallpaper!

At first he meant to repaper the room, but afterward he said that I was letting it get the better of me, and that nothing was worse for a nervous patient than to give way to such fancies.

He said that after the wallpaper was changed it would be the heavy bedstead, and then the barred windows, and then that gate at the head of the stairs, and so on.

"You know the place is doing you good," he said, "and really, dear, I don't care to renovate the house just for a three months' rental."

"Then do let us go downstairs," I said. "There are such pretty rooms there."

Then he took me in his arms and called me a blessed little goose, and said he would go down to the cellar, if I wished, and have it white-washed into the bargain.

But he is right enough about the beds and windows and things.

It is as airy and comfortable a room as anyone need wish, and, of course, I would not be so silly as to make him uncomfortable just for a whim.

I'm really getting quite fond of the big room, all but that horrid paper.

Out of one window I can see the garden—those mysterious deep-shaded arbors, the riotous old-fashioned flowers, and bushes and gnarly trees.

Out of another I get a lovely view of the bay and a little private wharf belonging to the estate. There is a beautiful shaded lane that runs down there from the house. I always fancy I see people walking in these numerous paths and arbors, but John has cautioned me not to give way to fancy in the least. He says that with my imaginative power and habit of storymaking, a nervous weakness like mine is sure to lead to all manner of excited fancies, and that I ought to use my will and good sense to check the tendency. So I try.

I think sometimes that if I were only well enough to write a little it would relieve the press of ideas and rest me.

But I find I get pretty tired when I try.

It is so discouraging not to have any advice and companionship about my work. When I get really well, John says we will ask Cousin Henry and Julia down for a long visit; but he says he would as soon put fireworks in my pillow-case as to let me have those stimulating people about now.

I wish I could get well faster.

But I must not think about that. This paper looks to me as if it *knew* what a vicious influence it had!

There is a recurrent spot where the pattern lolls like a broken neck and two bulbous eyes stare at you upside down.

I get positively angry with the impertinence of it and the everlast-ingness. Up and down and sideways they crawl, and those absurd un-blinking eyes are everywhere. There is one place where two breadths didn't match, and the eyes go all up and down the line, one a little higher than the other.

I never saw so much expression in an inanimate thing before, and we all know how much expression they have! I used to lie awake as a child and get more entertainment and terror out of blank walls and plain furniture than most children could find in a toy-store.

I remember what a kindly wink the knobs of our big old bureau used to have, and there was one chair that always seemed like a strong friend.

I used to feel that if any of the other things looked too fierce I could always hop into that chair and be safe.

The furniture in this room is no worse than inharmonious, however, for we had to bring it all from downstairs. I suppose when this was used as a playroom they had to take the nursery things out, and no wonder! I never saw such ravages as the children have made here.

The wallpaper, as I said before, is torn off in spots, and it sticketh closer than a brother—they must have had perseverance as well as hatred.

Then the floor is scratched and gouged and splintered, the plaster itself is dug out here and there, and this great heavy bed, which is all we found in the room, looks as if it had been through the wars.

But I don't mind it a bit—only the paper.

There comes John's sister. Such a dear girl as she is, and so careful of me! I must not let her find me writing.

She is a perfect and enthusiastic housekeeper, and hopes for no better profession. I verily believe she thinks it is the writing which made me sick!

But I can write when she is out, and see her a long way off from these windows.

There is one that commands the road, a lovely shaded winding road, and one that just looks off over the country. A lovely country, too, full of great elms and velvet meadows.

This wallpaper has a kind of subpattern in a different shade, a particularly irritating one, for you can only see it in certain lights, and not clearly then.

But in the places where it isn't faded and where the sun is just so— I can see a strange, provoking, formless sort of figure that seems to skulk about behind that silly and conspicuous front design.

There's sister on the stairs!

Well, the Fourth of July is over! The people are all gone, and I am tired out. John thought it might do me good to see a little company, so we just had Mother and Nellie and the children down for a week.

Of course I didn't do a thing. Jennie sees to everything now.

But it tired me all the same.

John says if I don't pick up faster he shall send me to Weir Mitchell[1] in the fall.

But I don't want to go there at all. I had a friend who was in his hands once, and she says he is just like John and my brother, only more so!

Besides, it is such an undertaking to go so far.

I don't feel as if it was worthwhile to turn my hand over for anything, and I'm getting dreadfully fretful and querulous.

I cry at nothing, and cry most of the time.

Of course I don't when John is here, or anybody else, but when I am alone.

And I am alone a good deal just now. John is kept in town very often by serious cases, and Jennie is good and lets me alone when I want her to.

So I walk a little in the garden or down that lovely lane, sit on the porch under the roses, and lie down up here a good deal.

I'm getting really fond of the room in spite of the wallpaper. Perhaps *because* of the wallpaper.

It dwells in my mind so!

I lie here on this great immovable bed—it is nailed down, I believe—and follow that pattern about by the hour. It is as good as gymnastics, I assure you. I start, we'll say, at the bottom, down in the corner over there where it has not been touched, and I determine for the thousandth time that I *will* follow that pointless pattern to some sort of a conclusion.

I know a little of the principle of design, and I know this thing was not arranged on any laws of radiation,[2] or alternation, or repetition, or symmetry, or anything else that I ever heard of.

It is repeated, of course, by the breadths, but not otherwise.

Looked at in one way, each breadth stands alone; the bloated curves and flourishes—a kind of "debased Romanesque" with *delirium tremens*—go waddling up and down in isolated columns of fatuity.

[1]**Weir Mitchell** (1829–1914) famed nerve specialist who actually treated the author, Charlotte Perkins Gilman, for nervous prostration with his well-known "rest cure." (The cure was not successful.) Also the author of *Diseases of the Nervous System, Especially of Women* (1881).
[2]**laws of radiation** a principle of design in which all elements are arranged in some circular pattern around a center

But, on the other hand, they connect diagonally, and the sprawling outlines run off in great slanting waves of optic horror, like a lot of wallowing seaweeds in full chase.

The whole thing goes horizontally, too, at least it seems so, and I exhaust myself trying to distinguish the order of its going in that direction.

They have used a horizontal breadth for a frieze, and that adds wonderfully to the confusion.

There is one end of the room where it is almost intact, and there, when the crosslights fade and the low sun shines directly upon it, I can almost fancy radiation after all—the interminable grotesque seems to form around a common center and rush off in headlong plunges of equal distraction.

It makes me tired to follow it. I will take a nap, I guess.

I don't know why I should write this.

I don't want to.

I don't feel able.

And I know John would think it absurd. But I *must* say what I feel and think in some way—it is such a relief!

But the effort is getting to be greater than the relief.

Half the time now I am awfully lazy, and lie down ever so much. John says I mustn't lose my strength, and has me take cod liver oil and lots of tonics and things, to say nothing of ale and wines and rare meat.

Dear John! He loves me very dearly, and hates to have me sick. I tried to have a real earnest reasonable talk with him the other day, and tell him how I wish he would let me go and make a visit to Cousin Henry and Julia.

But he said I wasn't able to go, nor able to stand it after I got there; and I did not make out a very good case for myself, for I was crying before I had finished.

It is getting to be a great effort for me to think straight. Just this nervous weakness, I suppose.

And dear John gathered me up in his arms, and just carried me upstairs and laid me on the bed, and sat by me and read to me till it tired my head.

He said I was his darling and his comfort and all he had, and that I must take care of myself for his sake, and keep well.

He says no one but myself can help me out of it, that I must use my will and self-control and not let any silly fancies run away with me.

There's one comfort—the baby is well and happy, and does not have to occupy this nursery with the horrid wallpaper.

If we had not used it, that blessed child would have! What a fortunate escape! Why, I wouldn't have a child of mine, an impressionable little thing, live in such a room for worlds.

I never thought of it before, but it is lucky that John kept me here after all; I can stand it so much easier than a baby, you see.

Of course I never mention it to them any more—I am too wise—but I keep watch for it all the same.

There are things in the wallpaper that nobody knows about but me, or ever will.

Behind that outside pattern the dim shapes get clearer every day.

It is always the same shape, only very numerous.

And it is like a woman stooping down and creeping about behind that pattern. I don't like it a bit. I wonder—I begin to think—I wish John would take me away from here!

It is so hard to talk with John about my case, because he is so wise, and because he loves me so.

But I tried it last night.

It was moonlight. The moon shines in all around just as the sun does.

I hate to see it sometimes, it creeps so slowly, and always comes in by one window or another.

John was asleep and I hated to waken him, so I kept still and watched the moonlight on that undulating wallpaper till I felt creepy.

The faint figure behind seemed to shake the pattern, just as if she wanted to get out.

I got up softly and went to feel and see if the paper *did* move, and when I came back John was awake.

"What is it, little girl?" he said. "Don't go walking about like that—you'll get cold."

I thought it was a good time to talk, so I told him that I really was not gaining here, and that I wished he would take me away.

"Why, darling!" said he. "Our lease will be up in three weeks, and I can't see how to leave before.

"The repairs are not done at home, and I cannot possibly leave town just now. Of course, if you were in any danger, I could and would, but you really are better, dear, whether you can see it or not. I am a doctor, dear, and I know. You are gaining flesh and color, your appetite is better, I feel really much easier about you."

"I don't weigh a bit more," said I, "nor as much; and my appetite may be better in the evening when you are here but it is worse in the morning when you are away!"

"Bless her little heart!" said he with a big hug. "She shall be as sick as she pleases! But now let's improve the shining hours by going to sleep, and talk about it in the morning!"

"And you won't go away?" I asked gloomily.

"Why, how can I, dear? It is only three weeks more and then we will take a nice little trip for a few days while Jennie is getting the house ready. Really, dear, you are better!"

"Better in body perhaps—" I began, and stopped short, for he sat up straight and looked at me with such a stern, reproachful look that I could not say another word.

"My darling," said he, "I beg you, for my sake and for our child's sake, as well as for your own, that you will never for one instant let that idea enter your mind! There is nothing so dangerous, so fascinating, to a temperament like yours. It is a false and foolish fancy. Can you trust me as a physician when I tell you so?"

So of course I said no more on that score, and we went to sleep before long. He thought I was asleep first, but I wasn't, and lay there for hours trying to decide whether that front pattern and the back pattern really did move together or separately.

On a pattern like this, by daylight, there is a lack of sequence, a defiance of law, that is a constant irritant to a normal mind.

The color is hideous enough, and unreliable enough, and infuriating enough, but the pattern is torturing.

You think you have mastered it, but just as you get well under way in following, it turns a back-somersault and there you are. It slaps you in the face, knocks you down, and tramples upon you. It is like a bad dream.

The outside pattern is a florid arabesque,[3] reminding one of a fungus. If you can imagine a toadstool in joints, an interminable string of toadstools, budding and sprouting in endless convolutions—why, that is something like it.

That is, sometimes!

[3]**arabesque** a type of ornamental style (Arabic in origin) that uses flowers, foliage, fruit, or other figures to create an intricate pattern of interlocking shapes and lines

There is one marked peculiarity about this paper, a thing nobody seems to notice but myself, and that is that it changes as the light changes.

When the sun shoots in through the east window—I always watch for that first long, straight ray—it changes so quickly that I never can quite believe it.

That is why I watch it always.

By moonlight—the moon shines in all night when there is a moon—I wouldn't know it was the same paper.

At night in any kind of light, in twilight, candlelight, lamplight, and worst of all by moonlight, it becomes bars! The outside pattern, I mean, and the woman behind it is as plain as can be.

I didn't realize for a long time what the thing was that showed behind, that dim subpattern, but now I am quite sure it is a woman.

By daylight she is subdued, quiet. I fancy it is the pattern that keeps her so still. It is so puzzling. It keeps me quiet by the hour.

I lie down ever so much now. John says it is good for me, and to sleep all I can.

Indeed he started the habit by making me lie down for an hour after each meal.

It is a very bad habit, I am convinced, for you see, I don't sleep.

And that cultivates deceit, for I don't tell them I'm awake—oh, no!

The fact is I am getting a little afraid of John.

He seems very queer sometimes, and even Jennie has an inexplicable look.

It strikes me occasionally, just as a scientific hypothesis, that perhaps it is the paper!

I have watched John when he did not know I was looking, and come into the room suddenly on the most innocent excuses, and I've caught him several times *looking at the paper!* And Jennie too. I caught Jennie with her hand on it once.

She didn't know I was in the room, and when I asked her in a quiet, a very quiet voice, with the most restrained manner possible, what she was doing with the paper, she turned around as if she had been caught stealing, and looked quite angry—asked me why I should frighten her so!

Then she said that the paper stained everything it touched, that she had found yellow smooches[4] on all my clothes and John's and she wished we would be more careful!

---

[4]**smooches** smudges or smears

Did not that sound innocent? But I know she was studying that pattern, and I am determined that nobody shall find it out but myself!

Life is very much more exciting now than it used to be. You see, I have something more to expect, to look forward to, to watch. I really do eat better, and am more quiet than I was.

John is so pleased to see me improve! He laughed a little the other day, and said I seemed to be flourishing in spite of my wallpaper.

I turned it off with a laugh. I had no intention of telling him it was *because* of the wallpaper—he would make fun of me. He might even want to take me away.

I don't want to leave now until I have found it out. There is a week more, and I think that will be enough.

I'm feeling so much better!

I don't sleep much at night, for it is so interesting to watch developments; but I sleep a good deal during the daytime.

In the daytime it is tiresome and perplexing.

There are always new shoots on the fungus, and new shades of yellow all over it. I cannot keep count of them, though I have tried conscientiously.

It is the strangest yellow, that wallpaper! It makes me think of all the yellow things I ever saw—not beautiful ones like buttercups, but old, foul, bad yellow things.

But there is something else about that paper—the smell! I noticed it the moment we came into the room, but with so much air and sun it was not bad. Now we have had a week of fog and rain, and whether the windows are open or not, the smell is here.

It creeps all over the house.

I find it hovering in the dining-room, skulking in the parlor, hiding in the hall, lying in wait for me on the stairs.

It gets into my hair.

Even when I go to ride, if I turn my head suddenly and surprise it— there is that smell!

Such a peculiar odor, too! I have spent hours in trying to analyze it, to find what it smelled like.

It is not bad—at first—and very gentle, but quite the subtlest, most enduring odor I ever met.

In this damp weather it is awful. I wake up in the night and find it hanging over me.

It used to disturb me at first. I thought seriously of burning the house—to reach the smell.

But now I am used to it. The only thing I can think of that it is like is the *color* of the paper! A yellow smell.

There is a very funny mark on this wall, low down, near the mop-board. A streak that runs round the room. It goes behind every piece of furniture, except the bed, a long, straight, even *smooch*, as if it had been rubbed over and over.

I wonder how it was done and who did it, and what they did it for. Round and round and round—round and round and round—it makes me dizzy!

I really have discovered something at last.

Through watching so much at night, when it changes so, I have finally found out.

The front pattern *does* move—and no wonder! The woman behind shakes it!

Sometimes I think there are a great many women behind, and sometimes only one, and she crawls around fast, and her crawling shakes it all over.

Then in the very bright spots she keeps still, and in the very shady spots she just takes hold of the bars and shakes them hard.

And she is all the time trying to climb through. But nobody could climb through that pattern—it strangles so; I think that is why it has so many heads.

They get through and then the pattern strangles them off and turns them upside down, and makes their eyes white!

If those heads were covered or taken off it would not be half so bad.

I think that woman gets out in the daytime!

And I'll tell you why—privately—I've seen her!

I can see her out of every one of my windows!

It is the same woman, I know, for she is always creeping, and most women do not creep by daylight.

I see her in that long shaded lane, creeping up and down. I see her in those dark grape arbors, creeping all round the garden.

I see her on that long road under the trees, creeping along, and when a carriage comes she hides under the blackberry vines.

I don't blame her a bit. It must be very humiliating to be caught creeping by daylight!

I always lock the door when I creep by daylight. I can't do it at night, for I know John would suspect something at once.

And John is so queer now that I don't want to irritate him. I wish he would take another room! Besides, I don't want anybody to get that woman out at night but myself.

I often wonder if I could see her out of all the windows at once.

But, turn as fast as I can, I can only see out of one at one time.

And though I always see her, she may be able to creep faster than I can turn! I have watched her sometimes away off in the open country, creeping as fast as a cloud shadow in a wind.

If only that top pattern could be gotten off from the under one! I mean to try it, little by little.

I have found out another funny thing, but I shan't tell it this time! It does not do to trust people too much.

There are only two more days to get this paper off, and I believe John is beginning to notice. I don't like the look in his eyes.

And I heard him ask Jennie a lot of professional questions about me. She had a very good report to give.

She said I slept a good deal in the daytime.

John knows I don't sleep very well at night, for all I'm so quiet!

He asked me all sorts of questions too, and pretended to be very loving and kind.

As if I couldn't see through him!

Still, I don't wonder he acts so, sleeping under this paper for three months.

It only interests me, but I feel sure John and Jennie are affected by it.

Hurrah! This is the last day, but it is enough. John is to stay in town over night, and won't be out until this evening.

Jennie wanted to sleep with me—the sly thing; but I told her I should undoubtedly rest better for a night all alone.

That was clever, for really I wasn't alone a bit! As soon as it was moonlight and that poor thing began to crawl and shake the pattern, I got up and ran to help her.

I pulled and she shook, I shook and she pulled, and before morning we had peeled off yards of that paper.

A strip about as high as my head and half around the room.

And then when the sun came and that awful pattern began to laugh at me, I declared I would finish it today!

We go away tomorrow, and they are moving all my furniture down again to leave things as they were before.

Jennie looked at the wall in amazement, but I told her merrily that I did it out of pure spite at the vicious thing.

She laughed and said she wouldn't mind doing it herself, but I must not get tired.

How she betrayed herself that time!

But I am here, and no person touches this paper but Me—not *alive!*

She tried to get me out of the room—it was too patent! But I said it was so quiet and empty and clean now that I believed I would lie down again and sleep all I could, and not to wake me even for dinner—I would call when I woke.

So now she is gone, and the servants are gone, and the things are gone, and there is nothing left but that great bedstead nailed down, with the canvas mattress we found on it.

We shall sleep downstairs tonight, and take the boat home tomorrow.

I quite enjoy the room, now it is bare again.

How those children did tear about here!

This bedstead is fairly gnawed!

But I must get to work.

I have locked the door and thrown the key down into the front path.

I don't want to go out, and I don't want to have anybody come in, till John comes.

I want to astonish him.

I've got a rope up here that even Jennie did not find. If that woman does get out, and tries to get away, I can tie her!

But I forgot I could not reach far without anything to stand on!

This bed will *not* move!

I tried to lift and push it until I was lame, and then I got so angry I bit off a little piece at one corner—but it hurt my teeth.

Then I peeled off all the paper I could reach standing on the floor. It sticks horribly and the pattern just enjoys it! All those strangled heads and bulbous eyes and waddling fungus growths just shriek with derision!

I am getting angry enough to do something desperate. To jump out of the window would be admirable exercise, but the bars are too strong even to try.

Besides I wouldn't do it. Of course not. I know well enough that a step like that is improper and might be misconstrued.

I don't like to *look* out of the windows even—there are so many of those creeping women, and they creep so fast.

I wonder if they all come out of that wallpaper as I did!

But I am securely fastened now by my well-hidden rope—you don't get *me* out in the road there!

I suppose I shall have to get back behind the pattern when it comes night, and that is hard!

It is so pleasant to be out in this great room and creep around as I please!

I don't want to go outside. I won't, even if Jennie asks me to:

For outside you have to creep on the ground, and everything is green instead of yellow.

But here I can creep smoothly on the floor, and my shoulder just fits in that long smooch around the wall, so I cannot lose my way.

Why, there's John at the door!

It is no use, young man, you can't open it!

How he does call and pound!

Now he's crying to Jennie for an axe.

It would be a shame to break down that beautiful door!

"John, dear!" said I in the gentlest voice. "The key is down by the front steps, under a plantain leaf!"

That silenced him for a few moments.

Then he said, very quietly indeed, "Open the door, my darling!"

"I can't," said I. "The key is down by the front door under a plantain leaf!" And then I said it again, several times, very gently and slowly, and said it so often that he had to go and see, and he got it of course, and came in. He stopped short by the door.

"What is the matter?" he cried. "For God's sake, what are you doing!"

I kept on creeping just the same, but I looked at him over my shoulder.

"I've got out at last," said I, "in spite of you and Jane.[5] And I've pulled off most of the paper, so you can't put me back!"

Now why should that man have fainted? But he did, and right across my path by the wall, so that I had to creep over him every time!

—1892

---

[5]**Jane** presumably the given name of her sister-in-law, Jennie.

Edith Wharton was born into a socially prominent New York family and was privately educated at home and in Europe. A writer from her adolescence, Wharton received little encouragement from her parents or her husband, Edward Wharton, whom she married in 1885. Wharton's marriage was never happy, although it lasted until 1912, when her husband's serious mental illness made divorce imperative. Wharton's first publication was a book on interior decorating, but near the turn of the century her short fiction began to appear in magazines and was first collected in The Greater Inclination *(1899). Novels such as* The House of Mirth *(1905) and* The Age of Innocence *(1920) proved popular and have both been made into successful film versions. Wharton was awarded the Pulitzer Prize for* The Age of Innocence, *and the stage adaptation of another of her works,* The Old Maid, *also won a Pulitzer in 1935. Following her divorce, Wharton lived in France and was made a member of the Legion of Honor for her relief work during World War I. A longtime friend of Henry James, she shared some of the elder writer's interests as a keen observer and chronicler of the comedies (and tragedies) of manners among the American upper class. It is somewhat ironic that one of her best-known works today is the novella* Ethan Frome *(1911), a grimly naturalistic tale of a doomed love triangle set in rural New England.*

Roman Fever

I

From the table at which they had been lunching two American ladies of ripe but well-cared-for middle age moved across the lofty terrace of the Roman restaurant and, leaning on its parapet, looked first at each other, and then down on the outspread glories of the Palatine and the Forum, with the same expression of vague but benevolent approval.

As they leaned there a girlish voice echoed up gaily from the stairs leading to the court below. "Well, come along, then," it cried, not to them but to an invisible companion, "and let's leave the young things to their knitting," and a voice as fresh laughed back: "Oh, look here, Babs, not actually *knitting*—" "Well, I mean figuratively," rejoined the first. "After all, we haven't left our poor parents much else to do . . ." and at that point the turn of the stairs engulfed the dialogue.

The two ladies looked at each other again, this time with a tinge of smiling embarrassment; and the smaller and paler one shook her head and colored slightly.

"Barbara!" she murmured, sending an unheard rebuke after the mocking voice in the stairway.

The other lady, who was fuller, and higher in color, with a small determined nose supported by vigorous black eyebrows, gave a good-humoured laugh. "That's what our daughters think of us!"

Her companion replied by a deprecating gesture. "Not of us individually. We must remember that. It's just the collective modern idea of Mothers. And you see—" Half guiltily she drew from her handsomely mounted black hand-bag a twist of crimson silk run through by two fine knitting needles. "One never knows," she murmured. "The new system has certainly given us a good deal of time to kill; and sometimes I get tired just looking—even at this." Her gesture was now addressed to the stupendous scene at their feet.

The dark lady laughed again, and they both relapsed upon the view, contemplating it in silence, with a sort of diffused serenity which might have been borrowed from the spring effulgence of the Roman skies. The luncheon hour was long past, and the two had their end of the vast terrace to themselves. At its opposite extremity a few groups, detained by a lingering look at the outspread city, were gathering up guide-books and fumbling for tips. The last of them scattered, and the two ladies were alone on the air-washed height.

"Well, I don't see why we shouldn't just stay here," said Mrs. Slade, the lady of the high color and energetic brows. Two derelict basket chairs stood near, and she pushed them into the angle of the parapet, and settled herself in one, her gaze upon the Palatine. "After all, it's still the most beautiful view in the world."

"It will always be, to me," assented her friend Mrs. Ansley, with so slight a stress on the "me" that Mrs. Slade, though she noticed it, wondered if it were not merely accidental, like the random underlinings of old-fashioned letter writers.

"Grace Ansley was always old-fashioned," she thought; and added aloud, with a retrospective smile: "It's a view we've both been familiar with for a good many years. When we first met here we were younger than our girls are now. You remember?"

"Oh, yes, I remember," murmured Mrs. Ansley, with the same undefinable stress—"There's that headwaiter wondering," she interpolated.

She was evidently far less sure than her companion of herself and of her rights in the world.

"I'll cure him of wondering," said Mrs. Slade, stretching her hand toward a bag as discreetly opulent-looking as Mrs. Ansley's. Signing to the head-waiter, she explained that she and her friend were old lovers of Rome, and would like to spend the end of the afternoon looking down on the view—that is, if it did not disturb the service? The head-waiter, bowing over her gratuity, assured her that the ladies were most welcome, and would be still more so if they would condescend to remain for dinner. A full moon night, they would remember. . . .

Mrs. Slade's black brows drew together, as though references to the moon were out-of-place and even unwelcome. But she smiled away her frown as the head-waiter retreated. "Well, why not? We might do worse. There's no way of knowing, I suppose, when the girls will be back. Do you even know back from *where?* I don't!"

Mrs. Ansley again colored slightly. "I think those young Italian aviators we met at the Embassy invited them to fly to Tarquinia for tea. I suppose they'll want to wait and fly back by moonlight."

"Moonlight—moonlight! What a part it still plays. Do you suppose they're as sentimental as we were?"

"I've come to the conclusion that I don't in the least know what they are," said Mrs. Ansley. "And perhaps we didn't know much more about each other."

"No; perhaps we didn't."

Her friend gave her a shy glance. "I never should have supposed you were sentimental, Alida."

"Well, perhaps I wasn't." Mrs. Slade drew her lips together in retrospect; and for a few moments the two ladies, who had been intimate since childhood, reflected how little they knew each other. Each one, of course, had a label ready to attach to the other's name; Mrs. Delphin Slade, for instance, would have told herself, or any one who asked her, that Mrs. Horace Ansley, twenty-five years ago, had been exquisitely lovely—no, you wouldn't believe it, would you? . . . though, of course, still charming, distinguished. . . . Well, as a girl she had been exquisite; far more beautiful than her daughter Barbara, though certainly Babs, according to the new standards at any rate, was more effective—had more *edge*, as they say. Funny where she got it, with those two nullities as parents. Yes; Horace Ansley was—well, just the duplicate of his wife. Museum specimens of old New York. Good-looking, irreproachable, exemplary. Mrs. Slade and Mrs. Ansley had lived opposite each other—

actually as well as figuratively—for years. When the drawing-room curtains in No. 20 East 73rd Street were renewed, No. 23, across the way, was always aware of it. And of all the movings, buyings, travels, anniversaries, illnesses—the tame chronicle of an estimable pair. Little of it escaped Mrs. Slade. But she had grown bored with it by the time her husband made his big *coup* in Wall Street, and when they bought in upper Park Avenue had already begun to think: "I'd rather live opposite a speakeasy for a change; at least one might see it raided." The idea of seeing Grace raided was so amusing that (before the move) she launched it at a women's lunch. It made a hit, and went the rounds— she sometimes wondered if it had crossed the street, and reached Mrs. Ansley. She hoped not, but didn't much mind. Those were the days when respectability was at a discount, and it did the irreproachable no harm to laugh at them a little.

A few years later, and not many months apart, both ladies lost their husbands. There was an appropriate exchange of wreaths and condolences, and a brief renewal of intimacy in the half-shadow of their mourning; and now, after another interval, they had run across each other in Rome, at the same hotel, each of them the modest appendage of a salient daughter. The similarity of their lot had again drawn them together, lending itself to mild jokes, and the mutual confession that, if in old days it must have been tiring to "keep up" with daughters, it was now, at times, a little dull not to.

No doubt, Mrs. Slade reflected, she felt her unemployment more than poor Grace ever would. It was a big drop from being the wife of Delphin Slade to being his widow. She had always regarded herself (with a certain conjugal pride) as his equal in social gifts, as contributing her full share to the making of the exceptional couple they were: but the difference after his death was irremediable. As the wife of the famous corporation lawyer, always with an international case or two on hand, every day brought its exciting and unexpected obligation: the impromptu entertaining of eminent colleagues from abroad, the hurried dashes on legal business to London, Paris or Rome, where the entertaining was so handsomely reciprocated; the amusement of hearing in her wake: "What, that handsome woman with the good clothes and the eyes is Mrs. Slade—*the* Slade's wife? Really? Generally the wives of celebrities are such frumps."

Yes; being *the* Slade's widow was a dullish business after that. In living up to such a husband all her faculties had been engaged; now she had only her daughter to live up to, for the son who seemed to have inherited his father's gifts had died suddenly in boyhood. She had fought through that agony because her husband was there, to be helped and to help; now, after the father's death, the thought of the boy had become unbearable. There was nothing left but to mother her daughter; and dear Jenny was such a perfect daughter that she needed no excessive mothering. "Now with Babs Ansley I don't know that I *should* be so quiet," Mrs. Slade sometimes half-enviously reflected; but Jenny, who was younger than her brilliant friend, was that rare accident, an extremely pretty girl who somehow made youth and prettiness seem as safe as their absence. It was all perplexing—and to Mrs. Slade a little boring. She wished that Jenny would fall in love—with the wrong man, even; that she might have to be watched, out-maneuvered, rescued. And instead, it was Jenny who watched her mother, kept her out of draughts, made sure that she had taken her tonic. . . .

Mrs. Ansley was much less articulate than her friend, and her mental portrait of Mrs. Slade was slighter, and drawn with fainter touches. "Alida Slade's awfully brilliant; but not as brilliant as she thinks," would have summed it up; though she would have added, for the enlightenment of strangers, that Mrs. Slade had been an extremely dashing girl; much more so than her daughter, who was pretty, of course, and clever in a way, but had none of her mother's— well "vividness," someone had once called it. Mrs. Ansley would take up current words like this, and cite them in quotation marks, as unheard-of audacities. No; Jenny was not like her mother. Sometimes Mrs. Ansley thought Alida Slade was disappointed; on the whole she had had a sad life. Full of failures and mistakes; Mrs. Ansley had always been rather sorry for her. . . .

So these two ladies visualized each other, each through the wrong end of her little telescope.

II

For a long time they continued to sit side by side without speaking. It seemed as though, to both, there was a relief in laying down their somewhat futile activities in the presence of the vast Memento Mori[1] which faced them. Mrs. Slade sat quite still, her eyes fixed on the golden slope of the Palace of the Caesars, and after a while Mrs. Ansley

[1]**Memento Mori** The Latin means "remember you must die": it applies to any object that reminds one of mortality.

ceased to fidget with her bag, and she too sank into meditation. Like many intimate friends, the two ladies had never before had occasion to be silent together, and Mrs. Ansley was slightly embarrassed by what seemed, after so many years, a new stage in their intimacy, and one with which she did not yet know how to deal.

Suddenly the air was full of that deep clangor of bells which periodically covers Rome with a roof of silver. Mrs. Slade glanced at her wristwatch. "Five o'clock already," she said, as though surprised.

Mrs. Ansley suggested interrogatively: "There's bridge at the Embassy at five." For a long time Mrs. Slade did not answer. She appeared to be lost in contemplation, and Mrs. Ansley thought the remark had escaped her. But after a while she said, as if speaking out of a dream: "Bridge, did you say? Not unless you want to. . . . But I don't think I will, you know."

"Oh, no," Mrs. Ansley hastened to assure her. "I don't care to at all. It's so lovely here; and so full of old memories, as you say." She settled herself in her chair, and almost furtively drew forth her knitting. Mrs. Slade took sideway note of this activity, but her own beautifully cared-for hands remained motionless on her knee.

"I was just thinking," she said slowly, "what different things Rome stands for to each generation of travelers. To our grandmothers, Roman fever; to our mothers, sentimental danger—how we used to be guarded!—to our daughters, no more dangers than the middle of Main Street. They don't know it—but how much they're missing!"

The long golden light was beginning to pale, and Mrs. Ansley lifted her knitting a little closer to her eyes. "Yes; how we were guarded!"

"I always used to think," Mrs. Slade continued, "that our mothers had a much more difficult job than our grandmothers. When Roman fever stalked the streets it must have been comparatively easy to gather in the girls at the danger hour; but when you and I were young, with such beauty calling us, and the spice of disobedience thrown in, and no worse risk than catching cold during the cool hour after sunset, the mothers used to be put to it to keep us in—didn't they?"

She turned again toward Mrs. Ansley, but the latter had reached a delicate point in her knitting. "One, two, three—slip two; yes, they must have been," she assented, without looking up.

Mrs. Slade's eyes rested on her with a deepened attention. "She can knit—in the face of *this!* How like her. . . ."

Mrs. Slade leaned back, brooding, her eyes ranging from the ruins which faced her to the long green hollow of the Forum, the fading glow of the church fronts beyond it, and the outlying immensity of the Colosseum. Suddenly she thought: "It's all very well to say that our girls have done away with sentiment and moonlight. But if Babs Ansley isn't out to catch that young aviator—the one who's a Marchese—then I don't know anything. And Jenny has no chance beside her. I know that too. I wonder if that's why Grace Ansley likes the two girls to go everywhere together? My poor Jenny as a foil—!" Mrs. Slade gave a hardly audible laugh, and at the sound Mrs. Ansley dropped her knitting.

"Yes—?"

"I—oh, nothing. I was only thinking how your Babs carries everything before her. That Campolieri boy is one of the best matches in Rome. Don't look so innocent, my dear—you know he is. And I was wondering, ever so respectfully, you understand . . . wondering how two such exemplary characters as you and Horace had managed to produce anything quite so dynamic." Mrs. Slade laughed again, with a touch of asperity.

Mrs. Ansley's hands lay inert across her needles. She looked straight out at the accumulated wreckage of passion and splendor at her feet. But her small profile was almost expressionless. At length she said: "I think you overrate Babs, my dear."

Mrs. Slade's tone grew easier. "No; I don't. I appreciate her. And perhaps envy you. Oh, my girl's perfect; if I were a chronic invalid I'd—well, I think I'd rather be in Jenny's hands. There must be times . . . but there! I always wanted a brilliant daughter . . . and never quite understood why I got an angel instead."

Mrs. Ansley echoed her laugh in a faint murmur. "Babs is an angel too."

"Of course—of course! But she's got rainbow wings. Well, they're wandering by the sea with their young men; and here we sit . . . and it all brings back the past a little too acutely."

Mrs. Ansley had resumed her knitting. One might almost have imagined (if one had known her less well, Mrs. Slade reflected) that, for her also, too many memories rose from the lengthening shadows of those august ruins. But no; she was simply absorbed in her work. What was there for her to worry about? She knew that Babs would almost certainly come back engaged to the extremely eligible Campolieri. "And she'll sell the New York house, and settle down near them in Rome, and never be in their way . . . she's much too tactful. But she'll have an excellent cook, and just the right people in for bridge and cocktails . . . and a perfectly peaceful old age among her grandchildren."

Mrs. Slade broke off this prophetic flight with a recoil of self-disgust. There was no one of whom she had less right to think unkindly than of Grace Ansley. Would she never cure herself of envying her? Perhaps she had begun too long ago.

She stood up and leaned against the parapet, filling her troubled eyes with the tranquilizing magic of the hour. But instead of tranquilizing her the sight seemed to increase her exasperation. Her gaze turned toward the Colosseum. Already its golden flank was drowned in purple shadow, and above it the sky curved crystal clear, without light or color. It was the moment when afternoon and evening hang balanced in mid-heaven.

Mrs. Slade turned back and laid her hand on her friend's arm. The gesture was so abrupt that Mrs. Ansley looked up, startled.

"The sun's set. You're not afraid, my dear?"

"Afraid—?"

"Of Roman fever or pneumonia? I remember how ill you were that winter. As a girl you had a very delicate throat, hadn't you?"

"Oh, we're all right up here. Down below, in the Forum, it does get deathly cold, all of a sudden . . . but not here."

"Ah, of course you know because you had to be so careful." Mrs. Slade turned back to the parapet. She thought: "I must make one more effort not to hate her." Aloud she said: "Whenever I look at the Forum from up here I remember that story about a great-aunt of yours, wasn't she? A dreadfully wicked great-aunt?"

"Oh yes; Great-aunt Harriet. The one who was supposed to have sent her young sister out to the Forum after sunset to gather a night-blooming flower for her album. All of our great-aunts and grandmothers used to have albums of dried flowers."

Mrs. Slade nodded. "But she really sent her because they were in love with the same man—"

"Well, that was the family tradition. They said Aunt Harriet confessed it years afterward. At any rate, the poor little sister caught the fever and died. Mother used to frighten us with the story when we were children."

"And you frightened *me* with it, that winter when you and I were here as girls. The winter I was engaged to Delphin."

Mrs. Ansley gave a faint laugh. "Oh, did I? Really frightened you? I don't believe you're easily frightened."

"Not often; but I was then. I was easily frightened because I was too happy. I wonder if you know what that means?"

"I—yes. . . ." Mrs. Ansley faltered.

"Well, I suppose that was why the story of your wicked aunt made such an impression on me. And I thought: 'There's no more Roman fever, but the Forum is deathly cold after sunset—especially after a hot day. And the Colosseum's even colder and damper.'"

"The Colosseum—?"

"Yes. It wasn't easy to get in, after the gates were locked for the night. Far from easy. Still, in those days it could be managed; it was managed, often. Lovers met there who couldn't meet elsewhere. You knew that?"

"I—I daresay. I don't remember."

"You don't remember? You don't remember going to visit some ruins or other one evening, just after dark, and catching a bad chill? You were supposed to have gone to see the moon rise. People always said that expedition was what caused your illness."

There was a moment's silence; then Mrs. Ansley rejoined: "Did they? It was all so long ago."

"Yes. And you got well again—so it didn't matter. But I suppose it struck your friends—the reason given for your illness, I mean—because everybody knew you were so prudent on account of your throat, and your mother took such care of you. . . . You *had* been out late sightseeing, hadn't you, that night?"

"Perhaps I had. The most prudent girls aren't always prudent. What made you think of it now?"

Mrs. Slade seemed to have no answer ready. But after a moment she broke out: "Because I simply can't bear it any longer—!"

Mrs. Ansley lifted her head quickly. Her eyes were wide and very pale. "Can't bear what?"

"Why—your not knowing that I've always known why you went."

"Why I went—?"

"Yes. You think I'm bluffing, don't you? Well, you went to meet the man I was engaged to—and I can repeat every word of the letter that took you there."

While Mrs. Slade spoke Mrs. Ansley had risen unsteadily to her feet. Her bag, her knitting and gloves, slid in a panic-stricken heap to the ground. She looked at Mrs. Slade as though she were looking at a ghost.

"No, no—don't," she faltered out.

"Why not? Listen, if you don't believe me. 'My one darling, things can't go on like this. I must see you alone. Come to the Colosseum immediately after dark tomorrow. There will be somebody to let you in. No one whom you need fear will suspect'—but perhaps you've forgotten what the letter said?"

Mrs. Ansley met the challenge with unexpected composure. Steadying herself against the chair she looked at her friend, and replied: "No; I know it by heart too."

"And the signature? 'Only *your* D.S.' Was that it? I'm right, am I? That was the letter that took you out that evening after dark?"

Mrs. Ansley was still looking at her. It seemed to Mrs. Slade that a slow struggle was going on behind the voluntarily controlled mask of her small quiet face. "I shouldn't have thought she had herself so well in hand," Mrs. Slade reflected, almost resentfully. But at this moment Mrs. Ansley spoke. "I don't know how you knew. I burnt that letter at once."

"Yes; you would, naturally—you're so prudent!" The sneer was open now. "And if you burnt the letter you're wondering how on earth I know what was in it. That's it, isn't it?"

Mrs. Slade waited, but Mrs. Ansley did not speak.

"Well, my dear, I know what was in that letter because I wrote it!"

"You wrote it?"

"Yes."

The two women stood for a minute staring at each other in the last golden light. Then Mrs. Ansley dropped back into her chair. "Oh," she murmured, and covered her face with her hands.

Mrs. Slade waited nervously for another word or movement. None came, and at length she broke out: "I horrify you."

Mrs. Ansley's hands dropped to her knee. The face they uncovered was streaked with tears. "I wasn't thinking of you. I was thinking—it was the only letter I ever had from him!"

"And I wrote it. Yes; I wrote it! But I was the girl he was engaged to. Did you happen to remember that?"

Mrs. Ansley's head drooped again. "I'm not trying to excuse myself... I remembered...."

"And still you went?"

"Still I went."

Mrs. Slade stood looking down on the small bowed figure at her side. The flame of her wrath had already sunk, and she wondered why she had ever thought there would be any satisfaction in inflicting so purposeless a wound on her friend. But she had to justify herself.

"You do understand? I'd found out—and I hated you, hated you. I knew you were in love with Delphin—and I was afraid; afraid of you, of your quiet ways, your sweetness . . . your . . . well, I wanted you out of the way, that's all. Just for a few weeks; just till I was sure of him. So in a blind fury I wrote that letter . . . I don't know why I'm telling you now."

"I suppose," said Mrs. Ansley slowly, "it's because you've always gone on hating me."

"Perhaps. Or because I wanted to get the whole thing off my mind." She paused. "I'm glad you destroyed the letter. Of course I never thought you'd die."

Mrs. Ansley relapsed into silence, and Mrs. Slade, leaning above her, was conscious of a strange sense of isolation, of being cut off from the warm current of human communion. "You think me a monster!"

"I don't know. . . . It was the only letter I had, and you say he didn't write it?"

"Ah, how you care for him still!"

"I cared for that memory," said Mrs. Ansley.

Mrs. Slade continued to look down on her. She seemed physically reduced by the blow—as if, when she got up, the wind might scatter her like a puff of dust. Mrs. Slade's jealousy suddenly leapt up again at the sight. All these years the woman had been living on that letter. How she must have loved him, to treasure the mere memory of its ashes! The letter of the man her friend was engaged to. Wasn't it she who was the monster?

"You tried your best to get him away from me, didn't you? But you failed; and I kept him. That's all."

"Yes. That's all."

"I wish now I hadn't told you. I've no idea you'd feel about it as you do; I thought you'd be amused. It all happened so long ago, as you say; and you must do me the justice to remember that I had no reason to think you'd ever taken it seriously. How could I, when you were married to Horace Ansley two months afterward? As soon as you could get out of bed your mother rushed you off to Florence and married you. People were rather surprised—they wondered at its being done so quickly; but I thought I knew. I had an idea you did it out of *pique*—to be able to say you'd got ahead of Delphin and me. Girls have such silly reasons for doing the most serious things. And your marrying so soon convinced me that you'd never really cared."

"Yes. I suppose it would," Mrs. Ansley assented.

The clear heaven overhead was emptied of all its gold. Dusk spread over it, abruptly darkening the Seven Hills. Here and there lights began to twinkle through the foliage at their feet. Steps were coming and going on the deserted terrace—waiters looking out of the doorway at the head of the stairs, then reappearing with trays and napkins and flasks of wine. Tables were moved, chairs straightened. A feeble string of electric lights flickered out. Some vases of faded flowers were carried away, and brought back replenished. A stout lady in a dustcoat suddenly appeared, asking in broken Italian if anyone had seen the elastic band which held together her tattered Baedeker.[2] She poked with her stick under the table at which she had lunched, the waiters assisting.

The corner where Mrs. Slade and Mrs. Ansley sat was still shadowy and deserted. For a long time neither of them spoke. At length Mrs. Slade began again: "I suppose I did it as a sort of joke—"

"A joke?"

"Well, girls are ferocious sometimes, you know. Girls in love especially. And I remember laughing to myself all that evening at the idea that you were waiting around there in the dark, dodging out of sight, listening for every sound, trying to get in—Of course I was upset when I heard you were so ill afterward."

Mrs. Ansley had not moved for a long time. But now she turned slowly toward her companion. "But I didn't wait. He'd arranged everything. He was there. We were let in at once," she said.

Mrs. Slade sprang up from her leaning position. "Delphin there? They let you in?—Ah, now you're lying!" she burst out with violence.

Mrs. Ansley's voice grew clearer, and full of surprise. "But of course he was there. Naturally he came—"

"Came? How did he know he'd find you there? You must be raving!"

Mrs. Ansley hesitated, as though reflecting. "But I answered the letter. I told him I'd be there. So he came."

Mrs. Slade flung her hands up to her face. "Oh, God—you answered! I never thought of your answering. . . ."

"It's odd you never thought of it, if you wrote the letter."

---

[2]**Baedeker** a popular guidebook for tourists

"Yes. I was blind with rage."

Mrs. Ansley rose, and drew her fur scarf about her. "It is cold here. We'd better go. . . . I'm sorry for you," she said, as she clasped the fur about her throat.

The unexpected words sent a pang through Mrs. Slade. "Yes; we'd better go." She gathered up her bag and cloak. "I don't know why you should be sorry for me," she muttered.

Mrs. Ansley stood looking away from her toward the dusky secret mass of the Colosseum. "Well—because I didn't have to wait that night."

Mrs. Slade gave an unquiet laugh. "Yes; I was beaten there. But I oughtn't to begrudge it to you, I suppose. At the end of all these years. After all, I had everything; I had him for twenty-five years. And you had nothing but that one letter that he didn't write."

Mrs. Ansley was again silent. At length she turned toward the door of the terrace. She took a step, and turned back, facing her companion.

"I had Barbara," she said, and began to move ahead of Mrs. Slade toward the stairway.

—1936

WILLA CATHER ■ (1873–1947)

Willa Cather was born in rural Virginia but moved in childhood to the Nebraska farmlands. After graduating from the University of Nebraska she lived for a time in Pittsburgh (the hometown of the title character in "Paul's Case"), where she moved so that she, like Paul, could attend the theater and concerts. After some years as a drama critic for the Pittsburgh Daily Leader and a brief term as a high school English teacher, she moved to New York, where she eventually became managing editor of McClure's Magazine, a position she held from 1906 to 1912. Her novels about the settling of the Nebraska farmlands, O Pioneers! (1913) and My Ántonia (1918), proved successful, and for the rest of her life Cather devoted her full energies to writing fiction. In her later years she ranged further for her subjects—New Mexico for the setting of Death Comes to the Archbishop (1927) and Quebec for Shadows on the Rock (1931). "Paul's Case," one of the stories that helped her obtain a position with McClure's, casts an almost clinical eye on heredity and environment as influences on the protagonist's personality. This deterministic view of character and Paul's desperate attempt to escape the dreary trap of his hometown reflect important themes of naturalism, a literary movement with which Cather would later express dissatisfaction but that dominated much fiction written near the turn of the century.

Paul's Case[1]

It was Paul's afternoon to appear before the faculty of the Pittsburgh High School to account for his various misdemeanors. He had been suspended a week ago, and his father had called at the Principal's office and confessed his perplexity about his son. Paul entered the faculty room suave and smiling. His clothes were a trifle outgrown and the tan velvet on the collar of his open overcoat was frayed and worn; but for all that there was something of the dandy about him, and he wore an opal pin in his neatly knotted black four-in-hand, and a red carnation in his buttonhole. This latter adornment the faculty somehow felt was not properly significant of the contrite spirit befitting a boy under the ban of suspension.

Paul was tall for his age and very thin, with high, cramped shoulders and a narrow chest. His eyes were remarkable for a certain hysterical brilliancy and he continually used them in a conscious, theatrical sort of way, peculiarly offensive in a boy. The pupils were abnormally large, as though he were addicted to belladonna, but there was a glassy glitter about them which that drug does not produce.

When questioned by the Principal as to why he was there, Paul stated, politely enough, that he wanted to come back to school. This was a lie, but Paul was quite accustomed to lying; found it, indeed, indispensable for overcoming friction. His teachers were asked to state their respective charges against him, which they did with such a rancor and aggrievedness as evinced that this was not a usual case. Disorder and impertinence were among the offenses named, yet each of his instructors felt that it was scarcely possible to put into words the real cause of the trouble, which lay in a sort of hysterically defiant manner of the boy's; in the contempt which they all knew he felt for them, and which he seemingly made not the least effort to conceal. Once, when he had been making a synopsis of a paragraph at the blackboard, his English teacher had stepped to his side and attempted to guide his

---

[1] "A Study in Temperament" (Cather's subtitle)

hand. Paul had started back with a shudder and thrust his hands violently behind him. The astonished woman could scarcely have been more hurt and embarrassed had he struck at her. The insult was so involuntary and definitely personal as to be unforgettable. In one way and another, he had made all his teachers, men and women alike, conscious of the same feeling of physical aversion. In one class he habitually sat with his hand shading his eyes; in another he always looked out of the window during the recitation; in another he made a running commentary on the lecture, with humorous intention.

His teachers felt this afternoon that his whole attitude was symbolized by his shrug and his flippantly red carnation flower, and they fell upon him without mercy, his English teacher leading the pack. He stood through it smiling, his pale lips parted over his white teeth. (His lips were continually twitching, and he had a habit of raising his eyebrows that was contemptuous and irritating to the last degree.) Older boys than Paul had broken down and shed tears under that baptism of fire, but his set smile did not once desert him, and his only sign of discomfort was the nervous trembling of the fingers that toyed with the buttons of his overcoat, and an occasional jerking of the other hand that held his hat. Paul was always smiling, always glancing about him, seeming to feel that people might be watching him and trying to detect something. This conscious expression, since it was as far as possible from boyish mirthfulness, was usually attributed to insolence or "smartness."

As the inquisition proceeded, one of his instructors repeated an impertinent remark of the boy's, and the Principal asked him whether he thought that a courteous speech to have made a woman. Paul shrugged his shoulders slightly and his eyebrows twitched.

"I don't know," he replied. "I didn't mean to be polite or impolite, either. I guess it's a sort of way I have of saying things regardless."

The Principal, who was a sympathetic man, asked him whether he didn't think that a way it would be well to get rid of. Paul grinned and said he guessed so. When he was told that he could go, he bowed gracefully and went out. His bow was but a repetition of the scandalous red carnation.

His teachers were in despair, and his drawing master voiced the feeling of them all when he declared there was something about the boy which none of them understood. He added: "I don't really believe that smile of his comes altogether from insolence; there's something sort of haunted about it. The boy is not strong, for one thing. I happen to know that he was born in Colorado, only a few months before his mother died out there of a long illness. There is something wrong about the fellow."

The drawing master had come to realize that, in looking at Paul, one saw only his white teeth and the forced animation of his eyes. One warm afternoon the boy had gone to sleep at his drawing-board, and his master had noted with amazement what a white, blue-veined face it was; drawn and wrinkled like an old man's about the eyes, the lips twitching even in his sleep, and stiff with a nervous tension that drew them back from his teeth.

His teachers left the building dissatisfied and unhappy; humiliated to have felt so vindictive toward a mere boy, to have uttered this feeling in cutting terms, and to have set each other on, as it were, in the gruesome game of intemperate reproach. Some of them remembered having seen a miserable street cat set at bay by a ring of tormentors.

As for Paul, he ran down the hill whistling the Soldiers' Chorus from *Faust* looking wildly behind him now and then to see whether some of his teachers were not there to writhe under his light-heartedness. As it was now late in the afternoon and Paul was on duty that evening as usher at Carnegie Hall, he decided that he would not go home to supper. When he reached the concert hall the doors were not yet open and, as it was chilly outside, he decided to go up into the picture gallery— always deserted at this hour—where there were some of Raffaeli's gay studies of Paris streets and an airy blue Venetian scene or two that always exhilarated him. He was delighted to find no one in the gallery but the old guard, who sat in one corner, a newspaper on his knee, a black patch over one eye and the other closed. Paul possessed himself of the place and walked confidently up and down, whistling under his breath. After a while he sat down before a blue Rico and lost himself. When he bethought him to look at his watch, it was after seven o'clock, and he rose with a start and ran downstairs, making a face at Augustus, peering out from the cast-room, and an evil gesture at the Venus of Milo as he passed her on the stairway.

When Paul reached the ushers' dressing-room half-a-dozen boys were there already, and he began excitedly to tumble into his uniform. It was one of the few that at all approached fitting, and Paul thought it very becoming—though he knew that the tight, straight coat accentuated his narrow chest, about which he was exceedingly sensitive. He was always considerably excited while he dressed, twanging all over to the tuning of the strings and the preliminary flourishes of the horns in the music-room; but tonight he seemed quite beside himself, and he teased and plagued the boys until, telling him that he was crazy, they put him down on the floor and sat on him.

Somewhat calmed by his suppression, Paul dashed out to the front of the house to seat the early comers. He was a model usher; gracious and smiling he ran up and down the aisles; nothing was too much trouble for him; he carried messages and brought programmes as though it were his greatest pleasure in life, and all the people in his section thought him a charming boy, feeling that he remembered and admired them. As the house filled, he grew more and more vivacious and animated, and the color came to his cheeks and lips. It was very much as though this were a great reception and Paul were the host. Just as the musicians came out to take their places, his English teacher arrived with checks for the seats which a prominent manufacturer had taken for the season. She betrayed some embarrassment when she handed Paul the tickets, and a *hauteur* which subsequently made her feel very foolish. Paul was startled for a moment, and had the feeling of wanting to put her out; what business had she here among all these fine people and gay colors? He looked her over and decided that she was not appropriately dressed and must be a fool to sit downstairs in such togs. The tickets had probably been sent her out of kindness, he reflected as he put down a seat for her, and she had about as much right to sit there as he had.

When the symphony began Paul sank into one of the rear seats with a long sigh of relief, and lost himself as he had done before the Rico. It was not that symphonies, as such, meant anything in particular to Paul, but the first sigh of the instruments seemed to free some hilarious and potent spirit within him; something that struggled there like the Genius in the bottle found by the Arab fisherman. He felt a sudden zest of life; the lights danced before his eyes and the concert hall blazed into unimaginable splendor. When the soprano soloist came on, Paul forgot even the nastiness of his teacher's being there and gave himself up to the peculiar stimulus such personages always had for him. The soloist chanced to be a German woman, by no means in her first youth, and the mother of many children; but she wore an elaborate gown and a tiara, and above all she had that indefinable air of achievement, that world-shine upon her, which, in Paul's eyes, made her a veritable queen of Romance.

After a concert was over Paul was always irritable and wretched until he got to sleep, and tonight he was even more than usually restless. He had the feeling of not being able to let down, of its being impossible to give up this delicious excitement which was the only thing that could be called living at all. During the last number he withdrew and, after hastily changing his clothes in the dressing-room, slipped out to the side door where the soprano's carriage stood. Here he began pacing rapidly up and down the walk, waiting to see her come out.

Over yonder the Schenley, in its vacant stretch, loomed big and square through the fine rain, the windows of its twelve stories glowing like those of a lighted cardboard house under a Christmas tree. All the actors and singers of the better class stayed there when they were in the city, and a number of the big manufacturers of the place lived there in the winter. Paul had often hung about the hotel, watching the people go in and out, longing to enter and leave school-masters and dull care behind him forever.

At last the singer came out, accompanied by the conductor, who helped her into her carriage and closed the door with a cordial *auf wiedersehen*[2] which set Paul to wondering whether she were not an old sweetheart of his. Paul followed the carriage over to the hotel, walking so rapidly as not to be far from the entrance when the singer alighted and disappeared behind the swinging glass doors that were opened by a negro in a tall hat and a long coat. In the moment that the door was ajar it seemed to Paul that be, too, entered. He seemed to feel himself go after her up the steps, into the warm, lighted building, into an exotic, a tropical world of shiny, glistening surfaces and basking ease. He reflected upon the mysterious dishes that were brought into the dining-room, the green bottles in buckets of ice, as he had seen them in the supper party pictures of the *Sunday World* supplement. A quick gust of wind brought the rain down with sudden vehemence, and Paul was startled to find that he was still outside in the slush of the gravel driveway; that his boots were letting in the water and his scanty overcoat was clinging wet about him; that the lights in front of the concert hall were out, and that the rain was driving in sheets between him and the orange glow of the windows above him. There it was, what he wanted—tangibly before him, like the fairy world of a Christmas pantomime, but mocking spirits stood guard at the doors, and, as the rain

[2]*auf wiedersehen* good-bye

beat in his face, Paul wondered whether he were destined always to shiver in the black night outside, looking up at it.

He turned and walked reluctantly toward the car tracks. The end had to come sometime; his father in his night-clothes at the top of the stairs, explanations that did not explain, hastily improvised fictions that were forever tripping him up, his upstairs room and its horrible yellow wall-paper, the creaking bureau with the greasy plush collar-box, and over his painted wooden bed the pictures of George Washington and John Calvin, and the framed motto, "Feed my Lambs," which had been worked in red worsted by his mother.

Half an hour later, Paul alighted from his car and went slowly down one of the side streets off the main thoroughfare. It was a highly respectable street, where all the houses were exactly alike, and where businessmen of moderate means begot and reared large families of children, all of whom went to Sabbath-school and learned the shorter catechism, and were interested in arithmetic; all of whom were as exactly alike as their homes, and of a piece with the monotony in which they lived. Paul never went up Cordelia Street without a shudder of loathing. His home was next to the house of the Cumberland[3] minister. He approached it tonight with the nerveless sense of defeat, the hopeless feeling of sinking back forever into ugliness and commonness that he had always had when he came home. The moment he turned into Cordelia Street he felt the waters close above his head. After each of these orgies of living, he experienced all the physical depression which follows a debauch; the loathing of respectable beds, of common food, of a house penetrated by kitchen odors; a shuddering repulsion for the flavorless, colorless mass of everyday existence; a morbid desire for cool things and soft lights and fresh flowers.

The nearer he approached the house, the more absolutely unequal Paul felt to the sight of it all; his ugly sleeping chamber; the cold bathroom with the grimy zinc tub, the cracked mirror, the dripping spigots; his father, at the top of the stairs, his hairy legs sticking out from his night-shirt, his feet thrust into carpet slippers. He was so much later than usual that there would certainly be inquiries and reproaches. Paul stopped short before the door. He felt that he could not be accosted by his father tonight; that he could not toss again on that miserable bed. He would not go in. He would tell his father that he had

[3]**Cumberland** an offshoot of the Presbyterian Church

no car fare, and it was raining so hard he had gone home with one of the boys and stayed all night.

Meanwhile, he was wet and cold. He went around to the back of the house and tried one of the basement windows, found it open, raised it cautiously, and scrambled down the cellar wall to the floor. There he stood, holding his breath, terrified by the noise he had made, but the floor above him was silent, and there was no creak on the stairs. He found a soap-box, and carried it over to the soft ring of light that streamed from the furnace door, and sat down. He was horribly afraid of rats, so he did not try to sleep, but sat looking distrustfully at the dark, still terrified lest he might have awakened his father. In such re- actions, after one of the experiences which made days and nights out of the dreary blanks of the calendar, when his senses were deadened, Paul's head was always singularly clear. Suppose his father had heard him getting in at the window and had come down and shot him for a burglar? Then, again, suppose his father had come down, pistol in hand, and he had cried out in time to save himself, and his father had been horrified to think how nearly he had killed him? Then, again, suppose a day should come when his father would remember that night, and wish there had been no warning cry to stay his hand? With this last supposition Paul entertained himself until daybreak.

The following Sunday was fine; the sodden November chill was broken by the last flash of autumnal summer. In the morning Paul had to go to church and Sabbath-school, as always. On seasonable Sunday afternoons the burghers of Cordelia Street always sat out on their front "stoops," and talked to their neighbors on the next stoop, or called to those across the street in neighborly fashion. The men usually sat on gay cushions placed upon the steps that led down to the sidewalk, while the women, in their Sunday "waists,"[4] sat in rockers on the cramped porches, pretending to be greatly at their ease. The children played in the streets; there were so many of them that the place resembled the recreation grounds of a kindergarten. The men on the steps—all in their shirt sleeves, their vests unbuttoned—sat with their legs well apart, their stomachs comfortably protruding, and talked of the prices of things, or told anecdotes of the sagacity of their various chiefs and overlords. They occasionally looked over the multitude of squabbling children, listened affectionately to their high-pitched, nasal voices,

[4] **"waists"** shirtwaist dresses, fashionable at the time

smiling to see their own proclivities reproduced in their offspring, and interspersed their legends of the iron kings with remarks about their sons' progress at school, their grades in arithmetic, and the amounts they had saved in their toy banks.

On this last Sunday of November, Paul sat all the afternoon on the lowest step of his "stoop," staring into the street, while his sisters, in their rockers, were talking to the minister's daughters next door about how many shirt-waists they had made in the last week, and how many waffles some one had eaten at the last church supper. When the weather was warm, and his father was in a particularly jovial frame of mind, the girls made lemonade, which was always brought out in a red-glass pitcher, ornamented with forget-me-nots in blue enamel. This the girls thought very fine, and the neighbors always joked about the suspicious color of the pitcher.

Today Paul's father sat on the top step, talking to a young man who shifted a restless baby from knee to knee. He happened to be the young man who was daily held up to Paul as a model, and after whom it was his father's dearest hope that he would pattern. This young man was of a ruddy complexion, with a compressed, red mouth, and faded, near-sighted eyes, over which he wore thick spectacles, with gold bows that curved about his ears. He was clerk to one of the magnates of a great steel corporation, and was looked upon in Cordelia Street as a young man with a future. There was a story that, some five years ago— he was now barely twenty-six—he had been a trifle dissipated but in order to curb his appetites and save the loss of time and strength that a sowing of wild oats might have entailed, he had taken his chief's advice, oft reiterated to his employees, and at twenty-one had married the first woman whom he could persuade to share his fortunes. She happened to be an angular schoolmistress, much older than he, who also wore thick glasses, and who had now borne him four children, all near-sighted, like herself.

The young man was relating how his chief, now cruising in the Mediterranean, kept in touch with all the details of the business, arranging his office hours on his yacht just as though he were at home, and "knocking off work enough to keep two stenographers busy." His father told, in turn, the plan his corporation was considering, of putting in an electric railway plant at Cairo. Paul snapped his teeth; he had an awful apprehension that they might spoil it all before he got there. Yet he rather liked to hear these legends of the iron kings, that were told and retold on Sundays and holidays; these stories of palaces in Venice, yachts on the Mediterranean, and high play at Monte Carlo appealed to his fancy, and he was interested in the triumphs of these cash boys who had become famous, though he had no mind for the cash-boy stage.

After supper was over, and he had helped to dry the dishes, Paul nervously asked his father whether he could go to George's to get some help in his geometry, and still more nervously asked for car fare. This latter request he had to repeat, as his father, on principle, did not like to hear requests for money, whether much or little. He asked Paul whether he could not go to some boy who lived nearer, and told him that he ought not to leave his school work until Sunday; but he gave him the dime. He was not a poor man, but he had a worthy ambition to come up in the world. His only reason for allowing Paul to usher was, that he thought a boy ought to be earning a little.

Paul bounded upstairs, scrubbed the greasy odor of the dish-water from his hands with the ill-smelling soap he hated, and then shook over his fingers a few drops of violet water from the bottle he kept hidden in his drawer. He left the house with his geometry conspicuously under his arm, and the moment he got out of Cordelia Street and boarded a downtown car, he shook off the lethargy of two deadening days, and began to live again.

The leading juvenile of the permanent stock company which played at one of the downtown theatres was an acquaintance of Paul's, and the boy had been invited to drop in at the Sunday-night rehearsals whenever he could. For more than a year Paul had spent every available moment loitering about Charley Edwards's dressing-room. He had won a place among Edwards's following not only because the young actor, who could not afford to employ a dresser, often found him useful, but because he recognized in Paul something akin to what churchmen term "vocation."

It was at the theatre and at Carnegie Hall that Paul really lived; the rest was but a sleep and a forgetting. This was Paul's fairy tale, and it had for him all the allurement of a secret love. The moment he inhaled the gassy, painty, dusty odor behind the scenes, he breathed like a prisoner set free, and felt within him the possibility of doing or saying splendid, brilliant, poetic things. The moment the cracked orchestra beat out the overture from *Martha*, or jerked at the serenade from *Rigoletto*, all stupid and ugly things slid from him, and his senses were deliciously, yet delicately fired.

Perhaps it was because, in Paul's world, the natural nearly always wore the guise of ugliness, that a certain element of artificiality seemed to him necessary in beauty. Perhaps it was because his experience of life elsewhere was so full of Sabbath-school picnics, petty economies, wholesome advice as to how to succeed in life, and the unescapable odors of cooking, that he found this existence so alluring, these smartly-clad men and women so attractive, that he was so moved by these starry apple orchards that bloomed perennially under the limelight.

It would be difficult to put it strongly enough how convincingly the stage entrance of that theatre was for Paul the actual portal of Romance. Certainly none of the company ever suspected it, least of all Charley Edwards. It was very like the old stories that used to float about London of fabulously rich Jews, who had subterranean halls there, with palms, and fountains, and soft lamps and richly apparelled women who never saw the disenchanting light of London day. So, in the midst of that smoke-palled city, enamored of figures and grimy toil, Paul had his secret temple, his wishing carpet, his bit of blue-and-white Mediterranean shore bathed in perpetual sunshine.

Several of Paul's teachers had a theory that his imagination had been perverted by garish fiction, but the truth was that he scarcely ever read at all. The books at home were not such as would either tempt or corrupt a youthful mind, and as for reading the novels that some of his friends urged upon him—well, he got what he wanted much more quickly from music; any sort of music, from an orchestra to a barrel organ. He needed only the spark, the indescribable thrill that made his imagination master of his senses, and he could make plots and pictures enough of his own. It was equally true that he was not stage struck—not, at any rate, in the usual acceptation of that expression. He had no desire to become an actor, any more than he had to become a musician. He felt no necessity to do any of these things; what he wanted was to see, to be in the atmosphere, float on the wave of it, to be carried out, blue league after blue league, away from everything.

After a night behind the scenes, Paul found the school room more than ever repulsive; the bare floors and naked walls; the prosy men who never wore frock coats, or violets in their button-holes; the women with their dull gowns, shrill voices, and pitiful seriousness about prepositions that govern the dative. He could not bear to have the other pupils think, for a moment, that he took these people seriously; he must convey to them that he considered it all trivial, and was there only by way of a jest, anyway. He had autographed pictures of all the members of the stock company which he showed his classmates, telling them the most incredible stories of his familiarity with these people, of his acquaintance with the soloists who came to Carnegie Hall, his suppers with them and the flowers he sent them. When these stories lost their effect, and his audience grew listless, he became desperate and would bid all the boys good-bye, announcing that he was going to travel for a while; going to Naples, to Venice, to Egypt. Then, next Monday, he would slip back, conscious and nervously smiling; his sister was ill, and he should have to defer his voyage until spring.

Matters went steadily worse with Paul at school. In the itch to let his instructors know how heartily he despised them and their homilies, and how thoroughly he was appreciated elsewhere, he mentioned once or twice that he had no time to fool with theorems; adding—with a twitch of the eyebrows and a touch of that nervous bravado which so perplexed them—that he was helping the people down at the stock company; they were old friends of his.

The upshot of the matter was that the Principal went to Paul's father, and Paul was taken out of school and put to work. The manager at Carnegie Hall was told to get another usher in his stead; the doorkeeper at the theatre was warned not to admit him to the house; and Charley Edwards remorsefully promised the boy's father not to see him again.

The members of the stock company were vastly amused when some of Paul's stories reached them—especially the women. They were hard-working women, most of them supporting indigent husbands or brothers, and they laughed rather bitterly at having stirred the boy to such fervid and florid inventions. They agreed with the faculty and with his father that Paul's was a bad case.

The east-bound train was ploughing through a January snowstorm; the dull dawn was beginning to show grey when the engine whistled a mile out of Newark. Paul started up from the seat where he had lain curled in uneasy slumber, rubbed the breath-misted window glass with his hand, and peered out. The snow was whirling in curling eddies above the white bottom lands, and the drifts lay already deep in the fields and along the fences, while here and there the long dead grass and dried weed stalks protruded black above it. Lights shone from the scattered houses, and a gang of laborers who stood beside the track waved their lanterns.

Paul had slept very little, and he felt grimy and uncomfortable. He had made the all-night journey in a day coach, partly because he was ashamed, dressed as he was, to go into a Pullman, and partly because he was afraid of being seen there by some Pittsburgh businessman, who might have noticed him in Denny & Carson's office. When the whistle awoke him, he clutched quickly at his breast pocket, glancing about him with an uncertain smile. But the little, clay-bespattered Italians were still sleeping, the slatternly women across the aisle were in open-mouthed oblivion, and even the crumby, crying babies were for the nonce stilled. Paul settled back to struggle with his impatience as best as he could.

When he arrived at the Jersey City station, he hurried through his breakfast manifestly ill at ease and keeping a sharp eye about him. After he reached the Twenty-third Street station, he consulted a cabman, and had himself driven to a men's furnishing establishment that was just opening for the day. He spent upward of two hours there, buying with endless reconsidering and great care. His new street suit he put on in the fitting-room; the frock coat and dress clothes he had bundled into the cab with his linen. Then he drove to a hatter's and a shoe house. His next errand was at Tiffany's, where he selected his silver and a new scarf-pin. He would not wait to have his silver marked, he said. Lastly, he stopped at a trunk shop on Broadway, and had his purchases packed into various traveling bags.

It was a little after one o'clock when he drove up to the Waldorf, and after settling with the cabman, went into the office. He registered from Washington; said his mother and father had been abroad, and that he had come down to await the arrival of their steamer. He told his story plausibly and had no trouble, since he volunteered to pay for them in advance, in engaging his rooms; a sleeping-room, sitting-room and bath.

Not once, but a hundred times Paul had planned this entry into New York. He had gone over every detail of it with Charley Edwards, and in his scrap book at home there were pages of description about New York hotels, cut from the Sunday papers. When he was shown to his sitting-room on the eighth floor, he saw at a glance that everything was as it should be; there was but one detail in his mental picture that the place did not realize, so he rang for the bell boy and sent him down for flowers. He moved about nervously until the boy returned, putting away his new linen and fingering it delightedly as he did so. When the flowers came, he put them hastily into water, and then tumbled into a hot bath. Presently he came out of his white bathroom, resplendent in his new silk underwear, and playing with the tassels of his red robe. The snow was whirling so fiercely outside his windows that he could scarcely see across the street, but within the air was deliciously soft and fragrant. He put the violets and jonquils on the taboret beside the couch, and threw himself down, with a long sigh, covering himself with a Roman blanket. He was thoroughly tired; he had been in such haste, he had stood up to such a strain, covered so much ground in the last twenty-four hours, that he wanted to think how it had all come about. Lulled by the sound of the wind, the warm air, and the cool fragrance of the flowers, he sank into deep, drowsy retrospection.

It had been wonderfully simple; when they had shut him out of the theatre and concert hall, when they had taken away his bone, the whole thing was virtually determined. The rest was a mere matter of opportunity. The only thing that at all surprised him was his own courage—for he realized well enough that he had always been tormented by fear, a sort of apprehensive dread that, of late years, as the meshes of the lies he had told closed about him, had been pulling the muscles of his body tighter and tighter. Until now, he could not remember the time when he had not been dreading something. Even when he was a little boy, it was always there—behind him, or before, or on either side. There had always been the shadowed corner, the dark place into which he dared not look, but from which something seemed always to be watching him—and Paul had done things that were not pretty to watch, he knew.

But now he had a curious sense of relief, as though he had at last thrown down the gauntlet to the thing in the corner.

Yet it was but a day since he had been sulking in the traces; but yesterday afternoon that he had been sent to the bank with Denny & Carson's deposit, as usual—but this time he was instructed to leave the book to be balanced. There was above two thousand dollars in checks, and nearly a thousand in the bank notes which he had taken from the book and quietly transferred to his pocket. At the bank he had made out a new deposit slip. His nerves had been steady enough to permit of his returning to the office, where he had finished his work and asked for a full day's holiday tomorrow, Saturday, giving a perfectly reasonable pretext. The bank book, he knew, would not be returned before Monday or Tuesday, and his father would be out of town for the next week. From the time he slipped the bank notes into his pocket until he boarded the night train for New York, he had not known a moment's hesitation. It was not the first time Paul had steered through treacherous waters.

How astonishingly easy it had all been; here he was, the thing done; and this time there would be no awakening, no figure at the top of the stairs. He watched the snow flakes whirling by his window until he fell asleep.

When he awoke, it was three o'clock in the afternoon. He bounded up with a start; half of one of his precious days gone already! He spent more than an hour in dressing, watching every stage of his toilet carefully in the mirror. Everything was quite perfect; he was exactly the kind of boy he had always wanted to be.

When he went downstairs, Paul took a carriage and drove up Fifth Avenue toward the Park. The snow had somewhat abated; carriages and tradesmen's wagons were hurrying soundlessly to and fro in the winter twilight; boys in woollen mufflers were shovelling off the doorsteps; the avenue stages made fine spots of color against the white street. Here and there on the corners were stands, with whole flower gardens blooming under glass cases, against the sides of which the snow flakes stuck and melted; violets, roses, carnations, lilies of the valley—somehow vastly more lovely and alluring that they blossomed thus unnaturally in the snow. The Park itself was a wonderful stage winter-piece.

When he returned, the pause of the twilight had ceased, and the tune of the streets had changed. The snow was falling faster, lights streamed from the hotels that reared their dozen stories fearlessly up into the storm, defying the raging Atlantic winds. A long, black stream of carriages poured down the avenue, intersected here and there by other streams, tending horizontally. There were a score of cabs about the entrance of his hotel, and his driver had to wait. Boys in livery were running in and out of the awning stretched across the sidewalk, up and down the red velvet carpet laid from the door to the street. Above, about, within it all was the rumble and roar, the hurry and toss of thousands of human beings as hot for pleasure as himself, and on every side of him towered the glaring affirmation of the omnipotence of wealth.

The boy set his teeth and drew his shoulders together in a spasm of realization: the plot of all dramas, the text of all romances, the nerve-stuff of all sensations was whirling about him like the snow flakes. He burnt like a faggot in a tempest.

When Paul went down to dinner, the music of the orchestra came floating up the elevator shaft to greet him. His head whirled as he stepped into the thronged corridor, and he sank back into one of the chairs against the wall to get his breath. The lights, the chatter, the perfumes, the bewildering medley of color—he had, for a moment, the feeling of not being able to stand it. But only for a moment; these were his own people, he told himself. He went slowly about the corridors, through the writing-rooms, smoking-rooms, reception-rooms, as though he were exploring the chambers of an enchanted palace, built and peopled for him alone.

When he reached the dining-room he sat down at a table near a window. The flowers, the white linen, the many-colored wine glasses, the gay toilettes of the women, the low popping of corks, the undulating repetitions of the *Blue Danube* from the orchestra, all flooded Paul's dream with bewildering radiance. When the roseate tinge of his champagne was added—that cold, precious, bubbling stuff that creamed and foamed in his glass—Paul wondered that there were honest men in the world at all. This was what all the world was fighting for, he reflected; this was what all the struggle was about. He doubted the reality of his past. Had he ever known a place called Cordelia Street, a place where fagged-looking businessmen got on the early car; mere rivets in a machine they seemed to Paul—sickening men, with combings of children's hair always hanging to their coats, and the smell of cooking in their clothes. Cordelia Street—Ah! that belonged to another time and country; had he not always been thus, had he not sat here night after night, from as far back as he could remember, looking pensively over just such shimmering textures, and slowly twirling the stem of a glass like this one between his thumb and middle finger? He rather thought he had.

He was not in the least abashed or lonely. He had no especial desire to meet or to know any of these people; all he demanded was the right to look on and conjecture, to watch the pageant. The mere stage properties were all he contended for. Nor was he lonely later in the evening, in his loge at the Metropolitan. He was now entirely rid of his nervous misgivings, of his forced aggressiveness, of the imperative desire to show himself different from his surroundings. He felt now that his surroundings explained him. Nobody questioned the purple; he had only to wear it passively. He had only to glance down at his attire to reassure himself that here it would be impossible for anyone to humiliate him.

He found it hard to leave his beautiful sitting-room to go to bed that night, and sat long watching the raging storm from his turret window. When he went to sleep it was with the lights turned on in his bedroom;

partly because of his old timidity, and partly so that, if he should wake in the night, there would be no wretched moment of doubt, no horrible suspicion of yellow wallpaper, or of Washington and Calvin above his bed.

Sunday morning the city was practically snowbound. Paul breakfasted late, and in the afternoon he fell in with a wild San Francisco boy, a freshman at Yale, who said he had run down for a "little flyer" over Sunday. The young man offered to show Paul the night side of the town, and the two boys went out together after dinner, not returning to the hotel until seven o'clock the next morning. They had started out in the confiding warmth of a champagne friendship, but their parting in the elevator was singularly cool. The freshman pulled himself together to make his train, and Paul went to bed. He awoke at two o'clock in the afternoon, very thirsty and dizzy, and rang for ice-water, coffee, and the Pittsburgh papers.

On the part of the hotel management, Paul excited no suspicion. There was this to be said for him, that he wore his spoils with dignity and in no way made himself conspicuous. Even under the glow of his wine he was never boisterous, though he found the stuff like a magician's wand for wonder-building. His chief greediness lay in his ears and eyes, and his excesses were not offensive ones. His dearest pleasures were the grey winter twilights in his sitting-room; his quiet enjoyment of his flowers, his clothes, his wide divan, his cigarette, and his sense of power. He could not remember a time when he had felt so at peace with himself. The mere release from the necessity of petty lying, lying every day and every day, restored his self-respect. He had never lied for pleasure, even at school; but to be noticed and admired, to assert his difference from other Cordelia Street boys; and he felt a good deal more manly, more honest, even, now that he had no need for boastful pretensions, now that he could, as his actor friends used to say, "dress the part." It was characteristic that remorse did not occur to him. His golden days went by without a shadow, and he made each as perfect as he could.

On the the eighth day after his arrival in New York, he found the whole affair exploited in the Pittsburgh papers, exploited with a wealth of detail which indicated that local news of a sensational nature was at a low ebb. The firm of Denny & Carson announced that the boy's father had refunded the full amount of the theft, and that they had no intention of prosecuting. The Cumberland minister had been interviewed, and expressed his hope of yet reclaiming the motherless lad, and his Sabbath-school teacher declared that she would spare no effort to that end. The rumor had reached Pittsburgh that the boy had been seen in a New York hotel, and his father had gone East to find him and bring him home.

Paul had just come in to dress for dinner; he sank into a chair, weak to the knees, and clasped his head in his hands. It was to be worse than jail, even; the tepid waters of Cordelia Street were to close over him finally and forever. The grey monotony stretched before him in hopeless, unrelieved years; Sabbath-school, Young People's Meeting, the yellow-papered room, the damp dishtowels; it all rushed back upon him with a sickening vividness. He had the old feeling that the orchestra had suddenly stopped, the sinking sensation that the play was over. The sweat broke out on his face, and he sprang to his feet, looked about him with his white, conscious smile, and winked at himself in the mirror. With something of the old childish belief in miracles with which he had so often gone to class, all his lessons unlearned, Paul dressed and dashed whistling down the corridor to the elevator.

He had no sooner entered the dining-room and caught the measure of the music than his remembrance was lightened by his old elastic power of claiming the moment, mounting with it, and finding it all sufficient. The glare and glitter about him, the mere scenic accessories had again, and for the last time, their old potency. He would show himself that he was game, he would finish the thing splendidly. He doubted, more than ever, the existence of Cordelia Street, and for the first time he drank his wine recklessly. Was he not, after all, one of those fortunate beings born to the purple, was he not still himself and in his own place? He drummed a nervous accompaniment to the Pagliacci music and looked about him, telling himself over and over that it had paid.

He reflected drowsily, to the swell of the music and the chill sweetness of his wine, that he might have done it more wisely. He might have caught an outboard steamer and been well out of their clutches before now. But the other side of the world had seemed too far away and too uncertain then; he could not have waited for it; his need had been too sharp. If he had to choose over again, he would do the same thing tomorrow. He looked affectionately about the dining-room, now gilded with a soft mist. Ah, it had paid indeed!

Paul was awakened next morning by a painful throbbing in his head and feet. He had thrown himself across the bed without undressing, and had slept with his shoes on. His limbs and hands were lead heavy, and his tongue and throat were parched and burnt. There came upon him one of those fateful attacks of clearheadedness that never occurred except when he was physically exhausted and his nerves hung loose. He lay still and closed his eyes and let the tide of things wash over him.

His father was in New York; "stopping at some joint or other," he told himself. The memory of successive summers on the front stoop fell upon him like a weight of black water. He had not a hundred dollars left; and he knew now, more than ever, that money was everything, the wall that stood between all he loathed and all he wanted. The thing was winding itself up; he had thought of that on his first glorious day in New York, and had even provided a way to snap the thread. It lay on his dressing-table now; he had got it out last night when he came blindly up from dinner, but the shiny metal hurt his eyes, and he disliked the looks of it.

He rose and moved about with a painful effort, succumbing now and again to attacks of nausea. It was the old depression exaggerated; all the world had become Cordelia Street. Yet somehow he was not afraid of anything, was absolutely calm; perhaps because he had looked into the dark corner at last and knew. It was bad enough, what he saw there, but somehow not so bad as his long fear of it had been. He saw everything clearly now. He had a feeling that he had made the best of it, that he had lived the sort of life he was meant to live, and for half an hour he sat staring at the revolver. But he told himself that was not the way, so he went downstairs and took a cab to the ferry.

When Paul arrived at Newark, he got off the train and took another cab, directing the driver to follow the Pennsylvania tracks out of the town. The snow lay heavy on the roadways and had drifted deep in the open fields. Only here and there the dead grass or dried weed stalks projected, singularly black, above it. Once well into the country, Paul dismissed the carriage and walked, floundering along the tracks, his mind a medley of irrelevant things. He seemed to hold in his brain an actual picture of everything he had seen that morning. He remembered every feature of both his drivers, of the toothless old woman from whom he had bought the red flowers in his coat, the agent from whom he had got his ticket, and all of his fellow-passengers on the ferry. His mind, unable to cope with vital matters near at hand, worked feverishly and deftly at sorting and grouping these images. They made for him a part of the ugliness of the world, of the ache in his head, and the bitter burning on his tongue. He stooped and put a handful of snow into his mouth as he walked, but that, too, seemed hot. When he reached a little hillside, where the tracks ran through a cut some twenty feet below him, he stopped and sat down.

The carnations in his coat were drooping with the cold, he noticed; their red glory all over. It occurred to him that all the flowers he had seen in the glass cases that first night must have gone the same way, long before this. It was only one splendid breath they had, in spite of their brave mockery at the winter outside the glass; and it was a losing game in the end, it seemed, this revolt against the homilies by which the world is run. Paul took one of the blossoms carefully from his coat and scooped a little hole in the snow, where he covered it up. Then he dozed a while, from his weak condition, seemingly insensible to the cold.

The sound of an approaching train awoke him, and he started to his feet, remembering only his resolution, and afraid lest he should be too late. He stood watching the approaching locomotive, his teeth chattering, his lips drawn away from them in a frightened smile; once or twice he glanced nervously sidewise, as though he were being watched. When the right moment came, he jumped. As he fell, the folly of his haste occurred to him with merciless clearness, the vastness of what he had left undone. There flashed through his brain, clearer than ever before, the blue of Adriatic water, the yellow of Algerian sands.

He felt something strike his chest, and that his body was being thrown swiftly through the air, on and on, immeasurably far and fast, while his limbs were gently relaxed. Then, because the picture-making mechanism was crushed, the disturbing visions flashed into black, and Paul dropped back into the immense design of things.

—1904

JAMES JOYCE ■ (1882–1941)

James Joyce is best known for his masterpiece Ulysses, *the difficult modernist novel of a single day in the life of Dublin that shortly after its appearance in 1922 became both a classic and the subject of a landmark censorship case, which its publishers eventually won. Joyce's lifelong quarrel with the provincial concerns of Irish religious, cultural, and literary life led him to permanent continental self-exile in Zürich and Paris. Most readers would associate Joyce with his pioneering of experimental techniques such as the fragmentary observations found in his early Epiphanies (posthumously published in 1956), his use of interior monologue and stream of consciousness, and the complicated linguistic games of Finnegans Wake (1939), forgetting that his earlier works lie squarely in the realm of traditional fiction. Dubliners (1914), his collection of short stories of life in his native city, remains an imposing achievement, as does his autobiographical novel A Portrait of the Artist as a Young Man (1916).*

Araby

North Richmond Street, being blind,[1] was a quiet street except at the hour when the Christian Brothers' School set the boys free. An uninhabited house of two stories stood at the blind end, detached from its neighbors in a square ground. The other houses of the street, conscious of decent lives within them, gazed at one another with brown imperturbable faces.

The former tenant of our house, a priest, had died in the back drawing-room. Air, musty from having long been enclosed, hung in all the rooms, and the waste room behind the kitchen was littered with old useless papers. Among these I found a few paper-covered books, the pages of which were curled and damp: *The Abbot,* by Walter Scott, *The Devout Communicant* and *The Memoirs of Vidocq.*[2] I liked the last best because its leaves were yellow. The wild garden behind the house contained a central apple-tree and a few straggling bushes under one of which I found the late tenant's rusty bicycle-pump. He had been a very charitable priest: in his will he had left all his money to institutions and the furniture of his house to his sister.

When the short days of winter came dusk fell before we had well eaten our dinners. When we met in the street the houses had grown somber. The space of sky above us was the color of ever-changing violet and towards it the lamps of the street lifted their feeble lanterns. The cold air stung us and we played till our bodies glowed. Our shouts echoed in the silent street. The career of our play brought us through the dark muddy lanes behind the houses where we ran the gantlet of the rough tribes from the cottages, to the back doors of the dark dripping

[1]**being blind** dead-end
[2]**The Abbot** ... *Vidocq* A historical romance (1820); a book of mediations; and a book by François-Jules Vidocq (1775–1857), a criminal who later turned detective.

gardens where odors arose from the ashpits, to the dark odorous stables where a coachman smoothed and combed the horse or shook music from the buckled harness. When we returned to the street light from the kitchen windows had filled the areas. If my uncle was seen turning the corner we hid in the shadow until we had seen him safely housed. Or if Mangan's sister came out on the doorstep to call her brother in to his tea we watched her from our shadow peer up and down the street. We waited to see whether she would remain or go in and, if she remained, we left our shadow and walked up to Mangan's steps resignedly. She was waiting for us, her figure defined by the light from the half-opened door. Her brother always teased her before he obeyed and I stood by the railings looking at her. Her dress swung as she moved her body and the soft rope of her hair tossed from side to side.

Every morning I lay on the floor in the front parlor watching her door. The blind was pulled down within an inch of the sash so that I could not be seen. When she came out on the doorstep my heart leaped. I ran to the hall, seized my books and followed her. I kept her brown figure always in my eye and, when we came near the point at which our ways diverged, I quickened my pace and passed her. This happened morning after morning. I had never spoken to her, except for a few casual words, and yet her name was like a summons to all my foolish blood.

Her image accompanied me even in places the most hostile to romance. On Saturday evenings when my aunt went marketing I had to go to carry some of the parcels. We walked through the flaring streets, jostled by drunken men and bargaining women, amid the curses of laborers, the shrill litanies of shopboys who stood on guard by the barrels of pigs' cheeks, the nasal chanting of street singers, who sang a *come-all-you* about O'Donovan Rossa,[3] or a ballad about the troubles in our native land. These noises converged in a single sensation of life for me: I imagined that I bore my chalice safely through the throng of foes. Her name sprang to my lips at moments in strange prayers and praises which I myself did not understand. My eyes were often full of tears (I could not tell why) and at times a flood from my heart seemed to pour itself out into my bosom. I thought little of the future. I did not know whether I would ever speak to her or not or, if I spoke to her, how I could tell her of my confused adoration. But my body was like a harp and her words and gestures were like fingers running upon the wires.

[3]*come-all-you* about O'Donovan Rossa a popular ballad

One evening I went into the back drawing-room in which the priest had died. It was a dark rainy evening and there was no sound in the house. Through one of the broken panes I heard the rain impinge upon the earth, the fine incessant needles of water playing in the sodden beds. Some distant lamp or lighted window gleamed below me. I was thankful that I could see so little. All my senses seemed to desire to veil themselves and, feeling that I was about to slip from them, I pressed the palms of my hands together until they trembled, murmuring: *O love! O love!* many times.

At last she spoke to me. When she addressed the first words to me I was so confused that I did not know what to answer. She asked me was I going to *Araby.* I forget whether I answered yes or no. It would be a splendid bazaar, she said; she would love to go.

—And why can't you? I asked.

While she spoke she turned a silver bracelet round and round her wrist. She could not go, she said, because there would be a retreat that week in her convent.[4] Her brother and two other boys were fighting for their caps and I was alone at the railings. She held one of the spikes, bowing her head towards me. The light from the lamp opposite our door caught the white curve of her neck, lit up her hair that rested there and, falling, lit up the hand upon the railing. It fell over one side of her dress and caught the white border of a petticoat, just visible as she stood at ease.

—It's well for you, she said.

—If I go, I said, I will bring you something.

What innumerable follies laid waste my waking and sleeping thoughts after that evening! I wished to annihilate the tedious intervening days. I chafed against the work of school. At night in my bedroom and by day in the classroom her image came between me and the page I strove to read. The syllables of the word *Araby* were called to me through the silence in which my soul luxuriated and cast an Eastern enchantment over me. I asked for leave to go to the bazaar on Saturday night. My aunt was surprised and hoped it was not some Freemason[5] affair. I answered few questions in class. I watched my master's face pass from amiability to sternness; he hoped I was not beginning to idle. I could not call my wandering thoughts together. I had hardly any patience with the serious

---

[4]**a retreat . . . in her convent** *a week of religious services in the convent school*
[5]**Freemason** Catholics were not allowed to become masons

work of life which, now that it stood between me and my desire, seemed to me child's play, ugly monotonous child's play.

On Saturday morning I reminded my uncle that I wished to go to the bazaar in the evening. He was fussing at the hall-stand, looking for the hat-brush, and answered me curtly:

—Yes, boy, I know.

As he was in the hall I could not go into the front parlor and lie at the window. I left the house in bad humor and walked slowly towards the school. The air was pitilessly raw and already my heart misgave me.

When I came home to dinner my uncle had not yet been home. Still it was early. I sat staring at the clock for some time and, when its ticking began to irritate me, I left the room. I mounted the staircase and gained the upper part of the house. The high cold empty gloomy rooms liberated me and I went from room to room singing. From the front window I saw my companions playing below in the street. Their cries reached me weakened and indistinct and, leaning my forehead against the cool glass, I looked over at the dark house where she lived. I may have stood there for an hour, seeing nothing but the brown-clad figure cast by my imagination, touched discreetly by the lamplight at the curved neck, at the hand upon the railings and at the border below the dress.

When I came downstairs again I found Mrs. Mercer sitting at the fire. She was an old garrulous woman, a pawnbroker's widow, who collected used stamps for some pious purpose. I had to endure the gossip of the tea-table. The meal was prolonged beyond an hour and still my uncle did not come. Mrs. Mercer stood up to go: she was sorry she couldn't wait any longer, but it was after eight o'clock and she did not like to be out late, as the night air was bad for her. When she had gone I began to walk up and down the room, clenching my fists. My aunt said:

—I'm afraid you may put off your bazaar for this night of Our Lord.

At nine o'clock I heard my uncle's latchkey in the halldoor. I heard him talking to himself and heard the hall-stand rocking when it had received the weight of his overcoat. I could interpret these signs. When he was midway through his dinner I asked him to give me the money to go to the bazaar. He had forgotten.

—The people are in bed and after their first sleep now, he said.

I did not smile. My aunt said to him energetically:

—Can't you give him the money and let him go? You've kept him late enough as it is.

My uncle said he was very sorry he had forgotten. He said he believed in the old saying: *All work and no play makes Jack a dull boy.* He asked me where I was going and, when I had told him a second time he asked me did I know *The Arab's Farewell to His Steed.*[6] When I left the kitchen he was about to recite the opening lines of the piece to my aunt.

I held a florin tightly in my hands as I strode down Buckingham Street towards the station. The sight of the streets thronged with buyers and glaring with gas recalled to me the purpose of my journey. I took my seat in a third-class carriage of a deserted train. After an intolerable delay the train moved out of the station slowly. It crept onward among ruinous houses and over the twinkling river. At Westland Row Station a crowd of people pressed to the carriage doors; but the porters moved them back, saying that it was a special train for the bazaar. I remained alone in the bare carriage. In a few minutes the train drew up beside an improvised wooden platform. I passed out on to the road and saw by the lighted dial of a clock that it was ten minutes to ten. In front of me was a large building which displayed the magical name.

I could not find any sixpenny entrance and, fearing that the bazaar would be closed, I passed in quickly through a turnstile, handing a shilling to a weary-looking man. I found myself in a big hall girdled at half its height by a gallery. Nearly all the stalls were closed and the greater part of the hall was in darkness. I recognized a silence like that which pervades a church after a service. I walked into the center of the bazaar timidly. A few people were gathered about the stalls which were still open. Before a curtain, over which the words *Café Chantant*[7] were written in colored lamps, two men were counting money on a salver.[8] I listened to the fall of the coins.

Remembering with difficulty why I had come I went over to one of the stalls and examined porcelain vases and flowered tea-sets. At the door of the stall a young lady was talking and laughing with two young gentlemen. I remarked their English accents and listened vaguely to their conversation.

—O, I never said such a thing!

—O, but you did!

—O, but I didn't!

—Didn't she say that?

---

[6] *The Arab's Farewell to His Steed* a sentimental ballad by a popular poet, Caroline Norton (1808–1877)
[7] *Café Chantant* a Parisian night club
[8] **salver** a tray used to serve Holy Communion

—Yes. I heard her.

—O, there's a . . . fib!

Observing me the young lady came over and asked me did I wish to buy anything. The tone of her voice was not encouraging; she seemed to have spoken to me out of a sense of duty. I looked humbly at the great jars that stood like eastern guards at either side of the dark entrance to the stall and murmured:

—No, thank you.

The young lady changed the position of one of the vases and went back to the two young men. They began to talk of the same subject. Once or twice the young lady glanced at me over her shoulder.

I lingered before her stall, though I knew my stay was useless, to make my interest in her wares seem the more real. Then I turned away slowly and walked down the middle of the bazaar. I allowed the two pennies to fall against the sixpence in my pocket. I heard a voice call from one end of the gallery that the light was out. The upper part of the hall was now completely dark.

Gazing up into the darkness I saw myself as a creature driven and derided by vanity; and my eyes burned with anguish and anger.

—1914

ZORA NEALE HURSTON ■ (1891–1960)

Zora Neale Hurston was born in Eatonville, Florida, one of eight children of a father who was a carpenter and Baptist preacher and became mayor of the first all-black town incorporated in the United States. After her mother's death, Hurston moved north, eventually attending high school and taking courses at Howard University and Barnard College, where she earned a B.A. in anthropology, and Columbia University, where she did graduate work. Hurston published her first story while a student and became an important member of the Harlem Renaissance, a group of young black artists, musicians, and writers who explored African-American heritage and identity. Hurston's most famous story, "Sweat," appeared in the only issue of Fire!!, a 1926 avant-garde magazine, and displays her unerring ear for the country speech of blacks in her native Florida. The expert handling of dialect would become a trademark of her style. Hurston achieved only modest success during her lifetime, despite the publication of her controversial novel, Their Eyes Were Watching God (1937). Hurston made many contributions to the study of African-American folklore, traveling through the Caribbean and the South to transcribe black myths, fables, and folk tales, which were collected in Mules and Men *(1935). Hurston died in a Florida welfare home and was buried in an unmarked grave, with most of her works long out of print. In the 1970s the rebirth of her reputation began, spurred by novelist Alice Walker, and virtually all of her works have since been republished.*

Sweat

I

It was eleven o'clock of a Spring night in Florida. It was Sunday. Any other night, Delia Jones would have been in bed for two hours by this time. But she was a washwoman, and Monday morning meant a great deal to her. So she collected the soiled clothes on Saturday when she returned the clean things. Sunday night after church, she sorted and put the white things to soak. It saved her almost a half-day's start. A great hamper in the bedroom held the clothes that she brought home. It was so much neater than a number of bundles lying around.

She squatted on the kitchen floor beside the great pile of clothes, sorting them into small heaps according to color, and humming a song in a mournful key, but wondering through it all where Sykes, her husband, had gone with her horse and buckboard.[1]

Just then something long, round, limp, and black fell upon her shoulders and slithered to the floor beside her. A great terror took hold of her. It softened her knees and dried her mouth so that it was a full minute before she could cry out or move. Then she saw that it was the big bull whip her husband liked to carry when he drove.

She lifted her eyes to the door and saw him standing there bent over with laughter at her fright. She screamed at him.

"Sykes, what you throw dat whip on me like dat? You know it would skeer me—looks just like a snake, an' you knows how skeered Ah is of snakes."

"Course Ah knowed it! That's how come Ah done it." He slapped his leg with his hand and almost rolled on the ground in his mirth. "If you such a big fool dat you got to have a fit over a earth worm or a string, Ah don't keer how bad Ah skeer you."

---

[1]**buckboard** open wagon with a seat

"You ain't got no business doing it. Gawd knows it's a sin. Some day Ah'm gointuh drop dead from some of yo' foolishness. 'Nother thing, where you been wid mah rig? Ah feeds dat pony. He ain't fuh you to be drivin' wid no bull whip."

"You sho' is one aggravatin' nigger woman!" he declared and stepped into the room. She resumed her work and did not answer him at once. "Ah done tole you time and again to keep them white folks' clothes outa dis house."

He picked up the whip and glared at her. Delia went on with her work. She went out into the yard and returned with a galvanized tub and set it on the washbench. She saw that Sykes had kicked all of the clothes together again, and now stood in her way truculently, his whole manner hoping, *praying*, for an argument. But she walked calmly around him and commenced to re-sort the things.

"Next time, Ah'm gointer kick 'em outdoors," he threatened as he struck a match along the leg of his corduroy breeches.

Delia never looked up from her work, and her thin, stooped shoulders sagged further.

"Ah ain't for no fuss t'night Sykes. Ah just come from taking sacrament at the church house."

He snorted scornfully. "Yeah, you just come from de church house on a Sunday night, but heah you is gone to work on them clothes. You ain't nothing but a hypocrite. One of them amen-corner Christians— sing, whoop, and shout, then come home and wash white folks' clothes on the Sabbath."

He stepped roughly upon the whitest pile of things, kicking them helter-skelter as he crossed the room. His wife gave a little scream of dismay, and quickly gathered them together again.

"Sykes, you quit grindin' dirt into these clothes! How can Ah git through by Sat'day if Ah don't start on Sunday?"

"Ah don't keer if you never git through. Anyhow, Ah done promised Gawd and a couple of other men, Ah ain't gointer have it in mah house. Don't gimme no lip neither, else Ah'll throw 'em out and put mah fist up side yo' head to boot."

Delia's habitual meekness seemed to slip from her shoulders like a blown scarf. She was on her feet; her poor little body, her bare knuckly hands bravely defying the strapping hulk before her.

"Looka heah, Sykes, you done gone too fur. Ah been married to you fur fifteen years, and Ah been takin' in washin' fur fifteen years. Sweat, sweat, sweat! Work and sweat, cry and sweat, pray and sweat!"

"What's that got to do with me?" he asked brutally.

"What's it got to do with you, Sykes? Mah tub of suds is filled yo' belly with vittles more times than yo' hands is filled it. Mah sweat is done paid for this house and Ah reckon Ah kin keep on sweatin' in it."

She seized the iron skillet from the stove and struck a defensive pose, which act surprised him greatly, coming from her. It cowed him and he did not strike her as he usually did.

"Naw you won't," she panted, "that ole snaggle-toothed black woman you runnin' with ain't comin' heah to pile up on *mah* sweat and blood. You ain't paid for nothin' on this place, and Ah'm gointer stay right heah till Ah'm toted out foot foremost."

"Well, you better quit gittin' me riled up, else they'll be totin' you out sooner than you expect. Ah'm so tired of you Ah don't know whut to do. Gawd! How Ah hates skinny wimmen!"

A little awed by this new Delia, he sidled out of the door and slammed the back gate after him. He did not say where he had gone, but she knew too well. She knew very well that he would not return until nearly daybreak also. Her work over, she went on to bed but not to sleep at once. Things had come to a pretty pass!

She lay awake, gazing upon the debris that cluttered their matrimonial trail. Not an image left standing along the way. Anything like flowers had long ago been drowned in the salty stream that had been pressed from her heart. Her tears, her sweat, her blood. She had brought love to the union and he had brought a longing after the flesh. Two months after the wedding, he had given her the first brutal beating. She had the memory of his numerous trips to Orlando with all of his wages when he had returned to her penniless, even before the first year had passed. She was young and soft then, but now she thought of her knotty, muscled limbs, her harsh knuckly hands, and drew herself up into an unhappy little ball in the middle of the big feather bed. Too late now to hope for love, even if it were not Bertha it would be someone else. This case differed from the others only in that she was bolder than the others. Too late for everything except her little home. She had built it for her old days, and planted one by one the trees and flowers there. It was lovely to her, lovely.

Somehow, before sleep came, she found herself saying aloud: "Oh well, whatever goes over the Devil's back, is got to come under his belly. Sometime or ruther, Sykes, like everybody else, is gointer reap his sowing." After that she was able to build a spiritual earthworks against her husband. His shells could no longer reach her. AMEN. She went to sleep and slept until he announced his presence in bed by kicking her feet and rudely snatching the covers away.

"Gimme some kivah heah, an' git yo' damn foots over on yo' own side! Ah oughter mash you in yo' mouf fuh drawing dat skillet on me."

Delia went clear to the rail without answering him. A triumphant indifference to all that he was or did.

II

The week was full of work for Delia as all other weeks, and Saturday found her behind her little pony, collecting and delivering clothes.

It was a hot, hot day near the end of July. The village men on Joe Clarke's porch even chewed cane listlessly. They did not hurl the cane-knots as usual. They let them dribble over the edge of the porch. Even conversation had collapsed under the heat.

"Heah come Delia Jones," Jim Merchant said, as the shaggy pony came 'round the bend of the road toward them. The rusty buckboard was heaped with baskets of crisp, clean laundry.

"Yep," Joe Lindsay agreed. "Hot or col', rain or shine, jes'ez reg'lar ez de weeks rool roun' Delia carries 'em an' fetches 'em on Sat'day."

"She better if she wanter eat," said Moss. "Syke Jones ain't wuth de shot an' powder hit would tek tuh kill 'em. Not to *huh* he ain't."

"He sho' ain't," Walter Thomas chimed in. "It's too bad, too, cause she wuz a right pretty li'l trick when he got huh. Ah'd uh mah'ied huh mahself if he hadnter beat me to it."

Delia nodded briefly at the men as she drove past.

"Too much knockin' will ruin *any* 'oman. He done beat huh 'nough tuh kill three women, let 'lone change they looks," said Elijah Moseley. "How Syke kin stommuck dat big black greasy Mogul he's layin' roun' wid, gits me. Ah swear dat eight-rock couldn't kiss a sardine can Ah done thowed out de back do' 'way las' yeah."

"Aw, she's fat, thass how come. He's allus been crazy 'bout fat women," put in Merchant. "He'd a' been tied up wid one long time ago if he could a' found one tuh have him. Did Ah tell yuh 'bout him come sidlin' roun' *mah* wife—bringin' her a basket uh peecans outa his yard fuh a present? Yessir, mah wife! She tol' him tuh take 'em right straight back home, 'cause Delia works so hard ovah dat washtub she reckon everything on de place taste lak sweat an' soapsuds. Ah jus' wisht Ah'd a' caught 'im 'roun' dere! Ah'd a' made his hips ketch on fiah down dat shell road."

"Ah know he done it, too. Ah sees 'im grinnin' at every 'oman dat passes," Walter Thomas said. "But even so, he useter eat some mighty big hunks uh humble pie tuh git dat li'l 'oman he got. She wuz ez pritty ez a speckled pup! Dat wuz fifteen years ago. He useter be so skeered uh losin' huh, she could make him do some parts of a husband's duty. Dey never wuz de same in de mind."

"There oughter be a law about him," said Lindsay. "He ain't fit tuh carry guts tuh a bear."

Clarke spoke for the first time. "Tain't no law on earth dat kin make a man be decent if it ain't in 'im. There's plenty men dat takes a wife lak dey do a joint uh sugar-cane. It's round, juicy, an' sweet when dey gits it. But dey squeeze an' grind, squeeze an' grind an' wring tell dey wring every drop uh pleasure dat's in 'em out. When dey's satisfied dat dey is wrung dry, dey treats 'em jes' lak dey do a cane-chew. Dey thows 'em away. Dey knows whut dey is doin' while dey is at it, an' hates theirselves fuh it but they keeps on hangin' after huh tell she's empty. Den dey hates huh fuh bein' a cane-chew an' in de way."

"We oughter take Syke an' dat stray 'oman uh his'n down in Lake Howell swamp an' lay on de rawhide till they cain't say Lawd a' mussy. He allus wuz uh ovahbearin niggah, but since dat white 'oman from up north done teached 'im how to run a automobile, he done got too beggety to live—an' we oughter kill 'im," Old Man Anderson advised.

A grunt of approval went around the porch. But the heat was melting their civic virtue and Elijah Moseley began to bait Joe Clarke.

"Come on, Joe, git a melon outa dere an' slice it up for yo' customers. We'se all sufferin' wid de heat. De bear's done got *me!*"

"Thass right, Joe, a watermelon is jes' whut Ah needs tuh cure de eppizudicks," Walter Thomas joined forces with Moseley. "Come on dere, Joe. We all is steady customers an' you ain't set us up in a long time. Ah chooses dat long, bowlegged Floridy favorite."

"A god, an' be dough. You all gimme twenty cents and slice away," Clarke retorted. "Ah needs a col' slice m'self. Heah, everybody chip in. Ah'll lend y'all mah meat knife."

The money was all quickly subscribed and the huge melon brought forth. At that moment, Sykes and Bertha arrived. A determined silence fell on the porch and the melon was put away again.

Merchant snapped down the blade of his jackknife and moved toward the store door.

"Come on in, Joe, an' gimme a slab uh sow belly an' uh pound uh coffee—almost fuhgot 'twas Sat'day. Got to git on home." Most of the men left also.

Just then Delia drove past on her way home, as Sykes was ordering magnificently for Bertha. It pleased him for Delia to see.

"Git whutsoever yo' heart desires, Honey. Wait a minute, Joe. Give huh two bottles uh strawberry soda-water, uh quart parched ground-peas, an' a block uh chewin' gum."

With all this they left the store, with Sykes reminding Bertha that this was his town and she could have it if she wanted it.

The men returned soon after they left, and held their watermelon feast.

"Where did Syke Jones git da 'oman from nohow?" Lindsay asked.

"Ovah Apopka. Guess dey musta been cleanin' out de town when she lef'. She don't look lak a thing but a hunk uh liver wid hair on it."

"Well, she sho' kin squall," Dave Carter contributed. "When she gits ready tuh laff, she jes' opens huh mouf an' latches it back tuh de las' notch. No ole granpa alligator down in Lake Bell ain't got nothin' on huh."

III

Bertha had been in town three months now. Sykes was still paying her room-rent at Della Lewis'—the only house in town that would have taken her in. Sykes took her frequently to Winter Park to "stomps." He still assured her that he was the swellest man in the state.

"Sho' you kin have dat li'l ole house soon's Ah git dat 'oman outadere. Everything b'longs tuh me an' you sho' kin have it. Ah sho' 'bominates uh skinny 'oman. Lawdy, you sho' is got one portly shape on you! You kin git *anything* you wants. Dis is *mah* town an' you sho' kin have it."

Delia's work-worn knees crawled over the earth in Gethsemane[2] and up the rocks of Calvary[3] many, many times during these months. She avoided the villagers and meeting places in her efforts to be blind and deaf. But Bertha nullified this to a degree, by coming to Delia's house to call Sykes out to her at the gate.

Delia and Sykes fought all the time now with no peaceful interludes. They slept and ate in silence. Two or three times Delia had attempted a

[2]**Gethsemane** The garden that was the scene of Jesus' arrest (see Matthew 26:36–57); hence, any scene of suffering.
[3]**Calvary** hill outside Jerusalem where Jesus was crucified

timid friendliness, but she was repulsed each time. It was plain that the breaches must remain agape.

The sun had burned July to August. The heat streamed down like a million hot arrows, smiting all things living upon the earth. Grass withered, leaves browned, snakes went blind in shedding, and men and dogs went mad. Dog days!

Delia came home one day and found Sykes there before her. She wondered, but started to go on into the house without speaking, even though he was standing in the kitchen door and she must either stoop under his arm or ask him to move. He made no room for her. She noticed a soap box beside the steps, but paid no particular attention to it, knowing that he must have brought it there. As she was stooping to pass under his outstretched arm, he suddenly pushed her backward, laughingly.

"Look in de box dere Delia, Ah done brung yuh somethin'!"

She nearly fell upon the box in her stumbling, and when she saw what it held, she all but fainted outright.

"Syke! Syke, mah Gawd! You take dat rattlesnake 'way from heah! You *gottuh.* Oh, Jesus, have mussy!"

"Ah ain't got tuh do nuthin' uh de kin'—fact is Ah ain't got tuh do nothin' but die. Tain't no use uh you puttin' on airs makin' out lak you skeered uh dat snake—he's gointer stay right heah tell he die. He wouldn't bite me cause Ah knows how tuh handle 'im. Nohow he wouldn't risk breakin' out his fangs 'gin *yo* skinny laigs."

"Naw, now Syke, don't keep dat thing 'round tryin' tuh skeer me tuh death. You knows Ah'm even feared uh earth worms. Thass de biggest snake Ah evah did see. Kill 'im Syke, please."

"Doan ast me tuh do nothin' fuh yuh. Goin' 'round tryin' tuh be so damn asterperious.[4] Naw, Ah ain't gonna kill it. Ah think uh damn sight mo' uh him dan you! Dat's a nice snake an' anybody doan lak 'im kin jes' hit de grit."

The village soon heard that Sykes had the snake, and came to see and ask questions.

"How de hen-fire did you ketch dat six-foot rattler, Syke?" Thomas asked.

"He's full uh frogs so he cain't hardly move, thass how Ah eased up on 'm. But Ah'm a snake charmer an' knows how tuh handle 'em.

[4]**asterperious** haughty

Shux, dat ain't nothin'. Ah could ketch one eve'y day if Ah so wanted tuh."

"Whut he needs is a heavy hick'ry club leaned real heavy on his head. Dat's de bes' way tuh charm a rattlesnake."

"Naw, Walt, y'all jes' don't understand dese diamon' backs lak Ah do," said Sykes in a superior tone of voice.

The village agreed with Walter, but the snake stayed on. His box remained by the kitchen door with its screen wire covering. Two or three days later it had digested its meal of frogs and literally came to life. It rattled at every movement in the kitchen or the yard. One day as Delia came down the kitchen steps she saw his chalky-white fangs curved like scimitars hung in the wire meshes. This time she did not run away with averted eyes as usual. She stood for a long time in the doorway in a red fury that grew bloodier for every second that she regarded the creature that was her torment.

That night she broached the subject as soon as Sykes sat down to the table.

"Syke, Ah wants you tuh take dat snake 'way fum heah. You done starved me an' Ah put up widcher, you done beat me an Ah took dat, but you done kilt all mah insides bringin' dat varmint heah."

Sykes poured out a saucer full of coffee and drank it deliberately before he answered her.

"A whole lot Ah keer 'bout how you feels inside uh out. Dat snake ain't goin' no damn wheah till Ah gits ready fuh 'im tuh go. So fur as beatin' is concerned, yuh ain't took near all dat you gointer take ef yuh stay 'round *me*."

Delia pushed back her plate and got up from the table. "Ah hates you, Sykes," she said calmly. "Ah hates you tuh de same degree dat Ah useter love yuh. Ah done took an' took till mah belly is full up tuh mah neck. Dat's de reason Ah got mah letter fum de church an' moved mah membership tuh Woodbridge—so Ah don't haftuh take no sacrament wid yuh. Ah don't wantuh see yuh 'round me at all. Lay 'round wid dat 'oman all yuh wants tuh, but gwan 'way fum me an' mah house. Ah hates yuh lak uh suck-egg dog."

Sykes almost let the huge wad of corn bread and collard greens he was chewing fall out of his mouth in amazement. He had a hard time whipping himself up to the proper fury to try to answer Delia.

"Well, Ah'm glad you does hate me. Ah'm sho' tiahed uh you hangin' ontuh me. Ah don't want yuh. Look at yuh stringey ole neck! Yo' rawbony laigs an' arms is enough tuh cut uh man tuh death. You looks jes' lak de devvul's doll-baby tuh *me*. You cain't hate me no worse dan Ah hates you. Ah been hatin' *you* fuh years."

"Yo' ole black hide don't look lak nothin' tuh me, but uh passle uh wrinkled up rubber, wid yo' big ole yeahs flappin' on each side lak uh paih uh buzzard wings. Don't think Ah'm gointuh be run 'way fum mah house neither. Ah'm goin' tuh de white folks 'bout *you*, mah young man, de very nex' time you lay yo' han's on me. Mah cup is done run ovah." Delia said this with no signs of fear and Sykes departed from the house, threatening her, but made not the slightest move to carry out any of them.

That night he did not return at all, and the next day being Sunday, Delia was glad she did not have to quarrel before she hitched up her pony and drove the four miles to Woodbridge.

She stayed to the night service—"love feast"—which was very warm and full of spirit. In the emotional winds her domestic trials were borne far and wide so that she sang as she drove homeward,

Jurden water,[5] black an' col
Chills de body, not de soul
An' Ah wantah cross Jurden in uh calm time.

She came from the barn to the kitchen door and stopped.

"Whut's de mattah, ol' Satan, you ain't kickin' up yo' racket?" She addressed the snake's box. Complete silence. She went on into the house with a new hope in its birth struggles. Perhaps her threat to go to the white folks had frightened Sykes! Perhaps he was sorry! Fifteen years of misery and suppression had brought Delia to the place where she would hope *anything* that looked towards a way over or through her wall of inhibitions.

She felt in the match-safe behind the stove at once for a match. There was only one there.

"Dat niggah wouldn't fetch nothin' heah tuh save his rotten neck, but he kin run thew whut Ah brings quick enough. Now he done toted off nigh on tuh haff uh box uh matches. He done had dat 'oman heah in mah house, too."

[5] *Jurden water* the River Jordan

144

Nobody but a woman could tell how she knew this even before she struck the match. But she did and it put her into a new fury.

Presently she brought in the tubs to put the white things to soak. This time she decided she need not bring the hamper out of the bedroom; she would go in there and do the sorting. She picked up the pot-bellied lamp and went in. The room was small and the hamper stood hard by the foot of the white iron bed. She could sit and reach through the bedposts—resting as she worked.

"*Ah wantah cross Jurden in uh calm time.*" She was singing again. The mood of the "love feast" had returned. She threw back the lid of the basket almost gaily. Then, moved by both horror and terror, she sprang back toward the door. *There lay the snake in the basket!* He moved sluggishly at first, but even as she turned round and round, jumped up and down in an insanity of fear, he began to stir vigorously. She saw him pouring his awful beauty from the basket upon the bed, then she seized the lamp and ran as fast as she could to the kitchen. The wind from the open door blew out the light and the darkness added to her terror. She sped to the darkness of the yard, slamming the door after her before she thought to set down the lamp. She did not feel safe even on the ground, so she climbed up in the hay barn.

There for an hour or more she lay sprawled upon the hay a gibbering wreck.

Finally she grew quiet, and after that came coherent thought. With this stalked through her a cold, bloody rage. Hours of this. A period of introspection, a space of retrospection, then a mixture of both. Out of this an awful calm.

"Well, Ah done de bes' Ah could. If things ain't right, Gawd knows tain't mah fault."

She went to sleep—a twitch sleep—and woke up to a faint gray sky. There was a loud hollow sound below. She peered out. Sykes was at the wood-pile, demolishing a wire-covered box.

He hurried to the kitchen door, but hung outside there some minutes before he entered, and stood some minutes more inside before he closed it after him.

The gray in the sky was spreading. Delia descended without fear now, and crouched beneath the low bedroom window. The drawn shade shut out the dawn, shut in the night. But the thin walls held back no sound.

"Dat ol' scratch[6] is woke up now!" She mused at the tremendous whirr inside, which every woodsman knows, is one of the sound illusions. The rattler is a ventriloquist. His whirr sounds to the right, to the left, straight ahead, behind, close under foot—everywhere but where it is. Woe to him who guesses wrong unless he is prepared to hold up his end of the argument! Sometimes he strikes without rattling at all.

Inside, Sykes heard nothing until he knocked a pot lid off the stove while trying to reach the match-safe in the dark. He had emptied his pockets at Bertha's.

The snake seemed to wake up under the stove and Sykes made a quick leap into the bedroom. In spite of the gin he had had, his head was clearing now.

"Mah Gawd!" he chattered, "ef Ah could on'y strack uh light!"

The rattling ceased for a moment as he stood paralyzed. He waited. It seemed that the snake waited also.

"Oh, fuh de light! Ah thought he'd be too sick"—Sykes was muttering to himself when the whirr began again, closer, right underfoot this time. Long before this, Sykes' ability to think had been flattened down to primitive instinct and he leaped—onto the bed.

Outside Delia heard a cry that might have come from a maddened chimpanzee, a stricken gorilla. All the terror, all the horror, all the rage that man possibly could express, without a recognizable human sound.

A tremendous stir inside there, another series of animal screams, the intermittent whirr of the reptile. The shade torn violently down from the window, letting in the red dawn, a huge brown hand seizing the window stick, great dull blows upon the wooden floor punctuating the gibberish of sound long after the rattle of the snake had abruptly subsided. All this Delia could see and hear from her place beneath the window, and it made her ill. She crept over to the four o'clocks and stretched herself on the cool earth to recover.

She lay there. "Delia, Delia!" She could hear Sykes calling in a most despairing tone as one who expected no answer. The sun crept on up, and he called. Delia could not move—her legs had gone flabby. She never moved, he called, and the sun kept rising.

[6]**scratch** the devil

"Mah Gawd!" She heard him moan, "Mah Gawd fum Heben!" She heard him stumbling about and got up from her flower-bed. The sun was growing warm. As she approached the door she heard him call out hopefully, "Delia, is dat you Ah heah?"

She saw him on his hands and knees as soon as she reached the door. He crept an inch or two toward her—all that he was able, and she saw his horribly swollen neck and his one open eye shining with hope. A surge of pity too strong to support bore her away from that eye that must, could not fail to, see the tubs. He would see the lamp. Orlando with its doctors was too far. She could scarcely reach the chinaberry tree, where she waited in the growing heat while inside she knew the cold river was creeping up and up to extinguish that eye which must know by now that she knew.

—1926

WILLIAM FAULKNER ■ (1897–1962)

William Faulkner came from a family whose name was originally spelled "Falkner," but a misprint in an early book led him to change it. Faulkner spent long periods of his adult life in Hollywood, where he had some success as a screenwriter (a 1991 film, Barton Fink, *has a character obviously modeled on him), but always returned to Oxford, Mississippi, the site of his fictional Jefferson and Yoknapatawpha County. With Thomas Wolfe and others, he was responsible for the flowering of southern fiction in the early decades of the century, though for Faulkner fame came relatively late in life. Despite the success of* Sanctuary *(1931) and the critical esteem in which other early works like* The Sound and the Fury *(1929) and* As I Lay Dying *(1930) were held, Faulkner proved too difficult for most readers and failed to attract large audiences for what are now considered his best novels. By the late 1940s most of his books were out of print. His reputation was revived when Malcolm Cowley's edition of* The Portable Faulkner *appeared in 1946, but despite the success of* Intruder in the Dust *(1948) he was not as well known as many of his contemporaries when he won the Nobel Prize in 1950. A brilliant innovator of unusual narrative techniques in his novels, Faulkner created complex genealogies of characters to inhabit the world of his mythical South.*

A Rose for Emily

WILLIAM FAULKNER

I

When Miss Emily Grierson died, our whole town went to her funeral: the men through a sort of respectful affection for a fallen monument, the women mostly out of curiosity to see the inside of her house, which no one save an old manservant—a combined gardener and cook—had seen in at least ten years.

It was a big, squarish frame house that had once been white, decorated with cupolas and spires and scrolled balconies in the heavily lightsome style of the seventies, set on what had once been our most select street. But garages and cotton gins had encroached and obliterated even the august names of that neighborhood; only Miss Emily's house was left, lifting its stubborn and coquettish decay above the cotton wagons and the gasoline pumps—an eyesore among eyesores. And now Miss Emily had gone to join the representatives of those august names where they lay in the cedar-bemused cemetery among the ranked and anonymous graves of Union and Confederate soldiers who fell at the battle of Jefferson.

Alive, Miss Emily had been a tradition, a duty, and a care; a sort of hereditary obligation upon the town, dating from that day in 1894 when Colonel Sartoris, the mayor—he who fathered the edict that no Negro woman should appear on the streets without an apron—remitted her taxes, the dispensation dating from the death of her father on into perpetuity. Not that Miss Emily would have accepted charity. Colonel Sartoris invented an involved tale to the effect that Miss Emily's father had loaned money to the town, which the town, as a matter of business, preferred this way of repaying. Only a man of Colonel Sartoris' generation and thought could have invented it, and only a woman could have believed it.

When the next generation, with its more modern ideas, became mayors and aldermen, this arrangement created some little dissatisfaction. On the first of the year they mailed her a tax notice. February came, and there was no reply. They wrote her a formal letter, asking her to call at the sheriff's office at her convenience. A week later the mayor wrote her himself, offering to call or to send his car for her, and received in reply a note on paper of an archaic shape, in a thin, flowing calligraphy in faded ink, to the effect that she no longer went out at all. The tax notice was also enclosed, without comment.

They called a special meeting of the Board of Aldermen. A deputation waited upon her, knocked at the door through which no visitor had passed since she ceased giving china-painting lessons eight or ten years earlier. They were admitted by the old Negro into a dim hall from which a stairway mounted into still more shadow. It smelled of dust and disuse—a close, dank smell. The Negro led them into the parlor. It was furnished in heavy, leather-covered furniture. When the Negro opened the blinds of one window, they could see that the leather was cracked; and when they sat down, a faint dust rose sluggishly about their thighs, spinning with slow motes in the single sunray. On a tarnished gilt easel before the fireplace stood a crayon portrait of Miss Emily's father.

They rose when she entered—a small, fat woman in black, with a thin gold chain descending to her waist and vanishing into her belt, leaning on an ebony cane with a tarnished gold head. Her skeleton was small and spare; perhaps that was why what would have been merely plumpness in another was obesity in her. She looked bloated, like a body long submerged in motionless water, and of that pallid hue. Her eyes, lost in the fatty ridges of her face, looked like two small pieces of coal pressed into a lump of dough as they moved from one face to another while the visitors stated their errand.

She did not ask them to sit. She just stood in the door and listened quietly until the spokesman came to a stumbling halt. Then they could hear the invisible watch ticking at the end of the gold chain.

Her voice was dry and cold. "I have no taxes in Jefferson. Colonel Sartoris explained it to me. Perhaps one of you can gain access to the city records and satisfy yourselves."

"But we have. We are the city authorities, Miss Emily. Didn't you get a notice from the sheriff, signed by him?"

"I received a paper, yes," Miss Emily said. "Perhaps he considers himself the sheriff . . . I have no taxes in Jefferson."

"But there is nothing on the books to show that, you see. We must go by the—"

"See Colonel Sartoris. I have no taxes in Jefferson."

"But, Miss Emily—"

"See Colonel Sartoris." (Colonel Sartoris had been dead almost ten years.) "I have no taxes in Jefferson. Tobe!" The Negro appeared. "Show these gentlemen out."

II

So she vanquished them, horse and foot, just as she had vanquished their fathers thirty years before about the smell. That was two years after her father's death and a short time after her sweetheart—the one we believed would marry her—had deserted her. After her father's death she went out very little; after her sweetheart went away, people hardly saw her at all. A few of the ladies had the temerity to call, but were not received, and the only sign of life about the place was the Negro man—a young man then—going in and out with a market basket.

"Just as if a man—any man—could keep a kitchen properly," the ladies said; so they were not surprised when the smell developed. It was another link between the gross, teeming world and the high and mighty Griersons.

A neighbor, a woman, complained to the mayor, Judge Stevens, eighty years old.

"But what will you have me do about it, madam?" he said.

"Why, send her word to stop it," the woman said. "Isn't there a law?"

"I'm sure that won't be necessary," Judge Stevens said. "It's probably just a snake or a rat that nigger of hers killed in the yard. I'll speak to him about it."

The next day he received two more complaints, one from a man who came in diffident deprecation. "We really must do something about it, Judge. I'd be the last one in the world to bother Miss Emily, but we've got to do something." That night the Board of Aldermen met—three graybeards and one younger man, a member of the rising generation.

"It's simple enough," he said. "Send her word to have her place cleaned up. Give her a certain time to do it in, and if she don't . . ."

"Dammit, sir," Judge Stevens said, "will you accuse a lady to her face of smelling bad?"

So the next night, after midnight, four men crossed Miss Emily's lawn and slunk about the house like burglars, sniffing along the base of the brickwork and at the cellar openings while one of them performed a regular sowing motion with his hand out of a sack slung from his shoulder. They broke open the cellar door and sprinkled lime there, and in all the outbuildings. As they re-crossed the lawn, a window that had been dark was lighted and Miss Emily sat in it, the light behind her, and her upright torso motionless as that of an idol. They crept quietly across the lawn and into the shadow of the locusts that lined the street. After a week or two the smell went away.

That was when people had begun to feel really sorry for her. People in our town, remembering how old lady Wyatt, her great-aunt, had gone completely crazy at last, believed that the Griersons held themselves a little too high for what they really were. None of the young men were quite good enough for Miss Emily and such. We had long thought of them as a tableau, Miss Emily a slender figure in white in the background, her father a spraddled silhouette in the foreground, his back to her and clutching a horsewhip, the two of them framed by the back-flung front door. So when she got to be thirty and was still single, we were not pleased exactly, but vindicated; even with insanity in the family she wouldn't have turned down all of her chances if they had really materialized.

When her father died, it got about that the house was all that was left to her; and in a way, people were glad. At last they could pity Miss Emily. Being left alone, and a pauper, she had become humanized. Now she too would know the old thrill and the old despair of a penny more or less.

The day after his death all the ladies prepared to call at the house and offer condolence and aid, as is our custom. Miss Emily met them at the door, dressed as usual and with no trace of grief on her face. She told them that her father was not dead. She did that for three days, with the ministers calling on her, and the doctors, trying to persuade her to let them dispose of the body. Just as they were about to resort to law and force, she broke down, and they buried her father quickly.

We did not say she was crazy then. We believed she had to do that. We remembered all the young men her father had driven away, and we knew that with nothing left, she would have to cling to that which had robbed her, as people will.

She was sick for a long time. When we saw her again, her hair was cut short, making her look like a girl, with a vague resemblance to those angels in colored church windows—sort of tragic and serene.

The town had just let the contracts for paving the sidewalks, and in the summer after her father's death they began the work. The construction company came with niggers and mules and machinery, and a foreman named Homer Barron, a Yankee—a big, dark, ready man, with a big voice and eyes lighter than his face. The little boys would follow in groups to hear him cuss the niggers, and the niggers singing in time to the rise and fall of picks. Pretty soon he knew everybody in town. Whenever you heard a lot of laughing anywhere about the square, Homer Barron would be in the center of the group. Presently we began to see him and Miss Emily on Sunday afternoons driving in the yellow-wheeled buggy and the matched team of bays from the livery stable.

At first we were glad that Miss Emily would have an interest, because the ladies all said, "Of course a Grierson would not think seriously of a Northerner, a day laborer." But there were still others, older people, who said that even grief could not cause a real lady to forget *noblesse oblige*[1]—without calling it *noblesse oblige*. They just said, "Poor Emily. Her kinsfolk should come to her." She had some kin in Alabama; but years ago her father had fallen out with them over the estate of old lady Wyatt, the crazy woman, and there was no communication between the two families. They had not even been represented at the funeral.

And as soon as the old people said, "Poor Emily," the whispering began. "Do you suppose it's really so?" they said to one another. "Of course it is. What else could . . ." This behind their hands; rustling of craned silk and satin behind jalousies closed upon the sun of Sunday afternoon as the thin, swift clop-clop-clop of the matched team passed: "Poor Emily."

She carried her head high enough—even when we believed that she was fallen. It was as if she demanded more than ever the recognition of her dignity as the last Grierson; as if it had wanted that touch of earthiness to reaffirm her imperviousness. Like when she bought the rat poison, the arsenic. That was over a year after they

[1]**noblesse oblige** the obligation of members of the nobility to act with dignity

had begun to say "Poor Emily," and while the two female cousins were visiting her.

"I want some poison," she said to the druggist. She was over thirty then, still a slight woman, though thinner than usual, with cold, haughty black eyes in a face the flesh of which was strained across the temples and about the eye-sockets as you imagine a lighthouse-keeper's face ought to look. "I want some poison," she said.

"Yes, Miss Emily. What kind? For rats and such? I'd recom—"

"I want the best you have. I don't care what kind."

The druggist named several. "They'll kill anything up to an elephant. But what you want is—"

"Arsenic," Miss Emily said. "Is that a good one?"

"Is . . . arsenic? Yes, ma'am. But what you want—"

"I want arsenic."

The druggist looked down at her. She looked back at him, erect, her face like a strained flag. "Why, of course," the druggist said. "If that's what you want. But the law requires you to tell what you are going to use it for."

Miss Emily just stared at him, her head tilted back in order to look him eye for eye, until he looked away and went and got the arsenic and wrapped it up. The Negro delivery boy brought her the package; the druggist didn't come back. When she opened the package at home there was written on the box, under the skull and bones: "For rats."

IV

So the next day we all said, "She will kill herself"; and we said it would be the best thing. When she had first begun to be seen with Homer Barron, we had said, "She will marry him." Then we said, "She will persuade him yet," because Homer himself had remarked—he liked men, and it was known that he drank with the younger men in the Elks' Club—that he was not a marrying man. Later we said, "Poor Emily," behind the jalousies as they passed on Sunday afternoon in the glittering buggy, Miss Emily with her head high and Homer Barron with his hat cocked and a cigar in his teeth, reins and whip in a yellow glove.

Then some of the ladies began to say that it was a disgrace to the town and a bad example to the young people. The men did not want to interfere, but at last the ladies forced the Baptist minister—Miss Emily's people were Episcopal—to call upon her. He would never divulge what happened during that interview, but he refused to go back again. The next Sunday they again drove about the streets, and the following day the minister's wife wrote to Miss Emily's relations in Alabama.

So she had blood-kin under her roof again and we sat back to watch developments. At first nothing happened. Then we were sure that they were to be married. We learned that Miss Emily had been to the jeweler's and ordered a man's toilet set in silver, with the letters H.B. on each piece. Two days later we learned that she had bought a complete outfit of men's clothing, including a nightshirt, and we said, "They are married." We were really glad. We were glad because the two female cousins were even more Grierson than Miss Emily had ever been.

So we were not surprised when Homer Barron—the streets had been finished some time since—was gone. We were a little disappointed that there was not a public blowing-off, but we believed that he had gone on to prepare for Miss Emily's coming, or to give her a chance to get rid of the cousins. (By that time it was a cabal, and we were all Miss Emily's allies to help circumvent the cousins.) Sure enough, after another week they departed. And, as we had expected all along, within three days Homer Barron was back in town. A neighbor saw the Negro man admit him at the kitchen door at dusk one evening.

And that was the last we saw of Homer Barron. And of Miss Emily for some time. The Negro man went in and out with the market basket, but the front door remained closed. Now and then we would see her at a window for a moment, as the men did that night when they sprinkled the lime, but for almost six months she did not appear on the streets. Then we knew that this was to be expected too; as if that quality of her father which had thwarted her woman's life so many times had been too virulent and too furious to die.

When we next saw Miss Emily, she had grown fat and her hair was turning gray. During the next few years it grew grayer and grayer until it attained an even pepper-and-salt iron-gray, when it ceased turning. Up to the day of her death at seventy-four it was still that vigorous iron-gray, like the hair of an active man.

From that time on her front door remained closed, save for a period of six or seven years, when she was about forty, during which she gave lessons in china-painting. She fitted up a studio in one of the downstairs rooms, where the daughters and granddaughters of Colonel Sartoris' contemporaries were sent to her with the same regularity and in the same spirit that they were sent to church on Sundays with a twenty-five-cent piece for the collection plate. Meanwhile her taxes had been remitted.

Then the newer generation became the backbone and the spirit of the town, and the painting pupils grew up and fell away and did not send their children to her with boxes of color and tedious brushes and pictures cut from the ladies' magazines. The front door closed upon the last one and remained closed for good. When the town got free postal delivery, Miss Emily alone refused to let them fasten the metal numbers above her door and attach a mailbox to it. She would not listen to them.

Daily, monthly, yearly we watched the Negro grow grayer and more stooped, going in and out with the market basket. Each December we sent her a tax notice, which would be returned by the post office a week later, unclaimed. Now and then we would see her in one of the downstairs windows—she had evidently shut up the top floor of the house—like the carven torso of an idol in a niche, looking or not looking at us, we could never tell which. Thus she passed from generation to generation—dear, inescapable, impervious, tranquil, and perverse.

And so she died. Fell ill in the house filled with dust and shadows, with only a doddering Negro man to wait on her. We did not even know she was sick; we had long since given up trying to get any information from the Negro. He talked to no one, probably not even to her, for his voice had grown harsh and rusty, as if from disuse.

She died in one of the downstairs rooms, in a heavy walnut bed with a curtain, her gray head propped on a pillow yellow and moldy with age and lack of sunlight.

V

The Negro met the first of the ladies at the front door and let them in, with their hushed, sibilant voices and their quick, curious glances, and then he disappeared. He walked right through the house and out the back and was not seen again.

The two female cousins came at once. They held the funeral on the second day, with the town coming to look at Miss Emily beneath a mass of bought flowers, with the crayon face of her father musing profoundly above the bier and the ladies sibilant and macabre; and the very old men—some in their brushed Confederate uniforms—on the porch and the lawn, talking of Miss Emily as if she had been a contemporary of theirs, believing that they had danced with her and courted her perhaps, confusing time with its mathematical progression, as the old do, to whom all the past is not a diminishing road but, instead, a huge meadow which no winter ever quite touches, divided from them now by the narrow bottleneck of the most recent decade of years.

Already we knew that there was one room in that region above stairs which no one had seen in forty years, and which would have to be forced. They waited until Miss Emily was decently in the ground before they opened it.

The violence of breaking down the door seemed to fill this room with pervading dust. A thin, acrid pall as of the tomb seemed to lie everywhere upon this room decked and furnished as for a bridal: upon the valance curtains of faded rose color, upon the rose-shaded lights, upon the dressing table, upon the delicate array of crystal and the man's toilet things backed with tarnished silver, silver so tarnished that the monogram was obscured. Among them lay collar and tie, as if they had just been removed, which, lifted, left upon the surface a pale crescent in the dust. Upon a chair hung the suit, carefully folded; beneath it the two mute shoes and the discarded socks.

The man himself lay in the bed.

For a long while we just stood there, looking down at the profound and fleshless grin. The body had apparently once lain in the attitude of an embrace, but now the long sleep that outlasts love, that conquers even the grimace of love, had cuckolded him. What was left of him, rotted beneath what was left of the nightshirt, had become inextricable from the bed in which he lay; and upon him and upon the pillow beside him lay that even coating of the patient and biding dust.

Then we noticed that in the second pillow was the indentation of a head. One of us lifted something from it, and leaning forward, that faint and invisible dust dry and acrid in the nostrils, we saw a long strand of iron-gray hair.

—1930

Ernest Hemingway completely embodied the public image of the successful writer for so long that even today, more than four decades after his suicide, it is difficult to separate the celebrity from the serious artist, the sportsman and carouser from the stylist whose influence on the short story and novel continues to be felt. The complexity of his life and personality still fascinates biographers, even though a half-dozen major studies have already appeared. Born the son of a doctor in a middle-class suburb of Chicago, wounded as a volunteer ambulance driver in Italy during World War I, trained as a reporter on the Kansas City Star, *Hemingway moved to Paris in the early 1920s, where he was at the center of a brilliant generation of American expatriates that included Gertrude Stein and F. Scott Fitzgerald. His wide travels are reflected in his work. He spent much time in Spain, which provided material for his first novel,* The Sun Also Rises *(1926), and his many later articles on bullfighting. His early stories earned him a reputation for daring subject matter and made him one of the chief spokesperson for the so-called Lost Generation. In the 1930s he covered the Spanish Civil War, the backdrop for his most popular novel,* For Whom the Bell Tolls *(1940). His African safaris and residence in pre-Castro Cuba were also sources for his fiction. When all else is said, Hemingway's greatest contribution may lie in the terse, stripped-down quality of his early prose, which renders modern alienation with stark concrete details. Hemingway won the Nobel Prize in 1954. The decades since his death have seen the release of much unpublished material—a memoir of his Paris years,* A Moveable Feast *(1964); two novels,* Islands in the Stream *(1970) and* The Garden of Eden *(1986); and a "fictional memoir" of his final African safari,* True at First Light *(1999). None of these posthumously published works has advanced his literary reputation.*

Up in Michigan

Jim Gilmore came to Hortons Bay from Canada. He bought the blacksmith shop from old man Horton. Jim was short and dark with big mustaches and big hands. He was a good horseshoer and did not look much like a blacksmith even with his leather apron on. He lived upstairs above the blacksmith shop and took his meals at D. J. Smith's.

Liz Coates worked for Smith's. Mrs. Smith, who was a very large clean woman, said Liz Coates was the neatest girl she'd ever seen. Liz had good legs and always wore clean gingham aprons and Jim noticed that her hair was always neat behind. He liked her face because it was so jolly but he never thought about her.

Liz liked Jim very much. She liked it the way he walked over from the shop and often went to the kitchen door to watch for him to start down the road. She liked it about his mustache. She liked it about how white his teeth were when he smiled. She liked it very much that he didn't look like a blacksmith. She liked it how much D. J. Smith and Mrs. Smith liked Jim. One day she found that she liked it the way the hair was black on his arms and how white they were above the tanned line when he washed up in the washbasin outside the house. Liking that made her feel funny.

Hortons Bay, the town, was only five houses on the main road between Boyne City and Charlevoix. There was the general store and post office with a high false front and maybe a wagon hitched out in front, Smith's house, Stroud's house, Dillworth's house, Horton's house and Van Hoosen's house. The houses were in a big grove of elm trees and the road was very sandy. There was farming country and timber each way up the road. Up the road a ways was the Methodist church and down the road the other direction was the township school. The blacksmith shop was painted red and faced the school.

A steep sandy road ran down the hill to the bay through the timber. From Smith's back door you could look out across the woods that ran down to the lake and across the bay. It was very beautiful in the spring and summer, the bay blue and bright and usually whitecaps on the lake out beyond the point from the breeze blowing from Charlevoix and Lake Michigan. From Smith's back door Liz could see ore barges way out in the lake going toward Boyne City. When she looked at them they didn't seem to be moving at all but if she went in and dried some more dishes and then came out again they would be out of sight beyond the point.

All the time now Liz was thinking about Jim Gilmore. He didn't seem to notice her much. He talked about the shop to D. J. Smith and about the Republican Party and about James G. Blaine.[1] In the evenings he read *The Toledo Blade* and the Grand Rapids paper by the lamp in the front room or went out spearing fish in the bay with a jacklight with D. J. Smith. In the fall he and Smith and Charley Wyman took a wagon

[1] **James G. Blaine** (1830–1893) Republican politician and Presidential candidate in 1884

and tent, grub, axes, their rifles and two dogs and went on a trip to the pine plains beyond Vanderbilt deer hunting. Liz and Mrs. Smith were cooking for four days for them before they started. Liz wanted to make something special for Jim to take but she didn't finally because she was afraid to ask Mrs. Smith for the eggs and flour and afraid if she bought them Mrs. Smith would catch her cooking. It would have been all right with Mrs. Smith but Liz was afraid.

All the time Jim was gone on the deer hunting trip Liz thought about him. It was awful while he was gone. She couldn't sleep well from thinking about him but she discovered it was fun to think about him too. If she let herself go it was better. The night before they were to come back she didn't sleep at all, that is she didn't think she slept because it was all mixed up in a dream about not sleeping and really not sleeping. When she saw the wagon coming down the road she felt weak and sick sort of inside. She couldn't wait till she saw Jim and it seemed as though everything would be all right when he came. The wagon stopped outside under the big elm and Mrs. Smith and Liz went out. All the men had beards and there were three deer in the back of the wagon, their thin legs sticking stiff over the edge of the wagon box. Mrs. Smith kissed D. J. and he hugged her. Jim said "Hello, Liz," and grinned. Liz hadn't known just what would happen when Jim got back but she was sure it would be something. Nothing had happened. The men were just home, that was all. Jim pulled the burlap sacks off the deer and Liz looked at them. One was a big buck. It was stiff and hard to lift out of the wagon.

"Did you shoot it, Jim?" Liz asked.

"Yeah. Ain't it a beauty?" Jim got it onto his back to carry to the smokehouse.

That night Charley Wyman stayed to supper at Smith's. It was too late to get back to Charlevoix. The men washed up and waited in the front room for supper.

"Ain't there something left in that crock, Jimmy?" D. J. Smith asked, and Jim went out to the wagon in the barn and fetched in the jug of whiskey the men had taken hunting with them. It was a four-gallon jug and there was quite a little slopped back and forth in the bottom. Jim took a long pull on his way back to the house. It was hard to lift such a big jug up to drink out of it. Some of the whiskey ran down on his shirt front. The two men smiled when Jim came in with the jug. D. J. Smith sent for glasses and Liz brought them. D. J. poured out three big shots.

"Well, here's looking at you, D. J.," said Charley Wyman.

"That damn big buck, Jimmy," said D. J.

"Here's all the ones we missed, D. J.," said Jim, and downed his liquor.

"Tastes good to a man."

"Nothing like it this time of year for what ails you."

"How about another, boys?"

"Here's how, D. J."

"Down the creek, boys."

"Here's to next year."

Jim began to feel great. He loved the taste and the feel of whiskey. He was glad to be back to a comfortable bed and warm food and the shop. He had another drink. The men came in to supper feeling hilarious but acting very respectable. Liz sat at the table after she put on the food and ate with the family. It was a good dinner. The men ate seriously. After supper they went into the front room again and Liz cleaned off with Mrs. Smith. Then Mrs. Smith went upstairs and pretty soon Smith came out and went upstairs too. Jim and Charley were still in the front room. Liz was sitting in the kitchen next to the stove pretending to read a book and thinking about Jim. She didn't want to go to bed yet because she knew Jim would be coming out and she wanted to see him as he went out so she could take the way he looked up to bed with her.

She was thinking about him hard and then Jim came out. His eyes were shining and his hair was a little rumpled. Liz looked down at her book. Jim came over back of her chair and stood there and she could feel him breathing and then he put his arms around her. Her breasts felt plump and firm and the nipples were erect under his hands. Liz was terribly frightened, no one had ever touched her, but she thought, "He's come to me finally. He's really come."

She held herself stiff because she was so frightened and did not know anything else to do and then Jim held her tight against the chair and kissed her. It was such a sharp, aching, hurting feeling that she thought she couldn't stand it. She felt Jim right through the back of the chair and she couldn't stand it and then something clicked inside of her and the feeling was warmer and softer. Jim held her tight hard against the chair and she wanted it now and Jim whispered, "Come on for a walk."

Liz took her coat off the peg on the kitchen wall and they went out the door. Jim had his arm around her and every little way they stopped and pressed against each other and Jim kissed her. There was no moon and they walked ankle-deep in the sandy road through the trees down to the dock and the warehouse on the bay. The water was lapping in the piles and the point was dark across the bay. It was cold but Liz was hot all over from being with Jim. They sat down in the shelter of the warehouse and Jim pulled Liz close to him. She was frightened. One of Jim's hands went inside her dress and stroked over her breast and the other hand was in her lap. She was very frightened and didn't know how he was going to go about things but she snuggled close to him. Then the hand that felt so big in her lap went away and was on her leg and started to move up it.

"Don't, Jim," Liz said. Jim slid the hand further up.

"You mustn't, Jim. You mustn't." Neither Jim nor Jim's big hand paid any attention to her.

The boards were hard. Jim had her dress up and was trying to do something to her. She was frightened but she wanted it. She had to have it but it frightened her.

"You mustn't do it, Jim. You mustn't."

"I got to. I'm going to. You know we got to."

"No we haven't, Jim. We ain't got to. Oh, it isn't right. Oh, it's so big and it hurts so. You can't. Oh, Jim. Jim. Oh."

The hemlock planks of the dock were hard and splintery and cold and Jim was heavy on her and he had hurt her. Liz pushed him, she was so uncomfortable and cramped. Jim was asleep. He wouldn't move. She worked out from under him and sat up and straightened her skirt and coat and tried to do something with her hair. Jim was sleeping with his mouth a little open. Liz leaned over and kissed him on the cheek. He was still asleep. She lifted his head a little and shook it. He rolled his head over and swallowed. Liz started to cry. She walked over to the edge of the dock and looked down to the water. There was a mist coming up from the bay. She was cold and miserable and everything felt gone. She walked back to where Jim was lying and shook him once more to make sure. She was crying.

"Jim," she said, "Jim. Please, Jim."

Jim stirred and curled a little tighter. Liz took off her coat and leaned over and covered him with it. She tucked it around him neatly and carefully. Then she walked across the dock and up the steep sandy road to go to bed. A cold mist was coming up through the woods from the bay.

—*1923, revised 1938*

Richard Wright was the son of a Mississippi farm worker and mill hand who abandoned the family when the writer was 5 and a mother who was forced by poverty to place her son in orphanages during part of his childhood. As he relates in his autobiography, Black Boy *(1945), he was largely self-educated through extensive reading; while working for the post office in Memphis he discovered the essays of H. L. Mencken, whom he credited as the major influence on his decision to become a writer. In Chicago in the 1930s he became associated with the Federal Writers' Project and, briefly, with the Communist Party. He later lived in New York and, for the last fifteen years of his life, Paris, where he was associated with French existentialist writers like Jean-Paul Sartre. Wright's first novel,* Native Son *(1940), based on an actual 1938 murder case, describes the chain of circumstances that lead to a black chauffeur's being tried and executed for the accidental slaying of a wealthy white woman. The success of that book established Wright as the leading black novelist of his generation, and while none of his subsequent works attracted the same level of attention, he nevertheless helped define many of the themes that African-American writers continue to explore today. "The Man Who Was Almost a Man" was filmed as part of the* PBS American Short Story *series.*

The Man Who Was Almost a Man

Dave struck out across the fields, looking homeward through paling light. Whut's the use talkin wid em niggers in the field? Anyhow, his mother was putting supper on the table. Them niggers can't understan nothing. One of these days he was going to get a gun and practice shooting, then they couldn't talk to him as though he were a little boy. He slowed, looking at the ground. Shucks, Ah ain scareda them even if they are biggern me! Aw, Ah know what Ahma do. Ahm going by ol Joe's sto n git that Sears Roebuck catlog n look at them guns. Mebbe Ma will lemme buy one when she gits mah pay from ol man Hawkins. Ahma beg her t gimme some money. Ahm ol ernough to hava gun. Ahm seventeen. Almost a man. He strode, feeling his long loose-jointed limbs. Shucks, a man oughta hava little gun aftah he done worked hard all day.

He came in sight of Joe's store. A yellow lantern glowed on the front porch. He mounted steps and went through the screen door, hearing it bang behind him. There was a strong smell of coal oil and mackerel fish. He felt very confident until he saw fat Joe walk in through the rear door, then his courage began to ooze.

"Howdy, Dave! Whutcha want?"

"How yuh, Mistah Joe? Aw, Ah don wanna buy nothing. Ah jus wanted t see ef yuhd lemme look at tha catlog erwhile."

"Sure! You wanna see it here?"

"Nawsuh. Ah wants t take it home wid me. Ah'll bring it back ter-morrow when Ah come in from the fiels."

"You plannin on buying something?"

"Yessuh."

"Your ma lettin you have your own money now?"

"Shucks. Mistah Joe, Ahm gittin t be a man like anybody else!"

Joe laughed and wiped his greasy white face with a red bandanna.

"Whut you plannin on buyin?"

Dave looked at the floor, scratched his head, scratched his thigh, and smiled. Then he looked up shyly.

"Ah'll tell yuh, Mistah Joe, ef yuh promise yuh won't tell."

"I promise."

"Waal, Ahma buy a gun."

"A gun? What you want with a gun?"

"Ah wanna keep it."

"You ain't nothing but a boy. You don't need a gun."

"Aw, lemme have the catlog, Mistah Joe. Ah'll bring it back."

Joe walked through the rear door. Dave was elated. He looked around at barrels of sugar and flour. He heard Joe coming back. He craned his neck to see if he were bringing the book. Yeah, he's got it. Gawddog, he's got it!

"Here, but be sure you bring it back. It's the only one I got."

"Sho, Mistah Joe."

"Say, if you wanna buy a gun, why don't you buy one from me? I gotta gun to sell."

"Will it shoot?"

"Sure it'll shoot."

"Whut kind is it?"

"Oh, it's kinda old . . . a left-hand Wheeler. A pistol. A big one."

"Is it got bullets in it?"

"It's loaded."

"Kin Ah see it?"

"Where's your money?"

"Whut yuh wan fer it?"

"I'll let you have it for two dollars."

"Just two dollahs? Shucks, Ah could buy that when Ah git mah pay."

"I'll have it here when you want it."

"Awright, suh. Ah be in fer it."

He went through the door, hearing it slam again behind him. Ahma git some money from Ma n buy me a gun! Only two dollahs! He tucked the thick catalogue under his arm and hurried.

"Where yuh been, boy?" His mother held a steaming dish of black-eyed peas.

"Aw, Ma, Ah jus stopped down the road t talk wid the boys."

"Yuh know bettah t keep suppah waitin."

He sat down, resting the catalogue on the edge of the table.

"Yuh git up from there and git to the well n wash yosef! Ah ain feedin no hogs in mah house!"

She grabbed his shoulder and pushed him. He stumbled out of the room, then came back to get the catalogue.

"Whut this?"

"Aw, Ma, it's jusa catlog."

"Who yuh git it from?"

"From Joe, down at the sto."

"Waal, thas good. We kin use it in the outhouse."

"Naw, Ma." He grabbed for it. "Gimme ma catlog, Ma."

She held onto it and glared at him.

"Quit hollerin at me! Whut's wrong wid yuh? Yuh crazy?"

"But Ma, please. It ain mine! It's Joe's! He tol me t bring it back t im termorrow."

She gave up the book. He stumbled down the back steps, hugging the thick book under his arm. When he had splashed water on his face and hands, he groped back to the kitchen and fumbled in a corner for the towel. He bumped into a chair; it clattered to the floor. The catalogue sprawled at his feet. When he had dried his eyes he snatched up the book and held it again under his arm. His mother stood watching him.

"Now, ef yuh gonna act a fool over that ol book, Ah'll take it n burn it up."

"Naw, Ma, please."

"Waal, set down n be still!"

He sat down and drew the oil lamp close. He thumbed page after page, unaware of the food his mother set on the table. His father came in. Then his small brother.

"Whutcha got there, Dave?" his father asked.

"Jusa catlog," he answered, not looking up.

"Yeah, here they is!" His eyes glowed at blue-and-black revolvers. He glanced up, feeling sudden guilt. His father was watching him. He eased the book under the table and rested it on his knees. After the blessing was asked, he ate. He scooped up peas and swallowed fat meat without chewing. Buttermilk helped to wash it down. He did not want to mention money before his father. He would do much better by cornering his mother when she was alone. He looked at his father uneasily out of the edge of his eye.

"Boy, how come yuh don quit foolin wid tha book n eat yo suppah?"

"Yessuh."

"How you n ol man Hawkins gitten erlong?"

"Suh?"

"Can't yuh hear? Why don yuh lissen? Ah ast yu how wuz yuh n ol man Hawkins gittin erlong?"

"Oh, swell, Pa. Ah plows mo lan than anybody over there."

"Waal, yuh oughta keep you mind on what yuh doin."

"Yessuh."

He poured his plate full of molasses and sopped it up slowly with a chunk of cornbread. When his father and brother had left the kitchen, he still sat and looked again at the guns in the catalogue, longing to muster courage enough to present his case to his mother. Lawd, ef Ah only had tha pretty one! He could almost feel the slickness of the weapon with his fingers. If he had a gun like that he would polish it and keep it shining so it would never rust! N Ah'd keep it loaded, by Gawd!

"Ma?" His voice was hesitant.

"Hunh?"

"Ol man Hawkins give yuh mah money yit?"

"Yeah, but ain no usa yuh thinking bout throwin nona it erway. Ahm keeping tha money sos yuh kin have cloes t go to school this winter."

He rose and went to her side with the open catalogue in his palms. She was washing dishes, her head bent low over a pan. Shyly he raised the book. When he spoke, his voice was husky, faint.

"Ma, Gawd knows Ah wans one of these."

"One of whut?" she asked, not raising her eyes.

"One of these," he said again, not daring even to point. She glanced up at the page, then at him with wide eyes. "Nigger, is yuh gone plumb crazy?"

"Aw, Ma—"

"Git outta here! Don yuh talk t me bout no gun! Yuh a fool!"

"Ma, Ah kin buy one fer two dollahs."

"Not ef Ah knows it, yuh ain!"

"But yuh promised me one—"

"Ah don care what Ah promised! Yuh ain nothing but a boy yit!"

"Ma, ef yuh lemme buy one Ah'll *never* ast yuh fer nothing no mo."

"Ah tol yuh t git outta here! Yuh ain gonna toucha penny of tha money fer no gun! Thas how come Ah has Mistah Hawkins t pay yo wages t me, cause Ah knows yuh ain got no sense."

"But, Ma, we needa gun. Pa ain got no gun. We needa gun in the house. Yuh kin never tell whut might happen."

"Now don yuh try to maka fool outta me, boy! Ef we did hava gun, yuh wouldn't have it!"

He laid the catalogue down and slipped his arm around her waist.

"Aw, Ma, Ah done worked hard alla summer n ain ast yuh fer nothing, is Ah, now?"

"Thas what yuh spose t do!"

"But Ma, Ah wans a gun. Yuh kin lemme have two dollahs outta mah money. Please, Ma. I kin give it to Pa . . . Please, Ma! Ah loves yuh, Ma!"

When she spoke her voice came soft and low.

"What yu wan wida gun, Dave? Yuh don need no gun. Yuh'll git in trouble. N ef yo pa jus thought Ah let yuh have money t buy a gun he'd hava fit."

"Ah'll hide it, Ma. It ain but two dollahs."

"Lawd, chil, whut's wrong wid yuh?"

"Ain nothin wrong, Ma. Ahm almos a man now. Ah wans a gun."

"Who gonna sell yuh a gun?"

"Ol Joe at the sto."

"N it don cos but two dollahs?"

"Thas all, Ma. Jus two dollahs. Please, Ma."

She was stacking the plates away; her hands moved slowly, reflectively. Dave kept an anxious silence. Finally, she turned to him.

"Ah'll let yuh git tha gun if yuh promise me one thing."

"What's tha, Ma?"

"Yuh bring it straight back t me, yuh hear? It be fer Pa."

"Yessum! Lemme go now, Ma."

She stooped, turned slightly to one side, raised the hem of her dress, rolled down the top of her stocking, and came up with a slender wad of bills.

"Here," she said. "Lawd knows yuh don need no gun. But yer pa does. Yuh bring it right back t me, yuh hear? Ahma put it up. Now ef yuh don, Ahma have yuh pa lick yuh so hard yuh won fergit it."

"Yessum."

He took the money, ran down the steps, and across the yard.

"Dave! Yuuuuuh Daaaaave!"

He heard, but he was not going to stop now. "Naw, Lawd!"

The first movement he made the following morning was to reach under the pillow for the gun. In the gray light of dawn he held it loosely, feeling a sense of power. Could kill a man with a gun like this. Kill anybody, black or white. And if he were holding his gun in his hand, nobody could run over him; they would have to respect him. It was a big gun, with a long barrel and a heavy handle. He raised and lowered it in his hand, marveling at its weight.

He had not come straight home with it as his mother had asked; instead he had stayed out in the fields, holding the weapon in his hand, aiming it now and then at some imaginary foe. But he had not fired it; he had been afraid that his father might hear. Also he was not sure he knew how to fire it.

To avoid surrendering the pistol he had not come into the house until he knew that they were all asleep. When his mother had tiptoed to his bedside late that night and demanded the gun, he had first played possum; then he had told her that the gun was hidden outdoors, that he would bring it to her in the morning. Now he lay turning it slowly in his hands. He broke it, took out the cartridges, felt them, and then put them back.

He slid out of bed, got a long strip of old flannel from a trunk, wrapped the gun in it, and tied it to his naked thigh while it was still loaded. He did not go in to breakfast. Even though it was not yet daylight he started for Jim Hawkins' plantation. Just as the sun was rising he reached the barns where the mules and plows were kept.

"Hey! That you, Dave?"

He turned. Jim Hawkins stood eyeing him suspiciously.

"What're yuh doing here so early?"

"Ah didn't know Ah wuz gittin up so early, Mistah Hawkins. Ah was fixin t hitch up ol Jenny n take her t the fiels."

"Good. Since you're so early, how about plowing that stretch down by the woods?"

"Suits me, Mistah Hawkins."

"O.K. Go to it!"

He hitched Jenny to a plow and started across the fields. Hot dog! This was just what he wanted. If he could get down by the woods, he could shoot his gun and nobody would hear. He walked behind the plow, hearing the traces creaking, feeling the gun tied tight to his thigh.

When he reached the woods, he plowed two whole rows before he decided to take out the gun. Finally, he stopped, looked in all directions, then untied the gun and held it in his hand. He turned to the mule and smiled.

"Know whut this is, Jenny? Naw, yuh wouldn know! Yuhs jusa ol mule! Anyhow, this is a gun, n it kin shoot, by Gawd!"

He held the gun at arm's length. Whut t hell, Ahma shoot this thing! He looked at Jenny again.

"Lissen here, Jenny! When Ah pull this ol trigger, Ah don wan yuh t run n acka fool now!"

Jenny stood with head down, her short ears pricked straight. Dave walked off about twenty feet, held the gun far out from him at arm's length, and turned his head. Hell, he told himself, Ah ain afraid. The gun felt loose in his fingers; he waved it wildly for a moment. Then he shut his eyes and tightened his forefinger. Bloom! A report half deafened him and he thought his right hand was torn from his arm. He heard Jenny whinnying and galloping over the field, and he found himself on his knees, squeezing his fingers hard between his legs. His hand was numb; he jammed it into his mouth, trying to warm it, trying to stop the pain. The gun lay at his feet. He did not quite know what had happened. He stood up and stared at the gun as though it were a living thing. He gritted his teeth and kicked the gun. Yuh almos broke mah arm! He turned to look for Jenny; she was far over the fields, tossing her head and kicking wildly.

"Hol on there, ol mule!"

When he caught up with her she stood trembling, walling her big white eyes at him. The plow was far away; the traces had broken. Then

Dave stopped short, looking, not believing. Jenny was bleeding. Her left side was red and wet with blood. He went closer. Lawd, have mercy! Wondah did Ah shoot this mule? He grabbed for Jenny's mane. She flinched, snorted, whirled, tossing her head.

"Hol on now! Hol on."

Then he saw the hole in Jenny's side, right between the ribs. It was round, wet, red. A crimson stream streaked down the front leg, flowing fast. Good Gawd! Ah wuzn't shootin at tha mule. He felt panic. He knew he had to stop that blood, or Jenny would bleed to death. He had never seen so much blood in all his life. He chased the mule for half a mile, trying to catch her. Finally she stopped, breathing hard, stumpy tail half arched. He caught her mane and led her back to where the plow and gun lay. Then he stopped and grabbed handfuls of damp black earth and tried to plug the bullet hole. Jenny shuddered, whinnied, and broke from him.

"Hol on! Hol on now!"

He tried to plug it again, but blood came anyhow. His fingers were hot and sticky. He rubbed dirt into his palms, trying to dry them. Then again he attempted to plug the bullet hole, but Jenny shied away, kicking her heels high. He stood helpless. He had to do something. He ran at Jenny; she dodged him. He watched a red stream of blood flow down Jenny's leg and form a bright pool at her feet.

"Jenny . . . Jenny," he called weakly.

His lips trembled. She's bleeding t death! He looked in the direction of home, wanting to go back, wanting to get help. But he saw the pistol lying in the damp black clay. He had a queer feeling that if he only did something, this would not be; Jenny would not be there bleeding to death.

When he went to her this time, she did not move. She stood with sleepy, dreamy eyes; and when he touched her she gave a low-pitched whinny and knelt to the ground, her front knees slopping in blood.

"Jenny . . . Jenny . . ." he whispered.

For a long time she held her neck erect; then her head sank, slowly. Her ribs swelled with a mighty heave and she went over.

Dave's stomach felt empty, very empty. He picked up the gun and held it gingerly between his thumb and forefinger. He buried it at the foot of a tree. He took a stick and tried to cover the pool of blood with dirt—but what was the use? There was Jenny lying with her mouth open and her eyes walled and glassy. He could not tell Jim Hawkins he had shot his mule. But he had to tell something. Yeah, Ah'll tell em Jenny started gittin wil n fell on the joint of the plow . . . But that would hardly happen to a mule. He walked across the field slowly, head down.

It was sunset. Two of Jim Hawkins' men were over near the edge of the woods digging a hole in which to bury Jenny. Dave was surrounded by a knot of people, all of whom were looking down at the dead mule.

"I don't see how in the world it happened," said Jim Hawkins for the tenth time.

The crowd parted and Dave's mother, father, and small brother pushed into the center.

"Where Dave?" his mother called.

"There he is," said Jim Hawkins.

His mother grabbed him.

"Whut happened, Dave? Whut yuh done?"

"Nothin."

"C mon, boy, talk," his father said.

Dave took a deep breath and told the story he knew nobody believed.

"Waal," he drawled. "Ah brung ol Jenny down here sos Ah could do mah plowin. Ah plowed bout two rows, just like yuh see." He stopped and pointed at the long rows of upturned earth. "Then somethin musta been wrong wid ol Jenny. She wouldn ack right a-tall. She started snortin n kickin her heels. Ah tried t hol her, but she pulled erway, rearin n goin in. Then when the point of the plow was stickin up in the air, she swung erroun n twisted herself back on it . . . She stuck herself n started t bleed. N fo Ah could do anything, she wuz dead."

"Did you ever hear anything like that in all your life?" asked Jim Hawkins.

There were white and black standing in the crowd. They murmured. Dave's mother came close to him and looked hard into his face. "Tell the truth, Dave," she said.

"Looks like a bullet hole to me," said one man.

"Dave, whut yuh do wid the gun?" his mother asked.

The crowd surged in, looking at him. He jammed his hands into his pockets, shook his head slowly from left to right, and backed away. His eyes were wide and painful.

"Did he hava gun?" asked Jim Hawkins.

"By Gawd, Ah tol yuh tha wuz a gun wound," said a man, slapping his thigh.

His father caught his shoulders and shook him till his teeth rattled.

"Tell whut happened, yuh rascal! Tell whut . . ."

Dave looked at Jenny's stiff legs and began to cry.

"Whut yuh do wid tha gun?" his mother asked.

"What wuz he doin wida gun?" his father asked.

"Come on and tell the truth," said Hawkins. "Ain't nobody going to hurt . . ."

His mother crowded close to him.

"Did yuh shoot tha mule, Dave?"

Dave cried, seeing blurred white and black faces.

"Ahh ddinn gggo tt sshooot hher . . . Ah sssswear ffo Gawd Ahh ddin . . . Ah wuz a-tryin t sssee ef the old gggun would sshoot—"

"Where yuh git the gun from?" his father asked.

"Ah got it from Joe, at the sto."

"Where yuh git the money?"

"Ma give it t me."

"He kept worryin me, Bob. Ah had t. Ah tol im t bring the gun right back t me . . . It was fer yuh, the gun."

"But how yuh happen to shoot that mule?" asked Jim Hawkins.

"Ah wuzn shootin at the mule, Mistah Hawkins. The gun jumped when Ah pulled the trigger . . . N fo Ah knowed anythin Jenny was there a-bleedin."

Somebody in the crowd laughed. Jim Hawkins walked close to Dave and looked into his face.

"Well, looks like you have bought you a mule, Dave."

"Ah swear fo Gawd, Ah didn go t kill the mule, Mistah Hawkins!"

"But you killed her!"

All the crowd was laughing now. They stood on tiptoe and poked heads over one another's shoulders.

"Well, boy, looks like yuh done bought a dead mule! Hahaha!"

"Ain tha ershame."

"Hohohohoho."

Dave stood, head down, twisting his feet in the dirt.

"Well, you needn't worry about it, Bob," said Jim Hawkins to Dave's father. "Just let the boy keep on working and pay me two dollars a month."

"Whut yuh wan fer yo mule, Mistah Hawkins?"

Jim Hawkins screwed up his eyes.

"Fifty dollars."

"Whut yuh do wid tha gun?" Dave's father demanded.

Dave said nothing.

"Yuh wan me t take a tree n beat yuh till yuh talk!"

"Nawsuh!"

"Whut yuh do wid it?"

"Ah throwed it erway."

"Where?"

"Ah . . . Ah throwed it in the creek."

"Waal, c mon home. N firs thing in the mawnin git to tha creek n fin tha gun."

"Yessuh."

"Whut yuh pay fer it?"

"Two dollahs."

"Take tha gun n git yo money back n carry it to Mistah Hawkins, yuh hear? N don fergit Ahma lam you black bottom good fer this! Now march yosef on home, suh!"

Dave turned and walked slowly. He heard people laughing. Dave glared, his eyes welling with tears. Hot anger bubbled in him. Then he swallowed and stumbled on.

That night Dave did not sleep. He was glad that he had gotten out of killing the mule so easily, but he was hurt. Something hot seemed to turn over inside him each time he remembered how they had laughed. He tossed on his bed, feeling his hard pillow. N Pa says he's gonna beat me . . . He remembered other beatings, and his back quivered. Naw, naw, Ah sho don wan im t beat me tha way no mo. Dam em all! Nobody ever gave him anything. All he did was work. They treat me like a mule, n then they beat me. He gritted his teeth. N Ma had t tell on me.

Well, if he had to, he would take old man Hawkins that two dollars. But that meant selling the gun. And he wanted to keep that gun. Fifty dollars for a dead mule.

He turned over, thinking how he had fired the gun. He had an itch to fire it again. Ef other men kin shoota gun, by Gawd, Ah kin! He was still, listening. Mebbe they all sleepin now. The house was still. He heard the soft breathing of his brother. Yes, now! He would go down and get that gun and see if he could fire it! He eased out of bed and slipped into overalls.

The moon was bright. He ran almost all the way to the edge of the woods. He stumbled over the ground, looking for the spot where he had buried the gun. Yeah, here it is. Like a hungry dog scratching for a bone, he pawed it up. He puffed his black cheeks and blew dirt from the trigger and barrel. He broke it and found four cartridges unshot. He looked around; the fields were filled with silence and moonlight. He clutched the gun stiff and hard in his fingers. But, as soon as he wanted to pull the trigger, he shut his eyes and turned his head. Naw, Ah can't shoot wid mah eyes closed n mah head turned. With effort he held his eyes open; then he squeezed. *Blooooom!* He was stiff, not breathing. The gun was still in his hands. Dammit, he'd done it! He fired again. *Blooooom!* He smiled. *Blooooom! Blooooom! Click, click.* There! It was empty. If anybody could shoot a gun, he could. He put the gun into his hip pocket and started across the fields.

When he reached the top of a ridge he stood straight and proud in the moonlight, looking at Jim Hawkins' big white house, feeling the gun sagging in his pocket. Lawd, ef Ah had just one mo bullet Ah'd taka shot at tha house. Ah'd like t scare ol man Hawkins jusa little . . . Jusa enough t let im know Dave Saunders is a man.

To his left the road curved, running to the tracks of the Illinois Central. He jerked his head, listening. From far off come a faint *hoooof-hoooof; hoooof-hoooof* . . . He stood rigid. Two dollahs a mont. Les see now . . . Tha means it'll take bout two years. Shucks! Ah'll be dam!

He started down the road, toward the tracks. Yeah, here she comes! He stood beside the track and held himself stiffly. Here she comes, er-roun the ben . . . C mon, yuh slow poke! C mon! He had his hand on his gun; something quivered in his stomach. Then the train thundered past, the gray and brown box cars rumbling and clinking. He gripped the gun tightly; then he jerked his hand out of his pocket. Ah betcha Bill wouldn't do it! Ah betcha . . . The cars slid past, steel grinding upon steel. Ahm ridin yuh ternight, so hep me Gawd! He was hot all over. He hesitated just a moment; then he grabbed, pulled atop of a car, and lay flat. He felt his pocket; the gun was still there. Ahead the long rails were glinting in the moonlight, stretching away, away to somewhere, somewhere where he could be a man. . . .

—1937

John Cheever was associated with The New Yorker *for most of his creative life. It was the magazine that first published most of his short stories. Cheever's examinations of the tensions of life in white-collar suburbia take many forms—from naturalism to outright fantasy—but virtually all of his fiction is suffused with a melancholy that is often fueled by marital tensions, failed social aspirations, and what one story aptly calls "the sorrows of gin." Born in Quincy, Massachusetts, Cheever was expelled from Thayer Academy at age 17, an event that formed the subject of his first published story, and he worked almost exclusively as a writer of fiction for the rest of his life, with occasional periods spent teaching at universities and writing for television. His most original writing is arguably in his short stories, but novels like the National Book Award–winning* The Wapshot Chronicle *(1957),* The Wapshot Scandal *(1964),* Bullet Park *(1969), and* Falconer *(1977) brought him to the attention of large audiences.* The Stories of John Cheever *won the Pulitzer Prize in 1979. In recent years his daughter, Susan Cheever, published a memoir,* Home Before Dark, *and an edition of her father's journals, both of which chronicle Cheever's long struggles with alcoholism and questions of sexual identity.*

Reunion

The last time I saw my father was in Grand Central Station. I was going from my grandmother's in the Adirondacks to a cottage on the Cape that my mother had rented, and I wrote my father that I would be in New York between trains for an hour and a half, and asked if we could have lunch together. His secretary wrote to say that he would meet me at the information booth at noon, and at twelve o'clock sharp I saw him coming through the crowd. He was a stranger to me—my mother divorced him three years ago and I hadn't been with him since—but as soon as I saw him I felt that he was my father, my flesh and blood, my future and my doom. I knew that when I was grown I would be something like him; I would have to plan my campaigns within his limitations. He was a big, good-looking man, and I was terribly happy to see him again. He struck me on the back and shook my hand. "Hi, Charlie," he said. "Hi, boy. I'd like to take you up to my club, but it's in the Sixties, and if you have to catch an early train I guess we'd better get something to eat around here." He put his arm around me, and I smelled my father the way my mother sniffs a rose. It was a rich compound of whiskey, after-shave lotion, shoe polish, woolens, and the rankness of a mature male. I hoped that someone would see us together. I wished that we could be photographed. I wanted some record of our having been together.

We went out of the station and up a side street to a restaurant. It was still early, and the place was empty. The bartender was quarreling with a delivery boy, and there was one very old waiter in a red coat down by the kitchen door. We sat down, and my father hailed the waiter in a loud voice. "*Kellner!*" he shouted. "*Garçon! Cameriere! You!*" His boisterousness in the empty restaurant seemed out of place. "Could we have a little service here!" he shouted. "Chop-chop." Then he clapped his hands. This caught the waiter's attention, and he shuffled over to our table.

"Were you clapping your hands at me?" he asked.

"Calm down, calm down, *sommelier*," my father said. "If it isn't too much to ask of you—if it wouldn't be too much above and beyond the call of duty, we would like a couple of Beefeater Gibsons."

"I don't like to be clapped at," the waiter said.

"I should have brought my whistle," my father said. "I have a whistle that is audible only to the ears of old waiters. Now, take out your little pad and your little pencil and see if you can get this straight: two Beefeater Gibsons. Repeat after me: two Beefeater Gibsons."

"I think you'd better go somewhere else," the waiter said quietly.

"That," said my father, "is one of the most brilliant suggestions I have ever heard. Come on, Charlie, let's get the hell out of here!"

I followed my father out of that restaurant into another. He was not so boisterous this time. Our drinks came, and he cross-questioned me about the baseball season. He then struck the edge of his empty glass with his knife and began shouting again. "*Garçon! Kellner! Cameriere! You!* Could we trouble you to bring us two more of the same."

"How old is the boy?" the waiter asked.

"That," my father said, "is none of your God-damned business."

"I'm sorry, sir," the waiter said, "but I won't serve the boy another drink."

"Well, I have some news for you," my father said. "I have some very interesting news for you. This doesn't happen to be the only restaurant in New York. They've opened another on the corner. Come on, Charlie."

He paid the bill, and I followed him out of that restaurant into another. Here the waiters wore pink jackets like hunting coats, and there was a lot of horse tack on the walls. We sat down, and my father began to shout again. "Master of the hounds! Tallyhoo and all that sort of thing. We'd like a little something in the way of a stirrup cup. Namely, two Bibson Geefeaters."

"Two Bibson Geefeaters?" the waiter asked, smiling.

"You know damned well what I want," my father said angrily. "I want two Beefeater Gibsons, and make it snappy. Things have changed in jolly old England. So my friend the duke tells me. Let's see what England can produce in the way of a cocktail."

"This isn't England," the waiter said.

"Don't argue with me," my father said. "Just do as you're told."

"I just thought you might like to know where you are," the waiter said.

"If there is one thing I cannot tolerate," my father said, "it is an impudent domestic. Come on, Charlie."

The fourth place we went to was Italian. "*Buon giorno*," my father said. "*Per favore, possiamo avere due cocktail americani, forti, forti. Molto gin, poco vermut.*"[1]

"I don't understand Italian," the waiter said.

"Oh, come off it," my father said. "You understand Italian, and you know damned well you do. *Vogliamo due cocktail americani. Subito.*"

The waiter left us and spoke with the captain, who came over to our table and said, "I'm sorry, sir, but this table is reserved."

"All right," my father said. "Get us another table."

"All the tables are reserved," the captain said.

"I get it," my father said. "You don't desire our patronage. Is that it? Well, the hell with you. *Vada all' inferno*. Let's go, Charlie."

"I have to get my train," I said.

"I'm sorry, sonny," my father said. "I'm terribly sorry." He put his arm around me and pressed me against him. "I'll walk you back to the station. If there had only been time to go up to my club."

"That's all right, Daddy," I said.

"I'll get you a paper," he said. "I'll get you a paper to read on the train."

---

[1] The father is ordering drinks in Italian.

Then he went up to a newsstand and said, "Kind sir, will you be good enough to favor me with one of your God-damned, no-good, ten-cent afternoon papers?" The clerk turned away from him and stared at a magazine cover. "Is it asking too much, kind sir," my father said, "is it asking too much for you to sell me one of your disgusting specimens of yellow journalism?"

"I have to go, Daddy," I said. "It's late."

"Now, just wait a second, sonny," he said. "Just wait a second. I want to get a rise out of this chap."

"Goodbye, Daddy," I said, and I went down the stairs and got my train, and that was the last time I saw my father.

—1962

RALPH ELLISON ■ (1914–1995)

REUNION

177

Ralph Ellison was born in Oklahoma City, where his early interests were primarily musical; he played trumpet and knew many prominent jazz musicians of the Depression era. In 1933 he attended Tuskegee Institute, intending to study music, but he was drawn to literature through his study of contemporary writers (especially the poet T. S. Eliot). Ellison left school in 1936 for New York City, where he found work for a time with the Federal Writers' Project and began to publish stories and reviews in the later 1930s in progressive magazines like New Masses. *Tuskegee and Harlem provided him with material for* Invisible Man *(1952), a brilliant picaresque novel of African-American life that established him as a major force in American fiction.* Invisible Man *won the National Book Award in 1953 and in 1965 was voted in a* Book Week *poll the most distinguished novel of the postwar period. Ellison published little subsequently, with two collections of essays,* Shadow and Act *(1964) and* Going to the Territory *(1986), a posthumous volume of collected stories, and an unfinished novel,* Juneteenth *(1999), having to suffice for readers who long anticipated a second novel that might somehow help to define the changes four decades had wrought in the experience of black America. "A Party Down at the Square," a brutally direct account of a lynching, is based on true accounts of similar events that appeared primarily in African-American newspapers in the 1920s and 1930s. Uncollected and almost forgotten at Ellison's death, it was posthumously reprinted in* Esquire.

A Party Down at the Square

I don't know what started it. A bunch of men came by my Uncle Ed's place and said there was going to be a party down at the Square, and my uncle hollered for me to come on and I ran with them through the dark and rain and there we were at the Square. When we got there everybody was mad and quiet and standing around looking at the nigger. Some of the men had guns, and one man kept goosing the nigger in his pants with the barrel of a shotgun, saying he ought to pull the trigger, but he never did. It was right in front of the courthouse, and the old clock in the tower was striking twelve. The rain was falling cold and freezing as it fell. Everybody was cold, and the nigger kept wrapping his arms around himself trying to stop the shivers. 死了吧

Then one of the boys pushed through the circle and snatched off the nigger's shirt, and there he stood, with his black skin all shivering in the light from the fire, and looking at us with a scaired look on his face and putting his hands in his pants pockets. Folks started yelling to hurry up and kill the nigger. Somebody yelled: "Take your hands out of your pockets, nigger; we gonna have plenty heat in a minnit." But the nigger didn't hear him and kept his hands where they were.

I tell you the rain was cold. I had to stick my hands in my pockets they got so cold. The fire was pretty small, and they put some logs around the platform they had the nigger on and then threw on some gasoline, and you could see the flames light up the whole Square. It was late and the streetlights had been off for a long time. It was so bright that the bronze statue of the general standing there in the Square was like something alive. The shadows playing on his moldy green face made him seem to be smiling down at the nigger.

They threw on more gas, and it made the Square bright like it gets when the lights are turned on or when the sun is setting red. All the wagons and cars were standing around the curbs. Not like Saturday though—the niggers weren't there. Not a single nigger was there except this Bacote nigger and they dragged him there tied to the back of Jed Wilson's truck. On Saturday there's as many niggers as white folks.

Everybody was yelling crazy 'cause they were about to set fire to the nigger, and I got to the rear of the circle and looked around the Square to try to count the cars. The shadows of the folks was flickering on the trees in the middle of the Square. I saw some birds that the noise had woke up flying through the trees. I guess maybe they thought it was morning. The ice had started the cobblestones in the street to shine where the rain was falling and freezing. I counted forty cars before I lost count. I knew folks must have been there from Phenix City by all the cars mixed in with the wagons.

God, it was a hell of a night. It was some night all right. When the noise died down I heard the nigger's voice from where I stood in the back, so I pushed my way up front. The nigger was bleeding from his nose and ears, and I could see him all red where the dark blood was running down his black skin. He kept lifting first one foot and then the other, like a chicken on a hot stove. I looked down to the platform they had him on, and they had pushed a ring of fire up close to his feet. It must have been hot to him with the flames almost touching his big black toes. Somebody yelled for the nigger to say his prayers, but the nigger wasn't saying anything now. He just kinda moaned with his eyes shut and kept moving up and down on his feet, first one foot and then the other.

I watched the flames burning the logs up closer and closer to the nigger's feet. They were burning good now, and the rain had stopped and the wind was rising, making the flames flare higher. I looked, and there must have been thirty-five women in the crowd, and I could hear their voices clear and shrill mixed in with those of the men. Then it happened. I heard the noise about the same time everyone else did. It was like the roar of a cyclone blowing up from the gulf, and everyone was looking up into the air to see what it was. Some of the faces looked surprised and scaired, all but the nigger. He didn't even hear the noise. He didn't even look up. Then the roar came closer, right above our heads and the wind was blowing higher and higher and the sound seemed to be going in circles.

Then I saw her. Through the clouds and fog I could see a red and green light on her wings. I could see them just for a second; then she rose up into the low clouds. I looked out for the beacon over the tops of the buildings in the direction of the airfield that's forty miles away, and it wasn't circling around. You usually could see it sweeping around the sky at night, but it wasn't there. Then, there she was again, like a big bird lost in the fog. I looked for the red and green lights, and they weren't there anymore. She was flying even closer to the tops of the buildings than before. The wind was blowing harder, and leaves started flying about, making funny shadows on the ground, and tree limbs were cracking and falling.

It was a storm all right. The pilot must have thought he was over the landing field. Maybe he thought the fire in the Square was put there for him to land by. Gosh, but it scaired the folks. I was scaired too. They started yelling: "He's going to land. He's going to land." And: "He's going to fall." A few started for their cars and wagons. I could hear the wagons creaking and chains jangling and cars spitting and missing as they started the engines up. Off to my right, a horse started pitching and striking his hooves against a car.

I didn't know what to do. I wanted to run, and I wanted to stay and see what was going to happen. The plane was close as hell. The pilot must have been trying to see where he was at, and her motors were drowning out all the sounds. I could even feel the vibration, and my hair felt like it was standing up under my hat. I happened to look over at the statue of the general standing with one leg before the other and leaning back on a sword, and I was fixing to run over and climb between his legs and sit there and watch when the roar stopped some, and I looked up and she was gliding just over the top of the trees in the middle of the Square.

Her motors stopped altogether and I could hear the sound of branches cracking and snapping off below her landing gear. I could see her plain now, all silver and shining in the light of the fire with T.W.A. in black letters under her wings. She was sailing smoothly out of the Square when she hit the high power lines that follow the Birmingham highway through the town. It made a loud crash. It sounded like the wind blowing the door of a tin barn shut. She only hit with her landing gear, but I could see the sparks flying, and the wires knocked loose from the poles were spitting blue sparks and whipping around like a bunch of snakes and leaving circles of blue sparks in the darkness.

The plane had knocked five or six wires loose, and they were dangling and swinging, and every time they touched they threw off more sparks. The wind was making them swing, and when I got over there, there was a crackling and spitting screen of blue haze across the highway. I lost my hat running over, but I didn't stop to look for it. I was among the first and I could hear the others pounding behind me across the grass of the Square. They were yelling to beat all hell, and they came up fast, pushing and shoving, and someone got pushed against a swinging wire. It made a sound like when a blacksmith drops a red hot horseshoe into a barrel of water, and the steam comes up. I could smell the flesh burning. The first time I'd ever smelled it. I got up close and it was a woman. It must have killed her right off. She was lying in a puddle stiff as a board, with pieces of glass insulators that the plane had knocked off the poles lying all around her. Her white dress was torn, and I saw one of her tits hanging out in the water and her thighs. Some woman screamed and fainted and almost fell on a wire, but a man caught her. The sheriff and his men were yelling and driving folks back with guns shining in their hands, and everything was lit up blue by the sparks. The shock had turned the woman almost as black as the nigger. I was trying to see if she wasn't blue too, or if it was just the sparks, and the sheriff drove me away. As I backed off trying to see, I heard the motors of the plane start up again somewhere off to the right in the clouds.

The clouds were moving fast in the wind and the wind was blowing the smell of something burning over to me. I turned around, and the crowd was headed back to the nigger. I could see him standing there in the middle of the flames. The wind was making the flames brighter every minute. The crowd was running. I ran too. I ran back across the grass with the crowd. It wasn't so large now that so many had gone when the plane came. I tripped and fell over the limb of a tree lying in the grass and bit my lip. It ain't well yet I bit it so bad. I could taste the blood in my mouth as I ran over. I guess that's what made me sick. When I got there, the fire had caught the nigger's pants, and the folks were standing around watching, but not too close on account of the wind blowing the flames. Somebody hollered, "Well, nigger, it ain't so cold now, is it? You don't need to put your hands in your pockets now." And the nigger looked up with his great white eyes looking like they was 'bout to pop out of his head, and I had enough. I didn't want to see anymore. I wanted to run somewhere and puke, but I stayed. I stayed right there in the front of the crowd and looked.

The nigger tried to say something I couldn't hear for the roar of the wind in the fire, and I strained my ears. Jed Wilson hollered, "What you say there, nigger?" And it came back through the flames in his nigger voice: "Will one a you gentlemen please cut my throat?" he said. "Will somebody please cut my throat like a Christian?" And Jed hollered back, "Sorry, but ain't no Christians around tonight. Ain't no Jew-boys neither. We're just one hundred percent Americans."

Then the nigger was silent. Folks started laughing at Jed. Jed's right popular with the folks, and next year, my uncle says, they plan to run him for sheriff. The heat was too much for me, and the smoke was making my eyes to smart. I was trying to back away when Jed reached down and brought up a can of gasoline and threw it in the fire on the nigger. I could see the flames catching the gas in a puff as it went in in a silver sheet and some of it reached the nigger, making spurts of blue fire all over his chest.

Well, that nigger was tough. I have to give it to that nigger; he was really tough. He had started to burn like a house afire and was making the smoke smell like burning hides. The fire was up around his head, and the smoke was so thick and black we couldn't see him. And him not moving—we thought he was dead. Then he started out. The fire had burned the ropes they had tied him with, and he started jumping and kicking about like he was blind, and you could smell his skin burning. He kicked so hard that the platform, which was burning too, fell in, and he rolled out of the fire at my feet. I jumped back so he wouldn't get on me. I'll never forget it. Every time I eat barbeque I'll remember that nigger. His back was just like a barbecued hog. I could see the prints of his ribs where they start around from his backbone and curve down and around. It was a sight to see, that nigger's back. He was right at my feet, and somebody behind pushed me and almost made me step on him, and he was still burning.

I didn't step on him though, and Jed and somebody else pushed him back into the burning planks and logs and poured on more gas. I wanted to leave, but the folks were yelling and I couldn't move except to look around and see the statue. A branch the wind had broken was resting on his hat. I tried to push out and get away because my guts were gone, and all I got was spit and hot breath in my face from the woman and two men standing directly behind me. So I had to turn back around. The nigger rolled out of the fire again. He wouldn't stay put. It was on the other side this time. I couldn't see him very well through the flames and smoke. They got some tree limbs and held him there this time and he stayed there till he was ashes. I guess he stayed there. I know he burned to ashes because I saw Jed a week later, and he laughed and showed me some white finger bones still held together with little pieces of the nigger's skin. Anyway, I left when somebody moved around to see the nigger. I pushed my way through the crowd, and a woman in the rear scratched my face as she yelled and fought to get up close.

I ran across the Square to the other side, where the sheriff and his deputies were guarding the wires that were still spitting and making a blue fog. My heart was pounding like I had been running a long ways, and I bent over and let my insides go. Everything came up and spilled in a big gush over the ground. I was sick, and tired, and weak, and cold. The wind was still high, and large drops of rain were beginning to fall. I headed down the street to my uncle's place past a store where the wind had broken a window, and glass lay over the sidewalk. I kicked it as I went by. I remember somebody's fool rooster crowing like it was morning in all that wind.

The next day I was too weak to go out, and my uncle kidded me and called me "the gutless wonder from Cincinnati." I didn't mind. He said you get used to it in time. He couldn't go out himself. There was too much wind and rain. I got up and looked out of the window, and the rain was pouring down and dead sparrows and limbs of trees were scattered all over the yard. There had been a cyclone all right. It swept a path right through the county, and we were lucky we didn't get the full force of it.

It blew for three days steady, and put the town in a hell of a shape. The wind blew sparks and set fire to the white-and-green-rimmed house on Jackson Avenue that had the big concrete lions in the yard and burned it down to the ground. They had to kill another nigger who tried to run out of the county after they burned this Bacote nigger. My Uncle Ed said they always have to kill niggers in pairs to keep the other niggers in place. I don't know though, the folks seem a little skittish of the niggers. They all came back, but they act pretty sullen. They look mean as hell when you pass them down at the store. The other day I was down to Brinkley's store, and a white cropper said it didn't do no good to kill the niggers 'cause things don't get no better. He looked hungry as hell. Most of the croppers look hungry. You'd be surprised how hungry white folks can look. Somebody said that he'd better shut his damn mouth, and he shut up. But from the look on his face he won't stay shut long. He went out of the store muttering to himself and spit a big chew of tobacco right down on Brinkley's floor. Brinkley said he was sore 'cause he wouldn't let him have credit. Anyway, it didn't seem to help things. First it was the nigger and the storm, then the plane, then the woman and the wires, and now I hear the airplane line is investigating to find who set the fire that almost wrecked their plane. All that in one night, and all of it but the storm over one nigger. It was some night all right. It was some party too. I was right there, see. I was right there watching it all. It was my first party and my last. God, but that nigger was tough. That Bacote nigger was some nigger!

—1997

Shirley Jackson was born in San Francisco and educated at Syracuse University. With her husband, the literary critic Stanley Edgar Hyman, she lived in Bennington, Vermont. There she produced three novels and the popular Life Among the Savages *(1953), a "disrespectful memoir" of her four children, and a sequel to it,* Raising Demons *(1957). "The Lottery," which created a sensation when it appeared in* The New Yorker *in 1948, remains a fascinating example of an allegory whose ultimate meaning is open to debate. Many readers at the time, for obvious reasons, associated it with the Holocaust, although it should not be approached in such a restrictive manner. "The Lottery" is the only one of Jackson's many short stories that has been widely reprinted (it was also dramatized for television), but she was a versatile writer of humorous articles (for popular magazines), psychological novels, and authored a popular gothic horror novel,* The Haunting of Hill House *(1959), which was made into a motion picture called* The Haunting *(1963). Jackson published two collections of short stories,* The Lottery *(1949) and* The Magic of Shirley Jackson *(1966).*

The Lottery

The morning of June 27th was clear and sunny, with the fresh warmth of a full-summer day; the flowers were blossoming profusely and the grass was richly green. The people of the village began to gather in the square, between the post office and the bank, around ten o'clock; in some towns there were so many people that the lottery took two days and had to be started on June 26th, but in this village, where there were only about three hundred people, the whole lottery took less than two hours, so it could begin at ten o'clock in the morning and still be through in time to allow the villagers to get home for noon dinner.

The children assembled first, of course. School was recently over for the summer, and the feeling of liberty sat uneasily on most of them; they tended to gather together quietly for a while before they broke into boisterous play, and their talk was still of the classroom and the teacher, of books and reprimands. Bobby Martin had already stuffed his pockets full of stones, and the other boys soon followed his example, selecting the smoothest and roundest stones; Bobby and Harry Jones and Dickie Delacroix—the villagers pronounced this name

"Dellacroy"—eventually made a great pile of stones in one corner of the square and guarded it against the raids of the other boys. The girls stood aside, talking among themselves, looking over their shoulders at the boys, and the very small children rolled in the dust or clung to the hands of their older brothers or sisters.

Soon the men began to gather, surveying their own children, speaking of planting and rain, tractors and taxes. They stood together, away from the pile of stones in the corner, and their jokes were quiet and they smiled rather than laughed. The women, wearing faded house dresses and sweaters, came shortly after their menfolk. They greeted one another and exchanged bits of gossip as they went to join their husbands. Soon the women, standing by their husbands, began to call to their children, and the children came reluctantly, having to be called four or five times. Bobby Martin ducked under his mother's grasping hand and ran, laughing, back to the pile of stones. His father spoke up sharply, and Bobby came quickly and took his place between his father and his oldest brother.

The lottery was conducted—as were the square dances, the teenage club, the Halloween program—by Mr. Summers, who had time and energy to devote to civic activities. He was a roundfaced, jovial man and he ran the coal business, and people were sorry for him, because he had no children and his wife was a scold. When he arrived in the square, carrying the black wooden box, there was a murmur of conversation among the villagers and he waved and called, "Little late today, folks." The postmaster, Mr. Graves, followed him, carrying a three-legged stool, and the stool was put in the center of the square and Mr. Summers set the black box down on it. The villagers kept their distance, leaving a space between themselves and the stool, and when Mr. Summers said, "Some of you fellows want to give me a hand?" there was a hesitation before two men, Mr. Martin and his oldest son, Baxter, came forward to hold the box steady on the stool while Mr. Summers stirred up the papers inside it.

The original paraphernalia for the lottery had been lost long ago, and the black box now resting on the stool had been put into use even before Old Man Warner, the oldest man in town, was born. Mr. Summers spoke frequently to the villagers about making a new box, but no one liked to upset even as much tradition as was represented by the black box. There was a story that the present box had been made with some pieces of the box that had preceded it, the one that had been constructed when the first people settled down to make a village here. Every year, after the lottery, Mr. Summers began talking again about a new box, but every year the subject was allowed to fade off without anything's being done. The black box grew shabbier each year; by now it was no longer completely black but splintered badly along one side to show the original wood color, and in some places faded or stained.

Mr. Martin and his oldest son, Baxter, held the black box securely on the stool until Mr. Summers had stirred the papers thoroughly with his hand. Because so much of the ritual had been forgotten or discarded, Mr. Summers had been successful in having slips of paper substituted for the chips of wood that had been used for generations. Chips of wood, Mr. Summers had argued, had been all very well when the village was tiny, but now that the population was more than three hundred and likely to keep on growing, it was necessary to use something that would fit more easily into the black box. The night before the lottery, Mr. Summers and Mr. Graves made up the slips of paper and put them in the box, and it was then taken to the safe of Mr. Summers's coal company and locked up until Mr. Summers was ready to take it to the square next morning. The rest of the year, the box was put away, sometimes one place, sometimes another; it had spent one year in Mr. Graves's barn and another year underfoot in the post office, and sometimes it was set on a shelf in the Martin grocery and left there.

There was a great deal of fussing to be done before Mr. Summers declared the lottery open. There were lists to make up—of heads of families, heads of households in each family, members of each household in each family. There was the proper swearing-in of Mr. Summers by the postmaster, as the official of the lottery; at one time, some people remembered, there had been a recital of some sort, performed by the official of the lottery, a perfunctory, tuneless chant that had been rattled off duly each year; some people believed that the official of the lottery used to stand just so when he said or sang it, others believed that he was supposed to walk among the people, but years and years ago this part of the ritual had been allowed to lapse. There had been, also, a ritual salute, which the official of the lottery had had to use in addressing each person who came up to draw from the box, but this also had changed with time, until now it was felt necessary only for the official to speak to each person approaching. Mr. Summers was very good at all this; in his clean white shirt and blue jeans, with one hand resting carelessly on the black box, he seemed very proper and important as he talked interminably to Mr. Graves and the Martins.

Just as Mr. Summers finally left off talking and turned to the assembled villagers, Mrs. Hutchinson came hurriedly along the path to the square, her sweater thrown over her shoulders, and slid into place in the back of the crowd. "Clean forgot what day it was," she said to Mrs. Delacroix, who stood next to her, and they both laughed softly. "Thought my old man was out back stacking wood," Mrs. Hutchinson went on, "and then I looked out the window and the kids were gone, and then I remembered it was the twenty-seventh and came a-running." She dried her hands on her apron, and Mrs. Delacroix said, "You're in time, though. They're still talking away up there."

Mrs. Hutchinson craned her neck to see through the crowd and found her husband and children standing near the front. She tapped Mrs. Delacroix on the arm as a farewell and began to make her way through the crowd. The people separated good-humoredly to let her through; two or three people said, in voices just loud enough to be heard across the crowd, "Here comes your Missus, Hutchinson," and "Bill, she made it after all." Mrs. Hutchinson reached her husband, and Mr. Summers, who had been waiting, said cheerfully, "Thought we were going to have to get on without you, Tessie." Mrs. Hutchinson said, grinning, "Wouldn't have me leave m'dishes in the sink, now would you, Joe?," and soft laughter ran through the crowd as the people stirred back into position after Mrs. Hutchinson's arrival.

"Well, now," Mr. Summers said soberly, "guess we better get started, get this over with, so's we can go back to work. Anybody ain't here?"

"Dunbar," several people said. "Dunbar, Dunbar."

Mr. Summers consulted his list. "Clyde Dunbar," he said. "That's right. He's broke his leg, hasn't he? Who's drawing for him?"

"Me, I guess," a woman said, and Mr. Summers turned to look at her. "Wife draws for her husband," Mr. Summers said. "Don't you have a grown boy to do it for you, Janey?" Although Mr. Summers and everyone else in the village knew the answer perfectly well, it was the business of the official of the lottery to ask such questions formally. Mr. Summers waited with an expression of polite interest while Mrs. Dunbar answered.

"Horace's not but sixteen yet," Mrs. Dunbar said regretfully. "Guess I gotta fill in for the old man this year."

"Right," Mr. Summers said. He made a note on the list he was holding. Then he asked, "Watson boy drawing this year?"

A tall boy in the crowd raised his hand. "Here," he said. "I'm drawing for m'mother and me." He blinked his eyes nervously and ducked his head as several voices in the crowd said things like "Good fellow, Jack," and "Glad to see your mother's got a man to do it."

"Well," Mr. Summers said, "guess that's everyone. Old Man Warner make it?"

"Here," a voice said, and Mr. Summers nodded.

A sudden hush fell on the crowd as Mr. Summers cleared his throat and looked at the list. "All ready?" he called. "Now, I'll read the names—heads of families first—and the men come up and take a paper out of the box. Keep the paper folded in your hand without looking at it until everyone has had a turn. Everything clear?"

The people had done it so many times that they only half listened to the directions; most of them were quiet, wetting their lips, not looking around. Then Mr. Summers raised one hand high and said, "Adams." A man disengaged himself from the crowd and came forward. "Hi, Steve," Mr. Summers said, and Mr. Adams said, "Hi, Joe." They grinned at one another humorlessly and nervously. Then Mr. Adams reached into the black box and took out a folded paper. He held it firmly by one corner as he turned and went hastily back to his place in the crowd, where he stood a little apart from his family, not looking down at his hand.

"Allen," Mr. Summers said. "Anderson . . . Bentham."

"Seems like there's no time at all between lotteries any more," Mrs. Delacroix said to Mrs. Graves in the back row. "Seems like we got through with the last one only last week."

"Time sure goes fast," Mrs. Graves said.

"Clark . . . Delacroix."

"There goes my old man," Mrs. Delacroix said. She held her breath while her husband went forward.

"Dunbar," Mr. Summers said, and Mrs. Dunbar went steadily to the box while one of the women said, "Go on, Janey," and another said, "There she goes."

"We're next," Mrs. Graves said. She watched while Mr. Graves came around from the side of the box, greeted Mr. Summers gravely, and selected a slip of paper from the box. By now, all through the crowd there were men holding the small folded papers in their large hands, turning them over and over nervously. Mrs. Dunbar and her two sons stood together, Mrs. Dunbar holding the slip of paper.

"Harburt . . . Hutchinson."

"Get up there, Bill," Mrs. Hutchinson said, and the people near her laughed.

"Jones."

"They do say," Mr. Adams said to Old Man Warner, who stood next to him, "that over in the north village they're talking of giving up the lottery."

Old Man Warner snorted. "Pack of crazy fools," he said. "Listening to the young folks, nothing's good enough for *them*. Next thing you know, they'll be wanting to go back to living in caves, nobody work any more, live *that* way for a while. Used to be a saying about 'Lottery in June, corn be heavy soon.' First thing you know, we'd all be eating stewed chickweed and acorns. There's *always* been a lottery," he added petulantly. "Bad enough to see young Joe Summers up there joking with everybody."

"Some places have already quit lotteries," Mrs. Adams said.

"Nothing but trouble in *that*," Old Man Warner said stoutly. "Pack of young fools."

"Martin." And Bobby Martin watched his father go forward. "Overdyke . . . Percy."

"I wish they'd hurry," Mrs. Dunbar said to her older son. "I wish they'd hurry."

"They're almost through," her son said.

"You get ready to run tell Dad," Mrs. Dunbar said.

Mr. Summers called his own name and then stepped forward precisely and selected a slip from the box. Then he called, "Warner."

"Seventy-seventh year I been in the lottery," Old Man Warner said as he went through the crowd. "Seventy-seventh time."

"Watson." The tall boy came awkwardly through the crowd. Someone said, "Don't be nervous, Jack," and Mr. Summers said, "Take your time, son."

"Zanini."

After that, there was a long pause, a breathless pause, until Mr. Summers, holding his slip of paper in the air, said, "All right, fellows." For a minute, no one moved, and then all the slips of paper were opened. Suddenly, all women began to speak at once, saying, "Who is it?"

"Who's got it?" "Is it the Dunbars?" "Is it the Watsons?" Then the voices began to say, "It's Hutchinson. It's Bill." "Bill Hutchinson's got it."

"Go tell your father," Mrs. Dunbar said to her older son.

People began to look around to see the Hutchinsons. Bill Hutchinson was standing quiet, staring down at the paper in his hand. Suddenly, Tessie Hutchinson shouted to Mr. Summers, "You didn't give him time enough to take any paper he wanted. I saw you. It wasn't fair!"

"Be a good sport, Tessie," Mrs. Delacroix called, and Mrs. Graves said, "All of us took the same chance."

"Shut up, Tessie," Bill Hutchinson said.

"Well, everyone," Mr. Summers said, "that was done pretty fast, and now we've got to be hurrying a little more to get done in time." He consulted his next list. "Bill," he said, "you draw for the Hutchinson family. You got any other households in the Hutchinsons?"

"There's Don and Eva," Mrs. Hutchinson yelled. "Make *them* take their chance!"

"Daughters draw with their husbands' families, Tessie," Mr. Summers said gently. "You know that as well as anyone else."

"It wasn't fair," Tessie said.

"I guess not, Joe," Bill Hutchinson said regretfully. "My daughter draws with her husband's family, that's only fair. And I've got no other family except the kids."

"Then, as far as drawing for families is concerned, it's you," Mr. Summers said in explanation, "and as far as drawing for households is concerned, that's you, too. Right?"

"Right," Bill Hutchinson said.

"How many kids, Bill?" Mr. Summers asked formally.

"Three," Bill Hutchinson said. "There's Bill, Jr., and Nancy, and little Dave. And Tessie and me."

"All right, then," Mr. Summers said. "Harry, you got their tickets back?"

Mr. Graves nodded and held up the slips of paper. "Put them in the box, then," Mr. Summers directed. "Take Bill's and put it in."

"I think we ought to start over," Mrs. Hutchinson said, as quietly as she could. "I tell you it wasn't *fair*. You didn't give him time enough to choose. *Everybody* saw that."

Mr. Graves had selected the five slips and put them in the box, and he dropped all the papers but those onto the ground, where the breeze caught them and lifted them off.

"Listen, everybody," Mrs. Hutchinson was saying to the people around her.

"Ready, Bill?" Mr. Summers asked, and Bill Hutchinson, with one quick glance around at his wife and children, nodded.

"Remember," Mr. Summers said, "take the slips and keep them folded until each person has taken one. Harry, you help little Dave." Mr. Graves took the hand of the little boy, who came willingly with him up to the box. "Take a paper out of the box, Davy," Mr. Summers said. Davy put his hand into the box and laughed. "Take just *one* paper," Mr. Summers said. "Harry, you hold it for him." Mr. Graves took the child's hand and removed the folded paper from the tight fist and held it while little Dave stood next to him and looked up at him wonderingly.

"Nancy next," Mr. Summers said. Nancy was twelve, and her school friends breathed heavily as she went forward, switching her skirt, and took a slip daintily from the box. "Bill, Jr.," Mr. Summers said, and Billy, his face red and his feet overlarge, nearly knocked the box over as he got a paper out. "Tessie," Mr. Summers said. She hesitated for a minute, looking around defiantly, and then set her lips and went up to the box. She snatched a paper out and held it behind her.

"Bill," Mr. Summers said, and Bill Hutchinson reached into the box and felt around, bringing his hand out at last with the slip of paper in it.

The crowd was quiet. A girl whispered, "I hope it's not Nancy," and the sound of the whisper reached the edges of the crowd.

"It's not the way it used to be," Old Man Warner said clearly. "People ain't the way they used to be."

"All right," Mr. Summers said. "Open the papers. Harry, you open little Dave's."

Mr. Graves opened the slip of paper and there was a general sigh through the crowd as he held it up and everyone could see that it was blank. Nancy and Bill, Jr., opened theirs at the same time, and both beamed and laughed, turning around to the crowd and holding their slips of paper above their heads.

"Tessie," Mr. Summers said. There was a pause, and then Mr. Summers looked at Bill Hutchinson, and Bill unfolded his paper and showed it. It was blank.

"It's Tessie," Mr. Summers said, and his voice was hushed. "Show us her paper, Bill."

Bill Hutchinson went over to his wife and forced the slip of paper out of her hand. It had a black spot on it, the black spot Mr. Summers had made the night before with the heavy pencil in the coal-company office. Bill Hutchinson held it up, and there was a stir in the crowd.

"All right, folks," Mr. Summers said, "let's finish quickly."

Although the villagers had forgotten the ritual and lost the original black box, they still remembered to use stones. The pile of stones the boys had made earlier was ready; there were stones on the ground with the blowing scraps of paper that had come out of the box. Mrs. Delacroix selected a stone so large she had to pick it up with both hands and turned to Mrs. Dunbar. "Come on," she said. "Hurry up."

Mrs. Dunbar had small stones in both hands, and she said, gasping for breath, "I can't run at all. You'll have to go ahead and I'll catch up with you."

The children had stones already, and someone gave little Davy Hutchinson a few pebbles.

Tessie Hutchinson was in the center of a cleared space by now, and she held her hands out desperately as the villagers moved in on her. "It isn't fair," she said. A stone hit her on the side of the head.

Old Man Warner was saying, "Come on, come on, everyone." Steve Adams was in the front of the crowd of villagers, with Mrs. Graves beside him.

"It isn't fair, it isn't right," Mrs. Hutchinson screamed, and then they were upon her.

—*1948*

HISAYE YAMAMOTO ■ (b. 1921)

Yamamoto was born in Redondo Beach, California, the daughter of Japanese immigrants who were strawberry farmers. During World War II she was held for three years in an Arizona internment camp, where she wrote for the camp newspaper. After the war, she worked for a time as a journalist and began to publish her stories in national magazines and journals. The mother of five, Yamamoto eventually gathered her stories into a collection, Seventeen Syllables, *which was published in 1987. A Nisei, or second-generation Japanese-American woman, Yamamoto explores the cultural differences between her peers and the older Issei generation of their mothers. Asked in an interview about writing for an Asian-American audience, Yamamoto replied, "I've never*

thought of writing for anybody. I don't think you can write aiming at a specif-
ically Asian-American audience if you want to write freely. No, you just express
yourself without thinking of that angle."

Seventeen Syllables

The first Rosie knew that her mother had taken to writing poems was one
evening when she finished one and read it aloud for her daughter's approval. It was about cats, and Rosie pretended to understand it thoroughly
and appreciate it no end, partly because she hesitated to disillusion her
mother about the quantity and quality of Japanese she had learned in all
the years now that she had been going to Japanese school every Saturday
(and Wednesday, too, in the summer). Even so, her mother must have
been skeptical about the depth of Rosie's understanding, because she
explained afterwards about the kind of poem she was trying to write.

See, Rosie, she said, it was a *haiku*, a poem in which she must pack
all her meaning into seventeen syllables only, which were divided into
three lines of five, seven, and five syllables. In the one she had just
read, she had tried to capture the charm of a kitten, as well as comment
on the superstition that owning a cat of three colors meant good luck.

"Yes, yes, I understand. How utterly lovely,"

Rosie said, and her mother, either satisfied or seeing through the
deception and resigned, went back to composing.

The truth was that Rosie was lazy; English lay ready on the tongue
but Japanese had to be searched for and examined, and even then put
forth tentatively (probably to meet with laughter). It was so much easier
to say yes, yes, even when one meant no, no. Besides, this was what was
in her mind to say: I was looking through one of your magazines from
Japan last night, Mother, and towards the back I found some *haiku* in
English that delighted me. There was one that made me giggle off and
on until I fell asleep—

> *It is morning, and lo!*
> *I lie awake, comme il faut,*
> *sighing for some dough.*

Now, how to reach her mother, how to communicate the melancholy
song? Rosie knew formal Japanese by fits and starts, her mother had
even less English, no French. It was much more possible to say yes, yes.

It developed that her mother was writing the *haiku* for a daily newspaper, the *Mainichi Shimbun*, that was published in San Francisco. Los Angeles, to be sure, was closer to the farming community in which the Hayashi family lived and several Japanese vernaculars were printed there, but Rosie's parents said they preferred the tone of the northern paper. Once a week, the *Mainichi* would have a section devoted to *haiku*, and her mother became an extravagant contributor, taking for herself the blossoming pen name, Ume Hanazono.

So Rosie and her father lived for a while with two women, her mother and Ume Hanazono. Her mother (Tome Hayashi by name) kept house, cooked, washed, and, along with her husband and the Carrascos, the Mexican family hired for the harvest, did her ample share of picking tomatoes out in the sweltering fields and boxing them in tidy strata in the cool packing shed. Ume Hanazono, who came to life after the dinner dishes were done, was an earnest, muttering stranger who often neglected speaking when spoken to and stayed busy at the parlor table as late as midnight scribbling with pencil on scratch paper or carefully copying characters on good paper with her fat, pale green Parker.

The new interest had some repercussions on the household routine. Before, Rosie had been accustomed to her parents and herself taking their hot baths early and going to bed almost immediately afterwards, unless her parents challenged each other to a game of flower cards or unless company dropped in. Now if her father wanted to play cards, he had to resort to solitaire (at which he always cheated fearlessly), and if a group of friends came over, it was bound to contain someone who was also writing *haiku*, and the small assemblage would be split in two, her father entertaining the non-literary members and her mother comparing ecstatic notes with the visiting poet.

If they went out, it was more of the same thing. But Ume Hanazono's life span, even for a poet's, was very brief—perhaps three months at most.

One night they went over to see the Hayano family in the neighboring town to the west, an adventure both painful and attractive to Rosie. It was attractive because there were four Hayano girls, all lovely and each one named after a season of the year (Haru, Natsu, Aki, Fuyu), painful because something had been wrong with Mrs. Hayano ever since the birth of her first child. Rosie would sometimes watch Mrs. Hayano, reputed to have been the belle of her native village, making her way about a room, stooped, slowly shuffling, violently trembling (*always* trembling), and she would be reminded that this woman, in this same condition, had carried and given issue to three babies. She would look wonderingly at Mr. Hayano, handsome, tall, and strong, and she would look at her four pretty friends. But it was not a matter she could come to any decision about.

On this visit, however, Mrs. Hayano sat all evening in the rocker, as motionless and unobtrusive as it was possible for her to be, and Rosie found the greater part of the evening practically anaesthetic. Too, Rosie spent most of it in the girls' room, because Haru, the garrulous one, said almost as soon as the bows and other greetings were over, "Oh, you must see my new coat!"

It was a pale plaid of grey, sand, and blue, with an enormous collar, and Rosie, seeing nothing special in it, said, "Gee, how nice."

"Nice?" said Haru, indignantly. "Is that all you can say about it? It's gorgeous! And so cheap, too. Only seventeen-ninety eight, because it was a sale. The saleslady said it was twenty-five dollars regular."

"Gee," said Rosie. Natsu, who never said much and when she said anything said it shyly, fingered the coat covetously and Haru pulled it away.

"Mine," she said, putting it on. She minced in the aisle between the two large beds and smiled happily. "Let's see how your mother likes it."

She broke into the front room and the adult conversation and went to stand in front of Rosie's mother, while the rest watched from the door. Rosie's mother was properly envious. "May I inherit it when you're through with it?"

Haru, pleased, giggled and said yes, she could, but Natsu reminded gravely from the door, "You promised me, Haru."

Everyone laughed but Natsu, who shamefacedly retreated into the bedroom. Haru came in laughing, taking off the coat. "We were only kidding, Natsu," she said. "Here, you try it on now."

After Natsu buttoned herself into the coat, inspected herself solemnly in the bureau mirror, and reluctantly shed it, Rosie, Aki, and Fuyu got their turns, and Fuyu, who was eight, drowned in it while her sisters and Rosie doubled up in amusement. They all went into the front room later, because Haru's mother quaveringly called to her to fix the tea and rice cakes and open a can of sliced peaches for everybody. Rosie noticed that her mother and Mr. Hayano were talking together at the little table—they were discussing a *haiku* that Mr. Hayano was planning to send to the *Mainichi*, while her father was sitting at one end of the sofa looking through a copy of *Life,* the new picture magazine. Occasionally, her father would comment on a photograph, holding it toward Mrs. Hayano and speaking to her as he always did—loudly, as though he thought someone such as she must surely be at least a trifle deaf also.

The five girls had their refreshments at the kitchen table, and it was while Rosie was showing the sisters her trick of swallowing peach slices without chewing (she chased each slippery crescent down with a swig of tea) that her father brought his empty teacup and untouched saucer to the sink and said, "Come on, Rosie, we're going home now."

"Already?" asked Rosie.

"Work tomorrow," he said.

He sounded irritated, and Rosie, puzzled, gulped one last yellow slice and stood up to go, while the sisters began protesting, as was their wont.

"We have to get up at five-thirty," he told them, going into the front room quickly, so that they did not have their usual chance to hang onto his hands and plead for an extension of time.

Rosie, following, saw that her mother and Mr. Hayano were sipping tea and still talking together, while Mrs. Hayano concentrated, quivering, on raising the handleless Japanese cup to her lips with both her hands and lowering it back to her lap. Her father, saying nothing, went out the door, onto the bright porch, and down the steps. Her mother looked up and asked, "Where is he going?"

"Where is he going?" Rosie said. "He said we were going home now."

"Going home?" Her mother looked with embarrassment at Mr. Hayano and his absorbed wife and then forced a smile. "He must be tired," she said.

Haru was not giving up yet. "May Rosie stay overnight?" she asked, and Natsu, Aki, and Fuyu came to reinforce their sister's plea by helping her make a circle around Rosie's mother. Rosie, for once having no desire to stay, was relieved when her mother, apologizing to the perturbed Mr. and Mrs. Hayano for her father's abruptness at the same time, managed to shake her head no at the quartet, kindly but adamant, so that they broke their circle and let her go.

Rosie's father looked ahead into the windshield as the two joined him. "I'm sorry," her mother said. "You must be tired." Her father, stepping on the starter, said nothing. "You know how I get when it's *haiku,*" she continued, "I forget what time it is." He only grunted.

As they rode homeward silently, Rosie, sitting between, felt a rush of hate for both—for her mother for begging, for her father for denying her mother. I wish this old Ford would crash, right now, she thought, then immediately, no, no, I wish my father would laugh, but it was too late: already the vision had passed through her mind of the green pick-up crumpled in the dark against one of the mighty eucalyptus trees they were just riding past, of the three contorted, bleeding bodies, one of them hers.

Rosie ran between two patches of tomatoes, her heart working more rambunctiously than she had ever known it to. How lucky it was that Aunt Taka and Uncle Gimpachi had come tonight, though, how very lucky. Otherwise she might not have really kept her half-promise to meet Jesus Carrasco. Jesus was going to be a senior in September at the same school she went to, and his parents were the ones helping with the tomatoes this year. She and Jesus, who hardly remembered seeing each other at Cleveland High where there were so many other people and two whole grades between them, had become great friends this summer—he always had a joke for her when he periodically drove the loaded pick-up from the fields to the shed where she was usually sorting while her mother and father did the packing, and they laughed a great deal together over infinitesimal repartee during the afternoon break for chilled watermelon or ice cream in the shade of the shed.

What she enjoyed most was racing him to see who could finish picking a double row first. He, who could work faster, would tease her by slowing down until she thought she would surely pass him this time, then speeding up furiously to leave her several sprawling vines behind. Once he had made her screech hideously by crossing over, while her back was turned, to place atop the tomatoes in her green-stained bucket a truly monstrous, pale green worm (it had looked more like an infant snake). And it was when they had finished a contest this morning, after she had pantingly pointed a green finger at the immature tomatoes evident in the lugs at the end of his row and he had returned the accusation (with justice), that he had startlingly brought up the matter of their possibly meeting outside the range of both their parents' dubious eyes.

"What for?" she had asked.

"I've got a secret I want to tell you," he said.

"Tell me now," she demanded.

"It won't be ready till tonight," he said.

She laughed. "Tell me tomorrow then."

"It'll be gone tomorrow," he threatened.

"Well, for seven hakes, what is it?" she had asked, more than twice, and when he had suggested that the packing shed would be an appropriate place to find out, she had cautiously answered maybe. She had not been certain she was going to keep the appointment until the arrival of mother's sister and her husband. Their coming seemed a sort of signal of permission, of grace, and she had definitely made up her mind to lie and leave as she was bowing them welcome.

So as soon as everyone appeared settled back for the evening, she announced loudly that she was going to the privy outside, "I'm going to the *benjo!*" and slipped out the door. And now that she was actually on her way, her heart pumped in such an undisciplined way that she could hear it with her ears. It's because I'm running, she told herself, slowing to a walk. The shed was up ahead, one more patch away, in the middle of the fields. Its bulk, looming in the dimness, took on a sinisterness that was funny when Rosie reminded herself that it was only a wooden frame with a canvas roof and three canvas walls that made a slapping noise on breezy days.

Jesus was sitting on the narrow plank that was the sorting platform and she went around to the other side and jumped backwards to seat herself on the rim of a packing stand. "Well, tell me," she said without greeting, thinking her voice sounded reassuringly familiar.

"I saw you coming out the door," Jesus said. "I heard you running part of the way, too."

"Uh-huh," Rosie said. "Now tell me the secret."

"I was afraid you wouldn't come," he said.

Rosie delved around on the chicken-wire bottom of the stall for number two tomatoes, ripe, which she was sitting beside, and came up with a left-over that felt edible. She bit into it and began sucking out the pulp and seeds. "I'm here," she pointed out.

"Rosie, are you sorry you came?"

"Sorry? What for?" she said. "You said you were going to tell me something."

"I will, I will," Jesus said, but his voice contained disappointment, and Rosie fleetingly felt the older of the two, realizing a brand-new power which vanished without category under her recognition.

"I have to go back in a minute," she said. "My aunt and uncle are here from Wintersburg. I told them I was going to the privy."

Jesus laughed. "You funny thing," he said. "You slay me!"

"Just because you have a bathroom *inside*," Rosie said. "Come on, tell me."

Chuckling, Jesus came around to lean on the stand facing her. They still could not see each other very clearly, but Rosie noticed that Jesus became very sober again as he took the hollow tomato from her hand and dropped it back into the stall. When he took hold of her empty hand, she could find no words to protest; her vocabulary had become distressingly constricted and she thought desperately that all that remained intact now was yes and no and oh, and even these few sounds would not easily out. Thus, kissed by Jesus, Rosie fell for the first time entirely victim to a helplessness delectable beyond speech. But the terrible, beautiful sensation lasted no more than a second, and the reality of Jesus' lips and tongue and teeth and hands made her pull away with such strength that she nearly tumbled.

Rosie stopped running as she approached the lights from the windows of home. How long since she had left? She could not guess, but gasping yet, she went to the privy in back and locked herself in. Her own breathing deafened her in the dark, close space, and she sat and waited until she could hear at last the nightly calling of the frogs and crickets. Even then, all she could think to say was oh, my, and the pressure of Jesus' face against her face would not leave.

No one had missed her in the parlor, however, and Rosie walked in and through quickly, announcing that she was next going to take a bath. "Your father's in the bathhouse," her mother said, and Rosie, in her room, recalled that she had not seen him when she entered. There had been only Aunt Taka and Uncle Gimpachi with her mother at the table, drinking tea. She got her robe and straw sandals and crossed the parlor again to go outside. Her mother was telling them about the *haiku* competition in the *Mainichi* and the poem she had entered.

Rosie met her father coming out of the bathhouse. "Are you through, Father?" she asked. "I was going to ask you to scrub my back."

"Scrub your own back," he said shortly, going toward the main house.

"What have I done now?" she yelled after him. She suddenly felt like doing a lot of yelling. But he did not answer, and she went into the bathhouse. Turning on the dangling light, she removed her denims and T-shirt and threw them in the big carton for dirty clothes standing next to the washing machine. Her other things she took with her into the bath compartment to wash after her bath. After she had scooped a basin of hot water from the square wooden tub, she sat on the grey cement of the floor and soaped herself at exaggerated leisure, singing "Red Sails in the Sunset" at the top of her voice and using da-da-da where she suspected her words. Then, standing up, still singing, for she was possessed by the notion that any attempt now to analyze would result in spoilage and she believed that the larger her volume the less she would be able to hear herself think, she obtained more hot water and poured it on until she was free of lather. Only then did she allow herself to step into the steaming vat, one leg first, then the remainder of her body inch by inch until the water no longer stung and she could move around at will.

She took a long time soaking, afterwards remembering to go around outside to stoke the embers of the tin-lined fireplace beneath the tub and to throw on a few more sticks so that the water might keep its heat for her mother, and when she finally returned to the parlor, she found her mother still talking *haiku* with her aunt and uncle, the three of them on another round of tea. Her father was nowhere in sight.

At Japanese school the next day (Wednesday, it was), Rosie was grave and giddy by turns. Preoccupied at her desk in the row for students on Book Eight, she made up for it at recess by performing wild mimicry for the benefit of her friend Chizuko. She held her nose and whined a witticism or two in what she considered was the manner of Fred Allen; she assumed intoxication and a British accent to go over the climax of the Rudy Vallee recording of the pub conversation about William Ewart Gladstone; she was the child Shirley Temple piping, "On the Good Ship Lollipop"; she was the gentleman soprano of the Four Inkspots trilling, "If I Didn't Care." And she felt reasonably satisfied when Chizuko wept and gasped, "Oh, Rosie, you ought to be in the movies!"

Her father came after her at noon, bringing her sandwiches of minced ham and two nectarines to eat while she rode, so that she could pitch right into the sorting when they got home. The lugs were piling up, he said, and the ripe tomatoes in them would probably have to be taken to the cannery tomorrow if they were not ready for the produce haulers tonight. "This heat's not doing them any good. And we've got no time for a break today."

It *was* hot, probably the hottest day of the year, and Rosie's blouse stuck damply to her back even under the protection of the canvas. But she worked as efficiently as a flawless machine and kept the stalls heaped, with one part of her mind listening in to the parental murmuring about the heat and the tomatoes and with another part planning the exact words she would say to Jesus when he drove up with the first load of the afternoon. But when at last she saw that the pick-up was coming, her hands went berserk and the tomatoes started falling in the wrong stalls, and her father said, "Hey, hey! Rosie, watch what you're doing!"

"Well, I have to go to the *benjo*," she said, hiding panic.

"Go in the weeds over there," he said, only half-joking.

"Oh, Father!" she protested.

"Oh, go on home," her mother said. "We'll make out for a while."

In the privy Rosie peered through a knothole toward the fields, watching as much as she could of Jesus. Happily she thought she saw him look in the direction of the house from time to time before he finished unloading and went back toward the patch where his mother and father worked. As she was heading for the shed, a very presentable black car purred up the dirt driveway to the house and its driver motioned to her. Was this the Hayashi home, he wanted to know. She nodded. Was she a Hayashi? Yes, she said, thinking that he was a good-looking man. He got out of the car with a huge, flat package and she saw that he warmly wore a business suit. "I have something here for your mother then," he said, in a more elegant Japanese than she was used to.

She told him where her mother was and he came along with her, patting his face with an immaculate white handkerchief and saying something about the coolness of San Francisco. To her surprised mother and father, he bowed and introduced himself as, among other things, the *haiku* editor of the *Mainichi Shimbun*, saying that since he had been coming as far as Los Angeles anyway, he had decided to bring her the first prize she had won in the recent contest.

"First prize?" her mother echoed, believing and not believing, pleased and overwhelmed. Handed the package with a bow, she bobbed her head up and down numerous times to express her utter gratitude.

"It is nothing much," he added, "but I hope it will serve as a token of our great appreciation for your contributions and our great admiration of your considerable talent."

"I am not worthy," she said, falling easily into his style. "It is I who should make some sign of my humble thanks for being permitted to contribute."

"No, no, to the contrary," he said, bowing again.

But Rosie's mother insisted, and then saying that she knew she was being unorthodox, she asked if she might open the package because her curiosity was so great. Certainly she might. In fact, he would like her reaction to it, for personally, it was one of his favorite *Hiroshiges*.

Rosie thought it was a pleasant picture, which looked to have been sketched with delicate quickness. There were pink clouds, containing some graceful calligraphy, and a sea that was a pale blue except at the edges, containing four sampans with indications of people in them. Pines edged the water and on the far-off beach there was a cluster of thatched huts towered over by pine-dotted mountains of grey and blue. The frame was scalloped and gilt.

After Rosie's mother pronounced it without peer and somewhat prodded her father into nodding agreement, she said Mr. Kuroda must at least have a cup of tea after coming all this way, and although Mr. Kuroda did not want to impose, he soon agreed that a cup of tea would be refreshing and went along with her to the house, carrying the picture for her.

"Ha, your mother's crazy!" Rosie's father said, and Rosie laughed uneasily as she resumed judgment on the tomatoes. She had emptied six lugs when he broke into an imaginary conversation with Jesus to tell her to go and remind her mother of the tomatoes, and she went slowly.

Mr. Kuroda was in his shirtsleeves expounding some *haiku* theory as he munched a rice cake, and her mother was rapt. Abashed in the great man's presence, Rosie stood next to her mother's chair until her mother looked up inquiringly, and then she started to whisper the message, but her mother pushed her gently away and reproached, "You are not being very polite to our guest."

"Father says the tomatoes . . . ," Rosie said aloud, smiling foolishly.

"Tell him I shall only be a minute," her mother said, speaking the language of Mr. Kuroda.

When Rosie carried the reply to her father, he did not seem to hear and she said again, "Mother says she'll be back in a minute."

"All right, all right," he nodded, and they worked again in silence. But suddenly, her father uttered an incredible noise, exactly like the cork of a bottle popping, and the next Rosie knew, he was stalking angrily toward the house, almost running in fact, and she chased after him crying, "Father! Father! What are you going to do?"

He stopped long enough to order her back to the shed. "Never mind!" he shouted. "Get on with the sorting!"

And from the place in the fields where she stood, frightened and vacillating, Rosie saw her father enter the house. Soon Mr. Kuroda came out alone, putting on his coat. Mr. Kuroda got into his car and backed out down the driveway onto the highway. Next her father emerged, also alone, something in his arms (it was the picture, she realized), and, going over to the bathhouse woodpile, he threw the picture on the ground and picked up the axe. Smashing the picture, glass and all (she heard the explosion faintly), he reached over for the kerosene that was used to encourage the bath fire and poured it over the wreckage. I am dreaming, Rosie said to herself, I am dreaming, but her father, having made sure that his act of cremation was irrevocable, was even then returning to the fields.

Rosie ran past him and toward the house. What had become of her mother? She burst into the parlor and found her mother at the back window watching the dying fire. They watched together until there remained only a feeble smoke under the blazing sun. Her mother was very calm.

"Do you know why I married your father?" she said without turning.

"No," said Rosie. It was the most frightening question she had ever been called upon to answer. Don't tell me now, she wanted to say, tell me tomorrow, tell me next week, don't tell me today. But she knew she would be told now, that the telling would combine with the other violence of the hot afternoon to level her life, her world to the very ground.

It was like a story out of the magazines illustrated in sepia, which she had consumed so greedily for a period until the information had somehow reached her that those wretchedly unhappy autobiographies, offered to her as the testimonials of living men and women, were largely inventions: Her mother, at nineteen, had come to America and married her father as an alternative to suicide.

At eighteen she had been in love with the first son of one of the well-to-do families in her village. The two had met whenever and wherever they could, secretly, because it would not have done for his family to see him favor her—her father had no money; he was a drunkard and a gambler besides. She had learned she was with child; an excellent match had already been arranged for her lover. Despised by her family, she had given premature birth to a stillborn son, who would be seventeen now. Her family did not turn her out, but she could no longer project herself in any direction without refreshing in them the memory of her indiscretion. She wrote to Aunt Taka, her favorite sister in America, threatening to kill herself if Aunt Taka would not send for her. Aunt Taka hastily arranged a marriage with a young man of whom she knew, but lately arrived from Japan, a young man of simple mind, it was said, but of kindly heart. The young man was never told why his unseen betrothed was so eager to hasten the day of meeting.

The story was told perfectly, with neither groping for words nor untoward passion. It was as though her mother had memorized it by heart, reciting it to herself so many times over that its nagging vileness had long since gone.

"I had a brother then?" Rosie asked, for this was what seemed to matter now; she would think about the other later, she assured herself, pushing back the illumination which threatened all that darkness that had hitherto been merely mysterious or even glamorous. "A half-brother?"

"Yes."

"I would have liked a brother," she said.

Suddenly, her mother knelt on the floor and took her by the wrists. "Rosie," she said urgently, "promise me you will never marry!" Shocked more by the request than the revelation, Rosie stared at her mother's face. Jesus, Jesus, she called silently, not certain whether she was invoking the help of the son of the Carrascos or of God, until there returned sweetly the memory of Jesus' hand, how it had touched her and where. Still her mother waited for an answer, holding her wrists so tightly that her hands were going numb. She tried to pull free. Promise, her mother whispered fiercely, promise. Yes, yes, I promise, Rosie said. But for an instant she turned away, and her mother, hearing the familiar glib agreement, released her. Oh, you, you, you, her eyes and twisted mouth said, you fool. Rosie, covering her face, began at last to cry, and the embrace and consoling hand came much later than she expected.

—1988

Flannery O'Connor was one of the first of many important writers to emerge from the Writers' Workshop of the University of Iowa, where she received an M.F.A. in creative writing. Born in Savannah, Georgia, she attended Georgia State College for Women, graduating in 1945. Plagued by disseminated lupus, the same incurable illness that killed her father in 1941, O'Connor spent most of the last decade of her life living with her mother on a dairy farm near Milledgeville, Georgia, where she wrote and raised peacocks. Unusual among modern American writers in the seriousness of her Christianity (she was a devout Roman Catholic in the largely Protestant South), O'Connor focuses an uncompromising moral eye on the violence and spiritual disorder of the modern world. She is sometimes called a "southern gothic" writer because of her fascination with the grotesque, although today she seems far ahead of her time in depicting a region in which the social and religious certainties of the past are becoming extinct almost overnight. O'Connor's published work includes two short novels, Wise Blood *(1952) and* The Violent Bear It Away *(1960), and two collections of short stories,* A Good Man Is Hard to Find *(1955) and* Everything That Rises Must Converge, *published posthumously in 1965. A collection of essays and miscellaneous prose,* Mystery and Manners *(1969), and her selected letters,* The Habit of Being *(1979), reveal an engaging social side of her personality that is not always apparent in her fiction.*

Everything That Rises Must Converge

Her doctor had told Julian's mother that she must lose twenty pounds on account of her blood pressure, so on Wednesday nights Julian had to take her downtown on the bus for a reducing class at the Y. The reducing class was designed for working girls over fifty, who weighed from 165 to 200 pounds. His mother was one of the slimmer ones, but she said ladies did not tell their age or weight. She would not ride the buses by herself at night since they had been integrated, and because the reducing class was one of her few pleasures, necessary for her health, and free, she said Julian could at least put himself out to take her, considering all she did for him. Julian did not like to consider all she did for him, but every Wednesday night he braced himself and took her.

She was almost ready to go, standing before the hall mirror, putting on her hat, while he, his hands behind him, appeared pinned to the door frame, waiting like Saint Sebastian for the arrows to begin piercing him. The hat was new and had cost her seven dollars and a half. She kept saying, "Maybe I shouldn't have paid that for it. No, I shouldn't have. I'll take it off and return it tomorrow. I shouldn't have bought it."

Julian raised his eyes to heaven. "Yes, you should have bought it," he said. "Put it on and let's go." It was a hideous hat. A purple velvet flap came down on one side of it and stood up on the other; the rest of it was green and looked like a cushion with the stuffing out. He decided it was less comical than jaunty and pathetic. Everything that gave her pleasure was small and depressed him.

She lifted the hat one more time and set it down slowly on top of her head. Two wings of gray hair protruded on either side of her florid face, but her eyes, sky-blue, were as innocent and untouched by experience as they must have been when she was ten. Were it not that she was a widow who had struggled fiercely to feed and clothe and put him through school and who was supporting him still, "until he got on his feet," she might have been a little girl that he had to take to town.

"It's all right, it's all right," he said. "Let's go." He opened the door himself and started down the walk to get her going. The sky was a dying violet and the houses stood out darkly against it, bulbous liver-colored monstrosities of a uniform ugliness though no two were alike. Since this had been a fashionable neighborhood forty years ago, his mother persisted in thinking they did well to have an apartment in it. Each house had a narrow collar of dirt around it in which sat, usually, a grubby child. Julian walked with his hands in his pockets, his head down and thrust forward and his eyes glazed with the determination to make himself completely numb during the time he would be sacrificed to her pleasure.

The door closed and he turned to find the dumpy figure, surmounted by the atrocious hat, coming toward him. "Well," she said, "you only live once and paying a little more for it, I at least won't meet myself coming and going."

"Some day I'll start making money," Julian said gloomily—he knew he never would— "and you can have one of those jokes whenever you take the fit." But first they would move. He visualized a place where the nearest neighbors would be three miles away on either side.

"I think you're doing fine," she said, drawing on her gloves. "You've only been out of school a year. Rome wasn't built in a day."

She was one of the few members of the Y reducing class who arrived in hat and gloves and who had a son who had been to college. "It takes time," she said, "and the world is in such a mess. This hat looked better on me than any of the others, though when she brought it out I said, 'Take that thing back. I wouldn't have it on my head,' and she said, 'Now wait till you see it on,' and when she put it on me, I said, 'We-ull,' and she said, 'If you ask me, that hat does something for you and you do something for the hat, and besides,' she said, 'with that hat, you won't meet yourself coming and going.'"

Julian thought he could have stood his lot better if she had been selfish, if she had been an old hag who drank and screamed at him. He walked along, saturated in depression, as if in the midst of his *martyrdom* he had lost his faith. Catching sight of his long, hopeless, irritated face, she stopped suddenly with a grief-stricken look, and pulled back on his arm. "Wait on me," she said. "I'm going back to the house and take this thing off and tomorrow I'm going to return it. I was out of my head. I can pay the gas bill with that seven-fifty."

He caught her arm in a vicious grip. "You are not going to take it back," he said. "I like it."

"Well," she said, "I don't think I ought . . ."

"Shut up and enjoy it," he muttered, more depressed than ever.

"With the world in the mess it's in," she said, "it's a wonder we can enjoy anything. I tell you, the bottom rail is on the top."

Julian sighed.

"Of course," she said, "if you know who you are, you can go anywhere." She said this every time he took her to the reducing class. "Most of them in it are not our kind of people," she said, "but I can be gracious to anybody. I know who I am."

"They don't give a damn for your graciousness," Julian said savagely. "Knowing who you are is good for one generation only. You haven't the foggiest idea where you stand now or who you are."

She stopped and allowed her eyes to flash at him. "I most certainly do know who I am," she said, "and if you don't know who you are, I'm ashamed of you."

"Oh hell," Julian said.

"Your great-grandfather was a former governor of this state," she said. "Your grandfather was a prosperous landowner. Your grandmother was a Godhigh."

"Will you look around you," he said tensely, "and see where you are now?" and he swept his arm jerkily out to indicate the neighborhood, which the growing darkness at least made less dingy.

"You remain what you are," she said. "Your great-grandfather had a plantation and two hundred slaves."

"There are no more slaves," he said irritably.

"They were better off when they were," she said. He groaned to see that she was off on that topic. She rolled onto it every few days like a train on an open track. He knew every stop, every junction, every swamp along the way, and knew the exact point at which her conclusion would roll majestically into the station: "It's ridiculous. It's simply not realistic. They should rise, yes, but on their own side of the fence."

"Let's skip it," Julian said.

"The ones I feel sorry for," she said, "are the ones that are half white. They're tragic."

"Will you skip it?"

"Suppose we were half white. We would certainly have mixed feelings."

"I have mixed feelings now," he groaned.

"Well let's talk about something pleasant," she said. "I remember going to Grandpa's when I was a little girl. Then the house had double stairways that went up to what was really the second floor—all the cooking was done on the first. I used to like to stay down in the kitchen on account of the way the walls smelled. I would sit with my nose pressed against the plaster and take deep breaths. Actually the place belonged to the Godhighs but your grandfather Chestny paid the mortgage and saved it for them. They were in reduced circumstances," she said, "but reduced or not, they never forgot who they were."

"Doubtless that decayed mansion reminded them," Julian muttered. He never spoke of it without contempt or thought of it without longing. He had seen it once when he was a child before it had been sold. The double stairways had rotted and been torn down. Negroes were living it it. But it remained in his mind as his mother had known it. It appeared in his dreams regularly. He would stand on the wide porch, listening to the rustle of oak leaves, then wander through the high-ceilinged hall into the parlor that opened onto it and gaze at the worn rugs and faded draperies. It occurred to him that it was he, not she, who could have appreciated it. He preferred its threadbare elegance to anything he could name and it was because of it that all the neighborhoods they had lived in had been a torment to him—whereas she had hardly known the difference. She called her insensitivity "being adjustable."

"And I remember the old darky who was my nurse, Caroline. There was no better person in the world. I've always had a great respect for my colored friends," she said. "I'd do anything in the world for them and they'd . . ."

"Will you for God's sake get off that subject?" Julian said. When he got on a bus by himself, he made it a point to sit down beside a Negro, in reparation as it were for his mother's sins.

"You're mighty touchy tonight," she said. "Do you feel all right?"

"Yes I feel all right," he said. "Now lay off."

She pursed her lips. "Well, you certainly are in a vile humor," she observed. "I just won't speak to you at all."

They had reached the bus stop. There was no bus in sight and Julian, his hands still jammed in his pockets and his head thrust forward, scowled down the empty street. The frustration of having to wait on the bus as well as ride on it began to creep up his neck like a hot hand. The presence of his mother was borne in upon him as she gave a pained sigh. He looked at her bleakly. She was holding herself very erect under the preposterous hat, wearing it like a banner of her imaginary dignity. There was in him an evil urge to break her spirit. He suddenly unloosened his tie and pulled it off and put it in his pocket.

She stiffened. "Why must you look like *that* when you take me to town?" she said. "Why must you deliberately embarrass me?"

"If you'll never learn where you are," he said, "you can at least learn where I am."

"You look like a—thug," she said.

"Then I must be one," he murmured.

"I'll just go home," she said. "I will not bother you. If you can't do a little thing like that for me . . ."

Rolling his eyes upward, he put his tie back on. "Restored to my class," he muttered. He thrust his face toward her and hissed, "True culture is in the mind, the *mind*," he said, and tapped his head, "the mind."

"It's in the heart," she said, "and in how you do things and how you do things is because of who you *are*."

"Nobody in the damn bus cares who you are."

"I care who I am," she said icily.

The lighted bus appeared on top of the next hill and as it approached, they moved out into the street to meet it. He put his hand under her elbow and hoisted her up on the creaking step. She entered with a little smile, as if she were going into a drawing room where everyone had been waiting for her. While he put in the tokens, she sat down on one of the broad front seats for three which faced the aisle. A thin woman with protruding teeth and long yellow hair was sitting on the end of it. His mother moved up beside her and left room for Julian beside herself. He sat down and looked at the floor across the aisle where a pair of thin feet in red and white canvas sandals were planted.

His mother immediately began a general conversation meant to attract anyone who felt like talking. "Can it get any hotter?" she said and removed from her purse a folding fan, black with a Japanese scene on it, which she began to flutter before her.

"I reckon it might could," the woman with the protruding teeth said, "but I know for a fact my apartment couldn't get no hotter."

"It must get the afternoon sun," his mother said. She sat forward and looked up and down the bus. It was half filled. Everybody was white. "I see we have the bus to ourselves," she said. Julian cringed.

"For a change," said the woman across the aisle, the owner of the red and white canvas sandals. "I come on one the other day and they were thick as fleas—up front and all through."

"The world is in a mess everywhere," his mother said. "I don't know how we've let it get in this fix."

"What gets my goat is all those boys from good families stealing automobile tires," the woman with the protruding teeth said. "I told my boy, I said you may not be rich but you been raised right and if I ever catch you in any such mess, they can send you on to the reformatory. Be exactly where you belong."

"Training tells," his mother said. "Is your boy in high school?"

"Ninth grade," the woman said.

"My son just finished college last year. He wants to write but he's selling typewriters until he gets started," his mother said.

The woman leaned forward and peered at Julian. He threw her such a malevolent look that she subsided against the seat. On the floor across the aisle there was an abandoned newspaper. He got up and got it and opened it out in front of him. His mother discreetly continued the conversation in a lower tone but the woman across the aisle said in a loud voice, "Well that's nice. Selling typewriters is close to writing. He can go right from one to the other."

"I tell him," his mother said, "that Rome wasn't built in a day."

Behind the newspaper Julian was withdrawing into the inner compartment of his mind where he spent most of his time. This was a kind of mental bubble in which he established himself when he could not bear to be a part of what was going on around him. From it he could see out and judge but in it he was safe from any kind of penetration from without. It was the only place where he felt free of the general idiocy of his fellows. His mother had never entered it but from it he could see her with absolute clarity.

The old lady was clever enough and he thought that if she had started from any of the right premises, more might have been expected of her. She lived according to the laws of her own fantasy world, outside of which he had never seen her set foot. The law of it was to sacrifice herself for him after she had first created the necessity to do so by making a mess of things. If he had permitted her sacrifices, it was only because her lack of foresight had made them necessary. All of her life had been a struggle to act like a Chestny without the Chestny goods, and to give him everything she thought a Chestny ought to have; but since, said she, it was fun to struggle, why complain? And when you had won, as she had won, what fun to look back on the hard times! *He could not forgive her that she had enjoyed the struggle and that she thought she had won.*

What she meant when she said she had won was that she had brought him up successfully and had sent him to college and that he had turned out so well—good looking (her teeth had gone unfilled so that his could be straightened), intelligent (he realized he was too intelligent to be a success), and with a future ahead of him (there was of course no future ahead of him). She excused his gloominess on the grounds that he was still growing up and his radical ideas on his lack of practical experience. She said he didn't yet know a thing about "life," that he hadn't even entered the real world—when already he was as disenchanted with it as a man of fifty.

The further irony of all this was that in spite of her, he had turned out so well. In spite of going to only a third-rate college, he had, on his own initiative, come out with a first-rate education; in spite of growing up dominated by a small mind, he had ended up with a large one; in spite of all her foolish views, he was free of prejudice and unafraid to face facts. Most miraculous of all, instead of being blinded by love for her as she was for him, he had cut himself emotionally free of her and could see her with complete objectivity. He was not dominated by his mother.

The bus stopped with a sudden jerk and shook him from his meditation. A woman from the back lurched forward with little steps and barely escaped falling in his newspaper as she righted herself. She got off and a large Negro got on. Julian kept his paper lowered to watch. It gave him a certain satisfaction to see injustice in daily operation. It confirmed his view that with a few exceptions there was no one worth knowing within a radius of three hundred miles. The Negro was well dressed and carried a briefcase. He looked around and then sat down on the other end of the seat where the woman with the red and white canvas sandals was sitting. He immediately unfolded a newspaper and obscured himself behind it. Julian's mother's elbow at once prodded insistently into his ribs. "Now you see why I won't ride on these buses by myself," she whispered.

The woman with the red and white canvas sandals had risen at the same time the Negro sat down and had gone further back in the bus and taken the seat of the woman who had got off. His mother leaned forward and cast her an approving look.

Julian rose, crossed the aisle, and sat down in the place of the woman with the canvas sandals. From this position, he looked serenely across at his mother. Her face had turned an angry red. He stared at her, making his eyes the eyes of a stranger. He felt his tension suddenly lift as if he had openly declared war on her.

He would have liked to get in conversation with the Negro and to talk with him about art or politics or any subject that would be above the comprehension of those around them, but the man remained entrenched behind his paper. He was either ignoring the change of seating or had never noticed it. There was no way for Julian to convey his sympathy.

His mother kept her eyes fixed reproachfully on his face. The woman with the protruding teeth was looking at him avidly as if he were a type of monster new to her.

"Do you have a light?" he asked the Negro.

Without looking away from his paper, the man reached in his pocket and handed him a packet of matches.

"Thanks," Julian said. For a moment he held the matches foolishly. A NO SMOKING sign looked down upon him from over the door. This alone would not have deterred him; he had no cigarettes. He had quit smoking some months before because he could not afford it. "Sorry," he muttered and handed back the matches. The Negro lowered the paper and gave him an annoyed look. He took the matches and raised the paper again.

His mother continued to gaze at him but she did not take advantage of his momentary discomfort. Her eyes retained their battered look. Her face seemed to be unnaturally red, as if her blood pressure had risen. Julian allowed no glimmer of sympathy to show on his face. Having got the advantage, he wanted desperately to keep it and carry it through. He would have liked to teach her a lesson that would last her awhile, but there seemed no way to continue the point. The Negro refused to come out from behind his paper.

Julian folded his arms and looked stolidly before him, facing her but as if he did not see her, as if he had ceased to recognize her existence. He visualized a scene in which, the bus having reached their stop, he would remain in his seat and when she said, "Aren't you going to get off?" he would look at her as at a stranger who had rashly addressed him. The corner they got off on was usually deserted, but it was well lighted and it would not hurt her to walk by herself the four blocks to the Y. He decided to wait until the time came and then decide whether or not he would let her get off by herself. He would have to be at the Y at ten to bring her back, but he could leave her wondering if he was going to show up. There was no reason for her to think she could always depend on him.

He retired again into the high-ceilinged room sparsely settled with large pieces of antique furniture. His soul expanded momentarily but then he became aware of his mother across from him and the vision shriveled. He studied her coldly. Her feet in little pumps dangled like a child's and did not quite reach the floor. She was training on him an exaggerated look of reproach. He felt completely detached from her. At that moment he could with pleasure have slapped her as he would have slapped a particularly obnoxious child in his charge.

He began to imagine various unlikely ways by which he could teach her a lesson. He might make friends with some distinguished Negro professor or lawyer and bring him home to spend the evening. He would be entirely justified but her blood pressure would rise to 300. He could not push her to the extent of making her have a stroke, and moreover, he had never been successful at making any Negro friends. He had tried to strike up an acquaintance on the bus with some of the better types, with ones that looked like professors or ministers or lawyers. One morning he had sat down next to a distinguished-looking dark brown man who had answered his questions with a sonorous solemnity but who had turned out to be an undertaker. Another day he had sat down beside a cigar-smoking Negro with a diamond ring on his finger, but after a few stilted pleasantries, the Negro had rung the buzzer and risen, slipping two lottery tickets into Julian's hand as he climbed over him to leave.

He imagined his mother lying desperately ill and his being able to secure only a Negro doctor for her. He toyed with that idea for a few minutes and then dropped it for a momentary vision of himself participating as a sympathizer in a sit-in demonstration. This was possible but he did not linger with it. Instead, he approached the ultimate horror. He brought home a beautiful suspiciously Negroid woman. Prepare yourself, he said. There is nothing you can do about it. This is the woman I've chosen. She's intelligent, dignified, even good, and she's suffered and she hasn't thought it *fun*. Now persecute us, go ahead and persecute us. Drive her out of here, but remember, you're driving me too. His eyes were narrowed and through the indignation he had generated, he saw his mother across the aisle, purple-faced, shrunken to the dwarf-like proportions of her moral nature, sitting like a mummy beneath the ridiculous banner of her hat.

He was tilted out of his fantasy again as the bus stopped. The door opened with a sucking hiss and out of the dark a large, gaily dressed, sullen-looking colored woman got on with a little boy. The child, who might have been four, had on a short plaid suit and a Tyrolean hat with a blue feather in it. Julian hoped that he would sit down beside him and that the woman would push in beside his mother. He could think of no better arrangement.

As she waited for her tokens, the woman was surveying the seating possibilities—he hoped with the idea of sitting where she was least wanted. There was something familiar-looking about her but Julian could not place what it was. She was a giant of a woman. Her face was set not only to meet opposition but to seek it out. The downward tilt of her large lower lip was like a warning sign: DON'T TAMPER TITH ME. Her bulging figure was encased in a green crepe dress and her feet overflowed in red shoes. She had on a hideous hat. A purple velvet flap came down on one side of it and stood up on the other; the rest of it was green and looked like a cushion with the stuffing out. She carried a mammoth red pocketbook that bulged throughout as if it were stuffed with rocks.

To Julian's disappointment, the little boy climbed up on the empty seat beside his mother. His mother lumped all children, black and white, into the common category, "cute," and she thought little Negroes were on the whole cuter than little white children. She smiled at the little boy as he climbed on the seat.

Meanwhile the woman was bearing down upon the empty seat beside Julian. To his annoyance, she squeezed herself into it. He saw his mother's face change as the woman settled herself next to him and he realized with satisfaction that this was more objectionable to her than it was to him. Her face seemed almost gray and there was a look of dull recognition in her eyes, as if suddenly she had sickened at some awful confrontation. Julian saw that it was because she and the woman had, in a sense, swapped sons. Though his mother would not realize the symbolic significance of this, she would feel it. His amusement showed plainly on his face.

The woman next to him muttered something unintelligible to herself. He was conscious of a kind of bristling next to him, a muted growling like that of an angry cat. He could not see anything but the red pocketbook upright on the bulging green thighs. He visualized the woman as she had stood waiting for her tokens—the ponderous figure, rising from the red shoes upward over the solid hips, the mammoth bosom, the haughty face, to the green and purple hat.

His eyes widened.

The vision of the two hats, identical, broke upon him with the radiance of a brilliant sunrise. His face was suddenly lit with joy. He could not believe that Fate had thrust upon his mother such a lesson. He gave a loud chuckle so that she would look at him and see that he saw. She turned her eyes on him slowly. The blue in them seemed to have turned a bruised purple. For a moment he had an uncomfortable sense of her innocence, but it lasted only a second before principle rescued him. Justice entitled him to laugh. His grin hardened until it said to her as plainly as if he were saying aloud: Your punishment exactly fits your pettiness. This should teach you a permanent lesson.

Her eyes shifted to the woman. She seemed unable to bear looking at him and to find the woman preferable. He became conscious again of the bristling presence at his side. The woman was rumbling like a volcano about to become active. His mother's mouth began to twitch slightly at one corner. With a sinking heart, he saw incipient signs of recovery on her face and realized that this was going to strike her suddenly as funny and was going to be no lesson at all. She kept her eyes on the woman and an amused smile came over her face as if the woman were a monkey that had stolen her hat. The little Negro was looking up at her with large fascinated eyes. He had been trying to attract her attention for some time.

"Carver!" the woman said suddenly. "Come heah!"

When he saw that the spotlight was on him at last, Carver drew his feet up and turned himself toward Julian's mother and giggled.

"Carver!" the woman said. "You heah me? Come heah!"

Carver slid down from the seat but remained squatting with his back against the base of it, his head turned slyly around toward Julian's mother, who was smiling at him. The woman reached a hand across the aisle and snatched him to her. He righted himself and hung backwards on her knees, grinning at Julian's mother. "Isn't he cute?" Julian's mother said to the woman with the protruding teeth.

"I reckon he is," the woman said without conviction.

The Negress yanked him upright but he eased out of her grip and shot across the aisle and scrambled, giggling wildly, onto the seat beside his love.

"I think he likes me," Julian's mother said, and smiled at the woman. It was the smile she used when she was being particularly gracious to an inferior. Julian saw everything lost. The lesson had rolled off her like rain on a roof.

The woman stood up and yanked the little boy off the seat as if she were snatching him from contagion. Julian could feel the rage in her at having no weapon like his mother's smile. She gave the child a sharp slap across his leg. He howled once and then thrust his head into her stomach and kicked his feet against her shins. "Be-have," she said vehemently.

The bus stopped and the Negro who had been reading the newspaper got off. The woman moved over and set the little boy down with a thump between herself and Julian. She held him firmly by the knee. In a moment he put his hands in front of his face and peeped at Julian's mother through his fingers.

"I see yoooooooo!" she said and put her hand in front of her face and peeped at him.

The woman slapped his hand down. "Quit yo' foolishness," she said, "before I knock the living Jesus out of you!"

Julian was thankful that the next stop was theirs. He reached up and pulled the cord. The woman reached up and pulled it at the same time. Oh my God, he thought. He had the terrible intuition that when they got off the bus together, his mother would open her purse and give the little boy a nickel. The gesture would be as natural to her as breathing. The bus stopped and the woman got up and lunged to the front, dragging the child, who wished to stay on, after her. Julian and his mother got up and followed. As they neared the door, Julian tried to relieve her of her pocketbook.

"No," she murmured, "I want to give the little boy a nickel."

"No!" Julian hissed. "No!"

She smiled down at the child and opened her bag. The bus door opened and the woman picked him up by the arm and descended with him, hanging at her hip. Once in the street she set him down and shook him.

Julian's mother had to close her purse while she got down the bus step but as soon as her feet were on the ground, she opened it again and began to rummage inside. "I can't find but a penny," she whispered, "but it looks like a new one."

"Don't do it!" Julian said fiercely between his teeth. There was a streetlight on the corner and she hurried to get under it so that she could better see into her pocketbook. The woman was heading off rapidly down the street with the child still hanging backward on her hand.

"Oh little boy!" Julian's mother called and took a few quick steps and caught up with them just beyond the lamppost. "Here's a bright new penny for you," and she held out the coin, which shone bronze in the dim light.

The huge woman turned and for a moment stood, her shoulders lifted and her face frozen with frustrated rage, and stared at Julian's mother. Then all at once she seemed to explode like a piece of machinery that had been given one ounce of pressure too much. Julian saw the black fist swing out with the red pocketbook. He shut his eyes and cringed as he heard the woman shout, "He don't take nobody's pennies!" When he opened his eyes, the woman was disappearing down the street with the little boy staring wide-eyed over her shoulder. Julian's mother was sitting on the sidewalk.

"I told you not to do that," Julian said angrily. "I told you not to do that!"

He stood over her for a minute, gritting his teeth. Her legs were stretched out in front of her and her hat was on her lap. He squatted down and looked her in the face. It was totally expressionless. "You got exactly what you deserved," he said. "Now get up."

He picked up her pocketbook and put what had fallen out back in it. He picked the hat up off her lap. The penny caught his eye on the sidewalk and he picked that up and let it drop before her eyes into the purse. Then he stood up and leaned over and held his hands out to pull her up. She remained immobile. He sighed. Rising above them on either side were black apartment buildings, marked with irregular rectangles of light. At the end of the block a man came out of a door and walked off in the opposite direction. "All right," he said, "suppose somebody happens by and wants to know why you're sitting on the sidewalk?"

She took the hand and, breathing hard, pulled heavily up on it and then stood for a moment, swaying slightly as if the spots of light in the darkness were circling around her. Her eyes, shadowed and confused, finally settled on his face. He did not try to conceal his irritation. "I hope this teaches you a lesson," he said. She leaned forward and her eyes raked his face. She seemed trying to determine his identity. Then, as if she found nothing familiar about him, she started off with a headlong movement in the wrong direction.

"Aren't you going on to the Y?" he asked.

"Home," she muttered.

"Well, are we walking?"

For answer she kept going. Julian followed along, his hands behind him. He saw no reason to let the lesson she had had go without backing it up with an explanation of its meaning. She might as well be made to understand what had happened to her. "Don't think that was just an uppity Negro woman," he said. "That was the whole colored race which will no longer take your condescending pennies. That was your black double. She can wear the same hat as you, and to be sure," he added gratuitously (because he thought it was funny), "it looked better on her than it did on you. What all this means," he said, "is that the old world is gone. The old manners are obsolete and your graciousness is not worth a damn." He thought bitterly of the house that had been lost for him. "You aren't who you think you are," he said.

She continued to plow ahead, paying no attention to him. Her hair had come undone on one side. She dropped her pocketbook and took no notice. He stooped and picked it up and handed it to her but she did not take it.

"You needn't act as if the world had come to an end," he said, "because it hasn't. From now on you've got to live in a new world and face a few realities for a change. Buck up," he said, "it won't kill you."

She was breathing fast.

"Let's wait on the bus," he said.

"Home," she said thickly.

"I hate to see you behave like this," he said. "Just like a child. I should be able to expect more of you." He decided to stop where he was and make her stop and wait for a bus. "I'm not going any farther," he said, stopping. "We're going on the bus."

She continued to go on as if she had not heard him. He took a few steps and caught her arm and stopped her. He looked into her face and caught his breath. He was looking into a face he had never seen before. "Tell Grandpa to come get me," she said.

He stared, stricken.

"Tell Caroline to come get me," she said.

Stunned, he let her go and she lurched forward again, walking as if one leg were shorter than the other. A tide of darkness seemed to be sweeping her from him. "Mother!" he cried. "Darling, sweetheart, wait!" Crumpling, she fell to the pavement. He dashed forward and fell at her side, crying, "Mamma, Mamma!" He turned her over. Her face was fiercely distorted. One eye, large and staring, moved slightly to the left as if it had become unmoored. The other remained fixed on him, raked his face again, found nothing and closed.

"Wait here, wait here!" he cried and jumped up and began to run for help toward a cluster of lights he saw in the distance ahead of him. "Help, help!" he shouted, but his voice was thin, scarcely a thread of sound. The lights drifted farther away the faster he ran and his feet moved numbly as if they carried him nowhere. The tide of darkness seemed to sweep him back to her, postponing from moment to moment his entry into the world of guilt and sorrow.

—1965

Gabriel García Márquez is the author of a brilliant serio-comic historical novel, One Hundred Years of Solitude *(1967). It is one of the landmarks of contemporary fiction, and rapidly became an international bestseller. "Magic realism" is the term that is often used to describe the author's unique blend of folklore, historical fact, naturalism, and fantasy, much of it occurring in the fictional village of Macondo. A native of Colombia, García Márquez, the eldest of twelve children, was born in Aracataca, a small town that is the model for the isolated, decaying settlements found in his fiction. García Márquez was trained as a journalist, first coming to public attention in 1955 with his investigative reporting about the government cover-up that followed the sinking of a Colombian navy vessel. After residence in Paris during the late 1950s, he worked for a time as a correspondent for Fidel Castro's official news agency. He has also lived in Mexico and Spain. Other works include the short story collections* No One Writes to the Colonel *(1968),* Leaf Storm and Other Stories *(1972), and* Innocent Eréndira and Other Stories *(1978). His novel* Love in the Time of Cholera *was a major success in 1988. He was awarded the Nobel Prize in 1982. In recent years García Márquez has focused on nonfiction.* News of a Kidnapping *(1997) tells the true story of how Colombian drug kingpins took ten citizens hostage to extort favors from their government.*

A Very Old Man with Enormous Wings

Translated by Gregory Rabassa

On the third day of rain they had killed so many crabs inside the house that Pelayo had to cross his drenched courtyard and throw them into the sea, because the newborn child had a temperature all night and they thought it was due to the stench. The world had been sad since Tuesday. Sea and sky were a single ash-gray thing and the sands of the beach, which on March nights glimmered like powdered light, had become a stew of mud and rotten shellfish. The light was so weak at noon that when Pelayo was coming back to the house after throwing away the crabs, it was hard for him to see what it was that was moving and groaning in the rear of the courtyard. He had to go very close to see that it was an old man, a very old man, lying face down in the mud, who, in spite of his tremendous efforts, couldn't get up, impeded by his enormous wings.

Frightened by that nightmare, Pelayo ran to get Elisenda, his wife, who was putting compresses on the sick child, and he took her to the rear of the courtyard. They both looked at the fallen body with mute stupor. He was dressed like a ragpicker. There were only a few faded hairs left on his bald skull and very few teeth in his mouth, and his pitiful condition of a drenched great-grandfather had taken away any sense of grandeur he might have had. His huge buzzard wings, dirty and half-plucked, were forever entangled in the mud. They looked at him so long and so closely that Pelayo and Elisenda very soon overcame their surprise and in the end found him familiar. Then they dared speak to him, and he answered in an incomprehensible dialect with a strong sailor's voice. That was how they skipped over the inconvenience of the wings and quite intelligently concluded that he was a lonely castaway from some foreign ship wrecked by the storm. And yet, they called in a neighbor woman who knew everything about life and death to see him, and all she needed was one look to show them their mistake.

"He's an angel," she told them. "He must have been coming for the child, but the poor fellow is so old that the rain knocked him down."

On the following day everyone knew that a flesh-and-blood angel was held captive in Pelayo's house. Against the judgment of the wise neighbor woman, for whom angels in those times were the fugitive survivors of a celestial conspiracy, they did not have the heart to club him to death. Pelayo watched over him all afternoon from the kitchen, armed with his bailiff's club, and before going to bed he dragged him out of the mud and locked him up with the hens in the wire chicken coop. In the middle of the night, when the rain stopped, Pelayo and Elisenda were still killing crabs. A short time afterward the child woke up without a fever and with a desire to eat. Then they felt magnanimous and decided to put the angel on a raft with fresh water and provisions for three days and leave him to his fate on the high seas. But when they went out into the courtyard with the first light of dawn, they found the whole neighborhood in front of the chicken coop having fun with the angel, without the slightest reverence, tossing him things to eat through the openings in the wire as if he weren't a supernatural creature but a circus animal.

Father Gonzaga arrived before seven o'clock, alarmed at the strange news. By that time onlookers less frivolous than those at dawn had already arrived and they were making all kinds of conjectures concerning the captive's future. The simplest among them thought that he should be named mayor of the world. Others of sterner mind felt that he should be promoted to the rank of five-star general in order to win all wars. Some visionaries hoped that he could be put to stud in order to implant on earth a race of winged wise men who could take charge of the universe. But Father Gonzaga, before becoming a priest, had been a robust woodcutter. Standing by the wire, he reviewed his catechism in an instant and asked them to open the door so that he could take a close look at that pitiful man who looked more like a huge decrepit hen among the fascinated chickens. He was lying in a corner drying his open wings in the sunlight among the fruit peels and breakfast leftovers that the early risers had thrown him. Alien to the impertinences of the world, he only lifted his antiquarian eyes and murmured something in his dialect when Father Gonzaga went into the chicken coop and said good morning to him in Latin. The parish priest had his first suspicion of an impostor when he saw that he did not understand the language of God or know how to greet His ministers. Then he noticed that seen close up he was much too human: he had an unbearable smell of the outdoors, the back side of his wings was strewn with parasites and his main feathers had been mistreated by terrestrial winds, and nothing about him measured up to the proud dignity of angels. Then he came out of the chicken coop and in a brief sermon warned the curious against the risks of being ingenuous. He reminded them that the devil had the bad habit of making use of carnival tricks in order to confuse the unwary. He argued that if wings were not the essential element in determining the difference between a hawk and an airplane, they were even less so in the recognition of angels. Nevertheless, he promised to write a letter to his bishop so that the latter would write to his primate so that the latter would write to the Supreme Pontiff in order to get the final verdict from the highest courts.

His prudence fell on sterile hearts. The news of the captive angel spread with such rapidity that after a few hours the courtyard had the bustle of a marketplace and they had to call in troops with fixed bayonets to disperse the mob that was about to knock the house down. Elisenda, her spine all twisted from sweeping up so much marketplace trash, then got the idea of fencing in the yard and charging five cents admission to see the angel.

The curious came from far away. A traveling carnival arrived with a flying acrobat who buzzed over the crowd several times, but no one paid any attention to him because his wings were not those of an angel but, rather, those of a sidereal[1] bat. The most unfortunate invalids on earth came in search of health: a poor woman who since childhood had been counting her heartbeats and had run out of numbers, a Portuguese man who couldn't sleep because the noise of the stars disturbed him, a sleepwalker who got up at night to undo the things he had done while awake; and many others with less serious ailments. In the midst of that shipwreck disorder that made the earth tremble, Pelayo and Elisenda were happy with fatigue, for in less than a week they had crammed their rooms with money and the line of pilgrims waiting their turn to enter still reached beyond the horizon.

The angel was the only one who took no part in his own act. He spent his time trying to get comfortable in his borrowed nest, befuddled by the hellish heat of the oil lamps and sacramental candles that had been placed along the wire. At first they tried to make him eat some mothballs, which according to the wisdom of the wise neighbor woman, were the food prescribed for angels. But he turned them down, just as he turned down the papal lunches that the penitents brought him, and they never found out whether it was because he was an angel or because he was an old man that in the end he ate nothing but eggplant mush. His only supernatural virtue seemed to be patience. Especially during the first days, when the hens pecked at him, searching for the stellar parasites that proliferated in his wings, and the cripples pulled out feathers to touch their defective parts with, and even the most merciful threw stones at him, trying to get him to rise so they could see him standing. The only time they succeeded in arousing him was when they burned his side with an iron for branding steers, for he had been motionless for so many hours that they thought he was dead. He awoke with a start, ranting in his hermetic language and with tears in his eyes, and he flapped his wings a couple of times, which brought on a whirlwind of chicken dung and lunar dust and a gale of panic that did not seem to be of this world. Although many thought that his reaction had been one not of rage but of pain, from then on they were careful not to annoy him, because the

[1]**sidereal** coming from the stars.

majority understood that his passivity was not that of a hero taking his ease but that of a cataclysm in repose.

Father Gonzaga held back the crowd's frivolity with formulas of maidservant inspiration while awaiting the arrival of a final judgment on the nature of the captive. But the mail from Rome showed no sense of urgency. They spent their time finding out if the prisoner had a navel, if his dialect had any connection with Aramaic, how many times he could fit on the head of a pin, or whether he wasn't just a Norwegian with wings. Those meager letters might have come and gone until the end of time if a providential event had not put an end to the priest's tribulations.

It so happened that during those days, among so many other carnival attractions, there arrived in town the traveling show of the woman who had been changed into a spider for having disobeyed her parents. The admission to see her was not only less than the admission to see the angel, but people were permitted to ask her all manner of questions about her absurd state and to examine her up and down so that no one would ever doubt the truth of her honor. She was a frightful tarantula the size of a ram and with the head of a sad maiden. What was most heart-rending, however, was not her outlandish shape but the sincere affliction with which she recounted the details of her misfortune. While still practically a child she had sneaked out of her parents' house to go to a dance, and while she was coming back through the woods after having danced all night without permission, a fearful thunderclap rent the sky in two and through the crack came the lightning bolt of brimstone that changed her into a spider. Her only nourishment came from the meatballs that charitable souls chose to toss into her mouth. A spectacle like that, full of so much human truth and with such a fearful lesson, was found to defeat without even trying that of a haughty angel who scarcely deigned to look at mortals. Besides, the few miracles attributed to the angel showed a certain mental disorder, like the blind man who didn't recover his sight but grew three new teeth, or the paralytic who didn't get to walk, but almost won the lottery, and the leper whose sores sprouted sunflowers. Those consolation miracles, which were more like mocking fun, had already ruined the angel's reputation when the woman who had been changed into a spider finally crushed him completely. That was how Father Gonzaga was cured forever of his insomnia and Pelayo's courtyard went back to being as empty as during the time it had rained for three days and crabs walked through the bedrooms.

The owners of the house had no reason to lament. With the money they saved they built a two-story mansion with balconies and gardens and high netting so that crabs wouldn't get in during the winter, and with iron bars on the windows so that angels wouldn't get in. Pelayo also set up a rabbit warren close to town and gave up his job as bailiff for good, and Elisenda bought some satin pumps with high heels and many dresses of iridescent silk, the kind worn on Sunday by the most desirable women in those times. The chicken coop was the only thing that didn't receive any attention. If they washed it down with creolin and burned tears of myrrh inside it every so often, it was not in homage to the angel but to drive away the dungheap stench that still hung everywhere like a ghost and was turning the new house into an old one. At first, when the child learned to walk, they were careful that he not get too close to the chicken coop. But then they began to lose their fears and got used to the smell, and before the child got his second teeth he'd gone inside the chicken coop to play, where the wires were falling apart. The angel was no less standoffish with him than with other mortals, but he tolerated the most ingenious infamies with the patience of a dog who had no illusions. They both came down with chicken pox at the same time. The doctor who took care of the child couldn't resist the temptation to listen to the angel's heart, and he found so much whistling in the heart and so many sounds in his kidneys that it seemed impossible for him to be alive. What surprised him most, however, was the logic of his wings. They seemed so natural on that completely human organism that he couldn't understand why other men didn't have them too.

When the child began school it had been some time since the sun and rain had caused the collapse of the chicken coop. The angel went dragging himself about here and there like a stray dying man. They would drive him out of the bedroom with a broom and a moment later find him in the kitchen. He seemed to be in so many places at the same time that they grew to think that he'd been duplicated, that he was reproducing himself all through the house, and the exasperated and unhinged Elisenda shouted that it was awful living in that hell full of angels. He could scarcely eat and his antiquarian eyes had also become so foggy that he went about bumping into posts. All he had left were the bare cannulae[2] of his last feathers. Pelayo threw a blanket over him and extended him the charity of letting him sleep in the shed, and only then did they notice that

[2]**cannulae** the tubular pieces by which feathers are attached to a body.

he had a temperature at night, and was delirious with the tongue twisters of an old Norwegian. That was one of the few times they became alarmed, for they thought he was going to die and not even the wise neighbor woman had been able to tell them what to do with dead angels.

And yet he not only survived his worst winter, but seemed improved with the first sunny days. He remained motionless for several days in the farthest corner of the courtyard, where no one would see him, and at the beginning of December some large, stiff feathers began to grow on his wings, the feathers of a scarecrow, which looked more like another misfortune of decrepitude. But he must have known the reason for those changes, for he was quite careful that no one should notice them, that no one should hear the sea chanteys that he sometimes sang under the stars. One morning Elisenda was cutting some bunches of onions for lunch when a wind that seemed to come from the high seas blew into the kitchen. Then she went to the window and caught the angel in his first attempts at flight. They were so clumsy that his fingernails opened a furrow in the vegetable patch and he was on the point of knocking the shed down with the ungainly flapping that slipped on the light and he couldn't get a grip on the air. But he did manage to gain altitude. Elisenda let out a sigh of relief, for herself and for him, when she saw him pass over the last houses, holding himself up in some way with the risky flapping of a senile vulture. She kept watching him even when she was through cutting the onions and she kept on watching until it was no longer possible for her to see him, because then he was no longer an annoyance in her life but an imaginary dot on the horizon of the sea.

—1968

CHINUA ACHEBE ■ (b. 1930)

Chinua Achebe was born in Ogidi, Nigeria, and, after graduation from University College in Ibadan and study at London University, was employed by the Nigerian Broadcasting Service, where he served for years as a producer. After the appearance of his first novel, Things Fall Apart, *in 1958 (the title is taken from William Butler Yeats's apocalyptic poem "The Second Coming"), he became one of the most widely acclaimed writers to emerge from the former British colonies of Africa. The author of several novels as well as a collection of short stories, Achebe has taught in the United States at the University of California—Los Angeles, Stanford University, and the University of Massachusetts–Amherst. One of his chief services to contemporary literature was his editorship of the*

African Writers Series, which sponsored the first publications of many of his fellow Nigerian writers. Achebe draws heavily on the oral traditions of his native country, but he has been successful in adapting European fictional techniques to deal with subjects like the degradations imposed by colonialism and the relative failure of most post-colonial governments to improve on the past for the betterment of the lives of their citizens.

Dead Men's Path

Michael Obi's hopes were fulfilled much earlier than he had expected. He was appointed headmaster of Ndume Central School in January 1949. It had always been an unprogressive school, so the Mission authorities decided to send a young and energetic man to run it. Obi accepted this responsibility with enthusiasm. He had many wonderful ideas and this was an opportunity to put them into practice. He had had sound secondary school education which designated him a "pivotal teacher" in the official records and set him apart from the other headmasters in the mission field. He was outspoken in his condemnation of the narrow views of these older and often less-educated ones.

"We shall make a good job of it, shan't we?" he asked his young wife when they first heard the joyful news of his promotion.

"We shall do our best," she replied. "We shall have such beautiful gardens and everything will be just *modern* and delightful. . . ." In their two years of married life she had become completely infected by his passion for "modern methods" and his denigration of "these old and superannuated people in the teaching field who would be better employed as traders in the Onitsha market." She began to see herself already as the admired wife of the young headmaster, the queen of the school.

The wives of the other teachers would envy her position. She would set the fashion in everything. . . . Then, suddenly, it occurred to her that there might not be other wives. Wavering between hope and fear, she asked her husband, looking anxiously at him.

"All our colleagues are young and unmarried," he said with enthusiasm which for once she did not share. "Which is a good thing," he continued.

"Why?"

"Why? They will give all their time and energy to the school."

Nancy was downcast. For a few minutes she became skeptical about the new school; but it was only for a few minutes. Her little personal misfortune could not blind her to her husband's happy prospects. She looked at him as he sat folded up in a chair. He was stoop-shouldered and looked frail. But he sometimes surprised people with sudden bursts of physical energy. In his present posture, however, all his bodily strength seemed to have retired behind his deep-set eyes, giving them an extraordinary power of penetration. He was only twenty-six, but looked thirty or more. On the whole, he was not unhandsome.

"A penny for your thoughts, Mike," said Nancy after a while, imitating the woman's magazine she read.

"I was thinking what a grand opportunity we've got at last to show these people how a school should be run."

Ndume School was backward in every sense of the word. Mr. Obi put his whole life into the work, and his wife hers too. He had two aims. A high standard of teaching was insisted upon, and the school compound was to be turned into a place of beauty. Nancy's dream-gardens came to life with the coming of the rains, and blossomed. Beautiful hibiscus and allamanda hedges in brilliant red and yellow marked out the carefully tended school compound from the rank neighborhood bushes.

One evening as Obi was admiring his work he was scandalized to see an old woman from the village hobble right across the compound, through a marigold flower-bed and the hedges. On going up there he found faint signs of an almost disused path from the village across the school compound to the bush on the other side.

"It amazes me," said Obi to one of his teachers who had been three years in the school, "that you people allowed the villagers to make use of this footpath. It is simply incredible." He shook his head.

"The path," said the teacher apologetically, "appears to be very important to them. Although it is hardly used, it connects the village shrine with their place of burial."

"And what has that got to do with the school?" asked the headmaster.

"Well, I don't know," replied the other with a shrug of the shoulders. "But I remember there was a big row some time ago when we attempted to close it."

"That was some time ago. But it will not be used now," said Obi as he walked away. "What will the Government Education Officer think of this when he comes to inspect the school next week? The villagers might, for all I know, decide to use the schoolroom for a pagan ritual during the inspection."

Heavy sticks were planted closely across the path at the two places where it entered and left the school premises. These were further strengthened with barbed wire.

Three days later the village priest of *Ani* called on the headmaster. He was an old man and walked with a slight stoop. He carried a stout walking-stick which he usually tapped on the floor, by way of emphasis, each time he made a new point in his argument.

"I have heard," he said after the usual exchange of cordialities, "that our ancestral footpath has recently been closed. . . ."

"Yes," replied Mr. Obi. "We cannot allow people to make a highway of our school compound."

"Look here, my son," said the priest bringing down his walking-stick, "this path was here before you were born and before your father was born. The whole life of this village depends on it. Our dead relatives depart by it and our ancestors visit us by it. But most important, it is the path of children coming in to be born. . . ."

Mr. Obi listened with a satisfied smile on his face.

"The whole purpose of our school," he said finally, "is to eradicate just such beliefs as that. Dead men do not require footpaths. The whole idea is just fantastic. Our duty is to teach your children to laugh at such ideas."

"What you say may be true," replied the priest, "but we follow the practices of our fathers. If you reopen the path we shall have nothing to quarrel about. What I always say is: let the hawk perch and let the eagle perch." He rose to go.

"I am sorry," said the young headmaster. "But the school compound cannot be a thoroughfare. It is against our regulations. I would suggest your constructing another path, skirting our premises. We can even get our boys to help in building it. I don't suppose the ancestors will find the little detour too burdensome."

"I have no more words to say," said the old priest, already outside.

Two days later a young woman in the village died in childbed. A diviner was immediately consulted and he prescribed heavy sacrifices to propitiate ancestors insulted by the fence.

Obi woke up next morning among the ruins of his work. The beautiful hedges were torn up not just near the path but right round the school, the flowers trampled to death and one of the school buildings pulled down . . . . That day, the white Supervisor came to inspect the school and wrote a nasty report on the state of the premises but more seriously about the "tribal-war situation developing between the school and the village, arising in part from the misguided zeal of the new headmaster."

—*1953*

Alice Munro was born on a farm in Wingham, Ontario, and educated at the University of Ontario, where she received her degree in 1952. Her first book, Dance of the Happy Shades, *appeared in 1968, and she has continued regularly to publish collections of short stories. Asked about her devotion to short fiction, Munro told* Contemporary Authors: *"I never intended to be a short story writer—I started writing them because I didn't have time to write anything else—I had three children. And then I got used to writing short stories, so I see my materials that way, and now I don't think I'll ever write a novel." Parent-child relations and the discovery of personal freedom are constant themes in Munro's work, especially in* The Beggar Maid: Stories of Rose and Flo *(1979), a series of stories about a woman and her stepdaughter. Munro has won both the Governor General's Literary Award and the Canadian Booksellers' Award, befitting her status as one of her country's most distinguished writers.* Selected Stories *appeared in 1996, and* The Love of a Good Woman *was published in 1998. Munro's most recent story compilation is* The View from Castle Rock *(2006). "The Bear Came Over the Mountain" was adapted for the screen as* Away from Her *in 2007, earning an Academy Award nomination for its star, Julie Christie.*

The Bear Came Over the Mountain

Fiona lived in her parents' house, in the town where she and Grant went to university. It was a big, bay-windowed house that seemed to Grant both luxurious and disorderly, with rugs crooked on the floors and cup rings bitten into the table varnish. Her mother was Icelandic—a powerful woman with a froth of white hair and indignant far-left politics. The father was an important cardiologist, revered around the hospital but happily subservient at home, where he would listen to his wife's strange tirades with an absent-minded smile. Fiona had her own little car and a pile of cashmere sweaters, but she wasn't in a sorority, and her mother's political activity was probably the reason. Not that she cared. Sororities were a joke to her, and so was politics—though she liked to play "The Four Insurgent Generals" on the phonograph, and sometimes also the "Internationale," very loud, if there was a guest she thought she could make nervous. A curly-haired gloomy-looking foreigner was courting her—she said he was a Visigoth—and so were two or three quite respectable and uneasy young interns. She made fun of them all and of Grant as well. She would drolly repeat some of his small-town phrases. He thought maybe she was joking when she proposed to him, on a cold bright day on the beach at Port Stanley. Sand was stinging their faces and the waves delivered crashing loads of gravel at their feet.

"Do you think it would be fun—" Fiona shouted. "Do you think it would be fun if we got married?"

He took her up on it, he shouted yes. He wanted never to be away from her. She had the spark of life.

Just before they left their house Fiona noticed a mark on the kitchen floor. It came from the cheap black house shoes she had been wearing earlier in the day.

"I thought they'd quit doing that," she said in a tone of ordinary annoyance and perplexity, rubbing at the gray smear that looked as if it had been made by a greasy crayon.

She remarked that she'd never have to do this again, since she wasn't taking those shoes with her.

"I guess I'll be dressed up all the time," she said. "Or semi-dressed up. It'll be sort of like in a hotel."

She rinsed out the rag she'd been using and hung it on the rack inside the door under the sink. Then she put on her golden-brown, fur-collared ski jacket, over a white turtleneck sweater and tailored fawn slacks. She was a tall, narrow-shouldered woman, seventy years old but still upright and trim, with long legs and long feet, delicate wrists and ankles, and tiny, almost comical-looking ears. Her hair that was as light as milkweed fluff had gone from pale blond to white somehow without Grant's noticing exactly when, and she still wore it down to her shoulders, as her mother had done. (That was the thing that had alarmed Grant's own mother, a small-town widow who worked as a doctor's receptionist. The long white hair on Fiona's mother, even more than the state of the house, had told her all she needed to know about attitudes and politics.) But otherwise Fiona, with her fine bones and small sapphire eyes, was nothing like her mother. She had a slightly crooked mouth, which she emphasized now with red lipstick—usually the last thing she did before she left the house.

She looked just like herself on this day—direct and vague as in fact she was, sweet and ironic.

Over a year ago, Grant had started noticing so many little yellow notes stuck up all over the house. That was not entirely new. Fiona had always written things down—the title of a book she'd heard mentioned on the radio or the jobs she wanted to make sure she got done that day. Even her morning schedule was written down. He found it mystifying and touching in its precision: "7 a.m. yoga. 7:30–7:54 teeth face hair. 7:45–8:15 walk. 8:15 Grant and breakfast."

The new notes were different. Stuck onto the kitchen drawers—Cutlery, Dishtowels, Knives. Couldn't she just open the drawers and see what was inside?

Worse things were coming. She went to town and phoned Grant from a booth to ask him how to drive home. She went for her usual walk across the field into the woods and came home by the fence line—a very long way round. She said that she'd counted on fences always taking you somewhere.

It was hard to figure out. She'd said that about fences as if it were a joke, and she had remembered the phone number without any trouble.

"I don't think it's anything to worry about," she said. "I expect I'm just losing my mind."

He asked if she had been taking sleeping pills.

"If I am I don't remember," she said. Then she said she was sorry to sound so flippant. "I'm sure I haven't been taking anything. Maybe I should be. Maybe vitamins."

Vitamins didn't help. She would stand in doorways trying to figure out where she was going. She forgot to turn on the burner under the vegetables or put water in the coffeemaker. She asked Grant when they'd moved to this house.

"Was it last year or the year before?"

"It was twelve years ago," he said.

"That's shocking."

"She's always been a bit like this," Grant said to the doctor. He tried without success to explain how Fiona's surprise and apologies now seemed somehow like routine courtesy, not quite concealing a private amusement. As if she'd stumbled on some unexpected adventure. Or begun playing a game that she hoped he would catch on to.

"Yes, well," the doctor said. "It might be selective at first. We don't know, do we? Till we see the pattern of the deterioration, we really can't say."

In a while it hardly mattered what label was put on it. Fiona, who no longer went shopping alone, disappeared from the supermarket while Grant had his back turned. A policeman picked her up as she was walking down the middle of the road, blocks away. He asked her name and she answered readily. Then he asked her the name of the Prime Minister.

"If you don't know that, young man, you really shouldn't be in such a responsible job."

He laughed. But then she made the mistake of asking if he'd seen Boris and Natasha. These were the now dead Russian wolfhounds she had adopted many years ago, as a favor to a friend, then devoted herself to for the rest of their lives. Her taking them over might have coincided with the discovery that she was not likely to have children. Something about her tubes being blocked, or twisted—Grant could not remember now. He had always avoided thinking about all that female apparatus. Or it might have been after her mother died. The dogs' long legs and silky hair, their narrow, gentle, intransigent faces made a fine match for her when she took them out for walks. And Grant himself, in those days, landing his first job at the university (his father-in-law's money welcome there in spite of the political taint), might have seemed to some people to have been picked up on another of Fiona's eccentric whims, and groomed and tended and favored—though, fortunately, he didn't understand this until much later.

There was a rule that nobody could be admitted to Meadowlake during the month of December. The holiday season had so many emotional pitfalls. So they made the twenty-minute drive in January. Before they reached the highway the country road dipped through a swampy hollow now completely frozen over.

Fiona said, "Oh, remember."

Grant said, "I was thinking about that, too."

"Only it was in the moonlight," she said.

She was talking about the time that they had gone out skiing at night under the full moon and over the black-striped snow, in this place that you could get into only in the depths of winter. They had heard the branches cracking in the cold.

If she could remember that, so vividly and correctly, could there really be so much the matter with her? It was all he could do not to turn around and drive home.

There was another rule that the supervisor explained to him. New residents were not to be visited during the first thirty days. Most people needed that time to get settled in. Before the rule had been put in place, there had been pleas and tears and tantrums, even from those who had come in willingly. Around the third or fourth day they would start lamenting and begging to be taken home. And some relatives could be susceptible to that, so you would have people being carted home who would not get on there any better than they had before. Six months or sometimes only a few weeks later, the whole upsetting hassle would have to be gone through again.

"Whereas we find," the supervisor said, "we find that if they're left on their own the first month they usually end up happy as clams."

They had in fact gone over to Meadowlake a few times several years ago to visit Mr. Farquhar, the old bachelor farmer who had been their neighbor. He had lived by himself in a drafty brick house unaltered since the early years of the century, except for the addition of a refrigerator and a television set. Now, just as Mr. Farquhar's house was gone, replaced by a gimcrack sort of castle that was the weekend home of some people from Toronto, the old Meadowlake was gone, though it had dated only from the fifties. The new building was a spacious, vaulted place, whose air was faintly, pleasantly pine-scented. Profuse and genuine greenery sprouted out of giant crocks in the hallways.

Nevertheless, it was the old Meadowlake that Grant found himself picturing Fiona in, during the long month he had to get through without seeing her. He phoned every day and hoped to get the nurse whose name was Kristy. She seemed a little amused at his constancy, but she would give him a fuller report than any other nurse he got stuck with.

Fiona had caught a cold the first week, she said, but that was not unusual for newcomers. "Like when your kids start school," Kristy said. "There's a whole bunch of new germs they're exposed to and for a while they just catch everything."

Then the cold got better. She was off the antibiotics and she didn't seem as confused as she had been when she came in. (This was the first Grant had heard about either the antibiotics or the confusion.) Her appetite was pretty good and she seemed to enjoy sitting in the sunroom. And she was making some friends, Kristy said.

If anybody phoned, he let the machine pick up. The people they saw socially, occasionally, were not close neighbors but people who lived around the country, who were retired, as they were, and who often went away without notice. They would imagine that he and Fiona were away on some such trip at present.

Grant skied for exercise. He skied around and around in the field behind the house as the sun went down and left the sky pink over a countryside that seemed to be bound by waves of blue-edged ice. Then he came back to the darkening house, turning the television news on while he made his supper. They had usually prepared supper together. One of them made the drinks and the other the fire, and they talked about his work (he was writing a study of legendary Norse wolves and particularly of the great wolf Fenrir, which swallows up Odin at the end of the world) and about whatever Fiona was reading and what they had been thinking during their close but separate day. This was their time of liveliest intimacy, though there was also, of course, the five or ten minutes of physical sweetness just after they got into bed—something that did not often end in sex but reassured them that sex was not over yet.

In a dream he showed a letter to one of his colleagues. The letter was from the roommate of a girl he had not thought of for a while and was sanctimonious and hostile, threatening in a whining way. The girl herself was someone he had parted from decently and it seemed unlikely that she would want to make a fuss, let alone try to kill herself, which was what the letter was elaborately trying to tell him she had done.

He had thought of the colleague as a friend. He was one of those husbands who had been among the first to throw away their neckties and leave home to spend every night on a floor mattress with a bewitching young mistress—coming to their offices, their classes, bedraggled and smelling of dope and incense. But now he took a dim view. "I wouldn't laugh," he said to Grant—who did not think he had been laughing. "And if I were you I'd try to prepare Fiona."

So Grant went off to find Fiona in Meadowlake—the old Meadowlake—and got into a lecture hall instead. Everybody was waiting there for him to teach his class. And sitting in the last, highest row was a flock of cold-eyed young women all in black robes, all in mourning, who never took their bitter stares off him, and pointedly did not write down, or care about, anything he was saying.

Fiona was in the first row, untroubled. "Oh phooey," she said. "Girls that age are always going around talking about how they'll kill themselves."

He hauled himself out of the dream, took pills, and set about separating what was real from what was not.

There *had* been a letter, and the word "rat" had appeared in black paint on his office door, and Fiona, on being told that a girl had suffered from a bad crush on him, had said pretty much what she said in the dream. The colleague hadn't come into it, and nobody had committed suicide. Grant hadn't been disgraced. In fact, he had got off easy when you thought of what might have happened just a couple of years later. But word got around. Cold shoulders became conspicuous. They had few Christmas invitations and spent New Year's Eve alone. Grant got drunk, and without its being required of him—also, thank God, without making the error of a confession—he promised Fiona a new life.

Nowhere had there been any acknowledgment that the life of a philanderer (if that was what Grant had to call himself—he who had not had half as many conquests as the man who had reproached him in his dream) involved acts of generosity, and even sacrifice. Many times he had catered to a woman's pride, to her fragility, by offering more affection—or a rougher passion—than anything he really felt. All so that he could now find himself accused of wounding and exploiting and destroying self-esteem. And of deceiving Fiona—as, of course, he had. But would it have been better if he had done as others had done with their wives, and left her? He had never thought of such a thing. He had never stopped making love to Fiona. He had not stayed away from her for a single night. No making up elaborate stories in order to spend a weekend in San Francisco or in a tent on Manitoulin Island. He had gone easy on the dope and the drink, and he had continued to publish papers, serve on committees, make progress in his career. He had never had any intention of throwing over work and marriage and taking to the country to practice carpentry or keep bees.

But something like that had happened, after all. He had taken early retirement with a reduced pension. Fiona's father had died, after some bewildered and stoical time alone in the big house, and Fiona had inherited both that property and the farmhouse where her father had grown up, in the country near Georgian Bay.

It was a new life. He and Fiona worked on the house. They got cross-country skis. They were not very sociable but they gradually made some friends. There were no more hectic flirtations. No bare female toes creeping up under a man's pants leg at a dinner party. No more loose wives.

Just in time, Grant was able to think, when the sense of injustice had worn down. The feminists and perhaps the sad silly girl herself and his cowardly so-called friends had pushed him out just in time. Out of a life that was in fact getting to be more trouble than it was worth. And that might eventually have cost him Fiona.

On the morning of the day when he was to go back to Meadowlake, for the first visit, Grant woke early. He was full of a solemn tingling, as in the old days on the morning of his first planned meeting with a new woman. The feeling was not precisely sexual. (Later, when the meetings had become routine, that was all it was.) There was an expectation of discovery, almost a spiritual expansion. Also timidity, humility, alarm.

There had been a thaw. Plenty of snow was left, but the dazzling hard landscape of earlier winter had crumbled. These pocked heaps under a gray sky looked like refuse in the fields. In the town near Meadowlake he found a florist's shop and bought a large bouquet. He had never presented flowers to Fiona before. Or to anyone else. He entered the building feeling like a hopeless lover or a guilty husband in a cartoon.

"Wow. Narcissus this early," Kristy said. "You must've spent a fortune." She went along the hall ahead of him and snapped on the light in a sort of pantry, where she searched for a vase. She was a heavy young woman who looked as if she had given up on her looks in every department except her hair. That was blond and voluminous. All the puffed-up luxury of a cocktail waitress's style, or a stripper's, on top of such a workaday face and body.

"There now," she said, and nodded him down the hall. "Name's right on the door."

So it was, on a nameplate decorated with bluebirds. He wondered whether to knock, and did, then opened the door and called her name.

She wasn't there. The closet door was closed, the bed smoothed. Nothing on the bedside table, except a box of Kleenex and a glass of water. Not a single photograph or picture of any kind, not a book or a magazine. Perhaps you had to keep those in a cupboard.

He went back to the nurses' station. Kristy said, "No?" with a surprise that he thought perfunctory. He hesitated, holding the flowers. She said, "O.K., O.K.—let's set the bouquet down here." Sighing, as if he were a backward child on his first day at school, she led him down the hall toward a large central space with skylights which seemed to be a general meeting area. Some people were sitting along the walls, in easy chairs, others at tables in the middle of the carpeted floor. None of them looked too bad. Old—some of them incapacitated enough to need wheelchairs—but decent. There had been some unnerving sights when he and Fiona visited Mr. Farquhar. Whiskers on old women's chins, somebody with a bulged-out eye like a rotted plum. Dribblers, head wagglers, mad chatterers. Now it looked as if there'd been some weeding out of the worst cases.

"See?" said Kristy in a softer voice. "You just go up and say hello and try not to startle her. Just go ahead."

He saw Fiona in profile, sitting close up to one of the card tables, but not playing. She looked a little puffy in the face, the flab on one cheek hiding the corner of her mouth, in a way it hadn't done before. She was watching the play of the man she sat closest to. He held his cards tilted so that she could see them. When Grant got near the table she looked up. They all looked up—all the players at the table looked up, with displeasure. Then they immediately looked down at their cards, as if to ward off any intrusion.

But Fiona smiled her lopsided, abashed, sly, and charming smile and pushed back her chair and came round to him, putting her fingers to her mouth.

"Bridge," she whispered. "Deadly serious. They're quite rabid about it." She drew him toward the coffee table, chatting. "I can remember being like that for a while at college. My friends and I would cut class and sit in the common room and smoke and play like cutthroats. Can I get you anything? A cup of tea? I'm afraid the coffee isn't up to much here."

Grant never drank tea.

He could not throw his arms around her. Something about her voice and smile, familiar as they were, something about the way she seemed to be guarding the players from him—as well as him from their displeasure—made that impossible.

"I brought you some flowers," he said. "I thought they'd do to brighten up your room. I went to your room but you weren't there."

"Well, no," she said. "I'm here." She glanced back at the table.

Grant said, "You've made a new friend." He nodded toward the man she'd been sitting next to. At this moment that man looked up at Fiona and she turned, either because of what Grant had said or because she felt the look at her back.

"It's just Aubrey," she said. "The funny thing is I knew him years and years ago. He worked in the store. The hardware store where my grandpa used to shop. He and I were always kidding around and he couldn't get up the nerve to ask me out. Till the very last weekend and he took me to a ballgame. But when it was over my grandpa showed up to drive me home. I was up visiting for the summer. Visiting my grandparents—they lived on a farm."

"Fiona. I know where your grandparents lived. It's where we live. Lived."

"Really?" she said, not paying her full attention because the card-player was sending her his look, which was one not of supplication but of command. He was a man of about Grant's age, or a little older. Thick coarse white hair fell over his forehead and his skin was leathery but pale, yellowish-white like an old wrinkled-up kid glove. His long face was dignified and melancholy and he had something of the beauty of a powerful, discouraged, elderly horse. But where Fiona was concerned he was not discouraged.

"I better go back," Fiona said, a blush spotting her newly fattened face. "He thinks he can't play without me sitting there. It's silly, I hardly know the game anymore. If I leave you now, you can entertain yourself? It must all seem strange to you but you'll be surprised how soon you get used to it. You'll get to know who everybody is. Except that some of them are pretty well off in the clouds, you know—you can't expect them all to get to know who you are."

She slipped back into her chair and said something into Aubrey's ear. She tapped her fingers across the back of his hand.

Grant went in search of Kristy and met her in the hall. She was pushing a cart with pitchers of apple juice and grape juice.

"Well?" she said.

Grant said, "Does she even know who I am?" He could not decide. She could have been playing a joke. It would not be unlike her. She had given herself away by that little pretense at the end, talking to him as if she thought perhaps he was a new resident. If it was a pretense.

Kristy said, "You just caught her at sort of a bad moment. Involved in the game."

"She's not even playing," he said.

"Well, but her friend's playing. Aubrey."

"So who is Aubrey?"

"That's who he is. Aubrey. Her friend. Would you like a juice?"

Grant shook his head.

"Oh look," said Kristy. "They get these attachments. That takes over for a while. Best buddy sort of thing. It's kind of a phase."

"You mean she really might not know who I am?"

"She might not. Not today. Then tomorrow—you never know, do you? You'll see the way it is, once you've been coming here for a while. You'll learn not to take it all so serious. Learn to take it day by day."

Day by day. But things really didn't change back and forth and he didn't get used to the way they were. Fiona was the one who seemed to get used to him, but only as some persistent visitor who took a special interest in her. Or perhaps even as a nuisance who must be prevented, according to her old rules of courtesy, from realizing that he was one. She treated him with a distracted, social sort of kindness that was successful in keeping him from asking the most obvious, the most necessary question: did she remember him as her husband of nearly fifty years? He got the impression that she would be embarrassed by such a question—embarrassed not for herself but for him.

Kristy told him that Aubrey had been the local representative of a company that sold weed killer "and all that kind of stuff" to farmers. And then when he was not very old or even retired, she said, he had suffered some unusual kind of damage.

"His wife is the one takes care of him, usually at home. She just put him in here on temporary care so she could get a break. Her sister wanted her to go to Florida. See, she's had a hard time, you wouldn't ever have expected a man like him—they just went on a holiday somewhere and he got something, like some bug that gave him a terrible high fever? And it put him in a coma and left him like he is now."

Most afternoons the pair could be found at the card table. Aubrey had large, thick-fingered hands. It was difficult for him to manage his cards. Fiona shuffled and dealt for him and sometimes moved quickly to straighten a card that seemed to be slipping from his grasp. Grant would watch from across the room her darting move and quick laughing apology. He could see Aubrey's husbandly frown as a wisp of her hair touched his cheek. Aubrey preferred to ignore her, as long as she stayed close.

But let her smile her greeting at Grant, let her push back her chair and get up to offer him tea—showing that she had accepted his right to be there—and Aubrey's face took on its look of sombre consternation. He would let the cards slide from his fingers and fall on the floor to spoil the game. And Fiona then had to get busy and put things right.

If Fiona and Aubrey weren't at the bridge table they might be walking along the halls, Aubrey hanging on to the railing with one hand and clutching Fiona's arm or shoulder with the other. The nurses thought that it was a marvel, the way she had got him out of his wheelchair. Though for longer trips—to the conservatory at one end of the building or the television room at the other—the wheelchair was called for.

In the conservatory, the pair would find themselves a seat among the most lush and thick and tropical-looking plants—a bower, if you liked. Grant stood nearby, on occasion, on the other side of the greenery, listening. Mixed in with the rustle of the leaves and the sound of plashing water was Fiona's soft talk and her laughter. Then some sort of chortle. Aubrey could talk, though his voice probably didn't sound as it used to be. He seemed to say something now—a couple of thick syllables.

Take care. He's here. My love.

Grant made an effort, and cut his visits down to Wednesdays and Saturdays. Saturdays had a holiday bustle and tension. Families arrived in clusters. Mothers were usually in charge; they were the ones who kept the conversation afloat. Men seemed cowed, teen-agers affronted. No children or grandchildren appeared to visit Aubrey, and since they could not play cards—the tables being taken over for ice-cream parties—he and Fiona stayed clear of the Saturday parade. The conservatory was far too popular then for any of their intimate conversations. Those might be going on, of course, behind Fiona's closed door. Grant could not manage to knock when he found it closed, though he stood there for some time staring at the Disney-style nameplate with an intense, a truly malignant dislike.

Or they might be in Aubrey's room. But he did not know where that was. The more he explored this place the more corridors and seating spaces and ramps he discovered, and in his wanderings he was still apt to get lost. One Saturday he looked out a window and saw Fiona—it had to be her—wheeling Aubrey along one of the paved paths now cleared of snow and ice. She was wearing a silly wool hat and a jacket with swirls of blue and purple, the sort of thing he had seen on local women at the supermarket. It must be that they didn't bother to sort out the wardrobes of the women who were roughly the same size and counted on the women not to recognize their own clothes anyway. They had cut her hair, too. They had cut away her angelic halo.

On a Wednesday, when everything was more normal and card games were going on again and the women in the Crafts Room were making silk flowers or costumed dolls—and when Aubrey and Fiona were again in evidence, so that it was possible for Grant to have one of his brief and friendly and maddening conversations with his wife—he said to her, "Why did they chop off your hair?"

Fiona put her hands up to her head, to check.

"Why—I never missed it," she said.

When Grant had first started teaching Anglo-Saxon and Nordic literature he got the regular sort of students in his classes. But after a few years he noticed a change. Married women had started going back to school. Not with the idea of qualifying for a better job, or for any job, but simply to give themselves something more interesting to think about than their usual housework and hobbies. To enrich their lives. And perhaps it followed naturally that the men who taught them these things became part of the enrichment, that these men seemed to these women more mysterious and desirable than the men they still cooked for and slept with.

Those who signed up for Grant's courses might have a Scandinavian background or they might have learned something about Norse mythology from Wagner or historical novels. There were also a few who thought he was teaching a Celtic language and for whom everything Celtic had a mystic allure. He spoke to such aspirants fairly roughly from his side of the desk.

"If you want to learn a pretty language go and learn Spanish. Then you can use it if you go to Mexico."

Some took his warning and drifted away. Others seemed to be moved in a personal way by his demanding tone. They worked with a will and brought into his office, into his regulated satisfactory life, the great surprising bloom of their mature female compliance, their tremulous hope of approval.

He chose a woman named Jacqui Adams. She was the opposite of Fiona—short, cushiony, dark-eyed, effusive. A stranger to irony. The affair lasted for a year, until her husband was transferred. When they were saying goodbye in her car, she began to shake uncontrollably. It was as if she had hypothermia. She wrote to him a few times, but he found the tone of her letters overwrought and could not decide how to answer. He let the time for answering slip away while he became magically and unexpectedly involved with a girl who was young enough to be Jacqui's daughter.

For another and more dizzying development had taken place while he was busy with Jacqui. Young girls with long hair and sandalled feet were coming into his office and all but declaring themselves ready for sex. The cautious approaches, the tender intimations of feeling required with Jacqui were out the window. A whirlwind hit him, as it did many others. Scandals burst wide open, with high and painful drama all round but a feeling that somehow it was better so. There were reprisals; there were firings. But those fired went off to teach at smaller, more tolerant colleges or Open Learning Centers, and many wives left behind got over the shock and took up the costumes, the sexual nonchalance of the girls who had tempted their men. Academic parties, which used to be so predictable, became a minefield. An epidemic had broken out, it was spreading like the Spanish flu. Only this time people ran after contagion, and few between sixteen and sixty seemed willing to be left out.

That was exaggeration, of course. Fiona was quite willing. And Grant himself did not go overboard. What he felt was mainly a gigantic increase in well-being. A tendency to pudginess which he had had since he was twelve years old disappeared. He ran up steps two at a time. He appreciated as never before a pageant of torn clouds and winter sunsets seen from his office window, the charm of antique lamps glowing between his neighbors' living-room curtains, the cries of children in the park, at dusk, unwilling to leave the hill where they'd been tobogganing. Come summer, he learned the names of flowers. In his classroom, after being coached by his nearly voiceless mother-in-law (her affliction was cancer in the throat), he risked reciting the majestic and gory Icelandic ode, the Höfudlausn, composed to honor King Erik Blood-axe by the skald whom that king had condemned to death.

Fiona had never learned Icelandic and she had never shown much respect for the stories that it preserved—the stories that Grant had taught and written about. She referred to their heroes as "old Njal" or "old Snorri." But in the last few years she had developed an interest in the country itself and looked at travel guides. She read about William Morris's trip, and Auden's. She didn't really plan to travel there. She said there ought to be one place you thought about and knew about and maybe longed for but never did get to see.

Nonetheless, the next time he went to Meadowlake, Grant brought Fiona a book he'd found of nineteenth-century watercolors made by a lady traveller to Iceland. It was a Wednesday. He went looking for her at the card tables but didn't see her. A woman called out to him, "She's not here. She's sick."

Her voice sounded self-important and excited—pleased with herself for having recognized him when he knew nothing about her. Perhaps also pleased with all she knew about Fiona, about Fiona's life here, thinking it was maybe more than he knew.

"He's not here, either," she added.

Grant went to find Kristy, who didn't have much time for him. She was talking to a weepy woman who looked like a first-time visitor.

"Nothing really," she said, when he asked what was the matter with Fiona. "She's just having a day in bed today, just a bit of an upset."

Fiona was sitting straight up in the bed. He hadn't noticed, the few times that he had been in this room, that this was a hospital bed and could be cranked up in such a way. She was wearing one of her high-necked maidenly gowns, and her face had a pallor that was like flour paste.

Aubrey was beside her in his wheelchair, pushed as close to the bed as he could get. Instead of the nondescript open-necked shirts he usually wore, he was wearing a jacket and tie. His natty-looking tweed hat was resting on the bed. He looked as if he had been out on important business.

Whatever he'd been doing, he looked worn out by it. He, too, was gray in the face.

They both looked up at Grant with a stony grief-ridden apprehension that turned to relief, if not to welcome, when they saw who he was. Not who they thought he'd be. They were hanging on to each other's hands and they did not let go.

The hat on the bed. The jacket and tie.

It wasn't that Aubrey had been out. It wasn't a question of where he'd been or whom he'd been to see. It was where he was going.

Grant set the book down on the bed beside Fiona's free hand.

"It's about Iceland," he said. "I thought may be you'd like to look at it."

"Why, thank you," said Fiona. She didn't look at the book.

"Iceland," he said.

She said, "Ice-land." The first syllable managed to hold a tinkle of interest, but the second fell flat. Anyway, it was necessary for her to turn her attention back to Aubrey, who was pulling his great thick hand out of hers.

"What is it?" she said. "What is it, dear heart?"

Grant had never heard her use this flowery expression before.

"Oh all right," she said. "Oh here." And she pulled a handful of tissues from the box beside her bed. Aubrey had begun to weep.

"Here. Here," she said, and he got hold of the Kleenex as well as he could and made a few awkward but lucky swipes at his face. While he was occupied, Fiona turned to Grant.

"Do you by any chance have any influence around here?" she said in a whisper. "I've seen you talking to them . . ."

Aubrey made a noise of protest or weariness or disgust. Then his upper body pitched forward as if he wanted to throw himself against her. She scrambled half out of bed and caught him and held on to him. It seemed improper for Grant to help her.

"Hush," Fiona was saying. "Oh, honey. Hush. We'll get to see each other. We'll have to. I'll go and see you. You'll come and see me."

Aubrey made the same sound again with his face in her chest and there was nothing Grant could decently do but get out of the room.

"I just wish his wife would hurry up and get here," Kristy said when he ran into her. "I wish she'd get him out of here and cut the agony short. We've got to start serving supper before long and how are we supposed to get her to swallow anything with him still hanging around?"

Grant said, "Should I stay?"

"What for? She's not sick, you know."

"To keep her company," he said.

Kristy shook her head.

"They have to get over these things on their own. They've got short memories, usually. That's not always so bad."

Grant left without going back to Fiona's room. He noticed that the wind was actually warm and the crows were making an uproar. In the parking lot a woman wearing a tartan pants suit was getting a folded-up wheelchair out of the trunk of her car.

Fiona did not get over her sorrow. She didn't eat at mealtimes, though she pretended to, hiding food in her napkin. She was being given a supplementary drink twice a day—someone stayed and watched while she swallowed it down. She got out of bed and dressed herself, but all she wanted to do then was sit in her room. She wouldn't have had any exercise at all if Kristy, or Grant during visiting hours, hadn't walked her up and down in the corridors or taken her outside. Weeping had left her eyes raw-edged and dim. Her cardigan—if it was hers—would be buttoned crookedly. She had not got to the stage of leaving her hair unbrushed or her nails uncleaned, but that might come soon. Kristy said that her muscles were deteriorating, and that if she didn't improve they would put her on a walker.

"But, you know, once they get a walker they start to depend on it and they never walk much anymore, just get wherever it is they have to go," she said to Grant. "You'll have to work at her harder. Try to encourage her."

But Grant had no luck at that. Fiona seemed to have taken a dislike to him, though she tried to cover it up. Perhaps she was reminded, every time she saw him, of her last minutes with Aubrey, when she had asked him for help and he hadn't helped her.

He didn't see much point in mentioning their marriage now.

The supervisor called him in to her office. She said that Fiona's weight was going down even with the supplement.

"The thing is, I'm sure you know, we don't do any prolonged bed care on the first floor. We do it temporarily if someone isn't feeling well, but if they get too weak to move around and be responsible we have to consider upstairs."

He said he didn't think that Fiona had been in bed that often.

"No. But if she can't keep up her strength she will be. Right now she's borderline."

Grant said that he had thought the second floor was for people whose minds were disturbed.

"That, too," she said.

The street Grant found himself driving down was called Blackhawks Lane. The houses all looked to have been built around the same time, perhaps thirty or forty years ago. The street was wide and curving and there were no sidewalks. Friends of Grant and Fiona's had moved to places something like this when they began to have their children, and young families still lived here. There were basketball hoops over garage doors and tricycles in the driveways. Some of the houses had gone downhill. The yards were marked by tire tracks, the windows plastered with tinfoil or hung with faded flags. But a few seemed to have been kept up as well as possible by the people who had moved into them when they were new—people who hadn't had the money or perhaps hadn't felt the need to move on to some place better.

The house that was listed in the phone book as belonging to Aubrey and his wife was one of these. The front walk was paved with flagstones and bordered by hyacinths that stood as stiff as china flowers, alternately pink and blue.

He hadn't remembered anything about Aubrey's wife except the tartan suit he had seen her wearing in the parking lot. The tails of the jacket had flared open as she bent into the trunk of the car. He had got the impression of a trim waist and wide buttocks.

She was not wearing the tartan suit today. Brown belted slacks and a pink sweater. He was right about the waist—the tight belt showed she made a point of it. It might have been better if she didn't, since she bulged out considerably above and below.

She could be ten or twelve years younger than her husband. Her hair was short, curly, artificially reddened. She had blue eyes—a lighter blue than Fiona's—a flat robin's-egg or turquoise blue, slanted by a slight puffiness. And a good many wrinkles, made more noticeable by a walnut-stain makeup. Or perhaps that was her Florida tan.

He said that he didn't quite know how to introduce himself.

"I used to see your husband at Meadowlake. I'm a regular visitor there myself."

"Yes," said Aubrey's wife, with an aggressive movement of her chin.

"How is your husband doing?"

The "doing" was added on at the last moment.

"He's O.K.," she said.

"My wife and he struck up quite a close friendship."

"I heard about that."

"I wanted to talk to you about something if you had a minute."

"My husband did not try to start anything with your wife if that's what you're getting at," she said. "He did not molest her. He isn't capable of it and he wouldn't anyway. From what I heard it was the other way round."

Grant said, "No. That isn't it at all. I didn't come here with any complaints about anything."

"Oh," she said. "Well, I'm sorry. I thought you did. You better come in then. It's blowing cold in through the door. It's not as warm out today as it looks."

So it was something of a victory for him even to get inside.

She took him past the living room, saying, "We'll have to sit in the kitchen, where I can hear Aubrey."

Grant caught sight of two layers of front-window curtains, both blue, one sheer and one silky, a matching blue sofa and a daunting pale carpet, various bright mirrors and ornaments. Fiona had a word for those sort of swooping curtains—she said it like a joke, though the women she'd picked it up from used it seriously. Any room that Fiona fixed up was bare and bright. She would have deplored the crowding of all this fancy stuff into such a small space. From a room off the kitchen—a sort of sunroom, though the blinds were drawn against the afternoon brightness—he could hear the sounds of television.

The answer to Fiona's prayers sat a few feet away, watching what sounded like a ballgame. His wife looked in at him.

She said, "You O.K.?" and partly closed the door.

"You might as well have a cup of coffee," she said to Grant. "My son got him on the sports channel a year ago Christmas. I don't know what we'd do without it."

On the kitchen counters there were all sorts of contrivances and appliances—coffeemaker, food processor, knife sharpener, and some things Grant didn't know the names or uses of. All looked new and expensive, as if they had just been taken out of their wrappings, or were polished daily.

He thought it might be a good idea to admire things. He admired the coffeemaker she was using and said that he and Fiona had always meant to get one. This was absolutely untrue—Fiona had been devoted to a European contraption that made only two cups at a time.

"They gave us that," she said. "Our son and his wife. They live in Kamloops. B.C. They send us more stuff than we can handle. It wouldn't hurt if they would spend the money to come and see us instead."

Grant said philosophically, "I suppose they're busy with their own lives."

"They weren't too busy to go to Hawaii last winter. You could understand it if we had somebody else in the family, closer at hand. But he's the only one."

She poured the coffee into two brown-and-green ceramic mugs that she took from the amputated branches of a ceramic tree trunk that sat on the table.

"People do get lonely," Grant said. He thought he saw his chance now. "If they're deprived of seeing somebody they care about, they do feel sad. Fiona, for instance. My wife."

"I thought you said you went and visited her."

"I do," he said. "That's not it."

Then he took the plunge, going on to make the request he'd come to make. Could she consider taking Aubrey back to Meadowlake, maybe just one day a week, for a visit? It was only a drive of a few miles. Or if she'd like to take the time off—Grant hadn't thought of this before and was rather dismayed to hear himself suggest it—then he himself could take Aubrey out there, he wouldn't mind at all. He was sure he could manage it. While he talked she moved her closed lips and her hidden tongue as if she were trying to identify some dubious flavor. She brought milk for his coffee and a plate of ginger cookies.

"Homemade," she said as she set the plate down. There was challenge rather than hospitality in her tone. She said nothing more until she had sat down, poured milk into her coffee, and stirred it.

Then she said no.

"No. I can't do that. And the reason is, I'm not going to upset him."

"Would it upset him?" Grant said earnestly.

"Yes, it would. It would. That's no way to do. Bringing him home and taking him back. That would just confuse him."

"But wouldn't he understand that it was just a visit? Wouldn't he get into the pattern of it?"

"He understands everything all right." She said this as if he had offered an insult to Aubrey. "But it's still an interruption. And then I've got to get him all ready and get him into the car, and he's a big man, he's not so easy to manage as you might think. I've got to maneuver him into the car and pack his chair and all that and what for? If I go to all that trouble I'd prefer to take him someplace that was more fun."

"But even if I agreed to do it?" Grant said, keeping his tone hopeful and reasonable. "It's true, you shouldn't have the trouble."

"You couldn't," she said flatly. "You don't know him. You couldn't handle him. He wouldn't stand for you doing for him. All that bother and what would he get out of it?"

Grant didn't think he should mention Fiona again.

"It'd make more sense to take him to the mall," she said. "Or now the lake boats are starting to run again, he might get a charge out of going and watching that."

She got up and fetched her cigarettes and lighter from the window above the sink.

"You smoke?" she said.

He said no, thanks, though he didn't know if a cigarette was being offered.

"Did you never? Or did you quit?"

"Quit," he said.

"How long ago was that?"

He thought about it.

"Thirty years. No—more."

He had decided to quit around the time he started up with Jacqui. But he couldn't remember whether he quit first, and thought a big reward was coming to him for quitting, or thought that the time had come to quit, now that he had such a powerful diversion.

"I've quit quitting," she said, lighting up. "Just made a resolution to quit quitting, that's all."

Maybe that was the reason for the wrinkles. Somebody—a woman— had told him that women who smoked developed a special set of fine facial wrinkles. But it could have been from the sun, or just the nature of her skin—her neck was noticeably wrinkled as well. Wrinkled neck, youthfully full and uptilted breasts. Women of her age usually had these contradictions. The bad and good points, the genetic luck or lack of it, all mixed up together. Very few kept their beauty whole, though shadowy, as Fiona had done. And perhaps that wasn't even true. Perhaps he only thought that because he'd known Fiona when she was young. When Aubrey looked at his wife did he see a high-school girl full of scorn and sass, with a tilt to her blue eyes, pursing her fruity lips around a forbidden cigarette?

"So your wife's depressed?" Aubrey's wife said. "What's your wife's name? I forget."

"It's Fiona."

"Fiona. And what's yours? I don't think I was ever told that."

Grant said, "It's Grant."

She stuck her hand out unexpectedly across the table.

"Hello, Grant. I'm Marian."

"So now we know each other's names," she said, "there's no point in not telling you straight out what I think. I don't know if he's still so stuck on seeing your—on seeing Fiona. Or not. I don't ask him and he's not telling me.

"Maybe just a passing fancy. But I don't feel like taking him back there in case it turns out to be more than that. I can't afford to risk it. I don't want him upset and carrying on. I've got my hands full with him as it is. I don't have any help. It's just me here. I'm it."

"Did you ever consider—I'm sure it's very hard for you—" Grant said. "Did you ever consider his going in there for good?"

He had lowered his voice almost to a whisper but she did not seem to feel a need to lower hers.

"No," she said. "I'm keeping him right here."

Grant said, "Well. That's very good and noble of you." He hoped the word "noble" had not sounded sarcastic. He had not meant it to be.

"You think so?" she said. "Noble is not what I'm thinking about."

"Still. It's not easy."

"No, it isn't. But the way I am, I don't have much choice. I don't have the money to put him in there unless I sell the house. The house is what we own outright. Otherwise I don't have anything in the way of resources. Next year I'll have his pension and my pension, but even so I couldn't afford to keep him there and hang on to the house. And it means a lot to me, my house does."

"It's very nice," said Grant.

"Well, it's all right. I put a lot into it. Fixing it up and keeping it up. I don't want to lose it."

"No. I see your point."

"The company left us high and dry," she said. "I don't know all the ins and outs of it but basically he got shoved out. It ended up with them saying he owed them money and when I tried to find out what was what he just went on saying it's none of my business. What I think is he did something pretty stupid. But I'm not supposed to ask so I shut up. You've been married. You are married. You know how it is. And in the middle of me finding out about this we're supposed to go on this trip and can't get out of it. And on the trip he takes sick from this virus you never heard of and goes into a coma. So that pretty well gets him off the hook."

Grant said, "Bad luck."

"I don't mean he got sick on purpose. It just happened. He's not mad at me anymore and I'm not mad at him. It's just life. You can't beat life."

She flicked her tongue in a cat's businesslike way across her top lip, getting the cookie crumbs. "I sound like I'm quite the philosopher, don't I? They told me out there you used to be a university professor."

"Quite a while ago," Grant said.

"I bet I know what you're thinking," she said. "You're thinking there's a mercenary type of a person."

"I'm not making judgments of that sort. It's your life."

"You bet it is."

He thought they should end on a more neutral note. So he asked her if her husband had worked in a hardware store in the summers, when he was going to school.

"I never heard about it," she said. "I wasn't raised here."

Grant realized he'd failed with Aubrey's wife. Marian. He had thought that what he'd have to contend with would be a woman's natural sexual jealousy—or her resentment, the stubborn remains of sexual jealousy. He had not had any idea of the way she might be looking at things. And yet in some depressing way the conversation had not been unfamiliar to him. That was because it reminded him of conversations he'd had with people in his own family. His relatives, probably even his mother, had thought the way Marian thought. Money first. They had believed that when other people did not think that way it was because they had lost touch with reality. That was how Marian would see him, certainly. A silly person, full of boring knowledge and protected by some fluke from the truth about life. A person who didn't have to worry about holding on to his house and could go around dreaming up the fine generous schemes that he believed would make another person happy. What a jerk, she would be thinking now.

Being up against a person like that made him feel hopeless, exasperated, finally almost desolate. Why? Because he couldn't be sure of holding on to himself, against people like that? Because he was afraid that in the end they were right? Yet he might have married her. Or some girl like that. If he'd stayed back where he belonged. She'd have been appetizing enough. Probably a flirt. The fussy way she had of shifting her buttocks on the kitchen chair, her pursed mouth, a slightly contrived air of menace—that was what was left of the more or less innocent vulgarity of a small-town flirt.

She must have had some hopes when she picked Aubrey. His good looks, his salesman's job, his white-collar expectations. She must have believed that she would end up better off than she was now. And so it often happened with those practical people. In spite of their calculations, their survival instincts, they might not get as far as they had quite reasonably expected. No doubt it seemed unfair.

In the kitchen the first thing he saw was the light blinking on his answering machine. He thought the same thing he always thought now. Fiona. He pressed the button before he took his coat off.

"Hello, Grant. I hope I got the right person. I just thought of something. There is a dance here in town at the Legion supposed to be for singles on Saturday night and I am on the lunch committee, which means I can bring a free guest. So I wondered whether you would happen to be interested in that? Call me back when you get a chance."

A woman's voice gave a local number. Then there was a beep and the same voice started talking again.

"I just realized I'd forgotten to say who it was. Well, you probably recognized the voice. It's Marian. I'm still not so used to these machines. And I wanted to say I realize you're not a single and I don't mean it that way. I'm not either, but it doesn't hurt to get out once in a while. If you are interested you can call me and if you are not you don't need to bother. I just thought you might like the chance to get out. It's Marian speaking. I guess I already said that. O.K. then. Goodbye."

Her voice on the machine was different from the voice he'd heard a short time ago in her house. Just a little different in the first message, more so in the second. A tremor of nerves there, an affected nonchalance, a hurry to get through and a reluctance to let go.

Something had happened to her. But when had it happened? If it had been immediate, she had concealed it very successfully all the time he was with her. More likely it came on her gradually, maybe after he'd gone away. Not necessarily as a blow of attraction. Just the realization that he was a possibility, a man on his own. More or less on his own. A possibility that she might as well try to follow up.

But she'd had the jitters when she made the first move. She had put herself at risk. How much of herself he could not yet tell. Generally a woman's vulnerability increased as time went on, as things progressed. All you could tell at the start was that if there was an edge of it then, there'd be more later. It gave him a satisfaction—why deny it?—to have brought that out in her. To have roused something like a shimmer, a blurring, on the surface of her personality. To have heard in her testy broad vowels this faint plea.

He set out the eggs and mushrooms to make himself an omelette. Then he thought he might as well pour a drink.

Anything was possible. Was that true—was anything possible? For instance, if he wanted to, would he be able to break her down, get her to the point where she might listen to him about taking Aubrey back to Fiona? And not just for visits but for the rest of Aubrey's life. And what would become of him and Marian after he'd delivered Aubrey to Fiona?

Marian would be sitting in her house now, waiting for him to call. Or probably not sitting. Doing things to keep herself busy. She might have fed Aubrey while Grant was buying the mushrooms and driving home. She might now be preparing him for bed. But all the time she would be conscious of the phone, of the silence of the phone. Maybe she would have calculated how long it would take Grant to drive home. His address in the phone book would have given her a rough idea of where he lived. She would calculate how long, then add to that the time it might take him to shop for supper (figuring that a man alone would shop every day). Then a certain amount of time for him to get around to listening to his messages. And as the silence persisted she'd think of other things. Other errands he might have had to do before he got home. Or perhaps a dinner out, a meeting that meant he would not get home at suppertime at all.

What conceit on his part. She was above all things a sensible woman. She would go to bed at her regular time thinking that he didn't look as if he'd be a decent dancer anyway. Too stiff, too professorial.

He stayed near the phone, looking at magazines, but he didn't pick it up when it rang again.

"Grant. This is Marian. I was down in the basement putting the wash in the dryer and I heard the phone and when I got upstairs whoever it was had hung up. So I just thought I ought to say I was here. If it was you and if you are even home. Because I don't have a machine, obviously, so you couldn't leave a message. So I just wanted. To let you know." The time was now twenty-five after ten.

"Bye."

He would say that he'd just got home. There was no point in bringing to her mind the picture of his sitting here weighing the pros and cons.

Drapes. That would be her word for the blue curtains—drapes. And why not? He thought of the ginger cookies so perfectly round that she had to announce they were homemade, the ceramic coffee mugs on their ceramic tree, a plastic runner, he was sure, protecting the hall carpet. A high-gloss exactness and practicality that his mother had never achieved but would have admired—was that why he could feel this twinge of bizarre and unreliable affection? Or was it because he'd had two more drinks after the first?

The walnut-stain tan—he believed now that it was a tan—of her face and neck would most likely continue into her cleavage, which would be deep, crêpey-skinned, odorous and hot. He had that to think of as he dialled the number that he had already written down. That and the practical sensuality of her cat's tongue. Her gemstone eyes.

Fiona was in her room but not in bed. She was sitting by the open window, wearing a seasonable but oddly short and bright dress. Through the window came a heady warm blast of lilacs in bloom and the spring manure spread over the fields.

She had a book open in her lap.

She said, "Look at this beautiful book I found. It's about Iceland. You wouldn't think they'd leave valuable books lying around in the rooms. But I think they've got the clothes mixed up—I never wear yellow."

"Fiona," he said.

"Are we all checked out now?" she said. He thought the brightness of her voice was wavering a little. "You've been gone a long time."

"Fiona, I've brought a surprise for you. Do you remember Aubrey?"

She stared at Grant for a moment, as if waves of wind had come beating into her face. Into her face, into her head, pulling everything to rags. All rags and loose threads.

"Names elude me," she said harshly.

Then the look passed away as she retrieved, with an effort, some bantering grace. She set the book down carefully and stood up and lifted her arms to put them around him. Her skin or her breath gave off a faint new smell, a smell that seemed to Grant like green stems in rank water.

"I'm happy to see you," she said, both sweetly and formally. She pinched his earlobes, hard.

"You could have just driven away," she said. "Just driven away without a care in the world and forsook me. Forsooken me. Forsaken."

He kept his face against her white hair, her pink scalp, her sweetly shaped skull.

He said, "Not a chance."

RAYMOND CARVER ■ (1938–1988)

As a master of the contemporary short story, Raymond Carver built a reputa-tion that was still growing at the end of his life, which came prematurely after a long struggle with cancer. A native of Clatskanie, Oregon, Carver worked at a number of unskilled jobs in his early years. Married and the father of two before he was 20, he knew the working class more intimately than have most American writers. Carver worked his way through Hum-boldt State College (now the University of California–Humboldt) and, like many major figures in contemporary American writing, was a graduate of the Writers' Workshop of the University of Iowa. Carver's publishing career is bracketed by collections of poetry; his earliest publications were poems, and A New Path to the Waterfall appeared posthumously in 1989. The compression of language he learned as a poet may in part account for the lean quality of his prose, which has been called, perhaps unfairly and inaccurately, "minimalist." Carver's last years were spent with his second wife, poet Tess Gallagher, and he taught at a number of universities. His personal victory over alcoholism paralleled the remarkable triumphs of his final years, which included receipt of a prestigious MacArthur Foundation Fellowship. Where I'm Calling From: New and Selected Stories was prepared by Carver shortly before his death and appeared in 1988, and Call If You Need Me, a volume of his uncollected stories and prose, was published in 2000. Several Carver stories were filmed by Robert Altman in his 1993 movie Short Cuts.

Cathedral

This blind man, an old friend of my wife's, he was on his way to spend the night. His wife had died. So he was visiting the dead wife's relatives in Connecticut. He called my wife from his in-laws'. Arrangements were made. He would come by train, a five-hour trip, and my wife would meet him at the station. She hadn't seen him since she worked for him one summer in Seattle ten years ago. But she and the blind man had kept in touch. They made tapes and mailed them back and forth. I wasn't enthusiastic about his visit. He was no one I knew. And his being blind bothered me. My idea of blindness came from the movies. In the movies, the blind moved slowly and never laughed. Sometimes they were led by seeing-eye dogs. A blind man in my house was not something I looked forward to.

That summer in Seattle she had needed a job. She didn't have any money. The man she was going to marry at the end of the summer was in officers' training school. He didn't have any money, either. But she was in love with the guy, and he was in love with her, etc. She'd seen something in the paper: HELP—*Reading to Blind Man*, and a telephone number. She phoned and went over, was hired on the spot. She'd worked with this blind man all summer. She read stuff to him, case studies, reports, that sort of thing. She helped him organize his little office in the county social-service department. They'd become good friends, my wife and the blind man. How do I know these things? She told me. And she told me something else. On her last day in the office, the blind man asked if he could touch her face. She agreed to this. She told me he touched his fingers to every part of her face, her nose—even her neck! She never forgot it. She even tried to write a poem about it. She was always trying to write a poem. She wrote a poem or two every year, usually after something really important had happened to her.

When we first started going out together, she showed me the poem. In the poem, she recalled his fingers and the way they had moved around over her face. In the poem, she talked about what she had felt at the time, about what went through her mind when the blind man touched her nose and lips. I can remember I didn't think much of the poem. Of course, I didn't tell her that. Maybe I just don't understand poetry. I admit it's not the first thing I reach for when I pick up something to read.

Anyway, this man who'd first enjoyed her favors, the officer-to-be, he'd been her childhood sweetheart. So okay. I'm saying that at the end of the summer she let the blind man run his hands over her face, said good-bye to him, married her childhood sweetheart etc., who was now a commissioned officer, and she moved away from Seattle. But they'd kept in touch, she and the blind man. She made the first contact after a year or so. She called him up one night from an Air Force base in Alabama. She wanted to talk. They talked. He asked her to send a tape and tell him about her life. She did this. She sent the tape. On the tape, she told the blind man about her husband and about their life together in the military. She told the blind man she loved her husband but she didn't like it where they lived and she didn't like it that he was part of the military-industrial thing. She told the blind man she'd written a poem and he was in it. She told him that she was writing a poem about what it was like to be an Air Force officer's wife. The poem wasn't finished yet. She was still writing it. The blind man made a tape. He sent her the tape. She made a tape. This went on for years. My wife's officer was posted to one base and then another. She sent tapes from Moody AFB, McGuire, McConnell, and finally Travis, near Sacramento, where one night she got to feeling lonely and cut off from people she kept losing in that moving-around life. She got to feeling she couldn't go it another step. She went in and swallowed all the pills and capsules in the medicine chest and washed them down with a bottle of gin. Then she got into a hot bath and passed out.

But instead of dying, she got sick. She threw up. Her officer—why should he have a name? he was the childhood sweetheart, and what more does he want?—came home from somewhere, found her, and called the ambulance. In time, she put it all on a tape and sent the tape to the blind man. Over the years, she put all kinds of stuff on tapes and sent the tapes off lickety-split. Next to writing a poem every year, I think it was her chief means of recreation. On one tape, she told the blind man she'd decided to live away from her officer for a time. On another tape, she told him about her divorce. She and I began going out, and of course she told her blind man about it. She told him everything, or so it seemed to me. Once she asked me if I'd like to hear the latest tape from the blind man. This was a year ago. I was on the tape, she said. So I said okay, I'd listen to it. I got us drinks and we settled down in the living room. We made ready to listen. First she inserted the tape into the player and adjusted a couple of dials. Then she pushed a lever. The tape squeaked and someone began to talk in this loud voice. She lowered the volume. After a few minutes of harmless chitchat, I heard my own name in the mouth of this stranger, this blind man I didn't even know! And then this: "From all you've said about him, I can only conclude—" But we were interrupted, a knock at the door, something, and we didn't ever get back to the tape. Maybe it was just as well. I'd heard all I wanted to.

Now this same blind man was coming to sleep in my house.

"Maybe I could take him bowling," I said to my wife. She was at the draining board doing scalloped potatoes. She put down the knife she was using and turned around.

"If you love me," she said, "you can do this for me. If you don't love me, okay. But if you had a friend, any friend, and the friend came to visit, I'd make him feel comfortable." She wiped her hands with the dish towel.

"I don't have any blind friends," I said.

"You don't have *any* friends," she said. "Period. Besides," she said, "goddamn it, his wife's just died! Don't you understand that? The man's lost his wife!"

I didn't answer. She'd told me a little about the blind man's wife. Her name was Beulah. Beulah! That's a name for a colored woman.

"Was his wife a Negro?" I asked.

"Are you crazy?" my wife said. "Have you just flipped or something?" She picked up a potato. I saw it hit the floor, then roll under the stove. "What's wrong with you?" she said. "Are you drunk?"

"I'm just asking," I said.

Right then my wife filled me in with more detail than I cared to know. I made a drink and sat at the kitchen table to listen. Pieces of the story began to fall into place.

Beulah had gone to work for the blind man the summer after my wife had stopped working for him. Pretty soon Beulah and the blind man had themselves a church wedding. It was a little wedding—who'd want to go to such a wedding in the first place?—just the two of them, plus the minister and the minister's wife. But it was a church wedding just the same. It was what Beulah had wanted, he'd said. But even then Beulah must have been carrying the cancer in her glands. After they had been inseparable for eight years—my wife's word, *inseparable*—Beulah's health went into a rapid decline. She died in a Seattle hospital room, the blind man sitting beside the bed and holding on to her hand. They'd married, lived and worked together, slept together—had sex, sure—and then the blind man had to bury her. All this without his having ever seen what the goddamned woman looked like. It was beyond my understanding. Hearing this, I felt sorry for the blind man for a little bit. And then I found myself thinking what a pitiful life this woman must have led. Imagine a woman who could never see herself as she was seen in the eyes of her loved one. A woman who could go on day after day and never receive the smallest compliment from her beloved. A woman whose husband could never read the expression on her face, be it misery or something better. Someone who could wear makeup or not—what difference to him? She could, if she wanted, wear green eyeshadow around one eye, a straight pin in her nostril, yellow slacks, and purple shoes, no matter. And then to slip off into death, the blind man's hand on her hand, his blind eyes streaming tears—I'm imagining now—her last thought maybe this: that he never even knew what she looked like, and she on an express to the grave. Robert was left with a small insurance policy and a half of a twenty-peso Mexican coin. The other half of the coin went into the box with her. Pathetic.

So when the time rolled around, my wife went to the depot to pick him up. With nothing to do but wait—sure, I blamed him for that—I was having a drink and watching the TV when I heard the car pull into the drive. I got up from the sofa with my drink and went to the window to have a look.

I saw my wife laughing as she parked the car. I saw her get out of the car and shut the door. She was still wearing a smile. Just amazing. She went around to the other side of the car to where the blind man was already starting to get out. This blind man, feature this, he was wearing a full beard! A beard on a blind man! Too much, I say. The blind man reached into the backseat and dragged out a suitcase. My wife took his arm, shut the car door, and, talking all the way, moved him down the drive and then up the steps to the front porch. I turned off the TV. I finished my drink, rinsed the glass, dried my hands. Then I went to the door.

My wife said, "I want you to meet Robert. Robert, this is my husband. I've told you all about him." She was beaming. She had this blind man by his coat sleeve.

The blind man let go of his suitcase and up came his hand.

I took it. He squeezed hard, held my hand, and then he let it go.

"I feel like we've already met," he boomed.

"Likewise," I said. I didn't know what else to say. Then I said, "Welcome. I've heard a lot about you." We began to move then, a little group, from the porch into the living room, my wife guiding him by the arm. The blind man was carrying his suitcase in his other hand. My wife said things like, "To your left here, Robert. That's right. Now watch it, there's a chair. That's it. Sit down right here. This is the sofa. We just bought this sofa two weeks ago."

I started to say something about the old sofa. I'd liked that old sofa. But I didn't say anything. Then I wanted to say something else, small-talk, about the scenic ride along the Hudson. How going *to* New York, you should sit on the right-hand side of the train, and coming *from* New York, the left-hand side.

"Did you have a good train ride?" I said. "Which side of the train did you sit on, by the way?"

"What a question, which side!" my wife said. "What's it matter which side?" she said.

"I just asked," I said.

"Right side," the blind man said. "I hadn't been on a train in nearly forty years. Not since I was a kid. With my folks. That's been a long time. I'd nearly forgotten the sensation. I have winter in my beard now," he said. "So I've been told, anyway. Do I look distinguished, my dear?" the blind man said to my wife.

"You look distinguished, Robert," she said. "Robert," she said. "Robert, it's just so good to see you."

My wife finally took her eyes off the blind man and looked at me. I had the feeling she didn't like what she saw. I shrugged.

I've never met, or personally known, anyone who was blind. This blind man was late forties, a heavy-set, balding man with stooped shoulders, as if he carried a great weight there. He wore brown slacks, brown shoes, a light-brown shirt, a tie, a sports coat. Spiffy. He also had this full beard. But he didn't use a cane and he didn't wear dark glasses. I'd always thought dark glasses were a must for the blind. Fact was, I wished he had a pair. At first glance, his eyes looked like anyone else's eyes. But if you looked close, there was something different about them. Too much white in the iris, for one thing, and the pupils seemed to move around in the sockets without his knowing it or being able to stop it. Creepy. As I stared at his face, I saw the left pupil turn in toward his nose while the other made an effort to keep in one place. But it was only an effort, for that eye was on the roam without his knowing it or wanting it to be.

I said, "Let me get you a drink. What's your pleasure? We have a little of everything. It's one of our pastimes."

"Bub, I'm a Scotch man myself," he said fast enough in this big voice.

"Right," I said. Bub! "Sure you are. I knew it."

He let his fingers touch his suitcase, which was sitting alongside the sofa. He was taking his bearings. I didn't blame him for that.

"I'll move that up to your room," my wife said.

"No, that's fine," the blind man said loudly. "It can go up when I go up."

"A little water with the Scotch?" I said.

"Very little," he said.

"I knew it," I said.

He said, "Just a tad. The Irish actor, Barry Fitzgerald? I'm like that fellow. When I drink water, Fitzgerald said, I drink water. When I drink whiskey, I drink whiskey." My wife laughed. The blind man brought his hand up under his beard. He lifted his beard slowly and let it drop.

I did the drinks, three big glasses of Scotch with a splash of water in each. Then we made ourselves comfortable and talked about Robert's travels. First the long flight from the West Coast to Connecticut, we covered that. Then from Connecticut up here by train. We had another drink concerning that leg of the trip.

I remembered having read somewhere that the blind didn't smoke because, as speculation had it, they couldn't see the smoke they exhaled. I thought I knew that much and that much only about blind people. But this blind man smoked his cigarette down to the nubbin and then lit another one. This blind man filled his ashtray and my wife emptied it.

When we sat down at the table for dinner, we had another drink. My wife heaped Robert's plate with cube steak, scalloped potatoes, green beans. I buttered him up two slices of bread. I said, "Here's bread and butter for you." I swallowed some of my drink. "Now let us pray," I said, and the blind man lowered his head. My wife looked at me, her mouth agape. "Pray the phone won't ring and the food doesn't get cold," I said.

We dug in. We ate everything there was to eat on the table. We ate like there was no tomorrow. We didn't talk. We ate. We scarfed. We grazed that table. We were into serious eating. The blind man had right away located his foods, he knew just where everything was on his plate. I watched with admiration as he used his knife and fork on the meat. He'd cut two pieces of meat, fork the meat into his mouth, and then go all out for the scalloped potatoes, the beans next, and then he'd tear off a hunk of buttered bread and eat that. He'd follow this up with a big drink of milk. It didn't seem to bother him to use his fingers once in a while, either.

We finished everything, including half a strawberry pie. For a few moments, we sat as if stunned. Sweat beaded on our faces. Finally, we got up from the table and left the dirty plates. We didn't look back. We took ourselves into the living room and sank into our places again. Robert and my wife sat on the sofa. I took the big chair. We had us two or three more drinks while they talked about the major things that had come to pass for them in the past ten years. For the most part, I just listened. Now and then I joined in. I didn't want him to think I'd left the room, and I didn't want her to think I was feeling left out. They talked of things that had happened to them—to them!—these past ten years. I waited in vain to hear my name on my wife's sweet lips: "And then my dear husband came into my life"—something like that. But I heard nothing of the sort. More talk of Robert. Robert had done a little of everything, it seemed, a regular blind jack-of-all-trades. But most recently he and his wife had had an Amway distributorship, from which, I gathered, they'd earned their living, such as it was. The blind man was also a ham radio operator. He talked in his loud voice about conversations he'd had with fellow operators in Guam, in the Philippines, in Alaska, and even in Tahiti. He said he'd have a lot of friends there if he ever wanted to go visit those places. From time to time, he'd turn his blind face toward me, put his hand under his beard, ask me something. How long had I been in my present position? (Three years.) Did I like my work? (I didn't.) Was I going to stay with it? (What were the options?) Finally, when I thought he was beginning to run down, I got up and turned on the TV.

My wife looked at me with irritation. She was heading toward a boil. Then she looked at the blind man and said, "Robert, do you have a TV?"

The blind man said, "My dear, I have two TVs. I have a color set and a black-and-white thing, an old relic. It's funny, but if I turn the TV on, and I'm always turning it on, I turn on the color set. It's funny, don't you think?"

I didn't know what to say to that. I had absolutely nothing to say to that. No opinion. So I watched the news program and tried to listen to what the announcer was saying.

"This is a color TV," the blind man said. "Don't ask me how, but I can tell."

"We traded up a while ago," I said.

The blind man had another taste of his drink. He lifted his beard, sniffed it, and let it fall. He leaned forward on the sofa. He positioned his ashtray on the coffee table, then put the lighter to his cigarette. He leaned back on the sofa and crossed his legs at the ankles.

My wife covered her mouth, and then she yawned. She stretched. She said, "I think I'll go upstairs and put on my robe. I think I'll change into something else. Robert, you make yourself comfortable," she said.

"I'm comfortable," the blind man said.

"I want you to feel comfortable in this house," she said.

"I am comfortable," the blind man said.

After she'd left the room, he and I listened to the weather report and then to the sports roundup. By that time, she'd been gone so long I didn't know if she was going to come back. I thought she might have gone to bed. I wished she'd come back downstairs. I didn't want to be left alone with a blind man. I asked him if he wanted another drink, and he said sure. Then I asked if he wanted to smoke some dope with me. I said I'd just rolled a number. I hadn't, but I planned to do so in about two shakes.

"I'll try some with you," he said.

"Damn right," I said. "That's the stuff."

I got our drinks and sat down on the sofa with him. Then I rolled us two fat numbers. I lit one and passed it. I brought it to his fingers. He took it and inhaled.

"Hold it as long as you can," I said. I could tell he didn't know the first thing.

My wife came back downstairs wearing her pink robe and her pink slippers.

"What do I smell?" she said.

"We thought we'd have us some cannabis," I said.

My wife gave me a savage look. Then she looked at the blind man and said, "Robert, I didn't know you smoked."

He said, "I do now, my dear. There's a first time for everything. But I don't feel anything yet."

"This stuff is pretty mellow," I said. "This stuff is mild. It's dope you can reason with," I said. "It doesn't mess you up."

"Not much it doesn't, bub," he said, and laughed.

My wife sat on the sofa between the blind man and me. I passed her the number. She took it and toked and then passed it back to me. "Which way is this going?" she said. Then she said, "I shouldn't be smoking this. I can hardly keep my eyes open as it is. That dinner did me in. I shouldn't have eaten so much."

"It was the strawberry pie," the blind man said. "That's what did it," he said, and he laughed his big laugh. Then he shook his head.

"There's more strawberry pie," I said.

"Do you want some more, Robert?" my wife said.

"Maybe in a little while," he said.

We gave our attention to the TV. My wife yawned again. She said, "Your bed is made up when you feel like going to bed, Robert. I know you must have had a long day. When you're ready to go to bed, say so." She pulled his arm. "Robert?"

He came to and said, "I've had a real nice time. This beats tapes, doesn't it?"

I said, "Coming at you," and I put the number between his fingers. He inhaled, held the smoke, and then let it go. It was like he'd been doing it since he was nine years old.

"Thanks, bub," he said. "But I think this is all for me. I think I'm beginning to feel it," he said. He held the burning roach out for my wife.

"Same here," she said. "Ditto. Me, too." She took the roach and passed it to me. "I may just sit here for a while between you two guys with my eyes closed. But don't let me bother you, okay? Either one of you. If it bothers you, say so. Otherwise, I may just sit here with my eyes closed until you're ready to go to bed," she said. "Your bed's made up, Robert, when you're ready. It's right next to our room at the top of the stairs. We'll show you up when you're ready. You wake me up now, you guys, if I fall asleep." She said that and then she closed her eyes and went to sleep.

The news program ended. I got up and changed the channel. I sat back down on the sofa. I wished my wife hadn't pooped out. Her head lay across the back of the sofa, her mouth open. She'd turned so that her robe slipped away from her legs, exposing a juicy thigh. I reached to draw her robe back over her, and it was then that I glanced at the blind man. What the hell! I flipped the robe open again.

"You say when you want some strawberry pie," I said.

"I will," he said.

I said, "Are you tired? Do you want me to take you up to your bed? Are you ready to hit the hay?"

"Not yet," he said. "No, I'll stay up with you, bub. If that's all right. I'll stay up until you're ready to turn in. We haven't had a chance to talk. Know what I mean? I feel like me and her monopolized the evening." He lifted his beard and he let it fall. He picked up his cigarettes and his lighter.

"That's all right," I said. Then I said, "I'm glad for the company."

And I guess I was. Every night I smoked dope and stayed up as long as I could before I fell asleep. My wife and I hardly ever went to bed at the same time. When I did go to sleep, I had these dreams. Sometimes I'd wake up from one of them, my heart going crazy.

Something about the church and the Middle Ages was on the TV. Not your run-of-the-mill TV fare. I wanted to watch something else. I turned to the other channels. But there was nothing on them, either. So I turned back to the first channel and apologized.

"Bub, it's all right," the blind man said. "It's fine with me. Whatever you want to watch is okay. I'm always learning something. Learning never ends. It won't hurt me to learn something tonight. I got ears," he said.

We didn't say anything for a time. He was leaning forward with his head turned at me, his right ear aimed in the direction of the set. Very disconcerting. Now and then his eyelids drooped and then they snapped open again. Now and then he put his fingers into his beard and tugged, like he was thinking about something he was hearing on the television.

On the screen, a group of men wearing cowls was being set upon and tormented by men dressed in skeleton costumes and men dressed as devils. The men dressed as devils wore devil masks, horns, and long tails. This pageant was part of a procession. The Englishman who was narrating the thing said it took place in Spain once a year. I tried to explain to the blind man what was happening.

"Skeletons," he said. "I know about skeletons," he said, and he nodded.

The TV showed this one cathedral. Then there was a long, slow look at another one. Finally, the picture switched to the famous one in Paris, with its flying buttresses and its spires reaching up to the clouds. The camera pulled away to show the whole of the cathedral rising above the skyline.

There were times when the Englishman who was telling the thing would shut up, would simply let the camera move around the cathedrals. Or else the camera would tour the countryside, men in fields walking behind oxen. I waited as long as I could. Then I felt I had to say something. I said, "They're showing the outside of this cathedral now. Gargoyles. Little statues carved to look like monsters. Now I guess they're in Italy. Yeah, they're in Italy. There's paintings on the walls of this one church."

"Are those fresco paintings, bub?" he asked, and he sipped from his drink.

I reached for my glass. But it was empty. I tried to remember what I could remember. "You're asking me are those frescoes?" I said. "That's a good question. I don't know."

The camera moved to a cathedral outside Lisbon. The differences in the Portuguese cathedral compared with the French and Italian were not that great. But they were there. Mostly the interior stuff. Then something occurred to me, and I said, "Something has occurred to me. Do you have any idea what a cathedral is? What they look like, that is? Do you follow me? If somebody says cathedral to you, do you have any notion what they're talking about? Do you know the difference between that and a Baptist church, say?"

He let the smoke dribble from his mouth. "I know they took hundreds of workers fifty or a hundred years to build," he said. "I just heard the man say that, of course. I know generations of the same families worked on a cathedral. I heard him say that, too. The men who began their life's work on them, they never lived to see the completion of their work. In that wise, bub, they're no different from the rest of us, right?" He laughed. Then his eyelids drooped again. His head nodded. He seemed to be snoozing. Maybe he was imagining himself in Portugal. The TV was showing another cathedral now. This one was in Germany. The Englishman's voice droned on. "Cathedrals," the blind man said. He sat up and rolled his head back and forth. "If you want the truth, bub, that's about all I know. What I just said. What I heard him say. But maybe you could describe one to me? I wish you'd do it. I'd like that. If you want to know. I really don't have a good idea."

I stared hard at the shot of the cathedral on the TV. How could I even begin to describe it? But say my life depended on it. Say my life was being threatened by an insane guy who said I had to do it or else.

I stared some more at the cathedral before the picture flipped off into the countryside. There was no use. I turned to the blind man and said, "To begin with, they're very tall." I was looking around the room for clues. "They reach way up. Up and up. Toward the sky. They're so big, some of them, they have to have these supports. To help hold them up, so to speak. These supports are called buttresses. They remind me of viaducts, for some reason. But maybe you don't know viaducts, either? Sometimes the cathedrals have devils and such carved into the front. Sometimes lords and ladies. Don't ask me why this is," I said.

He was nodding. The whole upper part of his body seemed to be moving back and forth.

"I'm not doing so good, am I?" I said.

He stopped nodding and leaned forward on the edge of the sofa. As he listened to me, he was running his fingers through his beard. I wasn't getting through to him, I could see that. But he waited for me to go on just the same. He nodded, like he was trying to encourage me. I tried to think what else to say. "They're really big," I said. "They're massive. They're built of stone. Marble, too, sometimes. In those olden days, when they built cathedrals, men wanted to be close to God. In those olden days, God was an important part of everyone's life. You could tell this from their cathedral-building. I'm sorry," I said, "but it looks like that's the best I can do for you. I'm just no good at it."

"That's all right, bub," the blind man said. "Hey, listen. I hope you don't mind my asking you. Can I ask you something? Let me ask you a simple question, yes or no. I'm just curious and there's no offense. You're my host. But let me ask if you are in any way religious? You don't mind my asking?"

I shook my head. He couldn't see that, though. A wink is the same as a nod to a blind man. "I guess I don't believe in it. In anything. Sometimes it's hard. You know what I'm saying?"

"Sure, I do," he said.

"Right," I said.

The Englishman was still holding forth. My wife sighed in her sleep. She drew a long breath and went on with her sleeping.

"You'll have to forgive me," I said. "But I can't tell you what a cathedral looks like. It just isn't in me to do it. I can't do any more than I've done."

The blind man sat very still, his head down, as he listened to me.

I said, "The truth is, cathedrals don't mean anything special to me. Nothing. Cathedrals. They're something to look at on late-night TV. That's all they are."

It was then that the blind man cleared his throat. He brought something up. He took a handkerchief from his back pocket. Then he said, "I get it, bub. It's okay. It happens. Don't worry about it," he said. "Hey, listen to me. Will you do me a favor? I got an idea. Why don't you find us some heavy paper? And a pen. We'll do something. We'll draw one together. Get us a pen and some heavy paper. Go on, bub, get the stuff," he said.

So I went upstairs. My legs felt like they didn't have any strength in them. They felt like they did after I'd done some running. In my wife's room, I looked around. I found some ballpoints in a little basket on her table. And then I tried to think where to look for the kind of paper he was talking about.

Downstairs, in the kitchen. I found a shopping bag with onion skins in the bottom of the bag. I emptied the bag and shook it. I brought it into the living room and sat down with it near his legs. I moved some things, smoothed the wrinkles from the bag, spread it out on the coffee table.

The blind man got down from the sofa and sat next to me on the carpet.

He ran his fingers over the paper. He went up and down the sides of the paper. The edges, even the edges. He fingered the corners.

"All right," he said. "All right, let's do her."

He found my hand, the hand with the pen. He closed his hand over my hand. "Go ahead, bub, draw," he said. "Draw. You'll see. I'll follow along with you. It'll be okay. Just begin now like I'm telling you. You'll see. Draw," the blind man said.

So I began. First I drew a box that looked like a house. It could have been the house I lived in. Then I put a roof on it. At either end of the roof. I drew spires. Crazy.

"Swell," he said, "Terrific. You're doing fine," he said. "Never thought anything like this could happen in your lifetime, did you, bub? Well, it's a strange life, we all know that. Go on now. Keep it up."

I put in windows with arches. I drew flying buttresses. I hung great doors. I couldn't stop. The TV station went off the air. I put down the pen and closed and opened my fingers. The blind man felt around over the paper. He moved the tips of his fingers over the paper, all over what I had drawn, and he nodded.

"Doing fine," the blind man said.

I took up the pen again, and he found my hand. I kept at it. I'm no artist. But I kept drawing just the same.

My wife opened up her eyes and gazed at us. She sat up on the sofa, her robe hanging open. She said, "What are you doing? Tell me, I want to know."

I didn't answer her.

The blind man said, "We're drawing a cathedral. Me and him are working on it. Press hard," he said to me. "That's right. That's good," he said. "Sure. You got it, bub, I can tell. You didn't think you could. But you can, can't you? You're cooking with gas now. You know what I'm saying? We're going to really have us something here in a minute. How's the old arm?" he said. "Put some people in there now. What's a cathedral without people?"

My wife said, "What's going on? Robert, what are you doing? What's going on?"

"It's all right," he said to her. "Close your eyes now," the blind man said to me.

I did it. I closed them just like he said.

"Are they closed?" he said. "Don't fudge."

"They're closed," I said.

"Keep them that way," he said. He said, "Don't stop now. Draw."

So we kept on with it. His fingers rode my fingers as my hand went over the paper. It was like nothing else in my life up to now.

Then he said, "I think that's it. I think you got it," he said. "Take a look. What do you think?"

But I had my eyes closed. I thought I'd keep them that way for a little longer. I thought it was something I ought to do.

"Well?" he said. "Are you looking?"

My eyes were still closed. I was in my house. I knew that. But I didn't feel like I was inside anything.

"It's really something," I said.

—1983

Joyce Carol Oates is a prolific writer who has published over 100 books since her first one appeared in 1963, and she shows few signs of slowing her output. Her new books—whether novels, books of poems, collections of stories, or nonfiction memoirs on subjects like boxing—always draw serious critical attention and more often than not land on the bestseller lists, and she has even written suspense novels pseudonymously as Rosamond Smith. Born in Lockport, New York, she holds degrees from Syracuse and the University of Wisconsin, and she is writer-in-residence at Princeton University, where she also codirected, with her late husband, the Ontario Review Press. Oates's work is often violent, a fact for which she has been criticized on numerous occasions. In response, she has remarked that these comments are "always ignorant, always sexist," implying that different standards are often applied to the work of women authors whose realism may be too strong for some tastes. Few readers would argue that her stories and novels exceed the violence of the society they depict. Them, a novel of African-American life in Detroit, won a National Book Award in 1970, and Oates has since garnered many other honors. "Where Are You Going, Where Have You Been?" is based on a Life magazine story about a serial rapist and killer known as "The Pied Piper of Tucson." In 1985 Oates's story was filmed by Joyce Chopra as Smooth Talk, starring Laura Dern and Treat Williams. Indicating the long popularity of this story, Oates published a collection of prose pieces in 1999 titled Where I've Been, and Where I'm Going.

Where Are You Going, Where Have You Been?

To Bob Dylan

Her name was Connie. She was fifteen and she had a quick nervous giggling habit of craning her neck to glance into mirrors or checking other people's faces to make sure her own was all right. Her mother, who noticed everything and knew everything and who hadn't much reason any longer to look at her own face, always scolded Connie about it. "Stop gawking at yourself, who are you? You think you're so pretty?" she would say. Connie would raise her eyebrows at these familiar complaints and look right through her mother, into a shadowy vision of herself as she was right at that moment: she knew she was pretty and that was everything. Her mother had been pretty once too, if you could believe those old snapshots in the album, but now her looks were gone and that was why she was always after Connie.

"Why don't you keep your room clean like your sister? How've you got your hair fixed—what the hell stinks? Hair spray? You don't see your sister using that junk."

Her sister June was twenty-four and still lived at home. She was a secretary in the high school Connie attended, and if that wasn't bad enough—with her in the same building—she was so plain and chunky and steady that Connie had to hear her praised all the time by her mother and her mother's sisters. June did this, June did that, she saved money and helped clean the house and cooked and Connie couldn't do a thing, her mind was all filled with trashy daydreams. Their father was away at work most of the time and when he came home he wanted supper and he read the newspaper at supper and after supper he went to bed. He didn't bother talking much to them, but around his bent head Connie's mother kept picking at her until Connie wished her mother was dead and she herself was dead and it was all over. "She makes me want to throw up sometimes," she complained to her friends. She had a high, breathless, amused voice which made everything she said sound a little forced, whether it was sincere or not.

There was one good thing: June went places with girlfriends of hers, girls who were just as plain and steady as she, and so when Connie wanted to do that her mother had no objections. The father of Connie's best girlfriend drove the girls the three miles to town and left them off at a shopping plaza, so that they could walk through the stores or go to a movie, and when he came to pick them up again at eleven he never bothered to ask what they had done.

They must have been familiar sights, walking around that shopping plaza in their shorts and flat ballerina slippers that always scuffed the sidewalk, with charm bracelets jingling on their thin wrists; they would lean together to whisper and laugh secretly if someone passed by who amused or interested them. Connie had long dark blond hair that drew anyone's eye to it, and she wore part of it pulled up on her head and puffed out and the rest of it she let fall down her back. She wore a pull over jersey blouse that looked one way when she was at home and another way when she was away from home. Everything about her had two sides to it, one for home and one for anywhere that was not home:

her walk that could be childlike and bobbing, or languid enough to make anyone think she was hearing music in her head, her mouth which was pale and smirking most of the time, but bright and pink on these evenings out, her laugh which was cynical and drawling at home—"Ha, ha, very funny"—but high-pitched and nervous anywhere else, like the jingling of the charms on her bracelet.

Sometimes they did go shopping or to a movie, but sometimes they went across the highway, ducking fast across the busy road, to a drive-in restaurant where older kids hung out. The restaurant was shaped like a big bottle, though squatter than a real bottle, and on its cap was a revolving figure of a grinning boy who held a hamburger aloft. One night in midsummer they ran across, breathless with daring, and right away someone leaned out a car window and invited them over, but it was just a boy from high school they didn't like. It made them feel good to be able to ignore him. They went up through the maze of parked and cruising cars to the bright-lit, fly-infested restaurant, their faces pleased and expectant as if they were entering a sacred building that loomed out of the night to give them what haven and what blessing they yearned for. They sat at the counter and crossed their legs at the ankles, their thin shoulders rigid with excitement, and listened to the music that made everything so good: the music was always in the background like music at a church service, it was something to depend upon.

A boy named Eddie came in to talk with them. He sat backward on his stool, turning himself jerkily around in semicircles and then stopping and turning again, and after a while he asked Connie if she would like something to eat. She said she did and so she tapped her friend's arm on her way out—her friend pulled her face up into a brave droll look—and Connie said she would meet her at eleven, across the way. "I just hate to leave her like that," Connie said earnestly, but the boy said that she wouldn't be alone for long. So they went out to his car and on the way Connie couldn't help but let her eyes wander over the windshields and faces all around her, her face gleaming with a joy that had nothing to do with Eddie or even this place; it might have been the music. She drew her shoulders up and sucked in her breath with the pure pleasure of being alive, and just at that moment she happened to glance at a face just a few feet from hers. It was a boy with shaggy black hair, in a convertible jalopy painted gold. He stared at her and then his lips widened into a grin. Connie slit her eyes at him and turned away, but she couldn't help glancing back and there he was still watching her. He wagged a finger and laughed and said, "Gonna get you, baby," and Connie turned away again without Eddie noticing anything.

She spent three hours with him, at the restaurant where they ate hamburgers and drank Cokes in wax cups that were always sweating, and then down an alley a mile or so away, and when he left her off at five to eleven only the movie house was still open at the plaza. Her girlfriend was there, talking with a boy. When Connie came up the two girls smiled at each other and Connie said, "How was the movie?" and the girl said, "You should know." They rode off with the girl's father, sleepy and pleased, and Connie couldn't help but look at the darkened shopping plaza with its big empty parking lot and its signs that were faded and ghostly now, and over at the drive-in restaurant where cars were still circling tirelessly. She couldn't hear the music at this distance.

Next morning June asked her how the movie was and Connie said, "So-so."

She and that girl and occasionally another girl went out several times a week that way, and the rest of the time Connie spent around the house—it was summer vacation—getting in her mother's way and thinking, dreaming, about the boys she met. But all the boys fell back and dissolved into a single face that was not even a face, but an idea, a feeling, mixed up with the urgent insistent pounding of the music and the humid night air of July. Connie's mother kept dragging her back to the daylight by finding things for her to do or saying, suddenly, "What's this about the Pettinger girl?"

And Connie would say nervously, "Oh, her. That dope." She always drew thick clear lines between herself and such girls, and her mother was simple and kindly enough to believe her. Her mother was so simple, Connie thought, that it was maybe cruel to fool her so much. Her mother went scuffling around the house in old bedroom slippers and complained over the telephone to one sister about the other, then the other called up and the two of them complained about the third one. If June's name was mentioned her mother's tone was approving, and if Connie's name was mentioned it was disapproving. This did not really mean she disliked Connie and actually Connie thought that her mother preferred her to June because she was prettier, but the two of them kept up a pretense of exasperation, a sense that they were tugging and struggling over something of little value to either of them.

Sometimes, over coffee, they were almost friends, but something would come up—some vexation that was like a fly buzzing suddenly around their heads—and their faces went hard with contempt.

One Sunday Connie got up at eleven—none of them bothered with church—and washed her hair so that it could dry all day long, in the sun. Her parents and sister were going to a barbecue at an aunt's house and Connie said no, she wasn't interested, rolling her eyes to let her mother know just what she thought of it. "Stay home alone then," her mother said sharply. Connie sat out back in a lawn chair and watched them drive away, her father quiet and bald, hunched around so that he could back the car out, her mother with a look that was still angry and not at all softened through the windshield, and in the back seat poor old June all dressed up as if she didn't know what a barbecue was, with all the running yelling kids and the flies. Connie sat with her eyes closed in the sun, dreaming and dazed with the warmth about her as if this were a kind of love, the caresses of love, and her mind slipped over onto thoughts of the boy she had been with the night before and how nice he had been, how sweet it always was, not the way someone like June would suppose but sweet, gentle, the way it was in movies and promised in songs; and when she opened her eyes she hardly knew where she was, the back yard ran off into weeds and a fence line of trees and behind it the sky was perfectly blue and still. The asbestos "ranch house" that was now three years old startled her—it looked small. She shook her head as if to get awake.

It was too hot. She went inside the house and turned on the radio to drown out the quiet. She sat on the edge of her bed, barefoot, and listened for an hour and a half to a program called XYZ Sunday Jamboree, record after record of hard, fast, shrieking songs she sang along with, interspersed by exclamations from "Bobby King": "An' look here you girls at Napoleon's—Son and Charley want you to pay real close attention to this song coming up!"

And Connie paid close attention herself, bathed in a glow of slow-pulsed joy that seemed to rise mysteriously out of the music itself and lay languidly about the airless little room, breathed in and breathed out with each gentle rise and fall of her chest.

After a while she heard a car coming up the drive. She sat up at once, startled, because it couldn't be her father so soon. The gravel kept crunching all the way in from the road—the driveway was long—and Connie ran to the window. It was a car she didn't know. It was an open jalopy, painted a bright gold that caught the sunlight opaquely. Her heart began to pound and her fingers snatched at her hair, checking it, and she whispered "Christ, Christ," wondering how bad she looked. The car came to a stop at the side door and the horn sounded four short taps as if this were a signal Connie knew.

She went into the kitchen and approached the door slowly, then hung out the screen door, her bare toes curling down off the step. There were two boys in the car and now she recognized the driver: he had shaggy, shabby black hair that looked crazy as a wig and he was grinning at her.

"I ain't late, am I?" he said.

"Who the hell do you think you are?" Connie said.

"Toldja I'd be out, didn't I?"

"I don't even know who you are."

She spoke sullenly, careful to show no interest or pleasure, and he spoke in a fast bright monotone. Connie looked past him to the other boy, taking her time. He had fair brown hair, with a lock that fell onto his forehead. His sideburns gave him a fierce, embarrassed look, but so far he hadn't even bothered to glance at her. Both boys wore sunglasses. The driver's glasses were metallic and mirrored everything in miniature.

"You wanta come for a ride?" he said.

Connie smirked and let her hair fall loose over one shoulder.

"Don'tcha like my car? New paint job," he said. "Hey."

"What?"

"You're cute."

She pretended to fidget, chasing flies away from the door.

"Don'tcha believe me, or what?" he said.

"Look, I don't even know who you are," Connie said in disgust.

"Hey, Ellie's got a radio, see. Mine's broke down." He lifted his friend's arm and showed her the little transistor the boy was holding, and now Connie began to hear the music. It was the same program that was playing inside the house.

"Bobby King?" she said.

"I listen to him all the time. I think he's great."

"He's kind of great," Connie said reluctantly.

"Listen, that guy's *great*. He knows where the action is."

Connie blushed a little, because the glasses made it impossible for her to see just what this boy was looking at. She couldn't decide if she liked him or if he was just a jerk, and so she dawdled in the doorway and wouldn't come down or go back inside. She said, "What's all that stuff painted on your car?"

"Can'tcha read it?" He opened the door very carefully, as if he was afraid it might fall off. He slid out just as carefully, planting his feet firmly on the ground, the tiny metallic world in his glasses slowing down like gelatine hardening and in the midst of it Connie's bright green blouse. "This here is my name, to begin with," he said. ARNOLD FRIEND was written in tarlike black letters on the side, with a drawing of a round grinning face that reminded Connie of a pumpkin, except it wore sunglasses. "I wanta introduce myself, I'm Arnold Friend and that's my real name and I'm gonna be your friend, honey, and inside the car's Ellie Oscar, he's kinda shy." Ellie brought his transistor radio up to his shoulder and balanced it there. "Now these numbers are a secret code, honey," Arnold Friend explained. He read off the numbers 33, 19, 17 and raised his eyebrows at her to see what she thought of that, but she didn't think much of it. The left rear fender had been smashed and around it was written, on the gleaming gold background—DONE BY CRAZY WOMAN DRIVER. Connie had to laugh at that. Arnold Friend was pleased at her laughter and looked up at her. "Around the other side's a lot more—you wanta come and see them?"

"No."

"Why not?"

"Why should I?"

"Don'tcha wanta see what's on the car? Don'tcha wanta go for a ride?"

"I don't know."

"Why not?"

"I got things to do."

"Like what?"

"Things."

He laughed as if she had said something funny. He slapped his thighs. He was standing in a strange way, leaning back against the car as if he were balancing himself. He wasn't tall, only an inch or so taller than she would be if she came down to him. Connie liked the way he was dressed, which was the way all of them dressed: tight faded jeans stuffed into black, scuffed boots, a belt that pulled his waist in and showed how lean he was, and a white pullover shirt that was a little soiled and showed the hard small muscles of his arms and shoulders. He looked as if he probably did hard work, lifting and carrying things. Even his neck looked muscular. And his face was a fa-miliar face, somehow—the jaw and chin and cheeks slightly darkened, because he hadn't shaved for a day or two, and the nose long and hawklike, sniffing as if she were a treat he was going to gobble up and it was all a joke.

"Connie, you ain't telling the truth. This is your day set aside for a ride with me and you know it," he said, still laughing. The way he straightened and recovered from his fit of laughing showed that it had been all fake.

"How do you know what my name is?" she said suspiciously.

"It's Connie."

"Maybe and maybe not."

"I know my Connie," he said, wagging his finger. Now she remem-bered him even better, back at the restaurant, and her cheeks warmed at the thought of how she sucked in her breath just at the moment she passed him—how she must have looked to him. And he had remem-bered her. "Ellie and I come out here especially for you," he said. "Ellie can sit in back. How about it?"

"Where?"

"Where what?"

"Where're we going?"

He looked at her. He took off the sunglasses and she saw how pale the skin around his eyes was, like holes that were not in shadow but in-stead in light. His eyes were like chips of broken glass that catch the light in an amiable way. He smiled. It was as if the idea of going for a ride somewhere, to some place, was a new idea to him.

"Just for a ride, Connie sweetheart."

"I never said my name was Connie," she said.

"But I know what it is. I know your name and all about you, lots of things," Arnold Friend said. He had not moved yet but stood still lean-ing back against the side of his jalopy. "I took a special interest in you, such a pretty girl, and found out all about you like I know your parents and sister are gone somewheres and I know where and how long they're going to be gone, and I know who you were with last night, and your best girlfriend's name is Betty. Right?"

He spoke in a simple lilting voice, exactly as if he were reciting the words to a song. His smile assured her that everything was fine. In the car Ellie turned up the volume on his radio and did not bother to look around at them.

"Ellie can sit in the back seat," Arnold Friend said. He indicated his friend with a casual jerk of his chin, as if Ellie did not count and she should not bother with him.

"How'd you find out all that stuff?" Connie said.

"Listen: Betty Schultz and Tony Fitch and Jimmy Pettinger and Nancy Pettinger," he said, in a chant. "Raymond Stanley and Bob Hutter—"

"Do you know all those kids?"

"I know everybody."

"Look, you're kidding. You're not from around here."

"Sure."

"But—how come we never saw you before?"

"Sure you saw me before," he said. He looked down at his boots, as if he were a little offended. "You just don't remember."

"I guess I'd remember you," Connie said.

"Yeah?" He looked up at this, beaming. He was pleased. He began to mark time with the music from Ellie's radio, tapping his fists lightly together. Connie looked away from his smile to the car, which was painted so bright it almost hurt her eyes to look at it. She looked at that name, ARNOLD FRIEND. And up at the front fender was an expression that was familiar—MAN THE FLYING SAUCERS. It was an expression kids had used the year before, but didn't use this year. She looked at it for a while as if the words meant something to her that she did not yet know.

"What're you thinking about? Huh?" Arnold Friend demanded. "Not worried about your hair blowing around in the car, are you?"

"No."

"Think I maybe can't drive good?"

"How do I know?"

"You're a hard girl to handle. How come?" he said. "Don't you know I'm your friend? Didn't you see me put my sign in the air when you walked by?"

"What sign?"

"My sign." And he drew an X in the air, leaning out toward her. They were maybe ten feet apart. After his hand fell back to his side the X was still in the air, almost visible. Connie let the screen door close and stood perfectly still inside it, listening to the music from her radio and the boy's blend together. She stared at Arnold Friend. He stood there so stiffly relaxed, pretending to be relaxed, with one hand idly on the door handle as if he were keeping himself up that way and had no intention of ever moving again. She recognized most things about him, the tight jeans that showed his thighs and buttocks and the greasy leather boots and the tight shirt, and even that slippery friendly smile of his, that sleepy dreamy smile that all the boys used to get across ideas they didn't want to put into words. She recognized all this and also the singsong way he talked, slightly mocking, kidding, but serious and a little melancholy, and she recognized the way he tapped one fist against the other in homage to the perpetual music behind him. But all these things did not come together.

She said suddenly, "Hey, how old are you?"

His smile faded. She could see then that he wasn't a kid, he was much older—thirty, maybe more. At this knowledge her heart began to pound faster.

"That's a crazy thing to ask. Can'tcha see I'm your own age?"

"Like hell you are."

"Or maybe a coupla years older, I'm eighteen."

"Eighteen?" she said doubtfully.

He grinned to reassure her and lines appeared at the corners of his mouth. His teeth were big and white. He grinned so broadly his eyes became slits and she saw how thick the lashes were, thick and black as if painted with a black tarlike material. Then he seemed to become embarrassed, abruptly, and looked over his shoulder at Ellie. "*Him*, he's crazy," he said. "Ain't he a riot, he's a nut, a real character." Ellie was still listening to the music. His sunglasses told nothing about what he was thinking. He wore a bright orange shirt unbuttoned halfway to show his chest, which was a pale, bluish chest and not muscular like Arnold Friend's. His shirt collar was turned up all around and the very tips of the collar pointed out past his chin as if they were protecting him. He was pressing the transistor radio up against his ear and sat there in a kind of daze, right in the sun.

"He's kinda strange," Connie said.

"Hey, she says you're kinda strange! Kinda strange!" Arnold Friend cried. He pounded on the car to get Ellie's attention. Ellie turned for the first time and Connie saw with shock that he wasn't a kid either— he had a fair, hairless face, cheeks reddened slightly as if the veins grew too close to the surface of his skin, the face of a forty-year-old baby. Connie felt a wave of dizziness rise in her at this sight and she stared at him as if waiting for something to change the shock of the moment, make it all right again. Ellie's lips kept shaping words, mumbling along, with the words blasting in his ear.

"Maybe you two better go away," Connie said faintly.

"What? How come?" Arnold Friend cried. "We come out here to take you for a ride. It's Sunday." He had the voice of the man on the radio now. It was the same voice, Connie thought. "Don'tcha know it's Sunday all day and honey, no matter who you were with last night today you're with Arnold Friend and don't you forget it!—Maybe you better step out here," he said, and this last was in a different voice. It was a little flatter, as if the heat was finally getting to him.

"No. I got things to do."

"Hey."

"You two better leave."

"We ain't leaving until you come with us."

"Like hell I am—"

"Connie, don't fool around with me. I mean, I mean, don't fool *around*," he said, shaking his head. He laughed incredulously. He placed his sunglasses on top of his head, carefully, as if he were indeed wearing a wig, and brought the stems down behind his ears. Connie stared at him, another wave of dizziness and fear rising in her so that for a moment he wasn't even in focus but was just a blur, standing there against his gold car, and she had the idea that he had driven up the driveway all right but had come from nowhere before that and belonged nowhere and that everything about him and even about the music that was so familiar to her was only half real.

"If my father comes and sees you—"

"He ain't coming. He's at the barbecue."

"How do you know that?"

"Aunt Tillie's. Right now they're—uh—they're drinking. Sitting around," he said vaguely, squinting as if he were staring all the way to town and over to Aunt Tillie's back yard. Then the vision seemed to get clear and he nodded energetically. "Yeah. Sitting around. There's your sister in a blue dress, huh? And high heels, the poor sad bitch—nothing like you, sweetheart! And your mother's helping some fat woman with the corn, they're cleaning the corn—husking the corn—"

"What fat woman?" Connie cried.

"How do I know what fat woman. I don't know every goddam fat woman in the world!" Arnold Friend laughed.

"Oh, that's Mrs. Hornby . . . Who invited her?" Connie said. She felt a little light-headed. Her breath was coming quickly.

"She's too fat. I don't like them fat. I like them the way you are, honey," he said, smiling sleepily at her. They stared at each other for a while, through the screen door. He said softly, "Now what you're going to do is this: you're going to come out that door. You're going to sit up front with me and Ellie's going to sit in the back, the hell with Ellie, right? This isn't Ellie's date. You're my date. I'm your lover, honey."

"What? You're crazy—"

"Yes, I'm your lover. You don't know what that is but you will," he said. "I know that too. I know all about you. But look: it's real nice and you couldn't ask for nobody better than me, or more polite. I always keep my word. I'll tell you how it is, I'm always nice at first, the first time. I'll hold you so tight you won't think you have to try to get away or pretend anything because you'll know you can't. And I'll come inside you where it's all secret and you'll give in to me and you'll love me—"

"Shut up! You're crazy!" Connie said. She backed away from the door. She put her hands against her ears as if she'd heard something terrible, something not meant for her. "People don't talk like that, you're crazy," she muttered. Her heart was almost too big now for her chest and its pumping made sweat break out all over her. She looked out to see Arnold Friend pause and then take a step toward the porch lurching. He almost fell. But, like a clever drunken man, he managed to catch his balance. He wobbled in his high boots and grabbed hold of one of the porch posts.

"Honey?" he said. "You still listening?"

"Get the hell out of here!"

"Be nice, honey. Listen."

"I'm going to call the police—"

He wobbled again and out of the side of his mouth came a fast spat curse, an aside not meant for her to hear. But even this "Christ!" sounded forced. Then he began to smile again. She watched this smile come, awkward as if he were smiling from inside a mask. His whole face was a mask, she thought wildly, tanned down onto his throat but then running out as if he had plastered makeup on his face but had forgotten about his throat.

"Honey—? Listen, here's how it is. I always tell the truth and I promise you this: I ain't coming in that house after you."

"You better not! I'm going to call the police if you—if you don't—"

"Honey," he said, talking right through her voice, "honey, I'm not coming in there but you are coming out here. You know why?"

She was panting. The kitchen looked like a place she had never seen before, some room she had run inside but which wasn't good enough, wasn't going to help her. The kitchen window had never had a curtain, after three years, and there were dishes in the sink for her to do—probably—and if you ran your hand across the table you'd probably feel something sticky there.

"You listening, honey? Hey?"

"—going to call the police—"

"Soon as you touch the phone I don't need to keep my promise and can come inside. You won't want that."

She rushed forward and tried to lock the door. Her fingers were shaking. "But why lock it," Arnold Friend said gently, talking right into her face. "It's just a screen door. It's just nothing." One of his boots was at a strange angle, as if his foot wasn't in it. It pointed out to the left, bent at the ankle. "I mean, anybody can break through a screen door and glass and wood and iron or anything else if he needs to, anybody at all and specially Arnold Friend. If the place got lit up with a fire honey you'd come runnin' out into my arms, right into my arms an' safe at home—like you knew I was your lover and'd stopped fooling around. I don't mind a nice shy girl but I don't like no fooling around." Part of those words were spoken with a slight rhythmic lilt, and Connie somehow recognized them—the echo of a song from last year, about a girl rushing into her boyfriend's arms and coming home again—

Connie stood barefoot on the linoleum floor, staring at him. "What do you want?" she whispered.

"I want you," he said.

"What?"

"Seen you that night and thought, that's the one, yes sir. I never needed to look any more."

"But my father's coming back. He's coming to get me. I had to wash my hair first—" She spoke in a dry, rapid voice, hardly raising it for him to hear.

"No, your Daddy is not coming and yes, you had to wash your hair and you washed it for me. It's nice and shining and all for me, I thank you, sweetheart," he said, with a mock bow, but again he almost lost his balance. He had to bend and adjust his boots. Evidently his feet did not go all the way down; the boots must have been stuffed with something so that he would seem taller. Connie stared out at him and behind him Ellie in the car, who seemed to be looking off toward Connie's right, into nothing. This Ellie said, pulling the words out of the air one after another as if he were just discovering them, "You want me to pull out the phone?"

"Shut your mouth and keep it shut," Arnold Friend said, his face red from bending over or maybe from embarrassment because Connie had seen his boots. "This ain't none of your business."

"What—what are you doing? What do you want?" Connie said. "If I call the police they'll get you, they'll arrest you—"

"Promise was not to come in unless you touch that phone, and I'll keep that promise," he said. He resumed his erect position and tried to force his shoulders back. He sounded like a hero in a movie, declaring something important. He spoke too loudly and it was as if he were speaking to someone behind Connie. "I ain't made plans for coming in that house where I don't belong but just for you to come out to me, the way you should. Don't you know who I am?"

"You're crazy," she whispered. She backed away from the door but did not want to go into another part of the house, as if this would give him permission to come through the door. "What do you . . . You're crazy, you . . ."

"Huh? What're you saying, honey?"

Her eyes darted everywhere in the kitchen. She could not remember what it was, this room.

"This is how it is, honey: you come out and we'll drive away, have a nice ride. But if you don't come out we're gonna wait till your people come home and then they're all going to get it."

"You want that telephone pulled out?" Ellie said. He held the radio away from his ear and grimaced, as if without the radio the air was too much for him.

"I toldja shut up, Ellie," Arnold Friend said, "you're deaf, get a hearing aid, right? Fix yourself up. This little girl's no trouble and's gonna be nice to me, so Ellie keep to yourself, this ain't your date—right? Don't hem in on me. Don't hog. Don't crush. Don't bird dog. Don't trail me," he said in a rapid meaningless voice, as if he were running through all the expressions he'd learned but was no longer sure which one of them was in style, then rushing on to new ones, making them up with his eyes closed, "Don't crawl under my fence, don't squeeze in my chipmunk hole, don't sniff my glue, suck my popsicle, keep your own greasy fingers on yourself!" He shaded his eyes and peered in at Connie, who was backed against the kitchen table. "Don't mind him honey he's just a creep. He's a dope. Right? I'm the boy for you and like I said you come out here nice like a lady and give me your hand, and nobody else gets hurt, I mean, your nice old bald-headed daddy and your mummy and your sister in her high heels. Because listen: why bring them in this?"

"Leave me alone," Connie whispered.

"Hey, you know that old woman down the road, the one with the chickens and stuff—you know her?"

"She's dead!"

"Dead? What? You know her?" Arnold Friend said.

"She's dead—"

"Don't you like her?"

"She's dead—she's—she isn't here any more—"

"But don't you like her, I mean, you got something against her? Some grudge or something?" Then his voice dipped as if he were conscious of a rudeness. He touched the sunglasses perched on top of his head as if to make sure they were still there. "Now you be a good girl."

"What are you going to do?"

"Just two things, or maybe three," Arnold Friend said. "But I promise it won't last long and you'll like me the way you get to like people you're close to. You will. It's all over for you here, so come on out. You don't want your people in any trouble, do you?"

She turned and bumped against a chair or something, hurting her leg, but she ran into the back room and picked up the telephone. Something roared in her ear, a tiny roaring, and she was so sick with fear that she could do nothing but listen to it—the telephone was clammy and very heavy and her fingers groped down to the dial but were too weak to touch it. She began to scream into the phone, into the roaring. She cried out, she cried for her mother, she felt her breath start jerking back and forth in her lungs as if it were something Arnold Friend were stabbing her with again and again with no tenderness. A noisy sorrowful wailing rose all about her and she was locked inside it the way she was locked inside the house.

After a while she could hear again. She was sitting on the floor with her wet back against the wall.

Arnold Friend was saying from the door, "That's a good girl. Put the phone back."

She kicked the phone away from her.

"No, honey. Pick it up. Put it back right."

She picked it up and put it back. The dial tone stopped.

"That's a good girl. Now, you come outside."

She was hollow with what had been fear, but what was now just an emptiness. All that screaming had blasted it out of her. She sat, one leg cramped under her, and deep inside her brain was something like a pinpoint of light that kept going and would not let her relax. She thought, I'm not going to see my mother again. She thought, I'm not going to sleep in my bed again. Her bright green blouse was all wet.

Arnold Friend said, in a gentle-loud voice that was like a stage voice, "The place where you came from ain't there any more, and where you had in mind to go is canceled out. This place you are now—inside your daddy's house—is nothing but a cardboard box I can knock down any time. You know that and always did know it. You hear me?"

She thought, I have got to think. I have to know what to do.

"We'll go out to a nice field, out in the country here where it smells so nice and it's sunny," Arnold Friend said. "I'll have my arms tight around you so you won't need to try to get away and I'll show you what love is like, what it does. The hell with this house! It looks solid all right," he said. He ran a fingernail down the screen and the noise did not make Connie shiver, as it would have the day before. "Now put your hand on your heart, honey. Feel that? That feels solid too but we know better, be nice to me, be sweet like you can because what else is there for a girl like you but to be sweet and pretty and give in?—and get away before her people come back?"

She felt her pounding heart. Her hand seemed to enclose it. She thought for the first time in her life that it was nothing that was hers, that belonged to her, but just a pounding, living thing inside this body that wasn't really hers either.

"You don't want them to get hurt," Arnold Friend went on. "Now get up, honey. Get up all by yourself."

She stood.

"Now turn this way. That's right. Come over here to me—Ellie, put that away, didn't I tell you? You dope. You miserable creepy dope," Arnold Friend said. His words were not angry but only part of an incantation. The incantation was kindly. "Now come out through the kitchen to me honey, and let's see a smile, try it, you're a brave sweet little girl and now they're eating corn and hot dogs cooked to bursting over an outdoor fire, and they don't know one thing about you and never did and honey you're better than them because not a one of them would have done this for you."

Connie felt the linoleum under her feet; it was cool. She brushed her hair back out of her eyes. Arnold Friend let go of the post tentatively and opened his arms for her, his elbows pointing in toward each other and his wrists limp, to show that this was an embarrassed embrace and a little mocking, he didn't want to make her self-conscious.

She put out her hand against the screen. She watched herself push the door slowly open as if she were safe back somewhere in the other doorway, watching this body and this head of long hair moving out into the sunlight where Arnold Friend waited.

"My sweet little blue-eyed girl," he said, in a half-sung sigh that had nothing to do with her brown eyes but was taken up just the same by the vast sunlit reaches of the land behind him and on all sides of him, so much land that Connie had never seen before and did not recognize except to know that she was going to it.

—1966

MARGARET ATWOOD ■ (b. 1939)

Margaret Atwood is a leading figure among Canadian writers, and she is equally skilled as a poet and fiction writer. She is also an internationally known feminist spokesperson in great demand for appearances at symposia on women's issues, and she was named by Ms. magazine as Woman of the Year for 1986. Born in Ottawa, Ontario, she graduated from University of Toronto in 1962, the same year that her first book appeared, and she later did graduate work at Radcliffe and Harvard. She has published two volumes of selected poems, over a dozen novels and collections of short stories, and a book of literary criticism. In addition, she served as editor of two anthologies of Canadian literature and wrote Survival: A Thematic Guide to Canadian Literature (1972), influential work that challenged Canadian writers to explore their own unique cultural heritage. Atwood has served as writer in residence at universities in Canada, the United States, and abroad. The Handmaid's Tale (1985), a work that presents a future dystopia controlled by a fundamentalist patriarchy, was a bestseller and was filmed in 1990. The Tent, a collection of "mini-fictions and micro-dramas," appeared in 2006, and a new collection of poems, The Door, appeared the following year.

Happy Endings

John and Mary meet.
What happens next?
If you want a happy ending, try A.

A

John and Mary fall in love and get married. They both have worthwhile and remunerative jobs which they find stimulating and challenging. They buy a charming house. Real estate values go up. Eventually, when they can afford live-in help, they have two children, to whom they are devoted. The children turn out well. John and Mary have a stimulating and challenging sex life and worthwhile friends. They go on fun vacations together. They retire. They both have hobbies which they find stimulating and challenging. Eventually they die. This is the end of the story.

B

Mary falls in love with John but John doesn't fall in love with Mary. He merely uses her body for selfish pleasure and ego gratification of a tepid kind. He comes to her apartment twice a week and she cooks him dinner, you'll notice that he doesn't even consider her worth the price of a dinner out, and after he's eaten the dinner he fucks her and after that he falls asleep, while she does the dishes so he won't think she's untidy, having all those dirty dishes lying around, and puts on fresh lipstick so she'll look good when he wakes up, but when he wakes up he doesn't even notice, he puts on his socks and his shorts and his pants and his shirt and his tie and his shoes, the reverse order from the one in which he took them off. He doesn't take off Mary's clothes, she takes them off herself, she acts as if she's dying for it every time, not because she likes sex exactly, she doesn't, but she wants John to think she does because if they do it often enough surely he'll get used to her, he'll come to depend on her and they will get married, but John goes out the door with hardly so much as a good-night and three days later he turns up at six o'clock and they do the whole thing over again.

Mary gets run-down. Crying is bad for your face, everyone knows that and so does Mary but she can't stop. People at work notice. Her friends tell her John is a rat, a pig, a dog, he isn't good enough for her, but she can't believe it. Inside John, she thinks, is another John, who is much nicer. This other John will emerge like a butterfly from a cocoon, a Jack from a box, a pit from a prune, if the first John is only squeezed enough.

One evening John complains about the food. He has never complained about the food before. Mary is hurt.

Her friends tell her they've seen him in a restaurant with another woman, whose name is Madge. It's not even Madge that finally gets to Mary: it's the restaurant. John has never taken Mary to a restaurant. Mary collects all the sleeping pills and aspirins she can find, and takes them and a half a bottle of sherry. You can see what kind of a woman she is by the fact that it's not even whiskey. She leaves a note for John. She hopes he'll discover her and get her to the hospital in time and repent and then they can get married, but this fails to happen and she dies.

John marries Madge and everything continues as in A.

C

John, who is an older man, falls in love with Mary, and Mary, who is only twenty-two, feels sorry for him because he's worried about his hair falling out. She sleeps with him even though she's not in love with him. She met him at work. She's in love with someone called James, who is twenty-two also and not yet ready to settle down.

John on the contrary settled down long ago: this is what is bothering him. John has a steady, respectable job and is getting ahead in his field, but Mary isn't impressed by him, she's impressed by James, who has a motorcycle and a fabulous record collection. But James is often away on his motorcycle, being free. Freedom isn't the same for girls, so in the meantime Mary spends Thursday evenings with John. Thursdays are the only days John can get away.

John is married to a woman called Madge and they have two children, a charming house which they bought just before the real estate values went up, and hobbies which they find stimulating and challenging, when they have the time. John tells Mary how important she is to him, but of course he can't leave his wife because a commitment is a commitment. He goes on about this more than is necessary and Mary finds it boring, but older men can keep it up longer so on the whole she has a fairly good time.

One day James breezes in on his motorcycle with some top-grade California hybrid and James and Mary get higher than you'd believe possible and they climb into bed. Everything becomes very underwater, but along comes John, who has a key to Mary's apartment. He finds them stoned and entwined. He's hardly in any position to be jealous, considering Madge, but nevertheless he's overcome with despair. Finally he's middle-aged, in two years he'll be bald as an egg and he can't stand it. He purchases a handgun, saying he needs it for target practice—this is the thin part of the plot, but it can be dealt with later—and shoots the two of them and himself.

Madge, after a suitable period of mourning, marries an understanding man called Fred and everything continues as in A, but under different names.

D

Fred and Madge have no problems. They get along exceptionally well and are good at working out any little difficulties that may arise. But their charming house is by the seashore and one day a giant tidal wave approaches. Real estate values go down. The rest of the story is about what caused the tidal wave and how they escape from it. They do, though thousands drown, but Fred and Madge are virtuous and lucky. Finally on high ground they clasp each other, wet and dripping and grateful, and continue as in A.

E

Yes, but Fred has a bad heart. The rest of the story is about how kind and understanding they both are until Fred dies. Then Madge devotes herself to charity work until the end of A. If you like, it can be "Madge," "cancer," "guilty and confused," and "bird watching."

F

If you think this is all too bourgeois, make John a revolutionary and Mary a counterespionage agent and see how far that gets you. Remember, this is Canada. You'll still end up with A, though in between you may get a lustful brawling saga of passionate involvement, a chronicle of our times, sort of.

You'll have to face it, the endings are the same however you slice it. Don't be deluded by any other endings, they're all fake, either deliberately fake, with malicious intent to deceive, or just motivated by excessive optimism if not by downright sentimentality.

The only authentic ending is the one provided here:

John and Mary die. John and Mary die. John and Mary die.

So much for endings. Beginnings are always more fun. True connoisseurs, however, are known to favor the stretch in between, since it's the hardest to do anything with.

That's about all that can be said for plots, which anyway are just one thing after another, a what and a what and a what.

Now try How and Why.

—*1983*

BOBBIE ANN MASON ■ (b. 1940)

Bobbie Ann Mason was born in Mayfield, Kentucky, and grew up on a dairy farm run by her parents. The rural background of her youth figures in many of her best stories, and one of Mason's favorite subjects is the assimilation of the countryside and the South into a larger American culture. Mason's characters may dream of living in log cabins, but they also take adult education courses, watch TV talk shows, and shop in supermarkets and malls. After taking degrees from the University of Kentucky and the University of Connecticut, Mason published her first two books, both works of literary criticism, in the mid-1970s. One of them, The Girl Sleuth, was a feminist guide to the exploits of fictional detectives like Nancy Drew that Mason read as a child. After years of attempts, Mason's stories began to appear in prestigious magazines, most prominently The New Yorker, and the publication of Shiloh and Other Stories (1982) established her as an important new voice in American fiction. She has since published a second collection of short stories and four novels, one of which, In Country (1985), was filmed in 1989. "Shiloh," like several of the stories in the collection from which it is taken, gains considerable immediacy from Mason's use of present tense and her sure sense of regional speech patterns. In recent years, Mason has published a story collection, Zigzagging Down a Wild Trail (2001), a biography, Elvis Presley (2003), and a short story collection, Nancy Culpepper (2006).

Shiloh

Leroy Moffitt's wife, Norma Jean, is working on her pectorals. She lifts three-pound dumbbells to warm up, then progresses to a twenty-pound barbell. Standing with her legs apart, she reminds Leroy of Wonder Woman.

"I'd give anything if I could just get these muscles to where they're real hard," says Norma Jean. "Feel this arm. It's not as hard as the other one."

"That's 'cause you're right-handed," says Leroy, dodging as she swings the barbell in an arc.

"Do you think so?"

"Sure."

Leroy is a truckdriver. He injured his leg in a highway accident four months ago, and his physical therapy, which involves weights and a pulley, prompted Norma Jean to try building herself up. Now she is attending a body-building class. Leroy has been collecting temporary disability since his tractor-trailer jackknifed in Missouri, badly twisting his left leg in its socket. He has a steel pin in his hip. He will probably not be able to drive his rig again. It sits in the backyard, like a gigantic bird that has flown home to roost. Leroy has been home in Kentucky for three months, and his leg is almost healed, but the accident frightened him and he does not want to drive any more long hauls. He is not sure what to do next. In the meantime, he makes things from craft kits. He started by building a miniature log cabin from notched Popsicle sticks. He varnished it and placed it on the TV set, where it remains. It reminds him of a rustic Nativity scene. Then he tried string art (sailing ships on black velvet), a macramé owl kit, a snap-together B-17 Flying Fortress, and a lamp made out of a model truck, with a light fixture screwed in the top of the cab. At first the kits were diversions, something to kill time, but now he is thinking about building a full-scale log house from a kit. It would be considerably cheaper than building a regular house, and besides, Leroy has grown to appreciate how things are put together. He has begun to realize that in all the years he was on the road he never took time to examine anything. He was always flying past scenery.

"They won't let you build a log cabin in any of the new subdivisions," Norma Jean tells him.

"They will if I tell them it's for you," he says, teasing her. Ever since they were married, he has promised Norma Jean he would build her a new home one day. They have always rented, and the house they live in is small and nondescript. It does not even feel like a home, Leroy realizes now.

Norma Jean works at the Rexall drugstore, and she has acquired an amazing amount of information about cosmetics. When she explains to Leroy the three stages of complexion care, involving creams, toners, and moisturizers, he thinks happily of other petroleum products—axle grease, diesel fuel. This is a connection between him and Norma Jean. Since he has been home, he has felt unusually tender about his wife and guilty over his long absences. But he can't tell what she feels about him. Norma Jean has never complained about his traveling; she has never made hurt remarks, like calling his truck a "widow-maker." He is reasonably certain she has been faithful to him, but he wishes she would celebrate his permanent home-coming more happily. Norma Jean is often startled to find Leroy at home, and he thinks she seems a little disappointed about it. Perhaps he reminds her too much of the early days of their marriage, before he went on the road. They had a child who died as an infant, years ago. They never speak about their memories of Randy, which have almost faded, but now that Leroy is home all the time, they sometimes feel awkward around each other, and Leroy wonders if one of them should mention the child. He has the feeling that they are waking up out of a dream together—that they must create a new marriage, start afresh. They are lucky they are still married. Leroy has read that for most people losing a child destroys the marriage—or else he heard this on *Donahue*. He can't always remember where he learns things anymore.

At Christmas, Leroy bought an electric organ for Norma Jean. She used to play the piano when she was in high school. "It don't leave you," she told him once. "It's like riding a bicycle."

The new instrument had so many keys and buttons that she was bewildered by it at first. She touched the keys tentatively, pushed some buttons, then pecked out "Chopsticks." It came out in an amplified foxtrot rhythm, with marimba sounds.

"It's an orchestra!" she cried.

The organ had a pecan-look finish and eighteen preset chords, with optional flute, violin, trumpet, clarinet, and banjo accompaniments. Norma Jean mastered the organ almost immediately. At first she played Christmas songs. Then she bought *The Sixties Songbook* and learned every tune in it, adding variations to each with the rows of brightly colored buttons.

"I didn't like these old songs back then," she said. "But I have this crazy feeling I missed something."

"You didn't miss a thing," said Leroy.

Leroy likes to lie on the couch and smoke a joint and listen to Norma Jean play "Can't Take My Eyes Off You" and "I'll Be Back." He is back again. After fifteen years on the road, he is finally settling down with the woman he loves. She is still pretty. Her skin is flawless. Her frosted curls resemble pencil trimmings.

Now that Leroy has come home to stay, he notices how much the town has changed. Subdivisions are spreading across western Kentucky like an oil slick. The sign at the edge of town says "Pop: 11,500"—only seven hundred more than it said twenty years before. Leroy can't figure out who is living in all the new houses. The farmers who used to gather around the courthouse square on Saturday afternoons to play checkers and spit tobacco juice have gone. It has been years since Leroy has thought about the farmers, and they have disappeared without his noticing.

Leroy meets a kid named Stevie Hamilton in the parking lot at the new shopping center. While they pretend to be strangers meeting over a stalled car, Stevie tosses an ounce of marijuana under the front seat of Leroy's car. Stevie is wearing orange jogging shoes and a T-shirt that says CHATTAHOOCHEE SUPER-RAT. His father is a prominent doctor who lives in one of the expensive subdivisions in a new white-columned brick house that looks like a funeral parlor. In the phone book under his name there is a separate number, with the listing "Teenagers."

"Where do you get this stuff?" asks Leroy. "From your pappy?"

"That's for me to know and you to find out," Stevie says. He is slit-eyed and skinny.

"What else you got?"

"What you interested in?"

"Nothing special. Just wondered."

Leroy used to take speed on the road. Now he has to go slowly. He needs to be mellow. He leans back against the car and says, "I'm aiming to build me a log house, soon as I get time. My wife, though, I don't think she likes the idea."

"Well, let me know when you want me again," Stevie says. He has a cigarette in his cupped palm, as though sheltering it from the wind. He takes a long drag, then stomps it on the asphalt and slouches away.

Stevie's father was two years ahead of Leroy in high school. Leroy is thirty-four. He married Norma Jean when they were both eighteen, and their child Randy was born a few months later, but he died at the age of four months and three days. He would be about Stevie's age now. Norma Jean and Leroy were at the drive-in, watching a double feature (*Dr. Strangelove* and *Lover Come Back*), and the baby was sleeping in the back seat. When the first movie ended, the baby was dead. It was the sudden infant death syndrome. Leroy remembers handing Randy to a nurse at the emergency room, as though he were offering her a large doll as a present. A dead baby feels like a sack of flour. "It just happens sometimes," said the doctor, in what Leroy always recalls as a nonchalant tone. Leroy can hardly remember the child anymore, but he still sees vividly a scene from *Dr. Strangelove* in which the President of the United States was talking in a folksy voice on the hot line to the Soviet premier about the bomber accidentally headed toward Russia. He was in the War Room, and the world map was lit up. Leroy remembers Norma Jean standing catatonically beside him in the hospital and himself thinking: Who is this strange girl? He had forgotten who she was. Now scientists are saying that crib death is caused by a virus. Nobody knows anything, Leroy thinks. The answers are always changing.

When Leroy gets home from the shopping center, Norma Jean's mother, Mabel Beasley, is there. Until this year, Leroy has not realized how much time she spends with Norma Jean. When she visits, she inspects the closets and then the plants, informing Norma Jean when a plant is droopy or yellow. Mabel calls the plants "flowers," although there are never any blooms. She also notices if Norma Jean's laundry is piling up. Mabel is a short, overweight woman whose tight, brown-dyed curls look more like a wig than the actual wig she sometimes wears. Today she has brought Norma Jean an off-white dust ruffle she made for the bed; Mabel works in a custom-upholstery shop.

"This is the tenth one I made this year," Mabel says. "I got started and couldn't stop."

"It's real pretty," says Norma Jean.

"Now we can hide things under the bed," says Leroy, who gets along with his mother-in-law primarily by joking with her. Mabel has never really forgiven him for disgracing her by getting Norma Jean pregnant. When the baby died, she said that fate was mocking her.

"What's that thing?" Mabel says to Leroy in a loud voice, pointing to a tangle of yarn on a piece of canvas.

Leroy holds it up for Mabel to see. "It's my needlepoint," he explains. "This is a *Star Trek* pillow cover."

"That's what a woman would do," says Mabel. "Great day in the morning!"

"All the big football players on TV do it," he says.

"Why, Leroy, you're always trying to fool me. I don't believe you for one minute. You don't know what to do with yourself—that's the whole trouble. Sewing!"

"I'm aiming to build us a log house," says Leroy. "Soon as my plans come."

"Like *heck* you are," says Norma Jean. She takes Leroy's needlepoint and shoves it into a drawer. "You have to find a job first. Nobody can afford to build now anyway."

Mabel straightens her girdle and says, "I still think before you get tied down y'all ought to take a little run to Shiloh."

"One of these days, Mama," Norma Jean says impatiently.

Mabel is talking about Shiloh, Tennessee. For the past few years, she has been urging Leroy and Norma Jean to visit the Civil War battleground there. Mabel went there on her honeymoon—the only real trip she ever took. Her husband died of a perforated ulcer when Norma Jean was ten, but Mabel, who was accepted into the United Daughters of the Confederacy in 1975, is still preoccupied with going back to Shiloh.

"I've been to kingdom come and back in that truck out yonder," Leroy says to Mabel, "but we never yet set foot in that battleground. Ain't that something? How did I miss it?"

"It's not even that far," Mabel says.

After Mabel leaves, Norma Jean reads to Leroy from a list she has made. "Things you could do," she announces. "You could get a job as a guard at Union Carbide, where they'd let you set on a stool. You could get on at the lumberyard. You could do a little carpenter work, if you want to build so bad. You could—"

"I can't do something where I'd have to stand up all day."

"You ought to try standing up all day behind a cosmetics counter. It's amazing that I have strong feet, coming from two parents that never had strong feet at all." At the moment Norma Jean is holding on to the kitchen counter, raising her knees one at a time as she talks. She is wearing two-pound ankle weights.

"Don't worry," says Leroy. "I'll do something."

"You could truck calves to slaughter for somebody. You wouldn't have to drive any big old truck for that."

"I'm going to build you this house," says Leroy. "I want to make you a real home."

"I don't want to live in any log cabin."

"It's not a cabin. It's a house."

"I don't care. It looks like a cabin."

"You and me together could lift those logs. It's just like lifting weights."

Norma Jean doesn't answer. Under her breath, she is counting. Now she is marching through the kitchen. She is doing goose steps.

Before his accident, when Leroy came home he used to stay in the house with Norma Jean, watching TV in bed and playing cards. She would cook fried chicken, picnic ham, chocolate pie—all his favorites. Now he is home alone much of the time. In the mornings, Norma Jean disappears, leaving a cooling place in the bed. She eats a cereal called Body Buddies, and she leaves the bowl on the table, with the soggy tan balls floating in a milk puddle. He sees things about Norma Jean that he never realized before. When she chops onions, she stares off into a corner, as if she can't bear to look. She puts on her house slippers almost precisely at nine o'clock every evening and nudges her jogging shoes under the couch. She saves bread heels for the birds. Leroy watches the birds at the feeder. He notices the peculiar way goldfinches fly past the window. They close their wings, then fall, then spread their wings to catch and lift themselves. He wonders if they close their eyes when they fall. Norma Jean closes her eyes when they are in bed. She wants the lights turned out. Even then, he is sure she closes her eyes.

He goes for long drives around town. He tends to drive a car rather carelessly. Power steering and an automatic shift make a car feel so small and inconsequential that his body is hardly involved in the driving process. His injured leg stretches out comfortably. Once or twice he has almost hit something, but even the prospect of an accident seems minor in a car. He cruises the new subdivisions, feeling like a criminal rehearsing for a robbery. Norma Jean is probably right about a log house being inappropriate here in the new subdivision. All the houses look grand and complicated. They depress him.

One day when Leroy comes home from a drive he finds Norma Jean in tears. She is in the kitchen making a potato and mushroom-soup casserole, with grated-cheese topping. She is crying because her mother caught her smoking.

"I didn't hear her coming. I was standing here puffing away pretty as you please," Norma Jean says, wiping her eyes.

"I knew it would happen sooner or later," says Leroy, putting his arm around her.

"She don't know the meaning of the word 'knock,'" says Norma Jean. "It's a wonder she hadn't caught me years ago."

"Think of it this way," Leroy says. "What if she caught me with a joint?"

"You better not let her!" Norma Jean shrieks. "I'm warning you, Leroy Moffitt!"

"I'm just kidding. Here, play me a tune. That'll help you relax."

Norma Jean puts the casserole in the oven and sets the timer. Then she plays a ragtime tune, with horns and banjo, as Leroy lights up a joint and lies on the couch, laughing to himself about Mabel's catching him at it. He thinks of Stevie Hamilton—a doctor's son pushing grass. Everything is funny. The whole town seems crazy and small. He is reminded of Virgil Mathis, a boastful policeman Leroy used to shoot pool with. Virgil recently led a drug bust in a back room at a bowling alley, where he seized ten thousand dollars' worth of marijuana. The newspaper had a picture of him holding up the bags of grass and grinning widely. Right now, Leroy can imagine Virgil breaking down the door and arresting him with a lungful of smoke. Virgil would probably have been alerted to the scene because of all the racket Norma Jean is making. Now she sounds like a hard-rock band. Norma Jean is terrific. When she switches to a Latin-rhythm version of "Sunshine Superman," Leroy hums along. Norma Jean's foot goes up and down, up and down.

"Well, what do you think?" Leroy says, when Norma Jean pauses to search through her music.

"What do I think about what?"

His mind has gone blank. Then he says, "I'll sell my rig and build us a house." That wasn't what he wanted to say. He wanted to know what she thought—what she *really* thought—about them.

"Don't start in on that again," says Norma Jean. She begins playing "Who'll Be the Next in Line?"

Leroy used to tell hitchhikers his whole life story—about his travels, his hometown, the baby. He would end with a question: "Well, what do you think?" It was just a rhetorical question. In time, he had the feeling that he'd been telling the same story over and over to the same hitchhikers. He quit talking to hitchhikers when he realized how his voice sounded—whining and self-pitying, like some teenage-tragedy song. Now Leroy has the sudden impulse to tell Norma Jean about himself, as if he had just met her. They have known each other so long they have forgotten a lot about each other. They could become reacquainted. But when the oven timer goes off and she runs to the kitchen, he forgets why he wants to do this.

The next day, Mabel drops by. It is Saturday and Norma Jean is clean-ing. Leroy is studying the plans of his log house, which have finally come in the mail. He has them spread out on the table—big sheets of stiff blue paper, with diagrams and numbers printed in white. While Norma Jean runs the vacuum, Mabel drinks coffee. She sets her coffee cup on a blueprint.

"I'm just waiting for time to pass," she says to Leroy, drumming her fingers on the table.

As soon as Norma Jean switches off the vacuum, Mabel says in a loud voice, "Did you hear about the datsun dog that killed the baby?"

Norma Jean says, "The word is 'dachshund.'"

"They put the dog on trial. It chewed the baby's legs off. The mother was in the next room all the time." She raises her voice. "They thought it was neglect."

Norma Jean is holding her ears. Leroy manages to open the refrig-erator and get some Diet Pepsi to offer Mabel. Mabel still has some coffee and she waves away the Pepsi.

"Datsuns are like that," Mabel says. "They're jealous dogs. They'll tear a place to pieces if you don't keep an eye on them."

"You better watch out what you're saying, Mabel," says Leroy.

"Well, facts is facts."

Leroy looks out the window at his rig. It is like a huge piece of fur-niture gathering dust in the backyard. Pretty soon it will be an antique. He hears the vacuum cleaner. Norma Jean seems to be cleaning the living room rug again.

Later, she says to Leroy, "She just said that about the baby because she caught me smoking. She's trying to pay me back."

"What are you talking about?" Leroy says, nervously shuffling blue-prints.

"You know good and well," Norma Jean says. She is sitting in a kitchen chair with her feet up and her arms wrapped around her knees. She looks small and helpless. She says, "The very idea, her bringing up a subject like that! Saying it was neglect."

"She didn't mean that," Leroy says.

"She might not have *thought* she meant it. She always says things like that. You don't know how she goes on."

"But she didn't really mean it. She was just talking."

Leroy opens a king-sized bottle of beer and pours it into two glasses, dividing it carefully. He hands a glass to Norma Jean and she takes it from him mechanically. For a long time, they sit by the kitchen window watching the birds at the feeder.

Something is happening. Norma Jean is going to night school. She has graduated from her six-week body-building course and now she is taking an adult-education course in composition at Paducah Community College. She spends her evenings outlining paragraphs.

"First, you have a topic sentence," she explains to Leroy. "Then you divide it up. Your secondary topic has to be connected to your primary topic."

To Leroy, this sounds intimidating. "I never was any good in English," he says.

"It makes a lot of sense."

"What are you doing this for, anyhow?"

She shrugs. "It's something to do." She stands up and lifts her dumbbells a few times.

"Driving a rig, nobody cared about my English."

"I'm not criticizing your English."

Norma Jean used to say, "If I lose ten minutes' sleep, I just drag all day." Now she stays up late, writing compositions. She got a B on her first paper—a how-to theme on soup-based casseroles. Recently Norma Jean has been cooking unusual foods—tacos, lasagna, Bombay chicken. She doesn't play the organ anymore, though her second paper was called "Why Music Is Important to Me." She sits at the kitchen table, concentrating on her outlines, while Leroy plays with his log house plans, practicing with a set of Lincoln Logs. The thought of getting a truckload of notched, numbered logs scares him, and he wants to be prepared. As he and Norma Jean work together at the kitchen table, Leroy has the hopeful thought that they are sharing something, but he knows he is a fool to think this. Norma Jean is miles away. He knows he is going to lose her. Like Mabel, he is just waiting for time to pass.

One day, Mabel is there before Norma Jean gets home from work, and Leroy finds himself confiding in her. Mabel, he realizes, must know Norma Jean better than he does.

"I don't know what's got into that girl," Mabel says. "She used to go to bed with the chickens. Now you say she's up all hours. Plus her a-smoking. I like to died."

"I want to make her this beautiful home," Leroy says, indicating the Lincoln Logs. "I don't think she even wants it. Maybe she was happier with me gone."

"She don't know what to make of you, coming home like this."

"Is that it?"

Mabel takes the roof off his Lincoln Log cabin. "You couldn't get me in a log cabin," she says. "I was raised in one. It's no picnic, let me tell you."

"They're different now," says Leroy.

"I tell you what," Mabel says, smiling oddly at Leroy.

"What?"

"Take her on down to Shiloh. Y'all need to get out together, stir a little. Her brain's all balled up over them books."

Leroy can see traces of Norma Jean's features in her mother's face. Mabel's worn face has the texture of crinkled cotton, but suddenly she looks pretty. It occurs to Leroy that Mabel has been hinting all along that she wants them to take her with them to Shiloh.

"Let's all go to Shiloh," he says. "You and me and her. Come Sunday."

Mabel throws up her hand in protest. "Oh, no, not me. Young folks want to be by theirselves."

When Norma Jean comes in with groceries, Leroy says excitedly, "Your mama here's been dying to go to Shiloh for thirty-five years. It's about time we went, don't you think?"

"I'm not going to butt in on anybody's second honeymoon," Mabel says.

"Who's going on a honeymoon, for Christ's sake?" Norma Jean says loudly.

"I never raised no daughter of mine to talk that-a-way," Mabel says.

"You ain't seen nothing yet," says Norma Jean. She starts putting away boxes and cans, slamming cabinet doors.

"There's a log cabin at Shiloh," Mabel says. "It was there during the battle. There's bullet holes in it."

"When are you going to *shut up* about Shiloh, Mama?" asks Norma Jean.

"I always thought Shiloh was the prettiest place, so full of history," Mabel goes on. "I just hoped y'all could see it once before I die, so you could tell me about it." Later, she whispers to Leroy, "You do what I said. A little change is what she needs."

"Your name means 'the king,'" Norma Jean says to Leroy that evening. He is trying to get her to go to Shiloh, and she is reading a book about another century.

"Well, I reckon I ought to be right proud."

"I guess so."

"Am I still king around here?"

Norma Jean flexes her biceps and feels them for hardness. "I'm not fooling around with anybody, if that's what you mean," she says.

"Would you tell me if you were?"

"I don't know."

"What does *your* name mean?"

"It was Marilyn Monroe's real name."

"No kidding!"

"Norma comes from the Normans. They were invaders," she says. She closes her book and looks hard at Leroy. "I'll go to Shiloh with you if you'll stop staring at me."

On Sunday, Norma Jean packs a picnic and they go to Shiloh. To Leroy's relief Mabel says she does not want to come with them. Norma Jean drives, and Leroy, sitting beside her, feels like some boring hitchhiker she has picked up. He tries some conversation, but she answers him in monosyllables. At Shiloh, she drives aimlessly through the park, past bluffs and trails and steep ravines. Shiloh is an immense place, and Leroy cannot see it as a battleground. It is not what he expected. He thought it would look like a golf course. Monuments are everywhere, showing through the thick clusters of trees. Norma Jean passes the log cabin Mabel mentioned. It is surrounded by tourists looking for bullet holes.

"That's not the kind of log house I've got in mind," says Leroy apologetically.

"I know *that*."

"This is a pretty place. Your mama was right."

"It's O.K.," says Norma Jean. "Well, we've seen it. I hope she's satisfied."

They burst out laughing together.

At the park museum, a movie on Shiloh is shown every half hour, but they decide that they don't want to see it. They buy a souvenir Confederate flag for Mabel, and then they find a picnic spot near the cemetery. Norma Jean has brought a picnic cooler, with pimiento sandwiches, soft drinks, and Yodels. Leroy eats a sandwich and then smokes a joint, hiding it behind the picnic cooler. Norma Jean has quit smoking altogether. She is picking cake crumbs from the cellophane wrapper, like a fussy bird.

Leroy says, "So the boys in gray ended up in Corinth. The Union soldiers zapped 'em finally. April 7, 1862."

They both know that he doesn't know any history. He is just talking about some of the historical plaques they have read. He feels awkward, like a boy on a date with an older girl. They are still just making conversation.

"Corinth is where Mama eloped to," says Norma Jean.

They sit in silence and stare at the cemetery for the Union dead and, beyond, at a tall cluster of trees. Campers are parked nearby, bumper to bumper, and small children in bright clothing are cavorting and squealing. Norma Jean wads up the cake wrapper and squeezes it tightly in her hand. Without looking at Leroy, she says, "I want to leave you."

Leroy takes a bottle of Coke out of the cooler and flips off the cap. He holds the bottle poised near his mouth but cannot remember to take a drink. Finally he says, "No, you don't."

"Yes, I do."

"I won't let you."

"You can't stop me."

"Don't do me that way."

Leroy knows Norma Jean will have her own way. "Didn't I promise to be home from now on?" he says.

"In some ways, a woman prefers a man who wanders," says Norma Jean. "That sounds crazy, I know."

"You're not crazy." Leroy remembers to drink from his Coke. Then he says, "Yes, you *are* crazy. You and me could start all over again. Right back at the beginning."

"We *have* started all over again," says Norma Jean. "And this is how it turned out."

"What did I do wrong?"

"Nothing."

"Is this one of those women's lib things?" Leroy asks.

"Don't be funny."

The cemetery, a green slope dotted with white markers, looks like a subdivision site. Leroy is trying to comprehend that his marriage is breaking up, but for some reason he is wondering about white slabs in a graveyard.

"Everything was fine till Mama caught me smoking," says Norma Jean, standing up. "That set something off."

"What are you talking about?"

"She won't leave me alone—*you* won't leave me alone." Norma Jean seems to be crying, but she is looking away from him. "I feel eighteen again. I can't face that all over again." She starts walking away. "No, it *wasn't* fine. I don't know what I'm saying. Forget it."

Leroy takes a lungful of smoke and closes his eyes as Norma Jean's words sink in. He tries to focus on the fact that thirty-five hundred soldiers died on the grounds around him. He can only think of that war as a board game with plastic soldiers. Leroy almost smiles, as he compares the Confederates' daring attack on the Union camps and Virgil Mathis's raid on the bowling alley. General Grant, drunk and furious, shoved the Southerners back to Corinth, where Mabel and Jet Beasley were married years later, when Mabel was still thin and good-looking. The next day, Mabel and Jet visited the battleground, and then Norma Jean was born, and then she married Leroy and they had a baby, which they lost, and now Leroy and Norma Jean are here at the same battleground. Leroy knows he is leaving out a lot. He is leaving out the insides of history. History was always just names and dates to him. It occurs to him that building a house of logs is similarly empty—too simple. And the real inner workings of a marriage, like most of history, have escaped him. Now he sees that building a log house is the dumbest idea he could have had. It was clumsy of him to think Norma Jean would want a log house. It was a crazy idea. He'll have to think of something else, quickly. He will wad the blueprints into tight balls and fling them into the lake. Then he'll get moving again. He opens his eyes. Norma Jean has moved away and is walking through the cemetery, following a serpentine brick path.

Leroy gets up to follow his wife, but his good leg is asleep and his bad leg still hurts him. Norma Jean is far away, walking rapidly toward the bluff by the river, and he tries to hobble toward her. Some children run past him, screaming noisily. Norma Jean has reached the bluff, and she is looking out over the Tennessee River. Now she turns toward Leroy and waves her arms. Is she beckoning to him? She seems to be doing an exercise for her chest muscles. The sky is unusually pale—the color of the dust ruffle Mabel made for their bed.

—1982

ALICE WALKER ■ (b. 1944)

Alice Walker wrote the Pulitzer Prize–winning epistolary novel The Color Purple *(1982). The book and its 1985 film version have made her the most famous living African-American woman writer, perhaps the most widely read of any American woman of color. A native of Eatonton, Georgia, Walker was the eighth child of an impoverished farm couple. She attended Spelman College in Atlanta and Sarah Lawrence College on scholarships, graduating in 1965. Walker began her literary career as a poet, eventually publishing six volumes of verse. Walker's short story collections and novels, including* The Temple of My Familiar *(1989) and* Possessing the Secret of Joy *(1992), which takes as its subject the controversial practice of female circumcision among African tribes, have continued to reach large audiences and have solidified her reputation as one of the major figures in contemporary literature. Walker has coined the term "womanist" to stand for the black feminist concerns of much of her fiction. "Everyday Use," a story from the early 1970s, is simultaneously a satisfying piece of realistic social commentary and a subtly satirical variation on the ancient fable of "The City Mouse and the Country Mouse." In recent years, Walker has published a novel,* Now Is the Time to Open Your Heart *(2004), and* A Poem Traveled Down My Arm *(2003), a collection of poems and drawings.*

Everyday Use

For your grandmama

I will wait for her in the yard that Maggie and I made so clean and wavy yesterday afternoon. A yard like this is more comfortable than most people know. It is not just a yard. It is like an extended living room. When the hard clay is swept clean as a floor and the fine sand around the edges lined with tiny, irregular grooves anyone can come and sit and look up into the elm tree and wait for the breezes that never come inside the house.

Maggie will be nervous until after her sister goes: she will stand hopelessly in corners homely and ashamed of the burn scars down her arms and legs, eyeing her sister with a mixture of envy and awe. She thinks her sister has held life always in the palm of one hand, that "no" is a word the world never learned to say to her.

You've no doubt seen those TV shows where the child who has "made it" is confronted, as a surprise, by her own mother and father, tottering in weakly from backstage. (A pleasant surprise, of course: What would they do if parent and child came on the show only to curse out and insult each other?) On TV mother and child embrace and smile into each other's faces. Sometimes the mother and father weep, the child wraps them in her arms and leans across the table to tell how she would not have made it without their help. I have seen these programs.

Sometimes I dream a dream in which Dee and I are suddenly brought together on a TV program of this sort. Out of a dark and soft-seated limousine I am ushered into a bright room filled with many people. There I meet a smiling, gray, sporty man like Johnny Carson who shakes my hand and tells me what a fine girl I have.* Then we are on the stage and Dee is embracing me with tears in her eyes. She pins on my dress a large orchid, even though she has told me once that she thinks orchids are tacky flowers.

In real life I am a large, big-boned woman with rough, man-working hands. In the winter I wear flannel nightgowns to bed and overalls during the day. I can kill and clean a hog as mercilessly as a man. My fat keeps me hot in zero weather. I can work outside all day, breaking ice to get water for washing. I can eat pork liver cooked over the open fire minutes after it comes steaming from the hog. One winter I knocked a bull calf straight in the brain between the eyes with a sledge hammer and had the meat hung up to chill before nightfall. But of course all this does not show on television. I am the way my daughter would want me to be: a hundred pounds lighter, my skin like an uncooked barley pancake. My hair glistens in the hot bright lights. Johnny Carson has much to do to keep up with my quick and witty tongue.

But that is a mistake. I know even before I wake up. Who ever knew a Johnson with a quick tongue? Who can even imagine me looking a strange white man in the eye? It seems to me I have talked to them always with one foot raised in flight, with my head turned in whichever way is farthest from them. Dee, though. She would always look anyone in the eye. Hesitation was no part of her nature.

"How do I look, Mama?" Maggie says, showing just enough of her thin body enveloped in pink skirt and red blouse for me to know she's there, almost hidden by the door.

"Come out into the yard," I say.

Have you ever seen a lame animal, perhaps a dog run over by some careless person rich enough to own a car, sidle up to someone who is ignorant enough to be kind to him? That is the way my Maggie walks. She has been like this, chin on chest, eyes on ground, feet in shuffle, ever since the fire that burned the other house to the ground.

Dee is lighter than Maggie, with nicer hair and a fuller figure. She's a woman now, though sometimes I forget. How long ago was it that the other house burned? Ten, twelve years? Sometimes I can still hear the flames and feel Maggie's arms sticking to me, her hair smoking and her dress falling off her in little black papery flakes. Her eyes seemed stretched open, blazed open by the flames reflected in them. And Dee. I see her standing off under the sweet gum tree she used to dig gum out of; a look of concentration on her face as she watched the last dingy gray board of the house fall in toward the red-hot brick chimney. Why don't you do a dance around the ashes? I'd wanted to ask her. She had hated the house that much.

I used to think she hated Maggie, too. But that was before we raised the money, the church and me, to send her to Augusta to school. She used to read to us without pity; forcing words, lies, other folks' habits, whole lives upon us two, sitting trapped and ignorant underneath her voice. She washed us in a river of make-believe, burned us with a lot of knowledge we didn't necessarily need to know. Pressed us to her with the serious way she read, to shove us away at just the moment, like dimwits, we seemed about to understand.

Dee wanted nice things. A yellow organdy dress to wear to her graduation from high school; black pumps to match a green suit she'd made from an old suit somebody gave me. She was determined to stare down any disaster in her efforts. Her eyelids would not flicker for minutes at a time. Often I fought off the temptation to shake her. At sixteen she had a style of her own: and knew what style was.

I never had an education myself. After second grade the school was closed down. Don't ask me why: in 1927 colored asked fewer questions than they do now. Sometimes Maggie reads to me. She stumbles along good-naturedly but can't see well. She knows she is not bright. Like good looks and money, quickness passed her by. She will marry John Thomas (who has mossy teeth in an earnest face) and then I'll be free to sit here and I guess just sing church songs to myself. Although I never was a good singer. Never could carry a tune. I was always better at a man's job. I used to love to milk till I was hoofed in the side in '49. Cows are soothing and slow and don't bother you, unless you try to milk them the wrong way.

I have deliberately turned my back on the house. It is three rooms, just like the one that burned, except the roof is tin; they don't make shingle roofs any more. There are no real windows, just some holes cut in the sides, like the portholes in a ship, but not round and not square, with rawhide holding the shutters up on the outside. This house is in a pasture, too, like the other one. No doubt when Dee sees it she will want to tear it down. She wrote me once that no matter where we "choose" to live, she will manage to come see us. But she will never bring her friends. Maggie and I thought about this and Maggie asked me, "Mama, when did Dee ever *have* any friends?"

She had a few. Furtive boys in pink shirts hanging about on wash-day after school. Nervous girls who never laughed. Impressed with her they worshiped the well-turned phrase, the cute shape, the scalding humor that erupted like bubbles in lye. She read to them.

When she was courting Jimmy T she didn't have much time to pay to us, but turned all her faultfinding power on him. He *flew* to marry a cheap gal from a family of ignorant flashy people. She hardly had time to recompose herself.

When she comes I will meet—but there they are!

Maggie attempts to make a dash for the house, in her shuffling way, but I stay her with my hand. "Come back here," I say. And she stops and tries to dig a well in the sand with her toe.

It is hard to see them clearly through the strong sun. But even the first glimpse of leg out of the car tells me it is Dee. Her feet were always neat-looking, as if God himself had shaped them with a certain style. From the other side of the car comes a short, stocky man. Hair is all over his head a foot long and hanging from his chin like a kinky mule tail. I hear Maggie suck in her breath. "Uhnnnh," is what it sounds like. Like when you see the wriggling end of a snake just in front of your foot on the road. "Uhnnnh."

Dee next. A dress down to the ground, in this hot weather. A dress so loud it hurts my eyes. There are yellows and oranges enough to throw back the light of the sun. I feel my whole face warming from the heat waves it throws out. Earrings, too, gold and hanging down to her shoulders. Bracelets dangling and making noises when she moves her arm up to shake the folds of the dress out of her armpits. The dress is loose and flows, and as she walks closer, I like it. I hear Maggie go "Uhnnnh" again. It is her sister's hair. It stands straight up like the wool on a sheep. It is black as night and around the edges are two long pigtails that rope about like small lizards disappearing behind her ears.

"Wa-su-zo-Tean-o!" she says, coming on in that gliding way the dress makes her move. The short stocky fellow with the hair to his navel is all grinning and he follows up with "Asalamalakim, my mother and sister!" He moves to hug Maggie but she falls back, right up against the back of my chair. I feel her trembling there and when I look up I see the perspiration falling off her chin.

"Don't get up," says Dee. Since I am stout it takes something of a push. You can see me trying to move a second or two before I make it. She turns, showing white heels through her sandals, and goes back to the car. Out she peeks next with a Polaroid. She stoops down quickly and lines up picture after picture of me sitting there in front of the house with Maggie cowering behind me. She never takes a shot without making sure the house is included. When a cow comes nibbling around the edge of the yard she snaps it and me and Maggie and the house. Then she puts the Polaroid in the back seat of the car, and comes up and kisses me on the forehead.

Meanwhile Asalamalakim is going through the motions with Maggie's hand. Maggie's hand is as limp as a fish, and probably as cold, despite the sweat, and she keeps trying to pull it back. It looks like Asalamalakim wants to shake hands but wants to do it fancy. Or maybe he don't know how people shake hands. Anyhow, he soon gives up on Maggie.

"Well," I say. "Dee."

"No, Mama," she says. "Not 'Dee,' Wangero Leewanika Kemanjo!"

"What happened to 'Dee'?" I wanted to know.

"She's dead," Wangero said. "I couldn't bear it any longer being named after the people who oppress me."

"You know as well as me you was named after your aunt Dicie," I said. Dicie is my sister. She named Dee. We called her "Big Dee" after Dee was born.

"But who was *she* named after?" asked Wangero.

"I guess after Grandma Dee," I said.

"And who was she named after?" asked Wangero.

"Her mother," I said, and saw Wangero was getting tired. "That's about as far back as I can trace it," I said. Though, in fact, I probably could have carried it back beyond the Civil War through the branches.

"Well," said Asalamalakim, "there you are."

"Uhnnnh," I heard Maggie say.

"There I was not," I said, "before 'Dicie' cropped up in our family, so why should I try to trace it that far back?"

He just stood there grinning, looking down on me like somebody inspecting a Model A car. Every once in a while he and Wangero sent eye signals over my head.

"How do you pronounce this name?" I asked.

"You don't have to call me by it if you don't want to," said Wangero.

"Why shouldn't I?" I asked. "If that's what you want us to call you, we'll call you."

"I know it might sound awkward at first," said Wangero.

"I'll get used to it," I said. "Ream it out again."

Well, soon we got the name out of the way. Asalamalakim had a name twice as long and three times as hard. After I tripped over it two or three times he told me to just call him Hakim-a-barber. I wanted to ask him was he a barber, but I didn't really think he was, so I didn't ask.

"You must belong to those beef-cattle peoples down the road," I said. They said "Asalamalakim" when they met you, too, but they didn't shake hands. Always too busy: feeding the cattle, fixing the fences, putting up salt-lick shelters, throwing down hay. When the white folks poisoned some of the herd the men stayed up all night with rifles in their hands. I walked a mile and a half just to see the sight.

Hakim-a-barber said, "I accept some of their doctrines, but farming and raising cattle is not my style." (They didn't tell me, and I didn't ask, whether Wangero [Dee] had really gone and married him.)

We sat down to eat and right away he said he didn't eat collards and pork was unclean. Wangero, though, went on through the chitlins and corn bread, the greens and everything else. She talked a blue streak over the sweet potatoes. Everything delighted her. Even the fact that we still used the benches her daddy made for the table when we couldn't afford to buy chairs.

"Oh, Mama!" she cried. Then turned to Hakim-a-barber. "I never knew how lovely these benches are. You can feel the rump prints," she said, running her hands underneath her and along the bench. Then she gave a sigh and her hand closed over Grandma Dee's butter dish. "That's it!" she said. "I knew there was something I wanted to ask you if I could have." She jumped up from the table and went over in the corner where the churn stood, the milk in it clabber by now. She looked at the churn and looked at it.

"This churn top is what I need," she said. "Didn't Uncle Buddy whittle it out of a tree you all used to have?"

"Yes," I said.

"Uh huh," she said happily. "And I want the dasher, too."

"Uncle Buddy whittle that, too?" asked the barber.

Dee (Wangero) looked up at me.

"Aunt Dee's first husband whittled the dash," said Maggie so low you almost couldn't hear her. "His name was Henry, but they called him Stash."

"Maggie's brain is like an elephant's," Wangero said, laughing. "I can use the churn top as a centerpiece for the alcove table," she said, sliding a plate over the churn, "and I'll think of something artistic to do with the dasher."

When she finished wrapping the dasher the handle stuck out. I took it for a moment in my hands. You didn't even have to look close to see where hands pushing the dasher up and down to make butter had left a kind of sink in the wood. In fact, there were a lot of small sinks; you could see where thumbs and fingers had sunk into the wood. It was beautiful light yellow wood, from a tree that grew in the yard where Big Dee and Stash had lived.

After dinner Dee (Wangero) went to the trunk at the foot of my bed and started rifling through it. Maggie hung back in the kitchen over the dishpan. Out came Wangero with two quilts. They had been pieced by Grandma Dee and then Big Dee and me had hung them on the quilt frames on the front porch and quilted them. One was in the Lone Star pattern. The other was Walk Around the Mountain. In both of them were scraps of dresses Grandma Dee had worn fifty and more years ago. Bits and pieces of Grandpa Jarrell's paisley shirts. And one teeny faded blue piece, about the size of a penny matchbox, that was from Great Grandpa Ezra's uniform that he wore in the Civil War.

"Mama," Wangero said sweet as a bird. "Can I have these old quilts?"

I heard something fall in the kitchen, and a minute later the kitchen door slammed.

"Why don't you take one or two of the others?" I asked. "These old things was just done by me and Big Dee from some tops your grandma pieced before she died."

"No," said Wangero. "I don't want those. They are stitched around the borders by machine."

"That's make them last better," I said.

"That's not the point," said Wangero. "These are all pieces of dresses Grandma used to wear. She did all this stitching by hand. Imagine!" She held the quilts securely in her arms, stroking them.

"Some of the pieces, like those lavender ones, come from old clothes her mother handed down to her," I said, moving up to touch the quilts. Dee (Wangero) moved back just enough so that I couldn't reach the quilts. They already belonged to her.

"Imagine!" she breathed again, clutching them closely to her bosom.

"The truth is," I said, "I promised to give them quilts to Maggie, for when she marries John Thomas."

She gasped like a bee had stung her.

"Maggie can't appreciate these quilts!" she said. "She'd probably be backward enough to put them to everyday use."

"I reckon she would," I said. "God knows I been saving 'em for long enough with nobody using 'em. I hope she will!" I didn't want to bring up how I had offered Dee (Wangero) a quilt when she went away to college. Then she had told me they were old-fashioned, out of style.

"But they're *priceless*!" she was saying now, furiously; for she has a temper. "Maggie would put them on the bed and in five years they'd be in rags. Less than that!"

"She can always make some more," I said. "Maggie knows how to quilt."

Dee (Wangero) looked at me with hatred. "You just will not understand. The point is these quilts, *these* quilts!"

"Well," I said, stumped. "What would *you* do with them?"

"Hang them," she said. As if that was the only thing you *could* do with quilts.

Maggie by now was standing in the door. I could almost hear the sound her feet made as they scraped over each other.

"She can have them, Mama," she said, like somebody used to never winning anything, or having anything reserved for her. "I can 'member Grandma Dee without the quilts."

I looked at her hard. She had filled her bottom lip with checker-berry snuff and it gave her face a kind of dopey, hangdog look. It was Grandma Dee and Big Dee who taught her how to quilt herself. She stood there with her scarred hands hidden in the folds of her skirt. She looked at her sister with something like fear but she was-n't mad at her. This was Maggie's portion. This was the way she knew God to work.

When I looked at her like that something hit me in the top of my head and ran down to the soles of my feet. Just like when I'm in church and the spirit of God touches me and I get happy and shout. I did something I never had done before: hugged Maggie to me, then dragged her on into the room, snatched the quilts out of Miss Wangero's hands and dumped them into Maggie's lap. Maggie just sat there on my bed with her mouth open.

"Take one or two of the others," I said to Dee.

But she turned without a word and went out to Hakim-a-barber.

"You just don't understand," she said, as Maggie and I came out to the car.

"What don't I understand?" I wanted to know.

"Your heritage," she said. And then she turned to Maggie, kissed her, and said, "You ought to try to make something of yourself, too, Maggie. It's really a new day for us. But from the way you and Mama still live you'd never know it."

She put on some sunglasses that hid everything above the tip of her nose and her chin.

Maggie smiled; maybe at the sunglasses. But a real smile, not scared. After we watched the car dust settle I asked Maggie to bring me a dip of snuff. And then the two of us sat there just enjoying, until it was time to go in the house and go to bed.

—1973

Tobias Wolff had an unusual childhood. His father was a noted con-artist who managed to work as an aeronautical engineer for over fifteen years despite having no formal training in the field. Wolff's elder brother, the journalist Geoffrey Wolff, wrote an autobiography about growing up with his father, and Tobias Wolff's memoir of growing up with his mother and step-father in Washington state, This Boy's Life, was made into a memorable film starring Robert De Niro and the young Leonardo diCaprio. Since 1997, Wolff has taught writing at his graduate alma mater, Stanford University, and many of his former students have gone onto make their mark as writers. Our Story Begins: New and Selected Stories was published in 2009.

Hunters in the Snow

Tub had been waiting for an hour in the falling snow. He paced the sidewalk to keep warm and stuck his head out over the curb whenever he saw lights approaching. One driver stopped for him but before Tub could wave the man on he saw the rifle on Tub's back and hit the gas. The tires spun on the ice.

The fall of snow thickened. Tub stood below the overhang of a building. Across the road the clouds whitened just above the rooftops, and the street lights went out. He shifted the rifle strap to his other shoulder. The whiteness seeped up the sky.

A truck slid around the corner, horn blaring, rear end sashaying. Tub moved to the sidewalk and held up his hand. The truck jumped the curb and kept coming, half on the street and half on the sidewalk. It wasn't slowing down at all. Tub stood for a moment, still holding up his hand, then jumped back. His rifle slipped off his shoulder and clattered on the ice, a sandwich fell out of his pocket. He ran for the steps of the building. Another sandwich and a package of cookies tumbled onto the new snow. He made the steps and looked back.

The truck had stopped several feet beyond where Tub had been standing. He picked up his sandwiches and his cookies and slung the rifle and went up to the driver's window. The driver was bent against the steering wheel, slapping his knees and drumming his feet on the floorboards. He looked like a cartoon of a person laughing, except that his eyes watched the man on the seat beside him. "You ought to see yourself," the driver said. "He looks just like a beach ball with a hat on, doesn't he? Doesn't he, Frank?"

The man beside him smiled and looked off.

"You almost ran me down," Tub said. "You could've killed me."

"Come on, Tub," said the man beside the driver. "Be mellow. Kenny was just messing around." He opened the door and slid over to the middle of the seat.

Tub took the bolt out of his rifle and climbed in beside him. "I waited an hour," he said. "If you meant ten o'clock why didn't you say ten o'clock?"

"Tub, you haven't done anything but complain since we got here," said the man in the middle. "If you want to piss and moan all day you might as well go home and bitch at your kids. Take your pick." When Tub didn't say anything he turned to the driver. "Okay, Kenny, let's hit the road."

Some juvenile delinquents had heaved a brick through the windshield on the driver's side, so the cold and snow tunneled right into the cab. The heater didn't work. They covered themselves with a couple of blankets Kenny had brought along and pulled down the muffs on their caps. Tub tried to keep his hands warm by rubbing them under the blanket but Frank made him stop.

They left Spokane and drove deep into the country, running along black lines offences. The snow let up, but still there was no edge to the land where it met the sky. Nothing moved in the chalky fields. The cold bleached their faces and made the stubble stand out on their cheeks and along their upper lips. They stopped twice for coffee before they got to the woods where Kenny wanted to hunt.

Tub was for trying someplace different; two years in a row they'd been up and down this land and hadn't seen a thing. Frank didn't care one way or the other, he just wanted to get out of the goddamned truck. "Feel that," Frank said, slamming the door. He spread his feet and closed his eyes and leaned his head way back and breathed deeply. "Tune in on that energy."

"Another thing," Kenny said. "This is open land. Most of the land around here is posted."

"I'm cold," Tub said.

Frank breathed out. "Stop bitching, Tub. Get centered."

"I wasn't bitching."

"Centered," 'Kenny said. "Next thing you'll be wearing a nightgown, Frank. Selling flowers out at the airport."

TOBIAS WOLFF

"Kenny," Frank said, "you talk too much."

"Okay," Kenny said. "I won't say a word. Like I won't say anything about a certain babysitter."

"What babysitter?" Tub asked.

"That's between us," Frank said, looking at Kenny. "That's confidential. You keep your mouth shut."

Kenny laughed.

"You're asking for it," Frank said.

"Asking for what?"

"You'll see."

"Hey," Tub said, "are we hunting or what?"

They started off across the field. Tub had trouble getting through the fences. Frank and Kenny could have helped him; they could have lifted up on the top wire and stepped on the bottom wire, but they didn't. They stood and watched him. There were a lot of fences and Tub was puffing when they reached the woods.

They hunted for over two hours and saw no deer, no tracks, no sign. Finally they stopped by the creek to eat. Kenny had several slices of pizza and a couple of candy bars: Frank had a sandwich, an apple, two carrots, and a square of chocolate; Tub ate one hard-boiled egg and a stick of celery.

"You ask me how I want to die today," Kenny said, "I'll tell you burn me at the stake." He turned to Tub. "You still on that diet?" He winked at Frank.

"What do you think? You think I like hard-boiled eggs?"

"All I can say is, it's the first diet I ever heard of where you gained weight from it."

"Who said I gained weight?"

"Oh, pardon me. I take it back. You're just wasting away before my very eyes. Isn't he, Frank?"

Frank had his fingers fanned out, tips against the bark of the stump where he'd laid his food. His knuckles were hairy. He wore a heavy wedding band and on his right pinky another gold ring with a flat face and an "F" in what looked like diamonds. He turned the ring this way and that. "Tub," he said, "you haven't seen your own balls in ten years."

Kenny doubled over laughing. He took off his hat and slapped his leg with it.

"What am I supposed to do?" Tub said. "It's my glands."

They left the woods and hunted along the creek. Frank and Kenny worked one bank and Tub worked the other, moving upstream. The snow was light but the drifts were deep and hard to move through. Wherever Tub looked the surface was smooth, undisturbed, and after a time he lost interest. He stopped looking for tracks and just tried to keep up with Frank and Kenny on the other side. A moment came when he realized he hadn't seen them in a long time. The breeze was moving from him to them; when it stilled he could sometimes hear Kenny laughing but that was all. He quickened his pace, breasting hard into the drifts, fighting away the snow with his knees and elbows. He heard his heart and felt the flush on his face but he never once stopped.

Tub caught up with Frank and Kenny at a bend of the creek. They were standing on a log that stretched from their bank to his. Ice had backed up behind the log. Frozen reeds stuck out, barely nodding when the air moved.

"See anything?" Frank asked.

Tub shook his head.

There wasn't much daylight left and they decided to head back toward the road. Frank and Kenny crossed the log and they started downstream, using the trail Tub had broken. Before they had gone very far Kenny stopped, "Look at that," he said, and pointed to some tracks going from the creek back into the woods. Tub's footprints crossed right over them. There on the bank, plain as day, were several mounds of deer sign. "What do you think that is, Tub?" Kenny kicked at it. "Walnuts on vanilla icing?"

"I guess I didn't notice."

Kenny looked at Frank.

"I was lost."

"You were lost. Big deal."

They followed the tracks into the woods. The deer had gone over a fence half buried in drifting snow. A no hunting sign was nailed to the top of one of the posts. Frank laughed and said the son of a bitch could read. Kenny wanted to go after him but Frank said no way, the people out here didn't mess around. He thought maybe the farmer who owned the land would let them use it if they asked. Kenny wasn't so sure. Anyway, he figured that by the time they walked to the truck and drove up the road and doubled back it would be almost dark.

"Relax," Frank said. "You can't hurry nature. If we're meant to get that deer, we'll get it. If we're not, we won't."

They started back toward the truck. This part of the woods was mainly pine. The snow was shaded and had a glaze on it. It held up Kenny and Frank but Tub kept falling through. As he kicked forward, the edge of the crust bruised his shins. Kenny and Frank pulled ahead of him, to where he couldn't even hear their voices any more. He sat down on a stump and wiped his face. He ate both the sandwiches and half the cookies, taking his own sweet time. It was dead quiet.

When Tub crossed the last fence into the road the truck started moving. Tub had to run for it and just managed to grab hold of the tailgate and hoist himself into the bed. He lay there, panting. Kenny looked out the rear window and grinned. Tub crawled into the lee of the cab to get out of the freezing wind. He pulled his earflaps low and pushed his chin into the collar of his coat. Someone rapped on the window but Tub would not turn around.

He and Frank waited outside while Kenny went into the farmhouse to ask permission. The house was old and paint was curling off the sides. The smoke streamed westward off the top of the chimney, fanning away into a thin gray plume. Above the ridge of the hills another ridge of blue clouds was rising.

"You've got a short memory," Tub said.

"What?" Frank said. He had been staring off.

"I used to stick up for you."

"Okay, so you used to stick up for me. What's eating you?"

"You shouldn't have just left me back there like that."

"You're a grown-up, Tub. You can take care of yourself. Anyway, if you think you're the only person with problems I can tell you that you're not."

"Is something bothering you, Frank?"

Frank kicked at a branch poking out of the snow. "Never mind," he said.

"What did Kenny mean about the babysitter?"

"Kenny talks too much," Frank said. "You just mind your own business."

Kenny came out of the farmhouse and gave the thumbs-up and they began walking back toward the woods. As they passed the barn a large black hound with a grizzled snout ran out and barked at them. Every time he barked he slid backwards a bit, like a cannon recoiling. Kenny got down on all fours and snarled and barked back at him, and the dog slunk away into the barn, looking over his shoulder and peeing a little as he went.

"That's an old-timer," Frank said. "A real graybeard. Fifteen years if he's a day."

"Too old," Kenny said.

Past the barn they cut off through the fields. The land was unfenced and the crust was freezing up thick and they made good time. They kept to the edge of the field until they picked up the tracks again and followed them into the woods, farther and farther back toward the hills. The trees started to blur with the shadows and the wind rose and needled their faces with the crystals it swept off the glaze. Finally they lost the tracks.

Kenny swore and threw down his hat. "This is the worst day of hunting I ever had, bar none." He picked up his hat and brushed off the snow. "This will be the first season since I was fifteen I haven't got my deer."

"It isn't the deer," Frank said. "It's the hunting. There are all these forces out here and you just have to go with them."

"You go with them," Kenny said. "I came out here to get me a deer, not listen to a bunch of hippie bullshit. And if it hadn't been for dimples here I would have, too."

"That's enough," Frank said.

"And you—you're so busy thinking about that little jailbait of yours you wouldn't know a deer if you saw one."

"Drop dead," Frank said, and turned away.

Kenny and Tub followed him back across the fields. When they were coming up to the barn Kenny stopped and pointed. "I hate that post," he said. He raised his rifle and fired. It sounded like a dry branch cracking. The post splintered along its right side, up towards the top. "There," Kenny said. "It's dead."

"Knock it off," Frank said, walking ahead.

Kenny looked at Tub. He smiled. "I hate that tree," he said, and fired again. Tub hurried to catch up with Frank. He started to speak but just then the dog ran out of the barn and barked at them. "Easy, boy," Frank said.

"I hate that dog." Kenny was behind them.

"That's enough," Frank said. "You put that gun down."

Kenny fired. The bullet went in between the dog's eyes. He sank right down into the snow, his legs splayed out on each side, his yellow eyes open and staring. Except for the blood he looked like a small bearskin rug. The blood ran down the dog's muzzle into the snow.

They all looked at the dog lying there.

"What did he ever do to you?" Tub asked. "He was just barking."

Kenny turned to Tub. "I hate you."

Tub shot from the waist. Kenny jerked backward against the fence and buckled to his knees. He folded his hands across his stomach. "Look," he said. His hands were covered with blood. In the dusk his blood was more blue than red. It seemed to belong to the shadows. It didn't seem out of place. Kenny eased himself onto his back. He sighed several times, deeply. "You shot me," he said.

"I had to," Tub said. He knelt beside Kenny. "Oh God," he said. "Frank. Frank."

Frank hadn't moved since Kenny killed the dog.

"Frank!" Tub shouted.

"I was just kidding around," Kenny said. "It was a joke. Oh!" he said, and arched his back suddenly. "Oh!" he said again, and dug his heels into the snow and pushed himself along on his head for several feet. Then he stopped and lay there, rocking back and forth on his heels and head like a wrestler doing warm-up exercises.

Frank roused himself. "Kenny," he said. He bent down and put his gloved hand on Kenny's brow. "You shot him," he said to Tub.

"He made me," Tub said.

"No no no," Kenny said.

Tub was weeping from the eyes and nostrils. His whole face was wet. Frank closed his eyes, then looked down at Kenny again. "Where does it hurt?"

"Everywhere," Kenny said, "just everywhere."

"Oh God," Tub said.

"I mean where did it go in?" Frank said.

"Here." Kenny pointed at the wound in his stomach. It was welling slowly with blood.

"You're lucky," Frank said. "It's on the left side. It missed your appendix. If it had hit your appendix you'd really be in the soup." He turned and threw up onto the snow, holding his sides as if to keep warm.

"Are you all right?" Tub said.

"There's some aspirin in the truck," Kenny said.

"I'm all right," Frank said.

"We'd better call an ambulance," Tub said.

"Jesus," Frank said. "What are we going to say?"

"Exactly what happened," Tub said. "He was going to shoot me but I shot him first."

"No sir!" Kenny said. "I wasn't either!"

Frank patted Kenny on the arm. "Easy does it, partner." He stood. "Let's go."

Tub picked up Kenny's rifle as they walked down toward the farmhouse. "No sense leaving this around," he said. "Kenny might get ideas."

"I can tell you one thing," Frank said. "You've really done it this time. This definitely takes the cake."

They had to knock on the door twice before it was opened by a thin man with lank hair. The room behind him was filled with smoke. He squinted at them, "You get anything?" he asked.

"No," Frank said.

"I knew you wouldn't. That's what I told the other fellow."

"We've had an accident."

The man looked past Frank and Tub into the gloom. "Shoot your friend, did you?"

Frank nodded.

"I did," Tub said.

"I suppose you want to use the phone."

"If it's okay."

The man in the door looked behind him, then stepped back. Frank and Tub followed him into the house. There was a woman sitting by the stove in the middle of the room. The stove was smoking badly. She looked up and then down again at the child asleep in her lap. Her face was white and damp; strands of hair were pasted across her forehead. Tub warmed his hands over the stove while Frank went into the kitchen to call. The man who had let them in stood at the window, his hands in his pockets.

"My friend shot your dog," Tub said.

The man nodded without turning around. "I should have done it myself. I just couldn't."

"He loved that dog so much," the woman said. The child squirmed and she rocked it.

"You asked him to?" Tub said. "You asked him to shoot your dog?"

"He was old and sick. Couldn't chew his food any more. I would have done it myself but I don't have a gun."

"You couldn't have anyway," the woman said. "Never in a million years."

The man shrugged.

Frank came out of the kitchen. "We'll have to take him ourselves. The nearest hospital is fifty miles from here and all their ambulances are out anyway."

The woman knew a shortcut but the directions were complicated and Tub had to write them down. The man told them where they could find some boards to carry Kenny on. He didn't have a flashlight but he said he would leave the porch light on.

It was dark outside. The clouds were low and heavy-looking and the wind blew in shrill gusts. There was a screen loose on the house and it banged slowly and then quickly as the wind rose again. They could hear it all the way to the barn. Frank went for the boards while Tub looked for Kenny, who was not where they had left him. Tub found him farther up the drive, lying on his stomach. "You okay?" Tub said.

"It hurts."

"Frank says it missed your appendix."

"I already had my appendix out."

"All right," Frank said, coming up to them. "We'll have you in a nice warm bed before you can say Jack Robinson." He put the two boards on Kenny's right side.

"Just as long as I don't have one of those male nurses," Kenny said.

"Ha ha," Frank said. "That's the spirit. Get ready, set, *over you go*," and he rolled Kenny onto the boards. Kenny screamed and kicked his legs in the air. When he quieted down Frank and Tub lifted the boards and carried him down the drive. Tub had the back end, and with the snow blowing into his face he had trouble with his footing. Also he was tired and the man inside had forgotten to turn the porch light on. Just past the house Tub slipped and threw out his hands to catch himself. The boards fell and Kenny tumbled out and rolled to the bottom of the drive, yelling all the way. He came to rest against the right front wheel of the truck.

"You fat moron," Frank said. "You aren't good for diddly."

Tub grabbed Frank by the collar and backed him hard up against the fence. Frank tried to pull his hands away but Tub shook him and snapped his head back and forth and finally Frank gave up.

"What do you know about fat," Tub said, "What do you know about glands." As he spoke he kept shaking Frank. "What do you know about me."

"All right," Frank said.

"No more," Tub said.

"All right."

"No more talking to me like that. No more watching. No more laughing."

"Okay, Tub. I promise."

Tub let go of Frank and leaned his forehead against the fence. His arms hung straight at his sides.

"I'm sorry, Tub." Frank touched him on the shoulder. "I'll be down at the truck."

Tub stood by the fence for a while and then got the rifles off the porch. Frank had rolled Kenny back onto the boards and they lifted him into the bed of the truck. Frank spread the seat blankets over him. "Warm enough?" he asked.

Kenny nodded.

"Okay. Now how does reverse work on this thing?"

"All the way to the left and up." Kenny sat up as Frank started forward to the cab. "Frank!"

"What?"

"If it sticks don't force it."

The truck started right away. "One thing," Frank said, "you've got to hand it to the Japanese. A very ancient, very spiritual culture and they can still make a hell of a truck." He glanced over at Tub. "Look, I'm sorry. I didn't know you felt that way, honest to God I didn't. You should have said something."

"I did."

"When? Name one time."

"A couple of hours ago."

"I guess I wasn't paying attention."

"That's true, Frank," Tub said. "You don't pay attention very much."

"Tub," Frank said, "what happened back there, I should have been more sympathetic. I realize that. You were going through a lot. I just want you to know it wasn't your fault. He was asking for it."

"You think so?"

"Absolutely. It was him or you. I would have done the same thing in your shoes, no question."

The wind was blowing into their faces. The snow was a moving white wall in front of their lights; it swirled into the cab through the hole in the windshield and settled on them. Tub clapped his hands and shifted around to stay warm, but it didn't work.

"I'm going to have to stop," Frank said. "I can't feel my fingers."

Up ahead they saw some lights off the road. It was a tavern. Outside in the parking lot there were several jeeps and trucks. A couple of them had deer strapped across their hoods. Frank parked and they went back to Kenny. "How you doing, partner," Frank said.

"I'm cold."

"Well, don't feel like the Lone Ranger. It's worse inside, take my word for it. You should get that windshield fixed."

"Look," Tub said, "he threw the blankets off." They were lying in a heap against the tailgate.

"Now look, Kenny," Frank said, "it's no use whining about being cold if you're not going to try and keep warm. You've got to do your share." He spread the blankets over Kenny and tucked them in at the corners.

"They blew off."

"Hold on to them then."

"Why are we stopping, Frank?"

"Because if me and Tub don't get warmed up we're going to freeze solid and then where will you be?" He punched Kenny lightly in the arm. "So just hold your horses."

The bar was full of men in colored jackets, mostly orange. The waitress brought coffee. "Just what the doctor ordered," Frank said, cradling the steaming cup in his hand. His skin was bone white. "Tub, I've been thinking. What you said about me not paying attention, that's true."

"It's okay."

"No. I really had that coming. I guess I've just been a little too interested in old number one. I've had a lot on my mind. Not that that's any excuse."

"Forget it, Frank. I sort of lost my temper back there. I guess we're all a little on edge."

Frank shook his head. "It isn't just that."

"Yon want to talk about it?"

"Just between us, Tub?"

"Sure, Frank. Just between us."

"Tub, I think I'm going to be leaving Nancy."

"Oh, Frank. Oh, Frank." Tub sat back and shook his head.

Frank reached out and laid his hand on Tub's arm. "Tub, have you ever been really in love?"

"Well—"

"I mean *really* in love." He squeezed Tub's wrist. "With your whole being."

"I don't know. When you put it like that, I don't know."

"You haven't then. Nothing against you, but you'd know it if you had." Frank let go of Tub's arm. "This isn't just some bit of fluff I'm talking about."

"Who is she, Frank?"

Frank paused. He looked into his empty cup. "Roxanne Brewer."

"Cliff Brewer's kid? The babysitter?"

"You can't just put people into categories like that, Tub. That's why the whole system is wrong. And that's why this country is going to hell in a rowboat."

"But she can't be more than—" Tub shook his head.

"Fifteen. She'll be sixteen in May." Frank smiled. "May fourth, three twenty-seven p.m. Hell, Tub, a hundred years ago she'd have been an old maid by that age. Juliet was only thirteen."

"Juliet? Juliet Miller? Jesus, Frank, she doesn't even have breasts. She doesn't even wear a top to her bathing suit. She's still collecting frogs."

"Not Juliet Miller. The real Juliet. Tub, don't you see how you're dividing people up into categories? He's an executive, she's a secretary, he's a truck driver, she's fifteen years old. Tub, this so-called babysitter, this so-called fifteen-year-old has more in her little finger than most of us have in our entire bodies. I can tell you this little lady is something special."

Tub nodded. "I know the kids like her."

"She's opened up whole worlds to me that I never knew were there."

"What does Nancy think about all of this?"

"She doesn't know."

"You haven't told her?"

"Not yet. It's not so easy. She's been damned good to me all these years. Then there's the kids to consider." The brightness in Frank's eyes trembled and he wiped quickly at them with the back of his hand. "I guess you think I'm a complete bastard."

"No, Frank. I don't think that."

"Well, you *ought* to."

"Frank, when you've got a friend it means you've always got someone on your side, no matter what. That's the way I feel about it, anyway."

"You mean that, Tub?"

"Sure I do."

Frank smiled. "You don't know how good it feels to hear you say that."

Kenny had tried to get out of the truck but he hadn't made it. He was jackknifed over the tailgate, his head hanging above the bumper. They lifted him back into the bed and covered him again. He was sweating and his teeth chattered. "It hurts, Frank."

"It wouldn't hurt so much if you just stayed put. Now we're going to the hospital. Got that? Say it—I'm going to the hospital."

"I'm going to the hospital."

"Again."

"I'm going to the hospital."

"Now just keep saying that to yourself and before you know it we'll be there."

After they had gone a few miles Tub turned to Frank. "I just pulled a real boner," he said.

"What's that?"

"I left the directions on the table back there."

"That's okay. I remember them pretty well."

The snowfall lightened and the clouds began to roll back off the fields, but it was no warmer and after a time both Frank and Tub were bitten through and shaking. Frank almost didn't make it around a curve, and they decided to stop at the next road-house.

There was an automatic hand-dryer in the bathroom and they took turns standing in front of it, opening their jackets and shirts and letting the jet of hot air breathe across their faces and chests.

"You know," Tub said, "what you told me back there, I appreciate it. Trusting me."

Frank opened and closed his fingers in front of the nozzle. "The way I look at it, Tub, no man is an island. You've got to trust someone."

"Frank—"

Frank waited.

"When I said that about my glands, that wasn't true. The truth is I just shovel it in."

"Well, Tub—"

"Day and night, Frank. In the shower. On the freeway." He turned and let the air play over his back. "I've even got stuff in the paper towel machine at work."

"There's nothing wrong with your glands at all?" Frank had taken his boots and socks off. He held first his right, then his left foot up to the nozzle.

"No. There never was."

"Does Alice know?" The machine went off and Frank started lacing up his boots.

"Nobody knows. That's the worst of it, Frank. Not the being fat, I never got any big kick out of being thin, but the lying. Having to lead a double life like a spy or a hit man. This sounds strange but I feel sorry for those guys, I really do. I know what they go through. Always having to think about what you say and do. Always feeling like people are watching you, trying to catch you at something. Never able to just be yourself. Like when I make a big deal about only having an orange for breakfast and then scarf all the way to work. Oreos, Mars Bars, Twinkies. Sugar Babies. Snickers." Tub glanced at Frank and looked quickly away. "Pretty disgusting, isn't it?"

"Tub. Tub." Frank shook his head. "Come on." He took Tub's arm and led him into the restaurant half of the bar. "My friend is hungry," he told the waitress. "Bring four orders of pancakes, plenty of butter and syrup."

"Frank—"

"Sit down."

When the dishes came Frank carved out slabs of butter and just laid them on the pancakes. Then he emptied the bottle of syrup, moving it back and forth over the plates. He leaned forward on his elbows and rested his chin in one hand. "Go on, Tub."

Tub ate several mouthfuls, then started to wipe his lips. Frank took the napkin away from him. "No wiping," he said. Tub kept at it. The syrup covered his chin; it dripped to a point like a goatee. "Weigh in, Tub," Frank said, pushing another fork across the table. "Get down to business." Tub took the fork in his left hand and lowered his head and started really chowing down. "Clean your plate," Frank said when the pancakes were gone, and Tub lifted each of the four plates and licked it clean. He sat back, trying to catch his breath.

"Beautiful," Frank said. "Are you full?"

"I'm full," Tub said. "I've never been so full."

Kenny's blankets were bunched up against the tailgate again.

"They must have blown off," Tub said.

"They're not doing him any good," Frank said. "We might as well get some use out of them."

Kenny mumbled. Tub bent over him. "What? Speak up."

"I'm going to the hospital," Kenny said.

"Attaboy," Frank said.

The blankets helped. The wind still got their faces and Frank's hands but it was much better. The fresh snow on the road and the trees sparkled under the beam of the headlight. Squares of light from farmhouse windows fell onto the blue snow in the fields.

"Frank," Tub said after a time, "you know that farmer? He told Kenny to kill the dog."

"You're kidding!" Frank leaned forward, considering. "That Kenny. What a card." He laughed and so did Tub. Tub smiled out the back window. Kenny lay with his arms folded over his stomach, moving his lips at the stars. Right overhead was the Big Dipper, and behind, hanging between Kenny's toes in the direction of the hospital, was the North Star, Pole Star, Help to Sailors. As the truck twisted through the gentle hills the star went back and forth between Kenny's boots, staying always in his sight. "I'm going to the hospital," Kenny said. But he was wrong. They had taken a different turn a long way back.

—1981

TIM GAUTREAUX ■ (b. 1947)

Tim Gautreaux was born in Morgan City, Louisiana, a port that grew prosperous in the early days of the offshore oil industry and declined as the industry waned. Gautreaux's fiction captures the regional speech patterns and "American dreams" of working-class members of the Cajun (Acadian) culture of southern Louisiana. Educated at Nicholls State University and the University of South Carolina, Gautreaux is a retired professor of English at Southeastern Louisiana University in Hammond.

Waiting for the Evening News

Jesse McNeil was running a locomotive while he was drunk, and he was doing a fine job of it, charging up the main line at fifty with the chemical train, rattling through the hot Louisiana night like a thunderstorm.

He watched the headlight brighten the rails to mile-long silver spears sailing through the sandy pine wastelands of the parish. Another nameless hamlet was rolling up in the distance, one in a row of asbestos-siding-and-tin communities strung along the railroad like ticks on a dog's backbone. He had roared through it a thousand times with a hundred cars of propane and vinyl chloride and had never so much as touched the air brake, had only to blow a signal for the one crossing, and then was gone like a gas pain in the bowel, discomfort and noise for a moment, soon forgotten by the few hundred folks who lived in wherever-it-was, Louisiana. He reached for the whistle lever in the dark cab and missed it, remembering the half-pint of whiskey he had gulped behind the engine house thirty minutes earlier. He was fifty years old today, and he wanted to do something wild and woolly, like get half-lit and pull the chemical train, known by enginemen as the "rolling bomb," up to the Mississippi line on time for a change. He could make this run in his sleep. After he got the train stretched out and up to the speed limit, all he had to do was blow the damned whistle. The train was on tracks and couldn't get lost or wander off among somebody's cows.

Jesse looked over at his brakeman, who was watching for automobiles on his side of the train. A highway followed along the tracks and at least once every trip a noodlehead with the windows rolled up and the radio blasting would turn in front of the engine at a crossing, notice the train, maybe mess in his britches, and then shoot on across to safety. Jesse reached again for the whistle lever and pulled it, sending a five-chime-whistle note crashing off all the tin and asbestos for a mile around. The gravel crossing winked in the moonlight and was gone, the train invaded the town, and Jesse looked out his window at the black air, listening to the hollow thunder in his head and laughing at how free he felt, how nobody cared what he was doing, how lost he was in the universe. He was the anonymous taxi driver of ethylene oxide and caustic soda, chlorine and ethyl antiknock compound, a man known intimately only by his menopausal wife and the finance company.

Then with a jolt, loose wrenches and lunch boxes flew forward in a convulsion of iron, and Jesse was knocked from his seat, his thermos flying over his head and sailing out into the thundering darkness. The locomotive lurched as though a giant hand had grabbed it from behind and wiggled it like a toy. Leaning out the window and looking back along the mile-long trail of tankers, he saw a whirlwind of sparks thirty cars back, and his heart divided in two and hid up under his shoulder blades. Somewhere an air hose parted, and the brakes jammed on with a squeal. He remembered to shut off the throttle, and as the engines bucked and ground rails for a quarter mile, he saw a white tanker turn sideways in the distance. Then he knew the train was breaking apart, the rear section running in like an accordion, and here he was in the dark woods at the edge of town, more than half-drunk, witnessing a catastrophe that would have happened even if he had been stone-sober and riding the rails with a Bible in his back pocket.

The black locomotives trembled to a stop, jumping as derailing cars smacked into those tankers still on the tracks. The brakeman and conductor hit the ground, running toward all the thunder. Jesse McNeil climbed down the engine steps carefully and put his hands in his pockets, wondering what he would do, what he would tell everybody. Then the first chemical tanker exploded, pinwheeling up into the night sky, slinging its wheels and coming down into a roadside 7-Eleven, the building disappearing in an unholy orange fireball. The strange pounding Jesse heard was the sound of his own feet running north along the railroad, scattering rocks and dust until he reached a spot where he could get down to the highway and lope along the blacktop. He ran until he had no wind and his heart pounded like a fist. Then he turned and saw the sky lit up a smoky yellow. He began to stumble backward through an unnameable fear, and when an old pickup pulled out of a side road and drove north toward him, he stuck out his thumb.

Jesse hitched to the next jerkwater town up the line, and even there he could see a poisonous glow on the horizon. A log-truck driver gave him a lift to the interstate, and he was faced with the choice of going north, farther into the trash-woods and hills where he was raised, the land of clapboard fundamentalist churches and mildewed trailers, or south toward the alien swamps and that Sodom of all Sodoms, New Orleans. He crossed the median to the southbound lane. No one would look for him in New Orleans.

After a while, a black sedan approached, and he stuck up his thumb, thinking that if he could get away long enough for his system to clear of bourbon, maybe he could tell the company officials that he'd had an attack of amnesia, or anxiety, or stupidity, and had run off like a fool to sort things out for a day. What could they do to him for being stupid? Fire him? He didn't need much money anyway. His frame house was paid for, and the only reason he worked at all was to spend time away from Lurleen, his prune-skin wife, who was always after him to paint or fix something. But if they had found him stumbling around by the engine, drunk, maybe the law would get involved. Maybe it would mean a great big fine, and if he ever did want to work for a railroad again, they wouldn't hire him to run a windup locomotive around a Christmas tree.

To his surprise the black sedan stopped, and soon he was cruising south in the company of an old Catholic priest, a Father Lambrusco, semiretired, who was filling in for a vacationing assistant pastor at St. Louis Cathedral.

"You out of work?" the priest asked, speeding past a gravel truck.

"Yeah," Jesse said, studying the eastern sky through the windshield. "I'm a carpenter,"

"Ah. Joseph was a carpenter."

"Joseph who?"

The priest checked his rearview. "Joseph, the father of Jesus."

Jesse frowned at himself. A priest talks about Joseph the carpenter, and Jesse thinks at first that maybe he's talking about Joseph Wiggins from McComb, Mississippi. "Oh yeah, that Joseph," Jesse said.

"You go to church?"

"Well, some. I'm sort of a fundamentalist."

"Isn't going to church fundamental? No, never mind. I didn't pick you up to preach. To tell the truth, I was falling asleep at the wheel," He turned his bald head toward Jesse and smiled, keeping his mouth closed, as though he had bad teeth. "Tell me, Mr. Carpenter, do you believe Catholics worship statues?"

Jesse assured him he did not, that one friend he had made in the service had been a Catholic chaplain.

"Were you baptized by total immersion in your church?" the priest asked.

"All the way under. We got our own special tank."

"Was your life changed?" The priest swung around a Volkswagen. Jesse pursed his lips and looked far down the road, as if he might see his life changing up ahead. "The minister said it might take some time in my case."

He and the priest talked for an hour and a half about snake-handler preachers and why nuns didn't have any spare time.

At two in the morning Jesse checked into the Night O' Delight Motel on Airline Highway in New Orleans. The desk clerk, a young Asian man, asked him if he wanted a fifteen-dollar room or a sixty-dollar room with a bed warmer. "What fool would pay sixty dollars just to sleep in a room?" he told him. He gave the man three fives, plus the tax, thankful that he had just cashed his paycheck and held back a few hundred to pay Lurleen's cousin to come over and paint the house. When he got to the room he turned on the television to check for news, flipping through channels until he reached the last station on the dial, which was showing a vividly pornographic scene.

Jesse mashed the off switch and drew back his finger as though it had been burned.

He looked around at the warped paneling and the window unit, which labored without a grille in its hole near the ceiling. Tomorrow he would call in his story. Things would go fairly rough with him for running off, but he would worry about that the next day. He pulled off his coveralls and climbed into the bed, which jittered and rang, sagging badly in the middle.

The next morning his bladder woke him in time for the eight o'clock news, and as he fumbled with the dials, he wondered if the wreck would even be mentioned. The fire probably had been put out by now. The railroad would have to buy somebody's 7-Eleven, but they could have the line clear by late afternoon.

However, on Channel 4 was a helicopter view of Satan's living room, fifty tank cars crashed together and burning. Black-and-green smoke rose a mile into the air, and on both sides of the track, seed elevators, storehouses, and shops flamed in fierce amber heaps. Jesse stepped back and cupped a hand to his forehead. He tried to say something like "What in God's name?" but he couldn't make a sound. The voice narrating the video told that the town had been evacuated and that fire-fighting teams were driven back by a mix of a dozen chemicals spilled from ruptured tankers, that the town's ditches were running with vinyl chloride and paint stripper. Then the voice told the world that Jesse P. McNeil, the train's engineer, had disappeared from the scene and it was thought that he had run off into the woods east of the derailment, where parish posse members were searching for him with teams of dogs.

When he heard his name fly out of the television, Jesse sat down hard on the creaking bed. Hardly forty people knew he existed, and now his name had sailed out into the region like parts of his exploded train. Why, he wondered, was it important to name him at all? And sheriff's officers were in the woods searching for him like he was a criminal. When the news report ended, he turned off the television and wondered if his blood would now test free of alcohol. He decided to eat a big breakfast. Stepping out of his room, he walked over to a run-down strip of glass and blond-colored brick businesses across the highway, entered a smoky cafe, and sat at the counter. On a shelf over the coffee urn, a grease-stained television blinked and buzzed. A local channel was showing the wreck from ground level. A handsome announcer listed twenty evil-sounding names of chemicals that were burning, spilling, or threatening to explode. He also mentioned that the engineer was a man of average build, with red hair combed straight back, last seen hitching a ride north of the wreck site. The waitresses were absorbed in the broadcast and didn't see Jesse slowly turn away from the counter and head for the door. Outside, he stood on the curb and felt light-headed, anxious that the next person to lay eyes on him might recognize who he was. He looked up and down the neon-infested highway for escape. Next to the cafe was a cubbyhole-sized barbershop, and he sidled over to its door and backed inside. Jesse found an Italian-looking gentleman stropping his razor and watching a TV mounted on a rack in the corner. The engineer sat in the chair and wondered how he could ask for his hair to be combed in some new way, maybe with a part on the side, anything different from the straight-back crimson mane he sported at the moment. The barber smiled and clicked his scissors in the air twice.

"Hey, what you think of the train wreck? Some mess, right?" He ran a comb through Jesse's hair slowly, as though admiring it.

Jesse looked at him warily. He hated the big-city accent of New Orleans folks. They sounded like New Yorkers to his piney woods ear. "I ain't heard of a wreck," Jesse said.

The barber bobbed his head. "Aw yeah. You just come in from the forest, hey? You from Mississippi, right? Hay-baling time and all that shit."

Jesse found himself nodding, glad to be given some kind of identity. Just then the television screen flashed a stern company photograph of his face. "Look here," he said, grabbing the barber's arm and pulling his attention away from the TV, "can't you give me kind of a modern look? Something maybe a little younger?"

The barber sucked in his cheeks and studied Jesse's head the way an expensive artist might. "Yeah, man. I could wash all that oil out, shorten everything up, and kinda spike it." He clicked his scissors once. "But your friends back in the woods gonna think you a Communist rock star or somethin'."

Jesse took in a deep breath and watched the white-hot center of the chemical train pulse over the barber's shoulder. "Do it to me," he said.

After his haircut, he spent the entire morning in the cafe next door, reading the newspapers. The noon TV news devoted a full five minutes to the train wreck. At that point he decided he would not call in for a while, that he would wait a few days until this was past and everyone would begin to forget, that he would lie low along Airline Highway in the Night O' Delight Motel until everyone and every thing cooled off and the poisonous fumes of his train wreck had blown clear of the unlucky town. It took him a good while to decide this, because out-of-the-ordinary decisions seldom came up in his life. The engineer had been running the same routes with the same trains for so many years that lately he found it hard to pay attention to the usual telegraph poles and sweet-gum trees sailing past his cab window. In the same way, the stunted pines along the road to his house, and the little house itself, had become unseeable. Sometimes he imagined himself an unseen part of this faded, repetitive background.

The sense of being invisible made Jesse think he could not be taken seriously, which was why he never voted, hardly ever renewed his driver's license, and paid attention in church only once a year at revival time. He thought of the plywood church at the end of the dirt lane and wondered what Father Lambrusco would think of it.

During the afternoon he watched soap operas, amazed at all the little things the characters could get upset about. He laughed as he thought of Lurleen watching the same shows, a cup of coffee in her lap, a cigarette mashed in the saucer. He began to feel some of the gloom brought on by the noon newscast evaporate, and he looked forward to the five o'clock news because he knew it would tell that the crisis was over, people were returning to their homes, and the railroad would be repaired in a day or so. Waiting for the evening news, Jesse pondered life's good points, how most injuries healed up, most people changed for the better, and whatever was big news today was small potatoes on page thirty tomorrow. He lay back on his bed and studied the rain-stained ceiling and the mismatched paneling on the walls. Even this room would be remodeled some-day and no one would suspect how ugly it had been. Things would improve.

But when the local news theme began to play over his scratched motel television, his face froze in a disbelieving stare. A black sky coiled and spread for miles above a crossroads town, and an evil-looking copper blaze flashed at the heart of a mountain of wreckage. The announcer stated that the train's brakeman had accused the en-gineer of being intoxicated at the time of the accident. Jesse balled up a fist. "Son of a bitch," he shouted at the television, "that hop-head smokes weed day and night." The announcer went on to say that the parish sheriff's department had a warrant out for the engineer's arrest and that railroad officials were hiring private investigators to locate the runaway employee. Meanwhile, firefighters were having to let the wreck burn because of an overheated propane tanker and the danger that two cars of chemicals would rupture and mix, producing mustard gas. Jesse's mouth fell open at this last awful announcement, and he began to fear that somehow everything was being blamed on him. He watched aerial shots of the fire spreading into the town, and as he did, another propane tanker went off like the end of the world, skyborne rills of fire torching a poor neighborhood of wooden houses to the east of the tracks. He sat on the floor, gathering fistfuls of cheap shag carpet, holding on, anchoring himself against the TV's revelations.

At the end of the report, he was shaking, so he snapped off the set. His name was on the air again, broadcast all over two states. And why did they want to arrest *him*? The train had come apart on its own. A wheel rim had cracked off, or a rail broke. He hadn't been speeding. Nobody knew what went wrong. Billy Graham could have been at the throttle of that locomotive and the same thing would have happened. He left the room, crossed the highway, and bought a deck of cards, returning to the little table by the window and dealing a hand of solitaire. He hoped the game would take his mind off the wreck, but after a while he began placing red eights on red nines, and he wished for his wife's face over his shoulder, telling him where he'd missed a play.

The next day he woke up and glared at the dark set a long time before deciding to shave. He refused to watch the news. Each broadcast injured his notion of who he was, and he would have no more of that. He caught a bus to the French Quarter and in Jackson Square sat on a wrought-iron bench, amazed that no one looked like his friends from his shriveled-up hometown. Jesse missed the red clay ditches and the boiled turpentine smell of Gumwood, Louisiana. He had never seen so many weak-looking men dressed in baggy, strange clothes, but he envied their anonymity, for at the moment he felt as obvious as the soaring statue of Andrew Jackson that rose before him, splattered by pigeons.

He spent all day in the Quarter, poking his sharp face into the doors of antique shops and bars, hankering for a hot charge of supermarket whiskey but holding back. Whenever he passed a newspaper vending machine, he saw a smoky photograph on the front page and felt a twinge of remorse. He wondered if he should turn himself in.

At the motel, he avoided the local news, deciding to turn the set on only for the national stuff, where, he was thinking, he would see the really important events, nothing about some local train burning a pissant town off the map. But as the CBS evening news played its intro theme over a film snippet of the main story, Jesse let out a pained yelp.

There on the screen was his wife, Lurleen, shaking her rat-gray hair and telling a reporter, "I don't know where he run off to leaving a blowed-up train behind like that." She sniffed and pointed a finger toward the camera. "But it don't surprise me one bit," she said to the world. "No sir, not one thing that man would do would surprise a jumpy cat." Jesse interlaced his fingers and placed his hands on top of his brushy head. On the screen, Lurleen looked powerful and almost attractive, in a dirt road kind of way. The program cut to an anchorman, and Jesse was thankful, for he half-expected Lurleen to start telling about him not paying her nephew for painting the house, and then everyone in red-white-and-blue America would know he was too lazy to paint his own damned living room. The announcer, low-voiced and serious in a blue sport coat, told how a white cloud of escaped chemical had rolled over a chicken farm and killed ten thousand hens, how three firemen were seriously injured when the wind shifted and they were overtaken by a toxic blanket.

"But the real mystery," the announcer continued, "is Jesse McNeil, the fifty-year-old engineer from Gumwood, Louisiana, who ran away from the scene of the accident. There are many speculations about his disappearance. Fellow workers suggest that McNeil was depressed because of his fiftieth birthday and was having marital and family problems. Whatever the reasons, he left behind a growing scene of destruction and pollution perhaps unequaled in American railroad history. Our live coverage continues from southeast Louisiana." And there it was. Jesse's eyes widened as a camera did a slow pan of his home on Loblolly Road, and he watched his partially bald yard, his house, which from this angle looked like a masonite-covered shoe box, and his carport, which seemed wobbly and anemic under its load of pine straw. He imagined voices all over America saying, "Is that the best he could do after fifty years?" And there was Lurleen, sitting on the sofa in front of the big picture of the ocean surf, talking to the reporter about her husband. What could be worse than this, Jesse wondered, to be introduced to the English-speaking world by Lurleen McNeil, a chain-smoking canasta dragon whose biggest ambition in life was to have everything they owned painted sea-foam green by a dopehead nephew who never got out of the sixth grade? He listened as Lurleen told the world about him.

She leaned back on the couch and he saw her checkered shirt tighten at the shoulders. She looked thoughtful and not as dowdy as usual; he had never seen her like this. "Sometimes he's a little out of it," Lurleen said, blowing a stream of smoke from the side of her mouth and looking off in the opposite direction. "I don't mean to say he's a bad man, but whenever he gets upset he tends to drink a little too much, if you know what I mean."

Jesse jumped up straight as a rail. "And who the hell wouldn't take a drink if they was married to a slave-driving snapping turtle?"

Lurleen looked into the camera as though she had heard the remark. "I just wish he could put all this mess behind him and come home to help paint the living room."

"The living room," Jesse yelled, jerking his fists out from his sides. "My name is on national TV and all you can think about is hiding that cheap paneling you put up last year."

Lurleen gave the camera a wry smile and she was off; more footage of the wreck followed, more details of chemicals, casualties, government inspection teams. Agents from the Environmental Protection Agency were now looking for Jesse McNeil. The president of the local Sierra Club, a fashionably dressed thirtyish woman, stated flatly that Jesse should be hunted down like a dangerous criminal.

"What have I done to you?" he yelled, holding his outstretched palms toward the screen. "You don't even know me. I'm nobody important."

After the news report, Jesse went into the bathroom to splash water on his face, a face framed in the mirror by a spiked crown of hair shaped like a thistle bloom. He should have stayed at the site of the wreck, he told himself. He would have been fired and fined, but there would have been nothing like the publicity he was generating.

In his absence, what he had done was growing like a thunderstorm feeding on hot air and invisible moisture, or bigger, like a tropical storm, spinning out of control, created by TV people just because it was good business. He could not for the life of him imagine how drinking a half-pint of whiskey could generate such a hurricane of interest in who he was, or why the people of the United States had been brought into his unpainted living room to find out about him. He went back to the bed, sat down, and put his head in his hands. "No more news for me," he said aloud. "Not for a while."

For four days he avoided the newspapers and television. He rode the bus downtown, watching the faces of his fellow riders for any trace of recognition, for now he felt as famous as Johnny Carson, guilty as Hitler, and half-expected the next old lady he saw to throw up her arms and exclaim, "It's him. It's the train wrecker." He slouched on a bench in Jackson Square, across from the cathedral, again wondering at all the tourists, worried that even some Korean or German might recognize him. He wondered once more why a man's mistake grows with importance according to how many people know about it.

He was so deep in thought, he didn't notice when an old priest sat next to him and unfurled a fresh copy of the *Times-Picayune*. The priest, a bald man with a silver ring of hair above the ears, was on Jesse's right, so the engineer had a good view of the open front page, which carried a photo of a blazing boxcar. The priest looked over the page at Jesse. "Are you still out of work?" It was Father Lambrusco.

"Uh, yeah. Sort of," Jesse growled.

"Would you like a section?" he asked, shaking the paper at him.

"Uh, naw. I was just reading about the train wreck."

The priest folded the paper half-size in his lap, studying the photograph. "That's a big mess. I hope they get the fellow who did it."

The phrase "the fellow who did it" gave Jesse a brief chill, He felt obligated to mount a defense. "The engineer was just in the cab when it happened. He might not've had anything to do with why the train came apart."

The priest turned to him then, his dewlap flowing over his Roman collar. "He'd been drinking and he ran away. You've got to admit that looks bad."

Jesse scowled and kicked at a pigeon wandering too close to his shoe. "Maybe the newspeople are blowing this thing up too much. You know, the more they yak about it, the worse it gets."

The priest sucked a tooth and thought a moment. "You mean, if someone does something wrong, and no one finds out, then it's not really all that wrong?"

Jesse sat back on the bench as though the priest had touched him in a sore spot, "I didn't say that, exactly."

"Secrecy is not innocence," the priest said. "If the engineer is not responsible, the facts should be brought out to that effect. But he's gone into hiding somewhere locally. . . ."

Jesse lurched forward, sending two pigeons fluttering off toward General Jackson's statue. "Does the paper say that?"

"The police think he's been sighted in New Orleans," the priest said, picking up the paper and opening it again,

Jesse stood up then, pretending to dust off his pants, casually looking around. "I've got to get going. So long."

"So long," the priest said, turning a page. "You had lunch yet?"

"No," he said, walking backward a couple steps. "I've got to go."

"Well, if you come around this time of day and I'm here, I'll buy you lunch." The priest raised up the front page and began reading an article on the back of it.

Another day dragged by. Jesse was seated in the grim motel room, rubbing his hands together, staring at the dead television. The statement "Secrecy is not innocence" kept running through his head, and he now wondered whether the newspeople were right in exposing his drunkenness, whether he might have noticed something wrong with his train had he been completely sober. Jesse McNeil looked back over his whole life much as a newscaster would do in a thumb-nail sketch, and he shuddered to think that he had been guilty of many mistakes. He craved the television set, but he would not let himself touch the knobs that would bring him more bad news to feed his growing guilt. He pulled his wallet and saw that he was nearly out of money. He guessed it would not be long before they would find him.

Then he called his wife in Gumwood, figuring that she would tear into his shortcomings like a tent preacher. But she didn't. She was worried about him.

"Jesse," she whispered, "they're all around here in the woods waiting for you to come home. I know you messed up big, but please don't come back here. If you turn yourself in, find a single policeman somewhere and do it. Baby, these people think you're something awful, and I'm worried they might hurt you." She told him what it had been like for the past few days, and he listened, moved by her care for him. For a moment he thought he had the wrong number, and then with a pang he realized that there might be more to Lurleen than he'd noticed. While she pleaded with him to be careful, he worried that she had become one of the details of his life that he no longer saw, like a telegraph pole flying by his engine window for the thousandth time. A series of clicks sounded in the background, and his wife cried for him to hang up because the line might be tapped. He slammed down the receiver and thought of her voice wavering on the wire. It took a lot to shake his wife's confidence, and it scared him to think of what she had been told.

He got off a bus at midday and found the old priest reading *The Catholic Commentator* on a bench in front of the cathedral. They had lunch in a cafe facing the square. Jesse marveled at the hamburger he was served, a domed giant with pickle spears on the side, nothing like the flat, bland burgers he bought at the Gumwood Cafe. The priest made him taste one of his french fries, which was as big as a spike. "Go on," he said, "have another. I love it when they leave the skin on." He and Father Lambrusco talked vaguely about the weather and then the priest spoke about guilt, as though the two were somehow related. Eventually, Jesse twisted the conversation like a stiff wire back to the train wreck. "Now take that poor engineer we were talking about the other day," he told the priest. "What he did might have been bad, all right, but the press blew the dang thing up so much, he seems like some sort of public enemy number one."

Father Lambrusco took a sip of wine and looked off toward the square. He suddenly laughed. "I once saw a cartoon in which someone had installed loudspeakers on top of a church and a microphone in the confessional, and all over town these sins were being broad-cast."

"Good Lord," Jesse said, wincing.

The priest put down his glass, a strange small grin on his lips. "Now that I think of it, I wonder what the newspapers would do with some of the things I hear in the confessional. What would the sinner's employers do, his neighbors?" He gave Jesse a piercing look with his dark, earnest eyes. "What would you think of me if you knew what was in my heart? Would you even talk to me?"

Jesse put down his hamburger. It was so big it took away his appetite. "I'm the one wrecked the train," he said in a low voice, glancing quickly at the diners at a small table near them.

"The train in the paper? The burning train?"

"Yes."

The priest sat back and sucked his lower lip. "What are you going to do?"

Jesse wagged his head. "I thought the longer I stayed put, the more people would forget. But it's the other way around. If I stay out one more week, I'll be right up there with Charlie Manson."

The priest sniffed and looked again toward the square. "You know, one of our missions burned to the ground in that little village."

"I didn't carry a torch to it," Jesse whined.

Father Lambrusco closed his eyes. "When you throw a rock in a pond, you make ripples."

Now Jesse stared off toward the cathedral, where he noticed a white pigeon perched on a gatepost. According to the priest, he was directly responsible for every poisoned and burned board in the ruined crossroads. "What can I do?" he asked.

"Nothing," the priest said. "It can't be undone. Just turn yourself in. Ask forgiveness."

Jesse scratched his jaw. Forgiveness from whom? he thought. The railroad? The crossroads town? The millions and millions who followed his mistake on television? For some reason he thought of Judas and wondered if he realized as he climbed the limbs of the fig tree, the hanging rope slung over his shoulder, how many people would come to know about him down through the years, how many would grow to hate his name. "Do me a favor, Father. About news time tonight, ten o'clock, call somebody and turn me in." He explained where he was staying and the priest bobbed his head, closed his eyes, and tasted a french fry. Jesse walked out onto the sidewalk and blended with the tourists. He wandered, distracted and haunted by a need for a drink, until he found a liquor store near Canal Street, where he purchased a fifth of Old Overholt rye. He told himself he needed one stiff shot to calm his nerves.

By news time that night, he was staggering drunk. He found the Gideon Bible next to the telephone and started reading Genesis for some clue to how everybody's troubles began. At news time he swayed from the bed and turned on the local station. The first story showed the train wreck. Additional cars had become involved, one new leak in a tanker of chlorine was keeping fire crews away still, and the little town was now a smudge on the map, a garden of chimneys and iron pipe rising from plots of ash. The screen showed a man in a lab coat standing a mile from the wreck, the smoke plume blossoming over his shoulder. He announced that such a deadly stew of chemicals had been spilled that the town could never be inhabited again, that all the soil for one square mile would have to be removed down to six feet, treated, and hauled off to a toxic-waste pit at a cost of tens of millions. The numbers spun slowly in Jesse's head.

There was a loud knock at the door, but he ignored it, turning the volume up high. The anchorman came back on with a somber comment: "Rumor has it he was spotted in New Orleans, but so far he has eluded the many agencies seeking his arrest. But what kind of person is Jesse Mc-Neil, a man who would father such devastation and disappear?" Following the question was Jesse's biography, starting with a bucktoothed photograph from his grammar school yearbook and ending, after a one-minute narrative of the main events of his life, with a photo of him seated on a bar stool, a detached, ordinary smile given to the world at large.

He stood and slammed his palm against the side of the television, which bobbled toward the door on its wheeled rack.

"Everybody knows me," he roared, waving his fists toward the ceiling. "Everybody knows who I am or what happened." He lurched to the scratched metal door of his room and pulled it open. "You know me," he shouted into the parking lot. Two policemen were standing a few feet away, cradling shotguns. Jesse held out his hands to them. "I read in the Bible where Noah got drunk in his tent, yet he was the one they let run the ark." Five men wearing suits walked in briskly from the highway. Behind Jesse, the announcer told of an upcoming live scene in a late-breaking story.

"The Lord trusted him to save our bacon," he told them all. To the left Jesse saw men in military garb or SWAT uniforms trotting out of sight behind a building. More policemen walked stiff-legged out of the darkness. Above him, on the roof, was the sound of boots stirring gravel. He heard a helicopter somewhere and soon a spotlight lit up the parking lot, casting Jesse's hair in a bristly glow. What do they all know? he wondered. They think I'm the most dangerous man alive.

Another brutal light fired up in the parking lot and a news camera poked between two worried-looking sheriff's deputies. No one said anything and no one touched him. They seemed to be looking past him into the motel room, and he turned to see on the television most of the law officers and a pitiful figure in the center, staggering in wilted coveralls and a botched haircut like the most worthless old drunk imaginable. Everyone was frozen, watching the screen to see what would happen next. Could he say something to the world? He shook his head. Everyone knew it all, or nobody knew the first thing.

The announcer's voice was underlined with the adventure of the capture: "Jesse McNeil has been surrounded by local, state, and federal agents at the Night O' Delight Motel on Airline Highway in New Orleans. He appears intoxicated and unable to speak now at the end of a nationwide search for the man who is at the heart of one of the largest ecological and industrial disasters the country has ever known." For all the policemen, the truth was in the bright eye of the television. Only Jesse turned away, ashamed of the drunk on the set, yet able to stare defiantly at the crowd of officers around him. He wavered in the peeling doorway, feeling as empty-handed and innocent as every man on earth.

The cop nearest him finally touched his arm. "Are you Jesse McNeil?" he asked.

"I feel like I'm two different people," Jesse said feebly.

The cop began to close handcuffs around his wrists. "Well, bud, we'll just have to put both of you in jail." A mean-spirited crackle of laughter ringed the parking lot, and a dozen more camera lights flooded on. Jesse was pulled through the fierce blaze until he felt a policeman's moist hand on the top of his head, shoving him under the river of light and into the backseat of a cruiser, which at once moved onto the highway, bathed by strobes and headlights and stares, locked in inescapable beams.

Sandra Cisneros received a MacArthur Foundation Fellowship in 1995. A native of Chicago and longtime resident of San Antonio, she is a graduate of the University of Iowa Writers' Workshop. My Wicked, Wicked Ways *(1987), a collection of poetry that contains several poems about Cisneros's experiences as the only daughter among her parents' seven children, has gone through several editions and was followed by a second collection,* Loose Woman *(1994). Her two collections of short fiction are* The House on Mango Street *(1984) and* Woman Hollering Creek *(1991), which is named after a real creek in the Texas Hill Country. Two nonfiction books on which Cisneros collaborated with other writers,* Days and Nights of Love and War *and* The Future Is Mestizo: Life Where Cultures Meet, *were published in 2000, and* Caramelo, *a novel, appeared in 2002.*

Woman Hollering Creek

The day Don Serafín gave Juan Pedro Martínez Sánchez permission to take Cleófilas Enriqueta DeLeón Hernández as his bride, across her father's threshold, over several miles of dirt road and several miles of paved, over one border and beyond to a town *en el otro lado*—on the other side—already did he divine the morning his daughter would raise her hand over her eyes, look south, and dream of returning to the chores that never ended, six good-for-nothing brothers, and one old man's complaints.

He had said, after all, in the hubbub of parting: I am your father, I will never abandon you. He *had* said that, hadn't he, when he hugged and then let her go. But at the moment Cleófilas was busy looking for Chela, her maid of honor, to fulfill their bouquet conspiracy. She would not remember her father's parting words until later. *I am your father, I will never abandon you.*

Only now as a mother did she remember. Now, when she and Juan Pedrito sat by the creek's edge. How when a man and a woman love each other, sometimes that love sours. But a parent's love for a child, a child's for its parents, is another thing entirely.

This is what Cleófilas thought evenings when Juan Pedro did not come home, and she lay on her side of the bed listening to the hollow roar of the interstate, a distant dog barking, the pecan trees rustling like ladies in stiff petticoats—*shh-shh-shh, shh-shh-shh*—soothing her to sleep.

In the town where she grew up, there isn't very much to do except accompany the aunts and godmothers to the house of one or the other to play cards. Or walk to the cinema to see this week's film again, speckled and with one hair quivering annoyingly on the screen. Or to the center of town to order a milk shake that will appear in a day and a half as a pimple on her backside. Or to the girlfriend's house to watch the latest *telenovela* episode and try to copy the way the women comb their hair, wear their makeup.

But what Cleófilas has been waiting for, has been whispering and sighing and giggling for, has been anticipating since she was old enough to lean against the window displays of gauze and butterflies and lace, is passion. Not the kind on the cover of the *¡Alarma!* magazines, mind you, where the lover is photographed with the bloody fork she used to salvage her good name. But passion in its purest crystalline essence. The kind the books and songs and *telenovelas* describe when one finds, finally, the great love of one's life, and does whatever one can, must do, at whatever the cost.

Tú o Nadie. "You or No One." The title of the current favorite *telenovela.* The beautiful Lucía Méndez having to put up with all kinds of hardships of the heart, separation and betrayal, and loving, always loving no matter what, because *that* is the most important thing, and did you see Lucía Méndez on the Bayer aspirin commercials—wasn't she lovely? Does she dye her hair do you think? Cleófilas is going to go to the *farmacia* and buy a hair rinse; her girlfriend Chela will apply it— it's not that difficult at all.

Because you didn't watch last night's episode when Lucía confessed she loved him more than anyone in her life. In her life! And she sings the song "You or No One" in the beginning and end of the show. *Tú o Nadie.* Somehow one ought to live one's life like that, don't you think? You or no one. Because to suffer for love is good. The pain all sweet somehow. In the end.

Seguín. She had liked the sound of it. Far away and lovely. Not like *Monclova. Coahuila.* Ugly.

Seguín, Tejas. A nice sterling ring to it. The tinkle of money. She would get to wear outfits like the women on the *tele*, like Lucía Méndez. And have a lovely house, and wouldn't Chela be jealous.

And yes, they will drive all the way to Laredo to get her wedding dress. That's what they say. Because Juan Pedro wants to get married right away, without a long engagement since he can't take off too much time from work. He has a very important position in Seguin with, with . . . a beer company, I think. Or was it tires? Yes, he has to be back. So they will get married in the spring when he can take off work, and then they will drive off in his new pickup—did you see it?—to their new home in Seguin. Well, not exactly new, but they're going to repaint the house. You know newlyweds. New paint and new furniture. Why not? He can afford it. And later on add maybe a room or two for the children. May they be blessed with many.

Well, you'll see. Cleófilas has always been so good with her sewing machine. A little *rrrr, rrrr, rrrr* of the machine and ¡zas! Miracles. She's always been so clever, that girl. Poor thing. And without even a mama to advise her on things like her wedding night. Well, may God help her. What with a father with a head like a burro, and those six clumsy brothers. Well, what do you think! Yes, I'm going to the wedding. Of course! The dress I want to wear just needs to be altered a teensy bit to bring it up to date. See, I saw a new style last night that I thought would suit me. Did you watch last night's episode of *The Rich Also Cry?* Well, did you notice the dress the mother was wearing?

La Gritona. Such a funny name for such a lovely *arroyo*. But that's what they called the creek that ran behind the house. Though no one could say whether the woman had hollered from anger or pain. The natives only knew the *arroyo* one crossed on the way to San Antonio, and then once again on the way back, was called Woman Hollering, a name no one from these parts questioned, little less understood. *Pues, allá de los indios,*[1] *quién sabe*—who knows, the townspeople shrugged, because it was of no concern to their lives how this trickle of water received its curious name.

"What do you want to know for?" Trini the laundromat attendant asked in the same gruff Spanish she always used whenever she gave Cleófilas change or yelled at her for something. First for putting too much soap in the machines. Later, for sitting on a washer. And still later, after Juan Pedrito was born, for not understanding that in this country you cannot let your baby walk around with no diaper and his pee-pee hanging out, it wasn't nice, *¿entiendes? Pues.*[2]

---

[1]**Pues, allá de los indios** Well, that came from the Indians
[2]*¿entiendes? Pues.* You understand?

How could Cleófilas explain to a woman like this why the name Woman Hollering fascinated her. Well, there was no sense talking to Trini.

On the other hand there were the neighbor ladies, one on either side of the house they rented near the *arroyo*. The woman Soledad on the left, the woman Dolores on the right.

The neighbor lady Soledad liked to call herself a widow, though how she came to be one was a mystery. Her husband had either died, or run away with an ice-house floozie, or simply gone out for cigarettes one afternoon and never came back. It was hard to say which since Soledad, as a rule, didn't mention him.

In the other house lived *la señora* Dolores, kind and very sweet, but her house smelled too much of incense and candles from the altars that burned continuously in memory of two sons who had died in the last war and one husband who had died shortly after from grief. The neighbor lady Dolores divided her time between the memory of these men and her garden, famous for its sunflowers—so tall they had to be supported with broom handles and old boards; red red cockscombs, fringed and bleeding a thick menstrual color; and, especially, roses whose sad scent reminded Cleófilas of the dead. Each Sunday *la señora* Dolores clipped the most beautiful of these flowers and arranged them on three modest headstones at the Seguin cemetery.

The neighbor ladies, Soledad, Dolores, they might've known once the name of the *arroyo* before it turned English but they did not know now. They were too busy remembering the men who had left through either choice or circumstance and would never come back.

Pain or rage, Cleófilas wondered when she drove over the bridge the first time as a newlywed and Juan Pedro had pointed it out. *La Gritona*, he had said, and she had laughed. Such a funny name for a creek so pretty and full of happily ever after.

The first time she had been so surprised she didn't cry out or try to defend herself. She had always said she would strike back if a man, any man, were to strike her.

But when the moment came, and he slapped her once, and then again, and again; until the lip split and bled an orchid of blood, she didn't fight back, she didn't break into tears, she didn't run away as she imagined she might when she saw such things in the *telenovelas*.

In her own home her parents had never raised a hand to each other or to their children. Although she admitted she may have been brought up a little leniently as an only daughter—*la consentida*, the princess— there were some things she would never tolerate. Ever.

Instead, when it happened the first time, when they were barely man and wife, she had been so stunned, it left her speechless, motion-less, numb. She had done nothing but reach up to the heat on her mouth and stare at the blood on her hand as if even then she didn't understand.

She could think of nothing to say, said nothing. Just stroked the dark curls of the man who wept and would weep like a child, his tears of repentance and shame, this time and each.

The men at the ice house. From what she can tell, from the times during her first year when still a newlywed she is invited and accompanies her husband, sits mute beside their conversation, waits and sips a beer until it grows warm, twists a paper napkin into a knot, then another into a fan, one into a rose, nods her head, smiles, yawns, politely grins, laughs at the appropriate moments, leans against her husband's sleeve, tugs at his el-bow, and finally becomes good at predicting where the talk will lead, from this Cleófilas concludes each is nightly trying to find the truth lying at the bottom of the bottle like a gold doubloon on the sea floor.

They want to tell each other what they want to tell themselves. But what is bumping like a helium balloon at the ceiling of the brain never finds its way out. It bubbles and rises, it gurgles in the throat, it rolls across the surface of the tongue, and erupts from the lips—a belch.

If they are lucky, there are tears at the end of the long night. At any given moment, the fists try to speak. They are dogs chasing their own tails before lying down to sleep, trying to find a way, a route, an out, and—finally—get some peace.

In the morning sometimes before he opens his eyes. Or after they have finished loving. Or at times when he is simply across from her at the table putting pieces of food into his mouth and chewing. Cleófilas thinks. This is the man I have waited my whole life for.

Not that he isn't a good man. She has to remind herself why she loves him when she changes the baby's Pampers, or when she mops the bathroom floor, or tries to make the curtains for the doorways without doors, or whiten the linen. Or wonder a little when he kicks the refrigerator and says he hates this shitty house and is going out where he won't be bothered with the baby's howling and her suspicious questions, and her requests to fix this and this and this because if she had any brains in her head she'd realize he's been up before the rooster earning his living to pay for the food in her belly and the roof over her head and would have to wake up again early the next day so why can't you just leave me in peace, woman.

He is not very tall, no, and he doesn't look like the men on the *telenovelas*. His face still scarred from acne. And he has a bit of a belly from all the beer he drinks. Well, he's always been husky.

This man who farts and belches and snores as well as laughs and kisses and holds her. Somehow this husband whose whiskers she finds each morning in the sink, whose shoes she must air each evening on the porch, this husband who cuts his fingernails in public, laughs loudly, curses like a man, and demands each course of dinner be served on a separate plate like at his mother's, as soon as he gets home, on time or late, and who doesn't care at all for music or *telenovelas* or romance or roses or the moon floating pearly over the *arroyo*, or through the bedroom window for that matter, shut the blinds and go back to sleep, this man, this father, this rival, this keeper, this lord, this master, this husband till kingdom come.

A doubt. Slender as a hair. A washed cup set back on the shelf wrong-side-up. Her lipstick, and body talc, and hairbrush all arranged in the bathroom a different way.

No. Her imagination. The house the same as always. Nothing.

Coming home from the hospital with her new son, her husband. Something comforting in discovering her house slippers beneath the bed, the faded housecoat where she left it on the bathroom hook. Her pillow. Their bed.

Sweet sweet homecoming. Sweet as the scent of face powder in the air, jasmine, sticky liquor.

Smudged fingerprint on the door. Crushed cigarette in a glass. Wrinkle in the brain crumpling to a crease.

Sometimes she thinks of her father's house. But how could she go back there? What a disgrace. What would the neighbors say? Coming home like that with one baby on her hip and one in the oven. Where's your husband?

The town of gossips. The town of dust and despair. Which she has traded for this town of gossips. This town of dust, despair. Houses farther apart perhaps, though no more privacy because of it. No leafy zócalo³ in the center of the town, though the murmur of talk is clear enough all the same. No huddled whispering on the church steps each Sunday. Because here the whispering begins at sunset at the ice house instead.

This town with its silly pride for a bronze pecan the size of a baby carriage in front of the city hall. TV repair shop, drugstore, hardware, dry cleaner's, chiropractor's, liquor store, bail bonds, empty storefront, and nothing, nothing, nothing of interest. Nothing one could walk to, at any rate. Because the towns here are built so that you have to depend on husbands. Or you stay home. Or you drive. If you're rich enough to own, allowed to drive, your own car.

There is no place to go. Unless one counts the neighbor ladies. Soledad on one side, Dolores on the other. Or the creek.

Don't go out there after dark, mi'jita. Stay near the house. *No es bueno para la salud.*⁴ *Mala suerte. Bad luck. Mal aire.*⁵ You'll get sick and the baby too. You'll catch a fright wandering about in the dark, and then you'll see how right we were.

The stream sometimes only a muddy puddle in the summer, though now in the springtime, because of the rains, a good-size alive thing, a thing with a voice all its own, all day and all night calling in its high, silver voice. Is it La Llorona, the weeping woman? La Llorona, who drowned her own children. Perhaps La Llorona is the one they named the creek after, she thinks, remembering all the stories she learned as a child.

La Llorona calling to her. She is sure of it. Cleófilas sets the baby's Donald Duck blanket on the grass. Listens. The day sky turning to night. The baby pulling up fistfuls of grass and laughing. La Llorona. Wonders if something as quiet as this drives a woman to the darkness under the trees.

What she needs is . . . and made a gesture as if to yank a woman's buttocks to his groin. Maximiliano, the foul-smelling fool from across the

---

³**zócalo** central square
⁴**No es bueno para la salud** It's bad for the health
⁵**Mal aire** bad air

road, said this and set the men laughing, but Cleófilas just muttered. *Grosero,*[6] and went on washing dishes.

She knew he said it not because it was true, but more because it was he who needed to sleep with a woman, instead of drinking each night at the ice house and stumbling home alone.

Maximiliano who was said to have killed his wife in an ice-house brawl when she came at him with a mop. I had to shoot, he had said— she was armed.

Their laughter outside the kitchen window. Her husband's, his friends'. Manolo, Beto, Efraín, el Perico. Maximiliano.

Was Cleófilas just exaggerating as her husband always said? It seemed the newspapers were full of such stories. This woman found on the side of the interstate. This one pushed from a moving car. This one's cadaver, this one unconscious, this one beaten blue. Her ex-husband, her husband, her lover, her father, her brother, her uncle, her friend, her co-worker. Always. The same grisly news in the pages of the dailies. She dunked a glass under the soapy water for a moment—shivered.

He had thrown a book. Hers. From across the room. A hot welt across the cheek. She could forgive that. But what stung more was the fact it was *her* book, a love story by Corín Tellado, what she loved most now that she lived in the U.S., without a television set, without the *telenovelas.*

Except now and again when her husband was away and she could manage it, the few episodes glimpsed at the neighbor lady Soledad's house because Dolores didn't care for that sort of thing, though Soledad was often kind enough to retell what had happened on what episode of *María de Nadie,* the poor Argentine country girl who had the ill fortune of falling in love with the beautiful son of the Arrocha family, the very family she worked for, whose roof she slept under and whose floors she vacuumed, while in that same house, with the dust brooms and floor cleaners as witnesses, the square-jawed Juan Carlos Arrocha had uttered words of love, I love you, María, listen to me, *mi querida,*[7] but it was she who had to say No, no, we are not of the same class, and remind him it was not his place nor hers to fall in love, while all the while her heart was breaking, can you imagine.

---

[6]**Grosero** gross
[7]**mi querida** my darling

350

Cleófilas thought her life would have to be like that, like a *telenovela*, only now the episodes got sadder and sadder. And there were no commercials in between for comic relief. And no happy ending in sight. She thought this when she sat with the baby out by the creek behind the house. Cleófilas de . . . ? But somehow she would have to change her name to Topazio, or Yesenia. Cristal, Adriana, Stefania, Andrea, something more poetic than Cleófilas. Everything happened to women with names like jewels. But what happened to a Cleófilas? Nothing. But a crack in the face.

Because the doctor has said so. She has to go. To make sure the new baby is all right, so there won't be any problems when he's born, and the appointment card says next Tuesday. Could he please take her. And that's all.

No, she won't mention it. She promises. If the doctor asks she can say she fell down the front steps or slipped when she was out in the backyard, slipped out back, she could tell him that. She has to go back next Tuesday, Juan Pedro, please, for the new baby. For their child.

She could write to her father and ask maybe for money, just a loan, for the new baby's medical expenses. Well then if he'd rather she didn't. All right, she won't. Please don't anymore. Please don't. She knows it's difficult saving money with all the bills they have, but how else are they going to get out of debt with the truck payments? And after the rent and the food and the electricity and the gas and the water and the who-knows-what, well, there's hardly anything left. But please, at least for the doctor visit. She won't ask for anything else. She has to. Why is she so anxious? Because.

Because she is going to make sure the baby is not turned around backward this time to split her down the center. Yes. Next Tuesday at five-thirty. I'll have Juan Pedrito dressed and ready. But those are the only shoes he has. I'll polish them, and we'll be ready. As soon as you come from work. We won't make you ashamed.

Felice? It's me, Graciela.

No, I can't talk louder. I'm at work.

Look, I need kind of a favor. There's a patient, a lady here who's got a problem.

Well, wait a minute. Are you listening to me or what?

I can't talk real loud 'cause her husband's in the next room.

Well, would you just listen?

I was going to do this sonogram on her—she's pregnant, right?—
and she just starts crying on me. *Híjole*,[8] Felice! This poor lady's got
black-and-blue marks all over. I'm not kidding.

From her husband. Who else? Another one of those brides from
across the border. And her family's all in Mexico.

Shit. You think they're going to help her? Give me a break. This lady
doesn't even speak English. She hasn't been allowed to call home or
write or nothing. That's why I'm calling you.

She needs a ride.

Not to Mexico, you goof. Just to the Greyhound. In San Anto.

No, just a ride. She's got her own money. All you'd have to do is
drop her off in San Antonio on your way home. Come on, Felice.
Please? If we don't help her, who will? I'd drive her myself, but she
needs to be on that bus before her husband gets home from work.
What do you say?

I don't know. Wait.

Right away, tomorrow even.

Well, if tomorrow's no good for you . . .

It's a date, Felice. Thursday. At the Cash N Carry off I-10. Noon.
She'll be ready.

Oh, and her name's Cleófilas.

I don't know. One of those Mexican saints, I guess. A martyr or
something.

Cleófilas. C-L-E-O-F-I-L-A-S. Cle. O. Fi. Las. Write it down.

Thanks, Felice. When her kid's born she'll have to name her after
us, right?

Yeah, you got it. A regular soap opera sometimes. *Qué vida, comadre.
Bueno*[9] bye.

All morning that flutter of half-fear, half-doubt. At any moment Juan
Pedro might appear in the doorway. On the street. At the Cash N Carry.
Like in the dreams she dreamed.

There was that to think about, yes, until the woman in the pickup
drove up. Then there wasn't time to think about anything but the
pickup pointed toward San Antonio. Put your bags in the back and
get in.

---

[8]*Híjole* a mild interjection
[9]*Qué vida, comadre. Bueno* What a life, friend. Good.

But when they drove across the *arroyo*, the driver opened her mouth and let out a yell as loud as any mariachi. Which startled not only Cleófilas, but Juan Pedrito as well.

Pues, look how cute. I scared you two, right? Sorry. Should've warned you. Every time I cross that bridge I do that. Because of the name, you know. Woman Hollering. *Pues*, I holler. She said this in a Spanish pocked with English and laughed. Did you ever notice, Felice continued, how nothing around here is named after a woman? Really. Unless she's the Virgin. I guess you're only famous if you're a virgin. She was laughing again.

That's why I like the name of that *arroyo*. Makes you want to holler like Tarzan, right?

Everything about this woman, this Felice, amazed Cleófilas. The fact that she drove a pickup. A pickup, mind you, but when Cleófilas asked if it was her husband's, she said she didn't have a husband. The pickup was hers. She herself had chosen it. She herself was paying for it.

I used to have a Pontiac Sunbird. But those cars are for *viejas*.[10] Pussy cars. Now this here is a *real* car.

What kind of talk was that coming from a woman? Cleófilas thought. But then again, Felice was like no woman she'd ever met. Can you imagine, when we crossed the *arroyo* she just started yelling like a crazy, she would say later to her father and brothers. Just like that. Who would've thought?

Who would've? Pain or rage, perhaps, but not a hoot like the one Felice had just let go. Makes you want to holler like Tarzan, Felice had said.

Then Felice began laughing again, but it wasn't Felice laughing. It was gurgling out of her own throat, a long ribbon of laughter, like water.

—1992

LOUISE ERDRICH ■ (b. 1954)

Louise Erdrich was born in Little Falls, Minnesota, and grew up in North Dakota. Her father was a teacher with the Bureau of Indian Affairs, and both he and her mother encouraged her to write stories from an early age. Erdrich holds degrees from Dartmouth College and Johns Hopkins University, where she studied creative writing. Her novel Love Medicine, *from which "The Red Convertible" is taken, is a sequence of fourteen connected*

---

[10]*viejas* old people

stories told by seven narrators. Love Medicine won the National Book Critics Circle Award for 1984. Much of Erdrich's fiction draws on her childhood on the Great Plains and her mixed cultural heritage (her ancestry is German American and Chippewa). In addition to Love Medicine, she has published novels, including The Beet Queen (1986) and Tracks (1988), several prizewinning short stories, and three books of poetry. Erdrich and her late husband Michael Dorris, another Native American writer, appeared in two documentary films shown on PBS and collaborated on a novel, The Crown of Columbus (1991). Along with James Welch and Leslie Marmon Silko, Erdrich has helped to redefine Native American fiction. According to the Columbia Literary History of the United States, "These authors have had to resist the formulaic approaches favored by the publishing industry, which has its own opinions about what constitutes the 'proper' form and content of minority fiction." The Birchbark House, a novel for young readers, and The Antelope Wife, a novel employing the techniques of magic realism, both appeared in 1999. Her most recent novel is The Plague of Doves (2008).

The Red Convertible

Lyman Lamartine

I was the first one to drive a convertible on my reservation. And of course it was red, a red Olds. I owned that car along with my brother Henry Junior. We owned it together until his boots filled with water on a windy night and he bought out my share. Now Henry owns the whole car, and his younger brother Lyman (that's myself), Lyman walks everywhere he goes.

How did I earn enough money to buy my share in the first place? My one talent was I could always make money. I had a touch for it, unusual in a Chippewa. From the first I was different that way, and everyone recognized it. I was the only kid they let in the American Legion Hall to shine shoes, for example, and one Christmas I sold spiritual bouquets for the mission door to door. The nuns let me keep a percentage. Once I started, it seemed the more money I made the easier the money came. Everyone encouraged it. When I was fifteen I got a job washing dishes at the Joliet Cafe, and that was where my first big break happened.

It wasn't long before I was promoted to bussing tables, and then the short-order cook quit and I was hired to take her place. No sooner than you know it I was managing the Joliet. The rest is history. I went on managing. I soon became part owner, and of course there was no stopping me then. It wasn't long before the whole thing was mine.

After I'd owned the Joliet for one year, it blew over in the worst tornado ever seen around here. The whole operation was smashed to bits. A total loss. The fryalator was up in a tree, the grill torn in half like it was paper. I was only sixteen. I had it all in my mother's name, and I lost it quick, but before I lost it I had every one of my relatives, and their relatives, to dinner, and I also bought that red Olds I mentioned, along with Henry.

The first time we saw it! I'll tell you when we first saw it. We had gotten a ride up to Winnipeg, and both of us had money. Don't ask me why, because we never mentioned a car or anything, we just had all our money. Mine was cash, a big bankroll from the Joliet's insurance. Henry had two checks—a week's extra pay for being laid off, and his regular check from the Jewel Bearing Plant.

We were walking down Portage anyway, seeing the sights, when we saw it. There it was, parked, large as life. Really as *if* it was alive. I thought of the word *repose*, because the car wasn't simply stopped, parked, or whatever. That car reposed, calm and gleaming, a FOR SALE sign in its left front window. Then, before we had thought it over at all, the car belonged to us and our pockets were empty. We had just enough money for gas back home.

We went places in that car, me and Henry. We took off driving all one whole summer. We started off toward the Little Knife River and Mandaree in Fort Berthold and then we found ourselves down in Wakpala somehow, and then suddenly we were over in Montana on the Rocky Boys, and yet the summer was not even half over. Some people hang on to details when they travel, but we didn't let them bother us and just lived our everyday lives here to there.

I do remember this one place with willows. I remember I laid under those trees and it was comfortable. So comfortable. The branches bent down all around me like a tent or a stable. And quiet, it was quiet, even though there was a powwow close enough so I could see it going on. The air was not too still, not too windy either. When the dust rises up and hangs in the air around the dancers like that, I feel good. Henry was asleep with his arms thrown wide. Later on, he woke up and we started driving again. We were somewhere in Montana, or maybe on the Blood Reserve—it could have been anywhere. Anyway it was where we met the girl.

All her hair was in buns around her ears, that's the first thing I noticed about her. She was posed alongside the road with her arm out, so we stopped. That girl was short, so short her lumber shirt looked comical on her, like a nightgown. She had jeans on and fancy moccasins and she carried a little suitcase.

"Hop on in," says Henry. So she climbs in between us.

"We'll take you home," I says. "Where do you live?"

"Chicken," she says.

"Where the hell's that?" I ask her.

"Alaska."

"Okay," says Henry, and we drive.

We got up there and never wanted to leave. The sun doesn't truly set there in summer, and the night is more a soft dusk. You might doze off, sometimes, but before you know it you're up again, like an animal in nature. You never feel like you have to sleep hard or put away the world. And things would grow up there. One day just dirt or moss, the next day flowers and long grass. The girl's name was Susy. Her family really took to us. They fed us and put us up. We had our own tent to live in by their house, and the kids would be in and out of there all day and night. They couldn't get over me and Henry being brothers, we looked so different. We told them we knew we had the same mother, anyway.

One night Susy came in to visit us. We sat around in the tent talking of this thing and that. The season was changing. It was getting darker by that time, and the cold was even getting just a little mean. I told her it was time for us to go. She stood up on a chair.

"You never seen my hair," Susy said.

That was true. She was standing on a chair, but still, when she unclipped her buns the hair reached all the way to the ground. Our eyes opened. You couldn't tell how much hair she had when it was rolled up so neatly. Then my brother Henry did something funny. He went up to the chair and said, "Jump on my shoulders." So she did that, and her hair reached down past his waist, and he started twirling, this way and that, so her hair was flung out from side to side.

"I always wondered what it was like to have long pretty hair," Henry says. Well we laughed. It was a funny sight, the way he did it. The next morning we got up and took leave of those people.

On to greener pastures, as they say. It was down through Spokane and
across Idaho then Montana and very soon we were racing the weather
right along under the Canadian border through Columbus, Des Lacs,
and then we were in Bottineau County and soon home. We'd made
most of the trip, that summer, without putting up the car hood at all.
We got home just in time, it turned out, for the army to remember
Henry had signed up to join it.

I don't wonder that the army was so glad to get my brother that they
turned him into a Marine. He was built like a brick outhouse anyway. We
liked to tease him that they really wanted him for his Indian nose. He had
a nose big and sharp as a hatchet, like the nose on Red Tomahawk, the Indian who killed Sitting Bull, whose profile is on signs all along the North
Dakota highways. Henry went off to training camp, came home once
during Christmas, then the next thing you know we got an overseas letter
from him. It was 1970, and he said he was stationed up in the northern
hill country. Wherebouts I did not know. He wasn't such a hot letter
writer, and only got off two before the enemy caught him. I could never
keep it straight, which direction those good Vietnam soldiers were from.
I wrote him back several times, even though I didn't know if those
letters would get through. I kept him informed all about the car. Most
of the time I had it up on blocks in the yard or half taken apart, because
that long trip did a hard job on it under the hood.

I always had good luck with numbers, and never worried about the
draft myself. I never even had to think about what my number was. But
Henry was never lucky in the same way as me. It was at least three
years before Henry came home. By then I guess the whole war was
solved in the government's mind, but for him it would keep on going.
In those years I'd put his car into almost perfect shape. I always thought
of it as his car while he was gone, even though when he left he said,
"Now it's yours," and threw me his key.

"Thanks for the extra key," I'd said. "I'll put it up in your drawer just
in case I need it." He laughed.

When he came home, though, Henry was very different, and I'll say
this: the change was no good. You could hardly expect him to change
for the better, I know. But he was quiet, so quiet, and never comfortable
sitting still anywhere but always up and moving around. I thought back
to times we'd sat still for whole afternoons, never moving a muscle, just
shifting our weight along the ground, talking to whoever sat with us,

watching things. He'd always had a joke, then, too, and now you couldn't get him to laugh, or when he did it was more the sound of a man chok-ing, a sound that stopped up the throats of other people around him. They got to leaving him alone most of the time, and I didn't blame them. It was a fact: Henry was jumpy and mean.

I'd bought a color TV set for my mom and the rest of us while Henry was away. Money still came very easy. I was sorry I'd ever bought it though, because of Henry. I was also sorry I'd bought color, because with black-and-white the pictures seem older and farther away. But what are you going to do? He sat in front of it, watching it, and that was the only time he was completely still. But it was the kind of stillness that you see in a rabbit when it freezes and before it will bolt. He was not easy. He sat in his chair gripping the armrests with all his might, as if the chair itself was moving at a high speed and if he let go at all he would rocket forward and maybe crash right through the set.

Once I was in the room watching TV with Henry and I heard his teeth click at something. I looked over, and he'd bitten through his lip. Blood was going down his chin. I tell you right then I wanted to smash that tube to pieces. I went over to it but Henry must have known what I was up to. He rushed from his chair and shoved me out of the way, against the wall. I told myself he didn't know what he was doing.

My mom came in, turned the set off real quiet, and told us she had made something for supper. So we went and sat down. There was still blood going down Henry's chin, but he didn't notice it and no one said anything, even though every time he took a bite of his bread his blood fell onto it until he was eating his own blood mixed in with the food.

While Henry was not around we talked about what was going to hap-pen to him. There were no Indian doctors on the reservation, and my mom was afraid of trusting Old Man Pillager because he courted her long ago and was jealous of her husbands. He might take revenge through her son. We were afraid that if we brought Henry to a regular hospital they would keep him.

"They don't fix them in those places," Mom said; "they just give them drugs."

"We wouldn't get him there in the first place," I agreed, "so let's just forget about it."

Then I thought about the car.

Henry had not even looked at the car since he'd gotten home, though like I said it was in tip-top condition and ready to drive. I thought the car might bring the old Henry back somehow. So I bided my time and waited for my chance to interest him in the vehicle.

One night Henry was off somewhere. I took myself a hammer. I went out to that car and I did a number on its underside. Whacked it up. Bent the tail pipe double. Ripped the muffler loose. By the time I was done with the car it looked worse than any typical Indian car that has been driven all its life on reservation roads, which they always say are like government promises—full of holes. It just about hurt me, I'll tell you that! I threw dirt in the carburetor and I ripped all the electric tape off the seats. I made it look just as beat up as I could. Then I sat back and waited for Henry to find it.

Still, it took him over a month. That was all right, because it was just getting warm enough, not melting, but warm enough to work outside.

"Lyman," he says, walking in one day, "that red car looks like shit."

"Well it's old," I says. "You got to expect that."

"No way!" says Henry. "That car's a classic! But you went and ran the piss right out of it, Lyman, and you know it don't deserve that. I kept that car in A-one shape. You don't remember. You're too young. But when I left, that car was running like a watch. Now I don't even know if I can get it to start again, let alone get it anywhere near its old condition."

"Well you try," I said, like I was getting mad, "but I say it's a piece of junk."

Then I walked out before he could realize I knew he'd strung together more than six words at once.

After that I thought he'd freeze himself to death working on that car. He was out there all day, and at night he rigged up a little lamp, ran a cord out the window, and had himself some light to see by while he worked. He was better than he had been before, but that's still not saying much. It was easier for him to do the things the rest of us did. He ate more slowly and didn't jump up and down during the meal to get this or that or look out the window. I put my hand in the back of the TV set, I admit, and fiddled around with it good, so that it was almost impossible now to get a clear picture. He didn't look at it very often anyway. He was always out with that car or going off to get parts for it. By the time it was really melting outside, he had it fixed.

I had been feeling down in the dumps about Henry around this time. We had always been together before. Henry and Lyman. But he was such a loner now that I didn't know how to take it. So I jumped at the chance one day when Henry seemed friendly. It's not that he smiled or anything. He just said, "Let's take that old shitbox for a spin." Just the way he said it made me think he could be coming around.

We went out to the car. It was spring. The sun was shining very bright. My only sister, Bonita, who was just eleven years old, came out and made us stand together for a picture. Henry leaned his elbow on the red car's windshield, and he took his other arm and put it over my shoulder, very carefully, as though it was heavy for him to lift and he didn't want to bring the weight down all at once.

"Smile," Bonita said, and he did.

That picture. I never look at it anymore. A few months ago, I don't know why, I got his picture out and tacked it on the wall. I felt good about Henry at the time, close to him. I felt good having his picture on the wall, until one night when I was looking at television. I was a little drunk and stoned. I looked up at the wall and Henry was staring at me. I don't know what it was, but his smile had changed, or maybe it was gone. All I know is I couldn't stay in the same room with that picture. I was shaking. I got up, closed the door, and went into the kitchen. A little later my friend Ray came over and we both went back into that room. We put the picture in a brown bag, folded the bag over and over tightly, then put it way back in a closet.

I still see that picture now, as if it tugs at me, whenever I pass that closet door. The picture is very clear in my mind. It was so sunny that day Henry had to squint against the glare. Or maybe the camera Bonita held flashed like a mirror, blinding him, before she snapped the picture. My face is right out in the sun, big and round. But he might have drawn back, because the shadows on his face are deep as holes. There are two shadows curved like little hooks around the ends of his smile, as if to frame it and try to keep it there—that one, first smile that looked like it might have hurt his face. He has his field jacket on and the worn-in clothes he'd come back in and kept wearing ever since. After Bonita took the picture, she went into the house and we got into the car. There was a full cooler in the trunk. We started off, east, toward Pembina and the Red River because Henry said he wanted to see the high water.

The trip over there was beautiful. When everything starts changing, drying up, clearing off, you feel like your whole life is starting. Henry felt it, too. The top was down and the car hummed like a top. He'd really put it back in shape, even the tape on the seats was very carefully put down and glued back in layers. It's not that he smiled again or even joked, but his face looked to me as if it was clear, more peaceful. It looked as though he wasn't thinking of anything in particular except the bare fields and windbreaks and houses we were passing.

The river was high and full of winter trash when we got there. The sun was still out, but it was colder by the river. There were still little clumps of dirty snow here and there on the banks. The water hadn't gone over the banks yet, but it would, you could tell. It was just at its limit, hard swollen, glossy like an old gray scar. We made ourselves a fire, and we sat down and watched the current go. As I watched it I felt something squeezing inside me and tightening and trying to let go all at the same time. I knew I was not just feeling it myself; I knew I was feeling what Henry was going through at that moment. Except that I couldn't stand it, the closing and opening. I jumped to my feet. I took Henry by the shoulders and I started shaking him. "Wake up," I says, "wake up, wake up, wake up!" I didn't know what had come over me. I sat down beside him again.

His face was totally white and hard. Then it broke, like stones break all of a sudden when water boils up inside them.

"I know it," he says. "I know it. I can't help it. It's no use."

We start talking. He said he knew what I'd done with the car. It was obvious it had been whacked out of shape and not just neglected. He said he wanted to give the car to me for good now, it was no use. He said he'd fixed it just to give it back and I should take it.

"No way," I says, "I don't want it."

"That's okay," he says, "you take it."

"I don't want it, though," I says back to him, and then to emphasize, just to emphasize, you understand, I touch his shoulder. He slaps my hand off.

"Take that car," he says.

"No," I say, "make me," I say, and then he grabs my jacket and rips the arm loose. That jacket is a class act, suede with tags and zippers. I push Henry backwards, off the log. He jumps up and bowls me over. We go down in a clinch and come up swinging hard, for all we're worth, with our fists. He socks my jaw so hard I feel like it swings loose. Then I'm at his ribcage and land a good one under his chin so his head snaps back. He's dazzled. He looks at me and I look at him and then his eyes are full of tears and blood and at first I think he's crying. But no, he's laughing. "Ha! Ha!" he says. "Ha! Ha! Take good care of it."

"Okay," I says, "okay, no problem. Ha! Ha!"

I can't help it, and I start laughing, too. My face feels fat and strange, and after a while I get a beer from the cooler in the trunk, and when I hand it to Henry he takes his shirt and wipes my germs off. "Hoof-and-mouth disease," he says. For some reason this cracks me up, and so we're really laughing for a while, and then we drink all the rest of the beers one by one and throw them in the river and see how far, how fast, the current takes them before they fill up and sink.

"You want to go on back?" I ask after a while. "Maybe we could snag a couple nice Kashpaw girls."

He says nothing. But I can tell his mood is turning again.

"They're all crazy, the girls up here, every damn one of them."

"You're crazy too," I say, to jolly him up. "Crazy Lamartine boys!"

He looks as though he will take this wrong at first. His face twists, then clears, and he jumps up on his feet. "That's right!" he says. "Crazier 'n hell. Crazy Indians!"

I think it's the old Henry again. He throws off his jacket and starts swinging his legs out from the knees like a fancy dancer. He's down doing something between a grouse dance and a bunny hop, no kind of dance I ever saw before, but neither has anyone else on all this green growing earth. He's wild. He wants to pitch whoopee! He's up and at me and all over. All this time I'm laughing so hard, so hard my belly is getting tied up in a knot.

"Got to cool me off!" he shouts all of a sudden. Then he runs over to the river and jumps in.

There's boards and other things in the current. It's so high. No sound comes from the river after the splash he makes, so I run right over. I look around. It's getting dark. I see he's halfway across the water already, and I know he didn't swim there but the current took him. It's far. I hear his voice, though, very clearly across it.

"My boots are filling," he says.

He says this in a normal voice, like he just noticed and he doesn't know what to think of it. Then he's gone. A branch comes by. Another branch. And I go in.

By the time I get out of the river, off the snag I pulled myself onto, the sun is down. I walk back to the car, turn on the high beams, and drive it up the bank. I put it in first gear and then I take my foot off the clutch. I get out, close the door, and watch it plow softly into the water. The headlights reach in as they go down, searching, still lighted even after the water swirls over the back end. I wait. The wires short out. It is all finally dark. And then there is only the water, the sound of it going and running and going and running and running.

—1984

GISH JEN ■ (b. 1955)

Gish Jen grew up in Scarsdale, New York, where her immigrant parents presided over "almost the only Asian-American family in town." After attending Harvard University and Stanford Business School, she entered the University of Iowa Writers' Workshop and earned an M.F.A. Jen's first novel, Typical American *(1991), continues the story of the Chang family, who were introduced in "In the American Society." This was followed by a second novel about a second generation of the Chang family,* Mona in the Promised Land *(1996), and a collection of short stories,* Who's Irish? *(1999). Jen's fiction may be "typically American" in that it largely deals with the immigrant experience, but the Chang family's saga of cultural assimilation takes place in the upper-middle-class milieu of suburban New York, the "WASP" territory that earlier writers like John O'Hara and John Cheever claimed as their own.* The Love Wife, *a novel, was published in 2004.*

In the American Society

1. His Own Society

When my father took over the pancake house, it was to send my little sister Mona and me to college. We were only in junior high at the time, but my father believed in getting a jump on things. "Those Americans always saying it," he told us. "Smart guys thinking in advance." My mother elaborated, explaining that businesses took bringing up, like children. They could take years to get going, she said, years.

In this case, though, we got rich right away. At two months we were breaking even, and at four, those same hotcakes that could barely withstand the weight of butter and syrup were supporting our family with ease. My mother bought a station wagon with air conditioning, my father an oversized, red vinyl recliner for the back room: and as time went on and the business continued to thrive, my father started to talk about his grandfather and the village he had reigned over in China— things my father had never talked about when he worked for other people. He told us about the bags of rice his family would give out to the poor at New Years, and about the people who came to beg, on their hands and knees, for his grandfather to intercede for the more wayward of their relatives. "Like that Godfather in the movie," he would tell us as, his feet up, he distributed paychecks. Sometimes an employee would get two green envelopes instead of one, which meant that Jimmy needed a tooth pulled, say, or that Tiffany's husband was in the clinker again.

"It's nothing, nothing," he would insist, sinking back into his chair. "Who else is going to take care of you people?"

My mother would mostly just sigh about it. "Your father thinks this is China," she would say, and then she would go back to her mending. Once in a while, though, when my father had given away a particularly large sum, she would exclaim, outraged, "But this here is the U-S-of-A!"—this apparently having been what she used to tell immigrant stock boys when they came in late.

She didn't work at the supermarket anymore; but she had made it to the rank of manager before she left, and this had given her not only new words and phrases, but new ideas about herself, and about America, and about what was what in general. She had opinions, now, on how downtown should be zoned; she could pump her own gas and check her own oil; and for all she used to chide Mona and me for being "copycats," she herself was now interested in espadrilles, and wallpaper, and most recently, the town country club.

"So join already," said Mona, flicking a fly off her knee.

My mother enumerated the problems as she sliced up a quarter round of watermelon: there was the cost. There was the waiting list. There was the fact that no one in our family played either tennis or golf.

"So what?" said Mona.

"It would be waste," said my mother.

"Me and Callie can swim in the pool."

"Plus you need that recommendation letter from a member."

"Come *on*," said Mona. "Annie's mom'd write you a letter in a *sec*."

My mother's knife glinted in the early summer sun. I spread some more newspaper on the picnic table.

"*Plus* you have to eat there twice a month. You know what that means." My mother cut another, enormous slice of fruit.

"No, I *don't* know what that means," said Mona.

"It means Dad would have to wear a jacket, dummy," I said.

"Oh! Oh! Oh!" said Mona, clasping her hand to her breast. "Oh! Oh! Oh! Oh! Oh!"

We all laughed: my father had no use for nice clothes, and would wear only ten-year-old shirts, with grease-spotted pants, to show how little he cared what anyone thought.

"Your father doesn't believe in joining the American society," said my mother. "He wants to have his own society."

"So go to dinner without him." Mona shot her seeds out in long arcs over the lawn. "Who cares what he thinks?"

But of course we all did care, and knew my mother could not simply up and do as she pleased. For in my father's mind, a family owed its head a degree of loyalty that left no room for dissent. To embrace what he embraced was to love; and to embrace something else was to betray him.

He demanded a similar sort of loyalty of his workers, whom he treated more like servants than employees. Not in the beginning, of course. In the beginning all he wanted was for them to keep on doing what they used to do, and to that end he concentrated mostly on leaving them alone. As the months passed, though, he expected more and more of them, with the result that for all his largesse, he began to have trouble keeping help. The cooks and busboys complained that he asked them to fix radiators and trim hedges, not only at the restaurant, but at our house; the waitresses that he sent them on errands and made them chauffeur him around. Our head waitress, Gertrude, claimed that he once even asked her to scratch his back.

"It's not just the blacks don't believe in slavery," she said when she quit.

My father never quite registered her complaint, though, nor those of the others who left. Even after Eleanor quit, then Tiffany, then Gerald, and Jimmy, and even his best cook, Eureka Andy, for whom he had bought new glasses, he remained mostly convinced that the fault lay with them.

"All they understand is that assembly line," he lamented. "Robots, they are. They want to be robots."

There *were* occasions when the clear running truth seemed to eddy, when he would pinch the vinyl of his chair up into little peaks and wonder if he were doing things right. But with time he would always smooth the peaks back down; and when business started to slide in the spring, he kept on like a horse in his ways.

By the summer our dishboy was overwhelmed with scraping. It was no longer just the hashbrowns that people were leaving for trash, and the service was as bad as the food. The waitresses served up French pancakes instead of German, apple juice instead of orange, spilt things on laps, on coats. On the Fourth of July some greenhorn sent an entire side of fries slaloming down a lady's *massif centrale*.[1] Meanwhile in the back room, my father labored through articles on the economy.

"What is housing starts?" he puzzled. "What is GNP?"

Mona and I did what we could, filling in as busgirls and bookkeepers and, one afternoon, stuffing the comments box that hung by the cashier's desk. That was Mona's idea. We rustled up a variety of pens and pencils, checked boxes for an hour, smeared the cards up with coffee and grease, and waited. It took a few days for my father to notice that the box was full, and he didn't say anything about it for a few days more. Finally, though, he started to complain of fatigue; and then he began to complain that the staff was not what it could be. We encouraged him in this—pointing out, for instance, how many dishes got chipped—but in the end all that happened was that, for the first time since we took over the restaurant, my father got it into his head to fire someone. Skip, a skinny busboy who was saving up for a sports car, said nothing as my father mumbled on about the price of dishes. My father's hands shook as he wrote out the severance check; and he spent the rest of the day napping in his chair once it was over.

As it was going on midsummer, Skip wasn't easy to replace. We hung a sign in the window and advertised in the paper, but no one called the first week, and the person who called the second didn't show up for his interview. The third week, my father phoned Skip to see if he would come back, but a friend of his had already sold him a Corvette for cheap.

Finally a Chinese guy named Booker turned up. He couldn't have been more than thirty, and was wearing a lighthearted seersucker suit,

[1] *massif centrale* Central mountain range (French); as a comic way of describing a woman's bosom.

but he looked as though life had him pinned: his eyes were bloodshot and his chest sunken, and the muscles of his neck seemed to strain with the effort of holding his head up. In a single dry breath he told us that he had never bussed tables but was willing to learn, and that he was on the lam from the deportation authorities.

"I do not want to lie to you," he kept saying. He had come to the United States on a student visa, had run out of money, and was now in a bind. He was loath to go back to Taiwan, as it happened—he looked up at this point, to be sure my father wasn't pro-KMT[2]—but all he had was a phony social security card and a willingness to absorb all blame, should anything untoward come to pass.

"I do not think, anyway, that it is against law to hire me, only to be me," he said, smiling faintly.

Anyone else would have examined him on this, but my father conceived of laws as speed bumps rather than curbs. He wiped the counter with his sleeve, and told Booker to report the next morning.

"I will be good worker," said Booker.

"Good," said my father.

"Anything you want me to do, I will do."

My father nodded.

Booker seemed to sink into himself for a moment. "Thank you," he said finally. "I am appreciate your help. I am very, very appreciate for everything." He reached out to shake my father's hand.

My father looked at him. "Did you eat today?" he asked in Mandarin.

Booker pulled at the hem of his jacket.

"Sit down," said my father. "Please, have a seat."

My father didn't tell my mother about Booker, and my mother didn't tell my father about the country club. She would never have applied, except that Mona, while over at Annie's, had let it drop that our mother wanted to join. Mrs. Lardner came by the very next day.

"Why, I'd be honored and delighted to write you people a letter," she said. Her skirt billowed around her.

"Thank you so much," said my mother. "But it's too much trouble for you, and also my husband is . . ."

---

[2]**KMT** the abbreviation for Kuomintang, the Chinese Nationalist Party, which fled to Taiwan after their defeat by Communists on mainland China in 1949

"Oh, it's no trouble at all, no trouble at all. I tell you." She leaned forward so that her chest freckles showed. "I know just how it is. It's a secret of course, but you know, my natural father was Jewish. Can you see it? Just look at my skin."

"My husband," said my mother.

"I'd be honored and delighted," said Mrs. Lardner with a little wave of her hands. "Just honored and delighted."

Mona was triumphant. "See, Mom," she said, waltzing around the kitchen when Mrs. Lardner left. "What did I tell you? 'I'm just honored and delighted, just honored and delighted.'" She waved her hands in the air.

"You know, the Chinese have a saying," said my mother. "To do nothing is better than to overdo. You mean well, but you tell me now what will happen."

"I'll talk Dad into it," said Mona, still waltzing. "Or I bet Callie can. He'll do anything Callie says."

"I can try, anyway," I said.

"Did you hear what I said?" said my mother. Mona bumped into the broom closet door. "You're not going to talk anything; you've already made enough trouble." She started on the dishes with a clatter.

Mona poked diffidently at a mop.

I sponged off the counter. "Anyway," I ventured. "I bet our name'll never even come up."

"That's if we're lucky," said my mother.

"There's all these people waiting," I said.

"Good," she said. She started on a pot.

I looked over at Mona, who was still cowering in the broom closet. "In fact, there's some black family's been waiting so long, they're going to sue," I said.

My mother turned off the water. "Where'd you hear that?"

"Patty told me."

She turned the water back on, started to wash a dish, then put it back down and shut the faucet.

"I'm sorry," said Mona.

"Forget it," said my mother. "Just forget it."

Booker turned out to be a model worker, whose boundless gratitude translated into a willingness to do anything. As he also learned quickly, he soon knew not only how to bus, but how to cook, and how to wait tables, and how to keep the books. He fixed the walk-in door so that it stayed shut, reupholstered the torn seats in the dining room, and devised a system for tracking inventory. The only stone in the rice was that he tended to be sickly; but, reliable even in illness, he would always send a friend to take his place. In this way we got to know Ronald, Lynn, Dirk, and Cedric, all of whom, like Booker, had problems with their legal status and were anxious to please. They weren't all as capable as Booker, though, with the exception of Cedric, whom my father often hired even when Booker was well. A round wag of a man who called Mona and me *shou hou*—skinny monkeys—he was a professed nonsmoker who was nevertheless always begging drags off of other people's cigarettes. This last habit drove our head cook, Fernando, crazy, especially since, when refused a hit, Cedric would occasionally snitch one. Winking impishly at Mona and me, he would steal up to an ashtray, take a quick puff, and then break out laughing so that the smoke came rolling out of his mouth in a great incriminatory cloud. Fernando accused him of stealing fresh cigarettes too, even whole packs.

"Why else do you think he's weaseling around in the back of the store all the time," he said. His face was blotchy with anger. "The man is a frigging thief."

Other members of the staff supported him in this contention and joined in on an "Operation Identification," which involved numbering and initialing their cigarettes—even though what they seemed to fear for wasn't so much their cigarettes as their jobs. Then one of the cooks quit; and rather than promote someone, my father hired Cedric for the position. Rumors flew that he was taking only half the normal salary, that Alex had been pressured to resign, and that my father was looking for a position with which to placate Booker, who had been bypassed because of his health.

The result was that Fernando categorically refused to work with Cedric.

"The only way I'll cook with that piece of slime," he said, shaking his huge tattooed fist, "is if it's his ass frying on the grill."

My father cajoled and cajoled, to no avail, and in the end was simply forced to put them on different schedules.

The next week Fernando got caught stealing a carton of minute steaks. My father would not tell even Mona and me how he knew to be standing by the back door when Fernando was on his way out, but everyone suspected Booker. Everyone but Fernando, that is, who was sure Cedric had been the tip-off. My father held a staff meeting in which he tried to reassure everyone that Alex had left on his own, and that he had no intention of firing anyone. But though he was careful not to mention Fernando, everyone was so amazed that he was being allowed to stay that Fernando was incensed nonetheless.

"Don't you all be putting your bug eyes on me," he said. "*He's* the frigging crook." He grabbed Cedric by the collar.

Cedric raised an eyebrow. "Cook, you mean," he said.

At this Fernando punched Cedric in the mouth; and the words he had just uttered notwithstanding, my father fired him on the spot.

With everything that was happening, Mona and I were ready to be getting out of the restaurant. It was almost time: the days were still stuffy with summer, but our window shade had started flapping in the evening as if gearing up to go out. That year the breezes were full of salt, as they sometimes were when they came in from the East, and they blew anchors and docks through my mind like so many tumbleweeds, filling my dreams with wherries and lobsters and grainy-faced men who squinted, day in and day out, at the sky.

It was time for a change, you could feel it; and yet the pancake house was the same as ever. The day before school started my father came home with bad news.

"Fernando called police," he said, wiping his hand on his pant leg.

My mother naturally wanted to know what police; and so with much coughing and hawing, the long story began, the latest installment of which had the police calling immigration, and immigration sending an investigator. My mother sat stiff as whalebone as my father described how the man summarily refused lunch on the house and how my father had admitted, under pressure, that he knew there were "things" about his workers.

"So now what happens?"

My father didn't know. "Booker and Cedric went with him to the jail," he said. "But me, here I am." He laughed uncomfortably.

The next day my father posted bail for "his boys" and waited apprehensively for something to happen. The day after that he waited again, and the day after that he called our neighbor's law student son, who suggested my father call the immigration department under an alias. My father took his advice; and it was thus that he discovered that Booker was right: it was illegal for aliens to work, but it wasn't to hire them.

In the happy interval that ensued, my father apologized to my mother, who in turn confessed about the country club, for which my father had no choice but to forgive her. Then he turned his attention back to "his boys."

My mother didn't see that there was anything to do.

"I like to talking to the judge," said my father.

"This is not China," said my mother.

"I'm only talking to him. I'm not give him money unless he wants it."

"You're going to land up in jail."

"So what else I should do?" My father threw up his hands. "Those are my boys."

"Your boys!" exploded my mother. "What about your family? What about your wife?"

My father took a long sip of tea. "You know," he said finally. "In the war my father sent our cook to the soldiers to use. He always said it— the province comes before the town, the town comes before the family."

"A restaurant is not a town," said my mother.

My father sipped at his tea again. "You know, when I first come to the United States, I also had to hide-and-seek with those deportation guys. If people did not helping me, I'm not here today."

My mother scrutinized her hem.

After a minute I volunteered that before seeing a judge, he might try a lawyer.

He turned. "Since when did you become so afraid like your mother?"

I started to say that it wasn't a matter of fear, but he cut me off.

"What I need today," he said, "is a son."

My father and I spent the better part of the next day standing in lines at the immigration office. He did not get to speak to a judge, but with much persistence he managed to speak to a judge's clerk, who tried to persuade him that it was not her place to extend him advice. My father, though, shamelessly plied her with compliments and offers of free pancakes until she finally conceded that she personally doubted anything would happen to either Cedric or Booker.

"Especially if they're 'needed workers,'" she said, rubbing at the red marks her glasses left on her nose. She yawned. "Have you thought about sponsoring them to become permanent residents?"

Could he do that? My father was overjoyed. And what if he saw to it right away? Would she perhaps put in a good word with the judge?

She yawned again, her nostrils flaring. "Don't worry," she said. "They'll get a fair hearing."

My father returned jubilant. Booker and Cedric hailed him as their savior, their Buddha incarnate. He was like a father to them, they said; and laughing and clapping, they made him tell the story over and over, sorting over the details like jewels. And how old was the assistant judge? And what did she say?

That evening my father tipped the paperboy a dollar and bought a pot of mums for my mother, who suffered them to be placed on the dining room table. The next night he took us all out to dinner. Then on Saturday, Mona found a letter on my father's chair at the restaurant.

> Dear Mr. Chang,
>
> You are the grat boss. But, we do not like to trial, so will runing away now. Plese to excus us. People saying the law in America is fears like dragon. Here is only $140. We hope some day we can pay back the rest bale. You will getting interest, as you diserving, so grat a boss you are. Thank you for every thing. In next life you will be burn in rich family, with no more pancaks.
>
> Yours truley,
Booker + Cedric

In the weeks that followed my father went to the pancake house for crises, but otherwise hung around our house, fiddling idly with the sump pump and boiler in an effort, he said, to get ready for winter. It was as though he had gone into retirement, except that instead of moving South, he had moved to the basement. He even took to showering my mother with little attentions, and to calling her "old girl," and when we finally heard that the club had entertained all the applications it could for the year, he was so sympathetic that he seemed more disappointed than my mother.

2. In the American Society

Mrs. Lardner tempered the bad news with an invitation to a bon voyage "bash" she was throwing for a friend of hers who was going to Greece for six months.

"Do come," she urged. "You'll meet everyone, and then, you know, if things open up in the spring . . ." She waved her hands.

My mother wondered if it would be appropriate to show up at a party for someone they didn't know, but "the honest truth" was that this was an annual affair. "If it's not Greece, it's Antibes," sighed Mrs. Lardner. "We really just do it because his wife left him and his daughter doesn't speak to him, and poor Jeremy just feels so *unloved*."

She also invited Mona and me to the going on, as *"demi-guests"* to keep Annie out of the champagne. I wasn't too keen on the idea, but before I could say anything, she had already thanked us for so generously agreeing to honor her with our presence.

"A pair of little princesses, you are!" she told us. "A pair of princesses!"

The party was that Sunday. On Saturday, my mother took my father out shopping for a suit. As it was the end of September, she insisted that he buy a worsted rather than a seersucker, even though it was only ten, rather than fifty percent off. My father protested that it was as hot out as ever, which was true—a thick Indian summer had cozied murderously up to us—but to no avail. Summer clothes, said my mother, were not properly worn after Labor Day.

The suit was unfortunately as extravagant in length as it was in price, which posed an additional quandary, since the tailor wouldn't be in until Monday. The salesgirl, though, found a way of tacking it up temporarily.

"Maybe this suit not fit me," fretted my father.

"Just don't take your jacket off," said the salesgirl.

He gave her a tip before they left, but when he got home refused to remove the price tag.

"I like to asking the tailor about the size," he insisted.

"You mean you're going to *wear* it and then return it?" Mona rolled her eyes.

"I didn't say I'm return it," said my father stiffly. "I like to asking the tailor, that's all."

The party started off swimmingly, except that most people were wearing bermudas or wrap skirts. Still, my parents carried on, sharing with great feeling the complaints about the heat. Of course my father tried to eat a cracker full of shallots and burnt himself in an attempt to help Mr. Lardner turn the coals of the barbeque; but on the whole he seemed to be doing all right. Not nearly so well as my mother, though, who had accepted an entire cupful of Mrs. Lardner's magic punch, and seemed indeed to be under some spell. As Mona and Annie skirmished over whether some boy in their class inhaled when he smoked, I watched my mother take off her shoes, laughing and laughing as a man with a beard regaled her with Navy stories by the pool. Apparently he had been stationed in the

Orient and remembered a few words of Chinese, which made my mother laugh still more. My father excused himself to go to the men's room then drifted back and weighed anchor at the hors d'oeuvres table, while my mother sailed on to a group of women, who tinkled at length over the clarity of her complexion. I dug out a book I had brought.

Just when I'd cracked the spine, though, Mrs. Lardner came by to bewail her shortage of servers. Her caterers were criminals, I agreed; and the next thing I knew I was handing out bits of marine life, making the rounds as amicably as I could.

"Here you go, Dad," I said when I got to the hors d'oeuvres table.

"Everything is fine," he said.

I hesitated to leave him alone; but then the man with the beard zeroed in on him, and though he talked of nothing but my mother, I thought it would be okay to get back to work. Just that moment, though, Jeremy Brothers lurched our way, an empty, albeit corked, wine bottle in hand. He was a slim, well-proportioned man, with a Roman nose and small eyes and a nice manly jaw that he allowed to hang agape.

"Hello," he said drunkenly. "Pleased to meet you."

"Pleased to meeting you," said my father.

"Right," said Jeremy. "Right. Listen. I have this bottle here, this most recalcitrant bottle. You see that it refuses to do my bidding. I bid it open sesame, please, and it does nothing." He pulled the cork out with his teeth, then turned the bottle upside down.

My father nodded.

"Would you have a word with it, please?" said Jeremy. The man with the beard excused himself. "Would you please have a goddamned word with it?"

My father laughed uncomfortably.

"Ah!" Jeremy bowed a little. "Excuse me, excuse me, excuse me. You are not my man, not my man at all." He bowed again and started to leave, but then circled back. "Viticulture is not your forte, yes I can see that, see that plainly. But may I trouble you on another matter? Forget the damned bottle." He threw it into the pool, and winked at the people he splashed. "I have another matter. Do you speak Chinese?"

My father said he did not, but Jeremy pulled out a handkerchief with some characters on it anyway, saying that his daughter had sent it from Hong Kong and that he thought the characters might be some secret message.

"Long life," said my father.

"But you haven't looked at it yet."

"I know what it says without looking." My father winked at me.

"You do?"

"Yes, I do."

"You're making fun of me, aren't you?"

"No, no, no," said my father, winking again.

"Who are you anyway?" said Jeremy.

His smile fading, my father shrugged.

"*Who are you?*"

My father shrugged again.

Jeremy began to roar. "This is my party, *my party*, and I've never seen you before in my life." My father backed up as Jeremy came toward him. "*Who are you? WHO ARE YOU?*"

Just as my father was going to step back into the pool, Mrs. Lardner came running up. Jeremy informed her that there was a man crashing his party.

"Nonsense," said Mrs. Lardner. "This is Ralph Chang, who I invited extra especially so he could meet you." She straightened the collar of Jeremy's peach-colored polo shirt for him.

"Yes, well we've had a chance to chat," said Jeremy.

She whispered in his ear; he mumbled something; she whispered something more.

"I do apologize," he said finally.

My father didn't say anything.

"I do." Jeremy seemed genuinely contrite. "Doubtless you've seen drunks before, haven't you? You must have them in China."

"Okay," said my father.

As Mrs. Lardner glided off, Jeremy clapped his arm over my father's shoulders. "You know, I really am quite sorry, quite sorry."

My father nodded.

"What can I do, how can I make it up to you?"

"No thank you."

"No, tell me, tell me," wheedled Jeremy. "Tickets to casino night?" My father shook his head. "You don't gamble. Dinner at Bartholomew's?" My father shook his head again. "You don't eat." Jeremy scratched his chin. "You know, my wife was like you. Old Annabelle could never let me make things up—never, never, never, never, never."

My father wriggled out from under his arm.

"How about sport clothes? You are rather overdressed, you know, excuse me for saying so. But here." He took off his polo shirt and folded it up. "You can have this with my most profound apologies." He ruffled his chest hairs with his free hand.

"No thank you," said my father.

"No, take it, take it. Accept my apologies." He thrust the shirt into my father's arms. "I'm so very sorry, so very sorry. Please, try it on."

Helplessly holding the shirt, my father searched the crowd for my mother.

"Here, I'll help you off with your coat."

My father froze.

Jeremy reached over and took his jacket off. "Milton's one hundred twenty-five dollars reduced to one hundred twelve-fifty," he read. "What a bargain, what a bargain!"

"Please give it back," pleaded my father. "Please."

"Now for your shirt," ordered Jeremy.

Heads began to turn.

"Take off your shirt."

"I do not take orders like a servant," announced my father.

"Take off your shirt, or I'm going to throw this jacket right into the pool, just right into this little pool here." Jeremy held it over the water.

"Go ahead."

"One hundred twelve-fifty," taunted Jeremy. "One hundred twelve . . ."

My father flung the polo shirt into the water with such force that part of it bounced back up into the air like a fluorescent fountain. Then it settled into a soft heap on top of the water. My mother hurried up.

"You're a sport!" said Jeremy, suddenly breaking into a smile and slapping my father on the back. "You're a sport! I like that. A man with spirit, that's what you are. A man with panache. Allow me to return to you your jacket." He handed it back to my father. "Good value you got on that, good value."

My father hurled the coat into the pool too. "We're leaving," he said grimly. "Leaving!"

"Now, Ralphie," said Mrs. Lardner, bustling up; but my father was already stomping off.

"Get your sister," he told me. To my mother: "Get your shoes."

"That was *great*, Dad," said Mona as we walked down to the car. "You were *stupendous*."

"Way to show 'em," I said.

"What?" said my father offhandedly.

Although it was only just dusk, we were in a gulch, which made it hard to see anything except the gleam of his white shirt moving up the hill ahead of us.

"It was all my fault," began my mother.

"Forget it," said my father grandly. Then he said, "The only trouble is I left those keys in my jacket pocket."

"Oh no," said Mona.

"Oh no is right," said my mother.

"So we'll walk home," I said.

"But how're we going to get into the *house*," said Mona.

The noise of the party churned through the silence.

"Someone has to going back," said my father.

"Let's go to the pancake house first," suggested my mother. "We can wait there until the party is finished, and then call Mrs. Lardner."

Having all agreed that that was a good plan, we started walking again.

"God, just think," said Mona. "We're going to have to *dive* for them."

My father stopped a moment. We waited.

"You girls are good swimmers," he said finally. "Not like me."

Then his shirt started moving again, and we trooped up the hill after it, into the dark.

—*[1986] 1999*

HELEN SIMPSON ■ (b. 1959)

English student Helen Simpson grew up in London and studied at Oxford. While a university student, she won a contest sponsored by Vogue *and went on to work for the magazine for five years. Her first collection,* Four Bare Legs in a Bed and Other Stories, *won the* Sunday Times Young Writer of the Year Award *in 1990, She has since published six more collections, including* In-Flight Entertainment *in 2010. "Diary of an Interesting Year" originally appeared in* The New Yorker.

Diary of an Interesting Year

February 12, 2040. My thirtieth birthday. G. gave me this little spiral-bound notebook and a Biro. It's a good present, hardly any rust on the spiral and no water damage to the paper. I'm going to start a diary. Ill keep my handwriting tiny to make the paper go further.

February 15th. G. is really getting me down. He's in his element. They should carve it on his tombstone: "I Was Right."

February 23rd. Glad we don't live in London. The Hatchwells have got cousins stayingwith them—they trekked up from Peckham (three days). Went round this afternoon and the cousins were saying the thing that finally drove them out was the sewage system—when the drains backed up, it overflowed everywhere. They said the smell was unbelievable. The pavements were swimming in it, and of course the hospitals are down, so there's nothing to be done about the cholera. Didn't get too close to them in case they were carrying it. They lost their two sons like that last year.

"You see," G. said to me on the way home, "capitalism cared more about its children as accessories and demonstrations of earning power than for their future."

"Oh, shut up" I said.

March 2nd. Can't sleep. I'm writing this instead of staring at the ceiling. There's a mosquito in the room, I can hear it whining close to my ear. Very humid, air like filthy soup, plus we're supposed to wear our face masks in bed, too, but I was running with sweat, so I ripped mine off just now. Got up and looked at myself in the mirror on the landing—ribs like a fence, hair in greasy rats' tails. Yesterday the rats in the kitchen were busy gnawing away at the bread bin, they didn't even look up when I came in.

March 6th. Another quarrel with G. O.K., "yes, he was right, but why crow about it? That's what you get when you marry your tutor from Uni—wall-to-wall pontificating from an older man. "I saw it coming, any fool could see it coming, especially after the Big Melt," he brags. "Thresholds crossed, cascade effect, hopelessly optimistic to assume we had till 2060, blahdyblahdy blah, the plutonomy as lemming, democracy's massive own goal." No wonder we haven't got any friends.

He cheered when rationing came in. He's the one who volunteered first as car-share warden for our road; one piddling little Peugeot for the entire road. He gets a real kick out of the camaraderie round the standpipe.

—Ill swap my big tin of chickpeas for your little tin of sardines.

—No, no, my sardines are protein. —Chickpeas are protein, too, plus they fill you up more. Anyway, I thought you still had some tuna.

—No, I swapped that with Violet Huggins for a tin of tomato soup.

Really sick of bartering, but hard to know how to earn money since the Internet went down. "Also, money's no use unless you've got shed-loads of it," as I said to him in bed last night. "The top layer hanging on inside their plastic bubbles of filtered air while the rest of us shuffle about with goiters and tumors and bits of old sheet tied over our mouths. Plus, we're soaking wet the whole time. We've given up on umbrellas, we just go round permanently drenched." I stopped ranting only when I heard a snore and clocked that he was asleep.

April 8th. Boring morning washing out rags. No wood for hot water, so had to use ashes and lye again. Hands very sore, even though I put plastic bags over them. Did the face masks first, then the rags from my period. Took forever. At least I haven't got to do nappies, like Lexi or Esme—that would send me right over the edge.

April 27th. Just back from Maia's. Seven months. She's very fright-ened. I don't blame her. She tried to make me promise I'd take care of the baby if anything happens to her. I havered (mostly at the thought of coming between her and that throwback Martin—she had a new black eye, I didn't ask). I suppose there's no harm in promising if it makes her feel better. After all, it wouldn't exactly be taking on a responsibil-ity—I give a new baby three months max in these conditions. Diar-rhea, basically.

May 14th. Can't sleep. Bites itching, trying not to scratch. Heavy thumps and squeaks just above, in the ceiling. Think of something nice. Soap and hot water. Fresh air. Condoms! Sick of being perma-nently on knife edge re pregnancy.

Start again. Wandering round a supermarket—warm, gorgeously lit—corridors of open fridges full of tiger prawns and fillet steak. Glid-ing off down the fast lane in a sports car, stopping to fill up with thirty litres of petrol. Online, booking tickets for "The Mousetrap," *click,* order-ing a crate of wine, *click,* a vacation home, *click,* a pair of patent-leather boots, *click,* a gap year, *click.* I go to iTunes and download "The Marriage of Figaro," then I chat face to face in real time with G.'s parents in Syd-ney, No, don't think about what happened to them. Horrible. Go to sleep.

May 21st. Another row with G. He blew my second candle out, he said one was enough. It wasn't, though. I couldn't see to read anymore. He drives me mad—it's like living with a policeman. It always was, even before the Collapse. "The earth has enough for everyone's need, but not for everyone's greed" was his favorite. Nobody likes being labelled greedy. I called him Killjoy and he didn't like that. "Every one of us takes about twenty-five thousand breaths a day," he told me. "Each breath removes oxygen from the atmosphere and replaces it with carbon dioxide," Well, pardon me for breathing! What was I supposed to do—turn into a tree?

June 6th. Went round to the Lumleys' for the news last night. Whole road there squashed into front room, straining to listen to radio—batteries very low (no new ones in the last government delivery). Big news, though: compulsory billeting imminent. The Shorthouses were up in arms, Kai shouting and red in the face, Lexi in tears. "You work all your life," etc., etc. What planet is he on? None of us too keen, but nothing to be done about it. When we got back, G. checked our stash of tins under the bedroom floorboards. A big rat shot out and I screamed my head off. G. held me till I stopped crying, then we had sex. Woke in the night and prayed not to be pregnant, though God knows who I was praying to.

June 12th. Visited Maia this afternoon. She was in bed, her legs have swollen up like balloons. On at me again to promise about the baby, and this time I said yes. She said Violet Huggins was going to help her when it started—Violet was a nurse once, apparently, not really the hands-on sort but better than nothing. Nobody else on the road will have a clue what to do now that we can't Google it. "All I remember from old films *is* that you're supposed to boil a kettle," I said. We started to laugh, we got a bit hysterical. Knuckle-dragger Martin put his head round the door and growled at us to shut up.

July 1st. First billet arrived today by Army truck. We've got a Spanish group of eight, including one old lady, her daughter, and twin toddler grandsons (all pretty feral), plus four unsmiling men of fighting age. A bit much, since we have only two bedrooms. G. and I tried to show them round but they ignored us. The grandmother bagged our bedroom straight off. We're under the kitchen table tonight. I might try to sleep on top of it because of the rats. We couldn't think of anything to say—the only Spanish we could remember was *"Muchas gracias,"* and, as G. snapped, we're certainly not saying that.

July 2nd. Fell off the table in my sleep. Bashed my elbow. Covered in bruises.

July 3rd. G. depressed. The four Spaniards are bigger than him, and he's worried that the biggest one, Miguel, has his eye on me (with reason, I have to say).

July 4th. G. depressed. The grandmother found our tins under the floor-boards and all but danced a flamenco Miguel punched G. when he tried to reclaim a tin of sardines and since then his nose won't stop bleeding.

July 6tb. Last night under the table G. came up with a plan. He thinks we should head north. Now that this lot are in the flat and a new group from Tehran promised next week, we might as well cut and run. Scotland's heaving—everyone else has already had the same idea—so he thinks we should get on one, of the ferries to Stavanger, then aim for Russia.

"I don't know," I said. "Where would we stay?"

"I've got the pop-up tent packed in a rucksack behind the shed," he said. "Plus our sleeping bags and my windup radio."

"Camping in the mud," I said.

"Look on the bright side," he said. 'We have a huge mortgage and we're just going to walk away from it."

"Oh, shut up," I said.

July 17th, Maia died yesterday. It was horrible. The baby got stuck two weeks ago, it died inside her. Violet Huggins was useless, she didn't have a clue. Martin started waving his Swiss Army knife around on the second day and yelling about a Cesarean—he had to be dragged off her. He's round at ours now drinking the last of our precious brandy with the Spaniards. That's it. We've got to go. Now, says G. Yes.

August 1st, Somewhere in Shropshire, or possibly Cheshire. We're staying off the beaten track. Heavy rain. This notebook's pages have gone all wavy. At least Biro doesn't run. I'm lying inside the tent now. G. is out foraging. We got away in the middle of the night. G. slung our two rucksacks across the bike. We took turns wheeling it, then on the fourth morning we woke up and looked outside the tent flap and it was gone, even though we'd covered it with leaves the night before.

"Could be worse," G. said. "We could have had our throats cut while we slept."

"Oh, shut up," I said.

August 3rd. Rivers and streams all toxic—fertilizers, typhoid, etc. So we're following G.'s D.I.Y. system. Dip billycan into stream or river. Add three drops of bleach. Boil up on camping stove with T-shirt stretched over billycan. Only moisture squeezed from the T-shirt is safe to drink; nothing else. "You're joking," I said, when G. first showed me how to do this. But no.

August 9th. Radio news in muddy sleeping bags—skeleton government obviously struggling, they keep playing the "Enigma Variations." Last night they announced the end of fuel for civilian use and the compulsory disabling of all remaining civilian cars. From now on we must all stay at home, they said, and not travel without permission. There's talk of martial law. We're going cross-country as much as possible—less chance of being arrested or mugged—trying to cover ten miles a day, but the weather slows us down. Torrential rain, often horizontal in gusting winds.

August 16th. Rare dry afternoon. Black lace clouds over yellow sky. Brown grass, frowsty gray mold, fungal frills. Dead trees come crashing down without warning—one nearly got us today, it made us jump. G. was hoping we'd find stuff growing in the fields, but all the farmland round here is surrounded by razor wire and armed guards. He says he knows how to grow vegetables from his gardening days, but so what. They take too long. We're hungry now—we can't wait till March for some old carrots to get ripe.

August 22nd. G. broke a front crown cracking a beechnut, there's a black hole and he whistles when he talks. "Dam-sons, blackberries, young green nettles for soup," he said at the start of all this, smacking his lips. He's not so keen now. No damsons or blackberries, of course—only chickweed and.

He's just caught a lame squirrel, so I suppose I'll have to do something with it. No creatures left except squirrels, rats, and pigeons, unless you count the insects. The news says they're full of protein—you're meant to grind them into a paste—but so far we haven't been able to face that.

August 24th. We met a pig this morning. It was a bit thin for a pig, and it didn't look well. G. said, "Quick! We've got to kill it."

"Why?" I said. "How?"

"With a knife," he said. "Bacon. Sausages."

I pointed out that even if we managed to stab it to death with our old kitchen knife, which seemed unlikely, we wouldn't be able just to open it up and find bacon and sausages inside.

"Milk, then!" G. said wildly. "It's a mammal, isn't it?"

Meanwhile, the pig walked off.

August 25th. Ravenous. We've both got streaming colds. Jumping with fleas, itching like crazy. Weeping sores on hands and faces—unfortunate side effects from cloud seeding, the news says. What with all this and his toothache (back molar, swollen jaw) and the malaria, G. is in a bad way.

August 27th. Found a dead hedgehog. Tried to peel offits spines and barbecue it over the last briquette. Disgusting. Both sick as dogs. Why did I moan about the barter system? Foraging is MUCH worse.

August 29th. Dreamed of Maia and the Swiss Army knife and woke up crying. G. held me in his shaky arms and talked about Russia, how it's the new land of milk and honey since the Big Melt. "Some really good farming opportunities opening up in Siberia," he said through chattering teeth. "We're like in 'Three Sisters,'" I said. "If only we could get to Moscow. Do you remember that production at the National? We walked by the river afterward, we stood and listened to Big Ben chime midnight." Hugged each other and carried on like this until sleep came.

August 31st. G. woke up crying. I held him and hushed him and asked what was the matter. "I wish I had a gun," he said.

September 15th. Can't believe this notebook was still at the bottom of the rucksack. And the Biro. Murderer wasn't interested in them. He's turned everything else inside out (including me). G. didn't have a gun. This one has a gun.

September 19th. M. speaks another language. Norwegian? Dutch? Croatian? We can't talk, so he hits me instead. He smells like an abandoned fridge, his breath stinks of rot. What he does to me is horrible. I don't want to think about it. I won't think about it. There's a tent and cooking stuff on the ground, but half the time we're up a tree with the gun. There's a big plank platform and a tarpaulin roped to the branches above. At night he pulls the rope ladder up after us. It's quite high—you can see for miles. He uses the platform for storing stuff he brings back from his mugging expeditions. I'm surrounded by tins of baked beans.

October 3rd. M. can't seem to get through the day without at least two blow jobs. I'm always sick afterward (sometimes during).

October 8th. M. beat me up yesterday. I'd tried to escape. I shan't do that again, he's too fast.

October 14th. If we run out of beans I think he might kill me for food. There were warnings about it on the news a while back. This one wouldn't think twice. I'm just meat on legs to him. He bit me all over last night, hard. I'm covered in bite marks. I was literally licking my wounds afterward when I remembered how nice the taste of blood is, how I miss it. Strength. Calves liver for iron. How I haven't had a period for ages. When that thought popped out I missed a beat. Then my blood ran cold.

October 15th. Wasn't it juniper berries they used to use? As in gin? Even if it was, I wouldn't know what they looked like—I remember only mint and basil. I can't be pregnant. I won't be pregnant.

October 17th. Very sick after drinking rank juice off random stewed herbs. Nothing else, though, worse luck.

October 20th. Can't sleep. Dreamed of G. I was moving against him, it started to go up a little way, so I thought he wasn't really dead. Dreadful waking to find M. there instead.

October 23rd. Can't sleep. Very bruised and scratched after today. They used to throw themselves downstairs to get rid of it. The trouble is the gravel pit just wasn't deep enough, plus the bramble bushes kept breaking my fall. There was some sort of body down there, too, seething with white vermin. Maybe it was a goat or a pig or something, but I don't think it was. I keep thinking it might have been G.

October 31st. This baby will be the death of me. Would have been. Let's make that a subjunctive. "Would have been," not "will."

November 7th. It's all over. I'm still here. Too tired to

November 8th. Slept for hours. Stronger. I've got all the food and drink, and the gun. There's still some shouting from down there but it's weaker now. I think he's almost finished.

November 9th. Slept for hours. Fever gone. Baked beans for breakfast. More groans started up just now. Never mind. I can wait

November 10th. It's over. I got stuck into his bottle of vodka—it was the demon drink that saved me. He was out mugging—left me up the tree as usual—I drank just enough to raise my courage. Nothing else had worked, so I thought I'd get him to beat me up. When he came back and saw me waving the bottle he was beside himself. I pretended to be drunker than I was and I lay down on the wooden platform with my arms round my head while he got the boot in. It worked. Not right away but that night. Meanwhile, M. decided he fancied a drink himself, and very soon he'd polished off the rest of it—more than three-quarters of a bottle. He was singing and sobbing and carrying on, out of his tree with alcohol, and then, when he was standing pissing off the side of the platform, I crept along and gave him a gigantic shove and he really was out of his tree. Crash.

November 13th. I've wrapped your remains in my good blue shirt; sorry I couldn't let you stay on board, but there's no future now for any baby aboveground. I'm the end of the line!

This is the last page of my thirtieth-birthday present. When I've finished it I'll wrap the notebook up in six plastic bags, sealing each one with duct tape against the rain, then I'll bury it in a hole on top of the blue shirt. I don't know why, as I'm not mad enough to think anybody will ever read it. After that I'm going to buckle on this rucksack of provisions and head north with my gun. Wish me luck Last line: Good luck, good luck, good luck, good luck, good luck."

—2009

SHERMAN ALEXIE ■ (b. 1966)

Sherman Alexie is a Spokane/Coeur d'Alene Indian and grew up on a reservation in Wellpinit, Washington. While at Washington State University as a pre-med major, Alexie attended a poetry workshop, and soon began to publish his work. Two collections of poetry were followed by The Lone Ranger and Tonto Fight in Heaven *(1993) and a first novel,* Reservation Blues *(2005). "This Is What It Means to Say Phoenix, Arizona" was made into a 1998 film,* Smoke Signals, *and won two awards at the Sundance Film Festival. A prolific author and frequent guest on radio and television talk shows, Alexie has also performed professionally as a stand-up comedian. A young adult novel,* The Absolutely True Diary of a Part-Time Indian, *appeared in 2007 and received a National Book Award.*

This Is What It Means to Say Phoenix, Arizona

Just after Victor lost his job at the BIA,[1] he also found out that his father had died of a heart attack in Phoenix, Arizona. Victor hadn't seen his father in a few years, only talked to him on the telephone once or twice, but there still was a genetic pain, which was soon to be pain as real and immediate as a broken bone.

Victor didn't have any money. Who does have money on a reservation, except the cigarette and fireworks salespeople? His father had a savings account waiting to be claimed, but Victor needed to find a way to get to Phoenix. Victor's mother was just as poor as he was, and the rest of his family didn't have any use at all for him. So Victor called the Tribal Council.

[1]**BIA** The Bureau of Indian Affairs

"Listen," Victor said. "My father just died. I need some money to get to Phoenix to make arrangements."

"Now, Victor," the council said. "You know we're having a difficult time financially."

"But I thought the council had special funds set aside for stuff like this."

"Now, Victor, we do have some money available for the proper return of tribal members' bodies. But I don't think we have enough to bring your father all the way back from Phoenix."

"Well," Victor said. "It ain't going to cost all that much. He had to be cremated. Things were kind of ugly. He died of a heart attack in his trailer and nobody found him for a week. It was really hot, too. You get the picture."

"Now, Victor, we're sorry for your loss and the circumstances. But we can really only afford to give you one hundred dollars."

"That's not even enough for a plane ticket."

"Well, you might consider driving down to Phoenix."

"I don't have a car. Besides, I was going to drive my father's pickup back up here."

"Now, Victor," the council said. "We're sure there is somebody who could drive you to Phoenix. Or is there somebody who could lend you the rest of the money?"

"You know there ain't nobody around with that kind of money."

"Well, we're sorry, Victor, but that's the best we can do."

Victor accepted the Tribal Council's offer. What else could he do? So he signed the proper papers, picked up his check, and walked over to the Trading Post to cash it.

While Victor stood in line, he watched Thomas Builds-the-Fire standing near the magazine rack, talking to himself. Like he always did. Thomas was a story-teller that nobody wanted to listen to. That's like being a dentist in a town where everybody has false teeth.

Victor and Thomas Builds-the-Fire were the same age, had grown up and played in the dirt together. Ever since Victor could remember, it was Thomas who always had something to say.

Once, when they were seven years old, when Victor's father still lived with the family, Thomas closed his eyes and told Victor this story: "Your father's heart is weak. He is afraid of his own family. He is afraid of you. Late at night he sits in the dark. Watches the television until there's nothing but that white noise. Sometimes he feels like he wants to buy a motorcycle and ride away. He wants to run and hide. He doesn't want to be found."

Thomas Builds-the-Fire had known that Victor's father was going to leave, knew it before anyone. Now Victor stood in the Trading Post with a one-hundred-dollar check in his hand, wondering if Thomas knew that Victor's father was dead, if he knew what was going to happen next.

Just then Thomas looked at Victor, smiled, and walked over to him.

"Victor, I'm sorry about your father," Thomas said.

"How did you know about it?" Victor asked.

"I heard it on the wind. I heard it from the birds. I felt it in the sunlight. Also, your mother was just in here crying."

"Oh," Victor said and looked around the Trading Post. All the other Indians stared, surprised that Victor was even talking to Thomas. Nobody talked to Thomas anymore because he told the same damn stories over and over again. Victor was embarrassed, but he thought that Thomas might be able to help him. Victor felt a sudden need for tradition.

"I can lend you the money you need," Thomas said suddenly. "But you have to take me with you."

"I can't take your money," Victor said. "I mean, I haven't hardly talked to you in years. We're not really friends anymore."

"I didn't say we were friends. I said you had to take me with you."

"Let me think about it."

Victor went home with his one hundred dollars and sat at the kitchen table. He held his head in his hands and thought about Thomas Builds-the-Fire, remembered little details, tears and scars, the bicycle they shared for a summer, so many stories.

Thomas Builds-the-Fire sat on the bicycle, waited in Victor's yard. He was ten years old and skinny. His hair was dirty because it was the Fourth of July.

"Victor," Thomas yelled. "Hurry up. We're going to miss the fireworks."

After a few minutes, Victor ran out of his house, jumped the porch railing, and landed gracefully on the sidewalk.

"And the judges award him a 9.95, the highest score of the summer," Thomas said, clapped, laughed.

"That was perfect, cousin," Victor said. "And it's my turn to ride the bike."

Thomas gave up the bike and they headed for the fairgrounds. It was nearly dark and the fireworks were about to start.

"You know," Thomas said. "It's strange how us Indians celebrate the Fourth of July. It ain't like it was *our* independence everybody was fighting for."

"You think about things too much," Victor said. "It's just supposed to be fun. Maybe Junior will be there."

"Which Junior? Everybody on this reservation is named Junior."

And they both laughed.

The fireworks were small, hardly more than a few bottle rockets and a fountain. But it was enough for two Indian boys. Years later, they would need much more.

Afterwards, sitting in the dark, fighting off mosquitoes, Victor turned to Thomas Builds-the-Fire.

"Hey," Victor said. "Tell me a story."

Thomas closed his eyes and told this story: "There were these two Indian boys who wanted to be warriors. But it was too late to be warriors in the old way. All the horses were gone. So the two Indian boys stole a car and drove to the city. They parked the stolen car in front of the police station and then hitchhiked back home to the reservation. When they got back, all their friends cheered and their parents' eyes shone with pride. *You were very brave*, everybody said to the two Indian boys. *Very brave*."

"Ya-hey," Victor said. "That's a good one. I wish I could be a warrior."

"Me, too," Thomas said.

They went home together in the dark, Thomas on the bike now, Victor on foot. They walked through shadows and light from streetlamps.

"We've come a long ways," Thomas said. "We have outdoor lighting."

"All I need is the stars," Victor said. "And besides, you still think about things too much."

They separated then, each headed for home, both laughing all the way.

Victor sat at his kitchen table. He counted his one hundred dollars again and again. He knew he needed more to make it to Phoenix and back. He knew he needed Thomas Builds-the-Fire. So he put his money in his wallet and opened the front door to find Thomas on the porch.

"Ya-hey, Victor," Thomas said. "I knew you'd call me."

Thomas walked into the living room and sat down on Victor's favorite chair.

"I've got some money saved up," Thomas said. "It's enough to get us down there, but you have to get us back."

"I've got this hundred dollars," Victor said. "And my dad had a savings account I'm going to claim."

"How much in your dad's account?"

"Enough. A few hundred."

"Sounds good. When we leaving?"

When they were fifteen and had long since stopped being friends, Victor and Thomas got into a fistfight. That is, Victor was really drunk and beat Thomas up for no reason at all. All the other Indian boys stood around and watched it happen. Junior was there and so were Lester, Seymour, and a lot of others. The beating might have gone on until Thomas was dead if Norma Many Horses hadn't come along and stopped it.

"Hey, you boys," Norma yelled and jumped out of her car. "Leave him alone."

If it had been someone else, even another man, the Indian boys would've just ignored the warnings. But Norma was a warrior. She was powerful. She could have picked up any two of the boys and smashed their skulls together. But worse than that, she would have dragged them all over to some tipi and made them listen to some elder tell a dusty old story.

The Indian boys scattered, and Norma walked over to Thomas and picked him up.

"Hey, little man, are you okay?" she asked.

Thomas gave her a thumbs up.

"Why they always picking on you?"

Thomas shook his head, closed his eyes, but no stories came to him, no words or music. He just wanted to go home, to lie in his bed and let his dreams tell his stories for him.

Thomas Builds-the-Fire and Victor sat next to each other in the airplane, coach section. A tiny white woman had the window seat. She was busy twisting her body into pretzels. She was flexible.

"I have to ask," Thomas said, and Victor closed his eyes in embarrassment.

"Don't," Victor said.

"Excuse me, miss," Thomas asked. "Are you a gymnast or something?"

"There's no something about it," she said. "I was first alternate on the 1980 Olympic team."

"Really?" Thomas asked.

"Really."

"I mean, you used to be a world-class athlete?" Thomas asked.

"My husband still thinks I am."

Thomas Builds-the-Fire smiled. She was a mental gymnast, too. She pulled her leg straight up against her body so that she could've kissed her kneecap.

"I wish I could do that," Thomas said.

Victor was ready to jump out of the plane. Thomas, that crazy Indian storyteller with ratty old braids and broken teeth, was flirting with a beautiful Olympic gymnast. Nobody back home on the reservation would ever believe it.

"Well," the gymnast said. "It's easy. Try it."

Thomas grabbed at his leg and tried to pull it up into the same position as the gymnast. He couldn't even come close, which made Victor and the gymnast laugh.

"Hey," she asked. "You two are Indian, right?"

"Full-blood," Victor said.

"Not me," Thomas said. "I'm half magician on my mother's side and half clown on my father's."

They all laughed.

"What are your names?" she asked.

"Victor and Thomas."

"Mine is Cathy. Pleased to meet you all."

The three of them talked for the duration of the flight. Cathy the gymnast complained about the government, how they screwed the 1980 Olympic team by boycotting.[2]

"Sounds like you all got a lot in common with Indians," Thomas said.

---

[2]**1980 Olympic team** . . . the United States boycotted the Olympics in Moscow over the Soviet Union's 1979 invasion of Afghanistan

Nobody laughed.

After the plane landed in Phoenix and they had all found their way to the terminal, Cathy the gymnast smiled and waved good-bye.

"She was really nice," Thomas said.

"Yeah, but everybody talks to everybody on airplanes," Victor said. "It's too bad we can't always be that way."

"You always used to tell me I think too much," Thomas said. "Now it sounds like you do."

"Maybe I caught it from you."

"Yeah."

Thomas and Victor rode in a taxi to the trailer where Victor's father died.

"Listen," Victor said as they stopped in front of the trailer. "I never told you I was sorry for beating you up that time."

"Oh, it was nothing. We were just kids and you were drunk."

"Yeah, but I'm still sorry."

"That's all right."

Victor paid for the taxi and the two of them stood in the hot Phoenix summer. They could smell the trailer.

"This ain't going to be nice," Victor said. "You don't have to go in."

"You're going to need help."

Victor walked to the front door and opened it. The stink rolled out and made them both gag. Victor's father had lain in that trailer for a week in hundred-degree temperatures before anyone found him. And the only reason anyone found him was because of the smell. They needed dental records to identify him. That's exactly what the coroner said. They needed dental records.

"Oh, man," Victor said. "I don't know if I can do this."

"Well, then don't."

"But there might be something valuable in there."

"I thought his money was in the bank."

"It is. I was talking about pictures and letters and stuff like that."

"Oh," Thomas said as he held his breath and followed Victor into the trailer.

When Victor was twelve, he stepped into an underground wasp nest. His foot was caught in the hole, and no matter how hard he struggled, Victor couldn't pull free. He might have died there, stung a thousand times, if Thomas Builds-the-Fire had not come by.

"Run," Thomas yelled and pulled Victor's foot from the hole. They ran then, hard as they ever had, faster than Billy Mills, faster than Jim Thorpe, faster than the wasps could fly.

Victor and Thomas ran until they couldn't breathe, ran until it was cold and dark outside, ran until they were lost and it took hours to find their way home.

All the way back, Victor counted his stings.

"Seven," Victor said. "My lucky number."

Victor didn't find much to keep in the trailer. Only a photo album and a stereo. Everything else had that smell stuck in it or was useless anyway.

"I guess this is all," Victor said. "It ain't much."

"Better than nothing," Thomas said.

"Yeah, and I do have the pickup."

"Yeah," Thomas said. "It's in good shape."

"Dad was good about that stuff."

"Yeah, I remember your dad."

"Really?" Victor asked. "What do you remember?"

Thomas Builds-the-Fire closed his eyes and told this story: "I remember when I had this dream that told me to go to Spokane, to stand by the Falls in the middle of the city and wait for a sign. I knew I had to go there but I didn't have a car. Didn't have a license. I was only thirteen. So I walked all the way, took me all day, and I finally made it to the Falls. I stood there for an hour waiting. Then your dad came walking up. *What the hell are you doing here?* he asked me. I said, *Waiting for a vision.* Then your father said, *All you're going to get here is mugged.* So he drove me over to Denny's, bought me dinner, and then drove me home to the reservation. For a long time I was mad because I thought my dreams had lied to me. But they didn't. Your dad was my vision. *Take care of each other* is what my dreams were saying. *Take care of each other.*"

Victor was quiet for a long time. He searched his mind for memories of his father, found the good ones, found a few bad ones, added it all up, and smiled.

"My father never told me about finding you in Spokane," Victor said.

"He said he wouldn't tell anybody. Didn't want me to get in trouble. But he said I had to watch out for you as part of the deal."

"Really?"

"Really. Your father said you would need the help. He was right."

"That's why you came down here with me, isn't it?" Victor asked.

"I came because of your father."

Victor and Thomas climbed into the pickup, drove over to the bank, and claimed the three hundred dollars in the savings account.

Thomas Builds-the-Fire could fly.

Once, he jumped off the roof of the tribal school and flapped his arms like a crazy eagle. And he flew. For a second, he hovered, suspended above all the other Indian boys who were too smart or too scared to jump.

"He's flying," Junior yelled, and Seymour was busy looking for the trick wires or mirrors. But it was real. As real as the dirt when Thomas lost altitude and crashed to the ground.

He broke his arm in two places.

"He broke his wing," Victor chanted, and the other Indian boys joined in, made it a tribal song.

"He broke his wing, he broke his wing, he broke his wing," all the Indian boys chanted as they ran off, flapping their wings, wishing they could fly, too. They hated Thomas for his courage, his brief moment as a bird. Everybody has dreams about flying. Thomas flew.

One of his dreams came true for just a second, just enough to make it real.

Victor's father, his ashes, fit in one wooden box with enough left over to fill a cardboard box.

"He always was a big man," Thomas said.

Victor carried part of his father and Thomas carried the rest out to the pickup. They set him down carefully behind the seats, put a cowboy hat on the wooden box and a Dodgers cap on the cardboard box. That's the way it was supposed to be.

"Ready to head back home?" Victor asked.

"It's going to be a long drive."

"Yeah, take a couple days, maybe."

"We can take turns," Thomas said.

"Okay," Victor said, but they didn't take turns. Victor drove for sixteen hours straight north, made it halfway up Nevada toward home before he finally pulled over.

"Hey, Thomas," Victor said. "You got to drive for a while."

"Okay."

Thomas Builds-the-Fire slid behind the wheel and started off down the road. All through Nevada, Thomas and Victor had been amazed at the lack of animal life, at the absence of water, of movement.

"Where is everything?" Victor had asked more than once.

Now when Thomas was finally driving they saw the first animal, maybe the only animal in Nevada. It was a long-eared jackrabbit.

"Look," Victor yelled. "It's alive."

Thomas and Victor were busy congratulating themselves on their discovery when the jackrabbit darted out into the road and under the wheels of the pickup.

"Stop the goddamn car," Victor yelled, and Thomas did stop, backed the pickup to the dead jackrabbit.

"Oh, man, he's dead," Victor said as he looked at the squashed animal.

"Really dead."

"The only thing alive in this whole state and we just killed it."

"I don't know," Thomas said. "I think it was suicide."

Victor looked around the desert, sniffed the air, felt the emptiness and loneliness, and nodded his head.

"Yeah," Victor said. "It had to be suicide."

"I can't believe this," Thomas said. "You drive for a thousand miles and there ain't even any bugs smashed on the windshield. I drive for ten seconds and kill the only living thing in Nevada."

"Yeah," Victor said. "Maybe I should drive."

"Maybe you should."

Thomas Builds-the-Fire walked through the corridors of the tribal school by himself. Nobody wanted to be anywhere near him because of all those stories. Story after story.

Thomas closed his eyes and this story came to him: "We are all given one thing by which our lives are measured, one determination. Mine are the stories which can change or not change the world. It doesn't matter which as long as I continue to tell the stories. My father, he died on Okinawa in World War II, died fighting for this country, which had tried to kill him for years. My mother, she died giving birth to me, died while I was still inside her. She pushed me out into the world with her last breath. I have no brothers or sisters. I have only my stories which came to me before I even had the words to speak. I learned a thousand stories before I took my first thousand steps. They are all I have. It's all I can do."

Thomas Builds-the-Fire told his stories to all those who would stop and listen. He kept telling them long after people had stopped listening.

Victor and Thomas made it back to the reservation just as the sun was rising. It was the beginning of a new day on earth, but the same old shit on the reservation.

"Good morning," Thomas said.

"Good morning."

The tribe was waking up, ready for work, eating breakfast, reading the newspaper, just like everybody else does. Willene LeBret was out in her garden wearing a bathrobe. She waved when Thomas and Victor drove by.

"Crazy Indians made it," she said to herself and went back to her roses.

Victor stopped the pickup in front of Thomas Builds-the-Fire's HUD house.[3] They both yawned, stretched a little, shook dust from their bodies.

"I'm tired," Victor said.

"Of everything," Thomas added.

They both searched for words to end the journey. Victor needed to thank Thomas for his help, for the money, and make the promise to pay it all back.

"Don't worry about the money," Thomas said. "It don't make any difference anyhow."

"Probably not, enit?"

"Nope."

Victor knew that Thomas would remain the crazy storyteller who talked to dogs and cars, who listened to the wind and pine trees. Victor knew that he couldn't really be friends with Thomas, even after all that had happened. It was cruel but it was real. As real as the ashes, as Victor's father, sitting behind the seats.

"I know how it is," Thomas said. "I know you ain't going to treat me any better than you did before. I know your friends would give you too much shit about it."

Victor was ashamed of himself. Whatever happened to the tribal ties, the sense of community? The only real thing he shared with anybody was a bottle and broken dreams. He owed Thomas something, anything.

[3]**HUD** The Department of Housing and Urban Development

"Listen," Victor said and handed Thomas the cardboard box which contained half of his father. "I want you to have this."

Thomas took the ashes and smiled, closed his eyes, and told this story: "I'm going to travel to Spokane Falls one last time and toss these ashes into the water. And your father will rise like a salmon, leap over the bridge, over me, and find his way home. It will be beautiful. His teeth will shine like silver, like a rainbow. He will rise, Victor, he will rise."

Victor smiled.

"I was planning on doing the same thing with my half," Victor said. "But I didn't imagine my father looking anything like a salmon. I thought it'd be like cleaning the attic or something. Like letting things go after they've stopped having any use."

"Nothing stops, cousin," Thomas said. "Nothing stops."

Thomas Builds-the-Fire got out of the pickup and walked up his driveway. Victor started the pickup and began the drive home.

"Wait," Thomas yelled suddenly from his porch. "I just got to ask one favor."

Victor stopped the pickup, leaned out the window, and shouted back. "What do you want?"

"Just one time when I'm telling a story somewhere, why don't you stop and listen?" Thomas asked.

"Just once?"

"Just once."

Victor waved his arms to let Thomas know that the deal was good. It was a fair trade, and that was all Victor had ever wanted from his whole life. So Victor drove his father's pickup toward home while Thomas went into his house, closed the door behind him, and heard a new story come to him in the silence afterwards.

—1993

JHUMPA LAHIRI ■ (1899–1961)

Born in London to immigrants from Bengal, at the age of three Lahiri moved to the United States, where her father was a college librarian. After earning degrees as Barnard and Boston University, Lahiri held a two-year fellowship at the Provincetown Arts Center, during which time she tried, with little success, to publish her short fiction. Her first collection of stories, The Interpreter of Maladies was published in 1999, selling over 600,000 copies and winning the Pulitzer Prize. Since then, a novel, The Namesake, and a second collection of short stories, Unaccustomed Earth, *have appeared, and* Lahiri's fiction appears regularly in The New Yorker. *Focusing mainly on the experiences of Indian-Americans, Lahiri has said, "What drew me to my craft was the desire to force the two worlds I occupied to mingle on the page as I was not brave enough, or mature enough, to allow in life."*

A Temporary Matter

The notice informed them that it was a temporary matter: for five days their electricity would be cut off for one hour, beginning at 8 P.M. A line had gone down in the last snowstorm, and the repairmen were going to take advantage of the milder evenings to set it right. The work would affect only the houses on their quiet tree-lined street, within walking distance of a row of brick-faced stores and a trolley stop, where Shoba and Shukumar had lived for three years.

"It's good of them to warn us," Shoba conceded after reading the notice aloud, more for her own benefit than for Shukumar's. She let the strap of her leather satchel, plump with files, slip from her shoulders, and left it in the hallway as she walked into the kitchen. She wore a navy-blue poplin raincoat over gray sweatpants and white sneakers, looking, at thirty-three, like the type of woman she'd once claimed she would never resemble.

She'd come from the gym. Her cranberry lipstick was visible only on the outer reaches of her mouth, and her eyeliner had left charcoal patches beneath her lashes. She used to look this way sometimes, Shukumar thought, on mornings after a party or a night at a bar, when she'd been too lazy to wash her face, too eager to collapse into his arms. She dropped a sheaf of mail on the table without a glance. Her eyes were still fixed on the notice in her other hand. "But they should do this sort of thing during the day,"

"When I'm here, you mean," Shukumar said. He put a glass lid on a pot of lamb, adjusting it so only the slightest bit of steam could escape. Since January he'd been working at home, trying to complete the final chapters of his dissertation on agrarian revolts in India. "When do the repairs start?"

"It says March 19th. Is today the nineteenth?" Shoba went ewer to the framed corkboard that hung on the wall by the fridge, bare except for a calendar—a Christmas gift from a friend, even though Shoba and Shukumar hadn't celebrated Christmas last year.

"Today then," Shoba announced. "You have a dentist appointment next Friday, by the way."

Shukumar ran his tongue over the tops of his teeth; he'd forgotten to brush them that morning. He hadn't left the house all day. The more Shoba stayed out, and the more she began putting in extra hours at work and taking on additional projects, the more he wanted to stay in, not even leaving to get the mail, or to buy fruit or wine at the stores by the trolley stop.

Six months ago, in September, Shukumar was at an academic conference in Baltimore when Shoba went into labor, three weeks before her due date. He hadn't wanted to go to the conference, but she had insisted; it was important to make contracts, and he would be entering the Job market next year. She told him that she had his number at the hotel, and a copy of his schedule and flight numbers, and she had arranged with her friend Gillian for a ride to the hospital in the event of an emergency. When the cab had pulled away that morning for the airport, Shoba stood waving goodbye in her robe, with one arm resting on the mound of her belly as if it were a perfectly natural part of her body.

Each time be thought of that moment, the last moment he saw Shoba Pregnant, it was the cab he remembered most, a station wagon, painted red with blue lettering. It was cavernous compared with their own car. Although Shukumar was six feet tall, with hands too big ever to rest comfortably in the pockets of his jeans, he felt dwarfed in the back seat. As the cab sped down Beacon Street, he imagined a day when he and Shoba might need a station wagon of their own. He pictured himself gripping the wheel, as Shoba turned around to hand their children juice boxes. Once, these images of parenthood had troubled Shukumar, adding to his anxiety that he was still a student at thirty-five. But that early-autumn morning, the trees heavy with bronze leaves, he welcomed the image for the first time.

A member of the hotel staff had handed him a stiff square of stationery. It was only a telephone number, but Shukumar knew it was the hospital. When he got back to Boston it was over. The baby had been born dead. Shoba was lying on a bed, asleep, in a private room so small there was barely enough space to stand beside her, in a wing of the hospital they hadn't been to on the tour for expectant parents. Her placenta had weakened and she'd had a cesarean, though not quickly enough. The doctor explained that these things happen. He smiled in the kindest way it was possible to smile at people one knew only professionally.

Shoba would be back on her feet in a few weeks. There was nothing to indicate that she would not be able to have children in the future.

Shukumar gathered onion skins in his hands and let them drop into the garbage, on top of the ribbons of fat he'd trimmed from the lamb. He ran the water in the sink, soaking the knife and the cutting board, and rubbed a lemon half along his fingertips to get rid of the garlic smell, a trick he'd learned from Shoba. It was seven-thirty. Through the window he saw the sky, like soft black pitch. Uneven banks of snow still lined the sidewalks, though it was warm enough for people to walk about without hats or gloves. Nearly three feet had fallen in the last storm, and for a weak people had to walk in single file, in narrow trenches. For a week, that was Shukumar's excuse for not leaving the house. But now the paths were widening, and water drained steadily into grates in the pavement.

"The lamb won't be done by eight," Shukumar said. "We may have to eat in the dark."

"We can light candles," Shoba said, She unclipped her hair, coiled neatly at her nape during the days, and pried the sneakers from her feet. "I'm going to shower before the lights go," she said, heading for the staircase. "I'll be down,"

Shukumar moved her satchel and her sneakers to the side of the fridge. She wasn't this way before. She used to put her coat on a hanger, her sneakers in the closet, and she paid bills as soon as they came. But now she treated the house as if it were a hotel. The fact that the yellow chintz armchair in the living room clashed with the blue-and-maroon. Turkish carpet no longer bothered her. On the enclosed porch at the back of the house, a crisp white bag still sat on the wicker chaise, filled with lace she had once planned to turn into curtains.

With no lights, they would have to eat together. For months now they'd served themselves from the stove, and he'd take his plate into his study, letting the meal grow cold on his desk before shoving it into his mouth without pause, while Shoba took her plate to the living room and watched game shows, or proofread files with her arsenal of colored pencils at hand.

At some point in the evening the visited him. When he heard her approach he began typing sentences. She would rest her hands on his shoulders and stare with him into the blue glow of the computer screen. "Don't work too hard," she would say after a minute or two, and head off to bed. It was the one time in the day she sought him out, and yet he'd come to dread it. He knew it was something she forced herself to do. She would look around the walls of the room, which they had decorated together last summer with a border of marching ducks and rabbits playing trumpets and drums. By the end of August there was a cherry crib under the window, and a rocking chair with checkered cushions. Shukumar had disassembled it all before bringing Shoba back from the hospital, scraping off the rabbits and ducks with a spatula. For some reason the room did not haunt him the way it haunted Shoba. In January, when he stopped working at his carrel in the library, he set up his desk there deliberately, partly because the room soothed him, and partly because it was a place Shoba avoided.

In the kitchen, Shukumar began to open drawers. He tried to find a candle among the scissors, the eggbeaters and whisks, the mortar and pestle she'd bought in a bazaar in Calcutta and had used to pound garlic cloves and cardamom pods, back when she used to cook. He found a flashlight, but no batteries, and a half-empty box of birthday candles. Shoba had thrown him a surprise birthday party last May. There had been a hundred and twenty people crammed into the house—all the friends and the friends of friends they now systematically avoided. Bottles of Vinho Verde had nested in a bed of ice in the bathtub. Shoba was in her fifth month, drinking ginger ale from a Martini glass. She had made a vanilla cream cake with custard and spun sugar. All night she kept Shukumar's long fingers linked with hers as they walked among the guests at the party.

Since September their only guest had been Shoba's mother. She came from Arizona and stayed with them for two months after Shoba returned from the hospital. She cooked dinner every night, drove herself to the supermarket, washed their clothes, put them away. She was a religious woman. She set up a small shrine, a framed picture of a lavenderfaced goddess and a plate of marigold petals, on the bedside table in the guest room, and prayed twice a day for healthy grandchildren in the future. She was polite to Shukumar without being friendly. She folded his sweaters with an expertise she had learned from her job in a department store. She replaced a missing button on his winter coat and knit him a beige and brown scarf, presenting it to him without the least bit of ceremony, as if he had only dropped it and hadn't noticed. She never talked to him about Shoba; once, when he mentioned the baby's death, she looked up from her knitting and said, "But you weren't even there."

He looked for something to put the birthday candles in and settled on the soil of a potted ivy that normally sat on the windowsill over the sink. Even though the plant was inches from the tap, the soil was so dry that he had to water it first before the candles would stand straight. He pushed aside the things on the Kitchen table, the piles of mail, the unread library books. He remembered their first meals there, when they were so thrilled to be married, to be living together at last, that they would just reach for each other foolishly, more eager to make love than to eat. He put down two embroidered placemats, a wedding gift from an uncle in Lucknow, and set out the plates and wine-glasses they usually saved for guests. He put the ivy in the middle, the white-edged, star-shaped leaves girded by ten little candles. He tuned the radio to a jazz station.

"What's all this?" Shoba asked when she came downstairs. Her hair was wrapped in a thick white towel. She undid the towel and draped it over a chair, allowing her hair, damp and dark, to fall across her back. As she walked absently toward the stove she took out a few tangles with her fingers. She wore a clean pair of sweat-pants, a T-shirt, an old flannel robe. Her stomach was flat again, her waist narrow before the flare of her hips, the belt of the robe tied in a floppy knot.

It was nearly eight. Shukumar put some lentils from the night before into the microwave oven, punching the numbers on the timer. "You made rogan josh," Shoba observed, looking through the glass lid at the bright paprika stew.

Shukumar took out a piece of lamb, pinching it quickly between his fingers so as not to scald himself. He prodded a larger piece with a serving spoon to make sure the meat slipped easily from the bone. "It's ready," he announced.

Once she had done all the cooking. Now he combed through her cookbooks every afternoon, following her pencilled-in instructions to use two teaspoons of ground coriander seeds instead of one, or red lentils instead of yellow. Each of the recipes was dated, telling when they had first eaten the dish together. April 2nd, cauliflower with fennel. January 14th, chicken with almonds and sultanas. He had no memory of eating those meals, and yet there they were recorded in her neat proofreader's hand. Shukumar enjoyed cooking now. It was the one thing that made him productive. If it weren't for him, he knew, Shoba would eat a bowl of cereal for her dinner.

The microwave had just beeped when the lights went out, and the music disappeared. "Perfect timing," Shoba said.

"All I could find were birthday candles." He lit up the ivy, keeping the rest of the candles and a book of matches by his plate.

"It doesn't matter," she said, running a finger along the stem of her wineglass. "It looks lovely."

In the dimness, he knew how she sat, a bit forward in her chair, ankles crossed against the lowest rung, left elbow on the table. During his search for the candles, Shukumar had found a bottle of wine in a crate he had thought was empty. Every few minutes he lit a few more birthday candles and drove them into the soil of the pot.

"It's like India," Shoba said, "Sometimes the current disappears for hours at a stretch. I once had to attend an entire rice ceremony in the dark. The baby just cried and cried. It must have been so hot."

Their baby would never have a rice ceremony, Shukumar considered. Shoba had made the guest list, and decided on which of her three brothers she was going to ask to feed the child its first taste of solid food, at six months if it was a boy, seven if it was a girl.

"Are you hot?" he asked her. He pushed the blazing ivy pot to the other end of the table, making it even more difficult for them to see each other. He was suddenly irritated that he couldn't go upstairs and sit in front of the computer.

"No, it's delicious," she said, tapping her plate with her fork. "It really is."

He refilled the wine in her glass. She thanked him.

They weren't like this before. Now he had to struggle to say something that interested her, something that made her look up from her plate, or from her proofreading files. Eventually he had given up trying to amuse her. He learned not to mind the silences.

"I remember during power failures at my grandmother's house, we all had to say something," Shoba continued. He could barely see her face, but from her tone he knew her eyes were narrowed, as if trying to focus on a distant object. It was a habit of hers.

"Like what?"

"I don't know. A little poem. A joke. A fact about the world. For some reason my relatives always wanted me to tell them the names of my friends in America. I don't know why the information was so interesting to them. The last time I saw my aunt, she asked after four girls I went to elementary school with in Tucson. I barely remember them now."

JHUMPA LAHIRI

402

Shukumar hadn't spent as much time in India as Shoba had. His parents, who settled in New Hampshire, used to go back without him. The first time he'd gone as an infant he'd nearly died of amebic dysentery. His father, a nervous type, was afraid to take him again, in case something were to happen, and left him with his aunt and uncle in Concord. As a teen-ager he preferred sailing camp or scooping ice cream during the summers rather than going to Calcutta. It wasn't until after his father died, in his last year of college, that the country began to interest him, and he studied its history from course books as if it were any other subject. He wished now that he had his own childhood story of India.

"Let's do that," she said suddenly.

"Do what?"

"Say something to each other in the dark."

"Like what? I don't know any jokes."

"No, no jokes." She thought for a minute. "How about telling each other something we've never told before."

"I used to play this game in high school," Shukumar recalled. "When I got drunk."

"You're thinking of Truth or Dare. This is different. O.K., I'll start." She took a sip of wine. "The first time I was alone in your apartment, I looked in your address book to see if you'd written me in. I think we'd known each other two weeks."

"Where was I?"

"You went to answer the telephone in the other room. It was your mother, and I figured it would be a long call. I wanted to know if you'd promoted me from the margins of your newspaper."

"Had I?"

"No. But I didn't give up on you. Now it's your turn."

He couldn't think of anything, but Shoba was waiting for him to speak. She hadn't appeared so determined in months. He through back to their first meeting, four years earlier at a lecture hall in Cambridge, where a group of Bengali poets were giving a recital. They'd ended up side by side, on folding wooden chairs. Shukumar was soon bored; he was unable to decipher the literary diction, and couldn't join the rest of the audience as they sighed and nodded solemnly after certain phrases. Peering at the newspaper folded in his lap, he studied the temperatures of cities around the world. Ninety-one degrees in Singapore yesterday, fifty-one in Stockholm.

When he turned his head to the left, he saw a woman next to him making a grocery list on the back of a folder, and was startled to find that she was beautiful.

"O.K.," he said, remembering. "The first time we went out to dinner, to the Portuguese place, I forgot to tip the waiter. I went back the next morning, found out his name, left money with the manager."

"You went all the way back to Somerville just to tip a waiter?"

"I took a cab."

"Why did you forget to tip the waiter?"

The birthday candles had run out, but he pictured her face clearly in the dark, the wide tilting eyes, the full grape-toned lips, the fall at age two from her high chair still visible as a comma on her chin. Each day, Shukumar noticed, her beauty, which had once overwhelmed him, seemed to fade. The cosmetics that had seemed superfluous were necessary now—not to improve her but to define her somehow.

"By the end of the meal I had a funny feeling that I might marry you," he said, admitting it to himself as well as to her for the first time. "I must have distracted me."

The next night Shoba came home earlier than usual. There was lamb left over from the evening before, and Shukumar heated it up so that they were able to eat by seven. He'd gone out that day, through the melting snow, and bought a packet of taper candles from the corner store, and batteries to fit the flashlight. He had the candles ready on the countertop, standing in brass holders shaped like lotuses, but they are under the glow of a copper-shaded ceiling lamp that hung over the table.

When they had finished eating, Shukumar was surprised to see that Shoba was stacking her plate on top of his, and then carrying them toward the sink. He had assumed that she would retreat to the living room, behind her barricade of files.

"Don't worry about the dishes," he said, taking them from her hands.

"It seems silly not to," she replied, pouring a drop of detergent onto a sponge. "It's nearly eight o'clock."

His heart quickened. All day Shukumar had looked forward to the lights going out. He thought about what Shoba had said the night before, about looking in his address book. It felt good to remember her as she was then, how bold yet nervous she'd been when they first met, how hopeful. They stood side by side at the sink, their reflections fitting together in the frame of the window. It made him shy, the way he felt the first time they stood before a mirror. He couldn't recall the last time they'd been photographed. They had stopped attending parties, went nowhere together. The film in his camera still contained pictures of Shoba, in the yard, when she was pregnant.

After finishing the dishes, they learned against the counter, drying their hands on either end of a towel. At eight o'clock the house went black. Shukumar lit the wicks of the candles, impressed by their long, steady flames. "Let's sit outside," Shoba said. "I think it's warm still."

They each took a candle and sat down on the steps. It seemed strange to be sitting outside with patches of snow still on the ground. But everyone was out of their houses tonight, the air fresh enough to make people restless. Screen doors opened and closed. A small parade of neighbors passed by with flashlights.

"We're going to the bookstore to browse," a silver-haired man called out. He was walking with his wife, a thin woman in a windbreaker, and holding a dog on a leash. They were the Bradfords, and they had tucked a sympathy card into Shoba and Shukumar's mail-box back in September. "I hear they've got their power."

"They'd better," Shukumar said. "Or you'll be browsing in the dark."

The woman laughed, slipping her arm through the crook of her husband's elbow. "Want to join us?"

"No thanks," Shoba and Shukumar called out together. It surprised Shukumar that his words matched hers.

He wondered what Shoba would tell him in the dark. The worst possibilities had already run through his head. That she'd had an affair. That she didn't respect him for being thirty-five and still a student. That she blamed him for being in Baltimore, the way her mother did. But he knew those things weren't true. She'd been faithful, as had he. She believed in him. It was she who had insisted he go to Baltimore. What didn't they know about each other? He knew she curled her fingers rightly when she slept, that her body twitched during bad dreams. He knew she favored honeydew over cantaloupe. He knew that when they returned from the hospital the first thing she did as she walked into the house was to pick out objects of theirs and toss them into a pile in the hallway; books from the shelves, plants from windowsills, paintings from walls, photos from tables, pots and pans that hung from the hooks over the stove. Shukumar had stepped out of her way, watching as she moved methodically from room to room. When she was satisfied, she stood staring at the pile she'd made, her lips drawn back in such distaste that Shukumar had thought she would spit. Then she'd started to cry.

He began to feel cold as he sat there on the steps. He felt that he needed her to talk first, in order to reciprocate.

"That time when your mother came to visit us," she said finally. "When I said one night that I had to stay late at work, I went out with Gillian and had a Martini."

He looked at her profile, the slender nose, the slightly masculine set of her jaw. He remembered that night well; eating with his mother, tired from teaching two classes back to back, wishing Shoba were there to say more of the right things, because he could come up only with wrong ones. It had been twelve years since his father had died, and his mother had come to spend two weeks with him and Shoba, to honor his memory together. Each night his mother cooked something his father had liked, but she was too upset to eat the dishes herself, and her eyes would well up as Shoba stroked her hand. "It's so touching," Shoba had said to him at the time. Now he saw Shoba with Gillian, in the bar with striped velvet sofas, the one they used to go to after the movies, making sure she got her extra olive, asking Gillian for a cigarette. He imagined her complaining, and Gillian sympathizing about visit from in-laws. It was Gillian who had driven Shoba to the hospital.

"Your turn," she said, stopping his thoughts.

At the end of their street Shukumar heard sounds of a drill and the electricians shouting over it. He looked at the darkened façades of the houses lining the street. Candles glowed in the windows of one. Smoke rose from a chimney.

"I cheated on my Oriental Civilization exam in college," he said. "It was my last semester, my last set of exams. My father had died a few months before. I could see the blue book of the guy next to me. He was an American guy, a maniac. He knew Urdu and Sanskrit. I couldn't remember if the verse we had to identify was an example of a *ghazal* or not. I looked at his answer and copied it down."

It had happened over fifteen years ago. He felt a relief now, having told her.

She turned to him, looking not at his face but at his shoes—old moccasins he wore as if they were slippers, the leather at the back permanently flattened. She took his hand and pressed it. "You didn't have to tell me why you did it," she said, moving closer to him.

They sat together until nine o'clock, when the lights came on. They heard some people across the street clapping from their porch, and televisions being turned on. The Bradfords walked back down the street, eating ice-cream cones, and waving. Shoba and Shukumar waved back. Then they stood up, his hand still in hers, and went inside.

Somehow, without either of them saying anything, it had turned into this. Into an exchange of confessions—the little ways they'd hurt or disappointed each other, and themselves. The following day Shukumar thought for hours about what to say to her. He was torn between admitting that he had once ripped out a photo of a woman in one of the fashion magazines she used to subscribe to and carried it in his books for a week, or saying that he really hadn't lost the sweater-vest she bought him for their third wedding anniversary but had exchanged it at Filene's and that he had got drunk alone in the middle of the day at a hotel bar. For their previous anniversary, Shoba had cooked a ten-course dinner just for him. This gift depressed him. "My wife gave me a sweater-vest for our anniversary," he complained to the bartender, his head heavy with cognac. "What do you expect?" the bartender had replied. "You're married."

As for the picture of the woman, he didn't know why he'd ripped it out. She wasn't as pretty as Shoba. She wore a white sequined dress, and had a sullen face, and lean, mannish legs. Shoba had been pregnant at the time, her stomach suddenly immense, to the point where Shukumar no longer wanted to touch her. The first time he saw the picture he was lying in bed next to her, watching her as she read. When he noticed the magazine in the recycling pile he found the woman and tore out the page as carefully as he could. For about a week he allowed himself a glimpse each day. He felt an intense desire for the woman, but it was a desire that turned to disgust after a minute or two. It was the closest he'd come to infidelity.

He told Shoba about the sweater on the third night, the picture on the fourth. She said nothing as he spoke. She simply listened, and then she took his hand, pressing it as she had before. On the third night, she told him that once, after a lecture they'd attended, she let him speak to the chairman of his department even though there was a dab of pâté on his chin. She'd been irritated with him, and so she'd let him go on and on, about securing his fellowship for the following semester, without putting a finger to her own chin as a signal. The fourth night, she said that she never liked the one poem he'd ever published, in a literary magazine in Utah. He'd written the poem after meeting Shoba. She added that she found the poem sentimental.

Something happened when the house was dark. They were able to talk to each other again. The third night after supper they'd sat together on the sofa, and once it was dark he began kissing her awkwardly on her forehead and her face. The fourth night they walked carefully upstairs, to bed, feeling together for the final step with their feet before the landing, and making love with a desperation they had forgotten. she wept without sound, and whispered his name, and traced his eyebrows with her finger in the dark. As he made love to her he wondered what he would say to her the next night, and what she would say, the thought of it exciting him. "Hold me," he said. "Hold me in your arms." By the time the lights came back on downstairs, they'd fallen asleep.

The morning of the fifth night Shukumar found another notice from the electric company in the mailbox. The line had been repaired ahead of schedule, it said. He was disappointed. He had planned on making shrimp malai for Shoba, but when he arrived at the store he didn't feel like cooking anymore. It wasn't the same, he thought, knowing that the lights wouldn't go out. In the store the shrimp looked gray and thin. The coconut-milk tin was dusty and overpriced. Still, he bought them, along with a beeswax candle and two bottles of wine.

She came home at seven-thirty. "I suppose this is the end of our game," he said when he saw her reading the notice.

She looked at him. "You can still light candles if you want." She hadn't been to the gym tonight. She wore a suit beneath her raincoat. Her makeup had been retouched.

When she went upstairs to change. Shukumar poured himself some wine and put on a Thelonious Monk record that she liked.

When she came downstairs they are together. She didn't thank him or compliment him. They simply ate in a darkened room, in the glow of a beeswax candle. They had survived a difficult time. They finished off the shrimp. They finished off the first bottle of wine and moved on to the second. They sat together until the candle had nearly burned away. She shifted in her chair, and Shukumar thought that she was about to say something. But instead she blew out the candle, stood up, turned on the light switch, and sat down again.

"Shouldn't we keep the lights off?" Shukumar asked.

She set her plate aside and clasped her hands on the table. "I want you to see my face when I tell you this," she said gently.

His heart began to pound. The day she told him she was pregnant, she had used the very same words, saying them in the same gentle way, turning off the basketball game he'd been watching on television. He hadn't been prepared then. Now he was.

Only he didn't want her to be pregnant again. He didn't want to have to pretend to be happy.

"I've been looking for an apartment and I've found one," she said, narrowing her eyes on something, it seemed, behind his left shoulder. It was nobody's fault, she continued. They'd been through enough. She needed some time alone. She had money saved up for a security deposit. The apartment was on Beacon Hill, so she could walk to work. She had signed the lease that night before coming home.

She wouldn't look at him, but he stared at her. It was obvious that she'd rehearsed the lines. All this time she'd been looking for an apartment, testing the water pressure, asking a realtor if heat and hot water were included in the rent. It shocked Shukumar, knowing that she had spent these past days preparing for a life without him. He was relieved and yet he was sickened. This was what she'd been trying to tell him for the past four evenings. This was the point of her game.

Now it was his turn to speak. There was something he'd sworn he would never tell her, and for six months he had done his best to block it from his mind. Before the ultrasound she had asked the doctor not to tell her the sex of their child, and Shukumar had agreed. She had wanted it to be a surprise.

Later, those few times they talked about what had happened, she said at least they'd been spared that knowledge. In a way she almost took pride in her decision, for it enabled her to seek refuge in a mystery. He knew that she assumed it was a mystery for him, too. He'd arrived too late from Baltimore—when it was all over and she was lying on the hospital bed. But he hadn't. He'd arrived early enough to see their baby, and to hold him before they cremated him. At first he had recoiled at the suggestion, but the doctor said holding the baby might help him with the process of grieving. Shoba was asleep. The baby had been cleaned off, his bulbous lids shut tight to the world.

"Our baby was a boy," he said. "His skin was more red than brown. He had black hair on his head. He weighed almost five pounds. His fingers were curled shut, just like yours in the night."

Shoba looked at him now, her face contorted with sorrow. He had cheated on a college exam, ripped a picture of a woman out of a magazine. He had returned a sweater and got drunk in the middle of the day instead. These were the things he had told her. He had held his son, who had known life only within her, against his chest in a darkened room in an unknown wing of the hospital. He had held him until a nurse knocked and took him away, and he had promised himself that day that he would never tell Shoba, because he still loved her then, and it was the one thing in her life that she had wanted to be a surprise.

Shukumar stood up and stacked his plate on top of hers. He carried the plates to the sink, but instead of running the tap he looked out the window. Outside, the evening was still warm, and the Bradfords were walking arm in arm. As he watched the couple, the room went dark, and he spun around. Shoba had turned the lights off. She came back to the table and sat down, and after a moment Shukumar joined her. They wept together, for the first time in their lives, for the things they now knew.

—1999

SUSAN PERABO ■ (b.1969)

Susan Perabo was born in St. Louis and attended Webster College, where she was the first woman to play on an NCAA men's baseball team, a milestone that is commemorated on a plaque in the Baseball Hall of Fame. Following graduate school at the University of Arkansas, she published her first collection of stories, Who I Was Supposed to Be, *which was named by the* Los Angeles Times *as Book of the Year. A novel,* The Broken Places, *appeared in 2001. She teaches at Dickinson College in Carlisle, Pennsylvania.*

The Payoff

Cincinnati Review 3.2 (Winter 2007)

When they gave us lumps of clay in art class, I made a pencil holder in the shape of a giraffe, and Louise made an ashtray. She molded and baked it, lopsided and heavy as a brick, as a birthday present for her mom, who smoked Kents vigorously and ground them flat with a callused thumb. So Louise had made this poop-brown ashtray, but she'd left it in the art room cooling outside the kiln and didn't remember it until after school, halfway through softball. When practice ended I yelled to my mom to wait on us and we ran back into the building—the side door was always open until five, so kids with softball and soccer could pee—and thundered down the stairs to the basement where the art room was. We didn't know if it would be unlocked or not, but we thought we'd give it a shot.

Louise reached the door first—it was one of those doors with nine little windows, to give kids nine separate chances at breaking something. No sooner had she put her hand on the knob and her face to the middle pane when she reeled back from the door like someone had grabbed a fistful of her long red hair and *yanked* her back.

"Bullshit," she said, for this was our favorite swear word, and we used it indiscriminately.

"What?" I too stepped to the window and was repelled back a step by what I saw inside: our principal, Dr. Dunn, was standing in the archway of the supply closet with his pants crumpled at his ankles and his hands clawing through the short black hair of Ms. McDaniel, our art teacher, who knelt in front of him with her mouth—well, I'd seen enough. I turned to Louise and we both stared at each other in horror and mute shock for what must have been ten full seconds. Then, at once, we both exploded into riotous laughter and burst into motion away from the scene of the crime, ran full blast down the hall and up the stairs, laughing and gasping for air. By the time we slid into the back seat of my mother's paneled station wagon we had our poker faces set, but the image of what we'd witnessed was so vivid in my mind I couldn't believe my mother couldn't see it herself, reflected with perfect detail in the pools of my eyes.

I had two little brothers, Nick and Sam. Their lives revolved around farting, indian burns, and the time worn torture of repeating everything you said, repeating everything you said. Some day I would enjoy the company of them both, my mother assured me, but until then I would need to exercise tolerance.

"Time for *Grade Your Day*," my father said from behind the curtain of steam that rose from his baked potato. "Anne?"

Though research had not yet proven it, my parents were certain that a well-balanced dinner together and a thorough discussion of the days' events would make us confident and bright children. They didn't know it would actually raise our SAT scores, but they were on the right track.

"B," I said, forking a stalk of asparagus.

"D minus-plus-minus-and-a-half," said Sam. He was six.

"A triple plus!" exclaimed Nick.

My father raised his eyebrows. "Win the lottery?"

"Nuh-uh." Nick grinned. "Two fifth graders got in a fight. They were both named Ben, and one of 'ems tooth got knocked out and flew about fifty feet down the hall."

"How awful," my mother said.

"Did Ben start it?" my father asked, winking at me. Though I was only three years older than Nick, I got to be in on all my father's jokes. "How 'bout you, kiddo?" he asked me. "News of the day?"

"Mrs. Payne subbed in math."

"Oh no," my mother said. "I thought they'd finally gotten rid of her."

I shrugged. "She was there."

"Mrs. Payne is a pain in the butt," Nick said, and Sam snorted.

"That's original," I said. "Only every single person ever to go to our school for the last hundred years has said that."

"Learn anything?" my father asked, undeterred.

I had learned what a blow job (or bj, as Louise told me on the phone before dinner) looked like. I had learned that men didn't actually need to remove their underpants to have sex.

"I learned how to bunt," I said. "At practice."

"Just hold the bat out there," my father said, pretending his steak knife was a Louisville Slugger and wiggling it over his slab of meat. "Just let the ball hit the bat, right?"

"And keep your fingers out of the way," I added.

"That's the most important part," my mother agreed, for my mother was a dodger from way back. In supermarket aisles, she was always the one scooting her cart around to make room for everybody else.

I was regarded with bemused suspicion in the Hanley home, because when Louise and I were in first grade my parents had voted for Richard Nixon. They'd staked a big red sign in our front yard—

4 More Years!

—which is how the Hanleys even knew about it in the first place. Now, even with a democrat in the White House (a peanut farmer, my father was forever pointing out, with a brother on HeeHaw) Mrs. Hanley still couldn't let it drop.

"There she is again," she would say wryly, smoke puffing from her nostrils. "President of the Young Republicans."

"Mom..." Louise would sigh. "Anne is not—" "...anything," I would finish. "I'm not anything. I swear."

On the mantle, in the place where most people had photos of grinning offspring, Mr. and Mrs. Hanley had framed pictures of John and Bobby Kennedy, looking contemplative and doomed. There was a Spiro Agnew velcro dart board on the refrigerator and a faded bumper sticker slapped crookedly across the oven window which said **50 Americans Died Today In Vietnam.** The Hanleys got at least four different newspapers and apparently felt the need to keep them handy for quick reference; there were waist-high stacks of them in every room of the house except for Louise's bedroom. Mrs. Hanley always sat at the dining room table scouring the articles and smoking her Kents, and when Mr. Hanley came home from work he sat on a tattered lawn chair in the middle of the back yard with his feet soaking in a little yellow tub and read until dark.

My mother called them eccentric; she didn't like all the time I spent there, and she often pumped me to find out if Mrs. Hanley had said anything unusual or confusing, anything that had left me feeling *uneasy.* I never gave a thing away; I'd learned earlier than most that the less your parents knew about the concrete details of your day the better off you were. My father thought the Hanleys were lunatics, but unlike my mother he believed it was important for me to be exposed to lunatics—provided they were harmless—in order to be a well rounded adult.

The day after we saw what we saw in the art room, Louise and I holed up after school in the Hanley's basement Ever since Louise's sister had left for college we had the basement to ourselves: the paneled walls, the matted shag carpet, the stale air of twenty thousand cigarettes smoked by unhappy members of the generation that directly proceeded ours.

"Ms. McDaniel should watch out," Louise said. She was sucking on a Charms Blow Pop, twirling it back and forth over her tongue. "She could get a disease doing that."

Louise knew things. Her sister Donna was seven years older, a freshman in college and willing to talk. Plus, the Hanleys let Louise see R rated movies and read whatever books she wanted. I'd looked at *Playboy* at her house one time, right at the dining room table. My mother wouldn't even let me read *Seventeen* in checkout lines.

"What kind of disease?" I asked.

"You don't even want to know," Louise said, which was her answer when she herself didn't know. "I wonder if they do that every day."

"I bet they do other things, too," I said, and with no warning whatsoever a vivid picture flashed into my mind of Ms. McDaniel carefully painting Dr. Dunn's penis with the very same blue watercolors we'd used last week on our skyscapes. I blushed at my own fantasy: I hadn't even known I had the capacity to create such an image.

"Dr. Dunn," Louise said thoughtfully, tapping her Blowpop on her top teeth. "Dr. Dickdunn. Dr. Dunn Dick Dunderhead."

"Remember last year," I said, "when he yelled at Melanie Moon when she dropped her Rube Goldberg project in the hallway and spilled all that corn oil?"

She scoffed. "He's such an asshole. We could get him in big trouble, you know. We could turn him in to the school board."

"Would he get fired?"

"Sure he would. Plus his wife would divorce him and his kids would hate him and he'd lose all his friends. And everywhere he went people would make sucking sounds."

She slurped obscenely on her Blowpop and I laughed. On the wall behind her was a torn poster that said "What if they had a war and

SUSAN PERABO

414

nobody came?" which I had never understood because if "they" had a war then at the very least "they" would be there so it wasn't really accurate to say that *nobody* came.

"Hey," Louise said. "What about blackmail?"

I frowned. "What about it?"

"We could do blackmail on him. Say we'll turn him in unless he pays up."

"Pays *money?*"

"No, Anne—gum. Of course money. Jeez." She tossed her Blowpop stick in a nearby ashtray.

"How much you think we could ask for?" I said.

"We should start small," she said, her eyes narrowing. "That's how you do it. You get 'em on the hook. You make 'em think it's just one time. Then you start to squeeze a little more, and a little more, and—"

I shook my head. "You're making this up. You don't know bullshit."

"What's to know?" she asked. "It's easy money."

It was hard to look at Ms. McDaniel on Monday. Sitting at our art table—once a victim of the school cafeteria, now dying a slow death of scissor scars and clotted paste—Louise and I smirked at each other and in the general direction of the supply closet, but neither of us managed to look up to the front of the room for several minutes. We entirely missed the instructions for the day's project, so when everyone started climbing out of the table and filing out the door we had no idea why and had to ask around. Turned out we were supposed to go outside and search for nature; this week's project was a spring collage.

Ms. McDaniel oversaw our progress from the front steps of the school, and I found my eyes passing over her again and again. I wondered exactly what it was that Dr. Dunn saw in her that led him down the sinful path to the art room. She was new this year and it showed; she always seemed apprehensive when she talked to us as a group, as if at any moment we might all stand up and start squirting glue at her. She'd loosen up once we'd started working, when she could meander around the room murmuring words of encouragement and gentle direction. She wore short skirts and had bobbed hair just under her ears, like she was a tomboy before she became a teacher. She didn't have much in the way of boobs, hardly more than Louise and me, and we weren't even wearing bras yet.

Louise nudged me. "Check that out," she said. I followed her gaze to the window of the principal's office, which faced the front lawn. Dr. Dunn was standing at the window with his arms crossed over his chest, looking out at us. We could only see him from the waist up and for a moment I imagined he didn't have any pants on, that his penis was dangling just out of view. I shook the thought from my head.

"He's gross," Louise said. "He's practically licking his lips."

"Why do you think he likes her?"

"They always like young ones," Louise said. "Donna said she could pick any man out of a crowd and he'd have sex with her, whether he was married or a hundred years old."

"Not any man," I said, thinking of my father standing among the men in Donna's crowd, my father with his shaggy hair and laugh lines around his mouth. Then I imagined my brothers grown up, tall and bearded but making armpit farts in a frantic attempt to draw Donna's attention.

Louise shrugged. "Check this out," she said, handing me a piece of notebook paper. In wavy, capital letters was written:

> Dear Dr. Dunn,
> It has come to our attention that you are having sexual relations with the art teacher Laurie McDaniel. Do not ask how we have the information, we just do. Unless you want everyone to find out your secret, put twenty dollars in an envelope and leave it behind the toilet in the middle stall in the second floor girls bathroom. Do this tomorrow (Tuesday) or face the consequences.
> —x and y

"Am I X or Y?" I asked, handing the letter back. "You're Y," Louise said. "How come?" "Because I'm X."

"Y is stupid," I said. "Nobody ever heard of Y. How come we can't both be X?"

"Two X's," she said, rolling her eyes. "Uh-huh. That would look really cool, Anne, really professional."

"No, just one X," I said. "For both of us. Just because we're two people we don't have to be two letters."

"Girls!" Ms. McDaniel shouted. She was standing at the front door waving us in. Her hair was fluttering in the breeze and I recalled how it had moved hi waves under Dr. Dunn's thick fingers.

On our way to math after lunch, two more floppy salmon swept along in the river of students, I shrewdly allowed Louise's letter to fall from my fingers and onto the floor outside the main office. The letter was folded and taped closed and said DR DUNN in big block letters we tore from the library copy of *Ranger Rick*, so we assumed the secretary would discover it and simply pass it along to him. I sat in math class imagining him at his giant desk, unfolding the letter, staring at it for a moment, then slowly folding it again. Perhaps after school he'd go down to the art room, wave it in Ms. McDaniel's face.

They've got right where they want us
he'd say, or:
The jig's up.
Maybe she would kiss him, poke her tongue between his lips.
Darling, she would whisper against his teeth. *What will we do?*
We'll *think of something . . .*
He'd fit his hands over her small breasts, rub them with his thumbs.

"Anne?"

I looked up at Mrs. Payne. She was standing at the blackboard in her hideous orange and white flowered dress, her stomach and breasts an indistinguishable flowery lump. Her grotesque bottom lip trembled slightly, and her words came layered in saliva: "Problem 4?"

I didn't know anything about problem 4. That was problem one. Problem two was that thinking about Dr. Dunn and Ms. McDaniel together had made me feel like I had a bubble expanding in my stomach, emptying me of everything but its own strained vulnerability, filling me up with the most palpable absence I'd ever known. My face was numb below my cheekbones and I felt sad and happy at the same time.

"Problem 4," Mrs. Payne croaked.

A word about Mrs. Payne. My mother (and countless others) had complained to Dr. Dunn about her on several occasions, for Mrs. Payne was prone to catastrophic mood swings of blinding speed. One minute she'd be the sweetest old lady you'd ever known, a cuddle and a peppermint at the ready, and the next she'd turn on you like a viper, call you lazy, stupid, hopeless, slobber insults on you until you cried or (in the now famous case of Chris Brewster) wet your pants. Other times she'd seem positively adrift; at least once in a day she began a sentence with "When Mr. Payne was alive . . ." and then would launch into a story that might or might not have anything to do with the subject at hand or even with Mr. Payne himself. For instance, we'd be talking about fractions and suddenly Mrs. Payne would say "When Mr. Payne was alive you could buy a sporty car for five-hundred dollars. I had such a car myself that I drove all the way from Moline, Illinois to Boise, Idaho to visit my dear cousin Edith who was so distraught over a man that the only word she'd spoken for a year was *pecan*"

She'd pause. To remember? To consider? Why *pecan*? And then she'd move on as if no interruption had occurred.

"Fourteen," Louise whispered from behind me. In addition to her numerous other afflictions, Mrs. Payne was also half-deaf, so it was pretty easy to cheat on her.

"Fourteen," I said. My lips were dry and I licked them.

"Fourteen," Mrs. Payne said, as if mulling over the existence of the number itself. "Fourteen. Four-tee-een. Fourteen is correct"

"Space case," Louise said as we gathered our books at the end of class. "Thinking about how to spend the money?"

"Yeah," I said.

The payoff came as two ten dollar bills, perfectly crisp as the ones my grandmother always sent for my birthday. Louise and I hit the bathroom between second and third periods the next morning, when it was packed with primping sixth graders, so that if Dr. Dunn was casing the joint he wouldn't be able to tell who'd actually made the pick-up. It was me who went into the middle stall, me who with trembling fingers opened the envelope, certain it would contain a note which said **Anne Foster you are expelled from school for the rest of your life.** But no—there were the two stiff tens, Andrew Jackson with his sly grin—and I slid the envelope into my backpack and remembered to flush the toilet for cover, even though I hadn't used it, and when I emerged from the stall I gave Louise the sign, which was to brush the side of my nose with my index finger. We had seen this in *The Sting*.

"What're you gonna get?" Louise asked. "Think your mom'll take us to the mall this weekend?"

We were in the Hanley's basement again and I felt like I'd swallowed the twenty dollars—in pennies. My stomach seemed to be sagging to my thighs.

"What's wrong?" Louise asked.

"We're gonna get caught," I said. "We're gonna get caught and my parents are going to kill me."

She rolled her eyes. "They're not going to kill you. What's the worst thing they could do to you, legally?"

"They could be very disappointed," I said. In my mind I could see clearly my parents' Very Disappointed faces, the unique mixture of grief and ire and guilt and pity I was fairly sure the two of them had begun assembling the moment they met, so profound and effective it was.

"Tough life," Louise said. "World's smallest violin, Anne."

I had known for years that Louise envied what she perceived as my perfect life and family. What she didn't know was that sometimes—like today—I envied hers. Whenever I did something I knew was wrong I wished my parents would die in a tragic car accident ASAP, before the truth of my flawed character could be revealed. It was an extreme solution, but the only one I could conceive of. Lucky Louise . . . the news of her own flawed character would cause little disruption in the Hanley house. Her mother probably wouldn't even look up from the paper.

"We could get two records each," Louise said. "Or we could save it to spend at Six Flags this summer."

"What if we bought something for Ms. McDaniel?"

She stared at me. "What?"

"I don't know." I dug my hands into the shag carpet. "Just, you know. We could buy her something. You know, with part of it."

She shook her head slowly. "You're a freak, Anne. Do you know that?"

"So?" I said. "You're a freak too."

"But you're a different kind of freak than me," she said thoughtfully. She twisted some hair around her finger. "I come from freaks. But you, like, sprouted up all on your own."

"So?"

"So fine," she said. "I'm just making an observation. What'dya want to buy her, ya freak? Frilly underwear?"

"No," I said, my cheeks warming. "Something cool. Like, drawing pencils or something."

"Drawing pencils," she said flatly. "You've thought about this."

I shrugged.

She gazed at me impatiently, with the look of someone who in two or three years would no longer want to be my friend. We were two weird kids who had leapt from the ship of fools and splashed blindly toward each other, scrambled aboard the same life raft. Perhaps it was only a matter of time before we leapt again and made for separate shores.

She threw me one of the tens. "It's your money," she said.

The next day I ditched recess after lunch and ran with a full heart to the art room. Ms. McDaniel was sitting at her desk nibbling on celery sticks and reading a thick book that bore no title on its cover. I shifted from one foot to the other in the doorway until she noticed me.

"Hello, Anne," she said, sliding the book into a desk drawer. She cocked her head cheerfully in the way of young teachers and enthusiastic babysitters. "What can I do for you?"

"I found these," I said. I approached her desk with the pencils held at arm's length in front of me. "Yesterday my mom needed to go to Art Mart and she gave me five dollars to spend and the thing that I wanted cost three-fifty so I picked these up off the sale table that was right next to the cash register and I thought you might want them."

Exhausted from the lie—I'd practiced it a dozen times that morning in the shower—I dropped the pencils on the desk beside her lunch bag. She looked at them curiously, then at me.

"Well, thank you," she said. "That's quite a story."

"It's what happened," I said emphatically, thinking she was on to my lie, but shortly thereafter realizing she was merely making conversation.

"You're very thoughtful," she said. She brushed a wayward hair from her forehead. "I love working with pencils."

"I know," I said. "One time you said that. In class, I mean. You mentioned that."

"I don't think I realized you had such an interest in art," she said.

"Sure," I said. I looked at her smiling expectantly and I wanted to tell her that she didn't have to do all those things to Dr. Dunn, even if he was the principal. "Art's good," I said. "It's, you know, it's really... it's amazing."

"What did you get at Art Mart?" she asked.

"Paper," I said.

"Drawing paper?"

"Yes," I said. "White."

"Well, it's very thoughtful of you to think of me," she said again. She wadded up her brown paper bag and turned to throw it in the trash can, and when she did the collar of her shirt shifted so that I could see her bra strap. In a burst of vivid color I imagined Dr. Dunn sinking his teeth into that shoulder, tugging on that bra strap like a dog with a rope, and I felt so dizzy I had to hold onto the desk to keep from falling over.

"Anne?" Ms. McDaniel said, turning back to me. "Honey, are you okay?"

> Dear Dr. Dunn,
>
> If you want to keep your affair quiet, place forty dollars in the envelope and put it in the appointed place.
>
> The x's
>
> ps Don't you think you're a little old for Ms. McDaniel?

Louise frowned. "What the hell is this?"

We were sitting on the school bus in our usual seat, fourth from the back on the right. This particular bus, for reasons none of us understood, always smelled like tuna salad in the morning and Bit-O-Honey in the afternoon.

"What's wrong with it?" I asked.

She ripped the paper in two and dropped it in my lap. "This is about blackmail," she said. "This is not about you being the pope or something."

"She's nice," I said. The bus went in and out of a pothole and the boys in the back seats whooped. "He's just using her for sex."

"Anne," she said. "You don't know anything about this. You don't have any idea what it's like to be an adult."

"Neither do you," I said, though I was realizing more and more this wasn't really true.

"I'm the letter writer from now on," she said. "We're just gonna stick to blackmail. We're not going to get into stuff we don't know anything about."

We dropped off the note the next morning, with directions that $40 be left in the usual spot by 6ᵗʰ period. Right after lunch, Louise went to the nurses' office and according to another kid who was there with a splinter in his palm–barfed the Thursday Special (Sloppy Joe, Tator Tots) in a steaming pile at Nurse Carol's feet. So Louise got sent home to the loving arms of her mother, and I was left alone to secure the afternoon's payoff.

We had planned poorly; my sixth period class was in the west wing of the building, three halls and a flight of stairs away from the bathroom in question. By the time I reached it the warning bell for seventh period had already rung. A couple girls were drying their hands and rushing out when I bolted myself into the middle stall and reached behind the toilet. Despite my tardiness (the final bell was sounding as I grasped my prize), I remained in the stall and tore open the envelope. Inside was a 3×5 note card on which was printed, in tidy black letters:

> Anne, Louise: There is nothing to tell. This foolishness ends right now.

Something that felt like cold water rushed from behind my ears all the way down to my heels. My brain flailed about senselessly for at least ten seconds before lighting upon the first thing it could recognize—I *have to get to social studies.* Hands trembling, I started at the latch, then froze when I heard the door to the hallway whoosh open. Six footsteps on soft soled shoes, then silence

"Louise?" I whispered hopefully, though I knew full well that Louise was at home safe in bed, which is exactly where I wished I were.

"It's not Louise."

It was Ms. McDaniel. I stood in the stall, my knees quaking, wondering: if I didn't open the door, didn't come out willingly, how long would she stand there? An hour? Overnight? Until school let out for the summer? I imagined my family sitting around the dinner table waiting for me, years passing, my mother's patience waning, my father's smile turning melancholy, my brothers stealing away with their own Ms. McDaniels.

I slid the latch to the side, let the door swing open of its own accord. She was leaning against the wall next to the paper towel dispenser. Her face was all blotchy and her lips were somehow crooked, but she wasn't crying. She looked like she should be in the emergency room.

"Well?" she said.

"Hi," I said.

I was standing there holding the index card; I could have run but it seemed pointless. Suddenly she sprang from the wall and grabbed my wrist, twisted it until the note dropped to the floor. Still gripping my wrist, she leaned over and picked it up, read it once, then read it again. Then she straightened up, loosened her grasp, and regarded me coolly.

"Are you satisfied?" she asked.

I had no idea what she meant. More importantly, I didn't know which answer would get me out the door faster. "Yes," I said, then changed my mind. "I mean no. Yes and no. Not really. Sort of." I bit my lip.

"Some day you'll know what it's like to really love someone," she said. She said it kind of gently, like she was talking to a little kid. "Some day you'll know what it's like to look at a man, his neck and his knees and his warm hands, and know that everything that was missing in your life has come knocking."

"Ms. McDaniel—" I said. I'm not sure what I had it in my mind to say, but it didn't really matter, because she wasn't listening.

"And some day, Anne Foster," she said. "Some day some awful little girl you don't even know will ruin your life for no reason. And when that day comes I want you to think of me."

Louise called that night and my father came to get me. I buried my head in my math book and told him I had to study for a test tomorrow. When she called again I told him the same thing. He returned to my room a few minutes later.

"Louise says you don't have a test in math tomorrow."

"She wouldn't know," I said. "She had to go home early today."

He leaned in the doorway. "Everything okay?"

I wanted to tell him what had happened in the bathroom. I wanted him to sit on the edge of my bed and explain point for point what had transpired, help me understand what Ms McDaniel had said to me. But I knew, somehow more than I'd ever known anything, that even had I the courage to ask the questions (which I did not) that he would be unable to answer a single one of them. It was a realization that left me cold: the machinations of the human heart were inexplicable, not only to me, but to my parents as well, and thus, apparently, to anyone. Was this what Louise had known all along? I wondered. Was there truly no one in her life from whom she had ever, *ever*, expected a satisfying explanation?

"Everything's fine," I said.

"You're gonna to have to tell me sometime," Louise said from her seat at the desk behind me. We were in math class.

I turned to her, deliberately put my finger to my lips.

"What the hell?" she said. "What happened to you?"

"When Mr. Payne was alive. . ." Mrs. Payne began.

Mrs. Payne, a pain in the butt, a punch line to the joke of every fifth grader. Yesterday she'd been as flat and clear as a pane of glass. Today I gazed through her sagging breasts and jowls and saw her as a young woman, as young as Ms. McDaniel, a mystery slipping out of her nightgown and into the arms of her beloved.

—1999

SUSAN PERABO

424

POETRY

Introduction to Poetry

An Anecdote: Where Poetry Starts

The room is not particularly grand, a large lecture hall in one of the old buildings on the college campus, and the small group of first-year students whose literature class has been dismissed so that they can attend the poetry reading has taken seats near the back of the room. They have been encouraged to come for several weeks by their instructor, and when she enters she looks around the room and nods in their direction, smiling.

The seats gradually fill. The crowd is a mixed one—several men and women known by sight as senior faculty members; a scattering of other older visitors, many of them apparently from the community; a large contingent of instructors and graduate students from the English Department sitting in the front rows; and small clusters of undergraduates scattered throughout the room.

One of the students scans the crowd, wondering aloud which is the poet. On the walk to the reading, several fellow class members decided that the poet, a cadaverous gray-haired man wrapped in a black cloak, would recite his poems in a resonant baritone, preferably with a strong breeze tossing his hair. Speculating on how the wind effect might be managed inside a lecture hall made them laugh.

Now the crowd grows quiet as the students' instructor steps to the podium and adjusts the microphone. She makes a few complimentary remarks about the strong turnout and thanks several benefactors for their support of poetry at the university. Then she introduces the guest.

Her students know most of this information, for they have studied several of his poems in class that week, but they are still slightly surprised when he rises to polite applause and takes the lectern. The balding middle-age man wearing a golf shirt could be taken for a professor in any campus department, and when he adjusts his glasses and clears his throat, blinking at the audience, there is little about him that would fit anyone's romantic stereotype of a poet.

Surprisingly, he does not begin with a poem. Instead, in a relaxed voice he tells an anecdote about his younger daughter and an overdue science project. When he moves from the background story into reading the poem itself, there is little change in his volume level, and his tone remains conversational. The students find that the poem, which they had discussed in class only a couple of days before, takes on more meaning when its origins are explained by the poet himself. They find themselves listening attentively to his words, even laughing out loud several times. The hour goes by quickly, and at its end their applause, like that of the rest of the audience, is long and sincere.

At the next class meeting, the instructor asks for reactions to the reading. Although some of the class members are slightly critical, faulting the speaker for his informal manner and his failure to maintain eye contact with the room, most of the remarks are positive. The comments that surface most often have to do with how much more meaningful the poems in the textbook become when the poet explains how he came to write them. They now know that one poem is actually spoken in the voice of the poet's dead father and that another is addressed to a friend who was paralyzed in an automobile accident. Although these things could perhaps be inferred from the poems alone, the students are unanimous in their opinion that knowing the details beforehand adds a great deal to the first impression a poem makes. As one student puts it, "It's just that a poem makes a lot more sense when you know who's talking and when and where it's supposed to be taking place."

"It always helps to know where poetry starts," adds one of her classmates.

Speaker, Listener, and Context

The situation described above is hardly unique. Instructors have long been encouraging, even begging, their students to attend events like the one described, and the college poetry reading has become, for many American students, the closest encounter they will have with this complex and often perplexing art form. But what students often find at such readings, sometimes to their amazement, is that poetry need not be intimidating or obscure. Poems that are *performed* provide a gentle reminder that the roots of poetry, like those of all literature, were originally part of the **oral tradition**. In ancient societies, stories and poems were passed down from generation to generation and recited for all members of the tribe, from the wizened elders to the youngest children. For most of its long history, poetry has been a popular art form aimed at audiences (remember that the word *audience* means "hearers"). It is only recently, in the last four or five decades, that its most visible signs of life are to be found on college campuses. Still, it is perhaps worth noting that we are exposed daily to a great deal of poetry in oral form, primarily through the medium of recorded song lyrics. The unique qualities of poetry throughout the ages, that is, its ability to tell stories or summarize complicated emotions in a few well-chosen words, are demonstrated whenever we memorize the lines of a popular song and sing them to ourselves.

Of course, poetry written primarily for the page is usually more demanding than song lyrics. Writers of popular songs aim at a wide commercial audience, and this simple fact of economics, added to the fact that the lyrics are not intended primarily for publication but for being recorded with all the resources of studio technology, tends to make many song lyrics relatively uninteresting when they appear in print. But a poem will exist primarily as a printed text, although its effect may be enhanced greatly through a skillful oral performance in which the poet can also explain the background of the poem, its setting and speaker, and the circumstances under which it was written. In general, these details, so crucial to understanding a poem yet so often only implied when the poem appears in print, are called the **dramatic situation** of a poem. Dramatic situation can be summed up in a question: *Who is speaking to whom under what circumstances?* If the poet fails to provide us with clues or if we are careless in picking up the information that is provided, then we may begin reading with no sense of reference and, thus, may go far astray. Even such words as "on," "upon," or "to" in titles can be crucial to our understanding of dramatic situation, telling us something about an event or object that provided the stimulus for the poem or about the identity of the "you" addressed in the poem.

An illustration may be helpful. Suppose we look at what is unquestionably the most widely known poem ever written by an American. It is a poem that virtually all Americans can recite in part and, in fact, do so by the millions every week. Yet if we were told that this poem is unusual because its best-known section is a long, unanswered question, addressed by the speaker to a nearby companion, about whether or not the object named in the title even exists, then it is likely that most of us would be confused. Before going further, let us look at the poem.

The Star-Spangled Banner

O say, can you see, by the dawn's early light,
    What so proudly we hailed at the twilight's last gleaming?
Whose broad stripes and bright stars thro' the perilous fight,
    O'er the ramparts we watched, were so gallantly streaming!
And the rockets' red glare, the bombs bursting in air,
    Gave proof through the night that our flag was still there:
O say, does that star-spangled banner yet wave
    O'er the land of the free and the home of the brave?

On the shore, dimly seen thro' the mists of the deep,
    Where the foe's haughty host in dread silence reposes,
What is that which the breeze, o'er the towering steep,
    As it fitfully blows, now conceals, now discloses?
Now it catches the gleam of the morning's first beam,
    In full glory reflected now shines on the stream:
'Tis the star-spangled banner! O long may it wave
    O'er the land of the free and the home of the brave!

And where is that band who so vauntingly swore
    That the havoc of war and the battle's confusion
A home and a country should leave us no more?
    Their blood has washed out their foul footsteps' pollution.
No refuge could save the hireling and slave
    From the terror of flight, or the gloom of the grave:
And the star-spangled banner in triumph doth wave
    O'er the land of the free and the home of the brave!

Oh! thus be it ever, when freemen shall stand
    Between their loved homes and the war's desolation!

Blest with victory and peace, may the heav'n-rescued land
    Praise the Pow'r that hath made and preserved us a nation.
Then conquer we must, when our cause it is just,
    And this be our motto: "In God is our trust."
And the star-spangled banner in triumph shall wave
    O'er the land of the free and the home of the brave!

"Now wait a minute!" you may be complaining. "'The Star-Spangled Banner' is a *song*, not a poem. And what's this *question* business? Don't we always sing it while facing the flag? Besides, it's just a patriotic song. Nobody really worries about what it *means*."

In answer to the first comment, "The Star-Spangled Banner" *was* in fact written as a poem and was set to music only after its composition. Most of us will probably agree that the words are not particularly well-suited to the melody (which was taken, curiously, from a popular British barroom ballad) and the song remains notoriously difficult to sing, even for professional performers. In its original form, "The Star-Spangled Banner" (or "The Defense of Fort McHenry," the title under which it was first published) is an example of **occasional verse**, a poem that is written about or for an important event (or occasion), sometimes private but usually of some public significance. Although poems of this type are not often printed on the front pages of newspapers as they once were, they are still being written. Enough poems appeared after the assassination of President John F. Kennedy in 1963 to fill a book, *Of Poetry and Power*, and the *Challenger* disaster of 1986 stimulated a similar outpouring of occasional poems, one of them by Howard Nemerov, who served as poet laureate of the United States. In 1993, Maya Angelou recited "On the Pulse of Morning" at the first inauguration of President Clinton, and Miller Williams read "Of History and Hope" at the second, in 1997. The events of September 11, 2001, stimulated thousands of poems including "The Names" by then-U.S. Poet Laureate Billy Collins. The author of "The Star-Spangled Banner," Francis Scott Key (1779–1843), wrote poetry as an avocation. Yet like many men and women who are not professional writers, Key was so deeply moved by an event that he witnessed that occasional poetry was the only medium through which he could express his feelings.

Now let's go back to our question about dramatic situation, taking it one part at a time: Who is speaking? A technical word that is often used to designate the speaker of a poem is **persona** (plural: **personae**), a word that meant "mask" in ancient Greek. Even though the persona of "The Star-Spangled Banner" never uses the word "I" in the poem, the speaker seems to be Key himself, a fact that can be verified by biographical research. Still, it is probably safer to look at poems carefully to see if they give any evidence that the speaker is someone other than the poet. Poems like "Ulysses" by Alfred, Lord Tennyson or "Porphyria's Lover" by Robert Browning have titles that identify personae who are, respectively, a character from ancient epic poetry and an unnamed man who is confessing the murder of his lover, Porphyria. In neither case is the persona to be identified with the poet himself. Other poems may be somewhat more problematical. Edgar Allan Poe's famous "The Raven," like many of Poe's short stories, is spoken by a persona who is not to be identified directly with the author, even though he shares many of the same morbid preoccupations of Poe's other characters. Even Sylvia Plath, a poet usually associated with an extremely candid form of autobiographical poetry known as **confessional poetry**, on a radio broadcast identified the persona of her masterpiece "Daddy" as an invented character, "a girl with an Electra complex." Although it now is clear that Plath used many autobiographical details in her poem, readers who try to identify her as a victim of child abuse on its evidence should instead turn to Plath's journals and the many biographies that have been written about her. Sometimes poems have more than one persona, which is the case with Thomas Hardy's "The Ruined Maid" and Robert Frost's "Home Burial," two poems that consist almost entirely of dialogue. In other poems, for instance in many ballads, the voice may simply be a third-person **narrator** such as we might find in a short story or novel. Thus, although it is perhaps true that many poems (including the majority of those included here) are in fact spoken by the poet out of his or her most private feelings, it is not a good idea to leap too quickly to the assumption that the persona of a poem is identical to the poet and shares his or her views. Conclusions about the degree to which a poem is autobiographical can be verified only by research and familiarity with a poet's other works.

To return to our question: Who is speaking to whom? Another useful term is **auditor**, the person or persons spoken to in a poem. Some poems identify no auditor; others clearly do specify an auditor or auditors, in most cases identified by name or by the second-person pronoun "you" (or "thee/thou" in older poetry). Again, the title may give clues: Robert Herrick's "To the Virgins, to Make Much of Time" is addressed to a group of young women; William Cullen Bryant's "To the Fringed Gentian" is addressed to a common New England wildflower. (The figure of speech **apostrophe**—discussed later in this introduction—is used when a nonhuman, inanimate, or abstract thing is directly addressed.) Relatively few poems are addressed directly to the reader, so when we read the opening of William Shakespeare's Sonnet 18 ("Shall I compare thee to a summer's day?") we should keep in mind that he is not addressing us but another individual, in this case a young male friend who is referred to in many of the sonnets. Claude McKay's sonnet "If We Must Die" begins in this manner:

> If we must die, let it not be like hogs
> Hunted and penned in an inglorious spot,
> While round us bark the mad and hungry dogs,
> Making their mock at our accursed lot.

Later in the poem McKay identifies his auditors as "Kinsmen." Without outside help, about all we can say with certainty at first glance is that the poet seems to be addressing a group of companions who share his desperate situation; when we learn, possibly through research, that McKay was an African-American poet writing in reaction to the Harlem race riots of 1919, the symbolic nature of his exhortation becomes clearer.

Now the final part of the question: Who is speaking to whom *under what circumstances*? First, we might ask if there is a relationship, either implied or stated, between persona and auditor. Obviously many love poems take the form of verbal transactions between two parties and, because relationships have their ups and downs, these shifts of mood are reflected in the poetry. One famous example is Michael Drayton's "Idea: Sonnet 61" ("Since there's no help, come let us kiss and part . . ."), which begins with the persona threatening to end the relationship with the auditor but which ends with an apparent reconciliation. Such "courtship ritual" poems as John Donne's "The Flea" or Andrew Marvell's "To His Coy Mistress" are witty arguments in favor of the couple's setting aside their hesitations and engaging in sexual relations. An example from poetry about marital love is Matthew Arnold's "Dover Beach," which ends with the plea "Ah, love, let us be true / To one another" as the only hope for stability the persona can find in a world filled with uncertainty and fear. Even an age disparity between persona and auditor can lend meaning to a poem, which is the case with the

Herrick poem mentioned earlier and a dialogue poem like John Crowe Ransom's "Piazza Piece," a classic example of the debate between innocence and experience.

Other questions relating to circumstances of the dramatic situation might concern the poem's physical setting (if any), time (of day, year, historical era), even such matters as weather. Thomas Hardy's "Neutral Tones" provides a good example of a poem in which the setting, a gray winter day in a barren outdoor location, symbolically reinforces the persona's memory of the bitter end of a love affair. The shift in setting from the springtime idyll to the "cold hill side" in John Keats's "La Belle Dame sans Merci" cannot be overlooked in discussing the persona's disillusionment. Of course, many poems are explicitly occasional and may even contain an **epigraph** (see Gwendolyn Brooks's "We Real Cool"), a brief explanatory statement or quotation, or a **dedication**, which explains the setting. Sometimes footnotes or even outside research may be necessary. John Milton's "On the Late Massacre in Piedmont" will make little sense to readers if they do not know that the poet is reacting to the massacre of a group of Waldensian Protestants by Roman Catholic soldiers on Easter Sunday, 1655. Milton, an English Puritan, uses the occasion to attack the papacy as a "triple tyrant" and the "Babylonian woe."

To return, then, one final time to "The Star-Spangled Banner," let us apply our question to the poem. We have already determined that Key is the persona. Who is the "you" mentioned four words into the poem? It seems clear that Key is addressing an auditor standing close to him, either a single individual or a group, as he asks the auditor if he can see the flag that they both observed for the last time the previous day at sundown. Key tells us that it is now the first moment of dawn, and that even though the flag could be glimpsed periodically in the "rockets' red glare" of the bombardment throughout the night, it cannot be clearly seen now. It is a crucial question, for if the flag is no longer flying "o'er the ramparts," it will mean that the fort has fallen to the enemy. The tension mounts and moves into the second stanza, where at last, "thro' the mists of the deep," the flag can be discerned, "dimly seen" at first, then clearly as it "catches the gleam" of the full sunlight.

The full story of how Key came to write the poem is fairly well known and supports this reading. The events that the poem describes took place on September 13–14, 1814, during the War of 1812.

Key, a lawyer, came aboard a British warship anchored off Baltimore to argue for the release of a client and friend who had been taken hostage by the British. Key won his friend's release, but the British captain, fearing that he might reveal information he had learned on board, kept Key overnight, releasing him and his client in the morning. It was during that night that Key witnessed the bombardment and, with it, the failure of the British to take Baltimore. The final half of the poem celebrates the victory and offers a hopeful prayer that God will continue to smile on America "when our cause . . . is just." One might well argue that Key's phrase "conquer we must" contradicts the spirit of the earlier parts of the poem, but few people have argued that "The Star-Spangled Banner" is a consistently great poem. Still, it is an effective piece of patriotic verse that has a few moments of real drama, expressed in a vivid manner that lets its readers become eyewitnesses to an incident from American history.

Lyric, Narrative, Dramatic

The starting point for all literary criticism in Western civilization is Aristotle's *Poetics*, a work dating from the fourth century BC. Although Aristotle's remarks on drama, tragedy in particular, are more complete than his analysis of other types of literature, he does mention three main types of poetry: lyric, epic, and dithyrambic. In doing so, Aristotle outlines for the first time a theory of literature based on **genres**, or separate categories delineated by distinct style, form, and content. This threefold division remains useful today, although in two cases different terminology is employed. The first genre, **lyric poetry**, originally comprised brief poems that were meant to be sung or chanted to the accompaniment of a lyre. Today we still use the word "lyrics" in a specialized sense when referring to the words of a song, but lyric poetry has become such a large category that it includes virtually all poems that are primarily *about* a subject and contain little narrative content. The subject of a lyric poem may be the poet's emotions, an abstract idea, a satirical insight, or a description of a person or place. The persona in a lyric is usually closely identified with the poet himself or herself, and because we tend to identify the essence of poetry with personal, subjective expression of feelings or ideas, lyric poetry remains the largest genre, with a number of subtypes. Among them are the

epigram, a short, satirical lyric usually aimed at a specific person; the **elegy**, a lyric on the occasion of a death; and the **ode**, a long lyric in elevated language on a serious theme.

Aristotle's second genre, the epic, has been expanded to include all types of **narrative poetry**, that is, poetry whose main function is to tell a story. Like prose fiction, narrative poems have plots, characters, setting, and point-of-view, and may be discussed in roughly the same terms as, say, a short story. The **epic** is a long narrative poem about the exploits of a hero. **Folk epics** like *The Iliad* or *Beowulf* were originally intended for public recitation and existed in oral form for a long period of time before they were transcribed. Little or nothing is known about the authors of folk epics; even Homer, the purported author of the *Iliad* and the *Odyssey*, is primarily a legendary character. **Literary epics**, like Dante's *Inferno* or Henry Wadsworth Longfellow's *The Song of Hiawatha*, differ in that they are the products of known authors who *wrote* their poems for publication. **Ballads** generally are shorter narratives with song-like qualities which often include rhyme and repeated refrains. **Folk ballads**, like folk epics, come from the oral tradition and are anonymously authored; "Bonny Barbara Allan" and "Sir Patrick Spens" are typical examples. **Art** or **literary ballads** are conscious imitations of the ballad style by later poets and are generally somewhat more sophisticated than folk ballads in their techniques. Examples of this popular genre include Keats's "La Belle Dame sans Merci," Robert Burns's "John Barleycorn," and more recently, Marilyn Nelson's "The Ballad of Aunt Geneva." **Realistic narratives** of medium length (under 1000 lines) like Robert Frost's "Home Burial" have been popular since the early nineteenth century and are sometimes discussed as "poetic novels" or "short stories in verse."

There is no exact contemporary analogue for Aristotle's third category, **dithyrambic poetry**. This type of poem, composed to be chanted at religious rituals by a chorus, was the forerunner of tragedy. Today this third type is usually called **dramatic poetry**, because it has perhaps as much in common with the separate genre of drama as with lyric and narrative poetry. In general, the persona in a dramatic poem is an invented character not to be identified with the poet. The poem is presented as a speech or dialogue that might be acted out like a soliloquy or scene from a play. The **dramatic monologue** is a speech for a single character, usually delivered to a silent auditor. Notable examples are Tennyson's "Ulysses" and Browning's "My Last Duchess." A dramatic monologue sometimes implies, in the words of its persona, a distinct setting and interplay between persona and auditor. At the close of "Ulysses" the aged hero urges his "mariners" to listen closely and to observe the ship in the harbor waiting to take them off on a final voyage. Dramatic poetry can also take the form of **dialogue poetry**, in which two personae speak alternately. Examples are Christina Rossetti's "Up-Hill" and Hardy's "The Ruined Maid." A popular type of dialogue poem that originated in the Middle Ages was the **débat**, or mock-debate, in which two characters, usually personified abstractions like the Soul and the Body, argued their respective merits.

Although it is easy enough to find examples of "pure" lyrics, narratives, and dramatic monologues, sometimes the distinction between the three major types may become blurred, even in the same poem. "The Star-Spangled Banner," for example, contains elements of all three genres. The opening stanza, with its vivid re-creation of a question asked at dawn, is closest to dramatic poetry. The second and third stanzas, which tell of the outcome of the battle, are primarily narrative. The final stanza, with its patriotic effusion and religious sentiment, is lyrical. Still, the threefold division is useful in discussing a single author's various ways of dealing with subjects or in comparing examples of one type by separate authors. To cite three poems by the same poet in this collection, we might look at William Blake's "The Tyger," "A Poison Tree," and "The Chimney Sweeper." The first of these is a descriptive lyric, dwelling primarily on the symbolic meaning of the tiger's appearance; the second is a narrative that relates, in the first person and the allegorical manner of a parable, the events leading up to a murder; and the third is a short dramatic monologue spoken by the persona identified in the title.

The Language of Poetry

One of the most persistent myths about poetry is that its language is artificial, "flowery," and essentially different from the language that people speak every day. Although these beliefs may be true of some poetry, one can easily find numerous examples that demonstrate poetic diction of an entirely different sort. It is impossible to characterize poetic language narrowly, for poetry, which is after all the art of language, covers the widest possible range of linguistic possibilities. For example, here are several passages from different poets, all describing birds:

Hail to thee, blithe Spirit!
  Bird thou never wert—
That from Heaven, or near it,
  Pourest thy full heart
In profuse strains of unpremeditated art.

Higher still and higher
  From the earth thou springest
Like a cloud of fire;
  The blue deep thou wingest,
And singing still dost soar, and soaring ever singest.

Percy Bysshe Shelley, "To a Skylark"

I caught this morning morning's minion, king-
    dom of daylight's dauphin, dapple-dawn-drawn Falcon, in
      his riding
  Of the rolling level underneath him steady air, and striding
High there, how he rung upon the rein of a wimpling wing
In his ecstacy!

Gerard Manley Hopkins, "The Windhover"

When the lilac-scent was in the air and Fifth-month grass was
    growing,
Up this seashore in some briers,
Two feather'd guests from Alabama, two together,
And their nest, and four light-green eggs spotted with brown,
And every day the he-bird to and fro near at hand,
And every day the she-bird crouch'd on her nest, silent, with
    bright eyes,
And every day I, a curious boy, never too close, never disturbing
    them,
Cautiously peering, absorbing, translating.

Walt Whitman, "Out of the Cradle Endlessly Rocking"

At once a voice arose among
  The bleak twigs overhead
In a full-hearted evensong
  Of joy illimited;
An aged thrush, frail, gaunt, and small,
  In blast-beruffled plume,

Had chosen thus to fling his soul
    Upon the growing gloom.

Thomas Hardy, "The Darkling Thrush"

There is a singer everyone has heard,
Loud, a mid-summer and a mid-wood bird,
Who makes the solid tree trunks sound again.
He says that leaves are old and that for flowers
Mid-summer is to spring as one to ten.

Robert Frost, "The Oven Bird"

The blue booby lives
on the bare rocks
of Galápagos
and fears nothing.
It is a simple life:
they live on fish,
and there are few predators.

James Tate, "The Blue Booby"

Of these quotes, only Shelley's, from the early nineteenth century, possesses the stereotypical characteristics of what we mean when we use the term "poetic" in a negative sense. Poetry, like any other art form, follows fashions that change over the years; by Shelley's day, the use of "thee" and "thou" and their related verb forms ("wert" and "wingest") had come full circle from their original use as a familiar form of the second person employed to address intimates and servants to an artificially heightened grammatical form reserved for prayers and poetry. Hopkins's language, from a poem of the 1870s, is artificial in an entirely different way; here the poet's **idiom**, the personal use of words that marks his poetry, is highly individual; indeed, it would be hard to mistake a poem by Hopkins, with its muscular monosyllables and rich texture of sound patterns, with one by any other poet. Whitman's diction should present few difficulties; the only oddity here is the use of "Fifth-month" instead of "May," a linguistic inheritance, perhaps, from the poet's Quaker mother. Of course, one might argue that Whitman's "naturalness" results from his use of free verse, but both Hardy and Frost, who write rhymed, metrical verse, are hardly less natural. When we move to the contemporary period, we can find little difference between the language of many poems and conversational speech, as Tate's lines indicate.

Still, in reading a poem, particularly one from the past, we should be aware of certain problems that may impede our understanding. **Diction** refers to the individual words in a poem and may be classified in several ways. A poem's **level of diction** can range from slang at one extreme to formal usage at the other, although in an age in which most poems use a level of diction that stays in the middle of the scale, ranging from conversational and standard levels, these distinctions are useful only when a poet is being self-consciously formal (perhaps for ironic effect) or going to the opposite extreme to imitate the language of the streets. In past eras the term **poetic diction** was used to indicate a level of speech somehow refined above ordinary usage and, thus, somehow superior to it. Today the same term would most likely be used as a way of criticizing a poet's language. We should keep in mind that the slang of one era may become the standard usage of another, as is the case with "O.K." which has become a universal expression. In other cases, a poet may even "invent" an idiom for a poem, the case with Lewis Carroll's famous "Jabberwocky" and Stevie Smith's "Our Bog Is Dood."

A good dictionary is useful in many ways, particularly in dealing with **archaisms** (words that are no longer in common use) and other words that may not be familiar to the reader. Take, for example, the opening lines of Edgar Allan Poe's "To Helen":

> Helen, thy beauty is to me
>   Like those Nicean barks of yore,
>   That gently, o'er a perfumed sea,
>   The weary, way-worn wanderer bore
>   To his own native shore.

Several words here may give trouble to the average contemporary reader. First, "o'er," like "ne'er" or similar words like "falt'ring" and "glimm'ring," is simply a contraction; this dropping of a letter, called **syncope**, is done for the sake of maintaining the poem's meter; in the fourth stanza of "The Star-Spangled Banner," the words "Pow'r" and "heav'n" are contracted for the same reason. "Barks of yore" will probably send most of us to the dictionary, for our sense of "bark" as either the outer surface of a tree or the noise that a dog makes does not fit here; likewise, "yore" is unfamiliar, possibly archaic. Looking up the literal sense of a word in a dictionary discloses its **denotation**, or literal meaning. Thus, we find that "barks" are small sailing ships and that "yore" refers to the distant past. Of course, Poe could have said "ships of the past" or a similar phrase, but his word choice was perhaps dictated by **connotation**, the implied meaning or feel that some words have acquired; it may be that even in Poe's day "barks of yore" had a remote quality that somehow evoked ancient Greece in a way that, say, "ancient ships" would not. But what are we to make of "Nicean," a proper adjective that sounds geographical but does not appear in either the dictionary or gazetteer? In this case we have encountered an example of a **coinage**, or **neologism**, a word made up by the poet. Speculation on the source of "Nicean" has ranged from Nice, in the south of France, to Phoenician, but it is likely that Poe simply coined the word for its exotic sound. Similarly, we might note that the phrase "weary, way-worn wanderer" contains words that seem to have been chosen primarily for their alliterated sounds.

When we put a poem into our own words, we **paraphrase** it, a practice that is often useful when passages are hard to understand. Other than diction, **syntax**, the order of words in a sentence, may also give readers problems. Syntax in poetry, particularly in poems that use rhyme, is likely to be different from that of both speech and prose; if a poet decides to rhyme in a certain pattern, then word order must be modified to fit the formal design, and this may present difficulties to readers in understanding the grammar of a passage. Here is the opening of a familiar piece of American patriotic verse: "My country, 'tis of thee, / Sweet land of liberty, / Of thee I sing." What is the subject of this sentence? Would you be surprised to learn that the grammatical subject is "it" (contained in the contraction "'tis"—"It is of thee, my country, sweet land of liberty, of thee [that] I sing")? The passage from Poe's poem presents few difficulties of this order but does contain one example of **inversion**, words that fall out of their expected order (a related syntactical problem lies in **ellipsis**, words that are consciously omitted by the poet). If we do not allow for this, we are likely to be confused by "the weary, way-worn wanderer bore / To his own native shore." The wanderer bore *what?* A quick mental sentence diagram shows that "wanderer" is the direct object of "bore," not its subject. A good paraphrase should simplify both diction and syntax: "Helen, to me your beauty is like those Nicean (?) ships of the ancient past that carried the weary, travel-worn wanderer gently over a perfumed sea to his own native land." In paraphrasing, only the potentially troublesome words and phrases should be substituted, leaving the original language as intact as possible. Paraphrasing is a useful first step toward unfolding a poem's literal sense, but it obviously takes few of a poet's specific nuances of language into account; words like "cool," "cold," "chilly," and "frigid" may denote the same thing, but each has its own connotation. "Poetry," Robert Frost famously remarked, "is what is lost in translation." He might have extended the complaint to include paraphrase as well.

Several other matters relevant to poetic language are worth mentioning. **Etymology**, the study of the sources of words, is a particularly rewarding topic in English because our language has such an unusually rich history—just compare an unabridged French dictionary to its English counterpart. Old English (or Anglo-Saxon), the ancient language of the British Isles, was part of the Germanic family of languages. When the Norman French successfully invaded Britain in 1066 they brought with them their own language, part of the Romance language family (all originally derived from Latin). By the time of Chaucer's death in 1400 these two linguistic traditions had merged into a single language, Middle English, that can be read today, despite its differences in spelling, pronunciation, and vocabulary. We can still, however, distinguish the words that show their Germanic heritage from those of Latinate origin. English is rich in synonyms, and Germanic and Latinate words that "mean" the same thing often have different connotations. "Smart" (from the Old English *smeart*) is not quite the same as "intelligent" (from the Latin *intellegent*). A "mapmaker" is subtly different from a "cartographer"—ask yourself which would have ink on his fingers. Although a poet's preference for words of a certain origin is not always immediately clear, we can readily distinguish the wide gulf that separates a statement like "I live in a house with my folks" from "I occupy a residence with my parents."

A final tension exists in poems between their use of **concrete diction** and **abstract diction**. Concrete words denote that which can be perceived by the senses, and the vividness of a poem's language resides primarily in the way it uses **imagery**, sensory details denoting specific physical experiences. Because sight is the most important of the five senses, **visual imagery** ("a dim light"; "a dirty rag"; "a golden daffodil") predominates in poems, but we should also be alert for striking examples of the other types of imagery: **auditory** ("a pounding surf"), **tactile** ("a scratchy beard"), **olfactory** ("the scent of apple blossoms"), and **gustatory** ("the bitter tang of gin"). The use of specific imagery has always been crucial for poetry. Consider, for example, the way Chaucer uses brilliantly chosen concrete details—a nun's coral jewelry, a monk's hood lined with fur, a festering sore on a cook's shin—to bring his pilgrims to life in the prologue to *The Canterbury Tales*. In the early twentieth century, a group of poets led by Americans Ezra Pound and H. D. (Hilda Doolittle) pioneered a poetic movement called **imagism**, in which concrete details predominate in short descriptive poems (see H. D.'s "Sea Rose"). "Go in fear of abstractions," commanded Pound, and his friend William Carlos Williams modified the remark to become a poetic credo: "No ideas but in things."

Still, for most poets abstract words remain important because they carry the burden of a poem's overall meaning or theme. William Butler Yeats's "Leda and the Swan" provides a good example of how concrete and abstract diction coexists in a poem. In reading this account of the myth in which Zeus, in the form of a swan, rapes and impregnates a human woman and thus sets in action the chain of events that leads to the Trojan War (Leda was the mother of Helen of Troy), we will probably be struck at first by the way that tactile imagery ("a sudden blow," fingers attempting to "push / The feathered glory" away, "A shudder in the loins") is used to describe an act of sexual violation. Even though some abstract words ("terrified," "vague," "glory," "strange") appear in the first eight lines of the poem they are all linked closely to concrete words like "fingers," "feathered," and "heart." In the last two lines of the poem, Yeats uses three large abstractions—"knowledge," "power," and "indifferent"—to state his theme (or at least ask the crucial rhetorical question about the meaning of the myth). More often than not, one can expect to encounter the largest number of abstract words near the conclusion of poems. Probably the most famous abstract statement in English poetry—John Keats's "'Beauty is truth, truth beauty,' that is all / Ye know on earth, and all ye need to know"—appears in the last two lines of a fifty-line poem that is otherwise filled with lush, sensory details of description.

Two other devices sometimes govern a poet's choice of words. **Onomatopoeia** refers to individual words like "splash" or "thud" whose meanings are closely related to their sounds. Auditory imagery in a poem can often be enhanced by the use of onomatopoeic words. In some cases, however, a whole line can be called onomatopoeic, even if it contains no single word that illustrates the device. Thomas Hardy uses this line to describe the pounding of distant surf: "Where hill-hid tides throb, throe on throe." Here the repetition of similar sounds helps to imitate the sound of the ocean. A second device is the **pun**, the use of one word to imply the additional meaning of a similar-sounding word (the formal term is **paranomasia**). Thus, when Anne Bradstreet, in "The Author to Her Book," compares her first book to an illegitimate child, she addresses the book in this manner: "If for thy Father asked, say thou had'st none; / And for thy Mother, she alas is poor, / Which caused her thus to send thee out of door." The closeness of the interjection "alas" to the article and noun "a lass" is hardly coincidental. Poets in Bradstreet's day considered the pun a staple of their repertoire, even in serious poetry, but contemporary poets are more likely to use it primarily for comic effect:

> They have a dozen children; it's their diet,
> For they have bread too often. Please don't try it (Anonymous)

More often than not, puns like these will elicit a groan from the audience, a response that may be exactly what the poet desires.

Figurative Language

We use figurative language in everyday speech without thinking of the poetic functions of the same devices. We can always relate experience in a purely literal fashion: "His table manners were deplorable. Mother scolded him severely, and Dad said some angry words to him. He left the table embarrassed and with his feelings hurt." But a more vivid way of saying the same thing might employ language used not in the literal but in the figurative sense. Thus, another version might run, "He made an absolute pig of himself. Mother jumped on his back about it, and Dad scorched his ears. You should have seen him slink off like a scolded puppy." At least four comparisons are made here in an attempt to describe one character's table manners, his mother's scolding, his father's words, and the manner in which the character retreated from the table. In every case, the thing being described, what is called the **tenor** of the figure of speech, is linked with a concrete image or **vehicle**. All of the types of figurative language, what are called **figures of speech**, or **tropes**, involve some kind of comparison, either explicit or implied. Thus, two of the figures in the above example specifically compare aspects of the character's behavior to animal behavior. The other two imply parental words that were delivered with strong physical force or extreme anger. Some of the most common figures of speech are:

Metaphor: a direct comparison between two unlike things. Metaphors may take several forms.

> His words were sharp knives.
> The sharp knife of his words cut through the silence.
> He spoke sharp, cutting words with his knife-edged voice.
> His words knifed through the still air.

> *I will speak daggers to her but use none.* (Shakespeare, *Hamlet*)

Implied metaphor: a metaphor in which either the tenor or vehicle is implied, not stated.

> The running back gathered steam and chugged toward the end zone.

Here the player is compared to a steam locomotive without naming it explicitly.

> *While smoke on its chin, that slithering gun*
> *Coiled back from its windowsill* (X. J. Kennedy)

In this passage from a poem about the assassination of President John F. Kennedy, Lee Harvey Oswald's rifle is indirectly compared ("coiled back" and "slithering") to a snake that has struck its victim.

Simile: a comparison using "like," "as," or "than" as a connective device.

> *My love is like a red, red rose* (Robert Burns)

> My love smells as sweet as a rose.
> My love looks fresher than a newly budded rose.

Conceit: an extended or far-fetched metaphor, in most cases comparing things that apparently have almost nothing in common.

> *Make me, O Lord, thy spinning wheel complete. . . .* (Edward Taylor)

The poem, "Huswifery," draws an analogy between the process of salvation and the manufacture of cloth, ending with the persona attired in "holy robes for glory."

Petrarchan conceit: named after the first great master of the sonnet, is a clichéd comparison usually relating to a woman's beauty (see Thomas

Campion's "There Is a Garden in Her Face"; Shakespeare's Sonnet 130 parodies this type of trope). The **metaphysical conceit** refers to the extended comparisons favored by such so-called metaphysical poets as John Donne, George Herbert, and Edward Taylor. The conceit in the final three stanzas of Donne's "A Valediction: Forbidding Mourning" compares the poet and his wife with a pair of drafting compasses, hardly an image that most people would choose to celebrate marital fidelity.

Hyperbole: an overstatement, a comparison using conscious exaggeration.

He threw the ball so fast it caught the catcher's mitt on fire.

And I will love thee still, my dear,
Till a' the seas gang dry. (Robert Burns)

Understatement: the opposite of hyperbole.

"I don't think we're in Kansas anymore, Toto." (says Dorothy in
    The Wizard of Oz)

The space between, is but an hour,
The frail duration of a flower. (Philip Freneau)

Freneau is understating a wild honeysuckle's lifespan by saying it is "but an hour." Because, by implication, he is also talking about human life, the understatement is even more pronounced.

I watched him; and the sight was not so fair
As one or two that I have seen elsewhere. (Edwin Arlington
    Robinson)

In "How Annandale Went Out," the persona is a physician who is about to perform euthanasia on a friend dying in agony. Understatement is often used in conjunction with verbal irony (see below).

Allusion: a metaphor making a direct comparison to a historical or literary event or character, a myth, a biblical reference, and so forth.

He is a Samson of strength but a Judas of duplicity.

He dreamed of Thebes and Camelot,
And Priam's neighbors. (Edwin Arlington Robinson)

Metonymy: use of a related object to stand for the thing actually being talked about.

It's the only white-collar street in this blue-collar town.

And O ye high-flown quills that soar the skies,
And ever with your prey still catch your praise. (Anne Bradstreet)

Here, Bradstreet speaks of critics who may be hostile to her work. She identifies them as "quills," referring to their quill pens.

He stood among a crowd at Dromahair;
His heart hung all upon a silken dress. (William Butler Yeats)

The title character of "The Man Who Dreamed of Faeryland" was interested in the woman *in* the dress, not the dress itself.

Synecdoche: use of a part for the whole, or vice versa (very similar to metonymy).

The crowned heads of Europe were in attendance.
Before the indifferent beak could let her drop. (William Butler Yeats)

Personification: giving human characteristics to nonhuman things or to abstractions.

Justice weighs the evidence in her golden scales.
The ocean cursed and spat at us.

Of all her train, the hands of Spring
First plant thee in the watery mould. (William Cullen Bryant)

Bryant personifies spring by giving it hands with which to plant a yellow violet, which is one of the first wildflowers to appear in the season.

Apostrophe: a variety of personification in which a nonhuman thing, abstraction, or person not physically present is directly addressed as if it could respond.

Milton! Thou shouldst be living at this hour. (William Wordsworth)

Is it, O man, with such discordant noises,
With such accursed instruments as these,
Thou drownest Nature's sweet and kindly voices,
And jarrest the celestial harmonies? (Henry Wadsworth Longfellow)

Longfellow is addressing the human race in general.

Paradox: an apparent contradiction or illogical statement.

> I'll never forget old what's-his-name.

> *His hand hath made this noble work which Stands,*
> *His Glorious Handiwork not made by hands.* (Edward Taylor)

Taylor is describing God's creation of the universe, which He willed into being out of nothingness.

Oxymoron: a short paradox, usually consisting of an adjective and noun with conflicting meanings.

> The touch of her lips was sweet agony.

> *Progress is a comfortable disease* (e. e. cummings)

> *A terrible beauty is born.* (William Butler Yeats)

Synesthesia: a conscious mixing of two different types of sensory experience.

> A raw, red wind rushed from the north.

> *Leaves cast in casual potpourris*
> *Whisper their scents from pits and cellar-holes* (Richard Wilbur)

Transferred epithet: not, strictly speaking, a trope, it occurs when an adjective is "transferred" from the word it actually modifies to a nearby word.

> *The plowman homeward plods his weary way.* (Thomas Gray)

In this example, the plowman is weary, not the path ("way") he walks upon.

Allegory and Symbol

Related to the figurative devices are the various types of symbolism that may occur in poems. In many cases, a poem may seem so simple on the surface that we feel impelled to read deeper meanings into it. Robert Frost's famous lyric "Stopping by Woods on a Snowy Evening" is a classic case in point. There is nothing wrong with searching for larger significance in a poem, but the reader should perhaps be wary of leaping to conclusions about symbolic meanings before fully exhausting the literal sense of a poem. Whatever the case, both allegory and symbolism share the demand that the reader supply abstract or general meanings to the specific concrete details of the poem.

The simplest form that this substitution takes occurs in **allegory**. An allegory is usually a narrative that exists on at least two levels simultaneously, a concrete literal level and a second level of abstract meaning; throughout an allegory a consistent sequence of parallels exists between the literal and the abstract. Sometimes allegories may imply third or fourth levels of meaning as well, especially in long allegorical poems like Dante's *The Divine Comedy*, which has been interpreted on personal, political, ethical, and Christian levels. The characters and actions in an allegory explicitly signify the abstract level of meaning, and generally this second level of meaning is what the poet primarily intends to convey. For example, Robert Southwell's "The Burning Babe" is filled with fantastic incidents and paradoxical speech that are made clear in the poem's last line: "And straight I callèd unto mind that it was Christmas day." The literal burning babe of the title is the Christ child, who predicts his own future to the amazed watcher. Thus, in interpreting the poem, the reader must substitute theological terms like "redemption" or "original sin" for the literal details it contains.

Two types of prose allegories, the fable and parable, have been universally popular. A fable is a short, nonrealistic narrative that is told to illustrate a universal moral concept. A parable is similar but generally contains realistic characters and events. Thus, Aesop's fable of the tortoise and the hare, instead of telling us something about animal behavior, illustrates the virtue of persistence against seemingly unbeatable competition. Jesus's parable of the Good Samaritan tells the story of a man who is robbed and beaten and eventually rescued by a stranger of another race in order to define the concept of "neighbor" for a questioning lawyer. Poetic allegories like George Herbert's "Redemption" or Christina Rossetti's "Up-Hill" can be read in Christian terms as symbolic accounts of the process of salvation. Robert Burns's witty ballad "John Barleycorn" tells on the literal surface the story of a violent murder, but the astute reader quickly discovers that the underlying meaning involves the poet's native Scotland's legendary talent for distilling and consuming strong drink.

Many poems contain symbolic elements that are somewhat more elusive in meaning than the simple one-for-one equivalences presented by allegory. A **symbol**, then, is any concrete thing or any action in a poem that implies a meaning beyond its literal sense. Many of these things or actions are called **traditional symbols**, that is, symbols that hold roughly the same meanings for members of a given society.

Certain flowers, colors, natural objects, and religious emblems possess meanings that we can generally agree on. A white lily and a red rose suggest, respectively, mourning and passion. Few Western cultures would associate a black dress with a festive occasion or a red one with purity and innocence. Dawn and rainbows are traditional natural symbols of hope and new beginnings. It would be unlikely for a poet to mention a cross without expecting readers to think of its Christian symbolism. Other types of symbols can be identified in poems that are otherwise not allegorical. A **private symbol** is one that has acquired certain meanings from a single poet's repeated use of it. William Butler Yeats's use of "gyres" in several poems like "The Second Coming" is explained in some of his prose writings as a symbol for the turning of historical cycles, and his use of the word in his poems obviously goes beyond the literal level. Some visionary poets like Yeats and William Blake devised complicated private symbolic systems, a sort of alternative mythology, and understanding the full import of these symbols becomes primarily the task of critics who have specialized in these poets. Other poets may employ **incidental symbols**, things that are not usually considered symbolic but may be in a particular poem, or symbolic acts, a situation or response that seems of greater than literal import. As noted earlier, one of the most famous poems using these two devices is Robert Frost's "Stopping by Woods on a Snowy Evening." In this poem some readers see the "lovely, dark and deep" woods as both inviting and threatening and want to view the persona's rejection of their allure ("But I have promises to keep / And miles to go before I sleep") as some sort of life-affirming act. Frost himself was not particularly helpful in guiding his readers, often scoffing at those who had read too much metaphysical portent into such a simple lyric, although in other poems he presents objects such as a fork in the road or an abandoned woodpile in a manner that leads the reader to feel that these obviously possess some larger significance. Many modern poems remain so enigmatic that readers have consistently returned to them seeking new interpretations. Poems like these were to a degree influenced by the Symbolists, a group of French poets of the late nineteenth century, who deliberately wrote poems filled with vague nuances subject to multiple interpretations. Such American attempts at symbolist experiments as Wallace Stevens's "Anecdote of the Jar" or "The Emperor of Ice-Cream" continue to perplex and fascinate readers, particularly those who are versed in recent schools of interpretation that focus on the indeterminacy of a poetic text.

Tone of Voice

Even the simplest statement is subject to multiple interpretations if it is delivered in several different tones of voice. Consider the shift in emphasis between saying "*I* gave you the money," "I *gave* you the money," and "I gave *you* the money." Even a seemingly innocent compliment like "You look lovely this morning" takes on a different meaning if it is delivered by a woman on New Year's Day to her hungover husband. Still, these variations in **tone**, the speaker's implied attitude toward the words he or she says, depend primarily on vocal inflection. Because a poet only rarely gets the opportunity to elucidate his tones in a public performance, it is possible that readers may have difficulties in grasping the tone of a poem printed on the page. Still, many poems establish their tone quite clearly from the outset. The opening of Milton's sonnet "On the Late Massacre in Piedmont" ("Avenge, O Lord, thy slaughtered saints . . .") establishes a tone of righteous anger that is consistent throughout the poem. Thus, in many cases we can relate the tone of voice in poems to the emotions we employ in our own speech, and we would have to violate quite a few rules of common sense to argue that Milton is being flippant.

Irony is the element of tone by which a poet may imply an attitude that is in fact contrary to what his words appear to say. Of course, the simplest form of irony is **sarcasm**, the wounding tone of voice we use to imply exactly the opposite of what we say: "That's really a *great* excuse!" or "What a *wonderful* performance!" For obvious reasons, sarcasm is appropriate primarily to spoken language. It has become almost universal to follow a bit of gentle sarcasm in an e-mail message with a symbolic :) to indicate that the remark is not to be taken "straight." **Verbal irony** is the conscious manipulation of tone by which the poet's actual attitude is the opposite of what he says. In a poem like Thomas Hardy's "The Ruined Maid," it is obvious that one speaker considers the meaning of "ruined" to be somewhat less severe than the other, and the whole poem hinges on this ironic counterpoint of definitions and the different moral and social attitudes they imply. Consider the opening lines of Oliver Wendell Holmes's "Old Ironsides," a piece of propaganda verse that succeeded in raising enough money to save the U.S.S. *Constitution* from the scrapyard: "Ay, tear her tattered ensign down! / Long has it waved on high, / And many an eye has danced to see / That banner in the sky. . . ." Because Holmes's poetic mission is to *save* the ship, it is obvious that he is speaking ironically in the opening line; he emphatically *does not* want the ship's flag stripped from her, an attitude that is made clear in the third and fourth lines. Verbal irony is also a conspicuous feature of **verse satire**, poetry that exists primarily to mock or ridicule, although often with serious intent. One famous example, in the form of a short satirical piece, or **epigram**, is Sarah N. Cleghorn's "The Golf Links," a poem written before the advent of child labor laws:

> The golf links lie so near the mill
>> That almost every day
> The laboring children can look out
>> And see the men at play.

Here the weight of the verbal irony falls on two words, "laboring" and "play," and the way each is incongruously applied to the wrong group of people.

"The Golf Links," taken as a whole, also represents a second form of irony, **situational irony**, in which the setting of the poem (laboring children watching playing adults) contains a built-in incongruity. One master of ironic situation is Thomas Hardy, who used the title "Satires of Circumstance" in a series of short poems illustrating this sort of irony. Hardy's "Ah, Are You Digging on My Grave?" hinges on this kind of irony, with a ghostly persona asking questions of living speakers who end up offering little comfort to the dead woman. **Dramatic irony**, the third type of irony, occurs when the persona of a poem is less aware of the full import of his or her words than is the reader. William Blake's "The Chimney Sweeper" (from *Songs of Innocence*) is spoken by a child who does not seem to fully realize how badly he is being exploited by his employer, who has apparently been using the promises of religion as a way of keeping his underage workers in line. A similar statement could be made of the persona of Walter Savage Landor's short dramatic monologue "Mother, I Cannot":

> Mother, I cannot mind my wheel;
>> My fingers ache, my lips are dry:
> Oh! if you felt the pain I feel!
>> But oh, who ever felt as I?
>
> No longer could I doubt him true;
>> All other men may use deceit:
> He always said my eyes were blue,
>> And often swore my lips were sweet.

The young woman who speaks here apparently has not realized (or is deliberately unwilling to admit) that she has been sexually deceived and deserted by a scoundrel; "All other men may use deceit" gives the measure of her tragic naïvete. Dramatic irony, as the term implies, is most often found in dramatic monologues, where the gap between the speaker's perception of the situation and the reader's may be wide indeed.

Repetition: Sounds and Schemes

Because poetry uses language at its most intense level, we are aware of the weight of individual words and phrases to a degree that is usually lacking when we read prose. Poets have long known that the meanings that they attempt to convey often depend as much on the sound of the words as their meaning. We have already mentioned one sound device, onomatopoeia. Consider how much richer the experience of "the murmuring of innumerable bees" is than a synonymous phrase, "the faint sound of a lot of bees." It has often been said that all art aspires to the condition of music in the way that it affects an audience on some unconscious, visceral level. By carefully exploiting the repetition of sound devices, a poet may attempt to produce some of the same effects that the musical composer does.

Of course, much of this sonic level of poetry is subjective; what strikes one listener as pleasant may overwhelm the ear of another. Still, it is useful to distinguish between a poet's use of **euphony**, a series of pleasant sounds, and **cacophony**, sounds that are deliberately unpleasant. Note the following passages from Alexander Pope's "An Essay on Criticism," a didactic poem which attempts to illustrate many of the devices poets use:

> Soft is the strain when Zephyr gently blows,
> And the smooth stream in smoother numbers flows . . .

The repetition of the initial consonant sounds is called **alliteration**, and here Pope concentrates on the s sound. The vowel sounds are generally long: strain, blows, smooth, and flows. Here the description of the gentle west wind is assisted by the generally pleasing sense of euphony. But Pope, to illustrate the opposite quality, follows this couplet with a second:

But when loud surges lash the sounding shore,
The hoarse, rough verse should like the torrent roar.

Now the wind is anything but gentle, and the repetition of the r sounds in su*r*ges, sho*r*e, hoa*r*se, *r*ough, ve*r*se, to*r*rent, and *r*oar force the reader to speak from the back of the throat, making sounds that are anything but euphonious.

Repetition of sounds has no inherent meaning values (although some linguists may argue that certain sounds do stimulate particular emotions), but this repetition does call attention to itself and can be particularly effective when a poet wishes to emphasize a certain passage. We have already mentioned alliteration. Other sound patterns are **assonance**, the repetition of similar vowel sounds (st*ee*p, *e*ven, rec*ei*ve, v*ea*l), and **consonance**, the repetition of similar consonant sounds (du*ck*, tor*que*, stri*ke*, tri*ck*le). It should go without saying that spelling has little to do with any sound pattern; an initial *f* will alliterate with an initial *ph*.

Rhyme is the most important sound device, and our pleasure in deftly executed rhymes (consider the possibilities of rhyming "neighbor" with "sabre," as Richard Wilbur does in one of his translations) goes beyond mere sound to include the pleasure we take when an unexpected word is magically made to fit with another. There are several types of rhyme. **Masculine rhyme** occurs between single stressed syllables: *fleece, release, surcease, niece,* and so on. **Feminine rhyme**, also called **double rhyme**, matches two syllables, the first stressed and the second usually unstressed: *stinging, upbringing, flinging.* **Triple rhyme** goes further: *slithering, withering.* **Slant rhyme** (also called **near rhyme** and **off rhyme**) contains hints of sound repetition (sometimes related to assonance and consonance): *chill, dull,* and *sale* are possibilities, although contemporary poets often grant themselves considerable leeway in counting as rhyming words pairs that often have only the slightest similarity. When rhymes fall in a pattern in a poem and are **end rhymes**, occurring at the ends of lines, it is then convenient to assign letters to the sounds and speak of a **rhyme scheme**. Thus, a stanza of four lines ending with *heaven, hell, bell, eleven* would be said to have a rhyme scheme of *abba*. Rhymes may also occasionally be found in the interior of lines, which is called **internal rhyme**. Note how both end and internal rhymes work in the complex stanza which Poe uses in "The Raven."

More complicated patterns of repetition involve more than mere sounds but whole phrases and grammatical units. Ancient rhetoricians, teaching the art of public speaking, identified several of these, and they are also found in poetry. **Parallel structure** is simply the repetition of grammatically similar phrases or clauses: Tennyson's "To strive, to seek, to find, and not to yield." **Anaphora** and **epistrophe** are repeated words or phrases at, respectively, the beginning and end of lines. Walt Whitman uses these schemes extensively, often in the same lines. This passage from "Song of Myself" illustrates both anaphora and epistrophe:

> If they are not yours as much as mine they are nothing, or next
> to nothing,
> If they are not the riddle and the untying of the riddle they are
> nothing,
> If they are not just as close as they are distant they are nothing.

Antithesis is the matching of parallel units that contain contrasting meanings, such as Whitman's "I am of old and young, of the foolish as much as the wise, / Regardless of others, ever regardful of others, / Maternal as well as paternal, a child as well as a man. . . ." Although the rhetorical schemes are perhaps more native to the orator, the poet can still make occasional effective use of them. Whitman's poetry was influenced by many sources but by none perhaps so powerfully as the heavily schematic language of the King James Bible.

Meter and Rhythm

The subject of poetic meter and rhythm can be a difficult one, to say the least, and it is doubtless true that such phrases as *trochaic octameter* or *spondaic substitution* have an intimidating quality. Still, discussions of meter need not be limited to experts, and even beginning readers should be able to apply a few of the metrical principles that are commonly found in poetry written in English.

First, let us distinguish between two terms that are often used synonymously: **poetry** and **verse**. Poetry refers to a whole genre of literature and thus stands with fiction and drama as one of the three major types of writing, whereas verse refers to a mode of writing in lines of a certain length; thus, many poets still retain the old practice of capitalizing the first word of each line to indicate its integrity as a unit of composition. Virtually any piece of writing can be versified (and sometimes rhymed as well). Especially useful are bits of **mnemonic verse**, in which information like the number of days in the months (thirty days hath September . . .) or simple spelling rules ("I before E / Except after

C . . .") is cast in a form that is easy to remember. Although it is not strictly accurate to do so, many writers use verse to denote metrical writing that somehow does not quite measure up to the level of true poetry; phrases like **light verse** or **occasional verse** (lines written for a specific occasion, like a birthday or anniversary) are often used in this manner.

If a writer is unconcerned about the length of individual lines and is governed only by the width of the paper being used, then he or she is not writing verse but **prose**. All verse is metrical writing; prose is not. Surprisingly enough, there is a body of writing called **prose poetry**, which uses language in a poetic manner but avoids any type of meter; Carolyn Forché's "The Colonel" is one example. Perhaps the simplest way to think of **meter** in verse is to think of its synonym **measure** (think of the use of meter in words like odometer or kilometer). Thus, meter refers to the method by which a poet determines line length.

When we talk about meter in poetry we ordinarily mean that the poet is employing some kind of consistent **prosody** or system of measurement. There are many possible prosodies, depending on what the poet decides to count as the unit of measurement in the line, but only three of these systems are common in English poetry. Perhaps the simplest is **syllabic verse**. In verse of this type, the length of the line is determined by counting the total number of syllables the line contains (Sylvia Plath's "Metaphors," for one example, uses lines of nine syllables, a witty metaphor for the poem's subject, pregnancy). Much French poetry of the past was written in twelve-syllable lines, or **Alexandrines**, and in English a word like **octosyllabic** denotes a line of eight syllables. Because English is a language of strong stresses, most of our poets have favored other prosodic systems, but syllabic poetry has been attempted by many poets, among them Marianne Moore, Richard Wilbur, and Dylan Thomas. Moore, in particular, often wrote in **quantitative syllabics**, that is, stanzas containing the same number of lines with identical numbers of syllables in the corresponding lines of different stanzas. Moore's "The Fish" uses stanzas made of lines of one, three, eight, one, six, and eight syllables, respectively.

More natural to the English language is **accentual** verse, a prosodic system in which only accented or strongly stressed syllables are counted in a line, which can also contain a varying number of unaccented syllables. Much folk poetry, perhaps intended to be recited to the beat of a percussion instrument, retains this stress-based pattern, and the oldest verse in the British tradition, Anglo-Saxon poetry like *Beowulf*, is composed in four-stress lines which were recited to musical accompaniment. Many of the verses we re-call from nursery rhymes, children's chanting games ("Red rover, red rover, / Send [any name from one to four syllables can be substituted here—*Bill, Susan, Latisha, Elizabeth*] right over"), and sports cheers ("Two bits, four bits, six bits, a dollar! / All for the [*Owls, Cowboys, Cardinals, Thundering Herd*] stand up and holler!") retain the strong sense of rhythmical pulse that characterizes much accentual verse, a fact we recognize when we clap our hands and move rhythmically to the sound of the words. Indeed, the lyrics to much current rap music are actually composed to a four-stress accentual line, and the stresses or "beats" can be heard plainly when we listen or dance. Gerard Manley Hopkins, attempting to recapture some of the flavor of Anglo-Saxon verse, pioneered a type of accentual prosody that he called **sprung rhythm**, in which he counted only the strong stresses in his lines. Accentual meters still supply possibilities for contempo-rary poets; indeed, what often appears to be free verse is revealed, on closer inspection, to be a poem written in accentual meter. Richard Wilbur's "The Writer," for example, is written in a stanza containing lines of three, five, and three strong stresses, respectively, but the stresses do not overwhelm the reader's ear.

Accentual-syllabic verse is the most important prosodic system in English, dominating our poetry for the five centuries from Chaucer's time down to the early years of the twentieth century. Even though in the last seventy years or so free verse has become the prevailing style in which poetry is written, accentual-syllabic verse still has many able practitioners. An accentual-syllabic prosody is somewhat more compli-cated than the two systems we have mentioned because it requires that the poet count both the strongly stressed syllables and the total num-ber of syllables in the line. Because stressed and unstressed syllables al-ternate fairly regularly in this system, four **metrical feet**, representing the most common patterns, designate the subdivisions of rhythm that make up the line (think of a yardstick divided into three feet). These feet are the **iamb** (or **iambic foot**), one unstressed and one stressed syl-lable; the **trochee** (or **trochaic foot**), one stressed and one unstressed syllable; the **anapest** (or **anapestic foot**), two unstressed syllables and one stressed syllable; and the **dactyl** (or **dactylic foot**), one stressed and two unstressed syllables. The first two of these, iambic and trochaic, are called **double meters**; the second two, **triple meters**. Iambic and anapestic meters are sometimes called **rising meters** because they "rise" toward the stressed syllable; trochaic and dactylic meters are called **falling meters** for the opposite reason. Simple repetition of words or phrases can give us the sense of how these lines sound in a purely schematic sense. The **breve** (˘) and **ictus** (ˊ) are used to denote unstressed and stressed syllables, respectively.

Iambic:

rĕleáse / rĕleáse / rĕleáse
tŏ fáll / iňtó /dĕspáir
 Marĭe / dĭscóv /eřs cándy̆

Trochaic:

mélti̇ňg / mélti̇ňg / mélti̇ňg / mélti̇ňg
Pétĕr / disă /gréed eň / tírely̆
clevĕr / wŕiti̇ňg / filled the /páge

Anapestic:

uňcoňtrólled / uňcoňtrólled
ă rĕtríev / ĕr ăppéared
aňd ă tér / řible thúndĕr

Dactylic:

shíveri̇ňg / shíveri̇ňg / shíveri̇ňg / shíveri̇ňg /shíveri̇ňg
térřibly̆ / iĺl wi̇th the / sýmptoms̆ ŏf / virăl pňeu / mŏňiă
nóte hŏw the / miništĕr / whíspeřed ăt / Émily̆'s / gráve

Because each of these lines contains a certain number of feet, a second specialized term is used to denote how many times a pattern is repeated in a line:

one foot	**monometer**
two feet	**dimeter**
three feet	**trimeter**
four feet	**tetrameter**
five feet	**pentameter**
six feet	**hexameter**
seven feet	**heptameter**
eight feet	**octameter**

Thus, in the examples above, the first set of lines is iambic trimeter; the second, trochaic tetrameter; the third, anapestic dimeter; and the fourth, dactylic pentameter. The third lines in the iambic and anapestic examples are **hypermetrical**; that is, they contain an extra unstressed syllable or **feminine ending**. Conversely, the third lines in the trochaic and dactylic examples are missing one and two unstressed final syllables, respectively, a common practice called **catalexis**. Although over thirty combinations of foot type and number per line theoretically are possible, relatively few are ordinarily encountered in poetry. The iambic foot is most common in English, followed by the anapest and the trochee; the dactylic foot is relatively rare. Line lengths tend to be from three to five feet, with anything shorter or longer used only sparingly. Still, there are famous exceptions like Poe's "The Raven," which is composed in trochaic octameters and tetrameters, or Southwell's "The Burning Babe," written in iambic heptameter. Long trochaic and iambic lines sometimes exhibit a kind of rhythmical counterpoint. In the opening line of John Whitworth's "The Examiners," for example, the line of trochaic octameter really has only four strong stresses: "Where the HOUSE is cold and EMPty and the GARden's over-GROWN." Verse like this is called **dipodic** ("double-footed") because two feet (/u|/u) are combined into a single unit (uu/u).

Meter denotes regularity, the "blueprint" for a line from which the poet works. Because iambic pentameter is the most common meter used in English poetry, our subsequent discussion will focus on poems written in it. Most poets quickly learn that a metronomic regularity, five iambic feet marching in lockstep line after line, is not a virtue and quickly becomes predictable. Thus, there are several ways by which poets can add variety to their lines so that the actual **rhythm** of the line, what is actually heard, plays a subtle counterpoint against the regularity of the meter. One way is to vary the placement of the **caesura** (||) or pause within a line (usually indicated by a mark of punctuation). Another is by mixing **end-stopped lines**, which clearly pause at their conclusion, with **enjambed** lines, which run on into the next line with no pause. The following lines from Tennyson's "Ulysses" illustrate these techniques:

> This is my son, mine own Telemachus,
> To whom I leave the scepter and the isle,
> Well-loved of me, discerning to fulfill
> This labor, by slow prudence to make mild
> A rugged people, and through soft degrees
> Subdue them to the useful and the good.

Lines two and six have no caesurae; the others do, after either the third, fourth, or fifth syllable. Lines one, two, and six are end-stopped; the others are enjambed (or use **enjambment**).

Another technique of varying regularity is **metrical substitution**, where feet of a different type are substituted for what the meter calls for. In iambic meter, trochaic feet are often encountered at the beginnings of lines, or after a caesura. Two other feet, the **pyrrhic** (˘˘) consisting of two unstressed syllables, and the **spondee** (´´), consisting of two stressed syllables, are also commonly substituted. Here are Tennyson's lines with their scansion marked.

Thís iš / m̆y són, ‖ / mĭne ówn / T̆elém / ăchús,
T̆o whóm / Ĭ leáve / thĕ scép / tĕr aňd / thĕ ísle,
Wéll-lóved / ŏf m̆e, / ‖ / discérn / iňg tŏ / fŭlfíll
This lá / bŏr, ‖ by / slow prú / dĕnce t̆o máke míld
Ă rúg / gĕd peó / pl̆e, ‖ aňd / thrŏugh sóft / dĕgrées
Sŭbdúe / thĕm tŏ / thĕ uśe / fŭl aňd / thĕ góod.

Even though these are fairly regular iambic pentameter lines, it should be observed that no single line is without some substitution. Still, the dominant pattern of five iambic feet per line should be apparent (out of thirty total feet, about twenty are iambs); there is even a strong tendency on the reader's part to "promote" the middle syllable of three unstressed syllables ("Subdue / them *to* / the use / ful *and* / the good") to keep the sense of the iambic rhythm.

How far can a poet depart from the pattern without losing contact with the original meter? That is a question that is impossible to answer in general terms. The following scansion will probably strike us at first as a far departure from regular iambic pentameter:

´ ‖ ´/˘ ‖ ´/ ˘˘ ‖ ´´˘ / ˘´

Yet it is actually the opening line of one of Shakespeare's most often quoted passages, Mark Antony's funeral oration from *Julius Caesar*:

Fríends, ‖ Ró / măns, ‖ cóun, ‖ trȳmeň, ‖ / lénd m̆e / yŏur eárs

Poets who have learned to use the full resources of meter do not consider it a restraint; instead, they are able to stretch the pattern to its limits without breaking it. A good analogy might be made between poetry and dance. Beginning dancers watch their feet and count the steps while making them; after considerable practice, the movements become second nature, and a skillful pair of partners can add dips and passes without losing the basic step of the music.

Free Verse and Open Form

Nothing has been so exhaustively debated in English-language poetry as the exact nature of **free verse**. The simplest definition may be the best: free verse is verse with no consistent metrical pattern. In free verse, line length is a subjective decision made by the poet, and length may be determined by grammatical phrases, the poet's own sense of individual "breath-units," or even by the visual arrangement of lines on the page. Clearly, it is easier to speak of what free verse is not than to explain what it is. Even its practitioners do not seem very happy with the term free verse, which is derived from the French *vers libre*. The extensive use of free verse is a fairly recent phenomenon in the history of poetry. Even though there are many examples of free verse from the past (the Psalms, Ecclesiastes, and the Song of Solomon from the King James Bible), the modern history of free verse begins in 1855 with the publication of Walt Whitman's *Leaves of Grass*. Whitman, influenced by Ralph Waldo Emerson's statement that "it is not meters but meter-making argument that makes a poem," created a unique variety of long-line free verse based on grammatical units—phrases and clauses. Whitman's free verse is so distinctive that he has had few direct imitators, and subsequent poets who have used free verse have written lines that vary widely in syllable count. Good free verse, as T. S. Eliot remarked, still contains some kind of "ghost of meter," and its rhythms can be as terse and clipped as those of Philip Levine or as lushly sensuous as those of Pattiann Rogers. The poet who claims that free verse is somehow easier to write than metrical verse would find many arguments to the contrary. As Eliot said, "No verse is free for the poet who wants to do a good job."

All poems have form, the arrangement of the poem on the page that differentiates it from prose. Sometimes this arrangement indicates that the poet is following a preconceived plan—a metrical pattern, a rhyme scheme, a purely visual design like that of **concrete** or **spatial poetry**, or a scheme like that of **acrostic verse**, in which the first letters of the lines spell a message. An analysis of poetic form notes how the lines are arranged, how long they are, and how they are grouped into blocks or **stanzas**. Further analysis might reveal the existence of types of repetition, rhyme, or the use of a **refrain**, or a repeated line or groups of lines. A large number of the poems composed in the twentieth and twenty-first centuries have been written in **open form**, which simply means that there is no strict pattern of regularity in the elements mentioned above; that is, there is no consistent meter and no rhyme scheme. Still, even a famous poem in open form like William Carlos Williams's "The Red Wheelbarrow" can be described in formal terms:

so much depends
upon

a red wheel
barrow

glazed with rain
water

beside the white
chickens.

Here we observe that the eight-line poem is divided into **uniform stanzas** of two lines each (or couplets). Line length varies between four and two syllables per line. The odd-numbered lines each contain three words; the even, one. Although there is no apparent use of rhyme or repetition here, many poems in open form contain some rhyme and metrical regularity at their conclusions. Alan Dugan's "Love Song: I and Thou" falls into regular iambic tetrameter in its final lines, and a typical contemporary example of an open form poem, Naomi Shihab Nye's "The Traveling Onion," concludes with a closing rhyme on "career" and "disappear."

Closed form, unlike open form, denotes the existence of some kind of regular pattern of meter, stanza, rhyme, or repetition. **Stanza forms** are consistent patterns in the individual units of the poem (stanza means "room" in Italian); **fixed forms** are patterns that encompass a complete poem, for example, a sonnet or a villanelle. **Traditional forms** are patterns that have been used for long periods of time and thus may be associated with certain subjects, themes, or types of poems; the sonnet is one example, for it has been used primarily (but by no means exclusively) for lyric poetry. **Nonce forms** are patterns that originate in an individual poem and have not been widely used by other poets. Of course, it goes without saying that every traditional form was at first a nonce form; the Italian poet (now lost to memory) who first wrote a lyric consisting of fourteen rhymed eleven-syllable lines could not have foreseen that in subsequent centuries poets the world over would produce literally millions of sonnets that are all variations on the original model. Some of the most common stanza and fixed forms are briefly discussed herein.

Stanza Forms

Blank verse is not, strictly speaking, a stanza form because it consists of individual lines of iambic pentameter that do not rhyme. However, long poems in blank verse may be arranged into **verse paragraphs** or stanzas with a varying number of lines. Blank verse originally appeared in English with the Earl of Surrey's translation of the *Aeneid* in the fifteenth century; it has been used extensively for narrative and dramatic purposes since then, particularly in epics like Milton's *Paradise Lost* and in Shakespeare's plays. Also written in stanzas of varying lengths is the **irregular ode**, a poem which employs lines of varying lengths (although usually of a regular rhythm that is iambic or matches one of the other feet) and an irregular rhyme scheme.

Paired rhyming lines *(aabbcc . . .)* are called **couplets**, although they are only rarely printed as separate stanzas. **Short couplets** have a meter of iambic tetrameter (and are sometimes called **octosyllabic couplets**). If their rhymes are predominantly feminine and seem chosen for comic effect, they may be called **Hudibrastic couplets** after Samuel Butler's satirical poem *Hudibras* of the late 1600s. **Heroic couplets** have a meter of iambic pentameter and have often been used effectively in satirical poems like Alexander Pope's "mock heroic" poem *The Dunciad* and even in dramatic monologues like Robert Browning's "My Last Duchess," where the rhymes are so effectively buried by enjambment that the poem approximates speech. Two other couplet forms, both rare, are poulter's *measure,* rhyming pairs of alternating lines of iambic hexameter and iambic heptameter, and *fourteeners,* pairs of iambic heptameter (fourteen-syllable) lines which, because a natural caesura usually falls after the fourth foot, closely resemble common meter (see below).

A three-line stanza is called a **tercet**. If it rhymes in an *aaa bbb . . .* pattern, it is a **triplet**; sometimes triplets appear in poems written in heroic couplets, especially at the end of sections or where special emphasis is desired. Iambic pentameter tercets rhyming *aba bcb cdc . . .* form **terza rima**, a pattern invented by Dante for *The Divine Comedy.*

A four-line stanza is known as a **quatrain**. Alternating lines of tetrameter and trimeter in any foot, rhyming *abcb* or *abab*, make up a

ballad stanza; if the feet are strictly iambic, then the quatrain is called **common meter**, the form of many popular hymns like "Amazing Grace." **Long meter**, also widely used in hymns, consists of iambic tetrameter lines rhyming *abcb* or *abab*; **short meter** has a similar rhyme scheme but contains first, second, and fourth lines of iambic trimeter and a third line of iambic tetrameter. The **In Memoriam stanza**, named after Tennyson's long poetic sequence, is iambic tetrameter rhyming *abba*. The **Rubaiyat stanza**, used by Frost in "Stopping by Woods on a Snowy Evening," is an import from Persia; and it consists of lines of either iambic tetrameter or pentameter, rhyming *aaba bbcb*. Lines of iambic pentameter rhyming *abab* are known as an **English quatrain**; lines of the same meter rhyming *abba* make up an **Italian quatrain**. One other unusual quatrain stanza is an import from ancient Greece, the **Sapphic stanza**, named after the poet Sappho. The Sapphic stanza consists of three **hendecasyllabic** (eleven-syllable) lines of this pattern:

$$ \prime\,/\mid\prime\,/\mid\prime\,/\mid\prime\,/\mid\prime\,/\,\prime $$

and a fourth line called an **Adonic**, which is five syllables long and consists of one dactylic foot and one trochaic foot. The Sapphic stanza is usually unrhymed. The quatrain stanza is also used in another import, the **pantoum**, a poem in which the second and fourth lines of the first stanza become the first and third of the second, and the second and fourth of the second become the first and third of the fourth, and so on. Pantoums may be written in any meter and may or may not employ rhyme.

A five-line stanza is known as a **quintet** and is relatively rare in English poetry. The **sestet**, or six-line stanza, can be found with a number of different meters and rhyme schemes. A seven-line stanza is called a **septet**; one septet stanza form is **rime royal**, seven lines of iambic pentameter rhyming *ababbcc*. An eight-line stanza is called an **octave**; one widely used stanza of this length is **ottava rima**, iambic pentameter lines rhyming *abababcc*. Another octave form is the **Monk's Tale stanza**, named after one of Chaucer's tales. It is iambic pentameter and rhymes *ababbcbc*. The addition of a ninth line, rhyming *c* and having a meter of iambic hexameter, makes a **Spenserian stanza**, named after Edmund Spenser, the poet who invented it for *The Faerie Queene*, a long metrical romance.

Fixed Forms

Fixed forms are combinations of meter, rhyme scheme, and repetition that comprise complete poems. One familiar three-line fixed form is the **haiku**, a Japanese import consisting of lines of five, seven, and five syllables, respectively.

The **clerihew**, named after its inventor, Edward Clerihew Bentley, is a humorous form in which the first line is a person's name; the clerihew has a rhyme scheme of *aa bb*.

Two five-line fixed forms are the **limerick** and the **cinquain**. The common and comic limerick consists of anapestic trimeter in lines one, two, and five, and anapestic dimeter in lines three and four. The rhymes, *aabba*, are usually double rhymes used for comic effect. Robert Conquest, the great historian of the purges of the Soviet Union, is also a celebrated poet and an accomplished author of limericks. Conquest memorably summed up his political conclusions in five lines:

> There was a great Marxist called Lenin
> Who did two or three million men in
> —That's a lot to have done in
> —But where he did one in
> That grand Marxist Stalin did ten in.

A cinquain, the invention of American poet Adelaide Crapsey (1878–1914), consists of five unrhymed lines of two, four, six, eight, and two syllables, respectively.

Two other short fixed forms, the **triolet** and the **double-dactyl**, have also proven popular. The eight-line triolet, a French form, uses two repeating lines in the pattern *ABaAabAB* with all lines having the same meter. The double-dactyl, which also is an eight-line form, was invented by the poets Anthony Hecht and John Hollander. The meter is dactylic dimeter with a rhyme scheme of *abcd efgd*. The other "rules" for the double-dactyl include a nonsense phrase in the first line, a person's name in the second, and a single word in the sixth. Here is an example, Leon Stokesbury's "Room with a View":

> Higgledy-piggledy
> Emily Dickinson
> Looked out her front window
> Struggling for breath—

Suffering slightly from
Agoraphobia:
"Think I'll just—stay in and—
Write about—Death—"

The most important of the fixed forms is the **sonnet**, which consists of fourteen lines of rhymed iambic pentameter. The original form of the sonnet is called the **Italian sonnet** or the **Petrarchan sonnet** after the fourteenth-century poet who popularized it. An Italian sonnet is usually cast in two stanzas, an octave rhyming *abbaabba* and a sestet with a variable rhyme scheme; *cdcdcd, cdecde,* and *cddcee* are some of the possible patterns. A **volta** or "turn," usually a conjunction or conjunctive adverb like "but" or "then," may appear at the beginning of the sestet, signifying a slight change of direction in thought. Many Italian sonnets have a strong logical connection between octave and sestet problem/solution, cause/effect, question/answer and the volta helps to clarify the transition. The **English sonnet**, also known as the **Shakespearean sonnet** after its prime exemplar, was developed in the sixteenth century after the sonnet was imported to England and employs a different rhyme scheme that takes into consideration the relative scarcity of rhymes in English (compared with Italian). The English sonnet has a rhyme scheme of *ababcdcdefefgg* and is usually printed as a single stanza. The pattern of three English quatrains plus a heroic couplet often forces a slightly different organizational scheme on the poet, although many of Shakespeare's sonnets still employ a strong volta at the beginning of the ninth line. Other English sonnets may withhold the turn until the beginning of the closing couplet. A third sonnet type, relatively rare, is the **Spenserian sonnet**, named after Edmund Spenser, author of *Amoretti,* one of the earliest sonnet sequences in English. The Spenserian sonnet rhymes *ababbcbccdcdee.* Many other sonnets have been written over the years that have other rhyme schemes, often hybrids of the Italian and English types. These are usually termed **nonce sonnets**. Shelley's "Ozymandias," with its unusual rhyme scheme of *ababacdcedefef,* is one notable example. In "Ode to the West Wind," Shelley employs a fourteen-line stanza rhyming *aba bcb cdc ded ee,* which has been called a **terza rima sonnet**.

Several other fixed forms, all French imports, have appeared frequently in English poetry. The eight-line **triolet**, usually written in iambic tetrameter, uses two refrains: *ABaAabAB.* The **rondeau** has fifteen lines of iambic tetrameter or pentameter arranged in three stanzas: *aabba aabR aabbaR;* the *R* here stands for the unrhymed refrain, which repeats the first few words of the poem's first line. A maddeningly complex variation is the twenty-five line **rondeau redoublé**, through which Wendy Cope wittily maneuvers in her poem of the same name. The **villanelle** is a nineteen-line poem, usually written in iambic pentameter, employing two refrain lines, A_1 and A_2, in a pattern of five tercets and a final quatrain: $A_1bA_2\ abA_1\ abA_2\ abA_1\ abA_2\ abA_1A_2$. A related form, also nineteen lines long, is the **terzanelle**, which uses several more repeating lines (capitalized here): $A_1BA_2\ bCB\ cDC\ dED\ eFE\ f\ A_1FA_2$. The **ballade** is twenty-eight lines of iambic tetrameter employing a refrain that appears at the end of its three octaves and final quatrain, or **envoy:** *ababbcbC ababbcbC ababbcbC bcbC.* Obviously the rhyming demands of the villanelle, the terzanelle, and the ballade pose serious challenges to English-language poets. A final fixed form is the thirty-nine-line **sestina**, which may be either metrical or in free verse and uses a complicated sequence repeating, in different order, the six words that end the lines of the initial stanza. The sequence for the first six sestets is *123456 615243 364125 532614 451362 246531.* A final tercet uses three words in the interior of the lines and three at the ends in the pattern *(2)5(4)3(6)1.* Many sestinas hinge on the poet's choice of six end words that have multiple meanings and can serve as more than one part of speech.

Two contemporary poets, Billy Collins and Kim Addonizio, have recently created nonce forms. Collins's tongue-in-cheek description of the **paradelle** was taken seriously by many readers, and a whole anthology of poems in the form has been assembled. Addonizio's personalized variation on the sonnet, the **sonnenizio**, has also been imitated by other poets. There are many other less familiar types of stanza forms and fixed forms. Lewis Turco's *The Book of Forms* and Miller Williams's *Patterns of Poetry* are two reference sources that are useful in identifying them.

Literary History and Poetic Conventions

What a poet attempts to do in any given poem is always governed by the tension that exists between originality and convention, or between the poet's desire, in Ezra Pound's famous phrase, to "make it new," and the various stylistic devices that other poets and readers are familiar with through their understanding of the poetic tradition. If we look at some of the most obscure passages of Pound's *Cantos* (a single page may contain passages in several foreign languages), we may think that the poet has departed about as far from conventional modes of expression as possible, leaving his audience far behind him. Yet it is important to keep two facts in mind. First, this style was not arrived at overnight; Pound's early poetry is relatively traditional and should present little difficulty to most readers. He arrived at the style of the *Cantos* after a twenty-year apprenticeship to the styles of writers as different as Li-Po, Robert Browning, and William Butler Yeats. Second, by the time Pound was writing his mature poetry the modernist movement was in full flower, forcing the public not only to read poems but also to look at paintings and sculpture and to listen to music in ways that would have been unimaginable only a decade or two earlier. When we talk about the stylistic conventions of any given literary period, we should keep in mind that poets are rarely willing to go much beyond what they have educated their audiences to understand. This mutual sense of agreement is the essence of poetic convention.

One should be wary of making sweeping generalizations about "schools" of poetry or the shared conventions of literary periods. In any era, there is always a significant amount of diversity among individual poets. Further, an anthology of this limited scope, which by its very nature must exclude most long poems, is likely to contribute to a misleading view of literary history and the development of poetry in English. When we read Shakespeare's or Milton's sonnets, we should not forget that their major reputations rest on poetry of a very different sort. The neoclassical era in English poetry, stretching from the late seventeenth century until almost the end of the eighteenth, is poorly represented in this anthology because the satires of John Dryden and Alexander Pope and long philosophical poems like Pope's *An Essay on Man* do not readily lend themselves to being excerpted (an exception is the section on meter from Pope's *An Essay on Criticism*). Edgar Allan Poe once claimed that a long poem is "simply a contradiction in terms," but the continued high reputations of *The Faerie Queene, Paradise Lost, Don Juan,* and even a modern verse-novella like Robinson Jeffers's "The Roan Stallion" demonstrate that Poe's was far from the last word on the subject.

The earliest poems in this volume, all anonymous, represent poetry's links to the oral folk tradition. The American folk songs that children learn to sing in elementary school represent our own inheritance of this rich legacy. The poets of the Tudor (1485–1558) and Elizabethan (1558–1603) eras excelled at lyric poetry; Sir Thomas Wyatt and Henry Howard, Earl of Surrey, had imported the sonnet form from Italy, and the form was perfected during this period. Much of the love poetry of the age is characterized by conventional imagery, so-called Petrarchan conceits, which even a later poet like Thomas Campion employs in "There Is a Garden in Her Face" and which Shakespeare satirizes brilliantly in his Sonnet 130 ("My mistress' eyes are nothing like the sun").

The poetry of the first half of the seventeenth century has several major schools: A smooth lyricism influenced by Ben Jonson that can be traced through the work of Robert Herrick, Edmund Waller, and Richard Lovelace; a serious body of devotional poetry by John Donne, George Herbert, and John Milton; and the metaphysical style, which uses complex extended metaphors or metaphysical conceits—Donne and Herbert are its chief exemplars, followed by the early American poets Anne Bradstreet and Edward Taylor. Shortly after the English Restoration in 1660, a profound period of conservatism began in the arts, and the neoclassical era, lasting through most of the eighteenth century, drew heavily on Greek and Roman models. Poetry written during this period—the age of Jonathan Swift, Alexander Pope, and Thomas Gray—was dominated by one form, the heroic couplet; the genres of epic and satire; and an emphasis on human reason as the poet's chief guide. Never has the private voice been so subordinated to the public as in this period when, as Pope put it, a poet's highest aspiration should be to utter "What oft was thought, but ne'er so well expressed."

The first inklings of the romantic era coincide with the American and French revolutions, and poets of the latter half of the eighteenth century like Robert Burns and William Blake exhibit some of its characteristics. But it was not until the publication of *Lyrical Ballads*, a 1798 book containing the best early work of William Wordsworth and Samuel Taylor Coleridge, that the romantic era can be said to have truly flowered. Wordsworth's famous formulation of a poem as "the spontaneous overflow of powerful feeling recollected in tranquillity" remains one of romanticism's key definitions, with its emphasis on emotion and immediacy and reflection; Wordsworth's own poetry, with its focus on the natural world, was tremendously influential. Most of the English and American poets of the first half of the nineteenth century have ties to romanticism in its various guises, and even a poet as late as Walt Whitman (b. 1819) inherits many of its liberal, democratic attitudes. Poets of the Victorian era (1837–1901), such as Alfred, Lord Tennyson and Robert Browning, continued to explore many of the same themes and genres as their romantic forebears, but certainly much of the optimism of the early years of the century had dissipated by the time poets like Thomas Hardy, A. E. Housman, and William Butler Yeats, with their omnipresent irony and pessimism, arrived on the scene in the century's last decades.

The twentieth century and the beginning of the twenty-first have been ruled by the upheavals that modernism caused in every art form. If anything characterized the first half of the twentieth century, it was its tireless experimentation with the forms of poetry. There is a continuum in English-language poetry from Chaucer through Robert Frost and Edwin Arlington Robinson, but Ezra Pound, T. S. Eliot, William Carlos Williams, and Marianne Moore, to mention only four chief modernists, published poetry that would have totally mystified readers of their grandparents' day, just as Picasso and Matisse produced paintings that represented radical breaks with the visual forms of the past. Although many of the experiments of movements like imagism and surrealism seem not much more than historical curiosities today, they parallel the unusual directions that most of the other arts took during the same period.

For the sake of convenience more than anything else, it has been useful to refer to the era following the end of World War II as the postmodern era. Certainly many of the hard-won modernist gains—open form and increased candor in language and subject matter—have been taken for granted by poets writing in the contemporary period. The confessional poem, a frankly autobiographical narrative that reveals what poets in earlier ages might have striven desperately to conceal, surfaced in the late 1950s in the works of Robert Lowell, W. D. Snodgrass, Sylvia Plath, and Anne Sexton, and remains one of the chief postmodern genres. Still, as the selections here will attest, there is considerable variety to be found in the contemporary scene, and it will perhaps be many years before critics have the necessary historical distance to assess the unique characteristics of the present period.

ANONYMOUS

Some of the popular ballads and lyrics of England and Scotland, composed for the most part between 1300 and 1500, were first collected in their current forms by Thomas Percy, whose Reliques of Ancient English Poetry *(1765) helped to revive interest in folk poetry. Francis James Child (1825–1896), an American, gathered over a thousand variant versions of the three hundred-odd core of poems. The Romantic poets of the early nineteenth century showed their debt to the folk tradition by writing imitative "art ballads" (see Keats's "La Belle Dame sans Merci" or Burns's "John Barleycorn"), which incorporate many of their stylistic devices.*

Western Wind

Western wind, when will thou blow,
    The small rain down can rain?
Christ, if my love were in my arms
    And I in my bed again!

—1450?

Bonny Barbara Allan

It was in and about the Martinmas° time,
    When the green leaves were a falling,
That Sir John Græme, in the West Country,
    Fell in love with Barbara Allan.

He sent his men down through the town,   5
    To the place where she was dwelling.
"O haste and come to my master dear,
    Gin° ye be Barbara Allan."

O hooly,° hooly rose she up,
    To the place where he was lying,   10
And when she drew the curtain by:
    "Young man, I think you're dying."

1 Martinmas November 11   **8 Gin** if   **9 hooly** slowly

BONNY BARBARA ALLAN

471

"O it's I'm sick, and very, very sick,
  And 'tis a'° for Barbara Allan."
"O the better for me ye s'° never be,   15
  Though your heart's blood were a-spilling."

"O dinna° ye mind, young man," said she,
  "When ye was in the tavern a drinking,
That ye made the healths gae° round and round,
  And slighted Barbara Allan?"   20

He turned his face unto the wall,
  And death was with him dealing:
"Adieu, adieu, my dear friends all,
  And be kind to Barbara Allan."

And slowly, slowly raise she up,   25
  And slowly, slowly left him,
And sighing said she could not stay,
  Since death of life had reft him.

She had not gane° a mile but twa,°
  When she heard the dead-bell ringing,   30
And every jow° that the dead-bell geid,°
  It cried, "Woe to Barbara Allan!"

"O mother, mother, make my bed!
  O make it saft° and narrow!
Since my love died for me to-day,   35
  I'll die for him to-morrow."

                                                              —1500?

Sir Patrick Spens

The king sits in Dumferling town,
  Drinking the blude-reid° wine:
"O whar will I get guid sailor,
  To sail this ship of mine?"

---

14 **a'** all   15 **s'** shall   17 **dinna** do not   19 **gae** go   29 **gane** gone   9 **twa** two   31 **jow** stroke
11 **geid** gave   34 **saft** soft
2 **blude-reid** blood-red

Up and spak an eldern knicht,°
    Sat at the king's richt° knee:
"Sir Patrick Spens is the best sailor
    That sails upon the sea."

The king has written a braid° letter,
    And signed it wi' his hand,
And sent it to Sir Patrick Spens,
    Was walking on the sand.

The first line that Sir Patrick read,
    A loud lauch° lauched he;
The next line that Sir Patrick read,
    The tear blinded his ee.°

"O wha is this has done this deed,
    This ill deed done to me,
To send me out this time o' the year,
    To sail upon the sea?

"Mak haste, mak haste, my mirry men all,
    Our guid ship sails the morn."
"O say na sae,° my master dear,
    For I fear a deadly storm.

"Late, late yestre'en° I saw the new moon,
    Wi' the auld moon in hir arm,
And I fear, I fear, my dear master,
    That we will come to harm."

O our Scots nobles wer richt laith°
    To weet° their cork-heeled shoon,°
But lang or a'° the play were played,
    Their hats they swam aboon.°

O lang, lang may their ladies sit,
    Wi' their fans into their hand,
Or ere they see Sir Patrick Spens
    Come sailing to the land.

5

10

15

20

25

30

35

---

5 eldern knicht elderly knight   **6 richt** right   **9 braid** long   **14 lauch** laugh   **16 ee** eye   **23 na sae** not so   **25 yestre'en** last evening   **29 laith** loath   **30 weet** wet   **23 shoon** shoes   **31 lang or a'** long before   **32 Their hats they swam aboon** their hats swam above them

O lang, lang may the ladies stand,
   Wi' their gold kems° in their hair,
Waiting for their ain dear lords,
   For they'll see them na mair.

Half o'er, half o'er to Aberdour
   It's fifty fadom deep,
And there lies guid Sir Patrick Spens
   Wi' the Scots lords at his feet.

—1500?

SIR THOMAS WYATT ■ (1503?–1542)

Sir Thomas Wyatt served Henry VIII as a diplomat in Italy. Wyatt read the love poetry of Petrarch (1304–1374) and is generally credited with having imported both the fashions of these lyrics—hyperbolic "conceits" or metaphorical descriptions of the woman's beauty and the lover's suffering—and their form, the sonnet, to England. "They Flee from Me," an example of one of his original lyrics, displays Wyatt's unique grasp of the rhythms of speech.

They Flee from Me

They flee from me, that sometime did me seek,
With naked foot stalking in my chamber.
I have seen them gentle, tame and meek,
That now are wild, and do not remember
That sometime they put themself in danger   5
To take bread at my hand; and now they range,
Busily seeking with a continual change.

Thanke'd be Fortune it hath been otherwise,
Twenty times better; but once in special,
In thin array, after a pleasant guise,°   10
When her loose gown from her shoulders did fall,
And she me caught in her arms long and small,
And therewith all sweetly did me kiss
And softly said, "Dear heart, how like you this?"

38 kems combs
10 guise appearance

40

474

It was no dream, I lay broad waking. 15
But all is turned, thorough° my gentleness,
Into a strange fashion of forsaking;
And I have leave to go, of her goodness,
And she also to use newfangleness.
But since that I so kindely° am served, 20
I fain° would know what she hath deserved.

—1557

Whoso List to Hunt

Whoso list° to hunt, I know where is an hind,°
But as for me, alas, I may no more:
The vain travail hath wearied me so sore.
I am of them that farthest cometh behind;
Yet may I by no means my wearied mind 5
Draw from the deer: but as she fleeth afore,
Fainting I follow. I leave off therefore,
Since in a net I seek to hold the wind.
Who list her to hunt, I put him out of doubt,
As well as I, may spend his time in vain: 10
And, graven with diamonds, in letters plain
There is written her fair neck round about:
Noli me tangere, for Caesar's I am,°
And wild for to hold, though I seem tame.

—1557

EDMUND SPENSER ■ (1552–1599)

Edmund Spenser was born in London, and spent most of his adult life in Ire-land, where he held a variety of minor government posts. The Faerie Queene, a long allegorical romance about Elizabethan England, was un-completed at his death. The eighty-odd sonnets that make up the sequence called Amoretti are generally thought to detail his courtship of his second wife, Elizabeth Boyle, whom he married in 1594.

---

16 thorough through   20 kindely in this manner   21 fain gladly
1 list desire   32 hind doe   13 *Noli me tangere* Touch me not; the poem is said to refer to the second
wife of Henry VIII, Anne Boleyn.

Amoretti: Sonnet 75

One day I wrote her name upon the strand,
But came the waves and washèd it away:
Agayne I wrote it with a second hand,°
But came the tyde, and made my paynes his pray.
"Vayne man," sayd she, "that doest in vaine assay,°   5
A mortall thing so to immortalize,
For I my selve shall lyke° to this decay
And eek° my name bee wypèd out lykewize."
"Not so," quod° I, "let baser things devize
To dy in dust, but you shall live by fame: 10
My verse your vertues rare shall eternize,
And in the hevens wryte your glorious name.
Where whenas death shall all the world subdew
Our love shall live, and later life renew."

—1595

SIR PHILIP SIDNEY ■ (1554–1586)

Sir Philip Sidney embodied many of the aspects of the ideal man of the Renaissance; he was a courtier, scholar, patron of the arts, and soldier who died of wounds received at the battle of Zutphen. His sonnet sequence Astrophel and Stella *appeared in 1591, several years before Spenser's* Amoretti, *and helped to precipitate the fashion for sonnets that lasted in England well into the next century.*

Astrophel and Stella: Sonnet 1

1

Loving in truth, and fain° in verse my love to show,
That she dear she might take some pleasure of my pain,
Pleasure might cause her read, reading might make her know,
Knowledge might pity win, and pity grace obtain,

---

3 second hand second time   **5 assay** attempt   **7 lyke** be similar to   **8 eek** also   **9 quod** said
1 fain glad

I sought fit words to paint the blackest face of woe: 5
Studying inventions fine, her wits to entertain,
Oft turning others' leaves,° to see if thence would flow
Some fresh and fruitful showers upon my sunburned brain.
But words came halting forth, wanting Invention's stay;
Invention, Nature's child, fled stepdame Study's blows;   10
And others' feet° still seemed but strangers in my way.
Thus, great with child to speak, and helpless in my throes,
Biting my truant pen, beating myself for spite:
"Fool," said my Muse to me, "look in thy heart, and write."

—1582

ROBERT SOUTHWELL ■ (1561?–1595)

Robert Southwell was a Roman Catholic priest in Elizabeth's Protestant England, who was executed for his religious beliefs. His devotional poems, most of them on the subject of spiritual love, were largely written during his three years in prison. Southwell was declared a saint in the Roman Catholic Church in 1970.

The Burning Babe

As I in hoary winter's night stood shivering in the snow,
Surprised I was with sudden heat which made my heart to
    glow;
And lifting up a fearful eye to view what fire was near,
A pretty babe all burning bright did in the air appear;
Who, scorchèd with excessive heat, such floods of tears did
    shed   5
As though his floods should quench his flames which with his
    tears were fed.
"Alas," quoth he, "but newly born in fiery heats I fry,
Yet none approach to warm their hearts or feel my fire but I!
My faultless breast the furnace is, the fuel wounding thorns,

Love is the fire, and sighs the smoke, the ashes shame
    and scorns;   10
The fuel justice layeth on, and mercy blows the coals,
The metal in this furnace wrought are men's defilèd souls,
For which, as now on fire I am to work them to their good,
So will I melt into a bath to wash them in my blood."
With this he vanished out of sight and swiftly shrunk away,   15
And straight I callèd unto mind that it was Christmas day.

—1602

MICHAEL DRAYTON ■ (1563–1631)

Michael Drayton, like his contemporary, Shakespeare, excelled in several literary genres. He collaborated on plays with Thomas Dekker and wrote long poems on English history, biography, and topography. Drayton labored almost three decades on the sixty-three sonnets in Idea, *publishing them in their present form in 1619.*

Idea: Sonnet 61

Since there's no help, come let us kiss and part;
Nay, I have done, you get no more of me,
And I am glad, yea glad with all my heart
That thus so cleanly I myself can free;
Shake hands forever, cancel all our vows,   5
And when we meet at any time again,
Be it not seen in either of our brows
That we one jot of former love retain.
Now at the last gasp of love's latest breath,
When, his pulse failing, passion speechless lies,   10
When faith is kneeling by his bed of death,
And innocence is closing up his eyes,
    Now if thou wouldst, when all have given him over,
    From death to life thou mightst him yet recover.

—1619

WILLIAM SHAKESPEARE ■ (1564–1616)

William Shakespeare first printed his sonnets in 1609, during the last years of his active career as a playwright, but they had circulated privately a dozen years before. Given the lack of concrete details about Shakespeare's life outside the theatre, critics have found the sonnets fertile ground for biographical speculation, and the sequence of 154 poems does contain distinct characters—a handsome youth to whom most of the first 126 sonnets are addressed, a "Dark Lady" who figures strongly in the remaining poems, and the poet himself, whose name is the source of many puns in the poems. There is probably no definitive "key" to the sonnets, but there is also little doubt that their place is secure among the monuments of English lyric verse. Shakespeare's other nondramatic poems include narratives, allegories, and songs, of which "When Daisies Pied," the companion pieces from his early comedy Love's Labour's Lost, are perhaps the best examples.

Sonnet 18

Shall I compare thee to a summer's day?
Thou art more lovely and more temperate:
Rough winds do shake the darling buds of May,
And summer's lease hath all too short a date:
Sometimes too hot the eye of heaven shines,   5
And often is his gold complexion dimmed;
And every fair from fair° sometimes declines,
By chance or nature's changing course untrimmed;°
But thy eternal summer shall not fade,
Nor lose possession of that fair thou ow'st;°   10
Nor shall death brag thou wander'st in his shade,
When in eternal lines to time thou grow'st:
So long as men can breathe, or eyes can see,
So long lives this, and this gives life to thee.

—1609

7 **fair from fair** every fair thing from its fairness   8 **untrimmed** stripped   10 **ow'st** ownest

Sonnet 20

A woman's face, with nature's own hand painted,
Hast thou, the master mistress of my passion—
A woman's gentle heart, but not acquainted
With shifting change, as is false women's fashion;
An eye more bright than theirs, less false in rolling,°   5
Gilding the object whereupon it gazeth;
A man in hue all hues in his controlling,
Which steals men's eyes and women's souls amazeth.
And for a woman wert thou first created,
Till nature as she wrought thee fell a-doting,   10
And by addition me of thee defeated,
By adding one thing to my purpose nothing.
But since she pricked thee out for women's pleasure,
Mine be thy love and thy love's use their treasure.

—1609

Sonnet 29

When, in disgrace with fortune and men's eyes,
I all alone beweep my outcast state,
And trouble deaf heaven with my bootless° cries,
And look upon myself, and curse my fate,
Wishing me like to one more rich in hope,   5
Featured like him, like him with friends possessed,
Desiring this man's art and that man's scope,
With what I most enjoy contented least;
Yet in these thoughts myself almost despising,
Haply° I think on thee—and then my state,   10
Like to the lark at break of day arising
From sullen earth, sings hymns at heaven's gate;
For thy sweet love remembered such wealth brings
That then I scorn to change my state with kings.

—1609

5 **rolling** wandering
3 **bootless** useless   10 **Haply** fortunately

Sonnet 73

That time of year thou mayst in me behold
When yellow leaves, or none, or few, do hang
Upon those boughs which shake against the cold,
Bare ruined choirs, where late the sweet birds sang.
In me thou see'st the twilight of such day   5
As after sunset fadeth in the west;
Which by and by black night doth take away,
Death's second self, that seals up all in rest.
In me thou see'st the glowing of such fire,
That on the ashes of his youth doth lie,   10
As the deathbed whereon it must expire,
Consumed with that which it was nourished by.
This thou perceiv'st, which makes thy love more strong,
To love that well which thou must leave ere long.

—1609

Sonnet 116

Let me not to the marriage of true minds
Admit impediments. Love is not love
Which alters when it alteration finds,
Or bends with the remover to remove:
Oh, no! it is an ever-fixèd mark,   5
That looks on tempests and is never shaken:
It is the star to every wandering bark,°
Whose worth's unknown, although his height be taken.°
Love's not Time's fool, though rosy lips and cheeks
Within his bending sickle's compass° come;   10
Love alters not with his brief hours and weeks,
But bears it out even to the edge of doom.
If this be error and upon me proved,
I never writ, nor no man ever loved.

—1609

7 bark boat   8 height be taken elevation be measured   10 compass range
1 waste desert

Sonnet 130

My mistress' eyes are nothing like the sun;
Coral is far more red than her lips' red;
If snow be white, why then her breasts are dun;
If hairs be wires, black wires grow on her head.
I have seen roses damasked,° red and white,   5
But no such roses see I in her cheeks;
And in some perfumes is there more delight
Than in the breath that from my mistress reeks.
I love to hear her speak, yet well I know
That music hath a far more pleasing sound;   10
I grant I never saw a goddess go;
My mistress, when she walks, treads on the ground.
And yet, by heaven, I think my love as rare
As any she belied° with false compare.°

—1609

When Daisies Pied°

Spring

When daisies pied and violets blue
        And ladysmocks all silver-white
And cuckoobuds of yellow hue
        Do paint the meadows with delight,
The cuckoo then, on every tree,   5
Mocks married men;° for thus sings he,
                Cuckoo;
Cuckoo, cuckoo: Oh word of fear,
Unpleasing to a married ear!
When shepherds pipe on oaten straws,   10
        And merry larks are plowmen's clocks,
When turtles tread,° and rooks, and daws,
And maidens bleach their summer smocks,
The cuckoo then, on every tree,

---

5 **damasked** multi-colored   14 **belied** lied about   **compare** comparisons
Pied multi-colored   6 **Mocks married men** The pun is on the similarity between "cuckoo" and
"cuckold."   12 **turtles tread** turtledoves mate

Mocks married men; for thus sings he,   15
     Cuckoo;
Cuckoo, cuckoo: Oh word of fear,
Unpleasing to a married ear!

Winter

When icicles hang by the wall
And Dick the shepherd blows his nail°   20
And Tom bears logs into the hall,
    And milk comes frozen home in pail,
When blood is nipped and ways be foul,
Then nightly sings the staring owl,
     Tu-who;   25
Tu-whit, tu-who: a merry note,
While greasy Joan doth keel° the pot.

When all aloud the wind doth blow,
    And coughing drowns the parson's saw,°
And birds sit brooding in the snow,   30
    And Marian's nose looks red and raw,
When roasted crabs° hiss in the bowl,
Then nightly sings the staring owl,
     Tu-who;
Tu-whit, tu-who: a merry note   35
While greasy Joan doth keel the pot.

—1598

THOMAS CAMPION ■ (1567–1620)

Thomas Campion was a poet and physician who wrote music and lyrics in a manner that was "chiefly aimed to couple my words and notes lovingly together." The imagery in "There Is a Garden in Her Face" represents a late flowering of the conceits of Petrarchan love poetry, so wittily mocked by Shakespeare in "Sonnet 130."

20 nail fingernails   **27 keel** stir   **29 saw** saying   **32 crabs** crabapples

There Is a Garden in Her Face

There is a garden in her face,
Where roses and white lilies grow,
A heavenly paradise is that place,
Wherein all pleasant fruits do flow.
There cherries grow which none may buy   5
Till "Cherry-ripe!" themselves do cry.

Those cherries fairly do enclose
Of orient pearl a double row,
Which when her lovely laughter shows,
They look like rosebuds filled with snow.   10
Yet them nor peer nor prince can buy,
Till "Cherry-ripe!" themselves do cry.

Her eyes like angels watch them still;
Her brows like bended bows do stand,
Threatening with piercing frowns to kill   15
All that attempt with eye or hand
Those sacred cherries to come nigh,
Till "Cherry-ripe!" themselves do cry.

—1617

JOHN DONNE ■ (1572–1631)

*John Donne was trained in the law for a career in government service,
but Donne became the greatest preacher of his day, ending his life as
dean of St. Paul's Cathedral in London. Only two of Donne's poems and
a handful of his sermons were printed during his life, but both circulated
widely in manuscript and his literary reputation among his contemporaries was considerable. His poetry falls into two distinct periods: the
witty love poetry of his youth and the sober religious meditations of his
maturity. In both, however, Donne shows remarkable originality in
rhythm, diction, and the use of metaphor and conceit, which marks him
as the chief poet of what has become commonly known as the metaphysical style.*

The Flea

Mark but this flea, and mark in this,
How little that which thou deniest me is;
Me it sucked first, and now sucks thee,
And in this flea our two bloods mingled be;
Thou know'st that this cannot be said   5
A sin, or shame, or loss of maidenhead,
　　Yet this enjoys before it woo,
　　And pampered swells with one blood made of two,
　　And this, alas, is more than we would do.

Oh stay, three lives in one flea spare,   10
Where we almost, nay more than married are.
This flea is you and I, and this
Our marriage bed and marriage temple is;
Though parents grudge, and you, we are met,
And cloistered in these living walls of jet.°   15
　　Though use° make you apt to kill me
　　Let not to that, self-murder added be,
　　And sacrilege, three sins in killing three.

Cruel and sudden, hast thou since
Purpled thy nail° in blood of innocence?   20
Wherein could this flea guilty be,
Except in that drop which it sucked from thee?
Yet thou triumph'st, and say'st that thou
Find'st not thy self nor me the weaker now;
　　'Tis true; then learn how false fears be: 25
　　Just so much honor, when thou yield'st to me,
　　Will waste, as this flea's death took life from thee.

—1633

Holy Sonnet 10

Death, be not proud, though some have callèd thee
Mighty and dreadful, for thou art not so;
For those whom thou think'st thou dost overthrow

15 jet black   16 use familiarity, especially in the sexual sense   20 Purpled thy nail bloodied your fingernail

Die not, poor Death, nor yet canst thou kill me.
From rest and sleep, which but thy pictures be,   5
Much pleasure; then from thee much more must flow,
And soonest our best men with thee do go,
Rest of their bones, and soul's delivery.
Thou'art slave to fate, chance, kings, and desperate men,
And dost with poison, war, and sickness dwell,   10
And poppy° or charms can make us sleep as well
And better than thy stroke; why swell'st thou then?
One short sleep past, we wake eternally,
And death shall be no more; Death, thou shalt die.

—*1633*

Holy Sonnet 14

JOHN DONNE

Batter my heart, three-personed God; for You
As yet but knock, breathe, shine, and seek to mend;
That I may rise, and stand, o'erthrow me, and bend
Your force to break, blow, burn, and make me new.
I, like an usurped town, to another due,   5
Labor to admit You, but O, to no end;
Reason, Your viceroy in me, me should defend,
But is captived, and proves weak or untrue.
Yet dearly I love You, and would be lovèd fain,°
But am betrothed unto Your enemy.   10
Divorce me, untie or break that knot again;
Take me to You, imprison me, for I,
Except You enthrall me, never shall be free,
Nor ever chaste, except You ravish me.

—*1633*

The Sun Rising

Busy old fool, unruly sun,
        Why dost thou thus
Through windows and through curtains call on us?
Must to the motions lovers' seasons run?

11 **poppy** opium
9 **fain** gladly

Saucy pedantic wretch, go chide   5
  Late schoolboys and sour prentices,
Go tell court huntsmen that the King will ride,
  Call country ants to harvest offices;°
Love, all alike, no season knows nor clime,
Nor hours, days, months, which are the rags of time.   10

  Thy beams, so reverend and strong
  Why shouldst thou think?
I could eclipse and cloud them with a wink,
But that I would not lose her sight so long;
  If her eyes have not blinded thine,   15
  Look, and tomorrow late, tell me,
Whether both th' Indias of spice and mine°
Be where thou leftst them, or lie here with me.
Ask for those kings whom thou saw'st yesterday,
And thou shalt hear, All here in one bed lay.   20

  She is all states, and all princes I,
  Nothing else is.
Princes do but play us; compared to this,
All honor's mimic, all wealth alchemy.
  Thou, sun, art half as happy as we,   25
  In that the world's contracted thus;
Thine age asks ease, and since thy duties be
To warm the world, that's done in warming us.
Shine here to us, and thou art everywhere;
This bed thy center is, these walls thy sphere.   30

—1633

A Valediction:° Forbidding Mourning

As virtuous men pass mildly away,
  And whisper to their souls to go,
Whilst some of their sad friends do say
  The breath goes now, and some say, No;

8 offices duties   **17 Indias of spice and mine** the East and West ladies, respectively
Valediction farewell speech; Donne is addressing his wife before leaving on a diplomatic mission.

So let us melt, and make no noise,   5
      No tear-floods, nor sigh-tempests move,
'Twere profanation of our joys
      To tell the laity our love.

Moving of th' earth brings harms and fears,
      Men reckon what it did and meant;   10
But trepidation of the spheres,°
      Though greater far, is innocent.

Dull sublunary° lovers' love,
      (Whose soul is sense) cannot admit
Absence, because it doth remove   15
      Those things which elemented it.

But we by a love so much refined
      That our selves know not what it is,
Inter-assurèd of the mind,
      Care less, eyes, lips, and hands to miss.   20

Our two souls therefore, which are one,
      Though I must go, endure not yet
A breach, but an expansion,
      Like gold to airy thinness beat.

If they be two, they are two so   25
      As stiff twin compasses° are two;
Thy soul, the fixed foot, makes no show
      To move, but doth, if th' other do.

And though it in the center sit,
      Yet when the other far doth roam,   30
It leans and hearkens after it,
      And grows erect, as that comes home.

Such wilt thou be to me, who must
      Like th' other foot, obliquely run;
Thy firmness makes my circle just,°   35
      And makes me end where I begun.

—1633

11 **trepidation of the spheres** natural trembling of the heavenly spheres, a concept of Ptolemaic
astronomy   13 **sublunary** under the moon, hence, changeable (a Ptolemaic concept)   26 **stiff twin
compasses** drafting compasses   35 **just** complete

Ben Jonson was Shakespeare's chief rival on the stage, and their contentious friendship has been the subject of much speculation. Jonson became England's first unofficial poet laureate, receiving a royal stipend from James I, and was a great influence of a group of younger poets who became known as the "Tribe of Ben." His tragedies are little regarded today, and his comedies, while still performed occasionally, have nevertheless failed to hold the stage as brilliantly as Shakespeare's. Still, he was a poet of considerable talents, particularly in short forms. His elegy on Shakespeare contains a famous assessment: "He was not of an age, but for all time!"

On My First Son

Farewell, thou child of my right hand,° and joy;
My sin was too much hope of thee, loved boy:
Seven years thou'wert lent to me, and I thee pay,
Exacted by thy fate, on the just day.°
Oh, could I lose all father now! for why   5
Will man lament the state he should envy,
To have so soon 'scaped world's and flesh's rage,
And, if no other misery, yet age?
Rest in soft peace, and asked, say, "Here doth lie
Ben Jonson his best piece of poetry."   10
For whose sake henceforth all his vows be such
As what he loves may never like too much.

—1616

Slow, Slow, Fresh Fount

From Cynthia's Revels°

Slow, slow, fresh fount, keep time with my salt tears;
Yet slower, yet, O faintly, gentle springs!
List to the heavy part the music bears,

---

1 **child of my right hand** Benjamin, the child's name, means this in Hebrew.   **4 the just day** Jonson's son died on his seventh birthday.
Slow, Slow, Fresh Fount: From Cynthia's Revels spoken in this masque by the nymph Echo about the dead Narcissus

Woe weeps out her division,° when she sings.
    Droop herbs and flowers;   5
    Fall grief in showers;
Our beauties are not ours. O, I could still,
Like melting snow upon some craggy hill,
    Drop, drop, drop, drop,
Since nature's pride is now a withered daffodil.   10

—1600

MARY WROTH ▪ (1587?–1651)

Mary Wroth was the niece of Sir Philip Sidney and the cousin of Sir Walter Raleigh, both distinguished poets and courtiers. A friend of poet Ben Jonson, who dedicated The Alchemist *to her, she was prominent in the court of King James I. Her prose romance,* Urania *(1621), stirred controversy because of its similarities to actual people and events. Wroth may have fallen into disfavor at court after the publication of* Urania, *and few facts are known about her later life.*

In This Strange Labyrinth How Shall I Turn

In this strange labyrinth how shall I turn,
Ways° are on all sides, while the way I miss:
If to the right hand, there in love I burn,
Let me go forward, therein danger is.
If to the left, suspicion hinders bliss: 5
Let me turn back, shame cries I ought return:
Nor faint, though crosses° with my fortunes kiss.
Stand still is harder, although sure to mourn.
Thus let me take the right, or left hand way,
Go forward, or stand still, or back retire: 10
I must these doubts endure without allay°

---

4 **division** part of a song
2 **Ways** paths   7 **crosses** troubles   11 **allay** alleviation

Or help, but travail find for my best hire
Yet that which most my troubled sense doth move,
Is to leave all and take the thread of Love°

—1621

ROBERT HERRICK ■ (1591–1674)

*Robert Herrick was the most distinguished member of the "Tribe of Ben."
Herrick is grouped with the Cavalier poets, whose graceful lyrics are marked
by wit and gentle irony. Surprisingly, Herrick was a minister; his Royalist
sympathies during the English Civil War caused him hardship during the
Puritan era, but his position in the church was returned to him by Charles II
after the Restoration.*

To the Virgins, to Make Much of Time

Gather ye rosebuds while ye may,
    Old time is still a-flying;
And this same flower that smiles today
    Tomorrow will be dying.

The glorious lamp of heaven, the sun,   5
    The higher he's a-getting,
The sooner will his race be run,
    And nearer he's to setting.

That age is best which is the first,
    When youth and blood are warmer;   10
But being spent, the worse, and worst
    Times still succeed the former.

Then be not coy, but use your time,
    And, while ye may, go marry;
For, having lost but once your prime,   15
    You may forever tarry.

—1648

---

14 Love an allusion to the myth of Theseus, who, with the help of Ariadne, unrolled a thread behind
him as he entered the labyrinth of Crete.

George Herbert was the great master of the English devotional lyric. Herbert was born into a distinguished family which included his mother, the formidable literary patroness Lady Magdalen Herbert, and his brother, the poet and statesman Edward, Lord Herbert of Cherbury. Like John Donne, with whom he shares the metaphysical label, Herbert early aimed at a political career but turned to the clergy, spending several happy years as rector of Bemerton before his death at age 40. The Temple, which contains most of his poems, was published posthumously in 1633.

Easter Wings

Lord, who createdst man in wealth and store,°
  Though foolishly he lost the same,
    Decaying more and more
      Till he became
        Most poor: 5
        With Thee
      O let me rise
    As larks, harmoniously,
  And sing this day Thy victories:
Then shall the fall further the flight in me. 10

My tender age in sorrow did begin;
  And still with sicknesses and shame
    Thou didst so punish sin,
      That I became
        Most thin.   15
        With Thee
      Let me combine,
    And feel this day thy victory;
  For, if I imp my wing on thine,°
Affliction shall advance the flight in me. 20

—1633

---

1 store abundance   **19 imp my wing on thine** to graft feathers from a strong wing onto a weak one, a term from falconry

The Pulley

When God at first made man,
Having a glass of blessings standing by,
    "Let us," said he, "pour on him all we can.
Let the world's riches, which dispersèd lie,
        Contract into a span."°   5

    So strength first made a way;
Then beauty flowed, then wisdom, honor, pleasure.
    When almost all was out, God made a stay,
Perceiving that, alone of all his treasure,
        Rest in the bottom lay.   10

    "For if I should," said he,
"Bestow this jewel also on my creature,
    He would adore my gifts instead of me,
And rest in Nature, not the God of Nature;
        So both should losers be.   15

    "Yet let him keep the rest,
But keep them with repining restlessness.
    Let him be rich and weary, that at least,
If goodness lead him not, yet weariness
May toss him to my breast."   20

                                                 —1633

Redemption

Having been tenant long to a rich lord,
    Not thriving, I resolvèd to be bold,
    And make a suit° unto him, to afford°
A new small-rented lease, and cancel the old.
In heaven at his manor I him sought;   5
    They told me there that he was lately gone
    About some land, which he had dearly bought
Long since on earth, to take possession.

---

5 **span** the distance between thumb tip and the tip of the little finger
3 **make a suit** formally request **afford** grant (me)

I straight returned, and knowing his great birth,
    Sought him accordingly in great resorts;   10
    In cities, theaters, gardens, parks, and courts;
At length I heard a ragged noise and mirth
    Of thieves and murderers; there I him espied,°
    Who straight, *Your suit is granted*, said, and died.

—1633

EDMUND WALLER ■ (1606–1687)

Edmund Waller was another Royalist sympathizer who suffered after the English Civil War, during Oliver Cromwell's protectorate. Waller is noted for having pioneered the use of the heroic couplet as a popular verse form. He has been often praised for the smoothness of his rhythms and sound patterns.

Song

    Go, lovely rose!
Tell her that wastes her time and me
    That now she knows,
When I resemble° her to thee,
How sweet and fair she seems to be.   5

    Tell her that's young,
And shuns to have her graces spied,
    That hadst thou sprung
In deserts, where no men abide,
Thou must have uncommended died.   10

    Small is the worth
Of beauty from the light retired;
    Bid her come forth,
Suffer herself to be desired,
And not blush so to be admired.   15

13 **him espied** saw him
4 **resemble** compare

Then die! that she
The common fate of all things rare
    May read in thee;
How small a part of time they share
That are so wondrous sweet and fair!

20

—1645

JOHN MILTON ▪ (1608–1674)

John Milton is best known as the author of Paradise Lost, *the greatest English epic poem. His life included service in the Puritan government of Cromwell, pamphleteering for liberal political causes, and brief imprisonment after the Restoration. Milton suffered from blindness in his later years. He excelled in the sonnet, a form to which he returned throughout his long literary life.*

How Soon Hath Time

How soon hath Time, the subtle thief of youth,
    Stol'n on his wing my three and twentieth year!
    My hasting days fly on with full career,
    But my late spring no bud or blossom shew'th.°
Perhaps my semblance might deceive the truth,   5
    That I to manhood am arrived so near,
    And inward ripeness doth much less appear,
    That some more timely-happy spirits endu'th.°
Yet be it less or more, or soon or slow,
    It shall be still in strictest measure even°   10
    To that same lot, however mean or high,
Toward which Time leads me, and the will of Heaven;
    All is, if I have grace to use it so,
    As ever in my great Taskmaster's eye.

—1645

4 shew'th shows   8 endu'th endows   10 even equal

On the Late Massacre in Piedmont°

Avenge, O Lord, thy slaughtered saints, whose bones
    Lie scattered on the Alpine mountains cold,
    Even them who kept thy truth so pure of old
    When all our fathers worshiped stocks and stones,°
Forget not: in thy book record their groans   5
    Who were thy sheep and in their ancient fold
    Slain by the bloody Piedmontese that rolled
    Mother with infant down the rocks. Their moans
The vales redoubled to the hills, and they
    To Heaven. Their martyred blood and ashes sow   10
    O'er all th'Italian fields where still doth sway
The triple tyrant:° that from these may grow
    A hundredfold, who having learnt thy way
    Early may fly the Babylonian woe.°

—1655

JOHN MILTON

When I Consider How My Light Is Spent

When I consider how my light is spent
    Ere half my days, in this dark world and wide,
    And that one talent which is death to hide°
    Lodged with me useless, though my soul more bent
To serve therewith my Maker, and present   5
    My true account, lest he returning chide;
    "Doth God exact day-labor, light denied?"
    I fondly° ask; but Patience to prevent
That murmur, soon replies, "God doth not need
    Either man's work or his own gifts; who best   10
    Bear his mild yoke, they serve him best. His state

Massacre in Piedmont 1700 Protestants from this North Italian state were massacred by Papal forces on Easter Day, 1655. **4 stocks and stones** idols **12 triple tyrant** the Pope **14 Babylonian woe** Early Protestants often linked ancient Babylon to modern Rome as centers of vice.
3 talent which is death to hide See the Parable of the Talents, Matthew 25:14–30. **8 fondly** foolishly

Is kingly. Thousands at his bidding speed
And post o'er land and ocean without rest:
They also serve who only stand and wait."

—1673

ANNE BRADSTREET ■ (1612–1672)

Anne Bradstreet was an American Puritan who was one of the first settlers of the Massachusetts Bay Colony, along with her husband Simon, later governor of the colony. The Tenth Muse Lately Sprung Up in America, published abroad by a relative without her knowledge, was the first American book of poetry published in England, and the circumstances of its appearance lie behind the witty tone of "The Author to Her Book."

The Author to Her Book

Thou ill-formed offspring of my feeble brain,
Who after birth didst by my side remain,
Till snatched from thence by friends, less wise than true,
Who thee abroad, exposed to public view,
Made thee in rags, halting to th' press° to trudge,   5
Where errors were not lessened (all may judge).
At thy return my blushing was not small,
My rambling brat (in print) should mother call,
I cast thee by as one unfit for light,
Thy visage was so irksome in my sight;   10
Yet being mine own, at length affection would
Thy blemishes amend, if so I could:
I washed thy face, but more defects I saw,
And rubbing off a spot still made a flaw.
I stretched thy joints to make thee even feet,°   15
Yet still thou run'st more hobbling than is meet;
In better dress to trim thee was my mind,
But nought save homespun cloth i' th' house I find.
In this array 'mongst vulgars° may'st thou roam.

5 press printing press; also a clothes closet or chest   **15 even feet** a pun on metrical feet
19 vulgars common people, i.e., average readers

In critic's hands beware thou dost not come,   20
And take thy way where yet thou art not known;
If for thy Father asked, say thou had'st none;
And for thy Mother, she alas is poor,
Which caused her thus to send thee out of door.

—1678

RICHARD LOVELACE ■ (1618–1658)

Richard Lovelace was another Cavalier lyricist who was a staunch supporter of Charles I, serving as a soldier in Scotland and France. He composed many of his poems in prison following the English Civil War.

To Lucasta, Going to the Wars

Tell me not, sweet, I am unkind
That from the nunnery
Of thy chaste breast and quiet mind,
To war and arms I fly.

True, a new mistress now I chase,   5
The first foe in the field;
And with a stronger faith embrace
A sword, a horse, a shield.

Yet this inconstancy is such
As you too shall adore;   10
I could not love thee, dear, so much,
Loved I not honor more.

—1649

ANDREW MARVELL ■ (1621–1678)

Andrew Marvell was widely known for the playful sexual wit of this most famous example of the carpé diem poem in English. Marvell was a learned Latin scholar who moved in high circles of government under both the Puritans and Charles II, serving as a member of Parliament for two decades. Oddly, Marvell was almost completely forgotten as a lyric poet for almost two hundred years after his death, although today he is considered the last of the great exemplars of the metaphysical style.

To His Coy Mistress

Had we but world enough, and time,
This coyness,° lady, were no crime.
We would sit down, and think which way
To walk, and pass our long love's day.
Thou by the Indian Ganges' side   5
Shouldst rubies find; I by the tide
Of Humber° would complain. I would
Love you ten years before the flood,
And you should, if you please, refuse
Till the conversion of the Jews.°   10
My vegetable° love should grow
Vaster than empires, and more slow;
An hundred years should go to praise
Thine eyes, and on thy forehead gaze;
Two hundred to adore each breast,   15
But thirty thousand to the rest;
An age at least to every part,
And the last age should show your heart.
For, lady, you deserve this state,°
Nor would I love at lower rate.   20
    But at my back I always hear
Time's wingèd chariot hurrying near;
And yonder all before us lie
Deserts of vast eternity.
Thy beauty shall no more be found;   25
Nor, in thy marble vault, shall sound
My echoing song; then worms shall try°
That long-preserved virginity,
And your quaint° honor turn to dust,
And into ashes all my lust: 30
The grave's a fine and private place,
But none, I think, do there embrace.

---

2 coyness here, artificial sexual reluctance   **7 Humber** an English river near Marvell's home
10 conversion of the Jews at the end of time   **11 vegetable** flourishing   **19 state** estate   **27 try** test
29 quaint too subtle

Now therefore, while the youthful hue
Sits on thy skin like morning glow,
And while thy willing soul transpires   35
At every pore with instant fires,
Now let us sport us while we may,
And now, like amorous birds of prey,
Rather at once our time devour
Than languish in his slow-chapped° power.   40
Let us roll all our strength and all
Our sweetness up into one ball,
And tear our pleasures with rough strife
Thorough the iron gates of life:
Thus, though we cannot make our sun   45
Stand still, yet we will make him run.

—1681

JOHN DRYDEN ■ (1631–1700)

John Dryden excelled at long forms—verse dramas like All for Love, *his version
of Shakespeare's* Antony and Cleopatra, *his translation of Virgil's* Aeneid, *political allegories like* Absalom and Achitophel, *and* MacFlecknoe, *the first
great English literary satire. Dryden's balance and formal conservatism introduced the neoclassical style to English poetry, a manner that prevailed for a
century after his death. He became poet laureate of England in 1668.*

To the Memory of Mr. Oldham°

Farewell, too little, and too lately known,
Whom I began to think and call my own:
For sure our souls were near allied, and thine
Cast in the same poetic mold with mine.
One common note on either lyre did strike,   5
And knaves and fools we both abhorred alike.
To the same goal did both our studies drive;
The last set out the soonest did arrive.
Thus Nisus° fell upon the slippery place,

---

40 chapped jawed
John Oldham (1653–1683) was a poet and a satirist.   **9 Nisus** In Virgil's *Aeneid* he is defeated in a
footrace by Euryalus, his friend.

While his young friend performed and won the race.   10
O early ripe! to thy abundant store
What could advancing age have added more?
It might (what nature never gives the young)
Have taught the numbers° of thy native tongue.
But satire needs not those, and wit will shine   15
Through the harsh cadence of a rugged line:
A noble error, and but seldom made,
When poets are by too much force betrayed.
Thy generous fruits, though gathered ere their prime,
Still showed a quickness, and maturing time   20
But mellows what we write to the dull sweets of rhyme.
Once more, hail and farewell; farewell, thou young,
But ah too short, Marcellus° of our tongue;
Thy brows with ivy, and with laurels bound
But fate and gloomy night encompass thee around.   25

—1684

JONATHAN SWIFT ■ (1667–1745)

Jonathan Swift, the author of Gulliver's Travels, *stands unchallenged as the greatest English prose satirist, but his poetry too is remarkable in the unsparing realism of its best passages. Like many poets of the neoclassical era, Swift adds tension to his poetry by ironically emphasizing parallels between the heroic past and the familiar characters and scenes of contemporary London. A native of Dublin, Swift returned to Ireland in his maturity as dean of St. Patrick's Cathedral.*

A Description of a City Shower

Careful observers may foretell the hour
(By sure prognostics)° when to dread a shower:
While rain depends,° the pensive cat gives o'er
Her frolics, and pursues her tail no more.
Returning home at night, you'll find the sink°   5

---

14 numbers poetic meters   **23 Marcellus** Roman military leader who died at age twenty
2 prognostics forecasts   **3 depends** is imminent   **5 sink** sewer

Strike your offended sense with double stink.
If you be wise, then go not far to dine;
You'll spend in coach hire more than save in wine.
A coming shower your shooting corns presage,
Old achès throb, your hollow tooth will rage.   10
Sauntering in coffeehouse is Dulman° seen;
He damns the climate and complains of spleen.°
    Meanwhile the South, rising with dabbled wings,
A sable cloud athwart the welkin° flings,
That swilled more liquor than it could contain,   15
And, like a drunkard, gives it up again.
Brisk Susan whips her linen from the rope,
While the first drizzling shower is borne aslope:
Such is that sprinkling which some careless quean°
Flirts on you from her mop, but not so clean: 20
You fly, invoke the gods; then turning, stop
To rail; she singing, still whirls on her mop.
Not yet the dust had shunned the unequal strife,
But, aided by the wind, fought still for life,
And wafted with its foe by violent gust,   25
'Twas doubtful which was rain and which was dust.
Ah! where must needy poet seek for aid,
When dust and rain at once his coat invade?
Sole coat, where dust cemented by the rain
Erects the nap, and leaves a mingled stain.   30
    Now in contiguous drops the flood comes down,
Threatening with deluge this devoted° town.
To shops in crowds the daggled° females fly,
Pretend to cheapen° goods, but nothing buy.
The Templar° spruce, while every spout's abroach,°   35
Stays till 'tis fair, yet seems to call a coach.
The tucked-up sempstress walks with hasty strides,
While streams run down her oiled umbrella's sides.
Here various kinds, by various fortunes led,
Commence acquaintance underneath a shed.   40

---

11 Dulman i.e., dull man **12 spleen** mental depression **14 welkin** sky **19 quean** ill-mannered woman **32 devoted** doomed **33 daggled** spattered **34 cheapen** inspect prices of **35 Templar** law student **abroach** pouring

Triumphant Tories and desponding Whigs°
Forget their feuds, and join to save their wigs.

Boxed in a chair° the beau impatient sits,
While spouts run clattering o'er the roof by fits,
And ever and anon with frightful din   45
The leather sounds; he trembles from within.

So when Troy chairmen bore the wooden steed,
Pregnant with Greeks impatient to be freed
(Those bully Greeks, who, as the moderns do,
Instead of paying chairmen, run them through),   50
Laocoön° struck the outside with his spear,
And each imprisoned hero quaked for fear.

    Now from all parts the swelling kennels° flow,
And bear their trophies with them as they go:
Filth of all hues and odors seem to tell   55
What street they sailed from, by their sight and smell.
They, as each torrent drives with rapid force,
From Smithfield° or St. Pulchre's shape their course,
And in huge confluence joined at Snow Hill ridge,
Fall from the conduit prone to Holborn Bridge.   60
Sweepings from butchers' stalls, dung, guts, and blood,
Drowned puppies, stinking sprats,° all drenched in mud,
Dead cats, and turnip tops, come tumbling down the flood.

—1710

ALEXANDER POPE ■ (1688–1744)

*Alexander Pope was a tiny man who was afflicted in childhood by a crip-
pling disease. Pope was the dominant poet of eighteenth-century England,
particularly excelling as a master of mock-epic satire in "The Rape of the
Lock" and "The Dunciad." His translations of the Iliad and the Odyssey
made him famous and financially independent and remained the standard
versions of Homer for almost two hundred years. "An Essay on Criticism," a
long didactic poem modeled on Horace's Ars Poetica, remains the most
complete statement of the neoclassical aesthetic.*

---

41 Tories . . . Whigs rival political factions   **43 chair** sedan chair   **51 Laocoön** For his attempt to
warn the Trojans, he was crushed by sea serpents sent by Poseidon.   **53 kennels** storm drains
58 Smithfield site of London cattle exchange   **62 sprats** small fish

From An Essay on Criticism

ALEXANDER POPE

504

But most by numbers judge a poet's song,
And smooth or rough with them is right or wrong.
In the bright Muse though thousand charms conspire,
Her voice is all these tuneful fools admire,
Who haunt Parnassus° but to please their ear,   5
Not mend their minds; as some to church repair,
Not for the doctrine, but the music there.
These equal syllables alone require,
Though oft the ear the open vowels tire,
While expletives° their feeble aid do join,   10
And ten low words oft creep in one dull line:
While they ring round the same unvaried chimes,
With sure returns of still expected rhymes;
Where'er you find "the cooling western breeze,"
In the next line, it "whispers through the trees";   15
If crystal streams "with pleasing murmurs creep,"
The reader's threatened (not in vain) with "sleep";
Then, at the last and only couplet fraught
With some unmeaning thing they call a thought,
A needless Alexandrine° ends the song   20
That, like a wounded snake, drags its slow length along.
Leave such to tune their own dull rhymes, and know
What's roundly smooth or languishingly slow;
And praise the easy vigor of a line
Where Denham's strength and Waller's° sweetness join.   25
True ease in writing comes from art, not chance,
As those move easiest who have learned to dance.
'Tis not enough no harshness gives offense,
The sound must seem an echo to the sense.
Soft is the strain when Zephyr° gently blows,   30
And the smooth stream in smoother numbers flows;
But when loud surges lash the sounding shore,
The hoarse, rough verse should like the torrent roar.

---

5 Parnassus mountain of the Muses   **10 expletives** unnecessary filler words (like "do" in this line)
20 Alexandrine line of six iambic feet (as in the next line)   **25 Denham's . . . Waller's** earlier
English poets praised by Pope   **30 Zephyr** the west wind

When Ajax° strives some rock's vast weight to throw,
The line too labors, and the words move slow; 35
Not so when swift Camilla° scours the plain,
Flies o'er the unbending corn, and skims along the main.
Hear how Timotheus'° varied lays surprise,
And bid alternate passions fall and rise!
While at each change the son of Libyan Jove° 40
Now burns with glory, and then melts with love;
Now his fierce eyes with sparkling fury glow,
Now sighs steal out, and tears begin to flow:
Persians and Greeks like turns of nature found
And the world's victor stood subdued by sound! 45
The power of music all our hearts allow,
And what Timotheus was is Dryden now.
    Avoid extremes; and shun the fault of such
Who still are pleased too little or too much.
At every trifle scorn to take offense: 50
That always shows great pride, or little sense.
Those heads, as stomachs, are not sure the best,
Which nauseate all, and nothing can digest.
Yet let not each gay turn thy rapture move;
For fools admire, but men of sense approve: 55
As things seem large which we through mists descry,
Dullness is ever apt to magnify.

—1711

Ode on Solitude

Happy the man whose wish and care
    A few paternal acres bound,
Content to breathe his native air,
        In his own ground.

Whose herds with milk, whose fields with bread, 5
    Whose flocks supply him with attire,
Whose trees in summer yield him shade,
        In winter fire.

34 **Ajax** legendary strong man of the *Iliad*   36 **Camilla** messenger of the goddess Diana
38 **Timotheus** a legendary musician   40 **son of Libyan Jove** Alexander the Great

Blest, who can unconcernedly find
    Hours, days, and years slide soft away,   10
In health of body, peace of mind,
    Quiet by day,

Sound sleep by night; study and ease,
    Together mixed; sweet recreation;
And innocence, which most does please   15
    With meditation.

Thus let me live, unseen, unknown;
    Thus unlamented let me die;
Steal from the world, and not a stone
    Tell where I lie.   20

—*1736*

THOMAS GRAY ■ (1716–1771)

Thomas Gray possesses a contemporary reputation that rests primarily on a single poem, but it remains one of the most often quoted in the whole English canon, and the quatrain stanza is often called "elegiac" in its honor. Gray lived almost all of his adult life at Cambridge University, where he was a professor of history and languages. He declined the poet laureateship of England in 1757.

Elegy Written in a Country Churchyard

The curfew tolls the knell of parting day,
    The lowing herd wind slowly o'er the lea,
The plowman homeward plods his weary way,
    And leaves the world to darkness and to me.

Now fades the glimmering landscape on the sight,   5
    And all the air a solemn stillness holds,
Save where the beetle wheels his droning flight,
    And drowsy tinklings lull the distant folds;

Save that from yonder ivy-mantled tower
    The moping owl does to the moon complain   10
Of such, as wandering near her secret bower,
    Molest her ancient solitary reign.

Beneath those rugged elms, that yew tree's shade,
    Where heaves the turf in many a moldering heap,
Each in his narrow cell forever laid,   15
    The rude° forefathers of the hamlet sleep.

The breezy call of incense-breathing morn,
    The swallow twittering from the straw-built shed,
The cock's shrill clarion, or the echoing horn,
    No more shall rouse them from their lowly bed.   20

For them no more the blazing hearth shall burn,
    Or busy housewife ply her evening care;
No children run to lisp their sire's return,
    Or climb his knees the envied kiss to share.

Oft did the harvest to their sickle yield,   25
    Their furrow oft the stubborn glebe° has broke;
How jocund did they drive their team afield!
    How bowed the woods beneath their sturdy stroke!

Let not Ambition mock their useful toil,
    Their homely joys, and destiny obscure;   30
Nor Grandeur hear with a disdainful smile
    The short and simple annals of the poor.

The boast of heraldry, the pomp of power,
    And all that beauty, all that wealth e'er gave,
Awaits alike the inevitable hour.   35
    The paths of glory lead but to the grave.

Nor you, ye proud, impute to these the fault,
    If Memory o'er their tomb no trophies raise,
Where through the long-drawn aisle and fretted° vault
    The pealing anthem swells the note of praise.   40

Can storied urn or animated° bust
    Back to its mansion call the fleeting breath?
Can Honor's voice provoke the silent dust,
    Or Flattery soothe the dull cold ear of Death?

16 **rude** unlearned   26 **glebe** plot of farmland   39 **fretted** carved   41 **animated** lifelike

Perhaps in this neglected spot is laid 45
　　Some heart once pregnant with celestial fire;
Hands that the rod of empire might have swayed,
　　Or waked to ecstasy the living lyre.

But Knowledge to their eyes her ample page
　　Rich with the spoils of time did ne'er unroll; 50
Chill Penury repressed their noble rage,
　　And froze the genial current of the soul.

Full many a gem of purest ray serene,
　　The dark unfathomed caves of ocean bear:
Full many a flower is born to blush unseen, 55
　　And waste its sweetness on the desert air.

Some village Hampden,° that with dauntless breast
　　The little tyrant of his field withstood;
Some mute inglorious Milton here may rest,
　　Some Cromwell° guiltless of his country's blood. 60

The applause of listening senates to command,
　　The threats of pain and ruin to despise,
To scatter plenty o'er a smiling land,
　　And read their history in a nation's eyes,

Their lot forbade: nor circumscribed alone 65
　　Their growing virtues, but their crimes confined;
Forbade to wade through slaughter to a throne,
　　And shut the gates of mercy on mankind,

The struggling pangs of conscious truth to hide,
　　To quench the blushes of ingenuous shame, 70
Or heap the shrine of Luxury and Pride
　　With incense kindled at the Muse's flame.

Far from the madding° crowd's ignoble strife,
　　Their sober wishes never learned to stray;
Along the cool sequestered vale of life 75
　　They kept the noiseless tenor of their way.

Yet even these bones from insult to protect
　　Some frail memorial still erected nigh,

---

57 **Hampden** hero of the English Civil War   60 **Cromwell** Lord Protector of England from 1653 to
1658   73 **madding** frenzied

With uncouth rhymes and shapeless sculpture decked,
    Implores the passing tribute of a sigh.   80

Their name, their years, spelt by the unlettered Muse,
    The place of fame and elegy supply:
And many a holy text around she strews,
    That teach the rustic moralist to die.

For who to dumb Forgetfulness a prey,   85
    This pleasing anxious being e'er resigned,
Left the warm precincts of the cheerful day,
    Nor cast one longing lingering look behind?

On some fond breast the parting soul relies,
    Some pious drops the closing eye requires;   90
Even from the tomb the voice of Nature cries,
    Even in our ashes live their wonted fires.

For thee, who mindful of the unhonored dead
    Dost in these lines their artless tale relate;
If chance, by lonely contemplation led,   95
    Some kindred spirit shall inquire thy fate,

Haply some hoary°-headed swain° may say,
    "Oft have we seen him at the peep of dawn
Brushing with hasty steps the dews away
    To meet the sun upon the upland lawn.   100

"There at the foot of yonder nodding beech
    That wreathes its old fantastic roots so high,
His listless length at noontide would he stretch,
    And pore upon the brook that babbles by.

"Hard by yon wood, now smiling as in scorn,   105
    Muttering his wayward fancies he would rove,
Now drooping, woeful wan, like one forlorn,
    Or crazed with care, or crossed in hopeless love.

"One morn I missed him on the customed hill,
    Along the heath and near his favorite tree;   110
Another came; nor yet beside the rill,
    Nor up the lawn, nor at the wood was he;

97 hoary frosty, white   **swain** peasant

"The next with dirges due in sad array
Slow through the churchway path we saw him borne.
Approach and read (for thou canst read) the lay, 115
Graved on the stone beneath yon aged thorn."

The Epitaph

Here rests his head upon the lap of Earth
A youth to Fortune and to Fame unknown.
Fair Science frowned not on his humble birth,
And Melancholy marked him for her own. 120

Large was his bounty, and his soul sincere,
Heaven did a recompense as largely send:
He gave to Misery all he had, a tear,
He gained from Heaven ('twas all he wished) a friend.

No farther seek his merits to disclose, 125
Or draw his frailties from their dread abode
(There they alike in trembling hope repose),
The bosom of his Father and his God.

—1751

WILLIAM BLAKE ▪ (1757–1827)

William Blake was a poet, painter, engraver, and visionary. Blake does not fit easily into any single category, although his political sympathies link him to the later romantic poets. His first book, Poetical Sketches, *attracted little attention, but his mature works, starting with* Songs of Innocence *and* Songs of Experience, *combine poetry with his own remarkable illustrations and are unique in English literature. Thought mad by many in his own day, Blake anticipated many future directions of both literature and modern psychology.*

The Chimney Sweeper

When my mother died I was very young,
And my father sold me while yet my tongue
Could scarcely cry "'weep! 'weep! 'weep! 'weep!"
So your chimneys I sweep & in soot I sleep.

There's little Tom Dacre, who cried when his head 5
That curl'd like a lamb's back, was shav'd, so I said,

"Hush, Tom! never mind it, for when your head's bare,
You know that the soot cannot spoil your white hair."

And so he was quiet, & that very night,
As Tom was a-sleeping, he had such a sight!   10
That thousands of sweepers, Dick, Joe, Ned, & Jack,
Were all of them lock'd up in coffins of black;

And by came an Angel who had a bright key,
And he open'd the coffins & set them all free;
Then down a green plain, leaping, laughing, they run,   15
And wash in a river and shine in the Sun.

Then naked & white, all their bags left behind,
They rise upon clouds, and sport in the wind.
And the Angel told Tom, if he'd be a good boy,
He'd have God for his father, & never want joy.   20

And so Tom awoke; and we rose in the dark,
And got with our bags & our brushes to work.
Tho' the morning was cold, Tom was happy & warm;
So if all do their duty, they need not fear harm.

—1789

The Little Black° Boy

My mother bore me in the southern wild,
And I am black, but O! my soul is white;
White as an angel is the English child:
But I am black as if bereav'd of light.

My mother taught me underneath a tree,   5
And sitting down before the heat of day,
She took me on her lap and kissèd me,
And pointing to the east, began to say:

"Look on the rising sun: there God does live,
And gives his light, and gives his heat away;   10
And flowers and trees and beasts and men receive
Comfort in morning, joy in the noon day.

Black probably Indian rather than African

"And we are put on earth a little space,
That we may learn to bear the beams of love,
And these black bodies and this sun-burnt face   15
Is but a cloud, and like a shady grove.

"For when our souls have learn'd the heat to bear,
The cloud will vanish; we shall hear his voice,
Saying: 'Come out from the grove, my love & care,
And round my golden tent like lambs rejoice.'"   20

Thus did my mother say, and kissèd me;
And thus I say to little English boy:
When I from black and he from white cloud free,
And round the tent of God like lambs we joy,

I'll shade him from the heat till he can bear   25
To lean in joy upon our father's knee:
And then I'll stand and stroke his silver hair,
And be like him, and he will then love me.

—1789

WILLIAM BLAKE
512

A Poison Tree

I was angry with my friend:
I told my wrath, my wrath did end.
I was angry with my foe:
I told it not, my wrath did grow.

And I water'd it in fears,   5
Night & morning with my tears;
And I sunnèd it with smiles,
And with soft deceitful wiles.

And it grew both day and night,
Till it bore an apple bright;   10
And my foe beheld it shine,
And he knew that it was mine,

And into my garden stole
When the night had veil'd the pole;
In the morning glad I see   15
My foe outstretch'd beneath the tree.

—1794

The Tyger

Tyger! Tyger! burning bright
In the forests of the night,
What immortal hand or eye
Could frame thy fearful symmetry?

In what distant deeps or skies   5
Burnt the fire of thine eyes?
On what wings dare he aspire?
What the hand, dare seize the fire?

And what shoulder, & what art,
Could twist the sinews of thy heart?   10
And when thy heart began to beat,
What dread hand? & what dread feet?

What the hammer? what the chain?
In what furnace was thy brain?
What the anvil? what dread grasp   15
Dare its deadly terrors clasp?

When the stars threw down their spears,
And water'd heaven with their tears,
Did he smile his work to see?
Did he who made the Lamb make thee?   20

Tyger! Tyger! burning bright
In the forests of the night,
What immortal hand or eye,
Dare frame thy fearful symmetry?

—1794

ROBERT BURNS ■ (1759–1796)

Robert Burns was a Scot known in his day as the "Ploughman Poet" and was one of the first English poets to put dialect to serious literary purpose. Chiefly known for his realistic depictions of peasant life, he was also an important lyric poet who prefigured many of the later concerns of the romantic era.

A Red, Red Rose

O my luve's like a red, red rose,
    That's newly sprung in June;
O my luve's like the melodie
    That's sweetly played in tune.

As fair art thou, my bonnie lass,   5
    So deep in luve am I;
And I will luve thee still, my dear,
    Till a' the seas gang° dry.

Till a' the seas gang dry, my dear,
    And the rocks melt wi' the sun;   10
O I will luve thee still, my dear,
    While the sands o' life shall run.

And fare thee weel, my only luve,
    And fare thee weel awhile!
And I will come again, my luve   15
    Though it were ten thousand mile.

—1791

514

John Barleycorn

There were three kings into the east,
Three kings both great and high;
And they has sworn a solemn oath
John Barleycorn should die.

They took a plough and plough'd him down,   5
Put clods upon his head;
And they hae sworn a solemn oath
John Barleycorn was dead.

But the cheerful spring came kindly on,
And showers began to fall;   10
John Barleycorn got up again,
And sore surprised them all.

8 gang go

The sultry suns of summer came,
And he grew thick and strong;
His head well armed wi' point'd spears,
That no one should him wrong.   15

The sober autumn enter'd mild,
When he grew wan and pale;
His bending joints and drooping head
Show'd he began to fail.   20

His colour sicken'd more and more
He faded into age;
And then his enemies began
To show their deadly rage.

They've ta'en a weapon long and sharp,   25
And cut him by the knee;
Then tied him fast upon a cart,
Like a rogue for forgery.

They laid him down upon his back,
And cudgell'd him full sore;   30
They hung him up before the storm,
And turn'd him o'er and o'er.

They fill'd up a darksome pit
With water to the brim;
They heaved in John Barleycorn,   35
There let him sink or swim.

They laid him out upon the floor,
To work him further woe;
And still as signs of life appear'd,
They toss'd him to and fro.   40

They wasted o'er a scorching flame
The marrow of his bones;
But a miller used him worst of all
He crushed him 'tween two stones.

And they has ta'en his very heart's blood,   45
And drank it round and round,
And still the more and more they drank,
Their joy did more abound.

John Barleycorn was a hero bold,
Of noble enterprise;   50
For if you do but taste his blood,
'Twill make your courage rise.

'Twill make a man forget his woe;
'Twill heighten all his joy;
'Twill make the widow's heart to sing,   55
Though the tear were in her eye.

Then let us toast John Barleycorn,
Each man a glass in hand;
And may his great posterity
Ne'er fail in old Scotland!   60

—1786

William Wordsworth is generally considered the first of the English romantics. Lyrical Ballads, the 1798 volume that introduced both his poetry and
Samuel Taylor Coleridge's to a wide readership, remains one of the most influential collections of poetry ever published. Wordsworth's preface to the revised edition of 1800 contains the famous Romantic formulation of poetry
as the "spontaneous overflow of powerful feelings," a theory exemplified in
short lyrics like "I Wandered Lonely as a Cloud" and in longer meditative
pieces like "Tintern Abbey" (the title by which "Lines" is commonly known).
Wordsworth served as poet laureate from 1843 to his death.

I Wandered Lonely as a Cloud

I wandered lonely as a cloud
That floats on high o'er vales and hills,
When all at once I saw a crowd,
A host, of golden daffodils;
Beside the lake, beneath the trees,   5
Fluttering and dancing in the breeze.

Continuous as the stars that shine
And twinkle on the milky way,
They stretched in never-ending line
Along the margin of a bay: 10

Ten thousand saw I at a glance,
Tossing their heads in sprightly dance.

The waves beside them danced, but they
Outdid the sparkling waves in glee;
A poet could not but be gay,   15
In such a jocund company;
I gazed—and gazed—but little thought
What wealth the show to me had brought:

For oft, when on my couch I lie
In vacant or in pensive mood,   20
They flash upon that inward eye
Which is the bliss of solitude;
And then my heart with pleasure fills,
And dances with the daffodils.

—1807

It Is a Beauteous Evening

It is a beauteous evening, calm and free,
The holy time is quiet as a Nun
Breathless with adoration; the broad sun
Is sinking down in its tranquillity;
The gentleness of heaven broods o'er the Sea: 5
Listen! the mighty Being is awake,
And doth with his eternal motion make
A sound like thunder—everlastingly.
Dear Child! dear Girl!° that walkest with me here,
If thou appear untouched by solemn thought,   10
Thy nature is not therefore less divine:
Thou liest in Abraham's bosom° all the year,
And worship'st at the Temple's inner shrine,
God being with thee when we know it not.

—1807

IT IS A BEAUTEOUS EVENING

517

---

9 **Dear Child! dear Girl!** the poet's daughter   12 **Abraham's bosom** where souls rest in Heaven

Ode

Intimations of Immortality
from Recollections of Early Childhood

The Child is Father of the Man;
And I could wish my days to be
Bound each to each by natural piety.°

1

There was a time when meadow, grove, and stream,
The earth, and every common sight,
      To me did seem
      Appareled in celestial light,
The glory and the freshness of a dream.   5
It is not now as it hath been of yore;—
      Turn wheresoe'er I may,
      By night or day,
The things which I have seen I now can see no more.

2

      The Rainbow comes and goes,   10
      And lovely is the Rose,
      The Moon doth with delight
Look round her when the heavens are bare,
      Waters on a starry night
      Are beautiful and fair;
      The sunshine is a glorious birth;   15
      But yet I know, where'er I go,
That there hath past away a glory from the earth.

3

Now, while the birds thus sing a joyous song,
      And while the young lambs bound   20
      As to the tabor's° sound,
To me alone there came a thought of grief:

---

1 **The Child . . . natural piety** last three lines of the poet's "My Heart Leaps Up"   **21 tabor's** small drum's

A timely utterance gave that thought relief,
   And I again am strong:
The cataracts blow their trumpets from the steep;   25
No more shall grief of mine the season wrong;
I hear the Echoes through the mountains throng,
The Winds come to me from the fields of sleep,
   And all the earth is gay;
    Land and sea   30
   Give themselves up to jollity,
   And with the heart of May
   Doth every Beast keep holiday;—
    Thou Child of Joy,
Shout round me, let me hear thy shouts, thou happy
   Shepherd-boy!   35

4

Ye blessèd Creatures, I have heard the call
   Ye to each other make; I see
The heavens laugh with you in your jubilee;
   My heart is at your festival,   40
   My head hath its coronal,°
The fulness of your bliss, I feel—I feel it all.
    Oh evil day! if I were sullen
    While Earth herself is adorning,
     This sweet May-morning,   45
    And the Children are culling
     On every side,
    In a thousand valleys far and wide,
    Fresh flowers; while the sun shines warm,
And the Babe leaps up on his Mother's arm:—   50
    I hear, I hear, with joy I hear!
    —But there's a Tree, of many, one,
A single Field which I have looked upon,
Both of them speak of something that is gone:
    The Pansy at my feet   55
    Doth the same tale repeat:
Whither is fled the visionary gleam?
Where is it now, the glory and the dream?

41 coronal floral crown

5

Our birth is but a sleep and a forgetting:
The Soul that rises with us, our life's Star,   60
    Hath had elsewhere its setting,
        And cometh from afar:
    Not in entire forgetfulness,
    And not in utter nakedness,
But trailing clouds of glory do we come   65
    From God, who is our home:
Heaven lies about us in our infancy!
Shades of the prison-house begin to close
    Upon the growing Boy,
But he beholds the light, and whence it flows,   70
    He sees it in his joy;
The Youth, who daily farther from the east
    Must travel, still is Nature's Priest,
    And by the vision splendid
    Is on his way attended;   75
At length the Man perceives it die away,
And fade into the light of common day.

6

Earth fills her lap with pleasures of her own;
Yearnings she hath in her own natural kind,
And, even with something of a Mother's mind,   80
    And no unworthy aim,
    The homely Nurse doth all she can
To make her Foster-child, her Inmate Man,
    Forget the glories he hath known,
And that imperial palace whence he came.   85

7

Behold the Child among his new-born blisses,
A six years' Darling of a pigmy size!
See where 'mid work of his own hand he lies,
Fretted° by sallies of his mother's kisses,

89 Fretted annoyed or marked

With light upon him from his father's eyes!　　　　　90
See, at his feet, some little plan or chart,
Some fragment from his dream of human life,
Shaped by himself with newly-learnèd art;
　　　A wedding or a festival,
　　　A mourning or a funeral;　　　　　　　95
　　　　　And this hath now his heart,
　　　　　And unto this he frames his song:
　　　　　Then will he fit his tongue
To dialogues of business, love, or strife;
　　　　　But it will not be long　　　　　100
　　　　　Ere this be thrown aside,
　　　　　And with new joy and pride
The little Actor cons another part;
Filling from time to time his "humorous stage"°
With all the Persons, down to palsied Age,　　　105
That Life brings with her in her equipage;
　　　　　As if his whole vocation
　　　　　Were endless imitation.

8

Thou whose exterior semblance doth belie
　　　　　Thy Soul's immensity;
Thou best Philosopher, who yet dost keep　　　110
Thy heritage, thou Eye among the blind,
That, deaf and silent, read'st the eternal deep,
Haunted for ever by the eternal mind,—
　　　　　Mighty Prophet! Seer blest!　　　115
　　　　　On whom those truths do rest,
Which we are toiling all our lives to find,
In darkness lost, the darkness of the grave;
Thou, over whom thy Immortality
Broods like the Day, a Master o'er a Slave,　　　120
A Presence which is not to be put by;
Thou little Child, yet glorious in the might
Of heaven-born freedom on thy being's height,

521

104 **"humorous stage"** phrase from poet Samuel Daniel (1563–1619)

Why with such earnest pains dost thou provoke
The years to bring the inevitable yoke, 125
Thus blindly with thy blessedness at strife?
Full soon thy Soul shall have her earthly freight,
And custom lie upon thee with a weight,
Heavy as frost, and deep almost as life!

9

O joy! that in our embers 130
Is something that doth live,
That nature yet remembers
What was so fugitive!
The thought of our past years in me doth breed
Perpetual benediction: not indeed 135
For that which is most worthy to be blest;
Delight and liberty, the simple creed
Of Childhood, whether busy or at rest,
With new-fledged hope still fluttering in his breast:—
Not for these I raise 140
The song of thanks and praise;
But for those obstinate questionings
Of sense and outward things,
Fallings from us, vanishings;
Blank misgivings of a Creature 145
Moving about in worlds not realized,
High instincts before which our mortal Nature
Did tremble like a guilty Thing surprised:
But for those first affections,
Those shadowy recollections, 150
Which, be they what they may,
Are yet the fountain light of all our day,
Are yet a master light of all our seeing;
Uphold us, cherish, and have power to make
Our noisy years seem moments in the being 155
Of the eternal Silence: truths that wake,
To perish never;
Which neither listlessness, nor mad endeavour,
Nor Man nor Boy,

Nor all that is at enmity with joy,   160
Can utterly abolish or destroy!
     Hence in a season of calm weather
       Though inland far we be,
Our Souls have sight of that immortal sea
       Which brought us hither,   165
      Can in a moment travel thither,
And see the Children sport upon the shore,
And hear the mighty waters rolling evermore.

10

Then sing, ye Birds, sing, sing a joyous song!
      And let the young Lambs bound   170
      As to the tabor's sound!
We in thought will join your throng,
    Ye that pipe and ye that play,
    Ye that through your hearts to-day
    Feel the gladness of the May!   175
What though the radiance which was once so bright
Be now for ever taken from my sight,
     Though nothing can bring back the hour
Of splendour in the grass, of glory in the flower;
      We will grieve not, rather find   180
      Strength in what remains behind;
      In the primal sympathy
      Which having been must ever be;
      In the soothing thoughts that spring
      Out of human suffering;   185
      In the faith that looks through death,
In years that bring the philosophic mind.

11

And O, ye Fountains, Meadows, Hills, and Groves,
Forbode not any severing of our loves!
Yet in my heart of hearts I feel your might;   190
I only have relinquished one delight
To live beneath your more habitual sway.

I love the Brooks which down their channels fret,
Even more than when I tripped lightly as they;
The innocent brightness of a new-born Day   195
           Is lovely yet;
The Clouds that gather round the setting sun
Do take a sober colouring from an eye
That hath kept watch o'er man's mortality;
Another race hath been, and other palms are won.   200
Thanks to the human heart by which we live,
Thanks to its tenderness, its joys, and fears,
To me the meanest° flower that blows can give
Thoughts that do often lie too deep for tears.

—1807

SAMUEL TAYLOR COLERIDGE ■ (1772–1834)

Samuel Taylor Coleridge, inspired but erratic, did his best work, like Wordsworth, during the great first decade of their friendship, the period that produced Lyrical Ballads. *Coleridge's later life is a tragic tale of financial and marital problems, unfinished projects, and a ruinous addiction to opium. A brilliant critic, Coleridge lectured on Shakespeare and other writers and wrote the* Biographia Literaria, *perhaps the greatest literary autobiography ever written.*

Frost at Midnight

    The Frost performs its secret ministry,
Unhelped by any wind. The owlet's cry
Came loud—and hark, again! loud as before.
The inmates of my cottage, all at rest,
Have left me to that solitude, which suits   5
Abstruser musings: save that at my side
My cradled infant° slumbers peacefully.

203 **meanest** least significant
7 **My cradled infant** the poet's son Hartley (1796–1849)

'Tis calm indeed! so calm, that it disturbs
And vexes meditation, with its strange
And extreme silentness. Sea, hill, and wood,   10
This populous village! Sea, and hill, and wood,
With all the numberless goings-on of life,
Inaudible as dreams! the thin blue flame
Lies on my low-burnt fire, and quivers not;
Only that film,° which fluttered on the grate,   15
Still flutters there, the sole unquiet thing.
Methinks its motion in this hush of nature
Gives it dim sympathies with me who live,
Making it a companionable form,
Whose puny flaps and freaks the idling Spirit   20
By its own moods interprets, everywhere
Echo or mirror seeking of itself,
And makes a toy of Thought.

                       But O! how oft,
How oft, at school, with most believing mind,
Presageful,° have I gazed upon the bars,   25
To watch that fluttering *stranger!* and as oft
With unclosed lids, already had I dreamt
Of my sweet birthplace, and the old church tower,
Whose bells, the poor man's only music, rang
From morn to evening, all the hot Fair-day,   30
So sweetly, that they stirred and haunted me
With a wild pleasure, falling on mine ear
Most like articulate sounds of things to come!
So gazed I, till the soothing things, I dreamt,
Lulled me to sleep, and sleep prolonged my dreams!   35
And so I brooded all the following morn,
Awed by the stern preceptor's° face, mine eye
Fixed with mock study on my swimming book:
Save if the door half opened, and I snatched
A hasty glance, and still my heart leaped up,   40
For still I hoped to see the *stranger's* face,
Townsman, or aunt, or sister more beloved,
My playmate when we both were clothed alike!

15 film a piece of ash **25 Presageful** with hints of the future **37 preceptor** teacher

Dear Babe, that sleepest cradled by my side,
Whose gentle breathings, heard in this deep calm,   45
Fill up the interspersèd vacancies
And momentary pauses of the thought!
My babe so beautiful! it thrills my heart
With tender gladness, thus to look at thee,
And think that thou shalt learn far other lore,   50
And in far other scenes! For I was reared
In the great city, pent 'mid cloisters dim,
And saw nought lovely but the sky and stars.
But *thou*, my babe! shalt wander like a breeze
By lakes and sandy shores, beneath the crags   55
Of ancient mountain, and beneath the clouds,
Which image in their bulk both lakes and shores
And mountain crags: so shalt thou see and hear
The lovely shapes and sounds intelligible
Of that eternal language, which thy God   60
Utters, who from eternity doth teach
Himself in all, and all things in himself.
Great universal Teacher! he shall mold
Thy spirit, and by giving make it ask.

Therefore all seasons shall be sweet to thee,   65
Whether the summer clothe the general earth
With greenness, or the redbreast sit and sing
Betwixt the tufts of snow on the bare branch
Of mossy apple tree, while the nigh thatch
Smokes in the sun-thaw; whether the eave-drops fall   70
Heard only in the trances of the blast,
Or if the secret ministry of frost
Shall hang them up in silent icicles,
Quietly shining to the quiet Moon.

—1798

Kubla Khan°

OR A VISION IN A DREAM,° A FRAGMENT

In Xanadu did Kubla Khan
A stately pleasure-dome decree:
Where Alph, the sacred river, ran
Through caverns measureless to man

Down to a sunless sea.   5
So twice five miles of fertile ground
With walls and towers were girdled round:
And there were gardens bright with sinuous rills,
Where blossomed many an incense-bearing tree;
And here were forests ancient as the hills,   10
Enfolding sunny spots of greenery.

But oh! that deep romantic chasm which slanted
Down the green hill athwart a cedarn cover!
A savage place! as holy and enchanted
As e'er beneath a waning moon was haunted   15
By woman wailing for her demon lover!
And from this chasm, with ceaseless turmoil seething,
As if this earth in fast thick pants were breathing,
A mighty fountain momently was forced:
Amid whose swift half-intermitted burst   20
Huge fragments vaulted like rebounding hail,
Or chaffy grain beneath the thresher's flail:
And 'mid these dancing rocks at once and ever
It flung up momently the sacred river.
Five miles meandering with a mazy motion   25

KUBLA KHAN

Kubla Khan ruler of China (1216–1294)   **vision in a dream** Coleridge's own account tells how he took opium for an illness and slept for three hours, during which time he envisioned a complete poem of some 300 lines. When he awoke, he began to write down the details of his dream. "At this moment he was unfortunately called out by a person on business from Porlock, and detained by him above an hour, and on his return to the room found, to his no small surprise and mortification, that though he still retained some vague and dim recollection of the general purport of the vision, yet, with the exception of some eight or ten scattered lines and images on the surface of a stream into which a stone has been cast . . ." [Coleridge's note].

Through wood and dale the sacred river ran,
Then reached the caverns measureless to man,
And sank in tumult to a lifeless ocean:
And 'mid this tumult Kubla heard from far
Ancestral voices prophesying war!   30

    The shadow of the dome of pleasure
    Floated midway on the waves;
    Where was heard the mingled measure
    From the fountain and the caves.
It was a miracle of rare device,   35
A sunny pleasure-dome with caves of ice!

    A damsel with a dulcimer
    In a vision once I saw:
    It was an Abyssinian maid,
    And on her dulcimer she played,   40
    Singing of Mount Abora.
    Could I revive within me
    Her symphony and song,

    To such a deep delight 'twould win me,
That with music loud and long,   45
I would build that dome in air,
That sunny dome! those caves of ice!
And all who heard should see them there,
And all should cry, Beware! Beware!
His flashing eyes, his floating hair!   50
Weave a circle round him thrice,
And close your eyes with holy dread,
For he on honey-dew hath fed,
And drunk the milk of Paradise.

—1797–98

Work Without Hope

Lines Composed 21st February 1825

All Nature seems at work. Slugs leave their lair—
The bees are stirring—birds are on the wing—
And Winter slumbering in the open air

Wears on his smiling face a dream of Spring!
And I the while, the sole unbusy thing,   5
Nor honey make, nor pair, nor build, nor sing.

    Yet well I ken° the banks where amaranths° blow,
Have traced the fount whence streams of nectar flow.
Bloom, O ye amaranths! bloom for whom ye may,
For me ye bloom not! Glide, rich streams, away!   10
With lips unbrightened, wreathless brow, I stroll:
And would you learn the spells that drowse my soul?
Work without Hope draws° nectar in a sieve,
And Hope without an object cannot live.

—1828

GEORGE GORDON, LORD BYRON ■ (1788–1824)

George Gordon, Lord Byron attained flamboyant celebrity status, leading an unconventional lifestyle that contributed to his notoriety. Byron was the most widely read of all the English romantic poets, but his verse romances and mock-epic poems like Don Juan *have not proved as popular in our era. An English aristocrat who was committed to revolutionary ideals, Byron died while lending military assistance to the cause of Greek freedom.*

She Walks in Beauty

She walks in beauty, like the night
    Of cloudless climes and starry skies;
And all that's best of dark and bright
    Meet in her aspect and her eyes:
Thus mellowed to that tender light   5
    Which heaven to gaudy day denies.

7 ken know **amaranths** legendary flowers that never fade **13 draws** dips

One shade the more, one ray the less,
    Had half impaired the nameless grace
Which waves in every raven tress,
    Or softly lightens o'er her face;   10
Where thoughts serenely sweet express
    How pure, how dear their dwelling-place.

And on that cheek, and o'er that brow,
    So soft, so calm, yet eloquent,
The smiles that win, the tints that glow,   15
    But tell of days in goodness spent,
A mind at peace with all below,
    A heart whose love is innocent!

—1815

Stanzas

When A Man Hath No Freedom To Fight For At Home

When a man hath no freedom to fight for at home,
    Let him combat for that of his neighbors;
Let him think of the glories of Greece and of Rome,
    And get knocked on his head for his labors.

To do good to mankind is the chivalrous plan,   5
    And is always as nobly requited:
Then battle for freedom wherever you can,
    And, if not shot or hanged, you'll get knighted.

—1824

When We Two Parted

When we two parted
    In silence and tears,
Half broken-hearted
    To sever for years,
Pale grew thy cheek and cold,   5
    Colder thy kiss;
Truly that hour foretold
    Sorrow to this.

The dew of the morning
    Sunk chill on my brow—   10

It felt like the warning
　　Of what I feel now.
Thy vows are all broken,
　　And light is thy fame;
I hear thy name spoken,　　　　　　　　　　15
　　And share in its shame.

They name thee before me,
　　A knell to mine ear;
A shudder comes o'er me—
　　Why wert thou so dear?　　　　　　　　20
They know not I knew thee,
　　Who knew thee too well:—
Long, long shall I rue thee,
　　Too deeply to tell.

In secret we met—　　　　　　　　　　　25
　　In silence I grieve
That thy heart could forget,
　　Thy spirit deceive.
If I should meet thee
　　After long years,　　　　　　　　　　30
How should I greet thee?—
　　With silence and tears.

　　　　　　　　　　　　　　　　—1813

PERCY BYSSHE SHELLEY ■ (1792–1822)

Percy Bysshe Shelley, like his friend Byron, has not found as much favor in recent eras as the other English romantics, although his political liberalism anticipates many currents of our own day. Perhaps his unbridled emotionalism is sometimes too intense for modern readers. His wife, Mary Wollstonecraft Shelley, will be remembered as the author of the classic horror novel Frankenstein.

Ode to the West Wind

1

O wild West Wind, thou breath of Autumn's being,
Thou, from whose unseen presence the leaves dead
Are driven, like ghosts from an enchanter fleeing,

Yellow, and black, and pale, and hectic red,
Pestilence-stricken multitudes: O thou,   5
Who chariotest to their dark wintry bed

The wingèd seeds, where they lie cold and low,
Each like a corpse within its grave, until
Thine azure sister of the Spring° shall blow

Her clarion o'er the dreaming earth, and fill   10
(Driving sweet buds like flocks to feed in air)
With living hues and odors plain and hill:

Wild Spirit, which art moving everywhere;
Destroyer and preserver; hear, oh, hear!

2

Thou on whose stream, mid the steep sky's commotion,   15
Loose clouds like earth's decaying leaves are shed,
Shook from the tangled boughs of Heaven and Ocean,

Angels of rain and lightning: there are spread
On the blue surface of thine aëry surge,
Like the bright hair uplifted from the head   20

Of some fierce Mænad,° even from the dim verge
Of the horizon to the zenith's height,
The locks of the approaching storm. Thou dirge

Of the dying year, to which this closing night
Will be the dome of a vast sepulcher,   25
Vaulted with all thy congregated might

Of vapors, from whose solid atmosphere
Black rain, and fire, and hail will burst: oh, hear!

3

Thou who didst waken from his summer dreams
The blue Mediterranean, where he lay,   30
Lulled by the coil of his crystàlline streams,

Beside a pumice isle in Baiae's bay,°
And saw in sleep old palaces and towers
Quivering within the wave's intenser day,

---

9 azure sister of the Spring i.e., the South Wind   **21 Mænad** female worshipper of Bacchus, god
of wine   **32 Baiae's bay** near Naples

All overgrown with azure moss and flowers 35
So sweet, the sense faints picturing them! Thou
For whose path the Atlantic's level powers

Cleave themselves into chasms, while far below
The sea-blooms and the oozy woods which wear
The sapless foliage of the ocean, know 40

Thy voice, and suddenly grow gray with fear,
And tremble and despoil themselves: oh, hear!

4

If I were a dead leaf thou mightest bear;
If I were a swift cloud to fly with thee;
A wave to pant beneath thy power, and share 45

The impulse of thy strength, only less free
Than thou, O uncontrollable! If even
I were as in my boyhood, and could be

The comrade of thy wanderings over Heaven,
As then, when to outstrip thy skyey speed 50
Scarce seemed a vision; I would ne'er have striven

As thus with thee in prayer in my sore need.
Oh, lift me as a wave, a leaf, a cloud!
I fall upon the thorns of life! I bleed!

A heavy weight of hours has chained and bowed 55
One too like thee: tameless, and swift, and proud.

5

Make me thy lyre, even as the forest is:
What if my leaves are falling like its own!
The tumult of thy mighty harmonies

Will take from both a deep, autumnal tone, 60
Sweet though in sadness. Be thou, Spirit fierce,
My spirit! Be thou me, impetuous one!

Drive my dead thoughts over the universe
Like withered leaves to quicken a new birth!
And, by the incantation of this verse, 65

Scatter, as from an unextinguished hearth
Ashes and sparks, my words among mankind!
Be through my lips to unawakened earth

The trumpet of a prophecy! O Wind,
If Winter comes, can Spring be far behind? 70

—1820

Ozymandias°

I met a traveler from an antique land
Who said: Two vast and trunkless legs of stone
Stand in the desert. . . . Near them, on the sand,
Half sunk, a shattered visage lies, whose frown,
And wrinkled lip, and sneer of cold command, 5
Tell that its sculptor well those passions read
Which yet survive, stamped on these lifeless things,
The hand that mocked them, and the heart that fed:
And on the pedestal these words appear:
"My name is Ozymandias, king of kings: 10
Look on my works, ye Mighty, and despair!"
Nothing beside remains. Round the decay
Of that colossal wreck, boundless and bare
The lone and level sands stretch far away.

—1818

JOHN KEATS ■ (1795–1821)

John Keats is now perhaps the most admired of all the major romantics. Certainly his tragic death from tuberculosis in his twenties gives poignancy to thoughts of the doomed young poet writing feverishly in a futile race against time; "Here lies one whose name was writ in water" are the words he chose for his own epitaph. Many of Keats's poems are concerned with glimpses of the eternal, whether a translation of an ancient epic poem or a pristine artifact of a vanished civilization.

Ozymandias Ramses II of Egypt (c. 1250 BC)

Bright Star, Would I Were Stedfast as Thou Art°

Bright star, would I were stedfast as thou art—
    Not in lone splendor hung aloft the night,
And watching, with eternal lids apart,
    Like nature's patient, sleepless eremite°,
The moving waters at their priestlike task   5
    Of pure ablution° round earth's human shores,
Or gazing on the new soft-fallen mask
    Of snow upon the mountains and the moors;
No—yet still stedfast, still unchangeable,
    Pillow'd upon my fair love's ripening breast,   10
To feel for ever its soft swell and fall,
    Awake for ever in a sweet unrest,
Still, still to hear her tender-taken breath,
    And so live ever—or else swoon to death°.

                      —1821

La Belle Dame sans Merci°

O what can ail thee, Knight at arms,
    Alone and palely loitering?
The sedge has withered from the Lake
    And no birds sing!

O what can ail thee, Knight at arms,   5
    So haggard, and so woebegone?
The squirrel's granary is full
    And the harvest's done.

I see a lily on thy brow
    With anguish moist and fever dew,   10
And on thy cheeks a fading rose
    Fast withereth too.

Bright star, would I were stedfast as thou art While on a tour of the Lake District in 1818, Keats had said that the austere scenes "refine one's sensual vision into a sort of north star which can never cease to be open lidded and steadfast over the wonders of the great Power." The thought developed into this sonnet, which Keats drafted in 1819, then copied into his volume of Shakespeare's poems at the end of September or the beginning of October 1820, while on his way to Italy, where he died   **4 eremite** Hermit, religious solitary   **6 ablution** warhing, as part of a religious rite   **14 death** in the earlier version: "Half passionless, and so swoon on to death
La Belle Dame sans Merci "the beautiful lady without pity"

"I met a Lady in the Meads,
    Full beautiful, a faery's child,
Her hair was long, her foot was light,
    And her eyes were wild.   15

"I made a Garland for her head,
    And bracelets too, and fragrant Zone;°
She looked at me as she did love
    And made sweet moan.   20

"I set her on my pacing steed
    And nothing else saw all day long,
For sidelong would she bend and sing
    A faery's song.

"She found me roots of relish sweet,   25
    And honey wild, and manna dew,
And sure in language strange she said
    'I love thee true.'

"She took me to her elfin grot°
    And there she wept and sighed full sore, 30
And there I shut her wild wild eyes
    With kisses four.

"And there she lullèd me asleep,
    And there I dreamed, Ah Woe betide!
The latest dream I ever dreamt   35
    On the cold hill side.

"I saw pale Kings, and Princes too,
    Pale warriors, death-pale were they all;
They cried, 'La belle Dame sans merci
    Hath thee in thrall!'   40

"I saw their starved lips in the gloam
    With horrid warning gapèd wide,
And I awoke, and found me here
    On the cold hill's side.

"And this is why I sojourn here   45
    Alone and palely loitering;
Though the sedge is withered from the Lake,
    And no birds sing."

                          —1819

18 Zone belt   **29 grot** cave

Ode to a Nightingale

1

My heart aches, and a drowsy numbness pains
    My sense, as though of hemlock° I had drunk,
Or emptied some dull opiate to the drains
    One minute past, and Lethe-wards° had sunk.
'Tis not through envy of thy happy lot,   5
    But being too happy in thine happiness—
        That thou, light-wingèd Dryad° of the trees,
           In some melodious plot
Of beechen green, and shadows numberless,
        Singest of summer in full-throated ease.   10

2

O, for a draught of vintage! that hath been
    Cooled a long age in the deep-delvèd earth,
Tasting of Flora° and the country green,
    Dance, and Provençal° song, and sunburnt mirth!
O for a beaker full of the warm South,   15
    Full of the true, the blushful Hippocrene,°
        With beaded bubbles winking at the brim,
           And purple-stainèd mouth;
That I might drink, and leave the world unseen,
        And with thee fade away into the forest dim: 20

3

Fade far away, dissolve, and quite forget
    What thou among the leaves hast never known,
The weariness, the fever, and the fret
    Here, where men sit and hear each other groan;
Where palsy shakes a few, sad, last gray hairs,   25
    Where youth grows pale, and specter-thin, and dies;
        Where but to think is to be full of sorrow
           And leaden-eyed despairs,
Where Beauty cannot keep her lustrous eyes,
    Or new Love pine at them beyond tomorrow.   30

2 **hemlock** a deadly poison   4 **Lethe-wards** toward the waters of forgetfulness   7 **Dryad** tree
nymph   13 **Flora** Roman goddess of spring   14 **Provençal** of Provence, in South of France
16 **Hippocrene** fountain of the Muses

4

Away! away! for I will fly to thee,
    Not charioted by Bacchus° and his pards,°
But on the viewless wings of Poesy,°
    Though the dull brain perplexes and retards:
Already with thee! tender is the night,   35
    And haply the Queen-Moon is on her throne,
        Clustered around by all her starry Fays;°
            But here there is no light,
Save what from heaven is with the breezes blown
        Through verdurous glooms and winding mossy ways.   40

5

I cannot see what flowers are at my feet,
    Nor what soft incense hangs upon the boughs,
But, in embalmèd darkness, guess each sweet
    Wherewith the seasonable month endows
The grass, the thicket, and the fruit-tree wild;   45
    White hawthorn, and the pastoral eglantine;
        Fast fading violets covered up in leaves;
            And mid-May's eldest child,
The coming musk-rose, full of dewy wine,
        The murmurous haunt of flies on summer eves.   50

6

Darkling° I listen; and for many a time
    I have been half in love with easeful Death,
Called him soft names in many a musèd rhyme,
    To take into the air my quiet breath;
Now more than ever seems it rich to die,   55
    To cease upon the midnight with no pain,
        While thou art pouring forth thy soul abroad
            In such an ecstasy!
        Still wouldst thou sing, and I have ears in vain—
            To thy high requiem become a sod.   60

---

32 Bacchus Roman god of wine   **pards** leopards   **33 Poesy** poetry   **37 Fays** fairies   **51 Darkling** in the dark

7

Thou wast not born for death, immortal Bird!
    No hungry generations tread thee down;
The voice I hear this passing night was heard
    In ancient days by emperor and clown;
Perhaps the selfsame song that found a path   65
    Through the sad heart of Ruth, when, sick for home,
        She stood in tears amid the alien corn;°
           The same that ofttimes hath
    Charmed magic casements, opening on the foam
        Of perilous seas, in faery lands forlorn.   70

8

Forlorn! the very word is like a bell
    To toll me back from thee to my sole self!
Adieu! the fancy cannot cheat so well
    As she is famed to do, deceiving elf.
Adieu! adieu! thy plaintive anthem fades   75
    Past the near meadows, over the still stream,
        Up the hill side; and now 'tis buried deep
           In the next valley-glades:
Was it a vision, or a waking dream?
        Fled is that music:—Do I wake or sleep?   80

—1819

On First Looking into Chapman's Homer°

Much have I traveled in the realms of gold,
    And many goodly states and kingdoms seen;
    Round many western islands have I been
Which bards in fealty to Apollo° hold.
Oft of one wide expanse had I been told   5
    That deep-browed Homer ruled as his demesne;
    Yet did I never breathe its pure serene

66–67 Ruth . . . alien corn in the Old Testament she is a Moabite working in the grain fields of Boaz in Judah
Chapman's Homer translation of the *Iliad* and *Odyssey* by George Chapman (1559–1634) 4 Apollo here, the god of poetry

Till I heard Chapman speak out loud and bold:
Then felt I like some watcher of the skies
　　When a new planet swims into his ken;　　　　　　10
Or like stout Cortez° when with eagle eyes
　　He stared at the Pacific—and all his men
Looked at each other with a wild surmise—
　　Silent, upon a peak in Darien.°

—1816

ELIZABETH BARRETT BROWNING ▪ (1806–1861)

Elizabeth Barrett Browning was already a famous poet when she met her husband-to-be, Robert Browning, who had been corresponding with her on literary matters. She originally published her famous sonnet sequence, written in the first years of her marriage, in the guise of a translation of Portuguese poems, perhaps to mask their personal revelations.

Sonnets from the Portuguese, 18

I never gave a lock of hair away
To a man, dearest, except this to thee,
Which now upon my fingers thoughtfully,
I ring out to the full brown length and say
"Take it." My day of youth went yesterday;　　　　　5
My hair no longer bounds to my foot's glee,
Nor plant I it from rose or myrtle-tree,
As girls do, any more: it only may
Now shade on two pale cheeks the mark of tears,
Taught drooping from the head that hangs aside　　10
Through sorrow's trick. I thought the funeral-shears
Would take this first, but Love is justified,—
Take it thou,—finding pure, from all those years,
The kiss my mother left here when she died.

—1845–46

11 **Cortez** Balboa was actually the first European to see the Pacific　14 **Darien** in modern-day Panama

Sonnets from the Portuguese, 43

How do I love thee? Let me count the ways.
I love thee to the depth and breadth and height
My soul can reach, when feeling out of sight
For the ends of Being and ideal Grace.
I love thee to the level of everyday's   5
Most quiet need, by sun and candle-light.
I love thee freely, as men strive for Right;
I love thee purely, as they turn from Praise.
I love thee with the passion put to use
In my old griefs, and with my childhood's faith.   10
I love thee with a love I seemed to lose
With my lost saints—I love thee with the breath,
Smiles, tears, of all my life!—and, if God choose,
I shall but love thee better after death.

—*1845–46*

HENRY WADSWORTH LONGFELLOW ■ (1807–1882)

Henry Wadsworth Longfellow was by far the most prominent nineteenth-century American poet, and his international fame led to his bust being placed in Westminster Abbey after his death. The long epic poems like Evangeline and Hiawatha that were immensely popular among contemporary readers are seldom read today, but his shorter poems reveal a level of craftsmanship that few poets have equaled.

The Arsenal at Springfield

This is the Arsenal. From floor to ceiling,
    Like a huge organ, rise the burnished arms;
But from their silent pipes no anthem pealing
    Startles the villages with strange alarms.

Ah! what a sound will rise, how wild and dreary,   5
    When the death-angel touches those swift keys!
What loud lament and dismal Miserere°
    Will mingle with their awful symphonies!

7 **Miserere** Latin hymn from Psalm 1: "Have mercy on me, Lord."

I hear even now the infinite fierce chorus,
    The cries of agony, the endless groan,   10
Which, through the ages that have gone before us,
    In long reverberations reach our own.

On helm and harness rings the Saxon hammer,
    Through Cimbric° forest roars the Norseman's song,
And loud, amid the universal clamor,   15
    O'er distant deserts sounds the Tartar gong.

I hear the Florentine, who from his palace
    Wheels out his battle-bell with dreadful din,
And Aztec priests upon their teocallis°
    Beat the wild war-drums made of serpent's skin;   20

The tumult of each sacked and burning village;
    The shout that every prayer for mercy drowns;
The soldiers' revels in the midst of pillage;
    The wail of famine in beleaguered towns;

The bursting shell, the gateway wrenched asunder,   25
    The rattling musketry, the clashing blade;
And ever and anon, in tones of thunder
    The diapason° of the cannonade.

Is it, O man, with such discordant noises,
    With such accursed instruments as these,   30
Thou drownest Nature's sweet and kindly voices,
    And jarrest the celestial harmonies?

Were half the power, that fills the world with terror,
    Were half the wealth bestowed on camps and courts,
Given to redeem the human mind from error,   35
    There were no need of arsenals or forts:

The warrior's name would be a name abhorred!
    And every nation, that should lift again
Its hand against a brother, on its forehead
    Would wear forevermore the curse of Cain!   40

14 **Cimbric** in Denmark   19 **teocallis** temples atop pyramids   28 **diapason** full range of pipe organ

Down the dark future, through long generations,
  The echoing sounds grow fainter and then cease;
And like a bell, with solemn, sweet vibrations,
  I hear once more the voice of Christ say, "Peace!"
Peace! and no longer from its brazen portals   45
  The blast of War's great organ shakes the skies!
But beautiful as songs of the immortals,
  The holy melodies of love arise.

—1846

The Cross of Snow

In the long, sleepless watches of the night,
  A gentle face—the face of one long dead—
  Looks at me from the wall, where round its head
  The night-lamp casts a halo of pale light.
Here in this room she died; and soul more white   5
  Never through martyrdom of fire° was led
  To its repose; nor can in books be read
  The legend of a life more benedight.°
There is a mountain in the distant West
  That, sun-defying, in its deep ravines   10
  Displays a cross of snow upon its side.
Such is the cross I wear upon my breast
  These eighteen years, through all the changing scenes
  And seasons, changeless since the day she died.

—1886

EDGAR ALLAN POE ■ (1809–1849)

Edgar Allan Poe has survived his own myth as a deranged, drug-crazed ge-
nius, despite the wealth of evidence to the contrary that can be gleaned from
his brilliant, though erratic, career as a poet, short-story writer, critic, and ed-
itor. Poe's brand of romanticism seems at odds with that of other American
poets of his day, and is perhaps more in keeping with the spirit of Coleridge
than that of Wordsworth. "The Raven" has been parodied perhaps more than
any other American poem, yet it still retains a powerful hold on its audience.

6 martyrdom of fire Longfellow's second wife, Frances, died as the result of a household fire
in 1861.   **8 benedight** blessed

The Haunted Palace

EDGAR ALLAN POE

In the greenest of our valleys,
    By good angels tenanted,
Once a fair and stately palace—
    Radiant palace—reared its head.
In the monarch Thought's dominion—   5
    It stood there!
Never seraph spread a pinion
    Over fabric half so fair!

Banners yellow, glorious, golden,
    On its roof did float and flow,   10
(This—all this—was in the olden
    Time long ago,)
And every gentle air that dallied,
    In that sweet day,
Along the ramparts plumed and pallid,   15
    A wingéd odor went away.

Wanderers in that happy valley,
    Through two luminous windows, saw
Spirits moving musically
    To a lute's well-tunéd law,   20
Round about a throne where, sitting,
    Porphyrogene!°
In state his glory well befitting,
    The ruler of the realm was seen.

And all with pearl and ruby glowing   25
    Was the fair palace door,
Through which came flowing, flowing, flowing,
    And sparkling evermore,
A troop of Echoes, whose sweet duty
    Was but to sing,   30
In voices of surpassing beauty,
    The wit and wisdom of their king.

---

22 Porphyrogene born to the purple, i.e., royal

But evil things, in robes of sorrow,
　　Assailed the monarch's high estate.
(Ah, let us mourn!—for never morrow
　　Shall dawn upon him, desolate!)
And round about his home the glory
　　That blushed and bloomed,
Is but a dim-remembered story
　　Of the old time entombed.

and travellers, now, within that valley,
　　Through the red-litten windows see
Vast forms that move fantastically
　　To a discordant melody,
While, like a ghastly rapid river,
　　Through the pale door
A hideous throng rush out forever,
　　And laugh—but smile no more.

—1845

The Raven

Once upon a midnight dreary, while I pondered, weak
　　and weary,
Over many a quaint and curious volume of forgotten lore—
While I nodded, nearly napping, suddenly there came a tapping,
As of some one gently rapping, rapping at my chamber door.
"'Tis some visitor," I muttered, "tapping at my chamber door—
　　　　　　　　　　　　Only this and nothing more."

Ah, distinctly I remember it was in the bleak December;
And each separate dying ember wrought its ghost upon
　　the floor.
Eagerly I wished the morrow;—vainly I had sought to borrow
From my books surcease of sorrow—sorrow for the
　　lost Lenore—
For the rare and radiant maiden whom the angels name
　　Lenore—
　　　　　　　　　　　　Nameless *here* for evermore.
And the silken, sad, uncertain rustling of each purple curtain
Thrilled me—filled me with fantastic terrors never felt before;

So that now, to still the beating of my heart, I stood repeating   15
"'Tis some visitor entreating entrance at my chamber door;—
Some late visitor entreating entrance at my chamber door;—
          This it is and nothing more."

Presently my soul grew stronger; hesitating then no longer,
"Sir," said I, "or Madam, truly your forgiveness I implore;   20
But the fact is I was napping, and so gently you came rapping,
And so faintly you came tapping, tapping at my chamber door,
That I scarce was sure I heard you"—here I opened wide the
    door;—
          Darkness there and nothing more.

Deep into that darkness peering, long I stood there wondering,
    fearing,   25
Doubting, dreaming dreams no mortal ever dared to dream
    before;
But the silence was unbroken, and the stillness gave no token,
And the only word there spoken was the whispered word,
    "Lenore?"
This I whispered, and an echo murmured back the word,
    "Lenore!"
          Merely this and nothing more.   30

Back into the chamber turning, all my soul within me burning,
Soon again I heard a tapping somewhat louder than before.
"Surely," said I, "surely that is something at my window lattice;
Let me see, then, what thereat is, and this mystery explore—
Let my heart be still a moment and this mystery explore;—   35
          'Tis the wind and nothing more!"

Open here I flung the shutter, when, with many a flirt and flutter,
In there stepped a stately Raven of the saintly days of yore;
Not the least obeisance made he; not a minute stopped or
    stayed he;
But, with mien of lord or lady, perched above my chamber
    door—   40
Perched upon a bust of Pallas° just above my chamber door—
          Perched, and sat, and nothing more.

41 **Pallas** Athena, goddess of wisdom

Then this ebony bird beguiling my sad fancy into smiling,
By the grave and stern decorum of the countenance it wore,
"Though thy crest be shorn and shaven, thou," I said, "art sure
    no craven,   45
Ghastly grim and ancient Raven wandering from the Nightly
    shore—
Tell me what thy lordly name is on the Night's Plutonian° shore!"
                        Quoth the Raven, "Nevermore."

Much I marvelled this ungainly fowl to hear discourse so plainly,
Though its answer little meaning—little relevancy bore;   50
For we cannot help agreeing that no living human being
Ever yet was blessed with seeing bird above his chamber door—
Bird or beast upon the sculptured bust above his chamber door,
                    With such name as "Nevermore."

But the Raven, sitting lonely on the placid bust, spoke only   55
That one word, as if his soul in that one word he did outpour.
Nothing farther then he uttered—not a feather then he
    fluttered—
Till I scarcely more than muttered, "Other friends have flown
    before—
On the morrow *he* will leave me, as my Hopes have flown before."
                Then the bird said, "Nevermore."   60

Startled at the stillness broken by reply so aptly spoken,
"Doubtless," said I, "what it utters is its only stock and store
Caught from some unhappy master whom unmerciful Disaster
Followed fast and followed faster till his songs one burden bore—
Till the dirges of his Hope that melancholy burden bore   65
                  Of 'Never—nevermore.'"

But the Raven still beguiling all my sad fancy into smiling,
Straight I wheeled a cushioned seat in front of bird and bust
    and door;
Then, upon the velvet sinking, I betook myself to linking
Fancy unto fancy, thinking what this ominous bird of yore—   70
What this grim, ungainly, ghastly, gaunt, and ominous bird of yore
              Meant in croaking "Nevermore."

47 Plutonian after Pluto, Roman god of the underworld

This I sat engaged in guessing, but no syllable expressing
To the fowl whose fiery eyes now burned into my bosom's core;
This and more I sat divining, with my head at ease reclining   75
On the cushion's velvet lining that the lamp-light gloated o'er,
But whose velvet-violet lining with the lamp-light gloating o'er,
               She shall press, ah, nevermore!

Then, methought, the air grew denser, perfumed from an
    unseen censer
Swung by seraphim whose foot-falls tinkled on the tufted floor.   80
"Wretch," I cried, "thy God hath lent thee—by these angels he
    hath sent thee.
Respite—respite and nepenthe° from thy memories of
    Lenore;
Quaff, oh quaff this kind nepenthe and forget this lost
    Lenore!"
               Quoth the Raven, "Nevermore."

"Prophet!" said I, "thing of evil!—prophet still, if bird or
    devil!—   85
Whether Tempter sent, or whether tempest tossed thee here
    ashore,
Desolate yet all undaunted, on this desert land enchanted—
On this home by Horror haunted—tell me truly, I implore—
Is there—*is* there balm in Gilead?—tell me—tell me, I implore!"
               Quoth the Raven, "Nevermore."   90

"Prophet!" said I, "thing of evil!—prophet still, if bird or devil!
By that Heaven that bends above us—by that God we both
    adore—
Tell this soul with sorrow laden if, within the distant Aidenn,°
It shall clasp a sainted maiden whom the angels name
    Lenore—
Clasp a rare and radiant maiden whom the angels name
    Lenore."
                    95
               Quoth the Raven, "Nevermore."

"Be that word our sign of parting, bird or fiend!" I shrieked,
    upstarting—

EDGAR ALLAN POE

82 nepenthe drug causing forgetfulness   **93 Aidenn** Eden

"Get thee back into the tempest and the Night's Plutonian shore!
Leave no black plume as a token of that lie thy soul hath
    spoken!
Leave my loneliness unbroken!—quit the bust above my
    door!   100
Take thy beak from out my heart, and take thy form from off
    my door!"
                        Quoth the Raven, "Nevermore."

And the Raven, never flitting, still is sitting, *still* is sitting
On the pallid bust of Pallas just above my chamber door;
And his eyes have all the seeming of a demon's that is
    dreaming,   105
And the lamp-light o'er him streaming throws his shadow on
    the floor;
And my soul from out that shadow that lies floating on the floor
                    Shall be lifted—nevermore!

                                                              —1845

Sonnet: To Science

Science! true daughter of Old Time thou art!
    Who alterest all things with the peering eyes.
Why preyest thou thus upon the poet's heart,
    Vulture, whose wings are dull realities?
How should he love thee? or how deem thee wise?   5
    Who wouldst not leave him in his wandering
To seek for treasure in the jeweled skies,
    Albeit he soared with an undaunted wing?
Has thou not dragged Diana° from her car?
    And driven the Hamadryad from the wood   10
To seek a shelter in some happier star?
    Hast thou not torn the Naiad from her flood,
The Elfin from the green grass, and from me
    The summer dream beneath the tamarind tree?

                                                       —1829, 1845

9 **Diana** Roman goddess, whose chariot was the moon.

Alfred, Lord Tennyson became the most famous English poet with the 1850 publication of In Memoriam, *a sequence of poems on the death of his friend A. H. Hallam. In the same year he became poet laureate. Modern critical opinion has focused more favorably on Tennyson's lyrical gifts than on his talents for narrative or drama. T. S. Eliot and W. H. Auden, among other critics, praised Tennyson's rhythms and sound patterns but had reservations about his depth of intellect, especially when he took on the role of official apologist for Victorian England.*

The Lady of Shalott

Part I

On either side the river lie
Long fields of barley and of rye,
That clothe the wold° and meet the sky;
And through the field the road runs by
  To many-towered Camelot;   5
And up and down the people go,
Gazing where the lilies blow
Round an island there below,
  The island of Shalott.
Willows whiten, aspens quiver,   10
Little breezes dusk and shiver
Through the wave that runs forever
By the island in the river
  Flowing down to Camelot.
Four gray walls, and four gray towers,   15
Overlook a space of flowers,
And the silent isle embowers
  The Lady of Shalott.

By the margin, willow-veiled,
Slide the heavy barges trailed   20
By slow horses; and unhailed

---

3 wold plain

The shallop° flitteth silken-sailed
	Skimming down to Camelot:
But who hath seen her wave her hand?
Or at the casement seen her stand?
Or is she known in all the land,					25
	The Lady of Shalott?

Only reapers, reaping early
In among the bearded barley,
Hear a song that echoes cheerly						30
From the river winding clearly,
	Down to towered Camelot;
And by the moon the reaper weary,
Piling sheaves in uplands airy,
Listening, whispers, "'Tis the fairy					35
	Lady of Shalott."

Part II

There she weaves by night and day
A magic web with colors gay.
She has heard a whisper say,
A curse is on her if she stay						40
	To look down to Camelot.
She knows not what the curse may be,
And so she weaveth steadily,
And little other care hath she,
	The Lady of Shalott.							45

And moving through a mirror clear
That hangs before her all the year,
Shadows of the world appear.
There she sees the highway near
	Winding down to Camelot;						50
There the river eddy whirls,
And there the surly village-churls,
And the red cloaks of market girls,
	Pass onward from Shalott.

22 **shallop** open boat

Sometimes a troop of damsels glad,
An abbot on an ambling pad,°
Sometimes a curly shepherd-lad,
Or long-haired page in crimson clad,
    Goes by to towered Camelot;
And sometimes through the mirror blue
The knights come riding two and two;
She hath no loyal knight and true,
    The Lady of Shalott.

But in her web she still delights
To weave the mirror's magic sights,
For often through the silent nights
A funeral, with plumes and lights
    And music, went to Camelot;
Or when the moon was overhead,
Came two young lovers lately wed;
"I am half sick of shadows," said
    The Lady of Shalott.

Part III

A bow-shot from her bower eaves,
He rode between the barley sheaves;
The sun came dazzling through the leaves,
And flamed upon the brazen greaves°
    Of bold Sir Lancelot.
A red-cross knight forever kneeled
To a lady in his shield.
That sparkled on the yellow field,
    Beside remote Shalott.

The gemmy bridle glittered free,
Like to some branch of stars we see
Hung in the golden Galaxy.
The bridle bells rang merrily
    As he rode down to Camelot;
And from his blazoned baldric° slung
A mighty silver bugle hung,
And as he rode his armor rung,
    Beside remote Shalott.

55

60

65

70

75

80

85

90

56 pad horse   **76 greaves** armor for legs   **87 baldric** belt to support a sword

All in the blue unclouded weather
Thick-jeweled shone the saddle-leather,
The helmet and the helmet-feather
Burned like one burning flame together
    As he rode down to Camelot;   95
As often through the purple night,
Below the starry clusters bright,
Some bearded meteor, trailing light,
    Moves over still Shalott.

His broad clear brow in sunlight glowed;   100
On burnished hooves his war horse trode;
From underneath his helmet flowed
His coal-black curls as on he rode,
    As he rode down to Camelot.
From the bank and from the river   105
He flashed into the crystal mirror,
"Tirra lirra," by the river
    Sang Sir Lancelot.

She left the web, she left the loom,
She made three paces through the room,   110
She saw the water lily bloom,
She saw the helmet and the plume,
    She looked down to Camelot.
Out flew the web and floated wide;
The mirror cracked from side to side;   115
"The curse is come upon me," cried
    The Lady of Shalott.

Part IV

In the stormy east wind straining,
The pale yellow woods were waning,
The broad stream in his banks complaining.   120
Heavily the low sky raining
    Over towered Camelot;
Down she came and found a boat
Beneath a willow left afloat,
And round about the prow she wrote   125
    The Lady of Shalott.

And down the river's dim expanse
Like some bold seer in a trance,
Seeing all his own mischance—
With a glassy countenance   130
    Did she look to Camelot.
And at the closing of the day
She loosed the chain, and down she lay;
The broad stream bore her far away,
    The Lady of Shalott.   135

Lying, robed in snowy white
That loosely flew to left and right—
The leaves upon her falling light—
Through the noises of the night
    She floated down to Camelot;   140
And as the boat-head wound along
The willowy hills and fields among,
They heard her singing her last song,
    The Lady of Shalott.

Heard a carol, mournful, holy,   145
Chanted loudly, chanted lowly,
Till her blood was frozen slowly,
And her eyes were darkened wholly,
    Turned to towered Camelot.
For ere she reached upon the tide   150
The first house by the waterside,
Singing in her song she died,
    The Lady of Shalott.

Under tower and balcony,
By garden wall and gallery,   155
A gleaming shape she floated by,
Dead-pale between the houses high,
    Silent into Camelot.
Out upon the wharfs they came,
Knight and burgher, lord and dame,   160
And round the prow they read her name,
    The Lady of Shalott.

Who is this? And what is here?
And in the lighted palace near
Died the sound of royal cheer;   165
And they crossed themselves for fear,
        All the knights at Camelot.
But Lancelot mused a little space;
He said, "She has a lovely face;
God in his mercy lend her grace,   170
        The Lady of Shalott."

—1842

Tears, Idle Tears

from The Princess

Tears, idle tears, I know not what they mean,
Tears from the depth of some divine despair
Rise in the heart, and gather to the eyes,
In looking on the happy autumn-fields,
And thinking of the days that are no more.   5

Fresh as the first beam glittering on a sail,
That brings our friends up from the underworld,
Sad as the last which reddens over one
That sinks with all we love below the verge;
So sad, so fresh, the days that are no more.   10

Ah, sad and strange as in dark summer dawns
The earliest pipe of half-awakened birds
To dying ears, when unto dying eyes
The casement slowly grows a glimmering square;
So sad, so strange, the days that are no more.   15

Dear as remembered kisses after death,
And sweet as those by hopeless fancy feigned
On lips that are for others; deep as love,
Deep as first love, and wild with all regret;
O Death in Life, the days that are no more!   20

—1847

Ulysses°

It little profits that an idle king,
By this still hearth, among these barren crags,
Matched with an aged wife, I mete and dole
Unequal laws unto a savage race,
That hoard, and sleep, and feed, and know not me.   5
I cannot rest from travel; I will drink
Life to the lees. All times I have enjoyed
Greatly, have suffered greatly, both with those
That loved me, and alone; on shore, and when
Through scudding drifts the rainy Hyades°   10
Vexed the dim sea. I am become a name;
For always roaming with a hungry heart
Much have I seen and known—cities of men
And manners, climates, councils, governments,
Myself not least, but honored of them all—   15
And drunk delight of battle with my peers,
Far on the ringing plains of windy Troy.
I am a part of all that I have met;
Yet all experience is an arch wherethrough
Gleams that untraveled world whose margin fades   20
For ever and for ever when I move.
How dull it is to pause, to make an end,
To rust unburnished, not to shine in use!
As though to breathe were life! Life piled on life
Were all too little, and of one to me   25
Little remains; but every hour is saved
From that eternal silence, something more,
A bringer of new things; and vile it were
For some three suns to store and hoard myself,
And this gray spirit yearning in desire   30
To follow knowledge like a sinking star,
Beyond the utmost bound of human thought.
    This is my son, mine own Telemachus,
To whom I leave the scepter and the isle,

Ulysses Homer's *Odyssey* ends with the return of Odysseus (Ulysses) to his island kingdom, Ithaca. Tennyson's poem takes place some years later.   **10 Hyades** a constellation thought to predict rain

ALFRED, LORD TENNYSON

556

Well-loved of me, discerning to fulfill   35
This labor, by slow prudence to make mild
A rugged people, and through soft degrees
Subdue them to the useful and the good.
Most blameless is he, centered in the sphere
Of common duties, decent not to fail   40
In offices of tenderness, and pay
Meet adoration to my household gods,
When I am gone. He works his work, I mine.
    There lies the port; the vessel puffs her sail;
There gloom the dark, broad seas. My mariners,   45
Souls that have toiled, and wrought, and thought with me,
That ever with a frolic welcome took
The thunder and the sunshine, and opposed
Free hearts, free foreheads—you and I are old;
Old age hath yet his honor and his toil.   50
Death closes all; but something ere the end,
Some work of noble note, may yet be done,
Not unbecoming men that strove with gods.
The lights begin to twinkle from the rocks;
The long day wanes; the low moon climbs; the deep   55
Moans round with many voices. Come, my friends,
'Tis not too late to seek a newer world.
Push off, and sitting well in order smite
The sounding furrows; for my purpose holds
To sail beyond the sunset, and the baths   60
Of all the western stars, until I die.
It may be that the gulfs will wash us down;
It may be we shall touch the Happy Isles,°
And see the great Achilles, whom we knew.
Though much is taken, much abides; and though   65
We are not now that strength which in old days
Moved earth and heaven, that which we are, we are,
One equal temper of heroic hearts,
Made weak by time and fate, but strong in will
To strive, to seek, to find, and not to yield.   70

—1833

63 **Happy Isles** Elysium, the resting place of dead heroes

ULYSSES

557

ROBERT BROWNING ■ (1812–1889)

Robert Browning wrote many successful dramatic monologues that are his lasting legacy, for he brings the genre to a level of achievement rarely equaled. Less regarded during his lifetime than his contemporary Tennyson, he has consistently risen in the esteem of modern readers. Often overlooked in his gallery of often grotesque characters are his considerable metrical skills and ability to simulate speech while working in demanding poetic forms.

My Last Duchess

FERRARA°

That's my last duchess painted on the wall,
Looking as if she were alive. I call
That piece a wonder, now: Frà Pandolf's° hands
Worked busily a day, and there she stands.
Will't please you sit and look at her? I said   5
"Frà Pandolf" by design, for never read
Strangers like you that pictured countenance,
The depth and passion of its earnest glance,
But to myself they turned (since none puts by
The curtain I have drawn for you, but I)   10
And seemed as they would ask me, if they durst,
How such a glance came there; so, not the first
Are you to turn and ask thus. Sir, 'twas not
Her husband's presence only, called that spot
Of joy into the Duchess' cheek: perhaps   15
Frà Pandolf chanced to say "Her mantle laps
Over my lady's wrist too much," or "Paint
Must never hope to reproduce the faint
Half-flush that dies along her throat": such stuff
Was courtesy, she thought, and cause enough   20
For calling up that spot of joy. She had
A heart—how shall I say?—too soon made glad,

Ferrara The speaker is probably Alfonso II d'Este, Duke of Ferrara (1533–158?)   **3 Frà Pandolf** an imaginary painter

Too easily impressed; she liked whate'er
She looked on, and her looks went everywhere.
Sir, 'twas all one! My favor at her breast,   25
The dropping of the daylight in the West,
The bough of cherries some officious fool
Broke in the orchard for her, the white mule
She rode with round the terrace—all and each
Would draw from her alike the approving speech,   30
Or blush, at least. She thanked men—good! but thanked
Somehow—I know not how—as if she ranked
My gift of a nine-hundred-years-old name
With anybody's gift. Who'd stoop to blame
This sort of trifling? Even had you skill   35
In speech—which I have not—to make your will
Quite clear to such an one, and say, "Just this
Or that in you disgusts me; here you miss,
Or there exceed the mark"—and if she let
Herself be lessoned so, nor plainly set   40
Her wits to yours, forsooth, and made excuse,
—E'en then would be some stooping; and I choose
Never to stoop. Oh sir, she smiled, no doubt,
Whene'er I passed her; but who passed without
Much the same smile? This grew; I gave commands;   45
Then all smiles stopped together. There she stands
As if alive. Will't please you rise? We'll meet
The company below, then. I repeat,
The Count your master's° known munificence
Is ample warrant that no just pretense   50
Of mine for dowry will be disallowed;
Though his fair daughter's self, as I avowed
At starting, is my object. Nay, we'll go
Together down, sir. Notice Neptune, though,
Taming a sea horse, thought a rarity,   55
Which Claus of Innsbruck cast in bronze for me!

—1842

---

49 Count your master's The auditor is apparently an envoy sent to arrange a marriage between the
Duke of Ferrara and a count's daughter

Porphyria's° Lover

ROBERT BROWNING

The rain set early in tonight,
    The sullen wind was soon awake,
It tore the elm-tops down for spite,
    And did its worst to vex the lake:
    I listened with heart fit to break.   5
When glided in Porphyria; straight
    She shut the cold out and the storm,
And kneeled and made the cheerless grate
    Blaze up, and all the cottage warm;
    Which done, she rose, and from her form   10
Withdrew the dripping cloak and shawl,
    And laid her soiled gloves by, untied
Her hat and let the damp hair fall,
    And, last, she sat down by my side
    And called me. When no voice replied,   15
She put my arm about her waist,
    And made her smooth white shoulder bare,
And all her yellow hair displaced,
    And, stooping, made my cheek lie there,
    And spread, o'er all, her yellow hair,   20
Murmuring how she loved me—she
    Too weak, for all her heart's endeavor,
To set its struggling passion free
    From pride, and vainer ties dissever,
    And give herself to me forever.   25
But passion sometimes would prevail,
    Nor could tonight's gay feast restrain
A sudden thought of one so pale
    For love of her, and all in vain:
    So, she was come through wind and rain.   30
Be sure I looked up at her eyes
    Happy and proud; at last I knew
Porphyria worshipped me; surprise
    Made my heart swell, and still it grew
    While I debated what to do.   35

Porphyria name suggesting purple, the color of nobility and royalty

That moment she was mine, mine, fair,
    Perfectly pure and good: I found
A thing to do, and all her hair
    In one long yellow string I wound
    Three times her little throat around,   40
And strangled her. No pain felt she;
    I am quite sure she felt no pain.
As a shut bud that holds a bee,
    I warily oped her lids: again
    Laughed the blue eyes without a stain.   45
And I untightened next the tress
    About her neck; her cheek once more
Blushed bright beneath my burning kiss:
    I propped her head up as before,
    Only, this time my shoulder bore   50
Her head, which droops upon it still:
    The smiling rosy little head
So glad it has its utmost will,
    That all it scorned at once is fled,
    And I, its love, am gained instead!   55
Porphyria's love: she guessed not how
    Her darling one wish would be heard.
And thus we sit together now,
    And all night long we have not stirred,
    And yet God has not said a word!   60
                         —1842

WALT WHITMAN ■ (1819–1892)

Walt Whitman pioneered the use of free verse, which established him as one of the forebears of modern poetry, but his subject matter, often dealing with sexual topics, and his unsparing realism were equally controversial in his day. An admirer of Emerson, he adapted many of the ideas of transcendentalism in Song of Myself, *his first major sequence, and also incorporated many of Emerson's calls for poets to use American subjects and patterns of speech.* Leaves of Grass, *which he revised from 1855 until his death, expanded to include virtually all of his poems, including the graphic poems he wrote while serving as a volunteer in Civil War army hospitals.*

A Noiseless Patient Spider

A noiseless patient spider,
I mark'd where on a little promontory it stood isolated,
Mark'd how to explore the vacant vast surrounding,
It launch'd forth filament, filament, filament, out of itself,
Ever unreeling them, ever tirelessly speeding them.   5

And you O my soul where you stand,
Surrounded, detached, in measureless oceans of space,
Ceaselessly musing, venturing, throwing, seeking the spheres to
    connect them,
Till the bridge you will need be form'd, till the ductile anchor
    hold,
Till the gossamer thread you fling catch somewhere, O my soul.   10

                                                            —1876

O Captain! My Captain!°

1

O Captain! my Captain! our fearful trip is done;
The ship has weather'd every rack, the prize we sought is won;
The port is near, the bells I hear, the people all exulting,
While follow eyes the steady keel, the vessel grim and daring:
    But O heart! heart! heart!   5
        O the bleeding drops of red,
            Where on the deck my Captain lies,
                Fallen cold and dead.

2

O Captain! my Captain! rise up and hear the bells;
Rise up—for you the flag is flung—for you the bugle trills;   10
For you bouquets and ribbon'd wreaths—for you the shores
    a-crowding;

O Captain! My Captain! This atypical ballad was written after the assassination of Abraham
Lincoln and ironically became Whitman's most popular poem during his lifetime.

For you they call, the swaying mass, their eager faces turning;
  Here Captain! dear father!
    This arm beneath your head;
      It is some dream that on the deck,   15
        You've fallen cold and dead.

3

My Captain does not answer, his lips are pale and still;
My father does not feel my arm, he has no pulse nor will;
The ship is anchor'd safe and sound, its voyage closed and done;
From fearful trip, the victor ship, comes in with object won;   20
  Exult, O shores, and ring, O bells!
    But I, with mournful tread,
      Walk the deck my Captain lies,
        Fallen cold and dead.

                                                        —1865

A Sight in Camp in the Daybreak Gray and Dim

A sight in camp in the daybreak gray and dim,
As from my tent I emerge so early sleepless,
As slow I walk in the cool fresh air the path near by the
    hospital tent,
Three forms I see on stretchers lying, brought out there
    untended lying,
Over each the blanket spread, ample brownish woolen
    blanket,   5
Gray and heavy blanket, folding, covering all.

Curious I halt and silent stand,
Then with light fingers I from the face of the nearest the first
    just lift the blanket;
Who are you elderly man so gaunt and grim, with well-gray'd
    hair, and flesh all sunken about the eyes?
Who are you my dear comrade?   10

Then to the second I step—and who are you my child and darling?
Who are you sweet boy with cheeks yet blooming?

Then to the third—a face nor child nor old, very calm, as of
  beautiful yellow-white ivory;
Young man I think I know you—I think this face is the face
  of the Christ himself,
Dead and divine and brother of all, and here again he lies.

—1865

Song of Myself, 6

A child said *What is the grass?* fetching it to me with full hands;
How could I answer the child? I do not know what it is any
  more than he.

I guess it must be the flag of my disposition, out of hopeful
  green stuff woven.

Or I guess it is the handkerchief of the Lord,
A scented gift and remembrancer designedly dropped,   5
Bearing the owner's name someway in the corners, that we may
  see and remark, and say *Whose?*

Or I guess the grass is itself a child, the produced babe of
  the vegetation.

Or I guess it is a uniform hieroglyphic,
And it means, Sprouting alike in broad zones and narrow zones,
Growing among black folks as among white,   10
Kanuck,° Tuckahoe,° Congressman, Cuff,° I give them the same, I
  receive them the same.

And now it seems to me the beautiful uncut hair of graves.

Tenderly will I use you curling grass,
It may be you transpire from the breasts of young men,
It may be if I had known them I would have loved them,   15
It may be you are from old people, or from offspring taken soon
  out of their mothers' laps,
And here you are the mothers' laps.

11 Kanuck French-Canadian **Tuckahoe** coastal Virginian **Cuff** a black slave

This grass is very dark to be from the white heads of old
    mothers.
Darker than the colorless beards of old men.
Dark to come from under the faint red roofs of mouths.   20

O I perceive after all so many uttering tongues,
And I perceive they do not come from the roofs of mouths for
    nothing.

I wish I could translate the hints about the dead young men and
    women,
And the hints about old men and mothers, and the offspring
    taken soon out of their laps.

What do you think has become of the young and old men?   25
And what do you think has become of the women and children?

They are alive and well somewhere,
The smallest sprout shows there is really no death,
And if ever there was it led forward life, and does not wait at the
    end to arrest it.
And ceased the moment life appeared.

All goes onward and outward, nothing collapses.
And to die is different from what anyone supposed, and
    luckier.

—1855

Song of Myself, 11

Twenty-eight young men bathe by the shore,
Twenty-eight young men and all so friendly;
Twenty-eight years of womanly life and all so lonesome.

She owns the fine house by the rise of the bank,
She hides handsome and richly drest aft the blinds of the
    window.   5

Which of the young men does she like the best?
Ah the homeliest of them is beautiful to her.

Where are you off to, lady? for I see you,
You splash in the water there, yet stay stock still in your room.

Dancing and laughing along the beach came the twenty-ninth
    bather, 10
The rest did not see her, but she saw them and loved them.

The beards of the young men glisten'd with wet, it ran from
    their long hair,
Little streams pass'd all over their bodies.

An unseen hand also pass'd over their bodies,
It descended trembling from their temples and ribs. 15

The young men float on their backs, their white bellies bulge to
    the sun, they do not ask who seizes fast to them,
They do not know who puffs and declines with pendant and
    bending arch,
They do not think whom they souse with spray.

—1855

When I Heard the Learn'd Astronomer

When I heard the learn'd astronomer,
When the proofs, the figures, were ranged in columns before me,
When I was shown the charts and diagrams, to add, divide, and
    measure them,
When I sitting heard the astronomer where he lectured with
    much applause in the lecture-room,
How soon unaccountable I became tired and sick, 5
Till rising and gliding out I wander'd off by myself,
In the mystical moist night-air, and from time to time,
Look'd up in perfect silence at the stars.

—1865

MATTHEW ARNOLD ■ (1822–1888)

Matthew Arnold was the son of the headmaster of Rugby School and him-self served as an inspector of schools during much of his adult life. An influential essayist as well as a poet, Arnold was unsparing in his criticism of middle-class "Philistinism." At least part of "Dover Beach" is thought to date from his honeymoon in 1851.

Dover Beach

The sea is calm tonight.
The tide is full, the moon lies fair
Upon the straits; on the French coast the light
Gleams and is gone; the cliffs of England stand,
Glimmering and vast, out in the tranquil bay.   5
Come to the window, sweet is the night-air!
Only, from the long line of spray
Where the sea meets the moon-blanched land,
Listen! you hear the grating roar
Of pebbles which the waves draw back, and fling,   10
At their return, up the high strand,
Begin, and cease, and then again begin,
With tremulous cadence slow, and bring
The eternal note of sadness in.

Sophocles° long ago   15
Heard it on the Aegean, and it brought
Into his mind the turbid ebb and flow
Of human misery; we
Find also in the sound a thought,
Hearing it by this distant northern sea.   20

The Sea of Faith
Was once, too, at the full, and round earth's shore
Lay like the folds of a bright girdle° furled.
But now I only hear
Its melancholy, long, withdrawing roar,   25
Retreating, to the breath
Of the night-wind, down the vast edges drear
And naked shingles° of the world.

Ah, love, let us be true
To one another! for the world, which seems   30
To lie before us like a land of dreams,
So various, so beautiful, so new,

15 **Sophocles** Athenian tragic poet (496–406 BC)   23 **girdle** sash   28 **shingles** beach pebbles

Hath really neither joy, nor love, nor light,
Nor certitude, nor peace, nor help for pain;
And we are here as on a darkling plain   35
Swept with confused alarms of struggle and flight,
Where ignorant armies clash by night.

—1867

EMILY DICKINSON ■ (1830–1886)

*Emily Dickinson has been reinvented with each generation, and readers'
views of her have ranged between two extremes—one perceiving her as the
abnormally shy "Belle of Amherst" making poetry out of her own neuroses
and another seeing her as a proto-feminist carving out a world of her own in
self-willed isolation. What remains is her brilliant poetry—unique, original,
and marked with the stamp of individual talent. Dickinson published only
seven poems during her lifetime, but left behind hundreds of poems in manuscript at her death. Published by her relatives, they were immediately popular, but it was not until the edition of Thomas Johnson in 1955 that they were
read with Dickinson's unusual punctuation and capitalization intact.*

After Great Pain, a Formal Feeling Comes

After great pain, a formal feeling comes—
The Nerves sit ceremonious, like Tombs—
The stiff Heart questions was it He, that bore,
And Yesterday, or Centuries before?   5

The Feet, mechanical, go round—
Of Ground, or Air, or Ought—

A Wooden way
Regardless grown,
A Quartz contentment, like a stone—

This is the Hour of Lead—   10
Remembered, if outlived,
As Freezing persons, recollect the Snow—
First—Chill—then Stupor—then the letting go—

—1890

Because I Could Not Stop for Death

Because I could not stop for Death—
He kindly stopped for me—
The Carriage held but just Ourselves—
And Immortality.

We slowly drove—He knew no haste   5
And I had put away
My labor and my leisure too,
For His Civility—

We passed the School, where Children strove
At Recess—in the Ring—   10
We passed the Fields of Gazing Grain—
We passed the Setting Sun—

Or rather—He passed Us—
The Dews drew quivering and chill—
For only Gossamer, my Gown—   15
My Tippet°—only Tulle°—

We paused before a House that seemed
A Swelling of the Ground—
The Roof was scarcely visible—
The Cornice—in the Ground—   20

Since then—'tis Centuries—and yet
Feels shorter than the Day
I first surmised the Horses' Heads
Were toward Eternity—

—1890

The Brain Is Wider than the Sky

The Brain—is wider than the Sky—
For—put them side by side—
The one the other will contain
With ease—and You—beside—   5

16 **Tippet** shawl **Tulle** net-like fabric

The Brain is deeper than the sea—
For—hold them—Blue to Blue—
The one the other will absorb—
As Sponges—Buckets—do—

The Brain is just the weight of God— 10
For—Heft them—Pound for Pound—
And they will differ—if they do—
As Syllable from Sound—

—1896

A Narrow Fellow in the Grass

A narrow Fellow in the Grass
Occasionally rides—
You may have met Him—did you not
His notice sudden is—

The Grass divides as with a Comb— 5
A spotted shaft is seen—
And then it closes at your feet
And opens further on—

He likes a Boggy Acre
A Floor too cool for Corn— 10
Yet when a Boy, and Barefoot—
I more than once at Noon
Have passed, I thought, a Whip lash
Unbraiding in the Sun
When stooping to secure it 15
It wrinkled, and was gone—

Several of Nature's People
I know, and they know me—
I feel for them a transport
Of cordiality— 20

But never met this Fellow
Attended, or alone
Without a tighter breathing
And Zero at the Bone—

—1866

Some Keep the Sabbath Going to Church

Some keep the Sabbath going to Church—
I keep it, staying at Home—
With a Bobolink for a Chorister—
And an Orchard, for a Dome—

Some keep the Sabbath in Surplice—   5
I just wear my Wings—
And instead of tolling the Bell, for Church,
Our little Sexton—sings.

God preaches, a noted Clergyman—
And the sermon is never long,   10
So instead of getting to Heaven, at least—
I'm going, all along.

—1864

The Soul Selects Her Own Society

The Soul selects her own Society—
Then—shuts the Door—
To her divine Majority—
Present no more—

Unmoved—she notes the Chariots—pausing—   5
At her low Gate—
Unmoved—an Emperor be kneeling
Upon her Mat—

I've known her—from an ample nation—
Choose One—   10
Then—close the Valves° of her attention—
Like Stone—

—1890

11 **Valves** sliding doors

Tell All the Truth, But Tell It Slant

Tell all the Truth but tell it slant—
Success in Circuit lies
Too bright for our infirm Delight
The Truth's superb surprise

As Lightning to the Children eased   5
With explanation kind
The Truth must dazzle gradually
Or every man be blind—

—1868

Wild Nights— Wild Nights!

Wild Nights—Wild Nights!
Were I with thee
Wild Nights should be
Our luxury!

Futile—the Winds—   5
To a Heart in port—
Done with the Compass—
Done with the Chart!

Rowing in Eden—
Ah, the Sea!
Might I but moor—Tonight—   10
In Thee!

—1891

CHRISTINA ROSSETTI ■ (1830–1894)

Christina Rossetti was the younger sister of Dante Gabriel and William, also distinguished writers, and was the author of numerous devotional poems and prose works. Her collected poems, edited by her brother William, appeared posthumously in 1904.

Up-Hill

Does the road wind up-hill all the way?
    Yes, to the very end.
Will the day's journey take the whole long day?
    From morn to night, my friend.

But is there for the night a resting-place?   5
    A roof for when the slow dark hours begin.
May not the darkness hide it from my face?
    You cannot miss that inn.

Shall I meet other wayfarers at night?
    Those who have gone before.   10
Then must I knock, or call when just in sight?
    They will not keep you waiting at that door.

Shall I find comfort, travel-sore and weak?
    Of labor you shall find the sum.
Will there be beds for me and all who seek?   15
    Yea, beds for all who come.

—1858

THOMAS HARDY ■ (1840–1928)

Thomas Hardy, after the disappointing response to his novel Jude the Obscure *in 1895, returned to his first love, writing poetry, for the last thirty years
of his long life. The language and life of Hardy's native Wessex inform both
his novels and poems. His subject matter is very much of the nineteenth century, but his ironic, disillusioned point of view marks him as one of the chief
predecessors of modernism.*

Ah, Are You Digging on My Grave?

"Ah, are you digging on my grave
    My loved one?—planting rue?"°
—"No: yesterday he went to wed
One of the brightest wealth has bred.
'It cannot hurt her now,' he said,   5
    'That I should not be true.'"

2 **rue** yellow flower traditionally associated with sadness

"Then who is digging on my grave?
        My nearest dearest kin?"
—"Ah, no; they sit and think, 'What use!
What good will planting flowers produce?   10
No tendance of her mound can loose
        Her spirit from Death's gin.'"°

"But some one digs upon my grave?
        My enemy?—prodding sly?"
—"Nay: when she heard you had passed the Gate   15
That shuts on all flesh soon or late.
She thought you no more worth her hate,
        And cares not where you lie."

"Then who is digging on my grave?
        Say—since I have not guessed!"   20
—"O it is I, my mistress dear,
Your little dog, who still lives near,
And much I hope my movements here
        Have not disturbed your rest?"

"Ah, yes! *You* dig upon my grave . . .   25
        Why flashed it not on me
That one true heart was left behind!
What feeling do we ever find
To equal among human kind
        A dog's fidelity!"   30

"Mistress, I dug upon your grave
        To bury a bone, in case
I should be hungry near this spot
When passing on my daily trot.
I am sorry, but I quite forgot   35
        It was your resting-place."

—1914

Channel Firing

That night your great guns, unawares,
Shook all our coffins as we lay,
And broke the chancel window-squares,
We thought it was the Judgment-day

12 **gin** grip

And sat upright. While drearisome 5
Arose the howl of weakened hounds:
The mouse let fall the alter-crumb,
The worms drew back into the mounds,

The glebe° cow drooled. Till God called, 'No;
It's gunnery practice out at sea 10
Just as before you went below;
The world is as it used to be:

'All nations striving strong to make
Red war yet redder. Mad as hatters
They do no more for Christés sake 15
Than you who are helpless in such matters.

'That this is not the judgment-hour
For some of them's a blessed thing,
For if it were they'd have to scour
Hell's floor for so much threatening. . . . 20

'Ha, ha. It will be warmer when
I blow the trumpet (if indeed
I ever do; for you are men,
And rest eternal sorely need).'

So down we lay again. 'I wonder, 25
Will the world ever saner be,'
Said one, 'than when he sent us under
In our indifferent century!'

And many a skeleton shook his head.
'Instead of preaching forty year,' 30
My neighbour Parson Thirdly said,
'I wish I had stuck to pipes and beer.'

Again the guns disturbed the hour,
Roaring their readiness to avenge,
As far inland as Stourton Tower, 35
And Camelot, and starlit Stonehenge.°

—1914

9 glebe farmland belonging to a church 35–36 Stourton . . . Stonehenge Stourton Tower was
built in the late 1700s as a memorial to the Seven Years War; Camelot was the legendary Castle of
King Arthur; Stonehenge dates from prehistoric times.

Neutral Tones

We stood by a pond that winter day,
And the sun was white, as though chidden of God,
And a few leaves lay on the starving sod;
     —They had fallen from an ash, and were gray.

Your eyes on me were as eyes that rove   5
Over tedious riddles solved years ago;
And some words played between us to and fro
     On which lost the more by our love.

The smile on your mouth was the deadest thing
Alive enough to have strength to die;   10
And a grin of bitterness swept thereby
     Like an ominous bird a-wing . . .

Since then, keen lessons that love deceives,
And wrings with wrong, have shaped to me
Your face, and the God-curst sun, and a tree,   15
     And a pond edged with grayish leaves.

—1898

The Ruined Maid

"O 'Melia, my dear, this does everything crown!
Who could have supposed I should meet you in Town?
And whence such fair garments, such prosperity?"
"O didn't you know I'd been ruined?" said she.

"You left us in tatters, without shoes or socks,   5
Tired of digging potatoes, and spudding up docks;°
And now you've gay bracelets and bright feathers three!"
"Yes: that's how we dress when we're ruined," said she.

"At home in the barton° you said 'thee' and 'thou,'
And 'thik oon,' and 'theäs oon,'° and 't'other'; but now   10
Your talking quite fits 'ee for high compa-ny!"
"Some polish is gained with one's ruin," said she.

"Your hands were like paws then, your face blue and bleak
But now I'm bewitched by your delicate cheek,

---

6 **docks** weeds   9 **barton** barnyard   10 **thik oon and theäs oon** dialect: "that one and this one"

And your little gloves fit as on any la-dy!"   15
"We never do work when we're ruined," said she.

"You used to call home-life a hag-ridden dream,
And you'd sigh, and you'd sock; but at present you seem
To know not of megrims° or melancho-ly!"
"True. One's pretty lively when ruined," said she.   20

"I wish I had feathers, a fine sweeping gown,
And a delicate face, and could strut about Town!"
"My dear—a raw country girl, such as you be,
Cannot quite expect that. You ain't ruined," said she.

—1866

GERARD MANLEY HOPKINS ■ (1844–1889)

Gerard Manley Hopkins was an English Jesuit priest who developed elaborate theories of poetic meter (what he called "sprung rhythm") and language to express his own spiritual ardor. Most of his work was posthumously printed through the efforts of his Oxford friend and later correspondent Robert Bridges, who was poet laureate.

God's Grandeur

The world is charged with the grandeur of God.
    It will flame out, like shining from shook foil;°
    It gathers to a greatness, like the ooze of oil
Crushed.° Why do men then now not reck his rod?
Generations have trod, have trod, have trod;   5
    And all is seared with trade; bleared, smeared with toil;
    And wears man's smudge and shares man's smell: the soil
Is bare now, nor can foot feel, being shod.

And for all this, nature is never spent;
    There lives the dearest freshness deep down things;   10
And though the last lights off the black West went
    Oh, morning, at the brown brink eastward, springs—
Because the Holy Ghost over the bent
    World broods with warm breast and with ah! bright wings.

—1877

19 megrims migraines
2 foil gold leaf   **4 Crushed** Hopkins is referring to olive oil

Pied Beauty

Glory be to God for dappled things—
    For skies of couple-color as a brinded° cow;
        For rose-moles all in stipple upon trout that swim;
Fresh-firecoal chestnut-falls;° finches' wings;
    Landscape plotted and pieced—fold, fallow, and plough;   5
        And all trades, their gear and tackle and trim.
All things counter, original, spare, strange;
    Whatever is fickle, freckled (who knows how?)
        With swift, slow; sweet, sour; adazzle, dim;
He fathers-forth whose beauty is past change: 10
        Praise him.

—1877

Spring and Fall

to a young child

Márgarét, are you gríeving?
Over Goldengrove unleaving?
Leáves, líke the things of man, you
With your fresh thoughts care for, can you?
Ah! ás the heart grows older   5
It will come to such sights colder
By and by, nor spare a sigh
Though worlds of wanwood leafmeal lie;
And yet you wíll weep and know why.
Now no matter, child, the name: 10
Sórrow's spríngs áre the same.
Nor mouth had, no nor mind, expressed
What heart heard of, ghost guessed:
It ís the blight man was born for,
It is Margaret you mourn for.   15

—1880

GERARD MANLEY HOPKINS

578

2 **brinded** streaked   4 **Fresh-firecoal chestnut-falls** According to the poet, chestnuts have a red color

EMMA LAZARUS ■ (1849–1887)

Emma Lazarus was born in New York City, one of seven children of a wealthy Jewish-American sugar refiner. Her famous sonnet "The New Colossus" was written in 1883 for an art auction raising money to build a pedestal for the Statue of Liberty, which had been given to the United States by France. During Lazarus's short life she became a powerful spokesperson for the rights of immigrants and called on Jews to claim a homeland in Palestine. Sixteen years after her death, "The New Colossus" was engraved on a plaque for the statue's base.

The New Colossus

Not like the brazen giant of Greek fame,
With conquering limbs astride from land to land;
Here at our sea-washed, sunset gates shall stand
A mighty woman with a torch, whose flame
Is the imprisoned lightning, and her name   5
Mother of Exiles. From her beacon-hand
Glows world-wide welcome; her mild eyes command
The air-bridged harbor that twin cities frame.
"Keep, ancient lands, your storied pomp!" cries she
With silent lips. "Give me your tired, your poor,   10
Your huddled masses yearning to breathe free,
The wretched refuse of your teeming shore.
Send these, the homeless, tempest-tost to me,
I lift my lamp beside the golden door!"

—1883

A. E. HOUSMAN ■ (1859–1936)

A. E. Housman was educated in the classics at Oxford and was almost forty before he began to write verse seriously. His ballad-like poems of Shropshire (an area in which he never actually lived) have proved some of the most popular lyrics in English, despite their pervasive mood of bittersweet pessimism.

Eight o'Clock

He stood, and heard the steeple
    Sprinkle the quarters° on the morning town.
One, two, three, four, to market-place and people
    It tossed them down.

Strapped, noosed, nighing his hour,   5
    He stood and counted them and cursed his luck;
And then the clock collected in the tower
    Its strength, and struck.

—1922

Loveliest of Trees, the Cherry Now

Loveliest of trees, the cherry now
Is hung with bloom along the bough,
And stands about the woodland ride
Wearing white for Eastertide.

Now, of my threescore years and ten,   5
Twenty will not come again,
And take from seventy springs a score,
It only leaves me fifty more.

And since to look at things in bloom
Fifty springs are little room,   10
About the woodlands I will go
To see the cherry hung with snow.

—1896

Stars, I Have Seen Them Fall

Stars, I have seen them fall,
    But when they drop and die
No star is lost at all
    From all the star-sown sky.

2 **quarters** quarter hours

A. E. HOUSMAN

580

The toil of all that be   5
    Helps not the primal fault;
It rains into the sea
    And still the sea is salt.

—1936

"Terence, This Is Stupid Stuff . . ."

"Terence, this is stupid stuff:
You eat your victuals fast enough;
There can't be much amiss, 'tis clear,
To see the rate you drink your beer.
But oh, good Lord, the verse you make,   5
It gives a chap the belly-ache.
The cow, the old cow, she is dead;
It sleeps well, the hornèd head:
We poor lads, 'tis our turn now
To hear such tunes as killed the cow.   10
Pretty friendship 'tis to rhyme
Your friends to death before their time
Moping melancholy mad:
Come, pipe a tune to dance to, lad."

Why, if 'tis dancing you would be,   15
There's brisker pipes than poetry.
Say, for what were hop-yards meant,
Or why was Burton built on Trent?°
Oh many a peer of England brews
Livelier liquor than the Muse,   20
And malt does more than Milton can
To justify God's ways to man.
Ale, man, ale's the stuff to drink
For fellows whom it hurts to think:
Look into the pewter pot   25
To see the world as the world's not.

18 **Burton built on Trent** site of breweries

And faith, 'tis pleasant till 'tis past:
The mischief is that 'twill not last.
Oh I have been to Ludlow fair
And left my necktie God knows where,   30
And carried halfway home, or near,
Pints and quarts of Ludlow beer:
Then the world seemed none so bad,
And I myself a sterling lad;
And down in lovely muck I've lain,   35
Happy till I woke again.
Then I saw the morning sky:
Heigho, the tale was all a lie;
The world, it was the old world yet,
I was I, my things were wet,   40
And nothing now remained to do
But begin the game anew.

    Therefore, since the world has still
Much good, but much less good than ill,
And while the sun and moon endure   45
Luck's a chance, but trouble's sure,
I'd face it as a wise man would,
And train for ill and not for good.
'Tis true, the stuff I bring for sale
Is not so brisk a brew as ale: 50
Out of a stem that scored the hand
I wrung it in a weary land.
But take it: if the smack is sour,
The better for the embittered hour;
It should do good to heart and head   55
When your soul is in my soul's stead;
And I will friend you, if I may,
In the dark and cloudy day.

    There was a king reigned in the East:
There, when kings will sit to feast,   60
They get their fill before they think
With poisoned meat and poisoned drink.
He gathered all that springs to birth
From the many-venomed earth;

First a little, thence to more, 65
He sampled all her killing store;
And easy, smiling, seasoned sound,
Sate the king when healths went round.
They put arsenic in his meat
And stared aghast to watch him eat; 70
They poured strychnine in his cup
And shook to see him drink it up:
They shook, they stared as white's their shirt:
Them it was their poison hurt.
—I tell the tale that I heard told. 75
Mithridates,° he died old.

—1896

WILLIAM BUTLER YEATS ■ (1865–1939)

William Butler Yeats is considered the greatest Irish poet and provides an important link between the late romantic era and early modernism. His early poetry, focusing on Irish legend and landscape, is regional in the best sense of the term, but his later work, with its prophetic tone and symbolist texture, moves on a larger stage. Yeats lived in London for many years and was at the center of British literary life. He was awarded the Nobel Prize in 1923.

The Lake Isle of Innisfree

I will arise and go now, and go to Innisfree,
And a small cabin build there, of clay and wattles° made:
Nine bean-rows will I have there, a hive for the honey-bee,
And live alone in the bee-loud glade.

And I shall have some peace there, for peace comes dropping
     slow,   5
Dropping from the veils of the morning to where the cricket
     sings;
There midnight's all a glimmer, and noon a purple glow,
And evening full of the linnet's wings.

76 Mithridates legendary King of Pontus, he protected himself from poisons by taking small doses regularly
2 wattles woven poles and reeds

I will arise and go now, for always night and day
I hear lake water lapping with low sounds by the shore;   10
While I stand on the roadway, or on the pavements gray,
I hear it in the deep heart's core.

—1892

Leda° and the Swan

A sudden blow: the great wings beating still
Above the staggering girl, her thighs caressed
By the dark webs, her nape caught in his bill,
He holds her helpless breast upon his breast.

How can those terrified vague fingers push   5
The feathered glory from her loosening thighs?
And how can body, laid in that white rush,
But feel the strange heart beating where it lies?

A shudder in the loins engenders there
The broken wall, the burning roof and tower   10
And Agamemnon dead.°
              Being so caught up,
So mastered by the brute blood of the air,
Did she put on his knowledge with his power
Before the indifferent beak could let her drop?

—1923

Sailing to Byzantium°

1

That is no country for old men. The young
In one another's arms, birds in the trees
—Those dying generations—at their song,
The salmon-falls, the mackerel-crowded seas,

Leda mortal mother of Helen of Troy and Clytemnestra, wife and assassin of Agamemnon
10–11 The broken wall . . . Agamemnon dead events that occurred during and after the Trojan War
Byzantium Constantinople or Istanbul, capital of the Eastern Roman Empire

Fish, flesh, or fowl, commend all summer long 5
Whatever is begotten, born, and dies.
Caught in that sensual music all neglect
Monuments of unaging intellect.

2

An aged man is but a paltry thing,
A tattered coat upon a stick, unless 10
Soul clap its hands and sing, and louder sing
For every tatter in its mortal dress,
Nor is there singing school but studying
Monuments of its own magnificence;
And therefore I have sailed the seas and come 15
To the holy city of Byzantium.

3

O sages standing in God's holy fire
As in the gold mosaic of a wall,
Come from the holy fire, perne in a gyre,°
And be the singing-masters of my soul. 20
Consume my heart away; sick with desire
And fastened to a dying animal
It knows not what it is; and gather me
Into the artifice of eternity.

4

Once out of nature I shall never take 25
My bodily form from any natural thing,
But such a form as Grecian goldsmiths make
Of hammered gold and gold enamelling
To keep a drowsy Emperor awake;
Or set upon a golden bough to sing 30
To lords and ladies of Byzantium
Of what is past, or passing, or to come.

—1927

19 **perne in a gyre** descend in a spiral; the gyre for Yeats was a private symbol of historical cycles

The Second Coming

Turning and turning in the widening gyre°
The falcon cannot hear the falconer;
Things fall apart; the center cannot hold;
Mere anarchy is loosed upon the world,
The blood-dimmed tide is loosed, and everywhere   5
The ceremony of innocence is drowned;
The best lack all conviction, while the worst
Are full of passionate intensity.

Surely some revelation is at hand;
Surely the Second Coming is at hand.   10
The Second Coming! Hardly are those words out
When a vast image out of *Spiritus Mundi*°
Troubles my sight: somewhere in the sands of the desert
A shape with lion body and the head of a man,
A gaze blank and pitiless as the sun,   15
Is moving its slow thighs, while all about it
Reel shadows of the indignant desert birds.
The darkness drops again; but now I know
That twenty centuries of stony sleep
Were vexed to nightmare by a rocking cradle,   20
And what rough beast, its hour come round at last,
Slouches towards Bethlehem to be born?

—1921

The Song of
Wandering Aengus°

I went out to the hazel wood,
Because a fire was in my head,
And cut and peeled a hazel wand,
And hooked a berry to a thread;
And when white moths were on the wing,   5
And moth-like stars were flickering out,

1 **gyre** see note to "Sailing to Byzantium"   12 *Spiritus Mundi* World-Spirit
Aengus Among the Sidhe (native Irish deities), the god of youth, love, beauty, and poetry. Yeats
once also called him the "Master of Love." Here, however, he seems mortal.

I dropped the berry in a stream
And caught a little silver trout.

When I had laid it on the floor
I went to blow the fire aflame,   10
But something rustled on the floor,
And some one called me by my name:
It had become a glimmering girl
With apple blossom in her hair
Who called me by my name and ran   15
And faded through the brightening air.

Though I am old with wandering
Through hollow lands and hilly lands,
I will find out where she has gone,
And kiss her lips and take her hands;   20
And walk among long dappled grass,
And pluck till time and times are done
The silver apples of the moon,
The golden apples of the sun.

—1899

FIRELIGHT

EDWIN ARLINGTON ROBINSON ■ (1869–1935)

Edwin Arlington Robinson wrote many poems set in "Tilbury," a re-creation of his hometown of Gardiner, Maine. These poems continue to present readers with a memorable cast of eccentric characters who somehow manifest universal human desires. Robinson languished in poverty and obscurity for many years before his reputation began to flourish as a result of the interest taken in his work by President Theodore Roosevelt, who obtained a government job for Robinson and wrote a favorable review of one of his books.

Firelight

Ten years together without yet a cloud,
They seek each other's eyes at intervals
Of gratefulness to firelight and four walls
For love's obliteration of the crowd.
Serenely and perennially endowed   5
And bowered as few may be, their joy recalls

No snake, no sword; and over them there falls
The blessing of what neither says aloud.
Wiser for silence, they were not so glad
Were she to read the graven° tale of lines   10
On the wan face of one somewhere alone;
Nor were they more content could he have had
Her thoughts a moment since of one who shines
Apart, and would be hers if he had known.

—1920

The Mill

EDWIN ARLINGTON ROBINSON

The miller's wife had waited long,
 The tea was cold, the fire was dead;
And there might yet be nothing wrong
 In how he went and what he said:
"There are no millers any more,"   5
 Was all that she had heard him say;
And he had lingered at the door
 So long that it seemed yesterday.

Sick with a fear that had no form
 She knew that she was there at last;   10
And in the mill there was a warm
 And mealy fragrance of the past.
What else there was would only seem
 To say again what he had meant;
And what was hanging from a beam   15
 Would not have heeded where she went.

And if she thought it followed her,
 She may have reasoned in the dark
That one way of the few there were
 Would hide her and would leave no mark: 20
Black water, smooth above the weir
 Like starry velvet in the night,
Though ruffled once, would soon appear
 The same as ever to the sight.

—1920

10 graven engraved

Richard Cory

Whenever Richard Cory went down town,
We people on the pavement looked at him:
He was a gentleman from sole to crown,
Clean favored, and imperially slim.

And he was always quietly arrayed,   5
And he was always human when he talked;
But still he fluttered pulses when he said,
"Good-morning," and he glittered when he walked.

And he was rich—yes, richer than a king—
And admirably schooled in every grace: 10
In fine, we thought that he was everything
To make us wish that we were in his place.

So on we worked, and waited for the light,
And went without the meat, and cursed the bread;
And Richard Cory, one calm summer night,   15
Went home and put a bullet through his head.

—1896

STEPHEN CRANE ■ (1871–1900)

Stephen Crane was the brilliant young journalist who wrote The Red Badge
of Courage *and was also an unconventional poet whose skeptical epigrams
and fables today seem far ahead of their time. In many ways he mirrors the
cosmic pessimism of contemporaries like Hardy, Housman, and Robinson,
all of whom were influenced by the currents of determinism that ran so
strongly at the end of the nineteenth century.*

The Trees in the Garden Rained Flowers

The trees in the garden rained flowers.
Children ran there joyously.
They gathered the flowers
Each to himself.
Now there were some   5

Who gathered great heaps—
Having opportunity and skill—
Until, behold, only chance blossoms
Remained for the feeble.
Then a little spindling tutor   10
Ran importantly to the father, crying:
"Pray, come hither!
See this unjust thing in your garden!"
But when the father had surveyed,
He admonished the tutor: 15
"Not so, small sage!
This thing is just.
For, look you,
Are not they who possess the flowers
Stronger, bolder, shrewder   20
Than they who have none?
Why should the strong—
The beautiful strong—
Why should they not have the flowers?"
Upon reflection, the tutor bowed to the ground,   25
"My lord," he said,
"The stars are displaced
By this towering wisdom."

                                                            —1899

The Wayfarer

The wayfarer,
Perceiving the pathway to truth,
Was struck with astonishment.
It was thickly grown with weeds.
"Ha," he said,   5
"I see that none has passed here
In a long time."
Later he saw that each weed
Was a singular knife.
"Well," he mumbled at last,   10
"Doubtless there are other roads."

                                                            —1899

Paul Laurence Dunbar, a native of Dayton, Ohio, was one of the first black poets to make a mark in American literature. Many of his dialect poems reflect a sentimentalized view of life in the South, which he did not know directly. However, he was also capable of powerful expressions of racial protest.

We Wear the Mask

We wear the mask that grins and lies,
It hides our cheeks and shades our eyes,—
This debt we pay to human guile;
With torn and bleeding hearts we smile,
And mouth with myriad subtleties.   5
Why should the world be over-wise,
In counting all our tears and sighs?
Nay, let them only see us, while
    We wear the mask.

We smile, but, O great Christ, our cries   10
To thee from tortured souls arise.
We sing, but oh the clay is vile
Beneath our feet, and long the mile;
But let the world dream otherwise,
    We wear the mask!   15

—*1896*

ROBERT FROST ■ (1874–1963)

Robert Frost, during the second half of his long life, was a public figure who attained a popularity unmatched by any American poet of the last century. His reading at the inauguration of John F. Kennedy in 1961 capped an impressive career that included four Pulitzer Prizes. Unattracted by the more exotic aspects of modernism, Frost nevertheless remains a poet who speaks eloquently to contemporary uncertainties about humanity's place in a universe that does not seem to care much for its existence. While Frost is rarely directly an autobiographical poet ("Home Burial" may reflect the death of Frost's son Elliot at age three), his work always bears the stamp of his powerful personality and identification with the New England landscape.

Acquainted with the Night

I have been one acquainted with the night.
I have walked out in rain—and back in rain.
I have outwalked the furthest city light.

I have looked down the saddest city lane.
I have passed by the watchman on his beat   5
And dropped my eyes, unwilling to explain.

I have stood still and stopped the sound of feet
When far away an interrupted cry
Came over houses from another street,

But not to call me back or say good-bye;   10
And further still at an unearthly height
One luminary clock against the sky

Proclaimed the time was neither wrong nor right.
I have been one acquainted with the night.

—1928

After Apple-Picking

My long two-pointed ladder's sticking through a tree
Toward heaven still,
And there's a barrel that I didn't fill
Beside it, and there may be two or three
Apples I didn't pick upon some bough.   5
But I am done with apple-picking now.
Essence of winter sleep is on the night,
The scent of apples: I am drowsing off.
I cannot rub the strangeness from my sight
I got from looking through a pane of glass   10
I skimmed this morning from the drinking trough
And held against the world of hoary grass.
It melted, and I let it fall and break.
But I was well
Upon my way to sleep before it fell,   15
And I could tell
What form my dreaming was about to take.

Magnified apples appear and disappear,
Stem end and blossom end,
And every fleck of russet showing clear.   20
My instep arch not only keeps the ache,
It keeps the pressure of a ladder-round.
I feel the ladder sway as the boughs bend.
And I keep hearing from the cellar bin
The rumbling sound   25
Of load on load of apples coming in.
For I have had too much
Of apple-picking: I am overtired
Of the great harvest I myself desired.
There were ten thousand thousand fruit to touch,   30
Cherish in hand, lift down, and not let fall.
For all
That struck the earth,
No matter if not bruised or spiked with stubble,
Went surely to the cider-apple heap   35
As of no worth.
One can see what will trouble
This sleep of mine, whatever sleep it is.
Were he not gone,
The woodchuck could say whether it's like his   40
Long sleep, as I describe its coming on,
Or just some human sleep.

                                                                      —1914

Design

I found a dimpled spider, fat and white,
On a white heal-all,° holding up a moth
Like a white piece of rigid satin cloth—
Assorted characters of death and blight
Mixed ready to begin the morning right,   5
Like the ingredients of a witches' broth—
A snow-drop spider, a flower like a froth,
And dead wings carried like a paper kite.

---

2 **heal-all** a wildflower, usually blue

What had that flower to do with being white,
The wayside blue and innocent heal-all?   10
What brought the kindred spider to that height,
Then steered the white moth thither in the night?
What but design of darkness to appall?—
If design govern in a thing so small.

—1936

Home Burial

He saw her from the bottom of the stairs
Before she saw him. She was starting down,
Looking back over her shoulder at some fear.
She took a doubtful step and then undid it
To raise herself and look again. He spoke   5
Advancing toward her: "What is it you see
From up there always?—for I want to know."
She turned and sank upon her skirts at that,
And her face changed from terrified to dull.
He said to gain time: "What is it you see?"   10
Mounting until she cowered under him.
"I will find out now—you must tell me, dear."
She, in her place, refused him any help,
With the least stiffening of her neck and silence.
She let him look, sure that he wouldn't see,   15
Blind creature; and awhile he didn't see.
But at last he murmured, "Oh," and again, "Oh."

"What is it—what?" she said.

                              "Just that I see."

"You don't," she challenged. "Tell me what it is."

"The wonder is I didn't see at once.   20
I never noticed it from here before.
I must be wonted to it—that's the reason.
The little graveyard where my people are!
So small the window frames the whole of it.
Not so much larger than a bedroom, is it?   25

There are three stones of slate and one of marble,
Broad-shouldered little slabs there in the sunlight
On the sidehill. We haven't to mind *those*.
But I understand: it is not the stones,
But the child's mound—"

"Don't, don't, don't, don't," she cried.　　30

She withdrew, shrinking from beneath his arm
That rested on the banister, and slid downstairs;
And turned on him with such a daunting look,
He said twice over before he knew himself:
"Can't a man speak of his own child he's lost?"　　35

"Not you!—Oh, where's my hat? Oh, I don't need it!
I must get out of here. I must get air.—
I don't know rightly whether any man can."

"Amy! Don't go to someone else this time.
Listen to me. I won't come down the stairs."　　40
He sat and fixed his chin between his fists.
"There's something I should like to ask you, dear."

"You don't know how to ask it."

"Help me, then."

Her fingers moved the latch for all reply.

"My words are nearly always an offense.　　45
I don't know how to speak of anything
So as to please you. But I might be taught,
I should suppose. I can't say I see how.
A man must partly give up being a man
With womenfolk. We could have some arrangement　　50
By which I'd bind myself to keep hands off
Anything special you're a-mind to name.
Though I don't like such things 'twixt those that love.
Two that don't love can't live together without them.
But two that do can't live together with them."　　55
She moved the latch a little. "Don't—don't go.
Don't carry it to someone else this time.
Tell me about it if it's something human.

Let me into your grief. I'm not so much
Unlike other folks as your standing there   60
Apart would make me out. Give me my chance.
I do think, though, you overdo it a little.
What was it brought you up to think it the thing
To take your mother-loss of a first child
So inconsolably—in the face of love.   65
You'd think his memory might be satisfied—"

"There you go sneering now!"

                              "I'm not, I'm not!
You make me angry. I'll come down to you.
God, what a woman! And it's come to this,
A man can't speak of his own child that's dead."   70

"You can't because you don't know how to speak.
If you had any feelings, you that dug
With your own hand—how could you?—his little grave;
I saw you from that very window there,
Making the gravel leap and leap in air,   75
Leap up, like that, like that, and land so lightly
And roll back down the mound beside the hole.
I thought, Who is that man? I didn't know you.
And I crept down the stairs and up the stairs
To look again, and still your spade kept lifting.   80
Then you came in. I heard your rumbling voice
Out in the kitchen, and I don't know why,
But I went near to see with my own eyes.
You could sit there with the stains on your shoes
Of the fresh earth from your own baby's grave   85
And talk about your everyday concerns.
You had stood the spade up against the wall
Outside there in the entry, for I saw it."

"I shall laugh the worst laugh I ever laughed.
I'm cursed. God, if I don't believe I'm cursed."   90

"I can repeat the very words you were saying:
'Three foggy mornings and one rainy day
Will rot the best birch fence a man can build.'

Think of it, talk like that at such a time!
What had how long it takes a birch to rot   95
To do with what was in the darkened parlor?
You *couldn't* care! The nearest friends can go
With anyone to death, comes so far short
They might as well not try to go at all.
No, from the time when one is sick to death,   100
One is alone, and he dies more alone.
Friends make pretense of following to the grave,
But before one is in it, their minds are turned
And making the best of their way back to life
And living people, and things they understand.   105

But the world's evil. I won't have grief so
If I can change it. Oh, I won't, I won't!"

"There, you have said it all and you feel better.
You won't go now. You're crying. Close the door.
The heart's gone out of it: why keep it up?   110
Amy! There's someone coming down the road!"

"*You*—oh, you think the talk is all. I must go—
Somewhere out of this house. How can I make you—"

"If—you—do!" She was opening the door wider.
"Where do you mean to go? First tell me that.   115
I'll follow and bring you back by force. I *will!*—"

—1914

The Road Not Taken

Two roads diverged in a yellow wood,
And sorry I could not travel both
And be one traveler, long I stood
And looked down one as far as I could
To where it bent in the undergrowth;   5

Then took the other, as just as fair,
And having perhaps the better claim,
Because it was grassy and wanted wear;

Though as for that, the passing there
Had worn them really about the same,   10

And both that morning equally lay
In leaves no step had trodden black.
Oh, I kept the first for another day!
Yet knowing how way leads on to way,
I doubted if I should ever come back.   15

I shall be telling this with a sigh
Somewhere ages and ages hence:
Two roads diverged in a wood, and I,
I took the one less traveled by,
And that has made all the difference.   20

—1916

Stopping by Woods on a Snowy Evening

Whose woods these are I think I know.
His house is in the village though;
He will not see me stopping here
To watch his woods fill up with snow.

My little horse must think it queer   5
To stop without a farmhouse near
Between the woods and frozen lake
The darkest evening of the year.

He gives his harness bells a shake
To ask if there is some mistake.   10
The only other sound's the sweep
Of easy wind and downy flake.

The woods are lovely, dark and deep,
But I have promises to keep,
And miles to go before I sleep,   15
And miles to go before I sleep.

—1923

Adelaide Crapsey was born in Brooklyn, New York, the daughter of an Epis-copalian minister. After graduation from college and travel abroad, she be-came an instructor of poetics at Smith College, but her declining health forced her to resign after only one year of teaching, and she died three years later from tuberculosis. Chiefly remembered as the inventor of the cinquain form, Crapsey was influenced by Asian poetry and anticipated many of the practices of imagists, who were coming to prominence in her final years. Her poetry and criticism were published posthumously.

Amaze

I know
Not these my hands
And yet I think there was
A woman like me once had hands
Like these. 5

—1915

Languor After Pain

Pain ebbs,
And like cool balm,
An opiate weariness
Settles on eye-lids, on relaxed
Pale wrists. 5

—1915

Trapped

Well and
If day on day
Follows, and weary year
On year . . . and ever days and years . . .
Well? 5

—1915

Wallace Stevens was a lawyer specializing in surety bonds and rose to be a vice-president of the Hartford Accident and Indemnity Company. His poetry was collected for the first time in Harmonium *when he was forty-five, and while he published widely during his lifetime, his poetry was only slowly recognized as the work of a major modernist whose originality has not been surpassed. Stevens's idea of poetry as a force taking the place of religion has had a profound influence on poets and critics of this century.*

Anecdote of the Jar

I placed a jar in Tennessee,
And round it was, upon a hill.
It made the slovenly wilderness
Surround that hill.

The wilderness rose up to it,   5
And sprawled around, no longer wild.
The jar was round upon the ground
And tall and of a port in air.

It took dominion everywhere.
The jar was gray and bare.   10
It did not give of bird or bush,
Like nothing else in Tennessee.

     —1923

Disillusionment of Ten o'Clock

The houses are haunted
By white night-gowns.
None are green,
Or purple with green rings,
Or green with yellow rings,   5
Or yellow with blue rings.

None of them are strange,
With socks of lace
And beaded ceintures.°
People are not going   10
To dream of baboons and periwinkles.°
Only, here and there, an old sailor,
Drunk and asleep in his boots,
Catches tigers
In red weather.   15

—1923

The Emperor of Ice-Cream

Call the roller of big cigars,
The muscular one, and bid him whip
In kitchen cups concupiscent° curds.
Let the wenches dawdle in such dress
As they are used to wear, and let the boys   5
Bring flowers in last month's newspapers.
Let be be finale of seem.
The only emperor is the emperor of ice-cream.

Take from the dresser of deal,°
Lacking the three glass knobs, that sheet   10
On which she embroidered fantails° once
And spread it so as to cover her face.
If her horny feet protrude, they come
To show how cold she is, and dumb.
Let the lamp affix its beam.   15
The only emperor is the emperor of ice-cream.

—1923

---

9 ceintures sashes   **11 periwinkles** either wildflowers or small mollusks
3 concupiscent lustful   **9 deal** cheap wood   **11 fantails** pigeons

The Snow Man

One must have a mind of winter
To regard the frost and the boughs
Of the pine-trees crusted with snow;

And have been cold a long time
To behold the junipers shagged with ice,   5
The spruces rough in the distant glitter

Of the January sun; and not to think
Of any misery in the sound of the wind,
In the sound of a few leaves,

Which is the sound of the land   10
Full of the same wind
That is blowing in the same bare place

For the listener, who listens in the snow,
And, nothing himself, beholds
Nothing that is not there and the nothing that is. 15

                                                —1923

Sunday Morning

I

Complacencies of the peignoir,° and late
Coffee and oranges in a sunny chair,
And the green freedom of a cockatoo
Upon a rug mingle to dissipate
The holy hush of ancient sacrifice.   5
She dreams a little, and she feels the dark
Encroachment of that old catastrophe,
As a calm darkens among water-lights.
The pungent oranges and bright, green wings
Seem things in some procession of the dead,   10
Winding across wide water, without sound.

1 **peignoir** woman's dressing gown

The day is like wide water, without sound,
Stilled for the passing of her dreaming feet
Over the seas, to silent Palestine,
Dominion of the blood and sepulchre.   15

II

Why should she give her bounty to the dead?
What is divinity if it can come
Only in silent shadows and in dreams?
Shall she not find in comforts of the sun,
In pungent fruit and bright, green wings, or else   20
In any balm or beauty of the earth,
Things to be cherished like the thought of heaven?
Divinity must live within herself:
Passions of rain, or moods in falling snow;
Grievings in loneliness, or unsubdued   25
Elations when the forest blooms; gusty
Emotions on wet roads on autumn nights;
All pleasures and all pains, remembering
The bough of summer and the winter branch.
These are the measures destined for her soul.   30

III

Jove° in the clouds had his inhuman birth.
No mother suckled him, no sweet land gave
Large-mannered motions to his mythy mind.
He moved among us, as a muttering king,
Magnificent, would move among his hinds,°   35
Until our blood, commingling, virginal,
With heaven, brought such requital to desire
The very hinds discerned it, in a star.
Shall our blood fail? Or shall it come to be
The blood of paradise? And shall the earth   40
Seem all of paradise that we shall know?

31 **Jove** Roman name of Zeus   35 **hinds** inferiors or shepherds who saw the star of the nativity

The sky will be much friendlier then than now,
A part of labor and a part of pain,
And next in glory to enduring love,
Not this dividing and indifferent blue.   45

IV

She says, "I am content when wakened birds,
Before they fly, test the reality
Of misty fields, by their sweet questionings;
But when the birds are gone, and their warm fields
Return no more, where, then, is paradise?"   50
There is not any haunt of prophecy,
Nor any old chimera° of the grave,
Neither the golden underground, nor isle
Melodious, where spirits gat them home,
Nor visionary south, nor cloudy palm   55
Remote on heaven's hill, that has endured
As April's green endures; or will endure
Like her remembrance of awakened birds,
Or her desire for June and evening, tipped
By the consummation of the swallow's wings.   60

V

She says, "But in contentment I still feel
The need of some imperishable bliss."
Death is the mother of beauty; hence from her,
Alone, shall come fulfilment to our dreams
And our desires. Although she strews the leaves   65
Of sure obliteration on our paths,
The path sick sorrow took, the many paths
Where triumph rang its brassy phrase, or love
Whispered a little out of tenderness,
She makes the willow shiver in the sun   70
For maidens who were wont to sit and gaze
Upon the grass, relinquished to their feet.

52 **chimera** imagined monster

She causes boys to pile new plums and pears
On disregarded plate. The maidens taste
And stray impassioned in the littering leaves. 75

VI

Is there no change of death in paradise?
Does ripe fruit never fall? Or do the boughs
Hang always heavy in that perfect sky,
Unchanging, yet so like our perishing earth,
With rivers like our own that seek for seas 80
They never find, the same receding shores
That never touch with inarticulate pang?
Why set the pear upon those river-banks
Or spice the shores with odors of the plum?
Alas, that they should wear our colors there, 85
The silken weavings of our afternoons,
And pick the strings of our insipid lutes!
Death is the mother of beauty, mystical,
Within whose burning bosom we devise
Our earthly mothers waiting, sleeplessly. 90

VII

Supple and turbulent, a ring of men
Shall chant in orgy on a summer morn
Their boisterous devotion to the sun,
Not as a god, but as a god might be,
Naked among them, like a savage source. 95
Their chant shall be a chant of paradise,
Out of their blood, returning to the sky;
And in their chant shall enter, voice by voice,
The windy lake wherein their lord delights,
The trees, like serafin,° and echoing hills, 100
That choir among themselves long afterward.
They shall know well the heavenly fellowship

---

100 **serafin** seraphim, a type of angel

Of men that perish and of summer morn.
And whence they came and whither they shall go
The dew upon their feet shall manifest.   105

VIII

She hears, upon that water without sound,
A voice that cries, "The tomb in Palestine
Is not the porch of spirits lingering.
It is the grave of Jesus, where he lay."
We live in an old chaos of the sun,   110
Or old dependency of day and night,
Or island solitude, unsponsored, free,
Of that wide water, inescapable.
Deer walk upon our mountains, and the quail
Whistle about us their spontaneous cries;   115
Sweet berries ripen in the wilderness;
And, in the isolation of the sky,
At evening, casual flocks of pigeons make
Ambiguous undulations as they sink,
Downward to darkness, on extended wings.   120

—1923

The Worms at Heaven's Gate

Out of the tomb, we bring Badroulbadour,°
Within our bellies, we her chariot.
Here is an eye. And here are, one by one,
The lashes of that eye and its white lid.
Here is the cheek on which that lid declined,   5
And, finger after finger, here, the hand,
The genius of that cheek. Here are the lips,
The bundle of the body and feet.

.   .   .   .   .   .

Out of the tomb we bring Badroulbadour.   10

—1923

1 **Badroulbadour** a princess in *The Arabian Nights*

WILLIAM CARLOS WILLIAMS ■ (1883–1963)

William Carlos Williams, like his friend Wallace Stevens, followed an un-conventional career for a poet, working until his death as a pediatrician in Rutherford, New Jersey. Williams is modern poetry's greatest proponent of the American idiom. His plainspoken poems have been more widely imi-tated than those of any other American poet of the twentieth century, perhaps because he represents a homegrown modernist alternative to the intellectualized Europeanism of Eliot and Ezra Pound (a friend of his from college days). In his later years, Williams assisted many younger poets, among them Allen Ginsberg, for whose controversial book Howl *he wrote an introduction.*

The Last Words of My English Grandmother

There were some dirty plates
and a glass of milk
beside her on a small table
near the rank, disheveled bed—

Wrinkled and nearly blind   5
she lay and snored
rousing with anger in her tones
to cry for food,

Gimme something to eat—
They're starving me—   10
I'm all right—I won't go
to the hospital. No, no, no

Give me something to eat!
Let me take you
to the hospital, I said   15
and after you are well

you can do as you please.
She smiled, Yes
you do what you please first
then I can do what I please—   20

Oh, oh, oh! she cried
as the ambulance men lifted
her to the stretcher—
Is this what you call

making me comfortable?   25
By now her mind was clear—
Oh you think you're smart
you young people,

she said, but I'll tell you
you don't know anything.   30
Then we started.
On the way

We passed a long row
of elms. She looked at them
awhile out of   35
the ambulance window and said,

What are all those
fuzzy-looking things out there?
Trees? Well, I'm tired
of them and rolled her head away.   40

                                           —1920

The Red Wheelbarrow

so much depends
upon

a red wheel
barrow

glazed with rain   5
water

beside the white
chickens.

                                           —1923

Spring and All

By the road to the contagious hospital°
under the surge of the blue
mottled clouds driven from the
northeast—a cold wind. Beyond, the
waste of broad, muddy fields   5
brown with dried weeds, standing and fallen

patches of standing water
the scattering of tall trees
All along the road the reddish
purplish, forked, upstanding, twiggy   10
stuff of bushes and small trees
with dead, brown leaves under them
leafless vines—

Lifeless in appearance, sluggish
dazed spring approaches—   15

They enter the new world naked,
cold, uncertain of all
save that they enter. All about them
the cold, familiar wind—

Now the grass, tomorrow   20
the stiff curl of wildcarrot leaf
One by one objects are defined—
It quickens: clarity, outline of leaf

But now the stark dignity of
entrance—Still, the profound change   25
has come upon them: rooted, they
grip down and begin to awaken

—1923

1 **contagious hospital** a hospital for quarantine patients

*Ezra Pound was the greatest international proponent of modernist poetry.
Born in Idaho and reared in Philadelphia, he emigrated to England in 1909,
where he befriended Yeats, promoted the early work of Frost, and discovered
Eliot. Pound's early promotion of the imagist movement assisted a number
of important poetic principles and reputations, including those of H. D.
(Hilda Doolittle) and, later, William Carlos Williams. Pound's support of
Mussolini during World War II, expressed in controversial radio broadcasts,
caused him to be held for over a decade after the war as a mental patient in
the United States, after which he returned to Italy for the final years of his
long and controversial life.*

In a Station of the Metro

The apparition of these faces in the crowd;
Petals on a wet, black bough.

—1916

Portrait d'une Femme°

Your mind and you are our Sargasso Sea,°
London has swept about you this score years
And bright ships left you this or that in fee:
Ideas, old gossip, oddments of all things,
Strange spars of knowledge and dimmed wares of price.   5
Great minds have sought you—lacking someone else.
You have been second always. Tragical?
No. You preferred it to the usual thing:
One dull man, dulling and uxorious,°
One average mind—with one thought less, each year   10
Oh, you are patient, I have seen you sit
Hours, where something might have floated up.
And now you pay one. Yes, you richly pay.

Portrait d'une Femme Portrait of a Lady   **1 Sargasso Sea** area of seaweed in the mid-Atlantic
where flotsam accumulates   **9 uxorious** doting and submissive

You are a person of some interest, one comes to you
And takes strange gain away: 15
Trophies fished up; some curious suggestion;
Fact that leads nowhere; and a tale or two,
Pregnant with mandrakes,° or with something else
That might prove useful and yet never proves,
That never fits a corner or shows use,   20
Or finds its hour upon the loom of days:
The tarnished, gaudy, wonderful old work;
Idols and ambergris° and rare inlays,
These are your riches, your great store; and yet
For all this sea-hoard of deciduous things,   25
Strange woods half sodden, and new brighter stuff:
In the slow float of differing light and deep,
No! there is nothing! In the whole and all,
Nothing that's quite your own.
                    Yet this is you

                                                        —1912

The River-Merchant's
Wife: A Letter°

While my hair was still cut straight across my forehead
I played about the front gate, pulling flowers.
You came by on bamboo stilts, playing horse,
You walked about my seat, playing with blue plums.
And we went on living in the village of Chokan: 5
Two small people, without dislike or suspicion.
At fourteen I married My Lord you.
I never laughed, being bashful.
Lowering my head, I looked at the wall.
Called to, a thousand times, I never looked back.   10

---

18 mandrakes plants with roots shaped like the lower half of the human body   **23 ambergris**
intestinal secretion of the sperm whale; valuable and used in making perfumes
The River-Merchant's Wife: A Letter imitation of a poem by Li-Po (AD 701–762)

At fifteen I stopped scowling,
I desired my dust to be mingled with yours
Forever and forever and forever.
Why should I climb the lookout?

At sixteen you departed,   15
You went into far Ku-to-yen, by the river of swirling eddies,
And you have been gone five months.
The monkeys make sorrowful noise overhead.

You dragged your feet when you went out.
By the gate now, the moss is grown, the different mosses,   20
Too deep to clear them away!
The leaves fall early this autumn, in wind.
The paired butterflies are already yellow with August
Over the grass in the West garden;
They hurt me. I grow older.   25
If you are coming down through the narrows of the river Kiang,
Please let me know beforehand,
And I will come out to meet you
    As far as Cho-Fu-Sa.

—1915

ELINOR WYLIE ■ (1885–1928)

*Elinor Wylie, whose considerable lyrical skills found wide popularity during her
relatively brief career, has recently come to the notice of the present generation.
For many readers in the post–World War I era, Wylie, along with her slightly
younger contemporary Edna St. Vincent Millay, helped to define the literary
role of the New Woman of the 1920s. A poetic traditionalist whose lifestyle was
thoroughly modern, Wylie now seems overdue for a serious reassessment of her
place in the development of twentieth-century women's poetry.*

Let No Charitable Hope

Now let no charitable hope
Confuse my mind with images
Of eagle and of antelope:
I am in nature none of these.

I was, being human, born alone;
I am, being woman, hard beset;
I live by squeezing from a stone
The little nourishment I get.   5

In masks outrageous and austere
The years go by in single file;
But none has merited my fear,   10
And none has quite escaped my smile.

—1923

Ophelia°

My locks are shorn for sorrow
Of love which may not be;
Tomorrow and tomorrow
Are plotting cruelty.

The winter wind tangles   5
These ringlets half-grown,
The sun sprays with spangles
And rays like his own.

Oh, quieter and colder
Is the stream; he will wait;   10
When my curls touch my shoulder
He will comb them straight.

—1921

H. D. (HILDA DOOLITTLE) ■ (1886–1961)

*H. D. (Hilda Doolittle) was born in Bethlehem, Pennsylvania. Doolittle was
a college friend of both Williams and Pound, and moved to Europe permanently in 1911. With her husband Richard Aldington, H. D. was an important member of the imagist group promoted by Pound.*

Ophelia character in Shakespeare's *Hamlet* who drowns herself after her father, Polonius, is killed
by Hamlet

OPHELIA

613

Pear Tree

Silver dust,
lifted from the earth,
higher than my arms reach,
you have mounted,
O, silver,   5
higher than my arms reach,
you front us with great mass;

no flower ever opened
so staunch a white leaf,
no flower ever parted silver   10
from such rare silver;

O, white pear,
your flower-tufts
thick on the branch
bring summer and ripe fruits   15
in their purple hearts.

—1916

Sea Rose

Rose, harsh rose,
marred and with stint of petals,
meager flower, thin,
sparse of leaf,

more precious   5
than a wet rose
single on a stem—
you are caught in the drift.

Stunted, with small leaf,
you are flung on the sand,   10
you are lifted
in the crisp sand
that drives in the wind.

Can the spice-rose
drip such acrid fragrance   15
hardened in a leaf?

—1916

SIEGFRIED SASSOON ■ (1886–1967)

*Siegfried Sassoon was a decorated hero who publicly denounced World
War I and became a friend and supporter of other British war poets, including Robert Graves and Wilfred Owen. His sardonic, anti-heroic war
poems owe much to Thomas Hardy, whom he acknowledged as his chief
poetic influence.*

Dreamers

Soldiers are citizens of death's grey land,
    Drawing no dividend from time's tomorrows.
In the great hour of destiny they stand,
    Each with his feuds, and jealousies, and sorrows.

Soldiers are sworn to action; they must win   5
    Some flaming, fatal climax with their lives.
Soldiers are dreamers, when the guns begin
    They think of firelit homes, clean beds, and wives.

I see them in foul dug-outs, gnawed by rats,
    And in the ruined trenches, lashed with rain,   10
Dreaming of things they did with balls and bats,
    And mocked by hopeless longing to regain
Bank-holidays, and picture shows, and spats,°
    And going to the office in the train.

—1918

13 **spats** once-fashionable shoe coverings

Robinson Jeffers lived with his wife and children for many years in Carmel, California, in a rock house that he built himself by the sea. Many of his ideas about man's small place in the larger world of nature have gained in relevance through the years since his death. Largely forgotten for many years, his poetry, particularly his book-length verse narratives, is once more regaining the attention of serious readers.

The Purse-Seine°

Our sardine fishermen work at night in the dark of the moon;
    daylight or moonlight
They could not tell where to spread the net, unable to see the
    phosphorescence of the shoals of fish.
They work northward from Monterey, coasting Santa Cruz; off
    New Year's Point or off Pigeon Point
The look-out man will see some lakes of milk-color light on the
    sea's night-purple; he points, and the helmsman
Turns the dark prow, the motorboat circles the gleaming shoal
    and drifts out her seine-net. They close the circle   5
and purse the bottom of the net, then with great labor haul
    it in.
                                      I cannot tell you
How beautiful the scene is, and a little terrible, then, when the
    crowded fish
Know they are caught, and wildly beat from one wall to the other
    of their closing destiny the phosphorescent
Water to a pool of flame, each beautiful slender body sheeted
    with flame, like a live rocket   10
A comet's tail wake of clear yellow flame; while outside the
    narrowing
Floats and cordage of the net great sea-lions come up to
    watch, sighing in the dark; the vast walls of night
Stand erect to the stars.

Purse-Seine large circular fishing net; the bottom is closed (or pursed) before it is hauled in

Lately I was looking from a night mountain-top
On a wide city, the colored splendor, galaxies of light: how could
    I help but recall the seine-net   15
Gathering the luminous fish? I cannot tell you how beautiful
    the city appeared, and a little terrible.
I thought, We have geared the machines and locked all together
    into interdependence; we have built the great cities; now
There is no escape. We have gathered vast populations
    incapable of free survival, insulated
From the strong earth, each person in himself helpless, on
    all dependent. The circle is closed, and the net
Is being hauled in. They hardly feel the cords drawing, yet
    they shine already. The inevitable mass-disasters   20
Will not come in our time nor in our children's, but we and
    our children
Must watch the net draw narrower, government take all powers—
    or revolution, and the new government
Take more than all, add to kept bodies kept souls—or anarchy,
    the mass-disasters.

                        These things are Progress;
Do you marvel our verse is troubled or frowning, while it keeps
    its reason? Or it lets go, lets the mood flow   25
In the manner of the recent young men into mere hysteria,
    splintered gleams, crackled laughter. But they are quite wrong.
There is no reason for amazement: surely one always knew
    that cultures decay, and life's end is death.

                                  —1937

617

MARIANNE MOORE ■ (1887–1972)

*Marianne Moore called her own work poetry—unconventional and marked
with the stamp of a rare personality—because, as she put it, there was no
other category for it. For four years she was editor of the* Dial, *one of the
chief modernist periodicals. Moore's wide range of reference, which can leap
from the commonplace to the wondrous within a single poem, reflects her
unique set of personal interests—which range from exotic natural species to
baseball.*

The Fish

wade
through black jade.
   Of the crow-blue mussel-shells, one
      keeps
      adjusting the ash-heaps;   5
   opening and shutting itself like

an
injured fan.
   The barnacles which encrust the
      side   10
      of the wave, cannot hide
   there for the submerged shafts of the

sun,
split like spun
   glass, move themselves with spotlight swift-   15
      ness
      into the crevices—
   in and out, illuminating

the
turquoise sea   20
   of bodies. The water drives a
      wedge
      of iron through the iron edge
   of the cliff; whereupon the stars,

pink   25
rice-grains, ink-
   bespattered jelly-fish, crabs like
      green
      lilies, and submarine
   toadstools, slide each on the other.   30

All
external
   marks of abuse are present on

this
defiant edifice—   35
all the physical features of

ac-
cident—lack
of cornice, dynamite grooves, burns,
and   40
hatchet strokes, these things stand
out on it; the chasm-side is

dead.
Repeated
evidence has proved that it can   45
live
on what can not revive
its youth. The sea grows old in it.

—1921

Silence

My father used to say,
"Superior people never make long visits,
have to be shown Longfellow's grave
or the glass flowers at Harvard.
Self-reliant like the cat—   5
that takes its prey to privacy,
the mouse's limp tail hanging like a shoelace from its
mouth—
they sometimes enjoy solitude
and can be robbed of speech
by speech which has delighted them.   10
The deepest feeling always shows itself in silence;
not in silence, but restraint."
Nor was he insincere in saying, "Make my house your inn."
Inns are not residences.

—1935

T. S. ELIOT ■ (1888–1965)

T. S. Eliot was the author of The Waste Land, one of the most famous and difficult modernist poems, and became an international figure. Born in St. Louis and educated at Harvard, he moved to London in 1914, where he remained for the rest of his life, becoming a British subject in 1927. This chief prophet of modern despair turned to the Church of England in later life, and wrote successful dramas on religious themes. As a critic and influential editor, Eliot dominated poetic taste in England and America for over twenty-five years. He was awarded the Nobel Prize in 1948.

Journey of the Magi°

'A cold coming we had of it,
Just the worst time of the year
For a journey, and such a long journey:
The ways deep and the weather sharp,
The very dead of winter.'°   5
And the camels galled, sore-footed, refractory,
Lying down in the melting snow.
There were times we regretted
The summer palaces on slopes, the terraces,
And the silken girls bringing sherbet.   10
Then the camel men cursing and grumbling
And running away, and wanting their liquor and women,
And the night-fires going out, and the lack of shelters,
And the cities hostile and the towns unfriendly
And the villages dirty and charging high prices: 15
A hard time we had of it.
At the end we preferred to travel all night,
Sleeping in snatches,
With the voices singing in our ears, saying
That this was all folly.   20

Magi Wise Men mentioned in Matthew 2:1–2   **1–5 'A cold . . . winter'** The quotation marks indicated Eliot's source, a sermon by Lancelot Andrewes (1555–1626).

Then at dawn we came down to a temperate valley,
Wet, below the snow line, smelling of vegetation;
With a running stream and a water-mill beating the darkness,
And three trees on the low sky.
And an old white horse galloped away in the meadow. 25
Then we came to a tavern with vine-leaves over the lintel,
Six hands at an open door dicing for pieces of silver,
And feet kicking the empty wine-skins.
But there was no information, and so we continued
And arrived at evening, not a moment too soon 30
Finding the place; it was (you may say) satisfactory.

All this was a long time ago, I remember,
And I would do it again, but set down
This° set down
This: were we led all that way for 35
Birth or Death? There was a Birth, certainly,
We had evidence and no doubt. I had seen birth and death,
But had thought they were different; this Birth was
Hard and bitter agony for us, like Death, our death.
We returned to our places, these Kingdoms, 40
But no longer at ease here, in the old dispensation,°
With an alien people clutching their gods.
I should be glad of another death.

—1927

The Love Song of J. Alfred Prufrock

S'io credesse che mia risposta fosse
A persona che mai tornasse al mondo,
Questa fiamma staria senza più scosse.
Ma perciocche giammai di questo fondo
Non tornò vivo alcun, s'i'odo il vero,
Senza tema d'infamia ti rispondo.°

33–34 **set down . . . This** The Magus is dictating his memoirs to a scribe. **41 old dispensation**
world before the birth of Christ
S'io credesse . . . rispondo From Dante's *Inferno* (Canto 27). The speaker is Guido da Montefeltro: "If I
thought I spoke to someone who would return to the world, this flame would tremble no longer. But,
if what I hear is true, since no one has ever returned alive from this place I can answer you without
fear of infamy."

T. S. ELIOT

Let us go then, you° and I,
When the evening is spread out against the sky
Like a patient etherised upon a table;
Let us go, through certain half-deserted streets,
The muttering retreats   5
Of restless nights in one-night cheap hotels
And sawdust restaurants with oyster-shells:
Streets that follow like a tedious argument
Of insidious intent
To lead you to an overwhelming question . . .   10
Oh, do not ask, "What is it?"
Let us go and make our visit.

In the room the women come and go
Talking of Michelangelo.°

The yellow fog that rubs its back upon the window-panes,   15
The yellow smoke that rubs its muzzle on the window-panes,
Licked its tongue into the corners of the evening,
Lingered upon the pools that stand in drains,
Let fall upon its back the soot that falls from chimneys,
Slipped by the terrace, made a sudden leap,   20
And seeing that it was a soft October night,
Curled once about the house, and fell asleep.

And indeed there will be time
For the yellow smoke that slides along the street,

Rubbing its back upon the window-panes;   25
There will be time, there will be time
To prepare a face to meet the faces that you meet;
There will be time to murder and create,
And time for all the works and days of hands
That lift and drop a question on your plate: 30
Time for you and time for me,
And time yet for a hundred indecisions,
And for a hundred visions and revisions,
Before the taking of a toast and tea.

1 you Eliot said that the auditor of the poem was a male friend of Prufrock.   14 Michelangelo Italian
painter and sculptor (1475–1564)

In the room the women come and go   35
Talking of Michelangelo.

And indeed there will be time
To wonder, "Do I dare?" and, "Do I dare?"—
Time to turn back and descend the stair,
With a bald spot in the middle of my hair—   40
(They will say: "How his hair is growing thin!")
My morning coat, my collar mounting firmly to the chin,
My necktie rich and modest, but asserted by a simple pin—
(They will say: "But how his arms and legs are thin!")
Do I dare   45
Disturb the universe?
In a minute there is time
For decisions and revisions which a minute will reverse.

For I have known them all already, known them all:
Have known the evenings, mornings, afternoons,   50
I have measured out my life with coffee spoons;
I know the voices dying with a dying fall
Beneath the music from a farther room.
          So how should I presume?

And I have known the eyes already, known them all—   55
The eyes that fix you in a formulated phrase,
And when I am formulated, sprawling on a pin,
When I am pinned and wriggling on the wall,
Then how should I begin
To spit out all the butt-ends of my days and ways?   60
          And how should I presume?

And I have known the arms already, known them all—
Arms that are braceleted and white and bare
(But in the lamplight, downed with light brown hair!)
Is it perfume from a dress   65
That makes me so digress?
Arms that lie along a table, or wrap about a shawl.
          And should I then presume?
          And how should I begin?

          . . . . .

Shall I say, I have gone at dusk through narrow streets,   70
And watched the smoke that rises from the pipes
Of lonely men in shirtsleeves, leaning out of windows? . . .

I should have been a pair of ragged claws
Scuttling across the floors of silent seas.

                    . . . . .

And the afternoon, the evening, sleeps so peacefully!   75
Smoothed by long fingers,
Asleep . . . tired . . . or it malingers,
Stretched on the floor, here beside you and me.
Should I, after tea and cakes and ices,
Have the strength to force the moment to its crisis?   80
But though I have wept and fasted, wept and prayed,
Though I have seen my head (grown slightly bald) brought in
          upon a platter,
I am no prophet°—and here's no great matter;
I have seen the moment of my greatness flicker,
And I have seen the eternal Footman hold my coat, and snicker, 85
          And in short, I was afraid.

And would it have been worth it, after all,
After the cups, the marmalade, the tea,
Among the porcelain, among some talk of you and me,
Would it have been worth while,   90
To have bitten off the matter with a smile,
To have squeezed the universe into a ball
To roll it towards some overwhelming question,
To say: "I am Lazarus,° come from the dead,
Come back to tell you all, I shall tell you all"—   95
If one, settling a pillow by her head,
          Should say: "That is not what I meant at all;
          That is not it, at all."

And would it have been worth it, after all,
Would it have been worth while,   100
After the sunsets and the dooryards and the sprinkled streets,

82–83 my head . . . no prophet allusion to John the Baptist   94 Lazarus raised from the dead in
John 11:1–44

After the novels, after the teacups, after the skirts that trail
    along the floor—
And this, and so much more?—
It is impossible to say just what I mean!
But as if a magic lantern° threw the nerves in patterns on a
    screen: 105

Would it have been worth while
If one, settling a pillow or throwing off a shawl,
And turning toward the window, should say:
    "That is not it at all,
    That is not what I meant, at all."   110

    . . . . .

No! I am not Prince Hamlet, nor was meant to be;
Am an attendant lord, one that will do
To swell a progress, start a scene or two,
Advise the prince; no doubt, an easy tool,
Deferential, glad to be of use,   115
Politic, cautious, and meticulous;
Full of high sentence, but a bit obtuse;
At times, indeed, almost ridiculous—
Almost, at times, the Fool.°

I grow old . . . I grow old . . .   120
I shall wear the bottoms of my trousers rolled.

Shall I part my hair behind? Do I dare to eat a peach?
I shall wear white flannel trousers, and walk upon the beach.
I have heard the mermaids singing, each to each.

I do not think that they will sing to me.   125

I have seen them riding seaward on the waves
Combing the white hair of the waves blown back
When the wind blows the water white and black.

We have lingered in the chambers of the sea
By sea-girls wreathed with seaweed red and brown   130
Till human voices wake us, and we drown.

                                           —1917

105 magic lantern old-fashioned slide projector   **111–119 not Prince Hamlet . . . the Fool** The
allusion is probably to Polonius, a character in *Hamlet*.

Raised in the coastal village of Camden, Maine, Edna St. Vincent Millay was extremely popular in the 1920s, when her sonnets seemed the ultimate expression of the liberated sexuality of what was then called the New Woman. Neglected for many years, her poems have recently generated renewed interest, and it seems likely that she will eventually regain her status as one of the most important female poets of the twentieth century.

If I Should Learn, in Some Quite Casual Way

If I should learn, in some quite casual way,
That you were gone, not to return again—
Read from the back-page of a paper, say,
Held by a neighbor in a subway train,
How at the corner of this avenue   5
And such a street (so are the papers filled)
A hurrying man, who happened to be you,
At noon today had happened to be killed—
I should not cry aloud—I could not cry
Aloud, or wring my hands in such a place—   10
I should but watch the station lights rush by
With a more careful interest on my face;
Or raise my eyes and read with greater care
Where to store furs and how to treat the hair.

—1917

Oh, Oh, You Will Be Sorry for That Word

Oh, oh, you will be sorry for that word!
Give back my book and take my kiss instead.
Was it my enemy or my friend I heard,
"What a big book for such a little head!"
Come, I will show you now my newest hat,   5
And you may watch me purse my mouth and prink!°

6 **prink** primp

Oh, I shall love you still, and all of that.
I never again shall tell you what I think.
I shall be sweet and crafty, soft and sly;
You will not catch me reading any more: 10
I shall be called a wife to pattern by;
And some day when you knock and push the door,
Some sane day, not too bright and not too stormy,
I shall be gone, and you may whistle for me.

—1923

What Lips My Lips Have Kissed, and Where, and Why

What lips my lips have kissed, and where, and why,
I have forgotten, and what arms have lain
Under my head till morning; but the rain
Is full of ghosts tonight, that tap and sigh
Upon the glass and listen for reply,   5
And in my heart there stirs a quiet pain
For unremembered lads that not again
Will turn to me at midnight with a cry.
Thus in the winter stands the lonely tree,
Nor knows what birds have vanished one by one,   10
Yet knows its boughs more silent than before:
I cannot say what loves have come and gone,
I only know that summer sang in me
A little while, that in me sings no more.

—1923

WILFRED OWEN ■ (1893–1918)

Wilfred Owen was killed in the trenches only a few days before the armistice that ended World War I. Owen showed more promise than any other English poet of his generation. A decorated officer whose nerves broke down after exposure to battle, he met Siegfried Sassoon at Craiglockhart military hospital. His work was posthumously collected by his friend. A novel by Pat Barker, Regeneration *(also made into a film), deals with their poetic and personal relationship.*

Dulce et Decorum Est°

Bent double, like old beggars under sacks,
Knock-kneed, coughing like hags, we cursed through sludge,
Till on the haunting flares we turned our backs
And towards our distant rest began to trudge.

Men marched asleep. Many had lost their boots   5
But limped on, blood-shod. All went lame; all blind;
Drunk with fatigue; deaf even to the hoots
Of tired, outstripped Five-Nines° that dropped behind.

Gas! Gas! Quick, boys!—An ecstasy of fumbling
Fitting the clumsy helmets just in time;   10
But someone still was yelling out and stumbling
And floundʼring like a man in fire or lime . . .
Dim, through the misty panes and thick green light,°
As under a green sea, I saw him drowning.

In all my dreams, before my helpless sight,   15
He plunges at me, guttering, choking, drowning.
If in some smothering dreams you too could pace
Behind the wagon that we flung him in,
And watch the white eyes writhing in his face,
His hanging face, like a devil's sick of sin;   20
If you could hear, at every jolt, the blood
Come gargling from the froth-corrupted lungs,
Obscene as cancer, bitter as the cud
Of vile, incurable sores on innocent tongues,—
My friend,° you would not tell with such high zest   25
To children ardent for some desperate glory,
The old Lie: Dulce et decorum est
Pro patria mori.

—1920

WILFRED OWEN

628

Dulce et Decorum Est (pro patria mori) from the Roman poet Horace: "It is sweet and proper to die for one's country"   **8 Five-Nines** German artillery shells (59 mm)   **13 misty panes and thick green light** i.e., through the gas mask   **25 My friend** The poem was originally addressed to Jessie Pope, a writer of patriotic verse.

e. e. cummings was the son of a Harvard professor and Unitarian clergy-
man. Edward Estlin Cummings served as a volunteer ambulance driver
in France during World War I. cummings's experimentation with the ty-
pographical aspects of poetry reveals his serious interest in cubist paint-
ing, which he studied in Paris in the 1920s. A brilliant satirist, he also
excelled as a writer of lyrical poems whose unusual appearance and idio-
syncratic grammar, spelling, and punctuation often overshadow their
traditional themes.

pity this busy
monster, manunkind

pity this busy monster, manunkind,

not. Progress is a comfortable disease:
your victim (death and life safely beyond)

plays with the bigness of his littleness
—electrons° deify one razorblade   5
into a mountainrange; lenses extend

unwish through curving wherewhen till unwish
returns on its unself.
                    A world of made
is not a world of born—pity poor flesh

and trees, poor stars and stones, but never this   10
fine specimen of hypermagical

ultraomnipotence. We doctors know

a hopeless case if—listen: there's a hell
of a good universe next door; let's go

—1944

5 **electrons** in an electron microscope

plato told

plato told

him: he couldn't
believe it (jesus

told him; he
wouldn't believe   5
it) lao

tsze
certainly told
him, and general
(yes

mam)   10
sherman;°

and even
(believe it
Or   15

not) you
told him: i told

him; we told him
(he didn't believe it, no

sir) it took   20
a nipponized° bit of
the old sixth

avenue
el; in the top of his head: to tell
him   25

          1944

---

11 William Tecumseh Sherman (1820–1891), Union general in the American Civil War. cummings
alludes to his famous statement "War is hell," a sentiment presumably shared by Plato, the Greek
philosopher (427?–347 BC), Jesus, and Lao-tze (c. 604 BC), Chinese philosopher credited as the
founder of Taoism. 21 Scrap metal from the Sixth Avenue elevated railway in New York City, torn
down in the 1930s, was sold to Japan and turned into armaments used in World War II.

r-p-o-p-h-e-s-s-a-g-r

                    r-p-o-p-h-e-s-s-a-g-r
              who
        a)s w(e loo)k
        upnowgath
                    PPEGORHRASS   5
                            eringint(o-
        aThe):l
              eA
                 !p:
        S   a   10
                 (r
        rIvInG   .gRrEaPsPhOs)
                                    to
        rea(be)rran(com)gi(e)ngly
        ,grasshopper;   15

                                                      —1932

somewhere I have never travelled

    somewhere i have never travelled, gladly beyond
    any experience, your eyes have their silence:
    in your most frail gesture are things which enclose me,
    or which i cannot touch because they are too near

    your slightest look will easily unclose me   5
    though i have closed myself as fingers,
    you open always petal by petal myself as Spring opens
    (touching skilfully,mysteriously) her first rose

    or if your wish be to close me, i and
    my life will shut very beautifully ,suddenly,   10
    as when the heart of this flower imagines
    the snow carefully everywhere descending;

    nothing which we are to perceive in this world equals
    the power of your intense fragility:whose texture
    compels me with the color of its countries,   15
    rendering death and forever with each breathing

(i do not know what it is about you that closes
and opens;only something in me understands
the voice of your eyes is deeper than all roses)
nobody,not even the rain,has such small hands   20

—1931

JEAN TOOMER ■ (1894–1967)

*Jean Toomer was born in Washington, D.C., the grandson of a black man who
served as governor of Louisiana during Reconstruction. His book* Cane *(1923) is
a mixed collection of prose and verse based on his observations of life in rural
Georgia, where he was a schoolteacher. A complete edition of his poetry, most of
it unpublished during his life, was assembled over twenty years after his death.*

Georgia Dusk

The sky, lazily disdaining to pursue
   The setting sun, too indolent to hold
   A lengthened tournament for flashing gold,
Passively darkens for night's barbecue,

A feast of moon and men and barking hounds,   5
   An orgy for some genius of the South
   With blood-hot eyes and cane-lipped scented mouth,
Surprised in making folk-songs from soul sounds.

The sawmill blows its whistle, buzz-saws stop,
   And silence breaks the bud of knoll and hill,   10
Soft settling pollen where plowed lands fulfill
Their early promise of a bumper crop.

Smoke from the pyramidal sawdust pile
   Curls up, blue ghosts of trees, tarrying low
   Where only chips and stumps are left to show   15
The solid proof of former domicile.

Meanwhile, the men, with vestiges of pomp,
   Race memories of king and caravan,
   High-priests, an ostrich, and a juju-man,
Go singing through the footpaths of the swamp.   20

Their voices rise . . the pine trees are guitars,
   Strumming, pine-needles fall like sheets of rain . . .

Their voices rise . . the chorus of the cane
Is caroling a vesper to the stars . .

O singers, resinous and soft your songs   25
   Above the sacred whisper of the pines,
   Give virgin lips to cornfield concubines,
Bring dreams of Christ to dusky cane-lipped throngs.

—1923

LOUISE BOGAN ■ (1897–1970)

Louise Bogan was for many years the poetry editor and resident critic of The
New Yorker, *and the opinions expressed in her many book reviews have held
up well in the years since her death. In her later years, Bogan suffered from
severe bouts of clinical depression and wrote little poetry, but her relatively
slim output reveals a unique poetic voice.*

Women

Women have no wilderness in them,
They are provident instead,
Content in the tight hot cell of their hearts
To eat dusty bread.

They do not see cattle cropping red winter grass,   5
They do not hear
Snow water going down under culverts
Shallow and clear.

They wait, when they should turn to journeys,
They stiffen, when they should bend.   10
They use against themselves that benevolence
To which no man is friend.

They cannot think of so many crops to a field
Or of clean wood cleft by an axe.
Their love is an eager meaninglessness   15
Too tense, or too lax.

They hear in every whisper that speaks to them
A shout and a cry.

As like as not, when they take life over their door-sills
They should let it go by.   20

—1923

LANGSTON HUGHES ■ (1902–1967)

*Langston Hughes was a leading figure in the Harlem Renaissance of the
1920s, and he became the most famous black writer of his day. Phrases from
his poems and other writings have become deeply ingrained in the American
consciousness. An important experimenter with poetic form, Hughes is credited with incorporating the rhythms of jazz into poetry.*

Dream Boogie

Good morning, daddy!
Ain't you heard
The boogie-woogie rumble
Of a dream deferred?
Listen closely: 5
You'll hear their feet
Beating out and beating out a—

>   *You think*
>   *It's a happy beat?*

Listen to it closely: 10
Ain't you heard
something underneath
like a—

>   *What did I say?*

Sure,   15
I'm happy!
Take it away!

>   *Hey, pop!*
>   *Re-bop!*
>   *Mop!*   20
>   *Y-e-a-h!*

—1951

Harlem Sweeties

Have you dug the spill
Of Sugar Hill?
Cast your gims
On this sepia thrill:
Brown sugar lassie,   5
Caramel treat,
Honey-gold baby
Sweet enough to eat.
Peach-skinned girlie,
Coffee and cream,   10
Chocolate darling
Out of a dream.
Walnut tinted
Or cocoa brown,
Pomegranate-lipped   15
Pride of the town.
Rich cream-colored
To plum-tinted black,
Feminine sweetness
In Harlem's no lack.   20
Glow of the quince
To blush of the rose.
Persimmon bronze
To cinnamon toes.
Blackberry cordial,   25
Virginia Dare wine—
All those sweet colors
Flavor Harlem of mine!
Walnut or cocoa,
Let me repeat: 30
Caramel, brown sugar,
A chocolate treat.
Molasses taffy,
Coffee and cream,
Licorice, clove, cinnamon   35
To a honey-brown dream.
Ginger, wine-gold,

Persimmon, blackberry,
All through the spectrum
Harlem girls vary—   40
So if you want to know beauty's
Rainbow-sweet thrill,
Stroll down luscious,
Delicious, *fine* Sugar Hill.

—1940

The Weary Blues

Droning a drowsy syncopated tune,
Rocking back and forth to a mellow croon,
    I heard a Negro play.
Down on Lenox Avenue the other night
By the pale dull pallor of an old gas light   5
    He did a lazy sway. . . .
    He did a lazy sway. . . .
To the tune o' those Weary Blues.
With his ebony hands on each ivory key
He made that poor piano moan with melody.   10
    O Blues!
Swaying to and fro on his rickety stool
He played that sad raggy tune like a musical fool.
    Sweet Blues!
Coming from a black man's soul.   15
    O Blues!
In a deep song voice with a melancholy tone
I heard that Negro sing, that old piano moan—
    "Ain't got nobody in all this world,
    Ain't got nobody but ma self.   20
    I's gwine to quit ma frownin'
    And put ma troubles on the shelf."

Thump, thump, thump, went his foot on the floor.
He played a few chords then he sang some more—
    "I got the Weary Blues   25
    And I can't be satisfied.
    Got the Weary Blues

And can't be satisfied—
I ain't happy no mo'
And I wish that I had died." 30
And far into the night he crooned that tune.
The stars went out and so did the moon.
The singer stopped playing and went to bed
While the Weary Blues echoed through his head.
He slept like a rock or a man that's dead. 35

—1926

COUNTEE CULLEN ■ (1903–1946)

Countee Cullen, among black writers of the first half of the twentieth century, crafted poetry representing a more conservative style than that of his contemporary, Hughes. Although he wrote a number of lyrics on standard poetic themes, he is best remembered for his eloquent poems on racial subjects.

Incident

Once riding in old Baltimore,
Heart-filled, head-filled with glee,
I saw a Baltimorean
Keep looking straight at me.

Now I was eight and very small, 5
And he was no whit bigger,
And so I smiled, but he poked out
His tongue, and called me, "Nigger."

I saw the whole of Baltimore
From May until December; 10
Of all the things that happened there
That's all that I remember.

—1925

Yet Do I Marvel

I doubt not God is good, well-meaning, kind,
And did He stoop to quibble could tell why
The little buried mole continues blind,
Why flesh that mirrors Him must some day die,
Make plain the reason tortured Tantalus°   5
Is baited by the fickle fruit, declare
If merely brute caprice dooms Sisyphus°
To struggle up a never-ending stair.
Inscrutable His ways are, and immune
To catechism by a mind too strewn   10
With petty cares to slightly understand
What awful brain compels His awful hand.
Yet do I marvel at this curious thing:
To make a poet black and bid him sing!

—1925

W. H. AUDEN ■ (1907–1973)

W. H. Auden was already established as an important younger British poet before he moved to America in 1939 (he later became a U.S. citizen). As a transatlantic link between two literary cultures, Auden was one of the most influential literary figures and cultural spokespersons in the English-speaking world for almost forty years, giving a name to the postwar era when he dubbed it "The Age of Anxiety" in a poem. In his last years he returned briefly to Oxford, where he occupied the poetry chair.

As I Walked Out One Evening

As I walked out one evening,
        Walking down Bristol Street,
The crowds upon the pavement
        Were fields of harvest wheat.

---

5 Tantalus mythological character tortured by unreachable fruit   **7 Sisyphus** figure in myth who endlessly rolls a boulder uphill

W. H. AUDEN

And down by the brimming river
    I heard a lover sing
Under an arch of the railway:
    "Love has no ending.

"I'll love you, dear, I'll love you
    Till China and Africa meet,
And the river jumps over the mountain
    And the salmon sing in the street.

"I'll love you till the ocean
    Is folded and hung up to dry,
And the seven stars go squawking
    Like geese about the sky.

"The years shall run like rabbits,
    For in my arms I hold
The Flower of the Ages,
    And the first love of the world."

But all the clocks in the city
    Began to whirr and chime:
"O let not Time deceive you,
    You cannot conquer Time.

"In the burrows of the Nightmare
    Where Justice naked is,
Time watches from the shadow
    And coughs when you would kiss.

"In headaches and in worry
    Vaguely life leaks away,
And Time will have his fancy
    Tomorrow or to-day.

"Into many a green valley
    Drifts the appalling snow;
Time breaks the threaded dances
    And the diver's brilliant bow.

"O plunge your hands in water,
    Plunge them in up to the wrist;
Stare, stare in the basin
    And wonder what you've missed.

"The glacier knocks in the cupboard,
    The desert sighs in the bed,
And the crack in the tea-cup opens
    A lane to the land of the dead.

"Where the beggars raffle the banknotes   45
    And the Giant is enchanting to Jack,
And the Lily-white Boy is a Roarer,
    And Jill goes down on her back.

"O look, look in the mirror,
    O look in your distress;   50
Life remains a blessing
    Although you cannot bless.

"O stand, stand at the window
    As the tears scald and start;
You shall love your crooked neighbor   55
    With your crooked heart."

It was late, late in the evening,
    The lovers they were gone;
The clocks had ceased their chiming,
    And the deep river ran on.   60

—1940

Musée des Beaux Arts°

About suffering they were never wrong,
The Old Masters: how well they understood
Its human position; how it takes place
While someone else is eating or opening a window or just
    walking dully along;
How, when the aged are reverently, passionately waiting   5
For the miraculous birth, there always must be
Children who did not specially want it to happen, skating
On a pond at the edge of the wood:
They never forgot
That even the dreadful martyrdom must run its course   10

Musée des Beaux Arts Museum of Fine Arts

Anyhow in a corner, some untidy spot
Where the dogs go on with their doggy life and the torturer's horse
Scratches its innocent behind on a tree.

In Brueghel's *Icarus*,° for instance: how everything turns away
Quite leisurely from the disaster; the ploughman may   15
Have heard the splash, the forsaken cry,
But for him it was not an important failure; the sun shone
As it had to on the white legs disappearing into the green
Water; and the expensive delicate ship that must have seen
Something amazing, a boy falling out of the sky,   20
Had somewhere to get to and sailed calmly on.

—*1938*

The Unknown Citizen

To JS/07/M/378
This Marble Monument Is Erected by the State

He was found by the Bureau of Statistics to be
One against whom there was no official complaint,
And all the reports on his conduct agree
That, in the modern sense of an old-fashioned word, he was a saint,
For in everything he did he served the Greater Community.   5
Except for the War till the day he retired
He worked in a factory and never got fired,
But satisfied his employers, Fudge Motors Inc.
Yet he wasn't a scab or odd in his views,
For his Union reports that he paid his dues,   10
(Our report on his Union shows it was sound)
And our Social Psychology workers found
That he was popular with his mates and liked a drink.
The Press are convinced that he bought a paper every day
And that his reactions to advertisements were normal
     in every way.   15
Policies taken out in his name prove that he was fully insured,

---

14 Brueghel's *Icarus* In this painting (c. 1550) the famous event from Greek myth is almost
inconspicuous among the other details Auden mentions.

And his Health-card shows he was once in hospital but left
    it cured.
Both Producers Research and High-Grade Living declare
He was fully sensible to the advantages of the Installment Plan
And had everything necessary to the Modern Man,   20
A phonograph, a radio, a car and a frigidaire.
Our researchers into Public Opinion are content
That he held the proper opinions for the time of year;
When there was peace, he was for peace; when there was war,
    he went.
He was married and added five children to the population,   25
Which our Eugenist says was the right number for a parent
    of his generation,
And our teachers report that he never interfered with their
    education.
Was he free? Was he happy? The question is absurd:
Had anything been wrong, we should certainly have heard.

—1939

THEODORE ROETHKE ■ (1908–1963)

Theodore Roethke was born in Michigan. Roethke was an influential teacher of poetry at the University of Washington for many years. His father was the owner of a greenhouse, and Roethke's childhood closeness to nature was an important influence on his mature poetry. His periodic nervous breakdowns, the result of bipolar manic-depression, presaged his early death.

Dolor°

I have known the inexorable sadness of pencils,
Neat in their boxes, dolor of pad and paper-weight,
All of the misery of manilla folders and mucilage,
Desolation in immaculate public places,
Lonely reception room, lavatory, switchboard,   5
The unalterable pathos of basin and pitcher,
Ritual of multigraph, paper-clip, comma,

Dolor sadness

Endless duplication of lives and objects.
And I have seen dust from the walls of institutions,
Finer than flour, alive, more dangerous than silica,°   10
Sift, almost invisible, through long afternoons of tedium,
Dropping a fine film on nails and delicate eyebrows,
Glazing the pale hair, the duplicate grey standard faces.

                                                    —1948

My Papa's Waltz

The whiskey on your breath
Could make a small boy dizzy;
But I hung on like death:
Such waltzing was not easy.

We romped until the pans   5
Slid from the kitchen shelf;
My mother's countenance
Could not unfrown itself.

The hand that held my wrist
Was battered on one knuckle;   10
At every step you missed
My right ear scraped a buckle.

You beat time on my head
With a palm caked hard by dirt,
Then waltzed me off to bed   15
Still clinging to your shirt.

                                                    —1948

Root Cellar

Nothing would sleep in that cellar, dank as a ditch,
Bulbs broke out of boxes hunting for chinks in the dark,
Shoots dangled and drooped,
Lolling obscenely from mildewed crates,
Hung down long yellow evil necks, like tropical snakes.   5

10 **silica** rock dust, a cause of silicosis, an occupational disease of miners and quarry workers

And what a congress of stinks!—
Roots ripe as old bait,
Pulpy stems, rank, silo-rich,
Leaf-mold, manure, lime, piled against slippery planks.
Nothing would give up life: 10
Even the dirt kept breathing a small breath.

—1948

ELIZABETH BISHOP ■ (1911–1979)

*Elizabeth Bishop for most of her life was highly regarded as a "poet's poet,"
winning the Pulitzer Prize for* North and South *in 1956, but in the years
since her death she has gained a wider readership. She traveled widely and
lived in Brazil for a number of years before returning to the United States to
teach at Harvard during the last years of her life.*

ELIZABETH BISHOP

644

The Fish

I caught a tremendous fish
and held him beside the boat
half out of water, with my hook
fast in a corner of his mouth.
He didn't fight.   5
He hadn't fought at all.
He hung a grunting weight,
battered and venerable
and homely. Here and there
his brown skin hung in strips   10
like ancient wallpaper,
and its pattern of darker brown
was like wallpaper:
shapes like full-blown roses
stained and lost through age.   15
He was speckled with barnacles,
fine rosettes of lime,
and infested
with tiny white sea-lice,
and underneath two or three   20

rags of green weed hung down.
While his gills were breathing in
the terrible oxygen
—the frightening gills,
fresh and crisp with blood, 25
that can cut so badly—
I thought of the coarse white flesh
packed in like feathers,
the big bones and the little bones,
the dramatic reds and blacks 30
of his shiny entrails,
and the pink swim-bladder
like a big peony.
I looked into his eyes
which were far larger than mine 35
but shallower, and yellowed,
the irises backed and packed
with tarnished tinfoil
seen through the lenses
of old scratched isinglass.° 40
They shifted a little, but not
to return my stare.
—It was more like the tipping
of an object toward the light.
I admired his sullen face, 45
the mechanism of his jaw,
and then I saw
that from his lower lip
—if you could call it a lip—
grim, wet, and weapon-like, 50
hung five old pieces of fish-line,
or four and a wire leader
with the swivel still attached,
with all their five big hooks
grown firmly in his mouth. 55
A green line, frayed at the end
where he broke it, two heavier lines,

40 isinglass semitransparent material made from fish bladders

and a fine black thread
still crimped from the strain and snap
when it broke and he got away.   60
Like medals with their ribbons
frayed and wavering,
a five-haired beard of wisdom
trailing from his aching jaw.
I stared and stared   65
and victory filled up
the little rented boat,
from the pool of bilge
where oil had spread a rainbow
around the rusted engine   70
to the bailer° rusted orange,
the sun-cracked thwarts,
the oarlocks on their strings,
the gunnels°—until everything
was rainbow, rainbow, rainbow!   75
And I let the fish go.

                                                —1946

One Art

The art of losing isn't hard to master;
so many things seem filled with the intent
to be lost that their loss is no disaster.

Lose something every day. Accept the fluster
of lost door keys, the hour badly spent.   5
The art of losing isn't hard to master.

Then practice losing farther, losing faster:
places, and names, and where it was you meant
to travel. None of these will bring disaster.

I lost my mother's watch. And look! my last, or   10
next-to-last, of three loved houses went.
The art of losing isn't hard to master.

71 **bailer** bucket   74 **gunnels** gunwales

I lost two cities, lovely ones. And, vaster,
some realms I owned, two rivers, a continent.
I miss them, but it wasn't a disaster.   15

—Even losing you (the joking voice, a gesture
I love) I shan't have lied. It's evident
the art of losing's not too hard to master
though it may look like (*Write* it!) like disaster.

—*1976*

The Shampoo

The still explosions on the rocks,
the lichens, grow
by spreading, gray, concentric shocks.
They have arranged
to meet the rings around the moon, although   5
within our memories they have not changed.

And since the heavens will attend
as long on us,
you've been, dear friend,
precipitate and pragmatical;   10
and look what happens. For Time is
nothing if not amenable.

The shooting stars in your black hair
in bright formation
are flocking where,   15
so straight, so soon?
—Come, let me wash it in this big tin basin,
battered and shiny like the moon.

—*1976*

ROBERT HAYDEN ■ (1913–1980)

*Robert Hayden named Countee Cullen as one of the chief early influences on
his poetry. A native of Michigan, he taught for many years at Fisk University
in Nashville and at the University of Michigan. Although many of Hayden's
poems are on African-American subjects, he wished to be considered a poet
with strong links to the mainstream English-language tradition.*

Those Winter Sundays

Sundays too my father got up early
and put his clothes on in the blueblack cold,
then with cracked hands that ached
from labor in the weekday weather made
banked fires blaze. No one ever thanked him.   5

I'd wake and hear the cold splintering, breaking.
When the rooms were warm, he'd call,
and slowly I would rise and dress,
fearing the chronic angers of that house,

Speaking indifferently to him,   10
who had driven out the cold
and polished my good shoes as well.
What did I know, what did I know
of love's austere and lonely offices?°

—1962

648

DUDLEY RANDALL ■ (1914–2000)

Dudley Randall was the founder of Broadside Press, a black-owned publishing firm that eventually attracted important writers like Gwendolyn Brooks and Don L. Lee. For most of his life a resident of Detroit, Randall spent many years working in that city's library system before taking a similar position at the University of Detroit.

Ballad of Birmingham

(On the Bombing of a Church in
Birmingham, Alabama, 1963)°

"Mother dear, may I go downtown
Instead of out to play,
And march the streets of Birmingham
In a Freedom March today?"

14 offices daily religious ceremonies
Birmingham, Alabama, 1963 during the height of the civil rights movement

"No, baby, no, you may not go,   5
For the dogs are fierce and wild,
And clubs and hoses, guns and jail
Aren't good for a little child."

"But, mother, I won't be alone.
Other children will go with me,   10
And march the streets of Birmingham
To make our country free."

"No, baby, no, you may not go,
For I fear those guns will fire.
But you may go to church instead   15
And sing in the children's choir."

She has combed and brushed her night-dark hair,
And bathed rose petal sweet,
And drawn white gloves on her small brown hands,
And white shoes on her feet.   20

The mother smiled to know her child
Was in the sacred place,
But that smile was the last smile
To come upon her face.

For when she heard the explosion,   25
Her eyes grew wet and wild.
She raced through the streets of Birmingham
Calling for her child.

She clawed through bits of glass and brick,
Then lifted out a shoe.   30
"O, here's the shoe my baby wore,
But, baby, where are you?"

—1969

WILLIAM STAFFORD ■ (1914–1993)

William Stafford was one of the most prolific poets of the postwar era. Stafford published in virtually every magazine in the United States. Raised in Kansas as a member of the pacifist Church of the Brethren, Stafford served in a camp for conscientious objectors during World War II. His first

Traveling Through the Dark

Traveling through the dark I found a deer
dead on the edge of the Wilson River road.
It is usually best to roll them into the canyon:
that road is narrow; to swerve might make more dead.

By glow of the tail-light I stumbled back of the car   5
and stood by the heap, a doe, a recent killing;
she had stiffened already, almost cold.
I dragged her off; she was large in the belly.

My fingers touching her side brought me the reason—
her side was warm; her fawn lay there waiting,   10
alive, still, never to be born.
Beside that mountain road I hesitated.

The car aimed ahead its lowered parking lights;
under the hood purred the steady engine.
I stood in the glare of the warm exhaust turning red;   15
around our group I could hear the wilderness listen.

I thought hard for us all—my only swerving—
then pushed her over the edge into the river.

—*1960*

DYLAN THOMAS ■ (1914–1953)

Dylan Thomas was a legendary performer of his and others' poetry. His popularity in the United States led to several collegiate reading tours, punctuated with outrageous behavior and self-destructive drinking that led to his early death in New York City, the victim of what the autopsy report labeled "insult to the brain." The Wales of his childhood remained a constant source of inspiration for his poetry and for radio dramas like Under Milk Wood, *which was turned into a film by fellow Welshman Richard Burton and his then-wife, Elizabeth Taylor.*

Do Not Go Gentle into That Good Night

Do not go gentle into that good night,
Old age should burn and rave at close of day;
Rage, rage against the dying of the light.

Though wise men at their end know dark is right,
Because their words had forked no lightning they   5
Do not go gentle into that good night.

Good men, the last wave by, crying how bright
Their frail deeds might have danced in a green bay,
Rage, rage against the dying of the light.

Wild men who caught and sang the sun in flight,   10
And learn, too late, they grieved it on its way,
Do not go gentle into that good night.

Grave men, near death, who see with blinding sight
Blind eyes could blaze like meteors and be gay,
Rage, rage against the dying of the light.   15

And you, my father, there on the sad height,
Curse, bless, me now with your fierce tears, I pray,
Do not go gentle into that good night.
Rage, rage against the dying of the light.

—1952

Poem in October

It was my thirtieth year to heaven
Woke to my heating from harbour and neighbour wood
    And the mussel pooled and the heron
        Priested shore
        The morning beckon   5
With water praying and call of seagull and rock
And the knock of sailing boats on the net webbed wall
        Myself to set foot
        That second
    In the still sleeping town and set forth.   10

My birthday began with the water-
Birds and the birds of the winged trees flying my name
Above the farms and the white horses
        And I rose
    In the rainy autumn   15
And walked abroad in a shower of all my days.
High tide and the heron dived when I took the road
        Over the border
        And the gates
Of the town closed as the town awoke.   20

A springful of larks in a rolling
Cloud and the roadside bushes brimming with whistling
Blackbirds and the sun of October
        Summary
    On the hill's shoulder,   25
Here were fond climates and sweet singers suddenly
Come in the morning where I wandered and listened
        To the rain wringing
        Wind blow cold
    In the wood faraway under me.   30

Pale rain over the dwindling harbour
And over the sea wet church the size of a snail
    With its horns through mist and the castle
        Brown as owls
        But all the gardens   35
Of spring and summer were blooming in the tall tales
Beyond the border and under the lark full cloud.
        There could I marvel
        My birthday
Away but the weather turned around.   40

It turned away from the blithe country
And down the other air and the blue altered sky
    Streamed again a wonder of summer
        With apples
    Pears and red currants   45
And I saw in the turning so clearly a child's
Forgotten morning when he walked with his mother
        Through the parables

        Of sun light
    And the legends of the green chapels   50

    And the twice told fields of infancy
That his tears burned my cheeks and his heart moved in mine.
    These were the woods the river and sea
        Where a boy
        In the listening   55
Summertime of the dead whispered the truth of his joy
To tree and the stones and the fish in the tide.
        And the mystery
            Sang alive
    Still in the water and singingbirds.   60

    And there could I marvel my birthday
Away but the weather turned around. And the true
    Joy of the long dead child sang burning
        In the sun.
        It was my thirtieth   65
Year to heaven stood there then in the summer noon
Though the town below lay leaved with October blood.
        O may my heart's truth
            Still be sung
    On this high hill in a year's turning.   70

                                                        —1946

WELDON KEES ■ (1914–1955)

*Weldon Kees was a multitalented poet, painter, jazz musician, and film-
maker who went from the University of Nebraska to New York to California.
His reputation, aided by posthumous publication of his stories, criticism, letters, and novels, has grown steadily since his apparent suicide by leaping
from the Golden Gate Bridge.*

For My Daughter

    Looking into my daughter's eyes I read
    Beneath the innocence of morning flesh
    Concealed, hintings of death she does not heed.

Coldest of winds have blown this hair, and mesh
Of seaweed snarled these miniatures of hands;   5
The night's slow poison, tolerant and bland,
Has moved her blood. Parched years that I have seen
That may be hers appear; foul, lingering
Death in certain war, the slim legs green.
Or, fed on hate, she relishes the sting   10
Of others' agony; perhaps the cruel
Bride of a syphilitic or a fool.
These speculations sour in the sun.
I have no daughter. I desire none.

—*1943*

MARGARET WALKER ▪ (1915–1998)

Margaret Walker, as a female African-American poet, was perhaps overshadowed by Gwendolyn Brooks, even though Walker's receipt of the Yale Younger Poets Award in 1942 for For My People *came some years before Brooks's own recognition. A longtime teacher at Jackson State University, she influenced several generations of young writers.*

For Malcolm X

All you violated ones with gentle hearts;
You violent dreamers whose cries shout heartbreak;
Whose voices echo clamors of our cool capers,
And whose black faces have hollowed pits for eyes.
All you gambling sons and hooked children and bowery bums   5
Hating white devils and black bourgeoisie,
Thumbing your noses at your burning red suns,
Gather round this coffin and mourn your dying swan.

Snow-white moslem head-dress around a dead black face!
Beautiful were your sand-papering words against our skins!   10
Our blood and water pour from your flowing wounds.
You have cut open our breasts and dug scalpels in our brains.
When and Where will another come to take your holy place?
Old man mumbling in his dotage, or crying child, unborn?

—*1970*

Gwendolyn Brooks was the first African American to win a Pulitzer Prize for poetry. Brooks reflected many changes in black culture during her long career, and she wrote about the stages of her own life candidly in In the Mecca *(1968), her literary autobiography. Brooks was the last poetry consultant of the Library of Congress before that position became poet laureate of the United States. At the end of her life, Brooks was one of the most honored and beloved of American poets.*

the ballad of chocolate Mabbie

It was Mabbie without° the grammar school gates.
And Mabbie was all of seven.
And Mabbie was cut from a chocolate bar.
And Mabbie thought life was heaven.

The grammar school gates were the pearly gates,   5
For Willie Boone went to school.
When she sat by him in history class
Was only her eyes were cool.

It was Mabbie without the grammar school gates
Waiting for Willie Boone.   10
Half hour after the closing bell!
He would surely be coming soon.

Oh, warm is the waiting for joys, my dears!
And it cannot be too long.
Oh, pity the little poor chocolate lips   15
That carry the bubble of song!

Out came the saucily bold Willie Boone.
It was woe for our Mabbie now.
He wore like a jewel a lemon-hued lynx
With sand-waves loving her brow.   20

---

1 **without** outside

It was Mabbie alone by the grammar school gates.
Yet chocolate companions had she:
Mabbie on Mabbie with hush in the heart.
Mabbie on Mabbie to be.

—1945

the mother

Abortions will not let you forget.
You remember the children you got that you did not get,
The damp small pulps with a little or with no hair,
The singers and workers that never handled the air.
You will never neglect or beat   5
them, or silence or buy with a sweet.
You will never wind up the sucking-thumb
Or scuttle off ghosts that come.
You will never leave them, controlling your luscious sigh,
Return for a snack of them, with gobbling mother-eye.   10

I have heard in the voices of the wind the voices of my dim
    killed children.
I have contracted. I have eased
My dim dears at the breasts they could never suck.
I have said, Sweets, if I sinned, if I seized
Your luck   15
And your lives from your unfinished reach,
If I stole your births and your names,
Your straight baby tears and your games,
Your stilted or lovely loves, your tumults, your marriages,
    aches, and your deaths,
If I poisoned the beginnings of your breaths,   20
Believe that even in my deliberateness I was not deliberate.
Though why should I whine,
Whine that the crime was other than mine?—
Since anyhow you are dead.
Or rather, or instead,   25
You were never made.
But that too, I am afraid,
Is faulty: oh, what shall I say, how is the truth to be said?

You were born, you had body, you died.
It is just that you never giggled or planned or cried. 30
Believe me, I loved you all.
Believe me, I knew you, though faintly, and I loved, I
     loved you
All.

—1945

We Real Cool

> The Pool Players.
> Seven at the Golden Shovel.

We real cool. We
Left school. We

Lurk late. We
Strike straight. We

Sing sin. We   5
Thin gin. We

Jazz June. We
Die soon.

—1960

LAWRENCE FERLINGHETTI ■ (b. 1919)

Lawrence Ferlinghetti, first owner of a literary landmark, San Francisco's City Lights Bookstore, has promoted and published the voice of the American avant-garde since the early 1950s. His own output has been relatively small, but Ferlinghetti's A Coney Island of the Mind remains one of the quintessential documents of the Beat Generation.

A Coney Island of the Mind, #15

Constantly risking absurdity
                    and death
          whenever he performs
                    above the heads

                    of his audience   5
       the poet like an acrobat
            climbs on rime
              to a high wire of his own making
   and balancing on eyebeams
                above a sea of faces   10
       paces his way
            to the other side of day
      performing entrechats
           and sleight-of-foot tricks
   and other high theatrics   15
            and all without mistaking
      any thing
          for what it may not be
   For he's the super realist
            who must perforce perceive   20
     taut truth
         before the taking of each stance or step
  in his supposed advance
           toward that still higher perch
where Beauty stands and waits   25
       with gravity
          to start her death-defying leap
   And he
    a little charleychaplin man
         who may or may not catch   30
her fair eternal form
     spreadeagled in the empty air
  of existence

                    —*1958*

MAY SWENSON ■ (1919–1989)

May Swenson displayed an inventiveness in poetry that ranges from traditional formalism to many spatial or concrete poems. A careful observer of the natural world, Swenson often attempted to mimic directly the rhythms of the physical universe in her self-labeled "iconographs."

How Everything Happens

(Based on a Study of the Wave)

```
                                                    happen.
                                                 to
                                              up
                                        stacking
                                           is
                              something
When nothing is happening
When it happens
                        something
                                    pulls
                                       back
                                            not
                                               to
                                                  happen.
When                                    has happened.
        pulling back          stacking up
                    happens
            has happened                                stacks up.
When it               something              nothing
                          pulls back while
Then nothing is happening
                                              happens.
                                                 and
                                        forward
                                     pushes
                           up
                    stacks
          something
Then
```

—1967

HOWARD NEMEROV ■ (1920–1991)

Howard Nemerov served as poet laureate of the United States during 1988 and 1989. A poet of brilliant formal inventiveness, he was also a skilled satirist and observer of the American scene. His sister, Diane Arbus, was a famous photographer. His Collected Poems *won the Pulitzer Prize in 1978.*

A Primer of the Daily Round

A peels an apple, while B kneels to God,
C telephones to D, who has a hand
On E's knee, F coughs, G turns up the sod
For H's grave, I do not understand
But J is bringing one clay pigeon down   5
While K brings down a nightstick on L's head,
And M takes mustard, N drives into town,
O goes to bed with P, and Q drops dead,
R lies to S, but happens to be heard
By T, who tells U not to fire V   10
For having to give W the word
That X is now deceiving Y with Z,
    Who happens just now to remember A
    Peeling an apple somewhere far away.

—*1958*

RICHARD WILBUR ■ (b. 1921)

Richard Wilbur will be remembered by posterity as perhaps the most skillful metricist and exponent of wit that American poetry has produced. His highly polished poetry—against the grain of much contemporary writing—is a monument to his craftsmanship and intelligence. Perhaps the most honored of all living American poets, Wilbur served as poet laureate of the United States in 1987. His translations of the verse dramas of Molière and Racine are regularly performed throughout the world. Collected Poems, 1943–2004 *appeared in 2004.*

For C.

After the clash of elevator gates
And the long sinking, she emerges where,
A slight thing in the morning's crosstown glare,
She looks up toward the window where he waits,
Then in a fleeting taxi joins the rest   5
Of the huge traffic bound forever west.

On such grand scale do lovers say good-bye—
Even this other pair whose high romance
Had only the duration of a dance,
And who, now taking leave with stricken eye,   10
See each in each a whole new life forgone.
For them, above the darkling clubhouse lawn,

Bright Perseids flash and crumble; while for these
Who part now on the dock, weighed down by grief
And baggage, yet with something like relief,   15
It takes three thousand miles of knitting seas
To cancel out their crossing, and unmake
The amorous rough and tumble of their wake.

We are denied, my love, their fine tristesse
And bittersweet regrets, and cannot share   20
The frequent vistas of their large despair,
Where love and all are swept to nothingness;
Still, there's a certain scope in that long love
Which constant spirits are the keepers of,

And which, though taken to be tame and staid,   25
Is a wild sostenuto of the heart,
A passion joined to courtesy and art
Which has the quality of something made,
Like a good fiddle, like the rose's scent,
Like a rose window or the firmament.   30

—2000

The Writer

In her room at the prow of the house
Where light breaks, and the windows are tossed with linden,
My daughter is writing a story.

I pause in the stairwell, hearing
From her shut door a commotion of typewriter-keys   5
Like a chain hauled over a gunwale.

Young as she is, the stuff
Of her life is a great cargo, and some of it heavy:
I wish her a lucky passage.

But now it is she who pauses,   10
As if to reject my thought and its easy figure.
A stillness greatens, in which

The whole house seems to be thinking,
And then she is at it again with a bunched clamor
Of strokes, and again is silent.   15

I remember the dazed starling
Which was trapped in that very room, two years ago;
How we stole in, lifted a sash

And retreated, not to affright it;
And how for a helpless hour, through the crack of the door,   20
We watched the sleek, wild, dark

And iridescent creature
Batter against the brilliance, drop like a glove
To the hard floor, or the desk-top.

And wait then, humped and bloody,   25
For the wits to try it again; and how our spirits
Rose when, suddenly sure,

It lifted off from a chair-back,
Beating a smooth course for the right window
And clearing the sill of the world.   30

It is always a matter, my darling,
Of life or death, as I had forgotten. I wish
What I wished you before, but harder.

—1976

Year's End

Now winter downs the dying of the year,
And night is all a settlement of snow;
From the soft street the rooms of houses show
A gathered light, a shapen atmosphere,
Like frozen-over lakes whose ice is thin   5
And still allows some stirring down within.

I've known the wind by water banks to shake
The late leaves down, which frozen where they fell
And held in ice as dancers in a spell
Fluttered all winter long into a lake;   10
Graved on the dark in gestures of descent,
They seemed their own most perfect monument.

There was perfection in the death of ferns
Which laid their fragile cheeks against the stone
A million years. Great mammoths overthrown   15
Composedly have made their long sojourns,
Like palaces of patience, in the gray
And changeless lands of ice. And at Pompeii°

The little dog lay curled and did not rise
But slept the deeper as the ashes rose   20
And found the people incomplete, and froze
The random hands, the loose unready eyes
Of men expecting yet another sun
To do the shapely thing they had not done.

These sudden ends of time must give us pause.   25
We fray into the future, rarely wrought
Save in the tapestries of afterthought.
More time, more time. Barrages of applause
Come muffled from a buried radio.
The New-year bells are wrangling with the snow.   30

—1950

663

PHILIP LARKIN ■ (1922–1985)

Philip Larkin was perhaps the latest British poet to establish a significant body of readers in the United States. The general pessimism of his work is mitigated by a wry sense of irony and brilliant formal control. For many years he was a librarian at the University of Hull, and he was also a dedicated fan and critic of jazz.

18 Pompeii Roman city destroyed by volcanic eruption in AD 79.

Next, Please

Always too eager for the future, we
Pick up bad habits of expectancy.
Something is always approaching; every day
Till *then* we say,

Watching from a bluff the tiny, clear,   5
Sparkling armada of promises draw near.
How slow they are! And how much time they waste,
Refusing to make haste!

Yet still they leave us holding wretched stalks
Of disappointment, for, though nothing balks   10
Each big approach, leaning with brasswork prinked,
Each rope distinct,

Flagged, and the figurehead with golden tits
Arching our way, it never anchors; it's
No sooner present than it turns to past.   15
Right to the last

We think each one will heave to and unload
All good into our lives, all we are owed
For waiting so devoutly and so long.
But we are wrong: 20

Only one ship is seeking us, a black-
Sailed unfamiliar, towing at her back
A huge and birdless silence. In her wake
No waters breed or break.

—1951

This Be the Verse

They fuck you up, your mum and dad.
    They may not mean to, but they do.
They fill you with the faults they had
    And add some extra, just for you.

But they were fucked up in their turn   5
    By fools in old-style hats and coats,
Who half the time were soppy-stern
    And half at one another's throats.

Man hands on misery to man.
>It deepens like a coastal shelf.

Get out as early as you can,
>And don't have any kids yourself.

—1971

The Whitsun° Weddings

That Whitsun, I was late getting away:
>Not till about

One-twenty on the sunlit Saturday
Did my three-quarters-empty train pull out,
All windows down, all cushions hot, all sense   5
Of being in a hurry gone. We ran
Behind the backs of houses, crossed a street
Of blinding windscreens, smelt the fish-dock; thence
The river's level drifting breadth began,
Where sky and Lincolnshire and water meet.   10

All afternoon, through the tall heat that slept
>For miles inland,

A slow and stopping curve southwards we kept.
Wide farms went by, short-shadowed cattle, and
Canals with floatings of industrial froth;   15
A hothouse flashed uniquely: hedges dipped
And rose: and now and then a smell of grass
Displaced the reek of buttoned carriage-cloth
Until the next town, new and nondescript,
Approached with acres of dismantled cars.   20

At first, I didn't notice what a noise
>The weddings made

Each station that we stopped at: sun destroys
The interest of what's happening in the shade,
And down the long cool platforms whoops and skirls   25
I took for porters larking with the mails,
And went on reading. Once we started, though,
We passed them, grinning and pomaded, girls
In parodies of fashion, heels and veils,
All posed irresolutely, watching us go,   30

Whitsun the seventh Sunday after Easter

As if out on the end of an event
    Waving goodbye
To something that survived it. Struck, I leant
More promptly out next time, more curiously,
And saw it all again in different terms: 35
The fathers with broad belts under their suits
And seamy foreheads; mothers loud and fat;
An uncle shouting smut; and then the perms,
The nylon gloves and jewellery-substitutes,
The lemons, mauves, and olive-ochres that   40

Marked off the girls unreally from the rest.
    Yes, from cafés
And banquet-halls up yards, and bunting-dressed
Coach-party annexes,° the wedding-days
Were coming to an end. All down the line
Fresh couples climbed aboard: the rest stood round;   45
The last confetti and advice were thrown,
And, as we moved, each face seemed to define
Just what it saw departing: children frowned
At something dull; fathers had never known   50

Success so huge and wholly farcical;
    The women shared
The secret like a happy funeral;
While girls, gripping their handbags tighter, stared
At a religious wounding. Free at last,   55
And loaded with the sum of all they saw,
We hurried towards London, shuffling gouts of steam.
Now fields were building-plots, and poplars cast
Long shadows over major roads, and for
Some fifty minutes, that in time would seem   60

Just long enough to settle hats and say
    I nearly died,
A dozen marriages got under way.
They watched the landscape, setting side by side
—An Odeon° went past, a cooling tower,   65
And someone running up to bowl°—and none

PHILIP LARKIN

666

---

43 Coach-party annexes reception rooms in hotels or restaurants   **65 Odeon** a movie theatre **66
bowl** to throw a cricket ball

Thought of the others they would never meet
Or how their lives would all contain this hour.
I thought of London spread out in the sun,
Its postal districts packed like squares of wheat: 70

There we were aimed. And as we raced across
    Bright knots of rail
Past standing Pullmans, walls of blackened moss
Came close, and it was nearly done, this frail
Traveling coincidence; and what it held 75
Stood ready to be loosed with all the power
That being changed can give. We slowed again,
And as the tightened brakes took hold, there swelled
A sense of falling, like an arrow-shower
Sent out of sight, somewhere becoming rain. 80

—1964

JAMES DICKEY ■ (1923–1997)

James Dickey became a national celebrity with the success of his novel Deliverance *(1970) and the celebrated film version. There was a long background to
Dickey's success, with years spent in the advertising business before he devoted
himself fully to writing. Born in Atlanta and educated at Clemson, Vanderbilt,
and Rice Universities, Dickey rarely strayed long from the South and taught at
the University of South Carolina for over two decades.*

The Heaven of Animals

Here they are. The soft eyes open
If they have lived in a wood
It is a wood.
If they have lived on plains
It is grass rolling
Under their feet forever. 5

Having no souls, they have come,
Anyway, beyond their knowing.
Their instincts wholly bloom
And they rise.
The soft eyes open. 10

THE HEAVEN OF ANIMALS

667

To match them, the landscape flowers,
Outdoing, desperately
Outdoing what is required:
The richest wood,
The deepest field. 15

For some of these,
It could not be the place
It is, without blood.
These hunt, as they have done,
But with claws and teeth grown perfect, 20

More deadly than they can believe.
They stalk more silently,
And crouch on the limbs of trees,
And their descent
Upon the bright backs of their prey 25

May take years
In a sovereign floating of joy.
And those that are hunted
Know this as their life,
Their reward: to walk 30

Under such trees in full knowledge
Of what is in glory above them,
And to feel no fear,
But acceptance, compliance.
Fulfilling themselves without pain 35

At the cycle's center,
They tremble, they walk
Under the tree,
They fall, they are torn,
They rise, they walk again. 40

—1962

ALAN DUGAN ■ (1923–2003)

*Alan Dugan received the 1961 Yale Younger Poets Award, leading to the
publication of his first collection as he neared forty. His plainspoken poetic
voice, often with sardonic overtones, is appropriate for the anti-romantic*

stance of his most characteristic poems. For many years Dugan was associated with the Fine Arts Work Center in Provincetown, Massachusetts, on Cape Cod.

Love Song: I and Thou

Nothing is plumb, level or square:
 the studs are bowed, the joists
are shaky by nature, no piece fits
 any other piece without a gap
or pinch, and bent nails   5
 dance all over the surfacing
like maggots. By Christ
 I am no carpenter. I built
the roof for myself, the walls
 for myself, the floors   10
for myself, and got
 hung up in it myself. I
danced with a purple thumb
 at this house-warming, drunk
with my prime whiskey: rage.   15
 Oh I spat rage's nails
into the frame-up of my work:
 it held. It settled plumb,
level, solid, square and true
 for that great moment. Then   20
it screamed and went on through,
 skewing as wrong the other way.
God damned it. This is hell,
 but I planned it, I sawed it,
I nailed it, and I   25
 will live in it until it kills me.
I can nail my left palm
 to the left-hand cross-piece but
I can't do everything myself.
 I need a hand to nail the right,   30
a help, a love, a you, a wife.

—1961

ANTHONY HECHT ■ (1923–2004)

Anthony Hecht is most often linked with Richard Wilbur as one of the American poets of the postwar era who has most effectively utilized traditional poetic forms. The brilliance of Hecht's technique, however, must be set beside the powerful moral intelligence that informs his poetry. The Hard Hours, his second collection, won the Pulitzer Prize in 1968.

The Dover Bitch: *A Criticism of Life*

for Andrews Wanning

So there stood Matthew Arnold° and this girl
With the cliffs of England crumbling away behind them,
And he said to her, "Try to be true to me,
And I'll do the same for you, for things are bad
All over, etc., etc."   5
Well now, I knew this girl. It's true she had read
Sophocles° in a fairly good translation
And caught that bitter allusion to the sea,
But all the time he was talking she had in mind
The notion of what his whiskers would feel like   10
On the back of her neck. She told me later on
That after a while she got to look out
At the lights across the channel, and really felt sad,
Thinking of all the wine and enormous beds
And blandishments in French and the perfumes.   15
And then she got really angry. To have been brought
All the way down from London, and then be addressed
As a sort of mournful cosmic last resort
Is really tough on a girl, and she was pretty.
Anyway, she watched him pace the room   20
And finger his watch-chain and seem to sweat a bit,
And then she said one or two unprintable things.
But you mustn't judge her by that. What I mean to say is,
She's really all right. I still see her once in a while

---

1 Matthew Arnold Victorian poet, author of "Dover Beach"   **7 Sophocles** Ancient Greek playwright

And she always treats me right. We have a drink 25
And I give her a good time, and perhaps it's a year
Before I see her again, but there she is,
Running to fat, but dependable as they come.
And sometimes I bring her a bottle of *Nuit d'Amour*.

—1967

Third Avenue in Sunlight

Third Avenue in sunlight. Nature's error.
Already the bars are filled and John is there.
Beneath a plentiful lady over the mirror°
He tilts his glass in the mild mahogany air.

I think of him when he first got out of college, 5
Serious, thin, unlikely to succeed;
For several months he hung around the Village,
Boldly T-shirted, unfettered but unfreed.

Now he confides to a stranger, "I was first scout,
And kept my glimmers peeled till after dark. 10
Our outfit had as its sign a bloody knout,
We met behind the museum in Central Park.

Of course, we were kids." But still those savages,
War-painted, a flap of leather at the loins,
File silently against him. Hostages 15
Are never taken. One summer, in Des Moines,

They entered his hotel room, tomahawks
Flashing like barracuda. He tried to pray.
Three years of treatment. Occasionally he talks
About how he almost didn't get away. 20

Daily the prowling sunlight whets its knife
Along the sidewalk. We almost never meet.
In the Rembrandt dark he lifts his amber life.
My bar is somewhat further down the street.

—1967

3 lady over the mirror a painting

LOUIS SIMPSON ■ (b. 1923)

Louis Simpson was born in Jamaica to a colonial lawyer father and an American mother. Simpson came to the United States in his teens and served in the U.S. Army in World War II. He won the Pulitzer Prize in 1964 for At the End of the Open Road, *a volume that attempts to reexamine Walt Whitman's nineteenth-century definitions of the American experience. Subsequent collections have continued to demonstrate Simpson's unsentimental view of American suburban life.*

American Classic

It's a classic American scene—
a car stopped off the road
and a man trying to repair it.

The woman who stays in the car
in the classic American scene   5
stares back at the freeway traffic.

They look surprised, and ashamed
to be so helpless . . .
let down in the middle of the road!

To think that their car would do this!   10
They look like mountain people
whose son has gone against the law.

But every night they set out food
and the robber goes skulking back to the trees.
That's how it is with the car . . .   15

it's theirs, they're stuck with it.
Now they know what it's like to sit
and see the world go whizzing by.

In the fume of carbon monoxide and dust
they are not such good Americans   20
as they thought they were.

The feeling of being left out
through no fault of your own, is common.
That's why I say, an American classic.

—1980

My Father in the Night Commanding No

My father in the night commanding No
Has work to do. Smoke issues from his lips;
    He reads in silence.
The frogs are croaking and the street lamps glow.

And then my mother winds the gramophone: 5
The Bride of Lammermoor° begins to shriek—
    Or reads a story
About a prince, a castle, and a dragon.

The moon is glittering above the hill.
I stand before the gateposts of the King—   10
    So runs the story—
Of Thule, at midnight when the mice are still.

And I have been in Thule! It has come true—
The journey and the danger of the world,
    All that there is   15
To bear and to enjoy, endure and do.

Landscapes, seascapes . . . Where have I been led?
The names of cities—Paris, Venice, Rome—
    Held out their arms.
A feathered god, seductive, went ahead.   20

Here is my house. Under a red rose tree
A child is swinging; another gravely plays.
    They are not surprised
That I am here; they were expecting me.

6 Bride of Lammermoor *Lucia di Lammermoor*, opera by Donizetti

And yet my father sits and reads in silence,   25
My mother sheds a tear, the moon is still,
    And the dark wind
Is murmuring that nothing ever happens.

Beyond his jurisdiction as I move,
Do I not prove him wrong? And yet, it's true   30
    They will not change
There, on the stage of terror and of love.

The actors in that playhouse always sit
In fixed positions—father, mother, child
    With painted eyes.   35
How sad it is to be a little puppet!

Their heads are wooden. And you once pretended
To understand them! Shake them as you will,
    They cannot speak.
Do what you will, the comedy is ended.   40

Father, why did you work? Why did you weep,
Mother? Was the story so important?
    "Listen!" the wind
Said to the children, and they fell asleep.

—1963

VASSAR MILLER ■ (1924–1997)

Vassar Miller was a lifelong resident of Houston, born with cerebral palsy.
Miller published both traditional devotional verse and a large body of auto-
biographical poetry in open forms. If I Had Wheels or Love, her collected
poems, appeared in 1990.

Subterfuge

I remember my father, slight,
staggering in with his Underwood,°
bearing it in his arms like an awkward bouquet

---

2 **Underwood** popular brand of manual typewriter

for his spastic child who sits down
on the floor, one knee on the frame   5
of the typewriter, and holding her left wrist

with her right hand, in that precision known
to the crippled, pecks at the keys
with a sparrow's preoccupation.

Falling by chance on rhyme, novel and curious bubble   10
blown with a magic pipe, she tries them over and over,
spellbound by life's clashing in accord or against itself,

pretending pretense and playing at playing,
she does her childhood backward as children do,
her fun a delaying action against what she knows.   15

My father must lose her, his runaway on her treadmill,
will lose the terrible favor that life has done him
as she toils at tomorrow, tensed at her makeshift toy.

—1981

DONALD JUSTICE ■ (1925–2004)

*Donald Justice published more selectively than most of his contemporaries.
His Pulitzer Prize–winning volume of selected poems displays considerable
literary sophistication and reveals the poet's familiarity with the traditions
of contemporary European and Latin American poetry. As an editor, he was
responsible for rescuing the important work of Weldon Kees from obscurity.*

Counting the Mad

This one was put in a jacket,
This one was sent home,
This one was given bread and meat
But would eat none,
And this one cried No No No No   5
All day long.

This one looked at the window
As though it were a wall,
This one saw things that were not there,
This one things that were,   10
And this one cried No No No No
All day long.

This one thought himself a bird,
This one a dog,
And this one thought himself a man,   15
An ordinary man,
And this one cried No No No No
All day long.

—1960

CAROLYN KIZER ■ (b. 1925)

Carolyn Kizer has had a fascinating career that included a year's study in Tai-
wan and another year in Pakistan, where she worked for the U.S. State
Department. Her first collection, The Ungrateful Garden *(1961), demonstrates*
an equal facility with formal and free verse, but her subsequent books (in-
cluding the Pulitzer Prize–winning Yin *of 1985) have tended more toward*
the latter. A committed feminist, Kizer anticipated many of today's women's
issues as early as the mid-1950s, just as the poem "The Ungrateful Garden"
was published a decade before "ecology" became a household word.

The Ungrateful Garden

Midas watched the golden crust
That formed over his streaming sores,
Hugged his agues, loved his lust,
But damned to hell the out-of-doors

Where blazing motes of sun impaled   5
The serried° roses, metal-bright.
"Those famous flowers," Midas wailed,
"Have scorched my retina with light."

This gift, he'd thought, would gild his joys,
Silt up the waters of his grief;   10
His lawns a wilderness of noise,
The heavy clang of leaf on leaf.

Within, the golden cup is good
To heft, to sip the yellow mead.
Outside, in summer's rage, the rude   15
Gold thorn has made his fingers bleed.

6 serried crowded in rows

"I strolled my halls in golden shift,
As ruddy as a lion's meat.
Then I rushed out to share my gift,
And golden stubble cut my feet." 20

Dazzled with wounds, he limped away
To climb into his golden bed.
Roses, roses can betray.
"Nature is evil," Midas said.

—1961

MAXINE KUMIN ▪ (b. 1925)

Maxine Kumin was born in Philadelphia and educated at Radcliffe. Kumin was an early literary ally and friend of Anne Sexton, with whom she co-authored several children's books. The winner of the 1973 Pulitzer Prize, Kumin has preferred a rural life raising horses for some years. Her increased interest in the natural world has paralleled the environmental awareness of many of her readers. Her most recent poetry collection is Still to Mow.

Noted in the *New York Times*

Lake Buena Vista, Florida, June 16, 1987

Death claimed the last pure dusky seaside sparrow
today, whose coastal range was narrow,
as narrow as its two-part buzzy song.
From hummocks lost to Cape Canaveral
this mouselike skulker in the matted grass, 5
a six-inch bird, plain brown, once thousands strong,
sang *toodle-raeee azhee*, ending on a trill
before the air gave way to rocket blasts.

It laid its dull white eggs (brown specked) in small
neat cups of grass on plots of pickleweed, 10
bulrushes, or salt hay. It dined
on caterpillars, beetles, ticks, the seeds
of sedges. Unremarkable
the life it led with others of its kind.
Tomorrow we can put it on a stamp, 15
a first-day cover with Key Largo rat,

Schaus swallowtail, Florida swamp
crocodile, and fading cotton mouse.
How simply symbols replace habitat!
The tower frames of Aerospace   20
quiver in the flush of another shot
where, once indigenous, the dusky sparrow
soared trilling twenty feet above its burrow.

—1989

ALLEN GINSBERG ■ (1926–1997)

*Allen Ginsberg became the chief poetic spokesman of the Beat Generation. He
was a force—as poet and celebrity—who continued to outrage and delight four
decades after the appearance of* Howl, *the monumental poem describing how
Ginsberg saw "the best minds of my generation destroyed by madness." Ginsberg's
poems are cultural documents that provide a key to understanding the radical
changes in American life, particularly among youth, that began in the mid-1950s.*

A Supermarket in California

What thoughts I have of you tonight, Walt Whitman, for I
walked down the sidestreets under the trees with a headache self-
conscious looking at the full moon.

In my hungry fatigue, and shopping for images, I went into
the neon fruit supermarket, dreaming of your enumerations!

What peaches and what penumbras?° Whole families
shopping at night! Aisles full of husbands! Wives in the avocados,
babies in the tomatoes!—and you, García Lorca,° what were you
doing down by the watermelons?

I saw you, Walt Whitman, childless, lonely old grubber, poking
among the meats in the refrigerator and eyeing the grocery boys.

I heard you asking questions of each: Who killed the pork
chops? What price bananas? Are you my Angel?   5

I wandered in and out of the brilliant stacks of cans following
you, and followed in my imagination by the store detective.

We strode down the open corridors together in our solitary
fancy tasting artichokes, possessing every frozen delicacy, and
never passing the cashier.

---

3 penumbras shadows   **García Lorca** Federico García Lorca, Spanish poet (1899–1936)

Where are we going, Walt Whitman? The doors close in an hour. Which way does your beard point tonight?

(I touch your book and dream of our odyssey in the supermarket and feel absurd.)

Will we walk all night through solitary streets? The trees add shade to shade, lights out in the houses, we'll both be lonely.   10

Will we stroll dreaming of the lost America of love past blue automobiles in driveways, home to our silent cottage?

Ah, dear father, graybeard, lonely old courage-teacher, what America did you have when Charon° quit poling his ferry and you got out on a smoking bank and stood watching the boat disappear on the black waters of Lethe?°

—1956

JAMES MERRILL ■ (1926–1995)

James Merrill wrote "The Changing Light at Sandover," a long poem that resulted from many years of sessions with a Ouija board. The book became his major work and, among many other things, a remarkable memoir of a long-term gay relationship. Merrill's shorter poems, collected in 2001, reveal meticulous craftsmanship and a play of wit unequaled among contemporary American poets.

Casual Wear

Your average tourist: Fifty. 2.3
Times married. Dressed, this year, in Ferdi Plinthbower°
Originals. Odds 1 to 9^{10}
Against her strolling past the Embassy

Today at noon. Your average terrorist: 5
Twenty-five. Celibate. No use for trends,
At least in clothing. Mark, though, where it ends.
People have come forth made of colored mist

---

12 **Charon** ferryman of Hades   **Lethe** river in Hades, means forgetfulness
2 **Ferdi Plinthbower** a fictional designer

Unsmiling on one hundred million screens
To tell of his prompt phone call to the station,   10
"Claiming responsibility"—devastation
Signed with a flourish, like the dead wife's jeans.

—1984

FRANK O'HARA ■ (1926–1966)

*Frank O'Hara suffered an untimely death in a dune buggy accident on Fire
Island that robbed American poetry of one its most refreshing talents. An
authority on modern art, O'Hara incorporated many of the spontaneous
techniques of abstract painting in his own poetry, which was often written as
an immediate reaction to the events of his daily life.*

The Day Lady° Died

It is 12:20 in New York a Friday
three days after Bastille day,° yes
it is 1959 and I go get a shoeshine
because I will get off the 4:19 in Easthampton
at 7:15 and then go straight to dinner   5
and I don't know the people who will feed me

I walk up the muggy street beginning to sun
and have a hamburger and a malted and buy
an ugly NEW WORLD WRITING to see what the poets
in Ghana are doing these days   10
                              I go on to the bank
and Miss Stillwagon (first name Linda I once heard)
doesn't even look up my balance for once in her life
and in the GOLDEN GRIFFIN I get a little Verlaine
for Patsy with drawings by Bonnard although I do   15
think of Hesiod, trans. Richard Lattimore or
Brendan Behan's new play or *Le Balcon* or *Les Nègres*
of Genet, but I don't, I stick with Verlaine
after practically going to sleep with quandariness

Lady Billie Holiday (1915–1959), blues singer   **2 Bastille day** July 14

and for Mike I just stroll into the PARK LANE   20
Liquor Store and ask for a bottle of Strega and
then I go back where I came from to 6th Avenue
and the tobacconist in the Ziegfeld Theatre and
casually ask for a carton of Gauloises and a carton
of Picayunes, and a NEW YORK POST with her face on it   25
and I am sweating a lot by now and thinking of
leaning on the john door in the 5 SPOT
while she whispered a song along the keyboard
to Mal Waldron° and everyone and I stopped breathing.

—1964

W. D. SNODGRASS ■ (b. 1926–2009)

W. D. Snodgrass won the Pulitzer Prize for his first collection, Heart's Needle *(1959), and is generally considered one of the first important confessional poets. However, in his later career he has turned away from autobiographical subjects, writing, among other poems, a long sequence of
dramatic monologues spoken by leading Nazis during the final days of the
Hitler regime.*

Mementos, I

Sorting out letters and piles of my old
        Canceled checks, old clippings, and yellow note cards
That meant something once, I happened to find
        Your picture. *That* picture. I stopped there cold,
Like a man raking piles of dead leaves in his yard   5
        Who has turned up a severed hand.

Still, that first second, I was glad: you stand
        Just as you stood—shy, delicate, slender,
In that long gown of green lace netting and daisies
        That you wore to our first dance. The sight of you stunned   10
Us all. Well, our needs were different, then,
        And our ideals came easy.

---

29 Mal Waldron Holiday's accompanist.

Then through the war and those two long years
    Overseas, the Japanese dead in their shacks
Among dishes, dolls, and lost shoes; I carried   15
    This glimpse of you, there, to choke down my fear,
Prove it had been, that it might come back.
        That was before we got married.

—Before we drained out one another's force
    With lies, self-denial, unspoken regret   20
And the sick eyes that blame; before the divorce
    And the treachery. Say it: before we met. Still,
I put back your picture. Someday, in due course,
    I will find that it's still there.

—*1968*

JOHN ASHBERY ■ (b. 1927)

John Ashbery was born in upstate New York and educated at Harvard University. His first full-length book, Some Trees, *was chosen by W. H. Auden as winner of the Yale Younger Poets Award in 1956. His enigmatic poems have intrigued readers for so long that much contemporary literary theory seems to have been created expressly for explicating his poems. Impossible to dismiss, Ashbery is now seen as the chief inheritor of the symbolist tradition brought to American locales by Wallace Stevens.* Notes from the Air: Selected Later Poems *appeared in 2007.*

Farm Implements and Rutabagas in a Landscape

The first of the undecoded messages read: "Popeye sits in
    thunder,
Unthought of. From that shoebox of an apartment,
From livid curtain's hue, a tangram emerges: a country."
Meanwhile the Sea Hag was relaxing on a green couch: "How
    pleasant
To spend one's vacation *en la casa de Popeye*," she scratched   5
Her cleft chin's solitary hair. She remembered spinach

And was going to ask Wimpy if he had bought any spinach.
"M'love," he intercepted, "the plains are decked out in thunder
Today, and it shall be as you wish." He scratched
The part of his head under his hat. The apartment   10
Seemed to grow smaller. "But what if no pleasant
Inspiration plunge us now to the stars? *For this is my country.*"
Suddenly they remembered how it was cheaper in the country.
Wimpy was thoughtfully cutting open a number 2 can of spinach
When the door opened and Swee'pea crept in. "How pleasant!"   15
But Swee'pea looked morose. A note was pinned to his bib.
  "Thunder
And tears are unavailing," it read. "Henceforth shall Popeye's
  apartment
Be but remembered space, toxic or salubrious, whole or scratched."
Olive came hurtling through the window; its geraniums scratched
Her long thigh. "I have news!" she gasped. "Popeye, forced as
  you know to flee the country   20
One musty gusty evening, by the schemes of his wizened,
  duplicate father, jealous of the apartment
And all that it contains, myself and spinach
In particular, heaves bolts of loving thunder
At his own astonished becoming, rupturing the pleasant

Arpeggio of our years. No more shall pleasant   25
Rays of the sun refresh your sense of growing old, nor the
  scratched
Tree-trunks and mossy foliage, only immaculate darkness
  and thunder."
She grabbed Swee'pea. "I'm taking the brat to the country."
"But you can't do that—he hasn't even finished his spinach,"
Urged the Sea Hag, looking fearfully around at the apartment.   30

But Olive was already out of earshot. Now the apartment
Succumbed to a strange new hush. "Actually it's quite pleasant
Here," thought the Sea Hag. "If this is all we need fear from
  spinach
Then I don't mind so much. Perhaps we could invite Alice the
  Goon over"—she scratched
One dug pensively—"but Wimpy is such a country   35
Bumpkin, always burping like that." Minute at first, the thunder

Soon filled the apartment. It was domestic thunder,
The color of spinach. Popeye chuckled and scratched
His balls: it sure was pleasant to spend a day in the country.

—1966

Paradoxes and Oxymorons

The poem is concerned with language on a very plain level.
Look at it talking to you. You look out a window
Or pretend to fidget. You have it but you don't have it.
You miss it, it misses you. You miss each other.

The poem is sad because it wants to be yours, and cannot.   5
What's a plain level? It is that and other things,
Bringing a system of them into play. Play?
Well, actually, yes, but I consider play to be

A deeper outside thing, a dreamed role-pattern,
As in the division of grace these long August days   10
Without proof. Open-ended. And before you know
It gets lost in the steam and chatter of typewriters.

It has been played once more. I think you exist only
To tease me into doing it, on your level, and then you aren't there
Or have adopted a different attitude. And the poem   15
Has set me softly down beside you. The poem is you.

—1981

W. S. MERWIN ■ (b. 1927)

W. S. Merwin often displays environmental concerns that have motivated much poetry in recent years. Even in earlier work, his fears of the results of uncontrolled destruction of the environment are presented allegorically. Born in New York City, he currently resides in Hawaii. He was appointed U.S. Poet Laureate in 2010.

For the Anniversary of My Death

Every year without knowing it I have passed the day
When the last fires will wave to me
And the silence will set out
Tireless traveller
Like the beam of a lightless star   5

Then I will no longer
Find myself in life as in a strange garment
Surprised at the earth
And the love of one woman
And the shamelessness of men   10
As today writing after three days of rain
Hearing the wren sing and the falling cease
And bowing not knowing to what

—1969

The Last One

Well they'd made up their minds to be everywhere because
    why not.
Everywhere was theirs because they thought so.
They with two leaves they whom the birds despise.
In the middle of stones they made up their minds.
They started to cut.   5

Well they cut everything because why not.
Everything was theirs because they thought so.
It fell into its shadows and they took both away.
Some to have some for burning.

Well cutting everything they came to the water.   10
They came to the end of the day there was one left standing.
They would cut it tomorrow they went away.
The night gathered in the last branches.
The shadow of the night gathered in the shadow on the water.
The night and the shadow put on the same head.   15
And it said Now.

Well in the morning they cut the last one.
Like the others the last one fell into its shadow.
It fell into its shadow on the water.
They took it away its shadow stayed on the water.   20

Well they shrugged they started trying to get the shadow
    away.
They cut right to the ground the shadow stayed whole.
They laid boards on it the shadow came out on top.
They shone lights on it the shadow got blacker and clearer.

They exploded the water the shadow rocked.
They built a huge fire on the roots.
They sent up black smoke between the shadow and the sun.
The new shadow flowed without changing the old one.
They shrugged they went away to get stones.

They came back the shadow was growing.
They started setting up stones it was growing.
They looked the other way it went on growing.
They decided they would make a stone out of it.
They took stones to the water they poured them into the shadow.
They poured them in they poured them in the stones vanished.
The shadow was not filled it went on growing.
That was one day.

The next day was just the same it went on growing.
They did all the same things it was just the same.
They decided to take its water from under it.
They took away water they took it away the water went down.
The shadow stayed where it was before.
It went on growing it grew onto the land.
They started to scrape the shadow with machines.
When it touched the machines it stayed on them.
They started to beat the shadow with sticks.
Where it touched the sticks it stayed on them.
They started to beat the shadow with hands.
Where it touched the hands it stayed on them.
That was another day.

Well the next day started about the same it went on growing.
They pushed lights into the shadow.
Where the shadow got onto them they went out.
They began to stomp on the edge it got their feet.
And when it got their feet they fell down.
It got into eyes the eyes went blind.
The ones that fell down it grew over and they vanished.
The ones that went blind and walked into it vanished.
The ones that could see and stood still
It swallowed their shadows.
Then it swallowed them too and they vanished.
Well the others ran.

The ones that were left went away to live if it would let them.
They went as far as they could.
The lucky ones with their shadows.   65

—1969

JAMES WRIGHT ▪ (1927–1980)

James Wright showed compassion for losers and underdogs of all types, an
attitude evident everywhere in his poetry. A native of Martins Ferry, Ohio, he
often described lives of quiet desperation in the blue-collar towns of his
youth. Like many poets of his generation, Wright wrote formal verse in his
early career and shifted to open forms during the 1960s.

Autumn Begins in Martins Ferry, Ohio

In the Shreve High football stadium,
I think of Polacks nursing long beers in Tiltonsville,
And gray faces of Negroes in the blast furnace at Benwood,
And the ruptured night watchman of Wheeling Steel,
Dreaming of heroes.   5

All the proud fathers are ashamed to go home.
Their women cluck like starved pullets,
Dying for love.

Therefore,
Their sons grow suicidally beautiful   10
At the beginning of October
And gallop terribly against each other's bodies.

—1963

Saint Judas

When I went out to kill myself, I caught
A pack of hoodlums beating up a man.
Running to spare his suffering, I forgot
My name, my number, how my day began,

How soldiers milled around the garden stone   5
And sang amusing songs; how all that day
Their javelins measured crowds; how I alone
Bargained the proper coins, and slipped away.

Banished from heaven, I found this victim beaten,
Stripped, kneed, and left to cry. Dropping my rope   10
Aside, I ran, ignored the uniforms:
Then I remembered bread my flesh had eaten,
The kiss that ate my flesh. Flayed without hope,
I held the man for nothing in my arms.

—*1959*

PHILIP LEVINE ■ (b. 1928)

Philip Levine was born in Detroit, Michigan. He is one of many contemporary poets to hold a degree from the University of Iowa Writers' Workshop. The gritty urban landscapes and characters trapped in dead-end industrial jobs that provide Levine subjects for many poems match exactly with his unadorned, informal idiom. As teacher and mentor, Levine has influenced many younger poets.

You Can Have It

My brother comes home from work
and climbs the stairs to our room.
I can hear the bed groan and his shoes drop
one by one. You can have it, he says.

The moonlight streams in the window   5
and his unshaven face is whitened
like the face of the moon. He will sleep
long after noon and waken to find me gone.

Thirty years will pass before I remember
that moment when suddenly I knew each man   10
has one brother who dies when he sleeps
and sleeps when he rises to face this life,

and that together they are only one man
sharing a heart that always labors, hands
yellowed and cracked, a mouth that gasps
for breath and asks, Am I gonna make it?

All night at the ice plant he had fed
the chute its silvery blocks, and then I
stacked cases of orange soda for the children
of Kentucky, one gray box-car at a time

with always two more waiting. We were twenty
for such a short time and always in
the wrong clothes, crusted with dirt
and sweat. I think now we were never twenty.

In 1948 in the city of Detroit, founded
by de la Mothe Cadillac for the distant purposes
of Henry Ford, no one wakened or died,
no one walked the streets or stoked a furnace,

for there was no such year, and now
that year has fallen off all the old newspapers,
calendars, doctors' appointments, bonds,
wedding certificates, drivers licenses.

The city slept. The snow turned to ice.
The ice to standing pools or rivers
racing in the gutters. Then bright grass rose
between the thousands of cracked squares,

and that grass died. I give you back 1948.
I give you all the years from then
to the coming one. Give me back the moon
with its frail light falling across a face.

Give me back my young brother, hard
and furious, with wide shoulders and a curse
for God and burning eyes that look upon
all creation and say, You can have it.

—1979

Anne Sexton lived a tortured life of mental illness and family troubles, becoming the model of the confessional poet. A housewife with two small daughters, she began writing poetry as the result of a program on public television, later taking a workshop from Robert Lowell in which Sylvia Plath was a fellow student. For fifteen years until her suicide, she was a vibrant, exciting presence in American poetry. A controversial biography of Sexton by Diane Wood Middlebrook appeared in 1991.

Cinderella

You always read about it:
the plumber with twelve children
who wins the Irish Sweepstakes.
From toilets to riches.
That story.   5

Or the nursemaid,
some luscious sweet from Denmark
who captures the oldest son's heart.
From diapers to Dior.
That story.   10

Or a milkman who serves the wealthy,
eggs, cream, butter, yogurt, milk,
the white truck like an ambulance
who goes into real estate
and makes a pile.   15
From homogenized to martinis at lunch.

Or the charwoman
who is on the bus when it cracks up
and collects enough from the insurance.
From mops to Bonwit Teller.°   20
That story.

20 **Bonwit Teller** an upscale department store

Once
the wife of a rich man was on her deathbed
and she said to her daughter Cinderella:
Be devout. Be good. Then I will smile   5
down from heaven in the seam of a cloud.
The man took another wife who had
two daughters, pretty enough
but with hearts like blackjacks.
Cinderella was their maid.   30
She slept on the sooty hearth each night
and walked around looking like Al Jolson.°
Her father brought presents home from town,
jewels and gowns for the other women
but the twig of a tree for Cinderella.   35
She planted that twig on her mother's grave
and it grew to a tree where a white dove sat.
Whenever she wished for anything the dove
would drop it like an egg upon the ground.
The bird is important, my dears, so heed him.   40

Next came the ball, as you all know.
It was a marriage market.
The prince was looking for a wife.
All but Cinderella were preparing
and gussying up for the big event.   45
Cinderella begged to go too.
Her stepmother threw a dish of lentils
into the cinders and said: Pick them
up in an hour and you shall go.
The white dove brought all his friends;   50
all the warm wings of the fatherland came,
and picked up the lentils in a jiffy.
No, Cinderella, said the stepmother,
you have no clothes and cannot dance.
That's the way with stepmothers.   55

---

32 Al Jolson (1885–1950) American singer and entertainer who often performed in blackface

Cinderella went to the tree at the grave
and cried forth like a gospel singer:
Mama! Mama! My turtledove,
send me to the prince's ball!
The bird dropped down a golden dress   60
and delicate little gold slippers.
Rather a large package for a simple bird.
So she went. Which is no surprise.
Her stepmother and sisters didn't
recognize her without her cinder face   65
and the prince took her hand on the spot
and danced with no other the whole day.

As nightfall came she thought she'd
better get home. The prince walked her home
and she disappeared into the pigeon house   70
and although the prince took an axe and broke
it open she was gone. Back to her cinders.
These events repeated themselves for three days.
However on the third day the prince
covered the palace steps with cobbler's wax 75
And Cinderella's gold shoe stuck upon it.
Now he would find whom the shoe fit
and find his strange dancing girl for keeps.
He went to their house and the two sisters
were delighted because they had lovely feet. 80
The eldest went into a room to try the slipper on
but her big toe got in the way so she simply
sliced it off and put on the slipper.

The prince rode away with her until the white dove
told him to look at the blood pouring forth. 85
That is the way with amputations.
They don't just heal up like a wish.
The other sister cut off her heel
but the blood told as blood will.
The prince was getting tired.   90
He began to feel like a shoe salesman.
But he gave it one last try.
This time Cinderella fit into the shoe
like a love letter into its envelope.

At the wedding ceremony 95
the two sisters came to curry favor
and the white dove pecked their eyes out.
Two hollow spots were left
like soup spoons.

Cinderella and the prince 100
lived, they say, happily ever after,
like two dolls in a museum case
never bothered by diapers or dust,
never arguing over the timing of an egg,
never telling the same story twice, 105
never getting a middle-aged spread,
their darling smiles pasted on for eternity
Regular Bobbsey Twins.°
That story.

—1970

THOM GUNN ■ (1929–2004)

Thom Gunn was a British expatriate who lived in San Francisco for over
four decades. Gunn managed to retain his ties to the traditions of British
literature while writing about motorcycle gangs, surfers, gay bars, and drug
experiences. The Man with Night Sweats, his 1992 collection, contains a
number of forthright poems on AIDS, of which "Terminal" is one.

From the Wave

It mounts at sea, a concave wall
    Down-ribbed with shine,
And pushes forward, building tall
    Its steep incline.

Then from their hiding rise to sight 5
    Black shapes on boards
Bearing before the fringe of white
    It mottles towards.

108 **Bobbsey Twins** characters in a series of popular juvenile novels by Laura Lee Hope

Their pale feet curl, they poise their weight
    With a learn'd skill.
It is the wave they imitate
    Keeps them so still.   10

The marbling bodies have become
    Half wave, half men,
Grafted it seems by feet of foam   15
    Some seconds, then,

Late as they can, they slice the face
    In timed procession:
Balance is triumph in this place,
    Triumph possession.   20

The mindless heave of which they rode
    A fluid shelf
Breaks as they leave it, falls and, slowed,
    Loses itself.

Clear, the sheathed bodies slick as seals   25
    Loosen and tingle;
And by the board the bare foot feels
    The suck of shingle.

They paddle in the shallows still;
    Two splash each other;
Then all swim out to wait until   30
    The right waves gather.

—1971

Terminal

The eight years difference in age seems now
Disparity so wide between the two
That when I see the man who armoured stood
Resistant to all help however good
Now helped through day itself, eased into chairs,   5
Or else led step by step down the long stairs
With firm and gentle guidance by his friend,

Who loves him, through each effort to descend,
Each wavering, each attempt made to complete
An arc of movement and bring down the feet   10
As if with that spare strength he used to enjoy,
I think of Oedipus, old, led by a boy.

—1992

X. J. KENNEDY ■ (b. 1929)

X. J. Kennedy is one the few contemporary American poets who has not been attracted to free verse, preferring to remain what he calls a "dinosaur," one of those poets who continue to write in meter. He is also rare among his contemporaries in his commitment to writing poems with strong ties to song. Kennedy is also the author of Literature: An Introduction to Fiction, Poetry, and Drama, *perhaps the most widely used college literature text ever written.*

In a Prominent Bar in Secaucus One Day

To the tune of "The Old Orange Flute" or the tune of "Sweet Betsy from Pike"

In a prominent bar in Secaucus one day
Rose a lady in skunk with a topheavy sway,
Raised a knobby red finger—all turned from their beer—
While with eyes bright as snowcrust she sang high and clear:

"Now who of you'd think from an eyeload of me   5
That I once was a lady as proud as could be?
Oh I'd never sit down by a tumbledown drunk
If it wasn't, my dears, for the high cost of junk.

"All the gents used to swear that the white of my calf
Beat the down of the swan by a length and a half.   10
In the kerchief of linen I caught to my nose
Ah, there never fell snot, but a little gold rose.

"I had seven gold teeth and a toothpick of gold,
My Virginia cheroot° was a leaf of it rolled
And I'd light it each time with a thousand in cash—
Why the bums used to fight if I flicked them an ash.

"Once the toast of the Biltmore, the belle of the Taft,
I would drink bottle beer at the Drake,° never draft,
And dine at the Astor on Salisbury steak
With a clean tablecloth for each bite I did take.

"In a car like the Roxy I'd roll to the track,
A steel-guitar trio, a bar in the back,
And the wheels made no noise, they turned over so fast,
Still it took you ten minutes to see me go past.

"When the horses bowed down to me that I might choose,
I bet on them all, for I hated to lose.
Now I'm saddled each night for my butter and eggs
And the broken threads race down the backs of my legs.

"Let you hold in mind, girls, that your beauty must pass
Like a lovely white clover that rusts with its grass.
Keep your bottoms off barstools and marry you young
Or be left—an old barrel with many a bung.

"For when time takes you out for a spin in his car
You'll be hard-pressed to stop him from going too far
And be left by the roadside, for all your good deeds,
Two toadstools for tits and a face full of weeds."

All the house raised a cheer, but the man at the bar
Made a phonecall and up pulled a red patrol car
And she blew us a kiss as they copped her away
From that prominent bar in Secaucus, N.J.

—1961

14 **cheroot** a thin cigar 17–18 **Biltmore, Taft, Drake** famous hotels

Little Elegy

for a child who skipped rope

Here lies resting, out of breath,
Out of turns, Elizabeth
Whose quicksilver toes not quite
Cleared the whirring edge of night.

Earth whose circles round us skim   5
Till they catch the lightest limb,
Shelter now Elizabeth
And for her sake trip up Death.

—1961

ADRIENNE RICH ■ (b. 1929)

Adrienne Rich's most recent books of poetry are Telephone Ringing in
the Labyrinth: Poems 2004-2006 *and* The School Among the Ruins:
2000-2004. *She edited Muriel Rukeyser's* Selected Poems *for the Library of
America.* A Human Eye: Essays on Art in Society, *appeared in April 2009.*
Tonight No Poetry Will Serve: Poems 2007-2010, *will appear in 2011 from
Norton. She is a recipient of the National Book Foundation's 2006 Medal for
Distinguished Contribution to American Letters among other honors. She
lives in California.*

Aunt Jennifer's Tigers

Aunt Jennifer's tigers prance across a screen,
Bright topaz denizens of a world of green.
They do not fear the men beneath the tree;
They pace in sleek chivalric certainty.

Aunt Jennifer's fingers fluttering through her wool   5
Find even the ivory needle hard to pull.
The massive weight of Uncle's wedding band
Sits heavily upon Aunt Jennifer's hand.

When Aunt is dead, her terrified hands will lie
Still ringed with ordeals she was mastered by.   10
The tigers in the panel that she made
Will go on prancing, proud and unafraid.

—1950

Diving into the Wreck

First having read the book of myths,
and loaded the camera,
and checked the edge of the knife-blade,
I put on
the body-armor of black rubber   5
the absurd flippers
the grave and awkward mask.
I am having to do this
not like Cousteau° with his
assiduous team   10
aboard the sun-flooded schooner
but here alone.

There is a ladder.
The ladder is always there
hanging innocently   15
close to the side of the schooner.
We know what it is for,
we who have used it.
Otherwise
it is a piece of maritime floss   20
some sundry equipment.

I go down.
Rung after rung and still
the oxygen immerses me
the blue light   25
the clear atoms
of our human air.
I go down.
My flippers cripple me,
I crawl like an insect down the ladder   30
and there is no one
to tell me when the ocean
will begin.

---

9 Cousteau Jacques-Yves Cousteau (1910–1997), underwater explorer and inventor of the scuba tank

First the air is blue and then
it is bluer and then green and then   35
black I am blacking out and yet
my mask is powerful
it pumps my blood with power
the sea is another story
the sea is not a question of power   40
I have to learn alone
to turn my body without force
in the deep element.

And now: it is easy to forget
what I came for   45
among so many who have always
lived here
swaying their crenellated fans
between the reefs
and besides   50
you breathe differently down here.

I came to explore the wreck.
The words are purposes.
The words are maps.
I came to see the damage that was done   55
and the treasures that prevail.
I stroke the beam of my lamp
slowly along the flank
of something more permanent
than fish or weed   60

the thing I came for:
the wreck and not the story of the wreck
the thing itself and not the myth
the drowned face always staring
toward the sun   65
the evidence of damage
worn by salt and sway into this threadbare beauty
the ribs of the disaster
curving their assertion
among the tentative haunters.   70

This is the place.
And I am here, the mermaid whose dark hair
streams black, the merman in his armored body.
We circle silently
about the wreck   75
we dive into the hold.
I am she: I am he

whose drowned face sleeps with open eyes
whose breasts still bear the stress
whose silver, copper, vermeil cargo lies   80
obscurely inside barrels
half-wedged and left to rot
we are the half-destroyed instruments
that once held to a course
the water-eaten log°   85
the fouled compass

We are, I am, you are
by cowardice or courage
the one who find our way
back to this scene   90
carrying a knife, a camera
a book of myths
in which
our names do not appear.

—1972

ADRIENNE RICH

700

Rape

There is a cop who is both prowler and father:
he comes from your block, grew up with your brothers,
had certain ideals.
You hardly know him in his boots and silver badge,
on horseback, one hand touching his gun.   5

You hardly know him but you have to get to know him:
he has access to machinery that could kill you.
He and his stallion clop like warlords among the trash,
his ideals stand in the air, a frozen cloud
from between his unsmiling lips.   10

85 log log book

And so, when the time comes, you have to turn to him,
the maniac's sperm still greasing your thighs,
your mind whirling like crazy. You have to confess
to him, you are guilty of the crime
of having been forced.   15

And you see his blue eyes, the blue eyes of all the family
whom you used to know, grow narrow and glisten,
his hand types out the details
and he wants them all
but the hysteria in your voice pleases him best.   20

You hardly know him but now he thinks he knows you:
he has taken down your worst moment
on a machine and filed it in a file.
He knows, or thinks he knows, how much you imagined;
he knows, or thinks he knows, what you secretly wanted.   25

He has access to machinery that could get you put away;
and if, in the sickening light of the precinct,
and if, in the sickening light of the precinct,
your details sound like a portrait of your confessor,
will you swallow, will you deny them, will you lie your way   30
    home?

                                                         —1972

TED HUGHES ■ (1930–1998)

*Ted Hughes was a native of Yorkshire, England. Hughes never ventured far
from the natural world of his childhood for his subject matter. Hughes was
married to Sylvia Plath until her death in 1963. At the time of his death,
Hughes was the British poet laureate and had recently published* Birthday
Letters, *a collection of poems about Plath's and his marriage.*

Pike

Pike, three inches long, perfect
Pike in all parts, green tigering the gold.
Killers from the egg: the malevolent aged grin.
They dance on the surface among the flies.

Or move, stunned by their own grandeur,
Over a bed of emerald, silhouette
Of submarine delicacy and horror.
A hundred feet long in their world.

In ponds, under the heat-struck lily pads—
Gloom of their stillness:
Logged on last year's black leaves, watching upwards.
Or hung in an amber cavern of weeds

The jaw's hooked clamp and fangs
Not to be changed at this date;
A life subdued to its instrument;
The gills kneading quietly, and the pectorals.

Three we kept behind glass,
Jungled in weed: three inches, four,
And four and a half: fed fry to them—
Suddenly there were two. Finally one

With a sag belly and the grin it was born with.
And indeed they spare nobody.
Two, six pounds each, over two feet long,
High and dry and dead in the willow-herb—

One jammed past its gills down the other's gullet:
The outside eye stared: as a vice locks—
The same iron in this eye
Though its film shrank in death.

A pond I fished, fifty yards across,
Whose lilies and muscular tench°
Had outlasted every visible stone
Of the monastery that planted them—

Stilled legendary depth:
It was as deep as England. It held
Pike too immense to stir, so immense and old
That past nightfall I dared not cast

30 **tench** European freshwater fish

But silently cast and fished
With the hair frozen on my head
For what might move, for what eye might move.
The still splashes on the dark pond,   40

Owls hushing the floating woods
Frail on my ear against the dream
Darkness beneath night's darkness had freed,
That rose slowly towards me, watching.

—1960

GARY SNYDER ■ (b. 1930)

*Gary Snyder was deeply involved in poetic activity in his hometown, San
Francisco, when that city became the locus of the Beat Generation in the
mid-1950s. Yet Snyder, whose studies in Zen Buddhism and Oriental cultures
preceded his acquaintance with Allen Ginsberg and Jack Kerouac, has always exhibited a seriousness of purpose that sets him apart from his peers.
His long familiarity with the mountains of the Pacific Northwest dates from
his jobs with logging crews during his college days.*

A Walk

Sunday the only day we don't work:
Mules farting around the meadow,
    Murphy fishing,
The tent flaps in the warm
Early sun: I've eaten breakfast and I'll   5
    take a walk
To Benson Lake. Packed a lunch,
Goodbye. Hopping on creekbed boulders
Up the rock throat three miles
    Piute Creek—   10
In steep gorge glacier-slick rattlesnake country
Jump, land by a pool, trout skitter,
The clear sky. Deer tracks.
Bad place by a falls, boulders big as houses,
Lunch tied to belt,   15
I stemmed up a crack and almost fell

But rolled out safe on a ledge
     and ambled on.
Quail chicks freeze underfoot, color of stone
Then run cheep! away, hen quail fussing.   20
Craggy west end of Benson Lake—after edging
Past dark creek pools on a long white slope—
Lookt down in the ice-black lake
     lined with cliff
From far above: deep shimmering trout.   25
A lone duck in a gunsightpass
     steep side hill
Through slide-aspen and talus, to the east end
Down to grass, wading a wide smooth stream
Into camp. At last.   30
    By the rusty three-year-
Ago left-behind cookstove
Of the old trail crew,
Stoppt and swam and ate my lunch.

—1968

Miller Williams won the Poets' Prize in 1990 for Living on the Surface, *a volume of selected poems. A skillful translator of both Giuseppe Belli, a Roman poet of the early nineteenth century, and of Nicanor Parra, a contemporary Chilean, Williams has written many poems about his travels throughout the world yet has retained the relaxed idiom of his native Arkansas. He read a poem at the 1997 presidential inauguration.*

The Book

I held it in my hands while he told the story.

He had found it in a fallen bunker,
a book for notes with all the pages blank.
He took it to keep for a sketchbook and diary.

He learned years later, when he showed the book   5
to an old bookbinder, who paled, and stepped back
a long step and told him what he held,
what he had laid the days of his life in.
It's bound, the binder said, in human skin.

I stood turning it over in my hands,
turning it in my head. Human skin.   10

What child did this skin fit? What man, what woman?
Dragged still full of its flesh from what dream?

Who took it off the meat? Some other one
who stayed alive by knowing how to do this?   15

I stared at the changing book and a horror grew,
I stared and a horror grew, which was, which is,
how beautiful it was until I knew.

—1989

LINDA PASTAN ■ (b. 1932)

Linda Pastan served as poet laureate of Maryland, where she has lived and taught for many years. Her first book, A Perfect Circle of Sun, *appeared in 1971, and a dozen more collections have been published since.*

Ethics

In ethics class so many years ago
our teacher asked this question every fall:
if there were a fire in a museum
which would you save, a Rembrandt painting
or an old woman who hadn't many   5
years left anyhow? Restless on hard chairs
caring little for pictures or old age
we'd opt one year for life, the next for art
and always half-heartedly. Sometimes
the woman borrowed my grandmother's face   10
leaving her usual kitchen to wander
some drafty, half-imagined museum.
One year, feeling clever, I replied
why not let the woman decide herself?
Linda, the teacher would report, eschews   15
the burdens of responsibility.
This fall in a real museum I stand
Before a real Rembrandt, old woman,
or nearly so, myself. The colors

within this frame are darker than autumn,   20
darker even than winter—the browns of earth,
though earth's most radiant elements burn
through the canvas. I know now that woman
and painting and season are almost one   25
and all beyond saving by children.

—1998

SYLVIA PLATH ■ (1932–1963)

Sylvia Plath, whose personal life is often difficult to separate from her poetry, is almost always read as an autobiographical and confessional poet. Brilliant and precocious, she served a long apprenticeship to the tradition of modern poetry before attaining her mature style in the final two years of her life. Only one collection, The Colossus (1960), appeared in her lifetime, and her fame has mainly rested on her posthumous books of poetry and the success of her lone novel, The Bell Jar (1963). She committed suicide in 1963. Plath has been the subject of a half-dozen biographical studies and a feature film, Sylvia (2003), reflecting the intense interest that readers have in her life and work.

Daddy

You do not do, you do not do
Any more, black shoe
In which I have lived like a foot
For thirty years, poor and white,
Barely daring to breathe or Achoo.   5

Daddy, I have had to kill you.
You died before I had time—
Marble-heavy, a bag full of God,
Ghastly statue with one gray toe
Big as a Frisco seal   10

And a head in the freakish Atlantic
Where it pours bean green over blue
In the waters off beautiful Nauset.
I used to pray to recover you.
Ach, du.°   15

15 **Ach, du** "Oh, you"

In the German tongue, in the Polish town
Scraped flat by the roller
Of wars, wars, wars.
But the name of the town is common.
My Polack friend   20

Says there are a dozen or two.
So I never could tell where you
Put your foot, your root,
I never could talk to you.
The tongue stuck in my jaw.   25

It stuck in a barb wire snare.
Ich, ich, ich, ich,°
I could hardly speak.
I thought every German was you.
And the language obscene   30

An engine, an engine
Chuffing me off like a Jew.
A Jew to Dachau, Auschwitz, Belsen.°
I began to talk like a Jew.
I think I may well be a Jew.   35

The snows of the Tyrol, the clear beer of Vienna
Are not very pure or true.
With my gypsy ancestress and my weird luck
And my Taroc pack and my Taroc pack
I may be a bit of a Jew.   40

I have always been scared of *you*,
With your Luftwaffe,° your gobbledygoo.
And your neat mustache
And your Aryan eye, bright blue.
Panzer-man, panzer-man, O You—   45

Not God but a swastika
So black no sky could squeak through.
Every woman adores a Fascist,
The boot in the face, the brute
Brute heart of a brute like you.   50

27 **Ich, ich, ich, ich** "I, I, I, I"   33 **Dachau, Auschwitz, Belsen** German concentration camps
42 **Luftwaffe** German Air Force

You stand at the blackboard, daddy,
In the picture I have of you,
A cleft in your chin instead of your foot
But no less a devil for that, no not
Any less the black man who   55

Bit my pretty red heart in two.
I was ten when they buried you.
At twenty I tried to die
And get back, back, back to you.
I thought even the bones would do.   60

But they pulled me out of the sack,
And they stuck me together with glue.
And then I knew what to do.
I made a model of you,
A man in black with a Meinkampf° look   65

And a love of the rack and the screw.
And I said I do, I do.
So daddy, I'm finally through.
The black telephone's off at the root,
The voices just can't worm through.   70

If I've killed one man, I've killed two—
The vampire who said he was you
And drank my blood for a year,
Seven years, if you want to know.
Daddy, you can lie back now.   75

There's a stake in your fat black heart
And the villagers never liked you.
They are dancing and stamping on you.
They always *knew* it was you.
Daddy, daddy, you bastard, I'm through.   80

—1966

65 Meinkampf title of Hitler's autobiography ("My Struggle")

Edge

The woman is perfected.
Her dead

Body wears the smile of accomplishment,
The illusion of a Greek necessity

Flows in the scrolls of her toga,   5
Her bare

Feet seem to be saying:
We have come so far, it is over.

Each dead child coiled, a white serpent,
One at each little   10

Pitcher of milk, now empty.
She has folded

Them back into her body as petals
Of a rose close when the garden

Stiffens and odors bleed   15
From the sweet, deep throats of the night flower.

The moon has nothing to be sad about,
Staring from her hood of bone.

She is used to this sort of thing.
Her blacks crackle and drag.   20

—1965

Metaphors

I'm a riddle in nine syllables,
An elephant, a ponderous house,
A melon strolling on two tendrils.
O red fruit, ivory, fine timbers!
This loaf's big with its yeasty rising.   5
Money's new-minted in this fat purse.
I'm a means, a stage, a cow in calf.
I've eaten a bag of green apples,
Boarded the train there's no getting off.

—1960

Gerald Barrax served as the editor of Obsidian II: Black Literature in Review, *one of the most influential journals of African-American writing. The author of five collections of poetry, he taught at North Carolina State University.*

Strangers Like Us: Pittsburgh, Raleigh, 1945–1985

The sounds our parents heard echoing over
housetops while listening to evening radios
were the uninterrupted cries running and cycling
we sent through the streets and yards, where spring summer
fall we were entrusted to the night, boys   5
and girls together, to send us home for bath
and bed after the dark had drifted down and eased
contests between pitcher and batter, hider and seeker.

Our own children live imprisoned in light.
They are cycloned into our yards and hearts,   10
whose gates flutter shut on unfamiliar smiles.
At the rumor of a moon, we call them in
before the monsters who hunt, who hurt, who haunt
us, rise up from our own dim streets.

—1992

MARK STRAND ■ (b. 1934)

Mark Strand displays a simplicity in his best poems that reveals the influence of Spanish-language poets like Nicanor Parra, the father of "anti-poetry," and Rafael Alberti, whom Strand has translated. Strand was named U.S. poet laureate in 1990.

The Tunnel

A man has been standing
in front of my house
for days. I peek at him
from the living room

window and at night,
unable to sleep,
I shine my flashlight
down on the lawn.
He is always there.

After a while
I open the front door
just a crack and order
him out of my yard.
He narrows his eyes
and moans. I slam
the door and dash back
to the kitchen, then up
to the bedroom, then down.

I weep like a schoolgirl
and make obscene gestures
through the window. I
write large suicide notes
and place them so he
can read them easily.
I destroy the living
room furniture to prove
I own nothing of value.

When he seems unmoved
I decide to dig a tunnel
to a neighboring yard.
I seal the basement off
from the upstairs with
a brick wall. I dig hard
and in no time the tunnel
is done. Leaving my pick
and shovel below,

I come out in front of a house
and stand there too tired to
move or even speak, hoping
someone will help me.
I feel I'm being watched

and sometimes I hear
a man's voice,
but nothing is done
and I have been waiting for days.   45

—1968

RUSSELL EDSON ■ (b. 1935)

*Russell Edson is the son of a cartoonist, and his surrealistic poems (often
illustrated by himself) perhaps owe as much to the whimsical drawings
and essays of* New Yorker *writer James Thurber than to the direct influence of any modern poet. Edson has been called "the godfather of the
prose poem in America," and the sheer originality of his imagination and
his defiance of poetic "rules" set him apart from other poets and ally him
with such contemporary masters of cartooning as R. Crumb and Harvey
Pekar.*

Ape

You haven't finished your ape, said mother to father, who had
monkey hair and blood on his whiskers.

I've had enough monkey, cried father.

You didn't eat the hands, and I went to all the trouble to make
onion rings for its fingers, said mother.   5

I'll just nibble on its forehead, and then I've had enough, said father.

I stuffed its nose with garlic, just like you like it, said mother.

Why don't you have the butcher cut these apes up? You lay the whole
thing on the table every night; the same fractured skull, the same
singed fur; like someone who died horribly. These aren't dinners,   10
these are postmortem dissections.

Try a piece of its gum, I've stuffed its mouth with bread, said mother.

Ugh, it looks like a mouth full of vomit. How can I bite into its
cheek with bread spilling out of its mouth? cried father.

Break one of the ears off, they're so crispy, said mother.   15

I wish to hell you'd put underpants on these apes; even a
jockstrap, screamed father.

Father, how dare you insinuate that I see the ape as anything
more than simple meat, screamed mother.

Well, what's with this ribbon tied in a bow on its privates?
screamed father.   20

Are you saying that I am in love with this vicious creature? That I
would submit my female opening to this brute? That after we had
love on the kitchen floor I would put him in the oven, after breaking
his head with a frying pan; and then serve him to my husband, that
my husband might eat the evidence of my infidelity . . . ?   25

I'm just saying that I'm damn sick of ape every night, cried father.

—1994

MARY OLIVER ■ (b. 1935)

*Mary Oliver was born in Cleveland, Ohio, and educated at Ohio State
University and Vassar College. She has served as a visiting professor at a
number of universities and at the Fine Arts Work Center in Provincetown,
Massachusetts. She has won both the Pulitzer Prize and the National
Book Award for her work. Red Bird, a new collection of poems, appeared
in 2008.*

The Black Walnut Tree

My mother and I debate:
we could sell
the black walnut tree
to the lumberman,
and pay off the mortgage.   5
Likely some storm anyway
will churn down its dark boughs,
smashing the house. We talk
slowly, two women trying
in a difficult time to be wise.   10

Roots in the cellar drains,
I say, and she replies
that the leaves are getting heavier
every year, and the fruit
harder to gather away.   15
But something brighter than money
moves in our blood—an edge
sharp and quick as a trowel
that wants us to dig and sow.
So we talk, but we don't do   20
anything. That night I dream
of my fathers out of Bohemia
filling the blue fields
of fresh and generous Ohio
with leaves and vines and orchards.   25
What my mother and I both know
is that we'd crawl with shame
in the emptiness we'd made
in our own and our fathers' backyard.
So the black walnut tree   30
swings through another year
of sun and leaping winds,
of leaves and bounding fruit,
and, month after month, the whip-
crack of the mortgage.   35

—1979

FRED CHAPPELL ■ (b. 1936)

Fred Chappell wrote the epic-length poem Midquest *(1981), and his achievement was recognized when he was awarded the Bollingen Prize in 1985. A
four-part poem written over a decade,* Midquest *uses the occasion of the
poet's thirty-fifth birthday as a departure for a complex sequence of autobiographical poems that are heavily indebted to Dante for their formal structure. A versatile writer of both poetry and prose, Chappell displays his classical learning brilliantly and in unusual contexts.*

FRED CHAPPELL

714

Narcissus and Echo°

Shall the water not remember *Ember*
my hand's slow gesture, tracing above *of*
its mirror my half-imaginary *airy*
portrait? My only belonging *longing*
is my beauty, which I take *ache*   5
away and then return as love *of*
teasing playfully the one being *unbeing.*

whose gratitude I treasure *Is your*
moves me. I live apart *heart*
from myself, yet cannot *not*   10
live apart. In the water's tone, *stone?*
that brilliant silence, a flower *Hour,*
whispers my name with such slight *light,*
moment, it seems filament of air, *fare*
the world become cloudswell. *well.*   15

—1985

LUCILLE CLIFTON ■ (b. 1936–2010)

Lucille Clifton, a native of Depew, New York, was educated at SUNY–Fredonia and Howard University, and has taught at several colleges, including American University in Washington, D.C. About her own work, she has commented succinctly, "I am a Black woman poet, and I sound like one." Clifton won a National Book Award in 2000.

homage to my hips

these hips are big hips
they need space to
move around in.

Narcissus and Echo In the myth, the vain Narcissus drowned attempting to embrace his own reflection in the water. Echo, a nymph who loved him, pined away until only her voice remained.

they don't fit into little
petty places. these hips
are free hips.
they don't like to be held back.
these hips have never been enslaved,
they go where they want to go
they do what they want to do.
these hips are mighty hips.
these hips are magic hips.
i have known them
to put a spell on a man and
spin him like a top!

5

10

15

—1980

wishes for sons

i wish them cramps.
i wish them a strange town
and the last tampon.
I wish them no 7-11.

i wish them one week early
and wearing a white skirt.
i wish them one week late.

later i wish them hot flashes
and clots like you
wouldn't believe. let the
flashes come when they
meet someone special.
let the clots come
when they want to.

let them think they have accepted
arrogance in the universe,
then bring them to gynecologists
not unlike themselves.

5

10

15

—1991

Marge Piercy was a political radical during her student days at the University of Michigan. Piercy has continued to be outspoken on political, cultural, and sexual issues. Her phrase "to be of use" has become a key measure by which feminist writers and critics have gauged the meaning of their own life experiences.

What's That Smell in the Kitchen?

All over America women are burning dinners.
It's lambchops in Peoria; it's haddock
in Providence; it's steak in Chicago;
tofu delight in Big Sur; red
rice and beans in Dallas.   5
All over America women are burning
food they're supposed to bring with calico
smile on platters glittering like wax.
Anger sputters in her brainpan, confined
but spewing out missiles of hot fat.   10
Carbonized despair presses like a clinker
from a barbecue against the back of her eyes.
If she wants to grill anything, it's
her husband spitted over a slow fire.
If she wants to serve him anything   15
it's a dead rat with a bomb in its belly
ticking like the heart of an insomniac.
Her life is cooked and digested,
nothing but leftovers in Tupperware.
Look, she says, once I was roast duck   20
on your platter with parsley but now I am Spam.
Burning dinner is not incompetence but war.

—1982

Betty Adcock was born in San Augustine, Texas. Adcock has lived for many years in Raleigh, North Carolina, where she is poet-in-residence at Meredith College. Her volume of selected poems, Intervale, *appeared in 2001.*

Voyages

We were five girls prowling alleyways behind the houses,
having skipped math class for any and no reason.
Equipped with too many camelhair coats, too many
    cashmeres,
we were privileged and sure and dumb, isolated
without knowing it, smug in our small crime, playing   5
hooky from Miss Hockaday's Boarding School for young
    ladies.
Looking for anything that wouldn't be boring
as we defined that, we'd gone off exploring the going-
    downhill
neighborhoods around our tight Victorian schoolgrounds.
The houses were fronted with concrete porches,   10
venetian blinds drawn tight against the sun.
Somebody had told us an eccentric lived where one
back fence got strangely high and something stuck over
the top. We didn't care what it was, but we went anyway,
giggling with hope for the freakish: bodies stashed and
    decaying,   15
a madwoman pulling her hair, maybe a maniac in a cage.
Anything sufficiently awful would have done.

But when we came close enough to look through
the inch of space between two badly placed fenceboards,
we saw only the ordinary, grown grotesque and huge: 20
somebody was building a sailboat bigger than most city
    backyards,
bigger almost than the house it belonged to,
mast towering high in a brass-and-blue afternoon.
This was in the middle of Dallas, Texas—
the middle of the 1950s, which had us   25
(though we didn't yet know this) by the throat.
Here was a backyard entirely full of boat,
out of scale, out of the Bible, maybe out of a movie,
all rescue and ornament. It looked to be something between
a galleon and a Viking ship, larger than we could imagine   30

in such a space, with sails and riggings and a face on the prow
(about which we made much but which neither smiled nor
    frowned).
Gasping, overplaying the scene, we guessed at the kind
of old fool who would give a lifetime to building this thing.
Then one of us asked for a light for a cigarette   35
and we all knew how easy it would be to swipe
a newspaper, light it, and toss it onto the deck
of that great wooden landlocked ark, watch it go up.

But of course we didn't do it and nobody of course came out
of that house and we of course went back   40
in time for English and to sneak out of P.E. later
for hamburgers at Mitch's where the blue-collar boys
leaned in their ducktails against the bar.

But before we did that, we stood for a while clumped
and smoking, pushed into silence by palpable obsession   45
where it sat as if it belonged on parched Dallas grass,
a stunned, unfinished restlessness.

And didn't the ground just then, under our penny-
loafers, give the tiniest heave? Didn't we feel how thin
the grass was, like a coat of light paint, like green ice   50
over something unmanageable? How thin the sun
became for a minute, the rest of our future dimming
and wavy and vast, even tomorrow's pop quiz and softball
    practice—

as if all around us were depths we really could drown in.

          —1995

ROBERT PHILLIPS ■ (b. 1938)

*Robert Phillips labored for over thirty years as a New York advertising execu-
tive, a remarkable fact when one considers his many books of poetry, fiction,
and criticism and the numerous books he has edited. He currently lives in
Houston, where he teaches in the creative writing program at the University
of Houston.*

The Stone Crab: A Love Poem

Joe's serves approximately 1,000 pounds of crab
claws each day.
—*Florida Gold Coast Leisure Guide*

Delicacy of warm Florida waters,
his body is undesirable. One giant claw
is his claim to fame, and we claim it,

more than once. Meat sweeter than lobster,
less dear than his life, when grown that claw   5
is lifted, broken off at the joint.

Mutilated, the crustacean is thrown back
into the water, back upon his own resources.
One of nature's rarities, he replaces

an entire appendage as you or I   10
grow a nail. (No one asks how he survives
that crabby sea with just one claw;

two-fisted menaces real as night-
mares, ten-tentacled nights cold
as fright.) In time he grows another,   15

large, meaty, magnificent as the first.
And one astonished day, *snap!* it too
is twigged off, the cripple dropped

back into treachery. Unlike a twig,
it sprouts again. How many losses   20
can he endure? Well,

his shell is hard, the sea is wide.
Something vital broken off, he doesn't
nurse the wound; develops something new.

—1994

DABNEY STUART ■ (b. 1938)

*Dabney Stuart has written many poems populated by the supporting cast of
the American family romance—parents, wives and ex-wives, and children. A
Virginian who taught for many years at Washington and Lee University,
Stuart published* Light Years, *a volume of selected poems, in 1995.*

Discovering My Daughter

Most of your life we have kept our separate places:
After I left your mother you knew an island,
Rented rooms, a slow coastal slide northward
To Boston, and, in summer, another island
Hung at the country's tip. Would you have kept going   5
All the way off the map, an absolute alien?

Sometimes I shiver, being almost forgetful enough
To have let that happen. We've come the longer way
Under such pressure, from one person to
Another. Our trip proves again the world is   10
Round, a singular island where people may come
Together, as we have, making a singular place.

—1987

MARGARET ATWOOD ■ (b. 1939)

Margaret Atwood is the leading woman writer of Canada, and she excels at both poetry and prose fiction. Among her many novels, The Handmaid's Tale *is perhaps the best known, becoming a bestseller in the United States and the subject of a motion picture. Atwood's* Selected Poems *appeared in 1976.*

Siren° Song

This is the one song everyone
would like to learn: the song
that is irresistible:

the song that forces men
to leap overboard in squadrons   5
even though they see the beached skulls

the song nobody knows
because anyone who has heard it
is dead, and the others can't remember.

Siren in Greek myth, one of the women whose irresistible song lured sailors onto the rocks

Shall I tell you the secret
and if I do, will you get me
out of this bird suit?

I don't enjoy it here
squatting on this island
looking picturesque and mythical

with these two feathery maniacs,
I don't enjoy singing
this trio, fatal and valuable.

I will tell the secret to you,
to you, only to you.
Come closer. This song

is a cry for help: Help me!
Only you, only you can,
you are unique

at last. Alas
it is a boring song
but it works every time.

—1974

STEPHEN DUNN ■ (b. 1939)

Stephen Dunn is a graduate of the creative writing program at Syracuse University. Dunn teaches at The Richard Stockton College of New Jersey in Pomona, New Jersey. His attempt to blend ordinary experience with larger significance is illustrated in the duality of his book titles like Full of Lust and Good Usage, Work and Love, *and* Between Angels. *Dunn was awarded the Pulitzer Prize in 2001.*

The Sacred

After the teacher asked if anyone had
    a sacred place
and the students fidgeted and shrank

in their chairs, the most serious of them all
      said it was his car,   5
being in it alone, his tape deck playing

things he'd chosen, and others knew the truth
      had been spoken
and began speaking about their rooms,

their hiding places, but the car kept coming up,   10
      the car in motion,
music filling it, and sometimes one other person

who understood the bright altar of the dashboard
      and how far away
a car could take him from the need   15

to speak, or to answer, the key
      in having a key
and putting it in, and going.

—1989

SEAMUS HEANEY ■ (b. 1939)

Seamus Heaney was born in the troubled country of Northern Ireland.
Heaney has largely avoided the type of political divisions that have divided
his homeland. Instead, he has chosen to focus on the landscape of the rural
Ireland he knew while growing up as a farmer's son. Since 1982, Heaney has
taught part of the year at Harvard University. He was awarded the Nobel
Prize for Literature in 1995.

Punishment

I can feel the tug
of the halter at the nape
of her neck, the wind
on her naked front.

It blows her nipples   5
to amber beads,
it shakes the frail rigging
of her ribs.

I can see her drowned
body in the bog,
the weighing stone,
the floating rods and boughs.

Under which at first
she was a barked sapling
that is dug up
oak-bone, brain-firkin:°

her shaved head
like a stubble of black corn,
her blindfold a soiled bandage,
her noose a ring

to store
the memories of love.
Little adulteress,
before they punished you

you were flaxen-haired,
undernourished, and your
tar-black face was beautiful.
My poor scapegoat,

I almost love you
but would have cast, I know,
the stones of silence.
I am the artful voyeur

of your brain's exposed
and darkened combs,
your muscles' webbing
and all your numbered bones:

I who have stood dumb
when your betraying sisters,
cauled in tar,
wept by the railings,

16 **firkin** a small barrel

who would connive
in civilized outrage
yet understand the exact
and tribal, intimate revenge.

—1975

TED KOOSER ■ (b. 1939)

Ted Kooser, who lives in Nebraska, writes plainspoken poems about life in America's heartland. Born in Iowa, Kooser studied at Iowa State University and the University of Nebraska. His poetry collections include Winter Morning Walks: One Hundred Postcards to Jim Harrison, *which was written during Kooser's recovery from cancer surgery and radiation treatment. It received the 2001 Nebraska Book Award for poetry. Kooser is editor and publisher of Windflower Press, a small press specializing in contemporary poetry. A retired vice president of Lincoln Benefit Life, an insurance company, Kooser teaches at the University of Nebraska, Lincoln. In 2004, Kooser was appointed U.S. Poet Laureate.*

Abandoned Farmhouse

He was a big man, says the size of his shoes
on a pile of broken dishes by the house;
a tall man too, says the length of the bed
in an upstairs room; and a good, God-fearing man,
says the Bible with a broken back   5
on the floor below the window, dusty with sun;
but not a man for farming, say the fields
cluttered with boulders and the leaky barn.

A woman lived with him, says the bedroom wall
papered with lilacs and the kitchen shelves   10
covered with oilcloth, and they had a child,
says the sandbox made from a tractor tire.
Money was scarce, say the jars of plum preserves
and canned tomatoes sealed in the cellar hole.
And the winters cold, say the rags in the window frames.   15
It was lonely here, says the narrow country road.

Something went wrong, says the empty house
in the weed-choked yard. Stones in the fields
say he was not a farmer; the still-sealed jars
in the cellar say she left in a nervous haste.   20
And the child? Its toys are strewn in the yard
like branches after a storm—a rubber cow,
a rusty tractor with a broken plow,
a doll in overalls. Something went wrong, they say.

—1980

TOM DISCH ■ (b 1940–2008)

Tom Disch was a science-fiction writer, author of interactive computer fiction, resident critic for magazines as diverse as Playboy *and* The Nation, *and poet. Disch was possibly the most brilliant satirist in contemporary American poetry.* Yes, Let's, *a collection of his selected poems, appeared in 1989.*

Ballade of the New God

I have decided I'm divine.
Caligula and Nero knew
A godliness akin to mine,
But they are strictly hitherto.
They're dead, and what can dead gods do?   5
I'm here and now. I'm dynamite.
I'd worship me if I were you.
A new religion starts tonight!

No booze, no pot, no sex, no swine:
I have decreed them all taboo.   10
My words will be your only wine,
The thought of me your honeydew.
All other thoughts you will eschew
And call yourself a Thomasite
And hymn my praise with loud yahoo.   15
A new religion starts tonight.

But (you might think) that's asinine!
I'm just as much a god as you.
You may have built yourself a shrine
But I won't bend my knee. Who   20
Asked you to be my god? I do,
Who am, as god, divinely right.
Now you must join my retinue:
A new religion starts tonight.

All that I have said is true.   25
I'm god and you're my acolyte.
Surrender's bliss: I envy you.
A new religion starts tonight.

—1995

FLORENCE CASSEN MAYERS ■ (b. 1940)

Florence Cassen Mayers is a widely published poet and children's author. Her "ABC" books include children's guides to baseball and to the National Basketball Association.

All-American Sestina

One nation, indivisible
two-car garage
three strikes you're out
four-minute mile
five-cent cigar   5
six-string guitar

six-pack Bud
one-day sale
five-year warranty
two-way street   10
fourscore and seven years ago
three cheers

three-star restaurant
sixty-
four-dollar question   15
one-night stand
two-pound lobster
five-star general

five-course meal
three sheets to the wind   20
two bits
six-shooter
one-armed bandit
four-poster

four-wheel drive   25
five-and-dime
hole in one
three-alarm fire
sweet sixteen
two-wheeler   30

two-tone Chevy
four rms, hi flr, w/vu
six-footer
high five
three-ring circus   35
one-room schoolhouse

two thumbs up, five-karat diamond
Fourth of July, three-piece suit
six feet under, one-horse town

—1996

PATTIANN ROGERS ■ (b. 1940)

Pattiann Rogers is the foremost naturalist among contemporary American poets. Her poems resound with the rich names of unfamiliar species of plants and animals, most of which she seems to know on intimate terms. Song of the World Becoming: New and Collected Poems 1981–2001 *was published in 2001. A new collection,* Wayfare, *appeared in 2008.*

Foreplay

When it first begins, as you might expect,
the lips and thin folds are closed, the pouting
layers pressed, lapped lightly,
almost languidly, against one another
in a sealed bud.   5

However, with certain prolonged
and random strokings of care
along each binding line, with soft
intrusions traced beneath each pursed
gathering and edge, with inquiring   10
intensities of gesture—as the sun
swinging slowly from winter back

to spring, touches briefly,
between moments of moon and masking
clouds, certain stunning points   15
and inner nubs of earth—so
with such ministrations, a slight
swelling, a quiver of reaching,
a tendency toward space,
might be noticed to commence.   20

Then with dampness from the dark,
with moisture from the falling
night of morning, from hidden places
within the hills, each seal begins
to loosen, each recalcitrant clasp   25
sinks away into itself, and every tucked
grasp, every silk tack willingly relents,
releases, gives way, proclaims a turning,
declares a revolution, assumes,
in plain sight, a surging position   30
that offers, an audacious offering
that beseeches, every petal parted wide.

Remember the spiraling, blue
valerian, remember the violet, sucking
larkspur, the laurel and rosebay   35

and pea cockle flung backwards, remember
the fragrant, funnelling lily, the lifted
honeysuckle, the sweet, open pucker
of the ground ivy blossom?

Now even the darkest crease possessed,   40
the most guarded, pulsing, least drop
of pearl bead, moon grain trembling
deep within is fully revealed, fully exposed
to any penetrating wind or shaking fur
or mad hunger or searing, plunging surprise   45
the wild descending sky in delirium
has to offer.

—1994

BILLY COLLINS ■ (b. 1941)

*Billy Collins was born in New York City and continues to teach there. One of
the few contemporary poets to reach a wide popular audience, Collins has
been an enthusiastic performer, commentator on National Public Radio, and
advocate for poetry. Beginning in 2001, he served two years as U.S. poet laureate, establishing the online anthology "Poetry 180," a website that presents a poem for every day in the school year.* Sailing Alone Around the
Room: New and Selected Poems *was published in 2001. A new book,* The
Trouble with Poetry, *was published in 2007.*

Litany

> You are the bread and the knife,
> The crystal goblet and the wine.
> —*Jacques Crickillon*

You are the bread and the knife,
the crystal goblet and the wine.
You are the dew on the morning grass,
and the burning wheel of the sun.
You are the white apron of the baker   5
and the marsh birds suddenly in flight.

However, you are not the wind in the orchard,
the plums on the counter,
or the house of cards.
And you are certainly not the pine-scented air. 10
There is no way you are the pine-scented air.

It is possible that you are the fish under the bridge,
maybe even the pigeon on the general's head,
but you are not even close
to being the field of cornflowers at dusk. 15

And a quick look in the mirror will show
that you are neither the boots in the corner
nor the boat asleep in its boathouse.

It might interest you to know,
speaking of the plentiful imagery of the world, 20
that I am the sound of rain on the roof.

I also happen to be the shooting star,
the evening paper blowing down an alley,
and the basket of chestnuts on the kitchen table.

I am also the moon in the trees 25
and the blind woman's teacup.
But don't worry, I am not the bread and the knife.
You are still the bread and the knife.
You will always be the bread and the knife,
not to mention the crystal goblet and—somehow—the wine. 30

—2002

LITANY

731

ROBERT HASS ■ (b. 1941)

*Robert Hass was born and reared in San Francisco, and teaches at U. C.
Berkeley. His first book,* Field Guide, *was chosen for the Yale Series of
Younger Poets in 1973. Recently he has collaborated with Nobel Prize–winner
Czeslaw Milosz on English translations of the latter's poetry. He was ap-
pointed U.S. poet laureate in 1995.*

Meditation at Lagunitas°

All the new thinking is about loss.
In this it resembles all the old thinking.
The idea, for example, that each particular erases
the luminous clarity of a general idea. That the clown-
faced woodpecker probing the dead sculpted trunk   5
of that black birch is, by his presence,
some tragic falling off from a first world
of undivided light. Or the other notion that,
because there is in this world no one thing
to which the bramble of *blackberry* corresponds,   10
a word is elegy to what it signifies.
We talked about it late last night and in the voice
of my friend, there was a thin wire of grief, a tone
almost querulous. After a while I understood that,
talking this way, everything dissolves: *justice,*   15
pine, hair, woman, you and I. There was a woman
I made love to and I remembered how, holding
her small shoulders in my hands sometimes,
I felt a violent wonder at her presence
like a thirst for salt, for my childhood river   20
with its island willows, silly music from the pleasure boat,
muddy places where we caught the little orange-silver fish
called *pumpkinseed.* It hardly had to do with her.
Longing, we say, because desire is full
of endless distances. I must have been the same to her   25
But I remember so much, the way her hands dismantled bread,
the thing her father said that hurt her, what
she dreamed. There are moments when the body is as numinous
as words, days that are the good flesh continuing.
Such tenderness, those afternoons and evenings,   30
saying *blackberry, blackberry, blackberry.*

—1979

Lagunitas in California

SIMON J. ORTIZ ■ (b. 1941)

Simon J. Ortiz was born in the Pueblo of Acoma, near Albuquerque, New Mexico. Ortiz has explained why he writes: "Because Indians always tell a story. The only way to continue is to tell a story." The author of collections of poetry and prose and of several children's books, Ortiz has taught creative writing and Native American literature at many universities.

The Serenity in Stones

I am holding this turquoise
in my hands.
My hands hold the sky
wrought in this little stone.
There is a cloud   5
at the furthest boundary.
The world is somewhere underneath.

I turn the stone, and there is more sky.
This is the serenity possible in stones,
the place of a feeling to which one belongs.   10
I am happy as I hold this sky
in my hands, in my eyes, and in myself.

—1975

GIBBONS RUARK ■ (b. 1941)

Gibbons Ruark is a native of North Carolina. Ruark is the author of five collections of poetry. Passing Through Customs, a volume of new and selected poems, appeared in 1999. He recently retired from teaching at the University of Delaware.

The Visitor

Holding the arm of his helper, the blind
Piano tuner comes to our piano.
He hesitates at first, but once he finds
The keyboard, his hands glide over the slow

Keys, ringing changes finer than the eye   5
Can see. The dusty wires he touches, row
On row, quiver like bowstrings as he
Twists them one notch tighter. He runs his
Finger along a wire, touches the dry
Rust to his tongue, breaks into a pure bliss   10
And tells us, "One year more of damp weather
Would have done you in, but I've saved it this
Time. Would one of you play now, please? I hear
It better at a distance." My wife plays
Stardust. The blind man stands and smiles in her   15
Direction, then disappears into the blaze
Of new October. Now the afternoon,
The long afternoon that blurs in a haze
Of music . . . Chopin nocturnes, *Clair de Lune,*
All the old familiar, unfamiliar   20
Music-lesson pieces, *Papa Haydn's*
Dead and gone, gently down the stream . . . Hours later,
After the latest car has doused its beams,
Has cooled down and stopped its ticking, I hear
Our cat, with the grace of animals free   25
To move in darkness, strike one key only,
And a single lucid drop of water stars my dream.

—1971

GLADYS CARDIFF ■ (b. 1942)

*Gladys Cardiff is a member of the Cherokee nation. "Combing" is taken
from her first collection,* To Frighten a Storm, *which was originally published in 1976.*

Combing

Bending, I bow my head
And lay my hand upon
Her hair, combing, and think
How women do this for

Each other. My daughter's hair
Curls against the comb,
Wet and fragrant—orange
Parings. Her face, downcast,
Is quiet for one so young.

I take her place. Beneath
My mother's hands I feel
The braids drawn up tight
As a piano wire and singing,
Vinegar-rinsed. Sitting
Before the oven I hear
The orange coils tick
The early hour before school.

She combed her grandmother
Mathilda's hair using
A comb made out of bone.
Mathilda rocked her oak wood
Chair, her face downcast,
Intent on tearing rags
In strips to braid a cotton
Rug from bits of orange
and brown. A simple act,

Preparing hair. Something
Women do for each other,
Plaiting the generations.

—1976

COMBING

735

B. H. FAIRCHILD ■ (b. 1942)

B. H. Fairchild grew up in Liberal, Kansas, and his father's machine shop provides the title and the setting for his prize-winning collection, The Art of the Lathe. *Fairchild teaches at the California State University, San Bernardino. His most recent collection,* Early Occult Memory Systems of the Lower Midwest (2002), *won the National Book Critics Circle Award.*

Body and Soul

B. H. FAIRCHILD

Half-numb, guzzling bourbon and Coke from coffee mugs,
our fathers fall in love with their own stories, nuzzling
the facts but mauling the truth, and my friend's father begins
to lay out with the slow ease of a blues ballad a story
about sandlot baseball in Commerce, Oklahoma decades ago.   5
These were men's teams, grown men, some in their thirties
and forties who worked together in zinc mines or on oil rigs,
sweat and khaki and long beers after work, steel guitar music
whanging in their ears, little white rent houses to return to
where their wives complained about money and broken
     Kenmores°   10
and then said the hell with it and sang *Body and Soul*
in the bathtub and later that evening with the kids asleep
lay in bed stroking their husband's wrist tattoo and smoking
Chesterfields from a fresh pack until everything was O.K.
Well, you get the idea. Life goes on, the next day is Sunday,   15
another ball game, and the other team shows up one man short.

They say, we're one man short, but can we use this boy,
he's only fifteen years old, and at least he'll make a game.
They take a look at the kid, muscular and kind of knowing
the way he holds his glove, with the shoulders loose,   20
the thick neck, but then with that boy's face under
a clump of angelic blonde hair, and say, oh, hell, sure,
let's play ball. So it all begins, the men loosening up,
joking about the fat catcher's sex life, it's so bad
last night he had to hump his wife, that sort of thing,   25
pairing off into little games of catch that heat up into
throwing matches, the smack of the fungo bat, lazy jogging
into right field, big smiles and arcs of tobacco juice,
and the talk that gives a cool, easy feeling to the air,
talk among men normally silent, normally brittle and a little   30
angry with the empty promise of their lives. But they chatter
and say rock and fire, babe, easy out, and go right ahead
and pitch to the boy, but nothing fancy, just hard fastballs
right around the belt, and the kid takes the first two

10 Kenmores a brand of appliance

but on the third pops the bat around so quick and sure   35
that they pause a moment before turning around to watch
the ball still rising and finally dropping far beyond
the abandoned tractor that marks left field. Holy shit.
They're pretty quiet watching him round the bases,
but then, what the hell, the kid knows how to hit a ball,   40
so what, let's play some goddamned baseball here.
And so it goes. The next time up, the boy gets a look
at a very nifty low curve, then a slider, and the next one
is the curve again, and he sends it over the Allis Chalmers,°
high and big and sweet. The left fielder just stands there, frozen.   45
As if this isn't enough, the next time up he bats left-handed.
They can't believe it, and the pitcher, a tall, mean-faced
man from Okarche who just doesn't give a shit anyway
because his wife ran off two years ago leaving him with
three little ones and a rusted-out Dodge with a cracked block,   50
leans in hard, looking at the fat catcher like he was the
        sonofabitch
who ran off with his wife, leans in and throws something
out of the dark, green hell of forbidden fastballs, something
that comes in at the knees and then leaps viciously towards
the kid's elbow. He swings exactly the way he did right-handed,   55
and they all turn like a chorus line toward deep right field
where the ball loses itself in sagebrush and the sad burnt
dust of dustbowl Oklahoma. It is something to see.
But why make a long story long: runs pile up on both sides,
the boy comes around five times, and five times the pitcher   60
is cursing both God and His mother as his chew of tobacco sours
into something resembling horse piss, and a ragged and bruised
Spalding baseball disappears into the far horizon. Goodnight,
Irene. They have lost the game and some painful side bets
and they have been suckered. And it means nothing to them   65
though it should to you when they are told the boy's name is
Mickey Mantle.° And that's the story and those are the facts.
But the facts are not the truth. I think, though, as I scan
the faces of these old men now lost in the innings of their youth,

44 Allis Chalmers manufacturer of tractors and agricultural equipment   **67 Mickey Mantle**
(1931–1995) Oklahoma-born baseball star

I think I know what the truth of this story is, and I imagine   70
it lying there in the weeds behind that Allis Chalmers
just waiting for the obvious question to be asked: why, oh
why in hell didn't they just throw around the kid, walk him,
after he hit the third homer? Anybody would have,
especially nine men with disappointed wives and dirty socks   75
and diminishing expectations for whom winning at anything
meant everything. Men who know how to play the game,
who had talent when the other team had nothing except
        this ringer
who without a pitch to hit was meaningless, and they could
        go home
with their little two-dollar side bets and stride into the house   80
singing *If You've Got the Money, Honey, I've Got the Time*
with a bottle of Southern Comfort under their arms and grab
Dixie or May Ella up and dance across the gray linoleum
as if it were V-Day° all over again. But they did not.
And they did not because they were men, and this was a boy.   85
And they did not because sometimes after making love,
after smoking their Chesterfields in the cool silence and
listening to the big bands on the radio that sounded so
        glamorous,
so distant, they glanced over at their wives and noticed the lines
growing heavier around the eyes and mouth, felt what
        their wives   90
felt: that Les Brown and Glenn Miller and all those dancing
        couples
and in fact all possibility of human gaiety and light-heartedness
were as far away and unreachable as Times Square or the
        Avalon
ballroom. They did not because of the gray linoleum lying
        there
in the half-dark, the free calendar from the local mortuary   95
that said one day was pretty much like another, the work
        gloves
looped over the doorknob like dead squirrels. And they did not

---

84 V-Day V-E Day (May 8, 1945) marked the end of World War II in Europe; V-J Day (August 15, 1945) marked the end of the war in the Pacific

because they had gone through a depression and a war that
    had left
them with the idea that being a man in the eyes of their fathers
and everyone else had cost them just too goddamned much to
    lay it   100
at the feet of a fifteen year-old boy. And so they did not walk
    him,
and lost, but at least had some ragged remnant of themselves
to take back home. But there is one thing more, though it is not
a fact. When I see my friend's father staring hard into the
    bottomless
well of home plate as Mantle's fifth homer heads toward
    Arkansas,   105
I know that this man with the half-orphaned children and
worthless Dodge has also encountered for his first and possibly
only time that vast gap between talent and genius, has seen
as few have in the harsh light of an Oklahoma Sunday,
    the blonde
and blue-eyed bringer of truth, who will not easily be forgiven. 110

—1998

CHARLES MARTIN ■ (b. 1942)

*Charles Martin is a lifelong resident of New York City. Martin has taught for
many years at Queensborough College. "E.S.L." appeared as a prefatory
poem to Martin's sequence "Passages from Friday," an ironic retelling of the
Robinson Crusoe story from his servant's point of view. A respected classicist,
Martin has translated Ovid and Catullus.*

E.S.L.°

    My frowning students carve
    Me monsters out of prose:
This one—a gargoyle—thumbs its contemptuous nose
At how, in English, subject must agree

E.S.L. English as a Second Language

With verb—for any such agreement shows   5
    Too great a willingness to serve,
        A docility

        Which wiry Miss Choi
        Finds un-American.
She steals a hard look at me. I wink. Her grin   10
Is my reward. *In his will, our peace, our Pass:*
Gargoyle erased, subject and verb now in
        Agreement, reach object, enjoy
            Temporary truce.

        Tonight my students must   15
        Agree or disagree:
America is still a land of opportunity.
The answer is always, uniformly, *Yes*—even though
"It has no doubt that here were to much free,"
        As Miss Torrico will insist.   20
            She and I both know

    That Language binds us fast,
        And those of us without
Are bound and gagged by those within. Each fledgling
Polyglot must shake old habits: tapping her sneakered feet, 25
Miss Choi exorcises incensed ancestors, flout-
        ing the ghosts of her Chinese past.
            Writhing in the seat

        Next to Miss Choi, Mister
        Fedakis, in anguish   30
Labors to express himself in a tongue which
Proves *Linear B* to me, when I attempt to read it
Later. They're here for English as a Second Language,
        Which I'm teaching this semester.
                God knows they need it,   35

        And so, thank God, do they.
        The night's made easier
By our agreement: I am here to help deliver
Them into the good life they write me papers about.
English is pre-requisite for that endeavor,   40
        Explored in their nightly essays
                Boldly setting out

To reconnoiter the fair
New World they would enter:
Suburban Paradise, the endless shopping center   45
Where one may browse for hours before one chooses
Some new necessity—gold-flecked magenta
    Wallpaper to re-do the spare
        Bath no one uses,

    Or a machine which can,   50
        In seven seconds, crush
A newborn calf into such seamless mush
As a *mousse* might be made of—or our true sublime:
The gleaming counters where frosted cosmeticians brush
        Decades from the allotted span,   55
            Abrogating Time

        As the spring tide brushes
            A single sinister
Footprint from the otherwise unwrinkled shore
Of America the Blank. In absolute confusion   60
Poor Mister Fedakis rumbles with despair
        And puts the finishing smutches
            To his conclusion

    While Miss Choi erases:
        One more gargoyle routed.   65
Their pure, erroneous lines yield an illuminated
Map of the new found land. We will never arrive there,
Since it exists only in what we say about it,
        As all the rest of my class is
            Bound to discover.   70

                                            —1987

SHARON OLDS ■ (b. 1942)

*Sharon Olds displays a candor in dealing with the intimacies of family ro-
mance covering three generations that has made her one of the chief contemporary heirs to the confessional tradition. A powerful and dramatic
reader, she is much in demand on the lecture circuit. Born in San Francisco,
she currently resides in New York City.*

The One Girl at the Boys Party

When I take my girl to the swimming party
I set her down among the boys. They tower and
bristle, she stands there smooth and sleek,
her math scores unfolding in the air around her.
They will strip to their suits, her body hard and   5
indivisible as a prime number,
they'll plunge into the deep end, she'll subtract
her height from ten feet, divide it into
hundreds of gallons of water, the numbers
bouncing in her mind like molecules of chlorine   10
in the bright blue pool. When they climb out,
her ponytail will hang its pencil lead
down her back, her narrow silk suit
with hamburgers and french fries printed on it
will glisten in the brilliant air, and they will   15
see her sweet face, solemn and
sealed, a factor of one, and she will
see their eyes, two each,
their legs, two each, and the curves of their sexes,
one each, and in her head she'll be doing her   20
wild multiplying, as the drops
sparkle and fall to the power of a thousand from her body.

—1983

DIANE LOCKWARD ■ (b. 1943)

*Diane Lockward is a former high school English teacher who now works as
a poet-in-the-schools for both the New Jersey State Council on the Arts
and the Geraldine R. Dodge Foundation. She has received numerous
awards for her poetry, which has appeared in many literary journals, but
her first full-length collection,* Eve's Red Dress, *did not appear until 2003.
"My Husband Discovers Poetry" has been read by Garrison Keillor several
times on National Public Radio's* The Writer's Almanac. *Lockward has
commented that "My Husband Discovers Poetry" is, in fact, her husband's
favorite poem.*

My Husband Discovers Poetry

Because my husband would not read my poems,
I wrote one about how I did not love him.
In lines of strict iambic pentameter,
I detailed his coldness, his lack of humor.
It felt good to do this.   5

Stanza by stanza, I grew bolder and bolder.
Towards the end, struck by inspiration,
I wrote about my old boyfriend,
a boy I had not loved enough to marry
but who could make me laugh and laugh.   10
I wrote about a night years after we parted
when my husband's coldness drove me from the house
and back to my old boyfriend.
I even included the name of a seedy motel
well-known for hosting quickies.   15
I have a talent for verisimilitude.

In sensuous images, I described
how my boyfriend and I stripped off our clothes,
got into bed, and kissed and kissed,
then spent half the night telling jokes,   20
many of them about my husband.
I left the ending deliberately ambiguous,
then hid the poem away
in an old trunk in the basement.

You know how this story ends,   25
how my husband one day loses something,
goes into the basement,
and rummages through the old trunk,
how he uncovers the hidden poem
and sits down to read it.   30

But do you hear the strange sounds
that floated up the stairs that day,
the sounds of an animal, its paw caught
in one of those traps with teeth of steel?
Do you see the wounded creature   35

at the bottom of the stairs,
his shoulders hunched over and shaking,
fist in his mouth and choking back sobs?
It was my husband paying tribute to my art.

—2003

ELLEN BRYANT VOIGT ■ (b. 1943)

Ellen Bryant Voigt is a native of Virginia. Voigt was trained as a concert pianist before earning her creative writing degree from the University of Iowa. She has taught poetry at a number of colleges in New England and the South.

Daughter

There is one grief worse than any other.

When your small feverish throat clogged, and quit,
I knelt beside the chair on the green rug
and shook you and shook you,
but the only sound was mine shouting you back,   5
the delicate curls at your temples,
the blue wool blanket,
your face blue,
your jaw clamped against remedy—

how could I put a knife to that white neck?   10
With you in my lap,
my hands fluttering like flags,
I bend instead over your dead weight
to administer a kiss so urgent, so ruthless,
pumping breath into your stilled body,   15
counting out the rhythm for how long until
the second birth, the second cry
oh Jesus that sudden noisy musical inhalation
that leaves me stunned
by your survival.   20

—1983

Robert Morgan is a native of the mountains of North Carolina, and has re-
tained a large measure of regional ties in his poetry. One of his collections,
Sigodlin, *takes its title from an Appalachian word for things that are built*
slightly out of square. Gap Creek: The Story of a Marriage, *a novel of turn-*
of-the-century mountain life, was a bestseller in 2000.

Mountain Bride

They say Revis found a flatrock
on the ridge just
perfect for a natural hearth,
and built his cabin with a stick

and clay chimney right over it.   5
On their wedding night he lit
the fireplace to dry away the mountain
chill of late spring, and flung on

applewood to dye
the room with molten color while   10
he and Martha that was a Parrish
warmed the sheets between the tick

stuffed with leaves and its feather
cover. Under that wide hearth
a nest of rattlers,   15
they'll knot a hundred together,

had wintered and were coming awake.
The warming rock
flushed them out early.
It was she   20

who wakened to their singing near
the embers and roused him to go look.
Before he reached the fire
more than a dozen struck

and he died yelling her to stay   25
on the big four-poster.
Her uncle coming up the hollow
with a gift bearham two days later

found her shivering there
marooned above a pool   30
of hungry snakes,
and the body beginning to swell.

—1979

CRAIG RAINE ■ (b. 1944)

Craig Raine early in his career displayed a comic surrealism that was responsible for so many imitations that critic James Fenton dubbed him the founder of the "Martian School" of contemporary poetry. Born in Bishop Auckland, England, and educated at Oxford, Raine is publisher of the literary magazine Arete.

A Martian Sends a Postcard Home

Caxtons° are mechanical birds with many wings
and some are treasured for their markings—

they cause the eyes to melt
or the body to shriek without pain.

I have never seen one fly, but   5
sometimes they perch on the hand.

Mist is when the sky is tired of flight
and rests its soft machine on ground:

then the world is dim and bookish
like engravings under tissue paper.   10

Rain is when the earth is television.
It has the property of making colours darker.

Model T is a room with the lock inside—
a key is turned to free the world

for movement, so quick there is a film   15
to watch for anything missed.

But time is tied to the wrist
or kept in a box, ticking with impatience.

---

1 **Caxtons** i.e., books after William Caxton (1422–1491), first English printer

In homes, a haunted apparatus sleeps,
that snores when you pick it up.   20

If the ghost cries, they carry it
to their lips and soothe it to sleep

with sounds. And yet, they wake it up
deliberately, by tickling with a finger.

Only the young are allowed to suffer   25
openly. Adults go to a punishment room

with water but nothing to eat.
They lock the door and suffer the noises

alone. No one is exempt
and everyone's pain has a different smell.   30

At night, when all the colours die,
they hide in pairs

and read about themselves—
in colour, with their eyelids shut.

—1978

ENID SHOMER ■ (b. 1944)

Enid Shomer grew up in Washington, D.C., and lived for a number of years in Florida. Her first collection, Stalking the Florida Panther *(1987), explored both the Jewish traditions of her childhood and her adult attachment to her adopted state. In recent years she has published* Imaginary Men, *a collection of short stories, and* Black Drum, *a collection of poetry.*

Women Bathing at Bergen-Belsen°

April 24, 1945

Twelve hours after the Allies arrive
there is hot water, soap. Two women bathe
in a makeshift, open-air shower while nearby
fifteen thousand are flung naked into mass graves
by captured SS guards. Clearly legs and arms   5

Bergen-Belsen German concentration camp in WWII

are the natural handles of a corpse. The bathers,
taken late in the war, still have flesh
on their bones, still have breasts. Though nudity was
a death sentence here, they have undressed,
oblivious to the soldiers and the cameras.   10
The corpses push through the limed earth like upended
headstones. The bathers scrub their feet, bending
in beautiful curves, mapping the contours
of the body, that kingdom to which they've returned.

—1987

WENDY COPE ■ (b. 1945)

*Wendy Cope says, "I hardly ever tire of love or rhyme. / That's why I'm poor
and have a rotten time." Her first collection,* Making Cocoa for Kingsley
Amis *(1986), was a bestseller in England. Whether reducing T. S. Eliot's
modernist classic "The Waste Land" to a set of five limericks or chronicling
the life and loves of Jason Strugnell, her feckless poetic alter-ego, Cope remains one of the wisest and wittiest poets writing today. "I dislike the term
'light verse' because it is used as a way of dismissing poets who allow humor
into their work. I believe that a humorous poem can also be 'serious'; deeply
felt and saying something that matters." She lives in Winchester, England.*

Rondeau Redoublé

There are so many kinds of awful men—
One can't avoid them all. She often said
She'd never make the same mistake again:
She always made a new mistake instead.

The chinless type who made her feel ill-bred;   5
The practised charmer, less than charming when
He talked about the wife and kids and fled—
There are so many kinds of awful men.

The half-crazed hippy, deeply into Zen,
Whose cryptic homilies she came to dread;   10
The fervent youth who worshipped Tony Benn°—
'One can't avoid them all,' she often said.

11 **Tony Benn** British politician of the 1960s

The ageing banker, rich and overfed,
who held forth on the dollar and the yen—
Though there were many more mistakes ahead,   15
She'd never make the same mistake again.

The budding poet, scribbling in his den
Odes not to her but to his pussy, Fred;
The drunk who fell asleep at nine or ten—
She always made a new mistake instead.   20

And so the gambler was at least unwed
And didn't preach or sneer or wield a pen
Or hoard his wealth or take the Scotch to bed.
She'd lived and learned and lived and learned but then
There are so many kinds.   25

                                              —1986

DICK DAVIS ■ (b. 1945)

*Dick Davis was born in Portsmouth, England, and, following graduation
from Cambridge and the University of Manchester, taught for many years in
England and in Iran. A scholar and translator as well as a poet, he came to
the United States in the 1980s and is currently a professor of Persian at Ohio
State University.*

A Monorhyme for the Shower

Lifting her arms to soap her hair
Her pretty breasts respond—and there
The movement of that buoyant pair
Is like a spell to make me swear
Twenty-odd years have turned to air;   5
Now she's the girl I didn't dare
Approach, ask out, much less declare
My love to, mired in young despair.

Childbearing, rows, domestic care—
All the prosaic wear and tear   10
That constitute the life we share—

Slip from her beautiful and bare
Bright body as, made half aware
Of my quick surreptitious stare,
She wrings the water from her hair   15
And turning smiles to see me there.

—2002

KAY RYAN ■ (b. 1945)

*Kay Ryan has taught for many years in California. She published her first
collection at the age of thirty-eight in 1983, and her poems have appeared in
four subsequent books and numerous appearances in* Poetry *and* The New
Yorker. *Ryan has often been compared to Emily Dickinson and Marianne
Moore for her attention to details from the natural world and for her gentle,
often witty moralizing. She is a former U.S. Poet Laureate.*

Bestiary

A bestiary catalogs
bests. The mediocres
both higher and lower
are suppressed in favor
of the singularly savage   5
or clever, the spectacularly
pincered, the archest
of the arch deceivers
who press their advantage
without quarter even after   10
they've won as of course they would.
Best is not to be confused with *good*—
a different creature altogether,
and treated of in the goodiary—
a text alas lost now for centuries. 15

—1996

Leon Stokesbury, as an undergraduate at Lamar State College of Technology (now Lamar University), published a poem in The New Yorker. *The author of three collections of poetry, including* Autumn Rhythm: New and Selected Poems, *Stokesbury has also edited anthologies of contemporary Southern poetry and the poetry of World War II.*

The Day Kennedy Died

Suppose that on the day Kennedy died
you had a vision. But this was no inner movie
with a discernible plot or anything like it.
Not even very visual when you get down
to admitting what actually occurred.   5
About two-thirds of the way through 4th period
Senior Civics, fifteen minutes before
the longed-for lunchtime, suppose you stood up
for no good reason—no reason at all really—
and announced, as you never had before,   10
to the class in general and to yourself
as well, "Something. Something is happening.
I see. Something coming. I can see. I . . ."

And that was all. You stood there: blank.
The class roared. Even Phyllis Hoffpaur, girl   15
most worshipped by you from afar that year,
turned a vaguely pastel shade of red
and smiled, and Richard Head, your best friend,
Dick Head to the chosen few, pulled you down
to your desk whispering, "Jesus, man! Jesus   20
Christ!" Then you went numb. You did not know
for sure what had occurred. But less than one hour
later, when Stella (despised) Vandenburg, teacher
of twelfth grade English, came sashaying
into the auditorium, informing, left and right,   25
as many digesting members of the student body
as she could of what she had just heard,

several students began to glance at you,
remembering what you'd said. A few pointed,
whispering to their confederates, and on that
disturbing day they slinked away in the halls.
Even Dick Head did not know what to say.

In 5th period Advanced Math, Principal
Crawford played the radio over the intercom
and the school dropped deeper into history.
For the rest of that day, everyone slinked away—
except for the one moment Phyllis Hoffpaur
stared hard, the look on her face asking,
assuming you would know, "Will it be ok?"

And you did not know. No one knew.
Everyone staggered back to their houses
that evening aimless and lost, not knowing,
certainly sensing something had been
changed forever. *Silsbee High forever!*
That is our claim! Never, no never!
Will we lose our fame! you often sang.
But this was to be the class of 1964,
afraid of the future at last, who would select,
as the class song, Terry Stafford's *Suspicion.*
And this was November—even in Texas
the month of failings, month of sorrows—
from which there was no turning.
It would be a slow two-months slide until
the manic beginnings of the British Invasion,
three months before Clay's ascension to the throne,
but all you saw walking home that afternoon
were the gangs of gray leaves clotting the curbs
and culverts, the odors of winter forever
in the air: cold, damp, bleak, dead, dull:
dragging you toward the solstice like a tide.

—2004

30

35

40

45

50

55

60

John Whitworth was born in Nasik, India, the son of a civil servant, and grew up in Edinburgh. After graduating from Merton College, Oxford, he taught English as a foreign language for some years before becoming a full-time writer. The author of numerous collections of verse, including the children's book The Complete Poetical Works of Phoebe Flood, he lives in Canterbury. "The Examiners" was a finalist in a readers' poll run by the Times Literary Supplement.

The Examiners

Where the house is cold and empty and the garden's overgrown,
  They are there.
Where the letters lie unopened by a disconnected phone,
  They are there.
Where your footsteps echo strangely on each moonlit cobblestone, 5
Where a shadow streams behind you but the shadow's not
  your own,
You may think the world's your oyster but it's bone, bone, bone:
  They are there, they are there, they are there.

They can parse a Latin sentence; they're as learned as Plotinus,°
  They are there.   10
They're as sharp as Ockham's razor,° they're as subtle as Aquinas,°
  They are there.
They define us and refine us with their beta-query-minus,°
They're the wall-constructing Emperors of undiscovered Chinas,
They confine us, then malign us, in the end they undermine us,   15
  They are there, they are there, they are there.

They assume it as an impost or they take it as a toll,
  They are there.
The contractors grant them all that they incontinently stole,
  They are there.   20
They will shrivel your ambition with their quality control,

---

9 **Plotinus** neo-Platonic philosopher (204–270)   11 **Ockham 's razor** a philosophical proposition by William of Ockham (1288–1347) that the simplest solution to a problem is always the best choice   **Aquinas** (1225–1274) Italian Catholic philosopher and theologian   13 **beta-query-minus** in British universities a mediocre grade (B-)

They will dessicate your passion, then eviscerate your soul,
Wring your life out like a sponge and stuff your body down a hole,
	They are there, they are there, they are there.

In the desert of your dreaming they are humped behind the
	dunes, 25
	They are there.
On the undiscovered planet with its seven circling moons,
	They are there.
They are ticking all the boxes, making sure you eat your prunes,
They are sending secret messages by helium balloons,   30
They are humming Bach cantatas, they are playing looney tunes
	They are there, they are there, they are there.

They are there, they are there like a whisper on the air,
	They are there.
They are slippery and soapy with our hope and our despair,   35
	They are there.
So it's idle if we bridle or pretend we never care,
If the questions are superfluous and the marking isn't fair,
For we know they're going to get us, we just don't know when or
	where,
	They are there, they are there, they are there. 40

—2007

MARILYN NELSON ■ (b. 1946)

Marilyn Nelson is the author of The Homeplace, *a sequence of poems on family history.* The Homeplace *is remarkable for its sensitive exploration of the mixed white and black bloodlines in the poet's family history.* Carver: A Life in Poems, *a poetic biography of George Washington Carver, appeared in 2001 and won a National Book Award.* A Wreath for Emmett Till, *a sonnet sequence about a famous hate crime in 1995 Mississippi, appeared in 2005. Both of these books are for young readers.*

The Ballad of Aunt Geneva

Geneva was the wild one.
Geneva was a tart.
Geneva met a blue-eyed boy
and gave away her heart.

MARILYN NELSON

754

Geneva ran a roadhouse.
Geneva wasn't sent
to college like the others:
Pomp's pride her punishment.

She cooked out on the river,
watching the shore slide by,
her lips pursed into hardness,
her deep-set brown eyes dry.

They say she killed a woman
over a good black man
by braining the jealous heifer
with an iron frying pan.

They say, when she was eighty,
she got up late at night
and sneaked her old, white lover in
to make love, and to fight.

First, they heard the tell-tale
singing of the springs,
then Geneva's voice rang out:
I need to buy some things,

So next time, bring more money.
And bring more moxie, too.
I ain't got no time to waste
on limp white mens like you.

Oh yeah? Well, Mister White Man,
it sure might be stone-white,
but my thing's white as it is.
And you know damn well I'm right.

Now listen: take your heart pills
and pay the doctor mind.
If you up and die on me,
I'll whip your white behind.

They tiptoed through the parlor
on heavy, time-slowed feet.
She watched him, from her front door,
walk down the dawnlit street.

Geneva was the wild one.
Geneva was a tart.
Geneva met a blue-eyed boy
and gave away her heart.

—1990

AI ■ (b. 1947–2010)

Ai wrote a number of realistic dramatic monologues that often reveal the agonies of characters trapped in unfulfilling or even dangerous lives. With her gallery of social misfits, she was the contemporary heir to the tradition begun by Robert Browning.

Child Beater

Outside, the rain, pinafore of gray water, dresses the town
and I stroke the leather belt,
as she sits in the rocking chair,
holding a crushed paper cup to her lips.
I yell at her, but she keeps rocking;   5
back, her eyes open, forward, they close.
Her body, somehow fat, though I feed her only once a day,
reminds me of my own just after she was born.
It's been seven years, but I still can't forget how I felt.
How heavy it feels to look at her.   10

I lay the belt on a chair
and get her dinner bowl.
I hit the spoon against it, set it down
and watch her crawl to it,
pausing after each forward thrust of her legs   15
and when she takes her first bite,
I grab the belt and beat her across the back
until her tears, beads of salt-filled glass, falling,
shatter on the floor.

I move off. I let her eat,
while I get my dog's chain leash from the closet.
I whirl it around my head.
O daughter, so far, you've only had a taste of icing,
are you ready now for some cake?

JIM HALL ■ (b. 1947)

Jim Hall is one of the most brilliantly inventive comic poets in recent years.
He has also written a successful series of crime novels set in his native south
Florida, beginning with Under Cover of Daylight *in 1987.*

Maybe Dats Your
Pwoblem Too

All my pwoblems,
who knows, maybe evvybody's pwoblems
is due to da fact, due to da awful twuth
dat I am SPIDERMAN.
I know, I know. All da dumb jokes: 5
No flies on you, ha ha,
and da ones about what do I do wit all
doze extwa legs in bed. Well, dat's funny yeah.
But you twy being
SPIDERMAN for a month or two. Go ahead.   10

You get doze cwazy calls fwom da
Gubbener askin you to twap some booglar who's
only twying to wip off color T.V. sets.
Now, what do I cawre about T.V. sets?
But I pull on da suit, da stinkin suit,   15
wit da sucker cups on da fingers,
and get my wopes and wittle bundle of
equipment and den I go flying like cwazy
acwoss da town fwom woof top to woof top.

Till der he is. Some poor dumb color T.V. slob   20
and I fall on him and we westle a widdle
until I get him all woped. So big deal.

You tink when you SPIDERMAN
der's sometin big going to happen to you.
Well, I tell you what. It don't happen dat way.   25
Nuttin happens. Gubbener calls, I go.
Bwing him to powice, Gubbener calls again,
like dat over and over.
I tink I twy sometin diffunt. I tink I twy
sometin excitin like wacing cawrs. Sometin to make   30
my heart beat at a difwent wate.
But den you just can't quit being sometin like
SPIDERMAN.
You SPIDERMAN for life. Fowever. I can't even
buin my suit. It won't buin. It's fwame wesistent.   35
So maybe dat's youwr pwoblem too, who knows.
Maybe dat's da whole pwoblem wif evwytin.
Nobody can buin der suits, dey all fwame wesistent.
Who knows?

—1980

YUSEF KOMUNYAKAA ■ (b. 1947)

*Yusef Komunyakaa is a native of Bogulusa, Louisiana. Komunyakaa has
written memorably on a wide range of subjects, including jazz and his service during the Vietnam War.* Neon Vernacular: New and Selected Poems
(1993) *won the Pulitzer Prize in 1994, and* Pleasure Dome: New and Collected Poems *appeared in 2001.*

Facing It

My black face fades,
hiding inside the black granite.
I said I wouldn't,
dammit: No tears.
I'm stone. I'm flesh.   5

My clouded reflection eyes me
like a bird of prey, the profile of night
slanted against morning. I turn
this way—the stone lets me go.
I turn this way—I'm inside   10
the Vietnam Veterans Memorial
again, depending on the light
to make a difference.
I go down the 58,022 names,
half-expecting to find   15
my own in letters like smoke.
I touch the name Andrew Johnson;
I see the booby trap's white flash.
Names shimmer on a woman's blouse
but when she walks away   20
the names stay on the wall.
Brushstrokes flash, a red bird's
wings cutting across my stare.
The sky. A plane in the sky.
A white vet's image floats   25
closer to me, then his pale eyes
look through mine. I'm a window.
He's lost his right arm
inside the stone. In the black mirror
a woman's trying to erase names: 30
No, she's brushing a boy's hair.

—1988

TIMOTHY STEELE ■ (b. 1948)

*Timothy Steele has written a successful scholarly study of the rise of free
verse,* Missing Measures, *and is perhaps the most skillful craftsman of the
contemporary New Formalist poets. Born in Vermont, he has lived for a
number of years in Los Angeles, where he teaches at California State University, Los Angeles.*

Sapphics° Against Anger

Angered, may I be near a glass of water;
May my first impulse be to think of Silence,
Its deities (who are they? do, in fact, they
    Exist? etc.).

May I recall what Aristotle says of   5
The subject: to give vent to rage is not to
Release it but to be increasingly prone
    To its incursions.

May I imagine being in the Inferno,
Hearing it asked: "Virgilio mio,° who's   10
That sulking with Achilles there?" and hearing
    Virgil say: "Dante,

That fellow, at the slightest provocation,
Slammed phone receivers down, and waved his arms like
A madman. What Attila did to Europe,   15
    What Genghis Khan did

To Asia, that poor dope did to his marriage."
May I, that is, put learning to good purpose,
Mindful that melancholy is a sin, though
    Stylish at present.   20

Better than rage is the post-dinner quiet,
The sink's warm turbulence, the streaming platters,
The suds rehearsing down the drain in spirals
    In the last rinsing.

For what is, after all, the good life save that   25
Conducted thoughtfully, and what is passion
If not the holiest of powers, sustaining
    Only if mastered.

—1986

TIMOTHY STEELE

760

Sapphics stanza form named after Sappho (c. 650 BC)   10 Virgilio mio Dante is addressing Virgil, his guide through hell.

JAMES FENTON ■ (b. 1949)

*James Fenton was born in Lincoln, England, and educated at Oxford. Fenton
has worked extensively as a book and drama critic. A brilliant satirical poet,
he has also written lyrics for* Les Misérables, *the musical version of Victor
Hugo's novel, and has served as a journalist in Asia.*

God, a Poem

A nasty surprise in a sandwich,
A drawing-pin caught in your sock,
The limpest of shakes from a hand which
You'd thought would be firm as a rock,

A serious mistake in a nightie,   5
A grave disappointment all around
Is all that you'll get from th'Almighty.
Is all that you'll get underground.

Oh, he *said:* 'If you lay off the crumpet°
I'll see you alright in the end.   10
Just hang on until the last trumpet.
Have faith in me, chum—I'm your friend.'

But if you remind him, he'll tell you:
'I'm sorry, I must have been pissed°—
Though your name rings a sort of a bell. You   15
Should have guessed that I do not exist.

'I didn't exist at Creation,
I didn't exist at the Flood.
And I won't be around for Salvation
To sort out the sheep from the cud—   20

'Or whatever the phrase is. The fact is
In soteriological° terms
I'm a crude existential malpractice
And you are a diet of worms.

---

9 crumpet vulgar British slang for women   **14 pissed** drunk   **22 soteriological** relation to
salvation

'You're a nasty surprise in a sandwich.   25
You're a drawing-pin caught in my sock.
You're the limpest of shakes from a hand which
I'd have thought would be firm as a rock,

'You're a serious mistake in a nightie,
You're a grave disappointment all round—   30
That's all that you are,' says th'Almighty,
'And that's all that you'll be underground.'

—*1983*

SARAH CORTEZ ■ (b. 1950)

*Sarah Cortez grew up in Houston, Texas, and holds degrees in psychology
and religion, classical studies, and accounting. She also serves as Visiting
Scholar at the University of Houston's Center for Mexican-American Studies.
She is a deputy constable in Harris County, Texas.*

Tu Negrito

She's got to bail me out,
he says into the phone outside the holding cell.
She's going there tomorrow anyway for Mikey.
Tell her she's got to do this for me.

He says into the phone outside the holding cell,   5
Make sure she listens. Make her feel guilty, man.
Tell her she's got to do this for me.
She can have all my money, man.

Make sure she listens. Make her feel guilty, man.
Tell her she didn't bail me out the other times.   10
She can have all my money, man.
She always bails out Mikey.

Tell her she didn't bail me out the other times.
I don't got no one else to call, cousin.
She always bails out Mikey.   15
Make sure you write all this down, cousin.

I don't got no one else to call, cousin.
I really need her now.
Make sure you write this all down, cousin.
Page her. Put in code 333. That's me.   20

I really need her now.
Write down "Mommie." Change it from "Mom."
Page her. Put in code 333. That's me.
Write down "*Tu Negrito*." Tell her I love her.

Write down "Mommie." Change it from "Mom."   25
I'm her littlest. Remind her.
Write down "*Tu Negrito*."
Tell her I love her. She's got to bail me out.

—2000

CAROLYN FORCHÉ ■ (b. 1950)

Carolyn Forché won the Yale Younger Poets Award for her first collection,
Gathering the Tribes *(1975). The* Country Between Us, *Forché's second
collection, contains poems based on the poet's experiences in the war-torn
country of El Salvador in the early 1980s.*

The Colonel

What you have heard is true. I was in his house.° His wife carried
a tray of coffee and sugar. His daughter filed her nails, his son
went out for the night. There were daily papers, pet dogs, a pistol
on the cushion beside him. The moon swung bare on its black
cord over the house. On the television was a cop show. It was in
English. Broken bottles were embedded in the walls around the
house to scoop the kneecaps from a man's legs or cut his hands to
lace. On the windows there were gratings like those in liquor
stores. We had dinner, rack of lamb, good wine, a gold bell was on
the table for calling the maid. The maid brought green mangoes,
salt, a type of bread. I was asked how I enjoyed the country. There
was a brief commercial in Spanish. His wife took everything away.

1 **his house** in El Salvador

There was some talk then of how difficult it had become to govern. The parrot said hello on the terrace. The colonel told it to shut up, and pushed himself from the table. My friend said to me with his eyes: say nothing. The colonel returned with a sack used to bring groceries home. He spilled many human ears on the table. They were like dried peach halves. There is no other way to say this. He took one of them in his hands, shook it in our faces, dropped it into a water glass. It came alive there. I am tired of fooling around he said. As for the rights of anyone, tell your people they can go fuck themselves. He swept the ears to the floor with his arm and held the last of his wine in the air. Something for your poetry, no? he said. Some of the ears on the floor caught this scrap of his voice. Some of the ears on the floor were pressed to the ground.

—1978

DANA GIOIA ■ (b. 1950)

Dana Gioia grew up in the suburbs of Los Angeles. He took a graduate degree in English from Harvard but made a successful career in business before devoting his full time to writing. The editor of several textbooks and anthologies, he is also an influential critic whose essay "Can Poetry Matter?" stimulated much discussion when it appeared in The Atlantic. *Interrogations at Noon, his third collection of poetry, appeared in 2001. Gioia became chairman of the National Endowment for the Arts in 2002.*

Planting a Sequoia

All afternoon my brothers and I have worked in the orchard,
Digging this hole, laying you into it, carefully packing the soil.
Rain blackened the horizon, but cold winds kept it over the
    Pacific,
And the sky above us stayed the dull gray
Of an old year coming to an end.   5

In Sicily a father plants a tree to celebrate his first son's birth—
An olive or a fig tree—a sign that the earth has one more life
    to bear.

I would have done the same, proudly laying new stock into my
    father's orchard,
A green sapling rising among the twisted apple boughs,
A promise of new fruit in other autumns.   10

But today we kneel in the cold planting you, our native giant,
Defying the practical custom of our fathers,
Wrapping in your roots a lock of hair, a piece of an infant's
    birth cord,
All that remains above earth of a first-born son,
A few stray atoms brought back to the elements.   15

We will give you what we can—our labor and our soil,
Water drawn from the earth when the skies fail,
Nights scented with the ocean fog, days softened by the circuit
    of bees.
We plant you in the corner of the grove, bathed in western light,
A slender shoot against the sunset.   20

And when our family is no more, all of his unborn brothers dead,
Every niece and nephew scattered, the house torn down,
His mother's beauty ashes in the air,
I want you to stand among strangers, all young and ephemeral
    to you,
Silently keeping the secret of your birth.   25

—*1991*

RODNEY JONES ■ (b. 1950)

Rodney Jones was born in Alabama and received important national attention when Transparent Gestures won the Poets' Prize in 1990. Like many younger southern poets, he often deals with the difficult legacy of racism and the adjustments that a new era have forced on both whites and blacks.

Winter Retreat: Homage to Martin Luther King, Jr.

There is a hotel in Baltimore where we came together,
  we black and white educated and educators,
    for a week of conferences, for important counsel

sanctioned by the DOE° and the Carter administration,
to make certain difficult inquiries, to collate notes   5
on the instruction of the disabled, the deprived,
the poor, who do not score well on entrance tests,
who, failing school, must go with mop and pail
skittering across the slick floors of cafeterias,
or climb dewy girders to balance high above cities,   10
or, jobless, line up in the bone cold. We felt
substantive burdens lighter if we stated it right.
Very delicately, we spoke in turn. We walked
together beside the still waters of behaviorism.
Armed with graphs and charts, with new strategies   15
to devise objectives and determine accountability,
we empathetic black and white shone in seminar rooms.
We enunciated every word clearly and without accent.
We moved very carefully in the valley of the shadow
of the darkest agreement error. We did not digress.   20
We ascended the trunk of that loftiest cypress
of Latin grammar the priests could never
successfully graft onto the rough green chestnut
of the English language. We extended ourselves
with that sinuous motion of the tongue that is half   25
pain and almost eloquence. We black and white
politely reprioritized the parameters of our agenda
to impact equitably on the Seminole and the Eskimo.
We praised diversity and involvement, the sacrifices
of fathers and mothers. We praised the next white   30
Gwendolyn Brooks° and the next black Robert Burns.°
We deep made friends. In that hotel we glistened
over the *pommes au gratin*° and the *poitrine de veau.*°
The morsels of lamb flamed near where we talked.
The waiters bowed and disappeared among the ferns.   35
And there is a bar there, there is a large pool.
Beyond the tables of the drinkers and raconteurs,

RODNEY JONES

4 **DOE** Department of Education   31 **Gwendolyn Brooks** African-American poet (1917–2000)
Robert Burns Scottish poet (1759–1796)   33 *pommes au gratin* potatoes baked with cheese   *poitrine de veau* brisket of veal

beyond the hot tub brimming with Lebanese tourists
and the women in expensive bathing suits doing laps,
if you dive down four feet, swim out far enough,   40
and emerge on the other side, it is sixteen degrees.
It is sudden and very beautiful and colder
than thought, though the air frightens you at first,
not because it is cold, but because it is visible,
almost palpable, in the fog that rises from difference.   45
While I stood there in the cheek-numbing snow,
all Baltimore was turning blue. And what I remember
of that week of talks is nothing the record shows,
but the revelation outside, which was the city
many came to out of the fields, then the thought   50
that we had wanted to make the world kinder,
but, in speaking proudly, we had failed a vision.

—1989

TIMOTHY MURPHY ■ (b. 1951)

*Timothy Murphy, a former student of Robert Penn Warren at Yale, returned
to his native North Dakota to make a career as a venture capitalist in the
agricultural field. Unpublished until his mid-forties, Murphy has brought
four collections to print during the last decade.*

Case Notes

for Dr. Richard Kolotkin
March 7, 2002

Raped at an early age
by older altar boy.
"Damned by the Church to Hell,
never to sire a son,
perhaps man's greatest joy,"   5
said father in a rage.
Patient was twenty-one.
Handled it pretty well.

March 14, 2002

Curiously, have learned
patient was Eagle Scout.   10
Outraged that Scouts have spurned
each camper who is "out."
Questioned if taunts endured
are buried? "No, immured."

March 21, 2002

Immersed in verse and drink   15
when he was just sixteen,
turned to drugs at Yale.
Patient began to sink,
to fear he was a "queen,"
a "queer" condemned to fail   20
or detox in a jail.

April 1, 2002

Into a straight town
he brought a sober lover.
"Worked smarter, drank harder
to stock an empty larder,"   25
wrote poetry, the cover
for grief he cannot drown.

April 9, 2002

Uneasy with late father,
feared for by his mother,
lover, and younger brother.   30
Various neuroses,
but no severe psychosis.
Precarious prognosis.

—2004

Joy Harjo, a member of the Creek tribe, is one of the leading voices of contemporary Native American poetry. She is a powerful performer and was one of the poets featured on Bill Moyers's television series, The Power of the Word.

She Had Some Horses

She had some horses.
She had horses who were bodies of sand.
She had horses who were maps drawn of blood.
She had horses who were skins of ocean water.
She had horses who were the blue air of sky.   5
She had horses who were fur and teeth.
She had horses who were clay and would break.
She had horses who were splintered red cliff.

She had some horses.

She had horses with eyes of trains.   10
She had horses with full brown thighs.
She had horses who laughed too much.
She had horses who threw rocks at glass houses.
She had horses who licked razor blades.

She had some horses.   15

She had horses who danced in their mother's arms.
She had horses who thought they were the sun and
their bodies shone and burned like stars.
She had horses who waltzed nightly on the moon.
She had horses who were much too shy, and kept quiet   20
    in stalls of their own making.

She had some horses.

She had horses who liked Creek Stomp Dance songs.
She had horses who cried in their beer.
She had horses who spit at male queens who made   25
    them afraid of themselves.
She had horses who said they weren't afraid.
She had horses who lied.

She had horses who told the truth, who were stripped
    bare of their tongues.   30

She had some horses.

She had horses who called themselves "horse."
She had horses who called themselves "spirit,"
and kept their voices secret and to themselves.
She had horses who had no names.   35
She had horses who had books of names.

She had some horses.

She had horses who whispered in the dark, who were afraid
    to speak.
She had horses who screamed out of fear of the silence,
who carried knives to protect themselves from ghosts.   40
She had horses who waited for destruction.
She had horses who waited for resurrection.

She had some horses.

She had horses who got down on their knees for any savior.
She had horses who thought their high price had saved
    them.   45
She had horses who tried to save her,
who climbed in her bed at night and prayed as they raped her.

She had some horses.

She had some horses she loved.
She had some horses she hated.   50

They were the same horses.

—1983

ANDREW HUDGINS ■ (b. 1951)

Andrew Hudgins, reared in Montgomery, Alabama, has demonstrated his poetic skills in a wide variety of poems, including a book-length sequence of dramatic monologues, After the Lost War, *in the voice of Sidney Lanier, the greatest Southern poet of the late nineteenth century.*

Air View of an Industrial Scene

There is a train at the ramp, unloading people
who stumble from the cars and toward the gate.
The building's shadows tilt across the ground
and from each shadow juts a longer one
and from that shadow crawls a shadow of smoke   5
black as just-plowed earth. Inside the gate
is a small garden and someone on his knees.
Perhaps he's fingering the yellow blooms
to see which ones have set and will soon wither,
clinging to a green tomato as it swells.   10
The people hold back, but are forced to the open gate,
and when they enter they will see the garden
and some, gardeners themselves, will yearn
to fall to their knees there, untangling vines,
plucking at weeds, cooling their hands in damp earth.   15
They're going to die soon, a matter of minutes.
Even from our height, we see in the photograph
the shadow of the plane stamped dark and large
on Birkenau,° one black wing shading the garden.
We can't tell which are guards, which prisoners.   20
We're watchers. But if we had bombs we'd drop them.

—1985

ROBERT WRIGLEY ■ (b. 1951)

*Robert Wrigley grew up in an Illinois coal mining town and studied with poets
Madeline DeFrees, John Haines, and Richard Hugo at the University of Montana. A past recipient of the Kingsley Tufts Award and the Poets' Prize, he lives
on the Clearwater River in Idaho. Lives of the Animals appeared in 2003.*

Thatcher Bitchboy

She had brought home just a single white wing was all,
only that one through all the hellish August weeks
the fat man's chickens kept disappearing into,

---

19 Birkenau German concentration camp in World War II

and that one wing I buried myself in the manure pile
behind the barn, so that by the time he finally arrived, 5
Fat Man oozing from his high-backed truck
like a gristly hock onto the hot black skillet of the county
    road,
mostly all I felt was the least yawny pang of nerves.
I sat with my dog by the front porch.
"Thatcher bitchboy?" he asked, 10
and I allowed as how she was.
"Daddyhome?" he croaked,
and soon we all were there,
Daddy and me, that good bitch hound of mine sleeping
in a mottle of the day's last sun and shade, and the fat man 15
brandishing his blurred implicational snapshots.
There rose then a cloud of Daddy's might-could-bees
and a cloud also of Fat Man showly-izzes,
the sudden stormification of
which could have been why the sky itself 20
came on so holy and dark just then, a dreadnought cloak
I hoped the Goddumb damn dog would run off under,
but it was only when the light from Momma's
lamp in the living room window showed them there,
that it ended, and the fat man tied a rope 25
to the collar that convicted her,
and she licked his blunt and bulbous fingers with love
and servility ("tastez lack chickin doe-nit daug," he chortled to
    the dirt).
Good cur hound, your eyes on me leaving were a blue
I believed the starved-blood likes of God's own ledger, 30
all the betrayals in all the lands of earth and more
recorded therein, a blue like the lost unredeemable sky
I would myself be forever falling into,
some heaven of hellfires and ice
I have since that mouthhot night learned to breathe in 35
as though it were the exhalations of the finest funereal orchids,
an air I believed would teach me at last
how to pray, and most certainly
God help me
what for. 40

—2003

JUDITH ORTIZ COFER ■ (b. 1952)

Judith Ortiz Cofer was born in Puerto Rico, the daughter of a member of the United States Navy, and came to the United States at the age of four, when her father was posted to the Brooklyn Naval Yard. After college, she studied at Oxford and began her teaching career in the United States. A skilled writer of fiction and autobiography, she published The Year of Our Revolution: New and Selected Stories and Poems *in 1998.*

The Latin Deli: An Ars Poetica

Presiding over a formica counter,
plastic Mother and Child magnetized
to the top of an ancient register,
the heady mix of smells from the open bins
of dried codfish, the green plantains   5
hanging in stalks like votive offerings,
she is the Patroness of Exiles,
a woman of no-age who was never pretty,
who spends her days selling canned memories
while listening to the Puerto Ricans complain   10
that it would be cheaper to fly to San Juan
than to buy a pound of Bustelo coffee here,
and to Cubans perfecting their speech
of a "glorious return" to Havana—where no one
has been allowed to die and nothing to change until then,   15
to Mexicans who pass through, talking lyrically
of *dólares* to be made in El Norte—
                                                  all wanting the comfort
of spoken Spanish, to gaze upon the family portrait
of her plain wide face, her ample bosom   20
resting on her plump arms, her look of maternal interest
as they speak to her and each other
of their dreams and their disillusions—
how she smiles understanding,
when they walk down the narrow aisles of her store   25
reading the labels of packages aloud, as if
they were the names of lost lovers: *Suspiros,*
Merengues, the stale candy of everyone's childhood.
                                                  She spends her days

slicing *jamón y queso* and wrapping it in wax paper   30
tied with string: plain ham and cheese
that would cost less at the A&P, but it would not satisfy
the hunger of the fragile old man lost in the folds
of his winter coat, who brings her lists of items
that he reads to her like poetry, or the others,   35
whose needs she must divine, conjuring up products
from places that now exist only in their hearts—
closed ports she must trade with.

—1995

RITA DOVE ■ (b. 1952)

Rita Dove won the Pulitzer Prize in 1987 for Thomas and Beulah, *a sequence of poems about her grandparents' lives in Ohio. She is one of the most important voices of contemporary African-American poetry and served as poet laureate of the United States from 1993 to 1995. She is also a competitive ballroom dancer.*

American Smooth

We were dancing—it must have
been a foxtrot or a waltz,
something romantic but
requiring restraint,
rise and fall, precise   5
execution as we moved
into the next song without
stopping, two chests heaving
above a seven-league
stride—such perfect agony   10
one learns to smile through,
ecstatic mimicry
being the sine qua non°
of American Smooth.
And because I was distracted   15
by the effort of
keeping my frame

13 **sine qua non** an essential part (Latin)

(the leftward lean, head turned
just enough to gaze out
past your ear and always   20
smiling, smiling),
I didn't notice
how still you'd become until
we had done it
(for two measures?   25
four?)—achieved flight,
that swift and serene
magnificence, before the earth
remembered who we were
and brought us down.   30

—2004

MARK JARMAN ▪ (b. 1952)

Mark Jarman was born in Kentucky and has lived in California and Ten-
nessee, where he currently teaches at Vanderbilt University. With Robert
McDowell, he edited The Reaper, *a magazine specializing in narrative*
poetry. His most recent collection is To the Green Man *(2004).*

After Disappointment

To lie in your child's bed when she is gone
Is calming as anything I know. To fall
Asleep, her books arranged above your head,
Is to admit that you have never been
So tired, so enchanted by the spell   5
Of your grown body. To feel small instead
Of blocking out the light, to feel alone,
Not knowing what you should or shouldn't feel,
Is to find out, no matter what you've said
About the cramped escapes and obstacles   10
You plan and face and have to call the world,
That there remain these places, occupied
By children, yours if lucky, like the girl
Who finds you here and lies down by your side.

—1997

Julie Kane was born and raised in New Jersey and studied creative writing with Anne Sexton. For many years a resident of Louisiana, she has a Ph.D. from Louisiana State University and currently teaches at Northwestern State University in Natchitoches, Louisiana. Rhythm & Booze (2003) was selected for the National Poetry Series by Maxine Kumin. Skilled in such difficult forms as the villanelle (the subject of her dissertation), Kane recently co-edited (with Grace Bauer) Umpteen Ways of Looking at a Possum, *a collection of miscellaneous writings about Everette Maddox, a legendary New Orleans street poet.*

Alan Doll Rap

When I was ten
I wanted a Ken
to marry Barbie
I was into patriarchy
for plastic dolls   5
eleven inches tall
cuz the sixties hadn't yet
happened at all
Those demonstrations
assassinations   10
conflagrations across the nation
still nothin but a speck in the imagination
Yeah, Ken was the man
but my mama had the cash
and the boy doll she bought me   15
was ersatz
"Alan" was his name
from the discount store
He cost a dollar ninety-nine
Ken was two dollars more   20
Alan's hair was felt
stuck on with cheap glue
like the top of a pool table
scuffed up by cues

and it fell out in patches   25
when he was brand new
Ken's hair was plastic
molded in waves
coated with paint
no Ken bad-hair days   30
Well they wore the same size
and they wore the same clothes
but Ken was a player
and Alan was a boze
Barbie looked around   35
at all the other Barbies
drivin up in Dream Cars
at the Ken-and-Barbie party
and knew life had dealt her
a jack, not a king   40
knew if Alan bought her
an engagement ring
it wouldn't scratch glass
bet your ass
no class   45
made of cubic zirconia
or cubic Plexiglas
Kens would move Barbies
out of their townhouses
into their dreamhouses   50
Pepto-Bismol pink
from the rugs to the sink
wrap her in mink
but Alan was a bum
Our doll was not dumb   55
She knew a fronter from a chum
Take off that tuxedo
Alan would torpedo
for the Barcalounger
Bye-bye libido   60
Hello VCR
No job, no car
Drinkin up her home bar

Stinkin up her boudoir with his cigar
Shrinkin up the line of cash   65
on her MasterCard
Till she'd be pleading:
"Where's that giant *hand*
used to make him *stand*,
used to make him *walk*?"   70

—2004

NAOMI SHIHAB NYE ■ (b. 1952)

*Naomi Shihab Nye, a dedicated world traveler and humanitarian, has read
her poetry in Bangladesh and the Middle East. Many of her poems are informed by her Palestinian ancestry, and she has translated contemporary
Arabic poetry.*

The Traveling Onion

It is believed that the onion originally came from India. In Egypt
it was an object of worship—why I haven't been able to find out.
From Egypt the onion entered Greece and on to Italy, thence into
all of Europe.

—*Better Living Cookbook*

When I think how far the onion has traveled
just to enter my stew today, I could kneel and praise
all small forgotten miracles,
crackly paper peeling on the drainboard,
pearly layers in smooth agreement,   5
the way knife enters onion, straight
and onion falls apart on the chopping block,
a history revealed.

And I would never scold the onion
for causing tears.   10
It is right that tears fall
for something small and forgotten.

How at meal, we sit to eat,
commenting on texture of meat or herbal aroma
but never on the translucence of onion,   15
now limp, now divided,
or its traditionally honorable career:
For the sake of others,
disappear.

—1986

ALBERTO RÍOS ■ (b. 1952)

*Alberto Ríos was born in Nogales, Arizona, the son of a Mexican-American
father and an English-born mother. He won the Walt Whitman Award of
the Academy of American Poets for his first book,* Whispering to Fool the
Wind *(1982). He has also written a collection of short stories,* The Iguana
Killer: Twelve Stories of the Heart, *which won the Western States
Book Award.*

The Purpose of Altar Boys

Tonio told me at catechism
the big part of the eye
admits good, and the little
black part is for seeing
evil—his mother told him   5
who was a widow and so
an authority on such things.
That's why at night
the black part gets bigger.
That's why kids can't go out   10
at night, and at night
girls take off their clothes
and walk around their
bedrooms or jump on their
beds or wear only sandals   15
and stand in their windows.
I was the altar boy

who knew about these things,
whose mission on some Sundays
was to remind people of   20
the night before as they
knelt for Holy Communion.
To keep Christ from falling
I held the metal plate under chins,
while on the thick   25
red carpet of the altar
I dragged my feet
and waited for the precise
moment: plate to chin
I delivered without expression   30
the Holy Electric Shock,
the kind that produces
a really large swallowing
and makes people think.
I thought of it as justice.   35
But on other Sundays the fire
in my eyes was different,
my mission somehow changed.
I would hold the metal plate
a little too hard   40
against those certain same
nervous chins, and I
I would look
with authority down
the tops of white dresses.   45

—1982

JULIA ALVAREZ ■ (b. 1953)

Julia Alvarez published her first collection, Homecoming, *in 1984. It contained both free verse and "33," a sequence of 33 sonnets on the occasion of the poet's thirty-third birthday. She has gained acclaim for* In the Time of the Butterflies, *a work of fiction, and* The Other Side/El Otro Lado, *a collection of poems.*

Bilingual Sestina

Some things I have to say aren't getting said
in this snowy, blond, blue-eyed, gum-chewing English:
dawn's early light sifting through *persianas*° closed
the night before by dark-skinned girls whose words
evoke *cama,*° *aposento,*° *sueños*° in *nombres*°   5
from that first world I can't translate from Spanish.

Gladys, Rosario, Altagracia—the sounds of Spanish
wash over me like warm island waters as I say
your soothing names: a child again learning the *nombres*
of things you point to in the world before English   10
turned *sol,*°*sierra,*° *cielo,*° *luna*° to vocabulary words—
sun, earth, sky, moon. Language closed

like the touch-sensitive *morivivi*° whose leaves closed
when we kids poked them, astonished. Even Spanish
failed us back then when we saw how frail a word is   15
when faced with the thing it names. How saying
its name won't always summon up in Spanish or English
the full blown genie from the bottled *nombre.*

Gladys, I summon you back by saying your *nombre.*
Open up again the house of slatted windows closed   20
since childhood, where *palabras*° left behind for English
stand dusty and awkward in neglected Spanish.
Rosario, muse of *el patio,*° sing in me and through me say
that world again, begin first with those first words

you put in my mouth as you pointed to the world—   25
not Adam, not God, but a country girl numbering
the stars, the blades of grass, warming the sun by saying,
¡Qué calor!° as you opened up the morning closed
inside the night until you sang in Spanish,
Estas son las mañanitas,° and listening in bed, no English   30

---

3 **persianas** venetian blinds   5 **cama** bed   **aposento** apartment   **sueños** dreams   **nombres** names   11 **sol** sun   **sierra** mountain   **cielo** sky   **luna** moon   13 **morivivi** a type of Caribbean bush   21 **palabras** words   23 **el patio** outdoor terrace   28 **Qué calor** What heat!   30 **Estas son las mañanitas** These are birthday songs

yet in my head to confuse me with translations, no English
doubling the world with synonyms, no dizzying array of words
—the world was simple and intact in Spanish—
luna, sol, casa,°luz, flor,° as if the *nombres*
were the outer skin of things, as if words were so close   35
one left a mist of breath on things by saying
their names, an intimacy I now yearn for in English—
words so close to what I mean that I almost hear my Spanish
heart beating, beating inside what I say *en inglés.°*

—1995

HARRYETTE MULLEN ■ (b. 1953)

Harryette Mullen says, "I intend the poem to be meaningful: to allow, or
suggest, to open up, or insinuate possible meanings, even in those places
where the poem drifts between intentional utterance and improvisational
wordplay." Born in Florence, Alabama, Mullen grew up in Fort Worth, Texas,
and holds degrees from the University of Texas and the University of Califor-
nia, Santa Cruz. She currently teaches African-American literature and cre-
ative writing at the University of California, Los Angeles.

782

Dim Lady°

My honeybunch's peepers are nothing like neon. Today's special at
Red Lobster is redder than her kisser. If Liquid Paper is white, her
racks are institutional beige. If her mop were Slinkys, dishwater
Slinkys would grow on her noggin. I have seen tablecloths in
Shakey's Pizza Parlors, red and white, but no such picnic colors do
I see in her mug. And in some minty-fresh mouthwashes there is
more sweetness than in the garlic breeze my main squeeze
wheezes. I love to hear her rap, yet I'm aware that Muzak has a
hipper beat. I don't know any Marilyn Monroes. My ball and chain
is plain from head to toe. And yet, by gosh, my scrumptious
Twinkie has as much sex appeal for me as any lanky model or
platinum movie idol who's hyped beyond belief.

—2003

34 casa house   **flor** flower   **39 en inglés** in English
Dim Lady See Shakespeare's *Sonnet 130*

Kim Addonizio is the author of four books of poetry and a book of short stories. Born in Washington, D.C., Addonizio earned a B.A. and an M.A. from San Francisco State University and has worked as a waitress, tennis instructor, Kelly Girl, attendant for the disabled, and auto parts store bookkeeper. She currently teaches private writing workshops in the San Francisco Bay area. Addonizio's poems achieve a delicate balance between the confessional and the universal, and manage to be simultaneously lyrical and gritty.

Sonnenizio° on a Line from Drayton°

Since there's no help, come let us kiss and part;
or kiss anyway, let's start with that, with the kissing part,
because it's better than the parting part, isn't it—
we're good at kissing, we like how that part goes:
we part our lips, our mouths get near and nearer,   5
then we're close, my breasts, your chest, our bodies partway
to making love, so we might as well, part of me thinks—
the wrong part, I know, the bad part, but still
let's pretend we're at that party where we met
and scandalized everyone, remember that part? Hold me   10
like that again, unbutton my shirt, part of you
wants to I can tell, I'm touching that part and it says
yes, the ardent partisan, let it win you over,
it's hopeless, come, we'll kiss and part forever.

—2004

Sonnenizio The sonnenizio was originated in Florence in the thirteenth century by Vanni Fucci as an irreverent form whose subject was usually the impossibility of everlasting love. Dante retaliated by putting Fucci into the seventh chasm of the *Inferno* as a thief. Originally composed in hendeca-syllabics, the sonnenizio gradually moved away from metrical constraints and began to tackle a wider variety of subject matter. The sonnenizio is 14 lines long. It opens with a line from someone else's sonnet, repeats a word from that line in each succeeding line of the poem, and closes with a rhymed couplet. [Addonizio's note]   **Drayton** Michael Drayton (1563–1631) see *Idea: Sonnet 61*

DAVID MASON ■ (b. 1954)

David Mason is best known for the title poem of The Country I Remember, *a long narrative about the life of a Civil War veteran and his daughter. The poem has been performed in a theatrical version. Mason edited, with Mark Jarman,* Rebel Angels, *an anthology of recent poetry written in traditional forms. A recent verse-novel,* Ludlow (2007), *concerns a 1914 coal-miners' strike in Colorado.*

Fog Horns

The loneliest days,
damp and indistinct,
sea and land a haze.

And purple fog horns
blossomed over tides —   5
bruises being born

in silence, so slow,
so out there, around,
above and below.

In such hurts of sound   10
the known world became
neither flat nor round.

The steaming tea pot
was all we fathomed
of *is* and *is not*.   15

The hours were hallways
with doors at the ends
opened into days

fading into night
and the scattering   20
particles of light.

Nothing was done then.
Nothing was ever
done. Then it was done.

                                                        —*2004*

Mary Jo Salter has traveled widely with her husband, poet and novelist Brad Leithauser, and has lived in Japan, Italy, and Iceland. A student of Elizabeth Bishop at Harvard, Salter brings to her art a devotion to the poet's craft that mirrors that of her mentor. She has published five collections of poetry and The Moon Comes Home, *a children's book.*

Welcome to Hiroshima

is what you first see, stepping off the train:
a billboard brought to you in living English
by Toshiba Electric. While a channel
silent in the TV of the brain

projects those flickering re-runs of a cloud   5
that brims its risen columnful like beer
and, spilling over, hangs its foamy head,
you feel a thirst for history: what year

it started to be safe to breathe the air,
and when to drink the blood and scum afloat   10
on the Ohta River. But no, the water's clear,
they pour it for your morning cup of tea

in one of the countless sunny coffee shops
whose plastic dioramas advertise
mutations of cuisine behind the glass: 15
a pancake sandwich; a pizza someone tops

with a maraschino cherry. Passing by
the Peace Park's floral hypocenter (where
how bravely, or with what mistaken cheer,
humanity erased its own erasure),   20

you enter the memorial museum
and through more glass are served, as on a dish
of blistered grass, three mannequins. Like gloves
a mother clips to coatsleeves, strings of flesh

hang from their fingertips; or as if tied   25
to recall a duty for us, *Reverence*
the dead whose mourners too shall soon be dead,
but all commemoration's swallowed up

in questions of bad taste, how re-created
horror mocks the grim original,   30
and thinking at last *They should have left it all*
you stop. This is the wristwatch of a child.

Jammed on the moment's impact, resolute
to communicate some message, although mute,
it gestures with its hands at eight-fifteen   35
and eight-fifteen and eight-fifteen again

while tables of statistics on the wall
update the news by calling on a roll
of tape, death gummed on death, and in the case
adjacent, an exhibit under glass   40

is glass itself: a shard the bomb slammed in
a woman's arm at eight-fifteen, but some
three decades on—as if to make it plain
hope's only as renewable as pain,

and as if all the unsung   45
debasements of the past may one day come
rising to the surface once again—
worked its filthy way out like a tongue.

—*1985*

CATHY SONG ■ (b. 1955)

Cathy Song was born in Honolulu, Hawaii, and holds degrees from Welles-
ley College and Boston University. Her first book, Picture Bride, *won the*
Yale Series of Younger Poets Award in 1983. The Land of Bliss, her fourth
collection, appeared in 2001.

Stamp Collecting

The poorest countries
have the prettiest stamps
as if impracticality were a major export
shipped with the bananas, t-shirts, and coconuts.
Take Tonga, where the tourists,   5
expecting a dramatic waterfall replete with birdcalls
are taken to see the island's peculiar mystery:
hanging bats with collapsible wings
like black umbrellas swing upside down from fruit trees.
The Tongan stamp is a fruit.   10
The banana stamp is scalloped like a butter-varnished seashell.
The pineapple resembles a volcano, a spout of green on top,
and the papaya, a tarnished goat skull.

They look impressive,
these stamps of countries without a thing to sell   15
except for what is scraped, uprooted and hulled
from their mule-scratched hills.
They believe in postcards,
in portraits of progress: the new dam;
a team of young native doctors   20
wearing stethoscopes like exotic ornaments;
the recently constructed "Facultad de Medicina,"°
a building as lack-lustre as an American motel.

The stamps of others are predictable.
Lucky is the country that possesses indigenous beauty.   25
Say a tiger or a queen.
The Japanese can display to the world
their blossoms: a spray of pink on green.
Like pollen, they drift, airborne.
But pity the country that is bleak and stark.   30

22 **Facultad de Medicina** Medical Faculty (building)

Beauty and whimsey are discouraged as indiscreet.
Unbreakable as their climate, a monument of ice,
they issue serious statements, commemorating
factories, tramways and aeroplanes;
athletes marbled into statues.   35
They turn their noses upon the world, these countries,
and offer this: an unrelenting procession
of a grim, historic profile.

—1988

GINGER ANDREWS ■ (b. 1956)

Ginger Andrews won the 1999 Nicholas Roerich Poetry Prize for her first book, An Honest Answer, *which explores the difficulties of working-class life in a Northwestern lumber town. Born in North Bend, Oregon, she cleans houses for a living, and is a janitor and Sunday school teacher. Her poems have been featured many times on National Public Radio's "The Writer's Almanac."*

Primping in the Rearview Mirror

after a solid ten-minute bout of tears,
hoping that the Safeway man who stocks the shelves
and talked to you once for thirty minutes about specialty jams,
won't ask if you're all right, or tell you you look like shit
and then have to apologize as he remembers that you don't   5
like cuss words and you don't date ex-prison guards
because you're married. The truth is you're afraid
this blue-eyed charismatic sexist hunk of a reject just might
trigger another round of tears, that you'll lean into him
right in front of the eggs and milk, crying like a baby,   10
your face buried in his chest just below the two opened
buttons of his tight white knit shirt, his big cold hands
pressed to the small of your back, pulling you closer
to whisper that everything will be all right.

—2002

AMY GERSTLER ■ (b. 1956)

A resident of Los Angeles, Gerstler has published six collections of poetry since 1986. Her seventh, Animal Planet, *appeared in 2010. A prolific writer of art criticism and book reviews, Gerstler has also collaborated with visual artists. She has taught writing at a number of universities, including Bennington, her graduate alma mater.*

Advice from a Caterpillar

Chew your way into a new world.
Munch leaves. Molt. Rest. Molt
again. Self-reinvention is *everything*.
Spin many nests. Cultivate stinging
bristles. Don't get sentimental
about your discarded skins. Grow
quickly. Develop a yen for nettles.
Alternate crumpling and climbing. Rely
on your antennae. Sequester poisons
in your body for use at a later date.
When threatened, emit foul odors
in self-defense. Behave cryptically
to confuse predators: change colors, spit,
or feign death. If all else fails, taste terrible.

—2008

REBECCA FOUST ■ (b. 1957)

Born in Altoona, Pennsylvania, and educated at Smith College, Foust worked for some years as an attorney, leaving law for motherhood and full-time writing. Her chapbook of poems about raising her autistic son, Dark Card, *appeared in 2008, the winner of a competition sponsored by Texas Review Press; the next year a second chapbook,* Mom's Canoe, *won the same prize. Her first full-length collection,* All That Gorgeous Pitiless Song, *was published in 2010. She lives in Marin County, California.*

Family Story

Mom talked about how when the x-ray
they used in those day before the ultrasound
confirmed she was pregnant the second time
with twins, she buttoned up her best
going-out dress, wondering what are those dark spots,
adjusted her hat and left. Weeks later it occurred to her
they were tears, wept for the long year behind
the long years ahead of diapers, glass bottles,
nights without sleep, no help with wailing kids
but from wailing kids. She wept
like she lived; when tears dripped and bloomed
on the gray wool of her dress, she looked up
at the changing room ceiling, expecting to find rain.

—2009

CATHERINE TUFARIELLO ■ (b. 1963)

*Catherine Tufariello grew up in upstate New York and holds a Ph.D. from
Cornell University. Her first full-length collection, Keeping My Name,
appeared in 2004. A translator of the sonnets of Petrarch, she has taught at
Valparaiso University.*

Useful Advice

You're 37? Don't you think that maybe
It's time you settled down and had a baby?

No wine? You're pregnant, aren't you? I knew it!

Hey, are you sure you two know how to do it?

All Dennis has to do is look at me   5
And I'm knocked up.
                              Some things aren't meant to be.
It's sad, but try to see this as God's will.

I've heard that sometimes when you take the Pill—

A friend of mine got pregnant when she stopped   10
Working so hard.
                              Why don't you two adopt?
You'll have one of your own then, like my niece.

At work I heard about this herb from Greece—

My sister swears by dong quai. Want to try it?   15

Forget the high-tech stuff. Just change your diet.

It's true! Too much caffeine can make you sterile.

Yoga is good for that. My cousin Carol—

They have these ceremonies in Peru—

You mind my asking, is it him or you?   20

Have you tried acupuncture? Meditation?

It's in your head. Relax! Take a vacation
And have some fun. You think too much. Stop trying.

Did I say something wrong? Why are you crying?

                                                    —2004

SHERMAN ALEXIE ■ (b. 1966)

*Sherman Alexie is a Spokane/Coeur d'Alene Indian and grew up on a
reservation in Wellpinit, Washington. While attending Washington State
University as a pre-med major, Alexie attended a poetry workshop and
soon began to publish his work. A prolific author of novels, poems, and
short stories, Alexie has also performed professionally as a stand-up
comedian.*

The Exaggeration of Despair

I open the door

(this Indian girl writes that her brother tried to hang himself
with a belt just two weeks after her other brother did hang himself

and this Indian man tells us that back in boarding school,
five priests took him into a back room and raped him repeatedly   5

and this homeless Indian woman begs for quarters, and when I ask
her about her tribe, she says she's horny and bends over in front
   of me

and this homeless Indian man is the uncle of an Indian man
who writes for a large metropolitan newspaper, and so now
   I know them both

and this Indian child cries when he sits to eat at our table   10
because he had never known his own family to sit at the
   same table

and this Indian woman was born to an Indian woman
who sold her for a six-pack and a carton of cigarettes

and this Indian poet shivers beneath the freeway
and begs for enough quarters to buy pencil and paper   15

and this fancydancer passes out at the powwow
and wakes up naked, with no memory of the evening, all of
   his regalia gone

and this is my sister, who waits years for an eagle, receives it
and stores it with our cousins, who then tell her it has disappeared

and this is my father, whose own father died on Okinawa, shot   20
by a Japanese soldier who must have looked so much like him

and this is my father, whose mother died of tuberculosis
not long after he was born, and so my father must hear
   coughing ghosts

and this is my grandmother who saw, before the white men came,
three ravens with white necks, and knew our God was going
   to change)   25

and invite the wind inside.

—1996

NATASHA TRETHEWEY ■ (b. 1966)

*Pulitzer Prize winner Natasha Trethewey grew up on the Gulf Coast, the
child of an interracial marriage (her father is poet Eric Trethewey). Her
first collection,* Domestic Work, *appeared in 2000, and her second,*

Bellocq's Ophelia (2002), *focused on the life of a mixed-race prostitute in Storyville, New Orleans's notorious red-light district. A third collection, Native Guard, appeared in 2006. Trethewey teaches at Emory University in Atlanta.*

Domestic Work, 1937

All week she's cleaned
someone else's house,
stared down her own face
in the shine of copper-
bottomed pots, polished   5
wood, toilets she'd pull
the lid to—that look saying

Let's make a change, girl.

But Sunday mornings are hers—
church clothes starched   10
and hanging, a record spinning
on the console, the whole house
dancing. She raises the shades,
washes the rooms in light,
buckets of water, Octagon soap.   15

Cleanliness is next to godliness . . .

Windows and doors flung wide,
curtains two-stepping
forward and back, neck bones
bumping in the pot, a choir   20
of clothes clapping on the line.

Nearer my God to Thee . . .

She beats time on the rugs,
blows dust from the broom
like dandelion spores, each one   25
a wish for something better.

—2000

Craig Arnold's first book of poetry, Shells, *was selected by W.S. Merwin for the Yale Series of Younger Poets, and his second,* Made Flesh, *was published in 2008. Arnold won numerous awards and fellowships during his brief career, including a National Endowment for the Arts grant. He was in Japan on a U.S.–Japan Friendship Commission Creative Artists' Exchange grant, researching on the island of Kuchinoerabushima for his most recent project, a book of lyric essays focused on the trope of the volcano, when he disappeared, presumably the victim of a hiking accident. Despite extensive searches and world-wide concern, his body was never found.*

The Singers

They are threatening to leave us the nimble-throated singers
    the little murderers with the quick pulses
They perch at the ends of bare branches their tails
    are ragged and pitiful the long green
feathers are fallen out They go on eating and eating
    last autumn's yellow melia berries
They do not care that you approach cold corpses
    rot in the grass in the reeds
The gray-shouldered crows hobble about the wren
    barely a mouthful cocks her pert tail
and threatens to slaughter the white-footed cat in the bushes
    They do not understand that they are dying

They are threatening to leave us how quickly we forget
    the way they taught us how to play our voices
opening soul to weightlessness like the Spartan poet
    singing under the burden of his old bones
to the chorus girls with their honey songs and their holy voices
    how he wished he could scoot like a kingfisher
lightly over the flower of the waves who boasted
    I know the tunes of every bird but I Alcman
found my words and song in the tongue of the strident partridge
    Where will we find songs when the sleek-headed
mallards are gone who chase each other around the pond
    the reluctant duck and the lovesick drake

The way she turns her head to the side to scold him
　　whack whack whack whack whack the way her boyfriend
chases off his rival and then swims back reeb reeb
　　with feeble reassurances the way
he sits on top of her the way she flaps her wings
　　to keep above water the way they look
pleased with themselves wagging their tails smoothing
　　each feather back in its right place

They are threatening to leave but you may still catch them
　　saying goodbye stealthed in the cedar and cypress
at dawn in the dark clarity between sleep and waking
　　A run of five notes on a black flute
another and another buried deep in the mix
　　how many melodies can the air hold
And what they sing so lovely and so meaningless
　　may urge itself upon you with the ache
of something just beyond the point of being remembered
　　the trace of a brave thought in the face of sadness

　　　　　　　　　　　　　　　　　　　　　—2008

ALLISON JOSEPH ■ (b. 1967)

Allison Joseph was born in London, the child of immigrants from Jamaica and Grenada. When she was a child, her parents relocated to New York, where she attended the Bronx High School of Science. Following graduation from Kenyon College and the University of Indiana, she began college teaching and is now a member of the creative writing faculty at Southern Illinois University. She has recently published a sequence of sonnets about her father, who died in 1997.

The Athlete

　　would like to be my friend,
　　but between volleyball tryouts
　　and broad-jump practice,
　　there's just no time to chat,
　　no time to hang out at lunch,　　　　　　　　　　5
　　blushing and gossiping over boys.
　　Hell, there isn't anything boys

can do that she can't—she'll
throw a ball just as hard,
run gutsy miles on the track   10
to match their distances,
ski cross-country or downhill,
topping their speed and endurance.
I admire her toughness, her
out-of-my-way attitude, her   15
assignments in on time, grades
better than mine even though I'm
only on one committee. She even
works after school, selling shoes
at Lady Footlocker to weekend jocks,   20
slinky aerobics babes. And they have
no idea how fast that girl can move,
long legs trained to respond
to whatever command her brain
issues, whatever demand   25
she puts on her muscles.
Once she asked if I'd like
to run track, hoping to pull me
into her world, make me as swift
as she. And I had to laugh at that,   30
at her ability to see an athlete
when all I could see was a scrawny girl
with fallen arches. I told her no,
but thanks, glad that she saw something
to work with when she looked   35
at me, something to mold, shape.

—1998

BRIAN TURNER ■ (b. 1967)

After completing a degree in creative writing at the University of Oregon, Brian Turner served seven years in the U.S. Army, including service in Bosnia-Herzegovina and a year in Iraq. His book about his military experiences, Here, Bullet, was named an "Editor's Choice" by the New York Times and was the 2007 recipient of the Poets' Prize.

Here, Bullet

If a body is what you want,
then here is bone and gristle and flesh.
Here is the clavicle-snapped wish,
the aorta's opened valves, the leap
thought makes at the synaptic gap. 5
Here is the adrenaline rush you crave,
that inexorable flight, that insane puncture
into heat and blood. And I dare you to finish
what you've started. Because here, Bullet,
here is where I complete the word you bring 10
hissing through the air, here is where I moan
the barrel's cold esophagus, triggering
my tongue's explosives for the rifling I have
inside of me, each twist of the round
spun deeper, because here, Bullet, 15
here is where the world ends, every time.

—2005

SUJI KWOCK KIM ■ (b. 1968)

Kim received the 2002 Walt Whitman Award for Notes from the Divided
Country, *an exploration of the Japanese occupation of Korea, and of the
Korean War and its aftermath. Kim's family emigrated to Poughkeepsie,
New York, in the 1970s. She studied at Yale; the Iowa Writers' Workshop;
Seoul National University, where she was a Fulbright Scholar; and Stan-
ford University, where she was a Stegner Fellow. She lives in San Francisco
and New York.*

Occupation

The soldiers
are hard at work
building a house.
They hammer
bodies into the earth 5
like nails,

they paint the walls
with blood.
Inside the doors
stay shut, locked   10
as eyes of stone.
Inside the stairs
feel slippery,
all flights go down.
There is no floor: 15
only a roof,
where ash is falling—
dark snow,
human snow,
thickly, mutely   20
falling.
Come, they say.
This house will
last forever.
You must occupy it.   25
And you, and you—
And you, and you—
Come, they say.
There is room
for everyone.   30

—2003

A. E. STALLINGS ■ (b. 1968)

Alicia Stallings is the author of Archaic Smile, *chosen for the 1999 Richard Wilbur Award. Written exclusively in received forms, the book is noteworthy for the vigor and humor with which Stallings rewrites classical myths. Raised in Decatur, Georgia, Stallings studied at the University of Georgia and Oxford University. She composed the Latin lyrics for the opening music of the Paramount film,* The Sum of All Fears, *and has done a verse translation of Lucretius'* De Rerum Natura. *A second collection of poems,* Hapax, *appeared in 2006. She lives in Athens, Greece, with her husband, John Psaropoulos, editor of the* Athens News.

First Love: A Quiz

He came up to me:
    a. in his souped-up Camaro
    b. to talk to my skinny best friend
    c. and bumped my glass of wine so I wore the ferrous stain
       on my sleeve
    d. from the ground, in a lead chariot drawn by a team of
       stallions black as crude oil and breathing sulfur; at his
       heart, he sported a tiny golden arrow   5

He offered me:
    a. a ride
    b. dinner and a movie, with a wink at the cliché
    c. an excuse not to go back alone to the apartment with its
       sink of dirty knives
    d. a narcissus with a hundred dazzling petals that breathed a
       sweetness as cloying as decay

I went with him because: 10
    a. even his friends told me to beware
    b. I had nothing to lose except my virginity
    c. he placed his hand in the small of my back and I felt the
       tread of honeybees
    d. he was my uncle, the one who lived in the half-finished
       basement, and he took me by the hair

The place he took me to: 15
    a. was dark as my shut eyes
    b. and where I ate bitter seed and became ripe
    c. and from which my mother would never take me wholly
       back, though she wept and walked the earth and made the
       bearded ears of barley wither on their stalks and the blasted
       flowers drop from their sepals
    d. is called by some men hell and others love
    e. all of the above   20

—2006

ERNEST HILBERT ■ (b. 1970)

Hilbert was born in Philadelphia and educated at Rutgers University and Oxford. With founding editor Garrick Davis, he helped to establish Contemporary Poetry Review *as one of the most comprehensive online journals of literary criticism. He has been credited as one of several contemporary poets who had led a revitalization of the sonnet. He works as an antiquarian book dealer in his hometown.*

Domestic Situation

Maybe you've heard about this. Maybe not.
A man came home and chucked his girlfriend's cat
In the wood chipper. This really happened.
Dinner wasn't ready on time. A lot
Of other little things went wrong. He spat   5
On her father, who came out when he learned
About it. He also broke her pinky,
Stole her checks, and got her sister pregnant.
But she stood by him, stood strong, through it all,
Because she loved him. She loved him, you see.   10
She actually said that, and then she went
And married him. She felt some unique call.
Don't try to understand what another
Person means by love. Don't even bother.

—2009

SOPHIE HANNAH ■ (b. 1971)

The daughter of writers Norman and Adèle Geras, Hannah was born and educated in Manchester, England. Though she is primarily known as a writer of light verse, she has also published novels, short stories, and children's books. A collection of poetry, Pessimism for Beginners, *was published in 2007.*

SOPHIE HANNAH

The Guest Speaker

I have to keep myself awake
While the guest speaker speaks.
For his and for procedure's sake
I have to keep myself awake.
However long his talk might take   5
(And, Christ, it feels like weeks)
I have to keep myself awake
While the guest speaker speaks.

—2003

EMILY MOORE ■ (b. 1977)

Emily Moore teaches English at Stuyvesant High School in New York. Her poetry has been published in Ploughshares, The Paris Review, *and* The New Yorker, *where "Auld Lang Syne" originally appeared. She also performs with a three-woman band, Ménage à Twang.*

Auld Lang Syne

Here's to the rock star with the crooked teeth,
the cellist, banker, mezzo bearing gifts,
the teacher with the flask inside her jeans—
those girls who made us sweat and lick our lips.

To the *jeune fille* who broke my heart in France,   5
the tramp who warmed your lap and licked your ear,
the one who bought me shots at 2 A.M.
that night I tied your pink tie at the bar.

Who smoked. Who locked you out. Who kissed my eyes
then pulled my hair and left me for a boy.   10
The girl who bit my upper, inner thigh.
My raspy laugh when I first heard your voice

toasting through broken kisses sloppy drunk:
To women! To abundance! To enough!

—2008

Erica Dawson was born in Columbia, Maryland, and studied at Johns Hopkins, Ohio State, and the University of Cincinnati. Her first book, Big-Eyed Afraid, won the Anthony Hecht Poetry Prize. In a "self-interview," she says, "People, including me, feel comfortable with categories, labels. Some people feel comfortable saying, 'Erica keeps it real.' Sometimes they want to put me, and others, in a box based on our gender or race." Working largely in traditional poetic forms, Dawson writes "outside the box."

Somewhere Between Columbus and Cincinnati

If you die today, where will you spend eternity?

Jesus, it's stretch of few
And far between the repetitions: fenced-
In fields and Christ's billboard-dispensed
    Commandments. There **HELL IS REAL**
    Worn in the corners, peel-

ing like dead skins (**McRIB** beneath).
Fence posts decay like rotting teeth.
    Sun spreads dusk's morning *deux.*
    Pale pink eclipses blue

And it's all memorial, two brown
Bottles, the worms a wren will down.
    The shattered ambers burn.
    And if the salmon cloudlets turn

Pitch-black, I will believe in You.

—2007

Introduction to Drama

The Play's the Thing

The theater, located in the heart of a rejuvenated downtown business district, is a relic of the silent movie era that has been restored to something approaching its former glory. While only a few members of tonight's audience can actually remember it in its prime, the expertise of the organist seated at the antique Wurlitzer instills a sense of false nostalgia in the crowd, now settling by twos and threes into red, plush-covered seats and looking around in search of familiar faces. Just as the setting is somewhat out of the ordinary, so is this group. Unlike movie audiences, they are for the most part older and less casually dressed. There are few small children present, and even the teenagers seem to be on their best behavior. Oddly, no one is eating popcorn or noisily drawing on a soda straw. A mood of seriousness and anticipation hovers over the theater, and those who have lived in the town long enough can spot the spouse or partner of one of the principal actors nervously folding a program or checking a watch.

As the organ magically descends into the recesses of the orchestra pit, the lights dim, a hush falls over the crowd, and the curtain creakily rises. There is a general murmur of approval at the ingenuity and many hours of hard work that have transformed empty space into a remarkable semblance of an upper-class drawing room in the early 1900s. Dressed as a domestic servant, a young woman, known to the audience from her frequent appearances in local television commercials, enters and begins to dust a table. She hums softly to herself. A tall young man, in everyday life a junior partner in a local law firm, wanders in carrying a tennis racket. The maid turns, sees him, and catches her breath, startled. "Why Mr. Fenton!" she exclaims. . . .

And the world begins.

The full experience of drama—whether at an amateur production like the little theater performance described here or at a huge Broadway playhouse—is much more complex than that of any other form of literature. The word **drama** itself comes from a Greek word meaning "a thing that is done," and the roots of both **theater** and **audience** call to mind the acts of seeing and hearing, respectively. Like other communal public activities—religious services, sporting events, meetings of political or fraternal organizations—drama has evolved, over many centuries, its own set of customs, rituals, and rules. The exact shape of these characteristics—**dramatic conventions**—may differ from country to country or from period to period, but they all have one aim in common, namely to define and govern an art form whose essence is to be found in public performances of written texts. No other form of literature shares this primary goal. Before we can discuss drama purely as literature, we should first ponder some aspects of its unique status as "a thing that is done."

It is worth noting that dramatists are also called playwrights. Note the spelling—a "wright" is a maker, as old family names like Cartwright or Boatwright attest. If a play is in fact *made* rather than written, then a playwright is similar to an architect who has designed a unique building. The concept may be his or hers, but the construction project requires the contributions of many other hands before the sparkling steel and glass tower alters the city's skyline. In the case of a new play, money will have to be raised by a producer, a director chosen, a cast found, a crew assembled, a set designed and built, and many hours of rehearsal completed before the curtain can be raised for the first time. Along the way, modifications to the original play may become necessary, and it is possible that the author will listen to advice from the actors, director, or stage manager and incorporate their opinions into any revisions. Professional theater is, after all, a branch of show business, and no play will survive its premiere for long if it does not attract paying crowds. The dramatists we read and study so reverently today managed to reach large popular audiences in their time. Even ancient Greek playwrights like Sophocles and Euripides must have stood by surreptitiously "counting the house" as the open-air seats slowly filled, and Shakespeare prospered as part-owner of the Globe Theatre to the extent that he was able to retire to his hometown at the ripe old age of forty-seven.

Set beside this rich communal experience, the solitary act of reading a play seems a poor substitute, contrary to the play's very nature (only a small category known as **closet drama** comprises plays intended to be read instead of acted). Yet dramatists like Shakespeare and Ibsen are counted among the giants of world literature, and their works are annually read by far more people than actually see their plays performed. In reading a play, we are forced to pay close attention to such matters as **set description,** particularly with a playwright like Ibsen, who lavishes great attention on the design of his set; references to **properties** or "props" that will figure in the action of the play; physical description of characters and costumes; **stage directions** indicating the movements and gestures made by actors in scenes; and any other **stage business,** that is, action without dialogue. Many modern dramatists are very scrupulous in detailing these matters; writers of earlier periods, however, provided little or no instruction. Reading Sophocles or Shakespeare, we are forced to concentrate on the characters' words to envision how actions and other characters were originally conceived. Reading aloud, alone or in a group, or following along in the text while listening to or watching an audio or video performance is particularly recommended for verse plays such as *Antigone* or *Twelfth Night*. Also, versions of many of the plays contained in this book are currently available on videotape or DVD. While viewing a film is an experience of a different kind from seeing a live performance, film versions obviously provide a convenient insight into the ways in which great actors have interpreted their roles.

Origins of Drama

No consensus exists about the exact date of the birth of drama, but according to most authorities, it originated in Greece over 2500 years ago, an outgrowth of rites of worship of the god Dionysus, who was associated with male fertility, agriculture (especially the cultivation of vineyards), and seasonal renewal. In these Dionysian festivals a group of fifty citizens of Athens, known as a **chorus,** outfitted and trained by a leader, or *choragos,* would perform hymns of praise to the god, known as **dithyrambic poetry.** The celebration concluded with the ritual sacrifice of a goat, or *tragos.* The two main genres of drama originally took their names from these rituals; comedy comes from *kômos,* the Greek word for a festivity. These primitive revels were invariably accompanied with a union of the sexes (*gamos* in Greek, a word that survives in English words like "monogamy") celebrating fertility and continuance of the race, an ancient custom still symbolically observed in the "fade-out kiss" that concludes most comedies. Tragedy, on the other hand, literally means "song of the goat," taking its name from the animal that was killed on the altar **(thymele),** cooked, and shared by the celebrants with their god.

Around 600 B.C. certain refinements took place. In the middle of the sixth century B.C. an official springtime festival, known as the Greater or City Dionysia, was established in Athens, and prizes for the best dithyrambic poems were first awarded. At about the same time a special **orchestra,** or "dancing place," was constructed, a circular area surrounding the altar, and permanent seats, or a **theatron** ("seeing place"), arranged in a semicircle around the orchestra were added. At the back of the orchestra the façade of a temple (the **skene**) and a raised "porch" in front of it (the **proskenion,** in later theaters the **proscenium**) served as a backdrop, usually representing the palace of the ruler; walls extending to either side of the *skene,* the **parodoi,** served to conceal backstage activity from the audience. A wheeled platform, or **eccyclema,** could be pushed through the door of the *skene* to reveal the tragic consequences of a play's climax (there was no onstage "action" in Greek tragedy). Behind the *skene* a crane-like device called a **mechane** (or **deus ex machina**) could be used to lower a god from the heavens or represent a spectacular effect like the flying chariot drawn by dragons at the conclusion of Euripides' *Medea.*

In 535 B.C. a writer named Thespis won the annual competition with a startling innovation. Thespis separated one member of the chorus (called a *hypocrites,* or "actor") and had him engage in **dialogue,** spoken lines representing conversation, with the remaining members. If we define drama primarily as a story related through live action and recited dialogue, then Thespis may rightly be called the father of drama, and his name endures in "thespian," a synonym for actor.

The century after Thespis, from 500–400 B.C., saw many refinements in the way tragedies were performed and is considered the golden age of Greek drama. In this century, the careers of the three great tragic playwrights—Aeschylus (525–456 B.C.), Sophocles (496?–406 B.C.), and Euripides (c. 480–406 B.C.)—and the greatest comic playwright, Aristophanes (450?–385? B.C.) overlapped. It is no coincidence that in this remarkable period Athens, under the leadership of the general Pericles (495–429 B.C.), reached the height of its wealth, influence, and cultural development and was home to the philosophers Socrates (470–399 B.C.) and Plato (c. 427–347 B.C.). Aristotle (384–322 B.C.), the third of the great Athenian philosophers, was also a literary critic who wrote the first extended analysis of drama.

Aristotle on Tragedy

The earliest work of literary criticism in Western civilization is Aristotle's *Poetics*, an attempt to define and classify the different literary **genres** that use rhythm, language, and harmony. Aristotle identifies four genres—epic poetry, dithyrambic poetry, comedy, and tragedy—which have in common their attempts at imitation, or *mimesis*, of various types of human activity.

Aristotle comments most fully on tragedy, and his definition of the genre demands close examination:

> A tragedy, then, is the imitation of an action that is serious and also, as having magnitude, complete in itself; in language with pleasurable accessories, each kind brought in separately in the parts of the work; in a dramatic, not in a narrative form; with incidents arousing pity and fear, wherewith to accomplish its catharsis of such emotions.

First we should note that the imitation here is of *action*. Later in the passage, when Aristotle differentiates between narrative and dramatic forms of literature, it is clear that he is referring to tragedy as a type of literature written primarily for public performance. Furthermore, tragedy must be serious and must have magnitude. By this, Aristotle implies that issues of life and death must be involved and that these issues must be of public import. In many Greek tragedies, the fate of the *polis*, or city, of which the chorus is the voice, is bound up with the actions taken by the main character in the play. Despite their rudimentary form of democracy, the people of Athens would have been perplexed by a tragedy with an ordinary citizen at its center; magnitude in tragedy demands that only the affairs of persons of high rank are of sufficient importance for tragedy. Aristotle further requires that this imitated action possess a sense of completeness. At no point does he say that a tragedy has to end with a death or even in a state of unhappiness; he does require, however, that the audience sense that after the last words are spoken no further story cries out to be told.

The next part of the passage may confuse the modern reader. By "language with pleasurable accessories" Aristotle means the poetic devices of rhythm and, in the choral parts of the tragedy, music and dance as well. Reading the choral passages in a Greek tragedy, we are likely to forget that these passages were intended to be chanted or sung ("chorus" and "choir" share the same root) and danced as well ("choreography" comes from this root as well).

The rest of Aristotle's definition dwells on the emotional effects of tragedy on the audience. Pity and fear are to be evoked—pity because we must care for the characters and to some extent empathize with them, fear because we come to realize that the fate they endure involves acts—of which murder and incest are only two—that civilized men and women most abhor. Finally, Aristotle's word *catharsis* has proved controversial over the centuries. The word literally means "a purging," but readers have debated whether Aristotle is referring to a release of harmful emotions or a transformation of them. In either case, the implication is that viewing a tragedy has a beneficial effect on an audience, perhaps because the viewers' deepest fears are brought to light in a make-believe setting. How many of us, at the end of some particularly wrenching film, have turned to a companion and said, "Thank god, it was only a movie"? The sacrificial animal from whom tragedy took its name was, after all, only a stand-in whose blood was offered to the gods as a substitute for a human subject. The protagonist of a tragedy remains, in many ways, a "scapegoat" on whose head we project our own unconscious terrors.

Aristotle identifies six elements of a tragedy, and these elements are still useful in analyzing not only tragedies but other types of plays as well. In order of importance they are **plot, characterization, theme, diction, melody,** and **spectacle.** Despite the fact that the *Poetics* is over two thousand years old, Aristotle's elements still provide a useful way of understanding how plays work.

Plot

Aristotle considers plot the chief element of a play, and it is easy to see this when we consider that in discussing a film with a friend we usually give a brief summary, or **synopsis**, of the plot, stopping just short of "giving it away" by telling how the story concludes. Aristotle defines plot as "the combination of incidents, or things done in the story," and goes on to give the famous formulation that a plot "is that which has a beginning, middle, and end." Aristotle notes that the best plots are selective in their use of material and have an internal coherence and logic. Two opposite terms that Aristotle introduced are still in use, although with slightly different meanings. By a **unified plot** we generally mean one that takes place in roughly a twenty-four hour period; in a short play with a unified plot like Susan Glaspell's *Trifles*, the action is continuous. By **episodic plot** we mean one that spreads its action out over a longer period of time. A play which has a unified plot, a single setting, and no subplots is said to observe the **three unities**, which critics in some eras have virtually insisted on as ironclad rules. Although most plots are chronological, playwrights in the last half-century have experimented, sometimes radically, with such straightforward progression through time. Arthur Miller's *Death of a Salesman* effectively blend **flashbacks** to past events with the action, and David Ives's *Sure Thing* plays havoc with chronology, allowing his protagonist to "replay" his previous scenes until he has learned the way to the "sure thing" of the title.

Two other important elements of most successful plots that Aristotle mentions are **reversal** (*peripeteia* in Greek, also known as **peripety**), and **recognition** (*anagnorisis* in Greek, also known as **discovery**). By reversal he means a change "from one state of things within the play to its opposite." Aristotle cites one example from *Oedipus the King*, the tragedy he focuses on: "the Messenger, who, coming to gladden Oedipus and to remove his fears as to his mother, reveals the secret of his birth"; but an earlier reversal in the same play occurs when Jocasta, attempting to alleviate Oedipus's fears of prophecies, inadvertently mentions the "place where three roads meet" where Oedipus killed a man he took to be a stranger. Most plays have more than a single reversal; each episode or act builds on the main character's hopes that his or her problems will be solved, only to dash those expectations as the play proceeds. Recognition, the second term, is perhaps more properly an element of characterization because it involves a character's "change from ignorance to knowledge." If the events of the plot have not served to illuminate the character about his or her failings, then the audience is likely to feel that the story has lacked depth. The kind of self-knowledge that tragedies provide is invariably accompanied by suffering and won at great emotional cost. In comedy, on the other hand, reversals may bring relief to the characters, and recognition may bring about the happy conclusion of the play.

A typical plot may be broken down into several components. First comes the **exposition**, which provides the audience with essential information—who, what, when, where—that it needs to know before the play can continue. A novelist or short story writer can present information directly with some sort of variation on the "Once upon a time" opening. But dramatists have particular problems with exposition because facts must be presented in the form of dialogue and action. Greek dramatists used the first two parts of a tragedy, relying on the audience's familiarity with the myths being retold, to set up the initial situation of the play. Other types of drama use a single character to provide expository material. Medieval morality plays often use a "heavenly messenger" to deliver the opening speech, and some of Shakespeare's plays employ a single character named "Chorus" who speaks an introductory prologue and "sets the scene" for later portions of the plays as well. In *The Glass Menagerie*, Tom Wingfield fulfills this role in an unusual manner, telling the audience at the beginning, "I am the narrator of the play, and also a character in it." Occasionally, we even encounter the least elegant solution to the problem of dramatic exposition, employing minor characters whose sole function is to provide background information in the play's opening scene. Countless drawing-room comedies have raised the curtain on a pair of servants in the midst of a gossipy conversation which catches the audience up on the doings of the family members who comprise the rest of the cast.

The second part of a plot is called the **complication**, the interjection of some circumstance or event that shakes up the stable situation that has existed before the play's opening and begins the **rising action** of the play, during which the audience's tension and expectations become tightly intertwined and involved with the characters and the events they experience. Complication in a play may be both external and internal. A plague, a threatened invasion, or a conclusion of a war are typical examples of external complication, outside events which affect the characters' lives. Many other plays rely primarily on an internal complication, a single character's failure in business or love that comes from a weakness in his or her personality. Often the complication is heightened by **conflict** between two characters whom events have forced into collision with each other. Whatever the case, the complication of the plot usually introduces a problem that the characters cannot avoid. The rising action, which constitutes the body of the play, usually contains a number of **moments of crisis**, when solutions crop up momentarily but quickly disappear. These critical moments in the scenes may take the form of the kinds of reversals discussed above, and the audience's emotional involvement in the plot generally hinges on the characters' rising and falling hopes.

The central moment of crisis in the play is the **climax**, or the moment of greatest tension, which initiates the **falling action** of the plot. Perhaps "moments" of greatest tension would be a more exact phrase, for skillful playwrights know how to wring as much tension as possible from the audience. In the best plots, everything in earlier parts of the play has pointed to this scene. In tragedy, the climax is traditionally accompanied with physical action and violence—a duel, a suicide, a murder—and the play's highest pitch of emotion.

The final part of a plot is the **dénouement**, or **resolution**. The French word literally refers to the untying of a knot, and we might compare the emotional effects of climax and dénouement to a piece of cloth twisted tighter and tighter as the play progresses and then untwisted as the action winds down. The dénouement returns the play and its characters to a stable situation, although not the same one that existed at the beginning of the play, and gives some indication of what the future holds for them. A dénouement may be either closed or open. A **closed dénouement** ties up everything neatly and explains all unanswered questions the audience might have; an **open dénouement** leaves a few tantalizing loose ends.

Several other plot terms should also be noted. Aristotle mentions, not altogether favorably, plots with "double issues." The most common word for this is **subplot**, a less important story involving minor characters that may mirror the main plot of the play. Some plays may even have more than one subplot. Occasionally, a playwright finds it necessary to drop hints about coming events in the plot, perhaps to keep the audience from complaining that certain incidents have happened "out of the blue." This is called **foreshadowing**. If a climactic incident that helps to resolve the plot has not been adequately prepared for, the playwright may be accused of having resorted to a *deus ex machina* ending, which takes its name from the *mechane* that once literally lowered a god or goddess into the midst of the dramatic proceedings. An ending of this sort, like that of an old western movie in which the cavalry arrives out of nowhere just as the wagon train is about to be annihilated, is rarely satisfactory.

Finally, the difference between **suspense** and **dramatic irony** should be addressed. Both of these devices generate tension in the audience, although through opposite means—suspense when the audience does not know what is about to happen; dramatic irony, paradoxically, when it does. Much of our pleasure in reading a new play lies in speculating about what will happen next, but in Greek tragedy the original audience would be fully familiar with the basic outlines of the mythic story before the action even began. Thus, dramatic irony occurs at moments when the audience is more knowledgeable about events than the on-stage characters are. In some plays, our foreknowledge of certain events is so strong that we may want to cry out a warning to the characters.

Characterization

The Greek word *agon* means "debate" and refers to the central issue or conflict of a play. From *agon* we derive two words commonly used to denote the chief characters in a play: **protagonist**, literally the "first speaker," and **antagonist**, one who speaks against him. Often the word *hero* is used as a synonym for protagonist, but we should be careful in its application; indeed, in many modern plays it may be more appropriate to speak of the protagonist as an **anti-hero** because she or he may possess few, if any, of the traditional attributes of a hero. Similarly, the word *villain* brings to mind a black-mustached, sneering character in a top hat and opera cloak from an old-fashioned **melodrama** (a play whose complications are solved happily at the last minute by the "triumph of good over evil"), and usually has little application to the complex characters one encounters in a serious play.

Aristotle, in his discussion of characterization, stresses the complexity that marks the personages in the greatest plays. Nothing grows tiresome more quickly than a perfectly virtuous man or woman at the center of a play, and nothing is more offensive to the audience than seeing absolute innocence despoiled. Although Aristotle stresses that a successful protagonist must be better than ordinary men and women, he also insists that the protagonist be somewhat less than perfect:

> *There remains, then, the intermediate kind of personage, a man not preeminently virtuous and just, whose misfortune, however, is brought upon him not by vice and depravity but by some error of judgment. . . .*

Aristotle's word for this error is **hamartia**, which is commonly translated as "tragic flaw" but might more properly be termed a "great error." Whether he means some innate flaw, like a psychological defect, or simply a great mistake is open to question, but writers of tragedies have traditionally created deeply flawed protagonists. In ordinary circumstances, the protagonist's strength of character may allow him to prosper, but under the pressure of events he may crack when one small chink in his armor widens and leaves him vulnerable. A typical flaw in tragedies is **hubris**, arrogance or excessive pride, which leads the protagonist into errors that might have been avoided if he or she had listened to the advice of others. Although he does not use the term himself, Aristotle touches on the concept of **poetic justice**, the audience's sense that virtue and vice have been fairly dealt with in the play and that the protagonist's punishment is to some degree deserved.

We should bear in mind that the greatest burden of characterization in drama falls on the actor or actress who undertakes a role. No matter how well written a part is, in the hands of an incompetent or inappropriate performer the character will not be credible. Vocal inflection, gesture, and even the strategic use of silence are the stock in trade of actors, for it is up to them to convince us that we are involved in the sufferings and joys of real human beings. No two actors will play the same part in the same manner. We are lucky to have two excellent film versions of Shakespeare's *Henry the Fifth* available. Comparing the cool elegance of Laurence Olivier with the rough and ready exuberance of Kenneth Branagh is a wonderful short course in the equal validity of two radically different approaches to the same role.

In reading, there are several points to keep in mind about main characters. Physical description, while it may be minimal at best, is worth paying close attention to. Sometimes an author will give a character a name that is an indicator of his or her personality and appearance a device called a **characternym**.

Character motivation is another point of characterization to ponder. Why do characters act in a certain manner? What do they hope to gain from their actions? In some cases these motives are clear enough and may be discussed openly by the characters. In other plays, motivation is more elusive, as the playwright deliberately mystifies the audience by presenting characters who perhaps are not fully aware of the reasons for their compulsions. Modern dramatists, influenced by advances in psychology, have often refused to reduce characters' actions to simple equations of cause and effect.

Two conventions that the playwright may employ in revealing motivation are **soliloquy** and **aside**. A soliloquy is a speech made by a single character on stage alone. Hamlet's soliloquies, among them some of the most famous passages in all drama, show us the process of his mind as he toys with various plans of revenge but delays putting them into action. The aside is a brief remark (traditionally delivered to the side of a raised hand) that an actor makes directly to the audience and that the other characters on stage cannot hear. Occasionally, an aside reveals a reason for a character's behavior in a scene. Neither of these devices is as widely used in today's theater as in earlier periods, but they remain part of the dramatist's collection of techniques.

Minor characters are also of great importance in a successful play, and there are several different traditional types. A **foil**, a minor character with whom a major character sharply contrasts, is used primarily as a sounding board for ideas. A **confidant** is a trusted friend or servant to whom a major character speaks frankly and openly; confidants fulfill in some respects one role that the chorus plays in Greek tragedy. **Stock characters** are stereotypes that are useful for advancing the plot and fleshing out the scenes, particularly in comedies. Hundreds of plays have employed pairs of innocent young lovers, sharp-tongued servants, and meddling mothers-in-law as part of their casts. **Allegorical characters** in morality plays like *Everyman* are clearly labeled by their names and, for the most part, are personifications of human attributes (Beauty, Good Deeds) or of theological concepts (Confession). **Comic relief** in a tragedy may be provided by minor characters like Shakespeare's fools or clowns.

Theme

Aristotle has relatively little to say about the theme of a play, simply noting, "Thought of the personages is shown in everything to be effected by their language." Because he focuses to such a large degree on the emotional side of tragedy—its stimulation of pity and fear—he seems to give less importance to the role of drama as a serious forum for the discussion of ideas, referring his readers to another of his works, *The Art of Rhetoric*, where these matters have greater prominence. Nevertheless, **theme**, the central idea or ideas that a play discusses, is important in Greek tragedy and in the subsequent history of the theater. The trilogies of early playwrights were thematically unified around an *aition*, a Greek word for the origin of a custom, just as a typical elementary school Thanksgiving pageant portrays how the holiday traditions were first established in the Plymouth Colony.

Some dramas are explicitly **didactic** in their intent, existing with the specific aim of instructing the audience in ethical, religious, or political areas. A **morality play**, a popular type of drama in the late Middle Ages, is essentially a sermon on sin and redemption rendered in dramatic terms. More subtle in its didacticism is the **problem play** of the late nineteenth century, popularized by Ibsen, which uses the theater as a forum for the serious debate of social issues like industrial pollution or women's rights. The **drama of ideas** of playwrights like George Bernard Shaw does not merely present social problems; it goes further, actually advancing programs of reform. In the United States during the Great Depression of the 1930s, Broadway theaters featured a great deal of **social drama**, in which radical social and political programs were openly propagandized. In the ensuing decades, the theater has remained a popular site for examining issues of race, class, and gender.

Keep in mind, however, that plays are not primarily religious or political forums. If we are not entertained and moved by a play's language, action, and plot, then it is unlikely that we will respond to its message. The author who has to resort to long sermons from a *raisonneur*, the French word for a character who serves primarily as the voice of reason (i.e., the mouthpiece for the playwright's opinions), is not likely to hold the audience's sympathy or attention for long. The best plays are complex enough that they cannot be reduced to simple "thesis statements" that sum up their meaning in a few words.

Diction

Aristotle was also the author of the first important manual of public speaking, *The Art of Rhetoric*, so it should come as no surprise that he devotes considerable attention in the *Poetics* to the precise words, either alone or in combinations, that playwrights use. Instead of "diction," we would probably speak today of a playwright's "style," or discuss his or her handling of various levels of idiom in the dialogue. Much of what Aristotle has to say about parts of speech and the sounds of words in

Greek is of little interest to us; of chief importance is his emphasis on clarity and originality in the choice of words. For Aristotle, the language of tragedy should be "poetic" in the best sense, somehow elevated above the level of ordinary speech but not so ornate that it loses the power to communicate feelings and ideas to an audience. Realism in speech is largely a matter of illusion, and close inspection of the actual lines of modern dramatists like Miller and Williams reveals a discrepancy between the carefully chosen words that characters speak in plays, often making up lengthy **monologues,** and the halting, often inarticulate ("Ya know what I mean?") manner in which we express ourselves in everyday life. The language of the theater has always been an artificial one. The idiom of plays, whether by Shakespeare or by August Wilson, *imitates* the language of life; it does not duplicate it.

Ancient Greek is a language with a relatively small vocabulary and, even in translation, we encounter a great deal of repetition of key words. *Polis*, the Greek word for city, appears many times in Sophocles' *Antigone*, stressing the communal fate that the protagonist and the chorus, representing the citizens, share. Shakespeare's use of the full resources of the English language has been the standard against which all subsequent writers in the language can measure themselves. Shakespeare's language presents some special difficulties to the modern reader. His vocabulary is essentially the same as ours, but many words have changed in meaning or become obsolete over the last four hundred years. Shakespeare is also a master of different **levels of diction.** In the space of a few lines he can range from self-consciously flowery heights ("If after every tempest come such calms, / May the winds blow till they have waken'd death! / And let the labouring bark climb hills of seas / Olympus-high and duck again as low / As hell's to heaven!" exults Othello on being reunited with his bride in Cyprus) to the slangy level of the streets—he is a master of the off-color joke and the sarcastic put-down. We should remember that Shakespeare's poetic drama lavishly uses figurative language; his lines abound with similes, metaphors, personifications, and hyperboles, all characteristic devices of the language of poetry. Shakespeare's theater had little in the way of scenery and no "special effects," so a passage from *Hamlet* like "But, look, the morn, in russet mantle clad / Walks o'er the dew of yon high eastward hill" is not merely pretty or picturesque; it has the dramatic function of helping the audience visualize the welcome end of a long, fearful night.

It is true that playwrights since the middle of the nineteenth century have striven for more fidelity to reality, more verisimilitude, in the language their characters use, but even realistic dramatists often rise to rhetorical peaks that have little relationship to the way people actually speak. Both Ibsen and Williams began their careers as poets and, surprisingly, the first draft of Miller's "realistic" tragedy *Death of a Salesman* was largely written in verse.

Melody

Greek tragedy was accompanied by music. None of this music survives, and we cannot be certain how it was integrated into the drama. Certainly the choral parts of the play were sung and danced, and it is likely that even the dialogue involved highly rhythmical chanting, especially in passages employing **stichomythia**, rapid alternation of single lines between two actors, a device often encountered during moments of high dramatic tension. In the original language, the different poetic rhythms used in Greek tragedy are still evident, although these are for the most part lost in English translation. At any rate it is apparent that the skillful manipulation of a variety of **poetic meters**, combinations of line lengths and rhythms, for different types of scenes was an important part of the tragic poet's repertoire.

Both tragedies and comedies have been written in verse throughout the ages, often employing rhyme as well as rhythm. *Antigone* is written in a variety of poetic meters, some of which are appropriate for dialogue between actors and others for the choral odes. Shakespeare's *Othello* is composed, like all of his plays, largely in **blank verse**, that is, unrhymed lines of iambic pentameter (lines of ten syllables, alternating unstressed and stressed syllables). He also uses rhymed couplets, particularly for emphasis at the close of scenes; songs (there are three in *Othello*); and even prose passages, especially when dealing with comic or "low" characters. A study of Shakespeare's versification is beyond the scope of this discussion, but suffice it to say that a trained actor must be aware of the rhythmical patterns that Shakespeare utilized if she or he is to deliver the lines with anything approaching accuracy.

Of course, not only verse drama has rhythm. The last sentences of Tennessee Williams's prose drama *The Glass Menagerie* can be easily recast as blank verse that would not have embarrassed Shakespeare himself:

> Then all at once my sister touches my shoulder.
> I turn around and look into her eyes . . .
> Oh, Laura, Laura, I tried to leave you behind me,
> but I am more faithful than I intended to be!

> *I reach for a cigarette, I cross the street,*
> *I run into the movies or a bar,*
> *I buy a drink, I speak to the nearest stranger—*
> *anything that can blow your candles out!*
> *—for nowadays the world is lit by lightning!*
> *Blow your candles out, Laura—and so good-bye . . .*

The ancient verse heritage of tragedy lingers on in the modern theater and has proved resistant to even the prosaic rhythms of what Williams calls a "world lit by lightning."

Spectacle

Spectacle (sometimes called *mise en scène*, French for "putting on stage") is the last of Aristotle's elements of tragedy and, in his view, the least important. By spectacle we mean the purely visual dimension of a play; in ancient Greece, this meant costumes, a few props, and effects carried out by the use of the *mechane*. Costumes in Greek tragedy were simple but impressive. The tragic mask, or *persona*, and a high-heeled boot (*cothurnus*) were apparently designed to give characters a larger-than-life appearance. Historians also speculate that the mask might have additionally served as a crude megaphone to amplify the actors' voices, a necessary feature when we consider that the open-air theater in Athens could seat over 10,000 spectators.

Other elements of set decoration were kept to a minimum, although playwrights occasionally employed a few well-chosen spectacular effects like the triumphant entrance of the victorious king in Aeschylus's *Agamemnon*. Elizabethan drama likewise relied little on spectacular stage effects. Shakespeare's plays call for few props, and little attempt was made at historical accuracy in costumes, with a noble patron's cast-off clothing dressing Caesar one week, Othello the next.

Advances in technology since Shakespeare's day have obviously facilitated more elaborate effects in what we now call **staging** than patrons of earlier centuries could have envisioned. In the nineteenth century, first gas and then electric lighting not only made effects like sunrises possible but also, through the use of different combinations of color, added atmosphere to certain scenes. By Ibsen's day, realistic **box sets** were designed to resemble, in the smallest details, interiors of houses and apartments with an invisible "fourth wall" nearest the audience. Modern theater has experimented in all directions with set design, from the bare stage to barely suggested walls and furnishings, from revolving stages to scenes that "break the plane" by involving the audience in the drama. Tennessee Williams's *The Glass Menagerie* employs music, complicated lighting and sound effects, and semi-transparent **scrims** onto which images are projected, all to enhance the play's dream-like atmosphere. The most impressive uses of spectacle in today's Broadway productions may represent anything from the catacombs beneath the Paris Opera House to thirty-foot-high street barricades manned by soldiers firing muskets. Modern technology can create virtually any sort of stage illusion; the only limitations in today's professional theater are imagination and budget.

Before we leave our preliminary discussion, one further element should be mentioned—**setting.** Particular locales—Thebes, Corinth, and Mycenæ—are the sites of different tragedies, and each city has its own history; in the case of Thebes, this history involves a family curse that touches the members of three generations. But for the most part, specific locales in the greatest plays are less important than the universal currents that are touched. If we are interested in the particular features of Norwegian civic government in the late nineteenth century, we would perhaps do better going to history texts than to Ibsen's *An Enemy of the People.*

Still, every play implies a larger sense of setting, a sense of history that is called the **enveloping action.** The "southern belle" youth of Amanda Wingfield, in Williams's *The Glass Menagerie,* is a fading dream as anachronistic as the "gentlemen callers" she still envisions knocking on her daughter's door. Even though a play from the past may still speak eloquently today, it also provides a "time capsule" whose contents tell us how people lived and what they most valued during the period when the play was written and first performed.

Brief History and Description of Dramatic Conventions

Greek Tragedy

By the time of Sophocles, tragedy had evolved into an art form with a complex set of conventions. Each playwright would submit a **tetralogy,** or set of four plays, to the yearly competition. The first three plays, or

trilogy, would be tragedies, perhaps unified like those of Aeschylus's *Oresteia,* which deals with Agamemnon's tragic homecoming from the Trojan War. The fourth, called a **satyr-play,** was comic, with a chorus of goatmen engaging in bawdy revels that, oddly, mocked the serious content of the preceding tragedies. Only one complete trilogy, the *Oresteia* by Aeschylus, and one satyr-play, *The Cyclops* by Euripides, have survived. Three plays by Sophocles derived from the myths surrounding Oedipus and his family—*Oedipus the King, Oedipus at Colonus,* and *Antigone*—are still performed and read, but they were written at separate times and accompanied by other tragedies that are now lost. As tragedy developed during this period, it seems clear that playwrights thought increasingly of individual plays as complete in themselves; *Antigone* does not leave the audience with the feeling that there is more to be told, even though Creon is still alive at the end of the play.

Each tragedy was composed according to a prescribed formula, as ritualized as the order of worship in a contemporary church service. The tragedy begins with a **prologue** *(prologos),* "that which is said first." The prologue is an introductory scene that tells the audience important information about the play's setting, characters, and events immediately preceding the opening of the drama. The second part of the tragedy is called the *parodos,* the first appearance of the chorus in the play. As the members of the chorus enter the orchestra, they dance and sing more generally of the situation in which the city finds itself. Choral parts in some translations are divided into sections called **strophes** and **antistrophes,** indicating choral movements to left and right, respectively. The body of the play is made up of two types of alternating scenes. The first, an **episode** *(episodos)* is a passage of dialogue between two or more actors or between the actors and the chorus. Each of these "acts" of the tragedy is separated from the rest by a choral **ode** *(stasimon;* pl. *stasima)* during which the chorus is alone on the orchestra, commenting, as the voice of public opinion, about the course of action being taken by the main characters. Typically there are four pairs of episodes and odes in the play. The final scene of the play is called the *exodos.* During this part the climax occurs out of sight of the audience and a vivid description of this usually violent scene is sometimes delivered by a messenger or other witness. After the messenger's speech, the main character reappears and the resolution of his fate is determined. In some plays a wheeled platform called an *eccyclema* was used to move this fatal tableau into view of the spectators. A tragedy concludes with the exit of the main characters, sometimes leaving the chorus to deliver a brief speech or **epilogue,** a final summing up of the play's meaning.

While we may at first find such complicated rituals bizarre, we should keep in mind that dramatic conventions are primarily customary and artificial and have little to do with "reality" as we usually experience it. The role of the chorus (set by the time of Sophocles at fifteen members) may seem puzzling to modern readers, but in many ways, the conventions of Greek tragedy are no stranger than those of contemporary musical comedy, in which a pair of lovers burst into a duet and dance in the middle of a stroll in the park, soon to be joined by a host of other cast members. What is most remarkable about the history of drama is not how much these conventions have changed but how remarkably similar they have remained for over twenty-five centuries.

Medieval Drama

Drama flourished during Greek and Roman times, but after the fall of the Roman Empire (A.D. 476) it declined during four centuries of eclipse, and was kept alive throughout Europe only by wandering troupes of actors performing various types of **folk drama.** The "Punch and Judy" puppet show, still popular in parts of Europe, is a late survivor of this tradition, as are the ancient slapstick routines of circus clowns. Even though drama was officially discouraged by the Church for a long period, when it did reemerge it was as an outgrowth of the Roman Catholic mass, in the form of **liturgical drama.** Around the ninth century, short passages of sung dialogue between the priest and choir, called **tropes,** were added on special holidays to commemorate the event. These tropes grew more elaborate over the years until full-fledged religious pageants were being performed in front of the altar. In 1210, Pope Innocent III, wishing to restore the dignity of the services, banned such performances from the interior of the church. Moving them outside, first to the church porch and later entirely off church property, provided greater opportunity for inventiveness in action and staging.

In the fourteenth and fifteenth centuries, much of the work of putting on plays passed to the guilds, organizations of skilled craftsmen, and their productions became part of city-wide festivals in many continental and British cities. Several types of plays evolved. **Mystery plays** were derived from holy scripture. **Passion plays** (some of which survive unchanged today) focused on the crucifixion of Christ. **Miracle plays** dramatized the lives of the saints. The last and most complex, **morality plays,** were dramatized sermons with allegorical characters (e.g., Everyman, Death, Good Deeds) representing various generalized aspects of human life.

Elizabethan Drama

While the older morality plays were still performed throughout the sixteenth century, during the time of Queen Elizabeth I (b. 1533, reigned 1558–1603) a new type of drama, typical in many ways of other innovative types of literature developed during the Renaissance, began to be produced professionally by companies of actors not affiliated with any religious institutions. This **secular drama,** beginning in short pieces called **interludes** that may have been designed for entertainment during banquets or other public celebrations, eventually evolved into full-length tragedies and comedies designed for performance in large outdoor theaters like Shakespeare's famous Globe.

A full history of this fertile period would take many pages, but a few of its dramatic conventions are worth noting. We have already mentioned blank verse, the poetic line perfected by Shakespeare's contemporary Christopher Marlowe (1564–1593). Shakespeare wrote tragedies, comedies, and historical dramas with equal success, all characterized by passages that remain the greatest examples of poetic expression in English.

The raised platform stage in an Elizabethan theater used little or no scenery, with the author's descriptive talents setting the scene and indicating lighting and weather. The stage itself had two supporting columns, which might be used to represent trees or hiding places; a raised area at the rear, which could represent a balcony or upper story of a house; a small curtained alcove at its base; and a trap door, which could serve as a grave or hiding place. In contrast to the relatively bare stage, costumes were elaborate and acting was highly stylized. Female roles were played by young boys, and the same actor might play several different minor roles in the same play. The Oscar-winning film

Shakespeare in Love reveals a great amount of information about Elizabethan staging.

A few more brief words about Shakespeare's plays are in order. First, drama in Shakespeare's time was intended for performance, with publication being of only secondary importance. The text of many of Shakespeare's plays were published in cheap editions called **quartos** which were full of misprints and often contained different versions of the same play. Any play by Shakespeare contains words and passages that different editors have trouble agreeing on. Second, originality, in the sense that we value it, meant little to a playwright in a time before copyright laws; virtually every one of Shakespeare's plays is derived from an earlier source—Greek myth, history, another play or, in the case of *Twelfth Night,* a contemporary prose tale of questionable literary merit. The true test of Shakespeare's genius rests in his ability to transform these raw materials into art. Finally, we should keep in mind that Shakespeare's plays were designed to appeal to a wide audience—educated aristocrats and illiterate "groundlings" filled the theater—and this fact may account for the great diversity of tones and levels of language in the plays. Purists of later eras may have been dismayed by some of Shakespeare's wheezy clowns and bad puns, but for us the mixture of "high" and "low" elements gives his plays their remarkable texture.

The Comic Genres

Shakespeare's ability to move easily between "high" and "low," between tragic and comic, should be a reminder that comedy has developed along lines parallel to tragedy and has never been wholly separate from it. Most of Aristotle's remarks on comedy are lost, but he does make the observation that comedy differs from tragedy in that comedy depicts men and women as worse than they are, whereas tragedy generally stresses their best qualities. During the great age of Greek tragedy, comedies were regularly performed at Athenian festivals. The greatest of the early comic playwrights was Aristophanes (450?–385? B.C.). The plays of Aristophanes are classified as **Old Comedy** and share many of the same structural elements as tragedy. Old Comedy was always satirical and usually obscene; in *Lysistrata,* written during the devastating Athenian wars with Sparta, the men of both sides are brought to their knees by the women of the two cities, who engage in a sex strike until the men relent.

Features of Old Comedy included the use of two semi-choruses (in *Lysistrata*, old men and old women); an *agon*, an extended debate between the protagonist and an authority figure; and a *parabasis*, an ode sung by the chorus at an intermission in the action which reveals the author's own views on the play's subject. **New Comedy,** which evolved in the century after Aristophanes, tended to observe more traditional moral values and stressed romance. The New Comedy of Greece greatly influenced the writings of Roman playwrights like Plautus (254–184 B.C.) and Terence (190–159 B.C.). Plautus's *Pseudolus* (combined with elements from two of his other comedies) still finds favor in its modern musical adaptation *A Funny Thing Happened on the Way to the Forum.*

Like other forms of drama, comedy virtually vanished during the early Middle Ages. Its spirit was kept alive primarily by roving companies of actors who staged improvisational dramas in the squares of towns throughout Europe. The popularity of these plays is evidenced by certain elements in the religious dramas of the same period; the *Second Shepherd's Play* (c. 1450) involves a sheep-rustler with three shepherds in an uproarious parody of the Nativity that still evokes laughter today. Even a serious play such as *Everyman* contains satirical elements in the involved excuses that gods and other characters contrive for not accompanying the protagonist on his journey with Death.

On the continent, a highly stylized form of improvisational drama appeared in sixteenth-century Italy, apparently an evolution from earlier types of folk drama. **Commedia dell'arte** involved a cast of masked stock characters (the miserly old man, the young wife, the ardent seducer) in situations involving mistaken identity and cuckoldry. *Commedia dell'arte*, because it is an improvisational form, does not survive, but its popularity influenced the direction that comedy would take in the following century. The great French comic playwright Molière (1622–1673) incorporated many of its elements into his own plays, which combine elements of **farce,** a type of comedy which hinges on broadly drawn characters and embarrassing situations usually involving sexual misconduct, with serious social satire. Comedy such as Molière's, which exposes the hypocrisy and pretensions of people in social situations, is called **comedy of manners;** as Molière put it, the main purpose of his plays was "the correction of mankind's vices," words with which Yasmin Raza would doubtless agree.

Other types of comedy have also been popular in different eras. Shakespeare's comedies begin with the farcical complications of *The*

Comedy of Errors, progress through romantic **pastoral** comedies such as *As You Like It*, which present an idealized view of rural life, and end with the philosophical comedies of his final period, of which *The Tempest* is the greatest example. His contemporary Ben Jonson (1572–1637) favored a type known as **comedy of humours,** a type of comedy of manners in which the conduct of the characters is determined by their underlying dominant trait (the four humours were thought to be bodily fluids whose proportions determined personality). English plays of the late seventeenth and early eighteenth centuries tended to combine the hard-edged satire of comedy of manners with varying amounts of sentimental romance. A play of this type, usually hinging on matters of inheritance and marriage, is known as a **drawing-room comedy,** and its popularity, while peaking in the mid-nineteenth century, endures today.

Modern comedy in English can be said to begin with Oscar Wilde (1854–1900) and George Bernard Shaw (1856–1950). Wilde's brilliant wit and skillful incorporation of paradoxical **epigrams,** witty sayings that have made him one of the most quoted authors of the nineteenth century, have rarely been equaled. Shaw, who began his career as a drama critic, admired both Wilde and Ibsen, and succeeded in combining the best elements of the comedy of manners and the problem play in his works. *Major Barbara* (1905), a typical **comedy of ideas,** frames serious discussion of war, religion, and poverty with a search for an heir to a millionaire's fortune and a suitable husband for one of his daughters. Most subsequent writers of comedy, from Neil Simon to Wendy Wasserstein, reveal their indebtedness to Wilde and Shaw.

One striking development of comedy in recent times lies in its deliberate harshness. So-called **black humor,** an extreme type of satire in which barriers of taste are assaulted and pain seems the constant companion of laughter, has characterized much of the work of playwrights like Samuel Beckett (1906–1989), Eugene Ionesco (1912–1994), and Edward Albee (b. 1928).

Realistic Drama, the Modern Stage, and Beyond

Realism is a term that is loosely employed as a synonym for "true to life," but in literary history it denotes a style of writing that developed in the mid-nineteenth century, first in the novels of such masters as

Charles Dickens, Gustave Flaubert, and Leo Tolstoy, and later in the dramas of Ibsen and Anton Chekhov. Many of the aspects of dramatic realism have to do with staging and acting. The box set, with its invisible "fourth wall" facing the audience, could, with the added subtleties of artificial lighting, successfully mimic the interior of a typical middle-class home. Realistic prose drama dropped devices like the soliloquy in favor of more natural methods of acting such as that championed by Konstantin Stanislavsky (1863–1938), the Russian director who worked closely with Chekhov (1860–1904) to perfect a process whereby actors learned to identify with their characters' psychological problems from "inside out." This "method" acting often tries, as is the case in Chekhov's plays and, later, in those of Williams and Miller, to develop a play's **subtext,** the crucial issue in the play that no one can bear to address directly. Stanislavsky's theories have influenced several generations of actors and have become standard throughout the world of the theater. Ibsen's plays, which in fact ushered in the modern era of the theater, are often called **problem plays** because they deal with serious, even controversial or taboo, issues in society. Shaw said that Ibsen's great originality as a playwright lay in his ability to shock the members of the audience into thinking about their own lives. As the barriers of censorship have fallen over the years, the capacity of the theater to shock has perhaps been diminished, but writers still find it a forum admirably suited for debating the controversial issues which divide society.

American and world drama in the twentieth and the present centuries has gone far beyond realism to experiment with the dream-like atmosphere of **expressionism** (which may employ distorted sets to mirror the troubled, perhaps even unbalanced, psyches of the play's characters) or **theater of the absurd,** which depicts a world, like that of Samuel Beckett's *Waiting for Godot* or the early plays of Edward Albee, without meaning in which everything seems ridiculous. Nevertheless, realism is still the dominant style of today's theater, even if our definition of it has to be modified to take into account plays as diverse as *The Glass Menagerie, The Piano Lesson,* and *The God of Carnage.*

SOPHOCLES ■ (496?–406 B.C.)

Sophocles lived in Athens in the age of Pericles, during the city's greatest period of culture, power, and influence. Sophocles distinguished himself as an athlete, a musician, a military advisor, a politician and, most important, a dramatist. At sixteen, he was chosen to lead a chorus in reciting a poem on the Greek naval victory over the Persians at Salamis, and he won his first prizes as a playwright before he was thirty. Although both Aeschylus, his senior, and Euripides, his younger rival, have their champions, Sophocles, whose career spanned so long a period that he competed against both of them, is generally considered to be the most important Greek writer of tragedies; his thirty victories in the City Dionysia surpass the combined totals of his two great colleagues. Of his 123 plays, only seven survive intact, including three plays relating to Oedipus and his children, Oedipus the King, Antigone, and Oedipus at Colonus, which was produced after Sophocles' death by his grandson. He is generally credited with expanding the technical possibilities of drama by introducing a third actor in certain scenes (Aeschylus used only two) and by both reducing the number of lines given to the chorus and increasing its integration into his plays. Sophocles was intimately involved in both civic and military affairs, twice serving as a chief advisor to Pericles, and his sense of duty to the polis (Greek for "city") is apparent in many of his plays. Sophocles' importance can be judged by the many references that Aristotle makes to his works in his discussion of tragedy in the Poetics.

Antigone

Translated by Robert Fagles

Characters

Antigone, *daughter of Oedipus and Jocasta*
Ismene, *sister of Antigone*
A chorus, *of old Theban citizens and their leader*
Creon, *king of Thebes, uncle of Antigone and Ismene*
A sentry
Haemon, *son of Creon and Eurydice*
Tiresias, *a blind prophet*
A messenger

Eurydice, *wife of Creon*
Guards, attendants, and a boy

Time and Scene: The royal house of Thebes. It is still night, and the invading armies of Argos have just been driven from the city. Fighting on opposite sides, the sons of Oedipus, Eteocles and Polynices, have killed each other in combat. Their uncle, Creon, is now king of Thebes.

Enter Antigone, slipping through the central doors of the palace. She motions to her sister, Ismene, who follows her cautiously toward an altar at the center of the stage.[1]

ANTIGONE: My own flesh and blood—dear sister, dear Ismene,
how many griefs our father Oedipus handed down!
Do you know one, I ask you, one grief
that Zeus will not perfect for the two of us
while we still live and breathe! There's nothing,   5
no pain—our lives are pain—no private shame,
no public disgrace, nothing I haven't seen
in your griefs and mine. And now this:
an emergency decree, they say, the Commander[1]
has just declared for all of Thebes.   10
What, haven't you heard? Don't you see?
The doom reserved for enemies
marches on the ones we love the most.
ISMENE: Not I, I haven't heard a word, Antigone.
Nothing of loved ones,   15
no joy or pain has come my way, not since
the two of us were robbed of our two brothers,
both gone in a day, a double blow—
not since the armies of Argos vanished,
just this very night. I know nothing more,   20
whether our luck's improved or ruin's still to come.
ANTIGONE: I thought so. That's why I brought you out here,
past the gates, so you could hear in private.
ISMENE: What's the matter? Trouble, clearly . . .
you sound so dark, so grim.   25
ANTIGONE: Why not? Our own brothers' burial!
Hasn't Creon graced one with all the rites,

---

[1]Creon. In the original he is given a military title; Antigone will not defer to him as King.

disgraced the other? Eteocles, they say,
has been given full military honors,
rightly so—Creon has laid him in the earth   30
and he goes with glory down among the dead.
But the body of Polynices, who died miserably—
why, a city-wide proclamation, rumor has it,
forbids anyone to bury him, even mourn him.
He's to be left unwept, unburied, a lovely treasure   35
for birds that scan the field and feast to their heart's content.
Such, I hear, is the martial law our good Creon
lays down for you and me—yes, me, I tell you—
and he's coming here to alert the uninformed
in no uncertain terms,   40
and he won't treat the matter lightly. Whoever
disobeys in the least will die, his doom is sealed:
stoning to death inside the city walls!

There you have it. You'll soon show what you are,
worth your breeding, Ismene, or a coward—   45
for all your royal blood.

ISMENE: My poor sister, if things have come to this,
who am I to make or mend them, tell me,
what good am I to you?

ANTIGONE: Decide.
Will you share the labor, share the work?   50

ISMENE: What work, what's the risk? What do you mean?

ANTIGONE: [*Raising her hands.*]
Will you lift up his body with these bare hands
and lower it with me?

ISMENE: What? You'd bury him—
when a law forbids the city?

ANTIGONE: Yes!
He is my brother and—deny it as you will—   55
your brother too.
No one will ever convict me for a traitor.

ISMENE: So desperate, and Creon has expressly—

ANTIGONE: No,
he has no right to keep me from my own.

ISMENE: Oh my sister, think—   60

think how our own father died, hated,[2]
his reputation in ruins, driven on
by the crimes he brought to light himself
to gouge out his eyes with his own hands—
then mother . . . his mother and wife, both in one,   65
mutilating her life in the twisted noose—
and last, our two brothers dead in a single day,
both shedding their own blood, poor suffering boys,
battling out their common destiny hand-to-hand.
Now look at the two of us, left so alone . . .   70
think what a death we'll die, the worst of all
if we violate the laws and override
the fixed decree of the throne, its power—
we must be sensible. Remember we are women,
we're not born to contend with men. Then too,   75
we're underlings, ruled by much stronger hands,
so we must submit in this, and things still worse.

I, for one, I'll beg the dead to forgive me—
I'm forced, I have no choice—I must obey
the ones who stand in power. Why rush to extremes?   80
It's madness, madness.

ANTIGONE: I won't insist,
no, even if you should have a change of heart,
I'd never welcome you in the labor, not with me.
So, do as you like, whatever suits you best—
I will bury him myself.   85
And even if I die in the act, that death will be a glory.
I will lie with the one I love and loved by him—
an outrage sacred to the gods! I have longer
to please the dead than please the living here:
in the kingdom down below I'll lie forever.   90
Do as you like, dishonor the laws
the gods hold in honor.

ISMENE: I'd do them no dishonor . . .
but defy the city? I have no strength for that.

---

[2] This play was written before *Oedipus the King* and *Oedipus at Colonnus*; the latter gives us a
different picture of Oedipus's end.

SOPHOCLES

ANTIGONE: You have your excuses. I am on my way,
    I'll raise a mound for him, for my dear brother. 95

ISMENE: Oh Antigone, you're so rash—I'm so afraid for you!

ANTIGONE: Don't fear for me. Set your own life in order.

ISMENE: Then don't, at least, blurt this out to anyone.
    Keep it a secret. I'll join you in that, I promise.

ANTIGONE: Dear god, shout it from the rooftops. I'll hate you 100
    all the more for silence—tell the world!

ISMENE: So fiery—and it ought to chill your heart.

ANTIGONE: I know I please where I must please the most.

ISMENE: Yes, if you can, but you're in love with impossibility.

ANTIGONE: Very well then, once my strength gives out 105
    I will be done at last.

ISMENE: You're wrong from the start,
    you're off on a hopeless quest.

ANTIGONE: If you say so, you will make me hate you,
    and the hatred of the dead, by all rights,
    will haunt you night and day. 110
    But leave me to my own absurdity, leave me
    to suffer this—dreadful thing. I will suffer
    nothing as great as death without glory.

                                    [*Exit to the side.*]

ISMENE: Then go if you must, but rest assured,
    wild, irrational as you are, my sister, 115
    you are truly dear to the ones who love you.

[*Withdrawing to the palace. Enter a chorus*[3], *the old citizens of
Thebes, chanting as the sun begins to rise.*]

CHORUS: Glory!—great beam of sun, brightest of all
    that ever rose on the seven gates of Thebes,
        you burn through night at last!
            Great eye of the golden day, 120
    mounting the Dirce's[4] banks you throw him back—
    the enemy out of Argos, the white shield[5], the man of bronze—

---

[3]The chorus of old men celebrates the victory won over the Argive forces and Polynices.
[4]A river of the Theban plain.
[5]The Argive soldiers' shields were painted white.

he's flying headlong now
　　the bridle of fate stampeding him with pain!

　　　　And he had driven against our borders,　　　　125
　　　　launched by the warring claims of Polynices—
　　　　like an eagle screaming, winging havoc
　　　　over the land, wings of armor
　　　　shielded white as snow,
　　　　a huge army massing,　　　　　　　　　　　130
　　　　crested helmets bristling for assault.

He hovered above our roofs, his vast maw gaping
closing down around our seven gates,
　　his spears thirsting for the kill
　　　　but now he's gone, look,　　　　　　　135
before he could glut his jaws with Theban blood
or the god of fire put our crown of towers to the torch.
He grappled the Dragon[6] none can master—Thebes—
　　the clang of our arms like thunder at his back!

　　　　Zeus hates with a vengeance all bravado,　　140
　　　　the mighty boasts of men. He watched them
　　　　coming on in a rising flood, the pride
　　　　of their golden armor ringing shrill—
　　　　and brandishing his lightning
　　　　blasted the fighter[7] just at the goal,　　　145
　　　　rushing to shout his triumph from our walls.

Down from the heights he crashed, pounding down on the earth!
And a moment ago, blazing torch in hand—
　　mad for attack, ecstatic
he breathed his rage, the storm　　　　　　　150
　　of his fury hurling at our heads!
But now his high hopes have laid him low
and down the enemy ranks the iron god of war

---

[6]According to legend the Thebans sprang from the dragon's teeth sown by Cadmus.
[7]Capaneus, the most violent of the Seven against Thebes. He had almost scaled the wall when the lightning of Zeus threw him down.

deals his rewards, his stunning blows—Ares[8]
rapture of battle, our right arm in the crisis.   155

      Seven captains marshaled at seven gates
      seven against their equals, gave
      their brazen trophies[9] up to Zeus,
      god of the breaking rout of battle,
      all but two: those blood brothers,   160
      one father, one mother—matched in rage,
      spears matched for the twin conquest—
      clashed and won the common prize of death.

But now for Victory! Glorious in the morning,
joy in her eyes to meet our joy   165
      she is winging[10] down to Thebes,
our fleets of chariots wheeling in her wake—
      Now let us win oblivion from the wars,
thronging the temples of the gods
in singing, dancing choirs through the night!   170
      Lord Dionysus,[11] god of the dance
      that shakes the land of Thebes, now lead the way!

[*Enter Creon from the palace, attended by his guard.*]

      But look, the king of the realm is coming
      Creon, the new man for the new day,
      whatever the gods are sending now . . .   175
      what new plan will he launch?
      Why this, this special session?
      Why this sudden call to the old men
      summoned at one command?

CREON: My countrymen,
the ship of state is safe. The gods who rocked her,   180
after a long, merciless pounding in the storm,
have righted her once more.

---

[8]Not only the god of war but also one of the patron deities of Thebes.
[9]The victors in Greek battle set up a trophy consisting of the armor of one of the enemy dead, fixed to a post and set up at the place where the enemy turned to run away.
[10]Victory is portrayed in Greek painting and sculpture as a winged young woman.
[11]A god of the vine and of revel; his father was Zeus, and his mother, Semele, was a Theban princess.

                              Out of the whole city
I have called you here alone. Well I know,
first, your undeviating respect
for the throne and royal power of King Laius.   185
Next, while Oedipus steered the land of Thebes,
and even after he died, your loyalty was unshakable,
you still stood by their children. Now then,
since the two sons are dead—two blows of fate
in the same day, cut down by each other's hands,   190
both killers, both brothers stained with blood—
as I am next in kin to the dead,
I now possess the throne and all its powers.

Of course you cannot know a man completely,
his character, his principles, sense of judgment,   195
not till he's shown his colors, ruling the people,
making laws. Experience, there's the test.
As I see it, whoever assumes the task,
the awesome task of setting the city's course,
and refuses to adopt the soundest policies   200
but fearing someone, keeps his lips locked tight,
he's utterly worthless. So I rate him now,
I always have. And whoever places a friend
above the good of his own country, he is nothing:
I have no use for him. Zeus my witness,   205
Zeus who sees all things, always—
I could never stand by silent, watching destruction
march against our city, putting safety to rout,
nor could I ever make that man a friend of mine
who menaces our country. Remember this: 210
our country *is* our safety.
Only while she voyages true on course
can we establish friendships, truer than blood itself.
Such are my standards. They make our city great.

Closely akin to them I have proclaimed,   215
just now, the following decree to our people
concerning the two sons of Oedipus.
Eteocles, who died fighting for Thebes,

excelling all in arms: he shall be buried,
crowned with a hero's honors, the cups we pour[12]   220
to soak the earth and reach the famous dead.

But as for his blood brother, Polynices,
who returned from exile, home to his father-city
and the gods of his race, consumed with one desire—
to burn them roof to roots—who thirsted to drink   225
his kinsmen's blood and sell the rest to slavery:
that man—a proclamation has forbidden the city
to dignify him with burial, mourn him at all.
No, he must be left unburied, his corpse
carrion for the birds and dogs to tear,   230
an obscenity for the citizens to behold!

These are my principles. Never at my hands
will the traitor be honored above the patriot.
But whoever proves his loyalty to the state—
I'll prize that man in death as well as life.   235

LEADER: If this is your pleasure, Creon, treating
our city's enemy and our friend this way . . .
The power is yours, I suppose, to enforce it
with the laws, both for the dead and all of us,
the living.

CREON: Follow my orders closely then,   240
be on your guard.

LEADER: We're too old.
Lay that burden on younger shoulders.

CREON: No, no,
I don't mean the body—I've posted guards already.

LEADER: What commands for us then? What other service?

CREON: See that you never side with those who break my orders.   245

LEADER: Never. Only a fool could be in love with death.

CREON: Death is the price—you're right. But all too often
the mere hope of money has ruined many men.

[A sentry enters from the side.]

---

[12]Libations (liquid offerings—wine, honey, etc.) poured on the grave.

SENTRY: My lord,
    I can't say I'm winded from running, or set out
    with any spring in my legs either—no sir,   250
    I was lost in thought, and it made me stop, often,
    dead in my tracks, heeling, turning back,
    and all the time a voice inside me muttering,
    "Idiot, why? You're going straight to your death."
    Then muttering, "Stopped again, poor fool?   255
    If somebody gets the news to Creon first,
    what's to save your neck?"
                        And so,
    mulling it over, on I trudged, dragging my feet,
    you can make a short road take forever . . .
    but at last, look, common sense won out,   260
    I'm here, and I'm all yours,
    and even though I come empty-handed
    I'll tell my story just the same, because
    I've come with a good grip on one hope,
    what will come will come, whatever fate—   265
CREON: Come to the point!
    What's wrong—why so afraid?
SENTRY: First, myself, I've got to tell you,
    I didn't do it, didn't see who did—
    Be fair, don't take it out on me.   270
CREON: You're playing it safe, soldier,
    barricading yourself from any trouble.
    It's obvious, you've something strange to tell.
SENTRY: Dangerous too, and danger makes you delay
    for all you're worth.   275
CREON: Out with it—then dismiss!
SENTRY: All right, here it comes. The body—
    someone's just buried it, then run off . . .
    sprinkled some dry dust on the flesh,[13]
    given it proper rites.
CREON: What?   280
    What man alive would dare—
SENTRY: I've no idea, I swear it.

---

[13]A symbolic burial, all Antigone could do alone, without Ismene's help.

There was no mark of a spade, no pickaxe there,
no earth turned up, the ground packed hard and dry,
unbroken, no tracks, no wheelruts, nothing,
the workman left no trace. Just at sunup   285
the first watch of the day points it out—
it was a wonder! We were stunned . . .
a terrific burden too, for all of us, listen:
you can't see the corpse, not that it's buried,
really, just a light cover of road-dust on it,   290
as if someone meant to lay the dead to rest
and keep from getting cursed.
Not a sign in sight that dogs or wild beasts
had worried the body, even torn the skin.

But what came next! Rough talk flew thick and fast,   295
guard grilling guard—we'd have come to blows
at last, nothing to stop it; each man for himself
and each the culprit, no one caught red-handed,
all of us pleading ignorance, dodging the charges,
ready to take up red-hot iron in our fists,   300
go through fire,[14] swear oaths to the gods—
"I didn't do it, I had no hand in it either,
not in the plotting, not in the work itself!"

Finally, after all this wrangling came to nothing,
one man spoke out and made us stare at the ground,   305
hanging our heads in fear. No way to counter him,
no way to take his advice and come through
safe and sound. Here's what he said:
"Look, we've got to report the facts to Creon,
we can't keep this hidden." Well, that won out,   310
and the lot fell to me, condemned me,
unlucky as ever, I got the prize. So here I am,
against my will and yours too, well I know—
no one wants the man who brings bad news.

[14]Both traditional assertions of truthfulness, derived perhaps from some primitive ritual of ordeal—only the liar would get burned.

LEADER: My king,
    ever since he began I've been debating in my mind,   315
    could this possibly be the work of the gods?
CREON: Stop—
    before you make me choke with anger—the gods!
    You, you're senile, must you be insane?
    You say—why it's intolerable—say the gods
    could have the slightest concern for the corpse?   320
    Tell me, was it for meritorious service
    they proceeded to bury him, prized him so? The hero
    who came to burn their temples ringed with pillars,
    their golden treasures—scorch their hallowed earth
    and fling their laws to the winds.   325
    Exactly when did you last see the gods
    celebrating traitors? Inconceivable!
    No, from the first there were certain citizens
    who could hardly stand the spirit of my regime,
    grumbling against me in the dark, heads together,   330
    tossing wildly, never keeping their necks beneath
    the yoke, loyally submitting to their king.
    These are the instigators, I'm convinced—
    they've perverted my own guard, bribed them
    to do their work.
                        Money! Nothing worse   335
    in our lives, so current, rampant, so corrupting.
    Money—you demolish cities, root men from their homes,
    you train and twist good minds and set them on
    to the most atrocious schemes. No limit,
    you make them adept at every kind of outrage,   340
    every godless crime—money!
                              Everyone—
    the whole crew bribed to commit this crime,
    they've made one thing sure at least:
    sooner or later they will pay the price.

[*Wheeling on the sentry.*]

                                          You—
    I swear to Zeus as I still believe in Zeus,   345
    if you don't find the man who buried that corpse,

the very man, and produce him before my eyes,
simple death won't be enough for you,
not till we string you up alive
and wring the immorality out of you.   350
Then you can steal the rest of your days,
better informed about where to make a killing.
You'll have learned, at last, it doesn't pay
to itch for rewards from every hand that beckons.
Filthy profits wreck most men, you'll see—   355
they'll never save your life.

SENTRY: Please,
may I say a word or two, or just turn and go?

CREON: Can't you tell? Everything you say offends me.

SENTRY: Where does it hurt you, in the ears or in the heart?

CREON: And who are you to pinpoint my displeasure?   360

SENTRY: The culprit grates on your feelings,
I just annoy your ears.

CREON: Still talking?
You talk too much! A born nuisance—

SENTRY: Maybe so,
but I never did this thing, so help me!

CREON: Yes you did—
what's more, you squandered your life for silver!   365

SENTRY: Oh it's terrible when the one who does the judging
judges things all wrong.

CREON: Well now,
you just be clever about your judgments—
if you fail to produce the criminals for me,
you'll swear your dirty money brought you pain.   370

[*Turning sharply, reentering the palace.*]

SENTRY: I hope he's found. Best thing by far.
But caught or not, that's in the lap of fortune:
I'll never come back, you've seen the last of me.
I'm saved, even now, and I never thought,
I never hoped—   375
dear gods, I owe you all my thanks!

[*Rushing out.*]

CHORUS: Numberless wonders
terrible wonders walk the world but none the match for man—
that great wonder crossing the heaving gray sea,
        driven on by the blasts of winter
on through breakers crashing left and right,   380
        holds his steady course
and the oldest of the gods he wears away—
the Earth, the immortal, the inexhaustible—
as his plows go back and forth, year in, year out
        with the breed of stallions[15] turning up the furrows.   385

And the blithe, lightheaded race of birds he snares,
the tribes of savage beasts, the life that swarms the depths—
        with one fling of his nets
woven and coiled tight, he takes them all,
        man the skilled, the brilliant!   390
He conquers all, taming with his techniques
the prey that roams the cliffs and wild lairs,
training the stallion, clamping the yoke across
        his shaggy neck, and the tireless mountain bull.
And speech and thought, quick as the wind   395
and the mood and mind for law that rules the city—
        all these he has taught himself
and shelter from the arrows of the frost
when there's rough lodging under the cold clear sky
and the shafts of lashing rain—   400
        ready, resourceful man!
        Never without resources
never an impasse as he marches on the future—
only Death, from Death alone he will find no rescue
but from desperate plagues he has plotted his escapes.   405

Man the master, ingenious past all measure
past all dreams, the skills within his grasp—
        he forges on, now to destruction
now again to greatness. When he weaves in
the laws of the land, and the justice of the gods   410

---

[15]Mules—the working animal of a Greek farmer.

that binds his oaths together
   he and his city rise high—
      but the city casts out
that man who weds himself to inhumanity
thanks to reckless daring. Never share my hearth   415
never think my thoughts, whoever does such things.

[*Enter Antigone from the side, accompanied by the sentry.*]

Here is a dark sign from the gods—
what to make of this? I know her,
how can I deny it? That young girl's Antigone!
Wretched, child of a wretched father,   420
Oedipus. Look, is it possible?
They bring you in like a prisoner—
why? did you break the king's laws?
Did they take you in some act of mad defiance?

SENTRY: She's the one, she did it single-handed—   425
   we caught her burying the body. Where's Creon?

[*Enter Creon from the palace.*]

LEADER: Back again, just in time when you need him.

CREON: In time for what? What is it?

SENTRY: My king,
   there's nothing you can swear you'll never do—
   second thoughts make liars of us all.   430
   I could have sworn I wouldn't hurry back
   (what with your threats, the buffeting I just took),
   but a stroke of luck beyond our wildest hopes,
   what a joy, there's nothing like it. So,
   back I've come, breaking my oath, who cares?   435
   I'm bringing in our prisoner—this young girl—
   we took her giving the dead the last rites.
   But no casting lots this time, this is *my* luck,
   my prize, no one else's.
                 Now, my lord,
   here she is. Take her, question her,   440
   cross-examine her to your heart's content.
   But set me free, it's only right—
   I'm rid of this dreadful business once for all.

CREON: Prisoner! Her? You took her—where, doing what?
SENTRY: Burying the man. That's the whole story.
CREON: What?   445
     You mean what you say, you're telling me the truth?
SENTRY: She's the one. With my own eyes I saw her
     bury the body, just what you've forbidden.
     There. Is that plain and clear?
CREON: What did you see? Did you catch her in the act?   450
SENTRY: Here's what happened. We went back to our post,
     those threats of yours breathing down our necks—
     we brushed the corpse clean of the dust that covered it,
     stripped it bare . . . it was slimy, going soft,
     and we took to high ground, backs to the wind   455
     so the stink of him couldn't hit us;
     jostling, baiting each other to keep awake,
     shouting back and forth—no napping on the job,
     not this time. And so the hours dragged by
     until the sun stood dead above our heads,   460
     a huge white ball in the noon sky, beating,
     blazing down, and then it happened—
     suddenly, a whirlwind!
     Twisting a great dust-storm up from the earth,
     a black plague of the heavens, filling the plain,   465
     ripping the leaves off every tree in sight,
     choking the air and sky. We squinted hard
     and took our whipping from the gods.

     And after the storm passed—it seemed endless—
     there, we saw the girl!   470
     And she cried out a sharp, piercing cry,
     like a bird come back to an empty nest,
     peering into its bed, and all the babies gone . . .
     Just so, when she sees the corpse bare
     she bursts into a long, shattering wail   475
     and calls down withering curses on the heads
     of all who did the work. And she scoops up dry dust,
     handfuls, quickly, and lifting a fine bronze urn,
     lifting it high and pouring, she crowns the dead
     with three full libations.

we rushed her, closed on the kill like hunters,
and she, she didn't flinch. We interrogated her,
charging her with offenses past and present—
she stood up to it all, denied nothing. I tell you,
it made me ache and laugh in the same breath.   485
It's pure joy to escape the worst yourself,
it hurts a man to bring down his friends.
But all that, I'm afraid, means less to me
than my own skin. That's the way I'm made.
CREON: [*Wheeling on Antigone.*]   You,
with your eyes fixed on the ground—speak up.   490
Do you deny you did this, yes or no?
ANTIGONE: I did it. I don't deny a thing.
CREON: [*To the sentry.*]   You, get out, wherever you please—
you're clear of a very heavy charge.

[*He leaves; Creon turns back to Antigone.*]

You, tell me briefly, no long speeches—   495
were you aware a decree had forbidden this?
ANTIGONE: Well aware. How could I avoid it? It was public.
CREON: And still you had the gall to break this law?
ANTIGONE: Of course I did. It wasn't Zeus, not in the least,
who made this proclamation—not to me.   500
Nor did that Justice, dwelling with the gods
beneath the earth, ordain such laws for men.
Nor did I think your edict had such force
that you, a mere mortal, could override the gods,
the great unwritten, unshakable traditions.   505
They are alive, not just today or yesterday:
they live forever, from the first of time,
and no one knows when they first saw the light.

These laws—I was not about to break them,
not out of fear of some man's wounded pride,   510
and face the retribution of the gods.
Die I must, I've known it all my life—
how could I keep from knowing?—even without
your death-sentence ringing in my ears.

And if I am to die before my time   515
I consider that a gain. Who on earth,
alive in the midst of so much grief as I,
could fail to find his death a rich reward?
So for me, at least, to meet this doom of yours
is precious little pain. But if I had allowed   520
my own mother's son to rot, an unburied corpse—
that would have been an agony! This is nothing.
And if my present actions strike you as foolish,
let's just say I've been accused of folly
by a fool.

LEADER:

        Like father like daughter,   525
passionate, wild . . .
she hasn't learned to bend before adversity.

CREON: No? Believe me, the stiffest stubborn wills
fall the hardest; the toughest iron,
tempered strong in the white-hot fire,   530
you'll see it crack and shatter first of all.
And I've known spirited horses you can break
with a light bit—proud, rebellious horses.
There's no room for pride, not in a slave
not with the lord and master standing by.   535

This girl was an old hand at insolence
when she overrode the edicts we made public.
But once she had done it—the insolence,
twice over—to glory in it, laughing,
mocking us to our face with what she'd done.   540
I'm not the man, not now: she is the man
if this victory goes to her and she goes free.

Never! Sister's child or closer in blood
than all my family clustered at my altar
worshipping Guardian Zeus—she'll never escape,   545
she and her blood sister, the most barbaric death.
Yes, I accuse her sister of an equal part
in scheming this, this burial.

[*To his attendants.*]

Bring her here!

I just saw her inside, hysterical, gone to pieces.
It never fails: the mind convicts itself 550
in advance, when scoundrels are up to no good,
plotting in the dark. Oh but I hate it more
when a traitor, caught red-handed,
tries to glorify his crimes.

ANTIGONE: Creon, what more do you want 555
than my arrest and execution?

CREON: Nothing. Then I have it all.

ANTIGONE: Then why delay? Your moralizing repels me,
every word you say—pray god it always will.
So naturally all I say repels you too.

Enough. 560

Give me glory! What greater glory could I win
than to give my own brother decent burial?
These citizens here would all agree,

[*To the Chorus.*]

they would praise me too
if their lips weren't locked in fear. 565

[*Pointing to Creon.*]

Lucky tyrants—the perquisites of power!
Ruthless power to do and say whatever pleases *them*.

CREON: You alone, of all the people in Thebes,
see things that way.

ANTIGONE: They see it just that way
but defer to you and keep their tongues in leash. 570

CREON: And you, aren't you ashamed to differ so from them?
So disloyal!

ANTIGONE: Not ashamed for a moment,
not to honor my brother, my own flesh and blood.

CREON: Wasn't Eteocles a brother too—cut down, facing him?

ANTIGONE: Brother, yes, by the same mother, the same father. 575

CREON: Then how can you render his enemy such honors,
such impieties in his eyes?

ANTIGONE: He'll never testify to that,
Eteocles dead and buried.

ANTIGONE

847

CREON: He will—
    if you honor the traitor just as much as him.   580
ANTIGONE: But it was his brother, not some slave that died—
CREON: Ravaging our country!—
    but Eteocles died fighting in our behalf.
ANTIGONE: No matter—Death longs for the same rites for all.
CREON: Never the same for the patriot and the traitor.   585
ANTIGONE: Who, Creon, who on earth can say the ones below
    don't find this pure and uncorrupt?
CREON: Never. Once an enemy, never a friend,
    not even after death.
ANTIGONE: I was born to join in love, not hate—   590
    that is my nature.
CREON: Go down below and love,
    if love you must—love the dead! While I'm alive,
    no woman is going to lord it over me.

[*Enter Ismene from the palace, under guard.*]

SOPHOCLES

CHORUS: Look,
    Ismene's coming, weeping a sister's tears,
    loving sister, under a cloud . . .   595
    her face is flushed, her cheeks streaming.
    Sorrow puts her lovely radiance in the dark.
CREON: You—
    in my own house, you viper, slinking undetected,
    sucking my life-blood! I never knew
    I was breeding twin disasters, the two of you   600
    rising up against my throne. Come, tell me,
    will you confess your part in the crime or not?
    Answer me. Swear to me.
ISMENE: I did it, yes—
    if only she consents—I share the guilt,
    the consequences too.
ANTIGONE: No,   605
    Justice will never suffer that—not you,
    you were unwilling. I never brought you in.
ISMENE: But now you face such dangers . . . I'm not ashamed
    to sail through trouble with you,
    make your troubles mine.

ANTIGONE: Who did the work?   610
Let the dead and the god of death bear witness!
I have no love for a friend who loves in words alone.
ISMENE: Oh no, my sister, don't reject me, please,
let me die beside you, consecrating
the dead together.
ANTIGONE: Never share my dying,   615
don't lay claim to what you never touched.
My death will be enough.
ISMENE: What do I care for life, cut off from you?
ANTIGONE: Ask Creon. Your concern is all for him.
ISMENE: Why abuse me so? It doesn't help you now.
ANTIGONE: You're right—   620
if I mock you, I get no pleasure from it,
only pain.
ISMENE: Tell me, dear one,
what can I do to help you, even now?
ANTIGONE: Save yourself. I don't grudge you your survival.
ISMENE: Oh no, no, denied my portion in your death?   625
ANTIGONE: You chose to live, I chose to die.
ISMENE: Not, at least,
without every kind of caution I could voice.
ANTIGONE: Your wisdom appealed to one world—mine, another.
ISMENE: But look, we're both guilty, both condemned to death.
ANTIGONE: Courage! Live your life. I gave myself to death,   630
long ago, so I might serve the dead.
CREON: They're both mad, I tell you, the two of them.
One's just shown it, the other's been that way
since she was born.
ISMENE: True, my king,
the sense we were born with cannot last forever . . .   635
commit cruelty on a person long enough
and the mind begins to go.
CREON: Yours did,
when you chose to commit your crimes with her.
ISMENE: How can I live alone, without her?
CREON: Her?
Don't even mention her—she no longer exists.   640
ISMENE: What? You'd kill your own son's bride?

CREON: Absolutely:
    there are other fields for him to plow.
ISMENE: Perhaps,
    but never as true, as close a bond as theirs.
CREON: A worthless woman for my son? It repels me.
ISMENE: Dearest Haemon, your father wrongs you so!   645
CREON: Enough, enough—you and your talk of marriage!
ISMENE: Creon—you're really going to rob your son of Antigone?
CREON: Death will do it for me—break their marriage off.
LEADER: So, it's settled then? Antigone must die?
CREON: Settled, yes—we both know that.   650

[To the guards.]

    Stop wasting time. Take them in.
    From now on they'll act like women.
    Tie them up, no more running loose;
    even the bravest will cut and run,
    once they see Death coming for their lives.   655

[The guards escort Antigone and Ismene into the palace. Creon
remains while the old citizens form their chorus.]

CHORUS: Blest, they are the truly blest who all their lives
    have never tasted devastation. For others, once
    the gods have rocked a house to its foundations
        the ruin will never cease, cresting on and on
    from one generation on throughout the race—   660
    like a great mounting tide
    driven on by savage northern gales,
        surging over the dead black depths
    rolling up from the bottom dark heaves of sand
    and the headlands, taking the storm's onslaught full-force, 665
    roar, and the low moaning
                            echoes on and on
                                    and now
    as in ancient times I see the sorrows of the house,
    the living heirs of the old ancestral kings,
    piling on the sorrows of the dead
        and one generation cannot free the next—   670
    some god will bring them crashing down,

the race finds no release.
And now the light, the hope
  springing up from the late last root
in the house of Oedipus, that hope's cut down in turn   675
by the long, bloody knife swung by the gods of death
by a senseless word
     by fury at the heart.
        Zeus,
yours is the power, Zeus, what man on earth
can override it, who can hold it back?
Power that neither Sleep, the all-ensnaring   680
  no, nor the tireless months of heaven
can ever overmaster—young through all time,
mighty lord of power, you hold fast
  the dazzling crystal mansions of Olympus.
And throughout the future, late and soon   685
as through the past, your law prevails:
no towering form of greatness
  enters into the lives of mortals
    free and clear of ruin.
       True,
our dreams, our high hopes voyaging far and wide   690
bring sheer delight to many, to many others
  delusion, blithe, mindless lusts
and the fraud steals on one slowly . . . unaware
till he trips and puts his foot into the fire.
  He was a wise old man who coined   695
the famous saying: "Sooner or later
foul is fair, fair is foul
to the man the gods will ruin"—
  He goes his way for a moment only   700
  free of blinding ruin.

[*Enter Haemon from the palace.*]

Here's Haemon now, the last of all your sons.
Does he come in tears for his bride,
his doomed bride, Antigone—
bitter at being cheated of their marriage?
CREON: We'll soon know, better than seers could tell us.   705

[*Turning to Haemon.*]

Son, you've heard the final verdict on your bride?
Are you coming now, raving against your father?
Or do you love me, no matter what I do?

HAEMON: Father, I'm your *son* . . . you in your wisdom
set my bearings for me—I obey you.   710
No marriage could ever mean more to me than you,
whatever good direction you may offer.

CREON: Fine, Haemon.
That's how you ought to feel within your heart,
subordinate to your father's will in every way.
That's what a man prays for: to produce good sons—   715
a household full of them, dutiful and attentive,
so they can pay his enemy back with interest
and match the respect their father shows his friend.
But the man who rears a brood of useless children,
what has he brought into the world, I ask you?   720
Nothing but trouble for himself, and mockery
from his enemies laughing in his face.

                                                    Oh Haemon,
never lose your sense of judgment over a woman.
The warmth, the rush of pleasure, it all goes cold
in your arms, I warn you . . . a worthless woman   725
in your house, a misery in your bed.
What wound cuts deeper than a loved one
turned against you? Spit her out,
like a mortal enemy—let the girl go.
Let her find a husband down among the dead.   730
Imagine it: I caught her in naked rebellion,
the traitor, the only one in the whole city.
I'm not about to prove myself a liar,
not to my people, no, I'm going to kill her!
That's right—so let her cry for mercy, sing her hymns   735
to Zeus who defends all bonds of kindred blood.
Why, if I bring up my own kin to be rebels,
think what I'd suffer from the world at large.
Show me the man who rules his household well:
I'll show you someone fit to rule the state.   740

That good man, my son,
I have every confidence he and he alone
can give commands and take them too. Staunch
in the storm of spears he'll stand his ground,
a loyal, unflinching comrade at your side.   745

But whoever steps out of line, violates the laws
or presumes to hand out orders to his superiors,
he'll win no praise from me. But that man
the city places in authority, his orders
must be obeyed, large and small,   750
right and wrong.
                    Anarchy—
show me a greater crime in all the earth!
She, she destroys cities, rips up houses,
breaks the ranks of spearmen into headlong rout.
But the ones who last it out, the great mass of them   755
owe their lives to discipline. Therefore
we must defend the men who live by law,
never let some woman triumph over us.
Better to fall from power, if fall we must,
at the hands of a man—never be rated   760
inferior to a woman, never.

LEADER: To us,
unless old age has robbed us of our wits,
you seem to say what you have to say with sense.

HAEMON: Father, only the gods endow a man with reason,
the finest of all their gifts, a treasure.   765
Far be it from me—I haven't the skill,
and certainly no desire, to tell you when,
if ever, you make a slip in speech . . . though
someone else might have a good suggestion.

Of course it's not for you,   770
in the normal run of things, to watch
whatever men say or do, or find to criticize.
The man in the street, you know, dreads your glance,
he'd never say anything displeasing to your face.
But it's for me to catch the murmurs in the dark,   775

the way the city mourns for this young girl.
"No woman," they say, "ever deserved death less,
and such a brutal death for such a glorious action.
She, with her own dear brother lying in his blood—
she couldn't bear to leave him dead, unburied,
food for the wild dogs or wheeling vultures.
Death? She deserves a glowing crown of gold!"
So they say, and the rumor spreads in secret,
darkly . . .
        I rejoice in your success, father—
nothing more precious to me in the world.
What medal of honor brighter to his children
than a father's growing glory? Or a child's
to his proud father? Now don't, please,
be quite so single-minded, self-involved,
or assume the world is wrong and you are right.
Whoever thinks that he alone possesses intelligence,
the gift of eloquence, he and no one else,
and character too . . . such men, I tell you,
spread them open—you will find them empty.
                                    No,
it's no disgrace for a man, even a wise man,
to learn many things and not to be too rigid.
You've seen trees by a raging winter torrent,
how many sway with the flood and salvage every twig,
but not the stubborn—they're ripped out, roots and all.
Bend or break. The same when a man is sailing:
haul your sheets too taut, never give an inch,
you'll capsize, and go the rest of the voyage
keel up and the rowing-benches under.

Oh give way. Relax your anger—change!
I'm young, I know, but let me offer this:
it would be best by far, I admit,
if a man were born infallible, right by nature.
If not—and things don't often go that way,
it's best to learn from those with good advice.

LEADER: You'd do well, my lord, if he's speaking to the point,
to learn from him.

780

785

790

795

800

805

810

[*Turning to Haemon.*]

                 and you, my boy, from him.
You both are talking sense.

CREON: So,
men our age, we're to be lectured, are we?—
schooled by a boy his age?

HAEMON: Only in what is right. But if I seem young,   815
look less to my years and more to what I do.

CREON: Do? Is admiring rebels an achievement?

HAEMON: I'd never suggest that you admire treason.

CREON: Oh?—
isn't that just the sickness that's attacked her?

HAEMON: The whole city of Thebes denies it, to a man.   820

CREON: And is Thebes about to tell me how to rule?

HAEMON: Now, you see? Who's talking like a child?

CREON: Am I to rule this land for others—or myself?

HAEMON: It's no city at all, owned by one man alone.

CREON: What? The city *is* the king's—that's the law!   825

HAEMON: What a splendid king you'd make of a desert island—
you and you alone.

CREON: [*To the chorus.*]   This boy, I do believe,
is fighting on her side, the woman's side.

HAEMON: If you are a woman, yes;
my concern is all for you.   830

CREON: Why, you degenerate—bandying accusations,
threatening me with justice, your own father!

HAEMON: I see my father offending justice—wrong.

CREON: Wrong?
To protect my royal rights?

HAEMON: Protect your rights?   835
When you trample down the honors of the gods?

CREON: You, you soul of corruption, rotten through—
woman's accomplice!

HAEMON: That may be,
but you'll never find me accomplice to a criminal.

CREON: That's what *she* is,   840
and every word you say is a blatant appeal for her—

HAEMON: And you, and me, and the gods beneath the earth.

CREON: You will never marry her, not while she's alive.

HAEMON: Then she'll die . . . but her death will kill another.

CREON: What, brazen threats? You go too far!

HAEMON: What threat?   845
Combating your empty, mindless judgments with a word?

CREON: You'll suffer for your sermons, you and your empty wisdom!

HAEMON: If you weren't my father, I'd say you were insane.

CREON: Don't flatter me with Father—you woman's slave!

HAEMON: You really expect to fling abuse at me   850
and not receive the same?

CREON: Is that so!
Now, by heaven, I promise you, you'll pay—
taunting, insulting me! Bring her out,
that hateful—she'll die now, here,
in front of his eyes, beside her groom!   855

HAEMON: No, no, she will never die beside me—
don't delude yourself. And you will never
see me, never set eyes on my face again.
Rage your heart out, rage with friends
who can stand the sight of you.   860

[Rushing out.]

LEADER: Gone, my king, in a burst of anger.
A temper young as his . . . hurt him once,
he may do something violent.

CREON: Let him do—
dream up something desperate, past all human limit!
Good riddance. Rest assured,   865
he'll never save those two young girls from death.

LEADER: Both of them, you really intend to kill them both?

CREON: No, not her, the one whose hands are clean—
you're quite right.

LEADER: But Antigone—
what sort of death do you have in mind for her?   870

CREON: I'll take her down some wild, desolate path
never trod by men, and wall her up alive
in a rocky vault, and set out short rations,
just the measure piety demands

to keep the entire city free of defilement.[16]   875
There let her pray to the one god she worships:
Death—who knows?—may just reprieve her from death.
Or she may learn at last, better late than never,
what a waste of breath it is to worship Death.

[*Exit to the palace.*]

CHORUS: Love, never conquered in battle
Love the plunderer laying waste the rich!   880
Love standing the night-watch
        guarding a girl's soft cheek,
you range the seas, the shepherds' steadings off in the wilds—
not even the deathless gods can flee your onset,
nothing human born for a day—   885
whoever feels your grip is driven mad.

                                Love!—
you wrench the minds of the righteous into outrage,
swerve them to their ruin—you have ignited this,
this kindred strife, father and son at war
        and Love alone the victor—   890
warm glance of the bride triumphant, burning with desire!
Throned in power, side-by-side with the mighty laws!
Irresistible Aphrodite,[17] never conquered—
Love, you mock us for your sport.   895

[*Antigone is brought from the palace under guard.*]

        But now, even I'd rebel against the king,
        I'd break all bounds when I see this—
        I fill with tears, I cannot hold them back,
        not any more . . . I see Antigone make her way
        to the bridal vault where all are laid to rest.   900
ANTIGONE: Look at me, men of my fatherland,
                setting out on the last road

---

[16]The penalty originally proclaimed was death by stoning. But this demands the participation of
the citizens, and it may be that Creon, after listening to Haemon's remarks, is not as sure as he
once was of popular support. Creon proposed imprisonment in a tomb with a ration of food. Since
Antigone would die of starvation but not actually by anyone's hand, Creon seems to think that the
city will not be "defiled," that is, will not incur blood guilt.
[17]Goddess of sexual love.

looking into the last light of day
the last I will ever see . . .
the god of death who puts us all to bed   905
takes me down to the banks of Acheron[18] alive—
    denied my part in the wedding-songs,
no wedding-song in the dusk has crowned my marriage—
I go to wed the lord of the dark waters.

CHORUS: Not crowned with glory,[19] or with a dirge,   910
    you leave for the deep pit of the dead.
    No withering illness laid you low,
      no strokes of the sword—a law to yourself,
    alone, no mortal like you, ever, you go down
    to the halls of Death alive and breathing.   915

ANTIGONE: But think of Niobe[20]—well I know her story—
think what a living death she died,
Tantalus' daughter, stranger queen from the east:
there on the mountain heights, growing stone
binding as ivy, slowly walled her round   920
and the rains will never cease, the legends say
the snows will never leave her . . .
    wasting away, under her brows the tears
showering down her breasting ridge and slopes—
a rocky death like hers puts me to sleep.   925

CHORUS: But she was a god, born of gods,
    and we are only mortals born to die.
    And yet, of course, it's a great thing
    for a dying girl to hear, just to hear
    she shares a destiny equal to the gods,   930
    during life and later, once she's dead.

---

[18]A river in the underworld.

[19]The usual version of this line is "crowned with glory." The Greek word *oukoun* can be negative or positive, depending on the accent, which determines the pronunciation; because written accents were not yet in use in Sophocles' time, no one will ever know for sure which meaning he intended. The present version is based on the belief that the chorus is expressing pity for Antigone's ignominious and abnormal death; she has no funeral at which her fame and praise are recited; she will not die by either of the usual causes—violence and disease—but by a living death. It is as they say, her own choice: she is "a law to [herself]" (line 913).

[20]A Phrygian princess married to Amphion, king of Thebes. She boasted that she had borne more children than Leto, mother of Apollo and Artemis. As vengeance, Apollo and Artemis killed all of Niobe's children. She fled to Phrygia, where she was turned into a rock on Mount Sipylus; the melting of the snow on the mountain caused "tears" to flow down the rock formation, which resembles a woman's face. See *Iliad* 24.651–69.

ANTIGONE: O you mock me!
Why, in the name of all my fathers' gods
why can't you wait till I am gone—
    must you abuse me to my face?
O my city, all your fine rich sons!   935
And you, you springs of the Dirce,
holy grove of Thebes where the chariots gather,
        you at least, you'll bear me witness, look,
unmourned by friend and forced by such crude laws
I go to my rockbound prison, strange new tomb—   940
    always a stranger, O dear god,
    I have no home on earth and none below,
        not with the living, not with the breathless dead.

CHORUS: You went too far, the last limits of daring—
        smashing against the high throne of Justice!   945
        Your life's in ruins, child—I wonder . . .
        do you pay for your father's terrible ordeal?

ANTIGONE: There—at last you've touched it, the worst pain
the worst anguish! Raking up the grief for father
        three times over, for all the doom   950
that's struck us down, the brilliant house of Laius.
O mother, your marriage-bed
the coiling horrors, the coupling there—
        you with your own son, my father—doomstruck mother!
Such, such were my parents, and I their wretched child.   955
I go to them now, cursed, unwed, to share their home—
    I am a stranger! O dear brother, doomed
    in your marriage—your marriage murders mine,[21]
        your dying drags me down to death alive!

[*Enter Creon.*]

CHORUS: Reverence asks some reverence in return—   960
    but attacks on power never go unchecked,
        not by the man who holds the reins of power.
    Your own blind will, your passion has destroyed you.

---

[21]Polynices had married the daughter of Adrastus of Argos, to seal the alliance that enabled him to
march against Thebes.

ANTIGONE: No one to weep for me, my friends,
  no wedding-song—they take me away   965
  in all my pain . . . the road lies open, waiting.
  Never again, the law forbids me to see
  the sacred eye of day. I am agony!
  No tears for the destiny that's mine,
  no loved one mourns my death.

CREON: Can't you see?   970
  If a man could wail his own dirge *before* he dies,
  he'd never finish.

  [*To the guards.*]

                  Take her away, quickly!
  Wall her up in the tomb, you have your orders.
  Abandon her there, alone, and let her choose—
  death or a buried life with a good roof for shelter.   975
  As for myself, my hands are clean. This young girl—
  dead or alive, she will be stripped of her rights,
  her stranger's rights,[22] here in the world above.

ANTIGONE: O tomb, my bridal-bed—my house, my prison
  cut in the hollow rock, my everlasting watch!   980
  I'll soon be there, soon embrace my own,
  the great growing family of our dead
  Persephone[23] has received among her ghosts.

                                               I,
  the last of them all, the most reviled by far,
  go down before my destined time's run out.   985
  But still I go, cherishing one good hope:
  my arrival may be dear to father,
  dear to you, my mother,
  dear to you, my loving brother, Eteocles—
  When you died I washed you with my hands,   990
  I dressed you all, I poured the sacred cups
  across your tombs. But now, Polynices,
  because I laid your body out as well,

[22]The Greek words suggest that he sees her not as a citizen but as a resident alien; by her action she has forfeited citizenship. But now she will be deprived even of that inferior status.
[23]Queen of the underworld.

this, this is my reward. Nevertheless
I honored you—the decent will admit it—   995
well and wisely too.
                        Never, I tell you,
if I had been the mother of children
or if my husband died, exposed and rotting—
I'd never have taken this ordeal upon myself,
never defied our people's will. What law,   1000
you ask, do I satisfy with what I say?
A husband dead, there might have been another.
A child by another too, if I had lost the first.
But mother and father both lost in the halls of Death,
no brother could ever spring to light again.[24]   1005
For this law alone I held you first in honor.
For this, Creon, the king, judges me a criminal
guilty of dreadful outrage, my dear brother!
And now he leads me off, a captive in his hands,
with no part in the bridal-song, the bridal-bed,
denied all joy of marriage, raising children—   1010
deserted so by loved ones, struck by fate,
I descend alive to the caverns of the dead.

What law of the mighty gods have I transgressed?
Why look to the heavens any more, tormented as I am?   1015
Whom to call, what comrades now? Just think,
my reverence only brands me for irreverence!
Very well: if this is the pleasure of the gods,
once I suffer I will know that I was wrong.
But if these men are wrong, let them suffer   1020
nothing worse than they mete out to me—
these masters of injustice!

LEADER: Still the same rough winds, the wild passion
raging through the girl.

---

[24]This strange justification for her action has been considered unacceptable by many critics, and they have suspected that it was an interpolation by some later producer of the play. But Aristotle quotes it in the next century and appears to have no doubt of its authenticity. If genuine, it means that Antigone momentarily abandons the law she championed against Creon—that all people have a right to burial—and sees her motive as exclusive devotion to her dead brother. For someone facing the prospect of a slow and hideous death, such a self-examination and realization is not impossible. And it makes no difference to the courage and tenacity of her defiance of state power.

CREON: [*To the guards.*]   Take her away.
  You're wasting time—you'll pay for it too.   1025
ANTIGONE: Oh god, the voice of death. It's come, it's here.
CREON: True. Not a word of hope—your doom is sealed.
ANTIGONE: Land of Thebes, city of all my fathers—
  O you gods, the first gods of the race![25]
  They drag me away, now, no more delay.   1030
  Look on me, you noble sons of Thebes—
  the last of a great line of kings,
  I alone, see what I suffer now
  at the hands of what breed of men—
  all for reverence, my reverence for the gods!   1035

[*She leaves under guard; the chorus gathers.*]

CHORUS: Danaë,[26] Danaë—
  even she endured a fate like yours,
    in all her lovely strength she traded
  the light of day for the bolted brazen vault—
  buried within her tomb, her bridal-chamber,   1040
  wed to the yoke and broken.
      But she was of glorious birth
        my child, my child
  and treasured the seed of Zeus within her womb,
  the cloudburst streaming gold!   1045
        The power of fate is a wonder,
        dark, terrible wonder—
      neither wealth nor armies
      towered walls nor ships
      black hulls lashed by the salt   1050
      can save us from that force.

The yoke tamed him too
    young Lycurgus flaming in anger

---

[25]The Theban royal house traced its ancestry through Harmonia, wife of Cadmus, to Aphrodite and Ares, her parents. Cadmus's daughter was Semele.
[26]Daughter of Acrisius, king of Argos. It was prophesied that he would be killed by his daughter's son; so he shut her up in a bronze tower. But Zeus came to her in the form of a golden rain shower and she bore a son, Perseus, who did in the end accidentally kill his grandfather.

king of Edonia,[27] all for his mad taunts
Dionysus clamped him down, encased
in the chain-mail of rock
        and there his rage
            his terrible flowering rage burst—
sobbing, dying away . . . at last that madman
came to know his god—
            the power he mocked, the power
            he taunted in all his frenzy
            trying to stamp out
            the women strong with the god—
            the torch, the raving sacred cries—
            enraging the Muses who adore the flute.

And far north[28] where the Black Rocks
        cut the sea in half
and murderous straits
split the coast of Thrace
        a forbidding city stands
where once, hard by the walls
the savage Ares thrilled to watch
a king's new queen, a Fury rearing in rage
            against his two royal sons—
                her bloody hands, her dagger-shuttle
stabbing out their eyes—cursed, blinding wounds—
their eyes blind sockets screaming for revenge!

They wailed in agony, cries echoing cries
        the princes doomed at birth . . .
and their mother doomed to chains,
walled up in a tomb of stone[29]—

1055

1060

1065

1070

1075

1080

[27]Thrace Lycurgus opposed the introduction of Dionysiac religion into his kingdom and was imprisoned by the god.
[28]The whole story is difficult to follow, and its application to the case of Antigone is obscure. Cleopatra, the daughter of the Athenian princess Orithyia (whom Boreas, the North Wind, carried off to his home in Thrac), was married to Phineus, the Thracian king, and bore him two sons. He tired of her, abandoned her, and married Eidothea ("a king's new queen," line 1074), who put out the eyes of Cleopatra's two sons. Ares watched the savage act.
[29]Lines 1081–82 have no equivalent in the Greek text. They represent a belief that Sophocles' audience knew a version of the legend in which Cleopatra was imprisoned in a stone tomb (which is found in a later source). This would give a point of comparison to Antigone as did the imprisonment of Danaë and Lycurgus.

but she traced her own birth back
to a proud Athenian line and the high gods
and off in caverns half the world away, 1085
born of the wild North Wind

    she sprang on her father's gales,

        racing stallions up the leaping cliffs—
child of the heavens. But even on her the Fates
the gray everlasting Fates rode hard 1090
my child, my child.

[Enter Tiresias, the blind prophet, led by a boy.]

TIRESIAS: Lords of Thebes,
I and the boy have come together,
hand in hand. Two see with the eyes of one . . .
so the blind must go, with a guide to lead the way.

CREON: What is it, old Tiresias? What news now?

TIRESIAS: I will teach you. And you obey the seer.

CREON: I will, 1095
I've never wavered from your advice before.

TIRESIAS: And so you kept the city straight on course.

CREON: I owe you a great deal, I swear to that.

TIRESIAS: Then reflect, my son: you are poised, 1100
once more, on the razor-edge of fate.

CREON: What is it? I shudder to hear you.

TIRESIAS: You will learn
when you listen to the warnings of my craft.
As I sat on the ancient seat of augury,
in the sanctuary where every bird I know 1105
will hover at my hands[30]—suddenly I heard it,
a strange voice in the wingbeats, unintelligible,
barbaric, a mad scream! Talons flashing, ripping,
they were killing each other—that much I knew—
the murderous fury whirring in those wings 1110
made that much clear!

                I was afraid,
I turned quickly, tasted the burnt-sacrifice,
ignited the altar at all points—but no fire,

[30]A place where the birds gathered and Tiresias waited for omens.

the god in the fire never blazed.
Not from those offerings . . . over the embers   1115
slid a heavy ooze from the long thighbones,
smoking, sputtering out, and the bladder
puffed and burst—spraying gall into the air—
and the fat wrapping the bones slithered off
and left them glistening white. No fire!   1120
The rites failed that might have blazed the future
with a sign. So I learned from the boy here:
he is my guide, as I am guide to others.
                                 And it is you—
your high resolve that sets this plague on Thebes.
The public altars and sacred hearths are fouled,   1125
one and all, by the birds and dogs with carrion
torn from the corpse, the doomstruck son of Oedipus!
and so the gods are deaf to our prayers, they spurn
the offerings in our hands, the flame of holy flesh.
No birds cry out an omen clear and true—   1130
they're gorged with the murdered victim's blood and fat.
Take these things to heart, my son, I warn you.
All men make mistakes, it is only human.
But once the wrong is done, a man
can turn his back on folly, misfortune too,   1135
if he tries to make amends, however low he's fallen,
and stops his bullnecked ways. Stubbornness
brands you for stupidity—pride is a crime.
No, yield to the dead! Never stab the fighter when he's down. 1140

Where's the glory, killing the dead twice over?
I mean you well. I give you sound advice.
It's best to learn from a good adviser
when he speaks for your own good:
it's pure gain.

CREON: Old man—all of you! So,   1145
you shoot your arrows at my head like archers at the target—
I even have *him* loosed on me, this fortune-teller.
Oh his ilk has tried to sell me short
and ship me off for years. Well,

drive your bargains, traffic—much as you like— 1150
in the gold of India, silver-gold of Sardis.[31]
You'll never bury that body in the grave,
not even if Zeus's eagles rip the corpse
and wing their rotten pickings off to the throne of god!
Never, not even in fear of such defilement 1155
will I tolerate his burial, that traitor.
Well I know, we can't defile the gods—
no mortal has the power.
                              No,
reverend old Tiresias, all men fall,
it's only human, but the wisest fall obscenely 1160
when they glorify obscene advice with rhetoric—
all for their own gain.

TIRESIAS: Oh god, is there a man alive
    who knows, who actually believes . . .

CREON: What now?
    What earth-shattering truth are you about to utter? 1165

TIRESIAS: . . . just how much a sense of judgment, wisdom
    is the greatest gift we have?

CREON: Just as much, I'd say,
    as a twisted mind is the worst affliction known.

TIRESIAS: You are the one who's sick, Creon, sick to death.

CREON: I am in no mood to trade insults with a seer. 1170

TIRESIAS: You have already, calling my prophecies a lie.

CREON: Why not?
    You and the whole breed of seers are mad for money!

TIRESIAS: And the whole race of tyrants lusts for filthy gain.

CREON: This slander of yours—
    are you aware you're speaking to the king? 1175

TIRESIAS: Well aware. Who helped you save the city?

CREON: You—
    you have your skills, old seer, but you lust for injustice!

TIRESIAS: You will drive me to utter the dreadful secret in my heart.

CREON: Spit it out! Just don't speak it out for profit.

TIRESIAS: Profit? No, not a bit of profit, not for you. 1180

---

[31]In Asia Minor. Electrum, a natural alloy of gold and silver, was found in a nearby river.

CREON: Know full well, you'll never buy off my resolve.
TIRESIAS: Then know this too, learn this by heart!
The chariot of the sun will not race through
so many circuits more, before you have surrendered
one born of your own loins, your own flesh and blood,   1185
a corpse for corpses given in return, since you have thrust
to the world below a child sprung from the world above,
ruthlessly lodged a living soul within the grave—
then you've robbed the gods below the earth,
keeping a dead body here in the bright air,   1190
unburied, unsung, unhallowed by the rites.

You, you have no business with the dead,
nor do the gods above—this is violence
you have forced upon the heavens.
And so the avengers, the dark destroyers late   1195
but true to the mark, now lie in wait for you,
the Furies sent by the gods and the god of death
to strike you down with the pains that you perfected!

There. Reflect on that, tell me I've been bribed.
The day comes soon, no long test of time, not now,   1200
when the mourning cries for men and women break
throughout your halls. Great hatred rises against you—
cities in tumult, all whose mutilated sons
the dogs have graced with burial, or the wild beasts
or a wheeling crow that wings the ungodly stench of carrion   1205
back to each city, each warrior's heart and home.

These arrows for your heart! Since you've raked me
I loose them like an archer in my anger,
arrows deadly true. You'll never escape
their burning, searing force.   1210

[*Motioning to his escort.*]

Come, boy, take me home.
So he can vent his rage on younger men,
and learn to keep a gentler tongue in his head
and better sense than what he carries now.

LEADER: The old man's gone, my king—   1215
terrible prophecies. Well I know,
since the hair on this old head went gray,
he's never lied to Thebes.

CREON: I know it myself—I'm shaken, torn.
It's a dreadful thing to yield . . . but resist now?   1220
Lay my pride bare to the blows of ruin?
That's dreadful too.

LEADER: But good advice,
Creon, take it now, you must.

CREON: What should I do? Tell me . . . I'll obey.

LEADER: Go! Free the girl from the rocky vault   1225
and raise a mound for the body you exposed.

CREON: That's your advice? You think I should give in?

LEADER: Yes, my king, quickly. Disasters sent by the gods
cut short our follies in a flash.

CREON: Oh it's hard,
giving up the heart's desire . . . but I will do it—   1230
no more fighting a losing battle with necessity.

LEADER: Do it now, go, don't leave it to others.

CREON: Now—I'm on my way! Come, each of you,
take up axes, make for the high ground,
over there, quickly! I and my better judgment   1235
have come round to this—I shackled her,
I'll set her free myself. I am afraid . . .
it's best to keep the established laws
to the very day we die.

[*Rushing out, followed by his entourage. The chorus clusters around
the altar.*]

CHORUS: God of a hundred names!
                          Great Dionysus—   1240
Son and glory of Semele! Pride of Thebes—
Child of Zeus whose thunder rocks the clouds—
Lord of the famous lands of evening—
King of the Mysteries!

King of Eleusis, Demeter's[32] plain
her breasting hills that welcome in the world—   1245
Great Dionysus!
                        Bacchus, living in Thebes
the mother-city of all your frenzied women—
                                                  Bacchus
living along the Ismenus'[33] rippling waters
standing over the field sown with the Dragons' teeth!
You—we have seen you through the flaring smoky fires,   1250
        your torches blazing over the twin peaks[34]
where nymphs of the hallowed cave climb onward
        fired with you, your sacred rage—
we have seen you at Castalia's running spring
and down from the heights of Nysa[35] crowned with ivy   1255
the greening shore rioting vines and grapes
        down you come in your storm of wild women
                ecstatic, mystic cries—
                        Dionysus—
down to watch and ward the roads of Thebes!

First of all cities, Thebes you honor first   1260
you and your mother, bride of the lightning—
come, Dionysus! now your people lie
in the iron grip of plague,
come in your racing, healing stride
        down Parnassus'[36] slopes   1265
or across the moaning straits.
                        Lord of the dancing—
dance, dance the constellations breathing fire!
Great master of the voices of the night!
Child of Zeus, God's offspring, come, come forth!
Lord, king, dance with your nymphs, swirling, raving   1270

---

[32]The grain and harvest goddess. Eleusis, the site of the mysteries and the worship of Demeter, is near Athens.
[33]A river at Thebes. Dionysus (or Bacchus) was among the divinities worshipped by the initiates.
[34]The two cliffs above Delphi, where Dionysus was thought to reside in the winter months.
[35]A mountain associated with Dionysiac worship; several mountains are so named, but the reference here is probably to the one on the island of Euboea, off the Attic coast.
[36]Mountain in central Greece just north of the Gulf of Corinth; an important cult of Dionysus was located there, as was Apollo's oracle at Delphi.

> arm-in-arm in frenzy through the night
>> they dance you, Iacchus[37]—
>>> Dance, Dionysus
> giver of all good things!

[*Enter a messenger from the side.*]

MESSENGER: Neighbors,
friends of the house of Cadmus and the kings,
there's not a thing in this mortal life of ours   1275
I'd praise or blame as settled once for all.
Fortune lifts and Fortune fells the lucky
and unlucky every day. No prophet on earth
can tell a man his fate. Take Creon:
there was a man to rouse your envy once,   1280
as I see it. He saved the realm from enemies;
taking power, he alone, the lord of the fatherland,
he set us true on course—flourished like a tree
with the noble line of sons he bred and reared . . .
and now it's lost, all gone.
                         Believe me,   1285
when a man has squandered his true joys,
he's good as dead, I tell you, a living corpse.
Pile up riches in your house, as much as you like—
live like a king with a huge show of pomp,
but if real delight is missing from the lot,   1290
I wouldn't give you a wisp of smoke for it,
not compared with joy.
LEADER: What now?
What new grief do you bring the house of kings?
MESSENGER: Dead, dead—and the living are guilty of their death!
LEADER: Who's the murderer? Who is dead? Tell us.   1295
MESSENGER: Haemon's gone, his blood spilled by the very hand—
LEADER: His father's or his own?
MESSENGER: His own . . .
raging mad with his father for the death—
LEADER: Oh great seer,
you saw it all, you brought your word to birth!

---

[37]Dionysus.

MESSENGER: Those are the facts. Deal with them as you will.   1300

[*As he turns to go, Eurydice enters from the palace.*]

LEADER: Look, Eurydice. Poor woman, Creon's wife,
       so close at hand. By chance perhaps,
       unless she's heard the news about her son.

EURYDICE: My countrymen,
       all of you—I caught the sound of your words
       as I was leaving to do my part,   1305
       to appeal to queen Athena with my prayers.
       I was just loosing the bolts, opening the doors,
       when a voice filled with sorrow, family sorrow,
       struck my ears, and I fell back, terrified,
       into the women's arms—everything went black.   1310
       Tell me the news, again, whatever it is . . .
       sorrow and I are hardly strangers;
       I can bear the worst.

MESSENGER: I—dear lady,
       I'll speak as an eye-witness. I was there.
       And I won't pass over one word of the truth.   1315
       Why should I try to soothe you with a story,
       only to prove a liar in a moment?
       Truth is always best.
                       So,
       I escorted your lord, I guided him
       to the edge of the plain where the body lay,   1320
       Polynices, torn by the dogs and still unmourned.
       And saying a prayer to Hecate of the Crossroads,
       Pluto[38] too, to hold their anger and be kind,
       we washed the dead in a bath of holy water
       and plucking some fresh branches, gathering . . .   1325
       what was left of him, we burned them all together
       and raised a high mound of native earth, and then
       we turned and made for that rocky vault of hers,
       the hollow, empty bed of the bride of Death.
       And far off, one of us heard a voice,   1330

---

[38]Or Hades, god of the underworld. Hecate is a goddess associated with darkness and burial grounds; offerings to her were left at crossroads.

a long wail rising, echoing
out of that unhallowed wedding-chamber,
he ran to alert the master and Creon pressed on,
closer—the strange, inscrutable cry came sharper,
throbbing around him now, and he let loose   1335
a cry of his own, enough to wrench the heart,
"Oh god, am I the prophet now? going down
the darkest road I've ever gone? My son—
it's *his* dear voice, he greets me! Go, men,
closer, quickly! Go through the gap,   1340
the rocks are dragged back—
right to the tomb's very mouth—and look,
see if it's Haemon's voice I think I hear,
or the gods have robbed me of my senses."

The king was shattered. We took his orders,   1345
went and searched, and there in the deepest,
dark recesses of the tomb we found her . . .
hanged by the neck in a fine linen noose,
strangled in her veils—and the boy,
his arms flung around her waist,   1350
clinging to her, wailing for his bride,
dead and down below, for his father's crimes
and the bed of his marriage blighted by misfortune.
When Creon saw him, he gave a deep sob,
he ran in, shouting, crying out to him,   1355
"Oh my child—what have you done? what seized you,
what insanity? what disaster drove you mad?
Come out, my son! I beg you on my knees!"
But the boy gave him a wild burning glance,
spat in his face, not a word in reply,   1360
he drew his sword—his father rushed out,
running as Haemon lunged and missed!—
and then, doomed, desperate with himself,
suddenly leaning his full weight on the blade,
he buried it in his body, halfway to the hilt.   1365
And still in his senses, pouring his arms around her,
he embraced the girl and breathing hard,
released a quick rush of blood,

bright red on her cheek glistening white.
And there he lies, body enfolding body . . .   1370
he has won his bride at last, poor boy,
not here but in the houses of the dead.

Creon shows the world that of all the ills
afflicting men the worst is lack of judgment.

[*Eurydice turns and reenters the palace.*]

LEADER: What do you make of that? The lady's gone,   1375
  without a word, good or bad.

MESSENGER: I'm alarmed too
  but here's my hope—faced with her son's death,
  she finds it unbecoming to mourn in public.
  Inside, under her roof, she'll set her women
  to the task and wail the sorrow of the house.   1380
  She's too discreet. She won't do something rash.

LEADER: I'm not so sure. To me, at least,
  a long heavy silence promises danger,
  just as much as a lot of empty outcries.

MESSENGER: We'll see if she's holding something back,   1385
  hiding some passion in her heart.
  I'm going in. You may be right—who knows?
  Even too much silence has its dangers.

        [*Exit to the palace. Enter Creon from the side, escorted
        by attendants carrying Haemon's body on a bier.*]

LEADER: The king himself! Coming toward us,
  look, holding the boy's head in his hands.   1390
  Clear, damning proof, if it's right to say so—
  proof of his own madness, no one else's,
      no, his own blind wrongs.

CREON: Ohhh,
  so senseless, so insane . . . my crimes,
  my stubborn, deadly—   1395
  Look at us, the killer, the killed,
  father and son, the same blood—the misery!
  My plans, my mad fanatic heart,
  my son, cut off so young!

Ai, dead, lost to the world,   1400
        not through your stupidity, no, my own.

LEADER: Too late,
        too late, you see what justice means.

CREON: Oh I've learned
        through blood and tears! Then, it was then,
        when the god came down and struck me—a great weight
        shattering, driving me down that wild savage path,   1405
        ruining, trampling down my joy. Oh the agony,
                the heartbreaking agonies of our lives.

[*Enter the Messenger from the palace.*]

MESSENGER: Master,
        what a hoard of grief you have, and you'll have more.
        The grief that lies to hand you've brought yourself—

[*Pointing to Haemon's body.*]

        the rest, in the house, you'll see it all too soon.   1410

CREON: What now? What's worse than this?

MESSENGER: The queen is dead.
        The mother of this dead boy . . . mother to the end—
        poor thing, her wounds are fresh.

CREON: No, no,
        harbor of Death, so choked, so hard to cleanse!—
        why me? why are you killing me?   1415
        Herald of pain, more words, more grief?
        I died once, you kill me again and again!
        What's the report, boy . . . some news for me?
        My wife dead? O dear god!
        Slaughter heaped on slaughter?

[*The doors open; the body of Eurydice is brought out on her bier.*]

MESSENGER: See for yourself: 1420
        now they bring her body from the palace.

CREON: Oh no,
        another, a second loss to break the heart.
        What next, what fate still waits for me?
        I just held my son in my arms and now,
        look, a new corpse rising before my eyes—   1425
                wretched, helpless mother—O my son!

MESSENGER: She stabbed herself at the altar,
   then her eyes went dark, after she'd raised
   a cry for the noble fate of Megareus,[39] the hero
   killed in the first assault, then for Haemon,   1430
   then with her dying breath she called down
   torments on your head—you killed her sons.
CREON: Oh the dread,
   I shudder with dread! Why not kill me too?—
   run me through with a good sharp sword?
   Oh god, the misery, anguish—   1435
   I, I'm churning with it, going under.
MESSENGER: Yes, and the dead, the woman lying there,
   piles the guilt of all their deaths on you.
CREON: How did she end her life, what bloody stroke?
MESSENGER: She drove home to the heart with her own hand,   1440
   once she learned her son was dead . . . that agony.
CREON: And the guilt is all mine—
   can never be fixed on another man,
   no escape for me. I killed you,
   I, god help me, I admit it all!   1445

[To his attendants.]

   Take me away, quickly, out of sight.
   I don't even exist—I'm no one. Nothing.
LEADER: Good advice, if there's any good in suffering.
   Quickest is best when troubles block the way.
CREON: [Kneeling in prayer.]
   Come, let it come!—that best of fates for me   1450
   that brings the final day, best fate of all.
   Oh quickly, now—
   so I never have to see another sunrise.
LEADER: That will come when it comes;
   we must deal with all that lies before us.   1455
   The future rests with the ones who tend the future.
CREON: That prayer—I poured my heart into that prayer!

---

[39]Another son of Creon and Eurydice; he was killed during the siege of the city. Tiresias had prophesied that his death would save Thebes.

LEADER: No more prayers now. For mortal men
           there is no escape from the doom we must endure.

CREON: Take me away, I beg you, out of sight.   1460
           A rash, indiscriminate fool!
           I murdered you, my son, against my will—
           you too, my wife . . .

                              Wailing wreck of a man,
           whom to look to? where to lean for support?

[Desperately turning from Haemon to Eurydice on their biers.]

           Whatever I touch goes wrong—once more   1465
           a crushing fate's come down upon my head.

[The messenger and attendants lead Creon into the palace.]

CHORUS: Wisdom is by far the greatest part of joy,
           and reverence toward the gods must be safeguarded.
           The mighty words of the proud are paid in full
           with mighty blows of fate, and at long last   1470
           those blows will teach us wisdom.

                              [The old citizens exit to the side.]

William Shakespeare, the supreme writer of English, was born, baptized, and buried in the market town of Stratford-on-Avon, eighty miles from London. Son of a glove maker and merchant who was high bailiff (or mayor) of the town, he probably attended grammar school and learned to read Latin authors in the original. At eighteen, he married Anne Hathaway, twenty-six, by whom he had three children, including twins. By 1592, he had become well known and envied as an actor and playwright in London. From 1594 until he retired, he belonged to the same theatrical company, the Lord Chamberlain's Men (later renamed the King's Men in honor of their patron, James I), for whom he wrote thirty-six plays—some of them, such as Hamlet and King Lear, profound reworkings of old plays. As an actor, Shakespeare is believed to have played supporting roles, such as Hamlet's father's ghost. The company prospered, moved into the Globe Theatre in 1599, and in 1608 bought the fashionable Blackfriars as well; Shakespeare owned an interest in both theaters. When plagues shut down the theaters from 1592 to 1594, Shakespeare turned to story poems; his great sonnets (published only in 1609) probably also date from the 1590s. Plays were regarded as entertainments of little literary merit, and Shakespeare did not bother to supervise their publication. After The Tempest (1611), the last play entirely from his hand, he retired to Stratford, where since 1597 he had owned the second largest house in town.

Twelfth Night; or, What You Will

[Dramatis Personae

ORSINO, Duke (sometimes called Count) of Illyria
VALENTINE, gentleman attending on Orsino
CURIO, gentleman attending on Orsino
VIOLA, a shipwrecked lady, later disguised as Cesario
SEBASTIAN, twin brother of Viola
ANTONIO, a sea captain, friend to Sebastian
CAPTAIN of the shipwrecked vessel
OLIVIA, a rich countess of Illyria
MARIA, gentlewoman in Olivia's household
SIR TOBY BELCH, Olivia's uncle
SIR ANDREW AGUECHEEK, a companion of Sir Toby
MALVOLIO, steward of Olivia's household

FABIAN, *a member of Olivia's household*
FESTE, *a clown, also called* FOOL, *Olivia's jester*

A PRIEST
FIRST OFFICER
SECOND OFFICER

Lords, Sailors, Musicians, and other Attendants
        SCENE: *Illyria°*]

1.1

Enter Orsino Duke of Illyria, Curio, and other lords [with musicians].

ORSINO: If music be the food of love, play on;
    Give me excess of it, that surfeiting,
    The appetite may sicken and so die.
    That strain again! It had a dying fall;°
    Oh, it came o'er my ear like the sweet sound   5
    That breathes upon a bank of violets,
    Stealing and giving odor. Enough, no more.
    'Tis not so sweet now as it was before.
    O spirit of love, how quick and fresh° art thou,
    That, notwithstanding thy capacity   10
    Receiveth as the sea, naught enters there,
    Of what validity° and pitch° soe'er,
    But falls into abatement° and low price
    Even in a minute! So full of shapes° is fancy°
    That it alone is high fantastical.°   15
CURIO: Will you go hunt, my lord?
ORSINO: What, Curio?
CURIO: The hart.
ORSINO: Why, so I do, the noblest that I have.°
    Oh, when mine eyes did see Olivia first,
    Methought she purged the air of pestilence.
    That instant was I turned into a hart,   20

SCENE *Illyria* Nominally on the east coast of the Adriatic Sea, but with a suggestion also of "illusion" and "delirium." **4 fall** cadence **9 quick and fresh** keen and hungry **12 validity** value.
pitch superiority. (Literally, the highest point of a falcon's flight.) **13 abatement** depreciation. (The lover's brain entertains innumerable fantasies but soon tires of them all.) **14 shapes** imagined forms. **fancy** love **15 it ... fantastical** it surpasses everything else in imaginative power. **17 the noblest . . . have** i.e., my noblest part, my heart. (Punning on *hart*.)

And my desires, like fell° and cruel hounds,
E'er since pursue me.°

Enter Valentine.

                                    How now, what news from her?
VALENTINE: So please my lord, I might not be admitted,
But from her handmaid do return this answer:
The element° itself, till seven years' heat,°   25
Shall not behold her face at ample view;
But like a cloistress° she will veilèd walk,
And water once a day her chamber round
With eye-offending brine—all this to season°
A brother's dead love,° which she would keep fresh   30
And lasting in her sad remembrance.
ORSINO: Oh, she that hath a heart of that fine frame°
To pay this debt of love but to a brother,
How will she love, when the rich golden shaft°
Hath killed the flock of all affections else°   35
That live in her; when liver, brain, and heart,
These sovereign thrones, are all supplied, and filled
Her sweet perfections, with one self king!°
Away before me to sweet beds of flowers.
Love-thoughts lie rich when canopied with bowers.   40

                                                              Exeunt.

1.2

Enter Viola, a Captain, and sailors.

VIOLA: What country, friends, is this?
CAPTAIN: This is Illyria, lady.
VIOLA: And what should I do in Illyria?
My brother he is in Elysium.°
Perchance he is not drowned. What think you, sailors?   5

---

21 **fell** fierce   22 **pursue me** (Alludes to the story in Ovid of Actaeon, who, having seen Diana bathing, was transformed into a stag and killed by his own hounds.)   25 **element** sky.   **seven years' heat** seven summers   27 **cloistress** nun secluded in a religious community   29 **season** keep fresh. (Playing on the idea of the salt in her tears.)   30 **A brother's dead love** her love for her dead brother and the memory of his love for her   32 **frame** construction   34 **golden shaft** Cupid's golden-tipped arrow, causing love. (His lead-tipped arrow causes aversion.)   35 **affections else** other feelings   36–8 **when ... king** i.e., when passion, thought, and feeling all sit in majesty in their proper thrones (liver, brain, and heart), and her sweet perfections are brought to completion by her union with a single lord and husband.
4 **Elysium** classical abode of the blessed dead.

CAPTAIN: It is perchance that you yourself were saved.

VIOLA: Oh, my poor brother! And so perchance may he be.

CAPTAIN: True, madam, and to comfort you with chance,°
    Assure yourself, after our ship did split,
    When you and those poor number saved with you   10
    Hung on our driving° boat, I saw your brother,
    Most provident in peril, bind himself,
    Courage and hope both teaching him the practice,
    To a strong mast that lived° upon the sea;
    Where, like Arion° on the dolphin's back,   15
    I saw him hold acquaintance with the waves
    So long as I could see.

VIOLA: For saying so, there's gold. [*She gives money.*]
    Mine own escape unfoldeth to my hope,
    Whereto thy speech serves for authority,   20
    The like of him°. Know'st thou this country?

CAPTAIN: Ay, madam, well, for I was bred and born
    Not three hours' travel from this very place.

VIOLA: Who governs here?

CAPTAIN: A noble duke, in nature as in name.   25

VIOLA: What is his name?

CAPTAIN: Orsino.

VIOLA: Orsino! I have heard my father name him.
    He was a bachelor then.

CAPTAIN: And so is now, or was so very late;°   30
    For but a month ago I went from hence,
    And then 'twas fresh in murmur°—as, you know,
    What great ones do the less° will prattle of—
    That he did seek the love of fair Olivia.

VIOLA: What's she?   35

CAPTAIN: A virtuous maid, the daughter of a count
    That died some twelvemonth since, then leaving her
    In the protection of his son, her brother,

6-7 perchance ... perchance Perhaps ... by mere chance   **8 chance** i.e., what one may hope that chance will bring about   **11 driving** drifting, driven by the seas   **14 lived** i.e., kept afloat   **15 Arion** a Greek poet who so charmed the dolphins with his lyre that they saved him when he leaped into the sea to escape murderous sailors   **19-21 unfoldeth ... him** offers a hopeful example that he may have escaped similarly, to which hope your speech provides support.   **30 late** lately.   **32 murmur** rumor   **33 less** social inferiors

Who shortly also died; for whose dear love,
They say, she hath abjured the sight
And company of men. 40

VIOLA: Oh, that I served that lady,
And might not be delivered° to the world
Till I had made mine own occasion mellow,°
What my estate° is!

CAPTAIN: That were hard to compass,°
Because she will admit no kind of suit, 45
No, not° the Duke's.

VIOLA: There is a fair behavior in thee, Captain,
And though that° nature with a beauteous wall
Doth oft close in pollution, yet of thee
I will believe thou hast a mind that suits 50
With this thy fair and outward character.°
I prithee, and I'll pay thee bounteously,
Conceal me what I am, and be my aid
For such disguise as haply shall become
The form of my intent°. I'll serve this duke. 55
Thou shalt present me as an eunuch° to him.
It may be worth thy pains, for I can sing
And speak to him in many sorts of music
That will allow° me very worth his service.
What else may hap, to time I will commit; 60
Only shape thou thy silence to my wit.°

CAPTAIN: Be you his eunuch, and your mute° I'll be;
When my tongue blabs, then let mine eyes not see.

VIOLA: I thank thee. Lead me on. *Exeunt.*

1.3

Enter Sir Toby [Belch] and Maria.

SIR TOBY: What a plague means my niece to take the death of
her brother thus? I am sure care's an enemy to life.

---

42 delivered revealed, made known. (With suggestion of "born.") **43 Till ... mellow** until the time is
ripe for my purpose **44 estate** social rank. **compass** encompass, bring about **46 not** not even
48 though that though **51 character** face or features as indicating moral qualities. **54–5 as haply
... intent** as may suit the nature of my purpose. **56 eunuch** castrato, high-voiced singer **59 allow**
prove **61 wit** plan, invention. **62 mute** silent attendant. (Sometimes used of nonspeaking actors.)

MARIA: By my troth, Sir Toby, you must come in earlier o'nights. Your cousin°, my lady, takes great exceptions to your ill hours.

SIR TOBY: Why, let her except before excepted.°   5

MARIA: Ay, but you must confine yourself within the modest° limits of order.

SIR TOBY: Confine? I'll confine myself no finer° than I am. These clothes are good enough to drink in, and so be these boots too. An° they be not, let them hang them-selves in their   10 own straps.

MARIA: That quaffing and drinking will undo you. I heard my lady talk of it yesterday, and of a foolish knight that you brought in one night here to be her wooer.

SIR TOBY: Who, Sir Andrew Aguecheek?

MARIA: Ay, he.   15

SIR TOBY: He's as tall° a man as any's in Illyria.

MARIA: What's that to th' purpose?

SIR TOBY: Why, he has three thousand ducats° a year.

MARIA: Ay, but he'll have but a year in all these ducats.° He's a very fool and a prodigal.   20

SIR TOBY: Fie, that you'll say so! He plays o'th' viol-de-gamboys,° and speaks three or four languages word for word without book,° and hath all the good gifts of nature.

MARIA: He hath indeed, almost natural,° for, besides that he's a fool, he's a great quarreler, and but that he hath the gift° of a   25 coward to allay the gust° he hath in quarreling, 'tis thought among the prudent he would quickly have the gift of a grave.

SIR TOBY: By this hand, they are scoundrels and substractors° that say so of him. Who are they?

MARIA: They that add, moreover, he's drunk nightly in your company.   30

SIR TOBY: With drinking healths to my niece. I'll drink to her as long as there is a passage in my throat and drink in Illyria.

---

4 cousin kinswoman   **5 let . . . excepted** i.e., let her take exception to my conduct all she wants; I don't care. (Plays on the legal phrase *exceptis excipiendis,* "with the exceptions before named.")   **6 modest** moderate   **8 I'll . . . finer** (1) I'll constrain myself no more rigorously (2) I'll dress myself no more finely   **10 An** If   **16 tall** brave. (But Maria pretends to take the word in the common sense.)   **18 ducats** coins worth about four or five shillings   **19 ducats . . . ducats** he'll spend all his money within a year.   **21 viol-de-gamboys** viola da gamba, leg-viol, bass viol   **22–3 without book** by heart   **24 natural** (With a play on the sense "born idiot.")   **25 gift** natural ability. (But shifted to mean "present" in line 33.)   **26 allay the gust** moderate the taste   **28 substractors** detractors

He's a coward and a coistrel° that will not drink to my niece
till his brains turn o'th' toe like a parish top.° What, wench?
Castiliano vulgo!° For here comes Sir Andrew Agueface.°   35

> *Enter Sir Andrew [Aguecheek].*

SIR ANDREW: Sir Toby Belch! How now, Sir Toby Belch?

SIR TOBY: Sweet Sir Andrew!

SIR ANDREW: [*to Maria*] Bless you, fair shrew.°

MARIA: And you too, sir.

SIR TOBY: Accost,° Sir Andrew, accost.   40

SIR ANDREW: What's that?

SIR TOBY: My niece's chambermaid.°

SIR ANDREW: Good Mistress Accost, I desire better acquaintance.

MARIA: My name is Mary, sir.

SIR ANDREW: Good Mistress Mary Accost—   45

SIR TOBY: You mistake, knight. "Accost" is front° her, board° her,
woo her, assail her.

SIR ANDREW: By my troth, I would not undertake° her in this
company. Is that the meaning of "accost"?   50

MARIA: Fare you well, gentlemen. [*Going.*]

SIR TOBY: An thou let part° so, Sir Andrew, would thou mightst
never draw sword again.

SIR ANDREW: An you part so, mistress, I would I might never
draw sword again. Fair lady, do you think you have fools in   55
hand?°

MARIA: Sir, I have not you by the hand.

SIR ANDREW: Marry,° but you shall have, and here's my hand.

> *[He gives her his hand.]*

---

33 coistrel horse-groom, base fellow   **34 parish top** a large top provided by the parish to be spun
by whipping, apparently for exercise.   **35 Castiliano vulgo!** (Of uncertain meaning. Possibly Sir
Toby is saying "Speak of the devil!" Castiliano is the name adopted by a devil in Haughton's *Grim
the Collier of Croydon*.)   **35 Agueface** (Like *Aguecheek*, this name betokens the thin, pale
countenance of one suffering from an ague or fever.)   **38 shrew** i.e., diminutive creature. (But with
probably unintended suggestion of shrewishness.)   **40 Accost** Go alongside (a nautical term), i.e.,
greet her, address her   **42 chambermaid** lady-in-waiting (a gentlewoman, not one who would do
menial tasks).   **46 front** confront, come alongside.   **46 board** greet, approach (as though
preparing to board in a naval encounter)   **48 undertake** have to do with. (Here with unintended
sexual suggestion, to which Maria mirthfully replies with her jokes about *dry jests, barren,* and
buttery-bar.)   **51 An . . . part** If you let her leave   **54–5 have . . . hand** i.e., have to deal with fools.
(But Maria puns on the literal sense.)   **57 Marry** i.e., Indeed. (Originally, "By the Virgin Mary.")

MARIA: Now, sir, thought is free.° I pray you, bring your hand to th' buttery-bar,° and let it drink.

SIR ANDREW: Wherefore, sweetheart? What's your metaphor? 60

MARIA: It's dry,° sir.

SIR ANDREW: Why, I think so. I am not such an ass but I can keep my hand dry.° But what's your jest?

MARIA: A dry jest, sir.

SIR ANDREW: Are you full of them? 65

MARIA: Ay, sir, I have them at my fingers' ends.° Marry, now I let go your hand, I am barren.°

[She lets go his hand.] Exit Maria.

SIR TOBY: Oh, knight, thou lack'st a cup of canary!° When did I see thee so put down?

SIR ANDREW: Never in your life, I think, unless you see canary 70
put me down.° Methinks sometimes I have no more wit than a Christian or an ordinary man has. But I am a great eater of beef, and I believe that does harm to my wit.

SIR TOBY: No question.

SIR ANDREW: An I thought that, I'd forswear it. I'll ride home tomorrow, Sir Toby. 75

SIR TOBY: *Pourquoi,*° my dear knight?

SIR ANDREW: What is "*pourquoi*"? Do or not do? I would I had bestowed that time in the tongues° that I have in fencing, dancing, and bearbaiting.° Oh, had I but followed the arts!°

SIR TOBY: Then hadst thou had an excellent head of hair.
   80

SIR ANDREW: Why, would that have mended° my hair?

SIR TOBY: Past question, for thou see'st it will not curl by nature.

SIR ANDREW: But it becomes me well enough, does't not?

---

58 thought is free i.e., I may think what I like. (Proverbial; replying to *do you think . . . in hand,* above.)   **59 buttery-bar** ledge on top of the half-door to the buttery or the wine cellar. (Maria's language is sexually suggestive, though Sir Andrew seems oblivious to that.)   **61 dry** thirsty; also dried up, a sign of age and sexual debility   **63 dry** (1) ironic (2) dull, barren. (Referring to Sir Andrew.)   **66 at my fingers' ends** (1) at the ready (2) by the hand.   **66 barren** i.e., empty of jests and of Sir Andrew's hand.   **68 thou . . . canary** i.e., you look as if you need a drink. (*Canary* is a sweet wine from the Canary Islands.)   **71 put me down** (1) baffle my wits (2) lay me out flat.   **76 *Pourquoi*** Why   **78 tongues** languages. (Sir Toby then puns on "tongs," curling irons.)   **79 bearbaiting** the sport of setting dogs on a chained bear.   **the arts** the liberal arts, learning. (But Sir Toby plays on the phrase as meaning "artifice," the antithesis of *nature.*) **81 mended** improved

SIR TOBY: Excellent. It hangs like flax on a distaff;° and I hope to see a huswife take thee between her legs and spin it off.° 85

SIR ANDREW: Faith, I'll home tomorrow, Sir Toby. Your niece will not be seen, or if she be, it's four to one she'll none of me. The Count° himself here hard° by woos her.

SIR TOBY: She'll none o'th' Count. She'll not match above her degree,° neither in estate,° years, nor wit; I have heard her 90 swear't. Tut, there's life in't,° man.

SIR ANDREW: I'll stay a month longer. I am a fellow o'th' strangest mind i'th' world; I delight in masques and revels sometimes altogether.

SIR TOBY: Art thou good at these kickshawses,° knight? 95

SIR ANDREW: As any man in Illyria, whatsoever he be, under the degree of my betters,° and yet I will not compare with an old man.°

SIR TOBY: What is thy excellence in a galliard,° knight?

SIR ANDREW: Faith, I can cut a caper.°

SIR TOBY: And I can cut the mutton to't. 100

SIR ANDREW: And I think I have the back-trick° simply as strong as any man in Illyria.

SIR TOBY: Wherefore are these things hid? Wherefore have these gifts a curtain before 'em? Are they like to take dust, like Mistress Mall's picture?° Why dost thou not go to church in a 105 galliard° and come home in a coranto?° My very walk should be a jig; I would not so much as make water but in a sink-a-pace.° What dost thou mean? Is it a world to hide virtues° in? I did think, by the excellent constitution of thy leg, it was formed under the star of a galliard.° 110

---

84 distaff a staff for holding the flax, tow, or wool in spinning   **85 spin it off** i.e., (1) treat your flaxen hair as though it were flax on a distaff to be spun (2) cause you to lose hair as a result of venereal disease (3) make you ejaculate. (*Huswife* suggests "hussy," "whore.")   **88 Count** i.e., Duke Orsino, sometimes referred to as Count. **hard** near   **90 degree** social position. **estate** fortune, social position   **91 there's life in't** i.e., while there's life there's hope   **95 kickshawses** delicacies, fancy trifles. (From the French, *quelque chose*.)   **96–7 under . . . betters** excepting those who are above me   **97–8 old man** i.e., one experienced through age.   **98 galliard** lively dance in triple time   **99 cut a caper** make a lively leap. (But Sir Toby puns on the *caper* used to make a sauce served with mutton. *Mutton*, in turn, suggests "whore.")   **101 back-trick** backward step in the galliard. (With sexual innuendo; the back was associated with sexual vigor.)   **104 like to take** likely to collect   **105 Mistress Mall's picture** i.e., perhaps the portrait of some woman protected from light and dust, as many pictures were, by curtains. (*Mall* is a diminutive of *Mary*.)   **106 coranto** lively running dance.   **107–8 sink-a-pace** dance like the galliard. (French *cinquepace*. *Sink* also suggests a cesspool into which one might urinate.)   **108 virtues** talents   **110 under . . . galliard** i.e., under a star favorable to dancing.

SIR ANDREW: Ay, 'tis strong, and it does indifferent well° in a dun-colored stock.° Shall we set about some revels?

SIR TOBY: What shall we do else? Were we not born under Taurus?°

SIR ANDREW: Taurus? That's sides and heart.   115

SIR TOBY: No, sir, it is legs and thighs. Let me see thee caper. [*Sir Andrew capers.*] Ha, higher! Ha, ha, excel-lent!   *Exeunt.*

1.4

Enter Valentine, and Viola in man's attire.

VALENTINE: If the Duke continue these favors towards you, Cesario, you are like° to be much advanced. He hath known you but three days, and already you are no stranger.

VIOLA: You either fear his humor° or my negligence, that you call in question the continuance of his love. Is he inconstant, sir, in his favors?

VALENTINE: No, believe me.   5

Enter Duke [Orsino], Curio, and attendants.

VIOLA: I thank you. Here comes the Count.

ORSINO: Who saw Cesario, ho?

VIOLA: On your attendance,° my lord, here.

ORSINO: Stand you awhile aloof.° [*The others stand aside.*] Cesario,
Thou know'st no less but all. I have unclasped   10
To thee the book even of my secret soul.
Therefore, good youth, address thy gait° unto her;
Be not denied access, stand at her doors,
And tell them,° there thy fixèd foot shall grow
Till thou have audience.

VIOLA: Sure, my noble lord,   15
If she be so abandoned to her sorrow
As it is spoke, she never will admit me.

---

111 **indifferent well** well enough. (Said complacently.)   112 **dun-colored stock** mouse-colored stocking.   114 **Taurus** zodiacal sign. (Sir Andrew is mistaken, since Leo governed sides and hearts in medical astrology. Taurus governed legs and thighs, or, more commonly, neck and throat.)   2 **like** likely   3 **humor** changeableness   8 **On your attendance** Ready to do you service   9 **aloof** aside.   12 **address thy gait** go   14 **them** i.e., Olivia's servants

ORSINO: Be clamorous and leap all civil bounds°
           Rather than make unprofited return.

VIOLA: Say I do speak with her, my lord, what then?   20

ORSINO: Oh, then unfold the passion of my love;
           Surprise° her with discourse of my dear° faith.
           It shall become° thee well to act my woes;
           She will attend it better in thy youth
           Than in a nuncio's° of more grave aspect.   25

VIOLA: I think not so, my lord.

ORSINO: Dear lad, believe it;
           For they shall yet belie thy happy years
           That say thou art a man. Diana's lip
           Is not more smooth and rubious;° thy small pipe°   30
           Is as the maiden's organ, shrill and sound,°
           And all is semblative° a woman's part.
           I know thy constellation° is right apt
           For this affair.—Some four or five attend him.
           All, if you will, for I myself am best   35
           When least in company.—Prosper well in this,
           And thou shalt live as freely as thy lord,
           To call his fortunes thine.

VIOLA: I'll do my best
           To woo your lady. [Aside] Yet a barful strife!°   40
           Whoe'er I woo, myself would be his wife.   Exeunt.

1.5

Enter Maria and Clown [Feste].

MARIA: Nay, either tell me where thou hast been, or I will not
          open my lips so wide as a bristle may enter in way of thy ex-
          cuse. My lady will hang thee for thy absence.

FESTE: Let her hang me. He that is well hanged in this world
          needs to fear no colors.°   5

---

18 civil bounds bounds of civility   **22 Surprise** Take by storm. (A military term.)   **dear** heartfelt
23 become suit   **25 nuncio's** messenger's   **30 rubious** ruby red.   **pipe** voice, throat   **31 shrill and**
sound high and clear, uncracked   **32 semblative** resembling, like   **33 constellation** i.e., nature as
determined by your horoscope   **40 barful strife** endeavor full of impediments.
5 fear no colors i.e., fear no foe, fear nothing. (With pun on _colors_, worldly deceptions, and
"collars," halters or nooses.)

MARIA: Make that good.°

FESTE: He shall see none to fear.°

MARIA: A good Lenten° answer. I can tell thee where that saying was born, of "I fear no colors."

FESTE: Where, good Mistress Mary?

MARIA: In the wars,° and that may you be bold to say in your foolery.°   10

FESTE: Well, God give them wisdom that have it; and those that are fools, let them use their talents.°

MARIA: Yet you will be hanged for being so long absent; or to be turned away,° is not that as good as a hanging to you?

FESTE: Many a good hanging° prevents a bad marriage; and for° turning away, let summer bear it out.°   15

MARIA: You are resolute, then?

FESTE: Not so, neither, but I am resolved on two points.°

MARIA: That if one break, the other will hold; or if both break, your gaskins° fall.

FESTE: Apt, in good faith, very apt. Well, go thy way. If Sir Toby would leave drinking, thou wert as witty a piece of Eve's flesh   20 as any in Illyria.°

MARIA: Peace, you rogue, no more o' that. Here comes my lady. Make your excuse wisely, you were best.°   [Exit.]

Enter Lady Olivia with Malvolio, [and attendants].

FESTE: [aside] Wit, an't° be thy will, put me into good fooling! Those wits that think they have thee do very oft prove fools, and I that am sure I lack thee may pass for a wise man. For   25 what says Quinapalus?° "Better a witty fool than a foolish wit."—God bless thee, lady!

---

6 Make that good Explain that.   **7 He . . . fear** i.e., The hanged man will be dead and unable to see anything.   **8 Lenten** meager, scanty (like Lenten fare), and morbid   **9 In the wars** (Where *colors* would mean "military standards, enemy flags"—the literal meaning of the proverb.) **9–10 that . . . foolery** that's an answer you may be bold to use in your fool's conundrums. (*Colors* here refer to military banners and insignia used to align rows of fighting men in battle.) **11 talents** abilities. (Also alluding to the parable of the talents, Matthew 25:14–29, and to "talons," claws.)   **13 turned away** dismissed. (Possibly also meaning "turned off," "hanged.")   **14 good hanging** (With possible bawdy pun on "being well hung.")   **14 for** as for.   **15 let . . . out** i.e., let mild weather make dismissal endurable.   **17 points** (Maria plays on the meaning "laces used to hold up hose or breeches.")   **18 gaskins** wide breeches   **20 thou . . . Illyria** (Feste may be hinting ironically that Maria would be a suitable mate for Sir Toby.)   **22 you were best** it would be best for you.   **23 an't** if it   **26 Quinapalus** (Feste's invented authority.)

OLIVIA: [*to attendants*] Take the fool away.

FESTE: Do you not hear, fellows? Take away the lady.

OLIVIA: Go to,° you're a dry° fool. I'll no more of you. Besides, you grow dishonest. 30

FESTE: Two faults, madonna,° that drink and good counsel will amend. For give the dry fool drink, then is the fool not dry. Bid the dishonest man mend himself; if he mend, he is no longer dishonest; if he cannot, let the botcher° mend him. Anything that's mended is but patched;° virtue that trans- 35 gresses is but patched with sin, and sin that amends is but patched with virtue. If that this simple syllogism will serve, so;° if it will not, what remedy? As there is no true cuckold but calamity, so beauty's a flower.° The lady bade take away the fool; therefore I say again, take her away.

OLIVIA: Sir, I bade them take away you. 40

FESTE: Misprision° in the highest degree! Lady, *cucullus non facit monachum*;° that's as much to say as I wear not motley° in my brain. Good madonna, give me leave to prove you a fool.

OLIVIA: Can you do it?

FESTE: Dexteriously, good madonna.

OLIVIA: Make your proof. 45

FESTE: I must catechize you for it, madonna. Good my mouse of virtue,° answer me.

OLIVIA: Well, sir, for want of other idleness,° I'll bide° your proof.

FESTE: Good madonna, why mourn'st thou?

OLIVIA: Good fool, for my brother's death.

FESTE: I think his soul is in hell, madonna. 50

OLIVIA: I know his soul is in heaven, fool.

FESTE: The more fool, madonna, to mourn for your brother's soul, being in heaven.—Take away the fool, gentlemen.

---

29 **Go to** (An expression of annoyance or expostulation.) **dry** dull   31 **madonna** my lady
34 **botcher** mender of old clothes and shoes. (Playing on two senses of *mend*: "reform" and "repair.")   34–5 **Anything . . . patched** i.e., Life is patched or parti-colored like the Fool's garment, a mix of good and bad   37 **so** well and good   38–9 **As . . . flower** (Nonsense, yet with a suggestion that Olivia has wedded calamity but should not be faithful to it, for the natural course is to seize the moment of youth and beauty before we lose it.)   41 **Misprision** Mistake, misunderstanding. (A legal term meaning a wrongful action or misdemeanor.)   41–2 *cucullus . . . monachum* the cowl does not make the monk   42 **motley** the many-colored garment of jesters   46–47 **Good . . . virtue** My good, virtuous mouse. (A term of endearment.)   48 **idleness** pastime.
bide endure

OLIVIA: What think you of this fool, Malvolio? Doth he not mend?°

MALVOLIO: Yes, and shall do till the pangs of death shake him. 55
Infirmity, that decays the wise, doth ever make the better fool.

FESTE: God send you, sir, a speedy infirmity for the better increasing your folly! Sir Toby will be sworn that I am no fox, but
he will not pass° his word for two pence that you are no fool.

OLIVIA: How say you to that, Malvolio? 60

MALVOLIO: I marvel Your Ladyship takes delight in such a barren
rascal. I saw him put down the other day with° an ordinary
fool that has no more brain than a stone. Look you now, he's
out of his guard° already. Unless you laugh and minister occa-
sion° to him, he is gagged. I protest° I take these wise men 65
that crow° so at these set° kind of fools no better than the
fools' zanies.°

OLIVIA: Oh, you are sick of self-love, Malvolio, and taste with a
distempered° appetite. To be generous,° guiltless, and of free°
disposition is to take those things for bird-bolts° that you
deem cannon bullets. There is no slander in an allowed° fool, 70
though he do nothing but rail; nor no railing in a known discreet man, though he do nothing but reprove.°

FESTE: Now Mercury endue thee with leasing,° for thou speak'st
well of fools!

    Enter Maria.

MARIA: Madam, there is at the gate a young gentleman much
desires to speak with you.

OLIVIA: From the Count Orsino, is it? 75

MARIA: I know not, madam. 'Tis a fair young man, and well attended.

WILLIAM SHAKESPEARE

54 **mend** i.e., improve, grow more amusing. (But Malvolio uses the word to mean "grow more like a fool.") 59 **pass** give 62 **with** by 64 **out of his guard** defenseless, unprovided with a witty answer 64–65 **minister occasion** provide opportunity (for his fooling) 65 **protest** avow, declare. 67 **crow** laugh stridently **set** artificial, stereotyped. **zanies** assistants, aping attendants. 68 **distempered** diseased. **generous** noble-minded. **free** magnanimous 69 **bird-bolts** blunt arrows for shooting small birds 70 **allowed** licensed (to speak freely) 70–72 **There . . . reprove** Both a licensed fool and a man known for discretion can criticize freely without being accused of slander in the first instance or railing in the second. (In rebuking Malvolio here, Olivia implies that he is not behaving like a "known discreet man.") 73 **Now . . . leasing** i.e., May Mercury, the god of deception, make you a skillful liar

OLIVIA: Who of my people hold him in delay?

MARIA: Sir Toby, madam,° your kinsman.

OLIVIA: Fetch him off, I pray you. He speaks nothing but mad-man.° Fie on him! [*Exit Maria.*]
Go you, Malvolio. If it be a suit from the Count, I am 80
sick or not at home; what you will, to dismiss it.

Exit Malvolio. Now you see, sir, how your fooling grows old,° and people dislike it.

FESTE: Thou hast spoke for us, madonna, as if thy eldest son should be a fool; whose skull Jove cram with brains, for—here he comes—

Enter Sir Toby.

one of thy kin has a most weak *pia mater.*°

OLIVIA: By mine honor, half drunk.—What is he at the gate, cousin?°

SIR TOBY: A gentleman. 85

OLIVIA: A gentleman? What gentleman?

SIR TOBY: 'Tis a gentleman here—[*He belches.*] A plague o' these pickle-herring! [*To Feste*] How now, sot?°

FESTE: Good Sir Toby.

OLIVIA: Cousin,° cousin, how have you come so early by this lethargy?

SIR TOBY: Lechery? I defy lechery. There's one at the gate. 90

OLIVIA: Ay, marry, what is he?

SIR TOBY: Let him be the devil an he will, I care not. Give me faith,° say I. Well, it's all one.° *Exit.*

OLIVIA: What's a drunken man like, Fool? 95

FESTE: Like a drowned man, a fool, and a madman. One draft above heat° makes him a fool, the second mads him, and a third drowns him.

OLIVIA: Go thou and seek the crowner,° and let him sit o' my coz;° for he's in the third degree of drink, he's drowned. Go, look after him. 100

---

78 **madman** i.e., the words of madness.   81 **old** stale   83 *pia mater* i.e., brain. (Actually the soft membrane enclosing the brain.)   87 **sot** (1) fool (2) drunkard.   89 **Cousin** Kinsman. (Here, uncle.) 92–93 **Give me faith** i.e., to resist the devil.   93 **it's all one** it doesn't matter.   96–97 **draft above heat** helping of drink raising his temperature above normal bodily warmth.   98 **crowner** coroner 98–99 **sit o' my coz** hold an inquest on my kinsman (Sir Toby)

FESTE: He is but mad yet, madonna; and the fool shall look to the madman. [Exit.]

Enter Malvolio.

MALVOLIO: Madam, yond young fellow swears he will speak with you. I told him you were sick; he takes on him to understand so much, and therefore comes to speak with you. I told him you were asleep; he seems to have a foreknowl- 105 edge of that too, and therefore comes to speak with you. What is to be said to him, lady? He's fortified against any denial.

OLIVIA: Tell him he shall not speak with me.

MALVOLIO: He's been told so; and he says he'll stand at your door like a sheriff's post,° and be the supporter° to a bench, but he'll speak with you.

OLIVIA: What kind o' man is he? 110

MALVOLIO: Why, of mankind.

OLIVIA: What manner of man?

MALVOLIO: Of very ill manner. He'll speak with you, will you or no.

OLIVIA: Of what personage and years is he?

MALVOLIO: Not yet old enough for a man, nor young enough for 115 a boy; as a squash° is before 'tis a peascod,° or a codling° when 'tis almost an apple. 'Tis with him in standing water° between boy and man. He is very well-favored,° and he speaks very shrewishly.° One would think his mother's milk were scarce out of him.

OLIVIA: Let him approach. Call in my gentlewoman. 120

MALVOLIO: Gentlewoman, my lady calls. *Exit.*

Enter Maria.

OLIVIA: Give me my veil. Come, throw it o'er my face. We'll once more hear Orsino's embassy. [*Olivia veils.*]

Enter Viola.

---

108 sheriff's post post before the sheriff's door to mark a residence of authority, often elaborately carved and decorated. **supporter** prop **116 squash** unripe pea pod. **peascod** ripe pea pod. (The image suggests that the boy's testicles have not yet dropped.) **codling** unripe apple **117 in standing water** at the turn of the tide **118 well-favored** good-looking. **119 shrewishly** sharply.

VIOLA: The honorable lady of the house, which is she?

OLIVIA: Speak to me; I shall answer for her. Your will?

VIOLA: Most radiant, exquisite, and unmatchable beauty—I pray   125
you, tell me if this be the lady of the house, for I never saw her.
I would be loath to castaway my speech; for besides that it is
excellently well penned, I have taken great pains to con° it.
Good beauties, let me sustain no scorn; I am very comptible,°
even to the least sinister° usage.

OLIVIA: Whence came you, sir?   130

VIOLA: I can say little more than I have studied, and that question's out of my part. Good gentle one, give me modest° assurance if you be the lady of the house, that I may proceed in
my speech.

OLIVIA: Are you a comedian?°

VIOLA: No, my profound heart;° and yet, by the very fangs of   135
malice, I swear I am not that I play.° Are you the lady of the
house?

OLIVIA: If I do not usurp myself,° I am.

VIOLA: Most certain, if you are she, you do usurp your-self;° for
what is yours to bestow is not yours to reserve. But this is
from° my commission. I will on with my speech in your
praise, and then show you the heart of my message.

OLIVIA: Come to what is important in't. I forgive you° the praise.   140

VIOLA: Alas, I took great pains to study it, and 'tis poetical.

OLIVIA: It is the more like to be feigned. I pray you, keep it in.
I heard you were saucy at my gates, and allowed your
approach rather to wonder at you than to hear you. If you
be not mad,° begone; if you have reason,° be brief. 'Tis not
that time of moon° with me to make one° in so skipping a
dialogue.

MARIA: Will you hoist sail, sir? Here lies your way.   145

---

127 con memorize   **128 comptible** susceptible, sensitive   **129 least sinister** slightest discourteous
132 modest reasonable   **134 comedian** actor.   **135 my profound heart** my most wise lady; or, in all
sincerity **135–6 by . . . I play** (Viola hints at her true identity, which malice itself might not detect.)
137 do . . . myself am not an impostor   **138 usurp yourself** i.e., misappropriate yourself, by
withholding yourself from love and marriage   **139 from** outside of   **140 forgive you** excuse you
from repeating   **143 not mad** i.e., not altogether mad   **144 reason** sanity.   **moon** (The moon was
thought to affect lunatics according to its changing phases.)   **make one** take part.

VIOLA: No, good swabber,° I am to hull° here a little longer.— Some mollification for° your giant,° sweet lady. Tell me your mind; I am a messenger.

OLIVIA: Sure you have some hideous matter to deliver, when the courtesy° of it is so fearful. Speak your office.°

VIOLA: It alone concerns your ear. I bring no overture° of war, no   150 taxation of homage.° I hold the olive° in my hand; my words are as full of peace as matter.

OLIVIA: Yet you began rudely.° What are you? What would you?

VIOLA: The rudeness that hath appeared in me have I learned from my entertainment.° What I am and what I would are as secret as maidenhead°—to your ears, divinity;° to any other's,   155 profanation.

OLIVIA: [to the others] Give us the place here alone. We will hear this divinity. [Exeunt Maria and attendants.] Now, sir, what is your text?

VIOLA: Most sweet lady—

OLIVIA: A comfortable° doctrine, and much may be said of it. Where lies your text?   160

VIOLA: In Orsino's bosom.

OLIVIA: In his bosom? In what chapter of his bosom?

VIOLA: To answer by the method,° in the first of his heart.

OLIVIA: Oh, I have read it. It is heresy. Have you no more to say?

VIOLA: Good madam, let me see your face.   165

OLIVIA: Have you any commission from your lord to negotiate with my face? You are now out of° your text. But we will draw the curtain and show you the picture. [Unveiling.] Look you, sir, such a one I was this present.° Is't not well done?

VIOLA: Excellently done, if God did all.   170

---

146 **swabber** one in charge of washing the decks. (A nautical retort to *hoist sail.*) **hull** lie with sails furled   147 **Some . . . for** i.e., Please mollify, pacify.   **giant** i.e., the diminutive Maria who, like many giants in medieval romances, is guarding the lady   149 **courtesy** i.e., complimentary, "poetical" introduction. (Or Olivia may refer to Cesario's importunate manner at her gate, as reported by Malvolio.)   **office** commission, business.   150 **overture** declaration. (Literally, opening.)   151 **taxation of homage** demand for tribute.   **olive** olive-branch (signifying peace)   153 **Yet . . . rudely** i.e., Yet you were saucy at my gates.   154 **entertainment** reception.   155 **maidenhead** virginity   155 **divinity** sacred discourse   159 **comfortable** comforting   163 **To . . . method** i.e., To continue the metaphor of delivering a sermon, begun with *divinity* and *what is your text* and continued in *doctrine, heresy,* etc.   167 **out of** straying from   169 **such . . . present** this is a recent portrait of me. (Since it was customary to hang curtains in front of pictures, Olivia in unveiling speaks as if she were displaying a picture of herself.)

894

OLIVIA: 'Tis in grain,° sir; 'twill endure wind and weather.

VIOLA: 'Tis beauty truly blent,° whose red and white
Nature's own sweet and cunning° hand laid on.
Lady, you are the cruel'st she alive
If you will lead these graces to the grave   175
And leave the world no copy.°

OLIVIA: Oh, sir, I will not be so hard hearted. I will give out divers
schedules° of my beauty. It shall be inventoried, and every
particle and utensil° labeled° to my will: as, item, two lips,
indifferent° red; item, two gray eyes, with lids to them; item,   180
one neck, one chin, and so forth. Were you sent hither to
praise° me?

VIOLA: I see you what you are: you are too proud.
But, if° you were the devil, you are fair.
My lord and master loves you. Oh, such love
Could be but recompensed, though you were crowned   185
The nonpareil of beauty!°

OLIVIA: How does he love me?

VIOLA: With adorations, fertile° tears,
With groans that thunder love, with sighs of fire.

OLIVIA: Your lord does know my mind; I cannot love him.   190
Yet I suppose him virtuous, know him noble,
Of great estate, of fresh and stainless youth,
In voices well divulged,° free,° learned, and valiant,
And in dimension and the shape of nature°
A gracious° person. But yet I cannot love him.   195
He might have took his answer long ago.

VIOLA: If I did love you in my master's flame,°
With such a suff'ring, such a deadly° life,
In your denial I would find no sense;
I would not understand it.   200

OLIVIA: Why, what would you?

---

171 **in grain** fast dyed   172 **blent** blended   173 **cunning** skillful   176 **copy** i.e., a child. (But Olivia
uses the word to mean "transcript.")   178 **schedules** inventories   179 **utensil** article, item.   **labeled**
added as a codicil   180 **indifferent** somewhat   181 **praise** (With pun on "appraise.")   183 **if** even if
184–6 **Oh . . . beauty!** i.e., Even if you were the most beautiful woman alive, that beauty could do no
more than repay my master's love for you!   188 **fertile** copious   193 **In . . . divulged** well spoken of.
free generous   194 **in . . . nature** in his physical form   195 **gracious** graceful, attractive   197 **flame**
passion   198 **deadly** deathlike

VIOLA: Make me a willow cabin° at your gate
       And call upon my soul° within the house;
       Write loyal cantons° of contemnèd° love
       And sing them loud even in the dead of night;   205
       Hallow° your name to the reverberate hills,
       And make the babbling gossip of the air°
       Cry out "Olivia!" Oh, you should not rest
       Between the elements of air° and earth
       But you should pity me!   210

OLIVIA: You might do much.
       What is your parentage?

VIOLA: Above my fortunes, yet my state° is well:
       I am a gentleman.

OLIVIA: Get you to your lord.   215
       I cannot love him. Let him send no more—
       Unless, perchance, you come to me again
       To tell me how he takes it. Fare you well.
       I thank you for your pains. Spend this for me.

                                   [She offers a purse.]

VIOLA: I am no fee'd post,° lady. Keep your purse.   220
       My master, not myself, lacks recompense.
       Love make his heart of flint that you shall love,°
       And let your fervor, like my master's, be
       Placed in contempt! Farewell, fair cruelty.   *Exit.*

OLIVIA: "What is your parentage?"   225
       "Above my fortunes, yet my state is well:
       I am a gentleman." I'll be sworn thou art!
       Thy tongue, thy face, thy limbs, actions, and spirit
       Do give thee fivefold blazon.° Not too fast! Soft,° soft!
       Unless the master were the man.° How now?   230
       Even so quickly may one catch the plague?
       Methinks I feel this youth's perfections
       With an invisible and subtle stealth

---

202 willow cabin shelter, hut. (Willow was a symbol of unrequited love.)   **203 my soul** i.e., Olivia
204 cantons songs. **contemnèd** rejected **206 Hallow** (1) halloo (2) bless **207 babbling . . .
air** echo **209 Between . . . air** i.e., anywhere **213 state** social standing **220 fee'd post**
messenger to be tipped **223 Love . . . love** May Cupid make the heart of the man you love as
hard as flint **229 blazon** heraldic description. **Soft** Wait a minute **230 Unless . . . man** i.e.,
Unless Cesario and Orsino changed places.

To creep in at mine eyes. Well, let it be.—
What ho, Malvolio!   235

Enter Malvolio.

MALVOLIO: Here, madam, at your service.
OLIVIA: Run after that same peevish messenger,
The County's° man. He left this ring behind him,

[giving a ring]

Would I or not.° Tell him I'll none of it.   240
Desire him not to flatter with° his lord,
Nor hold him up with hopes; I am not for him.
If that the youth will come this way tomorrow,
I'll give him reasons for't. Hie thee,° Malvolio.
MALVOLIO: Madam, I will.   *Exit.*
OLIVIA: I do I know not what, and fear to find   245
Mine eye too great a flatterer for my mind.°
Fate, show thy force. Ourselves we do not owe.°
What is decreed must be; and be this so.   [*Exit.*]

2.1

Enter Antonio and Sebastian.

ANTONIO: Will you stay no longer? Nor will you not° that I go
with you?
SEBASTIAN: By your patience,° no. My stars shine darkly over
me. The malignancy° of my fate might perhaps distemper°
yours; therefore I shall crave of you your leave that I may bear
my evils alone. It were a bad recompense for your love to lay
any of them on you.   5
ANTONIO: Let me yet know of you whither you are bound.
SEBASTIAN: No, sooth,° sir; my determinate° voyage is mere extravagancy.° But I perceive in you so excellent a touch of modesty that you will not extort from me what I am willing° to

---

239 County's Count's, i.e., Duke's   **240 Would I or not** whether I wanted it or not.   **241 flatter with**
encourage   **243 Hie thee** Hasten   **246 Mine . . . mind** i.e., that my eyes (through which love
enters the soul) have deceived my reason.   **247 owe** own, control.
1 Nor will you not Do you not wish   **2 patience** leave   **3 malignancy** malevolence (of the stars;
also in a medical sense)   **distemper** infect   **7 sooth** truly.   **determinate** intended, determined
upon   **8 extravagancy** aimless wandering.   **9 am willing . . . in** wish to keep secret

keep in; therefore it charges me in manners° the rather to 10
express° myself. You must know of me then, Antonio, my
name is Sebastian, which I called Roderigo. My father was that
Sebastian of Messaline° whom I know you have heard of. He
left behind him myself and a sister, both born in an hour.° If
the heavens had been pleased, would we had so ended! But 15
you, sir, altered that, for some hour° before you took me from
the breach of the sea° was my sister drowned.

ANTONIO: Alas the day!

SEBASTIAN: A lady, sir, though it was said she much resembled
me, was yet of many accounted beautiful. But though I could 20
not with such estimable wonder° over-far believe that, yet
thus far I will boldly publish° her: she bore a mind that envy°
could not but call fair. She is drowned already, sir, with salt
water, though I seem to drown her remembrance again with
more.

ANTONIO: Pardon me, sir, your bad entertainment.° 25

SEBASTIAN: O good Antonio, forgive me your trouble.°

ANTONIO: If you will not murder° me for my love, let me be your
servant.

SEBASTIAN: If you will not undo what you have done, that is, kill
him whom you have recovered,° desire it not. Fare ye well at
once. My bosom is full of kindness,° and I am yet so near the 30
manners of my mother° that upon the least occasion more
mine eyes will tell tales of me. I am bound to the Count
Orsino's court. Farewell. *Exit.*

ANTONIO: The gentleness of all the gods go with thee!
I have many enemies in Orsino's court, 35
Else would I very shortly see thee there.
But come what may, I do adore thee so
That danger shall seem sport, and I will go. *Exit.*

---

10 **it . . . manners** it is incumbent upon me in all courtesy 11 **express** reveal 13 **Messaline**
possibly Messina, or, more likely, Massila (the modern Marseilles). In Plautus's *Menaechmi,*
Massilians and Illyrians are mentioned together. 14 **in an hour** in the same hour. 16 **some hour**
about an hour 17 **breach of the sea** surf 21 **estimable wonder** admiring judgment 22 **publish**
proclaim 22 **envy** even malice 25 **Pardon . . . entertainment** i.e., I'm sorry I cannot offer you
better hospitality and comfort. 26 **your trouble** the trouble I put you to. 27 **murder . . . love** i.e.,
cause me to die from lacking your love 29 **recovered** rescued, restored 30 **kindness** emotion,
affection 31 **manners of my mother** i.e., womanly inclination to weep

2.2

Enter Viola and Malvolio, at several° doors.

MALVOLIO: Were not you ev'n now with the Countess Olivia?

VIOLA: Even now, sir. On a moderate pace I have since arrived but hither.

MALVOLIO: She returns this ring to you, sir. You might have saved me my pains, to have taken° it away yourself. She adds, moreover, that you should put your lord into a desperate° as- 5 surance she will none of him. And one thing more: that you be never so hardy to come° again in his affairs, unless it be to report your lord's taking of this. Receive it so.

VIOLA: She took the ring of me. I'll none of it.°

MALVOLIO: Come, sir, you peevishly threw it to her, and her will is it 10 should be so returned. [*He throws down the ring.*] If it be worth stooping for, there it lies, in your eye;° if not, be it his that finds it. *Exit.*

VIOLA: [*picking up the ring*]
I left no ring with her. What means this lady?
Fortune forbid my outside have not charmed° her! 15
She made good view of me, indeed so much
That sure methought her eyes had lost her tongue,°
For she did speak in starts, distractedly.
She loves me, sure! The cunning of her passion
Invites me in° this churlish messenger. 20
None of my lord's ring? Why, he sent her none.
I am the man.° If it be so—as 'tis—
Poor lady, she were better love a dream.
Disguise, I see, thou art a wickedness
Wherein the pregnant enemy° does much. 25
How easy is it for the proper false°
In women's waxen° hearts to set their forms!°
Alas, our frailty is the cause, not we,

0.1 several different **4 to have taken** by taking **5 desperate** without hope **7 so hardy to come** so bold as to come **9 She . . . it** (Viola tells a quick and friendly lie to shield Olivia.) **12 in your eye** in plain sight **15 charmed** enchanted **17 her eyes . . . tongue** i.e., the sight of me had deprived her of speech **20 in** in the person of **22 the man** the man of her choice. **25 the pregnant enemy** the resourceful enemy (either Satan or Cupid) **26 the proper false** deceptively handsome men **27 waxen** i.e., malleable, impressionable. **set their forms** stamp their images (as of a seal).

For such as we are made of, such we be.°
How will this fadge?° My master loves her dearly,   30
And I, poor monster,° fond° as much on him;
And she, mistaken, seems to dote on me.
What will become of this? As I am man,
My state is desperate for my master's love;
As I am woman—now, alas the day!—   35
What thriftless° sighs shall poor Olivia breathe!
O Time, thou must untangle this, not I;
It is too hard a knot for me t'untie.   [*Exit.*]

2.3

Enter Sir Toby and Sir Andrew.

SIR TOBY: Approach, Sir Andrew. Not to be abed after midnight
is to be up betimes;° and *diluculo surgere,*° thou know'st—

SIR ANDREW: Nay, by my troth, I know not, but I know to be up
late is to be up late.

SIR TOBY: A false conclusion. I hate it as an unfilled can.° To be   5
up after midnight and to go to bed then, is early; so that to go
to bed after midnight is to go to bed betimes. Does not our
lives consist of the four elements?°

SIR ANDREW: Faith, so they say, but I think it rather consists of
eating and drinking.   10

SIR TOBY: Thou'rt a scholar; let us therefore eat and drink.—
Marian, I say, a stoup° of wine!

Enter Clown [Feste].

SIR ANDREW: Here comes the Fool, i'faith.

FESTE: How now, my hearts! Did you never see the picture of
"we three"°?

SIR TOBY: Welcome, ass. Now let's have a catch.°   15

SIR ANDREW: By my troth, the Fool has an excellent breast.° I
had rather than forty shillings I had such a leg,° and so sweet a

---

28–9 our . . . be i.e., the fault lies not in us as individuals, but in the frailty of female nature   **30 fadge**
turn out   **31 monster** i.e., being both man and woman. **fond** dote   **36 thriftless** unprofitable
2 betimes early.   *diluculo surgere* (*saluberrimum est*) to rise early is most healthful. (A sentence from
Lilly's *Latin Grammar.*)   **5 can** tankard   **8 four elements** i.e., fire, air, water, and earth, the elements
that were thought to make up all matter.   **12 stoup** drinking vessel   **13–4 picture of "we three"**
picture of two fools or asses inscribed "we three," the spectator being the third   **15 catch** round.
16 breast voice.   **17 leg** (for dancing)

breath to sing, as the Fool has. In sooth, thou wast in very gracious fooling last night, when thou spok'st of Pigrogromitus, of
the Vapians passing the equinoctial of Queubus°. 'Twas very   20
good, i'faith. I sent thee sixpence for thy leman.° Hadst it?

FESTE: I did impeticos thy gratillity;° for Malvolio's nose is no
whipstock.° My lady has a white hand,° and the Myrmidons°
are no bottle-ale houses.°

SIR ANDREW: Excellent! Why, this is the best fooling, when all is
done. Now, a song.   25

SIR TOBY: Come on, there is sixpence for you. [*He gives money.*]
Let's have a song.

SIR ANDREW: There's a testril° of me too. [*He gives money.*] If one
knight give a—

FESTE: Would you have a love song, or a song of good life?

SIR TOBY: A love song, a love song.   30

SIR ANDREW: Ay, ay, I care not for good life.°

FESTE: (*sings*)
O mistress mine, where are you roaming?
Oh, stay and hear, your true love 's coming,
That can sing both high and low.   35
Trip no further, pretty sweeting;
Journeys end in lovers' meeting,
Every wise man's son doth know.

SIR ANDREW: Excellent good, i'faith.

SIR TOBY: Good, good.   40

FESTE: [*sings*]
What is love? 'Tis not hereafter;
Present mirth hath present laughter;
What's to come is still° unsure.
In delay there lies no plenty.
Then come kiss me, sweet and twenty;°   45
Youth's a stuff will not endure.

19–20 Pigrogromitus . . . Queubus (Feste's mock erudition.)   **21 leman** sweetheart.   **22 impeticos thy gratillity** (Suggests "impetticoat, or pocket up, thy gratuity.")   **22–3 is no whipstock** is no whip-handle. (More nonsense, but perhaps suggesting that Malvolio's nose for smelling out faults does not give him the right to punish, so that he need not be feared.)   **23 has a white hand** i.e., is lady-like. (But Feste's speech may be mere nonsense.)   **Myrmidons** followers of Achilles.   **23–4 bottle-ale houses** (Used contemptuously of taverns because they sold low-class drink.)   **27 testril** tester, a coin worth sixpence   **31 good life** virtuous living. (Or perhaps Feste means simply "life's pleasures," but is misunderstood by Sir Andrew to mean "virtuous living.")   **43 still** always   **45 sweet and twenty** i.e., sweet and twenty times sweet, or twenty years old

SIR ANDREW: A mellifluous voice, as I am true knight.

SIR TOBY: A contagious° breath.

SIR ANDREW: Very sweet and contagious, i'faith.   50

SIR TOBY: To hear by the nose, it is dulcet in contagion.° But
   shall we make the welkin dance° indeed? Shall we rouse the
   night owl in a catch that will draw three souls° out of one
   weaver?° Shall we do that?

SIR ANDREW: An you love me, let's do't. I am dog at° a catch.°   55

FESTE: By'r Lady,° sir, and some dogs will catch well.

SIR ANDREW: Most certain. Let our catch be "Thou knave."°

FESTE: "Hold thy peace, thou knave," knight? I shall be
   constrained in't to call thee knave, knight.°

SIR ANDREW: 'Tis not the first time I have constrained one to   60
   call me knave. Begin, Fool. It begins, "Hold thy peace."

FESTE: I shall never begin if I hold my peace.

SIR ANDREW: Good, i'faith. Come, begin. *Catch sung.*

   Enter Maria.

MARIA: What a caterwauling do you keep° here! If my lady have
   not called up her steward Malvolio and bid him turn you out
   of doors, never trust me.   65

SIR TOBY: My lady's a Cataian,° we are politicians,° Malvolio's a
   Peg-o'-Ramsey,° and [*he sings*] "Three merry men be we."° Am
   not I consanguineous?° Am I not of her blood? Tillyvally!°
   Lady!° [*He sings.*] "There dwelt a man in Babylon, lady, lady."°

FESTE: Beshrew° me, the knight's in admirable fooling.   70

SIR ANDREW: Ay, he does well enough if he be disposed, and
   so do I too. He does it with a better grace, but I do it more
   natural.°

---

49 contagious infectiously delightful   **51 To . . . contagion** i.e., If we were to describe hearing
in olfactory terms, we could say it is sweet in stench. **52 make . . . dance** i.e., drink till the sky
seems to turn around   **53 draw three souls** (Refers to the threefold nature of the soul—
vegetal, sensible, and intellectual—or to the three singers of the three-part catch; or, just a
comic exaggeration.)   **54 weaver** (Weavers were often associated with psalm singing.)
55 dog at very clever at. (But Feste uses the word literally.)   **catch** round. (But Feste uses it to
mean "seize.")   **56 By 'r Lady** (An oath, originally, "by the Virgin Mary.")   **57 "Thou knave"**
(This popular round is arranged so that the three singers repeatedly accost one another with
"Thou knave.")   **58–9 "Hold . . . knight** ("Knight and knave" is a common antithesis, like "rich
and poor.")   **63 keep** keep up   **66 Cataian** Cathayan, i.e., Chinese, a trickster or inscrutable; or,
just nonsense. **politicians** schemers, intriguers   **67 Peg-o'-Ramsey** character in a popular song.
(Used here contemptuously.)   **"Three . . . we"** (A snatch of an old song.)   **68 consanguineous** i.e.,
a blood relative of Olivia.   **Tillyvally!** Nonsense, fiddle-faddle!   **69 "There . . . lady"** (The first
line of a ballad, "The Constancy of Susanna," together with the refrain, "Lady, lady.")   **70 Beshrew**
i.e., The devil take. (A mild curse.)   **73 natural** naturally. (But unconsciously suggesting idiocy.)

SIR TOBY: [*sings*]
"O' the twelfth day of December"°—

MARIA: For the love o' God, peace!

Enter Malvolio.

MALVOLIO: My masters, are you mad? Or what are you? Have   75
you no wit,° manners, nor honesty° but to gabble like tinkers
at this time of night? Do ye make an ale-house of my lady's
house, that ye squeak out your coziers'° catches without any
mitigation or remorse° of voice? Is there no respect of place,
persons, nor time in you?

SIR TOBY: We did keep time, sir, in our catches. Sneck up!°   80

MALVOLIO: Sir Toby, I must be round° with you. My lady bade
me tell you that though she harbors you as her kinsman, she's
nothing allied to your disorders. If you can separate yourself
and your misdemeanors, you are welcome to the house; if not,
an it would please you to take leave of her, she is very willing
to bid you farewell.   85

SIR TOBY: [*sings*]
"Farewell, dear heart, since I must needs be gone."°

MARIA: Nay, good Sir Toby.

FESTE: [*sings*]
"His eyes do show his days are almost done."

MALVOLIO: Is't even so?

SIR TOBY: [*sings*]
"But I will never die."   90

FESTE: "Sir Toby, there you lie."

MALVOLIO: This is much credit to you.

SIR TOBY: [*sings*]
"Shall I bid him go?"

FESTE: [*sings*]
"What an if you do?"

SIR TOBY: [*sings*]
"Shall I bid him go, and spare not?"   95

---

74 **"O' . . . December"** (Possibly part of a ballad about the Battle of Musselburgh Field, or Toby's
error for the "twelfth day of Christmas," i.e., Twelfth Night.) 76 **wit** common sense. **honesty**
decency 78 **coziers'** cobblers' 79 **mitigation or remorse** i.e., considerate lowering 80 **Sneck
up!** Go hang! 81 **round** blunt 86 **"Farewell . . . gone"** (From the ballad "Corydon's Farewell
to Phyllis.")

FESTE: [*sings*]
"Oh, no, no, no, no, you dare not."

SIR TOBY: Out o' tune,° sir? Ye lie. Art any more than a steward? Dost thou think, because thou art virtuous, there shall be no more cakes and ale?

FESTE: Yes, by Saint Anne,° and ginger° shall be hot i'th' mouth, too. 100

SIR TOBY: Thou'rt i'the right.—Go, sir, rub your chain with crumbs.°—A stoup of wine, Maria!

MALVOLIO: Mistress Mary, if you prized my lady's favor at anything more than contempt, you would not give means° for this uncivil rule.° She shall know of it, by this hand. *Exit.*

MARIA: Go shake your ears.° 105

SIR ANDREW: 'Twere as good a deed as to drink when a man's a-hungry to challenge him the field° and then to break promise with him and make a fool of him.

SIR TOBY: Do't, knight. I'll write thee a challenge, or I'll deliver thy indignation to him by word of mouth.

MARIA: Sweet Sir Toby, be patient for tonight. Since the youth of 110 the Count's was today with my lady, she is much out of quiet. For° Monsieur Malvolio, let me alone with him. If I do not gull° him into a nayword° and make him° a common recreation,° do not think I have wit enough to lie straight in my bed. I know I can do it.

SIR TOBY: Possess° us, possess us. Tell us something of him. 115

MARIA: Marry, sir, sometimes he is a kind of Puritan.°

SIR ANDREW: Oh, if I thought that, I'd beat him like a dog.

SIR TOBY: What, for being a Puritan? Thy exquisite reason, dear knight?

WILLIAM SHAKESPEARE

97 Out o' tune (Perhaps a quibbling reply—"We did too keep time in our tune"—to Malvolio's accusation of having no respect for place or time, line 91. Often emended to *Out o' time*, easily misread in secretary hand.) **99 Saint Anne** mother of the Virgin Mary. (Her cult was derided in the Reformation, much as Puritan reformers also derided the tradition of *cakes and ale* at church feasts.) **ginger** (Commonly used to spice ale.) **101–2 rub . . . crumbs** i.e., scour or polish your steward's chain; attend to your own business and remember your station. **104 give means** i.e., supply drink. **rule** conduct. **105 your ears** i.e., your ass's ears. **107 the field** i.e., to a duel **112 For** As for. **let . . . him** leave him to me. **113 gull** trick. **nayword** byword. (His name will be synonymous with "dupe.") **113–4 recreation** sport **115 Possess** Inform **116 puritan** (Maria's point is that Malvolio is sometimes a *kind* of Puritan, insofar as he is precise about moral conduct and censorious of others for immoral conduct, but that he is nothing consistently except a time-server. He is not, then, simply a satirical type of the Puritan sect. The extent of the resemblance is left unstated.)

SIR ANDREW: I have no exquisite reason for't, but I have reason good enough.

MARIA: The devil a Puritan that he is, or anything constantly,° 120
but a time-pleaser;° an affectioned° ass, that cons state without book° and utters it by great swaths;° the best persuaded°
of himself, so crammed, as he thinks, with excellencies, that it
is his grounds of faith° that all that look on him love him; and
on that vice in him will my revenge find notable cause to work.

SIR TOBY: What wilt thou do? 125

MARIA: I will drop in his way some obscure epistles° of love,
wherein by the color of his beard, the shape of his leg, the
manner of his gait, the expressure° of his eye, forehead, and
complexion, he shall find himself most feelingly personated.°
I can write very like my lady your niece; on a forgotten matter°
we can hardly make distinction of our hands.° 130

SIR TOBY: Excellent! I smell a device.

SIR ANDREW: I have't in my nose too.

SIR TOBY: He shall think, by the letters that thou wilt drop, that
they come from my niece, and that she's in love with him.

MARIA: My purpose is indeed a horse of that color.

SIR ANDREW: And your horse now would make him an ass. 135

MARIA: Ass,° I doubt not.

SIR ANDREW: Oh, 'twill be admirable!

MARIA: Sport royal, I warrant you. I know my physic° will work
with him. I will plant you two, and let the Fool make a third,
where he shall find the letter. Observe his construction° of it. 140
For this night, to bed, and dream on the event.° Farewell.
Exit.

SIR TOBY: Good night, Penthesilea.°

SIR ANDREW: Before me,° she's a good wench.

SIR TOBY: She's a beagle° true-bred and one that adores me.
What o' that? 145

---

120 constantly consistently   **121 time-pleaser** time-server, sycophant. **affectioned** affected
122–3 cons . . . book learns by heart the phrases and mannerisms of the great   **123 by great swaths**
in great sweeps, like rows of mown grain.   **the best persuaded** having the best opinion
124 grounds of faith creed, belief   **126 some obscure epistles** an ambiguously worded letter
127 expressure expression   **128 personated** represented.   **129 on a forgotten matter** when we've
forgotten which of us wrote something or what it was about   **130 hands** handwriting.   **136 Ass, I**
(With a pun on "as I.")   **138 physic** medicine   **140 construction** interpretation   **141 event**
outcome.   **142 Penthesilea** Queen of the Amazons. (Another ironical allusion to Maria's
diminutive stature.)   **143 Before me** i.e., On my soul. (A mild oath.) **144 beagle** a small, intelligent
hunting dog

SIR ANDREW: I was adored once, too.

SIR TOBY: Let's to bed, knight. Thou hadst need send for more money.

SIR ANDREW: If I cannot recover° your niece, I am a foul way out.°

SIR TOBY: Send for money, knight. If thou hast her not i'th' end, call me cut.°

SIR ANDREW: If I do not, never trust me, take it how you will.   150

SIR TOBY: Come, come, I'll go burn some sack.° 'Tis too late to go to bed now. Come, knight; come, knight.

Exeunt.°

2.4

Enter Duke [Orsino], Viola, Curio, and others.

ORSINO: Give me some music. Now, good morrow,° friends.
Now, good Cesario, but° that piece of song,
That old and antique° song we heard last night.
Methought it did relieve my passion much,
More than light airs and recollected terms°   5
Of these most brisk and giddy-pacèd times.
Come, but one verse.

CURIO: He is not here, so please Your Lordship, that should sing it.

ORSINO: Who was it?

CURIO: Feste the jester, my lord, a fool that the Lady Olivia's   10
father took much delight in. He is about the house.

ORSINO: Seek him out, and play the tune the while.

[Exit Curio.] Music plays.

[*To Viola*] Come hither, boy. If ever thou shalt love,
In the sweet pangs of it remember me;
For such as I am, all true lovers are,   15
Unstaid and skittish in all motions else°
Save in the constant image of the creature
That is beloved. How dost thou like this tune?

---

148 **recover** win.   **foul way out** i.e., miserably out of pocket. (Literally, out of my way and in the mire.)   149 **cut** A proverbial term of abuse: literally, a horse with a docked tail; also, a gelding, or the female genital organ.   151 **burn some sack** warm some Spanish wine.   157.1 *Exeunt* (Feste may have left earlier; he says nothing after line 117 and is perhaps referred to without his being present at 172–3.)
1 **morrow** morning   2 **but** i.e., I ask only   3 **antique** old, quaint, fantastic   5 **recollected terms** studied and artificial expressions   16 **all motions else** all other thoughts and emotions

VIOLA: It gives a very echo to the seat°
Where Love is throned.

ORSINO: Thou dost speak masterly.
My life upon't, young though thou art, thine eye
Hath stayed upon some favor° that it loves.
Hath it not, boy?

VIOLA: A little, by your favor.°

ORSINO: What kind of woman is't?

VIOLA: Of your complexion.

ORSINO: She is not worth thee, then. What years, i'faith?

VIOLA: About your years, my lord.

ORSINO: Too old, by heaven. Let still° the woman take
An elder than herself. So wears she° to him;
So sways she level° in her husband's heart.
For, boy, however we do praise ourselves,
Our fancies are more giddy and unfirm,
More longing, wavering, sooner lost and worn,°
Than women's are.

VIOLA: I think it well, my lord.

ORSINO: Then let thy love be younger than thyself,
Or thy affection cannot hold the bent;°
For women are as roses, whose fair flower
Being once displayed,° doth fall that very hour.

VIOLA: And so they are. Alas that they are so,
To die even when° they to perfection grow!

Enter Curio and Clown [Feste].

ORSINO: Oh, fellow, come, the song we had last night.
Mark it, Cesario, it is old and plain;
The spinsters° and the knitters in the sun,
And the free° maids that weave their thread with bones,°
Do use° to chant it. It is silly sooth,°
And dallies with° the innocence of love,
Like the old age.°

20

25

30

35

40

45

50

---

19 **the seat** i.e., the heart 23 **stayed . . . favor** rested upon some face 25 **by your favor** if you please. (But also hinting at "like you in feature.") 30 **still** always 31 **wears she** she adapts herself 32 **sways she level** she keeps a perfect equipoise and steady affection 35 **worn** exhausted. (Sometimes emended to *won*.) 39 **hold the bent** hold steady, keep the intensity (like the tension of a bow) 41 **displayed** full blown 43 **even when** just as 46 **spinsters** spinners 47 **free** carefree, innocent. **bones** bobbins on which bone-lace was made 48 **Do use** are accustomed. **silly sooth** simple truth 49 **dallies with** dwells lovingly on, sports with 50 **Like . . . age** as in the good old times.

FESTE: Are you ready, sir?

ORSINO: Ay, prithee, sing.   *Music.*

          The Song.

FESTE: [*sings*]
          Come away,° come away, death,
          And in sad cypress° let me be laid.   55
          Fly away, fly away, breath;
          I am slain by a fair cruel maid.
          My shroud of white, stuck all with yew,°
          Oh, prepare it!
          My part of death, no one so true   60
          Did share it.°
          Not a flower, not a flower sweet
          On my black coffin let there be strown;°
          Not a friend, not a friend greet
          My poor corpse, where my bones shall be thrown.   65
          A thousand thousand sighs to save,
          Lay me, oh, where
          Sad true lover never find my grave,
          To weep there!

ORSINO: [*offering money*] There's for thy pains.   70

FESTE: No pains, sir. I take pleasure in singing, sir.

ORSINO: I'll pay thy pleasure then.

FESTE: Truly, sir, and pleasure will be paid, one time or another.°

ORSINO: Give me now leave to leave° thee.

FESTE: Now, the melancholy god° protect thee, and the tailor   75
          make thy doublet° of changeable taffeta,° for thy mind is a
          very opal.° I would have men of such constancy put to sea,
          that their business might be everything and their intent
          everywhere,° for that's it that always makes a good voyage of
          nothing.° Farewell.   *Exit.*   80

---

54 Come away Come hither   **55 cypress** i.e., a coffin of cypress wood, or bier strewn with sprigs
of cypress   **58 yew** yew sprigs. (Emblematic of mourning, like cypress.)   **60–1 My . . . it** No one
died for love so true to love as I.   **63 strown** strewn   **73 pleasure . . . another** sooner or later one
must pay for indulgence.   **74 leave to leave** permission to take leave of, dismiss   **75 the melancholy
god** i.e., Saturn, whose planet was thought to control the melancholy temperament   **76 doublet**
close-fitting jacket.   **changeable taffeta** a silk so woven of various-colored threads that its color
shifts with changing perspective   **77 opal** an iridescent precious stone that changes color when
seen from various angles or in different lights.   **78–9 that . . . everywhere** i.e., so that in the
changeableness of the sea their inconstancy could always be exercised   **79–80 for . . . nothing**
because that's the quality that is satisfied with an aimless voyage.

ORSINO: Let all the rest give place.°

[Curio and attendants withdraw.]

Once more, Cesario,
Get thee to yond same sovereign cruelty.
Tell her, my love, more noble than the world,
Prizes not quantity of dirty lands;
The parts° that fortune hath bestowed upon her,   85
Tell her, I hold as giddily as fortune;°
But 'tis that miracle and queen of gems°
That nature pranks° her in attracts° my soul.

VIOLA: But if she cannot love you, sir?

ORSINO: I cannot be so answered.   90

VIOLA: Sooth,° but you must.
Say that some lady—as perhaps there is—
Hath for your love as great a pang of heart
As you have for Olivia. You cannot love her;
You tell her so. Must she not then be answered?°   95

ORSINO: There is no woman's sides
Can bide° the beating of so strong a passion
As love doth give my heart; no woman's heart
So big, to hold° so much. They lack retention.°
Alas, their love may be called appetite,   100
No motion° of the liver, but the palate,°
That suffer surfeit, cloyment,° and revolt;°
But mine is all as hungry as the sea,
And can digest as much. Make no compare°
Between that love a woman can bear me   105
And that I owe° Olivia.

VIOLA: Ay, but I know—

ORSINO: What dost thou know?

VIOLA: Too well what love women to men may owe.
In faith, they are as true of heart as we.   110
My father had a daughter loved a man

---

81 **give place** withdraw.   85 **parts** attributes such as wealth or rank   86 **I . . . fortune** I esteem as carelessly as I do fortune, that fickle goddess   87 **that miracle . . . gems** i.e., her beauty   88 **pranks** adorns.   **attracts** that attracts   91 **Sooth** In truth   95 **be answered** be satisfied with your answer.   97 **bide** withstand   99 **to hold** as to contain.   **retention** constancy, the power of retaining.   101 **motion** impulse.   **liver . . . palate** (Real love is a passion of the liver, whereas fancy, light love, is born in the eye and nourished in the palate.)   102 **cloyment** satiety.   **revolt** revulsion   104 **compare** comparison   106 **owe** have for

As it might be, perhaps, were I a woman,
I should Your Lordship.

ORSINO: And what's her history?   115

VIOLA: A blank, my lord. She never told her love,
But let concealment, like a worm i'th' bud,
Feed on her damask° cheek. She pined in thought,
And with a green and yellow° melancholy;
She sat like Patience on a monument,°   120
Smiling at grief. Was not this love indeed?
We men may say more, swear more, but indeed
Our shows° are more than will;° for still° we prove
Much in our vows, but little in our love.

ORSINO: But died thy sister of her love, my boy?   125

VIOLA: I am all the daughters of my father's house,
And all the brothers too—and yet I know not.
Sir, shall I to this lady?

ORSINO: Ay, that's the theme.
To her in haste; give her this jewel. [*He gives a jewel.*] Say   130
My love can give no place, bide no denay.°

                                                    Exeunt [separately].

2.5

Enter Sir Toby, Sir Andrew, and Fabian.

SIR TOBY: Come thy ways,° Signor Fabian.

FABIAN: Nay, I'll come. If I lose a scruple° of this sport, let me be
boiled° to death with melancholy.

SIR TOBY: Wouldst thou not be glad to have the niggardly ras-
cally sheep-biter° come by some notable shame?   5

FABIAN: I would exult, man. You know he brought me out o'favor
with my lady about a bearbaiting° here.

SIR TOBY: To anger him we'll have the bear again, and we will
fool him black and blue.° Shall we not, Sir Andrew?

---

118 **damask** pink and white like the damask rose   119 **green and yellow** pale and sallow
120 **on a monument** carved in statuary on a tomb   124 **shows** displays of passion. **more than will**
greater than our determination. **still** always   131 **can . . . denay** cannot yield or endure denial.
1 **Come thy ways** Come along   2 **a scruple** the least bit   3 **boiled** (With a pun on "biled"; black
bile was the "humor" of melancholy and was thought to be a cold humor.)   5 **sheep-biter** a dog
that bites sheep, i.e., a scoundrel   7 **bearbaiting** (A special target of Puritan disapproval.)
9 **fool . . . blue** mock him until he is figuratively black and blue.

SIR ANDREW: An° we do not, it is pity of our lives.°   10

    Enter Maria [with a letter].

SIR TOBY: Here comes the little villain°.—How now, my metal°
of India!

MARIA: Get ye all three into the boxtree.° Malvolio's coming
down this walk. He has been yonder i' the sun practicing behavior to his own shadow this half hour. Observe him, for the
love of mockery, for I know this letter will make a contempla-   15
tive° idiot of him. Close,° in the name of jesting! [*The others
hide.*] Lie thou there [*throwing down a letter*]; for here comes
the trout that must be caught with tickling.°   *Exit.*

    Enter Malvolio.

MALVOLIO: 'Tis but fortune; all is fortune. Maria once told me
she° did affect° me; and I have heard herself come thus near,   20
that should she fancy,° it should be one of my complexion.
Besides, she uses me with a more exalted respect than anyone
else that follows° her. What should I think on't?

SIR TOBY: Here's an overweening rogue!

FABIAN: Oh, peace! Contemplation makes a rare° turkey-cock of
him. How he jets° under his advanced° plumes!   25

SIR ANDREW: 'Slight,° I could so beat the rogue!

SIR TOBY: Peace, I say.

MALVOLIO: To be Count Malvolio.

SIR TOBY: Ah, rogue!

SIR ANDREW: Pistol him, pistol him.   30

SIR TOBY: Peace, peace!

MALVOLIO: There is example° for't. The lady of the Strachy°
married the yeoman of the wardrobe.

SIR ANDREW: Fie on him, Jezebel!°

FABIAN: Oh, peace! Now he's deeply in. Look how imagination
blows° him.

---

10 **An** If. **pity of our lives** a pity we should live. **11 villain** (Here, a term of endearment.)
metal gold, i.e., priceless one   **12 boxtree** an evergreen shrub.   **15–6 contemplative** i.e., from his
musings. **16 Close** i.e., Keep close, stay hidden   **18 tickling** (1) stroking gently about the gills—an
actual method of fishing (2) deception.   **20 she** Olivia. **affect** have fondness for   **21 fancy** fall in
love   **23 follows** serves   **25 rare** extraordinary   **26 jets** struts.   **advanced** prominent   **27 'Slight**
By His (God's) light   **32 example** precedent.   **lady of the Strachy** (Apparently a lady who had
married below her station; no certain identification.)   **33 Jezebel** the proud queen of Ahab, King of
Israel.   **34 blows** puffs up

MALVOLIO: Having been three months married to her, sitting in my state°— 35

SIR TOBY: Oh, for a stone-bow,° to hit him in the eye!

MALVOLIO: Calling my officers about me, in my branched° velvet gown; having come from a daybed,° where I have left Olivia sleeping—

SIR TOBY: Fire and brimstone!

FABIAN: Oh, peace, peace! 40

MALVOLIO: And then to have the humor of state;° and after a demure travel of regard,° telling them I know my place as I would they should do theirs, to ask for my kinsman Toby.°

SIR TOBY: Bolts and shackles!

FABIAN: Oh, peace, peace, peace! Now, now. 45

MALVOLIO: Seven of my people, with an obedient start, make out for him. I frown the while, and perchance wind up my watch, or play with my°—some rich jewel. Toby approaches; curtsies° there to me—

SIR TOBY: Shall this fellow live?

FABIAN: Though our silence be drawn from us with cars,° yet peace. 50

MALVOLIO: I extend my hand to him thus, quenching my familiar° smile with an austere regard of control°—

SIR TOBY: And does not Toby take° you a blow o' the lips then?

MALVOLIO: Saying, "Cousin Toby, my fortunes having cast me on your niece give me this prerogative of speech—" 55

SIR TOBY: What, what?

MALVOLIO: "You must amend your drunkenness."

SIR TOBY: Out, scab!°

FABIAN: Nay, patience, or we break the sinews of ° our plot.

MALVOLIO: "Besides, you waste the treasure of your time with a foolish knight—" 60

SIR ANDREW: That's me, I warrant you.

MALVOLIO: "One Sir Andrew."

---

35 **state** chair of state   36 **stone-bow** crossbow that shoots stones   37 **branched** adorned with a figured pattern suggesting branched leaves or flowers.   38 **daybed** sofa, couch   41 **have . . . state** adopt the imperious manner of authority   42 **demure . . . regard** grave survey of the company   43 **Toby** (Malvolio omits the title *Sir*.)   48 **play with my** (Malvolio perhaps means his steward's chain but checks himself in time; as "Count Malvolio," he would not be wearing it. A bawdy meaning of playing with himself is also suggested.)   **curtsies** bows   50 **with cars** with chariots, i.e., pulling apart by force   51 **familiar** (1) customary (2) friendly.   52 **regard of control** look of authority   53 **take** deliver   58 **scab** scurvy fellow.   59 **break . . . of** hamstring, disable

SIR ANDREW: I knew 'twas I, for many do call me fool.

MALVOLIO: What employment° have we here?

[Taking up the letter.]

FABIAN: Now is the woodcock° near the gin.°   65

SIR TOBY: Oh, peace, and the spirit of humors° intimate reading
aloud to him!

MALVOLIO: By my life, this is my lady's hand. These be her very
c's, her u's, and her t's;° and thus makes she her great° P's. It is
in contempt of° question her hand.

SIR ANDREW: Her c's, her u's, and her t's. Why that?   70

MALVOLIO: [reads] "To the unknown beloved, this, and my good
wishes."—Her very phrases! By your leave, wax.° Soft!° And
the impressure° her Lucrece,° with which she uses° to seal.
'Tis my lady. To whom should this be?   [He opens the letter.]

FABIAN: This wins him, liver° and all.   75

MALVOLIO: [reads]

"Jove knows I love,
But who?
Lips, do not move;
No man must know."   80

"No man must know." What follows? The numbers altered!°
"No man must know." If this should be thee, Malvolio?

SIR TOBY: Marry, hang thee, brock!°

MALVOLIO: [reads]

"I may command where I adore,   85
But silence, like a Lucrece knife,
With bloodless stroke my heart doth gore;
M.O.A.I. doth sway my life."

FABIAN: A fustian° riddle!

SIR TOBY: Excellent wench, say I.   90

MALVOLIO: "M.O.A.I. doth sway my life." Nay, but first, let me
see, let me see, let me see.

---

64 **employment** business   65 **woodcock** (A bird proverbial for its stupidity.)   **gin** snare.   66 **humors**
whim, caprice   68 **c's . . . t's** i.e., *cut*, slang for the female pudenda.   **great** (1) uppercase (2) copious.
(P suggests "pee.")   69 **in contempt of** beyond   72 **By . . . wax** (Addressed to the seal on the letter.)
Soft Softly, not so fast.   73 **impressure** device imprinted on the seal.   **Lucrece** Lucretia, chaste
matron who, ravished by Tarquin, committed suicide   **uses** is accustomed   75 **liver** i.e., the seat of
passion   81 **The numbers altered!** More verses, in a different meter!   83 **brock** badger. (Used
contemptuously.)   89 **fustian** bombastic, ridiculously pompous

FABIAN: What° dish o' poison has she dressed° him!

SIR TOBY: And with what wing° the staniel° checks at it!°

MALVOLIO: "I may command where I adore." Why, she may command me; I serve her, she is my lady. Why, this is evident to any formal capacity.° There is no obstruction in this. And 95 the end—what should that alphabetical position° portend? If I could make that resemble something in me! Softly! "M.O.A.I."—

SIR TOBY: Oh, ay,° make up° that. He is now at a cold scent.

FABIAN: Sowter° will cry upon't for all this, though it be as rank as a fox.

MALVOLIO: "M"—Malvolio. "M"! Why, that begins my name! 100

FABIAN: Did not I say he would work it out? The cur is excellent at faults.°

MALVOLIO: "M"—But then there is no consonancy in the sequel that suffers under probation:° "A" should follow, but "O" does.

FABIAN: And "O" shall end,° I hope.

SIR TOBY: Ay, or I'll cudgel him, and make him cry "Oh!" 105

MALVOLIO: And then "I" comes behind.

FABIAN: Ay, an you had any eye° behind you, you might see more detraction at your heels° than fortunes before you.

MALVOLIO: "M.O.A.I." This simulation° is not as the former. And yet, to crush this a little, it would bow to me, for every one of 110 these letters are in my name. Soft! Here follows prose.

[He reads.] "If this fall into thy hand, revolve.° In my stars° I am above thee, but be not afraid of greatness. Some are born great, some achieve greatness, and some have greatness thrust upon 'em. Thy Fates open their hands;° let thy blood 115 and spirit embrace them; and, to inure° thyself to what thou

92 What What a.   dressed prepared for   93 wing speed.   staniel kestrel, a sparrow hawk. (The word is used contemptuously because of the uselessness of the staniel for falconry.)   checks at it turns to fly at it.   95 formal capacity normal understanding.   96 position arrangement   97 Oh, ay (Playing on O.I. of M.O.A.I.)   make up work out   98–9 Sowter . . . fox The hound Sowter (literally, "Cobbler") will bay triumphantly at picking up this false scent, even though the smell is as rank as a fox. ("M.O.A.I." is a false lead that reeks.)   101 at faults i.e., at maneuvering his way past breaks in the line of scent—in this case, on a false trail.   102–3 no consonancy . . . probation no pattern in the following letters that stands up under examination. (In fact, the letters "M.O.A.I." represent the first, last, second, and next to last letters of Malvolio's name.)   104 "O" shall end (1) "O" ends Malvolio's name (2) omega ends the Greek alphabet and is thus a symbol for the ending of the world, alpha to omega (3) Malvolio's cry of pain will end the matter, as Sir Toby suggests in the next line.   107 eye (punning on the "I" of "Oh, ay" and "M.O.A.I.")   108 detraction . . . heels defamation pursuing you   109 simulation disguise, puzzle   112 revolve consider.   stars fortune   115 open their hands offer their bounty   116 inure accustom.

art like° to be, cast° thy humble slough° and appear fresh. Be
opposite° with a kinsman, surly with servants. Let thy tongue
tang° arguments of state;° put thyself into the trick of
singularity.° She thus advises thee that sighs for thee. 120
Remember who commended thy yellow stockings, and
wished to see thee ever cross-gartered.° I say, remember. Go
to,° thou art made, if thou desir'st to be so. If not, let me see
thee a steward still, the fellow of servants, and not worthy to
touch Fortune's fingers. Farewell. She that would alter 125
services° with thee, The Fortunate-Unhappy."
Daylight and champaign° discovers° not more! This is open. I will
be proud, I will read politic° authors, I will baffle° Sir Toby, I
will wash off gross° acquaintance, I will be point-devise° the
very man. I do not now fool myself, to let° imagination jade 130
me;° for every reason excites to this,° that my lady loves me.
She did commend my yellow stockings of late, she did praise
my leg being cross-gartered; and in this° she manifests
herself to my love, and with a kind of injunction drives me to
these habits° of her liking. I thank my stars, I am happy.° I will 135
be strange, stout,° in yellow stockings and cross-gartered, even
with the swiftness of putting on. Jove and my stars be praised!
Here is yet a post-script. [*He reads.*] "Thou canst not choose but
know who I am. If thou entertain'st° my love, let it appear in
thy smiling; thy smiles become thee well. Therefore in my 140
presence still° smile, dear my sweet, I prithee." Jove, I thank
thee. I will smile; I will do everything that thou wilt have me.

Exit.

[Sir Toby, Sir Andrew, and Fabian come from hiding.]

FABIAN: I will not give my part of this sport for a pension of
thousands to be paid from the Sophy.°

---

117 **like** likely. **cast** cast off. **slough** skin of a snake; hence, former demeanor of humbleness.
118 **opposite** contradictory 119 **tang** sound loud with. **state** politics, statecraft. **trick of
singularity** eccentricity of manner. 121 **cross-gartered** wearing garters above and below the knee
so as to cross behind it. 122 **Go to** (An expression of remonstrance.) 125–26 **alter services** i.e.,
exchange place of mistress and servant 127 **champaign** open country. **discovers** discloses
128 **politic** dealing with state affairs. **baffle** deride, degrade. (A technical chivalric term used to
describe the disgrace of a perjured knight.) 129 **gross** base. **point-devise** correct to the letter
130 **to let** by letting. 130–1 **jade me** trick me, make me look ridiculous (as an unruly horse
might do). 131 **excites to this** prompts this conclusion 133 **this** this letter 135 **these habits**
this attire **happy** fortunate. 136 **strange, stout** aloof, haughty 139 **thou entertain'st** you
accept 141 **still** continually 143 **Sophy** Shah of Persia.

SIR TOBY: I could marry this wench for this device.

SIR ANDREW: So could I too.   145

SIR TOBY: And ask no other dowry with her but such another jest.

        Enter Maria.

SIR ANDREW: Nor I neither.

FABIAN: Here comes my noble gull-catcher.°

SIR TOBY: Wilt thou set thy foot o' my neck?

SIR ANDREW: Or o' mine either?   150

SIR TOBY: Shall I play° my freedom at tray-trip,° and become
    thy bond slave?

SIR ANDREW: I'faith, or I either?

SIR TOBY: Why, thou hast put him in such a dream that when
    the image of it leaves him he must run mad.   155

MARIA: Nay, but say true, does it work upon him?

SIR TOBY: Like aqua vitae° with a midwife.

MARIA: If you will then see the fruits of the sport, mark his first
    approach before my lady. He will come to her in yellow stock-
    ings, and 'tis a color she abhors, and cross-gartered, a fashion   160
    she detests; and he will smile upon her, which will now be so
    unsuitable to her disposition, being addicted to a melancholy
    as she is, that it cannot but turn him into a notable contempt.°
    If you will see it, follow me.

SIR TOBY: To the gates of Tartar,° thou most excellent devil of wit!   165

SIR ANDREW: I'll make one° too.   *Exeunt.*

3.1

        Enter Viola, and Clown [Feste, playing his pipe and tabor].

VIOLA: Save° thee, friend, and thy music. Dost thou live by°
    thy tabor?°

FESTE: No, sir, I live by the church.

VIOLA: Art thou a churchman?

FESTE: No such matter, sir. I do live by the church, for I do live at
    my house, and my house doth stand by the church.   5

---

148 gull-catcher tricker of *gulls* or dupes.   **151 play** gamble. **tray-trip** a game of dice, success in which
depended on throwing a three (*tray*)   **157 aqua vitae** brandy or other distilled liquor   **163 notable
contempt** notorious object of contempt.   **165 Tartar** Tartarus, the infernal regions   **166 make one**
i.e., tag along

1 Save God save.   **live by** earn your living with. (But Feste uses the phrase to mean "dwell near.")
2 tabor small drum.

VIOLA: So thou mayst say the king lies by° a beggar if a beggar dwell near him, or the church stands by thy tabor if thy tabor stand by° the church.

FESTE: You have said,° sir. To see this age! A sentence° is but a cheveril° glove to a good wit. How quickly the wrong side may be turned outward! 10

VIOLA: Nay, that's certain. They that dally nicely° with words may quickly make them wanton.°

FESTE: I would therefore my sister had had no name, sir.

VIOLA: Why, man?

FESTE: Why, sir, her name's a word, and to dally with that word 15 might make my sister wanton. But indeed, words are very rascals since bonds disgraced them.°

VIOLA: Thy reason, man?

FESTE: Troth, sir, I can yield you none without words, and words are grown so false I am loath to prove reason with them.

VIOLA: I warrant thou art a merry fellow and car'st for nothing.° 20

FESTE: Not so, sir, I do care for something; but in my conscience, sir, I do not care for you. If that be to care for nothing, sir, I would it would make you invisible.°

VIOLA: Art not thou the Lady Olivia's fool?

FESTE: No indeed, sir. The Lady Olivia has no folly. She will keep no fool, sir, till she be married, and fools areas like husbands 25 as pilchers° are to herrings—the husband's the bigger.° I am indeed not her fool but her corrupter of words.

VIOLA: I saw thee late° at the Count Orsino's.

FESTE: Foolery, sir, does walk about the orb° like the sun; it shines everywhere. I would be sorry, sir, but the fool should be 30 as oft with your master as with my mistress.° I think I saw Your Wisdom° there.

---

6 lies by (1) lies sexually with (2) dwells near   **7–8 stands by ... stand by** (1) is maintained by (2) is placed near   **9 You have said** You've expressed your opinion.   **sentence** maxim, judgment, opinion   **10 cheveril** kidskin   **11 dally nicely** (1) play subtly (2) toy amorously   **21 wanton** (1) equivocal (2) licentious, unchaste. (Feste then "dallies" with the word in its sexual sense; see line 20.)   **17 since ... them** i.e., since bonds have been needed to make sworn statements good. (Words cannot be relied on since not even contractual promises are reliable.)   **20 car'st for nothing** are without any worries. (But Feste puns on *care for* in lines 29–30 in the sense of "like.")   **23 invisible** i.e., nothing; absent.   **26 pilchers** pilchards, fish resembling herring but smaller   **the bigger** (1) the larger (2) the bigger fool.   **28 late** recently   **29 orb** earth   **30–1 I would ... mistress** (1) I should be sorry not to visit Orsino's house often (2) It would be a shame if folly were no less common there than in Olivia's household.   **31 Your Wisdom** i.e., you. (A title of mock courtesy.)

VIOLA: Nay, an thou pass upon me,° I'll no more with thee. Hold, there's expenses for thee.

[*She gives a coin.*]

FESTE: Now Jove, in his next commodity° of hair, send thee a beard!

VIOLA: By my troth, I'll tell thee, I am almost sick for one°— [*aside*] though I would not have it grow on my chin.—Is thy   35
lady within?

FESTE: Would not a pair of these have bred, sir?

VIOLA: Yes, being kept together and put to use.°

FESTE: I would play Lord Pandarus° of Phrygia, sir, to bring a Cressida to this Troilus.

VIOLA: I understand you, sir. 'Tis well begged.

[*She gives another coin.*]

FESTE: The matter, I hope, is not great, sir, begging but a beggar;   40
Cressida was a beggar.° My lady is within, sir. I will conster° to them whence you come. Who you are and what you would are out of my welkin°—I might say "element,"° but the word is overworn.   *Exit.*

VIOLA: This fellow is wise enough to play the fool,
And to do that well craves a kind of wit.   45
He must observe their mood on whom he jests,
The quality° of persons, and the time,
Not, like the haggard,° check at every feather
That comes before his eye.° This is a practice°
As full of labor as a wise man's art;   50
For folly that he wisely shows is fit,
But wise men, folly-fall'n, quite taint their wit.°

Enter Sir Toby and [Sir] Andrew.

32 **an . . . me** if you fence (verbally) with me, pass judgment on me   33 **commodity** supply
34 **sick for one** (1) eager to have a beard (2) in love with a bearded man   37 **put to use** put out at interest.   38 **Pandarus** the go-between in the love story of Troilus and Cressida; uncle to Cressida   40–1 **begging . . . was a beggar** (A reference to Henryson's *Testament of Cresseid* in which Cressida became a leper and a beggar. Feste desires another coin to be the mate of the one he has, just as Cressida, the beggar, was mate to Troilus.)   41 **conster** construe, explain
43 **welkin** sky.   **element** (The word can be synonymous with *welkin*, but the common phrase *out of my element* means "beyond my scope.")   47 **quality** character, rank   48 **haggard** untrained adult hawk, hence unmanageable   48–9 **check . . . eye** strike at every bird it sees, i.e., dart from subject to subject.   49 **practice** exercise of skill   51–2 **For . . . wit** for the folly he judiciously displays is appropriate and clever, whereas when wise men fall into folly they utterly infect their own intelligence.

SIR TOBY: Save you, gentleman.

VIOLA: And you, sir.

SIR ANDREW: *Dieu vous garde, monsieur.*° 55

VIOLA: *Et vous aussi; votre serviteur.*°

SIR ANDREW: I hope, sir, you are, and I am yours.

SIR TOBY: Will you encounter° the house? My niece is desirous you should enter, if your trade° be to her.

VIOLA: I am bound° to your niece, sir; I mean, she is the list° of 60 my voyage.

SIR TOBY: Taste° your legs, sir. Put them to motion.

VIOLA: My legs do better understand° me, sir, than I understand what you mean by bidding me taste my legs.

SIR TOBY: I mean, to go, sir, to enter.

VIOLA: I will answer you with gait and entrance.°—But we are 65 prevented.°

Enter Olivia and gentlewoman [Maria].

Most excellent accomplished lady, the heavens rain odors on you!

SIR ANDREW: [*to Sir Toby*] That youth's a rare courtier. "Rain odors"—well.

VIOLA: [*to Olivia*] My matter hath no voice,° lady, but to your own most pregnant and vouchsafed° ear.

SIR ANDREW: [*to Sir Toby*] "Odors," "pregnant," and "vouch- 70 safed." I'll get 'em all three all ready.°

OLIVIA: Let the garden door be shut, and leave me to my hearing. [*Exeunt Sir Toby, Sir Andrew, and Maria.*] Give me your hand, sir.

VIOLA: My duty, madam, and most humble service.

OLIVIA: What is your name?

VIOLA: Cesario is your servant's name, fair princess. 75

OLIVIA: My servant, sir? 'Twas never merry world Since lowly feigning was called compliment.° You're servant to the Count Orsino, youth.

55 *Dieu . . . monsieur* God keep you, sir. 56 *Et . . . serviteur* And you, too; (I am) your servant. (Sir Andrew is not quite up to a reply in French.) 58 encounter (High-sounding word to express "approach.") 59 trade business. (Suggesting also a commercial venture.) 60 I am bound (1) I am on a journey. (Continuing Sir Toby's metaphor in *trade*.) (2) I am confined, obligated. list limit, destination 61 Taste Try 62 understand stand under, support 65 gait and entrance going and entering. (With a pun on *gate*:[1] stride [2] entryway.) prevented anticipated. 68 hath no voice cannot be uttered 69 pregnant and vouchsafed receptive and attentive 70 all ready committed to memory for future use. 75–6 'Twas . . . compliment Things have never been the same since affected humility (like calling oneself another's servant) began to be mistaken for courtesy.

VIOLA: And he is yours,° and his° must needs be yours;
Your servant's servant is your servant, madam.   80

OLIVIA: For° him, I think not on him. For his thoughts,
Would they were blanks,° rather than filled with me!

VIOLA: Madam, I come to whet your gentle thoughts
On his behalf.

OLIVIA: Oh, by your leave,° I pray you.   85
I bade you never speak again of him.
But, would you undertake another suit,
I had rather hear you to solicit that
Than music from the spheres.°

VIOLA: Dear lady—   90

OLIVIA: Give me leave, beseech you. I did send,
After the last enchantment you did here,
A ring in chase of you; so did I abuse°
Myself, my servant, and, I fear me, you.
Under your hard construction° must I sit,   95
To force that° on you in a shameful cunning
Which you knew none of yours. What might you think?
Have you not set mine honor at the stake°
And baited° it with all th' unmuzzled thoughts
That tyrannous heart can think? To one of your receiving°   100
Enough is shown; a cypress, not a bosom,
Hides my heart.° So, let me hear you speak.

VIOLA: I pity you.

OLIVIA: That's a degree to love.

VIOLA: No, not a grece;° for 'tis a vulgar proof°   105
That very oft we pity enemies.

OLIVIA: Why then, methinks 'tis time to smile° again.
Oh, world, how apt the poor are to be proud!°

---

79 is yours is your servant.   **his** those belonging to him   **81 For** As for   **82 blanks** blank coins ready to be stamped or empty sheets of paper   **85 by your leave** i.e., allow me to interrupt **89 music from the spheres** (The heavenly bodies were thought to be fixed in hollow concentric spheres that revolved one about the other, producing a harmony too exquisite to be heard by human ears.)   **93 abuse** wrong, mislead   **95 hard construction** harsh interpretation   **96 To force that** for forcing the ring   **98 at the stake** (The figure is from bearbaiting.)   **99 baited** harassed. (Literally, set the unmuzzled dogs on to bite the bear.)   **100 receiving** capacity, intelligence **101-2 a cypress . . . heart** i.e., I have shown my heart to you, veiled only with thin, gauzelike cypress cloth rather than the opaque flesh of my bosom.   **105 grece** step. (Synonymous with *degree* in the preceding line.)   **vulgar proof** common experience   **107 smile** i.e., cast off love's melancholy   **108 how . . . proud!** how ready the unfortunate and rejected (like myself) are to find something to be proud of in their distress! Or, how apt are persons of comparatively low social station like yourself to show pride in rejecting love!

If one should be a prey, how much the better
To fall before the lion than the wolf!°   *Clock strikes.*   110
The clock upbraids me with the waste of time.
Be not afraid, good youth, I will not have you;
And yet, when wit and youth is come to harvest
Your wife is like° to reap a proper° man.
There lies your way, due west.   115

VIOLA: Then westward ho!°
Grace and good disposition attend Your Ladyship.°
You'll nothing, madam, to my lord by me?

OLIVIA: Stay.
I prithee, tell me what thou think'st of me.   120

VIOLA: That you do think you are not what you are.°

OLIVIA: If I think so, I think the same of you.°

VIOLA: Then think you right. I am not what I am.

OLIVIA: I would you were as I would have you be!

VIOLA: Would it be better, madam, than I am?   125
I wish it might, for now I am your fool.°

OLIVIA: [*aside*]
Oh, what a deal of scorn looks beautiful
In the contempt and anger of his lip!
A murderous guilt shows not itself more soon   130
Than love that would seem hid; love's night is noon.°—
Cesario, by the roses of the spring,
By maidhood, honor, truth, and everything,
I love thee so that, maugre° all thy pride,
Nor° wit nor reason can my passion hide.   135
Do not extort thy reasons from this clause,
For that I woo, thou therefore hast no cause.°
But rather reason thus with reason fetter:°
Love sought is good, but given unsought is better.

---

110 To fall . . . wolf! i.e., to fall before a noble adversary rather than to a person like you who attacks me thus!   **114 like** likely. **proper** handsome, worthy   **116 westward ho** (The cry of Thames watermen to attract westward-bound passengers.)   **117 Grace . . . Ladyship** May you enjoy God's blessing and a happy frame of mind.   **120–1 That . . . are** i.e., That you think you are in love with a man, and you are mistaken.   **122 If . . . you** (Olivia may interpret Viola's cryptic statement as suggesting that Olivia "does not know herself," i.e., is distracted with passion; she may also hint at her suspicion that "Cesario" is higher born than he admits.)   **126 fool** butt.   **131 love's . . . noon** i.e., love, despite its attempt to be secret, reveals itself as plain as day.   **134 maugre** in spite of **135 Nor** neither   **136–7 Do . . . cause** Do not rationalize your indifference along these lines, that because I am the wooer you have no cause to reciprocate.   **138 But . . . fetter** But instead control your reasoning with the following reason

VIOLA: By innocence I swear, and by my youth,   140
        I have one heart, one bosom, and one truth,
        And that no woman has, nor never none
        Shall mistress be of it save I alone.
        And so adieu, good madam. Nevermore
        Will I my master's tears to you deplore.°   145
OLIVIA: Yet come again, for thou perhaps mayst move
        That heart, which now abhors, to like his love.

        Exeunt [separately].

3.2

        Enter Sir Toby, Sir Andrew, and Fabian.

SIR ANDREW: No, faith, I'll not stay a jot longer.
SIR TOBY: Thy reason, dear venom,° give thy reason.
FABIAN: You must needs yield your reason, Sir Andrew.
SIR ANDREW: Marry, I saw your niece do more favors to the
        Count's servingman than ever she bestowed upon me. I saw't   5
        i' th' orchard.°
SIR TOBY: Did she see thee the while, old boy? Tell me that.
SIR ANDREW: As plain as I see you now.
FABIAN: This was a great argument° of love in her toward you.
SIR ANDREW: 'Slight,° will you make an ass o' me?
FABIAN: I will prove it° legitimate, sir, upon the oaths° of judg-   10
        ment and reason.
SIR TOBY: And they have been grand-jurymen since before
        Noah was a sailor.
FABIAN: She did show favor to the youth in your sight only to ex-
        asperate you, to awake your dormouse° valor, to put fire in
        your heart and brimstone in your liver. You should then have   15
        accosted her, and with some excellent jests, fire-new from the
        mint,° you should have banged° the youth into dumbness.
        This was looked for at your hand, and this was balked.° The
        double gilt° of this opportunity you let time wash off, and you

---

145 **deplore** beweep.
2 **venom** i.e., person filled with venomous anger   6 **orchard** garden.   8 **argument** proof
9 **'Slight** By his (God's) light   10 **it** my contention.   **oaths** i.e., testimony under oath   14 **dormouse**
i.e., sleepy and timid   16–7 **fire-new . . . mint** newly coined   17 **banged** struck   18 **balked** missed,
neglected.   19 **double gilt** thick layer of gold, i.e., rare worth

are now sailed into the north of my lady's opinion,° where you
will hang like an icicle on a Dutchman's beard° unless you do
redeem it by some laudable attempt either of valor or policy.°

SIR ANDREW: An't be any way, it must be with valor, for policy I
hate. I had as lief be a Brownist° as a politician.°

SIR TOBY: Why, then, build me thy fortunes upon the basis of
valor. Challenge me° the Count's youth to fight with him; hurt
him in eleven places. My niece shall take note of it; and assure
thyself, there is no love-broker° in the world can more prevail
in man's commendation with woman than report of valor.

FABIAN: There is no way but this, Sir Andrew.

SIR ANDREW: Will either of you bear me a challenge to him?

SIR TOBY: Go, write it in a martial hand. Be curst° and brief; it is
no matter how witty, so it be eloquent and full of invention.
Taunt him with the license of ink.° If thou "thou"-est° him
some thrice, it shall not be amiss; and as many lies° as will lie
in thy sheet of paper, although the sheet were big enough for
the bed of Ware° in England, set 'em down. Go, about it. Let
there be gall° enough in thy ink, though thou write with a
goose pen,° no matter. About it.

SIR ANDREW: Where shall I find you?

SIR TOBY: We'll call thee° at the cubiculo.° Go.

Exit Sir Andrew.

FABIAN: This is a dear manikin° to you, Sir Toby.

SIR TOBY: I have been dear° to him, lad, some two thousand
strong or so.

FABIAN: We shall have a rare° letter from him; but you'll not
deliver't?

20

25

30

35

40

45

---

20 into . . . opinion i.e., out of the warmth and sunshine of Olivia's favor   **21 icicle . . . beard**
(Alludes to the arctic voyage of William Barents in 1596–1597.)   **22 policy** stratagem.   **24 Brownist**
(An early name of the Congregationalists, from the name of the founder, Robert Browne.)
politician intriguer. (Sir Andrew misinterprets Fabian's more neutral use of *policy*, "clever
stratagem.")   **25–6 build me . . . Challenge me** build . . . Challenge. ("Me" is idiomatic.)   **28 love-
broker** agent between lovers   **32 curst** fierce   **34 with . . . ink** i.e., with all the unfettered
eloquence at your disposal as a writer.   **"thou"-est** ("Thou" was used only between friends or
to inferiors.)   **35 lies** charges of lying   **37 bed of Ware** a famous bedstead capable of holding
twelve persons, about eleven feet square, said to have been at the Stag Inn in Ware, Hertfordshire
38 gall (1) bitterness, rancor (2) a growth found on certain oaks, used as an ingredient of ink
39 goose pen (1) goose quill (2) foolish style   **41 call thee** call for you. **cubiculo** little chamber,
bedchamber.   **42 manikin** puppet   **43 dear** expensive. (Playing on *dear*, "fond," in the previous
speech.)   **45 rare** extraordinary

SIR TOBY: Never trust me, then; and by all means stir on the
youth to an answer. I think oxen and wainropes° cannot hale°
them together. For° Andrew, if he were opened and you find
so much blood in his liver° as will clog the foot of a flea, I'll eat
the rest of th' anatomy.° 50

FABIAN: And his opposite,° the youth, bears in his visage no
great presage of cruelty.

Enter Maria.

SIR TOBY: Look where the youngest wren of nine° comes.

MARIA: If you desire the spleen,° and will laugh your-selves into
stitches, follow me. Yond gull Malvolio is turned heathen, a 55
very renegado;° for there is no Christian that means to be
saved by believing rightly can ever believe such impossible
passages of grossness.° He's in yellow stockings.

SIR TOBY: And cross-gartered?

MARIA: Most villainously,° like a pedant° that keeps a school i' th' 60
church. I have dogged him like his murderer. He does obey
every point of the letter that I dropped to betray him. He does
smile his face into more lines than is in the new map with the
augmentation of the Indies.° You have not seen such a thing
as 'tis. I can hardly for bear hurling things at him. I know my 65
lady will strike him. If she do, he'll smile and take't for a great
favor.

SIR TOBY: Come, bring us, bring us where he is.

Exeunt omnes.

3.3

Enter Sebastian and Antonio.

SEBASTIAN: I would not by my will have troubled you,
But since you make your pleasure of your pains,
I will no further chide you.

47 **wainropes** wagon ropes. **hale** haul. 48 **For** As for 49 **liver** (A pale and bloodless liver was a sign of cowardice.) 50 **th' anatomy** the cadaver. 51 **opposite** adversary 53 **youngest . . . nine** the last hatched and smallest of a nest of wrens 54 **the spleen** a laughing fit. (The spleen was thought to be the seat of immoderate laughter.) 56 **renegado** renegade, deserter of his religion 57–8 **impossible . . . grossness** gross impossibilities (i.e., in the letter). 60 **villainously** i.e., abominably. **pedant** schoolmaster 63–4 **the new . . . Indies** (Probably a reference to a map made by Emmeric Mollineux in 1599–1600 to be printed in Hakluyt's *Voyages*, showing more of the East indies, including Japan, than had ever been mapped before.)

ANTONIO: I could not stay behind you. My desire,
　　　More sharp than filèd steel, did spur me forth, 　　　　5
　　　And not all° love to see you—though so much°
　　　As might have drawn one to a longer voyage—
　　　But jealousy° what might befall your travel,
　　　Being skilless in° these parts, which to a stranger,
　　　Unguided and unfriended, often prove 　　　　10
　　　Rough and unhospitable. My willing love,
　　　The rather° by these arguments of fear,
　　　Set forth in your pursuit.

SEBASTIAN: My kind Antonio,
　　　I can no other answer make but thanks, 　　　　15
　　　And thanks; and ever oft good turns°
　　　Are shuffled off° with such uncurrent° pay.
　　　But were my worth,° as is my conscience,° firm,
　　　You should find better dealing.° What's to do?
　　　Shall we go see the relics° of this town? 　　　　20

ANTONIO: Tomorrow, sir. Best first go see your lodging.

SEBASTIAN: I am not weary, and 'tis long to night.
　　　I pray you, let us satisfy our eyes
　　　With the memorials and the things of fame
　　　That do renown° this city. 　　　　25

ANTONIO: Would you'd pardon me.
　　　I do not without danger walk these streets.
　　　Once in a sea fight 'gainst the Count his° galleys
　　　I did some service, of such note indeed
　　　That were I ta'en here it would scarce be answered.° 　　　　30

SEBASTIAN: Belike° you slew great number of his people?

ANTONIO: Th' offense is not of such a bloody nature,
　　　Albeit the quality of the time and quarrel
　　　Might well have given us bloody argument.°
　　　It might have since been answered° in repaying 　　　　35
　　　What we took from them, which for traffic's° sake

---

6 all only, merely. **so much** i.e., that was great enough　**8 jealousy** anxiety　**9 skilless in**
unacquainted with　**12 The rather** made all the more willing　**16 And . . . turns** (This probably
corrupt line is usually made to read, "And thanks and ever thanks; and oft good turns.")
17 shuffled off turned aside. **uncurrent** worthless (such as mere thanks)　**18 worth** wealth.
conscience i.e., moral inclination to assist　**19 dealing** treatment, payment.　**20 relics** antiquities
25 renown make famous　**28 Count his** Count's, i.e., Duke's　**30 it . . . answered** I'd be hard put to
offer a defense.　**31 Belike** Perhaps　**34 bloody argument** cause for bloodshed.　**35 answered**
compensated　**36 traffic's** trade's

Most of our city did. Only myself stood out,
For which, if I be lapsèd° in this place,
I shall pay dear.

SEBASTIAN: Do not then walk too open.

ANTONIO: It doth not fit me. Hold, sir, here's my purse. 40

[He gives his purse.]

In the south suburbs, at the Elephant,°
Is best to lodge. I will bespeak our diet,°
Whiles you beguile the time and feed your knowledge
With viewing of the town. There shall you have° me. 45

SEBASTIAN: Why I your purse?

ANTONIO: Haply° your eye shall light upon some toy°
You have desire to purchase; and your store°
I think is not for idle markets,° sir.

SEBASTIAN: I'll be your purse-bearer and leave you 50
For an hour.

ANTONIO: To th' Elephant.

SEBASTIAN: I do remember.

Exeunt [separately].

3.4

Enter Olivia and Maria.

OLIVIA: *[aside]*
I have sent after him; he says he'll come.°
How shall I feast him? What bestow of° him?
For youth is bought more oft than begged or borrowed.
I speak too loud.—
Where's Malvolio? He is sad and civil,° 5
And suits well for a servant with my fortunes.
Where is Malvolio?

MARIA: He's coming, madam, but in very strange manner. He is,
sure, possessed,° madam.

OLIVIA: Why, what's the matter? Does he rave? 10

---

38 **lapsèd** caught off guard, surprised 42 **Elephant** the name of an inn 43 **bespeak our diet**
order our food 45 **have** find 47 **Haply** Perhaps. **toy** trifle 48 **store** store of money 49 **is not
... markets** cannot afford luxuries
1 **he . . . come** i.e., suppose he says he'll come. 2 **of** on 5 **sad and civil** sober and decorous
9 **possessed** (1) possessed with an evil spirit (2) mad

MARIA: No, madam, he does nothing but smile. Your Ladyship
were best to have some guard about you if he come, for sure
the man is tainted in's° wits.

OLIVIA: Go call him hither. [*Maria summons Malvolio.*] I am as
mad as he,
If sad and merry madness equal be.°   15

Enter Malvolio, [cross-gartered and in yellow stockings].

How now, Malvolio?

MALVOLIO: Sweet lady, ho, ho!

OLIVIA: Smil'st thou? I sent for thee upon a sad° occasion.

MALVOLIO: Sad, lady? I could be sad.° This does make some obstruction in the blood, this cross-gartering, but what of that? If   20
it please the eye of one, it is with me as the very true sonnet°
is, "Please one and please all."°

OLIVIA: Why, how dost thou, man? What is the matter with thee?

MALVOLIO: Not black° in my mind, though yellow in my legs. It°
did come to his° hands, and commands shall be executed. I
think we do know the sweet roman hand.°   25

OLIVIA: Wilt thou go to bed,° Malvolio?

MALVOLIO: To bed! "Ay, sweetheart, and I'll come to thee."°

OLIVIA: God comfort thee! Why dost thou smile so and kiss thy
hand so oft?

MARIA: How do you, Malvolio?

MALVOLIO: At your request? Yes, nightingales answer daws.°   30

MARIA: Why appear you with this ridiculous boldness before my
lady?

MALVOLIO: "Be not afraid of greatness." 'Twas well writ.

OLIVIA: What mean'st thou by that, Malvolio?

MALVOLIO: "Some are born great—"

OLIVIA: Ha?   35

MALVOLIO: "Some achieve greatness—"

---

13 in's in his   **15 If . . . equal be** i.e., if love melancholy and smiling madness are essentially alike.
(Love melancholy was regarded as a kind of madness.)   **18 sad** serious   **19 sad** (1) serious
(2) melancholy.   **21 sonnet** song, ballad   **22 "Please . . . all"** "To please one special person is as good
as to please everybody." (The refrain of a ballad.)   **23 black** i.e., melancholic.   **It** i.e., The letter.
24 his Malvolio's   **25 roman hand** fashionable italic or Italian style of handwriting rather than
English "secretary" handwriting.   **26 go to bed** i.e., try to sleep off your mental distress. (But
Malvolio misinterprets as a sexual invitation.)   **27 "Ay . . . thee"** (Malvolio quotes from a popular
song of the day.)   **30 nightingales answer daws** i.e. (to Maria), do you suppose a fine fellow like
me would answer a lowly creature (a *daw*, a "jackdaw") like you?

OLIVIA: What say'st thou?

MALVOLIO: "And some have greatness thrust upon them."

OLIVIA: Heaven restore thee!

MALVOLIO: "Remember who commended thy yellow stockings—"   40

OLIVIA: Thy yellow stockings?

MALVOLIO: "And wished to see thee cross-gartered."

OLIVIA: Cross-gartered?

MALVOLIO: "Go to, thou art made, if thou desir'st to be so—"

OLIVIA: Am I made?   45

MALVOLIO: "If not, let me see thee a servant still."

OLIVIA: Why, this is very midsummer madness.°

Enter Servant.

SERVANT   Madam, the young gentleman of the Count Orsino's is
returned. I could hardly entreat him back. He attends Your
Ladyship's pleasure.

OLIVIA: I'll come to him. [*Exit Servant.*]   50
Good Maria, let this fellow be looked to. Where's my cousin
Toby? Let some of my people have a special care of him. I
would not have him miscarry° for the half of my dowry.

Exeunt [Olivia and Maria, different ways].

MALVOLIO: Oho, do you come near° me now? No worse man
than Sir Toby to look to me! This concurs directly with the let-   55
ter. She sends him on purpose that I may appear stubborn to
him, for she incites me to that in the letter. "Cast thy humble
slough," says she; "be opposite with a kinsman, surly with servants; let thy tongue tang with arguments of state; put thyself
into the trick of singularity." And consequently° sets down the   60
manner how: as, a sad° face, a reverend carriage, a slow
tongue, in the habit of some sir of note,° and so forth. I have
limed° her, but it is Jove's doing, and Jove make me thankful!
And when she went away now, "Let this fellow be looked to."
"Fellow!"° Not "Malvolio," nor after my degree,° but "fellow."   65
Why, everything adheres together, that no dram° of a scruple,

47 midsummer madness (A proverbial phrase; the midsummer moon was supposed to cause
madness.)   52 miscarry come to harm   53 come near understand, appreciate   60 consequently
thereafter   61 sad serious   62 habit . . . note attire suited to a man of distinction   63 limed
caught like a bird with birdlime (a sticky substance spread on branches)   65 Fellow (Malvolio takes
the basic meaning, "companion.")   65 after my degree according to my position   66 dram
(Literally, one-eighth of a fluid ounce.)

no scruple° of a scruple, no obstacle, no incredulous° or un-
safe° circumstance—what can be said?—nothing that can be
can come between me and the full prospect of my hopes.
Well, Jove, not I, is the doer of this, and he is to be thanked.   70

Enter [Sir] Toby, Fabian, and Maria.

SIR TOBY: Which way is he, in the name of sanctity? If all the
devils of hell be drawn in little,° and Legion° himself possessed him, yet I'll speak to him.

FABIAN: Here he is, here he is.—How is't with you, sir? How is't
with you, man?

MALVOLIO: Go off. I discard you. Let me enjoy my private.° Go   75
off.

MARIA: Lo, how hollow the fiend speaks within him! Did not I
tell you? Sir Toby, my lady prays you to have a care of him.

MALVOLIO: Aha, does she so?

SIR TOBY: Go to, go to! Peace, peace, we must deal gently with
him. Let me alone.°—How do you, Malvolio? How is't with   80
you? What, man, defy° the devil! Consider, he's an enemy to
mankind.

MALVOLIO: Do you know what you say?

MARIA: La you,° an you speak ill of the devil, how he takes it at
heart! Pray God he be not bewitched!

FABIAN: Carry his water° to th' wise woman.°   85

MARIA: Marry, and it shall be done tomorrow morning, if I live.
My lady would not lose him for more than I'll say.

MALVOLIO: How now, mistress?

MARIA: Oh, Lord!

SIR TOBY: Prithee, hold thy peace; this is not the way. Do you   90
not see you move° him? Let me alone with him.

FABIAN: No way but gentleness, gently, gently. The fiend is
rough, and will not be roughly used.

SIR TOBY: Why, how now, my bawcock!° How dost thou, chuck?°

MALVOLIO: Sir!   95

---

67 scruple (Literally, one-third of a dram.)   **incredulous** incredible   **67–8 unsafe** uncertain,
unreliable   **72 drawn in little** (1) portrayed in miniature (2) gathered into a small space.   **Legion**
an unclean spirit. ("My name is Legion, for we are many," Mark 5:9.)   **75 private** privacy.   **80 Let
me alone** Leave him to me.   **81 defy** renounce   **83 La you** Look you   **85 water** urine (for medical
analysis).   **wise woman** sorceress.   **91 move** upset, excite   **94 bawcock** fine fellow. (From the
French *beau-coq.*)   **95 chuck** (A form of "chick," term of endearment.)

SIR TOBY: Ay, biddy,° come with me. What, man, 'tis not for gravity° to play at cherry-pit° with Satan. Hang him, foul collier!°

MARIA: Get him to say his prayers, good Sir Toby, get him to pray.

MALVOLIO: My prayers, minx?

MARIA: No, I warrant you, he will not hear of godliness.   100

MALVOLIO: Go hang yourselves all! You are idle,° shallow things; I am not of your element.° You shall know more° hereafter.

Exit.

SIR TOBY: Is't possible?

FABIAN: If this were played upon a stage, now, I could condemn it as an improbable fiction.   105

SIR TOBY: His very genius° hath taken the infection of the device, man.

MARIA: Nay, pursue him now, lest the device take air and taint.°

FABIAN: Why, we shall make him mad indeed.

MARIA: The house will be the quieter.

SIR TOBY: Come, we'll have him in a dark room and bound.° My   110 niece is already in the belief that he's mad. We may carry° it thus for our pleasure and his penance till our very pastime, tired out of breath, prompt us to have mercy on him, at which time we will bring the device to the bar° and crown thee for a finder of madmen.° But see, but see!   115

Enter Sir Andrew [with a letter].

FABIAN: More matter for a May morning.°

SIR ANDREW: Here's the challenge. Read it. I warrant there's vinegar and pepper in't.

FABIAN: Is't so saucy?°

SIR ANDREW: Ay, is't, I warrant him.° Do but read.   120

SIR TOBY: Give me. [*He reads.*] "Youth, whatsoever thou art, thou art but a scurvy fellow."

FABIAN: Good, and valiant.

WILLIAM SHAKESPEARE

96 biddy chicken   **96–7 for gravity** suitable for a man of your dignity.   **97 cherry-pit** a children's game consisting of throwing cherry stones into a little hole.   **collier** i.e., Satan. (Literally, a coal vendor.)   **101 idle** foolish   **102 element** sphere.   **know more** i.e., hear about this   **106 genius** i.e., soul, spirit   **107 take . . . taint** become exposed to air (i.e., become known) and thus spoil.   **110 have . . . bound** (The standard treatment for insanity at this time.)   **111 carry** manage   **114 bar** i.e., bar of judgment   **115 finder of madmen** member of a jury changed with "finding" if the accused is insane.   **116 matter . . . morning** sport for Mayday plays or games.   **119 saucy** (1) spicy (2) insolent.   **120 him** it.

SIR TOBY: [*reads*] "Wonder not, nor admire° not in thy mind, why I do call thee so, for I will show thee no reason for't."

FABIAN: A good note,° that keeps you from the blow of the law. 125

SIR TOBY: [*reads*] "Thou com'st to the Lady Olivia, and in my sight she uses thee kindly. But thou liest in thy throat; that is not the matter I challenge thee for."

FABIAN: Very brief, and to exceeding good sense—less.

SIR TOBY: [*reads*] "I will waylay thee going home, where if it be 130 thy chance to kill me—"

FABIAN: Good.

SIR TOBY: [*reads*] "Thou kill'st me like a rogue and a villain."

FABIAN: Still you keep o' th' windy° side of the law. Good.

SIR TOBY: [*reads*] "Fare thee well, and God have mercy upon one 135 of our souls! He may have mercy upon mine, but my hope is better,° and so look to thyself. Thy friend, as thou usest him, and thy sworn enemy, Andrew Aguecheek." If this letter move° him not, his legs cannot. I'll give't him.

MARIA: You may have very fit occasion for't. He is now in some 140 commerce° with my lady, and will by and by depart.

SIR TOBY: Go, Sir Andrew. Scout me° for him at the corner of the orchard like a bum-baily.° So soon as ever thou see'st him, draw, and as thou draw'st, swear horrible;° for it comes to pass oft that a terrible oath, with a swaggering accent sharply 145 twanged off, gives manhood more approbation° than ever proof° itself would have earned him. Away!

SIR ANDREW: Nay, let me alone for swearing.° *Exit.*

SIR TOBY: Now will not I deliver his letter, for the behavior of the young gentleman gives him out to be of good capacity 150 and breeding; his employment between his lord and my niece confirms no less. Therefore this letter, being so excellently ignorant, will breed no terror in the youth. He will find it comes from a clodpoll.° But, sir, I will deliver his challenge by word of mouth, set upon Aguecheek a notable report of valor, and 155

---

123 **admire** marvel   125 **note** observation, remark   134 **windy** windward, i.e., safe, where one is less likely to be driven onto legal rocks and shoals   136–7 **my hope is better** (Sir Andrew's comically inept way of saying he hopes to be the survivor; instead, he seems to say, "May I be damned.")   139 **move** (1) stir up (2) set in motion   141 **commerce** transaction   142 **Scout me** Keep watch   143 **bum-baily** minor sheriff's officer employed in making arrests.   144 **horrible** horribly   146 **approbation** reputation (for courage).   147 **proof** performance   148 **let . . . swearing** don't worry about my ability in swearing.   154 **clodpoll** blockhead.

drive the gentleman—as I know his youth will aptly receive it°—into a most hideous opinion of his rage, skill, fury, and impetuosity. This will so fright them both that they will kill one another by the look, like cockatrices.°

Enter Olivia and Viola.

FABIAN: Here he comes with your niece. Give them way° till he   160
take leave, and presently° after him.

SIR TOBY: I will meditate the while upon some horrid° message
for a challenge.

[Exeunt Sir Toby, Fabian, and Maria.]

OLIVIA: I have said too much unto a heart of stone
And laid° mine honor too unchary on't.°   165
There's something in me that reproves my fault,
But such a headstrong potent fault it is
That it but mocks reproof.

VIOLA: With the same havior that your passion bears
Goes on my master's griefs.°   170

OLIVIA: *[giving a locket]*
Here, wear this jewel for me. 'Tis my picture.
Refuse it not; it hath no tongue to vex you.
And I beseech you come again tomorrow.
What shall you ask of me that I'll deny,   175
That honor, saved, may upon asking give?°

VIOLA: Nothing but this: your true love for my master.

OLIVIA: How with mine honor may I give him that
Which I have given to you?

VIOLA: I will acquit you.°   180

OLIVIA: Well, come again tomorrow. Fare thee well.
A fiend like thee might bear my soul to hell.°   *[Exit.]*

Enter [Sir] Toby and Fabian.

SIR TOBY: Gentleman, God save thee.

156–7 his . . . it his inexperience will make him all the more ready to believe it   **159 cockatrices**
basilisks, fabulous serpents reputed to be able to kill by a mere look.   **160 Give them way** Stay out
of their way   **161 presently** immediately   **162 horrid** terrifying. (Literally, "bristling.")   **165 laid**
hazarded.   **unchary on't** recklessly on it.   **169–70 With . . . griefs** i.e., Orsino's sufferings in love
are as reckless and uncontrollable as your feelings.   **176 That . . . give?** that can be granted
without compromising my honor?   **180 acquit you** release you of your promise.   **181 A fiend . . .**
hell i.e., You are my torment. (*Like thee* means "in your likeness.")

VIOLA: And you, sir.

SIR TOBY: That defense thou hast, be take thee to't.° Of what na- 185
ture the wrongs are thou hast done him, I know not, but thy
intercepter,° full of despite,° bloody as the hunter,° attends
thee at the orchard end. Dismount thy tuck,° be yare° in thy
preparation, for thy assailant is quick, skillful, and deadly.

VIOLA: You mistake sir. I am sure no man hath any quarrel to° 190
me. My remembrance is very free and clear from any image of
offense done to any man.

SIR TOBY: You'll find it otherwise, I assure you. Therefore, if you
hold your life at any price, be take you to your guard, for your
opposite° hath in him what° youth, strength, skill, and wrath 195
can furnish man withal.°

VIOLA: I pray you, sir, what is he?

SIR TOBY: He is knight, dubbed with unhatched° rapier and on
carpet consideration,° but he is a devil in private brawl. Souls and
bodies hath he divorced three, and his incensement at this mo- 200
ment is so implacable that satisfaction can be none but by pangs
of death and sepulchre. Hob, nob° is his word;° give't or take't.

VIOLA: I will return again into the house and desire some con-
duct° of the lady. I am no fighter. I have heard of some kind of
men that put quarrels purposely on others, to taste° their
valor. Belike° this is a man of that quirk.° 205

SIR TOBY: Sir, no. His indignation derives itself out of a very
competent° injury; therefore, get you on and give him his desire. Back you shall not to the house unless you undertake that
with me which with as much safety you might answer him.
Therefore, on, or strip your sword stark naked;° for meddle° 210
you must, that's certain, or for swear to wear iron° about you.

VIOLA: This is as uncivil as strange. I beseech you, dome this
courteous office as to know of° the knight what my offense

___

185 That . . . to't Get ready to deploy whatever skill you have in fencing.   187 intercepter he who
lies in wait.   despite defiance, ill will.   bloody as the hunter bloodthirsty as a hunting dog
188 Dismount thy tuck Draw your rapier.   yare ready, nimble   190 to with   195 opposite opponent.
what whatsoever.   196 withal with.   197 unhatched unhacked, unused in battle   198 carpet
consideration (A carpet knight was one whose title was obtained, not in battle, but through
connections at court.)   201 Hob, nob Have or have not, i.e., give it or take it, kill or be killed.   word
motto   202–3 conduct safe-conduct, escort   204 taste test, prove   205 Belike Probably.   quirk
peculiar humor.   207 competent sufficient   210 strip . . . naked draw your sword from its sheath.
meddle engage (in conflict)   211 forswear . . . iron give up your right to wear a sword   213 know
of inquire from

to him is. It is something of my negligence, nothing of my purpose.°

SIR TOBY: I will do so.—Signor Fabian, stay you by this gentle- ₂₁₅
man till my return. *Exit [Sir] Toby.*

VIOLA: Pray you, sir, do you know of this matter?

FABIAN: I know the knight is incensed against you, even to a mortal arbitrament,° but nothing of the circumstance more.

VIOLA: I beseech you, what manner of man is he? ₂₂₀

FABIAN: Nothing of that wonderful promise, to read him by his form,° as you are like° to find him in the proof of his valor. He is, indeed, sir, the most skillful, bloody, and fatal opposite that you could possibly have found in any part of Illyria. Will you° walk towards him, I will make your peace with him if I can. ₂₂₅

VIOLA: I shall be much bound to you for't. I am one that had rather go with° Sir Priest° than Sir Knight. I care not who knows so much of my mettle. *Exeunt.*

Enter [Sir] Toby and [Sir] Andrew.

SIR TOBY: Why, man, he's a very devil; I have not seen such a firago.° I had a pass° with him, rapier, scabbard, and all, and ₂₃₀ he gives me the stuck-in° with such a mortal motion that it is inevitable; and on the answer,° he pays you as surely as your feet hits the ground they step on. They say he has been fencer to° the Sophy.

SIR ANDREW: Pox on't, I'll not meddle with him.

SIR TOBY: Ay, but he will not now be pacified. Fabian can scarce ₂₃₅ hold him yonder.

SIR ANDREW: Plague on't, an I thought he had been valiant and so cunning in fence, I'd have seen him damned ere I'd have challenged him. Let him let the matter slip and I'll give him my horse, gray Capilet.°

SIR TOBY: I'll make the motion.° Stand here, make a good show on't. This shall end without the perdition of souls.° *[Aside, as* ₂₄₀

---

214 It is . . . purpose It is the result of some oversight, not anything I intended.   **219 mortal arbitrament** trial to the death   **221–2 read . . . form** judge him by his appearance   **222 like** likely   **224 Will you** If you will   **227 go with** associate with.   **Sir Priest** (*Sir* was a courtesy title for priests.)   **230 firago** virago.   **pass** bout   **231 stuck-in** stoccado, a thrust in fencing   **232 answer** return hit   **233 to** in the service of   **238 Capilet** i.e., "little horse." (From "capel," a nag.)   **239 motion** offer.   **240 perdition of souls** i.e., loss of lives.

he crosses to meet Fabian] Marry, I'll ride your horse as well as I ride you.

Enter Fabian and Viola.

[*Aside to Fabian*] I have his horse to take up° the quarrel. I have persuaded him the youth's a devil.

FABIAN: He is as horribly conceited of him,° and pants and looks pale as if a bear were at his heels.   245

SIR TOBY: [*to Viola*] There's no remedy, sir, he will fight with you for's oath's sake. Marry, he hath better be thought him of his quarrel, and he finds that now scarce to be worth talking of. Therefore draw, for the supportance° of his vow; he protests he will not hurt you.

VIOLA: [*aside*] Pray God defend me! A little thing would make me   250
tell them how much I lack of a man.°

FABIAN: Give ground, if you see him furious.

SIR TOBY: [*crossing to Sir Andrew*] Come, Sir Andrew, there's no remedy. The gentleman will, for his honor's sake, have one bout with you. He cannot by the *duello*° avoid it. But he has promised me, as   255
he is a gentleman and a soldier, he will not hurt you. Come on, to't.

SIR ANDREW: Pray God he keep his oath!

Enter Antonio.

VIOLA: [*to Fabian*] I do assure you, 'tis against my will.

[*They draw.*]

ANTONIO: [*drawing, to Sir Andrew*]
Put up your sword. If this young gentleman
Have done offense, I take the fault on me;   260
If you offend him, I for him defy you.

SIR TOBY: You, sir? Why, what are you?

ANTONIO: One, sir, that for his love dares yet do more
Than you have heard him brag to you he will.

SIR TOBY: [*drawing*]   265
Nay, if you be an undertaker,° I am for you.°

Enter Officers.

---

242 **take up** settle, make up   244 **He . . . him** i.e., Cesario has as horrible a conception of Sir Andrew   249 **supportance** upholding   250–1 **A little . . . man** (With bawdy suggestion of the penis.)   255 *duello* dueling code   266 **undertaker** one who takes upon himself a task or business; here, a challenger.   **for you** ready for you.

FABIAN: Oh, good Sir Toby, hold! Here come the officers.

SIR TOBY: [*to Antonio*] I'll be with you anon.

VIOLA: [*to Sir Andrew*] Pray, sir, put your sword up, if you please.

SIR ANDREW: Marry, will I, sir; and for that° I promised you, I'll 270
be as good as my word. He° will bear you easily, and reins well.

FIRST OFFICER This is the man. Do thy office.

SECOND OFFICER Antonio, I arrest thee at the suit
Of Count Orsino.

ANTONIO: You do mistake me, sir. 275

FIRST OFFICER No, sir, no jot. I know your favor° well,
Though now you have no sea-cap on your head.—
Take him away. He knows I know him well.

ANTONIO: I must obey. [*To Viola*] This comes with seeking you.
But there's no remedy; I shall answer it.° 280
What will you do, now my necessity
Makes me to ask you for my purse? It grieves me
Much more for what I cannot do for you
Than what befalls myself. You stand amazed,
But be of comfort. 285

SECOND OFFICER Come, sir, away.

ANTONIO: [*to Viola*]
I must entreat of you some of that money.

VIOLA: What money, sir?
For the fair kindness you have showed me here,
And part° being prompted by your present trouble, 290
Out of my lean and low ability
I'll lend you something. My having° is not much;
I'll make division of my present° with you.
Hold, there's half my coffer.° [*She offers money.*] 295

ANTONIO: Will you deny me now?
Is't possible that my deserts to you
Can lack persuasion?° Do not tempt° my misery,
Lest that it make me so unsound° a man
As to upbraid you with those kindnesses 300
That I have done for you.

---

270 for that as for what **271 He** i.e., The horse **276 favor** face **280 answer it** stand trial and
make reparation for it. **291 part** partly **293 having** wealth **294 present** present store
295 coffer purse. (Literally, strongbox.) **297–8 deserts . . . persuasion** claims on you can fail to
persuade me to help me. **298 tempt** try too severely **299 unsound** morally weak, lacking in
self-control

VIOLA: I know of none,
    Nor know I you by voice or any feature.
    I hate ingratitude more in a man
    Than lying, vainness,° babbling drunkenness,   305
    Or any taint of vice whose strong corruption
    Inhabits our frail blood.

ANTONIO: Oh, heavens themselves!

SECOND OFFICER   Come, sir, I pray you, go.

ANTONIO: Let me speak a little. This youth that you see here   310
    I snatched one half out of the jaws of death,
    Relieved him with such sanctity of love,°
    And to his image,° which methought did promise
    Most venerable worth,° did I devotion.

FIRST OFFICER   What's that to us? The time goes by. Away!   315

ANTONIO: But, oh, how vile an idol proves this god!
    Thou hast, Sebastian, done good feature shame.°
    In nature there's no blemish but the mind;
    None can be called deformed but the unkind.°
    Virtue is beauty, but the beauteous evil°   320
    Are empty trunks° o'erflourished° by the devil.

FIRST OFFICER   The man grows mad. Away with him! Come,
come, sir.

ANTONIO: Lead me on.   *Exit [with Officers].*

VIOLA: [aside]
    Methinks his words do from such passion fly
    That he believes himself. So do not I.°   325
    Prove true, imagination, oh, prove true,
    That I, dear brother, be now ta'en for you!

SIR TOBY: Come hither, knight. Come hither, Fabian.
    We'll whisper o'er a couplet or two of most sage saws.°

    [They gather apart from Viola.]

---

305 **vainness** vaingloriousness   312 **such . . . love** i.e., such veneration as is due to a sacred relic
313 **image** what he appeared to be. (Playing on the idea of a religious icon to be venerated.)
314 **venerable worth** worthiness of being venerated   317 **Thou . . . shame** i.e., You have shamed
physical beauty by showing that it does not always reflect inner beauty.   319 **unkind** ungrateful,
unnatural.   320 **beauteous evil** those who are outwardly beautiful but evil within   321 **trunks**
(1) chests (2) bodies.   **o'erflourished** (1) covered with ornamental carvings (2) made outwardly
beautiful 325 **So . . . I** i.e., I do not believe myself (in the hope that has arisen in me).   329 **We'll . . .
saws** i.e., Let's converse privately. (*Saws* are sayings.)

VIOLA: He named Sebastian. I my brother know
    Yet living in my glass;° even such and so
    In favor° was my brother, and he went
    Still° in this fashion, color, ornament,
    For him I imitate. Oh, if it prove,°
    Tempests are kind, and salt waves fresh in love! 335

    [Exit.]

SIR TOBY: A very dishonest° paltry boy, and more a coward than
a hare. His dishonesty° appears in leaving his friend here in
necessity and denying° him; and for his cowardship, ask
Fabian.

FABIAN: A coward, a most devout coward, religious in it.°

SIR ANDREW: 'Slid,° I'll after him again and beat him. 340

SIR TOBY: Do, cuff him soundly, but never draw thy sword.

SIR ANDREW: An I do not— *[Exit.]*

FABIAN: Come, let's see the event.°

SIR TOBY: I dare lay° any money 'twill be nothing yet.°

    Exeunt.

4.1

    Enter Sebastian and Clown [Feste].

FESTE: Will you make me believe that I am not sent for you?

SEBASTIAN: Go to, go to, thou art a foolish fellow. Let me be
clear of thee.

FESTE: Well held out,° i' faith! No, I do not know you, nor I am
not sent to you by my lady to bid you come speak with her,
nor your name is not Master Cesario, nor this is not my nose, 5
neither. Nothing that is so is so.

SEBASTIAN: I prithee, vent° thy folly somewhere else. Thou
know'st not me.

FESTE: Vent my folly! He has heard that word of° some great
man, and now applies it to a fool. Vent my folly! I am afraid

---

330–1 I . . . glass i.e., I know that my brother's likeness lives in me   **332 favor** appearance
333 Still always   **334 prove** prove true   **336 dishonest** dishonorable   **337 dishonesty** dishonor
338 denying refusing to acknowledge   **339 religious in it** making a religion of cowardice.
340 'Slid By his (God's) eyelid   **343 event** outcome.   **344 lay** wager.   **yet** nevertheless, after all.
3 held out kept up   **6 vent** (1) utter (2) void, excrete, get rid of   **7 of** from, suited to the diction
of; or, with reference to

this great lubber,° the world, will prove a cockney.° I prithee
now, ungird thy strangeness° and tell me what I shall vent to   10
my lady. Shall I vent to her that thou art coming?

SEBASTIAN: I prithee, foolish Greek,° depart from me. There's
money for thee. [*He gives money.*] If you tarry longer, I shall
give worse payment.

FESTE: By my troth, thou hast an open° hand. These wise men
that give fools money get themselves a good report°—after   15
fourteen years' purchase.°

Enter [Sir] Andrew, [Sir] Toby, and Fabian.

SIR ANDREW: Now, sir, have I met you again? There's for you!
[*He strikes Sebastian.*]

SEBASTIAN: Why, there's for thee, and there, and there!

[*He beats Sir Andrew with the hilt of his dagger.*]

Are all the people mad?

SIR TOBY: Hold, sir, or I'll throw your dagger o'er the house.

FESTE: This will I tell my lady straight.° I would not be in some   20
of your coats° for two pence.   [*Exit.*]

SIR TOBY: Come on, sir, hold!   [*He grips Sebastian.*]

SIR ANDREW: Nay, let him alone. I'll go another way to work with
him. I'll have an action of battery° against him, if there be any
law in Illyria. Though I struck him first, yet it's no matter for that.

SEBASTIAN: Let go thy hand!   25

SIR TOBY: Come, sir, I will not let you go. Come, my young soldier, put up your iron. You are well fleshed.° Come on.

SEBASTIAN: I will be free from thee. [*He breaks free and draws his
sword.*] What wouldst thou now?
If thou dar'st tempt° me further, draw thy sword.   30

SIR TOBY: What, what? Nay, then I must have an ounce or two of
this malapert° blood from you.   [*He draws.*]

Enter Olivia.

9 **lubber** lout.   **cockney** effeminate or foppish fellow. (Feste comically despairs of finding common
sense anywhere if people start using affected phrases like those Sebastian uses.)   **10 ungird thy
strangeness** put off your affectation of being a stranger. (Feste apes the kind of high-flown speech he
has just deplored.)   **12 Greek** (1) one who speaks gibberish (as in "It's all Greek to me") (2) buffoon (as
in "merry Greek")   **14 open** generous. (With money or with blows.)   **15 report** reputation.   **15–6 after
. . . purchase** i.e., at great cost and after long delays. (Land was ordinarily valued at the price of
twelve years' rental; the Fool adds two years to this figure.)   **20 straight** at once.   **20–21 in . . . coats**
i.e., in your shoes   **23 action of battery** lawsuit for physical assault   **27 fleshed** initiated into battle.
30 tempt make trial of   **32 malapert** saucy, impudent

OLIVIA: Hold, Toby! On thy life I charge thee, hold!

SIR TOBY: Madam—

OLIVIA: Will it be ever thus? Ungracious wretch,   35
    Fit for the mountains and the barbarous caves,
    Where manners ne'er were preached! Out of my sight!—
    Be not offended, dear Cesario.—
    Rudesby,° begone!

        [Exeunt Sir Toby, Sir Andrew, and Fabian.]

    I prithee, gentle friend,   40
    Let thy fair wisdom, not thy passion, sway
    In this uncivil and unjust extent°
    Against thy peace. Go with me to my house,
    And hear thou there how many fruitless pranks
    This ruffian hath botched up,° that thou thereby   45
    Mayst smile at this. Thou shalt not choose but go.°
    Do not deny.° Beshrew° his soul for me!°
    He started one poor heart of mine, in thee.°

SEBASTIAN: *[aside]*
What relish is in this?° How runs the stream?   50
    Or° I am mad, or else this is a dream.
    Let fancy still my sense in Let he steep;°
    If it be thus to dream, still let me sleep!

OLIVIA: Nay, come, I prithee. Would thou'dst be ruled by me!

SEBASTIAN: Madam, I will.   55

OLIVIA: Oh, say so, and so be!   *Exeunt.*

4.2

Enter Maria [carrying a gown and a false beard], and Clown [Feste].

MARIA: Nay, I prithee, put on this gown and this beard; make
    him believe thou art Sir° Topas° the curate. Do it quickly. I'll
    call Sir Toby the whilst.°   *[Exit.]*

---

39 Rudesby Ruffian   **42 extent** attack   **45 botched up** clumsily contrived **46 Thou . . . go** I insist
on your going with me.   **47 deny** refuse.   **Beshrew** Curse. (A mild oath.)   **for me** for my part.
48 He . . . thee i.e., He alarmed that part of my heart which lies in your bosom. (To *start* is also to
drive an animal such as a *hart [heart]* from its cover.)   **50 What . . . this?** i.e., What am I to make of
this? (*Relish* means "taste.")   **51 Or** Either   **52 Let . . . steep** i.e., Let this fantasy continue to steep
my senses in forgetfulness. (*Lethe* is the river of forgetfulness in the underworld.)
2 Sir (An honorific title for priests.) **Topas** (A name perhaps derived from Chaucer's comic knight
in the "Rime of Sir Thopas" or from a similar character in Lyly's *Endymion*. Topaz, a semiprecious
stone, was believed to be a cure for lunacy.)   **3 the whilst** in the meantime.

FESTE: Well, I'll put it on, and I will dissemble° myself in't, and I
would I were the first that ever dissembled in such a gown.   5
[*He disguises himself in gown and beard.*] I am not tall enough
to become the function° well, nor lean° enough to be thought
a good student;° but to be said an honest man and a good
housekeeper goes as fairly as to say a careful man and a great
scholar.° The competitors° enter.

        Enter [Sir] Toby [and Maria].

SIR TOBY: Jove bless thee, Master Parson.   10
FESTE: *Bonos dies,*° Sir Toby. For, as the old hermit of Prague,°
that never saw pen and ink, very wittily said to a niece of King
Gorboduc,° "That that is, is"; so I, being Master Parson, am
Master Parson; for what is "that" but "that," and "is" but "is"?
SIR TOBY: To him, Sir Topas.   15
FESTE: What, ho, I say! Peace in this prison!

        [*He approaches the door behind which Malvolio is
        confined.*]

SIR TOBY: The knave counterfeits well; a good knave.
MALVOLIO: (*within*) Who calls there?
FESTE: Sir Topas the curate, who comes to visit Malvolio the lunatic.
MALVOLIO: Sir Topas, Sir Topas, good Sir Topas, go to my lady—   20
FESTE: Out, hyperbolical° fiend!° How vexest thou this man!
Talkest thou nothing but of ladies?
SIR TOBY: Well said, Master Parson.
MALVOLIO: Sir Topas, never was man thus wronged. Good Sir
Topas, do not think I am mad. They have laid me here in   25
hideous darkness.
FESTE: Fie, thou dishonest Satan! I call thee by the most modest°
terms, for I am one of those gentle ones that will use the devil
himself with courtesy. Say'st thou that house° is dark?
MALVOLIO: As hell, Sir Topas.

---

4 dissemble disguise. (With a play on "feign.")   **7 become the function** adorn the priestly office
lean (Scholars were proverbially sparing of diet.)   **8 student** scholar (in divinity)   **8–9 to be . . .
scholar** to be accounted honest and hospitable is as good as being known as a painstaking scholar.
(Feste suggests that honesty and charity are found as often in ordinary men as in clerics.)
9 competitors associates, partners (in this plot)   **11 Bonos dies** Good day.   **hermit of Prague**
(Probably another invented authority.)   **12–3 King Gorboduc** a legendary king of ancient Britain,
protagonist in the English tragedy *Gorboduc* (1562)   **21 hyperbolical** vehement, boisterous.
fiend i.e., the devil supposedly possessing Malvolio.   **27 modest** moderate   **29 house** i.e., room

FESTE: Why, it hath bay windows transparent as barricadoes,° 30
and the clerestories° toward the south north are as lustrous as
ebony; and yet complainest thou of obstruction?

MALVOLIO: I am not mad, Sir Topas. I say to you this house is
dark.

FESTE: Madman, thou errest. I say there is no darkness but ignorance, in which thou art more puzzled than the Egyptians 35
in their fog.°

MALVOLIO: I say this house is as dark as ignorance, though ignorance were as dark as hell; and I say there was never man thus
abused. I am no more mad than you are. Make the trial of it in
any constant question.°

FESTE: What is the opinion of Pythagoras concerning wildfowl?° 40

MALVOLIO: That the soul of our grandam might haply° inhabit a
bird.

FESTE: What think'st thou of his opinion?

MALVOLIO: I think nobly of the soul, and no way approve his
opinion.

FESTE: Fare thee well. Remain thou still in darkness. Thou shalt
hold th' opinion of Pythagoras ere I will allow of thy wits,° and 45
fear to kill a woodcock° lest thou dispossess the soul of thy
grandam. Fare thee well.

[He moves away from Malvolio's prison.]

MALVOLIO: Sir Topas, Sir Topas!

SIR TOBY: My most exquisite Sir Topas!

FESTE: Nay, I am for all waters.° 50

MARIA: Thou mightst have done this without thy beard and
gown. He sees thee not.

SIR TOBY: To him in thine own voice, and bring me word how
thou find'st him.—I would we were well rid of this knavery. If
he may be conveniently delivered,° I would he were, for I am 55

---

30 barricadoes barricades. (Which are opaque. Feste speaks comically in impossible paradoxes,
but Malvolio seems not to notice.) **31 clerestories** windows in an upper wall **35 Egyptians . . .
fog** (Alluding to the darkness brought upon Egypt by Moses; see Exodus 10:21–3.) **39 constant
question** problem that requires consecutive reasoning. **40 Pythagoras . . . wildfowl** (An
opening for the discussion of transmigration of souls, a doctrine held by Pythagoras.) **41 haply**
perhaps **45 allow of thy wits** certify your sanity. **46 woodcock** (A proverbially stupid bird,
easily caught.) **50 Nay . . . waters** i.e., Indeed, I can turn my hand to anything. **55 delivered**
i.e., delivered from prison

now so far in offense with my niece that I cannot pursue with any safety this sport to the upshot.° Come by and by to my chamber.

> *Exit [with Maria].*

FESTE: [*singing as he approaches Malvolio's prison*]
"Hey, Robin, jolly Robin,
Tell me how thy lady does."° 60

MALVOLIO: Fool!

FESTE: "My lady is unkind, pardie."°

MALVOLIO: Fool!

FESTE: "Alas, why is she so?"

MALVOLIO: Fool, I say! 65

FESTE: "She loves another—" Who calls, ha?

MALVOLIO: Good Fool, as ever thou wilt deserve well at my hand, help me to a candle, and pen, ink, and paper. As I am a gentleman, I will live to be thankful to thee for't.

FESTE: Master Malvolio? 70

MALVOLIO: Ay, good Fool.

FESTE: Alas, sir, how fell you besides° your five wits?°

MALVOLIO: Fool, there was never man so notoriously abused.° I am as well in my wits, Fool, as thou art.

FESTE: But° as well? Then you are mad indeed, if you be no better in your wits than a fool. 75

MALVOLIO: They have here propertied me,° keep me in darkness, send ministers to me—asses—and do all they can to face me out of my wits.°

FESTE: Advise you° what you say. The minister is here. [*He speaks as Sir Topas.*] Malvolio, Malvolio, thy wits the heavens restore! Endeavor thyself to sleep, and leave thy vain bibble-babble. 80

MALVOLIO: Sir Topas!

FESTE: [*in Sir Topas's voice*] Maintain no words with him, good fellow. [*In his own voice*] Who, I, sir? Not I, sir. God b'wi'you, good

---

57 **upshot** conclusion.   59–60 **"Hey, Robin . . . does"** (Another fragment of an old song, a version of which is attributed to Sir Thomas Wyatt.)   62 **pardie** i.e., by God, certainly.   72 **besides** out of. **five wits** The intellectual faculties, usually listed as common wit, imagination, fantasy, judgment, and memory.   73 **notoriously abused** egregiously ill treated.   75 **But** Only   76 **propertied me** i.e., treated me as property and thrown me into the lumber-room   77 **face . . . wits** brazenly represent me as having lost my wits.   78 **Advise you** Take care.

Sir Topas. [*In Sir Topas's voice*] Marry, amen. [*In his own voice*] I
will, sir, I will.

MALVOLIO: Fool! Fool! Fool, I say!   85

FESTE: Alas, sir, be patient. What say you, sir? I am shent° for
speaking to you.

MALVOLIO: Good Fool, help me to some light and some paper. I
tell thee I am as well in my wits as any man in Illyria.

FESTE: Welladay° that you were, sir!

MALVOLIO: By this hand, I am. Good Fool, some ink, paper, and   90
light; and convey what I will set down to my lady. It shall advantage thee more than ever the bearing of letter did.

FESTE: I will help you to't. But tell me true, are you not mad indeed, or do you but counterfeit?

MALVOLIO: Believe me, I am not. I tell thee true.   95

FESTE: Nay, I'll ne'er believe a madman till I see his brains. I will
fetch you light and paper and ink.

MALVOLIO: Fool, I'll requite it in the highest degree. I prithee,
begone.

FESTE: [*sings*]
I am gone, sir,   100
And anon, sir,
I'll be with you again,
In a trice,
Like to the old Vice,°
Your need to sustain;   105
Who, with dagger of lath,°
In his rage and his wrath,
Cries, "Aha!" to the devil;
Like a mad lad,
"Pare thy nails,° dad?   110
Adieu, goodman° devil!"   *Exit.*

---

86 shent scolded, rebuked   **89 Welladay** Alas, would that   **104 Vice** comic tempter of the "old"
morality plays   **106 dagger of lath** comic weapon of the Vice in at least some morality plays
110 Pare thy nails (This may allude to the belief that evil spirits could use nail parings to get
control of their victims; cf. Dromio of Syracuse in *The Comedy of Errors*, 4.3.69, "Some devils ask
but the parings of one's nail," and the Boy's characterization of Pistol in *Henry V*, 4.4.72–3, as
"this roaring devil i'th' old play, that everyone may pare his nails with a wooden dagger.")
111 goodman title for a person of substance but not of gentle birth. (This line could be Feste's
farewell to Malvolio and his "devil.")

4.3

Enter Sebastian [with a pearl].

SEBASTIAN: This is the air; that is the glorious sun;
This pearl she gave me, I do feel't and see't;
And though 'tis wonder that enwraps me thus,
Yet 'tis not madness. Where's Antonio, then?
I could not find him at the Elephant;   5
Yet there he was,° and there I found this credit,°
That he did range the town to seek me out.
His counsel now might do me golden service;
For though my soul disputes well with my sense°
That this may be some error, but no madness,   10
Yet doth this accident° and flood of fortune
So far exceed all instance,° all discourse,°
That I am ready to distrust mine eyes
And wrangle with my reason that persuades me
To any other trust° but that I am mad,   15
Or else the lady's mad. Yet if 'twere so,
She could not sway° her house, command her followers,
Take and give back affairs and their dispatch°
With such a smooth, discreet, and stable bearing
As I perceive she does. There's something in't   20
That is deceivable.° But here the lady comes.

Enter Olivia and Priest.

OLIVIA: Blame not this haste of mine. If you mean well,
Now go with me and with this holy man
Into the chantry by.° There, before him,
And underneath that consecrated roof,   25
Plight me the full assurance of your faith,
That my most jealous° and too doubtful° soul
May live at peace. He shall conceal it
Whiles° you are willing it shall come to note,°

TWELFTH NIGHT; OR, WHAT YOU WILL

945

---

6 **was** was previously.   **credit** report   9 **my soul ... sense** i.e., both my rational faculties and my
physical senses come to the conclusion   11 **accident** unexpected event   12 **instance** precedent.
discourse reason   15 **trust** belief   17 **sway** rule   18 **Take ... dispatch** receive reports on matters
of household business and see to their execution   21 **deceivable** deceptive.   24 **chantry by** private
endowed chapel nearby (where mass would be said for the souls of the dead, including Olivia's
brother).   27 **jealous** anxious, mistrustful.   **doubtful** full of doubts   29 **Whiles** until.   **come to
note** become known

What time° we will our celebration° keep   30
According to my birth.° What do you say?
SEBASTIAN: I'll follow this good man, and go with you,
And having sworn truth, ever will be true.
OLIVIA: Then lead the way, good father, and heavens so shine
That they may fairly note° this act of mine!   *Exeunt.*   35

5.1

Enter Clown [Feste] and Fabian.

FABIAN: Now, as thou lov'st me, let me see his letter.
FESTE: Good Master Fabian, grant me another request.
FABIAN: Anything.
FESTE: Do not desire to see this letter.
FABIAN: This is to give a dog and in recompense desire my dog
again.°   5

Enter Duke [Orsino], Viola, Curio, and lords.

ORSINO: Belong you to the Lady Olivia, friends?
FESTE: Ay, sir, we are some of her trappings.°
ORSINO: I know thee well. How dost thou, my good fellow?
FESTE: Truly, sir, the better for° my foes and the worse for my
friends.
ORSINO: Just the contrary—the better for thy friends.   10
FESTE: No, sir, the worse.
ORSINO: How can that be?
FESTE: Marry, sir, they praise me, and make an ass of me.° Now
my foes tell me plainly I am an ass, so that by my foes, sir, I
profit in the knowledge of myself, and by my friends I am
abused;° so that, conclusions to be as kisses, if your four nega-   15
tives make your two affirmatives,° why then the worse for my
friends and the better for my foes.

---

30 What time at which time.   **our celebration** i.e., the actual marriage. (What they are about to
perform is a binding betrothal.)   **31 birth** social position.   **35 fairly note** look upon with favor
5 This . . . again (Apparently a reference to a well-known reply of Dr. Bulleyn when Queen
Elizabeth asked for his dog and promised a gift of his choosing in return; he asked to have his dog
back.)   **7 trappings** ornaments, decorations.   **9 for** because of   **13 make an ass of me** i.e., flatter
me into foolishly thinking well of myself.   **15 abused** flatteringly deceived   **15–6 conclusions . . .**
affirmatives i.e., as when a young lady, asked for a kiss, says "no, no" really meaning "yes"; or, as in
grammar, two negatives make an affirmative

ORSINO: Why, this is excellent.

FESTE: By my troth, sir, no, though° it please you to be one of my friends.°

ORSINO: Thou shalt not be the worse for me. There's gold. 20

[He gives a coin.]

FESTE: But° that it would be double-dealing,° sir, I would you could make it another.

ORSINO: Oh, you give me ill counsel.

FESTE: Put your grace in your pocket,° sir, for this once, and let your flesh and blood obey it.° 25

ORSINO: Well, I will be so much a sinner to be° a double-dealer. There's another. *[He gives another coin.]*

FESTE: *Primo, secundo, tertio,*° is a good play,° and the old saying is, the third pays for all.° The triplex,° sir, is a good tripping measure; or the bells of Saint Bennet,° sir, may put you in mind—one, two, three. 30

ORSINO: You can fool no more money out of me at this throw.° If you will let your lady know I am here to speak with her, and bring her along with you, it may awake my bounty further.

FESTE: Marry, sir, lullaby to your bounty till I come again. I go, sir, but I would not have you to think that my desire of having 35 is the sin of covetousness. But asyou say, sir, let your bounty take a nap. I will awake it anon. *Exit.*

Enter Antonio and Officers.

VIOLA: Here comes the man, sir, that did rescue me.

ORSINO: That face of his I do remember well,
Yet when I saw it last it was besmeared 40
As black as Vulcan° in the smoke of war.
A baubling° vessel was he captain of,

---

18 though even though   **19 friends** i.e., those who, according to Feste's syllogism, flatter him.
21 But Except for the fact.   **double-dealing** (1) giving twice (2) deceit, duplicity   **24 Put ... pocket** (1) Pay no attention to your honor, put it away (2) Reach in your pocket or purse and show your customary grace or munificence. (*Your Grace* is also the formal way of addressing a duke.)   **25 it** i.e., my "ill counsel."   **26 to be** as to be   **27 *Primo ... tertio*** Latin ordinals: first, second, third. **play** (Perhaps a mathematical game or game of dice.)   **28 the third ... all** the third time is lucky. (Proverbial.)   **triplex** triple time in music   **29 Saint Bennet** church of St. Benedict   **32 throw** (1) time (2) throw of the dice.   **41 Vulcan** Roman god of fire and smith to the other gods; his face was blackened by the fire   **42 baubling** insignificant, trifling

For° shallow draft° and bulk unprizable,°
With which such scatheful° grapple did he make
With the most noble bottom° of our fleet   45
That very envy° and the tongue of loss°
Cried fame and honor on him. What's the matter?

FIRST OFFICER   Orsino, this is that Antonio
That took the *Phoenix* and her freight from Candy,°
And this is he that did the *Tiger* board   50
When your young nephew Titus lost his leg.
Here in the streets, desperate of shame and state,°
In private brabble° did we apprehend him.

VIOLA: He did me kindness, sir, drew on my side,
But in conclusion put strange speech upon me.°   55
I know not what 'twas but distraction.°

ORSINO: Notable° pirate, thou saltwater thief,
What foolish boldness brought thee to their mercies
Whom thou in terms so bloody and so dear°
Hast made thine enemies?   60

ANTONIO: Orsino, noble sir,
Be pleased that I° shake off these names you give me.
Antonio never yet was thief or pirate,
Though, I confess, on base and ground° enough
Orsino's enemy. A witchcraft drew me hither.   65
That most ingrateful boy there by your side
From the rude sea's enraged and foamy mouth
Did I redeem; a wreck° past hope he was.
His life I gave him, and did thereto add
My love, without retention° or restraint,   70
All his in dedication.° For his sake
Did I expose myself—pure° for his love—
Into° the danger of this adverse° town,

43 For because of.   **draft** depth of water a ship draws.   **unprizable** of value too slight to be estimated, not worth taking as a "prize"   **44 scatheful** destructive   **45 bottom** ship   **46 very envy** i.e., even those who had most reason to hate him, his enemies.   **loss** i.e., the losers   **49 from Candy** on her return from Candia, or Crete   **52 desperate . . . state** recklessly disregarding the disgrace and danger to himself   **53 brabble** brawl   **55 put . . . me** spoke to me strangely.   **56 but distraction** unless (it was) madness.   **57 Notable** Notorious   **59 in terms . . . dear** in so bloodthirsty and so costly a manner   **62 Be pleased that I** Allow me to   **64 base and ground** solid grounds   **68 wreck** shipwrecked person   **70 retention** reservation   **71 All . . . dedication** devoted wholly to him.   **72 pure** entirely, purely   **73 Into** unto.   **adverse** hostile

Drew to defend him when he was beset;
Where being apprehended, his false cunning,   75
Not meaning to partake with me in danger,
Taught him to face me out of his acquaintance°
And grew a twenty years' removèd thing
While one would wink;° denied me mine own purse,
Which I had recommended° to his use   80
Not half an hour before.

VIOLA: How can this be?

ORSINO: When came he to this town?

ANTONIO: Today, my lord; and for three months before,
No interim, not a minute's vacancy,   85
Both day and night did we keep company.

Enter Olivia and attendants.

ORSINO: Here comes the Countess. Now heaven walks on earth.
But for° thee, fellow—fellow, thy words are madness.
Three months this youth hath tended upon me;
But more of that anon.—Take him aside.   90

OLIVIA: [*to Orsino*]
What would my lord—but that he may not have°—
Wherein Olivia may seem serviceable?—
Cesario, you do not keep promise with me.

VIOLA: Madam?   95

ORSINO: Gracious Olivia—

OLIVIA: What do you say, Cesario?—Good my lord°—

VIOLA: My lord would speak. My duty hushes me.

OLIVIA: If it be aught to the old tune, my lord,
It is as fat and fulsome° to mine ear   100
As howling after music.

ORSINO: Still so cruel?

OLIVIA: Still so constant, lord.

ORSINO: What, to perverseness? You uncivil lady,
To whose ingrate and unauspicious° altars   105

---

77 face . . . acquaintance brazenly deny he knew me   **78–9 grew . . . wink** in the twinkling of an
eye acted as though we had been estranged for twenty years   **80 recommended** consigned
88 for as for   **91 but . . . have** except that which he may not have—i.e., my love   **97 Good my lord**
(Olivia urges Orsino to listen to Cesario.)   **100 fat and fulsome** gross and offensive   **105 ingrate
and unauspicious** thankless and unpropitious

My soul the faithfull'st off'rings have breathed out
That e'er devotion tendered! What shall I do?

OLIVIA: Even what it please my lord that shall become° him.

ORSINO: Why should I not, had I the heart to do it,
Like to th' Egyptian thief° at point of death   110
Kill what I love?—a savage jealousy
That sometime savors nobly.° But hear me this:
Since you to nonregardance° cast my faith,
And that° I partly know the instrument
That screws° me from my true place in your favor,   115
Live you the marble-breasted tyrant still.
But this your minion,° whom I know you love,
And whom, by heaven I swear, I tender° dearly,
Him will I tear out of that cruel eye
Where he sits crownèd in his master's spite.°—   120
Come, boy, with me. My thoughts are ripe in mischief.
I'll sacrifice the lamb that I do love,
To spite a raven's heart within a dove.°   [*Going.*]

VIOLA: And I, most jocund, apt,° and willingly,
To do you rest,° a thousand deaths would die.   125

        [*Going.*]

OLIVIA: Where goes Cesario?

VIOLA: After him I love
More than I love these eyes, more than my life,
More by all mores° than e'er I shall love wife.
If I do feign, you witnesses above   130
Punish my life for tainting of my love!°

OLIVIA: Ay me, detested!° How am I beguiled!

VIOLA: Who does beguile you? Who does do you wrong?

---

108 become suit   **110 th' Egyptian thief** (An allusion to the story of Theagenes and Chariclea
in the *Ethiopica*, a Greek romance by Heliodorus. The robber chief, Thyamis of Memphis,
having captured Chariclea and fallen in love with her, is attacked by a larger band of robbers;
threatened with death, he attempts to slay her first.)   **112 savors nobly** is not without nobility.
113 nonregardance neglect   **114 that** since   **115 screws** pries, forces   **117 minion** darling, favorite
118 tender regard   **119–20 Him . . . spite** I will tear Cesario away from Olivia, in whose cruel
eye he sits like a king to spite me, his true master.   **122–3 I'll . . . dove** i.e., I'll kill Cesario, whom
I love, to revenge myself on this seemingly gracious but black-hearted lady.   **124 apt** readily
125 do you rest give you ease   **129 by all mores** by all such comparisons   **131 Punish . . . love!**
punish me with death for being disloyal to the love I feel!   **132 detested** hated and denounced
by another.

OLIVIA: Hast thou forgot thyself? Is it so long?
Call forth the holy father.   [*Exit an attendant.*]

ORSINO: [*to Viola*] Come, away!   135

OLIVIA: Whither, my lord?—Cesario, husband, stay.

ORSINO: Husband?

OLIVIA: Ay, husband. Can he that deny?

ORSINO: [*to Viola*]
Her husband, sirrah?°   140

VIOLA: No, my lord, not I.

OLIVIA: Alas, it is the baseness of thy fear
That makes thee strangle thy propriety.°
Fear not, Cesario, take thy fortunes up;
Be that° thou know'st thou art, and then thou art   145
As great as that thou fear'st.°

     Enter Priest.

Oh, welcome, father!
Father, I charge thee by thy reverence
Here to unfold—though lately we intended
To keep in darkness what occasion° now   150
Reveals before 'tis ripe—what thou dost know
Hath newly passed between this youth and me.

PRIEST   A contract of eternal bond of love,
Confirmed by mutual joinder° of your hands,
Attested by the holy close° of lips,   155
Strengthened by interchangement of your rings,
And all the ceremony of this compact
Sealed in my function,° by my testimony;
Since when, my watch hath told me, toward my grave
I have traveled but two hours.   160

ORSINO: [*to Viola*]
Oh, thou dissembling cub! What wilt thou be
When time hath sowed a grizzle° on thy case?°
Or will not else thy craft so quickly grow

---

140 sirrah (The normal way of addressing an inferior.)   **143 strangle thy propriety** i.e., deny what
is properly yours, disavow your marriage to me.   **145 that** that which   **146 as that thou fear'st** as
him you fear, i.e., Orsino.   **150 occasion** necessity   **154 joinder** joining   **155 close** meeting
158 Sealed . . . function ratified through my carrying out of my priestly office   **162 grizzle**
scattering of gray hair.   **case** skin.

That thine own trip° shall be thine overthrow?
Farewell, and take her, but direct thy feet   165
Where thou and I henceforth may never meet.

VIOLA: My Lord, I do protest—

OLIVIA: Oh, do not swear!
Hold little faith, though thou hast too much fear.°

Enter Sir Andrew.

SIR ANDREW: For the love of God, a surgeon! Send one presently°
to Sir Toby.   170

OLIVIA: What's the matter?

SIR ANDREW: He's broke° my head across, and has given
Sir Toby a bloody coxcomb° too. For the love of God, your
help! I had rather than forty pound I were at home.

OLIVIA: Who has done this, Sir Andrew?   175

SIR ANDREW: The Count's gentleman, one Cesario. We took him
for a coward, but he's the very devil incardinate.°

ORSINO: My gentleman, Cesario?

SIR ANDREW: 'Od's lifelings,° here he is!—You broke my head
for nothing, and that that I did I was set on to do't by Sir   180
Toby.

VIOLA: Why do you speak to me? I never hurt you.
You drew your sword upon me without cause,
But I bespake you fair,° and hurt you not.   185

SIR ANDREW: If a bloody coxcomb be a hurt, you have hurt me. I
think you set nothing by° a bloody cox-comb.

Enter [Sir] Toby and Clown [Feste].

Here comes Sir Toby, halting.° You shall hear more. But if he
had not been in drink, he would have tickled you othergates°
than he did.

ORSINO: How now, gentleman? How is't with you?   190

SIR TOBY: That's all one.° He's hurt me, and there's th'end
on't.°—Sot,° didst see Dick surgeon, sot?

---

164 trip wrestling trick used to throw an opponent. (You'll get overclever and trip yourself up.)
169 Hold . . . fear Keep to your oath as well as you can, even if you are frightened by Orsino's
threats. **170 presently** immediately **173 broke** broken the skin, cut **174 coxcomb** fool's cap
resembling the crest of a cock; here, head **178 incardinate** (For "incarnate.") **180 'Od's lifelings**
By God's little lives **185 bespake you fair** addressed you courteously **187 set nothing by** regard
as insignificant **188 halting** limping. **189 othergates** otherwise **191 That's all one** It doesn't
matter; never mind. **191–2 there's . . . on't** that's all there is to it. **192 Sot** (1) Fool (2) Drunkard

FESTE: Oh, he's drunk, Sir Toby, an hour agone;° his eyes were
set° at eight i'th' morning.

SIR TOBY: Then he's a rogue, and a passy measures pavane.° I 195
hate a drunken rogue.

OLIVIA: Away with him! Who hath made this havoc with them?

SIR ANDREW: I'll help you, Sir Toby, because we'll be dressed°
together.

SIR TOBY: Will you help? An ass-head and a coxcomb and a 200
knave, a thin-faced knave, a gull!

OLIVIA: Get him to bed, and let his hurt be looked to.

[*Exeunt Feste, Fabian, Sir Toby, and Sir Andrew.*]

Enter Sebastian.

SEBASTIAN: I am sorry, madam, I have hurt your kinsman;
But, had it been the brother of my blood,°
I must have done no less with wit and safety.°— 205
You throw a strange regard upon me,° and by that
I do perceive it hath offended you.
Pardon me, sweet one, even for the vows
We made each other but so late ago.

ORSINO: One face, one voice, one habit,° and two persons, 210
A natural perspective,° that is and is not!

SEBASTIAN: Antonio, O my dear Antonio!
How have the hours racked° and tortured me
Since I have lost thee!

ANTONIO: Sebastian are you? 215

SEBASTIAN: Fear'st thou that,° Antonio?

ANTONIO: How have you made division of yourself?
An apple cleft in two is not more twin
Than these two creatures. Which is Sebastian?

OLIVIA: Most wonderful! 220

SEBASTIAN: [*seeing Viola*]
Do I stand there? I never had a brother;
Nor can there be that deity in my nature

---

193 agone ago   **194 set** fixed or closed   **195 passy measures pavane** passe-measure pavane, a
slow-moving, stately dance. (Suggesting Sir Toby's impatience to have his wounds dressed.)
198 be dressed have our wounds surgically dressed   **204 the brother . . . blood** my own brother
205 with wit and safety with intelligent concern for my own safety.   **206 You . . . me** You look
strangely at me   **210 habit** dress   **211 A natural perspective** an optical device or illusion created
in this instance by nature   **213 racked** tortured   **216 Fear'st thou that** Do you doubt that

Of here and everywhere.° I had a sister,
Whom the blind° waves and surges have devoured.
Of charity,° what kin are you to me? 225
What countryman? What name? What parentage?

VIOLA: Of Messaline. Sebastian was my father.
Such a Sebastian was my brother, too.
So went he suited° to his watery tomb.
If spirits can assume both form and suit,° 230
You come to fright us.

SEBASTIAN: A spirit I am indeed,
But am in that dimension grossly clad°
Which from the womb I did participate.°
Were you a woman, as the rest goes even,° 235
I should my tears let fall upon your cheek
And say, "Thrice welcome, drownèd Viola!"

VIOLA: My father had a mole upon his brow.

SEBASTIAN: And so had mine.

VIOLA: And died that day when Viola from her birth 240
Had numbered thirteen years.

SEBASTIAN: Oh, that record° is lively in my soul!
He finishèd indeed his mortal act
That day that made my sister thirteen years.

VIOLA: If nothing lets° to make us happy both 245
But this my masculine usurped attire,
Do not embrace me till each circumstance
Of place, time, fortune, do cohere and jump°
That I am Viola—which to confirm
I'll bring you to a captain in this town 250
Where lie my maiden weeds,° by whose gentle help
I was preserved to serve this noble count.
All the occurrence of my fortune since
Hath been between this lady and this lord.

SEBASTIAN: [to Olivia]
So comes it, lady, you have been mistook. 255
But nature to her bias drew in that.°

---

223 here and everywhere omnipresence.   **224 blind** heedless, indiscriminate   **225 Of charity** (Tell me) in kindness   **229 suited** dressed; clad in human form   **230 form and suit** physical appearance and dress   **233 in . . . clad** clothed in that fleshly shape **234 participate** possess in common with all humanity.   **235 as . . . even** since everything else agrees   **242 record** recollection   **245 lets** hinders **248 jump** coincide, fit exactly   **251 weeds** clothes   **256 nature . . . that** nature followed her bent in that. (The metaphor is from the game of bowls.)

OLIVIA: Open't and read it.   285

FESTE: Look then to be well edified when the fool delivers° the
madman. [*He reads loudly.*] "By the Lord, madam—"

OLIVIA: How now, art thou mad?

FESTE: No, madam, I do but read madness. An Your Ladyship
will have it as it ought to be, you must allow *vox*.°   290

OLIVIA: Prithee, read i'thy right wits.

FESTE: So I do, madonna; but to read his right wits° is to read
thus. Therefore perpend,° my princess, and give ear.

OLIVIA: [*to Fabian*] Read it you, sirrah.

FABIAN: (*reads*) "By the Lord, madam, you wrong me, and the   295
world shall know it. Though you have put mein to darkness
and given your drunken cousin rule over me, yet have I the
benefit of my senses as well as Your Ladyship. I have your own
letter that induced me to the semblance I put on, with the
which° I doubt not but to do myself much right or you much   300
shame. Think of me as you please. I leave my duty a little unthought of, and speak out of my injury.° The madly used
Malvolio."

OLIVIA: Did he write this?

FESTE: Ay, madam.   305

ORSINO: This savors not much of distraction.

OLIVIA: See him delivered,° Fabian. Bring him hither.

[*Exit Fabian.*]

My lord, so please you, these things further thought on,°
To think me as well a sister as a wife,°
One day shall crown th' alliance on't,° so please you,   310
Here at my house and at my proper° cost.

ORSINO: Madam, I am most apt° t'embrace your offer.
[*To Viola*] Your master quits° you; and for your service done him,
So much against the mettle° of your sex,

---

286 delivers speaks the words of   **290 vox** voice, i.e., an appropriately loud voice.   **292 to read
. . . wits** to express his true state of mind   **293 perpend** consider, attend. (A deliberately lofty
word.)   **299–300 the which** i.e., the letter   **301–2 I leave . . . injury** I leave unsaid the
expressions of duty with which I would normally conclude, and convey instead my sense of
having been wronged.   **307 delivered** released   **308 so . . . on** if you are pleased on further
consideration of all that has happened   **309 To . . . wife** to regard me as favorably as a sister-in-
law as you had hoped to regard me as a wife   **310 crown . . . on't** i.e., serve as occasion for two
marriages confirming our new relationships   **311 proper** own   **312 apt** ready   **313 quits** releases
314 mettle natural disposition

You would have been contracted to a maid,°
Nor are you therein, by my life, deceived.
You are betrothed both to a maid and man.

ORSINO: [to Olivia]
Be not amazed; right noble is his blood.   260
If this be so, as yet the glass° seems true,
I shall have share in this most happy wreck.°
[To Viola] Boy, thou hast said to me a thousand times
Thou never shouldst love woman like to me.°

VIOLA: And all those sayings will I over swear,°   265
And all those swearings keep as true in soul
As doth that orbèd continent the fire°
That severs day from night.

ORSINO: Give me thy hand,
And let me see thee in thy woman's weeds.   270

VIOLA: The captain that did bring me first on shore
Hath my maid's garments. He upon some action°
Is now in durance,° at Malvolio's suit,
A gentleman and follower of my lady's.

OLIVIA: He shall enlarge° him. Fetch Malvolio hither.   275
And yet, alas, now I remember me,
They say, poor gentleman, he's much distract.

      Enter Clown [Feste] with a letter, and Fabian.

A most extracting° frenzy of mine own
From my remembrance clearly banished his.°
How does he, sirrah?   280

FESTE: Truly, madam, he holds Beelzebub at the stave's end° as
well as a man in his case may do. He's here writ a letter to you;
I should have given't you today morning. But as a madman's
epistles are no gospels,° so it skills° not much when they are
delivered.°

---

257 a maid i.e., a virgin man   **261 the glass** i.e., the *natural perspective* of line 216   **262 wreck**
shipwreck, accident.   **264 like to me** as well as you love me.   **265 over swear** swear again
267 As . . . fire i.e., as the sphere of the sun keeps the fire   **272 action** legal charge   **273 in durance**
imprisoned   **275 enlarge** release   **278 extracting** i.e., that obsessed me and drew all thoughts except
of Cesario from my mind   **279 his** i.e., his madness.   **281 holds . . . end** i.e., keeps the devil at a safe
distance. (The metaphor is of fighting with quarterstaffs or long poles.)   **283–4 a madman's . . .
gospels** i.e., there is no truth in a madman's letters. (An allusion to readings in the church
service of selected passages from the epistles and the gospels.)   **284 skills** matters.   **delivered**
(1) delivered to their recipient (2) read aloud.

So far beneath your soft and tender breeding,   315
And since you called me master for so long,
Here is my hand. You shall from this time be
Your master's mistress.

OLIVIA: A sister! You are she.

Enter [Fabian, with] Malvolio.

ORSINO: Is this the madman?   320

OLIVIA: Ay, my lord, this same.
How now, Malvolio?

MALVOLIO: Madam, you have done me wrong,
Notorious wrong.

OLIVIA: Have I, Malvolio? No.   325

MALVOLIO: [*showing a letter*]
Lady, you have. Pray you, peruse that letter.
You must not now deny it is your hand.
Write from it,° if you can, in hand or phrase,
Or say 'tis not your seal, not your invention.°   330
You can say none of this. Well, grant it then,
And tell me, in the modesty of honor,°
Why you have given me such clear lights° of favor,
Bade me come smiling and cross-gartered to you,
To put on yellow stockings, and to frown   335
Upon Sir Toby and the lighter° people?
And, acting this in an obedient hope,°
Why have you suffered me to be imprisoned,
Kept in a dark house, visited by the priest,°
And made the most notorious geck° and gull   340
That e'er invention played on?° Tell me why?

OLIVIA: Alas, Malvolio, this is not my writing,
Though, I confess, much like the character;°
But out of° question 'tis Maria's hand.
And now I do bethink me, it was she   345
First told me thou wast mad; then cam'st° in smiling,
And in such forms which here were presupposed°

---

329 from it differently **330 invention** composition.   **332 in . . . honor** in the name of all that is
decent and honorable   **333 clear lights** evident signs   **336 lighter** lesser   **337 acting . . . hope** when
I acted thus out of obedience to you and in hope of your favor   **339 priest** i.e., Feste   **340 geck**
dupe   **341 invention played on** contrivance sported with.   **343 the character** my handwriting
344 out of beyond   **346 cam'st** you came   **347 presupposed** specified beforehand

Upon thee in the letter. Prithee, be content.
This practice° hath most shrewdly passed° upon thee;
But when we know the grounds and authors of it,   350
Thou shalt be both the plaintiff and the judge
Of thine own cause.

FABIAN: Good madam, hear me speak,
And let no quarrel nor no brawl to come°
Taint the condition° of this present hour,   355
Which I have wondered at. In hope it shall not,
Most freely I confess, myself and Toby
Set this device against Malvolio here,
Upon° some stubborn and uncourteous parts°
We had conceived against him.° Maria writ   360
The letter at Sir Toby's great importance,°
In recompense whereof he hath married her.
How with a sportful malice it was followed°
May rather pluck on° laughter than revenge,
If that° the injuries be justly weighed   365
That have on both sides passed.

OLIVIA: [to Malvolio]
Alas, poor fool, how have they baffled° thee!

FESTE: Why, "Some are born great, some achieve greatness, and
some have greatness thrown upon them." I was one, sir, in
this interlude,° one Sir Topas, sir, but that's all one.° "By the   370
Lord, fool, I am not mad." But do you remember? "Madam,
why laugh you at such a barren rascal? An you smile not,
he's gagged." And thus the whirligig° of time brings in his
revenges.

MALVOLIO: I'll be revenged on the whole pack of you!   375

[Exit.]

OLIVIA: He hath been most notoriously abused.

ORSINO: Pursue him, and entreat him to a peace.
He hath not told us of the captain yet.
When that is known, and golden time convents,°

349 **practice** plot. **shrewdly passed** mischievously been perpetrated   354 **to come** in the future
355 **condition** (happy) nature   359 **Upon** on account of.   **parts** qualities, deeds   360 **conceived against
him** seen and resented in him.   361 **importance** importunity   363 **followed** carried out   364 **pluck on**
induce   365 **If that** if   367 **baffled** disgraced, quelled   370 **interlude** little play.   **that's all one** no
matter for that.   373 **whirligig** spinning top   379 **convents** (1) summons, calls together (2) suits

A solemn combination shall be made   380
Of our dear souls. Meantime, sweet sister,
We will not part from hence. Cesario, come—
For so you shall be, while you are a man;
But when in other habits° you are seen,
Orsino's mistress and his fancy's° queen.   385

   Exeunt [all, except Feste].

FESTE: (*sings*)
 When that I was and a little° tiny boy,
 With hey, ho, the wind and the rain,
 A foolish thing was but a toy,°
 For the rain it raineth every day.
 But when I came to man's estate,   390
 With hey, ho, the wind and the rain,
 'Gainst knaves and thieves men shut their gate,
 For the rain it raineth every day.
 But when I came, alas, to wive,
 With hey, ho, the wind and the rain,   395
 By swaggering could I never thrive,
 For the rain it raineth every day.
 But when I came unto my beds,°
 With hey, ho, the wind and the rain,
 With tosspots° still had drunken heads,   400
 For the rain it raineth every day.
 A great while ago the world begun,
 With hey, ho, the wind and the rain,
 But that's all one, our play is done,
 And we'll strive to please you every day.   405

   [Exit.]

---

384 habits attire **385 fancy's** love's **386 and a little** a little **388 toy** trifle **398 unto my beds** i.e., (1) drunk to bed, or, perhaps, (2) in the evening of life **400 tosspots** drunkards

Henrik Ibsen, universally acknowledged as the first of the great modern play-wrights, was born in Skien, a small town in Norway, the son of a merchant who went bankrupt during Ibsen's childhood. Ibsen first trained for a medical career, but drifted into the theater, gaining, like Shakespeare and Molière, important dramatic training through a decade's service as a stage manager and director. Ibsen was unsuccessful in establishing a theater in Oslo, and he spent almost thirty years living and writing in Germany and Italy. The fame he won through early poetic dramas like Peer Gynt *(1867), which is considered the supreme exploration of the Norwegian national character, was overshadowed by the realistic prose plays he began writing, starting with* Pillars of Society *(1877).* A Doll's House *(1879) and* Ghosts *(1881), which deal, respectively, with a woman's struggle for independence and self-respect and with the taboo subject of venereal disease, made Ibsen an internationally famous, if controversial, figure. In fact, Ibsen wrote* An Enemy of the People *as a response to the public outcry over* Ghosts, *whose subject was considered so controversial that it could not be performed in London until 1891, and then for only a single performance in a private subscription theater. Although Ibsen's type of realism, displayed in "problem plays" such as these and later psychological dramas like* The Wild Duck *(1885) and* Hedda Gabler *(1890), has become so fully assimilated into our literary heritage that now it is difficult to think of him as an innovator, his marriage of the tightly constructed plots of the conventional "well-made play" to serious discussion of social issues was one of the most significant developments in the history of drama. His most influential advocate in English-speaking countries was George Bernard Shaw, whose* The Quintessence of Ibsenism *(1891) is one of the earliest and most influential studies of Ibsen's dramatic methods and ideas.*

An Enemy of the People

Adapted by Arthur Miller

Characters

Morten Kiil
Billing
Mrs. Stockmann
Peter Stockmann

Hovstad
Dr. Stockmann
Morten
Ejlif
Captain Horster
Petra
Aslaksen
The drunk

Synopsis of Scenes

The Action Takes Place in a Norwegian Town

Throughout, in the stage directions, right and left mean stage right and stage left.

Act I

Scene I. Dr. Stockmann's living room

It is evening. Dr. Stockmann's living room is simply but cheerfully furnished. A doorway, upstage right, leads into the entrance hall, which extends from the front door to the dining room, running unseen behind the living room. At the left is another door, which leads to the Doctor's study and other rooms. In the upstage left corner is a stove. Toward the left foreground is a sofa with a table behind it. In the right foreground are two chairs, a small table between them, on which stand a lamp and a bowl of apples. At the back, to the left, an open doorway leads to the dining room, part of which is seen. The windows are in the right wall, a bench in front of them.

As the curtain rises, Billing and Morten Kiil are eating in the dining room. Billing is junior editor of the People's Daily Messenger. *Kiil is a slovenly old man who is feeding himself in a great hurry. He gulps his last bite and comes into the living room, where he puts on his coat and ratty fur hat. Billing comes in to help him.*

BILLING: You sure eat fast, Mr. Kiil. [*Billing is an enthusiast to the point of foolishness.*]

KIIL: Eating don't get you anywhere, boy. Tell my daughter I went home.

> *Kiil starts across to the front door. Billing returns to his food in the dining room. Kiil halts at the bowl of apples; he takes one,*

tastes it, likes it, takes another and puts it in his pocket, then continues on toward the door. Again he stops, returns, and takes another apple for his pocket. Then he sees a tobacco can on the table. He covers his action from Billing's possible glance, opens the can, smells it, pours some into his side pocket. He is just closing the can when Catherine Stockman enters from the dining room.

MRS. STOCKMANN: Father! You're not going, are you?

KIIL: Got business to tend to.

MRS. STOCKMANN: Oh, you're only going back to your room and you know it. Stay! Mr. Billing's here, and Hovstad's coming. It'll be interesting for you.

KIIL: Got all kinds of business. The only reason I came over was the butcher told me you bought roast beef today. Very tasty, dear.

MRS. STOCKMANN: Why don't you wait for Tom? He only went for a little walk.

KIIL [*taking out his pipe*]: You think he'd mind if I filled my pipe?

MRS. STOCKMANN: No, go ahead. And here—take some apples. You should always have some fruit in your room.

KIIL: No, no, wouldn't think of it.

The doorbell rings.

MRS. STOCKMANN: That must be Hovstad. [*She goes to the door and opens it.*]

Peter Stockmann, the Mayor, enters. He is a bachelor, nearing sixty. He has always been one of those men who make it their life work to stand in the center of the ship to keep it from overturning. He probably envies the family life and warmth of this house, but when he comes he never wants to admit he came and often sits with his coat on.

MRS. STOCKMANN: Peter! Well, this is a surprise!

PETER STOCKMANN: I was just passing by . . . [*He sees Kiil and smiles, amused.*] Mr. Kiil!

KIIL [*sarcastically*]: Your Honor! [*He bites into his apple and exits.*]

MRS. STOCKMANN: You mustn't mind him, Peter, he's getting terribly old. Would you like a bite to eat?

PETER STOCKMANN: No, no thanks. [*He sees Billing now, and Billing nods to him from the dining room.*]

MRS. STOCKMANN [*embarrassed*]:   He just happened to drop in.

PETER STOCKMANN: That's all right. I can't take hot food in the evening. Not with my stomach.

MRS. STOCKMANN: Can't I ever get you to eat anything in this house?

PETER STOCKMANN: Bless you, I stick to my tea and toast. Much healthier and more economical.

MRS. STOCKMANN [*smiling*]:   You sound as though Tom and I throw money out the window.

PETER STOCKMANN: Not you, Catherine. He wouldn't be home, would he?

MRS. STOCKMANN: He went for a little walk with the boys.

PETER STOCKMANN: You don't think that's dangerous, right after dinner? [*There is a loud knocking on the front door.*] That sounds like my brother.

MRS. STOCKMANN: I doubt it, so soon. Come in, please.

Hovstad enters. He is in his early thirties, a graduate of the peasantry struggling with a terrible conflict. For while he hates authority and wealth, he cannot bring himself to cast off a certain desire to partake of them. Perhaps he is dangerous because he wants more than anything to belong, and in a radical that is a withering wish, not easily to be borne.

MRS. STOCKMANN: Mr. Hovstad—

HOVSTAD: Sorry I'm late. I was held up at the printing shop. [*Surprised*]:   Good evening, Your Honor.

PETER STOCKMANN [*rather stiffly*]:   Hovstad. On business, no doubt.

HOVSTAD: Partly. It's about an article for the paper—

PETER STOCKMANN [*sarcastically*]: Ha! I don't doubt it. I understand my brother has become a prolific contributor to—what do you call it?—the *People's Daily Liberator?*

HOVSTAD [*laughing, but holding his ground*]:   The *People's Daily Messenger*, sir. The Doctor sometimes honors the *Messenger* when he wants to uncover the real truth of some subject.

PETER STOCKMANN: The truth! Oh, yes, I see.

MRS. STOCKMANN [*nervously to Hovstad*]:   Would you like to . . . [*She points to dining room.*]

PETER STOCKMANN: I don't want you to think I blame the Doctor for using your paper. After all, every performer goes for the audience that applauds him most. It's really not your paper I have anything against, Mr. Hovstad.

HOVSTAD: I really didn't think so, Your Honor.

PETER STOCKMANN: As a matter of fact, I happen to admire the spirit of tolerance in our town. It's magnificent. Just don't forget that we have it because we all believe in the same thing; it brings us together.

HOVSTAD: Kirsten Springs, you mean.

PETER STOCKMANN: The springs, Mr. Hovstad, our wonderful new springs. They've changed the soul of this town. Mark my words, Kirsten Springs are going to put us on the map, and there is no question about it.

MRS. STOCKMANN: That's what Tom says too.

PETER STOCKMANN: Everything is shooting ahead—real estate going up, money changing hands every hour, business humming—

HOVSTAD: And no more unemployment.

PETER STOCKMANN: Right. Give us a really good summer, and sick people will be coming here in carloads. The springs will turn into a regular fad, a new Carlsbad. And for once the well-to-do people won't be the only ones paying taxes in this town.

HOVSTAD: I hear reservations are really starting to come in?

PETER STOCKMANN: Coming in every day. Looks very promising, very promising.

HOVSTAD: That's fine. [*To Mrs. Stockmann*]: Then the Doctor's article will come in handy.

PETER STOCKMANN: He's written something again?

HOVSTAD: No, it's a piece he wrote at the beginning of the winter, recommending the water. But at the time I let the article lie.

PETER STOCKMANN: Why, some hitch in it?

HOVSTAD: Oh, no, I just thought it would have a bigger effect in the spring, when people start planning for the summer.

PETER STOCKMANN: That's smart, Mr. Hovstad, very smart.

MRS. STOCKMANN: Tom is always so full of ideas about the springs; every day he—

PETER STOCKMANN: Well, he ought to be, he gets his salary from the springs, my dear.

HOVSTAD: Oh, I think it's more than that, don't you? After all, Doctor Stockmann *created* Kirsten Springs.

PETER STOCKMANN: You don't say! I've been hearing that lately, but I did think I had a certain modest part—

MRS. STOCKMANN: Oh, Tom always says—

HOVSTAD: I only meant the original idea was—

PETER STOCKMANN: My good brother is never at a loss for ideas. All sorts of ideas. But when it comes to putting them into action you need another kind of man, and I did think that at least people in this house would—

MRS. STOCKMANN: But Peter, dear—we didn't mean to— Go get yourself a bite, Mr. Hovstad, my husband will be here any minute.

HOVSTAD: Thank you, maybe just a little something. [*He goes into the dining room and joins Billing at the table*].

PETER STOCKMANN, [*lowering his voice*]:   Isn't it remarkable? Why is it that people without background can never learn tact?

MRS. STOCKMANN: Why let it bother you? Can't you and Thomas share the honor like good brothers?

PETER STOCKMANN: The trouble is that certain men are never satisfied to share, Catherine.

MRS. STOCKMANN: Nonsense. You've always gotten along beautifully with Tom— That must be him now.

She goes to the front door, opens it. Dr. Stockmann is laughing and talking outside. He is in the prime of his life. He might be called the eternal amateur—a lover of things, of people, of sheer living, a man for whom the days are too short, and the future fabulous with discoverable joys. And for all this most people will not like him—he will not compromise for less than God's own share of the world while they have settled for less than Man's.

DR. STOCKMANN [*in the entrance hall*]:   Hey, Catherine! Here's another guest for you! Here's a hanger for your coat, Captain. Oh, that's right, you don't wear overcoats! Go on in, boys. You kids must be hungry all over again. Come here, Captain Horster, I want you to get a look at this roast. [*He pushes Captain Horster along the hallway to the dining room. Ejlif and Morten also go to the dining room*].

MRS. STOCKMANN: Tom, dear . . . [*She motions toward Peter in the living room*].

DR. STOCKMANN [*turns around in the doorway to the living room and sees Peter*]: Oh, Peter . . . [*He walks across and stretches out his hand.*] Say now, this is really nice.

PETER STOCKMANN: I'll have to go in a minute.

DR. STOCKMANN: Oh, nonsense, not with the toddy on the table. You haven't forgotten the toddy, have you, Catherine?

MRS. STOCKMANN: Of course not, I've got the water boiling. [*She goes into the dining room*].

PETER STOCKMANN: Toddy too?

DR. STOCKMANN: Sure, just sit down and make yourself at home.

PETER STOCKMANN: No, thanks, I don't go in for drinking parties.

DR. STOCKMANN: But this is no party.

PETER STOCKMANN: What else do you call it? [*He looks toward the dining room*]. It's extraordinary how you people can consume all this food and live.

DR. STOCKMANN [*rubbing his hands*]: Why? What's finer than to watch young people eat? Peter, those are the fellows who are going to stir up the whole future.

PETER STOCKMANN [*a little alarmed*]: Is that so! What's there to stir up? *He sits in a chair to the left.*

DR. STOCKMANN [*walking around*]: Don't worry, they'll let us know when the time comes. Old idiots like you and me, we'll be left behind like—

PETER STOCKMANN: I've never been called *that* before.

DR. STOCKMANN: Oh, Peter, don't jump on me every minute! You know your trouble, Peter? Your impressions are blunted. You ought to sit up there in that crooked corner of the north for five years, the way I did, and then come back here. It's like watching the first seven days of creation!

PETER STOCKMANN: Here!

DR. STOCKMANN: Things to work and fight for, Peter! Without that you're dead. Catherine, you sure the mailman came today?

MRS. STOCKMANN, [*from the dining room*]: There wasn't any mail today.

DR. STOCKMANN: And another thing, Peter—a good income; *that's* something you learn to value after you've lived on a starvation diet.

PETER STOCKMANN: When did you starve?

DR. STOCKMANN: Damned near! It was pretty tough going a lot of the time up there. And now, to be able to live like a prince! Tonight, for instance, we had roast beef for dinner, and, by God, there was enough left for supper too. Please have a piece—come here.

PETER STOCKMANN: Oh, no, no—please, certainly not.

DR. STOCKMANN: At least let me show it to you! Come in here—we even have a tablecloth. [*He pulls his brother toward the dining room.*]

PETER STOCKMANN: I saw it.

DR. STOCKMANN: Live to the hilt! that's my motto. Anyway, Catherine says I'm earning almost as much as we spend.

PETER STOCKMANN [*refusing an apple*]: Well, you are improving.

DR. STOCKMANN: Peter, that was a joke! You're supposed to laugh! [*He sits in the other chair to the left*].

PETER STOCKMANN: Roast beef twice a day is no joke.

DR. STOCKMANN: Why can't I give myself the pleasure of having people around me? It's a necessity for me to see young, lively, happy people, free people burning with a desire to do something. You'll see. When Hovstad comes in we'll talk and—

PETER STOCKMANN: Oh, yes, Hovstad. That reminds me. He told me he was going to print one of your articles.

DR. STOCKMANN: One of my articles?

PETER STOCKMANN: Yes, about the springs—an article you wrote during the winter?

DR. STOCKMANN: Oh, that one! In the first place, I don't want that one printed right now.

PETER STOCKMANN: No? It sounded to me like it would be very timely.

DR. STOCKMANN: Under normal conditions, maybe so. [*He gets up and walks across the floor*].

PETER STOCKMANN [*looking after him*]: Well, what is abnormal about the conditions now?

DR. STOCKMANN [*stopping*]: I can't say for the moment, Peter—at least not tonight. There could be a great deal abnormal about conditions; then again, there could be nothing at all.

PETER STOCKMANN: Well, you've managed to sound mysterious. Is there anything wrong? Something you're keeping from me? Because I wish once in a while you'd remind yourself that I am chairman of the board for the springs.

DR. STOCKMANN: And I would like *you* to remember that, Peter. Look, let's not get into each other's hair.

PETER STOCKMANN: I don't make a habit of getting into people's hair! But I'd like to underline that everything concerning Kirsten Springs must be treated in a businesslike manner, through the proper channels, and dealt with by the legally constituted authorities. I can't allow anything done behind my back in a roundabout way.

DR. STOCKMANN: When did I ever go behind your back, Peter?

PETER STOCKMANN: You have an ingrained tendency to go your own way, Thomas, and that simply can't go on in a well-organized society. The individual really must subordinate himself to the over-all, or [*groping for words, he points to himself*] to the authorities who are in charge of the general welfare. *He gets up.*

DR. STOCKMANN: Well, that's probably so. But how the hell does that concern me, Peter?

PETER STOCKMANN: My dear Thomas, this is exactly what you will never learn. But you had better watch out because someday you might pay dearly for it. Now I've said it. Good-bye.

DR. STOCKMANN: Are you out of your mind? You're absolutely on the wrong track.

PETER STOCKMANN: I am usually not. Anyway, may I be excused? [*He nods toward the dining room.*] Good-by, Catherine. Good evening, gentlemen. [*He leaves*].

MRS. STOCKMANN, [*entering the living room*]: He left?

DR. STOCKMANN: And burned up!

MRS. STOCKMANN: What did you do to him now?

DR. STOCKMANN: What does he want from me? He can't expect me to give him an accounting of every move I make, every thought I think, until I am ready to do it.

MRS. STOCKMANN: Why? What should you give him an accounting of?

DR. STOCKMANN [*hesitantly*]: Just leave that to me, Catherine. Peculiar the mailman didn't come today.

Hovstad, Billing, and Captain Horster have gotten up from the dining-room table and enter the living room. Ejlif and Morten come in a little later. Catherine exits.

BILLING [*stretching out his arms*]: After a meal like that, by God, I feel like a new man. This house is so—

HOVSTAD [*cutting him off*]: The Mayor certainly wasn't in a glowing mood tonight.

DR. STOCKMANN: It's his stomach. He has a lousy digestion.

HOVSTAD: I think two editors from the *People's Daily Messenger* didn't help either.

DR. STOCKMANN: No, it's just that Peter is a lonely man. Poor fellow, all he knows is official business and duties, and then all that damn weak tea that he pours into himself. Catherine, may we have the toddy?

MRS. STOCKMANN [*calling from the dining room*]:   I'm just getting it.

DR. STOCKMANN: Sit down here on the couch with me, Captain Horster—a rare guest like you—sit here. Sit down, friends.

HORSTER: This used to be such an ugly house. Suddenly it's beautiful!

Billing and Hovstad sit down at the right. Mrs. Stockmann brings a tray with pot, glasses, bottles, etc. on it, and puts it on the table behind the couch.

BILLING [*to Horster, intimately, indicating Stockmann*]:   Great man!

MRS. STOCKMANN: Here you are. Help yourselves.

DR. STOCKMANN [*taking a glass*]:   We sure will. [*He mixes the toddy.*] And the cigars, Ejlif—you know where the box is. And Morten, get my pipe. [*The boys go out to the left.*] I have a sneaking suspicion that Ejlif is snitching a cigar now and then, but I don't pay any attention. Catherine, you know where I put it? Oh, he's got it. Good boys! [*The boys bring the various things in.*] Help yourselves, fellows. I'll stick to the pipe. This one's gone through plenty of blizzards with me up in the north. Skol! [*He looks around.*] Home! What an invention, heh?

The boys sit down on the bench near the windows.

MRS. STOCKMANN [*who has sat down and is now knitting*]:   Are you sailing soon, Captain Horster?

HORSTER: I expect to be ready next week.

MRS. STOCKMANN: And then to America, Captain?

HORSTER: Yes, that's the plan.

BILLING: Oh, then you won't be home for the new election?

HORSTER: Is there going to be another election?

BILLING: Didn't you know?

HORSTER: No, I don't get mixed up in those things.

BILLING: But you are interested in public affairs, aren't you?

HORSTER: Frankly, I don't understand a thing about it.

He does, really, although not very much. Captain Horster is one of the longest silent roles in dramatic literature, but he is not to be thought of as characterless. It is not a bad thing to have a courageous, quiet man for a friend, even if it has gone out of fashion.

MRS. STOCKMANN [*sympathetically*]: Neither do I, Captain. Maybe that's why I'm always so glad to see you.

BILLING: Just the same, you ought to vote, Captain.

HORSTER: Even if I don't understand anything about it?

BILLING: Understand! What do you mean by that? Society, Captain, is like a ship—every man should do something to help navigate the ship.

HORSTER: That may be all right on shore, but on board a ship it doesn't work out so well.

Petra in hat and coat and with textbooks and notebooks under her arm comes into the entrance hall. She is Ibsen's clear-eyed hope for the future—and probably ours. She is forthright, determined, and knows the meaning of work, which to her is the creation of good on the earth.

PETRA [*from the hall*]: Good evening.

DR. STOCKMANN, *warmly*: Good evening, Petra!

BILLING [*to Horster*]: Great young woman!

There are mutual greetings. Petra removes her coat and hat and places the books on a chair in the entrance hall.

PETRA [*entering the living room*]: And here you are, lying around like lizards while I'm out slaving.

DR. STOCKMANN: Well, you come and be a lizard too. Come here, Petra, sit with me. I look at her and say to myself, "How did I do it?"

Petra goes over to her father and kisses him.

BILLING: Shall I mix a toddy for you?

PETRA [*coming up to the table*]: No, thanks, I had better do it myself—you always mix it too strong. Oh, Father, I forgot—I have a letter for you. [*She goes to the chair where her books are.*]

DR. STOCKMANN [*alerted*]: Who's it from?

PETRA: I met the mailman on the way to school this morning and he gave me your mail too, and I just didn't have time to run back.

DR. STOCKMANN [*getting up and walking toward her*]:   And you don't give it to me until now!

PETRA: I really didn't have time to run back, Father.

MRS. STOCKMANN: If she didn't have time . . .

DR. STOCKMANN: Let's see it—come on, child! [*He takes the letter and looks at the envelope.*] Yes, indeed.

MRS. STOCKMANN: Is that the one you've been waiting for?

DR. STOCKMANN: I'll be right back. There wouldn't be a light on in my room, would there?

MRS. STOCKMANN: The lamp is on the desk, burning away.

DR. STOCKMANN: Please excuse me for a moment. [*He goes into his study and quickly returns. Mrs. Stockmann hands him his glasses. He goes out again.*]

PETRA: What is that, Mother?

MRS. STOCKMANN: I don't know. The last couple of days he's been asking again and again about the mailman.

BILLING: Probably an out-of-town patient of his.

PETRA: Poor Father, he's got much too much to do. [*She mixes her drink.*] This ought to taste good.

HOVSTAD: By the way, what happened to that English novel you were going to translate for us?

PETRA: I started it, but I've gotten so busy—

HOVSTAD: Oh, teaching evening school again?

PETRA: Two hours a night.

BILLING: Plus the high school every day?

PETRA [*sitting down on the couch*]:   Yes, five hours, and every night a pile of lessons to correct!

MRS. STOCKMANN: She never stops going.

HOVSTAD: Maybe that's why I always think of you as kind of breathless and—well, breathless.

PETRA: I love it. I get so wonderfully tired.

BILLING [*to Horster*]:   She looks tired.

MORTEN: You must be a wicked woman, Petra.

PETRA [*laughing*]:   Wicked?

MORTEN: You work so much. My teacher says that work is a punishment for our sins.

EJLIF: And you believe that?

MRS. STOCKMANN: Ejlif! Of course he believes his teacher!

BILLING [smiling]:   Don't stop him . . .

HOVSTAD: Don't you like to work, Morten?

MORTEN: Work? No.

HOVSTAD: Then what will you ever amount to in this world?

MORTEN: Me? I'm going to be a Viking.

EJLIF: You can't! You'd have to be a heathen!

MORTEN: So I'll be a heathen.

MRS. STOCKMANN: I think it's getting late, boys.

BILLING: I agree with you, Morten. I think—

MRS. STOCKMANN [making signs to Billing]:   You certainly don't, Mr. Billing.

BILLING: Yes, by God, I do. I am a real heathen and proud of it. You'll see, pretty soon we're all going to be heathens!

MORTEN: And then we can do anything we want!

BILLING: Right! You see, Morten—

MRS. STOCKMANN, [interrupting]:   Don't you have any homework for tomorrow, boys? Better go in and do it.

EJLIF: Oh, can't we stay in here a while?

MRS. STOCKMANN: No, neither of you. Now run along.

The boys say good night and go off at the left.

HOVSTAD: You really think it hurts them to listen to such talk?

MRS. STOCKMANN: I don't know, but I don't like it.

Dr. Stockmann enters from his study, an open letter in his hand. He is like a sleepwalker, astonished, engrossed. He walks toward the front door.

MRS. STOCKMANN: Tom!

He turns, suddenly aware of them.

DR. STOCKMANN: Boys, there is going to be news in this town!

BILLING: News?

MRS. STOCKMANN: What kind of news?

DR. STOCKMANN: A terrific discovery, Catherine.

HOVSTAD: Really?

MRS. STOCKMANN: That you made?

DR. STOCKMANN: That I made. *He walks back and forth.* Now let the baboons running this town call me a lunatic! Now they'd better watch out. Oh, how the mighty have fallen!

PETRA: What is it, Father?

DR. STOCKMANN: Oh, if Peter were only here! Now you'll see how human beings can walk around and make judgments like blind rats.

HOVSTAD: What in the world's happened, Doctor?

DR. STOCKMANN [*stopping at the table*]: It's the general opinion, isn't it, that our town is a sound and healthy spot?

HOVSTAD: Of course.

MRS. STOCKMANN: What happened?

DR. STOCKMANN: Even a rather unusually healthy spot! Oh, God, a place that can be recommended not only to all people but to sick people!

MRS. STOCKMANN: But, Tom, what are you—

DR. STOCKMANN: And we certainly have recommended it. I myself have written and written, in the *People's Messenger*, pamphlets—

HOVSTAD: Yes, yes, but—

DR. STOCKMANN: The miraculous springs that cost such a fortune to build, the whole Health Institute, is a pesthole!

PETRA: Father! The springs?

MRS. STOCKMANN [*simultaneously*]: Our springs?

BILLING: That's unbelievable!

DR. STOCKMANN: You know the filth up in Windmill Valley? That stuff that has such a stinking smell? It comes down from the tannery up there, and the same damn poisonous mess comes right out into the blessed, miraculous water we're supposed to *cure* people with!

HORSTER: You mean actually where our beaches are?

DR. STOCKMANN: Exactly.

HOVSTAD: How are you so sure about this, Doctor?

DR. STOCKMANN: I had a suspicion about it a long time ago—last year there were too many sick cases among the visitors, typhoid and gastric disturbances.

MRS. STOCKMANN: That did happen. I remember Mrs. Svensen's niece—

DR. STOCKMANN: Yes, dear. At the time we thought that the visitors brought the bug, but later this winter I got a new idea and I started investigating the water.

MRS. STOCKMANN: So that's what you've been working on!

DR. STOCKMANN: I sent samples of the water to the University for an exact chemical analysis.

HOVSTAD: And that's what you have just received?

DR. STOCKMANN [*waving the letter again*]: This is it. It proves the existence of infectious organic matter in the water.

MRS. STOCKMANN: Well, thank God you discovered it in time.

DR. STOCKMANN: I think we can say that, Catherine.

MRS. STOCKMANN: Isn't it wonderful!

HOVSTAD: And what do you intend to do now, Doctor?

DR. STOCKMANN: Put the thing right, of course.

HOVSTAD: Do you think that can be done?

DR. STOCKMANN: Maybe. If not, the whole Institute is useless. But there's nothing to worry about—I am quite clear on what has to be done.

MRS. STOCKMANN: But, Tom, why did you keep it so secret?

DR. STOCKMANN: What did you want me to do? Go out and shoot my mouth off before I really knew? [*He walks around, rubbing his hands.*] You don't realize what this means, Catherine—the whole water system has got to be changed.

MRS. STOCKMANN: The *whole* water system?

DR. STOCKMANN: The whole water system. The intake is too low, it's got to be raised to a much higher spot. The whole construction's got to be ripped out!

PETRA: Well, Father, at last you can prove they should have listened to you!

DR. STOCKMANN: Ha, she remembers!

MRS. STOCKMANN: That's right, you did warn them—

DR. STOCKMANN: Of course I warned them. When they started the damned thing I told them not to build it down there! But who am I, a mere scientist, to tell politicians where to build a health institute! Well, now they're going to get it, both barrels!

BILLING: This is tremendous! (*To Horster*): He's a great man!

DR. STOCKMANN: It's bigger than tremendous. [*He starts toward his study.*] Wait'll they see this! (*He stops.*) Petra, my report is on my desk . . . [*Petra goes into his study.*] An envelope, Catherine! [*She goes for it.*] Gentlemen, this final proof from the University [*Petra comes out with the report, which he takes*] and my report [*he flicks the pages*] five solid, explosive pages . . .

MRS. STOCKMANN [*handing him an envelope*]: Is this big enough?

DR. STOCKMANN: Fine. Right to the Board of Directors! [*He inserts the report, seals the envelope, and hands it to Catherine.*] Will you give this to the maid—what's her name again?

MRS. STOCKMANN: Randine, dear, Randine.

DR. STOCKMANN: Tell our darling Randine to wipe her nose and run over to the Mayor right now.

Mrs. Stockmann just stands there looking at him.

DR. STOCKMANN: What's the matter, dear?

MRS. STOCKMANN: I don't know . . .

PETRA: What's Uncle Peter going to say about this?

MRS. STOCKMANN: That's what I'm wondering.

DR. STOCKMANN: What can he say! He ought to be damn glad that such an important fact is brought out before we start an epidemic! Hurry, dear!

Catherine exits at the left.

HOVSTAD: I would like to put a brief item about this discovery in the *Messenger.*

DR. STOCKMANN: Go ahead. I'd really be grateful for that now.

HOVSTAD: Because the public ought to know soon.

DR. STOCKMANN: Right away.

BILLING: By God, you'll be the leading man in this town, Doctor.

DR. STOCKMANN [*walking around with an air of satisfaction*]: Oh, there was nothing to it. Every detective gets a lucky break once in his life. But just the same I—

BILLING: Hovstad, don't you think the town ought to pay Dr. Stockmann some tribute?

DR. STOCKMANN: Oh, no, no . . .

HOVSTAD: Sure, let's all put in a word for—

BILLING: I'll talk to Aslaksen about it!

Catherine enters.

DR. STOCKMANN: No, no, fellows, no fooling around! I won't put up with any commotion. Even if the Board of Directors wants to give me an increase I won't take it—I just won't take it, Catherine.

MRS. STOCKMANN [*dutifully*]: That's right, Tom.

PETRA [*lifting her glass*]: Skol, Father!

EVERYBODY: Skol, Doctor!

HORSTER: Doctor, I hope this will bring you great honor and pleasure.

DR. STOCKMANN: Thanks, friends, thanks. There's one blessing above all others. To have earned the respect of one's neighbors is—is— Catherine, I'm going to dance!

He grabs his wife and whirls her around. There are shouts and struggles, general commotion. The boys in nightgowns stick their heads through the doorway at the right, wondering what is going on. Mrs. Stockmann, seeing them, breaks away and chases them upstairs as the curtain falls.

Scene II. The same, the following morning

Dr. Stockmann's living room the following morning. As the curtain rises, Mrs. Stockmann comes in from the dining room, a sealed letter in her hand. She goes to the study door and peeks in.

MRS. STOCKMANN: Are you there, Tom?

DR. STOCKMANN, [*from within*]: I just got in. [*He enters the living room.*] What's up?

MRS. STOCKMANN: From Peter. It just came. [*She hands him the envelope.*]

DR. STOCKMANN: Oh, let's see. [*He opens the letter and reads*]: "I am returning herewith the report you submitted . . ." [*He continues to read, mumbling to himself.*]

MRS. STOCKMANN: Well, what does he say? Don't stand there!

DR. STOCKMANN [*putting the letter in his pocket*]: He just says he'll come around this afternoon.

MRS. STOCKMANN: Oh. Well, maybe you ought to try to remember to be home then.

DR. STOCKMANN: Oh, I sure will. I'm through with my morning visits anyway.

MRS. STOCKMANN: I'm dying to see how he's going to take it.

DR. STOCKMANN: Why, is there any doubt? He'll probably make it look like he made the discovery, not I.

MRS. STOCKMANN: But aren't you a little bit afraid of that?

DR. STOCKMANN: Oh, underneath he'll be happy, Catherine. It's just that Peter is so afraid that somebody else is going to do something good for this town.

MRS. STOCKMANN: I wish you'd go out of your way and share the honors with him. Couldn't we say that he put you on the right track or something?

DR. STOCKMANN: Oh, I don't mind—as long as it makes everybody happy.

Morten Kiil sticks his head through the doorway. He looks around searchingly and chuckles. He will continue chuckling until he leaves the house. He is the archetype of the little twinkle-eyed man who sneaks into so much of Ibsen's work. He will chuckle you right over the precipice. He is the dealer, the man with the rat's finely tuned brain. But he is sometimes likable because he is without morals and announces the fact by laughing.

KIIL [*slyly*]: Is it really true?

MRS. STOCKMANN [*walking toward him*]: Father!

DR. STOCKMANN: Well, good morning!

MRS. STOCKMANN: Come on in.

KIIL: It better be true or I'm going.

DR. STOCKMANN: What had better be true?

KIIL: This crazy story about the water system. Is it true?

MRS. STOCKMANN: Of course it's true! How did you find out about it?

KIIL: Petra came flying by on her way to school this morning.

DR. STOCKMANN: Oh, she did?

KIIL: Ya. I thought she was trying to make a fool out of me—

MRS. STOCKMANN: Now why would she do that?

KIIL: Nothing gives more pleasure to young people than to make fools out of old people. But this is true, eh?

DR. STOCKMANN: Of course it's true. Sit down here. It's pretty lucky for the town, eh?

KIIL [*fighting his laughter*]: Lucky for the town!

DR. STOCKMANN: I mean, that I made the discovery before it was too late.

KIIL: Tom, I never thought you had the imagination to pull your own brother's leg like this.

DR. STOCKMANN: Pull his leg?

MRS. STOCKMANN: But, Father, he's not—

KIIL: How does it go now, let me get it straight. There's some kind of—like cockroaches in the waterpipes—

DR. STOCKMANN [*laughing*]: No, not cockroaches.

KIIL: Well, some kind of little animals.

MRS. STOCKMANN: Bacteria, Father.

KIIL [*who can barely speak through his laughter*]: Ah, but a whole mess of them, eh?

DR. STOCKMANN: Oh, there'd be millions and millions.

KIIL: And nobody can see them but you, is that it?

DR. STOCKMANN: Yes, that's—well, of course anybody with a micro— [*He breaks off.*] What are you laughing at?

MRS. STOCKMANN [*smiling at Kiil*]: You don't understand, Father. Nobody can actually see bacteria, but that doesn't mean they're not there.

KIIL: Good girl, you stick with him! By God, this is the best thing I ever heard in my life!

DR. STOCKMANN [*smiling*]: What do you mean?

KIIL: But tell me, you think you are actually going to get your brother to believe this?

DR. STOCKMANN: Well, we'll see soon enough!

KIIL: You really think he's that crazy?

DR. STOCKMANN: I hope the whole town will be that crazy, Morten.

KIIL: Ya, they probably are, and it'll serve them right too—they think they're so much smarter than us old-timers. Your good brother ordered them to bounce me out of the council, so they chased me out like a dog! Make jackasses out of all of them, Stockmann!

DR. STOCKMANN: Yes, but, Morten—

KIIL: Long-eared, short-tailed jackasses! [*He gets up.*] Stockmann, if you can make the Mayor and his elegant friends grab at this bait, I will give a couple of hundred crowns to charity, and right now, right on the spot.

DR. STOCKMANN: Well, that would be very kind of you, but I'm—

KIIL: I haven't got much to play around with, but if you can pull the rug out from under him with this cockroach business, I'll give at least fifty crowns to some poor people on Christmas Eve. Maybe this'll teach them to put some brains back in Town Hall!

Hovstad enters from the hall.

HOVSTAD: Good morning! Oh, pardon me . . .

KIIL [*enjoying this proof immensely*]: Oh, this one is in on it, too?

HOVSTAD: What's that, sir?

DR. STOCKMANN: Of course he's in on it.

KIIL: Couldn't I have guessed that! And it's going to be in the papers, I suppose. You're sure tying down the corners, aren't you? Well, lay it on thick. I've got to go.

DR. STOCKMANN: Oh, no, stay a while, let me explain it to you!

KIIL: Oh, I get it, don't worry! Only you can see them, heh? That's the best idea I've ever—damn it, you shouldn't do this for nothing! [*He goes toward the hall.*]

MRS. STOCKMANN [*following him out, laughing*]:   But, Father, you don't understand about bacteria.

DR. STOCKMANN [*laughing*]:   The old badger doesn't believe a word of it.

HOVSTAD: What does he think you're doing?

DR. STOCKMANN: Making an idiot out of my brother—imagine that?

HOVSTAD: You got a few minutes?

DR. STOCKMANN: Sure, as long as you like.

HOVSTAD: Have you heard from the Mayor?

DR. STOCKMANN: Only that he's coming over later.

HOVSTAD: I've been thinking about this since last night—

DR. STOCKMANN: Don't say?

HOVSTAD: For you as a medical man, a scientist, this is a really rare opportunity. But I've been wondering if you realize that it ties in with a lot of other things.

DR. STOCKMANN: How do you mean? Sit down. [*They sit at the right*]. What are you driving at?

HOVSTAD: You said last night that the pollution comes from impurities in the ground—

DR. STOCKMANN: It comes from the poisonous dump up in Windmill Valley.

HOVSTAD: Doctor, I think it comes from an entirely different dump.

DR. STOCKMANN: What do you mean?

HOVSTAD [*with growing zeal*]:   The same dump that is poisoning and polluting our whole social life in this town.

DR. STOCKMANN: For God's sake, Hovstad, what are you babbling about?

HOVSTAD: Everything that matters in this town has fallen into the hands of a few bureaucrats.

DR. STOCKMANN: Well, they're not all bureaucrats—

HOVSTAD: They're all rich, all with old reputable names, and they've got everything in the palm of their hands.

DR. STOCKMANN: Yes, but they happen to have ability and knowledge.

HOVSTAD: Did they show ability and knowledge when they built the water system where they did?

DR. STOCKMANN: No, of course not, but that happened to be a blunder, and we'll clear it up now.

HOVSTAD: You really imagine it's going to be as easy as all that?

DR. STOCKMANN: Easy or not easy, it's got to be done.

HOVSTAD: Doctor, I've made up my mind to give this whole scandal very special treatment.

DR. STOCKMANN: Now wait. You can't call it a scandal yet.

HOVSTAD: Doctor, when I took over the *People's Messenger* I swore I'd blow that smug cabal of old, stubborn, self-satisfied fogies to bits. This is the story that can do it.

DR. STOCKMANN: But I still think we owe them a deep debt of gratitude for building the springs.

HOVSTAD: The Mayor being your brother, I wouldn't ordinarily want to touch it, but I know you'd never let that kind of thing obstruct the truth.

DR. STOCKMANN: Of course not, but . . .

HOVSTAD: I want you to understand me. I don't have to tell you I come from a simple family. I know in my bones what the underdog needs—he's got to have a say in the government of society. That's what brings out ability, intelligence, and self-respect in people.

DR. STOCKMANN: I understand that, but . . .

HOVSTAD: I think a newspaperman who turns down any chance to give the underdog a lift is taking on a responsibility that I don't want. I know perfectly well that in fancy circles they call it agitation, and they can call it anything they like if it makes them happy, but I have my own conscience—

DR. STOCKMANN [*interrupting*]: I agree with you, Hovstad, but this is just the water supply and—[*There is a knock on the door.*] Damn it! Come in!

Mr. Aslaksen, the publisher, enters from the hall. He is simply but neatly dressed. He wears gloves and carries a hat and an umbrella in his hand. He is so utterly drawn it is unnecessary to say any-thing at all about him.

ASLAKSEN: I beg your pardon, Doctor, if I intrude . . .

HOVSTAD [*standing up*]:   Are you looking for me, Aslaksen?

ASLAKSEN: No, I didn't know you were here. I want to see the Doctor.

DR. STOCKMANN: What can I do for you?

ASLAKSEN: Is it true, Doctor, what I hear from Mr. Billing, that you intend to campaign for a better water system?

DR. STOCKMANN: Yes, for the Institute. But it's not a campaign.

ASLAKSEN: I just wanted to call and tell you that we are behind you a hundred percent.

HOVSTAD [*to Dr. Stockmann*]:   There, you see!

DR. STOCKMANN: Mr. Aslaksen, I thank you with all my heart. But you see—

ASLAKSEN: We can be important, Doctor. When the little business-man wants to push something through, he turns out to be the majority, you know, and it's always good to have the majority on your side.

DR. STOCKMANN: That's certainly true, but I don't understand what this is all about. It seems to me it's a simple straightforward busi-ness. The water—

ASLAKSEN: Of course we intend to behave with moderation, Doctor. I always try to be a moderate and careful man.

DR. STOCKMANN: You are known for that, Mr. Aslaksen, but—

ASLAKSEN: The water system is very important to us little business-men, Doctor. Kirsten Springs are becoming a gold mine for this town, especially for the property owners, and that is why, in my capacity as chairman of the Property Owners Association—

DR. STOCKMANN: Yes.

ASLAKSEN: And furthermore, as a representative of the Temperance Society—You probably know, Doctor, that I am active for prohibition.

DR. STOCKMANN: So I have heard.

ASLAKSEN: As a result, I come into contact with all kinds of people, and since I am known to be a law-abiding and solid citizen, I have a certain influence in this town—you might even call it a little power.

DR. STOCKMANN: I know that very well, Mr. Aslaksen.

ASLAKSEN: That's why you can see that it would be practically noth-ing for me to arrange a demonstration.

DR. STOCKMANN: Demonstration! What are you going to demonstrate about?

ASLAKSEN: The citizens of the town complimenting you for bringing this important matter to everybody's attention. Obviously it would have to be done with the utmost moderation so as not to hurt the authorities.

HOVSTAD: This could knock the big-bellies right into the garbage can!

ASLAKSEN: No indiscretion or extreme aggressiveness toward the authorities, Mr. Hovstad! I don't want any wild-eyed radicalism on this thing. I've had enough of that in my time, and no good ever comes of it. But for a good solid citizen to express his calm, frank, and free opinion is something nobody can deny.

DR. STOCKMANN [*shaking the publisher's hand*]: My dear Aslaksen, I can't tell you how it heartens me to hear this kind of support. I am happy—I really am—I'm happy. Listen! Wouldn't you like a glass of sherry?

ASLAKSEN: I am a member of the Temperance Society. I—

DR. STOCKMANN: Well, how about a glass of beer?

ASLAKSEN [*considers, then*]: I don't think I can go quite that far, Doctor. I never take anything. Well, good day, and I want you to remember that the little man is behind you like a wall.

DR. STOCKMANN: Thank you.

ASLAKSEN: You have the solid majority on your side, because when the little—

DR. STOCKMANN [*trying to stop Aslaksen's talk*]: Thanks for that, Mr. Aslaksen, and good day.

ASLAKSEN: Are you going back to the printing shop, Mr. Hovstad?

HOVSTAD: I just have a thing or two to attend to here.

ASLAKSEN: Very well. (*He leaves.*)

HOVSTAD: Well, what do you say to a little hypodermic for these fence-sitting deadheads?

DR. STOCKMANN [*surprised*]: Why? I think Aslaksen is a very sincere man.

HOVSTAD: Isn't it time we pumped some guts into these well-intentioned men of good will? Under all their liberal talk they still idolize authority, and that's got to be rooted out of this town. This blunder of the water system has to be made clear to every voter. Let me print your report.

DR. STOCKMANN: Not until I talk to my brother.

HOVSTAD: I'll write an editorial in the meantime, and if the Mayor won't go along with us—

DR. STOCKMANN: I don't see how you can imagine such a thing!

HOVSTAD: Believe me, Doctor, it's possible, and then—

DR. STOCKMANN: Listen, I promise you: he will go along, and then you can print my report, every word of it.

HOVSTAD: On your word of honor?

DR. STOCKMANN [giving Hovstad the manuscript]: Here it is. Take it. It can't do any harm for you to read it. Return it to me later.

HOVSTAD: Good day, Doctor.

DR. STOCKMANN: Good day. You'll see, it's going to be easier than you think, Hovstad!

HOVSTAD: I hope so, Doctor. Sincerely. Let me know as soon as you hear from His Honor. *He leaves.*

DR. STOCKMANN [goes to the dining room and looks in]: Catherine! Oh, you're home already, Petra!

PETRA [coming in]: I just got back from school.

MRS. STOCKMANN [entering]: Hasn't he been here yet?

DR. STOCKMANN: Peter? No, but I just had a long chat with Hovstad. He's really fascinated with my discovery, and you know, it has more implications that I thought at first. Do you know what I have backing me up?

MRS. STOCKMANN: What in heaven's name have you got backing you up?

DR. STOCKMANN: The solid majority.

MRS. STOCKMANN: Is that good?

DR. STOCKMANN: Good? It's wonderful. You can't imagine the feeling, Catherine, to know that your own town feels like a brother to you. I have never felt so at home in this town since I was a boy. *A noise is heard.*

MRS. STOCKMANN: That must be the front door.

DR. STOCKMANN: Oh, it's Peter then. Come in.

PETER STOCKMANN [entering from the hall]: Good morning!

DR. STOCKMANN: It's nice to see you, Peter.

MRS. STOCKMANN: Good morning. How are you today?

PETER STOCKMANN: Well, so so. [To Dr. Stockmann.] I received your thesis about the condition of the springs yesterday.

DR. STOCKMANN: I got your note. Did you read it?

PETER STOCKMANN: I read it.

DR. STOCKMANN: Well, what do you have to say?

Peter Stockmann clears his throat and glances at the women.

MRS. STOCKMANN: Come on, Petra. [*She and Petra leave the room at the left.*]

PETER STOCKMANN [*after a moment*]: Thomas, was it really necessary to go into this investigation behind my back?

DR. STOCKMANN: Yes. Until I was convinced myself, there was no point in—

PETER STOCKMANN: And now you are convinced?

DR. STOCKMANN: Well, certainly. Aren't you too, Peter? *Pause.* The University chemists corroborated . . .

PETER STOCKMANN: You intend to present this document to the Board of Directors, officially, as the medical officer of the springs?

DR. STOCKMANN: Of course, something's got to be done, and quick.

PETER STOCKMANN: You always use such strong expressions, Thomas. Among other things, in your report you say that we *guarantee* our guests and visitors a permanent case of poisoning.

DR. STOCKMANN: But, Peter, how can you describe it any other way? Imagine! Poisoned internally and externally!

PETER STOCKMANN: So you merrily conclude that we must build a waste-disposal plant—and reconstruct a brand-new water system from the bottom up!

DR. STOCKMANN: Well, do you know some other way out? I don't.

PETER STOCKMANN: I took a little walk over to the city engineer this morning and in the course of conversation I sort of jokingly mentioned these changes—as something we might consider for the future, you know.

DR. STOCKMANN: The future won't be soon enough, Peter.

PETER STOCKMANN: The engineer kind of smiled at my extravagance and gave me a few facts. I don't suppose you have taken the trouble to consider what your proposed changes would cost?

DR. STOCKMANN: No, I never thought of that.

PETER STOCKMANN: Naturally. Your little project would come to at least three hundred thousand crowns.

DR. STOCKMANN [*astonished*]: That expensive!

PETER STOCKMANN: Oh, don't look so upset—it's only money. The worst thing is that it would take some two years.

DR. STOCKMANN: Two years?

PETER STOCKMANN: At the least. And what do you propose we do about the springs in the meantime? Shut them up, no doubt! Because we would have to, you know. As soon as the rumor gets around that the water is dangerous, we won't have a visitor left. So that's the picture, Thomas. You have it in your power literally to ruin your own town.

DR. STOCKMANN: Now look, Peter! I don't want to ruin anything.

PETER STOCKMANN: Kirsten Springs are the blood supply of this town, Thomas—the only future we've got here. Now will you stop and think?

DR. STOCKMANN: Good God! Well, what do you think we ought to do?

PETER STOCKMANN: Your report has not convinced me that the conditions are as dangerous as you try to make them.

DR. STOCKMANN: Now listen; they are even worse than the report makes them out to be. Remember, summer is coming, and the warm weather!

PETER STOCKMANN: I think you're exaggerating. A capable physician ought to know what precautions to take.

DR. STOCKMANN: And what then?

PETER STOCKMANN: The existing water supply for the springs is a fact, Thomas, and has got to be treated as a fact. If you are reasonable and act with discretion, the directors of the Institute will be inclined to take under consideration any means to make possible improvements, reasonably and without financial sacrifices.

DR. STOCKMANN: Peter, do you imagine that I would ever agree to such trickery?

PETER STOCKMANN: Trickery?

DR. STOCKMANN: Yes, a trick, a fraud, a lie! A treachery, a downright crime, against the public and against the whole community!

PETER STOCKMANN: I said before that I am not convinced that there is any actual danger.

DR. STOCKMANN: Oh, you aren't? Anything else is impossible! My report is an absolute fact. The only trouble is that you and your administration were the ones who insisted that the water supply be built where it is, and now you're afraid to admit the blunder you committed. Damn it! Don't you think I can see through it all?

PETER STOCKMANN: All right, let's suppose that's true. Maybe I do care a little about my reputation. I still say I do it for the good of the town—without moral authority there can be no government.

And that is why, Thomas, it is my duty to prevent your report from reaching the Board. Some time later I will bring up the matter for discussion. In the meantime, not a single word is to reach the public.

DR. STOCKMANN: Oh, my dear Peter, do you imagine you can prevent that!

PETER STOCKMANN: It will be prevented.

DR. STOCKMANN: It can't be. There are too many people who already know about it.

PETER STOCKMANN, *angered:*   Who? It can't possibly be those people from the *Daily Messenger* who—

DR. STOCKMANN: Exactly. The liberal, free, and independent press will stand up and do its duty!

PETER STOCKMANN: You are an unbelievably irresponsible man, Thomas! Can't you imagine what consequences that is going to have for you?

DR. STOCKMANN: For me?

PETER STOCKMANN: Yes, for you and your family.

DR. STOCKMANN: What the hell are you saying now!

PETER STOCKMANN: I believe I have the right to think of myself as a helpful brother, Thomas.

DR. STOCKMANN: You have been, and I thank you deeply for it.

PETER STOCKMANN: Don't mention it. I often couldn't help myself. I had hoped that by improving your finances I would be able to keep you from running completely hog wild.

DR. STOCKMANN: You mean it was only for your own sake?

PETER STOCKMANN: Partly, yes. What do you imagine people think of an official whose closest relatives get themselves into trouble time and time again?

DR. STOCKMANN: And that's what I have done?

PETER STOCKMANN: You do it without knowing it. You're like a man with an automatic brain—as soon as an idea breaks into your head, no matter how idiotic it may be, you get up like a sleepwalker and start writing a pamphlet about it.

DR. STOCKMANN: Peter, don't you think it's a citizen's duty to share a new idea with the public?

PETER STOCKMANN: The public doesn't need new ideas—the public is much better off with old ideas.

DR. STOCKMANN: You're not even embarrassed to say that?

PETER STOCKMANN: Now look, I'm going to lay this out once and for all. You're always barking about authority. If a man gives you an order he's persecuting you. Nothing is important enough to respect once you decide to revolt against your superiors. All right then, I give up. I'm not going to try to change you any more. I told you the stakes you are playing for here, and now I am going to give you an order. And I warn you, you had better obey it if you value your career.

DR. STOCKMANN: What kind of an order?

PETER STOCKMANN: You are going to deny these rumors officially.

DR. STOCKMANN: How?

PETER STOCKMANN: You simply say that you went into the examination of the water more thoroughly and you find that you overestimated the danger.

DR. STOCKMANN: I see.

PETER STOCKMANN: And that you have complete confidence that whatever improvements are needed, the management will certainly take care of them.

DR. STOCKMANN [after a pause]: My convictions come from the condition of the water. My convictions will change when the water changes, and for no other reason.

PETER STOCKMANN: What are you talking about convictions? You're an official, you keep your convictions to yourself!

DR. STOCKMANN: To myself?

PETER STOCKMANN: As an official, I said. God knows, as a private person that's something else, but as a subordinate employee of the Institute, you have no right to express any convictions or personal opinions about anything connected with policy.

DR. STOCKMANN: Now you listen to me. I am a doctor and a scientist—

PETER STOCKMANN: This has nothing to do with science!

DR. STOCKMANN: Peter, I have the right to express my opinion on anything in the world!

PETER STOCKMANN: Not about the Institute—that I forbid.

DR. STOCKMANN: You forbid!

PETER STOCKMANN: I forbid you as your superior, and when I give orders you obey.

DR. STOCKMANN: Peter, if you weren't my brother—

PETRA [throwing the door at the left open]: Father! You aren't going to stand for this! [She enters.]

MRS. STOCKMANN [*coming in after her*]: Petra, Petra!

PETER STOCKMANN: What have you two been doing, eavesdropping?

MRS. STOCKMANN: You were talking so loud we couldn't help . . .

PETRA: Yes, I was eavesdropping!

PETER STOCKMANN: That makes me very happy.

DR. STOCKMANN [*approaching his brother*]: You said something to me about forbidding—

PETER STOCKMANN: You forced me to.

DR. STOCKMANN: So you want me to spit in my own face officially— is that it?

PETER STOCKMANN: Why must you always be so colorful?

DR. STOCKMANN: And if I don't obey?

PETER STOCKMANN: Then we will publish our own statement, to calm the public.

DR. STOCKMANN: Good enough! And I will write against you. I will stick to what I said, and I will prove that I am right and that you are wrong, and what will you do then?

PETER STOCKMANN: Then I simply won't be able to prevent your dismissal.

DR. STOCKMANN: What!

PETRA: Father!

PETER STOCKMANN: Dismissed from the Institute is what I said. If you want to make war on Kirsten Springs, you have no right to be on the Board of Directors.

DR. STOCKMANN (*after a pause*): You'd dare to do that?

PETER STOCKMANN: Oh, no, you're the daring man.

PETRA: Uncle, this is a rotten way to treat a man like Father!

MRS. STOCKMANN: Will you be quiet, Petra!

PETER STOCKMANN: So young and you've got opinions already—but that's natural. (*To Mrs. Stockmann.*) Catherine dear, you're probably the only sane person in this house. Knock some sense into his head, will you? Make him realize what he's driving his whole family into.

DR. STOCKMANN: My family concerns nobody but myself.

PETER STOCKMANN: His family and his own town.

DR. STOCKMANN: I'm going to show you who loves his town. The people are going to get the full stink of this corruption, Peter, and then we will see who loves his town!

PETER STOCKMANN: You love your town when you blindly, spitefully, stubbornly go ahead trying to cut off our most important industry?

DR. STOCKMANN: That source is poisoned, man. We are getting fat by peddling filth and corruption to innocent people!

PETER STOCKMANN: I think this has gone beyond opinions and convictions, Thomas. A man who can throw that kind of insinuation around is nothing but a traitor to society!

DR. STOCKMANN [*starting toward his brother in a fury*]: How dare you to—

MRS. STOCKMANN [*stepping between them*]: Tom!

PETRA [*grabbing her father's arm*]: Be careful, Father!

PETER STOCKMANN [*with dignity*]: I won't expose myself to violence. You have been warned. Consider what you owe yourself and your family! Good day! [*He exits.*]

DR. STOCKMANN [*walking up and down*]: He's insulted. *He's* insulted!

MRS. STOCKMANN: It's shameful, Tom.

PETRA: Oh, I would love to give him a piece of my mind!

DR. STOCKMANN: It was my own fault! I should have shown my teeth right from the beginning. He called me a traitor to society. Me! Damn it all, that's not going to stick!

MRS. STOCKMANN: Please, think! He's got all the power on his side.

DR. STOCKMANN: Yes, but I have the truth on mine.

MRS. STOCKMANN: Without power, what good is the truth?

PETRA: Mother, how can you say such a thing?

DR. STOCKMANN: That's ridiculous, Catherine. I have the liberal press with me, and the majority. If that isn't power, what is?

MRS. STOCKMANN: But, for heaven's sake, Tom, you aren't going to—

DR. STOCKMANN: What am I not going to do?

MRS. STOCKMANN: You aren't going to fight it out in public with your brother!

DR. STOCKMANN: What the hell else do you want me to do?

MRS. STOCKMANN: But it won't do you any earthly good. If they won't do it, they won't. All you'll get out of it is a notice that you're fired.

DR. STOCKMANN: I am going to do my duty, Catherine. Me, the man he calls a traitor to society!

MRS. STOCKMANN: And how about your duty toward your family— the people you're supposed to provide for?

PETRA: Don't always think of us first, Mother.

MRS. STOCKMANN [*to Petra*]: You can talk! If worst comes to worst, you can manage for yourself. But what about the boys, Tom, and you and me?

DR. STOCKMANN: What about you? You want me to be the miserable animal who'd crawl up the boots of that damn gang? Will you be happy if I can't face myself the rest of my life?

MRS. STOCKMANN: Tom, Tom, there's so much injustice in the world! You've simply got to learn to live with it. If you go on this way, God help us, we'll have no money again. Is it so long since the north that you've forgotten what it was to live like we lived? Haven't we had enough of that for one lifetime? [*The boys enter.*] What will happen to them? We've got nothing if you're fired!

DR. STOCKMANN: Stop it! [*He looks at the boys.*] Well, boys, did you learn anything in school today?

MORTEN [*looking at them, puzzled*]: We learned what an insect is.

DR. STOCKMANN: You don't say!

MORTEN: What happened here? Why is everybody—

DR. STOCKMANN: Nothing, nothing. You know what I'm going to do, boys? From now on I'm going to teach you what a man is. [*He looks at Mrs. Stockmann. She cries as the curtain falls.*]

Act II

Scene I. Editorial offices of the *People's Daily Messenger*

The editorial office of the People's Daily Messenger. *At the back of the room, to the left, is a door leading to the printing room. Near it, in the left wall, is another door. At the right of the stage is the entrance door. In the middle of the room there is a large table covered with papers, newspapers, and books. Around it are a few chairs. A writing desk stands against the right wall. The room is dingy and cheerless, the furniture shabby.*

As the curtain rises, Billing is sitting at the desk, reading the manuscript. Hovstad comes in after a moment from the printing room. Billing looks up.

BILLING: The Doctor not come yet?

HOVSTAD: No, not yet. You finish it?

Billing holds up a hand to signal "just a moment." He reads on, the last paragraph of the manuscript. Hovstad comes and stands over him, reading with him. Now Billing closes the manuscript, glances up at Hovstad with some trepidation, then looks off. Hovstad, looking at Billing, walks a few steps away.

HOVSTAD: Well? What do you think of it?

BILLING [*with some hesitation*]: It's devastating. The Doctor is a brilliant man. I swear, I myself never really understood how incompetent those fat fellows are, on top. [*He picks up the manuscript and waves it a little.*] I hear the rumble of revolution in this.

HOVSTAD [*looking toward the door*]: Sssh! Aslaksen's inside.

BILLING: Aslaksen's a coward. With all that moderation talk, all he's saying is, he's yellow. You're going to print this, aren't you?

HOVSTAD: Sure, I'm just waiting for the Doctor to give the word. If his brother hasn't given in, we put it on the press anyway.

BILLING: Yes, but if the Mayor's against this it's going to get pretty rough. You know that, don't you?

HOVSTAD: Just let him try to block the reconstruction—the little businessmen and the whole town'll be screaming for his head. Aslaksen'll see to that.

BILLING [*ecstatically*]: The stockholders'll have to lay out a fortune of money if this goes through!

HOVSTAD: My boy, I think it's going to bust them. And when the springs go busted, the people are finally going to understand the level of genius that's been running this town. Those five sheets of paper are going to put in a liberal administration once and for all.

BILLING: It's a revolution. You know that? [*With hope and fear.*] I mean it, we're on the edge of a real revolution!

DR. STOCKMANN (*entering*): Put it on the press!

HOVSTAD (*excited*): Wonderful! What did the Mayor say?

DR. STOCKMANN: The Mayor has declared war, so war is what it's going to be! [*He takes the manuscript from Billing.*] And this is only the beginning! You know what he tried to do?

BILLING [*calling into the printing room*]: Mr. Aslaksen, the Doctor's here!

DR. STOCKMANN [*continuing*]: He actually tried to blackmail me! He's got the nerve to tell me that I'm not allowed to speak my mind without his permission! Imagine the shameless effrontery!

HOVSTAD: He actually said it right out?

DR. STOCKMANN: Right to my face! The trouble with me was I kept giving them credit for being our kind of people, but they're dictators!

They're people who'll try to hold power even if they have to poison the town to do it.

Toward the last part of Dr. Stockmann's speech Aslaksen enters.

ASLAKSEN: Now take it easy, Doctor, you—you mustn't always be throwing accusations. I'm with you, you understand, but moderation—

DR. STOCKMANN [*cutting him off*]: What'd you think of the article, Hovstad?

HOVSTAD: It's a masterpiece. In one blow you've managed to prove beyond any doubt what kind of men are running us.

ASLAKSEN: May we print it now, then?

DR. STOCKMANN: I should say *so!*

HOVSTAD: We'll have it ready for tomorrow's paper.

DR. STOCKMANN: And listen, Mr. Aslaksen, do me a favor, will you? You run a fine paper, but supervise the printing personally, eh? I'd hate to see the weather report stuck into the middle of my article.

ASLAKSEN (*laughing*): Don't worry, that won't happen this time!

DR. STOCKMANN: Make it perfect, eh? Like you were printing money. You can't imagine how I'm dying to see it in print. After all the lies in the papers, the half-lies, the quarter-lies—to finally see the absolute, unvarnished truth about something important. And this is only the beginning. We'll go on to other subjects and blow up every lie we live by! What do you say, Aslaksen?

ASLAKSEN (*nodding in agreement*): But just remember . . .

BILLING *and* HOVSTAD *together with* ASLAKSEN: Moderation!

ASLAKSEN [*to Billing and Hovstad*]: I don't know what's so funny about that!

BILLING (*enthralled*): Doctor Stockmann, I feel as though I were standing in some historic painting. Goddammit, this is a historic day! Someday this scene'll be in a museum, entitled, "The Day the Truth Was Born."

DR. STOCKMANN [*suddenly*]: Oh! I've got a patient half-bandaged down the street. [*He leaves.*]

HOVSTAD [*to Aslaksen*]: I hope you realize how useful he could be to us.

ASLAKSEN: I don't like that business about "this is only the beginning." Let him stick to the springs.

BILLING: What makes you so scared all the time?

ASLAKSEN: I have to live here. It'd be different if he were attacking the national government or something, but if he thinks I'm going to start going after the whole town administration—

BILLING: What's the difference? Bad is bad!

ASLAKSEN: Yes, but there is a difference. You attack the national government, what's going to happen? Nothing. They go right on. But a town administration—they're liable to be overthrown or something! I represent the small property owners in this town—

BILLING: Ha! It's always the same. Give a man a little property and the truth can go to hell!

ASLAKSEN: Mr. Billing, I'm older than you are. I've seen fireeaters before. You know who used to work at that desk before you? Councilman Stensford—councilman!

BILLING: Just because I work at a renegade's desk, does that mean—

ASLAKSEN: You're a politician. A politician never knows where he's going to end up. And besides you applied for a job as secretary to the Magistrate, didn't you?

HOVSTAD [surprised, laughs]: Billing!

BILLING [to Hovstad]: Well, why not? If I get it I'll have a chance to put across some good things. I could put plenty of big boys on the spot with a job like that!

ASLAKSEN: All right, I'm just saying. [He goes to the printing-room door.] People change. Just remember when you call me a coward—I may not have made the hot speeches, but I never went back on my beliefs either. Unlike some of the big radicals around here, I didn't change. Of course, I am a little more moderate, but moderation is—

HOVSTAD: Oh, God!

ASLAKSEN: I don't see what's so funny about that! [He glares at Hovstad and goes out.]

BILLING: If we could get rid of him we—

HOVSTAD: Take it easy—he pays the printing bill, he's not that bad. [He picks up the manuscript.] I'll get the printer on this. [He starts out.]

BILLING: Say, Hovstad, how about asking Stockmann to back us? Then we could really put out a paper!

HOVSTAD: What would he do for money?

BILLING: His father-in-law.

HOVSTAD: Kiil? Since when has he got money?

BILLING: I think he's loaded with it.

HOVSTAD: No! Why, as long as I've known him he's worn the same overcoat, the same suit—

BILLING: Yeah, and the same ring on his right hand. You ever get a look at that boulder? [He points to his finger.]

HOVSTAD: No, I never—

BILLING: All year he wears the diamond inside, but on New Year's Eve he turns it around. Figure it out—when a man has no visible means of support, what is he living on? Money, right?

Petra enters, carrying a book.

PETRA: Hello.

HOVSTAD: Well, fancy seeing you here. Sit down. What—

PETRA [*walking slowly up to Hovstad*]:   I want to ask you a question. [*She starts to open the book.*]

BILLING: What's that?

PETRA: The English novel you wanted translated.

HOVSTAD: Aren't you going to do it?

PETRA [*with deadly seriousness and curiosity*]:   I don't get this.

HOVSTAD: You don't get what?

PETRA: This book is absolutely against everything you people believe.

HOVSTAD: Oh, it isn't that bad.

PETRA: But, Mr. Hovstad, it says if you're good there's a supernatural force that'll fix it so you end up happy. And if you're bad you'll be punished. Since when does the world work that way?

HOVSTAD: Yes, Petra, but this is a newspaper, people like to read that kind of thing. They buy the paper for that and then we slip in our political stuff. A newspaper can't buck the public—

PETRA [*astonished, beginning to be angry*]:   You don't say! [*She starts to go.*]

HOVSTAD [*hurrying after her*]:   Now, wait a minute, I don't want you to go feeling that way. [*He holds the manuscript out to Billing.*] Here, take this to the printer, will you?

BILLING [*taking the manuscript*]:   Sure. (*He goes.*)

HOVSTAD: I just want you to understand something: I never even read that book. It was Billing's idea.

PETRA [*trying to penetrate his eyes*]:   I thought he was a radical.

HOVSTAD: He is. But he's also a—

PETRA [*testily*]:   A newspaperman.

HOVSTAD: Well, that too, but I was going to say that Billing is trying to get the job as secretary to the Magistrate.

PETRA: What?

HOVSTAD: People are—people, Miss Stockmann.

PETRA: But the Magistrate! He's been fighting everything progressive in this town for thirty years.

HOVSTAD: Let's not argue about it, I just didn't want you to go out of here with a wrong idea of me. I guess you know that I—I happen to admire women like you. I've never had a chance to tell you, but I—well, I want you to know it. Do you mind? [*He smiles.*]

PETRA: No, I don't mind, but—reading that book upset me. I really don't understand. Will you tell me why you're supporting my father?

HOVSTAD: What's the mystery? It's a matter of principle.

PETRA: But a paper that'll print a book like this has no principle.

HOVSTAD: Why do you jump to such extremes? You're just like . . .

PETRA: Like what?

HOVSTAD: I simply mean that . . .

PETRA [*moving away from him*]:   Like my father, you mean. You really have no use for him, do you?

HOVSTAD: Now wait a minute!

PETRA: What's behind this? Are you just trying to hold my hand or something?

HOVSTAD: I happen to agree with your father, and that's why I'm printing his stuff.

PETRA: You're trying to put something over, I think. Why are you in this?

HOVSTAD: Who're you accusing? Billing gave you that book, not me!

PETRA: But you don't mind printing it, do you? What are you trying to do with my father? You have no principles—what are you up to here?

Aslaksen hurriedly enters from the printing shop, Stockmann's manuscript in his hand.

ASLAKSEN: My God! Hovstad! (*He sees Petra*). Miss Stockmann.

PETRA [*looking at Hovstad*]:   I don't think I've been so frightened in my life. [*She goes out.*]

HOVSTAD [*starting after her*]:   Please, you mustn't think I—

ASLAKSEN [*stopping him*]:   Where are you going? The Mayor's out there.

HOVSTAD: The Mayor!

ASLAKSEN: He wants to speak to you. He came in the back door. He doesn't want to be seen.

HOVSTAD: What does he want? [*He goes to the printing-room door, opens it, calls out with a certain edge of servility.*] Come in, Your Honor!

PETER STOCKMANN [*entering*]:   Thank you.

Hovstad carefully closes the door.

PETER STOCKMANN [*walking around*]: It's clean! I always imagined this place would look dirty. But it's clean. [*Commendingly.*] Very nice, Mr. Aslaksen. [*He puts his hat on the desk.*]

ASLAKSEN: Not at all, Your Honor—I mean to say, I always . . .

HOVSTAD: What can I do for you, Your Honor? Sit down?

PETER STOCKMANN [*sits, placing his cane on the table*]: I had a very annoying thing happen today, Mr. Hovstad.

HOVSTAD: That so?

PETER STOCKMANN: It seems my brother has written some sort of— memorandum. About the springs.

HOVSTAD: You don't say.

PETER STOCKMANN [*looking at Hovstad now*]: He mentioned it . . . to you?

HOVSTAD: Yes. I think he said something about it.

ASLAKSEN [*nervously starts to go out, attempting to hide the manuscript*]: Will you excuse me, gentlemen . . .

PETER STOCKMANN [*pointing to the manuscript*]: That's it, isn't it?

ASLAKSEN: This? I don't know, I haven't had a chance to look at it, the printer just handed it to me . . .

HOVSTAD: Isn't that the thing the printer wanted the spelling checked?

ASLAKSEN: That's it. It's only a question of spelling. I'll be right back.

PETER STOCKMANN: I'm very good at spelling. [*He holds out his hand.*] Maybe I can help you.

HOVSTAD: No, Your Honor, there's some Latin in it. You wouldn't know Latin, would you?

PETER STOCKMANN: Oh, yes. I used to help my brother with his Latin all the time. Let me have it.

Aslaksen gives him the manuscript. Peter Stockmann looks at the title on the first page, then glances up sarcastically at Hovstad, who avoids his eyes.

PETER STOCKMANN: You're going to print this?

HOVSTAD: I can't very well refuse a signed article. A signed article is the author's responsibility.

PETER STOCKMANN: Mr. Aslaksen, you're going to allow this?

ASLAKSEN: I'm the publisher, not the editor, Your Honor. My policy is freedom for the editor.

PETER STOCKMANN: You have a point—I can see that.

ASLAKSEN [*reaching for the manuscript*]: So if you don't mind . . .

PETER STOCKMANN: Not at all. [*But he holds on to the manuscript. After a pause.*] This reconstruction of the springs—

ASLAKSEN: I realize, Your Honor—it does mean tremendous sacrifices for the stockholders.

PETER STOCKMANN: Don't upset yourself. The first thing a Mayor learns is that the less wealthy can always be prevailed upon to demand a spirit of sacrifice for the public good.

ASLAKSEN: I'm glad you see that.

PETER STOCKMANN: Oh, yes. Especially when it's the wealthy who are going to do the sacrificing. What you don't seem to understand, Mr. Aslaksen, is that so long as I am Mayor, any changes in those springs are going to be paid for by a municipal loan.

ASLAKSEN: A municipal—you mean you're going to tax the people for this?

PETER STOCKMANN: Exactly.

HOVSTAD: But the springs are a private corporation!

PETER STOCKMANN: The corporation built Kirsten Springs out of its own money. If the people want them changed, the people naturally must pay the bill. The corporation is in no position to put out any more money. It simply can't do it.

ASLAKSEN [*to Hovstad*]: That's impossible! People will never stand for a new tax. [*To the Mayor.*] Is this a fact or your opinion?

PETER STOCKMANN: It happens to be a fact. Plus another fact—you'll forgive me for talking about facts in a newspaper office—but don't forget that the springs will take two years to make over. Two years without income for your small businessmen, Mr. Aslaksen, and a heavy new tax besides. And all because [*his private emotion comes to the surface; he throttles the manuscript in his hand*] because of this dream, this hallucination, that we live in a pesthole!

HOVSTAD: That's based on science.

PETER STOCKMANN [*raising the manuscript and throwing it down on the table.*] This is based on vindictiveness, on his hatred of authority and nothing else. [*He pounds on the manuscript.*] This is the mad dream of a man who is trying to blow up our way of life! It has nothing to do with reform or science or anything else, but pure and simple destruction! And I intend to see to it that the people understand it exactly so!

ASLAKSEN [*hit by this*]: My God! [*To Hovstad.*] Maybe . . . You sure you want to support this thing, Hovstad?

HOVSTAD [*nervously*]: Frankly I'd never thought of it in quite that way. I mean . . . [*To the Mayor.*] When you think of it psychologically it's completely possible, of course, that the man is simply out to—I don't know what to say, Your Honor. I'd hate to hurt the town in any way. I never imagined we'd have to have a new tax.

PETER STOCKMANN: You should have imagined it because you're going to have to advocate it. Unless, of course, liberal and radical newspaper readers enjoy high taxes. But you'd know that better than I. I happen to have here a brief story of the actual facts. It proves that, with a little care, nobody need be harmed at all by the water. [*He takes out a long envelope.*] Of course, in time we'd have to make a few minor structural changes and we'd pay for those.

HOVSTAD: May I see that?

PETER STOCKMANN: I want you to *study* it, Mr. Hovstad, and see if you don't agree that—

BILLING [*entering quickly*]: Are you expecting the Doctor?

PETER STOCKMANN [*alarmed*]: He's here?

BILLING: Just coming across the street.

PETER STOCKMANN: I'd rather not run into him here. How can I . . .

BILLING: Right this way, sir, hurry up!

ASLAKSEN, [*at the entrance door, peeking*]: Hurry up!

PETER STOCKMANN, [*going with Billing through the door at the left*]: Get him out of here right away! [*They exit.*]

HOVSTAD: Do something, do something!

Aslaksen pokes among some papers on the table. Hovstad sits at the desk, starts to "write." Dr. Stockmann enters.

DR. STOCKMANN: Any proofs yet? [*He sees they hardly turn to him.*] I guess not, eh?

ASLAKSEN [*without turning*]: No, you can't expect them for some time.

DR. STOCKMANN: You mind if I wait?

HOVSTAD: No sense in that, Doctor, it'll be quite a while yet.

DR. STOCKMANN [*laughing, places his hand on Hovstad's back*]: Bear with me, Hovstad, I just can't wait to see it in print.

HOVSTAD: We're pretty busy, Doctor, so . . .

DR. STOCKMANN [*starting toward the door*]: Don't let me hold you up. That's the way to be, busy, busy. We'll make this town shine like a jewel! [*He has opened the door, now he comes back.*] Just one thing. I—

HOVSTAD: Couldn't we talk some other time? We're very—

DR. STOCKMANN: Two words. Just walking down the street now, I looked at the people, in the stores, driving the wagons, and suddenly I was—well, touched, you know? By their innocence, I mean. What I'm driving at is, when this exposé breaks they're liable to start making a saint out of me or something, and I—Aslaksen, I want you to promise me that you're not going to try to get up any dinner for me or—

ASLAKSEN [*turning toward the Doctor*]: Doctor, there's no use concealing—

DR. STOCKMANN: I knew it. Now look, I will simply not attend a dinner in my honor.

HOVSTAD [*getting up*]: Doctor, I think it's time we—

Mrs. Stockmann enters.

MRS. STOCKMANN: I thought so. Thomas, I want you home. Now come. I want you to talk to Petra.

DR. STOCKMANN: What happened? What are you doing here?

HOVSTAD: Something wrong, Mrs. Stockmann?

MRS. STOCKMANN [*leveling a look of accusation at Hovstad*]: Doctor Stockmann is the father of three children, Mr. Hovstad.

DR. STOCKMANN: Now look, dear, everybody knows that. What's the—

MRS. STOCKMANN [*restraining an outburst at her husband*]: Nobody would *believe* it from the way you're dragging us into this disaster!

DR. STOCKMANN: What disaster?

MRS. STOCKMANN [*to Hovstad*]: He treated you like a son, now you make a fool of him?

HOVSTAD: *I'm* not making a—

DR. STOCKMANN: Catherine! (*He indicates Hovstad.*) How can you accuse—

MRS. STOCKMANN [*to Hovstad*]: He'll lose his job at the springs, do you realize that? You print the article, and they'll grind him up like a piece of flesh!

DR. STOCKMANN: Catherine, you're embarrassing me! I beg your pardon, gentlemen . . .

MRS. STOCKMANN: Mr. Hovstad, what are you up to?

DR. STOCKMANN: I won't have you jumping at Hovstad, Catherine!

MRS. STOCKMANN: I want you home! This man is not your friend!

DR. STOCKMANN: He is my friend! Any man who shares my risk is my friend! You simply don't understand that as soon as this breaks everybody in this town is going to come out in the streets and drive that gang of—[*He picks up the Mayor's cane from the table, notices what it is, and stops. He looks from it to Hovstad and Aslaksen.*] What's this? [*They don't reply. Now he notices the hat on the desk and picks it up with the tip of the cane. He looks at them again. He is angry, incredulous.*] What the hell is he doing here?

ASLAKSEN: All right, Doctor, now let's be calm and—

DR. STOCKMANN [*starting to move*]: Where is he? What'd he do, talk you out of it? Hovstad! [*Hovstad remains immobile.*] He won't get away with it! Where'd you hide him? [*He opens the door at the left.*]

ASLAKSEN: Be careful, Doctor!

Peter Stockmann enters with Billing through the door Dr. Stockmann opened. Peter Stockmann tries to hide his embarrassment.

DR. STOCKMANN: Well, Peter, poisoning the water was not enough! You're working on the press now, eh? [*He crosses to the entrance door.*]

PETER STOCKMANN: My hat, please. And my stick. [*Dr. Stockmann puts on the Mayor's hat.*] Now what's *this* nonsense! Take that off, that's official insignia!

DR. STOCKMANN: I just wanted you to realize, Peter, [*he takes off the hat and looks at it*] that anyone may wear this hat in a democracy, and that a free citizen is not afraid to touch it. [*He hands him the hat.*] And as for the baton of command, Your Honor, it can pass from hand to hand. [*He hands the cane to Peter Stockmann.*] So don't gloat yet. The people haven't spoken. [*He turns to Hovstad and Aslaksen.*] And I have the people because I have the truth, my friends!

ASLAKSEN: Doctor, we're not scientists. We can't judge whether your article is really true.

DR. STOCKMANN: Then print it under my name. Let *me* defend it!

HOVSTAD: I'm not printing it. I'm not going to sacrifice this newspaper. When the whole story gets out the public is not going to stand for any changes in the springs.

ASLAKSEN: His Honor just told us, Doctor—you see, there will have to be a new tax—

DR. STOCKMANN: Ahhhhh! Yes. I see. That's why you're not scientists suddenly and can't decide if I'm telling the truth. Well. So!

HOVSTAD: Don't take that attitude. The point is—

DR. STOCKMANN: The point, the point, oh, the point is going to fly through this town like an arrow, and I am going to fire it! *To Aslaksen:* Will you print this article as a pamphlet? I'll pay for it.

ASLAKSEN: I'm not going to ruin this paper and this town. Doctor, for the sake of your family—

MRS. STOCKMANN: You can leave his family out of this, Mr. Aslaksen. God help me, I think you people are horrible!

DR. STOCKMANN: My article, if you don't mind.

ASLAKSEN [*giving it to him*]:   Doctor, you won't get it printed in this town.

PETER STOCKMANN: Can't you forget it? [*He indicates Hovstad and Aslaksen.*] Can't you see now that everybody—

DR. STOCKMANN: Your Honor, I can't forget it, and you will never forget it as long as you live. I am going to call a mass meeting, and I—

PETER STOCKMANN: And who is going to rent you a hall?

DR. STOCKMANN: Then I will take a drum and go from street to street, proclaiming that the springs are befouled and poison is rotting the body politic! [*He starts for the door.*]

PETER STOCKMANN: And I believe you really are that mad!

DR. STOCKMANN: Mad? Oh, my brother, you haven't even heard me raise my voice yet. Catherine? [*He holds out his hand, she gives him her elbow. They go stiffly out.*]

Peter Stockmann looks regretfully toward the exit, then takes out his manuscript and hands it to Hovstad, who in turn gives it to Billing, who hands it to Aslaksen, who takes it and exits. Peter Stockmann puts his hat on and moves toward the door. Blackout. The curtain falls.

Act II

Scene II. A room in Captain Horster's house

A room in Captain Horster's house. The room is bare, as though unused for a long time. A large doorway is at the left, two shuttered windows at the back, and another door at the right. Upstage right, packing cases have been set together, forming a platform, on which are a chair and a small table.

There are two chairs next to the platform at the right. One chair stands downstage left.

The room is angled, thus making possible the illusion of a large crowd off in the wing to the left. The platform faces the audience at an angle, thus giving the speakers the chance to speak straight out front and creating the illusion of a large crowd by addressing "people" in the audience.

As the curtain rises the room is empty. Captain Horster enters, carrying a pitcher of water, a glass, and a bell. He is putting these on the table when Billing enters. A crowd is heard talking outside in the street.

BILLING: Captain Horster?

HORSTER [*turning*]: Oh, come in. I don't have enough chairs for a lot of people so I decided not to have chairs at all.

BILLING: My name is Billing. Don't you remember, at the Doctor's house?

HORSTER [*a little coldly*]: Oh, yes, sure. I've been so busy I didn't recognize you. [*He goes to a window and looks out.*] Why don't those people come inside?

BILLING: I don't know, I guess they're waiting for the Mayor or somebody important so they can be sure it's respectable in here. I wanted to ask you a question before it begins, Captain. Why are you lending your house for this? I never heard of you connected with anything political.

HORSTER [*standing still*]: I'll answer that. I travel most of the year and—did you ever travel?

BILLING: Not abroad, no.

HORSTER: Well, I've been in a lot of places where people aren't allowed to say unpopular things. Did you know that?

BILLING: Sure, I've read about it.

HORSTER [*simply*]: Well, I don't like it. [*He starts to go out.*]

BILLING: One more question. What's your opinion about the Doctor's proposition to rebuild the springs?

HORSTER [*turning, thinks, then*]: Don't understand a thing about it.

Three citizens enter.

HORSTER: Come in, come in. I don't have enough chairs so you'll just have to stand. [*He goes out.*]

FIRST CITIZEN: Try the horn.

SECOND CITIZEN: No, let him start to talk first.

THIRD CITIZEN [*a big beef of a man, takes out a horn*]: Wait'll they hear this! I could blow your mustache off with this!

Horster returns. He sees the horn and stops abruptly.

HORSTER: I don't want any roughhouse, you hear me?

Mrs. Stockmann and Petra enter.

HORSTER: Come in. I've got chairs just for you.

MRS. STOCKMANN [*nervously*]: There's quite a crowd on the sidewalk. Why don't they come in?

HORSTER: I suppose they're waiting for the Mayor.

PETRA: Are all those people on his side?

HORSTER: Who knows? People are bashful, and it's so unusual to come to a meeting like this, I suppose they—

BILLING [*going over to this group*]: Good evening, ladies. *They simply look at him.* I don't blame you for not speaking. I just wanted to say I don't think this is going to be a place for ladies tonight.

MRS. STOCKMANN: I don't remember asking your advice, Mr. Billing.

BILLING: I'm not as bad as you think, Mrs. Stockmann.

MRS. STOCKMANN: Then why did you print the Mayor's statement and not a word about my husband's report? Nobody's had a chance to find out what he really stands for. Why, everybody on the street there is against him already!

BILLING: If we printed his report it only would have hurt your husband.

MRS. STOCKMANN: Mr. Billing, I've never said this to anyone in my life, but I think you're a liar.

Suddenly the third citizen lets out a blast on his horn. The women jump, Billing and Horster turn around quickly.

HORSTER: You do that once more and I'll throw you out of here!

Peter Stockmann enters. Behind him comes the crowd. He pretends to be unconnected with them. He goes straight to Mrs. Stockmann, bows.

PETER STOCKMANN: Catherine? Petra?

PETRA: Good evening.

PETER STOCKMANN: Why so coldly? He wanted a meeting and he's got it. [*To Horster.*] Isn't he here?

HORSTER: The Doctor is going around town to be sure there's a good attendance.

PETER STOCKMANN: Fair enough. By the way, Petra, did you paint that poster? The one somebody stuck on the Town Hall?

PETRA: If you can call it painting, yes.

PETER STOCKMANN: You know I could arrest you? It's against the law to deface the Town Hall.

PETRA: Well, here I am. [*She holds out her hands for the handcuffs.*]

MRS. STOCKMANN [*taking it seriously*]: If you arrest her, Peter, I'll never speak to you!

PETER STOCKMANN [*laughing*]: Catherine, you have no sense of humor!

He crosses and sits down at the left. They sit right. A drunk comes out of the crowd.

DRUNK: Say, Billy, who's runnin'? Who's the candidate?

HORSTER: You're drunk, Mister, now get out of here!

DRUNK: There's no law says a man who's drunk can't vote!

HORSTER [*pushing the drunk toward the door as the crowd laughs*]: Get out of here! Get out!

DRUNK: I wanna vote! I got a right to vote!

Aslaksen enters hurriedly, sees Peter Stockmann, and rushes to him.

ASLAKSEN: Your Honor . . . [*He points to the door.*] He's . . .

DR. STOCKMANN [*offstage*]: Right this way, gentlemen! In you go, come on, fellows!

Hovstad enters, glances at Peter Stockmann and Aslaksen, then at Dr. Stockmann and another crowd behind him, who enter.

DR. STOCKMANN: Sorry, no chairs, gentlemen, but we couldn't get a hall, y'know, so just relax. It won't take long anyway. [*He goes to the platform, sees Peter Stockmann.*] Glad you're here, Peter!

PETER STOCKMANN: Wouldn't miss it for the world.

DR. STOCKMANN: How do you feel, Catherine?

MRS. STOCKMANN (*nervously*): Just promise me, don't lose your temper . . .

HORSTER [*seeing the drunk pop in through the door*]: Did I tell you to get out of here!

DRUNK: Look, if you ain't votin', what the hell's going on here? [*Horster starts after him.*] Don't push!

PETER STOCKMANN [to the drunk]: I order you to get out of here and stay out!

DRUNK: I don't like the tone of your voice! And if you don't watch your step I'm gonna tell the Mayor right now, and he'll throw yiz all in the jug! [To all]: What're you, a revolution here?

The crowd bursts out laughing; the drunk laughs with them, and they push him out. Dr. Stockmann mounts the platform.

DR. STOCKMANN [quieting the crowd]: All right, gentlemen, we might as well begin. Quiet down, please. [He clears his throat.] The issue is very simple—

ASLAKSEN: We haven't elected a chairman, Doctor.

DR. STOCKMANN: I'm sorry, Mr. Aslaksen, this isn't a meeting. I advertised a lecture and I—

A CITIZEN: I came to a meeting, Doctor. There's got to be some kind of control here.

DR. STOCKMANN: What do you mean, control? What is there to control?

SECOND CITIZEN: Sure, let him speak, this is no meeting!

THIRD CITIZEN: Your Honor, why don't you take charge of this—

DR. STOCKMANN: Just a minute now!

THIRD CITIZEN: Somebody responsible has got to take charge. There's a big difference of opinion here—

DR. STOCKMANN: What makes you so sure? You don't even know yet what I'm going to say.

THIRD CITIZEN: I've got a pretty good idea what you're going to say, and I don't like it! If a man doesn't like it here, let him go where it suits him better. We don't want any troublemakers here!

There is assent from much of the crowd. Dr. Stockmann looks at them with new surprise.

DR. STOCKMANN: Now look, friend, you don't know anything about me—

FOURTH CITIZEN: We know plenty about you, Stockmann!

DR. STOCKMANN: From what? From the newspapers? How do you know I don't like this town? [He picks up his manuscript.] I'm here to save the life of this town!

PETER STOCKMANN [quickly]: Now just a minute, Doctor, I think the democratic thing to do is to elect a chairman.

FIFTH CITIZEN: I nominate the Mayor!

Seconds are heard.

PETER STOCKMANN: No, no, no! That wouldn't be fair. We want a neutral person. I suggest Mr. Aslaksen—

SECOND CITIZEN: I came to a lecture, I didn't—

THIRD CITIZEN [*to second citizen*]: What're you afraid of, a fair fight? [*To the Mayor*]: Second Mr. Aslaksen!

The crowd assents.

DR. STOCKMANN: All right, if that's your pleasure. I just want to remind you that the reason I called this meeting was that I have a very important message for you people and I couldn't get it into the press, and nobody would rent me a hall. [*To Peter Stockmann:*] I just hope I'll be given time to speak here. Mr. Aslaksen?

As Aslaksen mounts the platform and Dr. Stockmann steps down, Kiil enters, looks shrewdly around.

ASLAKSEN: I just have one word before we start. Whatever is said tonight, please remember, the highest civic virtue is moderation. [*He can't help turning to Dr. Stockmann, then back to the crowd.*] Now if anybody wants to speak—

The drunk enters suddenly.

DRUNK, *pointing at Aslaksen:* I heard that! Since when you allowed to electioneer at the poles? [*Citizens push him toward the door amid laughter.*] I'm gonna report this to the Mayor, goddammit! [*They push him out and close the door.*]

ASLAKSEN: Quiet, please, quiet. Does anybody want the floor?

Dr. Stockmann starts to come forward, raising his hand, but Peter Stockmann also has his hand raised.

PETER STOCKMANN: Mr. Chairman!

ASLAKSEN [*quickly recognizing Peter Stockmann*]: His Honor the Mayor will address the meeting.

Dr. Stockmann stops, looks at Peter Stockmann, and, suppressing a remark, returns to his place. The Mayor mounts the platform.

PETER STOCKMANN: Gentlemen, there's no reason to take very long to settle this tonight and return to our ordinary, calm, and peaceful life. Here's the issue: Doctor Stockmann, my brother—and believe me, it is not easy to say this—has decided to destroy Kirsten Springs, our Health Institute—

DR. STOCKMANN: Peter!

ASLAKSEN [*ringing his bell*]: Let the Mayor continue, please. There mustn't be any interruptions.

PETER STOCKMANN: He has a long and very involved way of going about it, but that's the brunt of it, believe me.

THIRD CITIZEN: Then what're we wasting time for? Run him out of town!

Others join in the cry.

PETER STOCKMANN: Now wait a minute. I want no violence here. I want you to understand his motives. He is a man, always has been, who is never happy unless he is badgering authority, ridiculing authority, destroying authority. He wants to attack the springs so he can prove that the administration blundered in the construction.

DR. STOCKMANN [*to Aslaksen*]: May I speak? I—

ASLAKSEN: The Mayor's not finished.

PETER STOCKMANN: Thank you. Now there are a number of people here who seem to feel that the Doctor has a right to say anything he pleases. After all, we are a democratic country. Now, God knows, in ordinary times I'd agree a hundred per cent with anybody's right to say anything. But these are not ordinary times. Nations have crises, and so do towns. There are ruins of nations, and there are ruins of towns all over the world, and they were wrecked by people who, in the guise of reform, and pleading for justice, and so on, broke down all authority and left only revolution and chaos.

DR. STOCKMANN: What the hell are you talking about!

ASLAKSEN: I'll have to insist, Doctor—

DR. STOCKMANN: I called a lecture! I didn't invite him to attack me. He's got the press and every hall in town to attack me, and I've got nothing but this room tonight!

ASLAKSEN: I don't think you're making a very good impression, Doctor.

Assenting laughter and catcalls. Again Dr. Stockmann is taken aback by this reaction.

ASLAKSEN: Please continue, Your Honor.

PETER STOCKMANN: Now this is our crisis. We know what this town was without our Institute. We could barely afford to keep the streets in condition. It was a dead, third-rate hamlet. Today we're just on the verge of becoming internationally known as a resort. I predict that within five years the income of every man in this room will be immensely greater. I predict that our schools will be bigger and better. And in time this town will be crowded with fine carriages; great homes will be built here; first-class stores will open all along Main Street. I predict that if we are not defamed and maliciously attacked we will someday be one of the richest and most beautiful resort towns in the world. There are your choices. Now all you've got to do is ask yourselves a simple question: Has any one of us the right, the "democratic right," as they like to call it, to pick at minor flaws in the springs, to exaggerate the most picayune faults? [*Cries of No, No!*] And to attempt to publish these defamations for the whole world to see? We live or die on what the outside world thinks of us. I believe there is a line that must be drawn, and if a man decides to cross that line, we the people must finally take him by the collar and declare, "You cannot say that!"

There is an uproar of assent. Aslaksen rings the bell.

PETER STOCKMANN [*continuing*]: All right then. I think we all understand each other. Mr. Aslaksen, I move that Doctor Stockmann be prohibited from reading his report at this meeting! [*He goes back to his chair, which meanwhile Kiil has occupied.*]

Aslaksen rings the bell to quiet the enthusiasm. Dr. Stockmann is jumping to get up on the platform, the report in his hand.

ASLAKSEN: Quiet, please. Please now. I think we can proceed to the vote.

DR. STOCKMANN: Well, aren't you going to let me speak at all?

ASLAKSEN: Doctor, we are just about to vote on that question.

DR. STOCKMANN: But damn it, man, I've got a right to—

PETRA, *standing up:* Point of order, Father!

DR. STOCKMANN [*picking up the cue*]: Yes, point of order!

ASLAKSEN [*turning to him now*]: Yes, Doctor.

Dr. Stockmann, at a loss, turns to Petra for further instructions.

PETRA: You want to discuss the motion.

DR. STOCKMANN: That's right, damn it, I want to discuss the motion!

ASLAKSEN: Ah . . . [*He glances at Peter Stockmann.*] All right, go ahead.

DR. STOCKMANN, *to the crowd*:   Now, listen. [*He points at Peter Stockmann.*] He talks and he talks and he talks, but not a word about the facts! [*He holds up the manuscript.*]

THIRD CITIZEN: We don't want to hear any more about the water!

FOURTH CITIZEN: You're just trying to blow up everything!

DR. STOCKMANN: Well, judge for yourselves, let me read—

Cries of No, No, No! The man with the horn blows it. Aslaksen rings the bell. Dr. Stockmann is utterly shaken. Astonished, he looks at the maddened faces. He lowers the hand holding the manuscript and steps back, defeated.

ASLAKSEN: Please, please now, quiet. We can't have this uproar! [*Quiet returns.*] I think, Doctor, that the majority wants to take the vote before you start to speak. If they so will, you can speak. Otherwise, majority rules. You won't deny that.

DR. STOCKMANN   [*turns, tosses the manuscript on the floor, turns back to Aslaksen*]:   Don't bother voting. I understand everything now. Can I have a few minutes—

PETER STOCKMANN: Mr. Chairman!

DR. STOCKMANN [*to his brother*]:   I won't mention the Institute. I have a new discovery that's a thousand times more important than all the Institutes in the world. [*To Aslaksen*]:   May I have the platform.

ASLAKSEN [*to the crowd*]:   I don't see how we can deny him that, as long as he confines himself to—

DR. STOCKMANN: The springs are not the subject. [*He mounts the platform, looks at the crowd.*] Before I go into my subject I want to congratulate the liberals and radicals among us, like Mr. Hovstad—

HOVSTAD: What do you mean, radical! Where's your evidence to call me a radical!

DR. STOCKMANN: You've got me there. There isn't any evidence. I guess there never really was. I just wanted to congratulate you on your self-control tonight—you who have fought in every parlor for the principle of free speech these many years.

HOVSTAD: I believe in democracy. When my readers are overwhelmingly against something, I'm not going to impose my will on the majority.

DR. STOCKMANN: You have begun my remarks, Mr. Hovstad. [*He turns to the crowd.*] Gentlemen, Mrs. Stockmann, Miss Stockmann. Tonight

I was struck by a sudden flash of light, a discovery second to none. But before I tell it to you—a little story. I put in a good many years in the north of our country. Up there the rulers of the world are the great seal and the gigantic squadrons of duck. Man lives on ice, huddled together in little piles of stones. His whole life consists of grubbing for food. Nothing more. He can barely speak his own language. And it came to me one day that it was romantic and sentimental for a man of my education to be tending these people. They had not yet reached the stage where they needed a doctor. If the truth were to be told, a veterinary would be more in order.

BILLING: Is that the way you refer to decent hard-working people!

DR. STOCKMANN: I expected that, my friend, but don't think you can fog up my brain with that magic word—the People! Not any more! Just because there is a mass of organisms with the human shape, they do not automatically become a People. That honor has to be earned! Nor does one automatically become a Man by having human shape, and living in a house, and feeding one's face—and agreeing with one's neighbors. That name *also* has to be earned. Now, when I came to my conclusions about the springs—

PETER STOCKMANN: You have no right to—

DR. STOCKMANN: That's a picayune thing, to catch me on a word, Peter. I am not going into the springs. *To the crowd:* When I became convinced of my theory about the water, the authorities moved in at once, and I said to myself, I will fight them to the death, because—

THIRD CITIZEN: What're you trying to do, make a revolution here? He's a revolutionist!

DR. STOCKMANN: Let me finish. I thought to myself: The majority, I have the majority! And let me tell you, friends, it was a grand feeling. Because that's the reason I came back to this place of my birth. I wanted to give my education to this town. I loved it so, I spent months without pay or encouragement and dreamed up the whole project of the springs. And why? Not as my brother says, so that fine carriages could crowd our streets, but so that we might cure the sick, so that we might meet people from all over the world and learn from them, and become broader and more civilized. In other words, more like Men, more like A People.

A CITIZEN: You don't like anything about this town, do you?

ANOTHER CITIZEN: Admit it, you're a revolutionist, aren't you? Admit it!

DR. STOCKMANN: I don't admit it! I proclaim it now! I am a revolutionist! I am in revolt against the age-old lie that the majority is always right!

HOVSTAD: He's an aristocrat all of a sudden!

DR. STOCKMANN: And more! I tell you now that the majority is always wrong, and in this way!

PETER STOCKMANN: Have you lost your mind! Stop talking before—

DR. STOCKMANN: Was the majority right when they stood by while Jesus was crucified? [*Silence.*] Was the majority right when they refused to believe that the earth moved around the sun and let Galileo be driven to his knees like a dog? It takes fifty years for the majority to be right. The majority is never right until it *does* right.

HOVSTAD: I want to state right now, that although I've been this man's friend, and I've eaten at his table many times, I now cut myself off from him absolutely.

DR. STOCKMANN: Answer me this! Please, one more moment! A platoon of soldiers is walking down a road toward the enemy. Every one of them is convinced he is on the right road, the safe road. But two miles ahead stands one lonely man, the outpost. He sees that this road is dangerous, that his comrades are walking into a trap. He runs back, he finds the platoon. Isn't it clear that this man must have the right to warn the majority, to argue with the majority, to fight with the majority if he believes he has the truth? Before many can know something, *one* must know it! [*His passion has silenced the crowd.*] It's always the same. Rights are sacred until it hurts for somebody to use them. I beg you now—I realize the cost is great, the inconvenience is great, the risk is great that other towns will get the jump on us while we're rebuilding—

PETER STOCKMANN: Aslaksen, he's not allowed to—

DR. STOCKMANN: Let me prove it to you! The water is poisoned!

THIRD CITIZEN [*steps up on the platform, waves his fist in Dr. Stockmann's face*]: One more word about poison and I'm gonna take you outside!

The crowd is roaring; some try to charge the platform. The horn is blowing. Aslaksen rings his bell. Peter Stockmann steps forward, raising his hands. Kiil quietly exits.

PETER STOCKMANN: That's enough. Now stop it! Quiet! There is not going to be any violence here! [*There is silence. He turns to Dr. Stockmann*] Doctor, come down and give Mr. Aslaksen the platform.

DR. STOCKMANN [*staring down at the crowd with new eyes*]: I'm not through yet.

PETER STOCKMANN: Come down or I will not be responsible for what happens.

MRS. STOCKMANN: I'd like to go home. Come on, Tom.

PETER STOCKMANN: I move the chairman order the speaker to leave the platform.

VOICES: Sit down! Get off that platform!

DR. STOCKMANN: All right. Then I'll take this to out-of-town newspapers until the whole country is warned!

PETER STOCKMANN: You wouldn't dare!

HOVSTAD: You're trying to ruin this town—that's all; trying to ruin it.

DR. STOCKMANN: You're trying to build a town on a morality so rotten that it will infect the country and the world! If the only way you can prosper is this murder of freedom and truth, then I say with all my heart, "Let it be destroyed! Let the people perish!"

He leaves the platform.

FIRST CITIZEN [*to the Mayor*]: Arrest him! Arrest him!

SECOND CITIZEN: He's a traitor!

Cries of "Enemy! Traitor! Revolution!"

ASLAKSEN [*ringing for quiet*]: I would like to submit the following resolution: The people assembled here tonight, decent and patriotic citizens, in defense of their town and their country, declare that Doctor Stockmann, medical officer of Kirsten Springs, is an enemy of the people and of his community.

An uproar of assent starts.

MRS. STOCKMANN [*getting up*]: That's not true! He loves this town!

DR. STOCKMANN: You damned fools, you fools!

The Doctor and his family are all standing together, at the right, in a close group.

ASLAKSEN [*shouting over the din*]: Is there anyone against this motion! Anyone against!

HORSTER [*raising his hand*]: I am.

ASLAKSEN: One? [*He looks around.*]

DRUNK [*who has returned, raising his hand*]: Me too! You can't do without a doctor! Anybody'll . . . tell you . . .

ASLAKSEN: Anyone else? With all votes against two, this assembly formally declares Doctor Thomas Stockmann to be the people's enemy. In the future, all dealings with him by decent, patriotic citizens will be on that basis. The meeting is adjourned.

Shouts and applause. People start leaving. Dr. Stockmann goes over to Horster.

DR. STOCKMANN: Captain, do you have room for us on your ship to America?

HORSTER: Any time you say, Doctor.

DR. STOCKMANN: Catherine? Petra?

The three start for the door, but a gantlet has formed, dangerous and silent, except for . . .

THIRD CITIZEN: You'd better get aboard soon, Doctor!

MRS. STOCKMANN: Let's go out the back door.

HORSTER: Right this way.

DR. STOCKMANN: No, no. No back doors. *To the crowd:* I don't want to mislead anybody—the enemy of the people is not finished in this town—not quite yet. And if anybody thinks—

The horn blasts, cutting him off. The crowd starts yelling hysterically: "Enemy! Traitor! Throw him in the river! Come on, throw him in the river! Enemy! Enemy! Enemy!" The Stockmanns, erect, move out through the crowd, with Horster. Some of the crowd follow them out, yelling.

Downstage, watching, are Peter Stockmann, Billing, Aslaksen, and Hovstad. The stage is throbbing with the chant, "Enemy, Enemy, Enemy!" as the curtain falls.

Act III

Dr. Stockmann's living room the following morning. The windows are broken. There is great disorder. As the curtain rises, Dr. Stockmann enters, a robe over shirt and trousers—it's cold in the house. He picks up a stone from the floor, lays it on the table.

DR. STOCKMANN: Catherine! Tell what's-her-name there are still some rocks to pick up in here.

MRS. STOCKMANN [*from inside*]: She's not finished sweeping up the glass.

As Dr. Stockmann bends down to get at another stone under a chair a rock comes through one of the last remaining panes. He rushes to the window, looks out. Mrs. Stockmann rushes in.

MRS. STOCKMANN [*frightened*]: You all right?

DR. STOCKMANN [*looking out*]: A little boy. Look at him run! [*He picks up the stone.*] How fast the poison spreads—even to the children!

MRS. STOCKMANN [*looking out the window*]: It's hard to believe this is the same town.

DR. STOCKMANN [*adding this rock to the pile on the table*]: I'm going to keep these like sacred relics. I'll put them in my will. I want the boys to have them in their homes to look at every day. [*He shudders.*] Cold in here. Why hasn't what's-her-name got the glazier here?

MRS. STOCKMANN: She's getting him . . .

DR. STOCKMANN: She's been getting him for two hours! We'll freeze to death in here.

MRS. STOCKMANN [*unwillingly*]: He won't come here, Tom.

DR. STOCKMANN [*stops moving*]: No! The glazier's afraid to fix my windows?

MRS. STOCKMANN: You don't realize—people don't like to be pointed out. He's got neighbors, I suppose, and—[*She hears something.*] Is that someone at the door, Randine?

She goes to the front door. He continues picking up stones. She comes back.

MRS. STOCKMANN: Letter for you.

DR. STOCKMANN [*taking and opening it*]: What's this now?

MRS. STOCKMANN [*continuing his pick-up for him*]: I don't know how we're going to do any shopping with everybody ready to bite my head off and—

DR. STOCKMANN: Well, what do you know? We're evicted.

MRS. STOCKMANN: Oh, no!

DR. STOCKMANN: He hates to do it, but with public opinion what it is . . .

MRS. STOCKMANN [*frightened*]: Maybe we shouldn't have let the boys go to school today.

DR. STOCKMANN: Now don't get all frazzled again.

MRS. STOCKMANN: But the landlord is such a nice man. If he's got to throw us out, the town must be ready to murder us!

DR. STOCKMANN: Just calm down, will you? We'll go to America, and the whole thing'll be like a dream.

MRS. STOCKMANN: But I don't want to go to America— [*She notices his pants.*] When did this get torn?

DR. STOCKMANN [*examining the tear*]: Must've been last night.

MRS. STOCKMANN: Your best pants!

DR. STOCKMANN: Well, it just shows you, that's all—when a man goes out to fight for the truth he should never wear his best pants. [*He calms her*]. Stop worrying, will you? You'll sew them up, and in no time at all we'll be three thousand miles away.

MRS. STOCKMANN: But how do you know it'll be any different there?

DR. STOCKMANN: I don't know. It just seems to me, in a big country like that, the spirit must be bigger. Still, I suppose they must have the solid majority there too. I don't know, at least there must be more room to hide there.

MRS. STOCKMANN: Think about it more, will you? I'd hate to go half around the world and find out we're in the same place.

DR. STOCKMANN: You know, Catherine, I don't think I'm ever going to forget the face of that crowd last night.

MRS. STOCKMANN: Don't think about it.

DR. STOCKMANN: Some of them had their teeth bared, like animals in a pack. And who leads them? Men who call themselves liberals! Radicals! [*She starts looking around at the furniture, figuring.*] The crowd lets out one roar, and where are they, my liberal friends? I bet if I walked down the street now not one of them would admit he ever met me! Are you listening to me?

MRS. STOCKMANN: I was just wondering what we'll ever do with this furniture if we go to America.

DR. STOCKMANN: Don't you ever listen when I talk, dear?

MRS. STOCKMANN: Why must I listen? I know you're right.

Petra enters.

MRS. STOCKMANN: Petra! Why aren't you in school?

DR. STOCKMANN: What's the matter?

PETRA [*with deep emotion, looks at Dr. Stockmann, goes up and kisses him*]: I'm fired.

MRS. STOCKMANN: They wouldn't!

PETRA: As of two weeks from now. But I couldn't bear to stay there.

DR. STOCKMANN [*shocked*]: Mrs. Busk fired you?

MRS. STOCKMANN: Who'd ever imagine she could do such a thing!

PETRA: It hurt her. I could see it, because we've always agreed so about things. But she didn't dare do anything else.

DR. STOCKMANN: The glazier doesn't dare fix the windows, the landlord doesn't dare let us stay on—

PETRA: The landlord!

DR. STOCKMANN: Evicted, darling! Oh, God, on the wreckage of all the civilizations in the world there ought to be a big sign: "They Didn't Dare!"

PETRA: I really can't blame her, Father. She showed me three letters she got this morning—

DR. STOCKMANN: From whom?

PETRA: They weren't signed.

DR. STOCKMANN: Oh, naturally. The big patriots with their anonymous indignation, scrawling out the darkness of their minds onto dirty little slips of paper—that's morality, and *I'm* the traitor! What did the letters say?

PETRA: Well, one of them was from somebody who said that he'd heard at the club that somebody who visits this house said that I had radical opinions about certain things.

DR. STOCKMANN: Oh, wonderful! Somebody heard that somebody heard that she heard, that he heard . . . ! Catherine, pack as soon as you can. I feel as though vermin were crawling all over me.

Horster enters.

HORSTER: Good morning.

DR. STOCKMANN: Captain! You're just the man I want to see.

HORSTER: I thought I'd see how you all were.

MRS. STOCKMANN: That's awfully nice of you, Captain, and I want to thank you for seeing us through the crowd last night.

PETRA: Did you get home all right? We hated to leave you alone with that mob.

HORSTER: Oh, nothing to it. In a storm there's just one thing to remember: it will pass.

DR. STOCKMANN: Unless it kills you.

HORSTER: You mustn't let yourself get too bitter.

DR. STOCKMANN: I'm trying, I'm trying. But I don't guarantee how I'll feel when I try to walk down the street with "Traitor" branded on my forehead.

MRS. STOCKMANN: Don't think about it.

HORSTER: Ah, what's a word?

DR. STOCKMANN: A word can be like a needle sticking in your heart, Captain. It can dig and corrode like an acid, until you become what they want you to be—really an enemy of the people.

HORSTER: You mustn't ever let that happen, Doctor.

DR. STOCKMANN: Frankly, I don't give a damn any more. Let summer come, let an epidemic break out, then they'll know whom they drove into exile. When are you sailing?

PETRA: You really decided to go, Father?

DR. STOCKMANN: Absolutely. When do you sail, Captain?

HORSTER: That's really what I came to talk to you about.

DR. STOCKMANN: Why? Something happen to the ship?

MRS. STOCKMANN [*happily, to Dr. Stockmann*]: You see! We can't go!

HORSTER: No, the ship will sail. But I won't be aboard.

DR. STOCKMANN: No!

PETRA: You fired too? 'Cause I was this morning.

MRS. STOCKMANN: Oh, Captain, you shouldn't have given us your house.

HORSTER: Oh, I'll get another ship. It's just that the owner, Mr. Vik, happens to belong to the same party as the Mayor, and I suppose when you belong to a party, and the party takes a certain position . . . Because Mr. Vik himself is a very decent man.

DR. STOCKMANN: Oh, they're all decent men!

HORSTER: No, really, he's not like the others.

DR. STOCKMANN: He doesn't have to be. A party is like a sausage grinder: it mashes up clearheads, longheads, fatheads, block-heads—and what comes out? Meatheads!

There is a knock on the hall door. Petra goes to answer.

MRS. STOCKMANN: Maybe that's the glazier!

DR. STOCKMANN: Imagine, Captain! [*He points to the window.*] Refused to come all morning!

Peter Stockmann enters, his hat in his hand. Silence.

PETER STOCKMANN: If you're busy . . .

DR. STOCKMANN: Just picking up broken glass. Come in, Peter. What can I do for you this fine, brisk morning? [*He demonstratively pulls his robe tighter around his throat.*]

MRS. STOCKMANN: Come inside, won't you, Captain?

HORSTER: Yes, I'd like to finish our talk, Doctor.

DR. STOCKMANN: Be with you in a minute, Captain.

Horster follows Petra and Catherine out through the dining-room doorway. Peter Stockmann says nothing, looking at the damage.

DR. STOCKMANN: Keep your hat on if you like, it's a little drafty in here today.

PETER STOCKMANN: Thanks, I believe I will. *He puts his hat on.* I think I caught cold last night—that house was freezing.

DR. STOCKMANN: I thought it was kind of warm—suffocating, as a matter of fact. What do you want?

PETER STOCKMANN: May I sit down? *He indicates a chair near the window.*

DR. STOCKMANN: Not there. A piece of the solid majority is liable to open your skull. Here.

They sit on the couch. Peter Stockmann takes out a large envelope.

DR. STOCKMANN: Now don't tell me.

PETER STOCKMANN: Yes. [*He hands the Doctor the envelope.*]

DR. STOCKMANN: I'm fired.

PETER STOCKMANN: The Board met this morning. There was nothing else to do, considering the state of public opinion.

DR. STOCKMANN [*after a pause*]: You look scared, Peter.

PETER STOCKMANN: I—I haven't completely forgotten that you're still my brother.

DR. STOCKMANN: I doubt that.

PETER STOCKMANN: You have no practice left in this town, Thomas.

DR. STOCKMANN: Oh, people always need a doctor.

PETER STOCKMANN: A petition is going from house to house. Everybody is signing it. A pledge not to call you any more. I don't think a single family will dare refuse to sign it.

DR. STOCKMANN: You started that, didn't you?

PETER STOCKMANN: No. As a matter of fact, I think it's all gone a little too far. I never wanted to see you ruined, Thomas. This will ruin you.

DR. STOCKMANN: No, it won't.

PETER STOCKMANN: For once in your life, will you act like a responsible man?

DR. STOCKMANN: Why don't you say it, Peter? You're afraid I'm going out of town to start publishing about the springs, aren't you?

PETER STOCKMANN: I don't deny that. Thomas, if you really have the good of the town at heart, you can accomplish everything without damaging anybody, including yourself.

DR. STOCKMANN: What's this now?

PETER STOCKMANN: Let me have a signed statement saying that in your zeal to help the town you went overboard and exaggerated. Put it any way you like, just so you calm anybody who might feel nervous about the water. If you'll give me that, you've got your job. And I give you my word, you can gradually make all the improvements you feel are necessary. Now, that gives you what you want . . .

DR. STOCKMANN: You're nervous, Peter.

PETER STOCKMANN [*nervously*]: I am not nervous!

DR. STOCKMANN: You expect me to remain in charge while people are being poisoned? [*He gets up*].

PETER STOCKMANN: In time you can make your changes.

DR. STOCKMANN: When, five years, ten years? You know your trouble, Peter? You just don't grasp—even now—that there are certain men you can't buy.

PETER STOCKMANN: I'm quite capable of understanding that. But you don't happen to be one of those men.

DR. STOCKMANN [*after a slight pause*]: What do you mean by that now?

PETER STOCKMANN: You know damned well what I mean by that. Morten Kiil is what I mean by that.

DR. STOCKMANN: Morten Kiil?

PETER STOCKMANN: Your father-in-law, Morten Kiil.

DR. STOCKMANN: I swear, Peter, one of us is out of his mind! What are you talking about?

PETER STOCKMANN: Now don't try to charm me with that professional innocence!

DR. STOCKMANN: What are you talking about?

PETER STOCKMANN: You don't know that your father-in-law has been running around all morning buying up stock in Kirsten Springs?

DR. STOCKMANN [*perplexed*]: Buying up stock?

PETER STOCKMANN: Buying up stock, every share he can lay his hands on!

DR. STOCKMANN: Well, I don't understand, Peter. What's that got to do with—

PETER STOCKMANN [*walking around agitatedly*]:   Oh, come now, come now, come now!

DR. STOCKMANN: I hate you when you do that! Don't just walk around gabbling "Come now, come now!" What the hell are you talking about?

PETER STOCKMANN: Very well, if you insist on being dense. A man wages a relentless campaign to destroy confidence in a corporation. He even goes so far as to call a mass meeting against it. The very next morning, when people are still in a state of shock about it all, his father-in-law runs all over town, picking up shares at half their value.

DR. STOCKMANN [*realizing, turns away*]:   My God!

PETER STOCKMANN: And you have the nerve to speak to me about principles!

DR. STOCKMANN: You mean you actually believe that I . . . ?

PETER STOCKMANN: I'm not interested in psychology! I believe what I see! And what I see is nothing but a man doing a dirty, filthy job for Morten Kiil. And let me tell you—by tonight every man in this town'll see the same thing!

DR. STOCKMANN: Peter, you, you . . .

PETER STOCKMANN: Now go to your desk and write me a statement denying everything you've been saying, or . . .

DR. STOCKMANN: Peter, you're a low creature!

PETER STOCKMANN: All right then, you'd better get this one straight, Thomas. If you're figuring on opening another attack from out of town, keep this in mind: the morning it's published I'll send out a subpoena for you and begin a prosecution for conspiracy. I've been trying to make you respectable all my life; now if you want to make the big jump there'll be nobody there to hold you back. Now do we understand each other?

DR. STOCKMANN: Oh, we do, Peter! [*Peter Stockmann starts for the door.*] Get the girl—what the hell is her name—scrub the floors, wash down the walls, a pestilence has been here!

Kiil enters. Peter Stockmann almost runs into him. Peter turns to his brother.

PETER STOCKMANN, *pointing to Kiil*:   Ha! [*He turns and goes out.*]

Kiil, humming quietly, goes to a chair.

DR. STOCKMANN: Morten! What have you done? What's the matter with you? Do you realize what this makes me look like?

Kiil has started taking some papers out of his pocket. Dr. Stockmann breaks off on seeing them. Kiil places them on the table.

DR. STOCKMANN: Is that—them?

KIIL: That's them, yes. Kirsten Springs shares. And very easy to get this morning.

DR. STOCKMANN: Morten, don't play with me—what is this all about?

KIIL: What are you so nervous about? Can't a man buy some stock without . . . ?

DR. STOCKMANN: I want an explanation, Morten.

KIIL [*Nodding*]: Thomas, they hated you last night—

DR. STOCKMANN: You don't have to tell me that.

KIIL: But they also believed you. They'd love to murder you, but they believe you. [*Slight pause*]. The way they say it, the pollution is coming down the river from Windmill Valley.

DR. STOCKMANN: That's exactly where it's coming from.

KIIL: Yes. And that's exactly where my tannery is.

Pause. Dr. Stockmann sits down slowly.

DR. STOCKMANN: Well, Morten, I never made a secret to you that the pollution was tannery waste.

KIIL: I'm not blaming you. It's my fault. I didn't take you seriously. But it's very serious now. Thomas, I got that tannery from my father; he got it from his father; and his father got it from my great-grandfather. I do not intend to allow my family's name to stand for the three generations of murdering angels who poisoned this town.

DR. STOCKMANN: I've waited a long time for this talk, Morten. I don't think you can stop that from happening.

KIIL: No, but you can.

DR. STOCKMANN: I?

KIIL [*nudging the shares*]: I've bought these shares because—

DR. STOCKMANN: Morten, you've thrown your money away. The springs are doomed.

KIIL: I never throw my money away, Thomas. These were bought with your money.

DR. STOCKMANN: My money? What . . . ?

KIIL: You've probably suspected that I might leave a little something for Catherine and the boys?

DR. STOCKMANN: Well, naturally, I'd hoped you'd . . .

KIIL [*touching the shares*]: I decided this morning to invest that money in some stock.

DR. STOCKMANN [*slowly getting up*]: You bought that junk with Catherine's money!

KIIL: People call me "badger," and that's an animal that roots out things, but it's also some kind of a pig, I understand. I've lived a clean man and I'm going to die clean. You're going to clean my name for me.

DR. STOCKMANN: Morten . . .

KIIL: Now I want to see if you really belong in a strait jacket.

DR. STOCKMANN: How could you do such a thing? What's the matter with you!

KIIL: Now don't get excited, it's very simple. If you should make another investigation of the water—

DR. STOCKMANN: I don't *need* another investigation, I—

KIIL: If you think it over and decide that you ought to change your opinion about the water—

DR. STOCKMANN: But the water is poisoned! It is poisoned!

KIIL: If you simply go on insisting the water is poisoned [*he holds up the shares*] with these in your house, then there's only one explanation for you—you're absolutely crazy. [*He puts the shares down on the table again.*]

DR. STOCKMANN: You're right! I'm mad! I'm insane!

KIIL [*with more force*]: You're stripping the skin off your family's back! Only a madman would do a thing like that!

DR. STOCKMANN: Morten, Morten, I'm a penniless man! Why didn't you tell me before you bought this junk?

KIIL: Because you would understand it better if I told you after. [*He goes up to Dr. Stockmann, holds him by the lapels. With terrific force, and the twinkle still in his eye*]: And, goddammit, I think you do understand it now, don't you? Millions of tons of water come down that river. How do you know the day you made your tests there wasn't something unusual about the water?

DR. STOCKMANN [*not looking at Kiil*]: Yes, but I . . .

KIIL: How do you know? Why couldn't those little animals have clotted up only the patch of water you souped out of the river? How do you know the rest of it wasn't pure?

DR. STOCKMANN: It's not probable. People were getting sick last summer . . .

KIIL: They were sick when they came here or they wouldn't have come!

DR. STOCKMANN [*breaking away*]: Not intestinal diseases, skin diseases . . .

KIIL [*following him*]: The only place anybody gets a bellyache is here! There are no carbuncles in Norway? Maybe the food was bad. Did you ever think of the food?

DR. STOCKMANN [*with the desire to agree with him*]: No, I didn't look into the food . . .

KIIL: Then what makes you so sure it's the water?

DR. STOCKMANN: Because I tested the water and—

KIIL [*taking hold of him again*]: Admit it! We're all alone here. You have some doubt.

DR. STOCKMANN: Well, there's always a possible . . .

KIIL: Then part of it's imaginary.

DR. STOCKMANN: Well, nothing is a hundred per cent on this earth, but—

KIIL: Then you have a perfect right to doubt the other way! You have a scientific right! And did you ever think of some disinfectant? I bet you never even thought of that.

DR. STOCKMANN: Not for a mass of water like that, you can't . . .

KIIL: Everything can be killed. That's science! Thomas, I never liked your brother either, you have a perfect right to hate him.

DR. STOCKMANN: I didn't do it because I hate my brother.

KIIL: Part of it, part of it, don't deny it! You admit there's some doubt in your mind about the water, you admit there may be ways to disinfect it, and yet you went after your brother as though these doubts didn't exist; as though the only way to cure the thing was to blow up the whole Institute! There's hatred in that, boy, don't forget it. [*He points to the shares*]. These can belong to you now, so be sure, be sure! Tear the hatred out of your heart, stand naked in front of yourself—*are you sure?*

DR. STOCKMANN: What right have you to gamble my family's future on the strength of my convictions?

KIIL: Aha! Then the convictions are not really that strong!

DR. STOCKMANN: I am ready to hang for my convictions! But no man has a right to make martyrs of others; my family is innocent.

Sell back those shares, give her what belongs to her. I'm a penniless man!

KIIL: Nobody is going to say Morten Kiil wrecked this town.

[*He gathers up the shares.*] You retract your convictions—or these go to my charity.

DR. STOCKMANN: Everything?

KIIL: There'll be a little something for Catherine, but not much. I want my good name. It's exceedingly important to me.

DR. STOCKMANN [*bitterly*]: And charity . . .

KIIL: Charity will do it, or you will do it. It's a serious thing to destroy a town.

DR. STOCKMANN: Morten, when I look at you, I swear to God I see the devil!

The door opens, and before we see who is there . . .

DR. STOCKMANN: You!

Aslaksen enters, holding up his hand defensively.

ASLAKSEN: Now don't get excited! Please!

Hovstad enters. He and Aslaksen stop short and smile on seeing Kiil.

KIIL: Too many intellectuals here: I'd better go.

ASLAKSEN [*apologetically*]: Doctor, can we have five minutes of—

DR. STOCKMANN: I've got nothing to say to you.

KIIL [*going to the door*]: I want an answer right away. You hear? I'm waiting. [*He leaves.*]

DR. STOCKMANN: All right, say it quick, what do you want?

HOVSTAD: We don't expect you to forgive our attitude at the meeting, but . . .

DR. STOCKMANN [*groping for the word*]: Your attitude was prone . . . prostrated . . . prostituted!

HOVSTAD: All right, call it whatever you—

DR. STOCKMANN: I've got a lot on my mind, so get to the point. What do you want?

ASLAKSEN: Doctor, you should have told us what was in back of it all. You could have had the *Messenger* behind you all the way.

HOVSTAD: You'd have had public opinion with you now. Why didn't you tell us?

DR. STOCKMANN: Look, I'm very tired, let's not beat around the bush!

HOVSTAD [*gesturing toward the door where Kiil went out*]: He's been all over town buying up stock in the springs. It's no secret any more.

DR. STOCKMANN [*after a slight pause*]: Well, what about it?

HOVSTAD [*in a friendly way*]: You don't want me to spell it out, do you?

DR. STOCKMANN: I certainly wish you would. I—

HOVSTAD: All right, let's lay it on the table. Aslaksen, you want to . . . ?

ASLAKSEN: No, no, go ahead.

HOVSTAD: Doctor, in the beginning we supported you. But it quickly became clear that if we kept on supporting you in the face of public hysteria—

DR. STOCKMANN: Your paper created the hysteria.

HOVSTAD: One thing at a time, all right? [*Slowly, to drive it into Dr. Stockmann's head*]: We couldn't go on supporting you because, in simple language, we didn't have the money to withstand the loss in circulation. You're boycotted now? Well, the paper would have been boycotted too, if we'd stuck with you.

ASLAKSEN: You can see that, Doctor.

DR. STOCKMANN: Oh, yes. But what do you want?

HOVSTAD: *The People's Messenger* can put on such a campaign that in two months you will be hailed as a hero in this town.

ASLAKSEN: We're ready to go.

HOVSTAD: We will prove to the public that you had to buy up the stock because the management would not make the changes required for public health. In other words, you did it for absolutely scientific, public-spirited reasons. Now what do you say, Doctor?

DR. STOCKMANN: You want money from me, is that it?

ASLAKSEN: Well, now, Doctor . . .

HOVSTAD [*to Aslaksen*]: No, don't walk around it. [*To Dr. Stockmann.*] If we started to support you again, Doctor, we'd lose circulation for a while. We'd like you—or Mr. Kiil rather—to make up the deficit. [*Quickly.*] Now that's open and aboveboard, and I don't see anything wrong with it. Do you?

Pause. Dr. Stockmann looks at him, then turns and walks to the windows, deep in thought.

ASLAKSEN: Remember, Doctor, you need the paper, you need it desperately.

DR. STOCKMANN [*returning*]: No, there's nothing wrong with it at all. I—I'm not at all averse to cleaning up my name—although for myself it never was dirty. But I don't *enjoy* being hated, if you know what I mean.

ASLAKSEN: Exactly.

HOVSTAD: Aslaksen, will you show him the budget . . .

Aslaksen reaches into his pocket.

DR. STOCKMANN: Just a minute. There is one point. I hate to keep repeating the same thing, but the water is poisoned.

HOVSTAD: Now, Doctor . . .

DR. STOCKMANN: Just a minute. The Mayor says that he will levy a tax on everybody to pay for the reconstruction. I assume you are ready to support that tax at the same time you're supporting me.

ASLAKSEN: That tax would be extremely unpopular.

HOVSTAD: Doctor, with you back in charge of the baths, I have absolutely no fear that anything can go wrong.

DR. STOCKMANN: In other words, you will clean up my name—so that I can be in charge of the corruption.

HOVSTAD: But we can't tackle everything at once. A new tax—there'd be an uproar!

ASLAKSEN: It would ruin the paper!

DR. STOCKMANN: Then you don't intend to do anything about the water?

HOVSTAD: We have faith you won't let anyone get sick.

DR. STOCKMANN: In other words, gentlemen, you are looking for someone to blackmail into paying your printing bill.

HOVSTAD [*indignantly*]: We are trying to clear your name, Doctor Stockmann! And if you refuse to cooperate, if that's going to be your attitude . . .

DR. STOCKMANN: Yes? Go on. What will you do?

HOVSTAD [*to Aslaksen*]: I think we'd better go.

DR. STOCKMANN [*stepping in their way*]: What will you do? I would like you to tell me. Me, the man two minutes ago you were going to make into a hero—what will you do now that I won't pay you?

ASLAKSEN: Doctor, the public is almost hysterical . . .

DR. STOCKMANN: To my face, tell me what you are going to do!

HOVSTAD: The Mayor will prosecute you for conspiracy to destroy a corporation, and without a paper behind you, you will end up in prison.

DR. STOCKMANN: And you'll support him, won't you? I want it from your mouth, Hovstad. This little victory you will not deny me. [*Hovstad starts for the door. Dr. Stockmann steps into his way*]. Tell the hero, Hovstad. You're going to go on crucifying the hero, are you not? Say it to me! You will not leave here until I get this from your mouth!

HOVSTAD [*looking directly at Dr. Stockmann*]: You are a madman. You are insane with egotism. And don't excuse it with humanitarian slogans, because a man who'll drag his family through a lifetime of disgrace is a demon in his heart! [*He advances on Dr. Stockmann.*] You hear me? A demon who cares more for the purity of a public bath than the lives of his wife and children. Doctor Stockmann, you deserve everything you're going to get!

Dr. Stockmann is struck by Hovstad's ferocious conviction. Aslaksen comes toward him, taking the budget out of his pocket.

ASLAKSEN [*nervously*]: Doctor, please consider it. It won't take much money, and in two months' time I promise you your whole life will change and . . .

Offstage Mrs. Stockmann is heard calling in a frightened voice, "What happened? My God, what's the matter?" She runs to the front door. Dr. Stockmann, alarmed, goes quickly to the hallway. Ejlif and Morten enter. Morten's head is bruised. Petra and Captain Horster enter from the left.

MRS. STOCKMANN: Something happened! Look at him!

MORTEN: I'm all right, they just . . .

DR. STOCKMANN [*looking at the bruise*]: What happened here?

MORTEN: Nothing, Papa, I swear . . .

DR. STOCKMANN [*to Ejlif*]: What happened? Why aren't you in school?

EJLIF: The teacher said we better stay home the rest of the week.

DR. STOCKMANN: The boys hit him?

EJLIF: They started calling you names, so he got sore and began to fight with one kid, and all of a sudden the whole bunch of them . . .

MRS. STOCKMANN [*to Morten*]: Why did you answer!

MORTEN [*indignantly*]: They called him a traitor! My father is no traitor!

EJLIF: But you didn't have to answer!

MRS. STOCKMANN: You should've known they'd all jump on you! They could have killed you!

MORTEN: I don't care!

DR. STOCKMANN [*to quiet him—and his own heart*]: Morten . . .

MORTEN [*pulling away from his father*]: I'll kill them! I'll take a rock and the next time I see one of them I'll kill him!

Dr. Stockmann reaches for Morten, who, thinking his father will chastise him, starts to run. Dr. Stockmann catches him and grips him by the arm.

MORTEN: Let me go! Let me . . . !

DR. STOCKMANN: Morten . . . Morten . . .

MORTEN [*crying in his father's arms*]: They called you traitor, an enemy . . . [*He sobs.*]

DR. STOCKMANN: Sssh. That's all. Wash your face.

Mrs. Stockmann takes Morten. Dr. Stockmann stands erect, faces Aslaksen and Hovstad.

DR. STOCKMANN: Good day, gentlemen.

HOVSTAD: Let us know what you decide and we'll—

DR. STOCKMANN: I've decided. I am an enemy of the people.

MRS. STOCKMANN: Tom, what are you . . . ?

DR. STOCKMANN: To such people, who teach their own children to think with their fists—to them I'm an enemy! And my boy . . . my boys . . . my family . . . I think you can count us all enemies.

ASLAKSEN: Doctor, you could have everything you want!

DR. STOCKMANN: Except the truth. I could have everything but that—that the water is poisoned!

HOVSTAD: But you'll be in charge.

DR. STOCKMANN: But the children are poisoned, the people are poisoned! If the only way I can be a friend of the people is to take charge of that corruption, then I am an enemy! The water is poisoned, poisoned, poisoned! That's the beginning of it and that's the end of it! Now get out of here!

HOVSTAD: You know where you're going to end?

DR. STOCKMANN: I said get out of here! [*He grabs Aslaksen's umbrella out of his hand.*]

MRS. STOCKMANN: What are you doing?

Aslaksen and Hovstad back toward the door as Dr. Stockmann starts to swing.

ASLAKSEN: You're a fanatic, you're out of your mind!

MRS. STOCKMANN: [grabbing Dr. Stockmann to take the umbrella] What are you doing?

DR. STOCKMANN: They want me to buy the paper, the public, the pollution of the springs, buy the whole pollution of this town! They'll make a hero out of me for that! [Furiously, to Aslaksen and Hovstad:] But I'm not a hero, I'm the enemy—and now you're first going to find out what kind of enemy I am! I will sharpen my pen like a dagger—you, all you friends of the people, are going to bleed before I'm done! Go, tell them to sign the petitions! Warn them not to call me when they're sick! Beat up my children! And never let her [he points to Petra] in the school again or she'll destroy the immaculate purity of the vacuum there! See to all the barricades—the truth is coming! Ring the bells, sound the alarm! The truth, the truth is out, and soon it will be prowling like a lion in the streets!

HOVSTAD: Doctor, you're out of your mind.

He and Aslaksen turn to go. They are in the doorway.

EJLIF, *rushing at them:* Don't you say that to him!

DR. STOCKMANN [*as Mrs. Stockmann cries out, rushes them with the umbrella*]: Out of here!

They rush out. Dr. Stockmann throws the umbrella after them, then slams the door. Silence. He has his back pressed against the door, facing his family.

DR. STOCKMANN: I've had all the ambassadors of hell today, but there'll be no more. Now, now listen, Catherine! Children, listen. Now we're besieged. They'll call for blood now, they'll whip the people like oxen— [*A rock comes through a remaining pane. The boys start for the window.*] Stay away from there!

MRS. STOCKMANN: The Captain knows where we can get a ship.

DR. STOCKMANN: No ships.

PETRA: We're staying?

MRS. STOCKMANN: But they can't go back to school! I won't let them out of the house!

DR. STOCKMANN: We're staying.

PETRA: Good!

DR. STOCKMANN: We must be careful now. We must live through this. Boys, no more school. I'm going to teach you, and Petra will. Do you know any kids, street louts, hookey-players—

EJLIF: Oh, sure, we—

DR. STOCKMANN: We'll want about twelve of them to start. But I
want them good and ignorant, absolutely uncivilized. Can we use
your house, Captain?

HORSTER: Sure, I'm never there.

DR. STOCKMANN: Fine. We'll begin, Petra, and we'll turn out not tax-
payers and newspaper subscribers, but free and independent people, hungry for the truth. Oh, I forgot! Petra, run to Grandpa and
tell him—tell him as follows: No!

MRS. STOCKMANN [*puzzled*]: What do you mean?

DR. STOCKMANN [*going over to Mrs. Stockmann*]: It means, my dear,
that we are all alone. And there'll be a long night before it's
day—

*A rock comes through a paneless window. Horster goes to the
window. A crowd is heard approaching.*

HORSTER: Half the town is out!

MRS. STOCKMANN: What's going to happen? Tom! What's going to
happen?

DR. STOCKMANN [*holding his hands up to quiet her, and with a trembling
mixture of trepidation and courageous insistence*]: I don't know. But
remember now, everybody. You are fighting for the truth, and
that's why you're alone. And that makes you strong. We're the
strongest people in the world . . .

*The crowd is heard angrily calling outside. Another rock comes
through a window.*

DR. STOCKMANN: . . . and the strong must learn to be lonely!

*The crowd noise gets louder. He walks upstage toward the win-
dows as a wind rises and the curtains start to billow out toward
him. the curtain falls.*

—1882

SUSAN GLASPELL ■ [1882–1948]

Susan Glaspell was born in Iowa and educated at Drake University. Glaspell was one of the founders, with her husband George Cram Cook, of the Provincetown Players. This company, founded in the Cape Cod resort village, was committed to producing experimental drama, an alternative to the standard fare playing in Broadway theaters. Eventually it was relocated to New York. Along with Glaspell, Eugene O'Neill, America's only Nobel Prize–winning dramatist, wrote plays for this group. Trained as a journalist and the author of short stories and novels, Glaspell wrote Trifles *[1916], her first play, shortly after the founding of the Players, basing her plot on an Iowa murder case she had covered. The one-act play, with both Glaspell and her husband in the cast, premiered during the Players' second season and also exists in a short-story version. Glaspell won the Pulitzer Prize for Drama in 1930 for* Alison's House, *basing the title character on poet Emily Dickinson. A socialist and feminist, Glaspell lived in Provincetown in her last years, writing* The Road to the Temple, *a memoir of her husband's life, and novels.*

Trifles

Characters

George Henderson, *County Attorney*
Mrs. Peters
Henry Peters, *Sheriff*
Lewis Hale, *a neighbor*
Mrs. Hale

The kitchen in the now abandoned farmhouse of John Wright, a gloomy kitchen, and left without having been put in order—unwashed pans under the sink, a loaf of bread outside the breadbox, a dish towel on the table— other signs of incompleted work. At the rear the outer door opens, and the Sheriff comes in, followed by the County Attorney and Hale. The Sheriff and Hale are men in middle life, the County Attorney is a young man; all are much bundled up and go at once to the stove. They are followed by the two women—the Sheriff's Wife first; she is a slight wiry woman, a thin nervous face. Mrs. Hale is larger and would ordinarily be called more comfortable looking, but she is disturbed now and looks fearfully about as she enters. The women have come in slowly and stand close together near the door.

COUNTY ATTORNEY [*rubbing his hands*]: This feels good. Come up to the fire, ladies.

MRS. PETERS [*after taking a step forward*]: I'm not—cold.

SHERIFF [*unbuttoning his overcoat and stepping away from the stove as if to the beginning of official business*]: Now, Mr. Hale, before we move things about, you explain to Mr. Henderson just what you saw when you came here yesterday morning.

COUNTY ATTORNEY: By the way, has anything been moved? Are things just as you left them yesterday?

SHERIFF [*looking about*]: It's just the same. When it dropped below zero last night, I thought I'd better send Frank out this morning to make a fire for us—no use getting pneumonia with a big case on; but I told him not to touch anything except the stove—and you know Frank.

COUNTY ATTORNEY: Somebody should have been left here yesterday.

SHERIFF: Oh—yesterday. When I had to send Frank to Morris Center for that man who went crazy—I want you to know I had my hands full yesterday. I knew you could get back from Omaha by today, and as long as I went over everything here myself—

COUNTY ATTORNEY: Well, Mr. Hale, tell just what happened when you came here yesterday morning.

HALE: Harry and I had started to town with a load of potatoes. We came along the road from my place; and as I got here, I said, "I'm going to see if I can't get John Wright to go in with me on a party telephone." I spoke to Wright about it once before, and he put me off, saying folks talked too much anyway, and all he asked was peace and quiet—I guess you know about how much he talked himself; but I thought maybe if I went to the house and talked about it before his wife, though I said to Harry that I didn't know as what his wife wanted made much difference to John—

COUNTY ATTORNEY: Let's talk about that later, Mr. Hale. I do want to talk about that, but tell now just what happened when you got to the house.

HALE: I didn't hear or see anything; I knocked at the door, and still it was all quiet inside. I knew they must be up, it was past eight o'clock. So I knocked again, and I thought I heard somebody say, "Come in." I wasn't sure, I'm not sure yet, but I opened the door—this door [*indicating the door by which the two women are still standing*], and there in that rocker—[*pointing to it*] sat Mrs. Wright. [*They all look at the rocker.*]

COUNTY ATTORNEY: What—was she doing?

HALE: She was rockin' back and forth. She had her apron in her hand and was kind of—pleating it.

COUNTY ATTORNEY: And how did she—look?

HALE: Well, she looked queer.

COUNTY ATTORNEY: How do you mean—queer?

HALE: Well, as if she didn't know what she was going to do next. And kind of done up.

COUNTY ATTORNEY: How did she seem to feel about your coming?

HALE: Why, I don't think she minded—one way or other. She didn't pay much attention. I said, "How do, Mrs. Wright, it's cold, ain't it?" And she said, "Is it?"—and went on kind of pleating at her apron. Well, I was surprised; she didn't ask me to come up to the stove, or to set down, but just sat there, not even looking at me, so I said, "I want to see John." And then she—laughed. I guess you would call it a laugh. I thought of Harry and the team outside, so I said a little sharp: "Can't I see John?" "No," she says, kind o' dull like. "Ain't he home?" says I. "Yes," says she, "he's home." "Then why can't I see him?" I asked her, out of patience. "Cause he's dead," says she. "*Dead?*" says I. She just nodded her head, not getting a bit excited, but rockin' back and forth. "Why—where is he?" says I, not knowing what to say. She just pointed upstairs—like that [*himself pointing to the room above*]. I got up, with the idea of going up there. I walked from there to here—then I says, "Why, what did he die of?" "He died of a rope around his neck," says she, and just went on pleatin' at her apron. Well, I went out and called Harry. I thought I might—need help. We went upstairs, and there he was lyin'—

COUNTY ATTORNEY: I think I'd rather have you go into that upstairs, where you can point it all out. Just go on now with the rest of the story.

HALE: Well, my first thought was to get that rope off. I looked . . . [*Stops, his face twitches.*] . . . but Harry, he went up to him, and he said, "No, he's dead all right, and we'd better not touch anything." So we went back downstairs. She was still sitting that same way.

"Has anybody been notified?" I asked. "No," says she, unconcerned. "Who did this, Mrs. Wright?" said Harry. He said it businesslike— and she stopped pleatin' of her apron. "I don't know," she says. "You don't *know*?" says Harry. "No," says she, "Weren't you sleepin' in the bed with him?" says Harry. "Yes," says she, "but I was on the inside." "Somebody slipped a rope round his neck and strangled him, and you didn't wake up?" says Harry. "I didn't wake up," she said after him. We must 'a looked as if we didn't see how that could be, for after a minute she said, "I sleep sound." Harry was going to ask her more questions, but I said maybe we ought to let her tell her story first to the coroner, or the sheriff, so Harry went fast as he could to Rivers' place, where there's a telephone.

COUNTY ATTORNEY: And what did Mrs. Wright do when she knew that you had gone for the coroner?

HALE: She moved from that chair to this over here . . . [*Pointing to a small chair in the corner.*] . . . and just sat there with her hands held together and looking down. I got a feeling that I ought to make some conversation, so I said I had come in to see if John wanted to put in a telephone, and at that she started to laugh, and then she stopped and looked at me—scared. [*The County Attorney, who has had his notebook out, makes a note.*] I dunno, maybe it wasn't scared. I wouldn't like to say it was. Soon Harry got back, and then Dr. Lloyd came, and you, Mr. Peters, and so I guess that's all I know that you don't.

COUNTY ATTORNEY [*looking around*]: I guess we'll go upstairs first— and then out to the barn and around there. [*To the Sheriff.*] You're convinced that there was nothing important here—nothing that would point to any motive?

SHERIFF: Nothing here but kitchen things.

[*The County Attorney, after again looking around the kitchen, opens the door of a cupboard closet. He gets up on a chair and looks on a shelf. Pulls his hand away, sticky.*]

COUNTY ATTORNEY: Here's a nice mess.

[*The women draw nearer.*]

MRS. PETERS [*to the other woman*]: Oh, her fruit; it did freeze. [*To the Lawyer.*] She worried about that when it turned so cold. She said the fir'd go out and her jars would break.

SHERIFF: Well, can you beat the women! Held for murder and worryin' about her preserves.

COUNTY ATTORNEY: I guess before we're through she may have
something more serious than preserves to worry about.

HALE: Well, women are used to worrying over trifles.

[*The two women move a little closer together.*]

COUNTY ATTORNEY [*with the gallantry of a young politician*]: And yet,
for all their worries, what would we do without the ladies? [*The
women do not unbend. He goes to the sink, takes a dipperful of water
from the pail and, pouring it into a basin, washes his hands. Starts to
wipe them on the roller towel, turns it for a cleaner place.*] Dirty towels!
[*Kicks his foot against the pans under the sink.*] Not much of a housekeeper, would you say, ladies?

MRS. HALE [*stiffly*]: There's a great deal of work to be done on a farm.

COUNTY ATTORNEY: To be sure. And yet . . . [*With a little bow to her.*] . . .
I know there are some Dickson county farmhouses which do not
have such roller towels. [*He gives it a pull to expose its full length
again.*]

MRS. HALE: Those towels get dirty awful quick. Men's hands aren't
always as clean as they might be.

COUNTY ATTORNEY: Ah, loyal to your sex, I see. But you and Mrs.
Wright were neighbors. I suppose you were friends, too.

MRS. HALE [*shaking her head*]: I've not seen much of her of late years.
I've not been in this house—it's more than a year.

COUNTY ATTORNEY: And why was that? You didn't like her?

MRS. HALE: I liked her all well enough. Farmers' wives have their
hands full, Mr. Henderson. And then—

COUNTY ATTORNEY: Yes—?

MRS. HALE [*looking about*]: It never seemed a very cheerful place.

COUNTY ATTORNEY: No—it's not cheerful. I shouldn't say she had
the homemaking instinct.

MRS. HALE: Well, I don't know as Wright had, either.

COUNTY ATTORNEY: You mean that they didn't get on very well?

MRS. HALE: No, I don't mean anything. But I don't think a place'd be
any cheerfuler for John Wright's being in it.

COUNTY ATTORNEY: I'd like to talk more of that a little later. I want
to get the lay of things upstairs now. [*He goes to the left, where three
steps lead to a stair door.*]

SHERIFF: I suppose anything Mrs. Peters does'll be all right. She was to take in some clothes for her, you know, and a few little things. We left in such a hurry yesterday.

COUNTY ATTORNEY: Yes, but I would like to see what you take, Mrs. Peters, and keep an eye out for anything that might be of use to us.

MRS. PETERS: Yes, Mr. Henderson.

[*The women listen to the men's steps on the stairs, then look about the kitchen.*]

MRS. HALE: I'd hate to have men coming into my kitchen, snooping around and criticizing. [*She arranges the pans under the sink which the Lawyer had shoved out of place.*]

MRS. PETERS: Of course it's no more than their duty.

MRS. HALE: Duty's all right, but I guess that deputy sheriff that came out to make the fire might have got a little of this on. [*Gives the roller towel a pull.*] Wish I'd thought of that sooner. Seems mean to talk about her for not having things slicked up when she had to come away in such a hurry.

MRS. PETERS [*who has gone to a small table in the left rear corner of the room, and lifted one end of a towel that covers a pan*]:   She had bread set. [*Stands still.*]

MRS. HALE [*eyes fixed on a loaf of bread beside the breadbox, which is on a low shelf at the other side of the room. Moves slowly toward it*]:   She was going to put this in there. [*Picks up loaf, then abruptly drops it. In a manner of returning to familiar things.*] It's a shame about her fruit. I wonder if it's all gone. [*Gets up on the chair and looks.*] I think there's some here that's all right, Mrs. Peters. Yes—here; [*Holding it toward the window.*] this is cherries, too. [*Looking again.*] I declare I believe that's the only one. [*Gets down, bottle in her hand. Goes to the sink and wipes it off on the outside.*] She'll feel awful bad after all her hard work in the hot weather. I remember the afternoon I put up my cherries last summer. [*She puts the bottle on the big kitchen table, center of the room, front table. With a sigh, is about to sit down in the rocking chair. Before she is seated realizes what chair it is; with a slow look at it, steps back. The chair, which she has touched, rocks back and forth.*]

MRS. PETERS: Well, I must get those things from the front room closet. [*She goes to the door at the right, but after looking into the other room steps back.*] You coming with me, Mrs. Hale? You could help me carry them. [*They go into the other room; reappear, Mrs. Peters carrying a dress and skirt, Mrs. Hale following with a pair of shoes.*]

MRS. PETERS: My, it's cold in there. [*She puts the cloth on the big table, and hurries to the stove.*]

MRS. HALE [*examining the skirt*]: Wright was close. I think maybe that's why she kept so much to herself. She didn't even belong to the Ladies' Aid. I suppose she felt she couldn't do her part, and then you don't enjoy things when you feel shabby. She used to wear pretty clothes and be lively, when she was Minnie Foster, one of the town girls singing in the choir. But that—oh, that was thirty years ago. This all you was to take in?

MRS. PETERS: She said she wanted an apron. Funny thing to want, for there isn't much to get you dirty in jail, goodness knows. But I suppose just to make her feel more natural. She said they was in the top drawer in this cupboard. Yes, here. And then her little shawl that always hung behind the door. [*Opens stair door and looks.*] Yes, here it is. [*Quickly shuts door leading upstairs.*]

MRS. HALE [*abruptly moving toward her*]: Mrs. Peters?

MRS. PETERS: Yes, Mrs. Hale?

MRS. HALE: Do you think she did it?

MRS. PETERS [*in a frightened voice*]: Oh, I don't know.

MRS. HALE: Well, I don't think she did. Asking for an apron and her little shawl. Worrying about her fruit.

MRS. PETERS [*starts to speak, glances up, where footsteps are heard in the room above. In a low voice*]: Mr. Peters says it looks bad for her. Mr. Henderson is awful sarcastic in speech, and he'll make fun of her sayin' she didn't wake up.

MRS. HALE: Well, I guess John Wright didn't wake when they was slipping that rope under his neck.

MRS. PETERS: No, it's strange. It must have been done awful crafty and still. They say it was such a—funny way to kill a man, rigging it all up like that.

MRS. HALE: That's just what Mr. Hale said. There was a gun in the house. He says that's what he can't understand.

MRS. PETERS: Mr. Henderson said coming out that what was needed for the case was a motive; something to show anger, or—sudden feeling.

MRS. HALE [*who is standing by the table*]: Well, I don't see any signs of anger around here. [*She puts her hand on the dish towel which lies on* the table, stands looking down at the table, one half of which is clean, the other half messy.] It's wiped here. [Makes a move as if to finish work, then turns and looks at loaf of bread outside the breadbox. Drops towel. In that voice of coming back to familiar things.] Wonder how they are finding things upstairs? I hope she had it a little more red-up there. You know, it seems kind of *sneaking*. Locking her up in town and then coming out here and trying to get her own house to turn against her!

MRS. PETERS: But, Mrs. Hale, the law is the law.

MRS. HALE: I s'pose 'tis. [Unbuttoning her coat.] Better loosen up your things, Mrs. Peters. You won't feel them when you go out.

[Mrs. Peters takes off her fur tippet, goes to hang it on a hook at the back of room, stands looking at the under part of the small corner table.]

MRS. PETERS: She was piecing a quilt. [She brings the large sewing basket, and they look at the bright pieces.]

MRS. HALE: It's log cabin pattern. Pretty, isn't it? I wonder if she was goin' to quilt or just knot it?

[Footsteps have been heard coming down the stairs. The Sheriff enters, followed by Hale and the County Attorney.]

SHERIFF: They wonder if she was going to quilt it or just knot it. [The men laugh, the women look abashed.]

COUNTY ATTORNEY [rubbing his hands over the stove]:   Frank's fire didn't do much up there, did it? Well, let's go out to the barn and get that cleared up.

[The men go outside.]

MRS. HALE [resentfully]:   I don't know as there's anything so strange, our takin' up our time with little things while we're waiting for them to get the evidence. [She sits down at the big table, smoothing out a block with decision.] I don't see as it's anything to laugh about.

MRS. PETERS [apologetically]:   Of course they've got awful important things on their minds. [Pulls up a chair and joins Mrs. Hale at the table.]

MRS. HALE [examining another block]:   Mrs. Peters, look at this one. Here, this is the one she was working on, and look at the sewing! All the rest of it has been so nice and even. And look at this! It's all over the place! Why, it looks as if she didn't know what she was about! [*After she has said this, they look at each other, then started to glance back at the door. After an instant Mrs. Hale has pulled at a knot and ripped the sewing.*]

MRS. PETERS: Oh, what are you doing, Mrs. Hale?

MRS. HALE [*mildly*]:   Just pulling out a stitch or two that's not sewed very good. [*Threading a needle.*] Bad sewing always made me fidgety.

MRS. PETERS [*nervously*]:   I don't think we ought to touch things.

MRS. HALE: I'll just finish up this end. [*Suddenly stopping and leaning forward.*] Mrs. Peters?

MRS. PETERS: Yes, Mrs. Hale?

MRS. HALE: What do you suppose she was so nervous about?

MRS. PETERS: Oh—I don't know. I don't know as she was nervous. I sometimes sew awful queer when I'm just tired. [*Mrs. Hale starts to say something, looks at Mrs. Peters, then goes on sewing.*] Well, I must get these things wrapped up. They may be through sooner than we think. [*Putting apron and other things together.*] I wonder where I can find a piece of paper, and string.

MRS. HALE: In that cupboard, maybe.

MRS. PETERS [*looking in cupboard*]:   Why, here's a birdcage. [*Holds it up.*] Did she have a bird, Mrs. Hale?

MRS. HALE: Why, I don't know whether she did or not—I've not been here for so long. There was a man around last year selling canaries cheap, but I don't know as she took one; maybe she did. She used to sing real pretty herself.

MRS. PETERS [*glancing around*]:   Seems funny to think of a bird here. But she must have had one, or why should she have a cage? I wonder what happened to it?

MRS. HALE: I s'pose maybe the cat got it.

MRS. PETERS: No, she didn't have a cat. She's got that feeling some people have about cats—being afraid of them. My cat got in her room, and she was real upset and asked me to take it out.

MRS. HALE: My sister Bessie was like that. Queer, ain't it?

MRS. PETERS [*examining the cage*]:   Why, look at this door. It's broke. One hinge is pulled apart.

MRS. HALE [*looking, too*]:   Looks as if someone must have been rough with it.

MRS. PETERS: Why, yes. [*She brings the cage forward and puts it on the table.*]

MRS. HALE: I wish if they're going to find any evidence they'd be about it. I don't like this place.

MRS. PETERS: But I'm awful glad you came with me, Mrs. Hale. It would be lonesome for me sitting here alone.

MRS. HALE: It would, wouldn't it? [*Dropping her sewing.*] But I tell you what I do wish, Mrs. Peters. I wish I had come over sometimes when *she* was here. I—[*Looking around the room.*]—wish I had.

MRS. PETERS: But of course you were awful busy, Mrs. Hale—your house and your children.

MRS. HALE: I could've come. I stayed away because it weren't cheerful—and that's why I ought to have come. I—I've never liked this place. Maybe because it's down in a hollow, and you don't see the road. I dunno what it is, but it's a lonesome place and always was. I wish I had come over to see Minnie Foster sometimes. I can see now—[*Shakes her head.*]

MRS. PETERS: Well, you mustn't reproach yourself, Mrs. Hale. Somehow we just don't see how it is with other folks until—something comes up.

MRS. HALE: Not having children makes less work—but it makes a quiet house, and Wright out to work all day, and no company when he did come in. Did you know John Wright, Mrs. Peters?

MRS. PETERS: Not to know him; I've seen him in town. They say he was a good man.

MRS. HALE: Yes—good; he didn't drink, and kept his word as well as most, I guess, and paid his debts. But he was a hard man, Mrs. Peters. Just to pass the time of day with him. [*Shivers.*] Like a raw wind that gets to the bone. [*Pauses, her eye falling on the cage.*] I should think she would 'a wanted a bird. But what do you suppose went with it?

MRS. PETERS: I don't know, unless it got sick and died. [*She reaches over and swings the broken door, swings it again; both women watch it.*]

MRS. HALE: You weren't raised round here, were you? [*Mrs. Peters shakes her head.*] You didn't know—her?

MRS. PETERS: Not till they brought her yesterday.

MRS. HALE: She—come to think of it, she was kind of like a bird herself—real sweet and pretty, but kind of timid and—fluttery. How—she—did—change. [*Silence; then as if struck by a happy thought and relieved to get back to everyday things.*] Tell you what,

Mrs. Peters, why don't you take the quilt in with you? It might take up her mind.

MRS. PETERS: Why, I think that's a real nice idea, Mrs. Hale. There couldn't possibly be any objection to it, could there? Now, just what would I take? I wonder if her patches are in here—and her things. [*They look in the sewing basket.*]

MRS. HALE: Here's some red. I expect this has got sewing things in it [*Brings out a fancy box.*] What a pretty box. Looks like something somebody would give you. Maybe her scissors are in here. [*Opens box. Suddenly puts her hand to her nose.*] Why—[*Mrs. Peters bends nearer, then turns her face away.*] There's something wrapped up in this piece of silk.

MRS. PETERS: Why, this isn't her scissors.

MRS. HALE [*lifting the silk*]: Oh, Mrs. Peters—it's—[*Mrs. Peters bends closer.*]

MRS. PETERS: It's the bird.

MRS. HALE [*jumping up*]: But, Mrs. Peters—look at it. Its neck! Look at its neck! It's all—other side *to*.

MRS. PETERS: Somebody—wrung—its neck.

[*Their eyes meet. A look of growing comprehension of horror. Steps are heard outside. Mrs. Hale slips box under quilt pieces, and sinks into her chair. Enter Sheriff and County Attorney. Mrs. Peters rises.*]

COUNTY ATTORNEY [*as one turning from serious things to little pleasantries*]: Well, ladies, have you decided whether she was going to quilt it or knot it?

MRS. PETERS: We think she was going to—knot it.

COUNTY ATTORNEY: Well, that's interesting, I'm sure. [*Seeing the birdcage.*] Has the bird flown?

MRS. HALE [*putting more quilt pieces over the box*]: We think the—cat got it.

COUNTY ATTORNEY [*preoccupied*]: Is there a cat?

[*Mrs. Hale glances in a quick covert way at Mrs. Peters.*]

MRS. PETERS: Well, not now. They're superstitious, you know. They leave.

COUNTY ATTORNEY [*to Sheriff Peters, continuing an interrupted conversation*]: No sign at all of anyone having come from the outside.

Their own rope. Now let's go up again and go over it piece by piece. [*They start upstairs.*] It would have to have been someone who knew just the—

[*Mrs. Peters sits down. The two women sit there not looking at one another, but as if peering into something and at the same time holding back. When they talk now, it is the manner of feeling their way over strange ground, as if afraid of what they are saying, but as if they cannot help saying it.*]

MRS. HALE: She liked the bird. She was going to bury it in that pretty box.

MRS. PETERS [*in a whisper*]:   When I was a girl—my kitten—there was a boy took a hatchet, and before my eyes—and before I could get there—[*Covers her face an instant.*] If they hadn't held me back, I would have—[*Catches herself, looks upstairs where steps are heard, falters weakly.*]—hurt him.

MRS. HALE [*with a slow look around her*]:   I wonder how it would seem never to have had any children around. [*Pause.*] No, Wright wouldn't like the bird—a thing that sang. She used to sing. He killed that, too.

MRS. PETERS [*moving uneasily*]:   We don't know who killed the bird.

MRS. HALE: I knew John Wright.

MRS. PETERS: It was an awful thing was done in this house that night, Mrs. Hale. Killing a man while he slept, slipping a rope around his neck that choked the life out of him.

MRS. HALE: His neck. Choked the life out of him.

[*Her hand goes out and rests on the birdcage.*]

MRS. PETERS [*with a rising voice*]:   We don't know who killed him. We don't *know.*

MRS. HALE [*her own feeling not interrupted*]:   If there'd been years and years of nothing, then a bird to sing to you, it would be awful—still, after the bird was still.

MRS. PETERS [*something within her speaking*]:   I know what stillness is. When we homesteaded in Dakota, and my first baby died—after he was two years old, and me with no other then—

MRS. HALE [*moving*]:   How soon do you suppose they'll be through, looking for evidence?

MRS. PETERS: I know what stillness is. [*Pulling herself back.*] The law has got to punish crime, Mrs. Hale.

MRS. HALE [*not as if answering that*]:   I wish you'd seen Minnie Foster
when she wore a white dress with blue ribbons and stood up there
in the choir and sang. [*A look around the room.*] Oh, I *wish* I'd come
over here once in a while! That was a crime! That was a crime!
Who's going to punish that?

MRS. PETERS [*looking upstairs*]:   We mustn't—take on.

MRS. HALE: I might have known she needed help! I know how things
can be—for women. I tell you, it's queer, Mrs. Peters. We live close
together and we live far apart. We all go through the same
things—it's all just a different kind of the same thing. [*Brushes her
eyes, noticing the bottle of fruit, reaches out for it.*] If I was you, I
wouldn't tell her her fruit was gone. Tell her it *ain't*. Tell her it's all
right. Take this in to prove it to her. She—she may never know
whether it was broke or not.

MRS. PETERS [*takes the bottle, looks about for something to wrap it in;
takes petticoat from the clothes brought from the other room, very nervously begins winding this around the bottle. In a false voice*]:   My, it's
a good thing the men couldn't hear us. Wouldn't they just laugh!
Getting all stirred up over a little thing like a—dead canary. As if
that could have anything to do with—with—wouldn't they *laugh!*

[*The men are heard coming downstairs.*]

MRS. HALE [*under her breath*]:   Maybe they would—maybe they
wouldn't.

COUNTY ATTORNEY: No, Peters, it's all perfectly clear except a reason
for doing it. But you know juries when it comes to women. If there
was some definite thing. Something to show—something to make
a story about—a thing that would connect up with this strange
way of doing it.

[*The women's eyes meet for an instant. Enter Hale from outer door.*]

HALE: Well, I've got the team around. Pretty cold out there.

COUNTY ATTORNEY: I'm going to stay here awhile by myself. [*To the
Sheriff.*] You can send Frank out for me, can't you? I want to go over
everything. I'm not satisfied that we can't do better.

SHERIFF: Do you want to see what Mrs. Peters is going to take in?

[*The Lawyer goes to the table, picks up the apron, laughs.*]

COUNTY ATTORNEY: Oh I guess they're not very dangerous things
the ladies have picked up. [*Moves a few things about, disturbing the*

quilt pieces which cover the box. Steps back.] No, Mrs. Peters doesn't need supervising. For that matter, a sheriff's wife is married to the law. Ever think of it that way, Mrs. Peters?

MRS. PETERS: Not—just that way.

SHERIFF [chuckling]:   Married to the law. [Moves toward the other room.] I just want you to come in here a minute, George. We ought to take a look at these windows.

COUNTY ATTORNEY [scoffingly]:   Oh, windows!

SHERIFF: We'll be right out, Mr. Hale.

[Hale goes outside. The Sheriff follows the County Attorney into the other room. Then Mrs. Hale rises, hands tight together, look-ing intensely at Mrs. Peters, whose eyes take a slow turn, finally meeting, Mrs. Hale's. A moment Mrs. Hale holds her, then her own eyes point the way to where the box is concealed. Suddenly Mrs. Peters throws back quilt pieces and tries to put the box in the bag she is wearing. It is too big. She opens box, starts to take the bird out, cannot touch it, goes to pieces, stands there helpless. Sound of a knob turning in the other room. Mrs. Hale snatches the box and puts it in the pocket of her big coat. Enter County At-torney and Sheriff.]

COUNTY ATTORNEY [facetiously]:   Well, Henry, at least we found out that she was not going to quilt it. She was going to—what is it you call it, ladies?

MRS. HALE [her hand against her pocket]:   We call it—knot it, Mr. Henderson.

CURTAIN

—1917

Tennessee Williams was the first important American playwright to emerge in the post–World War II period. Born Thomas Lanier Williams and raised in St. Louis, he took his professional name from his mother's southern forebears. Williams studied at the University of Missouri and Washington University, ultimately completing a degree in drama at the University of Iowa. After staging some of his early one-act plays with the Group Theater (later known as the Actors Studio), Williams first came to larger public attention with The Glass Menagerie, which won a Drama Critics Circle award in 1945. The Glass Menagerie is clearly autobiographical, drawing on Williams's memories of life with his faded southern belle mother and his tragically disturbed sister, Rose, who ultimately had to be institutionalized. Subsequent plays draw on Williams's life and his southern roots. In 1947, A Streetcar Named Desire received the Pulitzer Prize, the first of two Williams would win in a forty-year career. A Streetcar Named Desire, which starred the young Marlon Brando on stage and film, is, in contrast to The Glass Menagerie, a brutally naturalistic tragedy in which no romantic illusions are allowed to survive. Both Jessica Tandy, who originated the stage role, and Vivien Leigh, who starred in the film, were acclaimed for their portrayals of Blanche DuBois. Williams's plays are constantly revived in little theaters and on Broadway. In the first decade of the twenty-first century, both A Streetcar Named Desire, with Alec Baldwin, and Cat on a Hot Tin Roof, starring Kathleen Turner, completed successful New York engagements, and 2005 saw yet another Broadway revival of The Glass Menagerie, starring Jessica Lange. Some of the film adaptations of Williams's plays, several of which have screenplays written by the author, remain main classics, especially Elia Kazan's version of A Streetcar Named Desire. Williams published his autobiography in 1975. A fascinating collection of his correspondence, which gives insight into both his concerns as a writer and his intensely troubled personal life, appeared in 2000.

The Glass Menagerie

nobody, not even the rain, has such small hands.

e. e. cummings

Characters

Amanda Wingfield, the mother.—A little woman of great but confused vitality clinging frantically to another time and place. Her characterization must be carefully created, not copied from type. She is not paranoiac, but her life is paranoia. There is much to admire in Amanda, and as much to love and pity as there is to laugh at. Certainly she has endurance and a kind of heroism, and though her foolishness makes her unwittingly cruel at times, there is tenderness in her slight person.

Laura Wingfield, her daughter.—Amanda, having failed to establish contact with reality, continues to live vitally in her illusions, but Laura's situation is even graver. A childhood illness has left her crippled, one leg slightly shorter than the other, and held in a brace. This defect need not be more than suggested on the stage. Stemming from this, Laura's separation increases till she is like a piece of her own glass collection, too exquisitely fragile to move from the shelf.

Tom Wingfield, her son.—And the narrator of the play. A poet with a job in a warehouse. His nature is not remorseless, but to escape from a trap he has to act without pity.

Jim O'Connor, the gentleman caller.—A nice, ordinary young man.

Scene: An alley in St. Louis.

Part 1. Preparation for a Gentleman Caller.

Part 2. The Gentleman Calls.

Part 3. Now and the Past.

Scene I

The Wingfield apartment is in the rear of the building, one of those vast hive-like conglomerations of cellular living-units that flower as warty growths in overcrowded urban centers of lower middle-class population and are symptomatic of the impulse of this largest and fundamentally enslaved section of American society to avoid fluidity and differentiation and to exist and function as one interfused mass of automatism.

The apartment faces an alley and is entered by a fire-escape, a structure whose name is a touch of accidental poetic truth, for all of these huge buildings are always burning with the slow and implacable fires of human desperation. The fire escape is included in the set—that is, the landing of it and steps descending from it.

The scene is memory and is therefore non-realistic. Memory takes a lot of poetic license. It omits some details; others are exaggerated, according to the *emotional value of the articles it touches, for memory is seated predominantly in the heart. The interior is therefore rather dim and poetic.*

At the rise of the curtain, the audience is faced with the dark, grim rear wall of the Wingfield tenement. This building, which runs parallel to the footlights, is flanked on both sides by dark, narrow alleys which run into murky canyons of tangled clotheslines, garbage cans and the sinister latticework of neighboring fire-escapes. It is up and down these side alleys that exterior entrances and exits are made, during the play. At the end of Tom's opening commentary, the dark tenement wall slowly reveals (by means of a transparency) the interior of the ground floor Wingfield apartment.

Downstage is the living room, which also serves as a sleeping room for Laura, the sofa unfolding to make her bed. Upstage, center, and divided by a wide arch or second proscenium with transparent faded portieres (or second curtain), is the dining room. In an old-fashioned what-not in the living room are seen scores of transparent glass animals. A blown-up photograph of the father hangs on the wall of the living room, facing the audience, to the left of the archway. It is the face of a very handsome young man in a doughboy's First World War cap. He is gallantly smiling, ineluctably smiling, as if to say, "I will be smiling forever."

The audience hears and sees the opening scene in the dining room through both the transparent wall of the building and the transparent gauze portieres of the diningroom arch. It is during this revealing scene that the fourth wall slowly ascends, out of sight.

This transparent exterior wall is not brought down again until the very end of the play, during Tom's final speech.

The narrator is an undisguised convention of the play. He takes whatever license with dramatic convention as is convenient to his purposes.

Tom enters dressed as a merchant sailor from alley, stage left, and strolls across the front of the stage to the fire-escape. There he stops and lights a cigarette. He addresses the audience.

TOM: Yes, I have tricks in my pocket, I have things up my sleeve. But I am the opposite of a stage magician. He gives you the illusion that has the appearance of truth. I give you truth in the pleasant disguise of illusion. To begin with, I turn back time. I reverse it to that quaint period, the thirties, when the huge middle class of America was matriculating in a school for the blind. Their eyes had failed them, or they had failed their eyes, and so they were having their fingers pressed forcibly down on the fiery Braille alphabet of a dissolving economy. In Spain there was revolution. Here there was only shouting and confusion. In Spain there was Guernica. Here there were disturbances of labor, sometimes pretty violent, in otherwise peaceful cities such as Chicago, Cleveland, Saint Louis . . . . This is the social background of the play.

[Music.]

The play is memory. Being a memory play, it is dimly lighted, it is sentimental, it is not realistic. In memory everything seems to happen to music. That explains the fiddle in the wings. I am the narrator of the play, and also a character in it. The other characters are my mother, Amanda, my sister, Laura, and a gentleman caller who appears in the final scenes. He is the most realistic character in the play, being an emissary from a world of reality that we were somehow set apart from. But since I have a poet's weakness for symbols, I am using this character also as a symbol; he is the long delayed but always expected something that we live for. There is a fifth character in the play who doesn't appear except in this larger-than-life photograph over the mantel. This is our father who left us a long time ago. He was a telephone man who fell in love with long distances; he gave up his job with the telephone company and skipped the light fantastic out of town . . . . The last we heard of him was a picture post-card from Mazatlan, on the Pacific coast of Mexico, containing a message of two words—"Hello—Good-bye!" and no address. I think the rest of the play will explain itself . . . .

Amanda's voice becomes audible through the portieres.

[Legend on Screen: "Où Sont Les Neiges?"]°

He divides the portieres and enters the upstage area. Amanda and Laura are seated at a drop-leaf table. Eating is indicated by gestures without food or utensils. Amanda faces the audience. Tom and Laura are seated in profile. The interior has lit up softly and through the scrim we see Amanda and Laura seated at the table in the upstage area.

Où Sont Les Neiges refrain from a poem by François Villion [1431–1463?]: "Where are the snows of yesteryear?"

AMANDA [calling]: Tom?

TOM: Yes, Mother.

AMANDA: We can't say grace until you come to the table!

TOM: Coming, Mother. [He bows slightly and withdraws, reappearing a few moments later in his place at the table.]

AMANDA [to her son]: Honey, don't push with your fingers. If you have to push with something, the thing to push with is a crust of bread. And chew—chew! Animals have sections in their stomachs which enable them to digest food without mastication, but human beings are supposed to chew their food before they swallow it down. Eat food leisurely, son, and really enjoy it. A well-cooked meal has lots of delicate flavors that have to be held in the mouth for appreciation. So chew your food and give your salivary glands a chance to function!

[Tom deliberately lays his imaginary fork down and pushes his chair back from the table.]

TOM: I haven't enjoyed one bite of this dinner because of your constant directions on how to eat it. It's you that makes me rush through meals with your hawk-like attention to every bite I take. Sickening—spoils my appetite—all this discussion of animals' secretion—salivary glands—mastication!

AMANDA [lightly]: Temperament like a Metropolitan star! [He rises and crosses downstage.] You're not excused from the table.

TOM: I am getting a cigarette.

AMANDA: You smoke too much. [Laura rises.]

LAURA: I'll bring in the blanc mange.

[He remains standing with cigarette by the portieres during the following.]

AMANDA [rising]: No, sister, no, sister—you be the lady this time and I'll be the darky.

LAURA: I'm already up.

AMANDA: Resume your seat, little sister—I want you to stay fresh and pretty—for gentlemen callers!

LAURA: I'm not expecting any gentlemen callers.

AMANDA [crossing out to kitchenette. Airily.]: Sometimes they come when they are least expected! Why, I remember one Sunday afternoon in the Blue Mountain—[Enters kitchenette.]

TOM: I know what's coming!

LAURA: Yes. But let her tell it.

TOM: Again?

LAURA: She loves to tell it.

[*Amanda returns with bowl of dessert.*]

AMANDA: One Sunday afternoon in Blue Mountain—your mother received—*seventeen!*—gentlemen callers! Why sometimes there weren't chairs enough to accommodate them all. We had to send the nigger over to bring in folding chairs from the parish house.

TOM [*remaining at portieres*]:   How did you entertain those gentlemen callers?

AMANDA: I understood the art of conversation!

TOM: I bet you could talk.

AMANDA: Girls in those days *knew* how to talk, I can tell you.

TOM: Yes?

[*Image: Amanda as a Girl on a Porch Greeting Callers.*]

AMANDA: They knew how to entertain their gentlemen callers. It wasn't enough for a girl to be possessed of a pretty face and a graceful figure—although I wasn't slighted in either respect. She also needed to have a nimble wit and a tongue to meet all occasions.

TOM: What did you talk about?

AMANDA: Things of importance going on in the world! Never anything coarse or common or vulgar. [*She addresses Tom as though he were seated in the vacant chair at the table though he remains by portieres. He plays this scene as though he held the book.*] My callers were gentlemen—all! Among my callers were some of the most prominent young planters of the Mississippi Delta—planters and sons of planters!

[*Tom motions for music and a spot of light on Amanda. Her eyes lift, her face glows, her voice becomes rich and elegiac.*]

[Screen Legend: "Où Sont Les Neiges?"]

There was young Champ Laughlin who later became vice-president of the Delta Planters Bank. Hadley Stevenson who was drowned in Moon Lake and left his widow one hundred and fifty thousand in Government bonds. There were the Cutrere brothers, Wesley and Bates. Bates was one of my bright particular beaux!

He got in a quarrel with that wild Wainright boy. They shot it out on the floor of Moon Lake Casino. Bates was shot through the stomach. Died in the ambulance on his way to Memphis. His widow was also well provided for, came into eight or ten thousand acres, that's all. She married him on the rebound—never loved her—carried my picture on him the night he died! And there was that boy that every girl in the Delta had set her cap for! That beautiful, brilliant young Fitzhugh boy from Green County!

TOM: What did he leave his widow?

AMANDA: He never married! Gracious, you talk as though all of my old admirers had turned up their toes to the daisies!

TOM: Isn't this the first you mentioned that still survives?

AMANDA: That Fitzhugh boy went North and made a fortune—came to be known as the Wolf of Wall Street! He had the Midas touch, whatever he touched turned to gold! And I could have been Mrs. Duncan J. Fitzhugh, mind you! But—I picked your *father*!

LAURA [*rising*]: Mother, let me clear the table.

AMANDA: No dear, you go in front and study your typewriter chart. Or practice your shorthand a little. Stay fresh and pretty!—It's almost time for our gentlemen callers to start arriving. [*She flounces girlishly toward the kitchenette.*] How many do you suppose we're going to entertain this afternoon?

[*Tom throws down the paper and jumps up with a groan.*]

LAURA [*alone in the dining room*]: I don't believe we're going to receive any, Mother.

AMANDA [*reappearing, airily*]: What? No one—not one? You must be joking! [*Laura nervously echoes her laugh. She slips in a fugitive manner through the half-open portieres and draws them gently behind her. A shaft of very clear light is thrown on her face against the faded tapestry of the curtain.*] [*Music: "The Glass Menagerie" Under Faintly.*] [*Lightly*] Not one gentleman caller? It can't be true! There must be a flood, there must have been a tornado!

LAURA: It isn't a flood, it's not a tornado, Mother. I'm just not popular like you were in Blue Mountain . . . . [*Tom utters another groan. Laura glances at him with a faint, apologetic smile. Her voice catching a little*] Mother's afraid I'm going to be an old maid.

[The Scene Dims Out with "Glass Menagerie" Music.]

Scene II. "Laura, Haven't You Ever Liked Some Boy?"

On the dark stage the screen is lighted with the image of blue roses. Gradually Laura's figure becomes apparent and the screen goes out. The music subsides. Laura is seated in the delicate ivory chair at the small clawfoot table. She wears a dress of soft violet material for a kimono—her hair tied back from her forehead with a ribbon. She is washing and polishing her collection of glass.

Amanda appears on the fire-escape steps. At the sound of her ascent, Laura catches her breath, thrusts the bowl of ornaments away and seats herself stiffly before the diagram of the typewriter keyboard as though it held her spellbound. Something has happened to Amanda. It is written in her face as she climbs to the landing: a look that is grim and hopeless and a little absurd.

She has one of those cheap or imitation velvety-looking cloth coats with imitation fur collar. Her hat is five or six years old, one of those dreadful cloche hats that were worn in the late twenties, and she is clasping an enormous black patent-leather pocketbook with nickel clasp and initials. This is her full-dress outfit, the one she usually wears to the D.A.R.

Before entering she looks through the door. She purses her lips, opens her eyes wide, rolls them upward and shakes her head. Then she slowly lets herself in the door. Seeing her mother's expression Laura touches her lips with a nervous gesture.

LAURA: Hello, Mother, I was—[*She makes a nervous gesture toward the chart on the wall. Amanda leans against the shut door and stares at Laura with a martyred look.*]

AMANDA: Deception? Deception? [*She slowly removes her hat and gloves, continuing the swift suffering stare. She lets the hat and gloves fall on the floor—a bit of acting.*]

LAURA [*shakily*]: How was the D.A.R. meeting? [*Amanda slowly opens her purse and removes a dainty white handkerchief which she shakes out delicately and delicately touches to her lips and nostrils.*] Didn't you go to the D.A.R. meeting, Mother?

AMANDA [*faintly, almost inaudibly*]: —No.—No. [*Then more forcibly*] I did not have the strength—to go to the D.A.R. In fact, I did not have the courage. I waited to find a hole in the ground and hide myself in it forever! [*She crosses slowly to the wall and removes the diagram of the typewriter keyboard. She holds it in front of her for a* *second, staring at it sweetly and sorrowfully—then bites her lips and tears it in two pieces.*]

LAURA [*faintly*]: Why did you do that, Mother? [*Amanda repeats the same procedure with the chart of the Gregg Alphabet.*] Why are you—

AMANDA: Why? Why? How old are you, Laura?

LAURA: Mother, you know my age.

AMANDA: I thought that you were an adult; it seems that I was mistaken. [*She crosses slowly to the sofa and sinks down and stares at Laura.*]

LAURA: Please don't stare at me, Mother.

[*Amanda closes her eyes and lowers her head. Count ten.*]

AMANDA: What are we going to do, what is going to become of us, what is the future?

[*Count ten.*]

LAURA: Has something happened, Mother? [*Amanda draws a long breath and takes out the handkerchief again. Dabbing process.*] Mother, has—something happened?

AMANDA: I'll be right in a minute. I'm just bewildered—[*count five*] — by life . . . .

LAURA: Mother, I wish you would tell me what's happened.

AMANDA: As you know, I was supposed to be inducted into my office at the D.A.R. this afternoon. [*Image: A Swarm of Typewriters.*] But I stopped off at Rubicam's Business College to speak to your teachers about your having a cold and ask them what progress they thought you were making down there.

LAURA: Oh . . . .

AMANDA: I went to the typing instructor and introduced myself as your mother. She didn't know who you were. Wingfield, she said. We don't have any such student enrolled at the school! I assured her she did, that you had been going to classes since early in January. "I wonder," she said, "if you could be talking about that terribly shy little girl who dropped out of school after only a few days' attendance?" "No," I said, "Laura, my daughter, has been going to school every day for the past six weeks!" "Excuse me," she said. She took the attendance book out and there was your name, unmistakably printed, and all the dates you were absent until they decided that you had dropped out of school. I still said, "No, there must have been some mistake! There must have been some mix-up in the records!" And she said, "No—I remember her perfectly now. Her hand shook so that she couldn't hit the right keys! The first time we gave a speed-test, she broke down completely—was sick at the stomach and almost had to be carried into the wash-room! After that morning she never showed up any more. We phoned the house but never got any answer"—while I was work-ing at Famous and Barr, I suppose demonstrating those—Oh! I felt so weak I could barely keep on my feet. I had to sit down while they got me a glass of water! Fifty dollars' tuition, all of our plans—my hopes and ambitions for you—just gone up the spout, just gone up the spout like that. [*Laura draws a long breath and gets awkwardly to her feet. She crosses to the victrola and winds it up.*] What are you doing?

LAURA: Oh! [*She releases the handle and returns to her seat.*]

AMANDA: Laura, where have you been going when you've gone out pretending that you were going to business college?

LAURA: I've just been going out walking.

AMANDA: That's not true.

LAURA: It is. I just went walking.

AMANDA: Walking? Walking? In winter? Deliberately courting pneu-monia in that light coat? Where did you walk to, Laura?

LAURA: It was the lesser of two evils, Mother. [*Image: Winter Scene in Park.*] I couldn't go back up. I—threw up—on the floor!

AMANDA: From half past seven till after five thirty every day you mean to tell me you walked around in the park, because you wanted to make me think that you were still going to Rubicam's Business College?

LAURA: It wasn't as bad as it sounds. I went inside places to get warmed up.

AMANDA: Inside where?

LAURA: I went in the art museum and the birdhouses at the Zoo. I visited the penguins every day! Sometimes I did without lunch and went to the movies. Lately I've been spending most of my after-noons in the Jewel-box, that big glass house where they raise the tropical flowers.

AMANDA: You did all this to deceive me, just for the deception? [*Laura looks down.*] Why?

LAURA: Mother, when you're disappointed, you get that awful suffering look on your face. Like the picture of Jesus' mother in the museum!

AMANDA: Hush!

LAURA: I couldn't face it.

[*Pause: A whisper of strings.*]

[Legend: "The Crust of Humility."]

AMANDA [*hopelessly fingering the huge pocketbook*]: So what are we going to do the rest of our lives? Stay home and watch the parades go by? Amuse ourselves with the glass menagerie, darling? Eternally play those worn-out phonograph records your father left as a painful reminder of him? We won't have a business career—we've given that up because it gave us nervous indigestion! [*Laughs wearily.*] What is there left but dependency all our lives? I know so well what becomes of unmarried women who aren't prepared to occupy a position. I've seen such pitiful cases in the South—barely tolerated spinsters living upon the grudging patronage of sister's husband or brother's wife!—stuck away in some little mousetrap of a room—encouraged by one inlaw to visit another—little bird-like women without any nest—eating the crust of humility all their life! Is that the future that we've mapped out for ourselves? I swear it's the only alternative I can think of! It isn't a very pleasant alternative, is it? Of course—some girls *do* marry. [*Laura twists her hands nervously.*] Haven't you ever liked some boy?

LAURA: Yes, I liked one once. [*Rises.*] I came across his picture a while ago.

AMANDA [*with some interest*]: He gave you his picture?

LAURA: No, it's in the year-book.

AMANDA [*disappointed*]: Oh—a high-school boy.

[Screen Image: Jim as a High-School Hero Bearing a Silver Cup.]

LAURA: Yes. His name was Jim. [*Laura lifts the heavy annual from the clawfoot table.*] Here he is in *The Pirates of Penzance*.

AMANDA [*absently*]: The what?

LAURA: The operetta the senior class put on. He had a wonderful voice and we sat across the aisle from each other Mondays, Wednesdays, and Fridays in the Aud. Here he is with the silver cup for debating! See his grin?

AMANDA [*absently*]: He must have had a jolly disposition.

LAURA: He used to call me—Blue Roses.

[Image: Blue Roses.]

AMANDA: Why did he call you such a name as that?

LAURA: When I had that attack of pleurosis—he asked me what was the matter when I came back. I said pleurosis—he thought I said Blue Roses! So that's what he always called me after that. Whenever he saw me, he'd holler, "Hello, Blue Roses!" I didn't care for the girl that he went out with. Emily Meisenbach. Emily was the best-dressed girl at Soldan. She never struck me, though, as being sincere . . . . It says in the Personal Section—they're engaged. That's—six years ago! They must be married by now.

AMANDA: Girls that aren't cut out for business careers usually wind up married to some nice man. [*Gets up with a spark of revival.*] Sister, that's what you'll do!

[*Laura utters a startled, doubtful laugh. She reaches quickly for a piece of glass.*]

LAURA: But, Mother—

AMANDA: Yes? [*Crossing to photograph.*]

LAURA [*in a tone of frightened apology*]:   I'm—crippled!

[Image: Screen.]

AMANDA: Nonsense! Laura, I've told you never, never to use that word. Why, you're not crippled, you just have a little defect—hardly noticeable, even! When people have some slight disadvantage like that, they cultivate other things to make up for it—develop charm—and vivacity—and—*charm!* That's all you have to do! [*She turns again to the photograph.*] One thing your father had *plenty of*—was *charm!*

[*Tom motions to the fiddle in the wings.*]

[The Scene Fades Out with Music.]

Scene III
(Legend on the Screen: "After the Fiasco—")

[*Tom speaks from the fire-escape landing.*]

TOM: After the fiasco at Rubicam's Business College, the idea of getting a gentleman caller for Laura began to play a more important part in Mother's calculations. It became an obsession.

Like some archetype of the universal unconscious, the image of the gentleman caller haunted our small apartment . . . . [*Image: Young Man at Door with Flowers.*] An evening at home rarely passed without some allusion to this image, this specter, this hope . . . . Even when he wasn't mentioned, his presence hung in Mother's preoccupied look and in my sister's frightened, apologetic manner—hung like a sentence passed upon the Wingfields! Mother was a woman of action as well as words. She began to take logical steps in the planned direction. Late that winter and in the early spring—realizing that extra money would be needed to properly feather the nest and plume the bird—she conducted a vigorous campaign on the telephone, roping in subscribers to one of those magazines for matrons called *The Home-maker's Companion,* the type of journal that features the serialized sublimation of ladies of letters who think in terms of delicate cup-like breasts, slim, tapering waists, rich, creamy thighs, eyes like wood-smoke in autumn, fingers that soothe and caress like strains of music, bodies as powerful as Etruscan sculpture.

[Screen Image: Glamour Magazine Cover.]

[*Amanda enters with phone on long extension cord. She is spotted in the dim stage.*]

AMANDA: Ida Scott? This is Amanda Wingfield! We *missed* you at the D.A.R. last Monday! I said to myself: She's probably suffering with that sinus condition! How is that sinus condition? Horrors! Heaven have mercy!—You're a Christian martyr, yes, that's what you are, a Christian martyr! Well, I just now happened to notice that your subscription to the *Companion's* about to expire! Yes, it expires with the next issue, honey!—just when that wonderful new serial by Bessie Mae Hopper is getting off to such an exciting start. Oh, honey, it's something that you can't miss! You remember how *Gone With the Wind* took everybody by storm? You simply couldn't go out if you hadn't read it. All everybody *talked* was Scarlett O'Hara. Well, this is a book that critics already compare to *Gone With the Wind.* It's the *Gone With the Wind* of the post-World War generation!—What?—Burning? Oh, honey, don't let them burn, go take a look in the oven and I'll hold the wire! Heavens—I think she's hung up!

[Legend on Screen: "You Think I'm in Love with Continental
Shoemakers?"]

*[Before the stage is lighted, the violent voices of Tom and
Amanda are heard. They are quarreling behind the portieres. In
front of them stands Laura with clenched hands and panicky
expression. A clear pool of light on her figure throughout this
scene.]*

TOM: What in Christ's name am I—

AMANDA [*shrilly*]: Don't you use that—

TOM: Supposed to do!

AMANDA: Expression! Not in my—

TOM: Ohhh!

AMANDA: Presence! Have you gone out of your senses?

TOM: I have, that's true, *driven* out!

AMANDA: What is the matter with you, you—big—big—IDIOT!

TOM: Look—I've got *no thing*, no single thing—

AMANDA: Lower your voice?

TOM: In my life here that I can call my OWN! Everything is—

AMANDA: Stop that shouting!

TOM: Yesterday you confiscated my books! You had the nerve to—

AMANDA: I took that horrible novel back to the library—yes! That
hideous book by that insane Mr. Lawrence. [*Tom laughs wildly.*] I
cannot control the output of diseased minds or people who cater
to them—[*Tom laughs still more wildly.*] BUT I WON'T ALLOW SUCH
FILTH BROUGHT INTO MY HOUSE! No, no, no, no, no!

TOM: House, house! Who pays rent on it, who makes a slave of himself to—

AMANDA [*fairly screeching*]: Don't you DARE to—

TOM: No, no, I mustn't say things! *I've* got to just—

AMANDA: Let me tell you—

TOM: I don't want to hear any more! [*He tears the portieres open. The
upstage area is lit with a turgid smoky red glow.*]

*Amanda's hair is in metal curlers and she wears a very old
bathrobe, much too large for her slight figure, a relic of the faith-
less Mr. Wingfield. An upright typewriter and a mild disarray of
manuscripts are on the drop-leaf table. The quarrel was probably
precipitated by Amanda's interruption of his creative labor. A*

chair lying overthrown on the floor. Their gesticulating shadows are cast on the ceiling by the fiery glow.

AMANDA: You *will* hear more, you—

TOM: No, I won't hear more, I'm going out!

AMANDA: You come right back in—

TOM: Out, out out! Because I'm—

AMANDA: Come back here, Tom Wingfield! I'm not through talking to you!

TOM: Oh, go—

LAURA [*desperately*]: Tom!

AMANDA: You're going to listen, and no more insolence from you! I'm at the end of my patience! [*He comes back toward her.*]

TOM: What do you think I'm at? Aren't I supposed to have any patience to reach the end of, Mother? I know, I know. It seems unimportant to you, what I'm *doing*—what I *want* to do—having a little *difference* between them! You don't think that—

AMANDA: I think you've been doing things that you're ashamed of. That's why you act like this. I don't believe that you go every night to movies. Nobody goes to the movies night after night. Nobody in their right minds goes to movies as often as you pretend to. People don't go to the movies at nearly midnight, and movies don't let out at two A.M. Come in stumbling. Muttering to yourself like a maniac! You get three hours' sleep and then go to work. Oh, I can picture the way you're doing down there. Moping, doping, because you're in no condition.

TOM [*wildly*]: No, I'm in no condition!

AMANDA: What right have you got to jeopardize your job? Jeopardize the security of us all? How do you think we'd manage if you were—

TOM: Listen! You think I'm crazy *about the warehouse?* [*He bends fiercely toward her slight figure.*] You think I'm in love with the Continental Shoemakers? You think I want to spend fifty-five *years* down there in that—*celotex interior!* with—*fluorescent—tubes!* Look! I'd rather somebody picked up a crowbar and battered out my brains than go back mornings! I *go!* Every time you come in yelling that God damn *"Rise and Shine!" "Rise and Shine!"* I say to myself *"How lucky dead people are!"* But I get up. I *go!* For sixty-five dollars a month I gave up all that I dream of doing and being *ever!* And you say self—*self's* all I ever think of. Why, listen, if self is what I thought of, Mother, I'd be where he is—GONE! [*Pointing to father's picture.*] As far as the system of transportation reaches! [*He starts past her. She grabs his arm.*] Don't grab at me, Mother!

AMANDA: Where are you going?

TOM: I'm going to the *movies*!

AMANDA: I don't believe that lie!

TOM [*crouching toward her, overtowering her tiny figure. She backs away, gasping*]: I'm going to opium dens! Yes, opium dens, dens of vice and criminals' hang-outs, Mother. I've joined the Hogan gang, I'm a hired assassin, I carry a tommy-gun in a violin case! I run a string of cat-houses in the Valley. They call me Killer, Killer Wingfield, I'm leading a double-life, a simple, honest warehouse worker by day, by night a dynamic *czar* of the *underworld, Mother.* I go to gambling casinos, I spin away fortunes on the roulette table! I wear a patch over one eye and a false mustache, sometimes I put on green whiskers. On those occasions they call me—*El Diablo!* Oh, I could tell you things to make you sleepless! My enemies plan to dynamite this place. They're going to blow us all sky-high some night! I'll be glad, very happy, and so will you! You'll go up, up on a broomstick, over Blue Mountain with seventeen gentlemen callers! You ugly—babbling old—*witch* . . . . [*He goes through a series of violent, clumsy movements, seizing his overcoat, lunging to the door, pulling it fiercely open. The women watch him, aghast. His arm catches in the sleeve of the coat as he struggles to pull it on. For a moment he is pinioned by the bulky garment. With an outraged groan he tears the coat off again, splitting the shoulders of it, and hurls it across the room. It strikes against the shelf of Laura's glass collection, there is a tinkle of shattering glass. Laura cries out as if wounded.*]

[Music Legend: "The Glass Menagerie."]

LAURA [*shrilly*]: My glass! —menagerie . . . . [*She covers her face and turns away.*]

[*But Amanda is still stunned and stupefied by the "ugly witch" so that she barely notices this occurrence. Now she recovers her speech.*]

AMANDA [*in an awful voice*]: I won't speak to you—until you apologize! [*She crosses through the portieres and draws them together behind her. Tom is left with Laura. Laura clings weakly to the mantel with* her face averted. Tom stares at her stupidly for a moment. Then he crosses to shelf. Drops awkwardly to his knees to collect the fallen glass, glancing at Laura as if he would speak but couldn't.]

["The Glass Menagerie" steals in as the Scene Dims Out.]

Scene IV

The interior is dark. Faint light in the alley. A deep-voiced bell in a church is tolling the hour by five as the scene commences.

Tom appears at the top of the alley. After each solemn boom of the bell in the tower, he shakes a little noise-maker or rattle as if to express the tiny spasm of man in contrast to the sustained power and dignity of the Almighty. This and the unsteadiness of his advance make it evident that he has been drinking.

As he climbs the few steps to the fire-escape landing light steals up inside. Laura appears in night-dress, observing Tom's empty bed in the front room.

Tom fishes in his pockets for the door-key, removing a motley assortment of articles in the search, including a perfect shower of movie-ticket stubs and an empty bottle. At last he finds the key, but just as he is about to insert it, it slips from his fingers. He strikes a match and crouches below the door.

TOM [bitterly]:   One crack—and it falls through!

[Laura opens the door.]

LAURA: Tom! Tom, what are you doing?

TOM: Looking for a door-key.

LAURA: Where have you been all this time?

TOM: I have been to the movies.

LAURA: All this time at the movies?

TOM: There was a very long program. There was a Garbo picture and a Mickey Mouse and a travelogue and a newsreel and a preview of coming attractions. And there was an organ solo and a collection for the milk-fund—simultaneously—which ended up in a terrible fight between a fat lady and an usher!

LAURA [innocently]:   Did you have to stay through everything?

TOM: Of course! And, oh, I forgot! There was a big stage show! The headliner on this stage show was Malvolio the Magician. He performed wonderful tricks, many of them, such as pouring water back and forth between pitchers. First it turned to wine and then it turned to beer and then it turned to whiskey. I know it was whiskey it finally turned into because he needed somebody to come up out of the audience to help him, and I came up—both shows! It was Kentucky Straight Bourbon. A very generous fellow, he gave souvenirs. [*He pulls from his back pocket a shimmering rainbow-colored scarf.*] He gave me this. This is his magic scarf. You can have it, Laura. You wave it over a canary cage and you get a bowl of gold-fish. You wave it over the goldfish bowl and they fly away canaries . . . . But the wonderfulest trick of all was the coffin trick. We nailed him into a coffin and he got out of the coffin without removing one nail. [*He has come inside.*] There is a trick that would come in handy for me—get me out of this 2 by 4 situation! [*Flops onto bed and starts removing shoes.*]

LAURA: Tom—Shhh!

TOM: What you shushing me for?

LAURA: You'll wake up Mother.

TOM: Goody, goody! Pay 'er back for those "Rise an' Shines." [*Lies down, groaning.*] You know it don't take much intelligence to get yourself into a nailed-up coffin, Laura. But who in hell ever got himself out of one without removing one nail?

[*As if in answer, the father's grinning photograph lights up.*]

[Scene Dims Out.]

Immediately following: The church bell is heard striking six. At the sixth stroke the alarm clock goes off in Amanda's room, and after a few moments we hear her calling: "Rise and Shine! Rise and Shine! Laura, go tell your brother to rise and shine!"

TOM [*sitting up slowly*]: I'll rise—but I won't shine.

[*The light increases.*]

AMANDA: Laura, tell your brother his coffee is ready.

[*Laura slips into the front room.*]

LAURA: Tom! it's nearly seven. Don't make Mother nervous. [*He stares at her stupidly. Beseechingly.*] Tom, speak to Mother this morning. Make up with her, apologize, speak to her!

TOM: She won't to me. It's her that started not speaking.

LAURA: If you just say you're sorry she'll start speaking.

TOM: Her not speaking—is that such a tragedy?

LAURA: Please—please!

AMANDA [*calling from kitchenette*]: Laura, are you going to do what I asked you to do, or do I have to get dressed and go out myself?

LAURA: Going, going—soon as I get on my coat! [*She pulls on a shapeless felt hat with nervous, jerky movement, pleadingly glancing at Tom. Rushes awkwardly for coat. The coat is one of Amanda's, inaccurately made-over, the sleeves too short for Laura.*] Butter and what else?

AMANDA [*entering upstage*]: Just butter. Tell them to charge it.

LAURA: Mother, they make such faces when I do that.

AMANDA: Sticks and stones may break my bones, but the expression of Mr. Garfinkel's face won't harm me! Tell your brother his coffee is getting cold.

LAURA [*at door*]: Do what I asked you, will you, will you, Tom?

[*He looks sullenly away.*]

AMANDA: Laura, go now or just don't go at all!

LAURA [*rushing out*]: Going—going! [*A second later she cries out. Tom springs up and crosses to the door. Amanda rushes anxiously in. Tom opens the door.*]

TOM: Laura?

LAURA: I'm all right. I slipped, but I'm all right.

AMANDA [*peering anxiously after her*]: If anyone breaks a leg on those fire-escape steps, the landlord ought to be sued for every cent he possesses! [*She shuts the door. Remembers she isn't speaking and returns to the other room.*]

[*As Tom enters listlessly for his coffee, she turns her back to him and stands rigidly facing the widow on the gloomy gray vault of the areaway. Its light on her face with its aged but childish features is cruelly sharp, satirical as a Daumier print.*]

[Music Under: "Ave Maria."]

[*Tom glances sheepishly but sullenly at her averted figure and slumps at the table. The coffee is scalding hot; he sips it and gasps and spits it back in the cup. At his gasp, Amanda catches her breath and half turns. Then catches herself and turns back to the window.*

Tom blows on his coffee, glancing sidewise at his mother. She clears her throat. Tom clears his. He starts to rise. Sinks back down again, scratches his head, clears his throat again. Amanda coughs. Tom raises his cup in both hands to blow on it, his eyes

staring over the rim of it at his mother for several moments. Then
he slowly sets the cup down and awkwardly and hesitantly rises
from the chair.]

TOM [*hoarsely*]: Mother. I—I apologize. Mother. [*Amanda draws a*
quick, shuddering breath. Her face works grotesquely. She breaks into
childlike tears.] I'm sorry for what I said, for everything that I said, I
didn't mean it.

AMANDA [*sobbingly*]: My devotion has made me a witch and so I
make myself hateful to my children!

TOM: No, you *don't.*

AMANDA: I worry so much, don't sleep, it makes me nervous!

TOM [*gently*]: I understand that.

AMANDA: I've had to put up a solitary battle all these years. But you're
my right-hand bower! Don't fall down, don't fail!

TOM [*gently*]: I try, Mother.

AMANDA [*with great enthusiasm*]: Try and you will SUCCEED! [*The*
notion makes her breathless.] Why, you—you're just *full* of natural
endowments! Both of my children—they're *unusual* children! Don't
you think I know it? I'm so—proud! Happy and—feel I've—so
much to be thankful for but—Promise me one thing, son!

TOM: What, Mother?

AMANDA: Promise, son, you'll—never be a drunkard!

TOM [*turns to her grinning*]: I will never be a drunkard!

AMANDA: That's what frightened me so, that you'd be drinking! Eat a
bowl of Purina!

TOM: Just coffee, Mother.

AMANDA: Shredded wheat biscuit?

TOM: No. No, Mother, just coffee.

AMANDA: You can't put in a day's work on an empty stomach. You've
got ten minutes—don't gulp! Drinking too-hot liquids makes cancer of the stomach . . . . Put cream in.

TOM: No, thank you.

AMANDA: To cool it.

TOM: No! No, thank you, I want it black.

AMANDA: I know, but it's not good for you. We have to do all that we
can to build ourselves up. In these trying times we live in, all that we
have to cling to is each other . . . . That's why it's so important to—
Tom, I—I sent out your sister so I could discuss something with
you. If you hadn't spoken I would have spoken to you. [*Sits down.*]

TOM [*gently*]:   What is it, Mother, that you want to discuss?

AMANDA: Laura!

[*Tom puts his cup down slowly.*]

[Legend on Screen: "Laura."]

[Music: "The Glass Menagerie."]

TOM: —Oh.—Laura . . .

AMANDA [*touching his sleeve*]:   You know how Laura is. So quiet but—
still water runs deep! She notices things and I think she—broods
about them. [*Tom looks up.*] A few days ago I came in and she was
crying.

TOM: What about?

AMANDA: You.

TOM: Me?

AMANDA: She has an idea that you're not happy here.

TOM: What gave her that idea?

AMANDA: What gives her any idea? However, you do act strangely.
I—I'm not criticizing, understand *that!* I know your ambitions do
not lie in the warehouse, that like everybody in the whole wide
world—you've had to—make sacrifices, but—Tom—Tom—life's
not easy, it calls for—Spartan endurance! There's so many things
in my heart that I cannot describe to you! I've never told you but
I—*loved* your father . . . .

TOM [*gently*]:   I know that, Mother.

AMANDA: And you—when I see you taking after his ways! Staying
out late—and—well, you *had* been drinking the night you were
in that—terrifying condition! Laura says that you hate the apartment and that you go out nights to get away from it! Is that true,
Tom?

TOM: No. You say there's so much in your heart that you can't describe to me. That's true of me, too. There's so much in my heart
that I can't describe to *you!* So let's respect each other's—

AMANDA: But, why—*why*, Tom—are you always so *restless?* Where do
you go to, nights?

TOM: I—go to the movies.

AMANDA: Why do you go to the movies so much, Tom?

TOM: I go to the movies because—I like adventure. Adventure is
something I don't have much of at work, so I go to the movies.

AMANDA: But, Tom, you go to the movies *entirely too much!*

TOM: I like a lot of adventure.

[*Amanda looks baffled, then hurt. As the familiar inquisition resumes he becomes hard and impatient again. Amanda slips back into her querulous attitude toward him.*]

[Image on Screen: Sailing Vessel with Jolly Roger.]

AMANDA: Most young men find adventure in their careers.

TOM: Then most young men are not employed in a warehouse.

AMANDA: The world is full of young men employed in warehouses and offices and factories.

TOM: Do all of them find adventure in their careers?

AMANDA: They do or they do without it! Not everybody has a craze for adventure.

TOM: Man is by instinct a lover, a hunter, a fighter, and none of these instincts are given much play at the warehouse!

ARMANDA: Man is by instinct! Don't quote instinct to me! Instinct is something that people have got away from! It belongs to animals! Christian adults don't want it!

TOM: What do Christian adults want, then, Mother?

AMANDA: Superior things! Things of the mind and the spirit! Only animals have to satisfy instincts! Surely your aims are somewhat higher than theirs! Than monkeys—pigs—

TOM: I reckon they're not.

AMANDA: You're joking. However, that isn't what I wanted to discuss.

TOM [*rising*]:   I haven't much time.

AMANDA [*pushing his shoulders*]:   Sit down.

TOM: You want me to punch in red at the warehouse, Mother?

AMANDA: You have five minutes. I want to talk about Laura.

[Legend: "Plans and Provisions."]

TOM: All right! What about Laura?

AMANDA: We have to be making plans and provisions for her. She's older than you, two years, and nothing has happened. She just drifts along doing nothing. It frightens me terribly how she just drifts along.

TOM: I guess she's the type that people call home girls.

AMANDA: There's no such type, and if there is, it's a pity! That is unless the home is hers, with a husband!

TOM: What?

AMANDA: Oh, I can see the handwriting on the wall as plain as I see the nose in front of my face! It's terrifying! More and more you re-mind me of your father! He was out all hours without explanation— Then *left! Good-bye!* And me with the bag to hold. I saw that letter you got from the Merchant Marine. I know what you're dreaming of. I'm not standing here blindfolded. Very well, then. Then *do* it! But not till there's somebody to take your place.

TOM: What do you mean?

AMANDA: I mean that as soon as Laura has got somebody to take care of her, married, a home of her own, independent—why, then you'll be free to go wherever you please, on land, on sea, whichever way the wind blows! But until that time you've got to look out for your sister. I don't say me because I'm old and don't matter! I say for your sister because she's young and dependent. I put her in business college—a dismal failure! Frightened her so it made her sick to her stomach. I took her over to the Young People's League at the church. Another fiasco. She spoke to nobody, nobody spoke to her. Now all she does is fool with those pieces of glass and play those worn-out records. What kind of life is that for a girl to lead!

TOM: What can I do about it?

AMANDA: Overcome selfishness! Self, self, self is all that you ever think of! [*Tom springs up and crosses to get his coat. It is ugly and bulky. He pulls on a cap with earmuffs.*] Where is your muffler? Put your wool muffler on! [*He snatches it angrily from the closet and tosses it around his neck and pulls both ends tight.*] Tom! I haven't said what I had in mind to ask you.

TOM: I'm too late to—

AMANDA [*catching his arms very importunately. Then shyly.*]: Down the warehouse, aren't there some—nice young men?

TOM: No!

AMANDA: There *must* be—*some.*

TOM: Mother—

[*Gesture.*]

AMANDA: Find out one that's clean-living—doesn't drink and—ask him out for sister?

TOM: What?

AMANDA: For *sister!* To *meet!* Get acquainted!

TOM [*stamping to door*]:   Oh, my *go-osh!*

AMANDA: Will you? [*He opens door. Imploringly*] Will you? [*He starts down.*] Will you? Will you, dear?

TOM [*calling back*]: YES!

[*Amanda closes the door hesitantly and with a troubled but faintly hopeful expression.*]

[Screen Image: Glamour Magazine Cover.]

[*Spot Amanda at phone.*]

AMANDA: Ella Cartwright? This is Amanda Wingfield! How are you, honey? How is that kidney condition? [*Count five.*] Horrors! [*Count five.*] You're a Christian martyr, yes, honey, that's what you are, a Christian martyr! Well, I just happened to notice in my little red book that your subscription to the *Companion* has just run out! I knew that you wouldn't want to miss out on the wonderful serial starting in this new issue. It's by Bessie Mae Hopper, the first thing she's written since *Honeymoon for Three*. Wasn't that a strange and interesting story? Well, this one is even lovelier, I believe. It has a sophisticated society background. It's all about the horsey set on Long Island!

[Fade Out.]

Scene V

[Legend on Screen: "Annunciation."] Fade With Music.

It is early dusk of a spring evening. Supper has just been finished in the Wingfield apartment. Amanda and Laura in light-colored dresses are removing dishes from the table, in the upstage area, which is shadowy, their movements formalized almost as a dance or ritual, their moving forms as pale and silent as moths. Tom, in white shirt and trousers, rises from the table and crosses toward the fire-escape.

AMANDA [*as he passes her*]: Son, will you do me a favor?

TOM: What?

AMANDA: Comb your hair! You look so pretty when your hair is combed! [*Tom slouches on the sofa with the evening paper. Enormous caption "Franco Triumphs."*] There is only one respect in which I would like you to emulate your father.

TOM: What respect is that?

AMANDA: The care he always took of his appearance. He never allowed himself to look untidy. [*He throws down the paper and crosses to the fire-escape.*] Where are you going?

TOM: I'm going out to smoke.

AMANDA: You smoke too much. A pack a day at fifteen cents a pack. How much would that amount to in a month? Thirty times fifteen is how much, Tom? Figure it out and you will be astounded at what you could save. Enough to give you a night-school course in accounting at Washington U! Just think what a wonderful thing that would be for you, son!

[*Tom is unmoved by the thought.*]

TOM: I'd rather smoke. [*He steps out on the landing, letting the screen door slam.*]

AMANDA [*sharply*]: I know! That's the tragedy of it . . . . [*Alone, she turns to look at her husband's picture.*]

[*Dance Music: "All the World Is Waiting for the Sunrise!"*]

TOM [*to the audience*]: Across the alley from us was the Paradise Dance Hall. On evenings in spring the windows and doors were open and the music came outdoors. Sometimes the lights were turned out except for a large glass sphere that hung from the ceiling. It would turn slowly about and filter the dusk with delicate rainbow colors. Then the orchestra played a waltz or a tango, something that had a slow and sensuous rhythm. Couples would come outside, to the relative privacy of the alley. You could see them kissing behind ashpits and telephone poles. This was the compensation for lives that passed like mine, without any change or adventure. Adventure and change were imminent in this year. They were waiting around the corner for all these kinds. Suspended in the mist over Berchtesgaden, caught in the folds of Chamberlain's umbrella—In Spain there was Guernica! But here there was only hot swing music and liquor, dance halls, bars, and movies, and sex that hung in the gloom like a chandelier and flooded the world with brief, deceptive rainbows . . . . All the world was waiting for bombardments!

[*Amanda turns from the picture and comes outside.*]

AMANDA [*sighing*]: A fire-escape landing's a poor excuse for a porch. [*She spreads a newspaper on a step and sits down, gracefully and*

demurely as if she were settling into a swing on a Mississippi veranda.]
What are you looking at?

TOM: The moon.

AMANDA: Is there a moon this evening?

TOM: It's rising over Garfinkel's Delicatessen.

AMANDA: So it is! A little silver slipper of a moon. Have you made a
wish on it yet?

TOM: Um-hum.

AMANDA: What did you wish for.

TOM: That's a secret.

AMANDA: A secret, huh? Well, I won't tell you mine either. I will be
just as mysterious as you.

TOM: I bet I can guess what yours is.

AMANDA: Is my head so transparent?

TOM: You're not a sphinx.

AMANDA: No, I don't have secrets. I'll tell you what I wished for on
the moon. Success and happiness for my precious children! I wish
for that whenever there's a moon, and when there isn't a moon,
I wish for it, too.

TOM: I thought perhaps you wished for a gentleman caller.

AMANDA: Why do you say that?

TOM: Don't you remember asking me to fetch one?

AMANDA: I remember suggesting that it would be nice for your sister
if you brought home some nice young man from the warehouse. I
think I've made that suggestion more than once.

TOM: Yes, you have made it repeatedly.

AMANDA: Well?

TOM: We are going to have one.

AMANDA: What?

TOM: A gentleman caller!

[The Annunciation Is Celebrated with Music.]

[*Amanda rises.*]

[Image on Screen: Caller with Bouquet.]

AMANDA: You mean you have asked some nice young man to come
over?

TOM: Yep. I've asked him to dinner.

AMANDA: You really did?

TOM: I did!

AMANDA: You did, and did he—*accept?*

TOM: He did!

AMANDA: Well, well—well, well! That's—lovely!

TOM: I thought that you would be pleased.

AMANDA: It's definite, then?

TOM: Very definite.

AMANDA: Soon?

TOM: Very soon.

AMANDA: For heaven's sake, stop putting on and tell me some things, will you?

TOM: What things do you want me to tell you?

AMANDA: Naturally I would like to know when he's *coming!*

TOM: He's coming tomorrow.

AMANDA: Tomorrow?

TOM: Yep. Tomorrow.

AMANDA: But, Tom!

TOM: Yes, Mother?

AMANDA: Tomorrow gives me no time!

TOM: Time for what?

AMANDA: Preparations! Why didn't you phone me at once, as soon as you asked him, the minute that he accepted? Then, don't you see, I could have been getting ready!

TOM: You don't have to make any fuss.

AMANDA: Oh, Tom, Tom, Tom, of course I have to make a fuss! I want things nice, not sloppy! Not thrown together. I'll certainly have to do some fast thinking, won't I?

TOM: I don't see why you have to think at all.

AMANDA: You just don't know. We can't have a gentleman caller in a pig-sty! All my wedding silver has to be polished, the monogrammed table linen ought to be laundered! The windows have to be washed and fresh curtains put up. And how about clothes? We have to *wear* something, don't we?

TOM: Mother, this boy is no one to make a fuss over!

AMANDA: Do you realize he's the first young man we've had introduced to your sister? It's terrible, dreadful, disgraceful that poor little sister has never received a single gentleman caller! Tom, come inside! [*She opens the screen door.*]

TOM: What for?

AMANDA: I want to ask you some things.

TOM: If you're going to make such a fuss, I'll call it off, I'll tell him not to come.

AMANDA: You certainly won't do anything of the kind. Nothing offends people worse than broken engagements. It simply means I'll have to work like a Turk! We won't be brilliant, but we'll pass inspection. Come on inside. [*Tom follows, groaning.*] Sit down.

TOM: Any particular place you would like me to sit?

AMANDA: Thank heavens I've got that new sofa! I'm also making payments on a floor lamp I'll have sent out! And put the chintz covers on, they'll brighten things up! Of course I'd hoped to have these walls re-papered . . . . What is the young man's name?

TOM: His name is O'Connor.

AMANDA: That, of course, means fish—tomorrow is Friday! I'll have that salmon loaf—with Durkee's dressing! What does he do? He works at the warehouse?

TOM: Of course! How else would I—

AMANDA: Tom, he—doesn't drink?

TOM: Why do you ask me that?

AMANDA: Your father *did!*

TOM: Don't get started on that!

AMANDA: He *does* drink, then?

TOM: Not that I know of!

AMANDA: Make sure, be certain! The last thing I want for my daughter's a boy who drinks?

TOM: Aren't you being a little premature? Mr. O'Connor has not yet appeared on the scene!

AMANDA: But will tomorrow. To meet your sister, and what do I know about his character? Nothing! Old maids are better off than wives of drunkards!

TOM: Oh, my God.

AMANDA: Be still!

TOM [*leaning forward to whisper*]: Lots of fellows meet girls whom they don't marry!

AMANDA: Oh, talk sensibly, Tom—and don't be sarcastic! [*She has gotten a hairbrush.*]

TOM: What are you doing?

AMANDA: I'm brushing that cow-lick down! What is this young man's position at the warehouse?

TOM [*submitting grimly to the brush and the interrogation*]: This young man's position is that of a shipping clerk, Mother.

AMANDA: Sounds to me like a fairly responsible job, the sort of a job *you* would be in if you just had more *get-up*. What is his salary? Have you got any idea?

TOM: I would judge it to be approximately eighty-five dollars a month.

AMANDA: Well—not princely, but—

TOM: Twenty more than I make.

AMANDA: Yes, how well I know! But for a family man, eighty-five dollars a month is not much more than you can just get by on . . . .

TOM: Yes, but Mr. O'Connor is not a family man.

AMANDA: He might be, mightn't he? Some time in the future?

TOM: I see. Plans and provisions.

AMANDA: You are the only young man that I know of who ignores the fact that the future becomes the present, the present the past, and the past turns into everlasting regret if you don't plan for it!

TOM: I will think that over and see what I can make of it.

AMANDA: Don't be supercilious with your mother! Tell me some more about this—what do you call him?

TOM: James D. O'Connor. The D. is for Delaney.

AMANDA: Irish on *both* sides! *Gracious!* And doesn't drink?

TOM: Shall I call him up and ask him right this minute?

AMANDA: The only way to find out about those things is to make discreet inquiries at the proper moment. When I was a girl in Blue Mountain and it was suspected that a young man drank, the girl whose attentions he had been receiving, if any girl *was*, would sometimes speak to the minister of his church, or rather her father would if her father was living, and sort of feel him out on the young man's character. That is the way such things are discreetly handled to keep a young woman from making a tragic mistake!

TOM: Then how did you happen to make a tragic mistake?

AMANDA: That innocent look of your father's had everyone fooled! He *smiled*—the world was *enchanted!* No girl can do worse than put herself at the mercy of a handsome appearance! I hope that Mr. O'Connor is not too good-looking.

TOM: No, he's not too good-looking. He's covered with freckles and hasn't too much of a nose.

AMANDA: He's not right-down homely, though?

TOM: Not right-down homely. Just medium homely, I'd say.

AMANDA: Character's what to look for in a man.

TOM: That's what I've always said, Mother.

AMANDA: You've never said anything of the kind and I suspect you would never give it a thought.

TOM: Don't be suspicious of me.

AMANDA: At least I hope he's the type that's up and coming.

TOM: I think he really goes in for self-improvement.

AMANDA: What reason have you to think so?

TOM: He goes to night school.

AMANDA [*beaming*]: Splendid! What does he do, I mean study?

TOM: Radio engineering and public speaking!

AMANDA: Then he has visions of being advanced in the world! Any young man who studies public speaking is aiming to have an executive job some day! And radio engineering? A thing for the future! Both of these facts are very illuminating. Those are the sort of things that a mother should know concerning any young man who comes to call on her daughter. Seriously or—not.

TOM: One little warning. He doesn't know about Laura. I didn't let on that we had dark ulterior motives. I just said, why don't you come have dinner with us? He said okay and that was the whole conversation.

AMANDA: I bet it was! You're eloquent as an oyster. However, he'll know about Laura when he gets here. When we sees how lovely and sweet and pretty she is, he'll thank his lucky stars he was asked to dinner.

TOM: Mother, you mustn't expect too much of Laura.

AMANDA: What do you mean?

TOM: Laura seems all those things to you and me because she's ours and we love her. We don't even notice she's crippled any more.

AMANDA: Don't say crippled! You know that I never allow that word to be used!

TOM: But face facts, Mother. She is and—that's not all—

AMANDA: What do you mean "not all"?

TOM: Laura is very different from other girls.

AMANDA: I think the difference is all to her advantage.

TOM: Not quite all—in the eyes of others—strangers—she's terribly shy and lives in a world of her own and those things make her seem a little peculiar to people outside the house.

AMANDA: Don't say peculiar.

TOM: Face the facts. She is.

[*The Dance-Hall Music Changes to a Tango That Has a Minor and Somewhat Ominous Tone.*]

AMANDA: In what way is she peculiar—may I ask?

TOM [*gently*]: She lives in a world of her own—a world of—little glass ornaments, Mother . . . . [*Gets up, Amanda remains holding the brush, looking at him, troubled.*] She plays old phonograph records and—that's about all—[*He glances at himself in the mirror and crosses to the door.*]

AMANDA [*sharply*]: Where are you going?

TOM: I'm going to the movies. [*Out screen door.*]

AMANDA: Not to the movies, every night to the movies! [*Follows quickly to screen door.*] I don't believe you always go to the movies! [*He is gone. Amanda looks worriedly after him for a moment. Then vitality and optimism return and she turns from the door. Crossing to portieres.*] Laura! Laura! [*Laura answers from kitchenette.*]

LAURA: Yes, Mother.

AMANDA: Let those dishes go and come in front! [*Laura appears with dish towel. Gaily*] Laura, come here and make a wish on the moon!

LAURA [*entering*]: Moon—moon?

AMANDA: A little silver slipper of a moon. Look over your left shoulder, Laura, and make a wish! [*Laura looks faintly puzzled as if called out of sleep. Amanda seizes her shoulders and turns her at angle by the door.*] Now! Now, darling, *wish*!

LAURA: What shall I wish for, Mother?

AMANDA [*her voice trembling and her eyes suddenly filling with tears*]: Happiness! Good Fortune!

[*The violin rises and the stage dims out.*]

Scene VI

[Image: High School Hero.]

TOM: And so the following evening I brought Jim home to dinner. I had known Jim slightly in high school. In high school Jim was a hero. He had tremendous Irish good nature and vitality with the scrubbed and polished look of white chinaware. He seemed to move in a continual spotlight. He was a star in basketball, captain of the debating club, president of the senior class and the glee club and he sang the male lead in the annual light operas. He was always running or bounding, never just walking. He seemed always at the point of defeating the law of gravity. He was shooting with such velocity through his adolescence that you would logically expect him to arrive at nothing short of the White House by the time he was thirty. But Jim apparently ran into more interference after his graduation from Soldan. His speed had definitely slowed. Six years after he left high school he was holding a job that wasn't much better than mine.

[Image: Clerk.]

He was the only one at the warehouse with whom I was on friendly terms. I was valuable to him as someone who could remember his former glory, who had seen him win basketball games and the silver cup in debating. He knew of my secret practice of retiring to a cabinet of the washroom to work on poems when business was slack in the warehouse. He called me Shakespeare. And while the other boys in the warehouse regarded me with suspicious hostility, Jim took a humorous attitude toward me. Gradually his attitude affected the others, their hostility wore off and they also began to smile at me as people smile at an oddly fashioned dog who trots across their path at some distance.

I knew that Jim and Laura had known each other at Soldan, and I had heard Laura speak admiringly of his voice. I didn't know if Jim remembered her or not. In high school Laura had been as unobtrusive as Jim had been astonishing. If he did remember Laura, it was not as my sister for when I asked him to dinner, he grinned and said, "You know, Shakespeare, I never thought of you as having folks!" He was about to discover that I did . . . .

[Light upstage.]
[Legend on Screen: "The Accent of a Coming Foot."]

[*Friday evening. It is about five o'clock of a late spring evening which comes "scattering poems in the sky." A delicate lemony light is in the Wingfield apartment. Amanda has worked like a Turk in preparation for the gentleman caller. The results are astonishing. The new floor lamp with its rose-silk shade is in place, a colored paper lantern conceals the broken light fixture in the ceiling, new billowing white curtains are at the windows, chintz covers are on chairs, and sofa, a pair of new sofa pillows make their initial appearance.*

Open boxes and tissue paper are scattered on the floor.

Laura stands in the middle with lifted arms while Amanda crouches before her, adjusting the hem of the new dress, devout and ritualistic. The dress is colored and designed by memory. The arrangement of Laura's hair is changed; it is softer and more becoming. A fragile, unearthly prettiness has come out in Laura: she is like a piece of translucent glass touched by light, given a momentary radiance, not actual, not lasting.]

AMANDA [*impatiently*]:   Why are you trembling?

LAURA: Mother, you've made me so nervous!

AMANDA: How have I made you nervous?

LAURA: By all this fuss! You make it seem so important?

AMANDA: I don't understand you, Laura. You couldn't be satisfied with just sitting home, and yet whenever I try to arrange something for you, you seem to resist it. [*She gets up.*] Now take a look at yourself. No, wait! Wait just a moment—I have an idea!

LAURA: What is it now?

[*Amanda produces two powder puffs which she wraps in handkerchiefs and stuffs in Laura's bosom.*]

LAURA: Mother, what are you doing?

AMANDA: They call them "Gay Deceivers"!

LAURA: I won't wear them!

AMANDA: You will!

LAURA: Why should I?

AMANDA: Because, to be painfully honest, your chest is flat.

LAURA: You make it seem like we were setting a trap.

AMANDA: All pretty girls are a trap, a pretty trap, and men expect them to be.

[Legend: "A Pretty Trap."]

Now look at yourself, young lady. This is the prettiest you will ever be! I've got to fix myself now! You're going to be surprised by your mother's appearance.

[*She crosses through portieres, humming gaily.*]

[*Laura moves slowly to the long mirror and stares solemnly at herself. A wind blows the white curtains inward in a slow, graceful motion and with a faint, sorrowful sighing.*]

AMANDA [*offstage*]:   It isn't dark enough yet. [*She turns slowly before the mirror with a troubled look.*]

[Legend on Screen: "This Is My Sister: Celebrate Her with Strings!"
Music.]

AMANDA [*laughing, off*]:   I'm going to show you something. I'm going to make a spectacular appearance!

LAURA: What is it, Mother?

AMANDA: Possess your soul in patience—you will see! Something I've resurrected from that old trunk! Styles haven't changed so terribly much after all . . . . [*She parts the portieres.*] Now just look at your mother! [*She wears a girlish frock of yellowed voile with a blue silk sash. She carries a bunch of jonquils—the legend of her youth is nearly revived. Feverishly*] This is the dress in which I led the cotillion. Won the cakewalk twice at Sunset Hill, wore one spring to the Governor's ball in Jackson! See how I sashayed around the ballroom, Laura? [*She raises her skirt and does a mincing step around the room.*] I wore it on Sundays for my gentleman callers! I had it on the day I met your father—I had malaria fever all that spring. The change of climate from East Tennessee to the Delta—weakened resistance—I had a little temperature all the time—not enough to be serious—just enough to make me restless and giddy! Invitations poured in parties all over the Delta!—"Stay in bed," said Mother, "you have fever!"—but I just wouldn't.—I took quinine but kept on going, going!—Evenings, dances!—Afternoon, long, long rides! Picnics—lovely!—So lovely, that country in May.—All lacy with dogwood, literally flooded with jonquils.—That was the spring I had the craze for jonquils. Jonquils became an absolute obsession. Mother said, "Honey, there's no more room for jonquils." And still I kept bringing in more jonquils. Whenever, wherever I saw them, I'd say, "Stop! Stop! I see jonquils!" I made the young men help me gather the jonquils! It was a joke, Amanda and her jonquils! Finally there were no more vases to hold them, every available space was filled with jonquils. No vases to hold them? All right, I'll hold them myself! And then I—[*She stops in front of the picture.*] [*Music.*] met your father! Malaria fever and jonquils and then—this—boy . . . . [*She switches on the rose-colored lamp.*] I hope they get here before it starts to rain. [*She crosses upstage* and places the jonquils in a bowl on the table.] I gave your brother a little extra change so he and Mr. O'Connor could take the service car home.

LAURA [with altered look]:   What did you say his name was?
AMANDA: O'Connor.
LAURA: What is his first name?
AMANDA: I don't remember. Oh, yes, I do. It was—Jim!

[Laura sways slightly and catches hold of a chair.]

[Legend on Screen: "Not Jim!"]

LAURA [faintly]:   Not—Jim!
AMANDA: Yes, that was it, it was Jim! I've never know a Jim that wasn't nice!

[Music: Ominous.]

LAURA: Are you sure his name is Jim O'Connor?
AMANDA: Yes. Why?
LAURA: Is he the one that Tom used to know in high school?
AMANDA: He didn't say so. I think he just got to know him at the warehouse.
LAURA: There was a Jim O'Connor we both knew in high school— [Then, with effort.] If that is the one that Tom is bringing to dinner— you'll have to excuse me, I won't come to the table.
AMANDA: What sort of nonsense is this?
LAURA: You asked me once if I'd ever liked a boy. Don't you remember I showed you this boy's picture?
AMANDA: You mean the boy you showed me in the year book?
LAURA: Yes, that boy.
AMANDA: Laura, Laura, were you in love with that boy?
LAURA: I don't know, Mother. All I know is I couldn't sit at the table if it was him!
AMANDA: It won't be him! It isn't the least bit likely. But whether it is or not, you will come to the table. You will not be excused.
LAURA: I'll have to be, Mother.
AMANDA: I don't intend to humor your silliness, Laura. I've had too much from you and your brother, both! So just sit down and compose yourself till they come. Tom has forgotten his key so you'll have to let them in, when they arrive.
LAURA [panicky]:   Oh, Mother—you answer the door!

AMANDA [*lightly*]: I'll be in the kitchen—busy!

LAURA: Oh, Mother, please answer the door, don't make me do it!

AMANDA [*crossing into kitchenette*]: I've got to fix the dressing for the salmon. Fuss, fuss—silliness!—over a gentleman caller!

[*Door swings shut. Laura is left alone.*]

[Legend: "Terror!"]

[*She utters a low moan and turns off the lamp—sits stiffly on the edge of the sofa, knotting her fingers together.*]

[Legend on Screen: "The Opening of a Door!"]

[*Tom and Jim appear on the fire-escape steps and climb to the landing. Hearing their approach, Laura rises with a panicky gesture. She retreats to the portieres.*

The doorbell. Laura catches her breath and touches her throat. Low drums.]

AMANDA [*calling*]: Laura, sweetheart! The door!

[*Laura stares at it without moving.*]

JIM: I think we just beat the rain.

TOM: Uh-huh. [*He rings again, nervously, Jim whistles and fishes for a cigarette.*]

AMANDA [*very, very gaily*]: Laura, that is your brother and Mr. O'Connor! Will you let them in, darling?

[*Laura crosses toward kitchenette door*].

LAURA [*breathlessly*]: Mother—you go to the door!

[*Amanda steps out of the kitchenette and stares furiously at Laura. She points imperiously at the door.*]

LAURA: Please, please!

AMANDA [*in a fierce whisper*]: What is the matter with you, you silly thing?

LAURA [*desperately*]: Please, you answer it, *please!*

AMANDA: I told you I wasn't going to humor you, Laura. Why have you chosen this time to lose your mind?

LAURA: Please, please, please, you go!

AMANDA: You'll have to go to the door because I can't.

LAURA [despairingly]: I can't either!

AMANDA: Why?

LAURA: I'm *sick*?

AMANDA: I'm sick, too—of your nonsense! Why can't you and your brother be normal people? Fantastic whims and behavior! [*Tom gives a long ring.*] Preposterous goings on! Can you give me one reason—[*Calls out lyrically.*] COMING! JUST ONE SECOND!—why should you be afraid to open a door? Now you answer it, Laura!

LAURA: Oh, oh, oh . . . [*She returns through the portieres. Darts to the victrola and winds it frantically and turns it on.*]

AMANDA: Laura Wingfield, you march right to that door!

LAURA: Yes—yes, Mother.

[*A faraway, scratchy rendition of "Dardanella" softens the air and gives her strength to move through it. She slips to the door and draws it cautiously open. Tom enters with the caller, Jim O'Connor.*]

TOM: Laura, this is Jim. Jim, this is my sister, Laura.

JIM [*stepping inside*]: I didn't know that Shakespeare had a sister!

LAURA [*retreating stiff and trembling from the door*]: How—how do you do?

JIM [*heartily extending his hand*]: Okay!

[*Laura touches it hesitantly with hers.*]

JIM: Your hand's *cold*, Laura!

LAURA: Yes, well—I've been playing the victrola . . . .

JIM: Must have been playing classical music on it! You ought to play a little hot swing music to warm you up!

LAURA: Excuse me—I haven't finished playing the victrola . . . .

[*She turns awkwardly and hurries onto the front room. She pauses a second by the victrola. Then catches her breath and darts through the portieres like a frightened deer.*]

JIM [*grinning*]: What was the matter?

TOM: Oh—with Laura? Laura is—terribly shy.

JIM: Shy, huh? It's unusual to meet a shy girl nowadays. I don't believe you ever mentioned you had a sister.

TOM: Well, now you know. I have one. Here is the *Post Dispatch*. You want a piece of it?

JIM: Uh-huh.

TOM: What piece? The comics?

JIM: Sports! [*Glances at it.*] Ole Dizzy Dean is on his bad behavior.

TOM [*disinterest*]: Yeah? [*Lights cigarette and crosses back to fire-escape door.*]

JIM: Where are *you* going?

TOM: I'm going out on the terrace.

JIM [*goes after him*]: You know, Shakespeare—I'm going to sell you a bill of goods!

TOM: What goods?

JIM: A course I'm taking.

TOM: Huh?

JIM: In public speaking! You and me, we're not the warehouse type.

TOM: Thanks—that's good news. But what has public speaking got to do with it?

JIM: It fits you for—executive positions!

TOM: Awww.

JIM: I tell you it's done a helluva lot for me.

[Image: Executive at Desk.]

TOM: In what respect?

JIM: In every! Ask yourself what is the difference between you an' me in the office down front? Brains?—No!—Ability?—No! Then what? Just one little thing—

TOM: What is that one little thing?

JIM: Primarily it amounts to—social poise! Being able to square up to people and hold your own on any social level!

AMANDA [*off stage*]: Tom?

TOM: Yes, Mother?

AMANDA: Is that you and Mr. O'Connor?

TOM: Yes, Mother.

AMANDA: Well, you just make yourselves comfortable in there.

TOM: Yes, Mother.

AMANDA: Ask Mr. O'Connor if he would like to wash his hands.

JIM: Aw—no—no—thank you—I took care of that at the warehouse. Tom—

TOM: Yes?

JIM: Mr. Mendoza was speaking to me about you.

TOM: Favorably?

JIM: What do you think?

TOM: Well—

JIM: You're going to be out of a job if you don't wake up.

TOM: I am waking up—

JIM: You show no signs.

TOM: The signs are interior.

[Image on Screen: The Sailing Vessel with Jolly Roger Again.]

TOM: I'm planning to change. [*He leans over the rail speaking with quiet exhilaration. The incandescent marquees and signs of the first-run movie houses light his face from across the alley. He looks like a voyager.*] I'm right at the point of committing myself to a future that doesn't include the warehouse and Mr. Mendoza or even a night-school course in public speaking.

JIM: What are you gassing about?

TOM: I'm tired of the movies.

JIM: Movies!

TOM: Yes, movies! Look at them—[*A wave toward the marvels of Grand Avenue.*] All of those glamorous people—having adventures—hogging it all, gobbling the whole thing up! You know what happens? People go to the *movies* instead of *moving*! Hollywood characters are supposed to have all the adventures for everybody in America, while everybody in America sits in a dark room and watches them have them! Yes, until there's a war. That's when adventure becomes available to the masses! *Everyone's* dish, not only Gable's! Then the people in the dark room come out of the dark room to have some adventures themselves—Goody, goody—It's our turn now, to go to the South Sea Island—to make a safari—to be exotic, far-off—But I'm not patient. I don't want to wait till then. I'm tired of the *movies* and I am *about* to move!

JIM [*incredulously*]: Move?

TOM: Yes.

JIM: When?

TOM: Soon!

JIM: Where? Where?

[*Theme Three: Music Seems to Answer the Question, While Tom Thinks It Over. He Searches Among His Pockets.*]

TOM: I'm starting to boil inside. I know I seem dreamy, but inside—well, I'm boiling! Whenever I pick up a shoe, I shudder a little thinking how short life is and what I am doing!—Whatever that means. I know it doesn't mean shoes—except as something to wear on a traveler's feet! [*Finds paper.*] Look—

JIM: What?

TOM: I'm a member.

JIM [*reading*]: The Union of Merchant Seamen.

TOM: I paid my dues this month, instead of the light bill.

JIM: You will regret it when they turn the lights off.

TOM: I won't be here.

JIM: How about your mother?

TOM: I'm like my father. The bastard son of a bastard! See how he grins? And he's been absent going on sixteen years!

JIM: You're just talking, you drip. How does your mother feel about it?

TOM: Shhh—Here comes Mother! Mother is not acquainted with my plans.

AMANDA [*enters portiere*]: Where are you all?

TOM: On the terrace, Mother.

[*They start inside. She advances to them. Tom is distinctly shocked at her appearance. Even Jim blinks a little. He is making his first contact with girlish Southern vivacity and in spite of the night-school course in public speaking is somewhat thrown off the beam by the unexpected outlay of social charm. Certain responses are attempted by Jim but are swept aside by Amanda's gay laughter and chatter. Tom is embarrassed but after the first shock Jim reacts very warmly. Grins and chuckles, is altogether won over.*]

[Image: Amanda as a Girl.]

AMANDA [*coyly smiling, shaking her girlish ringlets*]: Well, well, well, so this is Mr. O'Connor. Introductions entirely unnecessary. I've heard so much about you from my boy. I finally said to him, Tom—good gracious!—why don't you bring this paragon to supper? I'd like to meet this nice young man at the warehouse!— Instead of just hearing him sing your praises so much! I don't know why my son is so stand-offish—that's not Southern behavior! Let's sit down and—I think we could stand a little more air in here! Tom, leave the door open. I felt a nice fresh breeze a moment ago. Where has it gone? Mmm, so warm already! And not quite summer, even. We're going to burn up when summer really gets started. However, we're having—we're having a very light supper. I think light things are better fo' this time of year. The same as light clothes are. Light clothes an' light food are what warm weather calls fo'. You know our blood gets so thick during th' winter—it takes a while fo' us to *adjust* ou'selves!—when the season changes . . . It's come so quick this year. I wasn't prepared. All of a sudden—heavens! Already summer!—I ran to the trunk an' pulled out this light dress—Terribly old! Historical almost! But feels so good—so good an' co-ol, y'know . . . .

TOM: Mother—

AMANDA: Yes, honey?

TOM: How about—supper?

AMANDA: Honey, you go ask Sister if supper is ready! You know that Sister is in full charge of supper! Tell her you hungry boys are waiting for it. [*To Jim*] Have you met Laura?

JIM: She—

AMANDA: Let you in? Oh, good, you've met already! It's rare for a girl as sweet an' pretty as Laura to be domestic! But Laura is, thank heavens, not only pretty but also very domestic. I'm not at all. I never was a bit. I never could make a thing but angel-food cake. Well, in the South we had so many servants. Gone, gone, gone. All vestiges of gracious living! Gone completely! I wasn't prepared for what the future brought me. All of my gentleman callers were sons of planters and so of course I assumed that I would be married to one and raise my family on a large piece of land with plenty of servants. But man proposes—and woman accepts the proposal!—To vary that old, old saying a little bit—I married no planter! I married a man who worked for the telephone company!—that gallantly smiling gentleman over there! [*Points to the picture.*] A telephone man who—fell in love with long distance!—Now he travels and I don't even know where!—But what am I going on for about my—tribulations! Tell me yours—I hope you don't have any! Tom?

TOM [*returning*]: Yes, Mother?

AMANDA: Is supper nearly ready?

TOM: It looks to me like supper is on the table.

AMANDA: Let me look—[*She rises prettily and looks through portieres.*] Oh, lovely—but where is Sister?

TOM: Laura is not feeling well and she says that she thinks she'd better not come to the table.

AMANDA: What?—Nonsense!—Laura? Oh, Laura!

LAURA [*off stage, faintly*]: Yes, Mother.

AMANDA: You really must come to the table. We won't be seated until you come to the table! Come in, Mr. O'Connor. You sit over there and I'll—Laura? Laura Wingfield! You're keeping us waiting, honey! We can't say grace until you come to the table!

[*The back door is pushed weakly open and Laura comes in. She is obviously quite faint, her lips trembling, her eyes wide and staring. She moves unsteadily toward the table.*]

[Legend: "Terror!"]

[*Outside a summer storm is coming abruptly. The white curtains billow inward at the windows and there is a sorrowful murmur and deep blue dusk. Laura suddenly stumbles—She catches at a chair with a faint moan.*]

TOM: Laura!

AMANDA: Laura! [*There's a clap of thunder*]. [Legend: "Ah!"] [*Despairingly*] Why, Laura, you are sick, darling! Tom, help your sister into the living room, dear! Sit in the living room, Laura—rest on the sofa. Well! [*To the gentleman caller*] Standing over the hot stove made her ill! I told her that it was just too warm this evening, but—[*Tom comes back in. Laura is on the sofa.*] Is Laura all right now?

TOM: Yes.

AMANDA: What is that? Rain? A nice cool rain has come up? [*She gives the gentleman caller a frightened look.*] I think we may—have grace—now . . . [*Tom looks at her stupidly.*] Tom, honey—you say grace!

TOM: Oh . . . "For these and all thy mercies—" [*They bow their heads. Amanda stealing a nervous glance at Jim. In the living room Laura, stretched on the sofa, clenches her hands to her lips, to hold back a shuddering sob.*] God's Holy Name be praised—

[The Scene Dims Out.]

Scene VII. A souvenir

Half an hour later. Dinner is just being finished in the upstage area which is concealed by the drawn portieres.

As the curtain rises Laura is still huddled upon the sofa, her feet drawn under her, her head resting on a pale blue pillow, her eyes wide and mysteriously watchful. The new floor lamp with its shade of rose-colored silk gives a soft, becoming light to her face, bringing out the fragile, unearthly prettiness which usually escapes attention. There is a steady murmur of rain, but it is slackening and stops soon after the scene begins; the air outside becomes pale and luminous as the moon breaks out.

A moment after the curtain rises, the lights in both rooms flicker and go out.

JIM: Hey, there, Mr. Light Bulb!

[Amanda laughs nervously.]

[Legend: "Suspension of a Public Service."]

AMANDA: Where was Moses when the lights went out? Ha-ha. Do you know the answer to that one, Mr. O'Connor?

JIM: No, Ma'am, what's the answer?

AMANDA: In the dark! [Jim laughs appreciatively.] Everybody sit still. I'll light the candles. Isn't it lucky we have them on the table? Where's a match. Which of you gentlemen can provide a match?

JIM: Here.

AMANDA: Thank you, sir.

JIM: Not at all, Ma'am!

AMANDA: I guess the fuse has burnt out. Mr. O'Connor, can you tell a burnt-out fuse? I know I can't and Tom is a total loss when it comes to mechanics. [Sound: Getting Up: Voices Recede a Little to Kitchenette.] Oh, be careful, you don't bump into something. We don't want our gentleman caller to break his neck. Now wouldn't that be a fine howdy-do?

JIM: Ha-ha! Where is the fuse-box?

AMANDA: Right there next to the stove. Can you see anything?

JIM: Just a minute.

AMANDA: Isn't electricity a mysterious thing? Wasn't it Benjamin Franklin who tied a key to a kite? We live in such a mysterious universe, don't we? Some people say that science clears up all the mysteries for us. In my opinion it only creates more! Have you found it yet?

JIM: No, Ma'am. All these fuses look okay to me.

AMANDA: Tom!

TOM: Yes, Mother?

AMANDA: That light bill I gave you several days ago. The one I told you we got the notices about?

TOM: Oh.—Yeah.

[Legend: "Ha!"]

AMANDA: You didn't neglect to pay it by any chance.

TOM: Why, I—

AMANDA: Didn't! I might have known it!

JIM: Shakespeare probably wrote a poem on the light bill, Mrs. Wingfield.

AMANDA: I might have known better than to trust him with it! There's such a high price for negligence in this world!

JIM: Maybe the poem will win a ten-dollar prize.

AMANDA: We'll just have to spend the remainder of the evening in the nineteenth century, before Mr. Edison made the Mazda lamp!

JIM: Candlelight is my favorite kind of light.

AMANDA: That shows you're romantic! But that's no excuse for Tom. Well, we got through dinner. Very considerate of them to let us get through dinner before they plunged us into everlasting darkness, wasn't it, Mr. O'Connor?

JIM: Ha-ha!

AMANDA: Tom, as a penalty for your carelessness you can help me with the dishes.

JIM: Let me give you a hand.

AMANDA: Indeed you will not!

JIM: I ought to be good for something.

AMANDA: Good for something? [*Her tone is rhapsodic.*] You? Why, Mr. O'Connor, nobody, *nobody's* given me this much entertainment in years—as you have!

JIM: Aw, now, Mrs. Wingfield!

AMANDA: I'm not exaggerating, not one bit! But Sister is all by her lonesome. You go keep her company in the parlor! I'll give you this lovely old candelabrum that used to be on the altar at the church of the Heavenly Rest. It was melted a little out of shape when the church burnt down. Lightning struck it one spring. Gypsy Jones was holding a revival at the time and he estimated that the church was destroyed because the Episcopalians gave card parties.

JIM: Ha-ha.

AMANDA: And how about coaxing Sister to drink a little wine? I think it would be good for her! Can you carry both at once?

JIM: Sure, I'm Superman!

AMANDA: Now, Thomas, get into this apron!

[*The door of the kitchenette swings closed on Amanda's gay laughter; the flickering light approaches the portieres. Laura sits up nervously as he enters. Her speech at first is low and breathless from the almost intolerable strain of being alone with a stranger.*]

[Legend: "I Don't Suppose You Remember Me at All!"]

[*In her first speeches in this scene, before Jim's warmth overcomes her paralyzing shyness, Laura's voice is thin and breathless as though she has run up a steep flight of stairs. Jim's attitude is gently humorous. In playing this scene it should be stressed that while the incident is apparently unimportant, it is to Laura the climax of her secret life.*]

JIM: Hello, there, Laura.

LAURA [*faintly*]:   Hello. [*She clears her throat.*]

JIM: How are you feeling now? Better?

LAURA: Yes. Yes, thank you.

JIM: This is for you. A little dandelion wine. [*He extends it toward her with extravagant gallantry.*]

LAURA: Thank you.

JIM: Drink it—but don't get drunk! [*He laughs heartily. Laura takes the glass uncertainly; laughs shyly.*] Where shall I set the candles?

LAURA: Oh—oh, anywhere . . .

JIM: How about here on the floor? Any objections?

LAURA: No.

JIM: I'll spread a newspaper under to catch the drippings. I like to sit on the floor. Mind if I do?

LAURA: Oh, no.

JIM: Give me a pillow?

LAURA: What?

JIM: A pillow!

LAURA: Oh . . . [*Hands him one quickly.*]

JIM: How about you? Don't you like to sit on the floor?

LAURA: Oh—yes.

JIM: Why don't you, then?

LAURA: I—will.

JIM: Take a pillow! [*Laura does. Sits on the other side of the candelabrum. Jim crosses his legs and smiles engagingly at her.*] I can't
hardly see you sitting way over there.

LAURA: I can—see you.

JIM: I know, but that's not fair, I'm in the limelight. [*Laura moves her
pillow closer.*] Good! Now I can see you! Comfortable?

LAURA: Yes.

JIM: So am I. Comfortable as a cow. Will you have some gum?

LAURA: No, thank you.

JIM: I think that I will indulge, with your permission. [*Musingly un-
wraps it and holds it up.*] Think of the fortune made by the guy that
invented the first piece of chewing gum. Amazing, huh? The
Wrigley Building is one of the sights of Chicago.—I saw it summer
before last when I went up to the Century of Progress. Did you
take in the Century of Progress?

LAURA: No, I didn't.

JIM: Well, it was quite a wonderful exposition. What impressed me
most was the Hall of Science. Gives you an idea of what the future
will be in America, even more wonderful than the present time is!
[*Pause. Smiling at her*] Your brother tells me you're shy. Is that right,
Laura?

LAURA: I—don't know.

JIM: I judge you to be an old-fashioned type of girl. Well, I think
that's a pretty good type to be. Hope you don't think I'm being too
personal—do you?

LAURA [*hastily, out of embarrassment*]: I believe I will take a piece of
gum, if you—don't mind. [*Clearing her throat*] Mr. O'Connor, have
you—kept up with your singing?

JIM: Singing? Me?

LAURA: Yes. I remember what a beautiful voice you had.

JIM: When did you hear me sing?

[Voice Offstage in the Pause.]

VOICE [*offstage*]: O blow, ye winds, heigh-ho,
A-roving I will go!
I'm off to my love

With a boxing glove—
Ten thousand miles away!

JIM: You say you've heard me sing?

LAURA: Oh, yes! Yes, very often . . . I—don't suppose you remember me—at all?

JIM [*smiling doubtfully*]: You know I have an idea I've seen you before. I had that idea soon as you opened the door. It seemed almost like I was about to remember your name. But the name that I started to call you—wasn't a name! And so I stopped myself before I said it.

LAURA: Wasn't it—Blue Roses?

JIM [*springs up, grinning*]: Blue Roses! My gosh, yes—Blue Roses! That's what I had on my tongue when you opened the door! Isn't it funny what tricks your memory plays? I didn't connect you with the high school somehow or other. But that's where it was; it was high school. I didn't even know you were Shakespeare's sister! Gosh, I'm sorry.

LAURA: I didn't expect you to. You—barely knew me!

JIM: But we did have a speaking acquaintance, huh?

LAURA: Yes, we—spoke to each other.

JIM: When did you recognize me?

LAURA: Oh, right away!

JIM: Soon as I came in the door?

LAURA: When I heard your name I thought it was probably you. I knew that Tom used to know you a little in high school. So when you came in the door—Well, then I was—sure.

JIM: Why didn't you say something, then?

LAURA [*breathlessly*]: I didn't know what to say, I was—too surprised!

JIM: For goodness' sakes! You know, this sure is funny!

LAURA: Yes! Yes, isn't it, though . . .

JIM: Didn't we have a class in something together?

LAURA: Yes, we did.

JIM: What class was that?

LAURA: It was—singing—Chorus!

JIM: Aw!

LAURA: I sat across the aisle from you in the Aud.

JIM: Aw.

LAURA: Mondays, Wednesdays and Fridays.

JIM: Now I remember—you always came in late.

LAURA: Yes, it was so hard for me, getting upstairs. I had that brace on my leg—it clumped so loud!

JIM: I never heard any clumping.

LAURA [*wincing at the recollection*]:   To me it sounded like—thunder!

JIM: Well, well, well. I never even noticed.

LAURA: And everybody was seated before I came in. I had to walk in front of all those people. My seat was in the back row. I had to go clumping all the way up the aisle with everyone watching!

JIM: You shouldn't have been self-conscious.

LAURA: I know, but I was. It was always such a relief when the singing started.

JIM: Aw, yes. I've placed you now! I used to call you Blue Roses. How was it that I got started calling you that?

LAURA: I was out of school a little while with pleurosis. When I came back you asked me what was the matter. I said I had pleurosis— you thought I said Blue Roses. That's what you always called me after that!

JIM: I hope you didn't mind.

LAURA: Oh, no—I liked it. You see, I wasn't acquainted with many— people . . . .

JIM: As I remember you sort of stuck by yourself.

LAURA: I—I—never had much luck at—making friends.

JIM: I don't see why you wouldn't.

LAURA: Well, I—started out badly.

JIM: You mean being—

LAURA: Yes, it sort of—stood between me—

JIM: You shouldn't have let it!

LAURA: I know but it did, and—

JIM: You were shy with people!

LAURA: I tried not to be but never could—

JIM: Overcome it?

LAURA: No, I—I never could!

JIM: I guess being shy is something you have to work out of kind of gradually.

LAURA [*sorrowfully*]:   Yes—I guess it—

JIM: Takes time!

LAURA: Yes.

JIM: People are not so dreadful when you know them. That's what you have to remember! And everybody has problems, not just you, but practically everybody has got some problems. You think of yourself as having the only problems, as being the only one who is disappointed. But just look around you and you will see lots of people as disappointed as you are. For instance, I hoped when I was going to high school that I would be further along at this time, six years later, than I am now—You remember that wonderful write-up I had in *The Torch*?

LAURA: Yes! [*She rises and crosses to the table.*]

JIM: It said I was bound to succeed in anything I went into! [*Laura returns with the annual.*] Holy Jeez! *The Torch*! [*He accepts it reverently. They smiled across it with mutual wonder. Laura crouches beside him and they begin to turn through it. Laura's shyness is dissolving in his warmth.*]

LAURA: Here you are in *Pirates of Penzance*!

JIM [*wistfully*]:   I sang the baritone lead in that operatta.

LAURA [*rapidly*]:   So—*beautifully*!

JIM [*protesting*]:   Aw—

LAURA: Yes, yes—beautifully—beautifully!

JIM: You heard me?

LAURA: All three times!

JIM: No!

LAURA: Yes!

JIM: All three performances?

LAURA [*looking down*]:   Yes.

JIM: Why?

LAURA: I—wanted to ask you to—autograph my program.

JIM: Why didn't you ask me to?

LAURA: You were always surrounded by your own friends so much that I never had a chance to.

JIM: You should have just—

LAURA: Well, I—thought you might think I was—

JIM: Thought I might think you was—what?

LAURA: Oh—

JIM [*with reflective relish*]:   I was beleaguered by females in those days.

LAURA: You were terribly popular!

JIM: Yeah—

LAURA: You had such a—friendly way—

JIM: I was spoiled in high school.

LAURA: Everybody—liked you!

JIM: Including you?

LAURA: I—yes, I—I did, too—[*She gently closes the book in her lap.*]

JIM: Well, well, well!—Give me that program, Laura. [*She hands it to him. He signs it with a flourish.*] There you are—better late then never!

LAURA: Oh, I—what a—surprise!

JIM: My signature isn't worth very much right now. But some day— maybe—it will increase in value! Being disappointed is one thing and being discouraged is something else. I am disappointed but I'm not discouraged. I'm twenty-three years old. How old are you?

LAURA: I'll be twenty-four in June.

JIM: That's not old age!

LAURA: No, but—

JIM: You finished high school?

LAURA [*with difficulty*]: I didn't go back.

JIM: You mean you dropped out?

LAURA: I made bad grades in my final examinations. [*She rises and replaces the book and the program. Her voice strained.*] How is—Emily Meisenbach getting along?

JIM: Oh, that kraut-head!

LAURA: Why do you call her that?

JIM: That's what she was.

LAURA: You're not still—going with her?

JIM: I never see her.

LAURA: It said in the Personal Section that you were—engaged!

JIM: I know, but I wasn't impressed by that—propaganda!

LAURA: It wasn't—the truth?

JIM: Only in Emily's optimistic opinion!

LAURA: Oh—

[Legend: "What Have You Done Since High School?"]

[*Jim lights a cigarette and leans indolently back on his elbows smiling at Laura with a warmth and charm which light her inwardly with altar candles. She remains by the table and turns in her hands a piece of glass to cover her tumult.*]

JIM [*after several reflective puffs on a cigarette*]: What have you done since high school? [*She seems not to hear him.*] Huh? [*Laura looks up.*] I said what have you done since high school, Laura?

LAURA: Nothing much.

JIM: You must have been doing something these six long years.

LAURA: Yes.

JIM: Well, then, such as what?

LAURA: I took a business course at business college—

JIM: How did that work out?

LAURA: Well, not very—well—I had to drop out, it gave me—indigestion—

[*Jim laughs gently.*]

JIM: What are you doing now?

LAURA: I don't do anything—much. Oh, please don't think I sit around doing nothing! My glass collection takes up a good deal of my time. Glass is something you have to take good care of.

JIM: What did you say—about glass?

LAURA: Collection I said—I have one—[*She clears her throat and turns away again, acutely shy.*]

JIM [*abruptly*]: You know what I judge to be the trouble with you? Inferiority complex! Know what that is? That's what they call it when someone low-rates himself? I understand it because I had it, too. Although my case was not so aggravated as yours seems to be. I had it until I took up public speaking, developed my voice, and learned that I had an aptitude for science. Before that time I never thought of myself as being outstanding in any way whatsoever! Now I've never made a regular study of it, but I have a friend who says I can analyze people better than doctors that make a profession of it. I don't claim that to be necessarily true, but I can sure guess a person's psychology, Laura. [*Takes out his gum.*] Excuse me, Laura. I always take it out when the flavor is gone. I'll use this scrap of paper to wrap it in. I know how it is to get it stuck on a shoe. Yep—that's what I judge to be your principal trouble. A lack of confidence in yourself as a person. You don't have the proper amount of faith in yourself. I'm basing that fact on a number of your remarks and also on certain observations I've made. For instance that clumping you thought was so awful in high school. You say that you even dreaded to walk into class. You see what you did? You dropped out of school, you gave up an education because of a clump, which as far as I know was practically nonexistent! A little physical defect is what you have? Hardly noticeable even! Magnified thousands of times by imagination! You know what my strong advice to you is? Think of yourself as superior in some way!

LAURA: In what way would I think?

JIM: Why, man alive, Laura! Just look about you a little. What do you see? A world full of common people! All of 'em born and all of' em going to die! Which of them has one-tenth of your good points! Or mine! Or anyone else's, as far as that goes—Gosh! Everybody excels in some one thing. Some in many! [*Unconsciously glances at himself in the mirror.*] All you've got to do is discover in what! Take me, for instance. [*He adjusts his tie at the mirror.*] My interest happens to lie in electrodynamics. I'm taking a course in radio engineering at night school, Laura, on top of a fairly responsible job at the warehouse. I'm taking that course and studying public speaking.

LAURA: Ohhhh.

JIM: Because I believe in the future of television! [*Turning back to her.*] I wish to be ready to go up right along with it. Therefore I'm planning to get in on the ground floor. In fact, I've already made the right connections and all that remains is for the industry itself to get under way! Full steam—[*His eyes are starry.*] Knowledge—Zzzzzp! Money—Zzzzzzp! Power! That's the cycle democracy is built on! [*His attitude is convincingly dynamic. Laura stares at him, even her shyness eclipsed in her absolute wonder. He suddenly grins.*] I guess you think I think a lot of myself!

LAURA: No—o-o-o, I—

JIM: Now how about you? Isn't there something you take more interest in than anything else?

LAURA: Well, I do—as I said—have my—glass collection—

[*A peal of girlish laughter from the kitchen.*]

JIM: I'm not right sure I know what you're talking about. What kind of glass is it?

LAURA: Little articles of it, they're ornaments mostly! Most of them are little animals made out of glass, the tiniest little animals in the world. Mother calls them a glass menagerie! Here's an example of one, if you'd like to see it! This one is one of the oldest. It's nearly thirteen. [*He stretches out his hand.*] [*Music: "The Glass Menagerie."*] Oh, be careful—if you breathe, it breaks!

JIM: I'd better not take it. I'm pretty clumsy with things.

LAURA: Go on. I trust you with him! [*Places it in his palm.*] There now—you're holding him gently! Hold him over the light, he loves the light! You see how the light shines through him?

JIM: It sure does shine!

LAURA: I shouldn't be partial, but he is my favorite one.

JIM: What kind of thing is this one supposed to be?

LAURA: Haven't you noticed the single horn on his forehead?

JIM: A unicorn, huh?

LAURA: Mmm-hmmm!

JIM: Unicorns, aren't they extinct in the modern world?

LAURA: I know!

JIM: Poor little fellow, he must feel sort of lonesome.

LAURA [smiling]: Well, if he does he doesn't complain about it. He stays on a shelf with some horses that don't have horns and all of them seem to get along nicely together.

JIM: How do you know?

LAURA [lightly]: I haven't heard any arguments among them!

JIM [grinning]: No arguments, huh? Well, that's a pretty good sign! Where shall I set him?

LAURA: Put him on the table. They all like a change of scenery once in a while!

JIM [stretching]: Well, well, well, well—Look how big my shadow is when I stretch!

LAURA: Oh, oh, yes—it stretches across the ceiling!

JIM [crossing to door]: I think it's stopped raining. [Opens fire-escape door] Where does the music come from?

LAURA: From the Paradise Dance Hall across the alley.

JIM: How about cutting the rug a little, Miss Wingfield?

LAURA: Oh, I—

JIM: Or is your program filled up? Let me have a look at it. [Grasps imaginary card.] Why, every dance is taken! I'll just have to scratch some out. [Waltz Music: "La Golondrina."] Ahhh, a waltz! [He executes some sweeping turns by himself then holds his arms toward Laura.]

LAURA [breathlessly]: I—can't dance!

JIM: There you go, that inferiority stuff!

LAURA: I've never danced in my life!

JIM: Come on, try!

LAURA: Oh, but I'd step on you!

JIM: I'm not made out of glass.

LAURA: How—how—how do we start?

JIM: Just leave it to me. You hold your arms out a little.

LAURA: Like this?

JIM: A little bit higher. Right. Now don't tighten up, that's the main thing about it—relax.

LAURA [*laughing breathlessly*]: It's hard not to.

JIM: Okay.

LAURA: I'm afraid you can't budge me.

JIM: What do you bet I can't? [*He swings her into motion.*]

LAURA: Goodness, yes, you can!

JIM: Let yourself go, now, Laura, just let yourself go.

LAURA: I'm—

JIM: Come on!

LAURA: Trying!

JIM: Not so stiff—Easy does it!

LAURA: I know but I'm—

JIM: Loosen th' backbone! There now, that's a lot better.

LAURA: Am I?

JIM: Lots, lots better! [*He moves her about the room in a clumsy waltz.*]

LAURA: Oh, my!

JIM: Ha-ha!

LAURA: Goodness, yes you can!

JIM: Ha-ha-ha! [*They suddenly bump into the table, Jim stops.*] What did we hit on?

LAURA: Table.

JIM: Did something fall off it? I think—

LAURA: Yes.

JIM: I hope that it wasn't the little glass horse with the horn!

LAURA: Yes.

JIM: Aw, aw, aw. Is it broken?

LAURA: Now it is just like all the other horses.

JIM: It's lost its—

LAURA: Horn! It doesn't matter. Maybe it's a blessing in disguise.

JIM: You'll never forgive me. I bet that was your favorite piece of glass.

LAURA: I don't have favorites much. It's no tragedy, Freckles. Glass breaks so easily. No matter how careful you are. The traffic jars the shelves and things fall off them.

JIM: Still I'm awfully sorry that I was the cause.

LAURA [*smiling*]: I'll just imagine he had an operation. The horn was removed to make him feel less—freakish! [*They both laugh.*] Now he will feel more at home with the other horses, the ones that don't have horns . . .

JIM: Ha-ha, that's very funny! [*Suddenly serious.*] I'm glad to see that you have a sense of humor. You know—you're—well—very different! Surprisingly different from anyone else I know! [*His voice becomes soft and hesitant with a genuine feeling.*] Do you mind me telling you that? [*Laura is abashed beyond speech.*] You make me feel sort of—I don't know how to put it! I'm usually pretty good at expressing things, but—This is something that I don't know how to say! [*Laura touches her throat, clears it—turns the broken unicorn in her hands.*] [*Even softer.*] Has anyone ever told you that you were pretty? [*Pause: Music.*] [*Laura looks up slowly, with wonder, and shakes her head.*] Well, you are! In a very different way from anyone else. And all the nicer because of the difference, too. [*His voice becomes low and husky. Laura turns away, nearly faint with the novelty of her emotions.*] I wish that you were my sister. I'd teach you to have some confidence in yourself. The different people are not like other people, but being different is nothing to be ashamed of. Because other people are not such wonderful people. They're one hundred times one thousand. You're one times one! They walk all over the earth. You just stay here. They're common as—weeds, but—you—well, you're—Blue Roses!

[Image on Screen: Blue Roses.]
[Music Changes.]

LAURA: But blue is wrong for—roses . . .

JIM: It's right for you—You're—pretty!

LAURA: In what respect am I pretty?

JIM: In all respects—believe me! Your eyes—your hair—are pretty! Your hands are pretty! [*He catches hold of her hand.*] You think I'm making this up because I'm invited to dinner and have to be nice. Oh, I could do that! I could put on an act for you, Laura, and say lots of things without being very sincere. But this time I am. I'm talking to you sincerely. I happened to notice you had this inferiority complex that keeps you from feeling comfortable with people. Somebody needs to build your confidence up and make you proud instead of shy and turning away and—blushing—Somebody ought to—ought to—*kiss* you, Laura!

[*His hand slips slowly up her arm to her shoulder.*] [*Music Swells Tumultuously.*] [*He suddenly turns her about and kisses her on the* lips. When he releases her Laura sinks on the sofa with a bright, dazed look. Jim backs away and fishes in his pocket for a cigarette.] [Legend on Screen: "Souvenir."] Stumble-john! [He lights the cigarette, avoiding her look. There is a peal of girlish laughter from Amanda in the kitchen. Laura slowly raises and opens her hand. It still contains the little broken glass animal. She looks at it with a tender, bewildered expression.] Stumble-john! I shouldn't have done that—That was way off the beam. You don't smoke, do you? [She looks up, smiling, not hearing the question. He sits beside her a little gingerly. She looks at him speechlessly— waiting. He coughs decorously and moves a little farther aside as he considers the situation and senses her feelings, dimly, with perturbation. Gently.] Would you—care for a—mint? [She doesn't seem to hear him but her look grows brighter even.] Peppermint— Life Saver? My pocket's a regular drug store—wherever I go ... [He pops a mint in his mouth. Then gulps and decides to make a clean breast of it. He speaks slowly and gingerly.] Laura, you know, if I had a sister like you, I'd do the same thing as Tom. I'd bring out fellows—introduce her to them. The right type of boys of a type to—appreciate her. Only—well—he made a mistake about me. Maybe I've got no call to be saying this. This may not have been the idea in having me over. But what if it was? There's nothing wrong about that. The only trouble is that in my case—I'm not in a situation to—do the right thing. I can't take down your number and say I'll phone. I can't call up next week and—ask for a date. I thought I had better explain the situation in case you misunderstood it and—hurt your feelings .... [Pause. Slowly, very slowly, Laura's look changes, her eyes returning slowly from his to the ornament in her palm.]

[Amanda utters another gay laugh in the kitchen.]

LAURA [faintly]:   You—won't—call again?

JIM: No, Laura. I can't. [He rises from the sofa.] As I was just explaining, I've—got strings on me, Laura, I've—been going steady! I go out all the time with a girl named Betty. She's a home-girl like you, and Catholic, and Irish, and in a great many ways we—get along fine. I met her last summer on a moonlight boat trip up the river to Alton, on the Majestic. Well—right away from the start it was—

love! [*Legend: "Love!"*] [*Laura sways slightly forward and grips the arm of the sofa. He fails to notice, now enrapt in his own comfortable being.*] Being in love has made a new man of me! [*Leaning stiffly forward, clutching the arm of the sofa, Laura struggles visibly with her storm. But Jim is oblivious, she is a long way off.*] The power of love is really pretty tremendous! Love is something that—changes the whole world, Laura! [*The storm abates a little and Laura leans back. He notices her again.*] It happened that Betty's aunt took sick, she got a wire and had to go to Centralia. So Tom—when he asked me to dinner—I naturally just accepted the invitation, not knowing that you—that he—that I—[*He stops awkwardly.*] Huh—I'm a stumble-john! [*He flops back on the sofa. The holy candles in the altar of Laura's face have been snuffed out! There is a look of almost infinite desolation. Jim glances at her uneasily.*] I wish that you would—say something. [*She bites her lip which was trembling and then bravely smiles. She opens her hand again on the broken glass ornament. Then she gently takes his hand and raises it level to her own. She carefully places the unicorn in the palm of his hand, then pushes his fingers closed upon it.*] What are you—doing that for? You want me to have him?—Laura? [*She nods.*] What for?

LAURA: A—souvenir . . .

[*She rises unsteadily and crouches beside the victrola to wind it up.*]

[*Legend on Screen: "Things Have a Way of Turning Out So Badly."*]
    [*Or Image: "Gentleman Caller Waving Good-Bye—Gaily."*]

[*At this moment Amanda rushes brightly back in the front room. She bears a pitcher of fruit punch in an old-fashioned cut-glass pitcher and a plate of macaroons. The plate has a gold border and poppies painted on it.*]

AMANDA: Well, well, well! Isn't the air delightful after the shower? I've made you children a little liquid refreshment. [*Turns gaily to the gentleman caller.*] Jim, do you know that song about lemonade?
"Lemonade, lemonade
Made in the shade and stirred with a spade—
Good enough for any old maid!"
JIM [*uneasily*]: Ha-ha! No—I never heard it.
AMANDA: Why, Laura! You look so serious!
JIM: We were having a serious conversation.

AMANDA: Good! Now you're better acquainted!

JIM [*uncertainly*]: Ha-ha! Yes.

AMANDA: You modern young people are much more serious-minded than my generation. I was so gay as a girl!

JIM: You haven't changed, Mrs. Wingfield.

AMANDA: Tonight I'm rejuvenated! The gaiety of the occasion, Mr. O'Connor! [*She tosses her head with a peal of laughter. Spills lemonade.*] Oooo! I'm baptizing myself!

JIM: Here—let me—

AMANDA [*setting the pitcher down.*]: There now. I discovered we had some maraschino cherries. I dumped them in, juice and all!

JIM: You shouldn't have gone to that trouble, Mrs. Wingfield.

AMANDA: Trouble, trouble? Why it was loads of fun! Didn't you hear me cutting up in the kitchen? I bet your ears were burning! I told Tom how outdone with him I was for keeping you to himself so long a time! He should have brought you over much, much sooner! Well, now that you've found your way, I want you to be a very frequent caller! Not just occasional but all the time. Oh, we're going to have a lot of gay times together! I see them coming! Mmm, just breathe that air! So fresh, and the moon's so pretty! I'll skip back out—I know where my place is when young folks are having a—serious conversation!

JIM: Oh, don't go out, Mrs. Wingfield. The fact of the matter is I've got to be going.

AMANDA: Going, now? You're joking! Why, it's only the shank of the evening, Mr. O'Connor.

JIM: Well, you know how it is.

AMANDA: You mean you're a young workingman and have to keep workingmen's hours. We'll let you off early tonight. But only on the condition that next time you stay later. What's the best night for you? Isn't Saturday night the best night for you workingmen?

JIM: I have a couple of time-clocks to punch, Mrs. Wingfield. One at morning, another one at night.

AMANDA: My, but you are ambitious! You work at night, too?

JIM: No, Ma'am, not work but—Betty! [*He crosses deliberately to pick up his hat. The band at the Paradise Dance Hall goes into a tender waltz.*]

AMANDA: Betty? Betty? Who's—Betty! [*There is an ominous cracking sound in the sky.*]

JIM: Oh, just a girl. The girl I go steady with! [*He smiles charmingly. The sky falls.*]

[Legend: "The Sky Falls"]

AMANDA [*a long-drawn exhalation*]:   Ohhhh . . . Is it a serious romance, Mr. O'Connor?

JIM: We're going to be married the second Sunday in June.

AMANDA: Ohhhh—how nice! Tom didn't mention that you were engaged to be married.

JIM: The cat's not out of the bag at the warehouse yet. You know how they are. They call you Romeo and stuff like that. [*He stops at the oval mirror to put on his hat. He carefully shapes the brim and the crown to give a discreetly dashing effect.*] It's been a wonderful evening, Mrs. Wingfield. I guess this is what they mean by Southern hospitality.

AMANDA: It really wasn't anything at all.

JIM: I hope it don't seem like I'm rushing off. But I promised Betty I'd pick her up at the Wabash depot, an' by the time I get my jalopy down there her train'll be in. Some women are pretty upset if you keep 'em waiting.

AMANDA: Yes, I know—The tyranny of women! [*Extends her hand.*] Goodbye, Mr. O'Connor. I wish you luck—and happiness—and success! All three of them, and so does Laura!—Don't you, Laura?

LAURA: Yes!

JIM [*taking her hand*]:   Goodbye, Laura. I'm certainly going to treasure that souvenir. And don't you forget the good advice I gave you. [*Raises his voice to a cheery shout.*] So long, Shakespeare! Thanks again, ladies—Good night!

[*He grins and ducks jauntily out. Still bravely grimacing, Amanda closes the door on the gentleman caller. Then she turns back to the room with a puzzled expression. She and Laura don't dare to face each other. Laura crouches beside the victrola to wind it.*]

AMANDA [*faintly*]:   Things have a way of turning out so badly. I don't believe that I would play the victrola. Well, well—well—Our gentleman caller was engaged to be married! Tom!

TOM [*from back*]:   Yes, Mother?

AMANDA: Come in here a minute. I want to tell you something awfully funny.

TOM [*enters with macaroon and a glass of the lemonade*]: Has the gentleman caller gotten away already?

AMANDA: The gentleman caller has made an early departure. What a
wonderful joke you played on us!

TOM: How do you mean?

AMANDA: You didn't mention that he was engaged to be married.

TOM: Jim? Engaged?

AMANDA: That's what he just informed us.

TOM: I'll be jiggered! I didn't know about that.

AMANDA: That seems very peculiar.

TOM: What's peculiar about it?

AMANDA: Didn't you call him your best friend down at the warehouse?

TOM: He is, but how did I know?

AMANDA: It seems extremely peculiar that you wouldn't know your
best friend was going to be married!

TOM: The warehouse is where I work, not where I know things about
people!

AMANDA: You don't know things anywhere! You live in a dream; you
manufacture illusions! [*He crosses to door.*] Where are you going?

TOM: I'm going to the movies.

AMANDA: That's right, now that you've had us make such fools of
ourselves. The effort, the preparations, all the expense! The new
floor lamp, the rug, the clothes for Laura! All for what? To entertain
some other girl's fiancé! Go to the movies, go! Don't think about
us, a mother deserted, an unmarried sister who's crippled and has
no job! Don't let anything interfere with your selfish pleasure! Just
go, go, go—to the movies!

TOM: All right, I will! The more you shout about my selfishness to me
the quicker I'll go, and I won't go to the movies!

AMANDA: Go, then! Then go to the moon—you selfish dreamer!

*Tom smashes his glass on the floor. He plunges out on the fire-
escape, slamming the door. Laura screams—cut by door.*

*Dance-hall music up. Tom goes to the rail and grips it desper-
ately, lifting his face in the chill white moonlight penetrating the
narrow abyss of the alley.*

[Legend on Screen: "And So Good-Bye . . ."]

[Tom's closing speech is timed with the interior pantomime. The interior scene is played as though viewed through sound-proof glass. Amanda appears to be making a comforting speech to Laura who is huddled upon the sofa. Now that we cannot hear the mother's speech, her silliness is gone and she has dignity and tragic beauty. Laura's dark hair hides her face until at the end of the speech she lifts it to smile at her mother. Amanda's gestures are slow and graceful, almost dancelike, as she comforts her daughter. At the end of her speech she glances a moment at the father's picture—then withdraws through the portieres. At close of Tom's speech, Laura blows out the candles, ending the play.]

TOM: I didn't go to the moon, I went much further—for time is the longest distance between two places—Not long after that I was fired for writing a poem on the lid of a shoe-box. I left Saint Louis. I descended the steps of this fire-escape for a last time and followed, from then on, in my father's footsteps, attempting to find in motion what was lost in space—I traveled around a great deal. The cities swept about me like dead leaves, leaves that were brightly colored but torn away from the branches. I would have stopped, but I was pursued by something. It always came upon me unawares, taking me altogether by surprise. Perhaps it was a familiar bit of music. Perhaps it was only a piece of transparent glass— Perhaps I am walking along a street at night, in some strange city, before I have found companions. I pass the lighted window of a shop where perfume is sold. The window is filled with pieces of colored glass, tiny transparent bottles in delicate colors, like bits of a shattered rainbow. Then all at once my sister touches my shoulder. I turn around and look into her eyes . . . Oh, Laura, Laura, I tried to leave you behind me, but I am more faithful than I intended to be! I reach for a cigarette, I cross the street, I run into the movies or a bar, I buy a drink, I speak to the nearest stranger— anything that can blow your candles out! *[Laura bends over the candles.]*—for nowadays the world is lit by lightning! Blow out your candles, Laura—and so goodbye . . .

[She blows the candles out.]

[The Scene Dissolves.]

—1944

Athol Fugard was born in Middelburg, Cape Province, South Africa, and was educated at the University of Cape Town. Growing up during the period of South African apartheid, Fugard both resisted and participated in the segregationist policies of the government, even insisting, at one point, that the family servants call him Master Harold (his given first name) and, in a moment of anger, spitting on one with whom he had been especially close. As he later said to an interviewer, "I think at a fairly early age I became suspicious of what the system was trying to do to me. . . . I became conscious of what attitudes it was trying to implant in me and what prejudices it was trying to pass on to me." Fugard founded the first important black theatrical company in South Africa, and he gained early prominence in his native country by his exploration of racial issues. While Fugard does not consider himself a political writer, his depictions of the interplay of black and white lives made him a controversial figure as a critic of apartheid. "Master Harold". . . and the boys is clearly an autobiographical work, for Fugard's father was a wounded war veteran, and his mother helped to support the family by running a tea room. After leaving college to travel to the Far East as a crew member of a tramp steamer, Fugard at first attempted to write novels but soon turned to the theater. Fugard began to produce his plays in the mid-1950s, and the New York production of The Blood Knot *in 1964 established his American reputation.* "Master Harold" . . . and the boys *was first produced in New Haven, Connecticut, in 1982, and soon enjoyed a successful Broadway run. Since the end of the apartheid era, Fugard has continued to write plays and autobiographical memoirs. He has often been mentioned as a possible recipient of the Nobel Prize.*

"Master Harold" . . . and the boys

Characters

Hally
Sam
Willie

Scene: *The St. George's Park Tea Room on a wet and windy Port Elizabeth afternoon.*

Tables and chairs have been cleared and are stacked on one side except for one which stands apart with a single chair. On this table a knife, fork, spoon and side plate in anticipation of a simple meal, together with a pile of comic books.

Other elements: a serving counter with a few stale cakes under glass and a not very impressive display of sweets, cigarettes and cool drinks, etc.; a few cardboard advertising handouts—Cadbury's Chocolate, Coca-Cola—and a blackboard on which an untrained hand has chalked up the prices of Tea, Coffee, Scones, Milkshakes—all flavors—and Cool Drinks; a few sad ferns in pots; a telephone; an old-style jukebox.

There is an entrance on one side and an exit into a kitchen on the other.

Leaning on the solitary table, his head cupped in one hand as he pages through one of the comic books, is Sam. A black man in his mid-forties. He wears the white coat of a waiter. Behind him on his knees, mopping down the floor with a bucket of water and a rag, is Willie. Also black and about the same age as Sam. He has his sleeves and trousers rolled up.

The year: 1950

WILLIE [*Singing as he works*]:
"She was scandalizin' my name,
She took my money
She called me honey
But she was scandalizin' my name.
Called it love but was playin' a game . . ."

He gets up and moves the bucket. Stands thinking for a moment, then, raising his arms to hold an imaginary partner, he launches into an intricate ballroom dance step. Although a mildly comic figure, he reveals a reasonable degree of accomplishment.

Hey, Sam.

Sam, absorbed in the comic book, does not respond.

Hey, Boet Sam!

Sam looks up.

I'm getting it. The quickstep. Look now and tell me. [*He repeats the step*] Well?

SAM [*Encouragingly*]: Show me again.

WILLIE: Okay, count for me.

SAM: Ready?

WILLIE: Ready.

SAM: Five, six, seven, eight . . . [*Willie starts to dance*] A-n-d one two three four . . . and one two three four . . . [*Ad libbing as Willie dances*] Your shoulders, Willie . . . your shoulders! Don't look down! Look happy, Willie! Relax, Willie!

WILLIE [*Desperate but still dancing*]:   I am relax.

SAM: No, you're not.

WILLIE [*He falters*]:   Ag no man, Sam! Mustn't talk. You make me make mistakes.

SAM: But you're too stiff.

WILLIE: Yesterday I'm not straight . . . today I'm too stiff!

SAM: Well, you are. You asked me and I'm telling you.

WILLIE: Where?

SAM: Everywhere. Try to glide through it.

WILLIE: Glide?

SAM: Ja, make it smooth. And give it more style. It must look like you're enjoying yourself.

WILLIE [*Emphatically*]:   I wasn't.

SAM: Exactly.

WILLIE: How can I enjoy myself? Not straight, too stiff and now it's also glide, give it more style, make it smooth. . . . Haai! Is hard to remember all those things, Boet Sam.

SAM: That's your trouble. You're trying too hard.

WILLIE: I try hard because it *is* hard.

SAM: But don't let me see it. The secret is to make it look easy. Ballroom must look happy, Willie, not like hard work. It must . . . Ja! . . . it must look like romance.

WILLIE: Now another one! What's romance?

SAM: Love story with happy ending. A handsome man in tails, and in his arms, smiling at him, a beautiful lady in evening dress!

WILLIE: Fred Astaire, Ginger Rogers.

SAM: You got it. Tapdance or ballroom, it's the same. Romance. In two weeks' time when the judges look at you and Hilda, they must see a man and a woman who are dancing their way to a happy ending. What I saw was you holding her like you were frightened she was going to run away.

WILLIE: Ja! Because that is what she wants to do! I got no romance left for Hilda anymore, Boet Sam.

SAM: Then pretend. When you put your arms around Hilda, imagine she is Ginger Rogers.

WILLIE: With no teeth? You try.

SAM: Well, just remember, there's only two weeks left.

WILLIE: I know, I know! [*To the jukebox*] I do it better with music. You got sixpence for Sarah Vaughan?

SAM: That's a slow foxtrot. You're practicing the quick-step.

WILLIE: I'll practice slow foxtrot.

SAM [*Shaking his head*]: It's your turn to put money in the jukebox.

WILLIE: I only got bus fare to go home. [*He returns disconsolately to his work*] Love story and happy ending! She's doing it all right, Boet Sam, but is not me she's giving happy endings. Fuckin' whore! Three nights now she doesn't come practice. I wind up gramophone, I get record ready and I sit and wait. What happens? Nothing. Ten o'clock I start dancing with my pillow. You try and practice romance by yourself, Boet Sam. Struesgod, she doesn't come tonight I take back my dress and ballroom shoes and I find me new partner. Size twenty-six. Shoes size seven. And now she's also making trouble for me with the baby again. Reports me to Child Wellfed, that I'm not giving her money. She lies! Every week I am giving her money for milk. And how do I know is my baby? Only his hair looks like me. She's fucking around all the time I turn my back. Hilda Samuels is a bitch! [*Pause*] Hey, Sam!

SAM: Ja.

WILLIE: You listening?

SAM: Ja.

WILLIE: So what you say?

SAM: About Hilda?

WILLIE: Ja.

SAM: When did you last give her a hiding?

WILLIE [*Reluctantly*]: Sunday night.

SAM: And today is Thursday.

WILLIE [*He knows what's coming*]: Okay.

SAM: Hiding on Sunday night, then Monday, Tuesday and Wednesday she doesn't come to practice . . . and you are asking me why?

WILLIE: I said okay, Boet Sam!

SAM: You hit her too much. One day she's going to leave you for good.

WILLIE: So? She makes me the hell-in too much.

SAM [*Emphasizing his point*]: *Too* much and *too* hard. You had the same trouble with Eunice.

WILLIE: Because she also make the hell-in, Boet Sam. She never got the steps right. Even the waltz.

SAM: Beating her up every time she makes a mistake in the waltz? [*Shaking his head*] No, Willie! That takes the pleasure out of ball-room dancing.

WILLIE: Hilda is not too bad with the waltz, Boet Sam. Is the quick-step where the trouble starts.

SAM [*Teasing him gently*]: How's your pillow with the quickstep?

WILLIE [*Ignoring the tease*]: Good! And why? Because it got no legs. That's her trouble. She can't move them quick enough, Boet Sam. I start the record and before halfway Count Basie is already winning. Only time we catch up with him is when gramophone runs down.

Sam laughs.

Haaikona, Boet Sam, is not funny.

SAM [*Snapping his fingers*]: I got it! Give her a handicap.

WILLIE: What's that?

SAM: Give her a ten-second start and then let Count Basie go. Then I put my money on her. Hot favorite in the Ballroom Stakes: Hilda Samuels ridden by Willie Malopo.

WILLIE [*Turning away*]: I'm not talking to you no more.

SAM [*Relenting*]: Sorry, Willie . . .

WILLIE: It's finish between us.

SAM: Okay, okay . . . I'll stop.

WILLIE: You can also fuck off.

SAM: Willie, listen! I want to help you!

WILLIE: No more jokes?

SAM: I promise.

WILLIE: Okay. Help me.

SAM [*His turn to hold an imaginary partner*]: Look and learn. Feet to-gether. Back straight. Body relaxed. Right hand placed gently in the small of her back and wait for the music. Don't start worrying about making mistakes or the judges or the other competitors. It's just you, Hilda and the music, and you're going to have a good time. What Count Basie do you play?

WILLIE: "You the cream in my coffee, you the salt in my stew."

SAM: Right. Give it to me in strict tempo.

WILLIE: Ready?

SAM: Ready.

WILLIE: A-n-d . . . [*Singing*]
"You the cream in my coffee.
You the salt in my stew.

You will always be my necessity.
I'd be lost without
   you. . . ." [etc.]

Sam launches into the quickstep. He is obviously a much more accomplished dancer than Willie. Hally enters. A seventeen-year-old white boy. Wet raincoat and school case. He stops and watches Sam. The demonstration comes to an end with a flourish. Applause from Hally and Willie.

HALLY: Bravo! No question about it. First place goes to Mr. Sam Semela.
WILLIE [*In total agreement*]: You was gliding with style, Boet Sam.
HALLY [*Cheerfully*]: How's it, chaps?
SAM: Okay, Hally.
WILLIE [*Springing to attention like a soldier and saluting*]: At your service, Master Harold!
HALLY: Not long to the big event, hey!
SAM: Two weeks.
HALLY: You nervous?
SAM: No.
HALLY: Think you stand a chance?
SAM: Let's just say I'm ready to go out there and dance.
HALLY: It looked like it. What about you, Willie?

Willie groans.

What's the matter?
SAM: He's got leg trouble.
HALLY [*Innocently*]: Oh, sorry to hear that, Willie.
WILLIE: Boet Sam! You promised. [*Willie returns to his work*]

Hally deposits his school case and takes off his raincoat. His clothes are a little neglected and untidy: black blazer with school badge, gray flannel trousers in need of an ironing, khaki shirt and tie, black shoes. Sam has fetched a towel for Hally to dry his hair.

HALLY: God, what a lousy bloody day. It's coming down cats and dogs out there. Bad for business, chaps . . . [*Conspiratorial whisper*] . . . but it also means we're in for a nice quiet afternoon.
SAM: You can speak loud. Your Mom's not here.
HALLY: Out shopping?

SAM: No. The hospital.

HALLY: But it's Thursday. There's no visiting on Thursday afternoons. Is my Dad okay?

SAM: Sounds like it. In fact, I think he's going home.

HALLY [*Stopped short by Sam's remark*]:   What do you mean?

SAM: The hospital phoned.

HALLY: To say what?

SAM: I don't know. I just heard your Mom talking.

HALLY: So what makes you say he's going home?

SAM: It sounded as if they were telling her to come and fetch him.

Hally thinks about what Sam has said for a few seconds.

HALLY: When did she leave?

SAM: About an hour ago. She said she would phone you. Want to eat?

Hally doesn't respond.

Hally, want your lunch?

HALLY: I suppose so. [*His mood has changed*] What's on the menu? . . . as if I don't know.

SAM: Soup, followed by meat pie and gravy.

HALLY: Today's?

SAM: No.

HALLY: And the soup?

SAM: Nourishing pea soup.

HALLY: Just the soup. [*The pile of comic books on the table*] And these?

SAM: For your Dad. Mr. Kempston brought them.

HALLY: You haven't been reading them, have you?

SAM: Just looking.

HALLY [*Examining the comics*]:   Jungle Jim . . . Batman and Robin . . . Tarzan . . . God, what rubbish! Mental pollution. Take them away.

Sam exits waltzing into the kitchen. Hally turns to Willie.

HALLY: Did you hear my Mom talking on the telephone, Willie?

WILLIE: No, Master Hally. I was at the back.

HALLY: And she didn't say anything to you before she left?

WILLIE: She said I must clean the floors.

HALLY: I mean about my Dad.

WILLIE: She didn't say nothing to me about him, Master Hally.

HALLY [*With conviction*]:   No! It can't be. They said he needed at least another three weeks of treatment. Sam's definitely made a mistake.

[*Rummages through his school case, finds a book and settles down at the table to read*] So, Willie!

WILLIE: Yes, Master Hally! Schooling okay today?

HALLY: Yes, okay. . . . [*He thinks about it*] . . . No, not really. Ag, what's the difference? I don't care. And Sam says you've got problems.

WILLIE: Big problems.

HALLY: Which leg is sore?

Willie groans.

Both legs.

WILLIE: There is nothing wrong with my legs. Sam is just making jokes.

HALLY: So then you *will* be in the competition.

WILLIE: Only if I can find me a partner.

HALLY: But what about Hilda?

SAM [*Returning with a bowl of soup*]: She's the one who's got trouble with her legs.

HALLY: What sort of trouble, Willie?

SAM: From the way he describes it, I think the lady has gone a bit lame.

HALLY: Good God! Have you taken her to see a doctor?

SAM: I think a vet would be better.

HALLY: What do you mean?

SAM: What do you call it again when a racehorse goes very fast?

HALLY: Gallop?

SAM: That's it!

WILLIE: Boet Sam!

HALLY: "A gallop down the homestretch to the winning post." But what's that got to do with Hilda?

SAM: Count Basie always gets there first.

Willie lets fly with his slop rag. It misses Sam and hits Hally.

HALLY [*Furious*]: For Christ's sake, Willie! What the hell do you think you're doing!

WILLIE: Sorry, Master Hally, but it's him. . . .

HALLY: Act your bloody age! [*Hurls the rag back at Willie*] Cut out the nonsense now and get on with your work. And you too, Sam. Stop fooling around.

Sam moves away.

No. Hang on. I haven't finished! Tell me exactly what my Mom said.

SAM: I have. "When Hally comes, tell him I've gone to the hospital and I'll phone him."

HALLY: She didn't say anything about taking my Dad home?

SAM: No. It's just that when she was talking on the phone . . .

HALLY [Interrupting him]: No, Sam. They can't be discharging him. She would have said so if they were. In any case, we saw him last night and he wasn't in good shape at all. Staff nurse even said there was talk about taking more X-rays. And now suddenly today he's better? If anything, it sounds more like a bad turn to me . . . which I sincerely hope it isn't. Hang on . . . how long ago did you say she left?

SAM: Just before two . . . [His wrist watch] . . . hour and a half.

HALLY: I know how to settle it. [Behind the counter to the telephone. Talking as he dials] Let's give her ten minutes to get to the hospital, ten minutes to load him up, another ten, at the most, to get home and another ten to get him inside. Forty minutes. They should have been home for at least half an hour already. [Pause—he waits with the receiver to his ear] No reply, chaps. And you know why? Because she's at his bedside in hospital helping him pull through a bad turn. You definitely heard wrong.

SAM: Okay.

As far as Hally is concerned, the matter is settled. He returns to his table, sits down and divides his attention between the book and his soup. Sam is at his school case and picks up a textbook.

Modern Graded Mathematics for Standards Nine and Ten. [Opens it at random and laughs at something he sees] Who is this supposed to be?

HALLY: Old fart-face Prentice.

SAM: Teacher?

HALLY: Thinks he is. And believe me, that is not a bad likeness.

SAM: Has he seen it?

HALLY: Yes.

SAM: What did he say?

HALLY: Tried to be clever, as usual. Said I was no Leonardo da Vinci and that bad art had to be punished. So, six of the best, and his are bloody good.

SAM: On your bum?

HALLY: Where else? The days when I got them on my hands are gone forever, Sam.

SAM: With your trousers down!

HALLY: No. He's not quite that barbaric.

SAM: That's the way they do it in jail.

HALLY [*Flicker of morbid interest*]:   Really?

SAM: Ja. When the magistrate sentences you to "strokes with a light cane."

HALLY: Go on.

SAM: They make you lie down on a bench. One policeman pulls down your trousers and holds your ankles, another one pulls your shirt over your head and holds your arms . . .

HALLY: Thank you! That's enough.

SAM: . . . and the one that gives you the strokes talks to you gently and for a long time between each one. [*He laughs*]

HALLY: I've heard enough, Sam! Jesus! It's a bloody awful world when you come to think of it. People can be real bastards.

SAM: That's the way it is, Hally.

HALLY: It doesn't *have* to be that way. There is something called progress, you know. We don't exactly burn people at the stake anymore.

SAM: Like Joan of Arc.

HALLY: Correct. If she was captured today, she'd be given a fair trial.

SAM: And then the death sentence.

HALLY [*A world-weary sigh*]:   I know, I know! I oscillate between hope and despair for this world as well, Sam. But things will change, you wait and see. One day somebody is going to get up and give history a kick up the backside and get it going again.

SAM: Like who?

HALLY [*After thought*]:   They're called social reformers. Every age, Sam, has got its social reformer. My history book is full of them.

SAM: So where's ours?

HALLY: Good question. And I hate to say it, but the answer is: I don't know. Maybe he hasn't even been born yet. Or is still only a babe in arms at his mother's breast. God, what a thought.

SAM: So we just go on waiting.

HALLY: Ja, looks like it. [*Back to his soup and the book*]

SAM [*Reading from the textbook*]:   "Introduction: In some mathematical problems only the magnitude . . ." [*He mispronounces the word "magnitude"*]

HALLY [*Correcting him without looking up*]: Magnitude.

SAM: What's it mean?

HALLY: How big it is. The size of the thing.

SAM [*Reading*]: ". . . magnitude of the quantities is of importance. In other problems we need to know whether these quantities are negative or positive. For example, whether there is a debit or credit bank balance . . ."

HALLY: Whether you're broke or not.

SAM: ". . . whether the temperature is above or below Zero . . ."

HALLY: Naught degrees. Cheerful state of affairs! No cash and you're freezing to death. Mathematics won't get you out of that one.

SAM: "All these quantities are called . . ." [*Spelling the word*] . . . s-c-a-l . . .

HALLY: Scalars.

SAM: Scalars! [*Shaking his head with a laugh*] You understand all that?

HALLY [*Turning a page*]: No. And I don't intend to try.

SAM: So what happens when the exams come?

HALLY: Failing a maths exam isn't the end of the world, Sam. How many times have I told you that examination results don't measure intelligence?

SAM: I would say about as many times as you've failed one of them.

HALLY [*Mirthlessly*]: Ha, ha, ha.

SAM [*Simultaneously*]: Ha, ha, ha.

HALLY: Just remember Winston Churchill didn't do particularly well at school.

SAM: You've also told me that one many times.

HALLY: Well, it just so happens to be the truth.

SAM [*Enjoying the word*]: Magnitude! Magnitude! Show me how to use it.

HALLY [*After thought*]: An intrepid social reformer will not be daunted by the magnitude of the task he has undertaken.

SAM [*Impressed*]: Couple of jaw-breakers in there!

HALLY: I gave you three for the price of one. Intrepid, daunted and magnitude. I did that once in an exam. Put five of the words I had to explain in one sentence. It was half a page long.

SAM: Well, I'll put my money on you in the English exam.

HALLY: Piece of cake. Eighty percent without even trying.

SAM [*Another textbook from Hally's case*]: And history?

HALLY: So-so. I'll scrape through. In the fifties if I'm lucky.

SAM: You didn't do too badly last year.

HALLY: Because we had World War One. That at least had some action. You try to find that in the South African Parliamentary system.

SAM [*Reading from the history textbook*]: "Napoleon and the principle of equality." Hey! This sounds interesting. "After concluding peace with Britain in 1802, Napoleon used a brief period of calm to in-sti-tute . . ."

HALLY: Introduce.

SAM: ". . . many reforms. Napoleon regarded all people as equal be-fore the law and wanted them to have equal opportunities for ad-vancement. All ves-ti-ges of the feu-dal system with its oppression of the poor were abolished." Vestiges, feudal system and abolished. I'm all right on oppression.

HALLY: I'm thinking. He swept away . . . abolished . . . the last re-mains . . . vestiges . . . of the bad old days . . . feudal system.

SAM: Ha! There's the social reformer we're waiting for. He sounds like a man of some magnitude.

HALLY: I'm not so sure about that. It's a damn good title for a book, though. A man of magnitude!

SAM: He sounds pretty big to me, Hally.

HALLY: Don't confuse historical significance with greatness. But maybe I'm being a bit prejudiced. Have a look in there and you'll see he's two chapters long. And hell! . . . has he only got dates, Sam, all of which you've got to remember! This campaign and that campaign, and then, because of all the fighting, the next thing is we get Peace Treaties all over the place. And what's the end of the story? Battle of Waterloo, which he loses. Wasn't worth it. No, I don't know about him as a man of magnitude.

SAM: Then who would you say was?

HALLY: To answer that, we need a definition of greatness, and I sup-pose that would be somebody who . . . somebody who benefited all mankind.

SAM: Right. But like who?

HALLY [*He speaks with total conviction*]: Charles Darwin. Remember him? That big book from the library. *The Origin of the Species.*

SAM Him?

HALLY: Yes. For his Theory of Evolution.

SAM: You didn't finish it.

HALLY: I ran out of time. I didn't finish it because my two weeks was up. But I'm going to take it out again after I've digested what I read. It's safe. I've hidden it away in the Theology section. Nobody ever goes in there. And anyway who are you to talk? You hardly even looked at it.

SAM: I tried. I looked at the chapters in the beginning and I saw one called "The Struggle for an Existence." Ah ha, I thought. At last! But what did I get? Something called the mistletoe which needs the apple tree and there's too many seeds and all are going to die except one . . . ! No, Hally.

HALLY [*Intellectually outraged*]:   What do you mean, No! The poor man had to start somewhere. For God's sake, Sam, he revolutionized science. Now we know.

SAM: What?

HALLY: Where we come from and what it all means.

SAM: And that's a benefit to mankind? Anyway, I still don't believe it.

HALLY: God, you're impossible. I showed it to you in black and white.

SAM: Doesn't mean I got to believe it.

HALLY: It's the likes of you that kept the Inquisition in business. It's called bigotry. Anyway, that's my man of magnitude. Charles Darwin! Who's yours?

SAM [*Without hesitation*]:   Abraham Lincoln.

HALLY: I might have guessed as much. Don't get sentimental, Sam. You've never been a slave, you know. And anyway we freed your ancestors here in South Africa long before the Americans. But if you want to thank somebody on their behalf, do it to Mr. William Wilberforce. Come on. Try again. I want a real genius. [*Now enjoying himself, and so is Sam. Hally goes behind the counter and helps himself to a chocolate*]

SAM: William Shakespeare.

HALLY [*No enthusiasm*]:   Oh. So you're also one of them, are you? You're basing that opinion on only one play, you know. You've only read my *Julius Caesar* and even I don't understand half of what they're talking about. They should do what they did with the old Bible: bring the language up to date.

SAM: That's all you've got. It's also the only one *you've* read.

HALLY: I know. I admit it. That's why I suggest we reserve our judgment until we've checked up on a few others. I've got a feeling, though, that by the end of this year one is going to be enough for me, and I can give you the names of twenty-nine other chaps in the Standard Nine class of the Port Elizabeth Technical College who feel the same. But if you want him, you can have him. My turn now. [*Pacing*] This is a damned good exercise, you know! It started off looking like a simple question and here it's got us really probing into the intellectual heritage of our civilization.

SAM: So who is it going to be?

HALLY: My next man . . . and he gets the title on two scores: social reform and literary genius . . . is Leo Nikolaevich Tolstoy.

SAM: That Russian.

HALLY: Correct. Remember the picture of him I showed you?

SAM: With the long beard.

HALLY [*Trying to look like Tolstoy*]:   And those burning, visionary eyes. My God, the face of a social prophet if ever I saw one! And remember my words when I showed it to you? Here's a *man*, Sam!

SAM: Those were words, Hally.

HALLY: Not many intellectuals are prepared to shovel manure with the peasants and then go home and write a "little book" called *War and Peace*. Incidentally, Sam, he was somebody else who, to quote, ". . . did not distinguish himself scholastically."

SAM: Meaning?

HALLY: He was also no good at school.

SAM: Like you and Winston Churchill.

HALLY [*Mirthlessly*]:   Ha, ha, ha.

SAM [*Simultaneously*]:   Ha, ha, ha.

HALLY: Don't get clever, Sam. That man freed his serfs of his own free will.

SAM: No argument. He was a somebody, all right. I accept him.

HALLY: I'm sure Count Tolstoy will be very pleased to hear that. Your turn. Shoot. [*Another chocolate from behind the counter*] I'm waiting, Sam.

SAM: I've got him.

HALLY: Good. Submit your candidate for examination.

SAM: Jesus.

HALLY [*Stopped dead in his tracks*]:   Who?

SAM: Jesus Christ.

HALLY: Oh, come on, Sam!

SAM: The Messiah.

HALLY: Ja, but still . . . No, Sam. Don't let's get started on religion. We'll just spend the whole afternoon arguing again. Suppose I turn around and say Mohammed?

SAM: All right.

HALLY: You can't have them both on the same list!

SAM: Why not? You like Mohammed, I like Jesus.

HALLY: I *don't* like Mohammed. I never have. I was merely being hypothetical. As far as I'm concerned, the Koran is as bad as the Bible. No. Religion is out! I'm not going to waste my time again arguing with you about the existence of God. You know perfectly well I'm an atheist . . . and I've got homework to do.

SAM: Okay, I take him back.

HALLY: You've got time for one more name.

SAM [*After thought*]: I've got one I know we'll agree on. A simple straightforward great Man of Magnitude . . . and no arguments. And *he* really *did* benefit all mankind.

HALLY: I wonder. After your last contribution I'm beginning to doubt whether anything in the way of an intellectual agreement is possible between the two of us. Who is he?

SAM: Guess.

HALLY: Socrates? Alexandre Dumas? Karl Marx? Dostoevsky? Nietzsche?

Sam shakes his head after each name.

Give me a clue.

SAM: The letter P is important . . .

HALLY: Plato!

SAM: . . . and his name begins with an F.

HALLY: I've got it. Freud and Psychology.

SAM: No. I didn't understand him.

HALLY: That makes two of us.

SAM: Think of mouldy apricot jam.

HALLY [*After a delighted laugh*]: Penicillin and Sir Alexander Fleming! And the title of the book: *The Microbe Hunters*. [*Delighted*] Splendid, Sam! Splendid. For once we are in total agreement. The major breakthrough in medical science in the Twentieth Century. If it wasn't for him, we might have lost the Second World War. It's deeply gratifying, Sam, to know that I haven't been wasting my time in talking to you. [*Strutting around proudly*] Tolstoy may have educated his peasants, but I've educated you.

SAM: Standard Four to Standard Nine.

HALLY: Have we been at it as long as that?

SAM: Yep. And my first lesson was geography.

HALLY [*Intrigued*]:   Really? I don't remember.

SAM: My room there at the back of the old Jubilee Boarding House. I had just started working for your Mom. Little boy in short trousers walks in one afternoon and asks me seriously: "Sam, do you want to see South Africa?" Hey man! Sure I wanted to see South Africa!

HALLY: Was that me?

SAM: . . . So the next thing I'm looking at a map you had just done for homework. It was your first one and you were very proud of yourself.

HALLY: Go on.

SAM: Then came my first lesson. "Repeat after me, Sam: Gold in the Transvaal, mealies in the Free State, sugar in Natal and grapes in the Cape." I still know it!

HALLY: Well, I'll be buggered. So that's how it all started.

SAM: And your next map was one with all the rivers and the mountains they came from. The Orange, the Vaal, the Limpopo, the Zambezi . . .

HALLY: You've got a phenomenal memory!

SAM: You should be grateful. That is why you started passing your exams. You tried to be better than me.

They laugh together. Willie is attracted by the laughter and joins them.

HALLY: The old Jubilee Boarding House. Sixteen rooms with board and lodging, rent in advance and one week's notice. I haven't thought about it for donkey's years . . . and I don't think that's an accident. God, was I glad when we sold it and moved out. Those years are not remembered as the happiest ones of an unhappy childhood.

WILLIE [*Knocking on the table and trying to imitate a woman's voice*]: "Hally, are you there?"

HALLY: Who's that supposed to be?

WILLIE: "What you doing in there, Hally? Come out at once!"

HALLY [*To Sam*]:   What's he talking about?

SAM: Don't you remember?

WILLIE: "Sam, Willie . . . is he in there with you boys?"

SAM: Hiding away in our room when your mother was looking for you.

HALLY [*Another good laugh*]:   Of course! I used to crawl and hide under your bed! But finish the story, Willie. Then what used to happen?

You chaps would give the game away by telling her I was in there with you. So much for friendship.

SAM: We couldn't lie to her. She knew.

HALLY: Which meant I got another rowing for hanging around the "servants' quarters." I think I spent more time in there with you chaps than anywhere else in that dump. And do you blame me? Nothing but bloody misery wherever you went. Somebody was always complaining about the food, or my mother was having a fight with Micky Nash because she'd caught her with a petty officer in her room. Maud Meiring was another one. Remember those two? They were prostitutes, you know. Soldiers and sailors from the troopships. Bottom fell out of the business when the war ended. God, the flotsam and jetsam that life washed up on our shores! No joking, if it wasn't for your room, I would have been the first certified ten-year-old in medical history. Ja, the memories are coming back now. Walking home from school and thinking: "What can I do this afternoon?" Try out a few ideas, but sooner or later I'd end up in there with you fellows. I bet you I could still find my way to your room with my eyes closed. [*He does exactly that*]. Down the corridor . . . telephone on the right, which my Mom keeps locked because somebody is using it on the sly and not paying . . . past the kitchen and unappetizing cooking smells . . . around the corner into the backyard, hold my breath again because there are more smells coming when I pass your lavatory, then into that little passageway, first door on the right and into your room. How's that?

SAM: Good. But, as usual, you forgot to knock.

HALLY: Like that time I barged in and caught you and Cynthia . . . at it. Remember? God, was I embarrassed! I didn't know what was going on at first.

SAM: Ja, that taught you a lesson.

HALLY: And about a lot more than knocking on doors, I'll have you know, and I don't mean geography either. Hell, Sam, couldn't you have waited until it was dark?

SAM: No.

HALLY: Was it that urgent?

SAM: Yes, and if you don't believe me, wait until your time comes.

HALLY: No, thank you. I am not interested in girls. [*Back to his memories . . . Using a few chairs he recreates the room as he lists the items*] A gray little room with a cold cement floor. Your bed against that

wall . . . and I now know why the mattress sags so much! . . .
Willie's bed . . . it's propped up on bricks because one leg is broken
. . . that wobbly little table with the washbasin and jug of water . . .
Yes! . . . stuck to the wall above it are some pin-up pictures from
magazines. Joe Louis . . .

WILLIE: Brown Bomber. World Title. [*Boxing pose*] Three rounds and
knockout.

HALLY: Against who?

SAM: Max Schmeling.

HALLY: Correct. I can also remember Fred Astaire and Ginger Rogers,
and Rita Hayworth in a bathing costume which always made me
hot and bothered when I looked at it. Under Willie's bed is an old
suitcase with all his clothes in a mess, which is why I never hide
there. Your things are neat and tidy in a trunk next to your bed,
and on it there is a picture of you and Cynthia in your ballroom
clothes, your first silver cup for third place in a competition and an
old radio which doesn't work anymore. Have I left out anything?

SAM: No.

HALLY: Right, so much for the stage directions. Now the characters.
[*Sam and Willie move to their appropriate positions in the bedroom*]
Willie is in bed, under his blankets with his clothes on, complaining nonstop about something, but we can't make out a word of
what he's saying because he's got his head under the blankets as
well. You're on your bed trimming your toenails with a knife—not
a very edifying sight—and as for me . . . What am I doing?

SAM: You're sitting on the floor giving Willie a lecture about being a
good loser while you get the checker board and pieces ready for a
game. Then you go to Willie's bed, pull off the blankets and make
him play with you first because you know you're going to win, and
that gives you the second game with me.

HALLY: And you certainly were a bad loser, Willie!

WILLIE: Haai!

HALLY: Wasn't he, Sam? And so slow! A game with you almost took
the whole afternoon. Thank God I gave up trying to teach you how
to play chess.

WILLIE: You and Sam cheated.

HALLY: I never saw Sam cheat, and mine were mostly the mistakes of
youth.

WILLIE: Then how is it you two was always winning?

HALLY: Have you ever considered the possibility, Willie, that it was because we were better than you?

WILLIE: Every time better?

HALLY: Not every time. There were occasions when we deliberately let you win a game so that you would stop sulking and go on playing with us. Sam used to wink at me when you weren't looking to show me it was time to let you win.

WILLIE: So then you two didn't play fair.

HALLY: It was for your benefit, Mr. Malopo, which is more than being fair. It was an act of self-sacrifice. [*To Sam*] But you know what my best memory is, don't you?

SAM: No.

HALLY: Come on, guess. If your memory is so good, you must remember it as well.

SAM: We got up to a lot of tricks in there, Hally.

HALLY: This one was special, Sam.

SAM: I'm listening.

HALLY: It started off looking like another of those useless nothing-to-do afternoons. I'd already been down to Main Street looking for adventure, but nothing had happened. I didn't feel like climbing trees in the Donkin Park or pretending I was a private eye and following a stranger . . . so as usual: See what's cooking in Sam's room. This time it was you on the floor. You had two thin pieces of wood and you were smoothing them down with a knife. It didn't look particularly interesting, but when I asked you what you were doing, you just said, "Wait and see, Hally. Wait . . . and see" . . . in that secret sort of way of yours, so I knew there was a surprise coming. You teased me, you bugger, by being deliberately slow and not answering my questions!

Sam laughs.

And whistling while you worked away! God, it was infuriating! I could have brained you! It was only when you tied them together in a cross and put that down on the brown paper that I realized what you were doing. "Sam is making a kite?" And when I asked you and you said "Yes" . . . ! [*Shaking his head with disbelief*] The sheer audacity of it took my breath away. I mean, seriously, what the hell does a black man know about flying a kite? I'll be honest with you, Sam, I had no hopes for it. If you think I was excited and happy, you got another guess coming. In fact, I was shit-scared that we were going to make fools of ourselves. When we left the boarding house to go up onto the hill, I was praying quietly that there wouldn't be any other kids around to laugh at us.

SAM [*Enjoying the memory as much as Hally*]: Ja, I could see that.

HALLY: I made it obvious, did I?

SAM: Ja. You refused to carry it.

HALLY: Do you blame me? Can you remember what the poor thing looked like? Tomato-box wood and brown paper! Flour and water for glue! Two of my mother's old stockings for a tail, and then all those bits and pieces of string you made me tie together so that we could fly it! Hell, no, that was now only asking for a miracle to happen.

SAM: Then the big argument when I told you to hold the string and run with it when I let go.

HALLY: I was prepared to run, all right, but straight back to the boarding house.

SAM [*Knowing what's coming*]: So what happened?

HALLY: Come on, Sam, you remember as well as I do.

SAM: I want to hear it from you.

Hally pauses. He wants to be as accurate as possible.

HALLY: You went a little distance from me down the hill, you held it up ready to let it go. . . . "This is it," I thought. "Like everything else in my life, here comes another fiasco." Then you shouted, "Go, Hally!" and I started to run. [*Another pause*] I don't know how to describe it, Sam. Ja! The miracle happened! I was running, waiting for it to crash to the ground, but instead suddenly there was something alive behind me at the end of the string, tugging at it as if it wanted to be free. I looked back . . . [*Shakes his head*] . . . I still can't believe my eyes. It was flying! Looping around and trying to climb even higher into the sky. You shouted to me to let it have more string. I did, until there was none left and I was just holding that piece of wood we had tied it to. You came up and joined me. You were laughing.

SAM: So were you. And shouting, "It works, Sam! We've done it!"

HALLY: And we had! I was so proud of us! It was the most splendid thing I had ever seen. I wished there were hundreds of kids around to watch us. The part that scared me, though, was when you showed me how to make it dive down to the ground and then just when it was on the point of crashing, swoop up again!

SAM: You didn't want to try yourself.

HALLY: Of course not! I would have been suicidal if anything had happened to it. Watching you do it made me nervous enough. I was quite happy just to see it up there with its tail fluttering behind it. You left me after that, didn't you? You explained how to get it down, we tied it to the bench so that I could sit and watch it, and you went away. I wanted you to stay, you know. I was a little scared of having to look after it by myself.

SAM [*Quietly*]:   I had work to do, Hally.

HALLY: It was sort of sad bringing it down, Sam. And it looked sad again when it was lying there on the ground. Like something that had lost its soul. Just tomato-box wood, brown paper and two of my mother's old stockings! But, hell, I'll never forget that first moment when I saw it up there. I had a stiff neck the next day from looking up so much.

Sam laughs. Hally turns to him with a question he never thought of asking before.

Why did you make that kite, Sam?

SAM [*Evenly*]:   I can't remember.

HALLY: Truly?

SAM: Too long ago, Hally.

HALLY: Ja, I suppose it was. It's time for another one, you know.

SAM: Why do you say that?

HALLY: Because it feels like that. Wouldn't be a good day to fly it, though.

SAM: No. You can't fly kites on rainy days.

HALLY [*He studies Sam. Their memories have made him conscious of the man's presence in his life*]:   How old are you, Sam?

SAM: Two score and five.

HALLY: Strange, isn't it?

SAM: What?

HALLY: Me and you.

SAM: What's strange about it?

HALLY: Little white boy in short trousers and a black man old enough to be his father flying a kite. It's not every day you see that.

SAM: But why strange? Because the one is white and the other black?

HALLY: I don't know. Would have been just as strange, I suppose, if it had been me and my Dad . . . cripple man and a little boy! Nope!

There's no chance of me flying a kite without it being strange. [*Simple statement of fact—no self-pity*] There's a nice little short story there. "The Kite-Flyers." But we'd have to find a twist in the ending.

SAM: Twist?

HALLY: Yes. Something unexpected. The way it ended with us was too straightforward . . . me on the bench and you going back to work. There's no drama in that.

WILLIE: And me?

HALLY: You?

WILLIE: Yes me.

HALLY: You want to get into the story as well, do you? I got it! Change the title: "Afternoons in Sam's Room" . . . expand it and tell all the stories. It's on its way to being a novel. Our days in the old Jubilee. Sad in a way that they're over. I almost wish we were still in that little room.

SAM: We're still together.

HALLY: That's true. It's just that life felt the right size in there . . . not too big and not too small. Wasn't so hard to work up a bit of courage. It's got so bloody complicated since then.

The telephone rings. Sam answers it.

SAM: St. George's Park Tea Room . . . Hello, Madam . . . Yes, Madam, he's here. . . . Hally, it's your mother.

HALLY: Where is she phoning from?

SAM: Sounds like the hospital. It's a public telephone.

HALLY [*Relieved*]: You see! I told you. [*The telephone*] Hello, Mom . . . Yes . . . Yes no fine. Everything's under control here. How's things with poor old Dad? . . . Has he had a bad turn? . . . What? . . . Oh, God! . . . Yes, Sam told me, but I was sure he'd made a mistake. But what's this all about, Mom? He didn't look at all good last night. How can he get better so quickly? . . . Then very obviously you must say no. Be firm with him. You're the boss. . . . You know what it's go-ing to be like if he comes home. . . . Well then, don't blame me when I fail my exams at the end of the year. . . . Yes! How am I ex-pected to be fresh for school when I spend half the night massag-ing his gammy leg? . . . So am I! . . . So tell him a white lie. Say Dr. Colley wants more X-rays of his stump. Or bribe him. We'll sneak in double tots of brandy in future. . . . What? . . . Order him to get back into bed at once! If he's going to behave like a child, treat him like one. . . . All right, Mom! I was just trying to . . . I'm sorry. . . . I said I'm sorry. . . . Quick, give me your number. I'll phone you back. [*He hangs up and waits a few seconds*] Here we go again! [*He dials*] I'm sorry, Mom. . . . Okay . . . But now listen to me carefully. All it needs is for you to put your foot down. Don't take no for an answer. . . . Did you hear me? And whatever you do, don't discuss it with him. . . . Because I'm frightened you'll give in to him. . . . Yes, Sam gave me lunch. . . . I ate all of it! . . . No, Mom not a soul. It's still raining here. . . . Right, I'll tell them. I'll just do some homework and then lock up. . . . But remember now, Mom. Don't listen to anything he says. And phone me back and let me know what happens. . . . Okay. Bye, Mom. [*He hangs up. The men are staring at him*] My Mom says that when you're finished with the floors you must do the windows. [*Pause*] Don't misunderstand me, chaps. All I want is for him to get better. And if he was, I'd be the first person to say: "Bring him home." But he's not, and we can't give him the medical care and attention he needs at home. That's what hospitals are there for. [*Brusquely*] So don't just stand there! Get on with it!

Sam clears Hally's table.

You heard right. My Dad wants to go home.

SAM: Is he better?

HALLY [*Sharply*]: No! How the hell can he be better when last night he was groaning with pain? This is not an age of miracles!

SAM: Then he should stay in hospital.

HALLY [*Seething with irritation and frustration*]: Tell me something I don't know, Sam. What the hell do you think I was saying to my Mom? All I can say is fuck-it-all.

SAM: I'm sure he'll listen to your Mom.

HALLY: You don't know what she's up against. He's already packed his shaving kit and pajamas and is sitting on his bed with his crutches, dressed and ready to go. I know him when he gets in that mood. If she tries to reason with him, we've had it. She's no match for him when it comes to a battle of words. He'll tie her up in knots. [*Trying to hide his true feelings*]

SAM: I suppose it gets lonely for him in there.

HALLY: With all the patients and nurses around? Regular visits from the Salvation Army? Balls! It's ten times worse for him at home. I'm at school and my mother is here in the business all day.

SAM: He's at least got you at night.

HALLY [*Before he can stop himself*]: And we've got him! Please! I don't want to talk about it anymore. [*Unpacks his school case, slamming down books on the table*] Life is just a plain bloody mess, that's all. And people are fools.

SAM: Come on, Hally.

HALLY: Yes, they are! They bloody well deserve what they get.

SAM: Then don't complain.

HALLY: Don't try to be clever, Sam. It doesn't suit you. Anybody who thinks there's nothing wrong with this world needs to have his head examined. Just when things are going along all right, without fail someone or something will come along and spoil everything. Somebody should write that down as a fundamental law of the Universe. The principle of perpetual disappointment. If there is a God who created this world, he should scrap it and try again.

SAM: All right, Hally, all right. What you got for homework?

HALLY: Bullshit, as usual. [*Opens an exercise book and reads*] "Write five hundred words describing an annual event of cultural or historical significance."

SAM: That should be easy enough for you.

HALLY: And also plain bloody boring. You know what he wants, don't you? One of their useless old ceremonies. The commemoration of the landing of the 1820 Settlers, or if it's going to be culture, Carols by Candlelight every Christmas.

SAM: It's an impressive sight. Make a good description, Hally. All those candles glowing in the dark and the people singing hymns.

HALLY: And it's called religious hysteria. [*Intense irritation*] Please, Sam! Just leave me alone and let me get on with it. I'm not in the mood for games this afternoon. And remember my Mom's orders . . . you're to help Willie with the windows. Come on now, I don't want any more nonsense in here.

SAM: Okay, Hally, okay.

*Hally settles down to his homework; determined preparations . . .
pen, ruler, exercise book, dictionary, another cake . . . all of which
will lead to nothing.*

*Sam waltzes over to Willie and starts to replace tables and chairs.
He practices a ballroom step while doing so. Willie watches.
When Sam is finished, Willie tries.*

Good! But just a little bit quicker on the turn and only move in to her after she's crossed over. What about this one?

Another step. When Sam is finished, Willie again has a go.

Much better. See what happens when you just relax and enjoy yourself? Remember that in two weeks' time and you'll be all right.

WILLIE: But I haven't got partner, Boet Sam.

SAM: Maybe Hilda will turn up tonight.

WILLIE: No, Boet Sam. [*Reluctantly*] I gave her a good hiding.

SAM: You mean a bad one.

WILLIE: Good bad one.

SAM: Then you mustn't complain either. Now you pay the price for losing your temper.

WILLIE: I also pay two pounds ten shilling entrance fee.

SAM: They'll refund you if you withdraw now.

WILLIE [*Appalled*]:   You mean, don't dance?

SAM: Yes.

WILLIE: No! I wait too long and I practice too hard. If I find me new partner, you think I can be ready in two weeks? I ask Madam for my leave now and we practice every day.

SAM: Quickstep non-stop for two weeks. World record, Willie, but you'll be mad at the end.

WILLIE: No jokes, Boet Sam.

SAM: I'm not joking.

WILLIE: So then what?

SAM: Find Hilda. Say you're sorry and promise you won't beat her again.

WILLIE: No.

SAM: Then withdraw. Try again next year.

WILLIE: No.

SAM: Then I give up.

WILLIE: Haaikona, Boet Sam, you can't.

SAM: What do you mean, I can't? I'm telling you: I give up.

WILLIE [*Adamant*]:   No! [*Accusingly*] It was you who start me ballroom dancing.

SAM: So?

WILLIE: Before that I use to be happy. And is you and Miriam who bring me to Hilda and say here's partner for you.

SAM: What are you saying, Willie?

WILLIE: You!

SAM: But me what? To blame?

WILLIE: Yes.

SAM: Willie . . . ? [Bursts into laughter]

WILLIE: And now all you do is make jokes at me. You wait. When Miriam leaves you is my turn to laugh. Ha! Ha! Ha!

SAM [He can't take Willie seriously any longer]: She can leave me tonight! I know what to do. [Bowing before an imaginary partner] May I have the pleasure? [He dances and sings]
"Just a fellow with his pillow . . .
Dancin' like a willow . . .
In an autumn breeze . . ."

WILLIE: There you go again!

Sam goes on dancing and singing.

Boet Sam!

SAM: There's the answer to your problem! Judges' announcement in two weeks' time: "Ladies and gentlemen, the winner in the open section . . . Mr. Willie Malopo and his pillow!"

This is too much for a now really angry Willie. He goes for Sam, but the latter is too quick for him and puts Hally's table between the two of them.

HALLY [Exploding]: For Christ's sake, you two!

WILLIE [Still trying to get at Sam]: I donner you, Sam! Struesgod!

SAM [Still laughing]: Sorry, Willie . . . Sorry . . .

HALLY: Sam! Willie! [Grabs his ruler and gives Willie a vicious whack on the bum] How the hell am I supposed to concentrate with the two of you behaving like bloody children!

WILLIE: Hit him too!

HALLY: Shut up, Willie.

WILLIE: He started jokes again.

HALLY: Get back to your work. You too, Sam. [His ruler] Do you want another one, Willie?

Sam and Willie return to their work. Hally uses the opportunity to escape from his unsuccessful attempt at homework. He struts around like a little despot, ruler in hand, giving vent to his anger and frustration.

Suppose a customer had walked in then? Or the Park Superintendent. And seen the two of you behaving like a pair of hooligans. That would have been the end of my mother's license, you know. And your jobs! Well, this is the end of it. From now on there will be no more of your ballroom nonsense in here. This is a business establishment, not a bloody New Brighton dancing school. I've been far too lenient with the two of you. [*Behind the counter for a green cool drink and a dollop of ice cream. He keeps up his tirade as he prepares it*] But what really makes me bitter is that I allow you chaps a little freedom in here when business is bad and what do you do with it? The foxtrot! Specially you, Sam. There's more to life than trotting around a dance floor and I thought at least you knew it.

SAM: It's a harmless pleasure, Hally. It doesn't hurt anybody.

HALLY: It's also a rather simple one, you know.

SAM: You reckon so? Have you ever tried?

HALLY: Of course not.

SAM: Why don't you? Now.

HALLY: What do you mean? Me dance?

SAM: Yes. I'll show you a simple step—the waltz—then you try it.

HALLY: What will that prove?

SAM: That it might not be as easy as you think.

HALLY: I didn't say it was easy. I said it was simple—like in simpleminded, meaning mentally retarded. You can't exactly say it challenges the intellect.

SAM: It does other things.

HALLY: Such as?

SAM: Make people happy.

HALLY [*The glass in his hand*]:   So do American cream sodas with ice cream. For God's sake, Sam, you're not asking me to take ballroom dancing serious, are you?

SAM: Yes.

HALLY [*Sigh of defeat*]:   Oh, well, so much for trying to give you a decent education. I've obviously achieved nothing.

SAM: You still haven't told me what's wrong with admiring something that's beautiful and then trying to do it yourself.

HALLY: Nothing. But we happen to be talking about a foxtrot, not a thing of beauty.

SAM: But that is just what I'm saying. If you were to see two champions doing, two masters of the art . . . !

HALLY: Oh, God, I give up. So now it's also art!

SAM: Ja.

HALLY: There's a limit, Sam. Don't confuse art and entertainment.

SAM: So then what is art?

HALLY: You want a definition?

SAM: Ja.

HALLY [*He realizes he has got to be careful. He gives the matter a lot of thought before answering*]: Philosophers have been trying to do that for centuries. What is Art? What is Life? But basically I suppose it's . . . the giving of meaning to matter.

SAM: Nothing to do with beautiful?

HALLY: It goes beyond that. It's the giving of form to the formless.

SAM: Ja, well, maybe it's not art, then. But I still say it's beautiful.

HALLY: I'm sure the word you mean to use is entertaining.

SAM [*Adamant*]: No. Beautiful. And if you want proof, come along to the Centenary Hall in New Brighton in two weeks' time.

The mention of the Centenary Hall draws Willie over to them.

HALLY: What for? I've seen the two of you prancing around in here often enough.

SAM [*He laughs*]: This isn't the real thing, Hally. We're just playing around in here.

HALLY: So? I can use my imagination.

SAM: And what do you get?

HALLY: A lot of people dancing around and having a so-called good time.

SAM: That all?

HALLY: Well, basically it is that, surely.

SAM: No, it isn't. Your imagination hasn't helped you at all. There's a lot more to it than that. We're getting ready for the championships, Hally, not just another dance. There's going to be a lot of people, all right, and they're going to have a good time, but they'll only be spectators, sitting around and watching. It's just the competitors out there on the dance floor. Party decorations and fancy lights all around the walls! The ladies in beautiful evening dresses!

HALLY: My mother's got one of those, Sam, and, quite frankly, it's an embarrassment every time she wears it.

SAM [*Undeterred*]:   Your imagination left out the excitement.

Hally scoffs.

Oh, yes. The finalists are not going to be out there just to have a good time. One of those couples will be the 1950 Eastern Province Champions. And your imagination left out the music.

WILLIE: Mr. Elijah Gladman Guzana and his Orchestral Jazzonions.

SAM: The sound of the big band, Hally. Trombone, trumpet, tenor and alto sax. And then, finally, your imagination also left out the climax of the evening when the dancing is finished, the judges have stopped whispering among themselves and the Master of Ceremonies collects their scorecards and goes up onto the stage to announce the winners.

HALLY: All right. So you make it sound like a bit of a do. It's an occasion. Satisfied?

SAM [*Victory*]:   So you admit that!

HALLY: Emotionally yes, intellectually no.

SAM: Well, I don't know what you mean by that, all I'm telling you is that it is going to be *the* event of the year in New Brighton. It's been sold out for two weeks already. There's only standing room left. We've got competitors coming from Kingwilliamstown, East London, Port Alfred.

Hally starts pacing thoughtfully.

HALLY: Tell me a bit more.

SAM: I thought you weren't interested . . . intellectually.

HALLY [*Mysteriously*]:   I've got my reasons.

SAM: What do you want to know?

HALLY: It takes place every year?

SAM: Yes. But only every third year in New Brighton. It's East London's turn to have the championships next year.

HALLY: Which, I suppose, makes it an even more significant event.

SAM: Ah ha! We're getting somewhere. Our "occasion" is now a "significant event."

HALLY: I wonder.

SAM: What?

HALLY: I wonder if I would get away with it.

SAM: But what?

HALLY [*To the table and his exercise book*]: "Write five hundred words describing an annual event of cultural or historical significance." Would I be stretching poetic license a little too far if I called your ballroom championships a cultural event?

SAM: You mean . . . ?

HALLY: You think we could get five hundred words out of it, Sam?

SAM: Victor Sylvester has written a whole book on ballroom dancing.

WILLIE: You going to write about it, Master Hally?

HALLY: Yes, gentlemen, that is precisely what I am considering doing. Old Doc Bromely—he's my English teacher—is going to argue with me, of course. He doesn't like natives. But I'll point out to him that in strict anthropological terms the culture of a primitive black society includes its dancing and singing. To put my thesis in a nut-shell: The war-dance has been replaced by the waltz. But it still amounts to the same thing: the release of primitive emotions through movement. Shall we give it a go?

SAM: I'm ready.

WILLIE: Me also.

HALLY: Ha! This will teach the old bugger a lesson. [*Decision taken*] Right. Let's get ourselves organized. [*This means another cake on the table. He sits*] I think you've given me enough general atmosphere, Sam, but to build the tension and suspense I need facts. [*Pencil poised*]

WILLIE: Give him facts, Boet Sam.

HALLY: What you called the climax . . . how many finalists?

SAM: Six couples.

HALLY [*Making notes*]: Go on. Give me the picture.

SAM: Spectators seated right around the hall. [*Willie becomes a spectator*]

HALLY: . . . and it's a full house.

SAM: At one end, on the stage, Gladman and his Orchestral Jazz-onions. At the other end is a long table with the three judges. The six finalists go onto the dance floor and take up their positions. When they are ready and the spectators have settled down, the Master of Ceremonies goes to the microphone. To start with, he makes some jokes to get the people laughing . . .

HALLY: Good touch! [*As he writes*] ". . . creating a relaxed atmosphere which will change to one of tension and drama as the climax is approached."

SAM [*Onto a chair to act out the M.C.*]: "Ladies and gentlemen, we come now to the great moment you have all been waiting for this evening . . . . The finals of the 1950 Eastern Province Open Ballroom Dancing Championships. But first let me introduce the finalists! Mr. and Mrs. Welcome Tchabalala from Kingwilliamstown . . ."

WILLIE [*He applauds after every name*]: Is when the people clap their hands and whistle and make a lot of noise, Master Hally.

SAM: "Mr. Mulligan Njikelane and Miss Nomhle Nkonyeni of Grahamstown; Mr. and Mrs. Norman Nchinga from Port Alfred; Mr. Fats Bokolane and Miss Dina Plaatjies from East London; Mr. Sipho Dugu and Mrs. Mable Magada from Peddie; and from New Brighton our very own Mr. Willie Malopo and Miss Hilda Samuels."

Willie can't believe his ears. He abandons his role as spectator and scrambles into position as a finalist.

WILLIE: Relaxed and ready to romance!

SAM: The applause dies down. When everybody is silent, Gladman lifts up his sax, nods at the Orchestral Jazzonions . . .

WILLIE: Play the jukebox please, Boet Sam!

SAM: I also only got bus fare, Willie.

HALLY: Hold it, everybody. [*Heads for the cash register behind the counter*] How much is in the till, Sam?

SAM: Three shillings. Hally . . . your Mom counted it before she left.

Hally hesitates.

HALLY: Sorry, Willie. You know how she carried on the last time I did it. We'll just have to pool our combined imaginations and hope for the best. [*Returns to the table*] Back to work. How are the points scored, Sam?

SAM: Maximum of ten points each for individual style, deportment, rhythm and general appearance.

WILLIE: Must I start?

HALLY: Hold it for a second, Willie. And penalties?

SAM: For what?

HALLY: For doing something wrong. Say you stumble or bump into somebody . . . do they take off any points?

SAM [*Aghast*]: Hally . . . !

HALLY: When you're dancing. If you and your partner collide into another couple.

Hally can get no further. Sam has collapsed with laughter. He explains to Willie.

SAM: If me and Miriam bump into you and Hilda . . .

Willie joins him in another good laugh.

Hally, Hally . . . !

HALLY [*Perplexed*]: Why? What did I say?

SAM: There's no collisions out there, Hally. Nobody trips or stumbles or bumps into anybody else. That's what that moment is all about. To be one of those finalists on that dance floor is like . . . like being in a dream about a world in which accidents don't happen.

HALLY [*Genuinely moved by Sam's image*]: Jesus, Sam! That's beautiful!

WILLIE [*Can endure waiting no longer*]: I'm starting! [*Willie dances while Sam talks*]

SAM: Of course it is. That's what I've been trying to say to you all afternoon. And it's beautiful because that is what we want life to be like. But instead, like you said, Hally, we're bumping into each other all the time. Look at the three of us this afternoon: I've bumped into Willie, the two of us have bumped into you, you've bumped into your mother, she bumping into your Dad. . . . None of us knows the steps and there's no music playing. And it doesn't stop with us. The whole world is doing it all the time. Open a newspaper and what do you read? America has bumped into Russia, England is bumping into India, rich man bumps into poor man. Those are big collisions, Hally. They make for a lot of bruises. People get hurt in all that bumping, and we're sick and tired of it now. It's been going on for too long. Are we never going to get it right? . . . Learn to dance life like champions instead of always being just a bunch of beginners at it?

HALLY [*Deep and sincere admiration of the man*]: You've got a vision, Sam!

SAM: Not just me. What I'm saying to you is that everybody's got it. That's why there's only standing room left for the Centenary Hall in two weeks' time. For as long as the music lasts, we are going to see six couples get it right, the way we want life to be.

HALLY: But is that the best we can do, Sam . . . watch six finalists dreaming about the way it should be?

SAM: I don't know. But it starts with that. Without the dream we won't know what we're going for. And anyway I reckon there are a few people who have got past just dreaming about it and are trying for something real. Remember that thing we read once in the paper about the Mahatma Gandhi? Going without food to stop those riots in India?

HALLY: You're right. He certainly was trying to teach people to get the steps right.

SAM: And the Pope.

HALLY: Yes, he's another one. Our old General Smuts as well, you know. He's also out there dancing. You know, Sam, when you come to think of it, that's what the United Nations boils down to . . . a dancing school for politicians!

SAM: And let's hope they learn.

HALLY [*A little surge of hope*]: You're right. We mustn't despair. Maybe there's some hope for mankind after all. Keep it up, Willie. [*Back to his table with determination*] This is a lot bigger than I thought. So what have we got? Yes, our title: "A World Without Collisions."

SAM: That sounds good! "A World Without Collisions."

HALLY: Subtitle: "Global Politics on the Dance Floor." No. A bit too heavy, hey? What about "Ballroom Dancing as a Political Vision"?

The telephone rings. Sam answers it.

SAM: St. George's Park Tea Room . . . Yes, Madam . . . Hally, it's your Mom.

HALLY [*Back to reality*]: Oh, God, yes! I'd forgotten all about that. Shit! Remember my words, Sam? Just when you're enjoying yourself, someone or something will come along and wreck everything.

SAM: You haven't heard what she's got to say yet.

HALLY: Public telephone?

SAM: No.

HALLY: Does she sound happy or unhappy?

SAM: I couldn't tell. [*Pause*] She's waiting, Hally.

HALLY [*To the telephone*]: Hello, Mom . . . No, everything is okay here. Just doing my homework. . . . What's your news? . . . You've what? . . . [*Pause. He takes the receiver away from his ear for a few seconds. In the course of Hally's telephone conversation, Sam and Willie discretely posi-*

tion the stacked tables and chairs. *Hally places the receiver back to his ear*]
Yes, I'm still here. Oh, well, I give up now. Why did you do it,
Mom? . . . Well, I just hope you know what you've let us in
for. . . . [*Loudly*] I said I hope you know what you've let us in for! It's
the end of the peace and quiet we've been having. [*Softly*] Where is
he? [*Normal voice*] He can't hear us from in there. But for God's
sake, Mom, what happened? I told you to be firm with him. . . .
Then you and the nurses should have held him down, taken his
crutches away. . . . I know only too well he's my father! . . . I'm not
being disrespectful, but I'm sick and tired of emptying stinking
chamberpots full of phlegm and piss. . . . Yes, I do! When you're
not there, he asks *me* to do it. . . . If you really want to know the
truth, that's why I've got no appetite for my food. . . . Yes! There's a
lot of things you don't know about. For your information, I still
haven't got that science textbook I need. And you know why? He
borrowed the money you gave me for it. . . . Because I didn't want
to start another fight between you two. . . . He says that every
time. . . . All right, Mom! [*Viciously*] Then just remember to start
hiding your bag away again, because he'll be at your purse before
long for money for booze. And when he's well enough to come
down here, you better keep an eye on the till as well, because that
is also going to develop a leak. . . . Then don't complain to me when
he starts his old tricks. . . . Yes, you do. I get it from you on one side
and from him on the other, and it makes life hell for me. I'm not
going to be the peacemaker anymore. I'm warning you now: when
the two of you start fighting again, I'm leaving home. . . . Mom, if
you start crying, I'm going to put down the receiver. . . . Okay . . .
[*Lowering his voice to a vicious whisper*] Okay, Mom. I heard you.
[*Desperate*] No. . . . Because I don't want to. I'll see him when I get
home! Mom! . . . [*Pause. When he speaks again, his tone changes
completely. It is not simply pretense. We sense a genuine emotional conflict*] Welcome home, chum! . . . What's that? . . . Don't be silly,
Dad. You being home is just about the best news in the world. . . .
I bet you are. Bloody depressing there with everybody going on
about their ailments, hey! . . . How you feeling? . . . Good . . . Here
as well, pal. Coming down cats and dogs. . . . That's right. Just the
day for a kip and a toss in your old Uncle Ned. . . . Everything's
just hunky-dory on my side, Dad. . . . Well, to start with, there's a
nice pile of comics for you on the counter. . . . Yes, old Kemple

brought them in. *Batman and Robin, Submariner . . .* just your cup of tea . . . I will. . . . Yes, we'll spin a few yarns tonight. . . . Okay, chum, see you in a little while. . . . No, I promise. I'll come straight home. . . . *[Pause—his mother comes back on the phone]* Mom? Okay. I'll lock up now. . . . What? . . . Oh, the brandy . . . Yes, I'll remember! . . . I'll put it in my suitcase now, for God's sake. I know well enough what will happen if he doesn't get it. . . . *[Places a bottle of brandy on the counter]* I *was* kind to him, Mom. I didn't say anything nasty! . . . All right. Bye. *[End of telephone conversation. A desolate Hally doesn't move. A strained silence]*

SAM *[Quietly]*: That sounded like a bad bump, Hally.

HALLY *[Having a hard time controlling his emotions. He speaks carefully]*: Mind your own business, Sam.

SAM: Sorry. I wasn't trying to interfere. Shall we carry on? Hally? *[He indicates the exercise book. No response from Hally]*

WILLIE *[Also trying]*: Tell him about when they give out the cups, Boet Sam.

SAM: Ja! That's another big moment. The presentation of the cups after the winners have been announced. You've got to put that in.

Still no response from Hally.

WILLIE: A big silver one, Master Hally, called floating trophy for the champions.

SAM: We always invite some big-shot personality to hand them over. Guest of honor this year is going to be His Holiness Bishop Jabulani of the All African Free Zionist Church.

Hally gets up abruptly, goes to his table and tears up the page he was writing on.

HALLY: So much for a bloody world without collisions.

SAM: Too bad. It was on its way to being a good composition.

HALLY: Let's stop bullshitting ourselves, Sam.

SAM: Have we been doing that?

HALLY: Yes! That's what all our talk about a decent world has been . . . just so much bullshit.

SAM: We did say it was still only a dream.

HALLY: And a bloody useless one at that. Life's a fuck-up and it's never going to change.

SAM: Ja, maybe that's true.

HALLY: There's no maybe about it. It's a blunt and brutal fact. All we've done this afternoon is waste our time.

SAM: Not if we'd got your homework done.

HALLY: I don't give a shit about my homework, so, for Christ's sake, just shut up about it. [*Slamming books viciously into his school case*] Hurry up now and finish your work. I want to lock up and get out of here. [*Pause*] And then go where? Home-sweet-fucking-home. Jesus, I hate that word.

Hally goes to the counter to put the brandy bottle and comics in his school case. After a moment's hesitation, he smashes the bottle of brandy. He abandons all further attempts to hide his feelings. Sam and Willie work away as unobtrusively as possible.

Do you want to know what is really wrong with your lovely little dream, Sam? It's not just that we are all bad dancers. That does happen to be perfectly true, but there's more to it than just that. You left out the cripples.

SAM: Hally!

HALLY [*Now totally reckless*]: Ja! Can't leave them out, Sam. That's why we always end up on our backsides on the dance floor. They're also out there dancing . . . like a bunch of broken spiders trying to do the quick-step! [*An ugly attempt at laughter*] When you come to think of it, it's a bloody comical sight. I mean, it's bad enough on two legs . . . but one and a pair of crutches! Hell, no, Sam. That's guaranteed to turn that dance floor into a shambles. Why you shaking your head? Picture it, man. For once this afternoon let's use our imaginations sensibly.

SAM: Be careful, Hally.

HALLY: Of what? The truth? I seem to be the only one around here who is prepared to face it. We've had the pretty dream, it's time now to wake up and have a good long look at the way things really are. Nobody knows the steps, there's no music, the cripples are also out there tripping up everybody and trying to get into the act, and it's all called the All-Comers-How-to-Make-a-Fuckup-of-Life Championships. [*Another ugly laugh*] Hang on, Sam! The best bit is still coming. Do you know what the winner's trophy is? A beautiful big chamber-pot with roses on the side, and it's full to the brim with piss. And guess who I think is going to be this year's winner.

SAM [Almost shouting]:   Stop now!

HALLY [Suddenly appalled by how far he has gone]:   Why?

SAM: Hally? It's your father you're talking about.

HALLY: So?

SAM: Do you know what you've been saying?

Hally can't answer. He is rigid with shame. Sam speaks to him sternly.

No, Hally, you mustn't do it. Take back those words and ask for forgiveness! It's a terrible sin for a son to mock his father with jokes like that. You'll be punished if you carry on. Your father is your father, even if he is a . . . cripple man.

WILLIE: Yes, Master Hally. Is true what Sam say.

SAM: I understand how you are feeling, Hally, but even so . . .

HALLY: No, you don't!

SAM: I think I do.

HALLY: And I'm telling you you don't. Nobody does. [Speaking carefully as his shame turns to rage at Sam] It's your turn to be careful, Sam. Very careful! You're treading on dangerous ground. Leave me and my father alone.

SAM: I'm not the one who's been saying things about him.

HALLY: What goes on between me and my Dad is none of your business!

SAM: Then don't tell me about it. If that's all you've got to say about him, I don't want to hear.

For a moment Hally is at loss for a response.

HALLY: Just get on with your bloody work and shut up.

SAM: Swearing at me won't help you.

HALLY: Yes, it does! Mind your own fucking business and shut up!

SAM: Okay. If that's the way you want it, I'll stop trying.

He turns away. This infuriates Hally even more.

HALLY: Good. Because what you've been trying to do is meddle in something you know nothing about. All that concerns you in here, Sam, is to try and do what you get paid for—keep the place clean and serve the customers. In plain words, just get on with your job.

My mother is right. She's always warning me about allowing you to get too familiar. Well, this time you've gone too far. It's going to stop right now.

No response from Sam.

You're only a servant in here, and don't forget it.

Still no response. Hally is trying hard to get one.

And as far as my father is concerned, all you need to remember is that he is your boss.

SAM [*Needled at last*]:   No, he isn't. I get paid by your mother.

HALLY: Don't argue with me, Sam!

SAM: Then don't say he's my boss.

HALLY: He's a white man and that's good enough for you.

SAM: I'll try to forget you said that.

HALLY: Don't! Because you won't be doing me a favor if you do. I'm telling you to remember it.

A pause. Sam pulls himself together and makes one last effort.

SAM: Hally, Hally . . . ! Come on now. Let's stop before it's too late. You're right. We *are* on dangerous ground. If we're not careful, somebody is going to get hurt.

HALLY: It won't be me.

SAM: Don't be so sure.

HALLY: I don't know what you're talking about, Sam.

SAM: Yes, you do.

HALLY [*Furious*]:   Jesus, I wish you would stop trying to tell me what I do and what I don't know.

Sam gives up. He turns to Willie.

SAM: Let's finish up.

HALLY: Don't turn your back on me! I haven't finished talking.

He grabs Sam by the arm and tries to make him turn around. Sam reacts with a flash of anger.

SAM: Don't do that, Hally! [*Facing the boy*] All right, I'm listening. Well? What do you want to say to me?

HALLY [*Pause as Hally looks for something to say*]:   To begin with, why don't you also start calling me Master Harold, like Willie.

SAM: Do you mean that?

HALLY: Why the hell do you think I said it?

SAM: And if I don't?

HALLY: You might just lose your job.

SAM [*Quietly and very carefully*]: If you make me say it once, I'll never call you anything else again.

HALLY: So? [*The boy confronts the man*] Is that meant to be a threat?

SAM: Just telling you what will happen if you make me do that. You must decide what it means to you.

HALLY: Well, I have. It's good news. Because that is exactly what Master Harold wants from now on. Think of it as a little lesson in respect, Sam, that's long overdue, and I hope you remember it as well as you do your geography. I can tell you now that some-body who will be glad to hear I've finally given it to you will be my Dad. Yes! He agrees with my Mom. He's always going on about it as well. "You must teach the boys to show you more re-spect, my son."

SAM: So now you can stop complaining about going home. Every-body is going to be happy tonight.

HALLY: That's perfectly correct. You see, you mustn't get the wrong idea about me and my Dad, Sam. We also have our good times to-gether. Some bloody good laughs. He's got a marvelous sense of humor. Want to know what our favorite joke is? He gives out a big groan, you see, and says: "It's not fair, is it, Hally?" Then I have to ask: "What, chum?" And then he says: "A nigger's arse" . . . and we both have a good laugh.

The men stare at him with disbelief.

What's the matter, Willie? Don't you catch the joke? You always were a bit slow on the uptake. It's what is called a pun. You see, fair means both light in color and to be just and decent. [*He turns to Sam*] I thought you would catch it, Sam.

SAM: Oh ja, I catch it all right.

HALLY: But it doesn't appeal to your sense of humor.

SAM: Do you really laugh?

HALLY: Of course.

SAM: To please him? Make him feel good?

HALLY: No, for heaven's sake! I laugh because I think it's a bloody good joke.

SAM: You're really trying hard to be ugly, aren't you? And why drag poor old Willie into it? He's done nothing to you except show you the respect you want so badly. That's also not being fair, you know . . . and *I* mean just or decent.

WILLIE: It's all right, Sam. Leave it now.

SAM: It's me you're after. You should just have said "Sam's arse" . . . because that's the one you're trying to kick. Anyway, how do you know it's not fair? You've never seen it. Do you want to? [*He drops his trousers and underpants and presents his backside for Hally's inspection*] Have a good look. A real Basuto arse . . . which is about as nigger as they can come. Satisfied? [*Trousers up*] Now you can make your Dad even happier when you go home tonight. Tell him I showed you my arse and he is quite right. It's not fair. And if it will give him an even better laugh next time, I'll also let *him* have a look. Come, Willie, let's finish up and go.

Sam and Willie start to tidy up the tea room. Hally doesn't move. He waits for a moment when Sam passes him.

HALLY [*Quietly*]: Sam . . .

Sam stops and looks expectantly at the boy. Hally spits in his face. A long and heartfelt groan from Willie. For a few seconds Sam doesn't move.

SAM [*Taking out a handkerchief and wiping his face*]: It's all right, Willie.

To Hally.

Ja, well, you've done it . . . Master Harold. Yes, I'll start calling you that from now on. It won't be difficult anymore. You've hurt yourself, Master Harold. I saw it coming. I warned you, but you wouldn't listen. You've just hurt yourself *bad*. And you're a coward, Master Harold. The face you should be spitting in is your father's . . . but you used mine, because you think you're safe inside your fair skin . . . and this time I don't mean just or decent. [*Pause, then moving violently towards Hally*] Should I hit him, Willie?

WILLIE [*Stopping Sam*]: No, Boet Sam.

SAM [*Violently*]: Why not?

WILLIE: It won't help, Boet Sam.

SAM: I don't want to help! I want to hurt him.

WILLIE: You also hurt yourself.

SAM: And if he had done it to you, Willie?

WILLIE: Me? Spit at me like I was a dog? [*A thought that had not occurred to him before. He looks at Hally*] Ja. Then I want to hit him. I want to hit him hard!

A dangerous few seconds as the men stand staring at the boy. Willie turns away, shaking his head.

But maybe all I do is go cry at the back. He's little boy, Boet Sam. Little white boy. Long trousers now, but he's still little boy.

SAM [*His violence ebbing away into defeat as quickly as it flooded*]: You're right. So go on, then: groan again, Willie. You do it better than me. [*To Hally*] You don't know all of what you've just done . . . Master Harold. It's not just that you've made me feel dirtier than I've ever been in my life . . . I mean, how do I wash off yours and your father's filth? . . . I've also failed. A long time ago I promised myself I was going to try and do something, but you've just shown me . . . Master Harold . . . that I've failed. [*Pause*] I've also got a memory of a little white boy when he was still wearing short trousers and a black man, but they're not flying a kite. It was the old Jubilee days, after dinner one night. I was in my room. You came in and just stood against the wall, looking down at the ground, and only after I'd asked you what you wanted, what was wrong, I don't know how many times, did you speak and even then so softly I almost didn't hear you. "Sam, please help me to go and fetch my Dad." Remember? He was dead drunk on the floor of the Central Hotel Bar. They'd phoned for your Mom, but you were the only one at home. And do you remember how we did it? You went in first by yourself to ask permission for me to go into the bar. Then I loaded him onto my back like a baby and carried him back to the boarding house with you following behind carrying his crutches. [*Shaking his head as he remembers*] A crowded Main Street with all the people watching a little white boy following his drunk father on a nigger's back! I felt for that little boy . . . Master Harold. I felt for him. After that we still had to clean him up, remember? He'd messed in his trousers, so we had to clean him up and get him into bed.

HALLY [*Great pain*]:   I love him, Sam.

SAM: I know you do. That's why I tried to stop you from saying these things about him. It would have been so simple if you could have just despised him for being a weak man. But he's your father. You love him and you're ashamed of him. You're ashamed of so much! . . . And now that's going to include yourself. That was the promise I made to myself: to try and stop that happening. [*Pause*] After we got him to bed you came back with me to my room and sat in a corner and carried on just looking down at the ground. And for days after that! You hadn't done anything wrong, but you went around as if you owed the world an apology for being alive. I didn't like seeing that! That's not the way a boy grows up to be a man!. . . But the one person who should have been teaching you what that means was the cause of your shame. If you really want to know, that's why I made you that kite. I wanted you to look up, be proud of something, of yourself . . . [*Bitter smile at the memory*] . . . and you certainly were that when I left you with it up there on the hill. Oh, ja . . . something else! . . . If you ever do write it as a short story, there *was* a twist in our ending. I couldn't sit down there and stay with you. It was a "Whites Only" bench. You were too young, too excited to notice then. But not anymore. If you're not careful . . . Master Harold . . . you're going to be sitting up there by yourself for a long time to come, and there won't be a kite in the sky. [*Sam has got nothing more to say. He exits into the kitchen, taking off his waiter's jacket*]

WILLIE: Is bad. Is all all bad in here now.

HALLY [*Books into his school case, raincoat on*]:   Willie . . . [*It is difficult to speak*] Will you lock up for me and look after the keys?

WILLIE: Okay.

Sam returns. Hally goes behind the counter and collects the few coins in the cash register. As he starts to leave . . .

SAM: Don't forget the comic books.

Hally returns to the counter and puts them in his case. He starts to leave again.

SAM [*To the retreating back of the boy*]:   Stop . . . Hally . . .

Hally stops, but doesn't turn to face him.

Hally . . . I've got no right to tell you what being a man means if I don't behave like one myself, and I'm not doing so well at that this afternoon. Should we try again, Hally?

HALLY: Try what?

SAM: Fly another kite, I suppose. It worked once, and this time I need it as much as you do.

HALLY: It's still raining, Sam. You can't fly kites on rainy days, remember.

SAM: So what do we do? Hope for better weather tomorrow?

HALLY [*Helpless gesture*]: I don't know. I don't know anything anymore.

SAM: You sure of that, Hally? Because it would be pretty hopeless if that was true. It would mean nothing has been learnt in here this afternoon, and there was a hell of a lot of teaching going on . . . one way or the other. But anyway, I don't believe you. I reckon there's one thing you know. You don't *have* to sit up there by yourself. You know what that bench means now, and you can leave it any time you choose. All you've got to do is stand up and walk away from it.

Hally leaves. Willie goes up quietly to Sam.

WILLIE: Is okay, Boet Sam. You see. Is . . . [*He can't find any better words*] . . . is going to be okay tomorrow. [*Changing his tone*] Hey, Boet Sam! [*He is trying hard*] You right. I think about it and you right. Tonight I find Hilda and say sorry. And make promise I won't beat her no more. You hear me, Boet Sam?

SAM: I hear you, Willie.

WILLIE: And when we practice I relax and romance with her from beginning to end. Non-stop! You watch! Two weeks' time: "First prize for promising newcomers: Mr. Willie Malopo and Miss Hilda Samuels." [*Sudden impulse*] To hell with it! I walk home. [*He goes to the jukebox, puts in a coin and selects a record. The machine comes to life in the gray twilight, blushing its way through a spectrum of soft, romantic colors*] How did you say it, Boet Sam? Let's dream. [*Willie sways with the music and gestures for Sam to dance*]

Sarah Vaughan sings.

"Little man you're crying,
I know why you're blue,

ATHOL FUGARD

Someone took your kiddy car away;
Better go to sleep now,
Little man you've had a busy day." [*etc. etc.*]
You lead. I follow.

The men dance together.

"Johnny won your marbles,
Tell you what we'll do;
Dad will get you new ones right away;
Better go to sleep now,
Little man you've had a busy day."

—1982

August Wilson, whose birth name was Frederick August Kittel, was born in Pittsburgh's predominantly African-American Hill District, the setting of many of his plays. The child of a mixed-race marriage, he grew up fatherless and credits his real education in life and, incidentally, in language to the older men in his neighborhood, whose distinctive voices echo memorably in his plays. A school dropout at fifteen after a teacher unjustly accused him of plagiarism, he joined in the Black Power movement of the 1960s, eventually founding the Black Horizon on the Hill, an African-American theater company. Wilson admits to having had little confidence in his own ability to write dialogue during his early career, and his first publications were poems. A move to St. Paul, Minnesota, led to work with the Minneapolis Playwrights' Center. After his return to Pittsburgh he wrote Jitney *and* Fullerton Street, *which were staged by regional theaters. His career hit full stride with the successful debut of* Ma Rainey's Black Bottom *(1984), which was first produced at the Yale Repertory Theater and later moved to Broadway.* Joe Turner's Come and Gone *(1986) was his next success, and* Fences *(1987) and* The Piano Lesson *(1990) both won Pulitzer Prizes and other major awards, establishing Wilson as the most prominent African-American dramatist. In most of Wilson's plays a historical theme is prominent, as Wilson attempts to piece together the circumstances that led African Americans to northern cities, depicting how they remain united and sometimes divided by a common cultural heritage that transcends even the ties of friendship and family. But to these social concerns Wilson brings a long training in the theater and a poet's love of language. As he said to an interviewer in 1991, "[Poetry] is the bedrock of my playwriting. . . . The idea of metaphor is a very large idea in my plays and something that I find lacking in most contemporary plays. I think I write the kinds of plays that I do because I have twenty-six years of writing poetry underneath all of that."* Two Trains Running *(1992),* Seven Guitars *(1995), and* King Hedley II *(2001) are recent plays.*

The Piano Lesson

Characters

Doaker
Boy Willie
Lymon
Berniece

Maretha
Avery
Wining Boy
Grace

Scene: *The action of the play takes place in the kitchen and parlor of the house where Doaker Charles lives with his niece, Berniece, and her eleven-year-old daughter, Maretha. The house is sparsely furnished, and although there is evidence of a woman's touch, there is a lack of warmth and vigor. Berniece and Maretha occupy the upstairs rooms. Doaker's room is prominent and opens onto the kitchen. Dominating the parlor is an old upright piano. On the legs of the piano, carved in the manner of African sculpture, are mask-like figures resembling totems. The carvings are rendered with a grace and power of invention that lifts them out of the realm of craftsmanship and into the realm of art. At left is a staircase leading to the upstairs.*

Act I

Scene I

The lights come up on the Charles household. It is five o'clock in the morning. The dawn is beginning to announce itself, but there is something in the air that belongs to the night. A stillness that is a portent, a gathering, a coming together of something akin to a storm. There is a loud knock at the door.

BOY WILLIE: [*Off stage, calling.*] Hey, Doaker . . . Doaker! [*He knocks again and calls.*]
Hey, Doaker! Hey, Berniece! Berniece!

Doaker enters from his room. He is a tall, thin man of forty-seven, with severe features, who has for all intents and purposes retired from the world though he works full-time as a railroad cook.

DOAKER: Who is it?
BOY WILLIE: Open the door, nigger! It's me . . . Boy Willie!
DOAKER: Who?
BOY WILLIE: Boy Willie! Open the door!

Doaker opens the door and Boy Willie and Lymon enter. Boy Willie is thirty years old. He has an infectious grin and a boyishness that is apt for his name. He is brash and impulsive, talkative and somewhat crude in speech and manner. Lymon is twenty-nine. Boy Willie's partner, he talks little, and then with a straightforwardness that is often disarming.

DOAKER: What you doing up here?

BOY WILLIE: I told you, Lymon. Lymon talking about you might be sleep. This is Lymon. You remember Lymon Jackson from down home? This my Uncle Doaker.

DOAKER: What you doing up here? I couldn't figure out who that was. I thought you was still down in Mississippi.

BOY WILLIE: Me and Lymon selling watermelons. We got a truck out there. Got a whole truckload of watermelons. We brought them up here to sell. Where's Berniece?

Calls.

Hey, Berniece!

DOAKER: Berniece up there sleep.

BOY WILLIE: Well, let her get up.

Calls.

Hey, Berniece!

DOAKER: She got to go to work in the morning.

BOY WILLIE: Well she can get up and say hi. It's been three years since I seen her.

Calls.

Hey, Berniece! It's me . . . Boy Willie.

DOAKER: Berniece don't like all that hollering now. She got to work in the morning.

BOY WILLIE: She can go on back to bed. Me and Lymon been riding two days in that truck . . . the least she can do is get up and say hi.

DOAKER: [*Looking out the window.*] Where you all get that truck from?

BOY WILLIE: It's Lymon's. I told him let's get a load of watermelons and bring them up here.

LYMON: Boy Willie say he going back, but I'm gonna stay. See what it's like up here.

BOY WILLIE: You gonna carry me down there first.

LYMON: I told you I ain't going back down there and take a chance on that truck breaking down again. You can take the train. Hey, tell him Doaker, he can take the train back. After we sell them watermelons he have enough money he can buy him a whole railroad car.

DOAKER: You got all them watermelons stacked up there no wonder the truck broke down. I'm surprised you made it this far with a load like that. Where you break down at?

BOY WILLIE: We broke down three times! It took us two and a half days to get here. It's a good thing we picked them watermelons fresh.

LYMON: We broke down twice in West Virginia. The first time was just as soon as we got out of Sunflower. About forty miles out she broke down. We got it going and got all the way to West Virginia before she broke down again.

BOY WILLIE: We had to walk about five miles for some water.

LYMON: It got a hole in the radiator but it runs pretty good. You have to pump the brakes sometime before they catch. Boy Willie have his door open and be ready to jump when that happens.

BOY WILLIE: Lymon think that's funny. I told the nigger I give him ten dollars to get the brakes fixed. But he thinks that funny.

LYMON: They don't need fixing. All you got to do is pump them till they catch.

Berniece enters on the stairs. Thirty-five years old, with an eleven-year-old daughter, she is still in mourning for her husband after three years.

BERNIECE: What you doing all that hollering for?

BOY WILLIE: Hey, Berniece. Doaker said you was sleep. I said at least you could get up and say hi.

BERNIECE: It's five o'clock in the morning and you come in here with all this noise. You can't come like normal folks. You got to bring all that noise with you.

BOY WILLIE: Hell, I ain't done nothing but come in and say hi. I ain't got in the house good.

BERNIECE: That's what I'm talking about. You start all that hollering and carry on as soon as you hit the door.

BOY WILLIE: Aw hell, woman, I was glad to see Doaker. You ain't had to come down if you didn't want to. I come eighteen hundred miles to see my sister I figure she might want to get up and say hi. Other than that you can go back upstairs. What you got, Doaker? Where your bottle? Me and Lymon want a drink.

To Berniece.

This is Lymon. You remember Lymon Jackson from down home.

LYMON: How you doing, Berniece. You look just like I thought you looked.

BERNIECE: Why you all got to come in hollering and carrying on? Waking the neighbors with all that noise.

BOY WILLIE: They can come over and join the party. We fixing to have a party. Doaker, where your bottle? Me and Lymon celebrating. The Ghosts of the Yellow Dog got Sutter.

BERNIECE: Say what?

BOY WILLIE: Ask Lymon, they found him the next morning. Say he drowned in his well.

DOAKER: When this happen, Boy Willie?

BOY WILLIE: About three weeks ago. Me and Lymon was over in Stoner County when we heard about it. We laughed. We thought it was funny. A great big old three-hundred-and-forty-pound man gonna fall down his well.

LYMON: It remind me of Humpty Dumpty.

BOY WILLIE: Everybody say the Ghosts of the Yellow Dog pushed him.

BERNIECE: I don't want to hear that nonsense. Somebody down there pushing them people in their wells.

DOAKER: What was you and Lymon doing over in Stoner County?

BOY WILLIE: We was down there working. Lymon got some people down there.

LYMON: My cousin got some land down there. We was helping him.

BOY WILLIE: Got near about a hundred acres. He got it set up real nice. Me and Lymon was down there chopping down trees. We was using Lymon's truck to haul the wood. Me and Lymon used to haul wood all around them parts.

To Berniece.

Me and Lymon got a truckload of watermelons out there.

Berniece crosses to the window to the parlor.

Doaker, where your bottle? I know you got a bottle stuck up in your room. Come on, me and Lymon want a drink.

Doaker exits into his room.

BERNIECE: Where you all get that truck from?

BOY WILLIE: I told you it's Lymon's.

BERNIECE: Where you get the truck from, Lymon?

LYMON: I bought it.

BERNIECE: Where he get that truck from, Boy Willie?

BOY WILLIE: He told you he bought it. Bought it for a hundred and twenty dollars. I can't say where he got that hundred and twenty dollars from . . . but he bought that old piece of truck from Henry Porter. [*To* LYMON.] Where you get that hundred and twenty dollars from, nigger?

LYMON: I got it like you get yours. I know how to take care of money.

Doaker brings a bottle and sets it on the table.

BOY WILLIE: Aw hell, Doaker got some of that good whiskey. Don't give Lymon none of that. he ain't used to good whiskey. He liable to get sick.

LYMON: I done had good whiskey before.

BOY WILLIE: Lymon bought that truck so he have him a place to sleep. He down there wasn't doing no work or nothing. Sheriff looking for him. He bought that truck to keep away from the sheriff. Got Stovall looking for him too. He down there sleeping in that truck ducking and dodging both of them. I told him come on let's go up and see my sister.

BERNIECE: What the sheriff looking for you for, Lymon?

BOY WILLIE: The man don't want you to know all his business. He's my company. He ain't asking you no questions.

LYMON: It wasn't nothing. It was just a misunderstanding.

BERNIECE: He in my house. You say the sheriff looking for him, I wanna know what he looking for him for. Otherwise you all can go back out there and be where nobody don't have to ask you nothing.

LYMON: It was just a misunderstanding. Sometimes me and the sheriff we don't think alike. So we just got crossed on each other.

BERNIECE: Might be looking for him about that truck. He might have stole that truck.

BOY WILLIE: We ain't stole no truck, woman. I told you Lymon bought it.

DOAKER: Boy Willie and Lymon got more sense than to ride all the way up here in a stolen truck with a load of watermelons. Now they might have stole them watermelons, but I don't believe they stole that truck.

BOY WILLIE: You don't even know the man good and you calling him a thief. And we ain't stole them watermelons either. Them old man Pitterford's watermelons. He give me and Lymon all we could load for ten dollars.

DOAKER: No Wonder you got them stacked up out there. You must have five hundred watermelons stacked up out there.

BERNIECE: Boy Willie, when you and Lymon planning on going back?

BOY WILLIE: Lymon say he staying. As soon as we sell them watermelons I'm going on back.

BERNIECE: [*Starts to exit up the stairs.*] That's what you need to do. And you need to do it quick. Come in here disrupting the house. I don't want all that loud carrying on around here. I'm surprised you ain't woke Maretha up.

BOY WILLIE: I was fixing to get her now.

Calls.

Hey, Maretha!

DOAKER: Berniece don't like all that hollering now.

BERNIECE: Don't you wake that child up!

BOY WILLIE: You going up there . . . wake her up and tell her her uncle's here. I ain't seen her in three years. Wake her up and send her down here. She can go back to bed.

BERNIECE: I ain't waking that child up . . . and don't you be making all that noise. You and Lymon need to sell them watermelons and go on back.

Berniece exits up the stairs.

BOY WILLIE: I see Berniece still try to be stuck up.

DOAKER: Berniece alright. She don't want you making all that noise. Maretha up there sleep. Let her sleep until she get up. She can see you then.

BOY WILLIE: I ain't thinking about Berniece. You hear from Wining Boy? You know Cleotha died?

DOAKER: Yeah, I heard that. He come by here about a year ago. Had a whole sack of money. He stayed here about two weeks. Ain't offered nothing. Berniece asked him for three dollars to buy some food and he got mad and left.

LYMON: Who's Wining Boy?

BOY WILLIE: That's my uncle. That's Doaker's brother. You heard me talk about Wining Boy. He play piano. He done made some records and everything. He still doing that, Doaker?

DOAKER: He made one or two records a long time ago. That's the only ones I ever known him to make. If you let him tell it he a big recording star.

BOY WILLIE: He stopped down home about two years ago. That's what I hear. I don't know. Me and Lymon was up on Parchman Farm doing them three years.

DOAKER: He don't never stay in one place. Now, he been here about eight months ago. Back in the winter. Now, you subject not to see him for another two years. It's liable to be that long before he stop by.

BOY WILLIE: If he had a whole sack of money you liable never to see him. You ain't gonna see him until he get broke. Just as soon as that sack of money is gone you look up and he be on your doorstep.

LYMON: [Noticing the piano.] Is that the piano?

BOY WILLIE: Yeah . . . look here, Lymon. See how it got all those carvings on it. See, that's what I was talking about. See how it's carved up real nice and polished and everything? You never find you another piano like that.

LYMON: Yeah, that look real nice.

BOY WILLIE: I told you. See how it's polished? My mama used to polish it every day. See all them pictures carved on it? That's what I was talking about. You can get a nice price for that piano.

LYMON: That's all Boy Willie talked about the whole trip up here. I got tired of hearing him talk about the piano.

BOY WILLIE: All you want to talk about is women. You ought to hear this nigger, Doaker. Talking about all the women he gonna get when he get up here. He ain't had none down there but he gonna get a hundred when he get up here.

DOAKER: How your people doing down there, Lymon?

LYMON: They alright. They still there. I come up here to see what it's like up here. Boy Willie trying to get me to go back and farm with him.

BOY WILLIE: Sutter's brother selling the land. He say he gonna sell it to me. That's why I come up here. I got one part of it. Sell them watermelons and get me another part. Get Berniece to sell that piano and I'll have the third part.

DOAKER: Berniece ain't gonna sell that piano.

BOY WILLIE: I'm gonna talk to her. When she see I got a chance to get Sutter's land she'll come around.

DOAKER: You can put that thought out your mind. Berniece ain't gonna sell that piano.

BOY WILLIE: I'm gonna talk to her. She been playing on it?

DOAKER: You know she won't touch that piano. I ain't never known her to touch it since Mama Ola died. That's over seven years now. She say it got blood on it. She got Maretha playing on it though. Say Maretha can go on and do everything she can't do. Got her in an extra school down at the Irene Kaufman Settlement House. She want Maretha to grow up and be a schoolteacher. Say she good enough she can teach on the piano.

BOY WILLIE: Maretha don't need to be playing on no piano. She can play on the guitar.

DOAKER: How much land Sutter got left?

BOY WILLIE: Got a hundred acres. Good land. He done sold it piece by piece, he kept the good part for himself. Now he got to give that up. His brother come down from Chicago for the funeral . . . he up there in Chicago got some kind of business with soda fountain equipment. He anxious to sell the land, Doaker. He don't want to be bothered with it. He called me to him and said cause of how long our families done known each other and how we been good friends and all, say he wanted to sell the land to me. Say he'd rather see me with it than Jim Stovall. Told me he'd let me have it for two thousand dollars cash money. He don't know I found out the most Stovall would give him for it was fifteen hundred dollars. He trying to get that extra five hundred out of me telling me he doing me a favor. I thanked him just as nice. Told him what a good man Sutter was and how he had my sympathy and all. Told him to give me two weeks. He said he'd wait on me. That's why I come up here. Sell them watermelons. Get Berniece to sell that piano. Put them two parts with the part I done saved. Walk in there. Tip my hat. Lay my money down on the table. Get my deed and walk on out. This time I get to keep all the cotton. Hire me some men to work it for me. Gin my cotton. Get my seed. And I'll see you again next year. Might even plant some tobacco or some oats.

DOAKER: You gonna have a hard time trying to get Berniece to sell that piano. You know Avery Brown from down there don't you? He up here now. He followed Berniece up here trying to get her to marry him after Crawley got killed. He been up here about two years. He call himself a preacher now.

BOY WILLIE: I know Avery. I know him from when he used to work on the Willshaw place. Lymon know him too.

DOAKER: He after Berniece to marry him. She keep telling him no but he won't give up. He keep pressing her on it.

BOY WILLIE: Avery think all white men is bigshots. He don't know there some white men ain't got as much as he got.

DOAKER: He supposed to come past here this morning. Berniece going down to the bank with him to see if he can get a loan to start his church. That's why I know Berniece ain't gonna sell that piano. He tried to get her to sell it to help him start his church. Sent the man around and everything.

BOY WILLIE: What man?

DOAKER: Some white fellow was going around to all the colored people's houses looking to buy up musical instruments. He'd buy anything. Drums. Guitars. Harmonicas. Pianos. Avery sent him past here. He looked at the piano and got excited. Offered her a nice price. She turned him down and got on Avery for sending him past. The man kept on her about two weeks. He seen where she wasn't gonna sell it, he gave her his number and told her if she ever wanted to sell it to call him first. Say he'd go one better than what anybody else would give her for it.

BOY WILLIE: How much he offer her for it?

DOAKER: Now you know me. She didn't say and I didn't ask. I just know it was a nice price.

LYMON: All you got to do is find out who he is and tell him somebody else wanna buy it from you. Tell him you can't make up your mind who to sell it to, and if he like Doaker say, he'll give you anything you want for it.

BOY WILLIE: That's what I'm gonna do. I'm gonna find out who he is from Avery.

DOAKER: It ain't gonna do you no good. Berniece ain't gonna sell that piano.

BOY WILLIE: She ain't got to sell it. I'm gonna sell it. I own just as much of it as she does.

BERNIECE: [*Offstage, hollers.*] Doaker! Go on get away. Doaker!

DOAKER: [*Calling.*] Berniece?

Doaker and Boy Willie rush to the stairs, Boy Willie runs up the stairs, passing Berniece as she enters, running.

DOAKER: Berniece, what's the matter? You alright? What's the matter?

Berniece tries to catch her breath. She is unable to speak.

DOAKER: That's alright. Take your time. You alright. What's the matter?

He calls.

Hey, Boy Willie?

BOY WILLIE: [*Offstage.*] Ain't nobody up here.

BERNIECE: Sutter . . . Sutter's standing at the top of the steps.

DOAKER: [*Calls.*] Boy Willie!

Lymon crosses to the stairs and looks up. Boy Willie enters from the stairs.

BOY WILLIE: Hey Doaker, what's wrong with her? Berniece, what's wrong? Who was you talking to?

DOAKER: She say she seen Sutter's ghost standing at the top of the stairs.

BOY WILLIE: Seen what? Sutter? She ain't seen no Sutter.

BERNIECE: He was standing right up there.

BOY WILLIE: [*Entering on the stairs.*] That's all in Berniece's head. Ain't nobody up there. Go on up there, Doaker.

DOAKER: I'll take your word for it. Berniece talking about what she seen. She say Sutter's ghost standing at the top of the steps. She ain't just make all that up.

BOY WILLIE: She up there dreaming. She ain't seen no ghost.

LYMON: You want a glass of water, Berniece? Get her a glass of water, Boy Willie.

BOY WILLIE: She don't need no water. She ain't seen nothing. Go on up there and look. Ain't nobody up there but Maretha.

DOAKER: Let Berniece tell it.

BOY WILLIE: I ain't stopping her from telling it.

DOAKER: What happened, Berniece?

BERNIECE: I come out my room to come back down here and Sutter was standing there in the hall.

BOY WILLIE: What he look like?

BERNIECE: He look like Sutter. He look like he always look.

BOY WILLIE: Sutter couldn't find his way from Big Sandy to Little Sandy. How he gonna find his way all the way up here to Pittsburgh? Sutter ain't never even heard of Pittsburgh.

DOAKER: Go on, Berniece.

BERNIECE: Just standing there with the blue suit on.

BOY WILLIE: The man ain't never left Marlin County when he was living . . . and he's gonna come all the way up here now that he's dead?

DOAKER: Let her finish. I want to hear what she got to say.

BOY WILLIE: I'll tell you this. If Berniece had seen him like she think she seen him she'd still be running.

DOAKER: Go on, Berniece. Don't pay Boy Willie no mind.

BERNIECE: He was standing there . . . had his hand on top of his head. Look like he might have thought if he took his hand down his head might have fallen off.

LYMON: Did he have on a hat?

BERNIECE: Just had on that blue suit . . . I told him to go away and he just stood there looking at me . . . calling Boy Willie's name.

BOY WILLIE: What he calling my name for?

BERNIECE: I believe you pushed him in the well.

BOY WILLIE: Now what kind of sense that make? You telling me I'm gonna go out there and hide in the weeds with all them dogs and things he got around there . . . I'm gonna hide and wait till I catch him looking down his well just right . . . then I'm gonna run over and push him in. A great big old three-hundred-and-forty-pound man.

BERNIECE: Well, what he calling your name for?

BOY WILLIE: He bending over looking down his well, woman . . . how he know who pushed him? It could have been anybody. Where was you when Sutter fell in his well? Where was Doaker? Me and Lymon was over in Stoner County. Tell her, Lymon. The Ghosts of the Yellow Dog got Sutter. That's what happened to him.

BERNIECE: You can talk all that Ghosts of the Yellow Dog stuff if you want. I know better.

LYMON: The Ghosts of the Yellow Dog pushed him. That's what the people say. They found him in his well and all the people say it must be the Ghosts of the Yellow Dog. Just like all them other men.

BOY WILLIE: Come talking about he looking for me. What he come all the way up here for? If he looking for me all he got to do is wait. He could have saved himself a trip if he looking for me. That ain't nothing but in Berniece's head. Ain't no telling what she liable to come up with next.

BERNIECE: Boy Willie, I want you and Lymon to go ahead and leave my house. Just go on somewhere. You don't do nothing but bring trouble with you everywhere you go. If it wasn't for you Crawley would still be alive.

BOY WILLIE: Crawley what? I ain't had nothing to do with Crawley getting killed. Crawley three time seven. He had his own mind.

BERNIECE: Just go on and leave. Let Sutter go somewhere else looking for you.

BOY WILLIE: I'm leaving. Soon as we sell them watermelons. Other than that I ain't going nowhere. Hell, I just got here. Talking about Sutter looking for me. Sutter was looking for that piano. That's what he was looking for. He had to die to find out where that piano was at . . . If I was you I'd get rid of it. That's the way to get rid of Sutter's ghost. Get rid of that piano.

BERNIECE: I want you and Lymon to go on and take all this confusion out of my house!

BOY WILLIE: Hey, tell her, Doaker. What kind of sense that make? I told you, Lymon, as soon as Berniece see me she was gonna start something. Didn't I tell you that? Now she done made up that story about Sutter just so she could tell me to leave her house. Well, hell, I ain't going nowhere till I sell them watermelons.

BERNIECE: Well why don't you go out there and sell them! Sell them and go on back!

BOY WILLIE: We waiting till the people get up.

LYMON: Boy Willie say if you get out there too early and wake the people up they get mad at you and won't buy nothing from you.

DOAKER: You won't be waiting long. You done let the sun catch up with you. This the time everybody be getting up around here.

BERNIECE: Come on, Doaker, walk up here with me. Let me get Maretha up and get her started. I got to get ready myself. Boy Willie, just go on out there and sell them watermelons and you and Lymon leave my house.

Berniece and Doaker exit up the stairs.

BOY WILLIE: [*Calling after them.*] If you see Sutter up there . . . tell him I'm down here waiting on him.

LYMON: What if she see him again?

BOY WILLIE: That's all in her head. There ain't no ghost up there.

Calls.

Hey, Doaker . . . I told you ain't nothing up there.

LYMON: I'm glad he didn't say he was looking for me.

BOY WILLIE: I wish I would see Sutter's ghost. Give me a chance to put a whupping on him.

LYMON: You ought to stay up here with me. You be down there working his land . . . he might come looking for you all the time.

BOY WILLIE: I ain't thinking about Sutter. And I ain't thinking about staying up here. You stay up here. I'm going back and get Sutter's land. You think you ain't got to work up here. You think this the land of milk and honey. But I ain't scared of work. I'm going back and farm every acre of that land.

Doaker enters from the stairs.

I told you there ain't nothing up there, Doaker. Berniece dreaming all that.

DOAKER: I believe Berniece seen something. Berniece level-headed. She ain't just made all that up. She say Sutter had on a suit. I don't believe she ever seen Sutter in a suit. I believe that's what he was buried in, and that's what Berniece saw.

BOY WILLIE: Well, let her keep on seeing him then. As long as he don't mess with me.

Doaker starts to cook his breakfast.

I heard about you, Doaker. They say you got all the women looking out for you down home. They be looking to see you coming. Say you got a different one every two weeks. Say they be fighting one another for you to stay with them.

To Lymon.

Look at him, Lymon. He know it's true.

DOAKER: I ain't thinking about no women. They never get me tied up with them. After Coreen I ain't got no use for them. I stay up on Jack Slattery's place when I be down there. All them women want is somebody with a steady payday.

BOY WILLIE: That ain't what I hear. I hear every two weeks the women all put on their dresses and line up at the railroad station.

DOAKER: I don't get down there but once a month. I used to go down there every two weeks but they keep switching me around. They keep switching all the fellows around.

BOY WILLIE: Doaker can't turn that railroad loose. He was working the railroad when I was walking around crying for sugartit. My mama used to brag on him.

DOAKER: I'm cooking now, but I used to line track. I pieced together the Yellow Dog stitch by stitch. Rail by rail. Line track all up around there. I lined track all up around Sunflower and Clarksdale. Wining Boy worked with me. He helped put in some of that track. He'd work it for six months and quit. Go back to playing piano and gambling.

BOY WILLIE: How long you been with the railroad now?

DOAKER: Twenty-seven years. Now, I'll tell you something about the railroad. What I done learned after twenty-seven years. See, you got North. You got West. You look over here you got South. Over there you got East. Now, you can start from anywhere. Don't care where you at. You got to go one of them four ways. And whichever way you decide to go they got a railroad that will take you there. Now, that's something simple. You think anybody would be able to understand that. But you'd be surprised how many people trying to go North get on a train going West. They think the train's supposed to go where they going rather than where it's going.

Now, why people going? Their sister's sick. They leaving before they kill somebody . . . and they sitting across from somebody who's leaving to keep from getting killed. They leaving cause they can't get satisfied. They going to meet someone. I wish I had a dollar for every time that someone wasn't at the station to meet them. I done seen that a lot. In between the time they sent the telegram and the time the person get there . . . they done forgot all about them.

They got so many trains out there they have a hard time keeping them from running into each other. Got trains going every whichaway. Got people on all of them. Somebody going where somebody just left. If everybody stay in one place I believe this would be a better world. Now what I done learned after twenty-seven years of railroading is this . . . if the train stays on the track . . . it's going to get where it's going. It might not be where you going. If it ain't then all you got to do is sit and wait cause the train's coming back to get you. The train don't never stop. It'll come back every time. Now I'll tell you another thing . . .

BOY WILLIE: What you cooking over there, Doaker? Me and Lymon's hungry.

DOAKER: Go on down there to Wylie and Kirkpatrick to Eddie's restaurant. Coffee cost a nickel and you can get two eggs, sausage, and grits for fifteen cents. He even give you a biscuit with it.

BOY WILLIE: That look good what you got. Give me a little piece of that grilled bread.

DOAKER: Here . . . go on take the whole piece.

BOY WILLIE: Here you go, Lymon . . . you want a piece?

He gives Lymon a piece of toast. Maretha enters from the stairs.

BOY WILLIE: Hey, sugar. Come here and give me a hug. Come on give Uncle Boy Willie a hug. Don't be shy. Look at her, Doaker. She done got bigger. Ain't she got big?

DOAKER: Yeah, she getting up there.

BOY WILLIE: How you doing, sugar?

MARETHA: Fine.

BOY WILLIE: You was just a little old thing last time I seen you. You remember me, don't you? This your Uncle Boy Willie from down South. That there's Lymon. He my friend. We come up here to sell watermelons. You like watermelons?

Maretha nods.

We got a whole truckload out front. You can have as many as you want. What you been doing?

MARETHA: Nothing.

BOY WILLIE: Don't be shy now. Look at you getting all big. How old is you?

MARETHA: Eleven. I'm gonna be twelve soon.

BOY WILLIE: You like it up here? You like the North?

MARETHA: It's alright.

BOY WILLIE: That there's Lymon. Did you say hi to Lymon?

MARETHA: Hi.

LYMON: How you doing? You look just like your mama. I remember you when you was wearing diapers.

BOY WILLIE: You gonna come down South and see me? Uncle Boy Willie gonna get him a farm. Gonna get a great big old farm. Come down there and I'll teach you how to ride a mule. Teach you how to kill a chicken, too.

MARETHA: I seen my mama do that.

BOY WILLIE: Ain't nothing to it. You just grab him by his neck and twist it. Get you a real good grip and then you just wring his neck and throw him in the pot. Cook him up. Then you got some good eating. What you like to eat? What kind of food you like?

MARETHA: I like everything . . . except I don't like no black-eyed peas.

BOY WILLIE: Uncle Doaker tell me your mama got you playing that piano. Come on play something for me.

Boy Willie crosses over to the piano followed by Maretha.

Show me what you can do. Come on now. Here . . . Uncle Boy Willie give you a dime . . . show me what you can do. Don't be bashful now. That dime say you can't be bashful.

Maretha plays. It is something any beginner first learns.

Here, let me show you something.

Boy Willie sits and plays a simple boogie-woogie.

See that? See what I'm doing? That's what you call the boogie-woogie. See now . . . you can get up and dance to that. That's how good it sound. It sound like you wanna dance. You can dance to that. It'll hold you up. Whatever kind of dance you wanna do you can dance to that right there. See that? See how it go? Ain't nothing to it. Go on you do it.

MARETHA: I got to read it on the paper.

BOY WILLIE: You don't need no paper. Go on. Do just like that there.

BERNIECE: Maretha! You get up here and get ready to go so you be on time. Ain't no need you trying to take advantage of company.

MARETHA: I got to go.

BOY WILLIE: Uncle Boy Willie gonna get you a guitar. Let Uncle Doaker teach you how to play that. You don't need to read no paper to play the guitar. Your mama told you about that piano? You know how them pictures got on there?

MARETHA: She say it just always been like that since she got it.

BOY WILLIE: You hear that, Doaker? And you sitting up here in the house with Berniece.

DOAKER: I ain't got nothing to do with that. I don't get in the way of Berniece's raising her.

BOY WILLIE: You tell your mama to tell you about that piano. You ask her how them pictures got on there. If she don't tell you I'll tell you.

BERNIECE: Maretha!

MARETHA: I got to get ready to go.

BOY WILLIE: She getting big, Doaker. You remember her, Lymon?

LYMON: She used to be real little.

There is a knock on the door. Doaker goes to answer it. Avery enters. Thirty-eight years old, honest and ambitious, he has taken to the city like a fish to water, finding in it opportunities for growth and advancement that did not exist for him in the rural South. He is dressed in a suit and tie with a gold cross around his neck. He carries a small Bible.

DOAKER: Hey, Avery, come on in. Berniece upstairs.

BOY WILLIE: Look at him . . . look at him . . . he don't know what to say. He wasn't expecting to see me.

AVERY: Hey, Boy Willie. What you doing up here?

BOY WILLIE: Look at him, Lymon.

AVERY: Is that Lymon? Lymon Jackson?

BOY WILLIE: Yeah, you know Lymon.

DOAKER: Berniece be ready in a minute, Avery.

BOY WILLIE: Doaker say you a preacher now. What . . . we supposed to call you Reverend? You used to be plain old Avery. When you get to be a preacher, nigger?

LYMON: Avery say he gonna be a preacher so he don't have to work.

BOY WILLIE: I remember when you was down there on the Willshaw place planting cotton. You wasn't thinking about no Reverend then.

AVERY: That must be your truck out there. I saw that truck with them watermelons, I was trying to figure out what it was doing in front of the house.

BOY WILLIE: Yeah, me and Lymon selling watermelons. That's Lymon's truck.

DOAKER: Berniece say you all going down to the bank.

AVERY: Yeah, they give me a half day off work. I got an appointment to talk to the bank about getting a loan to start my church.

BOY WILLIE: Lymon say preachers don't have to work. Where you working at, nigger?

DOAKER: Avery got him one of them good jobs. He working at one of them skyscrapers downtown.

AVERY: I'm working down there at the Gulf Building running an elevator. Got a pension and everything. They even give you a turkey on Thanksgiving.

LYMON: How you know the rope ain't gonna break? Ain't you scared the rope's gonna break?

AVERY: That's steel. They got steel cables hold it up. It take a whole lot of breaking to break that steel. Naw, I ain't worried about nothing like that. It ain't nothing but a little old elevator. Now, I wouldn't get in none of them airplanes. You couldn't pay me to do nothing like that.

LYMON: That be fun. I'd rather do that than ride in one of them elevators.

BOY WILLIE: How many of them watermelons you wanna buy?

AVERY: I thought you was gonna give me one seeing as how you got a whole truck full.

BOY WILLIE: You can get one, get two. I'll give you two for a dollar.

AVERY: I can't eat but one. How much are they?

BOY WILLIE: Aw, nigger, you know I'll give you a watermelon. Go on, take as many as you want. Just leave some for me and Lymon to sell.

AVERY: I don't want but one.

BOY WILLIE: How you get to be a preacher, Avery? I might want to be a preacher one day. Have everybody call me Reverend Boy Willie.

AVERY: It come to me in a dream. God called me and told me he wanted me to be a shepherd for his flock. That's what I'm gonna call my church . . . The Good Shepherd Church of God in Christ.

DOAKER: Tell him what you told me. Tell him about the three hobos.

AVERY: Boy Willie don't want to hear all that.

LYMON: I do. Lots a people say your dreams can come true.

AVERY: Naw. You don't want to hear all that.

DOAKER: Go on. I told him you was a preacher. He didn't want to believe me. Tell him about the three hobos.

AVERY: Well, it come to me in a dream. See . . . I was sitting out in this railroad yard watching the trains go by. The train stopped and these three hobos got off. They told me they had come from Nazareth and was on their way to Jerusalem. They had three candles. They gave me one and told me to light it . . . but to be careful that it didn't go out. Next thing I knew I was standing in front of this house. Something told me to go knock on the door. This old woman opened the door and said they had been waiting on me. Then she led me into this room. It was a big room and it was full of all kinds of different people. They looked like anybody else except they all had sheep heads and was making noise like sheep make. I heard somebody call my name. I looked around and there was these same three hobos. They told me to take off my clothes and they give me a blue robe with gold thread. They washed my feet and combed my hair. Then they showed me these three doors and told me to pick one.

I went through one of them doors and that flame leapt off that candle and it seemed like my whole head caught fire. I looked around and there was four or five other men standing there with these same blue robes on. Then we heard a voice tell us to look out across this valley. We looked out and saw the valley was full of wolves. The voice told us that these sheep people that I had seen in the other room had to go over to the other side of this valley and somebody had to take them. Then I heard another voice say, "Who shall I send?" Next thing I knew I said, "Here I am. Send me." That's when I met Jesus. He say, "If you go, I'll go with you." Something told me to say, "Come on. Let's go." That's when I woke up. My head still felt like it was on fire . . . but I had a peace about myself that was hard to explain. I knew right then that I had been filled with the Holy Ghost and called to be a servant of the Lord. It took me a while before I could accept that. But then a lot of little ways God showed me that it was true. So I became a preacher.

LYMON: I see why you gonna call it the Good Shepherd Church. You dreaming about them sheep people. I can see that easy.

BOY WILLIE: Doaker say you sent some white man past the house to look at that piano. Say he was going around to all the colored people's houses looking to buy up musical instruments.

AVERY: Yeah, but Berniece didn't want to sell that piano. After she told me about it . . . I could see why she didn't want to sell it.

BOY WILLIE: What's this man's name?

AVERY: Oh, that's a while back now. I done forgot his name. He give Berniece a card with his name and telephone number on it, but I believe she throwed it away.

Berniece and Maretha enter from the stairs.

BERNIECE: Maretha, run back upstairs and get my pocketbook. And wipe that hair grease off your forehead. Go ahead, hurry up.

Maretha exits up the stairs.

How you doing, Avery? You done got all dressed up. You look nice. Boy Willie, I thought you and Lymon was going to sell them watermelons.

BOY WILLIE: Lymon done got sleepy. We liable to get some sleep first.

LYMON: I ain't sleepy.

DOAKER: As many watermelons as you got stacked up on that truck out there, you ought to have been gone.

BOY WILLIE: We gonna go in a minute. We going.

BERNIECE: Doaker. I'm gonna stop down there on Logan Street. You want anything?

DOAKER: You can pick up some ham hocks if you going down there. See if you can get the smoked ones. If they ain't got that get the fresh ones. Don't get the ones that got all that fat under the skin. Look for the long ones. They nice and lean.

He gives her a dollar.

Don't get the short ones lessen they smoked. If you got to get the fresh ones make sure that they the long ones. If they ain't got them smoked then go ahead and get the short ones.

Pause.

You may as well get some turnip greens while you down there. I got some buttermilk . . . if you pickup some cornmeal I'll make me some cornbread and cook up them turnip greens.

Maretha enters from the stairs.

MARETHA: We gonna take the streetcar?

BERNIECE: Me and Avery gonna drop you off at the settlement house. You mind them people down there. Don't be going down there showing your color. Boy Willie, I done told you what to do. I'll see you later, Doaker.

AVERY: I'll be seeing you again, Boy Willie.

BOY WILLIE: Hey, Berniece . . . what's the name of that man Avery sent past say he want to buy the piano?

BERNIECE: I knew it. I knew it when I first seen you. I knew you was up to something.

BOY WILLIE: Sutter's brother say he selling the land to me. He waiting on me now. Told me he'd give me two weeks. I got one part. Sell them watermelons get me another part. Then we can sell that piano and I'll have the third part.

BERNIECE: I ain't selling that piano, Boy Willie. If that's why you come up here you can just forget about it.

To Doaker.

Doaker, I'll see you later. Boy Willie ain't nothing but a whole lot of mouth. I ain't paying him no mind. If he come up here thinking he gonna sell that piano then he done come up here for nothing.

Berniece, Avery, and Maretha exit the front door.

BOY WILLIE: Hey, Lymon! You ready to go sell these watermelons.

Boy Willie and Lymon start to exit. At the door Boy Willie turns to Doaker.

Hey, Doaker . . . if Berniece don't want to sell that piano . . . I'm gonna cut it in half and go on and sell my half.

Boy Willie and Lymon exit.

The lights go down on the scene.

Scene II

The lights come up on the kitchen. It is three days later. Wining Boy sits at the kitchen table. There is a half-empty pint bottle on the table. Doaker busies himself washing pots. Wining Boy is fifty-six years old. Doaker's older brother, he tries to present the image of a successful musician and gambler, but his music, his clothes, and even his manner of presentation are old. He is a man who looking back over his life continues to live it with an odd mixture of zest and sorrow.

WINING BOY: So the Ghosts of the Yellow Dog got Sutter. That just go to show you I believe I always lived right. They say every dog gonna have his day and time it go around it sure come back to you. I done seen that a thousand times. I know the truth of that. But I'll tell you outright . . . if I see Sutter's ghost I'll be on the first thing I find that got wheels on it.

Doaker enters from his room.

DOAKER: Wining Boy!

WINING BOY: And I'll tell you another thing . . . Berniece ain't gonna sell that piano.

DOAKER: That's what she told him. He say he gonna cut it in half and go on and sell his half. They been around here three days trying to sell them watermelons. They trying to get out to where the white folks live but the truck keep breaking down. They go a block or two and it break down again. They trying to get out to Squirrel Hill and can't get around the corner. He say soon as he can get that truck empty to where he can set the piano up in there he gonna take it out of here and go sell it.

WINING BOY: What about them boys Sutter got? How come they ain't farming that land?

DOAKER: One of them going to school. He left down there and come North to school. The other one ain't got as much sense as that frying pan over yonder. That is the dumbest white man I ever seen. He'd stand in the river and watch it rise till it drown him.

WINING BOY: Other than seeing Sutter's ghost how's Berniece doing?

DOAKER: She doing alright. She still got Crawley on her mind. He been dead three years but she still holding on to him. She need to go out here and let one of these fellows grab a whole handful of whatever she got. She act like it done got precious.

WINING BOY: They always told me any fish will bite if you got good bait.

DOAKER: She stuck up on it. She think it's better than she is. I believe she messing around with Avery. They got something going. He a preacher now. If you let him tell it the Holy Ghost sat on his head and heaven opened up with thunder and lightning and God was calling his name. Told him to go out and preach and tend to his flock. That's what he gonna call his church. The Good Shepherd Church.

WINING BOY: They had that joker down in Spear walking around talking about he Jesus Christ. He gonna live the life of Christ. Went through the Last Supper and everything. Rented him a mule on Palm Sunday and rode through the town. Did everything . . . talking about he Christ. He did everything until they got up to that crucifixion part. Got up to that part and told everybody to go home and quit pretending. He got up to the crucifixion part and changed his mind. Had a whole bunch of folks come down there to see him get nailed to the cross. I don't know who's the worse fool. Him or them. Had all them folks come down there . . . even carried the cross up this little hill. People standing around waiting to see him get nailed to the cross and he stop everything and preach a little sermon and told everybody to go home. Had enough nerve to tell them to come to church on Easter Sunday to celebrate his resurrection.

DOAKER: I'm surprised Avery ain't thought about that. He trying every little thing to get him a congregation together. They meeting over at his house till he get him a church.

WINING BOY: Ain't nothing wrong with being a preacher. You got the preacher on one hand and the gambler on the other. Sometimes there ain't too much difference in them.

DOAKER: How long you been in Kansas City?

WINING BOY: Since I left here. I got tied up with some old gal down there.

Pause.

You know Cleotha died.

DOAKER: Yeah, I heard that last time I was down there. I was sorry to hear that.

WINING BOY: One of her friends wrote and told me. I got the letter right here.

He takes the letter out of his pocket.

I was down in Kansas City and she wrote and told me Cleotha had died. Name of Willa Bryant. She say she know cousin Rupert.

He opens the letter and reads.

Dear Wining Boy: I am writing this letter to let you know Miss Cleotha Holman passed on Saturday the first of May she departed this world in the loving arms of her sister Miss Alberta Samuels. I know you would want to know this and am writing as a friend of Cleotha. There have been many hardships since last you seen her but she survived them all and to the end was a good woman whom I hope have God's grace and is in His Paradise. Your cousin Rupert Bates is my friend also and he give me your address and I pray this reaches you about Cleotha. Miss Willa Bryant. A friend.

He folds the letter and returns it to his pocket.

They was nailing her coffin shut by the time I heard about it. I never knew she was sick. I believe it was that yellow jaundice. That's what killed her mama.

DOAKER: Cleotha wasn't but forty-some

WINING BOY: She was forty-six. I got ten years on her. I met her when she was sixteen. You remember I used to run around there. Couldn't nothing keep me still. Much as I loved Cleotha I loved to ramble.

Couldn't nothing keep me still. We got married and we used to fight about it all the time. Then one day she asked me to leave. Told me she loved me before I left. Told me, Wining Boy, you got a home as long as I got mine. And I believe in my heart I always felt that and that kept me safe.

DOAKER: Cleotha always did have a nice way about her.

WINING BOY: Man that woman was something. I used to thank the Lord. Many a night I sat up and looked out over my life. Said, well, I had Cleotha. When it didn't look like there was nothing else for me, I said, thank God, at least I had that. If ever I go anywhere in this life I done known a good woman. And that used to hold me till the next morning.

Pause.

What you got? Give me a little nip. I know you got something stuck up in your room.

DOAKER: I ain't seen you walk in here and put nothing on the table. You done sat there and drank up your whiskey. Now you talking about what you got.

WINING BOY: I got plenty money. Give me a little nip.

Doaker carries a glass into his room and returns with it half-filled. He sets it on the table in front of Wining Boy.

WINING BOY: You hear from Coreen?

DOAKER: She up in New York. I let her go from my mind.

WINING BOY: She was something back then. She wasn't too pretty but she had a way of looking at you made you know there was a whole lot of woman there. You got married and snatched her out from under us and we all got mad at you.

DOAKER: She up in New York City. That's what I hear.

The door opens and Boy Willie and Lymon enter.

BOY WILLIE: Aw hell . . . look here! We was just talking about you. Doaker say you left out of here with a whole sack of money. I told him we wasn't going see you till you got broke.

WINING BOY: What you mean broke? I got a whole pocketful of money.

DOAKER: Did you all get that truck fixed?

BOY WILLIE: We got it running and got halfway out there on Centre and it broke down again. Lymon went out there and messed it up some more. Fellow told us we got to wait till tomorrow to get it fixed. Say he have it running like new. Lymon going back down there and sleep in the truck so the people don't take the watermelons.

LYMON: Lymon nothing. You go down there and sleep in it.

BOY WILLIE: You was sleeping in it down home, nigger! I don't know nothing about sleeping in no truck.

LYMON: I ain't sleeping in no truck.

BOY WILLIE: They can take all the watermelons. I don't care. Wining Boy, where you coming from? Where you been?

WINING BOY: I been down in Kansas City.

BOY WILLIE: You remember Lymon? Lymon Jackson.

WINING BOY: Yeah, I used to know his daddy.

BOY WILLIE: Doaker say you don't never leave no address with nobody. Say he got to depend on your whim. See when it strike you to pay a visit.

WINING BOY: I got four or five addresses.

BOY WILLIE: Doaker say Berniece asked you for three dollars and you got mad and left.

WINING BOY: Berniece try and rule over you too much for me. That's why I left. It wasn't about no three dollars.

BOY WILLIE: Where you getting all these sacks of money from? I need to be with you. Doaker say you had a whole sack of money . . . turn some of it loose.

WINING BOY: I was just fixing to ask you for five dollars.

BOY WILLIE: I ain't got no money. I'm trying to get some. Doaker tell you about Sutter? The Ghosts of the Yellow Dog got him about three weeks ago. Berniece done seen his ghost and everything. He right upstairs.

Calls.

Hey Sutter! Wining Boy's here. Come on, get a drink!

WINING BOY: How many that make the Ghosts of the Yellow Dog done got?

BOY WILLIE: Must be about nine or ten, eleven or twelve. I don't know.

DOAKER: You got Ed Saunders. Howard Peterson. Charlie Webb.

WINING BOY: Robert Smith. That fellow that shot Becky's boy . . . say he was stealing peaches . . .

DOAKER: You talking about Bob Mallory.

BOY WILLIE: Berniece say she don't believe all that about the Ghosts of the Yellow Dog.

WINING BOY: She ain't got to believe. You go ask them white folks in Sunflower County if they believe. You go ask Sutter if he believe. I don't care if Berniece believe or not. I done been to where the Southern cross the Yellow Dog and called out their names. They talk back to you, too.

LYMON: What they sound like? The wind or something?

BOY WILLIE: You done been there for real, Wining Boy?

WINING BOY: Nineteen thirty. July of nineteen thirty I stood right there on that spot. It didn't look like nothing was going right in my life. I said everything can't go wrong all the time . . . let me go down there and call on the Ghosts of the Yellow Dog, see if they can help me. I went down there and right there where them two railroads cross each other . . . I stood right there on that spot and called out their names. They talk back to you, too.

LYMON: People say you can ask them questions. They talk to you like that?

WINING BOY: A lot of things you got to find out on your own. I can't say how they talked to nobody else. But to me it just filled me up in a strange sort of way to be standing there on that spot. I didn't want to leave. It felt like the longer I stood there the bigger I got. I seen the train coming and it seem like I was bigger than the train. I started not to move. But something told me to go ahead and get on out the way. The train passed and I started to go back up there and stand some more. But something told me not to do it. I walked away from there feeling like a king. Went on and had a stroke of luck that run on for three years. So I don't care if Berniece believe or not. Berniece ain't got to believe. I know cause I been there. Now Doaker'll tell you about the Ghosts of the Yellow Dog.

DOAKER: I don't try and talk that stuff with Berniece. Avery got her all tied up in that church. She just think it's a whole lot of nonsense.

BOY WILLIE: Berniece don't believe in nothing. She just think she believe. She believe in anything if it's convenient for her to believe. But when that convenience run out then she ain't got nothing to stand on.

WINING BOY: Let's not get on Berniece now. Doaker tell me you talking about selling that piano.

BOY WILLIE: Yeah . . . hey, Doaker, I got the name of that man Avery was talking about. The man what's fixing the truck gave me his name. Everybody know him. Say he buy up anything you can make music with. I got his name and his telephone number. Hey, Wining Boy, Sutter's brother say he selling the land to me. I got one part. Sell them watermelons get me the second part. Then . . . soon as I get them watermelons out that truck I'm gonna take and sell that piano and get the third part.

DOAKER: That land ain't worth nothing no more. The smart white man's up here in these cities. He cut the land loose and step back and watch you and the dumb white man argue over it.

WINING BOY: How you know Sutter's brother ain't sold it already? You talking about selling the piano and the man's liable to sold the land two or three times.

BOY WILLIE: He say he waiting on me. He say he give me two weeks. That's two weeks from Friday. Say if I ain't back by then he might gonna sell it to somebody else. He say he wanna see me with it.

WINING BOY: You know as well as I know the man gonna sell the land to the first one walk up and hand him the money.

BOY WILLIE: That's just who I'm gonna be. Look, you ain't gotta know he waiting on me. I know. Okay. I know what the man told me. Stoval already done tried to buy the land from him and he told him no. The man say he waiting on me . . . he waiting on me. Hey, Doaker . . . . give me a drink. I see Wining Boy got his glass.

Doaker exists into his room.

Wining Boy, what you doing in Kansas City? What they got down there?

LYMON: I hear they got some nice-looking women in Kansas City. I sure like to go down there and find out.

WINING BOY: Man, the women down there is something else.

Doaker enters with a bottle of whiskey. He sets it on the table with some glasses.

DOAKER: You wanna sit up here and drink up my whiskey, leave a dollar on the table when you get up.

BOY WILLIE: You ain't doing nothing but showing your hospitality. I know we ain't got to pay for your hospitality.

WINING BOY: Doaker say they had you and Lymon down on the Parchman Farm. Had you on my old stomping grounds.

BOY WILLIE: Me and Lymon was down there hauling wood for Jim Miller and keeping us a little bit to sell. Some white fellows tried to run us off of it. That's when Crawley got killed. They put me and Lymon in the penitentiary.

LYMON: They ambushed us right there where that road dip down and around that bend in the creek. Crawley tried to fight them. Me and Boy Willie got away but the sheriff got us. Say we was stealing wood. They shot me in my stomach.

BOY WILLIE: They looking for Lymon down there now. They rounded him up and put him in jail for not working.

LYMON: Fined me a hundred dollars. Mr. Stovall come and paid my hundred dollars and the judge say I got to work for him to pay him back his hundred dollars. I told them I'd rather take my thirty days but they wouldn't let me do that.

BOY WILLIE: As soon as Stovall turned his back, Lymon was gone. He down there living in that truck dodging the sheriff and Stovall. He got both of them looking for him. So I brought him up here.

LYMON: I told Boy Willie I'm gonna stay up here. I ain't going back with him.

BOY WILLIE: Ain't nobody twisting your arm to make you go back. You can do what you want to do.

WINING BOY: I'll go back with you. I'm on my way down there. You gonna take the train? I'm gonna take the train.

LYMON: They treat you better up here.

BOY WILLIE: I ain't worried about nobody mistreating me. They treat you like you let them treat you. They mistreat me I mistreat them right back. Ain't no difference in me and the white man.

WINING BOY: Ain't no difference as far as how somebody supposed to treat you. I agree with that. But I'll tell you the difference between the colored man and the white man. Alright. Now you take and eat some berries. They taste real good to you. So you say I'm gonna go out and get me a whole pot of these berries and cook them up to make a pie or whatever. But you ain't looked to see them berries is sitting in the white fellow's yard. Ain't got no fence around them. You figure anybody want something they'd fence it in. Alright. Now the white man come along and say that's my land. Therefore everything that grow on it belong to me. He tell the sheriff, "I want you to put this nigger in jail as a warning to all the other niggers. Otherwise first thing you know these niggers have everything that belong to us."

BOY WILLIE: I'd come back at night and haul off his whole patch while he was sleep.

WINING BOY: Alright. Now Mr. So and So, he sell the land to you. And he come to you and say, "John, you own the land. It's all yours now. But them is my berries. And come time to pick them I'm gonna send my boys over. You got the land . . . but them berries, I'm gonna keep them. They mine." And he go and fix it with the law that them is his berries. Now that's the difference between the colored man and the white man. The colored man can't fix nothing with the law.

BOY WILLIE: I don't go by what the law say. The law's liable to say anything. I go by if it's right or not. It don't matter to me what the law say. I take and look at it for myself.

LYMON: That's why you gonna end up back down there on the Parchman Farm.

BOY WILLIE: I ain't thinking about no Parchman Farm. You liable to go back before me.

LYMON: They work you too hard down there. All that weeding and hoeing and chopping down trees. I didn't like all that.

WINING BOY: You ain't got to like your job on Parchman. Hey, tell him, Doaker, the only one got to like his job is the waterboy.

DOAKER: If he don't like his job he need to set that bucket down.

BOY WILLIE: That's what they told Lymon. They had Lymon on water and everybody got mad at him cause he was lazy.

LYMON: That water was heavy.

BOY WILLIE: They had Lymon down there singing:

Sings.

O Lord Berta Berta O Lord gal oh-ah
O Lord Berta Berta O Lord gal well

[Lymon *and Wining Boy join in.*]

Go 'head marry don't you wait on me oh-ah
Go 'head marry don't you wait on me well
Might not want you when I go free oh-ah
Might not want you when I go free well

BOY WILLIE: Come on, Doaker. Doaker know this one.

As Doaker joins in the men stamp and clap to keep time. They sing in harmony with great fervor and style.

O Lord Berta Berta O Lord gal oh-ah
O Lord Berta Berta O Lord gal well

Raise them up higher, let them drop on down oh-ah
Raise them up higher, let them drop on down well
Don't know the difference when the sun go down oh-ah
Don't know the difference when the sun go down well

Berta in Meridan and she living at ease oh-ah
Berta in Meridan and she living at ease well
I'm on old Parchman, got to work or leave oh-ah
I'm on old Parchman, got to work or leave well

O Alberta, Berta, O Lord gal oh-ah
O Alberta, Berta, O Lord gal well

When you marry, don't marry no farming man oh-ah
When you marry, don't marry no farming man well
Everyday Monday, hoe handle in your hand oh-ah
Everyday Monday, hoe handle in your hand well

When you marry, marry a railroad man, oh-ah
When you marry, marry a railroad man, well
Everyday Sunday, dollar in your hand oh-ah
Everyday Sunday, dollar in your hand well

O Alberta, Berta, O Lord gal oh-ah
O Alberta, Berta, O Lord gal well

BOY WILLIE: Doaker like that part. He like that railroad part.

LYMON: Doaker sound like Tangleye. He can't sing a lick.

BOY WILLIE: Hey, Doaker, they still talk about you down on Parchman. They ask me, "You Doaker Boy's nephew?" I say, "Yeah, me and him is family." They treated me alright soon as I told them that. say, "Yeah, he my uncle."

DOAKER: I don't never want to see none of them niggers no more.

BOY WILLIE: I don't want to see them either. Hey, Wining Boy, come on play some piano. You a piano player, play some piano. Lymon wanna hear you.

WINING BOY: I give that piano up. That was the best thing that ever happened to me, getting rid of that piano. That piano got so big and I'm carrying it around on my back. I don't wish that on no-body. See, you think it's all fun being a recording star. Got to carrying that piano around and man did I get slow. Got just like mo-lasses. The world just slipping by me and I'm walking around with that piano. Alright. Now, there ain't but so many places you can go.

Only so many road wide enough for you and that piano. And that piano get heavier and heavier. Go to a place and they find out you play piano, the first thing they want to do is give you a drink, find you a piano, and sit you right down. And that's where you gonna be for the next eight hours. They ain't gonna let you get up! Now, the first three or four years of that is fun. You can't get enough whiskey and you can't get enough women and you don't never get tired of playing that piano. But that only last so long. You look up one day and you hate the whiskey, and you hate the women, and you hate the piano. But that's all you got. You can't do nothing else. All you know how to do is play that piano. Now, who am I? Am I me? Or am I the piano player? Sometime it seem like the only thing to do is shoot the piano player cause he the cause of all the trouble I'm having.

DOAKER: What you gonna do when your troubles get like mine?

LYMON: If I knew how to play it, I'd play it. That's a nice piano.

BOY WILLIE: Whoever playing better play quick. Sutter's brother say he waiting on me. I sell them watermelons. Get Berniece to sell that piano. Put them two parts with the part I done saved . . .

WINING BOY: Berniece ain't gonna sell that piano. I don't see why you don't know that.

BOY WILLIE: What she gonna do with it? She ain't doing nothing but letting it sit up there and rot. That piano ain't doing nobody no good.

LYMON: That's a nice piano. If I had it I'd sell it. Unless I knew how to play like Wining Boy. You can get a nice price for that piano.

DOAKER: Now I'm gonna tell you something, Lymon don't know this . . . but I'm gonna tell you why me and Wining Boy say Berniece ain't gonna sell that piano.

BOY WILLIE: She ain't got to sell it! I'm gonna sell it! Berniece ain't got no more rights to that piano than I do.

DOAKER: I'm talking to the man . . . let me talk to the man. See, now . . . to understand why we say that . . . to understand about that piano . . . you got to go back to slavery time. See, our family was owned by a fellow named Robert Sutter. That was Sutter's grandfather. Alright. The piano was owned by a fellow named Joel Nolander. He was one of the Nolander brothers from down in Georgia. It was coming up on Sutter's wedding anniversary and he was looking to buy his wife . . . Miss Ophelia was her name . . . he was looking to buy her an anniversary present. Only thing with him . . . he ain't had no money. But he had some niggers. So he asked Mr. Nolander to see if maybe he could trade off some of his niggers for that piano. Told him he would give him one and a half niggers for it. That's the way he told him. Say he could have one full grown and one half grown. Mr. Nolander agreed only he say he had to pick them. He didn't want Sutter to give him just any old nigger. He say he wanted to have the pick of the litter. So Sutter lined up his niggers and Mr. Nolander looked them over and out of the whole bunch he picked my grandmother . . . her name was Berniece . . . same like Berniece . . . and he picked my daddy when he wasn't nothing but a little boy nine years old. They made the trade off and Miss Ophelia was so happy with that piano that it got to be just about all she would do was play on that piano.

WINING BOY: Just get up in the morning, get all dressed up and sit down and play on that piano.

DOAKER: Alright. Time go along. Time go along. Miss Ophelia got to missing my grandmother . . . the way she would cook and clean the house and talk to her and what not. And she missed having my daddy around the house to fetch things for her. So she asked to see if maybe she could trade back that piano and get her niggers back. Mr. Nolander said no. Said a deal was a deal. Him and Sutter had a big falling out about it and Miss Ophelia took sick to the bed. Wouldn't get out of the bed in the morning. She just lay there. The doctor said she was wasting away.

WINING BOY: That's when Sutter called our granddaddy up to the house.

DOAKER: Now, our granddaddy's name was Boy Willie. That's who Boy Willie's named after . . . only they called him Willie Boy. Now, he was a worker of wood. He could make you anything you wanted out of wood. He'd make you a desk. A table. A lamp. Anything you wanted. Them white fellows around there used to come up to Mr. Sutter and get him to make all kinds of things for them. Then they'd pay Mr. Sutter a nice price. See, everything my granddaddy made Mr. Sutter owned cause he owned him. That's why when Mr. Nolander offered to buy him to keep the family together Mr. Sutter wouldn't sell him. Told Mr. Nolander he didn't have enough money to buy him. Now . . . am I telling it right, Wining Boy?

WINING BOY: You telling it.

DOAKER: Sutter called him up to the house and told him to carve my grandmother and my daddy's picture on the piano for Miss Ophelia. And he took and carved this . . .

Doaker crosses over to the piano.

See that right there? That's my grandmother, Berniece. She looked just like that. And he put a picture of my daddy when he wasn't nothing but a little boy the way he remembered him. He made them up out of his memory. Only thing . . . he didn't stop there. He carved all this. He got a picture of his mama . . . Mama Esther . . . and his daddy, Boy Charles.

WINING BOY: That was the first Boy Charles.

DOAKER: Then he put on the side here all kinds of things. See that? That's when him and Mama Berniece got married. They called it jumping the broom. That's how you got married in them days. Then he got here when my daddy was born . . . and here he got Mama Esther's funeral . . . and down here he got Mr. Nolander taking Mama Berniece and my daddy away down to his place in Georgia. He got all kinds of things what happened with our family. When Mr. Sutter seen the piano with all them carvings on it he got mad. He didn't ask for all that. But see . . . there wasn't nothing he could do about it. When Miss Ophelia seen it . . . she got excited. Now she had her piano and her niggers too. She took back to playing it and played on it right up till the day she died. Alright . . . now see, our brother Boy Charles . . . that's Berniece and Boy Willie's daddy . . . he was the oldest of us three boys. He's dead now. But he would have been fifty-seven if he had lived. He died in 1911 when he was thirty-one years old. Boy Charles used to talk about that piano all the time. He never could get it off his mind. Two or three months go by and he be talking about it again. He be talking about taking it out of Sutter's house. Say it was the story of our whole family and as long as Sutter had it . . . he had us. Say we was still in slavery. Me and wining Boy tried to talk him out of it but it wouldn't do any good. Soon as he quiet down about it he'd start up again. We seen where he wasn't gonna get it off his mind . . . so, on the Fourth of July, 1911 . . . when Sutter was at the picnic what the county give every year . . . me and Wining Boy went on down there with him and took that piano out of Sutter's house. We put it on a wagon and me and Wining Boy carried it over into the next county with Mama Ola's people. Boy Charles decided to stay around there and wait until Sutter got home to make it look like business as usual.

Now, I don't know what happened when Sutter came home and found that piano gone. But somebody went up to Boy Charles's house and set it on fire. But he wasn't in there. He must have seen them coming cause he went down and caught the 3:57 Yellow Dog. He didn't know they was gonna come down and stop the train. Stopped the train and found Boy Charles in the boxcar with four of them hobos. Must have got mad when they couldn't find the piano cause they set the boxcar afire and killed everybody. Now, nobody know who done that. Some people say it was Sutter cause it was his piano. Some people say it was Sheriff Carter. Some people say it was Robert Smith and Ed Saunders. But don't nobody know for sure. It was about two months after that that Ed Saunders fell down his well. Just upped and fell down his well for no reason. People say it was the ghost of them men who burned up in the boxcar that pushed him in his well. They started calling them the Ghosts of the Yellow Dog. Now, that's how all that got started and that's why we say Berniece ain't gonna sell that piano. Cause her daddy died over it.

BOY WILLIE: All that's in the past. If my daddy had seen where he could have traded that piano in for some land of his own, it wouldn't be sitting up here now. He spent his whole life farming on somebody else's land. I ain't gonna do that. See, he couldn't do no better. When he come along he ain't had nothing he could build on. His daddy ain't had nothing to give him. The only thing my daddy had to give me was that piano. And he died over giving me that. I ain't gonna let it sit up there and rot without trying to do something with it. If Berniece can't see that, then I'm gonna go ahead and sell my half. And you and Wining Boy know I'm right.

DOAKER: Ain't nobody said nothing about who's right and who's wrong. I was just telling the man about the piano. I was telling him why we say Berniece ain't gonna sell it.

LYMON: Yeah, I can see why you say that now. I told Boy Willie he ought to stay up here with me.

BOY WILLIE: You stay! I'm going back! That's what I'm gonna do with my life! Why I got to come up here and learn to do something I don't know how to do when I already know how to farm? You stay up here and make your own way if that's what you want to do. I'm going back and live my life the way I want to live it.

Wining Boy gets up and crosses to the piano.

WINING BOY: Let's see what we got here. I ain't played on this thing for a while.

DOAKER: You can stop telling that. You was playing on it the last time you was through here. We couldn't get you off of it. Go on and play something.

Wining Boy sits down at the piano and plays and sings. The song is one which has put many dimes and quarters in his pocket, long ago, in dimly remembered towns and way stations. He plays badly, without hesitation, and sings in a forceful voice.

WINING BOY: *Singing.*

> I am a rambling gambling man
> I gambled in many towns
> I rambled this wide world over
> I rambled this world around
> I had my ups and downs in life
> And bitter times I saw
> But I never knew what misery was
> Till I lit on old Arkansas.
>
> I started out one morning
> To meet that early train
> He said, "You better work for me
> I have some land to drain.
> I'll give you fifty cents a day,
> Your washing, board and all
> And you shall be a different man
> In the state of Arkansas."
>
> I worked six months for the rascal
> Joe Herrin was his name
> He fed me old corn dodgers
> They was hard as any rock
> My tooth is all got loosened
> And my knees begin to knock
> That was the kind of hash I got
> In the state of Arkansas.
>
> Traveling man
> I've traveled all around this world

Traveling man
I've traveled from land to land
Traveling man
I've traveled all around this world
Well it ain't no use
writing no news
I'm a traveling man.

The door opens and Berniece enters with Maretha.

BERNIECE: Is that . . . Lord, I know that ain't Wining Boy sitting there.

WINING BOY: Hey, Berniece.

BERNIECE: You all had this planned. You and Boy Willie had this planned.

WINING BOY: I didn't know he was gonna be here. I'm on my way down home. I stopped by to see you and Doaker first.

DOAKER: I told the nigger he left out of here with that sack of money, we thought we might never see him again. Boy Willie say he wasn't gonna see him till he got broke. I looked up and seen him sitting on the doorstep asking for two dollars. Look at him laughing. He know it's the truth.

BERNIECE: Boy Willie, I didn't see that truck out there. I thought you was out selling watermelons.

BOY WILLIE: We done sold them all. Sold the truck too.

BERNIECE: I don't want to go through none of your stuff. I done told you to go back where you belong.

BOY WILLIE: I was just teasing you, woman. You can't take no teasing?

BERNIECE: Wining Boy, when you get here?

WINING BOY: A little while ago. I took the train from Kansas City.

BERNIECE: Let me go upstairs and change and then I'll cook you something to eat.

BOY WILLIE: You ain't cooked me nothing when I come.

BERNIECE: Boy Willie, go on and leave me alone. Come on, Maretha, get up here and change your clothes before you get them dirty.

Berniece exits up the stairs, followed by Maretha.

WINING BOY: Maretha sure getting big, ain't she, Doaker. And just as pretty as she want to be. I didn't know Crawley had it in him.

Boy Willie crosses to the piano.

BOY WILLIE: Hey, Lymon . . . get up on the other side of this piano and let me see something.

WINING BOY: Boy Willie, what is you doing?

BOY WILLIE: I'm seeing how heavy this piano is. Get up over there, Lymon.

WINING BOY: Go on and leave that piano alone. You ain't taking that piano out of here and selling it.

BOY WILLIE: Just as soon as I get them watermelons out that truck.

WINING BOY: Well, I got something to say about that.

BOY WILLIE: This my daddy's piano.

WINING BOY: He ain't took it by himself. Me and Doaker helped him.

BOY WILLIE: He died by himself. Where was you and Doaker at then? Don't come telling me nothing about this piano. This is me and Berniece's piano. Am I right, Doaker?

DOAKER: Yeah, you right.

BOY WILLIE: Let's see if we can lift it up, Lymon. Get a good grip on it and pick it up on your end. Ready? Lift!

As they start to move the piano, the sound of Sutter's Ghost *is heard. Doaker is the only one to hear it. With difficulty they move the piano a little bit so it is out of place.*

BOY WILLIE: What you think?

LYMON: It's heavy . . . but you can move it. Only it ain't gonna be easy.

BOY WILLIE: It wasn't that heavy to me. Okay, let's put it back.

The sound of Sutter's Ghost is heard again. They all hear it as Berniece enters on the stairs.

BERNIECE: Boy Willie . . . you gonna play around with me one too many times. And then God's gonna bless you and West is gonna dress you. Now set that piano back over there. I done told you a hundred times I ain't selling that piano.

BOY WILLIE: I'm trying to get me some land, woman. I need that piano to get me some money so I can buy Sutter's land.

BERNIECE: Money can't buy what that piano cost. You can't sell your soul for money. It won't go with the buyer. It'll shrivel and shrink to know that you ain't taken on to it. But it won't go with the buyer.

BOY WILLIE: I ain't talking about all that, woman. I ain't talking about selling my soul. I'm talking about trading that piece of wood for some land. Get something under your feet. Land the only thing

God ain't making no more of. You can always get you another piano. I'm talking about some land. What you get something out the ground from. That's what I'm talking about. You can't do nothing with that piano but sit up there and look at it.

BERNIECE: That's just what I'm gonna do. Wining Boy, you want me to fry you some pork chops?

BOY WILLIE: Now, I'm gonna tell you the way I see it. The only thing that make that piano worth something is them carvings Papa Willie Boy put on there. That's what make it worth something. That was my great-granddaddy. Papa Boy Charles brought that piano into the house. Now, I'm supposed to build on what they left me. You can't do nothing with that piano sitting up here in the house. That's just like if I let them watermelons sit out there and rot. I'd be a fool. Alright now, if you say to me, Boy Willie, I'm using that piano. I give out lessons on it and that help me make my rent or whatever. Then that be something else. I'd have to go on and say, well, Berniece using that piano. She building on it. Let her go on and use it. I got to find another way to get Sutter's land. But Doaker say you ain't touched that piano the whole time it's been up here. So why you wanna stand in my way? See, you just looking at the sentimental value. See, that's good. That's alright. I take my hat off whenever somebody say my daddy's name. But I ain't gonna be no fool about no sentimental value. You can sit up here and look at the piano for the next hundred years and it's just gonna be a piano. You can't make more than that. Now I want to get Sutter's land with that piano. I get Sutter's land and I can go down and cash in the crop and get my seed. As long as I got the land and the seed then I'm alright. I can always get me a little something else. Cause that land give back to you. I can make me another crop and cash that in. I still got the land and the seed. But that piano don't put out nothing else. You ain't got nothing working for you. Now, the kind of man my daddy was he would have understood that. I'm sorry you can't see it that way. But that's why I'm gonna take that piano out of here and sell it.

BERNIECE: You ain't taking that piano out of my house.

She crosses to the piano.

Look at this piano. Look at it. Mama Ola polished this piano with her tears for seventeen years. For seventeen years she rubbed on it till her hands bled. Then she rubbed the blood in . . . mixed it up with the rest of the blood on it. Every day that God breathed life into her body she rubbed and cleaned and polished and prayed over it. "Play something for me, Berniece. Play something for me, Berniece." Every day. "I cleaned it up for you, play something for me, Berniece." You always talking about your daddy but you ain't never stopped to look at what his foolishness cost your mama. Seventeen years' worth of cold nights and an empty bed. For what? For a piano? For a piece of wood? To get even with somebody? I look at you and you're all the same. You, Papa Boy Charles, Wining Boy, Doaker, Crawley . . . you're all alike. All this thieving and killing and thieving and killing. And what it ever lead to? More killing and more thieving. I ain't never seen it come to nothing. People getting burned up. People getting shot. People falling down their wells. It don't never stop.

DOAKER: Come on now, Berniece, ain't no need in getting upset.

BOY WILLIE: I done a little bit of stealing here and there, but I ain't never killed nobody. I can't be speaking for nobody else. You all got to speak for yourself, but I ain't never killed nobody.

BERNIECE: You killed Crawley just as sure as if you pulled the trigger.

BOY WILLIE: See, that's ignorant. That's downright foolish for you to say something like that. You ain't doing nothing but showing your ignorance. If the nigger was here I'd whup his ass for getting me and Lymon shot at.

BERNIECE: Crawley ain't knew about the wood.

BOY WILLIE: We told the man about the wood. Ask Lymon. He knew all about the wood. He seen we was sneaking it. Why else we gonna be out there at night? Don't come telling me Crawley ain't knew about the wood. Them fellows come up on us and Crawley tried to bully them. Me and Lymon seen the sheriff with them and give in. Wasn't no sense in getting killed over fifty dollars' worth of wood.

BERNIECE: Crawley ain't knew you stole that wood.

BOY WILLIE: We ain't stole no wood. Me and Lymon was hauling wood for Jim Miller and keeping us a little bit on the side. We dumped our little bit down there by the creek till we had enough to make a load. Some fellows seen us and we figured we better get it before they did. We come up there and got Crawley to help us load it. Figured we'd cut him in. Crawley trying to keep the wolf from his door . . . we was trying to help him.

LYMON: Me and Boy Willie told him about the wood. We told him some fellows might be trying to beat us to it. He say let me go back and get my thirty-eight. That's what caused all the trouble.

BOY WILLIE: If Crawley ain't had the gun he'd be alive today.

LYMON: We had it about half loaded when they come up on us. We seen the sheriff with them and we tried to get away. We ducked around near the bend in the creek . . . but they was down there too. Boy Willie say let's give in. But Crawley pulled out his gun and started shooting. That's when they started shooting back.

BERNIECE: All I know is Crawley would be alive if you hadn't come up there and got him.

BOY WILLIE: I ain't had nothing to do with Crawley getting killed. That was his own fault.

BERNIECE: Crawley's dead and in the ground and you still walking around here eating. That's all I know. He went off to load some wood with you and ain't never come back.

BOY WILLIE: I told you, woman . . . I ain't had nothing to do with . . .

BERNIECE: He ain't here, is he? He ain't here!

Berniece hits Boy Willie.

I said he ain't here. Is he?

Berniece continues to hit Boy Willie, who doesn't move to defend himself, other than back up and turning his head so that most of the blows fall on his chest and arms.

DOAKER: [*Grabbing Berniece:*] Come on, Berniece . . . let it go, it ain't his fault.

BERNIECE: He ain't here, is he? Is he?

BOY WILLIE: I told you I ain't responsible for Crawley.

BERNIECE: He ain't here.

BOY WILLIE: Come on now, Berniece . . . don't' do this now. Doaker get her. I ain't had nothing to do with Crawley.

BERNIECE: You come up there and got him!

BOY WILLIE: I done told you now. Doaker, get her. I ain't playing.

DOAKER: Come on, Berniece.

Maretha is heard screaming upstairs. It is a scream of stark terror.

MARETHA: Mama! . . . Mama!

The lights go down to black. End of Act One.

Act II

Scene I

The lights come up on the kitchen. It is the following morning. Doaker is ironing the pants to his uniform. He has a pot cooking on the stove at the same time. He is singing a song. The song provides him with the rhythm for his work and he moves about the kitchen with the ease born of many years as a railroad cook.

DOAKER:

> Gonna leave Jackson Mississippi
> and go to Memphis
> and double back to Jackson
> Come on down to Hattiesburg
> Change cars on the Y.D.
> coming through the territory to
> Meridian
> and Meridian to Greenville
> and Greenville to Memphis
> I'm on my way and I know where
>
> Change cars on the Katy
> Leaving Jackson
> and going through Clarksdale
> Hello Winona!
> Courtland!
> Bateville!
> Como!
> Senitobia!
> Lewisberg!
> Sunflower!
> Glendora!
> Sharkey!
> And double back to Jackson
> Hello Greenwood
> I'm on my way Memphis
> Clarksdale
> Moorhead
> Indianola
> Can a highball pass through?

Highball on through sir
Grand Carson!
Thirty First Street Depot
Fourth Street Depot
Memphis!

Wining Boy enters carrying a suit of clothes.

DOAKER: I thought you took that suit to the pawnshop?

WINING BOY: I went down there and the man tell me the suit is too old. Look at this suit. This is one hundred percent silk! How a silk suit gonna get too old? I know what it was he just didn't want to give me five dollars for it. Best he wanna give me is three dollars. I figure a silk suit is worth five dollars all over the world. I wasn't gonna part with it for no three dollars so I brought it back.

DOAKER: They got another pawnshop up on Wylie.

WINING BOY: I carried it up there. He say he don't take no clothes. Only thing he take is guns and radios. Maybe a guitar or two. Where's Berniece?

DOAKER: Berniece still at work. Boy Willie went down there to meet Lymon this morning. I guess they got that truck fixed, they been out there all day and ain't come back yet. Maretha scared to sleep up there now. Berniece don't know, but I seen Sutter before she did.

WINING BOY: Say what?

DOAKER: About three weeks ago. I had just come back from down there. Sutter couldn't have been dead more than three days. He was sitting over there at the piano. I come out to go to work . . . and he was sitting right there. Had his hand on top of his head just like Berniece said. I believe he broke his neck when he fell in the well. I kept quiet about it. I didn't see no reason to upset Berniece.

WINING BOY: Did he say anything? Did he say he was looking for Boy Willie?

DOAKER: He was just sitting there. He ain't said nothing. I went on out the door and left him sitting there. I figure as long as he was on the other side of the room everything be alright. I don't know what I would have done if he had started walking toward me.

WINING BOY: Berniece say he was calling Boy Willie's name.

DOAKER: I ain't heard him say nothing. He was just sitting there when I seen him. But I don't believe Boy Willie pushed him in the well. Sutter here cause of that piano. I heard him playing on it one time. I thought it was Berniece but then she don't play that kind of music. I come out here and ain't seen nobody, but them piano keys was moving a mile a minute. Berniece need to go on and get rid of if. It ain't done nothing but cause trouble.

WINING BOY: I agree with Berniece. Boy Charles ain't took it to give it back. He took it cause he figure he had more right to it than Sutter did. If Sutter can't understand that . . . then that's just the way that go. Sutter dead and in the ground . . . don't care where his ghost is. He can hover around and play on the piano all he want. I want to see him carry it out the house. That's what I want to see. What time Berniece get home? I don't see how I let her get away from me this morning.

DOAKER: You up there sleep. Berniece leave out of here early in the morning. She out there in Squirrel Hill cleaning house for some bigshot down there at the steel mill. They don't like you to come late. You come late they won't give you your carfare. What kind of business you got with Berniece?

WINING BOY: My business. I ain't asked you what kind of business you got.

DOAKER: Berniece ain't got no money. If that's why you was trying to catch her. She having a hard enough time trying to get by as it is. If she go ahead and marry Avery . . . he working every day . . . she go ahead and marry him they could do alright for themselves. But as it stands she ain't got no money.

WINING BOY: Well, let me have five dollars.

DOAKER: I just give you a dollar before you left out of here. You ain't gonna take my five dollars out there and gamble and drink it up.

WINING BOY: Aw, nigger, give me five dollars. I'll give it back to you.

DOAKER: You wasn't looking to give me five dollars when you had that sack of money. You wasn't looking to throw nothing my way. Now you wanna come in here and borrow five dollars. If you going back with Boy Willie you need to be trying to figure out how you gonna get train fare.

WINING BOY: That's why I need the five dollars. If I had five dollars I could get me some money.

Doaker goes into his pocket.

Make it seven.

DOAKER: You take this five dollars . . . and you bring my money back here too.

Boy Willie and Lymon enter. They are happy and excited. They have money in all of their pockets and are anxious to count it.

DOAKER: How'd you do out there?

BOY WILLIE: They was lining up for them.

LYMON: Me and Boy Willie couldn't sell them fast enough. Time we got one sold we'd sell another.

BOY WILLIE: I seen what was happening and told Lymon to up the price on them.

LYMON: Boy Willie say charge them a quarter more. They didn't care. A couple of people give me a dollar and told me to keep the change.

BOY WILLIE: One fellow bought five. I say now what he gonna do with five watermelons? He can't eat them all. I sold him the five and asked him did he want to buy five more.

LYMON: I ain't never seen nobody snatch a dollar fast as Boy Willie.

BOY WILLIE: One lady asked me say, "Is they sweet?" I told her say, "Lady, where we grow these watermelons we put sugar in the ground." You know, she believed me. Talking about she had never heard of that before. Lymon was laughing his head off. I told her, "Oh, yeah, we put the sugar right in the ground with the seed." She say, "Well, give me another one." Them white folks is something else . . . ain't they, Lymon?

LYMON: Soon as you holler watermelons they come right out their door. Then they go and get their neighbors. Look like they having a contest to see who can buy the most.

WINING BOY: I got something for Lymon.

Wining Boy goes to get his suit. Boy Willie and Lymon continue to count their money.

BOY WILLIE: I know you got more than that. You ain't sold all them watermelons for that little bit of money.

LYMON: I'm still looking. That ain't all you got either. Where's all them quarters?

BOY WILLIE: You let me worry about the quarters. Just put the money on the table.

WINING BOY: [*Entering with his suit.*] Look here, Lymon . . . see this? Look at his eyes getting big. He ain't never seen a suit like this. This is one hundred percent silk. Go ahead . . . put it on. See if it fit you.

Lymon tries the suit coat on.

Look at that. Feel it. That's one hundred percent genuine silk. I got that in Chicago. You can't get clothes like that nowhere but New York and Chicago. You can't get clothes like that in Pittsburgh. These folks in Pittsburgh ain't never seen clothes like that.

LYMON: This is nice, feel real nice and smooth.

WINING BOY: That's a fifty-five-dollar suit. That's the kind of suit the bigshots wear. You need a pistol and a pocketful of money to wear that suit. I'll let you have it for three dollars. The women will fall out their windows they see you in a suit like that. Give me three dollars and go on and wear it down the street and get you a woman.

BOY WILLIE: That looks nice, Lymon. Put the pants on. Let me see it with the pants.

Lymon begins to try on the pants.

WINING BOY: Look at that . . . see how it fits you? Give me three dollars and go on and take it. Look at that, Doaker . . . don't he look nice?

DOAKER: Yeah . . . that's a nice suit.

WINING BOY: Got a shirt to go with it. Cost you an extra dollar. Four dollars you got the whole deal.

LYMON: How this look, Boy Willie?

BOY WILLIE: That look nice . . . if you like that kind of thing. I don't like them dress-up kind of clothes. If you like it, look real nice.

WINING BOY: That's the kind of suit you need for up here in the North.

LYMON: Four dollars for everything? The suit and the shirt?

WINING BOY: That's cheap. I should be charging you twenty dollars. I give you a break cause you a homeboy. That's the only way I let you have it for four dollars.

LYMON: [*Going into his pocket.*] Okay . . . here go the four dollars.

WINING BOY: You got some shoes? What size you wear?

LYMON: Size nine.

WINING BOY: That's what size I got! Size nine. I let you have them for three dollars.

LYMON: Where they at? Let me see them.

WINING BOY: They real nice shoes, too. Got a nice tip to them. Got pointy toe just like you want.

Wining Boy goes to get his shoes.

LYMON: Come on, Boy Willie, let's go out tonight. I wanna see what it looks like up here. Maybe we go to a picture show. Hey, Doaker, they got picture shows up here?

DOAKER: The Rhumba Theater. Right down there on Fullerton Street. Can't miss it. Got the speakers outside on the sidewalk. You can hear it a block away. Boy Willie know where it's at.

Doaker exits into his room.

LYMON: Let's go to the picture show, Boy Willie. Let's go find some women.

BOY WILLIE: Hey, Lymon, how many of them watermelons would you say we got left? We got just under a half a load . . . right?

LYMON: About that much. Maybe a little more.

BOY WILLIE: You think that piano will fit up in there?

LYMON: If we stack them watermelons you can sit it up in the front there.

BOY WILLIE: I'm gonna call that man tomorrow.

WINING BOY: [*Returns with his shoes.*] Here you go . . . size nine. Put them on. Cost you three dollars. That's a Florsheim shoe. That's the kind Staggerlee wore.

LYMON: [*Trying on the shoes.*] You sure these size nine?

WINING BOY: You can look at my feet and see we wear the same size. Man, you put on that suit and them shoes and you got something there. You ready for whatever's out there. But is they ready for you? With them shoes on you be the King of the Walk. Have everybody stop to look at your shoes. Wishing they had a pair. I'll give you a break. Go on and take them for two dollars.

Lymon pays Wining Boy two dollars.

LYMON: Come on, Boy Willie . . . let's go find some women. I'm gonna go upstairs and get ready. I'll be ready to go in a minute. Ain't you gonna get dressed?

BOY WILLIE: I'm gonna wear what I got on. I ain't dressing up for these city niggers.

Lymon exits up the stairs.

That's all Lymon think about is women.

WINING BOY: His daddy was the same way. I used to run around with him. I know his mama too. Two strokes back and I would have been his daddy! His daddy's dead now . . . but I got the nigger out of jail one time. They was fixing to name him Daniel and walk him through the Lion's Den. He got in a tussle with one of them white fellows and the sheriff lit on him like white on rice. That's how the whole thing come about between me and Lymon's mama. She knew me and his daddy used to run together and he got in jail and she went down there and took the sheriff a hundred dollars. Don't get me to lying about where she got it from. I don't know. The sheriff *looked at that hundred dollars and turned his nose up.* Told her, say, "That ain't gonna do him no good. You got to put another hundred on top of that." She come up *there and got me where I was playing at this saloon . . .* said she had all but fifty dollars and asked me if I could help. Now the way I figured it . . . without that fifty dollars the sheriff was gonna turn him over to Parchman. The sheriff turn him over to Parchman it be three years before anybody see him again. Now I'm gonna say it right . . . I will give anybody fifty dollars to keep them out of jail for three years. I give her the fifty dollars and she told me to come over to the house. I ain't asked her. I figure if she was nice enough to invite me I ought to go. I ain't had to say a word. She invited me over just as nice. Say, "Why don't you come over to the house?" She ain't had to say nothing else. Them words rolled off her tongue just as nice. I went on down there and sat about three hours. Started to leave and changed my mind. She grabbed hold to me and say, "Baby, it's all night long." That was one of the shortest nights I have ever spent on this earth! I could have used another eight hours. Lymon's daddy didn't even say nothing to me when he got out. He just looked at me funny. He had a good notion something had happened between me an' her. L. D. Jackson. That was one bad-luck nigger. Got killed at some dance. Fellow walked in and shot him thinking he was somebody else.

Doaker enters from his room.

Hey, Doaker, you remember L. D. Jackson?

DOAKER: That's Lymon's daddy. That was one bad-luck nigger.

BOY WILLIE: Look like you ready to railroad some.

DOAKER: Yeah, I got to make that run.

Lymon enters from the stairs. He is dressed in his new suit and shoes, to which he has added a cheap straw hat.

LYMON: How I look?

WINING BOY: You look like a million dollars. Don't he look good, Doaker? Come on, let's play some cards. You wanna play some cards?

BOY WILLIE: We ain't gonna play no cards with you. Me and Lymon gonna find some women. Hey, Lymon, don't play no cards with Wining Boy. He'll take all your money.

WINING BOY: [to Lymon.] You got a magic suit there. You can get you a woman easy with that suit . . . but you got to know the magic words. You know the magic words to get you a woman?

LYMON: I just talk to them to see if I like them and they like me.

WINING BOY: You just walk right up to them and say, "If you got the harbor I got the ship." If that don't work ask them if you can put them in your pocket. The first thing they gonna say is, "It's too small." That's when you look them dead in the eye and say, "Baby, ain't nothing small about me." If that don't work then you move on to another one. Am I telling him right, Doaker?

DOAKER: That man don't need you to tell him nothing about no women. These women these days ain't gonna fall for that kind of stuff. You got to buy them a present. That's what they looking for these days.

BOY WILLIE: Come on, I'm ready. You ready, Lymon? Come on, let's go find some women.

WINING BOY: Here, let me walk out with you. I wanna see the women fall out their window when they see Lymon.

They all exit and the lights go down on the scene.

Scene II

The lights come up on the kitchen. It is late evening of the same day. Berniece has set a tub for her bath in the kitchen. She is heating up water on the stove. There is a knock at the door.

BERNIECE: Who is it?

AVERY: It's me, Avery.

Berniece opens the door and lets him in.

BERNIECE: Avery, come on in. I was just fixing to take my bath.

AVERY: Where Boy Willie? I see that truck out there almost empty. They done sold almost all them watermelons.

BERNIECE: They was gone when I come home. I don't know where they went off to. Boy Willie around here about to drive me crazy.

AVERY: They sell them watermelons . . . he'll be gone soon.

BERNIECE: What Mr. Cohen say about letting you have the place?

AVERY: He say he'll let me have it for thirty dollars a month. I talked him out of thirty-five and he say he'll let me have it for thirty.

BERNIECE: That's a nice spot next to Benny Diamond's store.

AVERY: Berniece . . . I be at home and I get to thinking you up here an' I'm down there. I get to thinking how that look to have a preacher that ain't married. It makes for a better congregation if the preacher was settled down and married.

BERNIECE: Avery . . . not now. I was fixing to take my bath.

AVERY: You know how I feel about you, Berniece. Now . . . I done got the place from Mr. Cohen. I get the money from the bank and I can fix it up real nice. They give me a ten cents a hour raise down there on the job . . . now Berniece, I ain't got much in the way of comforts. I got a hole in my pockets near about as far as money is concerned. I ain't never found no way through life to a woman I care about like I care about you. I need that. I need somebody on my bond side. I need a woman that fits in my hand.

BERNIECE: Avery, I ain't ready to get married now.

AVERY: You too young a woman to close up, Berniece.

BERNIECE: I ain't said nothing about closing up. I got a lot of woman left in me.

AVERY: Where's it at? When's the last time you looked at it?

BERNIECE: [Stunned by his remark.] That's a nasty thing to say. And you call yourself a preacher.

AVERY: Anytime I get anywhere near you . . . you push me away.

BERNIECE: I got enough on my hands with Maretha. I got enough people to love and take care of.

AVERY: Who you got to love you? Can't nobody get close enough to you. Doaker can't half say nothing to you. You jump all over Boy Willie. Who you got to love you, Berniece?

BERNIECE: You trying to tell me a woman can't be nothing without a man. But you alright, huh? You can just walk out of here with-out me—without a woman—and still be a man. that's alright. Ain't nobody gonna ask you, "Avery, who you got to love you?" That's alright for you. But everybody gonna be worried about Berniece. "How Berniece gonna take care of herself? How she gonna raise that child without a man? Wonder what she do with herself. How she gonna live like that?" Everybody got all kinds of questions for Berniece. Everybody telling me I can't be a woman unless I got a man. Well, you tell me, Avery—you know—how much woman am I?

AVERY: It wasn't me, Berniece. You can't blame me for nobody else. I'll own up to my own shortcomings. But you can't blame me for Crawley or nobody else.

BERNIECE: I ain't blaming nobody for nothing. I'm just stating the facts.

AVERY: How long you gonna carry Crawley with you, Berniece? It's been over three years. At some point you got to let go and go on. Life's got all kinds of twists and turns. That don't mean you stop living. That don't mean you cut yourself off from life. You can't go through life carrying Crawley's ghost with you. Crawley's been dead three years. Three years, Berniece.

BERNIECE: I know how long Crawley's been dead. You ain't got to tell me that. I just ain't ready to get married right now.

AVERY: What is you ready for, Berniece? You just gonna drift along from day to day. Life is more than making it from one day to another. You gonna look up one day and it's all gonna be past you. Life's gonna be gone out of your hands—there won't be enough to make nothing with. I'm standing here now, Berniece—but I don't know how much longer I'm gonna be standing here waiting on you.

BERNIECE: Avery, I told you . . . when you get your church we'll sit down and talk about this. I got too many other things to deal with right now. Boy Willie and the piano . . . and Sutter's ghost. I thought I might have been seeing things, but Maretha done seen Sutter's ghost, too.

AVERY: When this happen, Berniece?

BERNIECE: Right after I came home yesterday. Me and Boy Willie was arguing about the piano and Sutter's ghost was standing at the top of the stairs. Maretha scared to sleep up there now. Maybe if you bless the house he'll go away.

AVERY: I don't know, Berniece. I don't know if I should fool around with something like that.

BERNIECE: I can't have Maretha scared to go to sleep up there. Seem like if you bless the house he would go away.

AVERY: You might have to be a special kind of preacher to do something like that.

BERNIECE: I keep telling myself when Boy Willie leave he'll go on and leave with him. I believe Boy Willie pushed him in the well.

AVERY: That's been going on down there a long time. The Ghosts of the Yellow Dog been pushing people in their wells long before Boy Willie got grown.

BERNIECE: Somebody down there pushing them people in their wells. They ain't just upped and fell. Ain't no wind pushed nobody in their well.

AVERY: Oh, I don't know. God works in mysterious ways.

BERNIECE: He ain't pushed nobody in their wells.

AVERY: He caused it to happen. God is the Great Causer. He can do anything. He parted the Red Sea. He say I will smite my enemies. Reverend Thompson used to preach on the Ghosts of the Yellow Dog as the hand of God.

BERNIECE: I don't care who preached what. Somebody down there pushing them people in their wells. Somebody like Boy Willie. I can see him doing something like that. You ain't gonna tell me that Sutter just upped and fell in his well. I believe Boy Willie pushed him so he could get his land.

AVERY: What Doaker say about Boy Willie selling the piano?

BERNIECE: Doaker don't want no part of that piano. He ain't never wanted no part of it. He blames himself for not staying behind with Papa Boy Charles. He washed his hands of that piano a long time ago. He didn't want me to bring it up here—but I wasn't gonna leave it down there.

AVERY: Well, it seems to me somebody ought to be able to talk to Boy Willie.

BERNIECE: You can't talk to Boy Willie. He been that way all his life. Mama Ola had her hands full trying to talk to him. He don't listen to nobody. He just like my daddy. He get his mind fixed on something and can't nobody turn him from it.

AVERY: You ought to start a choir at the church. Maybe if he seen you was doing something with it—if you told him you was gonna put it in my church—maybe he'd see it different. You ought to put it down in the church and start a choir. The Bible say, "Make a joyful noise unto the Lord." Maybe if Boy Willie see you was doing something with it he'd see it different.

BERNIECE: I done told you I don't play on that piano. Ain't no need in you to keep talking this choir stuff. When my mama died I shut the top on that piano and I ain't never opened it since. I was only playing it for her. When my daddy died seem like all her life went into that piano. She used to have me playing on it . . . had Miss Eula come in and teach me . . . say when I played it she could hear my daddy talking to her. I used to think them pictures came alive and walked through the house. Sometime late at night I could hear my mama talking to them. I said that wasn't gonna happen to me. I don't play that piano cause I don't want to wake them spirits. They never be walking around in this house.

AVERY: You got to put all that behind you, Berniece.

BERNIECE: I got Maretha playing on it. She don't know nothing about it. Let her go on and be a schoolteacher or something. She don't have to carry all of that with her. She got a chance I didn't have. I ain't gonna burden her with that piano.

AVERY: You got to put all of that behind you, Berniece. That's the same thing like Crawley. Everybody got stones in their passway. You got to step over them or walk around them. You picking them up and carrying them with you. All you got to do is set them down by the side of the road. You ain't got to carry them with you. You can walk over there right now and play that piano. You can walk over there right now and God will walk over there with you. Right now you can set that sack of stones down by the side of the road and walk away from it. You don't have to carry it with you. You can do it right now.

Avery crosses over to the piano and raises the lid.

Come on, Berniece . . . set it down and walk away from it. Come on, play "Old Ship of Zion." Walk over here and claim it as an instrument of the Lord. You can walk over here right now and make it into a celebration.

Berniece moves toward the piano.

BERNIECE: Avery . . . I done told you I don't want to play that piano. Now or no other time.

AVERY: The Bible say, "The Lord is my refuge . . . and my strength!" With the strength of God you can put the past behind you, Berniece. With the strength of God you can do anything! God got a bright tomorrow. God don't ask what you done . . . God ask what you gonna do. The strength of God can move mountains! God's got a bright tomorrow for you . . . all you got to do is walk over here and claim it.

BERNIECE: Avery, just go on and let me finish my bath. I'll see you tomorrow.

AVERY: Okay, Berniece. I'm gonna go home. I'm gonna go home and read up on my Bible. And tomorrow . . . if the good Lord give me strength tomorrow . . . I'm gonna come by and bless the house . . . and show you the power of the Lord.

Avery crosses to the door.

It's gonna be alright, Berniece. God say he will soothe the troubled waters. I'll come by tomorrow and bless the house.

The lights go down to black.

Scene III

Several hours later. The house is dark. Berniece has retired for the night. Boy Willie enters the darkened house with Grace.

BOY WILLIE: Come on in. This my sister's house. My sister live here. Come on, I ain't gonna bite you.

GRACE: Put some light on. I can't see.

BOY WILLIE: You don't need to see nothing, baby. This here is all you need to see. All you need to do is see me. If you can't see me you can feel me in the dark. How's that, sugar?

He attempts to kiss her.

GRACE: Go on now . . . wait!

BOY WILLIE: Just give me one little old kiss.

GRACE: [*Pushing him away.*] Come on, now. Where I'm gonna sleep at?

BOY WILLIE: We got to sleep out here on the couch. Come on, my sister don't mind. Lymon come back he just got to sleep on the floor. He run off with Dolly somewhere he better stay there. Come on, sugar.

GRACE: Wait now . . . you ain't told me nothing about no couch. I thought you had a bed. Both of us can't sleep on that little old couch.

BOY WILLIE: It don't make no difference. We can sleep on the floor. Let Lymon sleep on the couch.

GRACE: You ain't told me nothing about no couch.

BOY WILLIE: What difference it make? You just wanna be with me.

GRACE: I don't want to be with you on no couch. Ain't you got no bed?

BOY WILLIE: You don't need no bed, woman. My granddaddy used to take women on the backs of horses. What you need a bed for? You just want to be with me.

GRACE: You sure is country. I didn't know you was this country.

BOY WILLIE: There's a lot of things you don't know about me. Come on, let me show you what this country boy can do.

GRACE: Let's go to my place. I got a room with a bed if Leroy don't come back there.

BOY WILLIE: Who's Leroy? You ain't said nothing about no Leroy.

GRACE: He used to be my man. He ain't coming back. He gone off with some other gal.

BOY WILLIE: You let him have your key?

GRACE: He ain't coming back.

BOY WILLIE: Did you let him have your key?

GRACE: He got a key but he ain't coming back. He took off with some other gal.

BOY WILLIE: I don't wanna go nowhere he might come. Let's stay here. Come on, sugar.

He pulls her over to the couch.

Let me heist your hood and check your oil. See if your battery needs charged.

He pulls her to him. They kiss and tug at each other's clothing. In their anxiety they knock over a lamp.

BERNIECE: Who's that . . . Wining Boy?

BOY WILLIE: It's me . . . Boy Willie. Go on back to sleep. Everything's alright.

To Grace.

That's my sister. Everything's alright, Berniece. Go on back to sleep.

BERNIECE: What you doing down there? What you done knocked over?

BOY WILLIE: It wasn't nothing. Everything's alright. Go on back to sleep.

To Grace.

That's my sister. We alright. She gone back to sleep.

They begin to kiss. Berniece enters from the stairs dressed in a nightgown. She cuts on the light.

BERNIECE: Boy Willie, what you doing down here?

BOY WILLIE: It was just that there lamp. It ain't broke. It's okay. Everything's alright. Go on back to bed.

BERNIECE: Boy Willie, I don't allow that in my house. You gonna have to take your company someplace else.

BOY WILLIE: It's alright. We ain't doing nothing. We just sitting here talking. This here is Grace. That's my sister Berniece.

BERNIECE: You know I don't allow that kind of stuff in my house.

BOY WILLIE: Allow what? We just sitting here talking.

BERNIECE: Well, your company gonna have to leave. Come back and talk in the morning.

BOY WILLIE: Go on back upstairs now.

BERNIECE: I got an eleven-year-old girl upstairs. I can't allow that around here.

BOY WILLIE: Ain't nobody said nothing about that. I told you we just talking.

GRACE: Come on . . . let's go to my place. Ain't nobody got to tell me to leave but once.

BOY WILLIE: You ain't got to be like that, Berniece.

BERNIECE: I'm sorry, Miss. But he know I don't allow that in here.

GRACE: You ain't got to tell me but once. I don't stay nowhere I ain't wanted.

BOY WILLIE: I don't know why you want to embarrass me in front of my company.

GRACE: Come on, take me home.

BERNIECE: Go on, Boy Willie. Just go on with your company.

Boy Willie and Grace exit. Berniece puts the light on in the kitchen and puts on the teakettle. Presently there is a knock at the door. Berniece goes to answer it. Berniece opens the door. Lymon enters.

LYMON: How you doing, Berniece? I thought you'd be asleep. Boy Willie been back here?

BERNIECE: He just left out of here a minute ago.

LYMON: I went out to see a picture show and never got there. We always end up doing something else. I was with this woman she just wanted to drink up all my money. So I left her there and came back looking for Boy Willie.

BERNIECE: You just missed him. He just left out of here.

LYMON: They got some nice-looking women in this city. I'm gonna like it up here real good. I like seeing them with their dresses on. Got them high heels. I like that. Make them look like they real precious. Boy Willie met a real nice one today. I wish I had met her before he did.

BERNIECE: He come by here with some woman a little while ago. I told him to go on and take all that out of my house.

LYMON: What she look like, the woman he was with? Was she a brown-skinned woman about this high? Nice and healthy? Got nice hips on her?

BERNIECE: She had on a red dress.

LYMON: That's her! That's Grace. She real nice. Laugh a lot. Lot of fun to be with. She don't be trying to put on. Some of these woman act like they the Queen of Sheba. I don't like them kind. Grace ain't like that. She real nice with herself.

BERNIECE: I don't know what she was like. He come in here all drunk knocking over the lamp, and making all kind of noise. I told them to take that somewhere else. I can't really say what she was like.

LYMON: She real nice. I seen her before he did. I was trying not to act like I seen her. I wanted to look at her a while before I said something. She seen me when I come into the saloon. I tried to act like I didn't see her. Time I looked around Boy Willie was talking to her. She was talking to him kept looking at me. That's when her friend Dolly came. I asked her if she wanted to go to the picture show. She told me to buy her a drink while she thought about it. Next thing I knew she done had three drinks talking about she too tired to go. I bought her another drink, then I left. Boy Willie was gone and I thought he might have come back here. Doaker gone, huh? He say he had to make a trip.

BERNIECE: Yeah, he gone on his trip. This is when I can usually get me some peace and quiet, Maretha asleep.

LYMON: She look just like you. Got them big eyes. I remember her when she was in diapers.

BERNIECE: Time just keep on. It go on with or without you. She going on twelve.

LYMON: She sure is pretty. I like kids.

BERNIECE: Boy Willie say you staying . . . what you gonna do up here in this big city? You thought about that?

LYMON: They never get me back down there. The sheriff looking for me. All because they gonna try and make me work for somebody when I don't want to. They gonna try and make me work for Stovall when he don't pay nothing. It ain't like that up here. Up here you more or less do what you want to. I figure I find me a job and try to get set up and then see what the year brings. I tried to do that two or three times down there . . . but it never would work out. I was always in the wrong place.

BERNIECE: This ain't a bad city once you get to know your way around.

LYMON: Up here is different. I'm gonna get me a job unloading box-cars or something. One fellow told me say he know a place. I'm gonna go over there with him next week. Me and Boy Willie finish selling them watermelons I'll have enough money to hold me for a while. But I'm gonna go over there and see what kind of jobs they have.

BERNIECE: You shouldn't have too much trouble finding a job. It's all in how you present yourself. See now, Boy Willie couldn't get no job up here. Somebody hire him they got a pack of trouble on their hands. Soon as they find that out they fire him. He don't want to do nothing unless he do it his way.

LYMON: I know. I told him let's go to the picture show first and see if there was any women down there. They might get tired of sitting at home and walk down to the picture show. He say he wanna look around first. We never did get down there. We tried a couple of places and then we went to this saloon where he met Grace. I tried to meet her before he did but he beat me to her. We left Wining Boy sitting down there running his mouth. He told me if I wear this suit I'd find me a woman. He was almost right.

BERNIECE: You don't need to be out there in them saloons. Ain't no telling what you liable to run into out there. This one liable to cut you as quick as that one shoot you. You don't need to be out there. You start out that fast life you can't keep it up. It makes you old quick. I don't know what them women out there be thinking about.

LYMON: Mostly they be lonely and looking for somebody to spend the night with them. Sometimes it matters who it is and sometimes it don't. I used to be the same way. Now it got to matter. That's why I'm here now. Dolly liable not to even recognize me if she sees me again. I don't like women like that. I like my women to be with me in a nice and easy way. That way we can both enjoy ourselves. The way I see it we the only two people like us in the world. We got to see how we fit together. A woman that don't want to take the time to do that I don't bother with. Used to. Used to bother with all of them. Then I woke up one time with this woman and I didn't know who she was. She was the prettiest woman I had ever seen in my life. I spent the whole night with her and didn't even know it. I had never taken the time to look at her. I guess she kinda knew I ain't never really looked at her. She must have known that cause she ain't wanted to see me no more. If she had wanted to see me I believe we might have got married. How come you ain't married? It seem like to me you would be married. I remember Avery from down home. I used to call him plain old Avery. Now he Reverend Avery. That's kinda funny about him becoming a preacher. I like when he told about how that come to him in a dream about them sheep people and them hobos. Nothing ever come to me in a dream like that. I just dream about women. Can't never seem to find the right one.

BERNIECE: She out there somewhere. You just got to get yourself ready to meet her. That's what I'm trying to do. Avery's alright. I ain't really got nobody in mind.

LYMON: I get me a job and a little place and get set up to where I can make a woman comfortable I might get married. Avery's nice. You ought to go ahead and get married. You be a preacher's wife you won't have to work. I hate living by myself. I didn't want to be no strain on my mama so I left home when I was about sixteen. Everything I tried seem like it just didn't work out. Now I'm trying this.

BERNIECE: You keep trying it'll work out for you.

LYMON: You ever go down there to the picture show?

BERNIECE: I don't go in for all that.

LYMON: Ain't nothing wrong with it. It ain't like gambling and sinning. I went to one down in Jackson once. It was fun.

BERNIECE: I just stay home most of the time. Take care of Maretha.

LYMON: It's getting kind of late. I don't know where Boy Willie went off to. He's liable not to come back. I'm gonna take off these shoes. My feet hurt. Was you in bed? I don't mean to be keeping you up.

BERNIECE: You ain't keeping me up. I couldn't sleep after that Boy Willie woke me up.

LYMON: You got on that nightgown. I likes women when they wear them fancy nightclothes and all. It makes their skin look real pretty.

BERNIECE: I got this at the five-and-ten-cents store. It ain't so fancy.

LYMON: I don't too often get to see a woman dressed like that.

There is a long pause. Lymon takes off his suit coat.

Well, I'm gonna sleep here on the couch. I'm supposed to sleep on the floor but I don't reckon Boy Willie's coming back tonight. Wining Boy sold me this suit. Told me it was a magic suit. I'm gonna put it on again tomorrow. Maybe it bring me a woman like he say.

He goes into his coat pocket and takes out a small bottle of perfume.

I almost forgot I had this. Some man sold me this for a dollar. Say it come from Paris. This is the same kind of perfume the Queen of France wear. That's what he told me. I don't know if it's true or not. I smelled it. It smelled good to me. Here . . . smell it see if you like it. I was gonna give it to Dolly. But I didn't like her too much.

BERNIECE: [*Takes the bottle.*] It smells nice.

LYMON: I was gonna give it to Dolly if she had went to the picture with me. Go on, you take it.

BERNIECE: I can't take it. Here . . . go on you keep it. You'll find somebody to give it to.

LYMON: I wanna give it to you. Make you smell nice.

He takes the bottle and puts perfume behind Berniece's ear.

They tell me you supposed to put it right here behind your ear. Say if you put it there you smell nice all day.

Berniece stiffens at his touch. Lymon bends down to smell her.

There . . . you smell real good now.

He kisses her neck.

You smell real good for Lymon.

He kisses her again. Berniece returns the kiss, then breaks the embrace and crosses to the stairs. She turns and they look silently at each other. Lymon hands her the bottle of perfume. Berniece exits up the stairs. Lymon picks up his suit coat and strokes it lovingly with the full knowledge that it is indeed a magic suit. The lights go down on the scene.

Scene IV

It is late the next morning. The lights come up on the parlor. Lymon is asleep on the sofa. Boy Willie enters the front door.

BOY WILLIE: Hey, Lymon! Lymon, come on get up.

LYMON: Leave me alone.

BOY WILLIE: Come on, get up, nigger! Wake up, Lymon.

LYMON: What you want?

BOY WILLIE: Come on, let's go. I done called the man about the piano.

LYMON: What piano?

BOY WILLIE: [*Dumps Lymon on the floor.*] Come on, get up!

LYMON: Why you leave, I looked around and you was gone.

BOY WILLIE: I come back here with Grace, then I went looking for you. I figured you'd be with Dolly.

LYMON: She just want to drink and spend up your money. I come on back here looking for you to see if you wanted to go to the picture show.

BOY WILLIE: I been up at Grace's house. Some nigger named Leroy come by but I had a chair up against the door. He got mad when he couldn't get in. He went off somewhere and I got out of there before he could come back. Berniece got mad when we came here.

LYMON: She say you was knocking over the lamp busting up the place.

BOY WILLIE: That was Grace doing all that.

LYMON: Wining Boy seen Sutter's ghost last night.

BOY WILLIE: Wining Boy's liable to see anything. I'm surprised he found the right house. Come on, I done called the man about the piano.

LYMON: What he say?

BOY WILLIE: He say to bring it on out. I told him I was calling for my sister, Miss Berniece Charles. I told him some man wanted to buy it for eleven hundred dollars and asked him if he would go any better. He said yeah, he would give me eleven hundred and fifty dollars for it if it was the same piano. I described it to him again and he told me to bring it out.

LYMON: Why didn't you tell him to come and pick it up?

BOY WILLIE: I didn't want to have no problem with Berniece. This way we just take it on out there and it be out the way. He want to charge twenty-five dollars to pick it up.

LYMON: You should have told him the man was gonna give you twelve hundred for it.

BOY WILLIE: I figure I was taking a chance with that eleven hundred. If I had told him twelve hundred he might have run off. Now I wish I had told him twelve-fifty. It's hard to figure out white folks sometimes.

LYMON: You might have been able to tell him anything. White folks got a lot of money.

BOY WILLIE: Come on, let's get it loaded before Berniece come back. Get that end over there. All you got to do is pick it up on that side. Don't worry about this side. You wanna stretch you' back for a minute?

LYMON: I'm ready.

BOY WILLIE: Get a real good grip on it now.

The sound of Sutter's Ghost is heard. They do not hear it.

LYMON: I got this end. You get that end.

BOY WILLIE: Wait till I say ready now. Alright. You got it good? You got a grip on it?

LYMON: Yeah, I got it. You lift up on that end.

BOY WILLIE: Ready? Lift!

The piano will not budge.

LYMON: Man, this piano is heavy! It's gonna take more than me and you to move this piano.

BOY WILLIE: We can do it. Come on—we did it before.

LYMON: Nigger—you crazy! That piano weighs five hundred pounds!

BOY WILLIE: I got three hundred pounds of it! I know you can carry two hundred pounds! You be lifting them cotton sacks! Come on lift this piano!

They try to move the piano again without success.

LYMON: It's stuck. Something holding it.

BOY WILLIE: How the piano gonna be stuck? We just moved it. Slide you' end out.

LYMON: Naw—we gonna need two or three more people. How this big old piano get in the house?

BOY WILLIE: I don't know how it got in the house. I know how it's going out though! You get on this end. I'll carry three hundred and fifty pounds of it. All you got to do is slide your end out. Ready?

They switch sides and try again without success. Doaker enters from his room as they try to push and shove it.

LYMON: Hey, Doaker . . . how this piano get in the house?

DOAKER: Boy Willie, what you doing?

BOY WILLIE: I'm carrying this piano out the house. What it look like I'm doing? Come on, Lymon, let's try again.

DOAKER: Go on let the piano sit there till Berniece come home.

BOY WILLIE: You ain't got nothing to do with this, Doaker. This my business.

DOAKER: This is my house, nigger! I ain't gonna let you or nobody else carry nothing out of it. You ain't gonna carry nothing out of here without my permission!

BOY WILLIE: This is my piano. I don't need your permission to carry my belongings out of your house. This is mine. This ain't got nothing to do with you.

DOAKER: I say leave it over there till Berniece come home. She got part of it too. Leave it set there till you see what she say.

BOY WILLIE: I don't care what Berniece say. Come on, Lymon. I got this side.

DOAKER: Go on and cut it half in two if you want to. Just leave Berniece's half sitting over there. I can't tell you what to do with your piano. But I can't let you take her half out of here.

BOY WILLIE: Go on, Doaker. You ain't got nothing to do with this. I don't want you starting nothing now. Just go on and leave me alone. Come on, Lymon. I got this end.

Doaker goes into his room. Boy Willie and Lymon prepare to move the piano.

LYMON: How we gonna get it in the truck?

BOY WILLIE: Don't worry about how we gonna get it on the truck. You got to get it out the house first.

LYMON: It's gonna take more than me and you to move this piano.

BOY WILLIE: Just lift up on that end, nigger!

Doaker comes to the doorway of his room and stands.

DOAKER: [*Quietly with authority.*] Leave that piano set over there till Berniece come back. I don't care what you do with it then. But you gonna leave it sit over there right now.

BOY WILLIE: Alright . . . I'm gonna tell you this, Doaker. I'm going out of here . . . I'm gonna get me some rope . . . find me a plank and some wheels . . . and I'm coming back. Then I'm gonna carry that piano out of here . . . sell it and give Berniece half the money. See . . . now that's what I'm gonna do. And you . . . or nobody else is gonna stop me. Come on, Lymon . . . let's go get some rope and stuff. I'll be back, Doaker.

Boy Willie and Lymon exit. The lights go down on the scene.

Scene V

The lights come up. Boy Willie sits on the sofa, screwing casters on a wooden plank. Maretha is sitting on the piano stool. Doaker sits at the table playing solitaire.

BOY WILLIE: [*To Maretha.*] Then after that them white folks down around there started falling down their wells. You ever seen a well? A well got a wall around it. It's hard to fall down a well. You got to be leaning way over. Couldn't nobody figure out too much what was making these fellows fall down their well . . . so everybody says the Ghosts of the Yellow Dog must have pushed them. That's what everybody called them four men what got burned up in the boxcar.

MARETHA: Why they call them that?

BOY WILLIE: Cause the Yazoo Delta railroad got yellow boxcars. Sometime the way the whistle blow sound like an old dog howling so the people call it the Yellow Dog.

MARETHA: Anybody ever see the Ghosts?

BOY WILLIE: I told you they like the wind. Can you see the wind?

MARETHA: No.

BOY WILLIE: They like the wind you can't see them. But sometimes you be in trouble they might be around to help you. They say if you go where the Southern cross the Yellow Dog . . . you go to where them two railroads cross each other . . . and call out their names . . . they say they talk back to you. I don't know, I ain't never done that. But Uncle Wining Boy he say he been down there and talked to them. You have to ask him about that part.

Berniece has entered from the front door.

BERNIECE: Maretha, you go on and get ready for me to do your hair.

Maretha crosses to the steps.

Boy Willie, I done told you to leave my house.

To Maretha.

Go on, Maretha.

Maretha is hesitant about going up the stairs.

BOY WILLIE: Don't be scared. Here, I'll go up there with you. If we see Sutter's ghost I'll put a whupping on him. Come on, Uncle Boy Willie going with you.

Boy Willie and Maretha exit up the stairs.

BERNIECE: Doaker—what is going on here?

DOAKER: I come home and him and Lymon was moving the piano. I told them to leave it over there till you got home. He went out and got that board and them wheels. He say he gonna take that piano out of here and ain't nobody gonna stop him.

BERNIECE: I ain't playing with Boy Willie. I got Crawley's gun upstairs. He don't know but I'm through with it. Where Lymon go?

DOAKER: Boy Willie sent him for some rope just before you come in.

BERNIECE: I ain't studying Boy Willie or Lymon—or the rope. Boy Willie ain't taking that piano out this house. That's all there is to it.

Boy Willie and Maretha enter on the stairs. Maretha carries a hot comb and a can of hair grease. Boy Willie crosses over and continues to screw the wheels on the board.

MARETHA: Mama, all the hair grease is gone. There ain't but this little bit left.

BERNIECE: [*Gives her a dollar.*] Here . . . run across the street and get another can. You come straight back, too. Don't you be playing around out there. And watch the cars. Be careful when you cross the street.

Maretha exits out the front door.

Boy Willie, I done told you to leave my house.

BOY WILLIE: I ain't in you' house. I'm in Doaker's house. If he ask me to leave then I'll go on and leave. But consider me done left your part.

BERNIECE: Doaker, tell him to leave. Tell him to go on.

DOAKER: Boy Willie ain't done nothing for me to put him out of the house. I told you if you can't get along just go on and don't have nothing to do with each other.

BOY WILLIE: I ain't thinking about Berniece.

He gets up and draws a line across the floor with his foot.

There! Now I'm out of your part of the house. Consider me done left your part. Soon as Lymon come back with that rope. I'm gonna take that piano out of here and sell it.

BERNIECE: You ain't gonna touch that piano.

BOY WILLIE: Carry it out of here just as big and bold. Do like my daddy would have done come time to get Sutter's land.

BERNIECE: I got something to make you leave it over there.

BOY WILLIE: It's got to come better than this thirty-two-twenty.

DOAKER: Why don't you stop all that! Boy Willie, go on and leave her alone. You know how Berniece get. Why you wanna sit there and pick with her?

BOY WILLIE: I ain't picking with her. I told her the truth. She the one talking about what she got. I just told her what she better have.

BERNIECE: That's alright, Doaker. Leave him alone.

BOY WILLIE: She trying to scare me. Hell, I ain't scared of dying. I look around and see people dying every day. You got to die to make room for somebody else. I had a dog that died. Wasn't nothing but a puppy. I picked it up and put it in a bag and carried it up there to Reverend C. L. Thompson's church. I carried it up there and prayed and asked Jesus to make it live like he did the man in the Bible. I prayed real hard. Knelt down and everything. Say ask in Jesus' name. Well, I must have called Jesus' name two hundred times. I called his name till my mouth got sore. I got up and looked in the bag and the dog still dead. It ain't moved a muscle! I say, "Well, ain't nothing precious." And then I went out and killed me a cat. That's when I discovered the power of death. See, a nigger that ain't afraid to die is the worse kind of nigger for the white man. He can't hold that power over you. That's what I learned when I killed that cat. I got the power of death too. I can command him. I can call him up. The white man don't like to see that. He don't like for you to stand up and look him square in the eye and say, "I got it too." Then he got to deal with you square up.

BERNIECE: That's why I don't talk to him, Doaker. You try and talk to him and that's the only kind of stuff that comes out his mouth.

DOAKER: You say Avery went home to get his Bible?

BOY WILLIE: What Avery gonna do? Avery can't do nothing with me. I wish Avery would say something to me about this piano.

DOAKER: Berniece ain't said about that. Avery went home to get his Bible. He coming by to bless the house see if he can get rid of Sutter's ghost.

BOY WILLIE: Ain't nothing but a house full of ghosts down there at the church. What Avery look like chasing away somebody's ghost?

Maretha enters the front door.

BERNIECE: Light that stove and set that comb over there to get hot. Get something to put around your shoulders.

BOY WILLIE: The Bible say an eye for an eye, a tooth for a tooth, and a life for a life. Tit for tat. But you and Avery don't want to believe that. You gonna pass up that part and pretend it ain't in there. Everything else you gonna agree with. But if you gonna agree with part of it you got to agree with all of it. You can't do nothing halfway. You gonna go at the Bible halfway. You gonna act like that part ain't in there. But you pull out the Bible and open it and see what it say. Ask Avery. He a preacher. He'll tell you it's in there. He the Good Shepherd. Unless he gonna shepherd you to heaven with half the Bible.

BERNIECE: Maretha, bring me that comb. Make sure it's hot.

Maretha brings the comb. Berniece begins to do her hair.

BOY WILLIE: I will say this for Avery. He done figured out a path to go through life. I don't agree with it. But he done fixed it so he can go right through it real smooth. Hell, he liable to end up with a million dollars that he done got from selling bread and wine.

MARETHA: OWWWWWW!

BERNIECE: Be still, Maretha. If you was a boy I wouldn't be going through this.

BOY WILLIE: Don't you tell that girl that. Why you wanna tell her that?

BERNIECE: You ain't got nothing to do with this child.

BOY WILLIE: Telling her you wished she was a boy. How's that gonna make her feel?

BERNIECE: Boy Willie, go on and leave me alone.

DOAKER: Why don't you leave her alone? What you got to pick with her for? Why don't you go on out and see what's out there in the streets? Have something to tell the fellows down home.

BOY WILLIE: I'm waiting on Lymon to get back with that truck. Why don't you go on out and see what's out there in the streets? You ain't got to work tomorrow. Talking about me . . . why don't you go out there? It's Friday night.

DOAKER: I got to stay around here and keep you all from killing one another.

BOY WILLIE: You ain't got to worry about me. I'm gonna be here just as long as it takes Lymon to get back here with that truck. You ought to be talking to Berniece. Sitting up there telling Maretha she wished she was a boy. What kind of thing is that to tell a child? If you want to tell her something tell her about that piano. You ain't even told her about that piano. Like that's something to be ashamed of. Like she supposed to go off and hide somewhere about that piano. You ought to mark down on the calendar the day that Papa Boy Charles brought that piano into the house. You ought to mark that day down and draw a circle around it . . . and every year when it come up throw a party. Have a celebration. If you did that she wouldn't have no problem in life. She could walk around here with her head held high. I'm talking about a big party! Invite everybody! Mark that day down with a special meaning. That way she know where she at in the world. You got her going out here thinking she wrong in the world. Like there ain't no part of it belong to her.

BERNIECE: Let me take care of my child. When you get one of your own then you can teach it what you want to teach it.

Doaker exits into his room.

BOY WILLIE: What I want to bring a child into this world for? Why I wanna bring somebody else into all this for? I'll tell you this . . . If I was Rockefeller I'd have forty or fifty. I'd make one every day. Cause they gonna start out in life with all the advantages. I ain't got no advantages to offer nobody. Many is the time I looked at my daddy and seen him staring off at his hands. I got a little older I know what he was thinking. He sitting there saying, "I got these big old hands but what I'm gonna do with them? Best I can do is make a fifty-acre crop for Mr. Stovall. Got these big old hands capable of doing anything. I can take and build something with these hands. But where's the tools? All I got is these hands. Unless I go out here and kill me somebody and take what they got . . . it's a long row to hoe for me to get something of my own. So what I'm gonna do with these big old hands? What would you do?"

See now . . . if he had his own land he wouldn't have felt that way. If he had something under his feet that belonged to him he could stand up taller. That's what I'm talking about. Hell, the land is there for everybody. All you got to do is figure out how to get you a piece. Ain't no mystery to life. You just got to go out and meet it square on. If you got a piece of land you'll find everything else fall right into place. You can stand right up next to the white man and talk about the price of cotton . . . the weather, and anything else you want to talk about. If you teach that girl that she living at the bottom of life, she's gonna grow up and hate you.

BERNIECE: I'm gonna teach her the truth. That's just where she living. Only she ain't got to stay there.

To Maretha.

Turn you' head over to the other side.

BOY WILLIE: This might be your bottom but it ain't mine. I'm living at the top of life. I ain't gonna just take my life and throw it away at the bottom. I'm in the world like everybody else. The way I see it everybody else got to come up a little taste to be where I am.

BERNIECE: You right at the bottom with the rest of us.

BOY WILLIE: I'll tell you this . . . and ain't a living soul can put a come back on it. If you believe that's where you at then you gonna act that way. If you act that way then that's where you gonna be. It's as simple as that. Ain't no mystery to life. I don't know how you come to believe that stuff. Crawley didn't think like that. He wasn't living at the bottom of life. Papa Boy Charles and Mama Ola wasn't living at the bottom of life. You ain't never heard them say nothing like that. They would have taken a strap to you if they heard you say something like that.

Doaker enters from his room.

Hey, Doaker . . . Berniece say the colored folks is living at the bottom of life. I tried to tell her if she think that . . . that's where she gonna be. You think you living at the bottom of life? Is that how you see yourself?

DOAKER: I'm just living the best way I know how. I ain't thinking about no top or no bottom.

BOY WILLIE: That's what I tried to tell Berniece. I don't know where she got that from. That sound like something Avery would say. Avery think cause the white man give him a turkey for Thanksgiving that makes him better than everybody else. That's gonna raise him out of the bottom of life. I don't need nobody to give me a turkey. I can get my own turkey. All you have to do is get out my way. I'll get me two or three turkeys.

BERNIECE: You can't even get a chicken let alone two or three turkeys. Talking about get out your way. Ain't nobody in your way.

To Maretha.

Straighten your head, Maretha! Don't be bending down like that. Hold your head up!

To Boy Willie.

All you got going for you is talk. You' whole life that's all you ever had going for you.

BOY WILLIE: See now . . . I'll tell you something about me. I done strung along and strung along. Going this way and that. Whatever way would lead me to a moment of peace. That's all I want. To be as easy with everything. But I wasn't born to that. I was born to a time of fire.

The world ain't wanted no part of me. I could see that since I was about seven. The world say it's better off without me. See, Berniece accept that. She trying to come up to where she can prove something to the world. Hell, the world a better place cause of me. I don't see it like Berniece. I got a heart that beats here and it beats just as loud as the next fellow's. Don't care if he black or white. Sometime it beats louder. When it beats louder, then everybody can hear it. Some people get scared of that. Like Berniece. Some people get scared to hear a nigger's heart beating. They think you ought to lay low with that heart. Make it beat quiet and go along with everything the way it is. But my mama ain't birthed me for nothing. So what I got to do? I got to mark my passing on the road. Just like you write on a tree, "Boy Willie was here."

That's all I'm trying to do with that piano. Trying to put my mark on the road. Like my daddy done. My heart say for me to sell that piano and get me some land so I can make a life for myself to live in my own way. Other than that I ain't thinking about nothing Berniece got to say.

There is a knock at the door. Boy Willie crosses to it and yanks it open thinking it is Lymon. Avery enters. He carries a Bible.

BOY WILLIE: Where you been, nigger? Aw . . . I thought you was Lymon. Hey, Berniece, look who's here.

BERNIECE: Come on in, Avery. Don't you pay Boy Willie no mind.

BOY WILLIE: Hey . . . Hey, Avery . . . tell me this . . . can you get to heaven with half the Bible?

BERNIECE: Boy Willie . . . I done told you to leave me alone.

BOY WILLIE: I just ask the man a question. He can answer. He don't need you to speak for him. Avery . . . if you only believe on half the Bible and don't want to accept the other half . . . you think God let you in heaven? Or do you got to have the whole Bible? Tell Berniece . . . if you only believe in part of it . . . when you see God he gonna ask you why you ain't believed in the other part . . . then he gonna send you straight to Hell.

AVERY: You got to be born again. Jesus say unless a man be born again he cannot come unto the Father and who so ever heareth my words and believeth them not shall be cast into a fiery pit.

BOY WILLIE: That's what I was trying to tell Berniece. You got to believe in it all. You can't go at nothing halfway. She think she going to heaven with half the Bible.

To Berniece.

You hear that . . . Jesus say you got to believe in it all.

BERNIECE: You keep messing with me.

BOY WILLIE: I ain't thinking about you.

DOAKER: Come on in, Avery, and have a seat. Don't pay neither one of them no mind. They been arguing all day.

BERNIECE: Come on in, Avery.

AVERY: How's everybody in here?

BERNIECE: Here, set this comb back over there on that stove.

To Avery.

Don't pay Boy Willie no mind. He been around here bothering me since I come home from work.

BOY WILLIE: Boy Willie ain't bothering you. Boy Willie ain't bothering nobody. I'm just waiting on Lymon to get back. I ain't thinking about you. You heard the man say I was right and you still don't want to believe it. You just wanna go and make up anythin'. Well there's Avery . . . there's the preacher . . . go on and ask him.

AVERY: Berniece believe in the Bible. She been baptized.

BOY WILLIE: What about that part that say an eye for an eye a tooth for a tooth and a life for a life? Ain't that in there?

DOAKER: What they say down there at the bank, Avery?

AVERY: Oh, they talked to me real nice. I told Berniece . . . they say maybe they let me borrow the money. They done talked to my boss down at work and everything.

DOAKER: That's what I told Berniece. You working every day you ought to be able to borrow some money.

AVERY: I'm getting more people in my congregation every day. Berniece says she gonna be the Deaconess. I get me my church I can get married and settled down. That's what I told Berniece.

DOAKER: That be nice. You all ought to go ahead and get married. Berniece don't need to be by herself. I tell her that all the time.

BERNIECE: I ain't said nothing about getting married. I said I was thinking about it.

DOAKER: Avery get him his church you all can make it nice.

To Avery.

Berniece said you was coming by to bless the house.

AVERY: Yeah, I done read up on my Bible. She asked me to come by and see if I can get rid of Sutter's ghost.

BOY WILLIE: Ain't no ghost in this house. That's all in Berniece's head. Go on up there and see if you see him. I'll give you a hundred dollars if you see him. That's all in her imagination.

DOAKER: Well, let her find that out then. If Avery blessing the house is gonna make her feel better . . . what you got to do with it?

AVERY: Berniece say Maretha seen him too. I don't know, but I found a part in the Bible to bless the house. If he is here then that ought to make him go.

BOY WILLIE: You worse than Berniece believing all that stuff. Talking about . . . if he here. Go on up there and find out. I been up there I ain't seen him. If you reading from that Bible gonna make him leave out of Berniece imagination, well, you might be right. But if you talking about . . .

DOAKER: Boy Willie, why don't you just be quiet? Getting all up in the man's business. This ain't got nothing to do with you. Let him go ahead and do what he gonna do.

BOY WILLIE: I ain't stopping him. Avery ain't got no power to do nothing.

AVERY: Oh, I ain't got no power. God got the power! God got power over everything in His creation. God can do anything. God say, "As I commandeth so it shall be." God said, "Let there be light," and there was light. He made the world in six days and rested on the seventh. God's got a wonderful power. He got power over life and death. Jesus raised Lazareth from the dead. They was getting ready to bury him and Jesus told him say, "Rise up and walk." He got up and walked and the people made great rejoicing at the power of God. I ain't worried about him chasing away a little old ghost!

There is a knock at the door. Boy Willie goes to answer it. Lymon enters carrying a coil of rope.

BOY WILLIE: Where you been? I been waiting on you and you run off somewhere.

LYMON: I ran into Grace. I stopped and bought her drink. She say she gonna go to the picture show with me.

BOY WILLIE: I ain't thinking about no Grace nothing.

LYMON: Hi, Berniece.

BOY WILLIE: Give me that rope and get up on this side of the piano.

DOAKER: Boy Willie, don't start nothing now. Leave the piano alone.

BOY WILLIE: Get that board there, Lymon. Stay out of this, Doaker.

Berniece exits up the stairs.

DOAKER: You just can't take the piano. How you gonna take the piano? Berniece ain't said nothing about selling that piano.

BOY WILLIE: She ain't got to say nothing. Come on, Lymon. We got to lift one end at a time up on the board. You got to watch so that the board don't slide up under there.

LYMON: What we gonna do with the rope?

BOY WILLIE: Let me worry about the rope. You just get up on this side over here with me.

Berniece enters from the stairs. She has her hand in her pocket where she has Crawley's gun.

AVERY: Boy Willie . . . Berniece . . . why don't you all sit down and talk this out now?

BERNIECE: Ain't nothing to talk out.

BOY WILLIE: I'm through talking to Berniece. You can talk to Berniece till you get blue in the face, and it don't make no difference. Get up on that side, Lymon. Throw that rope around there and tie it to the leg.

LYMON: Wait a minute . . . wait a minute, Boy Willie. Berniece got to say. Hey, Berniece . . . did you tell Boy Willie he could take this piano?

BERNIECE: Boy Willie ain't taking nothing out of my house but himself. Now you let him go ahead and try.

BOY WILLIE: Come on, Lymon, get up on this side with me.

Lymon stands undecided.

Come on, nigger! What you standing there for?

LYMON: Maybe Berniece is right, Boy Willie. Maybe you shouldn't sell it.

AVERY: You all ought to sit down and talk it out. See if you can come to an agreement.

DOAKER: That's what I been trying to tell them. Seem like one of them ought to respect the other one's wishes.

BERNIECE: I wish Boy Willie would go on and leave my house. That's what I wish. Now, he can respect that. Cause he's leaving here one way or another.

BOY WILLIE: What you mean one way or another? What's that supposed to mean? I ain't scared of no gun.

DOAKER: Come on, Berniece, leave him alone with that.

BOY WILLIE: I don't care what Berniece say. I'm selling my half. I can't help it if her half got to go along with it. It ain't like I'm trying to cheat her out of her half. Come on, Lymon.

LYMON: Berniece . . . I got to do this . . . Boy Willie say he gonna give you half of the money . . . say he want to get Sutter's land.

BERNIECE: Go on, Lymon. Just go on . . . I done told Boy Willie what to do.

BOY WILLIE: Here, Lymon . . . put that rope up over there.

LYMON: Boy Willie, you sure you want to do this? The way I figure it . . . I might be wrong . . . but I figure she gonna shoot you first.

BOY WILLIE: She just gonna have to shoot me.

BERNIECE: Maretha, get on out the way. Get her out the way, Doaker.

DOAKER: Go on, do what your mama told you.

BERNIECE: Put her in your room.

Maretha exits to Doaker's room. Boy Willie and Lymon try to lift the piano. The door opens and Wining Boy enters. He has been drinking.

WINING BOY: Man, these niggers around here! I stopped down there at Seefus . . . . These folks standing around talking about Patchneck Red's coming. They jumping back and getting off the sidewalk talking about Patchneck Red this and Patchneck Red that. Come to find out . . . you know who they was talking about? Old John D. from up around Tyler! Used to run around with Otis Smith. He got everybody scared of him. Calling him Patchneck Red. They don't know I whupped the nigger's head in one time.

BOY WILLIE: Just make sure that board don't slide, Lymon.

LYMON: I got this side. You watch that side.

WINING BOY: Hey, Boy Willie, what you got? I know you got a pint stuck up in your coat.

BOY WILLIE: Wining Boy, get out the way!

WINING BOY: Hey, Doaker. What you got? Gimme a drink. I want a drink.

DOAKER: It look like you had enough of whatever it was. Come talking about "What you got?" You ought to be trying to find somewhere to lay down.

WINING BOY: I ain't worried about no place to lay down. I can always find me a place to lay down in Berniece's house. Ain't that right, Berniece?

BERNIECE: Wining Boy, sit down somewhere. You been out there drinking all day. Come in here smelling like an old polecat. Sit on down there, you don't need nothing to drink.

DOAKER: You know Berniece don't like all that drinking.

WINING BOY: I ain't disrespecting Berniece. Berniece, am I disrespecting you? I'm just trying to be nice. I been with strangers all day and they treated me like family. I come in here to family and you treat me like a stranger. I don't need your whiskey. I can buy my own. I wanted your company, not your whiskey.

DOAKER: Nigger, why don't you go upstairs and lay down? You don't need nothing to drink.

WINING BOY: I ain't thinking about no laying down. Me and Boy Willie fixing to party. Ain't that right, Boy Willie? Tell him. I'm fixing to play me some piano. Watch this.

Wining Boy sits down at the piano.

BOY WILLIE: Come on, Wining Boy! Me and Lymon fixing to move the piano.

WINING BOY: Wait a minute . . . wait a minute. This a song I wrote for Cleotha. I wrote this song in memory of Cleotha.

He begins to play and sing.

Hey little woman what's the matter with you now
Had a storm last night and blowed the line all down

Tell me how long
Is I got to wait
Can I get it now
Or must I hesitate

It takes a hesitating stocking in her hesitating shoe
It takes a hesitating woman wanna sing the blues

Tell me how long
Is I got to wait
Can I kiss you now
Or must I hesitate.

BOY WILLIE: Come on, Wining Boy, get up! Get up, Wining Boy! Me and Lymon's fixing to move the piano.

WINING BOY: Naw . . . Naw . . . you ain't gonna move this piano!

BOY WILLIE: Get out the way, Wining Boy.

Wining Boy, his back to the piano, spreads his arms out over the piano.

WINING BOY: You ain't taking this piano out the house. You got to take me with it!

BOY WILLIE: Get on out the way, Wining Boy! Doaker get him!

There is a knock on the door.

BERNIECE: I got him, Doaker. Come on, Wining Boy. I done told Boy Willie he ain't taking the piano.

Berniece tries to take Wining Boy away from the piano.

WINING BOY: He got to take me with it!

Doaker goes to answer the door. Grace enters.

GRACE: Is Lymon here?

DOAKER: Lymon.

WINING BOY: He ain't taking that piano.

BERNIECE: I ain't gonna let him take it.

GRACE: I thought you was coming back. I ain't gonna sit in that truck all day.

LYMON: I told you I was coming back.

GRACE: [Sees Boy Willie.] Oh, hi, Boy Willie. Lymon told me you was gone back down South.

LYMON: I said he was going back. I didn't say he had left already.

GRACE: That's what you told me.

BERNIECE: Lymon, you got to take your company someplace else.

LYMON: Berniece, this is Grace. That there is Berniece. That's Boy Willie's sister.

GRACE: Nice to meet you.

To Lymon.

I ain't gonna sit out in that truck all day. You told me you was gonna take me to the movie.

LYMON: I told you I had something to do first. You supposed to wait on me.

BERNIECE: Lymon, just go on and leave. Take Grace or whoever with you. Just go on get out my house.

BOY WILLIE: You gonna help me move this piano first, nigger!

LYMON: [To Grace.] I got to help Boy Willie move the piano first.

Everybody but Grace suddenly senses Sutter's presence.

GRACE: I ain't waiting on you. Told me you was coming right back. Now you got to move a piano. You just like all the other men.

Grace now senses something.

Something ain't right here. I knew I shouldn't have come back up in this house.

Grace exits.

LYMON: Hey, Grace! I'll be right back, Boy Willie.

BOY WILLIE: Where you going, nigger?

LYMON: I'll be back. I got to take Grace home.

BOY WILLIE: Come on, let's move the piano first!

LYMON: I got to take Grace home. I told you I'll be back.

Lymon exits. Boy Willie exits and calls after him.

BOY WILLIE: Come on, Lymon! Hey . . . Lymon! Lymon . . . come on!

Again, the presence of Sutter is felt.

WINING BOY: Hey, Doaker, did you feel that? Hey, Berniece . . . did you get cold? Hey, Doaker . . .

DOAKER: What you calling me for?

WINING BOY: I believe that's Sutter.

DOAKER: Well, let him stay up there. As long as he don't mess with me.

BERNIECE: Avery, go on and bless the house.

DOAKER: You need to bless that piano. That's what you need to bless. It ain't done nothing but cause trouble. If you gonna bless anything go on and bless that.

WINING BOY: Hey, Doaker, if he gonna bless something let him bless everything. The kitchen . . . the upstairs. Go on and bless it all.

BOY WILLIE: Ain't no ghost in this house. He need to bless Berniece's head. That's what he need to bless.

AVERY: Seem like that piano's causing all the trouble. I can bless that. Berniece, put me some water in that bottle.

Avery takes a small bottle from his pocket and hands it to Berniece, who goes into the kitchen to get water. Avery takes a candle from his pocket and lights it. He gives it to Berniece as she gives him the water.

Hold this candle. Whatever you do make sure it don't go out.

O Holy Father we gather here this evening in the Holy Name to cast out the spirit of one James Sutter. May this vial of water be empowered with thy spirit. May each drop of it be a weapon and a shield against the presence of all evil and may it be a cleansing and blessing of this humble abode.

Just as Our Father taught us how to pray so He say, "I will prepare a table for you in the midst of mine enemies," and in His hands we place ourselves to come unto his presence. Where there is Good so shall it cause Evil to scatter to the Four Winds.

He throws water at the piano at each commandment.

AVERY: Get thee behind me, Satan! Get thee behind the face of Righteousness as we Glorify His Holy Name! Get thee behind the Hammer of Truth that breaketh down the Wall of Falsehood! Father. Father. Praise. Praise. We ask in Jesus' name and call forth the power of the Holy Spirit as it is written. . . .

He opens the Bible and reads from it.

I will sprinkle clean water upon thee and ye shall be clean.

BOY WILLIE: All this old preaching stuff. Hell, just tell him to leave.

Avery continues reading throughout Boy Willie's outburst.

AVERY: I will sprinkle clean water upon you and you shall be clean: from all your uncleanliness, and from all your idols, will I cleanse you. A new heart also will I give you, and a new spirit will I put within you: and I will take out of your flesh the heart of stone, and I will give you a heart of flesh. And I will put my spirit within you, and cause you to walk in my statutes, and ye shall keep my judgments, and do them.

Boy Willie grabs a pot of water from the stove and begins to fling it around the room.

BOY WILLIE: Hey Sutter! Sutter! Get your ass out this house! Sutter! Come on and get some of this water! You done drowned in the well, come on and get some more of this water!

Boy Willie is working himself into a frenzy as he runs around the room throwing water and calling Sutter's name. Avery continues reading.

BOY WILLIE: Come on, Sutter!

He starts up the stairs.

Come on, get some water! Come on, Sutter!

The sound of Sutter's Ghost is heard. As Boy Willie approaches the steps he is suddenly thrown back by the unseen force, which is choking him. As he struggles he frees himself, then dashes up the stairs.

BOY WILLIE: Come on, Sutter!

AVERY: [*Continuing.*] A new heart also will I give you and a new spirit will I put within you: and I will take out of your flesh the heart of stone, and I will give you a heart of flesh. And I will put my spirit within you, and cause you to walk in my statutes, and ye shall keep my judgments, and do them.

There are loud sounds heard from upstairs as Boy Willie begins to wrestle with Sutter's Ghost. It is a life-and-death struggle fraught with perils and faultless terror. Boy Willie is thrown down the stairs. Avery is stunned into silence. Boy Willie picks himself up and dashes back upstairs.

AVERY: Berniece, I can't do it.

There are more sounds heard from upstairs. Doaker and Wining Boy stare at one another in stunned disbelief. It is in this moment, from somewhere old, that Berniece realizes what she must do. She crosses to the piano. She begins to play. The song is found piece by piece. It is an old urge to song that is both a commandment and a plea. With each repetition it gains in strength. It is intended as an exorcism and a dressing for battle. A rustle of wind blowing across two continents.

BERNIECE: [*Singing.*]

I want you to help me
I want you to help me
I want you to help me
I want you to help me
I want you to help me
I want you to help me
Mama Berniece
I want you to help me
Mama Esther
I want you to help me
Papa Boy Charles
I want you to help me
Mama Ola
I want you to help me

I want you to help me
I want you to help me
I want you to help me
I want you to help me
I want you to help me
I want you to help me
I want you to help me
I want you to help me

The sound of a train approaching is heard. The noise upstairs subsides.

BOY WILLIE: Come on, Sutter! Come back, Sutter!

Berniece begins to chant:

BERNIECE:

> *Thank you.*
> *Thank you.*
> *Thank you.*

> *A calm comes over the house. Maretha enters from Doaker's room.*
> *Boy Willie enters on the stairs. He pauses a moment to watch*
> *Berniece at the piano.*

BERNIECE:

> *Thank you.*
> *Thank you.*

BOY WILLIE: Wining Boy, you ready to go back down home? Hey, Doaker, what time the train leave?

DOAKER: You still got time to make it.

> *Maretha crosses and embraces Boy Willie.*

BOY WILLIE: Hey Berniece . . . if you and Maretha don't keep playing on that piano . . . ain't no telling . . . me and Sutter both liable to be back.

> *He exits.*

BERNIECE: Thank you.

> *The lights go down to black.*

—1990

DAVID IVES ■ (b. 1950)

David Ives grew up on Chicago's South Side, the son of working-class parents, and wrote his first play at the age of nine: "But then I realized you had to have a copy of the script for each person in the play, so that was the end of it." Impressed by theatrical productions he saw in his teens, Ives entered Northwestern University and after graduation attended Yale Drama School. After several attempts to become a "serious writer," he decided to "aspire to silliness on a daily basis" and began creating the short comic plays on which his reputation rests. An evening of six one-act comedies, All in the Timing, *had a successful off-Broadway production in 1994, running over two years. In 1996 it was the most performed contemporary play in the nation, and* Sure Thing, *its signature piece, remains popular, especially with student drama groups. A second collection of one acts,* Mere Mortals, *had a successful run at Primary Stages in 1997, and a third collection,* Lives of Saints, *was produced in 1999. A number of his collections—including* All in the Timing *(1995),* Time Flies *(2001), and* Polish Joke and Other Plays *(2004)—have been published. Ives's comedic skills range from a hilarious parody of David Mamet's plays (presented at an event honoring Mamet) to his witty revision of a legendary character in the full-length* Don Juan in Chicago *(1995). His short plays, in many cases, hinge on brilliant theatrical conceits; in* Mayflies, *a boy mayfly and girl mayfly must meet, court, and consummate their relationship before their one day of adult life ends.* Sure Thing, *a piece that plays witty tricks with time, resembles a scene in the Bill Murray film* Groundhog Day, *the script of which was written some years after Ives's play. Among many other activities, Ives has written the books for concert versions of a number of classic American musicals. In an article titled "Why I Shouldn't Write Plays," Ives notes, among other reasons, "All reviews should carry a Surgeon General's warning. The good ones turn your head, the bad ones break your heart."*

Sure Thing

Characters

Betty
Bill

Scene: *A café.*

Betty, a woman in her late twenties, is reading at a café table. An empty chair is opposite her. Bill, same age, enters.

BILL: Excuse me. Is this chair taken?

BETTY: Excuse me?
BILL: Is this taken?
BETTY: Yes it is.
BILL: Oh. Sorry.
BETTY: Sure thing.

A bell rings softly.

BILL: Excuse me. Is this chair taken?
BETTY: Excuse me?
BILL: Is this taken?
BETTY: No, but I'm expecting somebody in a minute.
BILL: Oh. Thanks anyway.
BETTY: Sure thing.

A bell rings softly.

BILL: Excuse me. Is this chair taken?
BETTY: No, but I'm expecting somebody very shortly.
BILL: Would you mind if I sit here till he or she or it comes?
BETTY [*glances at her watch*]: They do seem to be pretty late. . . .
BILL: You never know who you might be turning down.
BETTY: Sorry. Nice try, though.
BILL: Sure thing.

Bell.

Is this seat taken?
BETTY: No it's not.
BILL: Would you mind if I sit here?
BETTY: Yes I would.
BILL: Oh.

Bell.

Is this chair taken?
BETTY: No it's not.
BILL: Would you mind if I sit here?
BETTY: No. Go ahead.
BILL: Thanks. [*He sits. She continues reading.*] Everyplace else seems to
be taken.
BETTY: Mm-hm.
BILL: Great place.
BETTY: Mm-hm.

BILL: What's the book?

BETTY: I just wanted to read in quiet, if you don't mind.

BILL: No. Sure thing.

Bell.

BILL: Everyplace else seems to be taken.

BETTY: Mm-hm.

BILL: Great place for reading.

BETTY: Yes, I like it.

BILL: What's the book?

BETTY: *The Sound and the Fury.*

BILL: Oh. Hemingway.

Bell.

What's the book?

BETTY: *The Sound and the Fury.*

BILL: Oh. Faulkner.

BETTY: Have you read it?

BILL: Not . . . actually. I've sure read *about* it, though. It's supposed to be great.

BETTY: It is great.

BILL: I hear it's great. [*Small pause.*] Waiter?

Bell.

What's the book?

BETTY: *The Sound and the Fury.*

BILL: Oh. Faulkner.

BETTY: Have you read it?

BILL: I'm a Mets fan, myself.

Bell.

BETTY: Have you read it?

BILL: Yeah, I read it in college.

BETTY: Where was college?

BILL: I went to Oral Roberts University.

Bell.

BETTY: Where was college?

BILL: I was lying. I never really went to college. I just like to party.

Bell.

BETTY: Where was college?

BILL: Harvard.

BETTY: Do you like Faulkner?

BILL: I love Faulkner. I spent a whole winter reading him once.

BETTY: I've just started.

BILL: I was so excited after ten pages that I went out and bought everything else he wrote. One of the greatest reading experiences of my life. I mean, all that incredible psychological understanding. Page after page of gorgeous prose. His profound grasp of the mystery of time and human existence. The smells of the earth . . . What do you think?

BETTY: I think it's pretty boring.

Bell.

BILL: What's the book?

BETTY: *The Sound and the Fury.*

BILL: Oh! Faulkner!

BETTY: Do you like Faulkner?

BILL: I love Faulkner.

BETTY: He's incredible.

BILL: I spent a whole winter reading him once.

BETTY: I was so excited after ten pages that I went out and bought everything else he wrote.

BILL: All that incredible psychological understanding.

BETTY: And the prose is so gorgeous.

BILL: And the way he's grasped the mystery of time—

BETTY: —and human existence. I can't believe I've waited this long to read him.

BILL: You never know. You might not have liked him before.

BETTY: That's true.

BILL: You might not have been ready for him. You have to hit these things at the right moment or it's no good.

BETTY: That's happened to me.

BILL: It's all in the timing. [*Small pause.*] My name's Bill, by the way.

BETTY: I'm Betty.

BILL: Hi.

BETTY: Hi. [*Small pause.*]

BILL: Yes I thought reading Faulkner was . . . a great experience.

BETTY: Yes. [*Small pause.*]

BILL: *The Sound and the Fury . . . [Another small pause.]*

BETTY: Well. Onwards and upwards. [*She goes back to her book.*]

BILL: Waiter—?

Bell.

You have to hit these things at the right moment or it's no good.

BETTY: That's happened to me.

BILL: It's all in the timing. My name's Bill, by the way.

BETTY: I'm Betty.

BILL: Hi.

BETTY: Hi.

BILL: Do you come in here a lot?

BETTY: Actually I'm just in town for two days from Pakistan.

BILL: Oh. Pakistan.

Bell.

My name's Bill, by the way.

BETTY: I'm Betty.

BILL: Hi.

BETTY: Hi.

BILL: Do you come in here a lot?

BETTY: Every once in a while. Do you?

BILL: Not so much anymore. Not as much as I used to. Before my nervous breakdown.

Bell.

Do you come in here a lot?

BETTY: Why are you asking?

BILL: Just interested.

BETTY: Are you really interested, or do you just want to pick me up?

BILL: No, I'm really interested.

BETTY: Why would you be interested in whether I come in here a lot?

BILL: I'm just . . . getting acquainted.

BETTY: Maybe you're only interested for the sake of making small talk long enough to ask me back to your place to listen to some music, or because you've just rented this great tape for your VCR, or because you've got some terrific unknown Django Reinhardt record, only all you really want to do is fuck—which you won't do very well—after which you'll go into the bathroom and pee very loudly, then pad into the kitchen and get yourself a beer from the refrigerator without asking me whether I'd like anything, and then you'll proceed to lie back down beside me and confess that you've got a girlfriend named Stephanie who's away at medical school in Belgium for a year, and that you've been involved with her—*off and on*—in what you'll call a very "intricate" relationship, for the past *seven YEARS*. None of which *interests* me, mister!

BILL: Okay.

Bell.

Do you come in here a lot?

BETTY: Every other day, I think.

BILL: I come in here quite a lot and I don't remember seeing you.

BETTY: I guess we must be on different schedules.

BILL: Missed connections.

BETTY: Yes. Different time zones.

BILL: Amazing how you can live right next door to somebody in this town and never even know it.

BETTY: I know.

BILL: City life.

BETTY: It's crazy.

BILL: We probably pass each other in the street every day. Right in front of this place, probably.

BETTY: Yep.

BILL [*looks around*]: Well the waiters here sure seem to be in some different time zone. I can't seem to locate one anywhere. . . . Waiter! [*He looks back.*] So what do you—[*He sees that she's gone back to her book.*]

BETTY: I beg pardon?

BILL: Nothing. Sorry.

Bell.

BETTY: I guess we must be on different schedules.

BILL: Missed connections.

BETTY: Yes. Different time zones.

BILL: Amazing how you can live right next door to somebody in this town and never even know it.

BETTY: I know.

BILL: City life.

BETTY: It's crazy.

BILL: You weren't waiting for somebody when I came in, were you?

BETTY: Actually I was.
BILL: Oh. Boyfriend?
BETTY: Sort of.
BILL: What's a sort-of boyfriend?
BETTY: My husband.
BILL: Ah-ha.

Bell.

You weren't waiting for somebody when I came in, were you?
BETTY: Actually I was.
BILL: Oh. Boyfriend?
BETTY: Sort of.
BILL: What's a sort-of boyfriend?
BETTY: We were meeting here to break up.
BILL: Mm-hm . . .

Bell.

What's a sort-of boyfriend?
BETTY: My lover. Here she comes right now!

Bell.

BILL: You weren't waiting for somebody when I came in, were you?
BETTY: No, just reading.
BILL: Sort of a sad occupation for a Friday night, isn't it? Reading here, all by yourself?
BETTY: Do you think so?
BILL: Well sure. I mean, what's a good-looking woman like you doing out alone on a Friday night?
BETTY: Trying to keep away from lines like that.
BILL: No, listen—

Bell.

You weren't waiting for somebody when I came in, were you?
BETTY: No, just reading.
BILL: Sort of a sad occupation for a Friday night, isn't it? Reading here all by yourself?
BETTY: I guess it is, in a way.
BILL: What's a good-looking woman like you doing out alone on a Friday night anyway? No offense, but . . .

BETTY: I'm out alone on a Friday night for the first time in a very long time.

BILL: Oh.

BETTY: You see, I just recently ended a relationship.

BILL: Oh.

BETTY: Of rather long standing.

BILL: I'm sorry. [*Small pause.*] Well listen, since reading by yourself *is* such a sad occupation for a Friday night, would you like to go elsewhere?

BETTY: No . . .

BILL: Do something else?

BETTY: No thanks.

BILL: I was headed out to the movies in a while anyway.

BETTY: I don't think so.

BILL: Big chance to let Faulkner catch his breath. All those long sentences get him pretty tired.

BETTY: Thanks anyway.

BILL: Okay.

BETTY: I appreciate the invitation.

BILL: Sure thing.

Bell.

You weren't waiting for somebody when I came in, were you?

BETTY: No, just reading.

BILL: Sort of a sad occupation for a Friday night, isn't it? Reading here all by yourself?

BETTY: I guess I was trying to think of it as existentially romantic. You know—cappuccino, great literature, rainy night . . .

BILL: That only works in Paris. We *could* hop the late plane to Paris. Get on a Concorde. Find a café . . .

BETTY: I'm a little short on plane fare tonight.

BILL: Darn it, so am I.

BETTY: To tell you the truth, I was headed to the movies after I finished this section. Would you like to come along? Since you can't locate a waiter?

BILL: That's a very nice offer, but . . .

BETTY: Uh-huh. Girlfriend?

BILL: Two, actually. One of them's pregnant, and Stephanie—

Bell.

BETTY: Girlfriend?

BILL: No, I don't have a girlfriend. Not if you mean the castrating bitch I dumped last night.

Bell.

BETTY: Girlfriend?

BILL: Sort of. Sort of.

BETTY: What's a sort-of girlfriend?

BILL: My mother.

Bell.

I just ended a relationship, actually.

BETTY: Oh.

BILL: Of rather long standing.

BETTY: I'm sorry to hear it.

BILL: This is my first night out alone in a long time. I feel a little bit at sea, to tell you the truth.

BETTY: So you didn't stop to talk because you're a Moonie, or you have some weird political affiliation—?

BILL: Nope. Straight-down-the-ticket Republican.

Bell.

Straight-down-the-ticket Democrat.

Bell.

Can I tell you something about politics?

Bell.

I like to think of myself as a citizen of the universe.

Bell.

I'm unaffiliated.

BETTY: That's a relief. So am I.

BILL: I vote my beliefs.

BETTY: Labels are not important.

BILL: Labels are not important, exactly. Take me, for example. I mean, what does it matter if I had a two-point at—

Bell.

three-point at—

Bell.

four-point at college? Or if I did come from Pittsburgh—

Bell.

Cleveland—

Bell.

Westchester County?

BETTY: Sure.

BILL: I believe that a man is what he is.

Bell.

A person is what he is.

Bell.

A person is . . . what they are.

BETTY: I think so too.

BILL: So what if I admire Trotsky?

Bell.

So what if I once had a total-body liposuction?

Bell.

So what if I don't have a penis?

Bell.

So what if I spent a year in the Peace Corps? I was acting on my convictions.

BETTY: Sure.

BILL: You just can't hang a sign on a person.

BETTY: Absolutely. I'll bet you're a Scorpio.

Many bells ring.

Listen, I was headed to the movies after I finished this section. Would you like to come along?

BILL: That sounds like fun. What's playing?

BETTY: A couple of the really early Woody Allen movies.

BILL: Oh.

BETTY: You don't like Woody Allen?

BILL: Sure. I like Woody Allen.

BETTY: But you're not crazy about Woody Allen.

BILL: Those early ones kind of get on my nerves.

BETTY: Uh-huh.

Bell.

BILL: Y'know I was headed to the—

BETTY [*simultaneously*]: I was thinking about—

BILL: I'm sorry.

BETTY: No, go ahead.

BILL: I was going to say that I was headed to the movies in a little while, and . . .

BETTY: So was I.

BILL: The Woody Allen festival?

BETTY: Just up the street.

BILL: Do you like the early ones?

BETTY: I think anybody who doesn't ought to be run off the planet.

BILL: How many times have you seen *Bananas*?

BETTY: Eight times.

BILL: Twelve. So are you still interested? [*Long pause.*]

BETTY: Do you like Entenmann's crumb cake . . . ?

BILL: Last night I went out at two in the morning to get one. Did you have an Etch-a-Sketch as a child?

BETTY: Yes! And do you like Brussels sprouts? [*Pause.*]

BILL: No, I think they're disgusting.

BETTY: They *are* disgusting!

BILL: Do you still believe in marriage in spite of current sentiments against it?

BETTY: Yes.

BILL: And children?

BETTY: Three of them.

BILL: Two girls and a boy.

BETTY: Harvard, Vassar, and Brown.

BILL: And will you love me?

BETTY: Yes.

BILL: And cherish me forever?

BETTY: Yes.

BILL: Do you still want to go to the movies?

BETTY: Sure thing.

BILL AND BETTY [*together*]: Waiter!

Blackout   —1988

Milcha Sanchez-Scott was born in Bali of Indonesian and Colombian parents. She attended school in England and moved to California in her teens. Following college at the University of San Diego, she had her first plays produced in the early 1980s. The Cuban Swimmer, first performed in 1984, displays elements of the "magic realism" practiced in fiction by Colombian Nobel prize–winner Gabriel García Márquez. Her most successful full-length play is Roosters (1987), which was made into a 1995 film starring Edward James Olmos.

The Cuban Swimmer

Characters

Margarita Suárez, *the swimmer*
Eduardo Suárez, *her father, the coach*
Simón Suárez, *her brother*
Aída Suárez, *the mother*
Abuela, *her grandmother*
Voice of Mel Munson
Voice of Mary Beth White
Voice of Radio Operator

Scene: *The Pacific Ocean between San Pedro and Catalina Island.*

Time: Summer.

Live conga drums can be used to punctuate the action of the play.

Scene I

Pacific Ocean. Midday. On the horizon, in perspective, a small boat enters upstage left, crosses to upstage right, and exits. Pause. Lower on the horizon, the same boat, in larger perspective, enters upstage right, crosses and exits upstage left. Blackout.

Scene II

Pacific Ocean. Midday. The swimmer, Margarita Suárez, is swimming. On the boat following behind her are her father, Eduardo Suárez, holding a megaphone, and Simón, her brother, sitting on top of the cabin with his shirt off, punk sunglasses on, binoculars hanging on his chest.

EDUARDO: [*Leaning forward, shouting in time to Margarita's swimming.*] *Uno, dos, uno, dos. Y uno, dos* . . . keep your shoulders parallel to the water.

SIMÓN: I'm gonna take these glasses off and look straight into the sun.

EDUARDO: [*Through megaphone.*] *Muy bien, muy bien* . . . but punch those arms in, baby.

SIMÓN: [*Looking directly at the sun through binoculars.*] Come on, come on, zap me. Show me something. [*He looks behind at the shoreline and ahead at the sea.*] Stop! Stop, Papi! Stop!

Aída Suárez and Abuela, the swimmer's mother and grand-mother, enter running from the back of the boat.

AÍDA AND ABUELA: *Qué? Qué es?*

AÍDA: *Es un* shark?

EDUARDO: Eh?

ABUELA: *Que es un* shark *dicen?*

Eduardo blows whistle. Margarita looks up at the boat.

SIMÓN: No, *Papi,* no shark, no shark. We've reached the halfway mark.

ABUELA: [*Looking into the water.*] *A dónde está?*

AÍDA: It's not in the water.

ABUELA: Oh, no? Oh, no?

AÍDA: No! *A poco* do you think they're gonna have signs in the water to say you are halfway to Santa Catalina? No. It's done very scientific. *A ver, hijo,* explain it to your grandma.

SIMÓN: Well, you see, Abuela—[*He points behind.*] There's San Pedro. [*He points ahead.*] And there's Santa Catalina. Looks halfway to me.

Abuela shakes her head and is looking back and forth, trying to make the decision, when suddenly the sound of a helicopter is heard.

ABUELA: [*Looking up.*] Virgencita de la Caridad del Cobre. *Qué es eso?*

Sound of helicopter gets closer. Margarita looks up.

MARGARITA: *Papi, Papi!*

A small commotion on the boat, with Everybody pointing at the helicopter above. Shadows of the helicopter fall on the boat. Simón looks up at it through binoculars.

Papi—*qué es?* What is it?

EDUARDO: [*Through megaphone.*] Uh . . . uh . . . uh, *un momentico . . .
mi hija*. . . . Your *papi's* got everything under control, understand?
Uh . . . you just keep stroking. And stay . . . uh . . . close to the boat.

SIMÓN: Wow, *Papi!* We're on TV, man! Holy Christ, we're all over the
fucking U.S.A.! It's Mel Munson and Mary Beth White!

AÍDA: *Por Dios!* Simón, don't swear. And put on your shirt.

*Aída fluffs her hair, puts on her sunglasses and waves to the heli-
copter. Simón leans over the side of the boat and yells to
Margarita.*

SIMÓN: Yo, Margo! You're on TV, man.

EDUARDO: Leave your sister alone. Turn on the radio.

MARGARITA: Papi! *Qué está pasando?*

ABUELA: *Que es la televisión dicen?* [*She shakes her head.*] *Porque como yo
no puedo ver nada sin mis espejuelos.*

*Abuela rummages through the boat, looking for her glasses.
Voices of Mel Munson and Mary Beth White are heard over the
boat's radio.*

MEL'S VOICE: As we take a closer look at the gallant crew of *La Havana*
. . . and there . . . yes, there she is . . . the little Cuban swimmer
from Long Beach, California, nineteen-year-old Margarita Suárez.
The unknown swimmer is our Cinderella entry . . . a bundle of
tenacity, battling her way through the choppy, murky waters of the
cold Pacific to reach the Island of Romance . . . Santa Catalina . . .
where should she be the first to arrive, two thousand dollars and a
gold cup will be waiting for her.

AÍDA: Doesn't even cover our expenses.

ABUELA: *Qué dice?*

EDUARDO: Shhhh!

MARY BETH'S VOICE: This is really a family effort, Mel, and—

MEL'S VOICE: Indeed it is. Her trainer, her coach, her mentor, is her
father, Eduardo Suárez. Not a swimmer himself, it says here, Mr.
Suárez is head usher of the Holy Name Society and the owner-
operator of Suárez Treasures of the Sea and Salvage Yard. I guess
it's one of those places—

MARY BETH'S VOICE: If I might interject a fact here, Mel, assisting in
this swim is Mrs. Suárez, who is a former Miss Cuba.

MEL'S VOICE: And a beautiful woman in her own right. Let's try and
get a closer look.

Helicopter sound gets louder. Margarita, frightened, looks up again.

MARGARITA: *Papi!*

EDUARDO: [*Through megaphone.*] *Mi hija*, don't get nervous . . . it's the press. I'm handling it.

AÍDA: I see how you're handling it.

EDUARDO: [*Through megaphone.*] Do you hear? Everything is under control. Get back into your rhythm. Keep your elbows high and kick and kick and kick and kick . . .

ABUELA [*Finds her glasses and puts them on.*]: *Ay sí, es la televisión . . .* [*She points to helicopter.*] *Qué lindo mira . . .* [*She fluffs her hair, gives a big wave.*] *Aló América! Viva mi Margarita, viva todo los Cubanos en los Estados Unidos!*

AÍDA: *Ay por Dios*, Cecilia, the man didn't come all this way in his helicopter to look at you jumping up and down, making a fool of yourself.

ABUELA: I don't care. I'm proud.

AÍDA: He can't understand you anyway.

ABUELA: *Viva . . .* [*She stops.*] Simón, *cómo se dice viva?*

SIMÓN: Hurray.

ABUELA: Hurray for *mi* Margarita *y* for all the Cubans living *en* the United States, *y un abrazo . . .* Simón, *abrazo . . .*

SIMÓN: A big hug.

ABUELA: *Sí*, a big hug to all my friends in Miami, Long Beach, Union City, except for my son Carlos, who lives in New York in sin! He lives . . . [*She crosses herself.*] in Brooklyn with a Puerto Rican woman in sin! *No decente . . .*

SIMÓN: Decent.

ABUELA: Carlos, *no decente.* This family, *decente.*

AÍDA: Cecilia, *por Dios.*

MEL'S VOICE: Look at that enthusiasm. The whole family has turned out to cheer little Margarita on to victory! I hope they won't be too disappointed.

MARY BETH'S VOICE: She seems to be making good time, Mel.

MEL'S VOICE: Yes, it takes all kinds to make a race. And it's a testimonial to the all-encompassing fairness . . . the greatness of this, the Wrigley Invitational Women's Swim to Catalina, where among all the professionals there is still room for the amateurs . . . like these, the simple people we see below us on the ragtag *La Havana*, taking their long-shot chance to victory. *Vaya con Dios!*

Helicopter sound fading as family, including Margarita, watch silently. Static as Simón turns radio off. Eduardo walks to bow of boat, looks out on the horizon.

EDUARDO: [*To himself.*] Amateurs.

AÍDA: Eduardo, that person insulted us. Did you hear, Eduardo? That he called us a simple people in a ragtag boat? Did you hear ... ?

ABUELA [*Clenching her fist at departing helicopter.*]: *Mal-Rayo los parta!*

SIMÓN: [*Same gesture.*] Asshole!

Aída follows Eduardo as he goes to side of boat and stares at Margarita.

AÍDA: This person comes in his helicopter to insult your wife, your family, your daughter ...

MARGARITA [*Pops her head out of the water.*]: *Papi?*

AÍDA: Do you hear me, Eduardo? I am not simple.

ABUELA: *Sí.*

AÍDA: I am complicated.

ABUELA: *Sí, demasiada complicada.*

AÍDA: Me and my family are not so simple.

SIMÓN: Mom, the guy's an asshole.

ABUELA [*Shaking her fist at helicopter.*]: Asshole!

AÍDA: If my daughter was simple, she would not be in that water swimming.

MARGARITA: Simple? *Papi* ... ?

AÍDA: *Ahora,* Eduardo, this is what I want you to do. When we get to Santa Catalina, I want you to call the TV station and demand an apology.

EDUARDO: *Cállete mujer! Aquí mando yo.* I will decide what is to be done.

MARGARITA: *Papi,* tell me what's going on.

EDUARDO: Do you understand what I am saying to you, Aída?

SIMÓN [*Leaning over side of boat, to Margarita.*]: Yo Margo! You know that Mel Munson guy on TV? He called you a simple amateur and said you didn't have a chance.

ABUELA [*Leaning directly behind Simón.*]: *Mi hija, insultó a la familia. Desgraciado!*

AÍDA [*Leaning in behind Abuela.*]: He called us peasants! And your father is not doing anything about it. He just knows how to yell at me.

EDUARDO [*Through megaphone.*]: Shut up! All of you! Do you want to break her concentration? Is that what you are after? Eh?

Abuela, Aída, and Simón shrink back. Eduardo paces before them.

Swimming is rhythm and concentration. You win a race *aquí.* *[Pointing to his head.]* Now . . . *[To Simón.]* you, take care of the boat, Aída *y Mama* . . . do something. Anything. Something practical.

Abuela and Aída get on knees and pray in Spanish.

Hija, give it everything, eh? . . . *por la familia. Uno* . . . *dos.* . . . You must win.

Simón goes into cabin. The prayers continue as lights change to indicate bright sunlight, later in the afternoon.

Scene III

Tableau for a couple of beats. Eduardo on bow with timer in one hand as he counts strokes per minute. Simón is in the cabin steering, wearing his sunglasses, baseball cap on backward. Abuela and Aída are at the side of the boat, heads down, hands folded, still muttering prayers in Spanish.

AÍDA AND ABUELA: *[Crossing themselves.]* En el nombre del Padre, del Hijo y del Espíritu Santo amén.

EDUARDO: *[Through megaphone.]* You're stroking seventy-two!

SIMÓN: *[Singing.]* Mama's stroking, Mama's stroking seventy-two. . . .

EDUARDO: *[Through megaphone.]* You comfortable with it?

SIMÓN: *[Singing.]* Seventy-two, seventy-two, seventy-two for you.

AÍDA: *[Looking at the heavens.]* Ay, Eduardo, *ven acá,* we should be grateful that *Nuestro Señor* gave us such a beautiful day.

ABUELA: *[Crosses herself.]* Sí, gracias a Dios.

EDUARDO: She's stroking seventy-two, with no problem *[He throws a kiss to the sky.]* It's a beautiful day to win.

AÍDA: *Qué hermoso!* So clear and bright. Not a cloud in the sky. *Mira! Mira!* Even rainbows on the water . . . a sign from God.

SIMÓN: *[Singing.]* Rainbows on the water . . . you in my arms . . .

ABUELA AND EDUARDO: *[Looking the wrong way.]* Dónde?

AÍDA: *[Pointing toward Margarita.]* There, dancing in front of margarita, leading her on . . .

EDUARDO: Rainbows on . . . *Ay coño!* It's an oil slick! You . . . you . . . *[To Simón.]* Stop the boat. *[Runs to bow, yelling.]* Margarita! Margarita!

On the next stroke, Margarita comes up all covered in black oil.

MARGARITA: *Papi! Papi . . . !*

Everybody goes to the side and stares at Margarita, who stares back. Eduardo freezes.

AÍDA: *Apúrate,* Eduardo, move . . . what's wrong with you . . . *no me oíste,* get my daughter out of the water.

EDUARDO: [*Softly.*] We can't touch her. If we touch her, she's disqualified.

AÍDA: But I'm her mother.

EDUARDO: Not even by her own mother. Especially by her own mother. . . . You always want the rules to be different for you, you always want to be the exception. [*To Simón.*] And you . . . you didn't see it, eh? You were playing again?

SIMÓN: *Papi,* I was watching . . .

AÍDA: [*Interrupting.*] *Pues,* do something Eduardo. You are the big coach, the monitor.

SIMÓN: Mentor! Mentor!

EDUARDO: How can a person think around you? [*He walks off to bow, puts head in hands.*]

ABUELA: [*Looking over side.*] *Mira como todos los* little birds are dead. [*She crosses herself.*]

AÍDA: Their little wings are glued to their sides.

SIMÓN: Christ, this is like the La Brea tar pits.

AÍDA: They can't move their little wings.

ABUELA: *Esa niña tiene que moverse.*

SIMÓN: Yeah, Margo, you gotta move, man.

Abuela and Simón gesture for Margarita to move. Aída gestures for her to swim.

ABUELA: *Anda niña, muévete.*

AÍDA: Swim, *hija,* swim or the *aceite* will stick to your wings.

MARGARITA: *Papi?*

ABUELA: [*Taking megaphone.*] Your *papi* say "move it!"

Margarita with difficulty starts moving.

ABUELA, AÍDA AND SIMÓN [*Laboriously counting.*]: *Uno, dos . . . uno, dos . . . anda . . . uno, dos.*

EDUARDO: [*Running to take megaphone from Abuela.*] *Uno, dos . . .*

Simón races into cabin and starts the engine. Abuela, Aída and Eduardo count together.

SIMÓN: [*Looking ahead.*] *Papi,* it's over there!

EDUARDO: Eh?

SIMÓN: [Pointing ahead and to the right.] It's getting clearer over there.

EDUARDO: [Through megaphone.] Now pay attention to me. Go to the right.

Simón, Abuela, Aída and Eduardo all lean over side. They point ahead and to the right, except Abuela, who points to the left.

FAMILY: [Shouting together.] *Para yá! Para yá!*

Lights go down on boat. A special light on Margarita, swimming through the oil, and on Abuela, watching her.

ABUELA: *Sangre de mi sangre,* you will be another to save us. En Bolondron, where your great-grandmother Luz Suárez was born, they say one day it rained blood. All the people, they run into their houses. They cry, they pray, *pero* your great-grandmother Luz she had cojones like a man. She run outside. She look straight at the sky. She shake her fist. And she say to the evil one, "Mira . . . [Beating her chest.] *coño, Diablo, aquí estoy si me quieres.*" And she open her mouth, and she drunk the blood.

Blackout.

Scene IV

Lights up on boat. Aída and Eduardo are on deck watching Margarita swim. We hear the gentle, rhythmic lap, lap, lap of the water, then the sound of inhaling and exhaling as Margarita's breathing becomes louder. Then Margarita's heartbeat is heard, with the lapping of the water and the breathing under it. These sounds continue beneath the dialogue to the end of the scene.

AÍDA: *Dios mío.* Look how she moves through the water. . . .

EDUARDO: You see, it's very simple. It is a matter of concentration.

AÍDA: The first time I put her in water she came to life, she grew before my eyes. She moved, she smiled, she loved it more than me. She didn't want my breast any longer. She wanted the water.

EDUARDO: And of course, the rhythm. The rhythm takes away the pain and helps the concentration.

Pause. Aída and Eduardo watch Margarita.

AÍDA: Is that my child or a seal. . . .

EDUARDO: Ah, a seal, the reason for that is that she's keeping her arms very close to her body. She cups her hands, and then she reaches and digs, reaches and digs.

AÍDA: To think that a daughter of mine. . . .

EDUARDO: It's the training, the hours in the water. I used to tie weights around her little wrists and ankles.

AÍDA: A spirit, an ocean spirit, must have entered my body when I was carrying her.

EDUARDO: [*To Margarita.*] Your stroke is slowing down.

Pause. We hear Margarita's heartbeat with the breathing under, faster now.

AÍDA: Eduardo, that night, the night on the boat . . .

EDUARDO: Ah, the night on the boat again . . . the moon was . . .

AÍDA: The moon was full. We were coming to America. . . . *Qué romantico.*

Heartbeat and breathing continue.

EDUARDO: We were cold, afraid, with no money, and on top of everything, you were hysterical, yelling at me, tearing at me with your nails. [*Opens his shirt, points to the base of his neck.*] Look, I still bear the scars . . . telling me that I didn't know what I was doing . . . saying that we were going to die. . . .

AÍDA: You took me, you stole me from my home . . . you didn't give me a chance to prepare. You just said we have to go now, now! Now, you said. You didn't let me take anything. I left everything behind. . . . I left everything behind.

EDUARDO: Saying that I wasn't good enough, that your father didn't raise you so that I could drown you in the sea.

AÍDA: You didn't let me say even a good-bye. You took me, you stole me, you tore me from my home.

EDUARDO: I took you so we could be married.

AÍDA: That was in Miami. But that night on the boat, Eduardo. . . . We were not married, that night on the boat.

EDUARDO: *No pasó nada!* Once and for all get it out of your head, it was cold, you hated me, and we were afraid. . . .

AÍDA: *Mentiroso!*

EDUARDO: A man can't do it when he is afraid.

AÍDA: Liar! You did it very well.

EDUARDO: I did?

AÍDA: Sí. Gentle. You were so gentle and then strong . . . my passion for you so deep. Standing next to you . . . I would ache . . . looking at your hands I would forget to breathe, you were irresistible.

EDUARDO: I was?

AÍDA: You took me into your arms, you touched my face with your fingertips . . . you kissed my eyes . . . *la esquina de la boca y* . . .

EDUARDO: *Sí, Sí,* and then . . .

AÍDA: I look at your face on top of mine, and I see the lights of Havana in your eyes. That's when you seduced me.

EDUARDO: Shhh, they're gonna hear you.

Lights go down. Special on Aída.

AÍDA: That was the night. A woman doesn't forget those things . . . and later that night was the dream . . . the dream of a big country with fields of fertile land and big, giant things growing. And there by a green, slimy pond I found a giant pea pod and when I opened it, it was full of little, tiny baby frogs.

Aída crosses herself as she watches Margarita. We hear louder breathing and heartbeat.

MARGARITA: Santa Teresa. Little Flower of God, pray for me. San Martín de Porres, pray for me. Santa Rosa de Lima, *Virgencita de la Caridad del Cobre,* pray for me. . . . Mother pray for me.

Scene V

Loud howling of wind is heard, as lights change to indicate unstable weather, fog, and mist. Family on deck, braced and huddled against the wind. Simón is at the helm.

AÍDA: *Ay Dios mío, qué viento.*

EDUARDO: [*Through megaphone.*] Don't drift out . . . that wind is pushing you out. [*To Simón.*] You! Slow down. Can't you see your sister is drifting out?

SIMÓN: It's the wind, *Papi.*

AÍDA: Baby, don't go so far. . . .

ABUELA: [*To heaven.*] *Ay Gran Poder de Dios, quita este maldito viento.*

SIMÓN: Margo! Margo! Stay close to the boat.

EDUARDO: Dig in. Dig in hard . . . .Reach down from your guts and dig in.

ABUELA: [To heaven.] Ay Virgen de la Caridad del Cobre, por lo más tú
    quieres a pararla.
AÍDA: [Putting her hand out, reaching for Margarita.] Baby, don't go far.

    Abuela crosses herself. Action freezes. Lights get dimmer, special on
    Margarita. She keeps swimming, stops, starts again, stops, then,
    finally exhausted, stops altogether. The boat stops moving.

EDUARDO: What's going on here? Why are we stopping?
SIMÓN: Papi, she's not moving! Yo Margo!

    The family all run to the side.

EDUARDO: Hija! . . . Hijita! You're tired, eh?
AÍDA: Por supuesto she's tired. I like to see you get in the water, waving
    your arms and legs from San Pedro to Santa Catalina. A person
    isn't a machine, a person has to rest.
SIMÓN: Yo, Mama! Cool out, it ain't fucking brain surgery.
EDUARDO: [To Simón.] Shut up, you. [Louder to Margarita.] I guess your
    mother's right for once, huh? . . . I guess you had to stop, eh? . . .
    Give your brother, the idiot . . . a chance to catch up with you.
SIMÓN: [Clowning like Mortimer Snerd.] Dum dee dum dee dum ooops,
    ah shucks . . .
EDUARDO: I don't think he's Cuban.
SIMÓN: [Like Ricky Ricardo.] Oye, Lucy! I'm home! Ba ba lu!
EDUARDO: [Joins in clowning, grabbing Simón in a headlock.] What am I
    gonna do with this idiot, eh? I don't understand this idiot. He's not
    like us, Margarita. [Laughing.] You think if we put him into your
    bathing suit with a cap on his head . . . [He laughs hysterically.] You
    think anyone would know . . . huh? Do you think anyone would
    know? [Laughs.]
SIMÓN: [Vamping.] Ay, mi amor. Anybody looking for tits would know.

    Eduardo slaps Simón across the face, knocking him down. Aída
    runs to Simón's aid. Abuela holds Eduardo back.

MARGARITA: Mía culpa! Mía culpa!
ABUELA: Qué dices hija?
MARGARITA: Papi, it's my fault, it's all my fault. . . . I'm so cold, I can't
    move. . . . I put my face in the water . . . and I hear them whisper-
    ing . . . laughing at me. . . .
AÍDA: Who is laughing at you?

MARGARITA: The fish are all biting me . . . they hate me . . . they whisper about me. She can't swim, they say. She can't glide. She has no grace. . . . Yellowtails, bonita, tuna, man-o'-war, snub-nose sharks, *los baracudas* . . . they all hate me . . . only the dolphins care . . . and sometimes I hear the whales crying . . . she is lost, she is dead. I'm so numb, I can't feel. *Papi! Papi!* Am I dead?

EDUARDO: *Vamos,* baby, punch those arms in. Come on . . . do you hear me?

MARGARITA: *Papi . . . Papi . . .* forgive me. . . .

All is silent on the boat. Eduardo drops his megaphone, his head bent down in dejection. Abuela, Aída, Simón, all leaning over the side of the boat. Simón slowly walks away.

AÍDA: *Mi hija, qué tienes?*

SIMÓN: Oh, Christ, don't make her say it. Please don't make her say it.

ABUELA: Say what? *Qué cosa?*

SIMÓN: She wants to quit, can't you see she's had enough?

ABUELA: *Mira, para eso. Esta niña* is turning blue.

AÍDA: *Oyeme, mi hija.* Do you want to come out of the water?

MARGARITA: *Papi?*

SIMÓN: [*To Eduardo.*] She won't come out until *you* tell her.

AÍDA: Eduardo . . . answer your daughter.

EDUARDO: *Le dije* to concentrate . . . concentrate on your rhythm. Then the rhythm would carry her . . . ay, it's a beautiful thing, Aída. It's like yoga, like meditation, the mind over matter . . . the mind controlling the body . . . that's how the great things in the world have been done. I wish you . . . I wish my wife could understand.

MARGARITA: *Papi?*

SIMÓN: [*To Margarita.*] Forget him.

AÍDA: [*Imploring.*] Eduardo, *por favor.*

EDUARDO: [*Walking in circles.*] Why didn't you let her concentrate? Don't you understand, the concentration, the rhythm is everything. But no, you wouldn't listen. [*Screaming to the ocean.*] Goddamn Cubans, why, God, why do you make us go everywhere with our families? [*He goes to back of boat.*]

AÍDA: [*Opening her arms.*] Mi hija, ven, come to Mami. [*Rocking.*] Your mami knows.

Abuela has taken the training bottle, puts it in a net. She and Simón lower it to Margarita.

SIMÓN: Take this. Drink it. [*As Margarita drinks, Abuela crosses herself.*]
ABUELA: *Sangre de mi sangre.*

Music comes up softly. Margarita drinks, gives the bottle back, stretches out her arms, as if on a cross. Floats on her back. She begins a graceful backstroke. Lights fade on boat as special lights come up on Margarita. She stops. Slowly turns over and starts to swim, gradually picking up speed. Suddenly as if in pain she stops, tries again, then stops in pain again. She becomes disoriented and falls to the bottom of the sea. Special on Margarita at the bottom of the sea.

MARGARITA: *Ya no puedo* . . . I can't. . . . A person isn't a machine . . . *es mi culpa* . . . Father forgive me . . . *Papi! Papi!* One, two. *Uno, dos.* [*Pause.*] *Papi! A dónde estás?* [*Pause.*] One, two, one, two. *Papi! Ay, Papi!* Where are you . . . ? Don't leave me. . . . Why don't you answer me? [*Pause. She starts to swim, slowly.*] *Uno, dos, uno, dos.* Dig in, dig in. [*Stops swimming.*] *Por favor, Papi!* [*Starts to swim again.*] One, two, one, two. Kick from your hip, kick from your hip. [*Stops swimming. Starts to cry.*] Oh God, please. . . . [*Pause.*] Hail Mary, full of grace . . . dig in, dig in . . . the Lord is with thee. . . . [*She swims to the rhythm of her Hail Mary.*] Hail Mary, full of grace . . . dig in, dig in . . . the Lord is with thee . . . dig in, dig in. . . . Blessed art thou among women. . . . *Mami*, it hurts. You let go of my hand. I'm lost. . . . And blessed is the fruit of thy womb, now and at the hour of our death. Amen. I don't want to die, I don't want to die.

Margarita is still swimming. Blackout. She is gone.

Scene VI

Lights up on boat, we hear radio static. There is a heavy mist. On deck we see only black outline of Abuela with shawl over her head. We hear the voices of Eduardo, Aída, and Radio Operator.

EDUARDO'S VOICE: *La Havana!* Coming from San Pedro. Over.
RADIO OPERATOR'S VOICE: Right, DT6-6, you say you've lost a swimmer.
AÍDA'S VOICE: Our child, our only daughter . . . listen to me. Her name is Margarita Inez Suárez, she is wearing a black one-piece bathing suit cut high in the legs with a white racing stripe down the sides, a white bathing cap with goggles and her whole body covered with a . . . with a . . .

EDUARDO'S VOICE: With lanolin and paraffin.

AÍDA'S VOICE: *Sí . . . con lanolin and paraffin.*

More radio static. Special on Simón, on the edge of the boat.

SIMÓN: Margo! Yo Margo! [*Pause.*] Man don't do this. [*Pause.*] Come on. . . . Come on. . . . [*Pause.*] God, why does everything have to be so hard? [*Pause.*] Stupid. You know you're not supposed to die for this. Stupid. It's his dream and he can't even swim. [*Pause.*] Punch those arms in. Come home. Come home. I'm your little brother. Don't forget what Mama said. You're not supposed to leave me behind. *Vamos,* Margarita, take your little brother, hold his hand tight when you cross the street. He's so little. [*Pause.*] Oh Christ, give us a sign. . . . I know! I know! Margo, I'll send you a message . . . like mental telepathy. I'll hold my breath, close my eyes, and I'll bring you home. [*He takes a deep breath; a few beats.*] This time I'll beep . . . I'll send out sonar signals like a dolphin. [*He imitates dolphin sounds.*]

The sound of real dolphins takes over from Simón, then fades into sound of Abuela saying the Hail Mary in Spanish, as full lights come up slowly.

Scene VII

Eduardo coming out of cabin, sobbing, Aída holding him. Simón anxiously scanning the horizon. Abuela looking calmly ahead.

EDUARDO: *Es mi culpa, sí, es mi culpa.* [*He hits his chest.*]

AÍDA: *Ya, ya viejo.* . . . it was my sin . . . I left my home.

EDUARDO: Forgive me, forgive me. I've lost our daughter, our sister, our granddaughter, *mi carne, mi sangre, mis ilusiones.* [*To heaven.*] *Dios mío,* take me . . . take me, I say . . . Goddammit, take me!

SIMÓN: I'm going in.

AÍDA AND EDUARDO: No!

EDUARDO [*Grabbing and holding Simón, speaking to heaven*]: God, take me, not my children. They are my dreams, my illusions . . . and not this one, this one is my mystery . . . he has my secret dreams. In him are the parts of me I cannot see.

Eduardo embraces Simón. Radio static becomes louder.

AÍDA: I . . . I think I see her.

SIMÓN: No, it's just a seal.

ABUELA [*Looking out with binoculars.*]: *Mi nietacita, dónde estás?* [*She feels her heart.*] I don't feel the knife in my heart . . . my little fish is not lost.

Radio crackles with static. As lights dim on boat, Voices of Mel and Mary Beth are heard over the radio.

MEL'S VOICE: Tragedy has marred the face of the Wrigley Invitational Women's Race to Catalina. The Cuban swimmer, little Margarita Suárez, has reportedly been lost at sea. Coast Guard and divers are looking for her as we speak. Yet in spite of this tragedy the race must go on because . . .

MARY BETH'S VOICE: [*Interrupting loudly.*] Mel!

MEL'S VOICE: [*Startled.*] What!

MARY BETH'S VOICE: Ah . . . excuse me, Mel . . . we have a winner. We've just received word from Catalina that one of the swimmers is just fifty yards from the breakers . . . it's, oh, it's . . . Margarita Suárez!

Special on family in cabin listening to radio.

MEL'S VOICE: What? I thought she died!

Special on Margarita, taking off bathing cap, trophy in hand, walking on the water.

MARY BETH'S VOICE: Ahh . . . unless . . . unless this is a tragic . . . No . . . there she is, Mel. Margarita Suárez! The only one in the race wearing a black bathing suit cut high in the legs with a racing stripe down the side.

Family cheering, embracing.

SIMÓN: [*Screaming.*]Way to go, Margo!

MEL'S VOICE: This is indeed a miracle! It's a resurrection! Margarita Suárez, with a flotilla of boats to meet her, is now walking on the waters, through the breakers . . . onto the beach, with crowds of people cheering her on. What a jubilation! This is a miracle!

Sound of crowds cheering. Lights and cheering sounds fade.

Blackout.

—1984

A native Parisian, Reza combines in her ethnic background Hungarian, Iranian, and Jewish ancestry. She began her career as an actor but turned to writing in the late 1980s. Art won a Tony Award for best play in 1998. The God of Carnage (Le Dieu du Carnage) was first performed in Zurich. The London production, starring Ralph Fiennes and Janet McTeer, won the Laurence Olivier Award for best new comedy, and the New York production, starring James Gandolfini and Marcia Gay Harden, ran for over a year on Broadway, winning the 2009 Tony for best play. Reza has also published six novels, including Dawn Evening or Night (L 'Aube le Soir ou la Nuit), *which drew on her experience following the political campaigns of Nicolas Sarkozy.*

The God of Carnage

Translated by Christopher Hampton

Characters

Véronique Vallon
Michel Vallon
Annette Reille
Alain Reille
All are in their forties

A living room. No realism. Nothing superfluous.

    The Vallons and the Reilles, sitting down, facing one another. We need to sense right away that the place belongs to the Vallons and that the two couples have just met.

    In the centre, a coffee table, covered with art books. Two big bunches of tulips in vases.

    The prevailing mood is serious, friendly and tolerant.

VÉRONIQUE: So, this is our statement—you'll be doing your own, of course . . . 'At 5.30 p.m. on the 3rd November, in Aspirant Dunant Gardens, following a verbal altercation, Ferdinand Reille, eleven, armed with a stick, struck our son, Bruno Vallon, in the face. This action resulted in, apart from a swelling of the upper lip, the breaking of two incisors, including injury to the nerve in the right incisor.'

ALAIN: Armed?

VÉRONIQUE: Armed? You don't like 'armed'—what shall we say, Michel, furnished, equipped, furnished with a stick, is that all right?

ALAIN: Furnished, yes.

MICHEL: 'Furnished with a stick'.

VÉRONIQUE: (*making the correction*) Furnished. The irony is, we've always regarded Aspirant Dunant Gardens as a haven of security, unlike the Montsouris Park.

MICHEL: She's right. We've always said the Montsouris Park no, Aspirant Dunant Gardens yes.

VÉRONIQUE: Absolutely. Anyway, thank you for coming. There's nothing to be gained from getting stuck down some emotional cul-de-sac.

ANNETTE: We should be thanking you. We should.

VÉRONIQUE: I don't see that any thanks are necessary. Fortunately, there is still such a thing as the art of co-existence, is there not?

ALAIN: Which the children don't appear to have mastered. At least, not ours!

ANNETTE: Yes, not ours! . . . What's going to happen to the tooth with the affected nerve? . . .

VÉRONIQUE: We don't know yet. They're being cautious about the prognosis. Apparently the nerve hasn't been totally exposed.

MICHEL: Only a bit of it's been exposed.

VÉRONIQUE: Yes. Some of it's been exposed and some of it's still covered. That's why they've decided not to kill the nerve just yet.

MICHEL: They're trying to give the tooth a chance.

VÉRONIQUE: Obviously it would be best to avoid endodontic surgery.

ANNETTE: Well, yes . . .

VÉRONIQUE: So there'll be an interim period while they give the nerve a chance to recover.

MICHEL: In the meantime, they'll be giving him ceramic crowns.

VÉRONIQUE: Whatever happens, you can't have an implant before you're eighteen.

MICHEL: No.

VÉRONIQUE: Permanent implants can't be fitted until you finish growing.

ANNETTE: Of course. I hope . . . I do hope it all works out.

VÉRONIQUE: Let's hope so.

Slight hiatus.

ANNETTE: Those tulips are gorgeous.

VÉRONIQUE: It's that little florist's in the Mouton-Duvernet Market. You know, the one right up the top.

ANNETTE: Oh, yes.

VÉRONIQUE: They come every morning direct from Holland, ten euros for a bunch of fifty.

ANNETTE: Oh, really!

VÉRONIQUE: You know, the one right up the top.

ANNETTE: Yes, yes.

VÉRONIQUE: You know he didn't want to identify Ferdinand.

MICHEL: No, he didn't.

VÉRONIQUE: Impressive sight, that child, face bashed in, teeth missing, still refusing to talk.

ANNETTE: I can imagine.

MICHEL: He also didn't want to identify him for fear of looking like a sneak in front of his friends; we have to be honest, Véronique, it was nothing more than bravado.

VÉRONIQUE: Of course, but bravado is a kind of courage, isn't it?

ANNETTE: That's right . . . So how . . . ? What I mean is, how did you find out Ferdinand's name? . . .

VÉRONIQUE: Well, we explained to Bruno he wasn't helping this child by shielding him.

MICHEL: We said to him if this child thinks he can go on hitting people with impunity, why should he stop?

VÉRONIQUE: We said to him, if we were this boy's parents, we would definitely want to be told.

ANNETTE: Absolutely.

ALAIN: Yes . . .

His mobile vibrates.

Excuse me . . .

He moves away from the group; as he talks, he pulls a newspaper out of his pocket.

. . . Yes, Maurice, thanks for calling back. Right, in today's *Le Monde*, let me read it to you . . . 'According to a paper published in the *Lancet* and taken up yesterday in the *FT*, two Australian researchers have revealed the neurological side-effects of Antril, a hypertensive beta-blocker, manufactured at the Verenz-Pharma laboratories. These side-effects range from hearing loss to ataxia . . .' So who the hell is your media watchdog? . . . Yes, it's very bloody inconvenient . . . No, what's most inconvenient about it as far as I'm concerned is the AGM's in two weeks. Do you have an insurance contingency to cover litigation? . . . OK . . . Oh, and Maurice, Maurice, ask your DOC to find out if this story shows up anywhere else . . . Call me back.

He hangs up.

. . . Excuse me.

MICHEL: So you're . . .

ALAIN: A lawyer.

ANNETTE: What about you?

MICHEL: Me, I have a wholesale company, household goods, and Véronique's a writer and works part-time in an art-history bookshop.

ANNETTE: A writer?

VÉRONIQUE: I contributed to a collection on the civilisation of Sheba, based on the excavations that were restarted at the end of the Ethiopian–Eritrean war. And I have a book coming out in January on the Darfur tragedy.

ANNETTE: So you specialise in Africa.

VÉRONIQUE: I'm very interested in that part of the world.

ANNETTE: Do you have any other children?

VÉRONIQUE: Bruno has a nine-year-old sister, Camille. Who's furious with her father because last night her father got rid of the hamster.

ANNETTE: You got rid of the hamster?

MICHEL: Yes. That hamster made the most appalling racket all night. Then it spent the whole day fast asleep. Bruno was in a very bad way, he was driven crazy by the noise that hamster made. As for me, to tell you the truth, I've been wanting to get rid of it for ages, so I said to myself, right, that's it. I took it and put it out in the street. I thought they loved drains and gutters and so on, but not a bit of it, it just sat there paralysed on the pavement. Well, they're not domestic animals, they're not wild animals, I don't know where their natural habitat is. Dump them in the woods, they're probably just as unhappy. I don't know where you're meant to put them.

ANNETTE: You left it outside?

VÉRONIQUE: He left it there and tried to convince Camille it had run away. But she wasn't having it.

ALAIN: And had the hamster vanished this morning?

MICHEL: Vanished.

VÉRONIQUE: And you, what field are you in?

AMIETTE I'm in wealth-management.

VÉRONIQUE: Is it at all possible—forgive me for putting the question so bluntly—that Ferdinand might apologise to Bruno?

ALAIN: It'd be good if they talked.

ANNETTE: He has to apologise, Alain. He has to tell him he's sorry.

ALAIN: Yes, yes. Of course.

VÉRONIQUE: But is he sorry?

ALAIN: He realises what he's done. He just doesn't understand the implications. He's eleven.

VÉRONIQUE: If you're eleven, you're not a baby any more.

MICHEL: You're not an adult either! We haven't offered you anything —coffee, tea, is there any of that *clafoutis*° left, Ronnie? It's an extraordinary *clafoutis!*

ALAIN: I wouldn't mind an espresso.

ANNETTE: Just some water.

MICHEL: (*to Véronique, on her way out*) Espresso for me too, darling, and bring the *clafoutis* anyway. (*After a hiatus.*) What I always say is, we're a lump of potter's clay and it's up to us to fashion something out of it. Perhaps it won't take shape till the very end. Who knows?

ANNETTE: Mm.

MICHEL: You have to taste the *clafoutis*. Good *clafoutis* is an endangered species.

ANNETTE: You're right.

ALAIN: What is it you sell?

MICHEL: Domestic hardware. Locks, doorknobs, soldering irons, all sorts of household goods, saucepans, frying pans . . .

ALAIN: Money in that, is there?

MICHEL: Well, you know, it's never exactly been a bonanza, it was pretty hard when we started. But provided I'm out there every day pushing my product, it rubs along. At least it's not seasonal, like textiles. Although we do sell a lot of *foie gras* pots in the run-up to Christmas!

ALAIN: I'm sure . . .

ANNETTE: When you saw the hamster sitting there, paralysed, why didn't you bring it back home?

MICHEL: Because I couldn't pick it up.

ANNETTE: You put it on the pavement.

°**clafoutis** a tart with fresh fruit

MICHEL: I took it out in its cage and sort of tipped it out. I just can't touch rodents.

Véronique comes back with a tray. Drinks and the clafoutis.

VÉRONIQUE: I don't know who put the *clafoutis* in the fridge. Monica puts everything in the fridge, she won't be told. What's Ferdinand said to you? Sugar?

ALAIN: No, thanks. What's in the *clafoutis*?

VÉRONIQUE: Apples and pears.

ANNETTE: Apples and pears?

VÉRONIQUE: My own little recipe.

She cuts the clafoutis *and distributes slices.*

It's going to be too cold, shame.

ANNETTE: Apples and pears, this is a first.

VÉRONIQUE: Apples and pears, it's pretty textbook, but there's a trick to it.

ANNETTE: There is?

VÉRONIQUE: Pears need to be cut thicker than apples. Because pears cook faster than apples.

ANNETTE: Ah, of course.

MICHEL: But she's not telling you the real secret.

VÉRONIQUE: Let them try it.

ALAIN: Very good. It's very good.

ANNETTE: Tasty.

VÉRONIQUE: . . . Gingerbread crumbs!

ANNETTE: Brilliant!

VÉRONIQUE: It's a version of the way they make *clafoutis* in Picardy. To be quite honest, I got it from his mother.

ALAIN: Gingerbread, delicious . . . Well, at least all this has given us a new recipe.

VÉRONIQUE: I'd have preferred it if it hadn't cost my son two teeth.

ALAIN: Of course, that's what I meant.

ANNETTE: Strange way of expressing it.

ALAIN: Not at all, I . . .

His mobile vibrates, he looks at the screen.

I have to take this . . . Yes, Maurice . . . No, no, don't ask for right of reply, you'll only feed the controversy . . . Are you insured? . . . Mm, mm . . . What are these symptoms, what is ataxia? . . . What about on a standard dose? . . . How long have you known about this? . . . And all that time you never recalled it? . . . What's the turnover? . . . Ah, yes. I see . . . Right.

He hangs up and immediately dials another number, scoffing clafoutis *all the while.*

ANNETTE: Alain, do you mind joining us?

ALAIN: Yes, yes, I'm coming . . . *(To the mobile.)* Serge? . . . They've known about the risks for two years . . . An internal report, but it didn't formally identify any undesirable side-effects . . . No, they took no precautions, they didn't insure, not a word about it in the annual report . . . Impaired motor skills, stability problems, in short you look permanently pissed . . . *(He laughs along with his colleague.)* . . . Turnover, a hundred and fifty million dollars . . . Blanket denial . . . Idiot wanted to demand a right of reply. We certainly don't want a right of reply—on the other hand if the story spreads we could put out a press release, say it's disinformation put about two weeks before the AGM. . . . He's going to call me back . . . OK.

He hangs up.

Actually I hardly had any lunch.

MICHEL: Help yourself, help yourself.

ALAIN: Thanks. I'm incorrigible. What were we saying?

VÉRONIQUE: That it would have been nicer to meet under different circumstances.

ALAIN: Oh, yes, right.

So the *clafoutis*, it's your mother's?

MICHEL: The recipe is my mother's, but Ronnie made this one.

VÉRONIQUE: Your mother doesn't mix pears and apples!

MICHEL: NO.

VÉRONIQUE: Poor thing has to have an operation.

ANNETTE: Really? What for?

VÉRONIQUE: Her knee.

MICHEL: They're going to insert a rotatable prosthesis made of metal and polyethylene. She's wondering what's going to be left of it when she's cremated.

VÉRONIQUE: Don't be horrible.

MICHEL: She refuses to be buried next to my father. She wants to be cremated and put next to her mother who's all on her own down south. Two urns, looking out to sea, trying to get a word in edgeways. Ha, ha! . . .

Smiles all round. Hiatus.

ANNETTE: We're very touched by your generosity. We appreciate the fact you're trying to calm the situation down rather than exacerbate it.

VÉRONIQUE: Frankly, it's the least we can do.

MICHEL: Yes!

ANNETTE: Not at all. How many parents standing up for their children become infantile themselves? If Bruno had broken two of Ferdinand's teeth, I'm afraid Alain and I would have been a good deal more thin-skinned about it. I'm not certain we'd have been so broad-minded.

MICHEL: Course you would!

ALAIN: She's right. By no means certain.

MICHEL: Oh, yes. Because we all know very well it might easily have been the other way round.

Hiatus,

VÉRONIQUE: So what does Ferdinand have to say about it? How does he view the situation?

ANNETTE: He's not saying much. I think he's still slightly in shock.

VÉRONIQUE: He understands that he's disfigured his playmate?

ALAIN: No. No, he does not understand that he's disfigured his playmate.

ANNETTE: Why are you saying that? Ferdinand understands very well!

ALAIN: He understands he's behaved like a thug, he does not understand that he's disfigured his playmate.

VÉRONIQUE: You don't care for the word, but the word is unfortunately accurate.

ALAIN: My son has not disfigured your son.

VÉRONIQUE: Your son has disfigured my son. Come back at five and have a look at his mouth and teeth.

MICHEL: Temporarily disfigured.

ALAIN: The swelling on his lip will go down, and as for his teeth, take him to the best dentist—I'm prepared to chip in . . .

MICHEL: That's what the insurance is for. What we'd like is for the boys to make up so that this sort of thing never happens again.

ANNETTE: Let's arrange a meeting.

MICHEL: Yes. That's the answer.

VÉRONIQUE: Should we be there?

ALAIN: They don't need to be coached. Just let them do it man to man.

ANNETTE: Man to man? Alain, don't be ridiculous. Having said that, we don't necessarily have to be there. It'd probably be better if we weren't, wouldn't it?

VÉRONIQUE: The question isn't whether we should be there or not. The question is, do they want to talk to one another, do they want to have a reckoning?

MICHEL: Bruno wants to.

VÉRONIQUE: What about Ferdinand?

ANNETTE: It's no use asking his opinion.

VÉRONIQUE: But it has to come from him.

ANNETTE: Ferdinand has behaved like a hooligan, we're not interested in what mood he's in.

VÉRONIQUE: If Ferdinand is forced to meet Bruno in a punitive context, I can't see the results would be very positive.

ALAIN: Madame, our son is a savage. To hope for any kind of spontaneous repentance would be fanciful. Right, I'm sorry, I have to get back to the office. You stay, Annette, you'll tell me what you've decided, I'm no use whichever way you cut it. Women always think you need a man, you need a father, as if .they'd be the slightest use. Men are a dead weight, they're clumsy and maladjusted—oh, you can see a stretch of the overground metro, that's great!

ANNETTE: I'm really embarrassed, but I can't stay either . . . My husband has never exactly been a pushchair father!

VÉRONIQUE: What a pity. It's lovely, taking the baby for a walk. And it lasts such a short time. You always enjoyed taking care of the children, didn't you, Michel? You loved pushing the pushchair.

MICHEL: Yes, I did.

VÉRONIQUE: So what have we decided?

ANNETTE: Could you come by the house with Bruno about seven-thirty?

VÉRONIQUE: Seven-thirty? . . . What do you think, Michel?

MICHEL: Well . . . If I may . . .

ANNETTE: Go on.

MICHEL: I rather think Ferdinand ought to come here.

VÉRONIQUE: Yes, I agree.

MICHEL: I don't think it's for the victim to go traipsing around.

VÉRONIQUE: That's right.

ALAIN: Personally, I can't be anywhere at seven-thirty.

ANNETTE: Since you're no use, we won't be needing you.

VÉRONIQUE: All the same, it would be better if his father were here.

Alain's mobile vibrates.

ALAIN: All right, but then it can't be this evening. Hello? . . . There's no mention of this in the executive report. And no risk has been formally established. There's no evidence . . .

He hangs up.

VÉRONIQUE: Tomorrow?

ALAIN: I'm in The Hague tomorrow.

VÉRONIQUE: You're working in The Hague?

ALAIN: I have a case at the International Criminal Court.

ANNETTE: The main thing is that the children speak to one another. I'll bring Ferdinand here at seven-thirty and we can leave them to have their reckoning. No? You don't look very convinced.

VÉRONIQUE: If Ferdinand is not made aware of his responsibilities, they'll just look at each other like a pair of china dogs, it'll be a catastrophe.

ALAIN: What do you mean, madame? What do you mean, 'made aware of his responsibilities'?

VÉRONIQUE: I'm sure your son is not a savage.

ANNETTE: Of course Ferdinand isn't a savage.

ALAIN: Yes, he is.

ANNETTE: Alain, this is absurd, why say something like that?

ALAIN: He's a savage.

MICHEL: How does he explain his behaviour?

ANNETTE: He doesn't want to discuss it.

VÉRONIQUE: But he ought to discuss it.

ALAIN: He ought to do any number of things, madame. He ought to come here, he ought to discuss it, he ought to be sorry for it, clearly you have parenting skills that put us to shame, we hope to improve, but in the meantime, please bear with us.

MICHEL: Now, now! This is idiotic. Don't let's end up like this!

VÉRONIQUE: I'm only thinking of him, I'm only thinking of Ferdinand.

ALAIN: I got the message.

ANNETTE: Let's just sit down for another couple of minutes.

MICHEL: Another drop of coffee?

ALAIN: A coffee, OK.

ANNETTE: Then I'll have one too. Thanks.

MICHEL: That's all right, Ronnie, I'll do it.

Hiatus. Annette delicately shuffles some of the numerous art books dispersed around the coffee table.

ANNETTE: I see you're a great art-lover.

VÉRONIQUE: Art. Photographs. To some extent it's my job.

ANNETTE: I adore Bacon.

VÉRONIQUE: Ah, yes, Bacon.

ANNETTE: *(turning the pages)* . . . Cruelty. Majesty.

VÉRONIQUE: Chaos. Balance.

ANNETTE: That's right. . .

VÉRONIQUE: Is Ferdinand interested in art?

ANNETTE: Not as much as he should be . . . What about your children?

VÉRONIQUE: We try. We try to fill the gaps in the educational system.

ANNETTE: Yes . . .

VÉRONIQUE: We try to make them read. To take them to concerts and exhibitions. We're eccentric enough to believe in the pacifying abilities of culture!

ANNETTE: And you're right. . .

Michel comes back with the coffee.

MICHEL: *Clafoutis,* is it a cake or a tart? Serious question. I was just thinking in the kitchen—*Linzertorte,* for example, is that a tart? Come on, come on, you can't leave that one little slice.

VÉRONIQUE: *Clafoutis* is a cake. The pastry's not rolled out, it's mixed in with the fruit.

ALAIN: You really are a cook.

VÉRONIQUE: I love it. The thing about cooking is you have to love it. In my view, it's only the classic tart, that's to say on a pastry base, that deserves to be called a tart.

MICHEL: What about you, do you have other children?

ALAIN: A son from my first marriage.

MICHEL: I was wondering, not that it's at all important, what started the quarrel. Bruno won't say a blind word about it.

ANNETTE: Bruno refused to let Ferdinand join his gang.

VÉRONIQUE: Bruno has a gang?

ALAIN: He also called Ferdinand a grass.

VÉRONIQUE: Did you know Bruno had a gang?

MICHEL: No. Fantastic!

VÉRONIQUE: Why is it fantastic?

MICHEL: Because I had my own gang.

ALAIN: Me too.

VÉRONIQUE: And what does that entail?

MICHEL: There are five or six kids devoted to you and ready to sacrifice themselves. Like in *Spartacus*.

ALAIN: Absolutely, like in *Spartacus*!

VÉRONIQUE: Who knows about Spartacus these days?

ALAIN: They use a different model. Spiderman.

VÉRONIQUE: Anyway, clearly you know more than we do. Ferdinand hasn't been as silent as you led us to believe. And do we know why Bruno called him a grass? No, sorry, stupid, that's a stupid question. First of all, I couldn't care less, also it's beside the point.

ANNETTE: We can't get involved in children's quarrels.

VÉRONIQUE: And it's none of our business.

ANNETTE: No.

VÉRONIQUE: On the other hand, what is our business is what unfortunately happened. Violence is always our business.

MICHEL: When I was leader of my gang, when I was twelve, I fought Didier Leglu, who was bigger than me, in single combat.

VÉRONIQUE: What are you talking about, Michel? What's that got to do with it?

MICHEL: No, you're right, it's got nothing to do with it.

VÉRONIQUE: We're not discussing single combat. The children weren't fighting.

MICHEL: I know, I know. I just suddenly had this memory.

ALAIN: There's not that big a difference.

VÉRONIQUE: Oh, yes, there is. Excuse me, monsieur, there's a very big difference.

MICHEL: There's a very big difference.

ALAIN: What?

MICHEL: With Didier Leglu, we'd agreed to have a fight.

ALAIN: Did you beat the shit out of him?

MICHEL: Up to a point.

VÉRONIQUE: Right, shall we forget Didier Leglu? Would you allow me to speak to Ferdinand?

ANNETTE: By all means!

VÉRONIQUE: I wouldn't want to do it without your permission.

ANNETTE: Speak to him. What could be more natural?

ALAIN: Good luck.

ANNETTE: Stop it, Alain. I don't understand you.

ALAIN: Madame thinks . . .

VÉRONIQUE: Véronique. This will work out better if we stop calling each other 'madame' and 'monsieur'.

ALAIN: Véronique, you're motivated by an educational impulse, which is very sympathetic . . .

VÉRONIQUE: If you don't want me to speak to him, I won't speak to him.

ALAIN: No, speak to him, read him the riot act, do what you like.

VÉRONIQUE: I don't understand why you don't seem to care about this.

ALAIN: Madame . . .

MICHEL: Véronique.

ALAIN: Of course I care, Véronique, enormously. My son has injured another child . . .

VÉRONIQUE: On purpose.

ALAIN: See, that's the kind of remark that puts my back up. Obviously, on purpose.

VÉRONIQUE: But that makes *all the difference.*

ALAIN: The difference between what and what? That's what we're talking about. Our son picked up a stick and hit your son. That's why we're here, isn't it?

ANNETTE: This is pointless.

MICHEL: Yes, she's right, this kind of argument is pointless.

ALAIN: Why do you feel the need to slip in 'on purpose'? What kind of message is that supposed to be sending me?

ANNETTE: Listen, we're on a slippery slope, my husband is desperate about all sorts of other things. I'll come back this evening with Ferdinand and we'll let things sort themselves out naturally.

ALAIN: I'm not in the least desperate.

ANNETTE: Well, I am.

MICHEL: There's nothing to be desperate about.

ANNETTE: Yes, there is.

Alain's mobile vibrates.

ALAIN: Don't make any statement. . . No comment. . . No, of course you mustn't take it off the market! If you take it off the market, you become responsible . . . The minute you take Antril off the market, you're admitting liability! There's nothing in the annual accounts. If you want to be sued for falsifying the executive report and given the elbow in two weeks' time, take it off the market. . .

VÉRONIQUE: Last year, on Open Day, wasn't it Ferdinand who played Monsieur de . . .?

ANNETTE: Monsieur de Pourceaugnac.°

VÉRONIQUE: Monsieur de Pourceaugnac.

ALAIN: We'll think about the victims later, Maurice . . . Let's see what the shares do after the AGM . . .

VÉRONIQUE: He was extraordinary.

ANNETTE: Yes . . .

ALAIN: We are not going to take the medicine off the market just because two or three people are bumping into the furniture! . . . Don't make any statements for the time being . . . Yes. I'll call you back . . .

He cuts him off and phones his colleague.

VÉRONIQUE: I remember him very clearly in *Monsieur de Pourceaugnac.* Do you remember him, Michel?

MICHEL: Yes, yes . . .

VÉRONIQUE: He was hilarious when he was in drag.

ANNETTE: Yes . . .

ALAIN: *(to his colleague)* . . . They're panicking, they've got the media up their arse, you have to prepare a press release, not something defensive, not at all, on the contrary, go out all guns blazing, you insist that Verenz-Pharma is the victim of a destabilisation attempt two weeks before its Annual General Meeting, where does this paper come from, why should it have fallen out of the sky just now, etcetera and so on . . . Don't say anything about health problems, just ask one question: who's behind this report? . . . Right.

He hangs up. Brief hiatus.

MICHEL: They're terrible, these pharmaceutical companies. Profit, profit, profit.

°**Monsieur de Pourceaugnac** title character of a comedy by Molière (1622-1673)

ALAIN: You're not supposed to be listening to my conversation,

MICHEL: You're not obliged to have it in front of me.

ALAIN: Yes, I am. I'm absolutely obliged to have it here. Not my choice, I can assure you.

MICHEL: They dump any old crap on you without giving it a second thought.

ALAIN: In the therapeutic field, every advance brings with it risk as well as benefit.

MICHEL: Yes, I understand that. All the same. Funny job you've got.

ALAIN: Meaning?

VÉRONIQUE: Michel, this is nothing to do with us.

MICHEL: Funny job.

ALAIN: And what is it you do?

MICHEL: I have an ordinary job.

ALAIN: What is an ordinary job?

MICHEL: I told you, I sell saucepans.

ALAIN: And doorknobs.

MICHEL: And toilet fittings. Loads of other things.

ALAIN: Ah, toilet fittings. Now we're talking. That's really interesting.

ANNETTE: Alain.

ALAIN: It's really interesting. I'm interested in toilet fittings.

MICHEL: Why shouldn't you be?

ALAIN: How many types are there?

MICHEL: Two different systems. Push-button or overhead flush.

ALAIN: I see.

MICHEL: Depending on the feed.

ALAIN: Well, yes.

MICHEL: Either the water comes down from above or up from under.

ALAIN: Yes.

MICHEL: I could introduce you to one of my warehousemen who specialises in this kind of thing, if you like. You'd have to leg it out to Saint-Denis la Plaine.

ALAIN: You seem to be very much on top of the subject.

VÉRONIQUE: Are you intending to punish Ferdinand in any way? You can carry on with the plumbing in some more appropriate setting.

ANNETTE: I'm not feeling well.

VÉRONIQUE: What's the matter?

ALAIN: Yes, you're very pale, sweetheart.

MICHEL: Palish, certainly.

ANNETTE: I feel sick.

VÉRONIQUE: Sick?. . . I have some Moxalon . . .

ANNETTE: No, no . . . It'll be all right. . .

VÉRONIQUE: What could we . . . ? Coke. Coke's very good.

She immediately sets off in search of it.

ANNETTE: It'll be all right. . .

MICHEL: Walk around a bit. Take a few steps.

She takes a few steps. Véronique comes back with the Coca-Cola.

ANNETTE: Really? You think so? . . .

VÉRONIQUE: Yes, yes. Small sips.

ANNETTE: Thank you . . .

Alain has discreetly called his office.

ALAIN: . . . Give me Serge, will you, please? . . . Oh, right. . . Ask him to call me back, ask him to call me back right away . . .

He hangs up.

It's good, is it, Coca-Cola? I thought it was just supposed to be for diarrhoea.

VÉRONIQUE: Not only for that. (*To Annette.*) All right?

ANNETTE: All right . . . Véronique, if we want to reprimand our child, we'll do it in our own way and without having to account to anybody.

MICHEL: Absolutely.

VÉRONIQUE: What do you mean, 'absolutely', Michel?

MICHEL: They can do whatever they like with their son, it's their prerogative.

VÉRONIQUE: I don't think so.

MICHEL: What do you mean, you don't think so, Ronnie?

VÉRONIQUE: I don't think it is their prerogative.

ALAIN: Really? Explain.

His mobile vibrates.

I'm sorry . . . (*To his colleague.*) Excellent. . . But don't forget, nothing's been proved, there's nothing definite . . . Get this straight, if anyone fucks up, Maurice is a dead man in two weeks, and us with him.

ANNETTE: That's enough, Alain! That's enough now with the mobile! Will you pay attention to what's going on here, shit!

ALAIN: Yes . . . Call me back and read it to me.

He hangs up.

What's the matter with you, have you gone mad, shouting like that? Serge heard everything.

ANNETTE: Good! Drives me mad, that mobile, endlessly!

ALAIN: Listen, Annette, I'm already doing you a big favour being here in the first place . . .

VÉRONIQUE: Extraordinary thing to say.

ANNETTE: I'm going to throw up.

ALAIN: No, you're not, you are not going to throw up.

ANNETTE: Yes, I am . . .

MICHEL: Do you want to go to the lavatory?

ANNETTE: (to Alain) No one's forcing you to stay.

VÉRONIQUE: No, no one's forcing him to stay.

ANNETTE: I'm feeling dizzy . . .

ALAIN: Stare at a fixed point. Stare at a fixed point, Woof-woof.

ANNETTE: Go away, leave me alone.

VÉRONIQUE: She would be better off in the lavatory.

ALAIN: Go to the lavatory. Go to the lavatory if you want to throw up.

MICHEL: Give her some Moxalon.

ALAIN: You don't suppose it could be the clafoutis?

VÉRONIQUE: It was made yesterday!

ANNETTE: (to Alain) Don't touch me! . . .

ALAIN: Calm down, Woof-woof.

MICHEL: Please, why get worked up about nothing?

ANNETTE: According to my husband, everything to do with house, school or garden is my department.

ALAIN: No, it's not!

ANNETTE: Yes, it is. And I understand why. It's deathly, all that. It's deathly.

VÉRONIQUE: If it's so deathly, why have children in the first place?

MICHEL: Maybe Ferdinand senses your lack of interest.

ANNETTE: What lack of interest?

MICHEL: You just said . . .

Annette vomits violently. A brutal and catastrophic spray, part of which goes over Alain. The art books on the coffee table are likewise deluged.

Go and fetch a bowl, go and fetch a bowl!

Véronique runs out to look for a bowl and Michel hands her the coffee tray, just in case. Annette retches again, but nothing comes out.

ALAIN: You should have gone to the lavatory, Woof-woof, this is ridiculous!

MICHEL: Your suit's definitely copped it!

Very soon, Véronique is back with a basin and a cloth. The basin is given to Annette.

VÉRONIQUE: Well, it's certainly not the *clafoutis*, it couldn't possibly be.

MICHEL: It's not the *clafoutis*, it's nerves. This is pure nerves.

VÉRONIQUE: *(to Alain)* Would you like to clean up in the bathroom? Oh, no, the Kokoschka! Oh, my God!

Annette vomits bile into the basin.

MICHEL: Give her some Moxalon.

VÉRONIQUE: Not now, she can't keep anything down.

ALAIN: Where's the bathroom?

VÉRONIQUE: I'll show you.

Véronique and Alain leave.

MICHEL: It's nerves. It's a panic attack. You're a mum, Annette. Whether you want to be or not. I understand why you feel desperate.

ANNETTE: Mmm.

MICHEL: What I always say is, you can't control the things that control you.

ANNETTE: Mmm . . .

MICHEL: With me, it's the cervical vertebrae. The vertebrae seize up.

ANNETTE: Mmm . . .

She brings up a little more bile. Véronique returns with another basin, containing a sponge.

VÉRONIQUE: What are we going to do about the Kokoschka?

MICHEL: Well, I would spray it with Mr Clean . . . The problem is how to dry it. . . Or else you could sponge it down and put a bit of perfume on it.

VÉRONIQUE: Perfume?

MICHEL: Use my Kouros, I never wear it.

VÉRONIQUE: It'll warp.

MICHEL: We could run the hair-dryer over it and flatten it out under a pile of other books. Or iron it like they do with banknotes.

VÉRONIQUE: Oh, my God . . .

ANNETTE: I'll buy you another one.

VÉRONIQUE: You can't find it! It went out of print years ago!

ANNETTE: I'm terribly sorry . . .

MICHEL: We'll salvage it. Let me do it, Ronnie.

She hands him the basin of water and the sponge, disgusted. Michel gets started on cleaning up the book.

VÉRONIQUE: It's a reprint of the catalogue from the '53 London exhibition, more than twenty years old! . . .

MICHEL: Go and get the hair-dryer. And the Kouros. In the towel cupboard.

VÉRONIQUE: Her husband's in the bathroom.

MICHEL: Well, he's not stark naked, is he?

She goes out as he continues to clean up.

. . . There, that's the worst of it. *The People of the Tundra* needs a bit of a wipe . . . I'll be back.

He goes out with the used basin. Véronique and Michel return more or less simultaneously. She has the bottle of perfume, he has the basin containing fresh water. Michel finishes cleaning up.

VÉRONIQUE: *(to Annette)* Feeling better?

ANNETTE: Yes . . .

VÉRONIQUE: Shall I spray?

MICHEL: Where's the hair-dryer?

VÉRONIQUE: He's bringing it when he's finished with it.

MICHEL: We'll wait for him. We'll put the Kouros on last thing.

ANNETTE: Can I use the bathroom as well?

VÉRONIQUE: Yes. Yes, yes. Of course.

ANNETTE: I can't tell you how sorry I am . . .

Véronique takes her out and returns immediately.

VÉRONIQUE: What a nightmare! Horrible!

MICHEL: Tell you what, he'd better not push me much further.

VÉRONIQUE: She's dreadful as well.

MICHEL: Not as bad.

VÉRONIQUE: She's a phoney.

MICHEL: Less irritating.

VÉRONIQUE: They're both dreadful! Why do you keep siding with them?

She sprays the tulips.

MICHEL: I don't keep siding with them, what are you talking about?

VÉRONIQUE: You keep vacillating, trying to play both ends against the middle.

MICHEL: Not at all!

VÉRONIQUE: Yes, you do. Going on about your triumphs as a gang leader, telling them they're free to do whatever they like with their son when the child is a public menace—when a child's a public menace, it's everybody's concern, I can't believe she puked all over my books!

She sprays the Kokoschka.

MICHEL: *(pointing)* Put some on *The People of the Tundra*.

VÉRONIQUE: If you think you're about to spew, you go to the proper place.

MICHEL: . . . And the Foujita.

VÉRONIQUE: *(spraying everything)* This is disgusting.

MICHEL: I was pushing it a bit with the shithouse systems.

VÉRONIQUE: You were brilliant.

MICHEL: Good answers, don't you think?

VÉRONIQUE: Brilliant. The warehouseman was brilliant.

MICHEL: What an arsehole. And what did he call her?! . . .

VÉRONIQUE: Woof-woof.

MICHEL: That's right, 'Woof-woof'!

VÉRONIQUE: Woof-woof!

They both laugh. Alain returns, hair-dryer in hand.

ALAIN: That's right, I call her Woof-woof.

VÉRONIQUE: Oh . . . I'm sorry, I didn't mean to be rude . . . It's so easy to make fun of other people's nicknames! What about us, what do we call each other, Michel? Far worse, isn't it?

ALAIN: Were you wanting the hair-dryer?

VÉRONIQUE: Thank you.

MICHEL: Thank you.

He takes the hair-dryer.

We call each other 'darjeeling', like the tea. Far more ridiculous, if you ask me!

Michel switches on the machine and starts drying the books. Véronique flattens out the damp pages.

Smooth them out, smooth them out.

VÉRONIQUE: *(as she smooths out the pages, raising her voice above the noise)* How's the poor thing feeling, better?

ALAIN: Better.

VÉRONIQUE: I reacted very badly, I'm ashamed of myself.

ALAIN: Not at all.

VÉRONIQUE: I just steamrollered her about my catalogue, I can't believe I did that.

MICHEL: Turn the page. Stretch it out, stretch it out properly.

ALAIN: You're going to tear it.

VÉRONIQUE: You're right. . . That's enough, Michel, it's dry. Objects can become ridiculously important, half the time you can't even remember why.

Michel shuts the catalogue and they both cover it with a little cairn of heavy books. Michel finishes drying the Foujita, The People of the Tundra, etc. . . .

MICHEL: There we are! Good as new. Where does 'Woof-woof' come from?

ALAIN: 'How much is that doggie in the window?'

MICHEL: I know it! *(He sings.)* 'The one with the waggly tail.'

ALAIN: 'Woof-woof.'

MICHEL: Ha, ha! . . . Ours comes from our honeymoon in India. Idiotic, really!

VÉRONIQUE: Shouldn't I go and see how she is?

MICHEL: Off you go, darjeeling.

VÉRONIQUE: Shall I? . . .

Annette returns.

. . . Ah, Annette! I was worried about you . . . Are you feeling better?

ANNETTE: I think so.

ALAIN: If you're not sure, stay away from the coffee table.

ANNETTE: I left the towel in the bathtub, I wasn't sure where to put it.

VÉRONIQUE: Perfect.

ANNETTE: You've cleaned it all up. I'm so sorry.

MICHEL: Everything's great. Everything's in order.

VÉRONIQUE: Annette, forgive me, I've taken hardly any notice of you. I've been obsessed with my Kokoschka.

ANNETTE: Don't worry about it.

VÉRONIQUE: The way I reacted, very bad of me.

ANNETTE: Not at all . . . *(After an embarrassed hiatus.)* Something occurred to me in the bathroom . . .

VÉRONIQUE: Yes?

ANNETTE: Perhaps we skated too hastily over . . .
I mean, what I mean is . . .

MICHEL: Say it, Annette, say it,

ANNETTE: An insult is also a kind of assault.

MICHEL: Of course it is.

VÉRONIQUE: Well, that depends, Michel.

MICHEL: Yes, it depends.

ANNETTE: Ferdinand's never shown any signs of violence. He wouldn't have done that without a reason.

ALAIN: He got called a grass!

His mobile vibrates.

I'm sorry! . . .

He moves to one side, making elaborately apologetic signs to Annette.

. . . Yes . . . As long as there aren't any statements from victims. We don't want any victims. I don't want you being quoted alongside victims! . . . A blanket denial and if necessary attack the newspaper . . . They'll fax you a draft of the press release, Maurice.

He hangs up.

If anyone calls me a grass, I'm liable to get annoyed.

MICHEL: Unless it's true.

ALAIN: What did you say?

MICHEL: I mean, suppose it's justified?

ANNETTE: My son is a grass?

MICHEL: Course not, I was joking.

ANNETTE: Yours is as well, if that's to be the way of it.

MICHEL: What do you mean, ours is as well?

ANNETTE: Well, he did identify Ferdinand.

MICHEL: Because we insisted!

VÉRONIQUE: Michel, this is completely beside the point.

ANNETTE: What's the difference? Whether you insisted or not, he gave you the name.

ALAIN: Annette.

ANNETTE: Annette what? (*To Michel.*) You think my son is a grass?

MICHEL: I don't think anything.

ANNETTE: Well, if you don't think anything, don't say anything. Stop making these insinuations.

VÉRONIQUE: Let's stay calm, Annette. Michel and I are making an effort to be reasonable and moderate . . .

ANNETTE: Not that moderate.

VÉRONIQUE: Oh, really? What do you mean?

ANNETTE: Moderate on the surface.

ALAIN: I really have to go, Woof-woof . . .

ANNETTE: All right, go on, be a coward.

ALAIN: Annette, right now I'm risking my most important client, so this responsible parent routine . . .

VÉRONIQUE: My son has lost two teeth. Two incisors.

ALAIN: Yes, yes, I think we all got that.

VÉRONIQUE: One of them for good.

ALAIN: He'll have new ones, we'll give him new ones! Better ones! It's not as if he's burst an eardrum!

ANNETTE: We're making a mistake not to take into account the origin of the problem.

VÉRONIQUE: There's no origin. There's just an eleven-year-old child hitting someone. With a stick.

ALAIN: Armed with a stick.

MICHEL: We withdrew that word.

ALAIN: You withdrew it because we objected to it.

MICHEL: We withdrew it without any protest.

ALAIN: A word deliberately designed to rule out error or clumsiness, to rule out childhood.

VÉRONIQUE: I'm not sure I'm able to take much more of this tone of voice.

ALAIN: You and I have had trouble seeing eye to eye right from the start.

VÉRONIQUE: There's nothing more detestable than to be attacked for something you yourself consider a mistake. The word 'armed' was inappropriate, so we changed it. Although, if you stick to the strict definition of the word, its use is far from inaccurate.

ANNETTE: Ferdinand was insulted and he reacted. If I'm attacked, I defend myself, especially if I find myself alone, confronted by a gang.

MICHEL: Puking seems to have perked you up.

ANNETTE: Are you aware how crude that sounds?

MICHEL: We're people of good will. All four of us, I'm sure. Why let these irritants, these pointless aggravations push us over the edge? . . .

VÉRONIQUE: Oh, Michel, that's enough! Let's stop beating about the bush. If all we are is moderate on the surface, let's forget it, shall we!

MICHEL: No, no, I refuse to allow myself to slide down that slope.

ALAIN: What slope?

MICHEL: The deplorable slope those two little bastards have perched us on! There, I've said it!

ALAIN: I'm not sure Ronnie has quite the same outlook.

VÉRONIQUE: Véronique!

ALAIN: Sorry.

VÉRONIQUE: So Bruno's a little bastard' now, is he, poor child. That's the last straw!

ALAIN: Right, well, I really do have to leave you.

ANNETTE: Me too.

VÉRONIQUE: Go on, go, I give up.

The Vallon telephone rings.

MICHEL: Hello? . . . Oh, Mum . . . No, no, we're with some friends, but tell me about it . . . Yes, do whatever the doctor wants you to do . . . They've given you Antril?! Wait a minute, Mum, wait a minute, don't go away . . . *(To Alain.)* Antril's your crap, isn't it? My mother's taking it!

ALAIN: Thousands of people take it.

MICHEL: You stop taking that stuff right now. Do you hear what I'm saying, Mum? Immediately . . . Don't argue, I'll explain later . . . Tell Dr Perolo I'm forbidding you to take it. . . Why luminous? . . . So that you can be seen? . . . That's completely ridiculous . . . All right, we'll talk about it later. Lots of love, Mum. I'll call you back.

He hangs up.

She's hired luminous crutches, so she doesn't get knocked down by a truck. As if someone in her condition would be strolling down the motorway in the middle of the night. They've given her Antril for her blood pressure.

ALAIN: If she takes it and stays normal, I'll have her called as a witness. Didn't I have a scarf? Ah, there it is.

MICHEL: I do not appreciate your cynicism. If my mother displays the most minor symptom, I'll be initiating a class action.

ALAIN: Oh, that'll happen anyway.

MICHEL: So I should hope.

ANNETTE: Goodbye, madame . . .

VÉRONIQUE: Behaving well gets you nowhere. Courtesy is a waste of time, it weakens you and undermines you . . .

ALAIN: Right, come on, Annette, let's go, enough preaching and sermons for today.

MICHEL: Go on, go. But can I just say one thing: having met you two, it's pretty clear that for what's-his-name, Ferdinand, there are mitigating circumstances.

ANNETTE: When you murdered that hamster . . .

MICHEL: Murdered?!

ANNETTE: Yes.

MICHEL: I murdered the hamster?!

ANNETTE: Yes. You've done your best to make us feel guilty, but your virtue went straight out the window once you decided to be a killer.

MICHEL: I absolutely did not murder that hamster!

ANNETTE: Worse. You left it, shivering with terror, in a hostile environment. That poor hamster is bound to have been eaten by a dog or a rat.

VÉRONIQUE: It's true! That is true!

MICHEL: What do you mean, 'that is true'?

VÉRONIQUE: It's true. What do you expect me to say? It's appalling what must have happened to that creature.

MICHEL: I thought the hamster would be happy to be liberated. I thought it was going to run off down the gutter jumping for joy!

VÉRONIQUE: Well, it didn't.

ANNETTE: And you abandoned it.

MICHEL: I can't touch those things! For fuck's sake, Ronnie, you know very well, I'm incapable of touching that whole species!

VÉRONIQUE: He has a phobia about rodents.

MICHEL: That's right, I'm frightened of rodents, I'm terrified of snakes, anything close to the ground, I have absolutely no rapport with! So that's the end of it!

ALAIN: *(to Véronique)* And you, why didn't you go out and look for it?

VÉRONIQUE: Because I had no idea what had happened! Michel didn't tell us, me and the children, that the hamster had escaped till the following morning. I went out immediately, immediately, I walked round the block, I even went down to the cellar.

MICHEL: Véronique, I find it intolerable to be in the dock all of a sudden for this hamster saga that you've seen fit to reveal. It's a personal matter which is nobody else's business but ours and which has nothing to do with the present situation! And I find it incomprehensible to be called a killer! In my own home!

VÉRONIQUE: What's your home got to do with it?

MICHEL: My home, the doors of which I have opened' the doors of which I have opened wide in a spirit of reconciliation, to people who ought to be grateful to me for it!

ALAIN: It's wonderful the way you keep patting yourself on the back.

ANNETTE: Don't you feel any guilt?

MICHEL: I feel no guilt whatsoever. I've always found that creature repulsive. I'm ecstatic that it's gone.

VÉRONIQUE: Michel, that is ridiculous.

MICHEL: What's ridiculous? Have you gone crazy as well? Their son bashes up Bruno, and I get shat on because of a hamster?

VÉRONIQUE: You behaved very badly with that hamster, you can't deny it.

MICHEL: Fuck the hamster!

VÉRONIQUE: You won't be able to say that to your daughter this evening.

MICHEL: Bring her on! I'm not going to let myself be told how to behave by some nine-year-old bruiser.

ALAIN: Hundred per cent behind you there.

VÉRONIQUE: Pathetic.

MICHEL: Careful, Véronique, you be careful, I've been extremely restrained up to now, but I'm two inches away from crossing that line.

ANNETTE: And what about Bruno?

MICHEL: What about Bruno?

ANNETTE: Isn't he upset?

MICHEL: If you ask me, Bruno has other problems.

VÉRONIQUE: Bruno was less attached to Nibbles.

MICHEL: Grotesque name as well!

ANNETTE: If you feel no guilt, why do you expect our son to feel any?

MICHEL: Let me tell you this, I'm up to here with these idiotic discussions. We tried to be nice, we bought tulips, my wife passed me off as a lefty, but the truth is, I can't keep this up any more, I'm fundamentally uncouth.

ALAIN: Aren't we all?

VÉRONIQUE: No. No. I'm sorry, we are not all fundamentally uncouth.

ALAIN: Well, not you, obviously.

VÉRONIQUE: No, not me, thank the Lord.

MICHEL: Not you, darjee, not you, you're a fully evolved woman, you're skid-resistant.

VÉRONIQUE: Why are you attacking me?

MICHEL: I'm not attacking you. Quite the opposite.

VÉRONIQUE: Yes, you're attacking me, you know you are.

MICHEL: You organised this little get-together, I just let myself be recruited . . .

VÉRONIQUE: You let yourself be recruited?

MICHEL: Yes.

VÉRONIQUE: That's detestable.

MICHEL: Not at all. You stand up for civilisation, that's completely to your credit.

VÉRONIQUE: Exactly, I'm standing up for civilisation! And it's lucky there are people prepared to do that! *(She's on the brink of tears.)* You think being fundamentally uncouth's a better idea?

ALAIN: Come on now, come on . . .

VÉRONIQUE: *(as above)* Is it normal to criticise someone for not being fundamentally uncouth? . . .

ANNETTE: No one's saying that. No one's criticising you.

VÉRONIQUE: Yes, they are! . . .

She bursts into tears.

ALAIN: No, they're not!

VÉRONIQUE: What were we supposed to do? Sue you? Not speak to one another and try to slaughter each other with insurance claims?

MICHEL: Stop it, Ronnie . . .

VÉRONIQUE: Stop what?! . . .

MICHEL: You've got things out of proportion . . .

VÉRONIQUE: I don't give a shit! You force yourself to rise above petty-mindedness . . . and you finish up humiliated and completely on your own . . .

Alain's mobile has vibrated.

ALAIN: . . . Yes . . . 'Let them prove it!' . . . 'Prove it'. . . but if you ask me, best not to answer at all . . .

MICHEL: We're always on our own! Everywhere! Who'd like a drop of rum?

ALAIN: . . . Maurice, I'm in a meeting, I'll call you back from the office . . .

He cuts the line.

VÉRONIQUE: So there we are! I'm living with someone who's totally negative.

ALAIN: Who's negative?

MICHEL: I am.

VÉRONIQUE: This was the worst idea! We should never have arranged this meeting!

MICHEL: I told you.

VÉRONIQUE: You told me?

MICHEL: Yes.

VÉRONIQUE: You told me you didn't want to have this meeting?!

MICHEL: I didn't think it was a good idea.

ANNETTE: It was a good idea . . .

MICHEL: Oh, please! . . .

He raises the bottle of rum.

Anybody?

VÉRONIQUE: You told me it wasn't a good idea, Michel?!

MICHEL: Think so.

VÉRONIQUE: You think so!

ALAIN: Wouldn't mind a little drop.

ANNETTE: Didn't you have to go?

ALAIN: I could manage a small glass, now we've got this far.

Michel pours a glass for Alain.

VÉRONIQUE: You look me in the eye and tell me we weren't in complete agreement about this!

ANNETTE: Calm down, Véronique, calm down, this is pointless . . .

VÉRONIQUE: Who stopped anyone touching the *clafoutis* this morning? Who said, 'Let's keep the rest of the *clafoutis* for the Reilles'?! Who said it?!

ALAIN: That was nice.

MICHEL: What's that got to do with it?

VÉRONIQUE: What do you mean, 'what's that got to do with it'?

MICHEL: If you invite people, you invite people.

VÉRONIQUE: You're a liar, you're a liar! He's a liar!

ALAIN: You know, speaking personally, my wife had to drag me here. When you're brought up with a kind of John Wayne-ish idea of virility, you don't want to settle this kind of problem with a lot of yakking.

Michel laughs.

ANNETTE: I thought your model was Spartacus.

ALAIN: Same family.

MICHEL: Analogous.

VÉRONIQUE: Analogous! Are there no lengths you won't go to to humiliate yourself, Michel?

ANNETTE: Obviously it was pointless dragging you here.

ALAIN: What were you hoping for, Woof-woof? It's true, it's a ludicrous nickname—were you hoping for a glimpse of universal harmony? This rum is terrific.

MICHEL: It is, isn't it? *Coeur de Chauffe,* fifteen years old, direct from Santa Rosa.

VÉRONIQUE: And the tulips, whose idea was that? I said it's a shame the tulips are finished, I didn't say rush down to Mouton-Duvernet at the crack of dawn.

ANNETTE: Don't work yourself up into this state, Véronique, it's crazy.

VÉRONIQUE: The tulips were his idea! Entirely his idea! Aren't we allowed a drink?

ANNETTE: Yes, Véronique, and I would like one too. By the way, it's quite amusing, someone descended from Spartacus and John Wayne who can't even pick up a mouse.

MICHEL: Will you *shut up* about that hamster! Shut up! . . .

He gives Annette a glass of rum.

VÉRONIQUE: Ha, ha! You're right, it's laughable!

ANNETTE: What about her?

MICHEL: I don't think she needs any.

VÉRONIQUE: Give me a drink, Michel.

MICHEL: No.

VÉRONIQUE: Michel!

MICHEL: No.

Véronique tries to snatch the bottle out of his hands. Michel resists.

ANNETTE: What's the matter with you, Michel?!

MICHEL: All right, there you are, take it. Drink, drink, who cares?

ANNETTE: Is alcohol bad for you?

VÉRONIQUE: It's wonderful.

She slumps.

ALAIN: Right . . . Well, I don't know . . .

VÉRONIQUE: *(to Alain)* . . . Listen, monsieur . . .

ANNETTE: Alain.

VÉRONIQUE: Alain, we're not exactly soul-mates, you and me, but, you see, I live with a man who's decided, once and for all, that life is second rate, It's very difficult living with a man who comforts himself with that thought, who doesn't want anything to change, who can't work up any enthusiasm about anything . . .

MICHEL: He doesn't give a fuck. He doesn't give a fuck about any of that.

VÉRONIQUE: You have to believe . . . you have to believe in the possibility of improvement, don't you?

MICHEL: He's the last person you should be telling all this.

VÉRONIQUE: I'll talk to who I like, for fuck's sake!

The telephone rings.

MICHEL: Who the fuck's this now? . . . Yes, Mum . . . He's fine. I say he's fine, he's lost his teeth, but he's fine . . . Yes, he's in pain. He's in pain, but it'll pass. Mum, I'm busy, I'll call you back.

ANNETTE: He's still in pain?

VÉRONIQUE: No.

ANNETTE: Then why worry your mother?

VÉRONIQUE: He can't help himself. He always has to worry her.

MICHEL: Right, that's enough, Véronique! What is this psychodrama?

ALAIN: Véronique, are we ever interested in anything but ourselves? Of course we'd all like to believe in the possibility of improvement. Of which we could be the architect and which would be in no way self-serving. Does such a thing exist? Some people drag their feet, it's their strategy, others refuse to acknowledge the passing of time, and drive themselves demented—what difference does it make? People struggle until they're dead. Education, the miseries of the world . . . You're writing a book about Darfur, fine, I can understand you saying to yourself, right, I'm going to choose a massacre, what else does history consist of, and I'm going to write about it. You do what you can to save yourself.

VÉRONIQUE: I'm not writing the book to save myself. You haven't read it, you don't know what it's about.

ALAIN: It makes no difference.

Hiatus.

VÉRONIQUE: Terrible stink of Kouros!° . . .

MICHEL: Ghastly.

ALAIN: You certainly laid it on.

ANNETTE: I'm sorry.

VÉRONIQUE: Not your fault. I was the one spraying like a lunatic . . . Anyway, why can't we take things more lightly, why does everything always have to be so exhausting? . . .

ALAIN: You think too much. Women think too much.

ANNETTE: There's an original remark, I bet that's thrown you for a loop.

VÉRONIQUE: 'Think too much', I don't know what that means. And I don't see the point of existence without some kind of moral conception of the world.

MICHEL: See what I have to live with?

VÉRONIQUE: Shut up! Will you shut up?! I detest this pathetic complicity! You disgust me.

MICHEL: Come on, have a sense of humour.

VÉRONIQUE: I don't have a sense of humour. And I have no intention of acquiring one.

MICHEL: What I always say is, marriage: the most terrible ordeal God can inflict on you.

ANNETTE: Great.

MICHEL: Marriage and children.

°**Kouros** an Yves Saint Laurent cologne

ANNETTE: There's no call for you to share your views with us, Michel. As a matter of fact, I find it slightly indecent.

VÉRONIQUE: That's not going to worry him.

MICHEL: You mean you don't agree?

ANNETTE: These observations are irrelevant. Alain, say something.

ALAIN: He's entitled to his opinions.

ANNETTE: Yes, but he doesn't have to broadcast them.

ALAIN: Well, yes, perhaps . . .

ANNETTE: We don't give a damn about their marriage. We're here to settle a problem to do with our children, we don't give a damn about their marriage.

ALAIN: Yes, but. . .

ANNETTE: But what? What do you mean?

ALAIN: There's a connection.

MICHEL: There's a connection! Of course there's a connection.

VÉRONIQUE: There's a connection between Bruno having his teeth broken and our marriage?!

MICHEL: Obviously.

ANNETTE: We're not with you.

MICHEL: Children consume and fracture our lives. Children drag us towards disaster, it's unavoidable. When you see those laughing couples casting off into the sea of matrimony, you say to yourself, they have no idea, poor things, they just have no idea, they're happy. No one tells you anything when you start out. I have an old school pal who's just about to have a child with his new girlfriend. I said to him, 'A child, at our age, are you insane?' The ten or a dozen good years left to us before we get cancer or a stroke, and you're going to bugger yourself up with some brat?

ANNETTE: You don't really believe what you're saying.

VÉRONIQUE: He does.

MICHEL: Of course I believe it. Worse, even.

VÉRONIQUE: Yes.

ANNETTE: You're demeaning yourself, Michel.

MICHEL: Is that right? Ha, ha!

ANNETTE: Stop crying, Véronique, you can see it only encourages him.

MICHEL: *(to Alain, who's refilling his empty glass)* Help yourself, help yourself—exceptional, isn't it?

ALAIN: Exceptional.

MICHEL: Could I offer you a cigar? . . .

VÉRONIQUE: No, no cigars!

ALAIN: Pity.

ANNETTE: You're not proposing to smoke a cigar, Alain!

ALAIN: I shall do what I like, Annette, if I feel like accepting a cigar, I shall accept a cigar. If I'm not smoking, it's because I don't want to upset Véronique, who's already completely lost it. She's right, stop snivelling, when a woman cries, a man is immediately provoked to the worst excesses. Added to which, Michel's point of view is, I'm sorry to say, entirely sound.

His mobile vibrates.

. . . Yes, Serge . . . Go ahead . . . Put Paris, the date . . . and the exact time . . .

ANNETTE: This is hideous!

ALAIN: *(moving aside and muffling his voice to escape her fury)* . . . Whatever time you send it. It has to look piping hot straight out of the oven . . . No, not 'We're surprised'. 'We condemn'. 'Surprised' is feeble . . .

ANNETTE: This goes on from morning to night, from morning to night he's glued to that mobile! That mobile makes mincemeat of our lives!

ALAIN: Er . . . Just a minute . . .

He covers the mobile.

Annette, this is very important! . . .

ANNETTE: It's always very important. Anything happening somewhere else is always more important.

ALAIN: *(resuming)* Go ahead . . . Yes . . . Not 'procedure', 'manoeuvre'. 'A manoeuvre, timed for two weeks before the annual accounts,' etc. . . .

ANNETTE: In the street, at dinner, he doesn't care where . . .

ALAIN: A 'paper' in inverted commas! Put the word 'paper' in inverted commas . . .

ANNETTE: I'm not saying another word. Total surrender. I want to be sick again.

MICHEL: Where's the basin?

VÉRONIQUE: I don't know.

ALAIN: . . . You just have to quote me: 'This is simply a disgraceful attempt to manipulate share prices . . .'

VÉRONIQUE: Here it is. Go on, off you go.

MICHEL: Ronnie . . .

VÉRONIQUE: Everything's all right. We're fully equipped.

ALAIN: '. . . share prices and to undermine my client,' confirms Maître Reille, counsel for the Verenz-Pharma company'. . . AP, Reuters, general press, specialised press, Uncle Tom Cobley and all. . .

He hangs up.

VÉRONIQUE: She wants to throw up again.

ALAIN: What's the matter with you?

ANNETTE: I'm touched by your concern.

ALAIN: It's upsetting me!

ANNETTE: I am sorry. I must have misunderstood.

ALAIN: Oh, Annette, please! Don't let us start now! Just because they're quarrelling, just because their marriage is fucked, doesn't mean we have to compete!

VÉRONIQUE: What right do you have to say our marriage is fucked? Who gave you permission?

Alain's mobile vibrates.

ALAIN: . . . They just read it to me. We're sending it to you, Maurice . . . 'Manipulation', 'manipulate share prices.' It's on its way.

He hangs up.

. . . Wasn't me who said it, it was François.

VÉRONIQUE: Michel.

ALAIN: Michel, sorry.

VÉRONIQUE: I forbid you to stand in any kind of judgement over our relationship.

ALAIN: Then don't stand in judgement over my son.

VÉRONIQUE: That's got nothing to do with it! Your son injured ours!

ALAIN: They're young, they're kids, kids have always given each other a good drubbing during break. It's a law of life.

VÉRONIQUE: No, no, it isn't!

ALAIN: Course it is. You have to go through a kind of apprenticeship before violence gives way to what's right. Originally, let me remind you, might was right.

VÉRONIQUE: Possibly in prehistoric times. Not in our society.

ALAIN: Our society? Explain 'society'.

VÉRONIQUE: You're exhausting me, these conversations are exhausting.

ALAIN: You see, Véronique, I believe in the god of carnage. He has ruled, uninterruptedly, since the dawn of time. You're interested in Africa, aren't you? . . . (*To Annette, who retches.*) . . . Feeling bad?

ANNETTE: Don't worry about me.

ALAIN: I am worried.

ANNETTE: Everything's fine.

ALAIN: As a matter of fact, I just came back from the Congo. Over there, little boys are taught to kill when they're eight years old. During their childhood, they may kill hundreds of people, with a machete, with a 12.7,° with a Kalashnikov, with a grenade launcher, so you'll understand that when my son picks up a bamboo rod, hits his playmate and breaks a tooth, or even two, in Aspirant Dunant Gardens, I'm likely to be less disposed than you to horror and indignation.

VÉRONIQUE: You're wrong.

ANNETTE: (*mocking*) 12.7! . . .

ALAIN: Yes, that's what they're called.

Annette spits in the basin.

MICHEL: Are you all right?

ANNETTE: . . . Perfectly.

ALAIN: What's the matter with you? What's the matter with her?

ANNETTE: It's just bile! It's nothing!

VÉRONIQUE: Don't lecture me about Africa. I know all about Africa's martyrdom, I've been steeped in it for months . . .

ALAIN: I don't doubt it. Anyway, the Prosecutor of the International Criminal Court has opened an inquiry on Darfur . . .

VÉRONIQUE: You think I don't know about that?

MICHEL: Don't get her started on that! For God's sake!

Véronique throws herself at her husband and hits him several times, with an uncontrolled and irrational desperation. Alain pulls her off him.

ALAIN: You know what, I'm starting to like you!

VÉRONIQUE: Well, I don't like you!

MICHEL: She's a supporter of peace and stability in the world.

VÉRONIQUE: Shut up!

Annette retches. She picks up her glass of rum and lifts it to her mouth.

°**12.7** 12.7 mm., a .50 caliber weapon

MICHEL: Are you sure about that?

ANNETTE: Yes, yes, it'll do me good.

Véronique follows suit.

VÉRONIQUE: We're living in France. We're not living in Kinshasa! We're living in France according to the principles of Western society. What goes on in Aspirant Dunant Gardens reflects the values of Western society! Of which, if it's all the same to you, I am happy to be a member.

MICHEL: Beating up your husband is one of those principles, is it?

VÉRONIQUE: Michel, this is going to end badly.

ALAIN: She threw herself on you in such a frenzy. If I were you, I'd be rather touched.

VÉRONIQUE: I'll do it again in a minute.

ANNETTE: He's making fun of you, you do realise?

VÉRONIQUE: I don't give a shit.

ALAIN: I'm not making fun, on the contrary. Morality decrees we should control our impulses, but sometimes it's good not to control them. You don't want to be singing 'Ave Maria' when you're fucking. Where can you find this rum?

MICHEL: That vintage, I doubt you can.

ANNETTE: 12.7! Ha, ha! . . .

VÉRONIQUE: *(same tone)* 12.7, you're right!

ALAIN: That's right. 12.7.

ANNETTE: Why can't you just say gun?

ALAIN: Because 12.7 is correct. You don't just say gun.

ANNETTE: Who's this 'you'?

ALAIN: That's enough, Annette. That's enough.

ANNETTE: The great warriors, like my husband, you have to give them some leeway, they have trouble working up an interest in local events.

ALAIN: It's true.

VÉRONIQUE: I don't see why. I don't see why. We're citizens of the world. I don't see why we should give up the struggle just because it's on our doorstep.

MICHEL: Oh, Ronnie! Do stop shoving these thoughts for the day down our throat.

VÉRONIQUE: I'm going to kill him.

Alain's mobile has vibrated.

ALAIN: . . . Yes, all right, take out 'regrettable'. . . 'Crude'. 'A crude attempt to . . .' That's it. . .

VÉRONIQUE: She's right, this is becoming unbearable!

ALAIN: . . . Otherwise he approves the rest? . . . Fine, fine. Very good.

He hangs up.

What were we saying? . . . 12.7 millimetre? . . .

VÉRONIQUE: I was saying, whether my husband likes it or not, that no one place is more important than another when it comes to exercising vigilance.

ALAIN: Vigilance . . . well . . . Annette, it's ridiculous to drink, the state you're in.

ANNETTE: What state? On the contrary.

ALAIN: Vigilance, it's an interesting idea . . .

His mobile. It's Serge.

. . . Yes, no, no interviews before the circulation of the press release.

VÉRONIQUE: That's it. I insist you break off this horrendous conversation!

ALAIN: . . . Absolutely not. . . The shareholders won't give a fuck . . . Remind him, the shareholder is king . . .

Annette launches herself at Alain, snatches the mobile and after a brief look-round to see where she can put it, shoves it into the vase of tulips.

Annette, what the . . .!

ANNETTE: So there.

VÉRONIQUE: Ha, ha! Well done!

MICHEL: *(horrified)* Oh, my God!

ALAIN: Are you completely insane? Fuck!!

He rushes towards the vase, but Michel, who has got in ahead of him, fishes out the dripping object.

MICHEL: The hair-dryer! Where's the hair-dryer?

He finds it and turns it on at once, directing it towards the mobile.

ALAIN: You need locking up, poor love! This is incomprehensible! . . . I had everything in there! . . . It's brand new, it took me hours to set up!

MICHEL: *(to Annette, above the infernal din of the hair-dryer)* Really, I don't understand you. That was completely irresponsible.

ALAIN: Everything's on there, my whole life . . .

ANNETTE: His whole life! . . .

MICHEL: *(still fighting the noise)* Hang on, we might be able to fix it . . .

ALAIN: No chance! It's fucked! . . . .

MICHEL: We'll take out the battery and the SIM-card. Can you open it?

Alain tries to open it with no conviction.

ALAIN: I haven't a clue, I've only just got it.

MICHEL: Let's have a look.

ALAIN: It's fucked . . . And they think it's funny, they think it's funny! . . .

MICHEL: *(opening it easily)* There we are.

He goes back on the offensive with the hair-dryer, having laid out the various parts.

You, Véronique, you at least could have the manners not to laugh at this!

VÉRONIQUE: *(laughing heartily)* My husband will have spent his entire afternoon blow-drying!

ANNETTE: Ha, ha, ha!

Annette makes no bones about helping herself to more rum. Michel, immune to finding any of this amusing, keeps busy, concentrating intently.
For a moment, there's only the sound of the hair-dryer. Alain has slumped.

ALAIN: Leave it, mate. Leave it. There's nothing to be done . . .

Michel finally switches off the hair-dryer.

MICHEL: We'll have to wait a minute . . . *(Hiatus.)* You want to use our phone?

Alain gestures that he doesn't and that he couldn't care less.

I have to say . . .

ANNETTE: Yes, what is it you have to say, Michel?

MICHEL: No . . . I really can't think what to say.

ANNETTE: Well, if you ask me, everyone's feeling fine. If you ask me, everyone's feeling better. *(Hiatus.)* . . . Everyone's much calmer, don't you think? . . . Men are so wedded to their gadgets . . . It belittles them . . . It takes away all their authority . . . A man needs to keep his hands free . . . If you ask me. Even an attaché case is enough to put me off. There was a man, once, I found really attractive, then I saw him with a square shoulder-bag, a man's shoulder-bag, but that was it. There's nothing worse than a shoulder-bag. Although there's also nothing worse than a mobile phone. A man ought to give the impression that he's alone . . . If you ask me. I mean, that he's capable of being alone . . . ! I also have a John Wayne-ish idea of virility. And what was it he had? A Colt .45. A device for creating a vacuum . . . A man who can't give the impression that he's a loner has no texture . . . So, Michel, are you happy? It is somewhat fractured, our little . . . What was it you said? . . . I've forgotten the word . . . but in the end . . . everyone's feeling more or less all right . . . If you ask me.

MICHEL: I should probably warn you, rum drives you crazy.

ANNETTE: I've never felt more normal.

MICHEL: Right.

ANNETTE: I'm starting to feel rather pleasantly serene.

VÉRONIQUE: Ha, ha! That's wonderful! . . . 'Rather pleasantly serene'.

MICHEL: As for you, darjeeling, I fail to see what's to be gained by getting publicly pissed.

VÉRONIQUE: Get stuffed.

Michel goes to fetch the cigar box.

MICHEL: Choose one, Alain. Relax.

VÉRONIQUE: Cigars are not smoked in this house!

MICHEL: Those are Hoyo, those are Monte Cristo Number 3 and Number 4.

VÉRONIQUE: You don't smoke in a house with an asthmatic child!

ANNETTE: Who's asthmatic?

VÉRONIQUE: Our son.

MICHEL: Didn't stop you buying a fucking hamster.

ANNETTE: It's true, if somebody has asthma, keeping animals isn't recommended.

MICHEL: Totally unrecommended!

ANNETTE: Even a goldfish can prove counter-productive.

VÉRONIQUE: Do I have to listen to this fatuous nonsense?

She snatches the cigar box out of Michel's hands and slams it shut brutally.

I'm sorry, no doubt I'm the only one of us not feeling rather pleasantly serene. In fact, I've never been so unhappy. I think this is the unhappiest day of my life.

MICHEL: Drinking always makes you unhappy.

VÉRONIQUE: Michel, every word that comes out of your mouth is destroying me, I don't drink. I drank a mouthful of this shitty rum you're waving about as if you were showing the congregation the Turin Shroud. I don't drink and I bitterly regret it, it'd be a relief to be able to take refuge in a little drop at every minor setback.

ANNETTE: My husband's unhappy as well. Look at him. Slumped. He looks as if someone's left him by the side of the road. I think it's the unhappiest day of his life too.

ALAIN: Yes.

ANNETTE: I'm so sorry, Woof-woof.

Michel starts up the hair-dryer again, directing it at the various parts of the mobile.

VÉRONIQUE: Will you turn off the hair-dryer?! The thing is buggered.

The telephone rings.

MICHEL: Yes! . . . Mum, I told you we were busy . . . Because it could kill you! That medication is poison! Someone's going to explain it to you . . .

He hands the receiver to Alain.

Tell her.

ALAIN: Tell her what? . . .

MICHEL: Everything you know about that crap you're peddling.

ALAIN: . . . How are you, madame? . . .

ANNETTE: What can he tell her? He doesn't know the first thing about it!

ALAIN: Yes . . . And does it hurt? . . . Of course. Well, the operation will fix that . . And the other leg, I see. No, no I'm not an orthopaedist. . . *(Aside.)* She keeps calling me 'doctor'. . .

ANNETTE: Doctor, this is grotesque—hang up!

ALAIN: But you . . . I mean to say, you're not having any problems with your balance? . . . Oh, no. Not at all. Not at all. Don't listen to any of that. All the same, it'd probably be just as well to stop taking it for the moment. Until . . . until you've had a chance to get quietly through your operation . . . Yes, you sound as if you're on very good form . . .

Michel snatches the receiver from him.

MICHEL: All right, Mum, is that clear, stop taking the medication, why do you always have to argue, stop taking it, do what you're told, I'll call you back . . . Lots of love, love from us all.

He hangs up.

She's killing me. One pain in the arse after another!

ANNETTE: Right then, what have we decided? Shall I come back this evening with Ferdinand? No one seems to give a toss any more. All the same, I should point out, that's what we're here for.

VÉRONIQUE: Now I'm starting to feel sick. Where's the bowl?

Michel takes the bottle of rum out of Annette's reach.

MICHEL: That'll do.

ANNETTE: To my mind, there are wrongs on both sides. That's it. Wrongs on both sides.

VÉRONIQUE: Are you serious?

ANNETTE: What?

VÉRONIQUE: Are you aware of what you're saying?

ANNETTE: I am. Yes.

VÉRONIQUE: Our son Bruno, to whom I was obliged to give two Extra Strength Nurofen last night, is in the wrong?

ANNETTE: He's not necessarily innocent.

VÉRONIQUE: Fuck off! I've had quite enough of you.

She grabs Annette's handbag and hurls it towards the door.

Fuck off!

ANNETTE: My handbag! . . . (*Like a little girl.*) Alain! . . .

MICHEL: What's going on? They've slipped their trolley.

ANNETTE: (*gathering up her scattered possessions*) Alain, help! . . .

VÉRONIQUE: 'Alain, help!'

ANNETTE: Shut up!. . . She's broken my compact! And my atomiser! (*To Alain.*) Defend me, why aren't you defending me? . . .

ALAIN: We're going.

He prepares to gather up the parts of his mobile.

VÉRONIQUE: It's not as if I'm strangling her!

ANNETTE: What have I done to you?

VÉRONIQUE: There are not wrongs on both sides! Don't mix up the victims and the executioners!

ANNETTE: Executioners!

MICHEL: You're so full of shit, Véronique, all this simplistic claptrap, we're up to here with it!

VÉRONIQUE: I stand by everything I've said.

MICHEL: Yes, yes, you stand by what you've said, you stand by what you've said, your infatuation for a bunch of Sudanese coons is bleeding into everything now.

VÉRONIQUE: I'm appalled. Why are you choosing to show yourself in this horrible light?

MICHEL: Because I feel like it. I feel like showing myself in a horrible light.

VÉRONIQUE: One day you may understand the extreme gravity of what's going on in that part of the world and you'll be ashamed of this inertia and your repulsive nihilism.

MICHEL: You're just wonderful, darjeeling, you're the best of us all!

VÉRONIQUE: I am. Yes.

ANNETTE: Let's get out of here, Alain, these people are monsters!

She drains her glass and goes to pick up the bottle.

ALAIN: (*preventing her*) . . . Stop it, Annette.

ANNETTE: No, I want to drink some more, I want to get pissed out of my head, this bitch hurls my handbag across the room and no one bats an eyelid, I want to get drunk!

ALAIN: You already are.

ANNETTE: Why are you letting them call my son an executioner? You come to their house to settle things and you get insulted and bullied and lectured on how to be a good citizen of the planet—our son did well clout yours, and I wipe my arse with your charter of human rights!

MICHEL: A mouthful of grog and, bam, the real face appears.

VÉRONIQUE: I told you! Didn't I tell you?

ALAIN: What did you tell him?

VÉRONIQUE: That she was a phoney. This woman is a phoney. I'm sorry.

ANNETTE: (*upset*) Ha, ha, ha! . . .

ALAIN: When did you tell him?

VÉRONIQUE: When you were in the bathroom.

ALAIN: You'd known her for fifteen minutes but you could tell she was a phoney.

VÉRONIQUE: It's the kind of thing I pick up on right away.

MICHEL: It's true.

VÉRONIQUE: I have an instinct for that kind of thing.

ALAIN: And 'phoney', what does that mean?

ANNETTE: I don't want to hear any more! Why are you putting me through this, Alain?

ALAIN: Calm down, Woof-woof.

VÉRONIQUE: She's someone who tries to round off corners. Full stop. She's all front. She doesn't care any more than you do.

MICHEL: It's true.

ALAIN: It's true.

VÉRONIQUE: 'It's true'! Are you saying it's true?

MICHEL: They don't give a fuck! They haven't given a fuck since the start, it's obvious! Her too, you're right!

ALAIN: And you do, I suppose? (*To Annette.*) Let me say something, love. (*To Michel.*) Explain to me in what way you care, Michel. What does the word mean in the first place? You're far more authentic when you're showing yourself in a horrible light. To tell the truth, no one in this room cares, except for Véronique, whose integrity, it has to be said, must be acknowledged.

VÉRONIQUE: Don't acknowledge me! Don't acknowledge me!

ANNETTE: I care. I absolutely care.

ALAIN: We only care about our own feelings, Annette, we're not social crusaders, (*To Véronique.*) I saw your friend Jane Fonda on TV the other day, I was inches away from buying a Ku Klux Klan poster . . .

VÉRONIQUE: What do you mean, 'my friend'? What's Jane Fonda got to do with all this? . . .

ALAIN: You're the same breed. You're part of the same category of woman—committed, problem-solving. That's not what we like about women, what we like about women is sensuality, wildness, hormones. Women who make a song and dance about their intuition, women who are custodians of the world depress us—even him, poor Michel, your husband, he's depressed . . .

MICHEL: Don't speak for me!

VÉRONIQUE: Who gives a flying fuck what you like about women? Where does this lecture come from? A man like you, who could begin to give a fuck for your opinion?

ALAIN: She's yelling. She's a regimental sergeant major.

VÉRONIQUE: What about her, doesn't she yell?! When she said that little bastard had done well to clout our son?

ANNETTE: Yes, he did do well! At least he's not a snivelling little poof!

VÉRONIQUE: Yours is a grass, is that any better?

ANNETTE: Alain, let's go! What are we doing, staying in this dump?

She makes to leave, then returns towards the tulips which she lashes out at violently. Flowers fly, disintegrate and scatter all over the place.

There, there, that's what I think of your pathetic flowers, your hideous tulips! . . . Ha, ha, ha! *(She bursts into tears.)* . . . It's the worst day of my life as well.

Silence.

A long stunned pause.
Michel picks something up off the floor.

MICHEL: *(to Annette)* This yours?

Annette takes a spectacle case, opens it and takes out a pair of glasses.

ANNETTE: Thanks . . .

MICHEL: Not broken?. . .

ANNETTE: No . . .

Hiatus.

MICHEL: What I always say is . . .

Alain starts gathering up the stems and petals.

Leave it.

ALAIN: No . . .

The telephone rings. After some hesitation, Véronique picks up the receiver.

VÉRONIQUE: Yes, darling . . . Oh, good . . . Will you be able to do your homework at Annabelle's?. . . No, no, darling, we haven't found her . . . Yes, I went all the way to the supermarket. But you know, my love, Nibbles is very resourceful, I think you have to have faith in her. You think she was happy in a cage? . . . Daddy's very sad, he didn't mean to upset you . . . Of course you will. Yes, of course you'll speak to him again. Listen, darling, we're worried enough already about your brother . . . She'll eat. . . she'll eat leaves . . . acorns, conkers . . . she'll find things, she knows what food she needs . . . Worms, snails, stuff that drops out of rubbish bins, she's like us, she's omnivorous . . . See you soon, sweetheart.

Hiatus.

MICHEL: I dare say that creature's stuffing its face as we speak.
VÉRONIQUE: No.

Silence.

MICHEL: What do we know?

—2006

appendix A

WRITING ABOUT LITERATURE

First Considerations

You are in your first college-level literature class, and you have probably already completed a composition course in which you used different organizational schemes—example and illustration, comparison and contrast, cause and effect—in writing five-hundred-word essays that were drawn largely from your own personal experiences. When your first effort was returned by your instructor with a bewildering array of correction symbols and a grade that was lower than any you had ever received for your writing, you were at first discouraged. But then you noticed your classmates also shaking their heads in dismay, and you realized that there were certain skills that you would have to learn if you were ever going to get out of English Composition I. You corrected your spelling errors, matched your instructor's grading symbols to those in your handbook, revised mistakes in usage, punctuation, and grammar, and polished your first draft and handed it in again. This time, when it was returned, you were pleased to find fewer correction marks and a couple of encouraging bits of praise in your margins. If you weren't exactly assured that you had permanently mastered every fine point of composition, at least you now had some hope that, with practice, hard work, and careful application of the skills you were learning, your writing would improve and the improvement would be rewarded.

Everyone has been there. Even your instructor was once a student in a freshman writing class, and very few instructors are candid enough to have preserved their own early writing efforts to display to their students. But the problem is no longer your instructor's. She has survived the process to acquire an advanced degree, and her job now is teach you the writing skills that she has acquired. You have some confidence in your own ability, but you also have begun to suspect that writing about literature is quite a bit more demanding than writing about your own life. An introduction to literature course places equal weight on your demonstrated skills as a writer and on your ability to go beyond what you have discussed in the classroom to formulate critical responses to the works that you have read. You may have written thesis papers and completed research projects that you were assigned in high school, but you still do not feel entirely confident about your ability to write about literature. You enjoy reading stories, poems, and plays, but you may find expressing your thoughts about their meaning or their literary merit intimidating. With these thoughts in mind, here are a few general strategies that may help you to write successful critical papers.

Topic Into Thesis

Writing assignments differ greatly, and your instructions may range from general (**Discuss the roles of three minor characters in any of the plays we have read**) to very specific (**Contrast, in not less than five hundred words, the major differences in the plot, characterization, and setting between Joyce Carol Oates's short story "Where Are You Going, Where Have You Been?" and Joyce Chopra's** *Smooth Talk*, **the 1985 film version of the story**). In some cases, especially in essay-type examinations, your instructor may give the whole class the same topic; in others, you may be allowed considerable freedom in selecting one. Length requirements may range from a single paragraph to the standard five-hundred-word theme (in some cases, written during a single class period) to a full-scale research paper of three or four times that length. The assignment will probably ask you to support your assertions with quotes from the story, poem, or play; or it may require that you add further supporting evidence from secondary critical sources. There is no way to predict the precise kinds of papers you may have to write in a literature course; however, there are a few simple guidelines to remember that may help you make the prewriting process easier.

Consider a typical assignment for an essay on poetry: **Discuss any three poems in our textbook that share a similar theme.** Although this is a topic that allows you some latitude in selecting the poems you wish to write about, paradoxically it is just this type of assignment that may cause you the most distress. Why is this so? Simply because there are over three hundred poems in this book, and it is usually impossible for the typical class to cover more than a fraction of that number in the time allotted during the semester to the study of poetry. Before despairing, however, consider the different ways the topic could be limited. Instead of "three poems," you might narrow the field by selecting a more specific group, for example, "three ballads," "three war poems," or "three poems by contemporary African-American poets." Suppose you settle on a group that is limited yet still allows some selection. Choosing "three sonnets by Shakespeare" would allow you to pick from a total of six sonnets included here. In the same way, the second half of the assignment, to find three sonnets with a similar theme, can be limited in various ways. After reading the sonnets, you might observe that #18, #20, and #30 deal with friendship; after further consideration you might decide that #116, because it deals with a "marriage of true minds," is also about a type of friendship. Reading the same group of sonnets a second time, you might be struck by how #18, #73, and #130 deal with physical beauty and its loss. Or, a third time, you might notice that #29, #30, and #73 all possess a depressed tone that sometimes verges on self-pity. After weighing your options and deciding which three sonnets you feel most comfortable discussing, you might formulate a thesis sentence: "In three of his sonnets, Shakespeare stresses that ideal love should be based on more than mere physical beauty." Always keep in mind that the process of choosing, limiting, and developing a topic and thesis sentence should follow the same steps that you practiced in earlier composition courses. As an aid to locating stories, poems, and plays that share similarities, you will find at the end of this book an appendix that groups works thematically.

What is next? A certain amount of informal preparation is always useful: "brainstorming" by taking notes on random ideas and refining those ideas further through discussing them with your peers and instructor. Many composition and introduction to literature courses now include group discussion and peer review of rough drafts as part of the writing process. Even if your class does not use formal group discussion as part of its prewriting activities, there is still nothing to prevent you from talking over your ideas with your classmates or scheduling a conference with your instructor. The conference, especially, is a good idea, as it allows you to get a clearer sense of what is expected from you. In many cases, after a conference with your instructor, you may discover that you could have limited your topic even further or that you could have selected other more pertinent examples to support your thesis.

Explication, Analysis, Reviewing

In general, writing assignments on literature fall into three broad categories: explication, analysis, and reviewing. Explication, which literally means "an unfolding" and is also known as "close reading," is a painstaking analysis of the details of a piece of writing. Because of its extremely limited focus—only on the specific words that the author uses—explication is a consistent favorite for writing assignments on individual poems. In such assignments, the writer attempts to discuss every possible nuance of meaning that a poet has employed. The most useful aid to explication is the dictionary; a full-scale assignment of this type may even involve using the multivolume *Oxford English Dictionary* to demonstrate how a word in a poem may have once possessed a meaning different from what it presently has or to support your contention that a phrase may have several possible meanings. Explication assignments are also possible in writing about fiction and drama. You might be expected to focus closely on a single short passage from a story, for example, explicating the passages describing Arnold Friend in Joyce Carol Oates's "Where Are You Going, Where Have You Been?"; or you might be limited to one scene from a play, being asked to discuss how Othello's speeches in act 1, scene 3 reveal both his strengths of character and the weaknesses that will prove his undoing. There are many useful critical sources to support assignments of this type, and some of them are mentioned later in the section on research methods.

Analysis uses the same general techniques of explication, that is, the use of specific details from the text to support your statements. But where explication attempts to exhaust the widest possible range of meanings, analysis is more selective in its focus, requiring that you examine how a single element—a theme, a technique, a structural device—functions in a single work or in a related group of works. Instead of being assigned to explicate Thomas Gray's "Elegy Written in a Country Churchyard" (a formidable task given its length), you might be asked to analyze only the poet's use of various figures of speech or to examine his imagery or to focus exclusively on the structure of the verse form. Analysis assignments often take the form of comparison-contrast essays (**Compare and contrast the sacrifices and motivations for them of the female protagonists of "Mother Savage" and "Where Are You Going, Where Have You Been?"**) or essays that combine definition with example-illustration (**Define the ballad and discuss ballads written by three poets of this century, showing their links to the tradition of this type of poem**). In the case of these examples, general reference books such as William Harmon and C. Hugh Holman's *A Handbook to Literature* or the exhaustive *The New Princeton Encyclopedia of Poetry and Poetics* will help you to establish your definitions and an overall context for your examples.

The third category, reviewing, is less common in introductory literature courses. A review is a firsthand reaction to a performance or a publication and combines literary analysis with the techniques of journalism. A review of a play or film would evaluate the theatrical elements—acting, direction, sets, and so on—of the performance. Reviews are largely descriptive reporting, but they also should provide evaluation and recommendation. Many of the stories and plays in this volume have been filmed, and you could be asked to discuss how one of them has been adapted for a different medium. Even a local production of a play that you are reading in class is a possibility, and you might find yourself jotting down notes on how the outgoing young woman who sits beside you in a chemistry lab has transformed herself into the role of Williams's Laura. It is even possible that you might find yourself reviewing a public reading given by a poet or fiction writer whose works you first encountered in this book, and you may find yourself commenting on the distance between the image that the writer projects in the poems or stories and his or her actual "stage presence" as a performer. On the purely literary side, book reviews of new collections of stories and poems regularly appear in periodicals such as the *Hudson Review* or the literary sections of major newspapers (the *New York Times Book Review*, published as a separate section of the Sunday *Times*, is the most comprehensive of these), and it is simple enough to find many excellent models should you be assigned to write a paper of this type.

One last word of warning: Note that there are no primarily biographical essays about authors listed as possible writing assignments. Research assignments may ask you to discuss how the particular circumstances of a writer's life may have influenced his or her works, but for the most part biographical information should reside in the background, not the foreground, of literary analysis. An explication of a single poem that begins "Richard Wilbur was born in 1921 in New York City . . ." gives the erroneous impression that you are writing about the poet's life instead of about his work. Try to find a more direct (and original) way of opening your paper.

Critical Approaches

Although most instructors of introduction to literature classes stress a formalist approach (or "close reading") to literary works, other instructors may lecture from a distinct critical perspective and ask their students to employ these techniques in their writing. You might be encouraged to apply a certain kind of critical strategy—feminist criticism or a type of historical approach—to the works you have studied. An instructor might stress that you should emphasize the socioeconomic situation and concerns of a fiction writer and his characters. Or you may be asked to explore how female poets employ visual images that differ from those used by males. Appendix B, *Literature: Thematic and Critical Approaches*, provides suggestions about how works may be grouped together for analysis using various critical methods. Here you will find some brief notes on six of the most often used areas of literary criticism and some advice on how to use the thematic listings to find stories, poems, and plays that might best profit from analysis that employs a specific critical approach. Applying complicated critical theories to individual works is a demanding assignment, and frequent instructor-student conferences may not just be helpful, they may be essential.

Style and Content

Style is the major stumbling block that many students find in writing an effective piece of literary analysis. Aware perhaps that their vocabularies and sentence structures are less sophisticated than those found in the primary and secondary materials being discussed, they sometimes try to overcompensate by adopting, usually without much success, the language of professional critics. This practice can result in garbled sentences and jargon-filled writing. It is much better to write simple, direct sentences, avoiding slang and contractions and using only words with which you are familiar.

Writing in a style with which you are comfortable allows you to make clear transitions between your own writing and the sources that you are citing for supporting evidence. In introducing a quote from a critic, use a phrase such as "As so-and-so notes in his essay on . . ." to guide the reader from your own style into one that is very different. Never include a statement from a critical work that you do not understand yourself, and do not hesitate to go on for a sentence or two after a supporting quote to explain it in your own words. Remember that literary criticism has its own technical vocabulary and that many of these literary terms are discussed elsewhere in this book. Proper terminology should be used instead of homemade substitutes. Thus, to talk about the "highpoint of the story line" instead of "the climax of the plot" or the "style of the rhythm and rhyme" instead of "the formal strategies of the poem" is to invite an unfavorable response.

As far as the content of your paper is concerned, try to avoid eccentric personal responses for which you can find no critical support. This rule holds for all types of literature but is especially true if you are writing about poetry. Because poetry compresses language and detail, you may have to fill in more than a few blank spaces to make sense of a poem. Good poems often *suggest* information instead of explicitly stating it; the shorter the poem, the more that may be suggested. If you do not begin by determining a poem's dramatic situation—the basic *who*, *what*, *where*, and *when* of a poem—you will not have established the basis on which your subsequent remarks must be anchored. It is possible for a student to go far astray on a poem as simple as A. E. Housman's "Eight o'Clock" because he or she failed to notice the poem's most important detail, that the only character in it has a *noose* around his neck.

In writing about other genres, you may have a brilliant intuition that Emily Grierson's servant Tobe is the real murderer of Homer Barron in Faulkner's "A Rose for Emily," but you may encounter difficulty in finding support for these conclusions either in the text or in the work of critics. Also, unless you are specifically asked to take a biographical approach, don't try to make close connections between an author's work and the events of his or her life; literature and autobiography are not identical. Some perfectly decent people (poets Robert Browning and Ai are two examples) have relished creating characters who are masterpieces of madness or evil, and some perfectly awful people have created beautiful works of literature. It may be the professional biographer's job to judge literary merit on the basis of what he or she perceives as the moral virtues or lack thereof of a writer, but unless you are specifically asked to take a biographical approach you should probably limit your remarks to the text that you are analyzing.

Writing About Fiction

As mentioned earlier, an explication assignment on a single short story demands close attention to detail because it focuses on the subtleties of a writer's language. "Close reading" means exactly what it sounds like: you should carefully weigh every word in the passage you are explicating. Typically, an explication assignment might ask you to look carefully at a key section of a short story, explaining how it contains some element on which the whole story hinges and without which it could not succeed. Suppose, for example, that you are asked to explicate the opening paragraph of Cheever's "Reunion" and are explicitly requested to explain what the paragraph conveys beyond obvious expository information. After poring over the paragraph several times, you might decide that it contains ample foreshadowing of the disastrous events that are about to occur. In particular you might cite such tell-tale phrases as "his secretary wrote to say" or "my mother divorced him" as Cheever's way of dropping hints about the father's unstable personality. Then you might go on to mention Charlie's forebodings of his own "doom," all leading up to the aroma of prelunch cocktails that Charlie notices when he and his father embrace. Any explication demands that you quote extensively from the text, explaining why certain choices of words and details are important and speculating about why the writer made these choices.

Student Michelle Ortiz decided to examine the significance of the colors used in Alice Walker's "Everyday Use."

> Walker establishes the color contrasts carefully. The opening paragraph describes the clean-swept "hard clay" of the front yard, which the mother says "is like an extended living room." She describes how she wears "flannel nightgowns to bed and overalls during the day." Maggie, the stay-at-home daughter, wears a "pink skirt and red blouse," colors that perhaps relate to the house fire years ago that scarred her. The items in the house that Dee wants to take away are drably colored, an old wooden bench

and a wooden churn top. The handmade quilts, which become the chief bone of contention between the mother and Maggie and the acquisitive Dee are made from scraps of old clothing. The colors that Walker mentions are "one teeny faded blue piece" from an ancestor's Civil War uniform and some "lavender ones" from one of her great-grandmother's dresses. Contrasting with the bright colors ("yellows and oranges") of the flamboyant Dee's outfit ("so loud it *hurts* my eyes," the mother says), the colors associated with the family home are muted and soft, suggesting things that have faded from years of "everyday use."

A typical analysis assignment in short fiction might ask you to explain what a "rites of passage" story is and demonstrate that "Reunion" has most of the characteristics of the type. Here you might want to first define the initiation story, using your lecture notes, general literary reference books, and your familiarity with other stories from popular sources like fairy tales or motion pictures. After demonstrating that this type of story is indeed well established and having described its chief characteristics, you might then focus on such matters in "Reunion" as Charlie's age, his naive expectations, his disillusioning experience, and his eventual "passage" out of his father's life at the end of the story. A slightly more complicated analysis assignment might involve comparison and contrast. Generally, comparison seeks out common ground between two subjects, whereas contrast finds differences; most papers of this type will do both, first pointing out the similarities before going on to demonstrate how each story represents a variation on the theme. Comparison-contrast essays may examine a single story, analyzing two characters' approaches to a similar situation, or even a single character's "before and after" view of another character or event. Or these essays may compare and contrast two or more works that have common threads. If you are examining a single author in depth, you might be required to locate other stories that deal with similar themes. Because Cheever writes extensively about alcoholism, family tensions, and divorce, you might choose several of his stories that reflect the same basic themes as "Reunion." Even more demanding might be a topic asking you to find stories (or even poems or plays) by other authors to compare or contrast. Among the stories in this book, there are several examples of initiation stories and others that deal with tensions between parents and children. Assignments in comparative analysis require careful selection and planning, and it is essential to find significant examples of both similarities and differences to support your thesis.

Writing About Poetry

Because explication of a poem involves careful close reading on a line-by-line basis, an assignment of this type will usually deal with a relatively short poem or a passage from a longer one. Some poems yield most of their meaning on a single reading; others, however, may contain complexities and nuances that deserve a careful inspection of how the poet utilizes all of the resources at his or her command. A typical explication examines both form and content. Because assignments in analysis usually involve many of the same techniques as explication, we will look at explication more closely. Poetry explications usually require much more familiarity with the technical details of poems than do those about fiction and drama, so here is a checklist of questions that you might ask before explicating a poem. Student Marc Potter's answers apply to a poem from this book, Edwin Arlington Robinson's sonnet "Firelight."

Form

1. How many lines does the poem contain? How are they arranged into stanzas? Is either the whole poem or the stanza an example of a traditional poetic form?

   "Firelight" is an Italian sonnet. It is divided into two stanzas, an octave and sestet, and there is a shift, or what is known in sonnets as a "turn" or *volta*, at the beginning of line nine, though here there is no single word that signals the shift.

2. Is there anything worth noting in the visual arrangement of the poem—indentation, spacing, and so on? Are capitalization and punctuation unusual?

   Capitalization and punctuation are standard in the poem, and Robinson follows the traditional practice of capitalizing the first word of each line.

3. What meter, if any, is the poem written in? Does the poet use any notable examples of substitution in the meter? Are the lines primarily end-stopped or enjambed?

   The meter is regular iambic pentameter ("Hĕr thóughts/ ă mó / mĕnt sínce / ŏf one / whŏ shínes") with occasional substitutions of trochees ("Wísĕr / fŏr sí/ lĕnce") and spondees ("thĕir jóy / rĕcálls / Nó snáke, / nó swórd"). Enjambment, found at the ends of lines two, five, six, seven, nine, ten, twelve, and thirteen, has the effect of masking the regular meter and rhymes and enforcing a conversational tone, an effect that is assisted by the caesurae in lines six, seven, nine, and (most importantly) fourteen. The caesura in this last line calls attention to "Apart," which ironically contrasts with the poem's opening phrase: "Ten years together."

4. What is the rhyme scheme, if any, of the poem? What types of rhyme are used?

The rhyme scheme of this poem is abbaabba cdecde. Robinson uses exact masculine rhyme, with the rhyming sounds falling on single stressed syllables; the only possible exception is "intervals," where the meter forces a secondary stress on the third syllable.

5. Are significant sound patterns evident? Is there any repetition of whole lines, phrases, or words?

Alliteration is present in "*f*irelight" and "*f*our" in line three and "*w*an" and "*o*ne" in line eleven, and there are several instances of assonance ("W*i*ser for s*i*lence"; "end*ow*ed / And b*ow*ered") and consonance ("Se*ren*ely and pe*renn*ially *en*dowed"; the *w*an face of *one* somewhere a*lone*"). However, these sound patterns do not call excessive attention to themselves and depart from the poem's relaxed, conversational sound. "Firelight" contains no prominent use of repetition, with the possible exception of the pronoun "they" and its variant forms "their" and "them" and the related use of the third-person singular pronouns "he" and "she" in the last five lines of the poem. This pronoun usage, confusing at first glance, indirectly carries the poem's theme of the separateness of the couple's thoughts. The only notable instance of parallel phrasing occurs in line seven with "No snake, no sword."

Content

1. To what genre (lyric, narrative, dramatic) does the poem belong? Does it contain elements of more than one genre?

"Firelight" is a short narrative poem. Even though it has little plot in the conventional sense, it contains two characters in a specific setting who perform actions that give the reader insight into the true nature of their relationship. The sonnet form has traditionally been used for lyrical poetry.

2. Who is the persona of the poem? Is there an auditor? If so, who? What is the relationship between persona and auditor? Does the poem have a specific setting? If so, where and when is it taking place? Is there any

action that has taken place before the poem opens? What actions take place during the poem?

The persona here is a third-person omniscient narrator such as might be encountered in a short story; the narrator has the ability to read "Her thoughts a moment since" and directly comments that the couple is "Wiser for silence." The unnamed characters in the poem are a man and woman who have been married for ten years. The poem is set in their home, apparently in a comfortable room with a fireplace where they are spending a quiet evening together. Neither character speaks during the poem; the only action is their looking at "each other's eyes at intervals / Of gratefulness." Much of the poem's ironic meaning hinges on the couple's silence: "what neither says aloud."

3. Does the poem contain any difficulties with grammar or syntax? What individual words or phrases are striking because of their denotation or connotation?

The syntax of "Firelight" is straightforward and contains no inversions or ellipses. The poem's sentence structure is deceptively simple. The first four lines make up a single sentence with one main clause; the second four lines also make up a single sentence, this time with two main clauses; the final six lines also make up a single sentence, broken into two equal parts by the semicolon, and consisting of both main and dependent clauses. The vocabulary of "Firelight" is not unusual, though "obliteration" (literally an *erasure*) seems at first a curious choice to describe the effects of love. One should note the allusion to the book of Genesis that is implied by "bowered," "snake," and "sword" in the octave and the rather complicated use of the subjunctive "were" in lines nine, ten, and twelve. Again, this slight alteration in grammar bears indirectly on the theme of the poem. "Yet" in the first line provides an interesting touch since it injects a slight negative note into the picture of marital bliss.

4. Does the poem use any figures of speech? If so, how do they add to the overall meaning? Is the action of the poem to be taken literally, symbolically, or both ways?

"Firelight" uses several figures of speech. "Cloud" is a commonly employed metaphor for "foreboding." "Firelight" and "four walls" are a metonymy and synecdoche, respectively, for the couple's comfortable home. The allusion to the "snake" and "sword" make the reader think of the unhappy ending of the Garden of Eden story. It is significant that Robinson repeats "no" when referring to what the couple's "joy recalls."

"Wiser for silence" is a slight paradox. "The graven tale of lines / on the wan face" is an implied metaphor which compares the lines on a person's face to the written ("graven" means *engraved* and also sounds like a word with several negative connotations: *grave*) story of her life. To say that a person "shines" instead of "excels" is another familiar metaphor. "Firelight" is to be understood primarily on the literal level. The characters are symbolic only in that the man and woman are perhaps representative of many married couples, who outwardly express happiness yet inwardly carry regrets and fantasies from past relationships.

5. Is the title of the poem appropriate? What are its subject, tone of voice, and theme? Is the theme stated or implied?

"Firelight" is a good title since it carries both the connotation of domestic tranquility and a hint of danger. "To bring to the light" means to reveal the truth, and the narrator in this poem does this. Robinson's attitude toward the couple is ironic. On the surface they seem to be the picture of ideal happiness, but Robinson reveals that this happiness has been purchased, in the man's case, at the expense of an earlier lover and, in the woman's, by settling for someone who has achieved less than another man for whom she apparently had unrequited love. Robinson's ironic view of marital stability is summed up in the phrase "Wiser for silence." Several themes are implied: the difference between surface appearance and deeper insight; the cynical idea that in love ignorance of what one's partner is thinking may be the key to bliss; the sense that individual happiness is not without its costs. All of these are possible ways to state Robinson's bittersweet theme.

Your instructor may ask you to employ specific strategies in your explication and may require a certain type of organization for the paper. In writing the body of the explication, you will probably proceed through the poem from beginning to end, summarizing and paraphrasing some lines and quoting others fully when you feel an explanation is required. It should be stressed that there are many ways, in theory, to approach a poem and that no two explications of the same poem will agree in every detail.

A writing assignment in analysis might examine the way a single element—dramatic situation, meter, form, imagery, one or more figures of speech, theme—functions in poetry. An analysis would probably require that you write about two or more poems, using the organizational patterns of comparison-contrast or definition/example-illustration. Such an assignment might examine two or more related poems by the same poet, or it might inspect the way that several poets have used a poetic device or theme. Comparison-contrast essays might explore both similarities and differences found in two poems. Definition–illustration papers usually begin with a general discussion of the topic, say, a popular theme such as the *carpe diem* motif, and then go on to illustrate how it may be found in several different poems. Assignments in analysis often lead to longer papers that may require the use of secondary sources. These two paragraphs from Jennifer Haughton's research paper on A. D. Hope's uses of various quatrain forms in his poetry include parenthetical citations both to the poem and to works by two critics, Paul Fussell and Robert Darling, who have made comments relevant to her argument.

> Another poem in which Hope uses quatrains contrary to convention is "Imperial Adam," which is written in elegiac stanzas (*Selected* 44). Traditionally, the elegiac stanza was often (though not always) employed to lament someone's death; however, it became so associated with this function over time that modern poets may now use it for irony (Fussell 135). Hope said he intended the poem "Imperial Adam" to be a satire of the profane image of Eve (thus the use of the elegiac stanza), yet at least one critic believes that he did his job too well and ended up perpetuating Eve's wicked image (Darling 44). The extent to which "Imperial Adam" succeeds as a satire depends on whether its content or its form becomes dominant in the poem.

> The first two stanzas maintain a fairly regular iambic meter and show a "puzzled" Adam discovering the loss of his rib. By the fourth quatrain, Eve has been introduced, and a double spondaic substitution ("dark hairs winked crisp") in the last line spotlights a part of Eve's anatomy that will spark the fall. Instead of eating a forbidden apple, the taboo of this poem centers on sex: "She promised on the turf of Paradise / Delicious pulp of the forbidden fruit" (18-19). In the absence of a literal serpent in the poem tempting Adam and Eve, the origin of evil becomes the question.

Writing About Drama

A review of a play is an evaluation of an actual performance and will focus less on the text of the play itself (especially if it is a well-known one) than on the actors' performances, the overall direction of the production, and the elements of staging. Because reviews are, first, news stories, basic information about the time and place of production should be given at the beginning of the review. A short summary of the play's plot might follow, and subsequent paragraphs will evaluate the performers and the production. Remember that a review is chiefly a *recommendation*, either positive or negative, to readers. Films of most of the plays in this book are available on videotape, and you also might be asked to review one of these versions, paying attention to the ways in which directors have "opened up" the action by utilizing the complex technical resources of motion pictures. Excellent examples of drama and film reviews can be found in almost any major newspaper or in the pages of popular magazines such as *Time* or *The New Yorker*.

Explication assignments, such as, the examples from fiction and poetry given earlier, will probably require that you pay close attention to a selected passage, giving a detailed account of all the fine shadings of language in a scene or perhaps a single speech. Because Shakespeare's poetry is often full of figurative language that may not be fully understood until it has been subjected to explication, close reading of one of the monologues or soliloquies in Twelfth Night would be a likely choice for this type of writing assignment. For a short writing assignment in a Shakespeare class, Brandon Frank chose to explicate one speech from *Othello*, the title character's defense of himself to the Venetian senate against charges brought by his new bride Desdemona's father, Brabantio, that Othello has used witchcraft to seduce his daughter. Here are his remarks on the opening of Othello's speech in act 1, scene 3:

> Othello is a subtle and intelligent man. He realizes that the charges against him are serious, and he also knows that the Duke and other members of the senate are inclined to trust Brabantio, one of their own to whom the Duke has just said, "Welcome gentle signior, / We lacked your counsel and your help tonight" (1.3.50-51). Othello counters, first, by deferring to the "most potent, grave, and reverend signiors" whom he calls his "very noble and approved good masters" (1.3.76-77). Next, he freely admits to one part of Brabantio's charge, that he and Desdemona have married:
>
> > That I have ta'en away this old man's daughter,
> > It is most true—true, I have married her.
> > The very head and front of my offending
> > Hath this extent, no more. (1.3.78-81)
>
> Having at least partially defused Brabantio's charges by showing respect to the senate which will decide his fate and by stating that has in fact wed Desdemona, he makes a humble reference to how, because he has spent most of his life "in the tented field" (1.3.85) and then proceeds to the heart of his defense, in which he will "a round unvarnished tale deliver / Of my

whole course of love" (1.3.90-91). He will inform the senate that it was the power of love, not "what drugs, what charms, / What conjuration and mighty magic" (1.3.91-92), that brought him and Desdemona together.

Analysis assignments typically hinge on only one of the elements of the play like plot or characterization, or on a concept set forth by a critic. For example, you might be asked to explain Aristotle's statements about reversal and recognition and then apply his terminology to a modern play such as *The Piano Lesson*. Here you would attempt to locate relevant passages from the play to support Aristotle's contentions about the importance of these reversals in the best plots. Or you might be asked to provide a summary of his comments about the tragic hero and then apply this definition to a character like Othello. Again, comparison and contrast schemes are useful. You might be asked to contrast two or more characters in a single play (Antigone versus her sister Ismene in terms of women's role in society) or to compare characters in two different plays as undeserving victims of fate. In an extended essay on Tennessee Williams's play *Cat on a Hot Tin Roof*, Beverly Williams examines attitudes toward God and religion that are revealed by the characters. Here is her paragraph on the family patriarch, Big Daddy :

> For Big Daddy Pollitt, God does not exist in any religious order, and he tells Brick, "Church!—it bores the bejesus out of me but I go!" (1155). Instead, his God has two manifestations, money and his youngest son Brick. To Big Daddy, money means power and freedom from want, but there are some wants that money cannot buy, no matter how much a man acquires. Though he states his worth at "Close on ten million in cash an' blue-chip stocks" (1143), Big Daddy knows that "a man can't buy back his life with it when his life has been spent" (1143), and it cannot buy "life everlasting." No one can escape mortality. In *The Broken World of Tennessee Williams*, Esther Merle Jackson states it best, "Big Daddy has believed in the power of money. He speaks of its failure as a god" (142).

The Process of Research: The Library and the Internet

Research is a time-consuming and sometimes frustrating process, but a few general principles may help you to streamline it. First, bear in mind that about 90% of the time you spend on assembling research materials will take place in one section of the library, the reference room, and that a large amount of information about where to find certain materials and the critical materials themselves are now available on electronic databases. If you rush off to consult a book on the fifth-floor shelves every time you locate a mention of something that is potentially useful to you, you may gain more expertise in operating an elevator than in conducting effective research. Thus, use the reference room to assemble the "shopping list" of items you will have to find in other parts of the library. Also, remember that the online indexes and sources have greatly enhanced the mechanics of research. It may be frustrating to learn that an article you spotted in a musty index and found, after a long search, in a bound volume of a journal that could have been downloaded and printed out in seconds from an online database.

Most contemporary students have literally grown up writing with computers and are familiar with the Internet. Still, a few words about the use of the Internet for online research may be helpful. In recent years, the Internet has facilitated the chores of research, and many online databases, reference works, and periodicals may be quickly located using search engines including Yahoo! (**www.yahoo.com**) and Google (**www.google.com**). The Internet also holds a wealth of information in the form of individual Web sites devoted to authors. Many of these Web sites are run by universities or private organizations. Students should be aware, however, that Web sites vary widely in quality. Some are legitimate sources displaying sound scholarship; others are little more than "fan pages" that may contain erroneous or misleading information. Online information, like any other kind of research material, should be carefully evaluated before it is used.

Careful documentation of your sources is essential; if you use any material other than what is termed "common knowledge" you must cite it in your paper. Common knowledge includes biographical information, an author's publications, prizes and awards received, and other information that can be found in more than one reference book. Anything else—direct quotes or material you have put in your own words by paraphrasing—requires both a parenthetical citation in the body of your paper and an entry on your works cited pages.

The first step in successful research is very simple: read the assigned text before looking for secondary sources. After you have read the story, poem, or play that you have been assigned, you may have already begun to formulate a workable thesis sentence. If you have done this before beginning your research, you will eliminate any number of missteps and repetitions. Next, perform a subject search for books that will be useful to you. If, for example, you are writing on one of Keats's odes, a subject search may reveal one or more books devoted solely to this single type of poem. Computerized library databases are set up in different configurations, but many of them allow multiple "keyword" searches; a search command like KEATS AND ODE might automatically cross-reference all journal articles that mention both subjects. If you are unfamiliar with your terminology and do not know, for example, how an ode differs from other kinds of poems, you should consult a reference book containing a discussion of literary terms. After you have located books and reference sources that will be of use, check the journals that publish literary criticism. The standard index for these is the *MLA International Bibliography*, which is available both in bound volumes and in an online version, and many items listed after a search may exist in full-text electronic versions. A reference librarian also may direct you to other indexes such as the *Literary Criticism Index* and the *Essay and General Literature Index*. It is a good idea to check indexes like these early in your research. No single college library carries all of the journals listed in the *MLA International Bibliography*, and you may discover that getting a reprint through interlibrary services can take a week or more.

Once you have located and assembled your sources, you can decide which of them will be most valuable to you. Again, if you have already formulated your thesis and perhaps completed a tentative outline as well, you can move more swiftly. Two blessed additions to almost every library are the copying machine and the network printer, which remove the tedious chore of taking notes by hand on 3 × 5 cards. Note cards may still be useful if you want to try different arrangements of your material, but most students have happily discarded them as relics of the distant past.

It is impossible to guess what research materials will be available in any given library, but most college libraries contain many different kinds of indexes and reference books for literary research. If you are writing about a living writer, particularly recommended are three popular reference sets published by Gale Research: *Dictionary of Literary Biography* (DLB), *Contemporary Authors* (CA), and *Contemporary Literary Criticism* (CLC). Both of these two last reference works are also available in editions that cover the nineteenth and twentieth centuries. These will provide you both with useful overviews of careers and with generous samples of criticism about the authors. *DLB* and *CA* articles also contain extensive bibliographies of other relevant sources; *CLC* contains reprints of book reviews and relevant passages from critical works. Similar to these reference works are those in the *Critical Survey* series from Magill Publishers, multivolume sets that focus on short and long fiction, poetry, drama, and film. Another reliable source of information on individual writers can be found in several series of critical books published by Twayne Publishers, which can be located in a subject search.

For locating explications, several indexes are available, including *Poetry Explication: A Checklist of Interpretations since 1925 of British and American Poems Past and Present* and *The Explicator Cyclopedia*, which reprints explications originally appearing in the periodical of the same name. *Poetry Criticism* and *Short Story Criticism* are multivolume reference works that reprint excerpts from critical essays and books. There are several popular indexes of book reviews; one of these, the annual *Book Review Digest*, reprints brief passages from the most representative reviews. Two reference sources providing, respectively, examples of professional drama and film reviews are *The New York Times Theater Reviews, 1920–1970* (and subsequent volumes) and *The New York Times Film Reviews*. Popular magazines containing book, drama, and film reviews (and occasionally poetry reviews as well) include *Time*, *Newsweek*, and *The New Yorker*, and these reviews are indexed in the *Readers' Guide to Periodical Literature*, more recent volumes of which are available online. Also, yearbooks such as *Theatre World* or the *Dictionary of Literary Biography Yearbook* provide a wealth of information about the literary activities of a given year.

Plagiarism: Proper Quotation and Citation of Sources

First, a warning about plagiarism. Few students knowingly plagiarize, and those who do are usually not successful at it. An instructor who has read four or five weak papers from a student is likely to be suspicious if the same student suddenly begins to sound like an officer of the Modern Language Association, writing, with no citations, about "paradigms" or "*différance*" in the "*texte*." A definition of "common knowledge," the kind of information that does not require a citation, is given above. Otherwise, any *opinion* about a writer and his or her work must be followed by a citation indicating its source. If the opinion is directly quoted, paraphrased, or even summarized in passing you should still include a citation. Doing less than this is to commit an act of plagiarism, for which the penalties are usually severe. Internet materials, which are so easily cut and pasted into a manuscript, provide an easy temptation but are immediately noticeable, and there has been much media scrutiny in recent years about the widespread "epidemic" of Internet plagiarism. Nothing is easier to spot in a paper than an uncited "lift" from a source; in most cases the vocabulary and sentence structure will be radically different from the rest of the paper, and a simple text search with Google will probably reveal its source. Particularly bothersome are the numerous Web sites offering "free" research papers; a quick perusal of some of these papers indicates that even at a free price they are significantly overpriced. Additionally, many educational institutions have subscribed to "plagiarism-detection" software services that maintain huge, searchable files of research papers that have seen more than one user.

You should always support the general statements you make about a story, poem, or play by quoting directly from the text or, if required, by using secondary sources for additional critical opinion. The *MLA Handbook for Writers of Research Papers*, 7th ed., which you will find in the reference section of almost any library, contains standard formats for bibliographies and manuscripts; indeed, most of the writing handbooks used in college composition courses follow MLA style guidelines. Purdue University maintains a useful online source on MLA style at **http://owl.english.purdue.edu/owl/resource/747/01/**. However, if you have doubts or if you have not been directed to use a certain format, ask your instructor which one he or she prefers.

The type of parenthetical citation used in MLA-style format to indicate the source of quotations is simple to learn and dispenses with such tedious and repetitive chores as footnotes and endnotes. In using parenthetical citations, remember that your goal is to direct your reader from the quoted passage in the paper to the corresponding entry on your works cited pages and from there, if necessary, to the book or periodical from which the quote was taken. A good parenthetical citation gives only the *minimal* information needed to accomplish this task. Here are a few typical examples from student papers on fiction, poetry, and drama. The first discusses Cheever's "Reunion":

> Cheever moves very quickly to indicate that the "Reunion" may well be memorable but will not be happy. As soon as father and son enter the first restaurant and are seated, Charlie's father begins to act strangely: "We sat down, and my father hailed the waiter in a loud voice. '*Kellner!*' he shouted. '*Garçon! Cameriere! You!*' His boisterousness in the empty restaurant seemed out of place" (518).

Here you should note a couple of conventions of writing about fiction and literature in general. One is that the present tense is used in speaking of the events of the story; in general, use the present tense throughout your critical writing except when you are giving biographical or historical information. Second, note the use of single and double quotation marks. Double quotes from the story are changed to single quotes here, as they appear within the writer's own quotation marks. The parenthetical citation lists only a page number, for earlier in this paper the writer has mentioned Cheever by name and the context makes it clear that the quotation comes from the story. Only one work by Cheever appears among the works cited entries. If several works by Cheever had been listed there, the parenthetical citation would clarify which one was being referred to by adding a shortened form of the book's title: (*Stories* 518). The reader finds the following entry among the sources:

> Cheever, John. *The Stories of John Cheever*. New York: Knopf, 1978. Print.

Similarly, quotes and paraphrases from secondary critical sources should follow the same rules of common sense:

> Cheever's daughter Susan, in her candid memoir of her father, observes that the author's alcoholism followed an increasingly destructive pattern:
>
>> Long before I was even aware that he was alcoholic, there were bottles hidden all over the house, and even outside in the privet hedge and the garden shed. Drink was his crucible, his personal hell. As early as the 1950s . . . he

> spent a lot of energy trying not to drink before 4 p.m., and
> then before noon, and then before 10 a.m., and then before
> breakfast. (43)

But she goes on to observe that Cheever's drinking had not yet affected his skills as a writer.

This quotation is longer than four lines, so it is indented one inch. Indented quotes of this type do not require quotation marks. Also note how ellipses are used to omit extraneous information. Because the author of the quotation is identified, only the page number is included in the parenthetical citation. The reader knows where to look among the sources:

> Cheever, Susan. *Home Before Dark*. Boston: Houghton, 1984. Print.

Notice that a paraphrase of the same passage requires the citation as well:

> Cheever's daughter Susan, in her candid memoir of her father, observes that the author's alcoholism followed an increasingly destructive pattern. She notes that as a child she found bottles hidden in the house, in outbuildings, and even in the hedge. She recalls that he spent a great deal of energy simply trying not to drink before a certain hour, at first before 4 p.m. but eventually before breakfast (43).

To simplify parenthetical citations, it is recommended that quotes from secondary sources be introduced, whenever possible, in a manner that identifies the author so that only the page number of the quote is needed inside of the parentheses.

Slightly different conventions govern quotations from poetry. Here are a few examples from papers on Edwin Arlington Robinson's poetry:

> Robinson's insights into character are never sharper than in "Miniver Cheevy," a portrait of a town drunk who loves "the days of old / When swords were bright and steeds were prancing" and dreams incongruously "of Thebes and Camelot, / And Priam's neighbors" (5–6, 11–12).

Pay attention to how only parts of numbered lines are quoted here to support the sentence and how the parts fit smoothly into the writer's sentence structure. In general, ellipses (. . .) are not necessary at the beginning or end of these quotes because it is clear that they are quoted fragmentarily; they should, however, be used if something is omitted from the middle of a quote ("the days of old / When . . . steeds were prancing"). The virgule or slash (/) is used to indicate line breaks; a double slash (//) indicates stanza breaks. Quotes of up to three lines should be treated in this manner. If a quote is longer than three lines it should be indented one inch (with no quotation marks) and printed as it appears in the original poem:

> Robinson opens one of his most effective and pitiless character sketches
> with an unsparing portrait of failure and bitterness:
>
>> Miniver Cheevy, child of scorn,
>> Grew lean while he assailed the seasons;
>> He wept that he was ever born,
>> And he had reasons. (1–4)

As in the example from the Cheever story, the parenthetical citation here lists only a page number because only one work by Robinson appears in the bibliography. If you are dealing with a classic poem that can be found in many editions (an ode by Keats or a Shakespeare sonnet, for example) the *MLA Handbook* recommends using line numbers instead of page numbers inside the parentheses. This practice also should be followed if you have included a copy of the poem that you are explicating with the paper.

Quoting from a play follows similar procedures. These papers discuss Shakespeare's tragedy *Othello*:

> In a disarming display of modesty before the Venetian senators, Othello
> states that his military background has not prepared him to act as an eloquent spokesman in his own defense, readily admitting that "little shall I
> grace my cause / In speaking for myself" (1.3.90–91).

Classic poetic dramas such as *Othello* may be cited by act, scene, and line numbers instead of by page numbers. The reader knows that Shakespeare is the author, so the citation here will simply direct him or her to the edition of Shakespeare listed in the works cited pages at the end of the paper. Also note that verse dramas should be quoted in the same manner as poems; quotations of more than three lines should be indented one inch. In this paper, a scene involving dialogue is quoted:

In the climactic scene of *Othello*, Shakespeare's practice of fragmenting his blank verse lines into two or more parts emphasizes the violence that is about to occur:

Othello:		He hath confessed.
Desdemona:	What, my lord?	
Othello:	That he hath used thee.	
Desdemona:		How? Unlawfully?
Othello:		Ay.
Desdemona:	He will not say so. (5.2.73–75)	

If you are quoting from a prose drama, you would cite a page number from the edition of the play that you used:

> In *A Doll's House* Ibsen wants to demonstrate immediately that Nora and Helmer share almost childlike attitudes toward each other. "Is that my little lark twittering out there?" is Helmer's initial line in the play (43).

Remember that common sense is the best test to apply to any parenthetical citation. Have you given the reader enough information in the citation to locate the source from which the quote was taken?

Sample Works Cited Entries

Here are formats for some of the most commonly used types of materials used in literary research. More detailed examples may be found in the *MLA Handbook for Writers of Research Papers*, 7th ed.

Book by a Single Author

Finch, Annie. *The Ghost of Meter: Culture and Prosody in American Free Verse*. Ann Arbor: U of Michigan P, 1993. Print.

Ives, David. *All in the Timing: Fourteen Plays*. New York: Vintage, 1995. Print.

Reynolds, Clay. *Ars Poetica*. Lubbock: Texas Tech UP, 2003. Print.

Sanderson, Jim. *Semi-Private Rooms*. Youngstown: Pig Iron, 1994. Print.

Wilbur, Richard. *Collected Poems 1943–2004*. New York: Harcourt, 2004. Print.

Book with Author and Editor

Robinson, Edwin Arlington. *Edwin Arlington Robinson's Letters to Edith Brower*. Ed. Richard Cary. Cambridge: Harvard UP, 1968. Print.

Casebook or Edited Collection of Critical Essays

Dean, Leonard Fellows, ed. *A Casebook on Othello*. New York: Crowell, 1961. Print.

Snyder, Susan, ed. *Othello: Critical Essays*. New York: Garland, 1988. Print.

Individual Selection from a Casebook or Edited Collection

Urbanski, Marie Mitchell Oleson. "Existential Allegory: Joyce Carol Oates's 'Where Are You Going, Where Have You Been?'" *"Where Are You Going, Where Have You Been?": Joyce Carol Oates*. Ed. Elaine Showalter. New Brunswick: Rutgers UP, 1994. 75–79. Print.

Woodring, Carl R. "Once More The Windhover." *Gerard Manley Hopkins: The Windhover*. Ed. John Pick. Columbus: Merrill, 1969. 52–56. Print.

Story, Poem, or Play Reprinted in Anthology or Textbook

Cheever, John. "The Swimmer." *The Longman Anthology of Short Fiction: Stories and Authors in Context*. Ed. Dana Gioia and R. S. Gwynn. New York: Longman, 2001. 390–99. Print.

Hansberry, Lorraine. *A Raisin in the Sun*. *Black Theater: A Twentieth-Century Collection of the Work of Its Best Playwrights*. Ed. Lindsay Patterson. New York: Dodd, 1971. 221–76. Print.

Robinson, Edwin Arlington. "Richard Cory." *Literature: An Introduction to Poetry, Fiction, and Drama*. 11th ed. Ed. X. J. Kennedy and Dana Gioia. New York: Longman, 2010. 792. Print.

Article in Reference Book

Johnson, Richard A. "Auden, W. H." *Academic American Encyclopedia (Electronic Edition)*. 2002 ed. Danbury: Grolier, 2002. CD-ROM.

"Othello." *The Oxford Companion to English Literature*. Ed. Margaret Drabble. 5th ed. New York: Oxford UP, 1985. Print.

Seymour-Smith, Martin. "Cheever, John." *Who's Who in Twentieth Century Literature*. New York: McGraw, 1976. Print.

Article, Book Review, Story, or Poem in Scholarly Journal

Berry, Edward. "Othello's Alienation." *Studies in English Literature, 1500-1900* 30 (1990): 315–33. Print.

Horgan, Paul. "To Meet Mr. Eliot: Three Glimpses." *American Scholar* 60 (1991): 407–13. Web. 22 Feb. 2011.

McDonald, Walter. "Sandstorms." *Negative Capability* 3.4 (1983): 93. Print.

Read, Arthur M., II. "Robinson's 'The Man Against the Sky.'" *Explicator* 26 (1968): 49. Print.

Article, Book Review, Story, or Poem in Magazine

Becker, Alida. Rev. of *Morning, Noon, and Night*, by Sidney Sheldon. *New York Times Book Review* 15 Oct. 1995: 20. Print.

Iyer, Pico. "Magic Carpet Ride." Rev. of *The English Patient*, by Michael Ondattje. *Time* 2 Nov. 1992: 71. *Time Man of the Year*. Compact. 1993. CD-ROM.

Jones, Rodney. "TV." *Atlantic Monthly* Jan. 1993: 52. Web. 29 Mar. 2011.

Spires, Elizabeth. "One Life, One Art: Elizabeth Bishop in Her Letters." Rev. of *One Art: Letters*, by Elizabeth Bishop. *New Criterion* May 1994: 18–23. Web. 30 Jan. 2011.

Interview

Cheever, John. Interview. "John Cheever: The Art of Fiction LXII." By Annette Grant. *Paris Review* 17 (1976): 39–66. Print.

Review of Play Production

Brantley, Ben. "Big Daddy's Ego Defies Death and His Family." *New York Times*. 3 Nov. 2003: E1. Web. 13 Feb. 2011.

Film, Video, or Audio Recording

Harjo, Joy, and Poetic Justice. *The Woman Who Fell from the Sky*. Norton, 1994. Audiocassette.

Pygmalion. Dir. Anthony Asquith and Leslie Howard. Perf. Leslie Howard and Wendy Hiller. Paschal, 1938. DVD.

Online: Article or Review

Wasserstein, Wendy. "A Place They'd Never Been: The Theater." *Theater Development Fund*. 7 June 2000. Web. 6 Mar. 2011.

Online: Author or Critical Web Site

"August Wilson." *Literature Online*. Rev. 12 May. 2001. Web. 15 Mar. 2011.

"A Page for Edwin." 5 Feb. 1998. Web. 20 Feb. 2011.

Online: Play Production Web Site

"Death of a Salesman." 15 Nov. 2000. Web. 12 Jan. 2011.

Online: Reference Work

"Sophocles." *Britannica Online*. Web. 15 Feb. 2011.

Final Considerations

Finally, some basic matters of common sense are worth pondering. Consider the first impression that the paper that you are about to turn in will make on your instructor. He or she may teach as many as five composition classes and, with an average classroom load of thirty students writing six to eight essays per class, may have to read, mark, and grade something approaching a half-million words of student writing in a single semester. No instructor, with the clock ticking past midnight and the coffee growing cold, likes trying to read an essay in scrawled handwriting, with pieces of its torn edges, hastily ripped from a spiral notebook, drifting to the carpet. If your instructor does allow handwritten work (increasingly rare these days), try to present a copy that can be read without extensive training in cryptographic analysis; in other words, make sure your writing is legible. But don't go to the opposite extreme and present a masterpiece of computer wizardry, complete with multiple sizes, shapes, and colors of fonts. In a word, plain vanilla is always the safest flavor to choose. In most cases, it will be required that your work be computer-generated. Your final copy should be double-spaced, using a printer set at high resolution. Choose a standard font (Times Roman 12 pt is the most widely used), and do not expect a faint, smeared copy to receive as much attention as a readable manuscript printed on good-quality paper. Do not put your paper in any kind of folder or binder unless you are specifically asked to do so. You may have been given specific instructions about title pages and page numbering, so be sure to follow them. If you are required to submit your work electronically, make sure that your attachment is in the prescribed word-processing format.

It should go without saying that you should proofread your final draft carefully, paying particular attention to some of the special problems in writing mechanics (punctuation and verb tenses are two of the most common) that arise in critical papers. And, please, remember two things about the computer. One is that a paper that has not been spell-checked is absolute proof of lack of diligence. The other is that even the most sophisticated spell-checker cannot distinguish between "there" and "their" or "it's" and "its." Errors in proper nouns such as the names of authors or publishers also must be checked manually. Writing assignments are graded both for content and for their demonstration that the writer knows the basics of composition. A spelling error on the title page is not the best introduction to the body of your paper, and even the most original insights into a literary work will not receive due credit if the rules of standard English are consistently ignored.

Effective writing requires a long process involving topic selection, assembly of support, organization, rough drafts, and final adjustments. By the time you have finished printing out your final draft you may feel that not only have you exhausted the topic, it has exhausted *you*. Still, the most important element that you can bring to any assignment is the simplest one: *care*. May your efforts be rewarded!

THEMATIC APPROACHES TO LITERATURE

Because it is possible to classify the stories, poems, and plays in the anthology in many different ways, the following listings are not exhaustive. They should, however, provide suggestions for reading and writing about works from the same genre or about works from different genres that share thematic similarities. Works are listed by genre, and works in each genre are listed in chronological order. Consult the *Index of Authors, Titles, and First Lines of Poems* for their page numbers in the text.

Following the thematic listings is a brief discussion of several key critical approaches and their applications to the thematic groups.

Aging (See also Carpe Diem Poetry)

Stories

Faulkner, "A Rose for Emily"
García Márquez, "A Very Old Man with Enormous Wings"
Munro, "The Bear Came Over the Mountain"

Poems

Shakespeare, "Sonnet 73"
Milton, "How Soon Hath Time"
Tennyson, "Ulysses"

Williams, "The Last Words of My English Grandmother"
Eliot, "The Love Song of J. Alfred Prufrock"
Millay, "What Lips My Lips Have Kissed, and Where, and Why"
Thomas, "Poem in October"
Kennedy, "In a Prominent Bar in Secaucus One Day"
Pastan, "Ethics"

Plays

Williams, *The Glass Menagerie*
Wilson, *The Piano Lesson*

Allegorical and Symbolic Works

Stories

Hawthorne, "The Minister's Black Veil"

Jackson, "The Lottery"

García Márquez, "A Very Old Man with Enormous Wings"

Oates, "Where Are You Going, Where Have You Been?"

Poems

Southwell, "The Burning Babe"

Herbert, "Redemption"

Burns, "John Barleycorn"

Poe, "The Haunted Palace"

Tennyson, "The Lady of Shalott"

Dickinson, "Because I Could Not Stop for Death"

Rossetti, "Up-Hill"

Crane, "The Trees in the Garden Rained Flowers"

Crane, "The Wayfarer"

Frost, "The Road Not Taken"

Stevens, "Anecdote of the Jar"

Stevens, "The Emperor of Ice-Cream"

Stevens, "The Snow Man"

Eliot, "Journey of the Magi"

Ransom, "Piazza Piece"

Larkin, "Next, Please"

Kizer, "The Ungrateful Garden"

Merwin, "The Last One"

Rich, "Diving into the Wreck"

Animals

Stories

Jewett, "A White Heron"

Wolff, "Hunters in the Snow"

Poems

Blake, "The Tyger"

Tennyson, "The Eagle"

Dickinson, "A Narrow Fellow in the Grass"

Moore, "The Fish"

cummings, "r-p-o-p-h-e-s-s-a-g-r"

Bishop, "The Fish"

Stafford, "Traveling Through the Dark"

Dickey, "The Heaven of Animals"

Hughes, "Pike"

Harjo, "She Had Some Horses"

Plays

Glaspell, *Trifles*

Art

Poems

Spenser, "Amoretti: Sonnet 75"

Shakespeare, "Sonnet 18"

Shelley, "Ozymandias"

Yeats, "Sailing to Byzantium"

Stevens, "Anecdote of the Jar"

Auden, "Musée des Beaux Arts"

Ballads and Narrative Poetry

Plays

Anonymous, "Bonny Barbara Allan"

Anonymous, "Sir Patrick Spens"
Burns, "John Barleycorn"
Keats, "La Belle Dame sans Merci"
Poe, "The Haunted Palace"
Tennyson, "The Lady of Shalott"
Randall, "Ballad of Birmingham"
Fairchild, "Body and Soul"
Stokesbury, "The Day Kennedy Died"
Nelson, "The Ballad of Aunt Geneva"

Carpe Diem

Poems

Donne, "The Sun Rising"
Herrick, "To the Virgins, to Make Much of Time"
Waller, "Song"
Marvell, "To His Coy Mistress"
Housman, "Loveliest of Trees, the Cherry Now"
Stevens, "The Emperor of Ice-Cream"
Ransom, "Piazza Piece"

Childhood and Adolescence (Initiation)

Stories

Jewett, "A White Heron"
Joyce, "Araby"
Wright, "The Man Who Was Almost a Man"
Cheever, "Reunion"
Ellison, "A Party Down at the Square"

Yamamoto, "Seventeen Syllables"
Oates, "Where Are You Going, Where Have You Been?"
Perabo, "The Payoff"

Poems

Blake, "The Chimney Sweeper"
Blake, "The Little Black Boy"
Wordsworth, "Ode: Intimations of Immortality"
Kennedy, "Little Elegy"
Dunn, "The Sacred"
Olds, "The One Girl at the Boys Party"
Kane, "Alan Doll Rap"
Rios, "The Purpose of Altar Boys"
Stallings. "First Love: A Quiz"

Plays

Fugard, "Master Harold". . . and the boys
Sanchez-Scott, The Cuban Swimmer
Reza, The God of Carnage

Conceit and Extended Metaphor (Poetry)

Plays

Donne, "Holy Sonnet 14"
Donne, "A Valediction: Forbidding Mourning"
Herbert, "Easter Wings"
Herbert, "The Pulley"
Bradstreet, "The Author to Her Book"

Chappell, "Narcissus and
Echo"

Dramatic Monologues

Stories

Poe, "The Cask of Amontillado"

Poems

Blake, "The Chimney
Sweeper"
Blake, "The Little Black Boy"
Blake, "A Poison Tree"
Tennyson, "Ulysses"
Browning, "My Last Duchess"
Browning, "Porphyria's
Lover"
Pound, "The River-Merchant's
Wife: A Letter"
Eliot, "Journey of the Magi"
Eliot, "The Love Song of
J. Alfred Prufrock"
Brooks, "the mother"
Brooks, "We Real Cool"
Wright, "Saint Judas"
Kennedy, "In a Prominent Bar
in Secaucus One Day"
Atwood, "Siren Song"
Hall, "Maybe Dats Your
Pwoblem Too"
Cortez, "Tu Negrito"
Gertstler, "Advice from
a Caterpillar"

Duty

Stories

Jewett, "A White Heron"
Maupassant, "Mother Savage"

Poems

Anonymous, "Sir Patrick Spens"
Lovelace, "To Lucasta, Going
to the Wars"

Plays

Sophocles, *Antigone*

Elegy

Poems

Jonson, "On My First Son"
Dryden, "To the Memory of
Mr. Oldham"
Gray, "Elegy Written in a
Country Churchyard"
Longfellow, "The Cross of
Snow"
Millay, "If I Should Learn, in
Some Quite Casual Way"
O'Hara, "The Day Lady Died"
Sexton, "The Truth the Dead
Know"
Gunn, "Terminal"
Gioia, "Planting a Sequoia"

Ethnic/Racial Identity and Racism

Stories

Wright, "The Man Who Was
Almost a Man"
Ellison, "A Party Down at the
Square"
Yamamoto, "Seventeen
Syllables"
O'Connor, "Everything that
Rises Must Converge"
Walker, "Everyday Use"

Cisneros, "Woman Hollering
Creek"
Erdrich, "The Red Convertible"
Jen, "In the American Society"
Alexie, "This Is What It
Means to Say Phoenix,
Arizona"

Poems

Blake, "The Little Black Boy"
Lazarus, "The New Colossus"
Dunbar, "We Wear the Mask"
Toomer, "Georgia Dusk"
Hughes, "Dream Boogie"
Hughes, "Harlem Sweeties"
Hughes, "The Weary Blues"
Cullen, "Incident"
Cullen, "Yet Do I Marvel"
Randall, "Ballad of
Birmingham"
Walker, "For Malcolm X"
Nelson, "The Ballad of Aunt
Geneva"
Jones, "Winter Retreat:
Homage to Martin Luther
King, Jr."
Harjo, "She Had Some
Horses"
Cofer, "The Latin Deli: An Ars
Poetica"
Alexie, "The Exaggeration of
Despair"
Tretheway, "Domestic Work,
1937"
Kim, "Occupation"

Plays

Fugard, *"Master Harold"...
and the boys*

Wilson, *The Piano Lesson*
Sanchez-Scott, *The Cuban
Swimmer*

Fate

Stories

Jackson, "The Lottery"

Poems

Yeats, "Leda and the Swan"
Frost, "Design"
Auden, "The Unknown
Citizen"
Randall, "Ballad of
Birmingham"
Kooser, "Abandoned
Farmhouse"

Plays

Sophocles, *Antigone*
Ives, *Sure Thing*

History

Stories

Maupassant, "Mother Savage"
Faulkner, "A Rose for Emily"
Ellison, "A Party Down at the
Square"
Jackson, "The Lottery"
Achebe, "Dead Men's Path"
Walker, "Everyday Use"

Poems

Milton, "On the Late
Massacre in Piedmont"
Gray, "Elegy Written in a
Country Churchyard"

Love

Stories

Wharton, "Roman Fever"
Joyce, "Araby"
Hemingway, "Up in Michigan"
Munro, "The Bear Came Over the Mountain"
Atwood, "Happy Endings"
Perabo, "The Payoff"

Poems

Shakespeare, "Sonnet 29"
Shakespeare, "Sonnet 116"
Wroth, "In This Strange Labyrinth How Shall I Turn"
Donne, "The Sun Rising"
Burns, "A Red, Red Rose"
Browning, "Sonnets from the Portuguese, 18"
Browning, "Sonnets from the Portuguese, 43"
Bishop, "The Shampoo"
cummings, "somewhere I have never travelled, glad beyond"
Dugan, "Love Song; I and Thou"
Addonizio, "Sonnenizio on a Line from Drayton"
Stallings, "First Love: A Quiz"

Plays

Ives, *Sure Thing*

Love: Loss of

Stories

Faulkner, "A Rose for Emily"

Poems

Anonymous, "Western Wind"
Wyatt, "They Flee from Me"
Wyatt, "Whoso List to Hunt"
Byron, "When We Two Parted"
Keats, "La Belle Dame sans Merci"
Poe, "The Raven"
Hardy, "Neutral Tones"
Wylie, "Ophelia"
Millay, "What Lips My Lips Have Kissed, and Where, and Why"
Bishop, "One Art"
Snodgrass, "Mementos, I"
Phillips, "The Stone Crab: A Love Poem"
Moore, "Auld Lang Syne"
Hilbert, "Domestic Situation"
Shakespeare, *Twelfth Night*

Love: Marital Relationships

Stories

Irving, "Rip Van Winkle"
Hurston, "Sweat"
Munro, "The Bear Came Over the Mountain"
Atwood, "Happy Endings"
Mason, "Shiloh"
Cisneros, "Woman Hollering Creek"

Poems

Shakespeare, "Sonnet 116"
Donne, "A Valediction: Forbidding Mourning"
Longfellow, "The Cross of Snow"
Browning, "My Last Duchess"

Poetry: Inspiration

Poems

Sidney, "Astrophel and Stella: Sonnet 1"

Coleridge, "Kubla Khan"

Keats, "Ode to a Nightingale"

Hopkins, "Pied Beauty"

Wilbur, "The Writer"

Political and Social Themes

Stories

Maupassant, "Mother Savage"

Achebe, "Dead Men's Path"

Gautreaux, "Waiting for the Evening News"

Erdrich, "The Red Convertible"

Jen, "In the American Society"

Simpson, "Diary of an Interesting Year"

Poems

Milton, "On the Late Massacre in Piedmont"

Blake, "The Chimney Sweeper"

Whitman, "O Captain! My Captain!"

Lazarus, "The New Colossus"

Housman, "Eight O'Clock"

Robinson, "The Mill"

Auden, "The Unknown Citizen"

Roethke, "Dolor"

Brooks, "the mother"

Simpson, "American Classic"

Merrill, "Casual Wear"

Walcott, "Central America"

Ai, "Child Beater"

Cortez, "Tu Negrito"

Forché, "The Colonel"

Song, "Stamp Collecting"

Plays

Sophocles, *Antigone*

Ibsen, *An Enemy of the People*

Fugard, "*Master Harold*" . . . *and the boys*

Wilson, *The Piano Lesson*

Satire and Humor

Stories

Walker, "Everyday Use"

Gautreaux, "Waiting for the Evening News"

Poems

Byron, "Stanzas"

Swift, "A Description of a City Shower"

Hardy, "The Ruined Maid"

Stevens, "Disillusionment of Ten O'Clock"

cummings, "plato told"

Auden, "The Unknown Citizen"

Martin, "E.S.L."

Fenton, "God, a Poem"

Kane, "Alan Doll Rap"

Hannah, "The Guest Speaker"

Dawson, "Somewhere Between Columbus and Cincinnati"

Plays

Ives, *Time Flies*

Sexual Themes (See also Carpe Diem)

Stories

Wharton, "Roman Fever"
Faulkner, "A Rose for Emily"
Hemingway, "Up in Michigan"
Oates, "Where Are You Going, Where Have You Been?"
Parabo, "The Payoff"

Poems

Wyatt, "Whoso List to Hunt"
Shakespeare, "Sonnet 20"
Donne, "The Flea,"
Donne, "The Sun Rising"
Marvell, "To His Coy Mistress"
Whitman, "Song of Myself, 11"
Hardy, "The Ruined Maid"
Eliot, "The Love Song of J. Alfred Prufrock"
Hecht, "The Dover Bitch"
Rich, "Rape"
Rogers, "Foreplay"
Ríos, "The Purpose of Altar Boys"
Addonizio, "First Poem for You"
Moore, "Auld Lang Syne"

Plays

Shakespeare, *Twelfth Night*
Ives, *Sure Thing*

Solitude

Stories

Jewett, "A White Heron"
Faulkner, "A Rose for Emily"

Poems

Pope, "Ode on Solitude"
Dickinson, "The Soul Selects Her Own Society"
Yeats, "The Lake Isle of Innisfree"
Frost, "Acquainted with the Night"
Frost, "Home Burial"

Plays

Glaspell, *Trifles*
Williams, *The Glass Menagerie*

Sports and Games

Stories

Wolff, "Hunters in the Snow"

Poems

Wright, "Autumn Begins in Martins Ferry, Ohio"
Gunn, "From the Wave"
Gildner, "First Practice"
Fairchild, "Body and Soul"
Dove, "American Smooth"
Joseph, "The Athlete"

Play

Sanchez-Scott, *The Cuban Swimmer*

acknowledgments

Fiction

Chinua Achebe. "Dead Men's Path," copyright © 1972, 1973 by Chinua Achebe, from *Girls at War and Other Stories* by Chinua Achebe. Used by permission of Doubleday, a division of Random House, Inc.

Sherman Alexie. "This Is What It Means to Say Phoenix, Arizona" from *The Lone Ranger and Tonto Fistfight in Heaven* by Sherman Alexie. Copyright © 1993, 2005 by Sherman Alexie. Used by permission of Grove/Atlantic, Inc.

Margaret Atwood. "Happy Endings," from *Good Bones and Simple Murders* by Margaret Atwood, copyright © 1983, 1992, 1994, by O.W. Toad Ltd. A Nan A. Talese Book. Used by permission of Doubleday, a division of Random House, Inc.

Raymond Carver. "Cathedral" from *Cathedral* by Raymond Carver, copyright © 1981, 1982, 1983 by Raymond Carver. Used by permission of Alfred A. Knopf, a division of Random House, Inc.

John Cheever. "Reunion" from *The Stories of John Cheever* by John Cheever, copyright © 1978 by John Cheever. Used by permission of Alfred A. Knopf, a division of Random House, Inc.

Sandra Cisneros. "Woman Hollering Creek" from *Woman Hollering Creek* by Sandra Cisneros. Copyright © 1991 by Sandra Cisneros. Published by Vintage Books, a division of Random House, Inc., New York and originally in hardcover by Random House, Inc. Reprinted by permission of Susan Bergholz Literary Services, New York, NY and Lamy, NM. All rights reserved.

Ralph Ellison. "A Party Down at the Square," copyright © 1996 by Fanny Ellison, from *Flying Home and Other Stories* by Ralph Ellison. Used by permission of Random House, Inc.

Louise Erdrich. "The Red Convertible" from the book *Love Medicine,* New and Expanded Version, by Louise Erdrich. Copyright © 1984, 1993 by Louise Erdrich. Reprinted by permission of Henry Holt and Company, LLC.

William Faulkner. "A Rose for Emily," copyright 1930 and renewed 1958 by William Faulkner, from *Collected Stories of William Faulkner* by William Faulkner. Used by permission of Random House, Inc.

Tim Gautreaux. "Waiting for the Evening News" by Tim Gautreaux, from *Same Place, Same Things,* Copyright © 1997 by Tim Gautreax. Used with permission of Tor Books, a division of St. Martin's Press, LLC. All rights reserved.

Dagoberto Gilb. "Look on the Bright Side" from *The Magic of Blood* by Dagoberto Gilb. Copyright © 1993. Reprinted by permission of the University of New Mexico Press.

Ernest Hemingway. "Up in Michigan," reprinted with the permission of Scribner, a Division of Simon & Schuster, Inc., from *The Short Stories of Ernest Hemingway.* Copyright 1938 by Ernest Hemingway. Copyright renewed © 1966 by Mary Hemingway. All rights reserved.

Shirley Jackson. "The Lottery" from *The Lottery* by Shirley Jackson. Copyright © 1948, 1949 by Shirley Jackson. Copyright renewed 1976, 1977 by Laurence Hyman, Barry Hyman, Mrs. Sarah Webster and Mrs. Joanne Schnurer. Reprinted by permission of Farrar, Straus and Giroux, LLC.

Gish Jen. "In the American Society" by Gish Jen. Copyright © 1986 by Gish Jen. First published in The Southern Review. From the collection *Who's Irish?* (Alfred A. Knopf). Reprinted with permission by Melanie Jackson Agency, LLC.

Jamaica Kincaid. "Girl" from *At the Bottom of the River* by Jamaica Kincaid. Copyright

© 1983 by Jamaica Kincaid. Reprinted by permission of Farrar, Straus and Giroux, LLC.

Jhumpa Lahiri. "A Temporary Matter" from *Interpreter of Maladies* by Jhumpa Lahiri. Copyright © 1999 by Jhumpa Lahiri. Reprinted by permission of Houghton Mifflin Harcourt Publishing Company. All rights reserved.

Ursula K. Le Guin. "The Ones Who Walk Away from Omelas" by Ursula K. Le Guin. Copyright © 1975, 2003 by Ursula K. Le Guin. First appeared in *New Dimensions 3*; from *The Wind's Twelve Quarters*. Reprinted by permission of the author and the author's agents, the Virginia Kidd Agency, Inc.

Gabriel Garcia Márquez. All pages from "A Very Old Man with Enormous Wings" from *Leaf Storm and Other Stories* by Gabriel Garcia Márquez. Translated by Gregory Rabassa. Copyright © 1971 by Gabriel Garcia Márquez. Reprinted by permission of HarperCollins Publishers.

Bobbie Ann Mason. "Shiloh" from *Shiloh and Other Stories* by Bobbie Ann Mason. Reprinted by permission of International Creative Management, Inc. Copyright © 1982 by Bobbie Ann Mason.

Lorrie Moore. "How to Become a Writer" from *Self-Help* by Lorrie Moore, copyright © 1985 by M.L. Moore. Used by permission of Alfred A. Knopf, a division of Random House, Inc.

Alice Munro. "The Bear Came Over the Mountain" by Alice Munro, originally published in *The New Yorker*, Dec. 27, 1999. Copyright © 1999 by Alice Munro. Reprinted by permission of William Morris Endeavor Entertainment, LLC on behalf of the author.

Flannery O'Connor. "Everything That Rises Must Converge" from *Everything That Rises Must Converge* by Flannery O'Connor. Copyright © 1965 by the Estate of Mary Flannery O'Connor. Copyright renewed 1993 by Regina O'Connor. Reprinted by permission of Farrar, Straus and Giroux, LLC.

Joyce Carol Oates. "Where Are You Going, Where Have You Been?" by Joyce Carol Oates. Copyright © 1970 *Ontario Review*. Reprinted by permission of John Hawkins & Associates, Inc.

Grace Paley. "Wants" from *Enormous Changes at the Last Minute* by Grace Paley. Copyright © 1971, 1974 by Grace Paley. Reprinted by permission of Farrar, Straus and Giroux, LLC.

Susan Perabo. "The Payoff" by Susan Perabo, originally published in *The Cincinnati Review* 3.2 (Winter 2007) is reprinted by permission of the author.

Helen Simpson. "Diary of an Interesting Year" from *In-Flight Entertainment* by Helen Simpson. Reprinted by permission of United Agents on behalf of Helen Simpson.

Alice Walker. "Everyday Use" from *In Love & Trouble: Stories of Black Women*, copyright © 1973 by Alice Walker, reprinted by permission of Houghton Mifflin Harcourt Publishing Company.

Eudora Welty. "A Memory" from *A Curtain of Green and Other Stories*, copyright 1937 and renewed 1965 by Eudora Welty, reprinted by permission of Houghton Mifflin Harcourt Publishing Company.

Edith Wharton. "Roman Fever." Reprinted with the permission of Scribner, a Division of Simon & Schuster Adult Publishing Group, from *Roman Fever and Other Stories* by Edith Wharton. Copyright © 1934 by Liberty Magazine. Copyright renewed © 1962 by William R. Tyler. All rights reserved.

Tobias Wolff. "Hunters in the Snow" (p. 7–26) from *In the Garden of the North American Martyrs* by Tobias Wolff. Copyright © 1981 by Tobias Wolff. Reprinted by permission of HarperCollins Publishers.

Richard Wright. "The Man Who Was Almost a Man" (pp. 3–18) from *Eight Men* by Richard Wright. Copyright 1940, © 1961 by Richard Wright; renewed © 1989 by Ellen Wright. Introduction © 1996 by Paul Gilroy. Reprinted by permission of HarperCollins Publishers.

Yamamoto Hisaye. "Seventeen Syllables" from *Seventeen Syllables and Other Stories*. Copyright © 1988 by Hisaye Yamamoto DeSoto.

Richard Yates. "Doctor Jack-o'-Lantern" from *The Collected Stories of Richard Yates* by Richard Yates. Copyright © 2001 by The Estate of Richard Yates. Reprinted by arrangement with Henry Holt and Company, LLC.

Poetry

Betty Adcock, "Voyages" from *The Difficult Wheel: Poems* by Betty Adcock. Copyright © 1995 by Betty Adcock. Reprinted by permission of Louisiana State University Press.

Kim Addonizio, "Sonnenizio on a Line from Drayton," from *What Is This Thing Called Love: Poems* by Kim Addonizio. Copyright © 2004 by Kim Addonizio. Used by permission of W.W. Norton & Company, Inc.

Craig Arnold, "The Singers" by Craig Arnold, originally published in Poetry in 2007. Reprinted by permission of the Estate of Craig Arnold.

Ai, "Child Beater" from *Cruelty*, published by Houghton Mifflin Company. Reprinted by permission of the author.

Sherman Alexie, "The Exaggeration of Despair," reprinted from *The Summer of Black Widows* © 1996 by Sherman Alexie, by permission of Hanging Loose Press.

Julia Alvarez, "Bilingual Sestina" from *The Other Side/El Otro Lado* by Julia Alvarez. Copyright © 1995 by Julia Alvarez. Published by Plume/ Penguin, a division of Penguin Group (USA). Reprinted by permission of Susan Bergholz Literary Services, New York, NY, and Larry, NM. All rights reserved.

Ginger Andrews, "Primping in the Rearview Mirror" by Ginger Andrews. Reprinted by permission from *The Hudson Review*, Vol. LV, No. 2 (Summer 2002). Copyright © 2002 by Ginger Andrews.

John Ashbery, "Farm Implements and Rutabagas in a Landscape" from *The Double Dream of Spring* by John Ashbery. Copyright © 1966, 1970 by John Ashbery. Reprinted by permission of Georges Borchardt, Inc., on behalf of the author. "Paradoxes and Oxymorons" from *Shadow Train* by John Ashbery. Copyright © 1980, 1981 by John Ashbery. Reprinted by permission of Georges Borchardt, Inc., on behalf of the author.

Margaret Atwood, "Siren Song" from *Selected Poems 1965–1975* by Margaret Atwood. Copyright © 1976 by Margaret Atwood. Reprinted by permission of Houghton Mifflin Harcourt Publishing Company. All rights reserved.

W. H. Auden, "The Unknown Citizen," copyright 1940 and copyright renewed 1968 by W. H. Auden, "Musee des Beaux Arts," copyright 1940 and renewed 1968 by W. H. Auden, "As I Walked Out One Evening," copyright 1940 and renewed 1968 by W. H. Auden, from *Collected Poems* by W. H. Auden. Used by permission of Random House, Inc.

Gerald Barrax, "Strangers Like Us: Pittsburgh, Raleigh, 1945–1985" from *From a Person Sitting in Darkness: New and Selected Poems* by Gerald Barrax. Copyright © 1998 by Gerald Barrax. Reprinted by permission of Louisiana State University Press.

Elizabeth Bishop, "The Fish", "One Art," and "The Shampoo" from *The Complete Poems 1927–1979* by Elizabeth Bishop. Copyright © 1979, 1983 by Alice Helen Methfessel. Reprinted by permission of Farrar, Straus, and Giroux, LLC.

Louise Bogan, "Women" from *The Blue Estuaries* by Louise Bogan. Copyright © 1968 by Louise Bogan. Copyright renewed 1996 by Ruth Limmer. Reprinted by permission of Farrar, Straus, and Giroux, LLC.

Gwendolyn Brooks, "The Ballad of Chocolate Mabbie" from *Selected Poems* by Gwendolyn Brooks. "The Mother" and "We Real Cool" from *Blacks* by Gwendolyn Brooks. Reprinted by consent of Brooks Permissions.

Gladys Cardiff, "Combing" Copyright © 1971 by Gladys Cardiff. Reprinted from *To Frighten a Storm* (Copper Canyon Press, 1976) by permission of the author.

Fred Chappell, "Narcissus and Echo" from *Source* by Fred Chappell. Copyright © 1985 by Fred Chappell. Reprinted by permission of Louisiana State University Press.

Lucille Clifton, "homage to my hips" copyright © 1980 by Lucille Clifton. First appeared in *Two-Headed Woman*, published by University of Massachusetts Press. Reprinted by permission of Curtis Brown, Ltd. "wishes for sons" from *Quilting: Poems 1987–1990* by Lucille Clifton. Copyright © 1991 by Lucille Clifton. Reprinted with the permission of BOA Editions, Ltd., www.boaeditions.org.

Judith Ortiz Cofer, "The Latin Deli: An Ars Poetica" by Judith Ortiz Cofer is reprinted with permission from the publisher of *The Americas Review* (Houston: Arte Público Press—University of Houston, 1993).

Billy Collins, "Litany," copyright © 2002 by Billy Collins, from *Nine Horses* by Billy Collins. Used by permission of Random House, Inc.

Wendy Cope, "Rondeau Redoublé" from *Making Cocoa for Kingsley Amis* by Wendy Cope. Copyright © Wendy Cope 1986. Reprinted by permission of United Agents on behalf of Wendy Cope.

Sarah Cortez, "Tu Negrito" from *How to Undress a Cop* by Sarah Cortez is reprinted with permission from the publisher (Houston: Arte Público Press—University of Houston, 2000).

Amy Gerstler, "Advice from a Caterpillar" from *Dearest Creature* by Amy Gerstler, copyright © 2009 by Amy Gerstler. Used by permission of Penguin, a division of Penguin Group (USA) Inc.

Allen Ginsberg, All lines from "A Supermarket in California" from *Collected Poems 1947–1980* by Allen Ginsberg. Copyright © 1955 by Allen Ginsberg. Reprinted by permission of HarperCollins Publishers.

Dana Gioia, "Planting a Sequoia" from *The Gods of Winter* by Dana Gioia. Copyright © 1991 by Dana Gioia. Reprinted with the permission of Graywolf Press, Minneapolis, Minnesota, www.graywolfpress.org.

Thom Gunn, "From the Wave" and "Terminal" from *Collected Poems* by Thom Gunn. Copyright © 1944 by Thom Gunn. Reprinted by permission of Farrar, Straus and Giroux, LLC.

Jim Hall, "Maybe Dats Your Pwoblem Too" from *The Mating Reflex*. By permission of Carnegie Mellon University Press, © 1980 by Jim Hall.

Sophie Hannah, "The Guest Speaker" from *First of the Last Chances* by Sophie Hannah. Published by Carcanet Press, Limited, 2003. Reprinted by permission of the publisher.

Joy Harjo, "She Had Some Horses," copyright © 1983 by Joy Harjo, from *She Had Some Horses* by Joy Harjo. Used by permission of W.W. Norton & Company, Inc.

Robert Hass, "Meditations at Lagunitas" (31 l.) from *Praise* by Robert Hass. Copyright © 1979 by Robert Hass. Reprinted by permission of HarperCollins Publishers.

Robert Hayden, "Those Winter Sundays," copyright © 1966 by Robert Hayden, from *Collected Poems of Robert Hayden* by Robert Hayden, edited by Frederick Glaysher. Used by permission of Liveright Publishing Corporation.

Seamus Heaney, "Punishment" from *Opened Ground: Selected Poems 1966–1996* by Seamus Heaney. Copyright © 1998 by Seamus Heaney. Reprinted by permission of Farrar, Straus and Giroux, LLC.

Anthony Hecht, "The Dover Bitch" and "Third Avenue in Sunlight" from *Collected Earlier Poems* by Anthony Hecht, copyright © 1990 by Anthony E. Hecht. Used by permission of Alfred A. Knopf, a division of Random House, Inc.

Ernest Hilbert is an American poet, critic, and editor born in Philadelphia. Educated at Rutgers and Oxford, he served as the editor of the *Contemporary Poetry Review* from 2005 to 2010. Hilbert also edits a popular blog/podcast/web TV show, *E-Verse Radio*, and is a rare-book dealer. His collection *Sixty Sonnets* was published by *Red Hen Press* <http://www.redhen.org/> in February 2009.

A. E. Housman, "Stars, I Have Seen Them Fall," by A. E. Housman from *The Collected Poems of A. E. Housman*. Copyright © 1936 by Barclays Bank Ltd. Copyright © 1964 by Robert E. Symons. Reprinted by arrangement with Henry Holt and Company, LLC.

Andrew Hudgins, "Air View of an Industrial Scene" from *Saints and Strangers* by Andrew Hudgins. Copyright © 1985 by Andrew Hudgins. Reprinted by permission of Houghton Mifflin Harcourt Publishing Company. All rights reserved.

Langston Hughes, "Dream Boogie," "Harlem Sweeties," and "The Weary Blues" from *The Collected Poems of Langston Hughes* by Langston Hughes, edited by Arnold Rampersad, with David Roessel, Associate Editor, copyright © 1994 by the Estate of Langston Hughes. Used by permission of Alfred A. Knopf, a division of Random House, Inc.

Ted Hughes, "Pike" from *Collected Poems* by Ted Hughes. Copyright © 2003 by The Estate of Ted Hughes. Reprinted by permission of Farrar, Straus and Giroux, LLC.

Robinson Jeffers, "The Purse Seine," copyright 1938 & renewed 1966 by Donnan Jeffers and Garth Jeffers, from *Selected Poetry of Robinson Jeffers* by Robinson Jeffers. Used by permission of Random House, Inc.

Rodney Jones, "Winter Retreat: Homage to Martin Luther King, Jr." from *Transparent Gestures* by Rodney Jones. Copyright © 1989 by Rodney Jones. Reprinted by permission of Houghton Mifflin Harcourt Publishing Company. All rights reserved.

Allison Joseph, "The Athlete" from *Worldly Pleasures* by Allison Joseph. Reprinted by permission of WordTech Communications LLC.

Donald Justice, "Counting the Mad" from *Collected Poems* by Donald Justice, copyright © 2004 by Donald Justice. Used by permission of Alfred A. Knopf, a division of Random House, Inc.

Julie Kane, "Alan Doll Rap" by Julie Kane. Reprinted by permission of the author.

Weldon Kees, "For My Daughter," reprinted from *The Collected Poems of Weldon Kees* edited by Donald Justice by permission of the University of Nebraska Press. Copyright 1962, 1975 by the University of Nebraska Press. Copyright renewed 2003 by the University of Nebraska Press.

X. J. Kennedy, "In a Prominent Bar in Secaucus One Day" from *In a Prominent Bar in Secaucus: New and Selected Poems, 1955–2007*, pp. 11–12, by X. J. Kennedy. © 2007 X. J. Kennedy. Reprinted with permission of The Johns Hopkins University Press. "Little Elegy" from *In a Prominent Bar in Secaucus: New and Selected Poems, 1955–2007*, p 20, by X. J. Kennedy. © 2007 X. J. Kennedy. Reprinted with permission of The Johns Hopkins University Press.

Suji Kwock Kim, "Occupation" from *Notes from a Divided Country: Poems* by Suji Kwock Kim. Copyright © 2003 by Suji Kwock Kim. Reprinted by permission of Louisiana State University Press.

Carolyn Kizer, "The Ungrateful Garden" from *Midnight Was My Cry: New and Selected Poems* by Carolyn Kizer. Copyright © 1961. Reprinted by the permission of the author.

Yusef Komunyakaa, "Facing It" from *Pleasure Dome: New and Collected Poems* by Yusef Komunyakaa © 2001 by Yussef Komunyakaa. Reprinted by permission of Wesleyan University Press.

Ted Kooser, "Abandoned Farmhouse" from *Sure Signs: New and Collected Poems*, by Ted Kooser, © 1980. Reprinted by permission of the University of Pittsburgh Press.

Maxine Kumin, "Noted in the New York Times" from *Nurture* by Maxine Kumin. Copyright © 1989 by Maxine Kumin. Used by permission of Viking Penguin, a division of Penguin Books USA Inc.

Philip Larkin, "The Whitsun Weddings" and "This Be the Verse" from *Collected Poems* by Philip Larkin. Copyright © 1988, 1989 by the Estate of Philip Larkin. Reprinted by permission of Farrar, Straus and Giroux, LLC. "Next Please" by Philip Larkin is reprinted from *The Less Deceived* by permission of The Marvell Press, England and Australia.

Philip Levine, "You Can Have It" from *New Selected Poems* by Philip Levine, copyright © 1991 by Philip Levine. Used by permission of Alfred A. Knopf, a division of Random House, Inc.

Diane Lockward "My Husband Discovers Poetry" from *Eve's Red Dress*. Reprinted by permission of Wind Publications, Nicholasville, KY.

Charles Martin, "E.S.L." from *Steal the Bacon* by Charles Martin, pp. 21–23, © 1987. Reprinted by permission of the author.

David Mason, "Fog Horns" by David Mason, published in *Poetry* magazine, September 2004. Reprinted by permission of the author.

Florence Cassen Mayers, "All American Sestina" © 1996 Florence Cassen Mayers, as first published in *Atlantic Monthly*. Reprinted by permission of the author.

James Merrill, "Casual Wear" from *Selected Poems 1946–1985* by James Merrill, copyright © 1992 by James Merrill. Used by permission of Alfred A. Knopf, a division of Random House, Inc.

W. S. Merwin, "For the Anniversary of My Death" and "The Last One" from *Migrations* by W. S. Merwin. Copyright © 1967, 2005 by W. S. Merwin, reprinted with permission of The Wylie Agency, LLC.

Edna St. Vincent Millay, "Oh, Oh, You Will Be Sorry for That Word!," and "What Lips My Lips Have Kissed, and Where, and Why" from *Collected Poems* by Edna St. Vincent Millay. Copyright © 1923, 1951 by Edna St. Vincent Millay and Norma Millay Ellis. Reprinted with permission of Elizabeth Barnett, The Millay Society.

Vassar Miller, the text of "Subterfuge" (copyright © 1981 by Vassar Miller) from *If I Had Wheels or Love: Collected Poems of Vassar Miller* is reprinted with the permission of Southern Methodist University Press.

Emily Moore, "Auld Lang Syne" by Emily Moore, originally published in *The New Yorker*, April 14, 2008. Reprinted by permission of the author.

Marianne Moore, "Silence" reprinted with the permission of Scribner, a Division of Simon & Schuster Inc., from *The Collected Poems of Marianne Moore* by Marianne Moore. Copyright © 1935 by Marianne Moore, renewed 1963 by Marianne Moore and T. S. Eliot. All right reserved.

Robert Morgan, "Mountain Bride" from *Groundwork*, Gnomon Press. Copyright © 1979. Reprinted by permission of the author.

Harryette Mullen, "Dim Lady" from *Sleeping With the Dictionary* by Harryette Mullen. Copyright © 2002 The Regents of the University of California. Reprinted by permission.

Timothy Murphy, "Case Notes," by Timothy Murphy. Reprinted by permission from *The*

Hudson Review, Vol. LVI, No. 4 (Winter 2004). Copyright © 2004 by Timothy Murphy.

Marilyn Nelson, "The Ballad of Aunt Geneva" from *The Homeplace* by Marilyn Nelson Waniek. Copyright © 1990 by Marilyn Nelson Waniek. Reprinted by permission of Louisiana State University Press.

Howard Nemerov, "A Primer of the Daily Round" from *New and Selected Poems* by Howard Nemerov, copyright © 1960 by Howard Nemerov (Univeristy of Chicago Press). Reprinted by permission of Margaret Nemerov.

Naomi Shihab Nye, "The Traveling Onion," reprinted by permission of Naomi Shihab Nye from *Yellow Glove*, Breitenbush Books, Portland, OR. Copyright © 1986 by Naomi Shihab Nye.

Frank O'Hara, "The Day Lady Died" from *Lunch Poems* © 1964 by Frank O'Hara. Reprinted by permission of City Lights Books.

Sharon Olds, "The One Girl at the Boys Party" from *The Dead and the Living* by Sharon Olds, copyright © 1987 by Sharon Olds. Used by permission of Alfred A. Knopf, a division of Random House, Inc.

Mary Oliver, "The Black Walnut Tree" from *Twelve Moons* by Mary Oliver. Copyright © 1972, 1973, 1974, 1976, 1977, 1978, 1979 by Mary Oliver. By permission of Little, Brown & Company.

Simon J. Ortiz, "The Serenity in Stones." Permission to reprint given by author Simon J. Ortiz, Copyright 1975.

Linda Pastan, "Ethics," copyright © 1981 by Linda Pastan, from *Carnival Evening: New and Selected Poems 1968–1998* by Linda Pastan. Used by permission of W. W. Norton & Company, Inc.

Robert Phillips, "The Stone Crab: A Love Poem" from *Breakdown Lane*, p. 32, by Robert Phillips. Copyright © 1994 Robert Phillips. Reprinted with permission of The Johns Hopkins University Press.

Marge Piercy, "What's That Smell in the Kitchen?" from *Circles on the Water* by Marge Piercy, copyright © 1982 by Marge Piercy. Used by permission of Alfred A. Knopf, a division of Random House, Inc.

Sylvia Plath, "Daddy" and Edge" from *Ariel Poems* by Sylvia Plath. Copyright © 1961, 1962, 1963, 1964, 1965, 1966 by Ted Hughes. Reprinted by permission of HarperCollins Publishers. All lines from "Metaphors" from *Crossing the Water* by Sylvia Plath. Copyright © 1960 by Ted Hughes. Reprinted by permission of HarperCollins Publishers.

Craig Raine, "A Martian Sends a Postcard Home" from *A Martian Sends a Postcard Home*. Reprinted with kind permission of the author, Craig Raine.

Dudley Randall, "Ballad of Birmingham" from *Cities Burning* by Dudley Randall. Reprinted by permission of the Estate of Dudley Randall.

Adrienne Rich, "Aunt Jennifer's Tigers," copyright © 2002, 1951 by Adrienne Rich, "Diving into the Wreck," copyright © 2002 by Adrienne Rich. Copyright © 1973 by W. W. Norton & Company, Inc. "Rape," copyright © 2002 by Adrienne Rich. Copyright © 1973 by W. W. Norton & Company, Inc., from *The Fact of a Doorframe: Selected Poems 1950–2001* by Adrienne Rich. Used by permission of the author and W. W. Norton & Company, Inc.

Alberto Ríos, "The Purpose of Altar Boys" from *Whispering to Fool the Wind* (Sheep Meadow Press). Copyright © 1982 by Alberto Ríos. Reprinted by permission of the author.

Theodore Roethke, "Dolor" copyright 1943 by Modern Poetry Association, Inc., "My Papa's Waltz" copyright 1942 by Hearst Magazines, Inc., "Root Cellar" copyright 1943 by Modern Poetry Association, Inc., from *The Collected Poems of Theodore Roethke* by Theodore Roethke. Used by permission of Doubleday, a division of Random House, Inc.

Pattiann Rogers, "Foreplay" from *Firekeeper: New and Selected Poems* by Pattiann Rogers (Milkweed Editions, 1994). Copyright © 1994 by Pattiann Rogers. Reprinted by permission of Milkweed Editions and Pattiann Rogers.

Gibbons Ruark, "The Visitor" from *Passing Through Customs: New and Selected Poems* by Gibbons Ruark. Copyright © 1999 by Gibbons Ruark. Reprinted by permission of Louisiana State University Press.

Kay Ryan, "Bestiary" from *Elephant Rocks* by Kay Ryan. Copyright © 1996 by Kay Ryan. Used by permission of Grove/Atlantic, Inc.

Mary Jo Salter, "Welcome to Hiroshima," copyright © 1984 by Mary Jo Salter from *Henry Purcell in Japan* by Mary Jo Salter. Used by permission of Alfred A. Knopf, a division of Random House, Inc.

Drama

ACKNOWLEDGMENTS

index of critical terms

index of authors, titles, and first lines of poems

Note: Authors' names appear in boldface type. Titles of short stories appear in double quotation marks and italics. Titles of poems appear in double quotation marks. Titles of plays appear in italics.

pearson penguin packages

Instructors: The Pearson Humanities team is proud to offer a variety of Penguin paperbacks at a significant discount when packaged with any of our textbooks. For a complete list of titles available, as well as complete information about how to package these titles with your text, visit www.pearsonhighered.com/penguin.

MYLITERATURELAB

Save time and improve results with MyLiteratureLab . . .

MyLiteratureLab is a state-of-the-art, web-based, interactive learning system for use in literature courses, either as a media supplement or as a management system to completely administer a course online. MyLiteratureLab offers students numerous tools for critical reading, analysis, writing, and research—including Longman Lectures, richly illustrated audio readings of key literary pieces with advice on writing about them from Pearson's authors. Visit www.myliteraturelab.com for more information.